Human Adjustment

Human Adjustment

John W. Santrock

University of Texas at Dallas

Boston   Burr Ridge, IL   Dubuque, IA   Madison, WI   New York   San Francisco   St. Louis
Bangkok   Bogotá   Caracas   Kuala Lumpur   Lisbon   London   Madrid   Mexico City
Milan   Montreal   New Delhi   Santiago   Seoul   Singapore   Sydney   Taipei   Toronto

Higher Education

HUMAN ADJUSTMENT

 This book is printed on recycled, acid-free paper.

7 8 9 0 QPD/QPD 0 9

ISBN-13: 978-0-07-299059-1
ISBN-10: 0-07-299059-7

Editor in Chief: *Emily Barrosse*
Publisher: *Stephen Rutter*
Senior Sponsoring Editor: *John T. Wannemacher*
Marketing Manager: *Melissa Caughlin*
Director of Development: *Judith Kromm*
Developmental Editor: *Judith Kromm*
Managing Editor: *Jean Dal Porto*
Project Manager: *Richard H. Hecker*
Manuscript Editor: *Laurie McGee*
Art Director: *Jeanne Schreiber*
Art Managaer: *Robin Mouat*
Illustrators: *John and Judy Waller*
Senior Photo Research Coordinator: *Alexandra Ambrose*
Photo Researcher: *LouAnn Wilson*
Cover Credit: *Chuck Savage/CORBIS*
Senior Print Supplements Producer: *Louis Swaim*
Lead Media Project Manager: *Marc Mattson*
Senior Production Supervisor: *Carol A. Bielski*
Lead Media Producer: *Sean Crowley*
Permissions Editor: *Marty Granahan*
Composition: *9.5/12 Meridien by Cenveo*
Printer: *Quebecor World Dubuque Inc.*

The credits section for this book begins on page C–1 and is considered an extension of the copyright page.

Library of Congress Cataloging-in-Publication Data

Santrock, John W.
    Human adjustment / John W. Santrock.
      p. cm.
    Includes bibliographical references and index.
    ISBN 0-07-299059-7 (pbk. alk. paper)
    Adjustment (Psychology)—Textbooks. I. Title.
  BF335.S15 2006
  155.2'4—dc22   2004061082

www.mhhe.com

Dedication

*To Kathleen Field, whose words
and wisdom fill these pages*

About the Author

John W. Santrock

John Santrock received his Ph.D. from the University of Minnesota. He taught at the University of Charleston and the University of Georgia before joining the psychology department at the University of Texas at Dallas, where he currently teaches a number of undergraduate courses.

John has a long-standing interest in human adjustment through his work as a school psychologist, research on the effects of divorce, working with Ph.D. students in clinical psychology, and effort in improving the quality of self-help books and resources. In 1994, he wrote the widely acclaimed *Authoritative Guide to Self-Help Books* and, with John Norcross and others, *The Authoritative Guide to Mental Health Resources* in 2003, which recently received the *American Journal of Nursing's* award as the best consumer health book.

John also has authored these exceptional McGraw-Hill texts: *Psychology,* 7th edition; *Life-Span Development,* 10th edition; *Adolescence,* 10th edition; and *Educational Psychology,* 2nd edition. In addition, he has written (with Jane Halonen), *Your Guide to College Success,* 4th edition.

For many years, John was involved in tennis as a player, teaching professional, and coach of professional tennis players. In the last decade, he also has spent time painting expressionist art.

John has been married for more than 35 years to his wife, Mary Jo, who is a realtor. He and Mary Jo have two daughters—Tracy, a marketing technology specialist, and Jennifer, who is a medical sales specialist—and two grandchildren, Jordan and Alex. Tracy recently completed the Boston Marathon and Jennifer was ranked in the top 100 tennis players on the Women's Professional Tennis Tour.

Brief Contents

Contents

Chapter 3
The Self, Identity, and Values 78

Chapter 4

Stress 110

Chapter 5

Coping 140

Chapter 6
Social Thinking, Influence, and Intergroup Relations 170

Chapter 7
Communicating Effectively 200

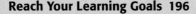

Chapter 8
Friendship and Love Relationships 232

Chapter 9
Adult Lifestyles 258

Chapter 10
Achievement, Careers, and Work 290

Chapter 11
Emerging Adulthood, Adult Development, and Aging 324

Chapter 12
Gender 364

Chapter 13
Sexuality 392

Chapter 14
Psychological Disorders 422

Chapter 15
Therapies 460

Chapter 16
Health 496

Appendex
Self-Assessment Scoring and Interpretation 530

Preface

What could be more important to us than our own adjustment and well-being and our ability to cope effectively with the challenges and stress we experience? Most students who take this course hope to learn how they personally can become happier, better-adjusted individuals. When they finish reading and studying this book, I believe that they will have the knowledge, strategies, and resources to cope effectively with the challenges they face.

Successful adjustment starts with an understanding of psychological principles and the underlying research. It requires learning to distinguish information based on research from personal opinions or easy solutions to personal problems publicized in the popular press. To meet these goals, *Human Adjustment* not only provides the necessary background in psychology in a very accessible and highly interesting way, but also challenges students to think critically about everything they read and hear.

In this text I present many examples and applications drawn from the experiences of individuals whose challenges mirror the ones students have faced or might one day encounter. They include positive examples of individuals, such as Lance Armstrong, who overcame cancer to win successive cycling trophies in the Tour de France, and those are representative of our economically and culturally diverse society. These stories will engage students' interest and encourage their own adjustment efforts.

To help students learn effectively and then apply what they have learned, I have provided proven study aids and opportunities for self-evaluation. The learning system in this book was developed with extensive feedback from instructors and students over two decades of teaching. This integrated system enables students to focus on key concepts and challenges them to think critically about them.

Additionally, each chapter contains self-assessment questionnaires and adjustment strategies to give students the resources to identify their own needs and improve their coping skills. These features, combined with an accessible, conversational writing style and a choice of highly interesting material, make *Human Adjustment* a very student-friendly text.

A SCIENTIFIC APPROACH

Human Adjustment presents psychology as a research-based science that can be applied successfully to students' own lives.

Students often have difficulty grasping the fact that the study of adjustment is a scientific endeavor supported by research. By frequently relating key ideas and concepts to studies, the book demonstrates this crucial idea. Not only do I cite classic psychological studies, but I also provide more than 500 references from 2004 and 2005 to illustrate that the field is continually evolving.

PERSONAL APPLICATIONS

Along with the real-world applications woven through the text, every chapter has at least two *Adjustment Strategies* and one or more *Self-Assessments* related to the topics being discussed. These sections provide important tools that allow students to apply their knowledge of psychology to their own benefit.

Human Adjustment contains more than 300 strategies that are described in Adjustment Strategies interludes. For example, there are strategies for thinking critically about adjustment, for achieving happiness and life satisfaction, for finding reliable human adjustment information on the Internet, for becoming a better listener, and for improving intercultural communication.

More than 30 Self-Assessments in the book encourage students to examine their own adjustment by answering a series of questions on a broad range of subjects. Chapter 5 (Coping), for example, includes the following Self-Assessments: How Emotionally Intelligent Am I? and My Coping Strategies. Information about how to score and interpret responses to the Self-Assessments is located in the appendix at the back of the book. Additional Self-Assessments and Adjustment Strategies can be found on the website for the book.

LEARNING TOOLS

Now more than ever, students struggle to find the main ideas in their courses. The learning system I have developed keeps the main ideas in front of the reader from the beginning to the end of each chapter.

Highlights of the learning system include the main headings, of which there are no more than six per chapter, and corresponding learning goals. At the beginning of the chapter, students will see the chapter outline and the learning goals presented side by side. Within the chapter, a mini-map with each main heading provides a visual overview of the main topics to be discussed in that section. At the end of each section, the learning goal for that section is repeated as part of a Review and Reflect summary, prompting students to review the key concepts in the section and answer a question that promotes critical thinking about the reading. At the end of the chapter, under the heading *Reach Your Learning Goals,* a complete map of the chapter topics appears, followed by a Summary that guides students through a bulleted review of the chapter's key concepts and ideas. The Summary answers the questions posed in the section Reviews within the chapter. The features of the learning system are illustrated in the Visual Student Preface that follows this preface.

Another very important tool, called Resources for Improving Adjustment, appears at the end of each chapter. This section lists the best self-help books and national support organizations related to topics covered in the chapter together with information about how to contact the organizations. Most of the recommended titles come from national surveys that I and my colleagues have conducted with more than 2,500 clinical and counseling psychologists affiliated with the American Psychological Association (Norcross, Santrock, & others, 2003).

I also selected the more than 400 websites referenced in the margins of the text. Links to these sites, as well as other learning tools, can be accessed by going to the website for *Human Adjustment* (www.mhhe.com/santrockha).

ACKNOWLEDGMENTS

Many people have played important roles in making this book a reality. In particular, I am indebted to Jane S. Halonen, my coauthor on a previous version of this text. A clinical psychologist who is now Dean of the College of Arts and Sciences at the University of Florida, Dr. Halonen was instrumental in developing for the other text applications that encourage students to hone their intellectual skills and actively engage with the concepts and principles of human adjustment, many of which have been retained in this book.

I am also especially grateful to Kathleen Field, an extraordinary developmental editor, who spent long hours improving the quality of *Human Adjustment.* In addition, I thank Steve Rutter, Psychology Publisher at McGraw-Hill, for asking me to write this book and John Wannemacher, Sponsoring Editor, for guiding its development. Judith Kromm, Director of Development, very competently coordinated many aspects of the project, as did Laura Kuhn, Editorial Assistant. Jane Dal Porto, Managing Editor, and Rick Hecker, Project Manager, superbly managed the production of the book. Laurie McGee did a great job of making the copyediting process as painless as possible. Laurie Entringer, Manager of Design, helped to make *Human Adjustment* a very attractive book, and Melissa Caughlin, Marketing Manager, contributed in many creative ways to the book.

I also owe special gratitude to the instructors teaching human adjustment courses who provided detailed feedback while the book was in development. Their comments have made *Human Adjustment* a much better book. In this regard, I thank the following individuals:

Ted Barker, *Walton Community College*
E. Thomas Dowd, *Kent State University*
Mary Beth Hartshorn, *Diablo Community College*
Ryan Kilmer, *University of North Carolina, Charlotte*
Bill Kohlmeyer, *Highland Community College*
R. McAnulty, *University of North Carolina, Charlotte*
Gary F. Meunier, *Ball State University*
Rebecca Rogers, *Augusta State University*
Jeffry Simpson, *Texas A & M University*
Marylou Robins, *San Jacinto College*
Sangeeta Singg, *Angelo State University*
Joseph Tloczynski, *Bloomsburg University*
Susan Weldon, *Eastern Michigan University*
Andrew Wenger, *University of Miami*

Supplements

My goal and that of McGraw-Hill was to create a student-oriented text and an integrated supplements package that will meet the unique needs of students and instructors. We hope that instructors will enjoy teaching with it and that it will not only motivate students to learn the material and think critically about what they read, but will also help them become well-adjusted individuals.

For the Instructor   The *Instructor's Manual* by Terry Pettijohn of Ohio State University provides many useful tools to enhance your teaching. For each chapter, the *Instructor's Manual* includes learning goals, an extended chapter outline, suggestions for teaching, lecture/discussion suggestions, video and film recommendations, classroom activities, and handouts. The *Instructor's Manual* is available on the Instructor's Resource CD-ROM and on the password-protected instructor's side of the website for the book (www.mhhe.com/santrockha).

The *Test Bank* by Jeannette Murphey of Meridian Community College contains more than 100 questions for each chapter of the book. The questions are available on the Instructor's Resource CD-ROM both as Word files and in computerized format. The Computerized Test Bank runs on both Macintosh and Windows computers and includes an editing feature that enables instructors to integrate their own questions, scramble items, and modify questions.

The **Instructor's Resource CD-ROM** enables instructors to customize materials for the course. This CD includes PowerPoint presentation slides prepared by Terry Pettijohn of Ohio State University, materials from the *Instructor's Manual,* the *Test Bank* and Computerized Test Bank, and a link to the text's website.

The **Classroom Performance System Guide and CD-ROM** allows instructors to gauge immediately what students are learning during lectures. With the Classroom Performance System (CPS) from **eInstruction,** instructors can ask questions, take polls, host classroom demonstrations, and get instant feedback. In addition, CPS makes it easy to take attendance, give and grade pop quizzes, or give formal paper-based class tests with multiple versions of the test using CPS for immediate grading.

For instructors who want to use CPS in the classroom, we offer a guide containing strategies for implementing the system, specific multiple-choice questions designed for in-class use, and classroom demonstrations for use with this system. For a quick, easy demonstration of CPS, go to www.mhhe.com/wmg/cps/psychology.

PageOut! makes it possible to build your own course website in less than an hour. You don't have to be a computer whiz to create a website with an exclusive McGraw-Hill product called PageOut! It requires no prior knowledge of HTML, no long hours of coding, and no design skills. For more information, visit the PageOut! website at www.pageout.net.

For the Student The **Student CD-ROM,** packaged free with each new copy of *Human Adjustment,* provides a dynamic set of interactivities and videos that will expand students' knowledge and understanding of how to become well adjusted. The CD includes additional self-assessments for most chapters. Also on the CD are short video segments, critical thinking exercises, and chapter quizzes with feedback. Accompanying each video segment is an overview, follow-up questions, and links to related websites, where students can find more information about the topic.

Student Study Guide by Kathleen Field includes the learning goals from the book, detailed chapter outlines, guided reviews, and multiple-choice practice tests. Answers to the practice tests are also provided.

The **Online Learning Center (www.mhhe.com/ santrockha)** is the website for *Human Adjustment.* On the student side of the website are additional chapter quizzes, the additional self-assessments, adjustment strategies, critical thinking exercises, as well as a glossary of terms used in the book and web links selected by John Santrock and referenced in the margins of the text.

Visual Student Preface

This book provides important study tools to help you learn more effectively about human adjustment. Especially important is the learning system that is integrated throughout each chapter. In the visual walk-through of features, be sure to pay attention to how the learning system works.

The Learning System

Key aspects of the learning system are the learning goals, chapter maps, and sections titled Review and Reflect, Reach Your Learning Goals, and Summary. All of these tools are linked together.

At the beginning of each chapter, you will see a page that includes both a chapter outline and three to six learning goals that preview the chapter's main themes and underscore the most important ideas in the chapter. Then, at the beginning of each major section of a chapter, you will see a mini–chapter map that provides a visual overview of the key topics in the section. At the end of each section is Review and Reflect, which restates the learning goal for the section, asks a series of review questions related to the mini–chapter map, and a question that encourages you to think critically about a topic related to the section appears. At the end of the chapter, you will come to a section titled Reach Your Learning Goals. This includes an overall chapter map that visually organizes all of the main headings, a statement of the chapter's learning goals, and a summary of the chapter's content that is directly linked to the chapter outline at the beginning of the chapter and the questions asked in the Review part of Review and Reflect within the chapter. The summary essentially answers the questions asked in the chapter Review sections.

A visual presentation of the learning goals system follows.

Chapter Opening Outline and Learning Goals

The outline show the organization of topics by headings. Primary topic headings are printed in blue capital letters. The Learning Goals highlight the main ideas in the chapter by section.

CHAPTER 3

The Self, Identity, and Values

Chapter Outline	Learning Goals
THE SELF Self-Concept Self-Esteem	**1** Discuss self-concept and self-esteem
IDENTITY Erikson's View The Four Statuses of Identity Developmental Changes Ethnic Identity Gender and Identity	**2** Describe what identity is and how it is formed
VALUES Exploring Values College Students' Values Meaning in Life Sociocultural Perspectives on Values	**3** Summarize some important aspects of value
RELIGION The Scope of Religion in People's Lives Religion and Health Religious Coping	**4** Characterize the role of religion in people's lives

Mini-Chapter Map

This visual preview displays the main headings and subheadings for each section of the chapter.

4 RELIGION

- The Scope of Religion in People's Lives
- Religious Coping
- Religion and Health

Religion is an important aspect of the self, identity, and values of many individuals. Recall from chapter 1 that happy people tend to have a meaningful religious faith (Diener, Lucas, & Oishi, 2002). Just how pervasive is religion in people's lives and how is it linked to their health? What is involved in religious coping.

The Scope of Religion in People's Lives

morita therapy Emphasizes accepting feelings, knowing one's purposes, and most important, doing what needs to be done.

Religion plays an important role in the lives of many people around the world. For example, 98 percent of respondents in India, 88 percent in Italy, 72 percent in France, and 63 percent in Scandinavia say that they believe in God (Gallup, 1987).

In the McArthur Study of Midlife Development, more than 70 percent of U.S. middle-aged adults said they are religious and consider spirituality a major part of

This approach—doing what needs to be done, rather than seeking pleasurable activity, and experiencing the task fully—is reflected in morita tasks. A therapy based on Zen Buddhism, **morita therapy** emphasizes accepting feelings, knowing one's purposes, and most important, doing what needs to be done. Morita exercises not only teach you to do constructive work with full attention but also decrease egocentrism and self-consciousness.

Review and Reflect

Review questions enable you to quiz yourself on the key ideas and find out whether you've met the learning goals for one section of a chapter before continuing to the next main topic. The question for reflection helps you to think about what you've just read and apply it. Answering these questions will help you to remember key points and concepts.

Review and Reflect

3 Summarize some important aspects of values

REVIEW

- What are values? Why is it important to clarify your values?
- What are college students' values? What is service learning and how does it influence people?
- What are some guidelines in searching for meaning in life?
- What are some sociocultural perspectives on values?

REFLECT

- What experiences have you had in volunteering and participating in community service? If you have had these experiences, what impact did they have on you? If you have not participated in volunteering and community service, what aspect interests you the most?

Reach Your Learning Goals

This section includes a complete chapter map and a summary restating the Learning Goals and answering the bulleted review question from the chapter. Use it as a guide to help you organize your study of the chapter, *not* as a substitute for reading and studying the chapter.

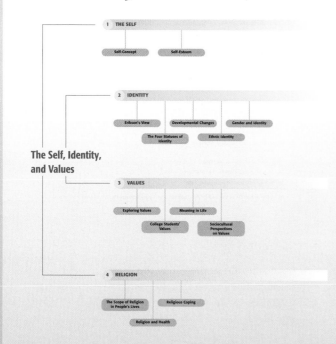

Reach Your Learning Goals

The Self, Identity, and Values

1 THE SELF
- Self-Concept
- Self-Esteem

2 IDENTITY
- Erikson's View
- Developmental Changes
- Gender and Identity
- The Four Statuses of Identity
- Ethnic Identity

3 VALUES
- Exploring Values
- Meaning in Life
- College Students' Values
- Sociocultural Perspectives on Values

4 RELIGION
- The Scope of Religion in People's Lives
- Religious Coping
- Religion and Health

Summary

1 Discuss self-concept and self-esteem

- Self-concept is an individual's perception of his or her abilities, personality, and other attributes; it consists of the overall thoughts and feelings about one's self. The self-concept includes representations of multiple selves—such as the real or actual self, the ideal self, the ought self, hoped-for possible selves, and dreaded possible selves—as well as representations of these selves from various viewpoints.

  Higgins' self-discrepancy theory argues that discrepancies between the actual and ideal selves tend to create dejection-relation emotions and discrepancies between the actual self and ought self tend to create agitated emotions.
- Self-esteem is a person's overall evaluation of his or her self-worth or self-image. This evaluation does not necessarily match reality. People have both a general level of self-esteem and fluctuating degrees of self-esteem related to specific domains of life. Self-esteem tends to be stable at least across a month or so. There is controversy about whether self-esteem varies according to the age of the individual. Researchers have found only moderate correlations between self-esteem and school performance and varying correlations between self-esteem and job performance. Self-esteem is strongly correlated with happiness. Some individuals who have high self-esteem are narcissistic. Strategies for enhancing self-esteem involve identifying sources of low self-esteem, facing a problem and coping with it, experiencing emotional support and social approval, taking responsibility for one's self-esteem, achieving, and exploring resources to improve self-understanding.

2 Describe what identity is and how it is formed

- Identity versus identity confusion is Erikson's fifth developmental stage, which individuals experience during adolescence and emerging adulthood. Youth enter a psychosocial moratorium during which they experiment with personalities and roles as they search for an identity. In technological societies like the United States, the vocational identity is especially important. Identity development is done in bits and pieces, and identity changes may occur throughout life.
- Marcia proposed four identity statuses: diffused, foreclosed, moratorium, and achieved. A combination of crisis (exploration) and commitment yields one of the statuses.
- Some experts believe that the main identity changes take place in late adolescence or emerging adulthood,

rather than in early adolescence. College upperclassmen are more likely to be identity achieved than are freshmen or high school students, although many college students are still wrestling with ideological commitments. Individuals often follow "moratorium–achievement–moratorium–achievement" cycles.
- Throughout the world ethnic minority groups have struggled to maintain their cultural identities while blending into majority culture. Adolescence and emerging adulthood often represent a special juncture in the identity development of ethnic minority individuals because for the first time they consciously confront their ethnic identity. Many ethnic minority individuals have a bicultural identity. Helms proposed a model of ethnic identity development.
- Erikson believed that males have a stronger vocational identity, females a stronger social identity. However, researchers are finding that these gender differences are disappearing.

3 Summarize some important aspects of values

- Values are standards that we maintain about the things we prefer or ideas that capture our allegiance. Without deeply exploring and reflecting about your values, you may spend too much time on things that aren't really important to you. Clarifying your values can help you identify the goals you want to pursue and where to direct your motivation and time.
- Over the past two decades U.S. college students have shown an increased concern for personal well-being and a decreased concern for the well-being of others, especially the disadvantaged. However, an increasing number of students are showing an interest in volunteer or community service work. Service learning is a form of education that promotes social responsibility and service to the community; participating in service learning is related to higher grades, increased goal setting, and higher self-esteem.
- Frankl believes that examining the finiteness of our existence leads to exploration of meaning in life. Baumeister argues that a quest for a meaningful life involves four main needs: purpose, values, efficacy, and self-worth.
- Some critics argue that Americans are too concerned with self-fulfillment and personal identity. Non-Western Zen Buddhism offers a negative perspective on the Western preoccupation with individuality and worrying so much about failure. Zen Buddhism emphasizes living in the present moment by focusing on the task at hand. This approach is reflected in morita therapy.

Other Learning System Features

Images of Adjustment

Each chapter opens with a high-interest story that is linked to the chapter's content.

Adjustment Strategies

Interludes appear after a topic is discussed to provide specific strategies for adjusting more effectively in life.

Adjustment Strategies
For Increasing Self-Esteem

Here are six strategies that can increase an individual's self-esteem:

1. **Identify your sources of self-esteem and what is causing low self-esteem.** A key first step in improving self-esteem is to determine what is contributing to low self-esteem. Is the source of low self-esteem academic performance? relationship problems? unrealistic insecurities? fear of losing your job? or possibly some combination of these or other problems?
2. **Face a problem and try to cope with it.** Self-esteem is often increased when individuals try to cope with a problem rather than avoiding it (Bednar, Wells, & Peterson, 1995). Facing problems realistically, honestly, and nondefensively leads to favorable thoughts about oneself, which lead to self-approval and higher self-esteem. In chapter 5, "Coping," we will describe a number of coping strategies that can benefit self-esteem.
3. **Seek emotional support.** Emotional support and social approval have a positive influence on self-esteem. However, some individuals experience little emotional support or social approval because their families are filled with conflict or their romantic relationships are marred by hostility. In some cases, alternative sources of emotional support can improve self-esteem. Quality friendships, counseling, or therapy can sometimes compensate for shortcomings in other sources of emotional support.
4. **Take responsibility for your self-esteem.** Assume that you have the ability to improve your self-esteem and take the initiative to do so (Crocker & Park, 2003).
5. **Look for opportunities to achieve.** Achievement can also improve self-esteem (Baumeister & others, 2003). Perhaps you can find a straightforward skill to master or a task to complete. If you know specific steps to take to

Self-Assessment

Self-Assessments provide you with an opportunity to evaluate yourself on a topic related to the discussion at that point in the text.

Images of Adjustment

Maxine Hong Kingston, Bridging Cultural Worlds

Maxine Hong Kingston's vivid portrayals of her Chinese ancestry and the struggles of Chinese immigrants have made her one of the world's leading Asian American writers. Kingston's parents were both Chinese immigrants. Born in California in 1940, she spent many hours working with her parents and five brothers and sisters in the family's laundry. As a youth, Kingston was profoundly influenced by her parents' struggle to adapt to American culture and descriptions of their Chinese heritage.

Growing up as she did, Kingston felt the pull of two very different cultures. She was especially intrigued by stories about Chinese women who were perceived as either privileged or degraded.

Her first book is titled *The Woman Warrior: Memoirs of a Girlhood among Ghosts*. According to a Chinese folk saying that Kingston (1976) recounts, "Better to raise geese than girls." In *The Woman Warrior*, Kingston also described her aunt, who gave birth to an illegitimate child. Because having a child outside of wedlock was taboo and perceived as a threat to the community's stability, the entire Chinese village condemned her, pushing her to kill herself and her child. From then on, even mentioning her name was forbidden.

In 1980, Kingston published *China Men*, which won the American Book Award for nonfiction and was runner-up for the Pulitzer Prize. Based on the experiences of her father and several generations of other male relatives, the book examines the lives of Chinese men who left their homeland to settle in the United States. It contains stories of loneliness and discrimination as well as determination and strength.

Kingston taught at the University of California at Berkeley. She says that she doesn't want to be viewed as an exotic writer but as someone who writes and teaches about Americans and what it means to be human. Kingston says she likes to guide people in how to find meaning in their lives, especially by exploring their

SELF-ASSESSMENT 3.1
My Self-Esteem

Below is a list of statements that deal with your general feelings about yourself. Place a check mark in the appropriate column for each item based on whether you strongly agree with it (1), agree with it (2), disagree with it (3), or strongly disagree with it (4).

Item	Strongly Agree (1)	Agree (2)	Disagree (3)	Strongly Disagree (4)
1. On the whole, I am satisfied with myself.				
2. At times, I think I'm no good at all.				
3. I feel that I have a number of good qualities.				
4. I am able to do things as well as most other people.				
5. I feel I do not have much to be proud of.				
6. I certainly feel useless at times.				
7. I feel that I'm a person of worth, at least on an equal plane with others.				
8. I wish I could have more respect for myself.				
9. All in all, I am inclined to feel that I am a failure.				
10. I take a positive attitude toward myself.				

Go to the appendix at the end of the book for scoring and interpretation of your responses.

Chapter 3

SELF-ASSESSMENT 3.1 MY SELF-ESTEEM

Scoring

Add up your scores for items 1, 2, 4, 6, and 7 = _____

Now reverse your scores on items 3, 5, 8, 9, and 10 (That is, if you had a 1—strongly agree–give yourself a 4 instead: if you had a 2 on item 1, give yourself a 3, and so on) = _____

Next, total your scores for the two sets of items to get your overall self-esteem score: _____

Interpretation

Your score can range from 10 to 40. If you scored 35 to 40 points, you likely have very high self-esteem. If you scored 30 to 34 points you likely have high self-esteem. If you scored 20 to 29 points, you likely have low self-esteem. And if you scored 10 to 19 points, you likely have very low self-esteem.

If your total self-esteem score was below 30 points, think about ways that you can improve your self-esteem. Go back and review the strategies described in chapter 3 for improving self-esteem. Also, if you feel that you have low self-esteem, consider talking with a counselor at your college about your self-esteem.

In an appendix at the end of the book, scoring and interpretation of your responses on the Self-Assessments are provided.

Key Terms and Glossary

Key terms appear in boldface. Their definitions appear in the margin near where they are introduced.

Key Terms

self-concept 81	self-esteem 83	psychological	ethnic identity 93
actual self 82	narcissism 87	moratorium 89	values 95
ideal self 82	identity 89	identity diffusion 90	value conflict 95
ought self 82	identity versus identity	identity foreclosure 90	service learning 97
self-discrepancy theory 82	confusion stage 89	identity moratorium 90	morita therapy 100
possible selves 82		identity achievement 90	

Key terms also are listed and page-referenced at the end of each chapter.

Glossary

A

abnormal behavior Behavior that is deviant, maladaptive, or personally distressful. 426

acculturative stress The negative consequences that result from contact between two distinctive cultural groups. 129

active-behavioral strategies Coping responses in which individuals take some type of action to improve their problem situation. 145

active-cognitive strategies Coping responses in which individuals actively think about a situation in an effort to adjust more effectively. 145

actual self Your representation of the attributes you believe or you actually possess. 82

gradual deterioration of memory, reasoning, language, and, eventually, physical function. 340

ambivalent attachment style The caregiver is inconsistently available and when present often overbearing with affection. These infants are typically anxious because they can't predict when and how the caregiver will respond to their needs. They may cling anxiously to the caregiver and fight against the closeness by pushing away. 241

androgens The class of hormones that predominate in males and are produced by the testes in males and by the adrenal glands in both males and females. 396

androgyny The presence of a high degree of feminine and masculine characteristics in the same individual. 378

anorexia nervosa An eating disorder that

archetypes The name Jung gave to the emotionally laden ideas and images in the collective unconscious that have rich meaning for all people. 43

attitudes Evaluations of people, objects, and ideas. 175

attributions Thoughts about why people behave the way they do. 173

authoritarian parenting A restrictive, punitive parenting style in which the parent exhorts the child to follow the parent's directions and to respect work and effort. Firm limits and controls are placed on the child, and little verbal exchange is allowed. This style is associated with children's socially incompetent behavior. 279

authoritative parenting A parenting style that encourages children to be independent but still places limits and controls on their

Key terms are alphabetically listed, defined, and page-referenced in a glossary at the end of the book.

The Self
Rogers' View of Self-Concept
Higgins' Self Research

- The **actual self** is your representation of the attributes you believe you actually possess.
- The **ideal self** is your representation of the attributes you would like to ideally possess—that is, a representation of your hopes, aspirations, and wishes.
- The **ought self** is your representation of the attributes you believe you should possess—that is, a representation of your duties, obligations, and responsibilities.

Each of these three domains of the self can be seen from either the individual's view or the view of a significant other such as a parent, spouse, or friend.

What happens when these representations do not match? According to Higgins' (1987, 1999, 2000) **self-discrepancy theory,** problems occur when representations from different viewpoints or from different domains are inconsistent, or discrepant. Two types of discrepancies are especially problematic and create different emotions:

- Discrepancies between the actual and ideal selves lead people to experience dejection-related emotions, such as sadness, disappointment, and shame. They feel dejected because they believe they have failed to reach the goals that they set for themselves and that others set for them.
- Second, discrepancies between the actual self and the ought self can produce agitated emotions, such as anxiety, fear, and guilt. In these instances, people believe that they have failed to live up to standards (established by themselves or others) for good, dutiful, and responsible behavior. The agitated emotions emerge because people feel they are being punished (by themselves or by others) for not doing what they ought to do.

To test these predictions about the effects of discrepancies, college students were asked to list traits or attributes that described their actual, ideal, and ought selves (Higgins, 1984). Then matches and mismatches in traits across the three domains were coded. For example, as part of a self-description a person might evaluate the actual self as "friendly," "sincere," and "hot-tempered," and the ought self as "friendly," "sincere," and "calm." These evaluations include two matches (friendly and sincere) and one mismatch (hot-tempered and calm). In this study, researchers also measured the students' levels of depression (which involves dejection-related emotions) and anxiety (which involves agitated-related emotions). As predicted, discrepancies between the actual self and ideal self were associated with depression (but not anxiety); discrepancies between the actual self and ought self were associated with anxiety (but not depression) (see figure 3.1).

Not all discrepancies produce the predicted emotional states. Self-discrepancies are most likely to lead to the expected outcomes (1) when the expectancies are large, (2) when you are aware of the discrepancy, (3) when the discrepancy is important to you, and (4) when the discrepancy is real rather than imagined (Dweck, Higgins, & Grant-Pillow, 2003; Higgins, 1999).

Possible Selves Another way of analyzing self-concept involves our **possible selves,** which are conceptions of what we might become, including what we would like to become and what we are afraid of becoming (Markus & Nurius, 1986). Thus, our possible selves reflect both the outcomes that we hope for and the ones that we dread (Bybee & Wells, 2003). Some possible selves are more important to us than others. For example, a person's possible selves might include being a doctor, being fit, and being an excellent pianist, but being a doctor might be far more important to the person than the other possible selves.

Each possible self is a construction by the person, and the person may spell it out in considerable detail (McAdams, 2001). For example, if one of a person's possible selves is the *unemployed self,* the person might develop a painfully clear picture of this

actual self Your representation of the attributes you believe you or you actually possess.

ideal self Your representation of the attributes you would like to ideally possess—that is, a representation of your hopes, aspirations, and wishes.

ought self Your representation of the attributes you believe you should possess—that is, a representation of your duties, obligations, and responsibilities.

self-discrepancy theory Higgins' theory that problems occur when representations from different viewpoints or from different domains are inconsistent or discrepant. Two types of discrepancies are especially problematic: between the actual and ideal selves (produces dejection-related emotions) and between the actual and ought selves (produces agitated emotions).

possible selves Individuals' conceptions of what they might become, including what they would like to become and what they are afraid of becoming.

Critical Thinking and Content Questions in Photograph Captions

Most photographs have a caption that ends with a critical thinking or knowledge question in italics to stimulate further thought about a topic.

Sociocultural Perspectives on Values

The values of Western culture are likely to encourage us to pursue needs for self-worth individually, by seeking to become our hoped-for possible selves and enhance our self-esteem. What are the consequences of emphasizing individuality over the collective good? Roy Baumeister (1991b) suggests that Americans are too concerned with self-fulfillment and personal identity, so much so that these have become burdens for many people. Because of the high priority Americans place on developing, maintaining, and enhancing a positive self-image, many of us are too self-critical, too motivated for change, and too stressed.

The pressures of seeking self-fulfillment can be overwhelming. Some people avoid these pressures by turning to activities that diminish self-preoccupation. Some turn on the television or read science fiction books. Others meditate or listen to classical music. Some people lose themselves in dance, others in a pitcher of beer. Society offers and endorses many ways to forget ourselves for a while. Unfortunately, many forms of escape have high costs. Some people develop substance-abuse problems, attempt suicide, or join radical cults. Escaping the burden of maintaining a personal identity can create even more serious challenges to the integrity of the self.

Non-Western Zen Buddhism offers a negative perspective on the Western preoccupation with individuality and worrying so much about failure. Zen Buddhism

Zen Buddhism being practiced. *What are some characteristics of Zen Buddhism?*

The Internet

Web icons appear a number of times in each chapter. They signal you to go to the book's website, where you will find connecting links that provide additional information on the topic discussed in the text. The labels under the web icon appear as web links at the Santrock *Human Adjustment*, 1st ed. website, under the chapter for easy access.

What are some of the personal benefits of volunteering?

less self-centered and more strongly motivated to help others. In service learning, adolescents and emerging adults engage in activities such as tutoring, helping older adults, working in a hospital, assisting at a child-care center, or cleaning up a vacant lot to make a play area. Thus, service learning takes education out into the community (Flanagan, 2004; Youniss & others, 2003).

A key feature of service learning is that it benefits both the student volunteers and the recipients of their help. For example, one college student worked as a reading tutor for students from low-income backgrounds with reading skills well below their grade levels. She commented that until she did the tutoring she did not realize how many students had not experienced the same opportunities that she had when she was growing up. An especially rewarding moment was when one young girl told her, "I want to learn to read like you so I can go to college when I grow up."

Volunteers tend to share certain characteristics, such as extraversion, a commitment to others, and a high degree of self-understanding (Eisenberg & Morris, 2004). Also, women are more likely to volunteer to engage in community service than men (Eisenberg & Morris, 2004).

Researchers have found that volunteering and community service benefit adolescents and emerging adults in a number of ways:

www.mhhe.com/santrockha

College Students' Values

- Their grades improve, they become more motivated, and set more goals (Johnson & others, 1998; Search Institute, 1995).
- Their self-esteem improves (Hamburg, 1997; Johnson & others, 1998).
- They have an improved sense of being able to make a difference for others (Search Institute, 1995).
- They become less alienated (Calabrese & Schumer, 1986).
- They increasingly reflect on society's political organization and moral order (Yates, 1995).

Meaning in Life

For some people, helping others is a value in itself; for others, it is a way of finding meaning in life. This value was the topic of a book by Austrian psychiatrist Viktor Frankl. Frankl's mother, father, brother, and wife died in the concentration camps and gas chambers in Auschwitz, Poland. Frankl survived the concentration camp and went on to write *Man's Search for Meaning* (1984).

Frankl emphasizes each person's uniqueness and the finiteness of life. He believes that examining the finiteness of our existence and the certainty of death adds meaning to life. If life were not finite, says Frankl, we could spend our life doing just about whatever we please because time would continue forever. Frankl proposed that people need to ask themselves such questions as why they exist, what they want from life, and what the meaning of their life is.

Roy Baumeister (1991b; Baumeister & Vohs, 2002) argues that the quest for a meaningful life can be understood in terms of four main needs that guide how people try to make sense out of their lives:

- *Need for purpose.* Present events draw meaning from their connection with future events. Purposes can be divided into (1) goals and (2) fulfillments. Life can be oriented toward a future anticipated state, such as living happily ever after or being in love.
- *Need for values.* This can lend a sense of life's goodness and justify certain courses of action. Values help to determine whether certain acts are right or wrong. Frankl (1984) emphasized value as the main form of meaning that people need.

www.mhhe.com/santrockha

Viktor Frankl

Resources for Improving Your Adjustment

Good self-help books and national support organizations related to the topics in the chapter are recommended.

Resources for Improving Your Adjustment

Self-Esteem

(2000) by Matthew McKay and Patrick Fanning. Oakland, CA: New Harbinger.

This book includes opportunities for you to evaluate your self-esteem and provides numerous strategies for increasing self-esteem. The authors especially emphasize the importance of countering negative self-statements.

Women & Self-Esteem

(1984) by Linda Sanford and Mary Donovan. New York: Anchor Doubleday.

Women & Self-Esteem explains why women often have low self-esteem and how they can improve the way they think about themselves. The authors provide readers with exercises that will help you engage in self-evaluation, reduce negative self-images, and decrease self-destructive behaviors. This is a good book for women with low self-esteem.

Man's Search for Meaning

(1984) by Viktor Frankl. New York: Pocket.

Frankl believes that the three most distinct human qualities are spirituality, freedom, and responsibility. The book will challenge you to think deeply about your values and the meaning of life.

Man's Search for Meaning was rated in the highest category (5 stars) in the national survey of self-help books (Norcross, Santrock, & others, 2003).

The Seven Habits of Highly Effective People

(1989) by Steven Covey. New York: Simon & Schuster.

Covey's best-selling book provides an in-depth examination of how people's perspectives and values determine how competent they are in their work and personal lives. This book was highly rated (5 stars) in the national survey of self-help books.

The Road Less Traveled

(1978) by M. Scott Peck. New York: Simon & Schuster.

The Road Less Traveled presents an approach to self-fulfillment based on spirituality and emotions. Peck begins by stating that life is difficult and that we all suffer pain and disappointment. He believes we should face up to life's difficulties, that people are thirsting for integrity in their lives, and that people need to move spirituality into all phases of their lives. Peck speaks of four important tools to use in life's journey: delaying gratification, accepting responsibility, dedication to the truth, and balancing. *The Road Less Traveled* received 4 of 5 stars in the national survey of self-help books (Norcross, Santrock, & others, 2003).

E-Learning Tools

To help you master the material in a chapter, you will find a number of valuable study tools on CD-ROM and the book's Online Learning Center, including self-assessments, critical thinking exercises, applications exercises, adjustment strategies assessment and planning, and video segments.

Resources for Improving Your Adjustment

Self-Esteem

(2000) by Matthew McKay and Patrick Fanning. Oakland, CA: New Harbinger.

This book includes opportunities for you to evaluate your self-esteem and provides numerous strategies for increasing self-esteem. The authors especially emphasize the importance of countering negative self-statements.

Women & Self-Esteem

(1984) by Linda Sanford and Mary Donovan. New York: Anchor Doubleday.

Women & Self-Esteem explains why women often have low self-esteem and how they can improve the way they think about themselves. The authors provide readers with exercises that will help you engage in self-evaluation, reduce negative self-images, and decrease self-destructive behaviors. This is a good book for women with low self-esteem.

Man's Search for Meaning

(1984) by Viktor Frankl. New York: Pocket.

Frankl believes that the three most distinct human qualities are spirituality, freedom, and responsibility. The book will challenge you to think deeply about your values and the meaning of life.

Man's Search for Meaning was rated in the highest category (5 stars) in the national survey of self-help books (Norcross, Santrock, & others, 2003).

The Seven Habits of Highly Effective People

(1989) by Steven Covey. New York: Simon & Schuster.

Covey's best-selling book provides an in-depth examination of how people's perspectives and values determine how competent they are in their work and personal lives. This book was highly rated (5 stars) in the national survey of self-help books.

The Road Less Traveled

(1978) by M. Scott Peck. New York: Simon & Schuster.

The Road Less Traveled presents an approach to self-fulfillment based on spirituality and emotions. Peck begins by stating that life is difficult and that we all suffer pain and disappointment. He believes we should face up to life's difficulties, that people are thirsting for integrity in their lives, and that people need to move spirituality into all phases of their lives. Peck speaks of four important tools to use in life's journey: delaying gratification, accepting responsibility, dedication to the truth, and balancing. *The Road Less Traveled* received 4 of 5 stars in the national survey of self-help books (Norcross, Santrock, & others, 2003).

 E-Learning Tools

www.mhhe.com/santrock

To help you master the material in this chapter, you will find a number of valuable study tools on the student CD-ROM that accompanies this book. In addition, visit the Online Learning Center for *Human Adjustment*, where you can find these valuable resources for Chapter 3, "The Self, Identity, and Values."

SELF-ASSESSMENT

In Text

You can complete these self-assessments in the text:
- Self-Assessment 3.1: *My Self-Esteem*
- Self-Assessment 3.2: *Do I Have Narcissistic Tendencies?*
- Self-Assessment 3.3: *What Is My Identity?*
- Self-Assessment 3.4: *What Are My Values?*
- Self-Assessment 3.5: *My Spiritual Well-Being*

Additional Self-Assessments

Complete these self-assessments on the Online Learning Center:
- Self-Assessment: *Comparing My Attitudes and Values with Those of Other College Students*
- Self-Assessment: *What Is My Purpose in Life?*

THINK CRITICALLY

To practice your critical thinking skills, complete these exercises on the Online Learning Center:
- *Advertising and Self-Enhancement* relates to commercials and self-esteem
- *Major Decisions and Identity Formation* focuses on the decisions you make and how they affect your identity
- *Value Billboards* involves T-shirt decorations and values
- *Faith and Evidence* deals with gender differences in religion

APPLY YOUR KNOWLEDGE

1. Self-Esteem and the Average Person.

Is the idea of self-esteem discussed by psychologists the same as the everyday person's perception of self-esteem? To find out, select the items that researchers have found to be associated with or characteristic of good self-esteem in your textbook. Write out each one and put "true" and "false" next to the characteristic. Then, ask five people to indicate whether they think the item is

privileged in another area. In addition, we often fail to recognize areas where we are privileged because we have learned to take it for granted. Although people can recognize that some are "under-privileged" we often have difficulty seeing other things as "over-privileged."

a. Begin by listing all the ways in which you are privileged. Think hard, remembering that we often fail to recognize areas of privilege.

b. After you have made your list, compare it with the list provided. Did you fail to identify any areas of privilege? Do you now recognize your privilege, or do you deny that people in the groups listed get better treatment than those against whom they would be compared?

c. Try this exercise on at least three friends. Did you notice any trends?

Privilege is increasingly an area of interest with regard to self-concept. How do your areas of privilege affect your self concept? How do they reflect your concept of people around you?

 VIDEO SEGMENT

Culture and the Self

If, as Hazel Markus argues, all selves are culture-specific, how does the sense of self fostered by individualist cultures differ from the self encouraged by collectivist cultures? The video for chapter 3 on the CD-ROM describes these two types of selves.

Self-Assessment

These include self-assessments from the text that you can fill out and have your scores automatically calculated and also additional self-assessments.

Think Critically

To practice your critical thinking skills, you can complete a number of exercises.

Apply Your Knowledge

This exercise consists of four situations in which you are asked to apply the knowledge you have learned in the chapter to the situations.

Video Segments

The CD-Rom has a number of video segments that focus on adjustment topics.

Adjusting to Life

Chapter Outline		*Learning Goals*

EXPLORING ADJUSTMENT   **1**
What Is Adjustment?
Contexts, Diversity, and Adjustment
Thinking Critically About Adjustment

1 Identify some key concepts that provide a foundation for understanding adjustment

SUBJECTIVE WELL-BEING AND ADJUSTMENT   **2**
Are Rich People Happier?
Who Is Happy?

2 Define subjective well-being and describe the factors related to it

THE SCIENTIFIC APPROACH TO ADJUSTMENT   **3**
Psychology and Adjustment
Adopting a Scientific Attitude
Using the Scientific Method
Experimental and Correlational Research
Being a Wise Consumer of Research Information

3 Characterize the scientific foundations of the study of adjustment

RESOURCES FOR IMPROVING ADJUSTMENT   **4**
Mental Health Professionals
National Support Groups
Self-Help Books
The Internet

4 Discuss some resources for improving adjustment and cautions in their use

Images of Adjustment

Ted Kaczynski and Alice Walker

Ted Kaczynski, the convicted Unabomber, traced his difficulties to growing up as a genius in a kid's body and not fitting in when he was a child.

Alice Walker won the Pulitzer Prize for her book *The Color Purple.* Like the characters in her book, Walker overcame pain and anger to triumph and celebrate the human spirit.

Ted Kaczynski sprinted through high school, not bothering with his junior year and making only passing efforts at social contact. Off to Harvard at age 16, Ted was a loner during his college years. One of his roommates at Harvard said that Ted had a special way of avoiding people: he would quickly shuffle by them and slam the door behind him.

After obtaining his Ph.D. in mathematics at the University of Michigan, Kaczynski became a professor at the University of California at Berkeley. His colleagues there remember him as hiding from situations—no friends, no allies, no networking. After several years at Berkeley, Kaczynski resigned and moved to a rural area of Montana where he lived as a hermit in a crude shack for 25 years. Town residents described him as a bearded eccentric. In 1996, he was arrested and charged with being the notorious Unabomber, America's most wanted killer who sent 16 mail bombs in 17 years that left 23 people wounded and maimed, and 3 people dead. In 1998, he pleaded guilty to the offenses and was sentenced to life in prison.

A decade before Kaczynski allegedly mailed his first bomb, Alice Walker spent her days battling racism in Mississippi. She had recently won her first writing fellowship, but rather than use the money to follow her dream of moving to Senegal, Africa, she put herself into the heart and heat of the civil rights movement. Walker grew up knowing the brutal effects of poverty and racism. Born in 1944, she was the eighth child of Georgia sharecroppers who earned $300 a year. When Walker was 8, her brother accidentally shot her in the left eye with a BB gun. By the time her parents got her to the hospital a week later (they had no car), she was blind in that eye, which had developed a disfiguring layer of scar tissue. Despite the odds against her, Walker went on to become an essayist, a poet, an award-winning novelist, a short-story writer, and a social activist who, like her characters (especially the women), has overcome pain and anger. She won a Pulitzer Prize for her book *The Color Purple.*

How can one individual, so full of promise, like Ted Kaczynski, adjust so poorly and commit brutal acts of violence and another, like Alice Walker, adjust so successfully and turn poverty and trauma into a rich literary harvest? Why can one individual pick up the pieces of a life shattered by tragedy, such as a loved one's death, whereas another one seems to come unhinged by life's minor hassles? Why are some individuals whirlwinds—successful in school, involved in a network of friends, and full of energy—while others stay on the sidelines, mere spectators of life? If you have ever wondered why some people adjust more effectively than others, you have asked yourself the central question we explore in this book.

In this chapter, we begin to examine some of the factors that might explain why people like Ted Kaczynski and Alice Walker differ so dramatically in the way they adjust to life's experiences. We explore the nature of adjustment, including strategies for thinking critically about adjustment; describe what makes people happy and satisfied with their lives; provide a scientific foundation for studying adjustment; and discuss resources for improving adjustment.

1   EXPLORING ADJUSTMENT

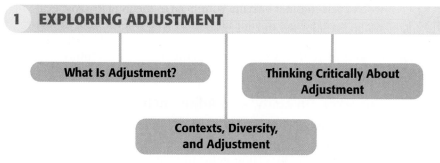

Does your lifestyle seem faster paced and more stressful than the lifestyles of your parents and grandparents? Indicative of the stressful times in which we live today, the U.S. divorce rate has doubled and depression has increased substantially since 1960 (Myers, 2000). In one recent survey, 40 percent of U.S. adults said they experience stress "frequently" (Saad, 2001).

The increasingly complex, fast-paced world produces overwhelming stress for some individuals, such as Ted Kaczynski. He decided to fight the system with bombs, adjusting to the challenges of our world by resorting to violence, and ended up losing his own freedom.

What Is Adjustment?

What can you do to cope with the stress of a fast-paced life? Answering this questions requires knowledge of **adjustment**, which is the psychological process of adapting to, coping with, and managing the challenges of everyday life. Adjustment is involved when a student develops better study habits; when an employee learns to get along better with co-workers; when a person redefines life after divorce; when a person remains calm enough to help family members after a disaster, such as the 9/11/01 terrorist attacks; when a workaholic executive adopts a more balanced and relaxed lifestyle; when a person in an ethnic conflict tries to view the problem from the other person's perspective; and when a self-centered adult learns how to be sensitive to another's feelings.

Sometimes the word *adjustment* is used with a negative tone. Adjustment can imply a passive acceptance of conditions, which allows the status quo to be maintained. During the long years of segregation, many people argued that African Americans should just "adjust" to second-class citizenship and that they should just learn to make the best they could of life within the limits set by White society. But Alice Walker is one of those who chose a different kind of adjustment. Rather than adapting to life as she found it, she challenged the society around her through the civil rights movement. In some circumstances, we probably should not adjust to conditions but instead foster changes in the circumstances themselves (Blonna, 2005; Maddux & Winstead, 2005).

Adjustment without growth is likely to be a hollow achievement. Growth involves learning, expanding your awareness, accepting new challenges, and coping effectively (Glidden-Tracey, 2005). This book is about adjustment and growth. Many of the concepts we will explore are useful in coping effectively with *hassles*—small, everyday stressful experiences such as being rudely interrupted, getting a parking ticket, or having someone cut in front of you when you are driving. However, you also will read

adjustment The psychological process of adapting to, coping with, and managing the challenges of everyday life.

Context is an important dimension of psychology. *Contexts* are settings, which are influenced by historical, economic, social, and cultural factors. Without reference to context, the racial tolerance of the college students shown here cannot be fully understood.

about how you can adjust effectively when you experience larger, more complex events, such as the death of a loved one, an illness, or the end of a long-standing relationship.

We all have the capacity to understand ourselves better, use better strategies to solve our personal problems, and think more clearly about how to adapt to stressful circumstances or overcome them (Blonna, 2005; Folkman & Moskowitz, 2004; Hankin & Abela, 2005). Thus, I hope that after finishing this book you won't even consider burying your head in the sand to avoid dealing with challenges in your life, but instead will use your knowledge to modify problematic aspects of your life. After all, what effort is more worthwhile than improving your own future?

Contexts, Diversity, and Adjustment

What is it that people adjust *to*? The study of adjustment highlights the fact we do not live in a vacuum. The settings in which we live affect our lives, presenting not only opportunities and rewards but also problems and demands that we must adjust to (López & Guarnaccia, 2005). **Contexts** refer to the historical, economic, social, and cultural factors and settings that influence us. Everything we think, say, and do is colored by where we come from, whom we have spent time with, and what has happened to us.

Ecological Theory   The contexts of our lives include our homes, schools, churches, cities, neighborhoods, communities, and colleges, as well as nations. The role that these contexts play in our development is the focus of ecological theory (Luster & Okaghi, 2005). Developed by Urie Bronfenbrenner (1986, 1995, 2000, 2004), **ecological theory** holds that people are influenced by five environmental systems, which are summarized in figure 1.1. These systems are the microsystem, mesosystem, exosystem, macrosystem, and chronosystem:

- *Microsystem* refers to the immediate setting in which you live and the people with whom you directly interact—family, romantic partner, spouse or life partner, peers, friends, college, and neighborhood.
- The *mesosystem* consists of connections between microsystems. Links are likely to exist, for example, between your family experiences and experiences with friends and between family experiences and romantic experiences.
- The *exosystem* refers to the influence that a social setting in which you do not have an active role exerts on your experiences in an immediate context. For example, you may have no contact with a friend's workplace, but trouble at that workplace may make your friend moody and irritable and ready to quarrel with you. Troubles at the workplace may spill over into your relationship.
- The *macrosystem* involves the culture in which individuals live. **Culture** refers to the behavior patterns, beliefs, and all other products of a group of people that are passed on from generation to generation. The attitudes of non-Latino White Americans toward African Americans were clearly a part of the macrosystem that affected the young Alice Walker.
- The *chronosystem* is the patterning of events and transitions over your life, as well as sociohistorical circumstances. For example, researchers have found that, on average, it takes about two years to adjust to a divorce and about five years to adjust to living in a stepfamily (Hetherington & Kelly, 2002). The changing life

contexts The historical, economic, social, and cultural factors and settings that influence us.

ecological theory Bronfenbrenner's theory that people's lives are influenced by five environmental systems: microsystem, mesosystem, exosystem, macrosystem, and chronosystem.

culture Refers to the behavior patterns, beliefs, and all other products of a group of people that are passed on from generation to generation.

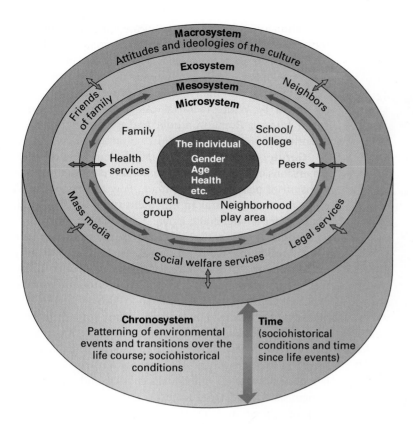

FIGURE 1.1 Bronfenbrenner's Ecological Theory of Development
Bronfenbrenner's ecological theory consists of five environmental systems: microsystem, mesosystem, exosystem, macrosystem, and chronosystem.

paths taken by U.S. women provide a striking example of the influence of sociohistorical circumstances: women are far more likely to pursue a career today than they were 40 years ago.

Contexts and Diversity   Your experience of the systems described by ecological theory depends partly on your sociocultural context—your culture, ethnicity, and gender. Recall that *culture* encompasses the behavior patterns, beliefs, and all other products of a particular group of people that are passed on from generation to generation. Thus, culture results from the interaction of people over many years. A cultural group can be as large as the United States or as small as an African village.

Whatever its size, the group's culture influences the behavior of its members (Matsumoto, 2004; Saraswathi & Mistry, 2003). Tourists sometimes discover the power of cultural influences when they fail to adapt to the cultural practices of the country they are visiting. For example, Jack was surprised when he admired the watch of his Japanese host. In keeping with the culture's custom, the host offered the watch to Jack—who refused it due to his discomfort at accepting such an expensive gift. By refusing the gift, Jack offended his host and set back their relationship.

Cross-cultural studies compare a culture with one or more other cultures. The comparison provides information about the degree to which a process or characteristic is universal across cultures or is instead culture-specific. For example, the United States is an achievement-oriented culture with a strong work ethic.

Ethnicity is rooted in cultural heritage, nationality, race, religion, and language. (The word *ethnic* comes from the Greek word for "nation.") In the United States we most often look at ethnicity in terms of ethnic groups such as African Americans, Latinos, Asian Americans, Native Americans, Polish Americans, Italian Americans, and so on. It is easy to fall into the trap of stereotyping and thinking that all members of an ethnic group are alike, but each ethnic group is diverse (Chun & Akutsu, 2003; Koppelman & Goodhart, 2005; Sheets, 2005). Latinos, for example, include people whose families have been in the United States for generations as well as people who have immigrated recently from countries such as Mexico, Cuba, and Puerto Rico.

cross-cultural studies Involve a comparison of a culture with one or more other cultures.

ethnicity Is rooted in cultural heritage, nationality characteristics, race, religion, and language.

In Xinjiang, China, a woman prepares for horseback courtship. Her suitor must chase her, kiss her, and evade her riding crop—all on the gallop. A new marriage law took effect in China in 1981. The law sets a minimum age for marriage—22 years for males, 20 years for females. Late marriage and late childbirth are critical efforts in China's attempt to control population growth. *What do you think about such laws?*

Ethnicity and race are sometimes misrepresented. *Race* is a controversial classification of people according to real or imagined biological characteristics such as skin color and blood group membership (Corsini, 1999). An individual's *ethnicity* may include his or her race but also many other characteristics. Thus, an individual might be White (a racial category) and a fifth-generation Texan who is a Roman Catholic and speaks English and Spanish fluently.

Gender encompasses the psychological and sociocultural dimensions of being female or male. *Sex* refers to the biological dimension of being female or male. Few aspects of our development are more central to our identity and social relationships than gender (Hyde, 2004; Lippa, 2005; Matlin, 2004).

Ethnicity, race, and gender have special significance for adjustment. Around the world, people experience prejudice and discrimination because of their ethnicity, race, or gender. Even among well-meaning people, diverse ethnic backgrounds may create unexpected obstacles to building relationships or even to carrying on pleasant interactions. For example, many Americans believe it is respectful to look a person in the eye when that person speaks to you (Axtell, 1992). However, Native Americans believe it is respectful to avoid eye contact. An important aspect of adjustment is being sensitive to an individual's cultural and ethnic background (Organista, Organista, & Kurasaki, 2003). We will weave discussions of contexts and diversity throughout the rest of this book.

Culture and Ethnicity
Counseling Across Cultures
Ethnic Groups
Diversity Resources
Women and Gender Resources

gender Involves the psychological and sociocultural dimensions of being female or male.

critical thinking The process of thinking reflectively, productively, and evaluating the evidence.

Thinking Critically About Adjustment

People don't change. Love is blind. Where there's a will there's a way. Choice is good. Such statements should spark both *curiosity* and *skepticism*, which is the tendency to doubt the validity of claims in the absence of evidence. Are these generalizations true? To sort fact from fancy, a first step is to think critically about the supposed fact.

Are you a critical thinker? **Critical thinking** is the process of thinking reflectively and productively, and evaluating the evidence. Thinking critically means asking yourself how you know something. Too often we tend to recite, define, describe, state, and list rather than analyze, infer, connect, synthesize, criticize, create, evaluate, think, and rethink (Brooks & Brooks, 2001). Here are some attitudes that can stimulate you to think reflectively and productively:

- *Be open-minded and curious.* Explore options and avoid narrow thinking. Wonder, probe, question, and inquire.
- *Be intellectually careful.* Check for inaccuracies and errors, be precise, and be organized.
- *Be skeptical.* Examine the evidence and be alert for problems and inconsistencies.

PEANUTS reprinted by permission of United Feature Syndicate.

Examining the evidence can be an exhausting process. At the very least, as a critical thinker, you should ask yourself the following questions:

www.mhhe.com/santrockha

Exploring Critical Thinking
Critical Thinking Resources
Critical Thinking Articles

- What is the source of the evidence? It is critical to look for biases. For example, a person who is wildly enthusiastic about the remarkable effects of exercise on health when responding to survey questions about health awareness might sell exercise videos on the side. Furthermore, critical thinkers recognize the limits of personal experience as the basis for persuasive evidence. They show a strong preference for objective evidence from scientific research.
- How strongly does the evidence support a position?
- Is there disconfirming evidence?
- Are there other possible factors and explanations? For example, some people believe that a full moon can cause an increase in crimes. Crime rates might be higher during a full moon, but it is unlikely that a rise in crime is directly due to any lunar influence. A plausible alternative explanation is that better lighting enhances both criminal activity and success by the police in capturing criminals.

Reasons for Critical Thinking   Advice about adjustment provides a rich ground for critical thinking. Headlines in tabloid newspapers routinely make outrageous claims about how to change behavior. Want to increase your intelligence? Eat cauliflower every day. Feel out of sorts? Buy some crystals. Want to enhance your sexual appeal? Check your horoscope. In fact, approximately 75 percent of Americans read their horoscopes, and many of them believe that it is personally meant for them (Lister, 1992).

Many people believe that it is possible to tap into unearthly forces besides the stars. In a survey of college students, virtually 100 percent believed in at least one of the following (Messer & Griggs, 1989):

- channeling (the ability to enter a trance state and communicate with someone in another place and time, even centuries ago)
- clairvoyance (the ability to perceive remote events that most people cannot perceive)
- precognition ("knowing" events before they occur)
- telepathy (the extrasensory transfer of thought from one person to another)
- psychic healing (performing miracle cures instantaneously through contact with a higher spiritual being)
- psychic surgery (a brand of faith healing in which sleight of hand is relied on to achieve a miracle, such as removing dead or diseased tissue)
- crystal power (use of quartz crystals for healing)
- psychokinesis (being able to move objects without actually touching them)
- astral travel
- levitation
- the Bermuda Triangle mystery
- unidentified flying objects (UFOs)
- plant consciousness
- auras
- ghosts

To explore your views about phenomena, complete Self-Assessment 1.1.

If you believe in any of these phenomena, psychologists urge you to be more skeptical. There is no scientific evidence for the existence of any of the previously listed phenomena, only personal anecdotes and coincidences.

When you think critically, you will be skeptical of anything that claims access to wondrous powers and supernatural forces (Ward & Grashial, 1995). If something sounds too good to be true, think through the claims logically and demand to see the evidence.

A failure to think critically often underlies our purchase and use of highly touted, ineffective products (Halpern, 1998, 2003; Halpern & Riggio, 2003). For example,

SELF-ASSESSMENT 1.1

My Beliefs About Psychic Phenomena

For each of the following items, indicate whether you believe in it, are not sure about it, or don't believe in it.

	Believe	Not Sure	Don't Believe
1. Channeling	_____	_____	_____
2. Clairvoyance	_____	_____	_____
3. Precognition	_____	_____	_____
4. Telepathy	_____	_____	_____
5. Psychic healing	_____	_____	_____
6. Psychic surgery	_____	_____	_____
7. Crystal power	_____	_____	_____
8. Psychokinesis	_____	_____	_____
9. Astral travel	_____	_____	_____
10. Levitation	_____	_____	_____
11. The Bermuda triangle mystery	_____	_____	_____
12. Unidentified Flying Objects (UFOs)	_____	_____	_____
13. Plant consciousness	_____	_____	_____
14. Auras	_____	_____	_____
15. Ghosts	_____	_____	_____

Go to the appendix at the end of the book for an interpretation of your responses.

Why should you be skeptical when you hear that eating a ground-up penis of a tiger will increase the human male's sexual potency?

there is a widespread belief around the world today that ingesting the ground-up penis of a tiger will increase man's sexual potency. The thinking behind this belief goes like this: tigers (presumably) have a great sex life; thus eating a tiger's sexual organ will improve my sex life. You should be able to see what is wrong with this kind of thinking, especially in the absence of any evidence to support it.

Adjustment Strategies
Involving Critical Thinking

Here are six critical-thinking strategies for effective adjustment.

1. ***Describe and interpret behavior carefully.*** Suppose you have just had a fight with your roommate. If someone asked you what was wrong, chances are good you would interpret the event rather than describe the behavior involved. "Casey's really crazy!" you might say, instead of saying, "Casey leaves books all over the apartment." The first statement is an interpretation, or inference. The second statement is a behavioral description. Most people can agree on the actions involved in a behavior, but they might not agree on the interpretation of the behavior. Interpretations tend to emphasize motivations (Why does Casey leave books around the apartment?) and promote the use of judgments and labels ("Casey must be crazy to engage in that behavior").

Critical thinkers are precise in their descriptions of behavior and cautious in their interpretations of behavior. They recognize that broad interpretations leave plenty of room for error, and they realize that they might not be aware of all the factors that would give rise to the behavior.

2. *Identify values and challenge assumptions about behavior.* We can acquire values and apply assumptions without being aware of them. Consider Marita's way of preparing a roast. Marita was taught by her mother to slice off the small end of her roast before placing it in the oven. Not until a dinner guest questioned her about this practice did she realize that she couldn't explain this step in the recipe. When she questioned her mother, she discovered the practice was a family tradition handed down from her grandmother, who didn't own a pan large enough to accommodate a roast. The tradition survived because no one thought to question the practice.

   Critical thinkers examine the role that values and assumptions can play in influencing behavior. They also avoid assuming that specific values automatically imply specific behaviors or vice versa. Critical thinkers explore how differing values contribute to varying perceptions and preferred solutions and behaviors.

3. *Examine the influence of context and culture on behavior.* Do you act the same in the company of your best friends as you do when you are with your grandparents? Do you act the same at a circus as you would at a funeral? Do people behave in certain ways because of their cultural background? Critical thinkers try to take context and culture into account in order to understand a particular behavior or situation.

4. *Seek multiple points of view and alternative explanations.* Have you ever disagreed with someone about the "facts" of an event? Although you both may have shared the event, your "realities" were different. Critical thinkers recognize that their own perspectives might be imperfect renditions of reality; they seek multiple perspectives. They recognize that one individual's viewpoint might not offer an accurate explanation.

   Remaining open to multiple interpretations obviously helps critical thinkers in interpersonal conflicts. They seek to understand the other person's perspective in order to resolve interpersonal problems.

5. *Appreciate individual and group differences.* Humans are alike in their basic anatomy and general genetic structure, yet their differences are remarkable. Many people are surprised to discover these differences in the pages of a novel, in tourism, in other neighborhoods, or even at play in their own backyards, or on the streets. Critical thinkers do not accept stereotypes and they are exhilarated by the differences among people.

6. *Engage in self-reflection to improve self-knowledge.* By taking this course, you are embarking on a journey that will give you many opportunities to understand yourself better. Each chapter contains self-assessments that will give you insight into your motives, values, preferences, and eccentricities. I hope that you will find these exercises to be fulfilling adventures that help you integrate your learning about adjustment with your daily life. Further, as you read about the many adjustment strategies throughout the book, reflect on which ones might benefit you the most.

Review and Reflect

1 **Identify some key concepts that provide a foundation for understanding adjustment**

REVIEW

- How can adjustment be defined?
- What are contexts? What is Bronfenbrenner's model? How can culture, cross-cultural studies, ethnicity, and gender be defined?
- What is critical thinking?

REFLECT

- Describe a situation in your life in the last several years that required adjustment on your part for each of Bronfenbrenner's five environmental systems.

2   SUBJECTIVE WELL-BEING AND ADJUSTMENT

| Are Rich People Happier? | | Who Is Happy? |

Ed Diener's Views on Subjective Well-Being

When you think critically about adjustment, what is your goal? How important is being happy to you? Ed Diener (2003) has found that college students rate life satisfaction and happiness as very important or extremely important in all 41 countries he has studied. In almost every country, college students rate life satisfaction and happiness as more important than money in their lives.

Happiness might seem out of reach for someone like Alice Walker, who grew up poor and disfigured. Perhaps for some people, her situation would have been a recipe for misery. But different people adjust to what may look like the same context in different ways. The relation between objective realities and happiness is not simple.

Subjective well-being is the scientific term for how people evaluate their lives in terms of their happiness and life satisfaction (Diener, 2003). People can evaluate their lives by making global judgments (such as describing whether they are satisfied with their lives overall or are generally happy) or by judging their ongoing feelings about what is happening to them. An important point is that it is the person who is making the life evaluation, not experts. Indeed, in judging subjective well-being, the individual is the expert, the best judge of how his or her life is going, according to the standard that person chooses.

Are Rich People Happier?

Many years ago, the French philosopher Jean-Jacques Rousseau described the subjective nature of happiness this way: "Happiness is a good bank account, a good cook, and a good digestion." A good cook and good digestion are not on most lists of factors that make people happy. But what about Rousseau's "good bank account"? Can winning the lottery or getting a substantial inheritance make you happier? Researchers have found that people who win the lottery or get a substantial inheritance typically get an initial surge of elation, but over the long term they are no happier than people who have not experienced these windfalls (Diener & Biswas-Diener, 2002; Gardner & Oswald, 2001).

Thus, winning a lottery does not appear to be the key to happiness. What is important, though, is having enough money to buy life's necessities. Extremely wealthy people are not happier than people who can purchase what they need. Even in the slums of Calcutta, India, and in Pakistan, people are more satisfied with their lives than would be expected (Diener & Oishi, 2000; Gardner & Oswald, 2001). The message is clear: If you believe money buys happiness, think again.

In fact, individuals who strive the most for wealth tend to have lower subjective well-being than those who do not strive for wealth (Ryan, 1999). This finding especially holds for people who seek money to gain power or show off rather than support their families (Srivastava, Locke, & Bartol, 2001). Instead, people who strive for intimacy, personal growth, and contribution to the community report a higher subjective well-being (Kasser, 2002).

Who Is Happy?

Subjective well-being is linked to many positive aspects of life. Happy people (those who rate themselves high in positive emotions over time) exhibit the following characteristics:

subjective well-being The scientific term for how people evaluate their lives in terms of their happiness and life satisfaction.

- Have good social relationships. More specifically, they have one or more close friends; they have successful marriages; other people like them more than unhappy people are liked; and they are more successful than unhappy people in leadership positions at work) (Diener, 2000; Diener, Lucas, & Oishi, 2002).
- Are mentally healthy and cope effectively with stressful situations (Diener, 2003).
- Have high levels of creativity, self-esteem, optimism, extraversion, and self-control (Lucas & Diener, 2000).
- Are good citizens at work; they help others more, skip work less, and so on (Lucas & Diener, 2000).
- Have a spirituality and faith that embodies purpose, social support, and in some individuals, religious attendance (Diener, 2003).
- Like other people, and others like them.
- Tend to be altruistic.

A recent study sought to find out what the happiest 10 percent of U.S. college students were like (Diener & Seligman, 2002). The very happy college students were highly social, more extraverted, and had stronger romantic and social relationships than the less happy college students (see figure 1.2).

Some characteristics that many people believe are involved in happiness have little or no link to subjective well-being:

- Age, gender, education level, and parenthood (having children or not) are not tied to happiness (DeNeve & Cooper, 1998; Myers, 2000).
- If people are satisfied with their health, this is moderately related to their life satisfaction.
- Physical attractiveness has a small positive link with subjective well-being (Diener, Wolsic, & Fujita, 1995). Thus, pretty and handsome individuals are only slightly happier than unattractive individuals.

In short, there seems to be no single key to happiness. No single factor guarantees that an individual will report that she or he has very high subjective well-being. However, the happiest people invariably say that they have good friends.

FIGURE 1.2 Characteristics of Very Happy College Students (Diener & Seligman, 2002)
Self-ratings were made on a scale of 1 to 7, with 1 being much below the average of college students on the campus studied (University of Illinois), and 7 being much above the average of college students on the campus. Daily activity scores reflect mean times with 1 representing no time, and 10 reflecting 8 hours per day.

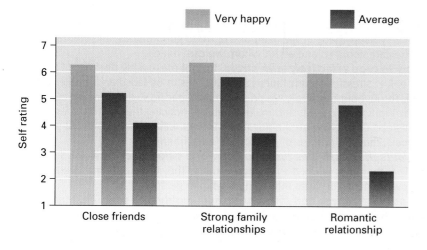

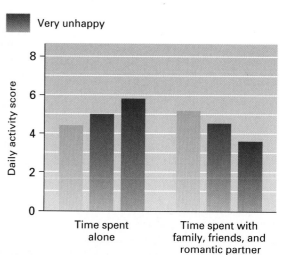

My Subjective Well-Being

Below are five statements that you may agree or disagree with. Using the 1 to 7 scale below, indicate your agreement with each item by placing the appropriate number on the line next to that item. Please be open and honest in making your responses.

7 = Strongly Agree, 6 = Agree, 5 = Slightly Agree, 4 = Neither Agree or Disagree, 3 = Slightly Disagree, 2 = Disagree, and 1 = Strongly Disagree

_____ In most ways my life is close to my ideal.

_____ The conditions of my life are excellent.

_____ I am satisfied with my life.

_____ So far I have gotten the important things I want in life.

_____ If I could live my life over, I would change almost nothing.

Go to the appendix at the end of the book for scoring and interpretation of your responses.

Diener, E., Emmons, R. A., Larsen, R. J., & Griffin, S. (1985). The Satisfaction with Life Scale. *Journal of Personality Assessment, 49*, 71–75.

On average, most people are slightly happy, although everyone has their up and down moods (Diener, 2003). Nobody is happy all of the time, not even the happiest people. To evaluate your subjective well-being, complete Self-Assessment 1.2.

Adjustment Strategies
For Happiness and Life Satisfaction

1. *Reflect on your responses to Self-Assessment 1.2.* If you rated yourself slightly happy or lower, develop a plan for improving your subjective well-being.
2. *Recognize that no single factor by itself produces a happy person; multiple factors are at work.*
3. *Develop good social relationships.* Good relationships consistently show up in profiles of very happy people. We need one or more good friends, and we need people who care about us and about whom we care deeply.
4. *Learn how to cope effectively with stress.* Do not make a big deal out of trivial hassles. Look at stressful circumstances as challenges to be faced and problems to be solved. Throughout this book, we present many specific suggestions for coping with stress. Work toward goals and make a habit of noticing the positive things in your life instead of dwelling on the negatives. Do not wait to be happy until you attain a goal. Enjoy the process of growth and adjustment.
5. *Involve yourself in activities that you enjoy and value, such as work.* People are usually at their best when they engage in things they value and find interesting, and this involvement translates into being a happier person.
6. *Develop purposefulness and incorporate spirituality into your life.* Many individuals who rate themselves as very happy find meaning in their life and say that they have spiritual or religious interests.

Review and Reflect

2 Define subjective well-being and describe the factors related to it

REVIEW

- Does subjective well-being depend on wealth?
- What factors are linked to subjective well-being?

REFLECT

- Who are the happiest people you know? What characteristics do they have? Why do you think they are so happy?

3 THE SCIENTIFIC APPROACH TO ADJUSTMENT

- Psychology and Adjustment
- Using the Scientific Method
- Being a Wise Consumer of Research Information
- Adopting a Scientific Attitude
- Experimental and Correlational Research

The previous discussion outlined many characteristics that are linked to happiness. How do I know these links exist? Where did this information come from? For this and other aspects of our analysis of adjustment, we depend primarily on the science of psychology.

Psychology and Adjustment

Psychology is not a cure-all for every knotty problem, and it doesn't reveal *the* meaning of life. It does, however, contribute enormously to our knowledge about why people are the way they are, why they think and act the way they do, and how they can cope more effectively with their lives. The study of psychology shows significant potential to improve our lives in the twenty-first century. **Psychology** is the scientific study of behavior and mental processes. Psychology emphasizes observing, describing, explaining, and predicting behavior. Three aspects of this definition need elaboration: behavior, mental processes, and science. Let's examine behavior first.

Behavior is everything we do that can be directly observed—such as two people *kissing*, a baby *crying*, a student *writing*. Psychologists strive to distinguish behavior from inferences we draw about behavior. Behaviors are usually described using verbs that communicate observable actions. In contrast, **inferences** are conclusions that we draw from behavior. If you observe a baby crying, you might infer that the baby is hungry or tired or afraid.

Mental processes are trickier to define and describe than behavior is. They encompass thoughts, feelings, and motives that each of us experiences privately but that cannot be observed directly. Although we cannot directly observe and describe thoughts and feelings, they are no less real because of that. For example, mental processes include *thoughts* about kissing someone, *feelings* a baby experiences when its mother leaves the room, and *memories* a college student has about a fine afternoon on a motorcycle.

Because we can't observe these processes directly in others, we often *infer* the mental processes that support observable behavior. For example, if we had been with

psychology The scientific study of behavior and mental processes.

behavior Everything that people do that can be directly observed.

inferences Conclusions that people draw from behavior.

mental processes Consist of thoughts, feelings, and motives that each person experiences privately but cannot be observed directly.

Describe the behaviors you see in this photograph. What verbs accurately describe it? What kinds of inferences can we draw about the meanings of these behaviors? Did you observe the behaviors closely by taking into account the contexts in which they are occurring? This example illustrates the fact that interpreting behavior involves three steps: (1) *making accurate observations,* (2) *describing the behavior,* and (3) *drawing inferences about the behavior.*

American Psychological Association
APA Help Center

Alice Walker when she received the good news that she had won the Pulitzer Prize, we might have observed her *smiling* or *crying,* but we would have had to infer her mental processes. Would she have been overjoyed? stunned? relieved? thinking about how long it had taken to receive the recognition? planning on calling her loved ones? We would *infer* the impact of the news on her from our observations of her behavior.

Describing behavior is a relatively straightforward process; drawing inferences about unobservable mental processes is not. We can usually reach agreement about how to describe behavior we observe, but our inferences often reflect wide variations in how we each experience and interpret behavior. In psychology, we make and test inferences through *scientific study,* which is the third component of our definition of psychology.

Consider the following statements:

Statement 1: Couples who live together before marriage have a better chance of making the marriage last.
Statement 2: Couples who do not live together before marriage tend to have a lower divorce rate than couples who do.

Which statement would you predict to be true? The common-sense notion that "practice makes perfect" suggests that the first statement is more likely to be accurate, but scientific studies have found a higher success rate for couples who do not live together before marriage (Centers for Disease Control and Prevention, 2002; Manning & Smock, 2002).

Because it is a science, psychology doesn't accept assumptions about human nature at face value, however reasonable they may sound. Rather, it is a rigorous discipline that tests assumptions and gathers evidence to support explanations of behavior. Psychology uses systematic methods to observe, describe, explain, and predict behavior and mental processes (Lammers & Badia, 2005; Rosnow & Rosenthal, 2005).

In short, because it is a science, psychology adopts scientific attitudes toward information and uses scientific methods when conducting research. These are the two ingredients of the scientific approach. Let's examine each.

Adopting a Scientific Attitude

Taking a scientific attitude means, first of all, thinking critically. As discussed earlier, critical thinkers are *curious* and *skeptical.* Skeptical people question things that other people take for granted. They wonder whether a supposed fact is really true. They ask what evidence there is for an idea and question whether the evidence is really strong enough to be accepted as accurate and factual.

Adopting a scientific attitude also means *being objective* (Pittenger, 2003; Rosnow & Rosenthal, 2005). It is sometimes said that experience is the most important teacher. We do get a great deal of knowledge from subjective, personal experience. We generalize from what we observe and frequently turn memorable encounters into lifetime "truths." But how valid are these conclusions? As individuals, we often misinterpret what we see and hear. Our personal judgments are often based on a need to protect our egos and self-esteem (McMillan, 2004).

Being objective means trying to see things as they really are, not just as we would like them to be. Scientists believe that one of the best ways to be objective is to conduct research studies (Beins, 2004; Christensen, 2004).

This description is depicted as ideal. No scientist possesses all of these at every moment in life. But the closer we embrace these scientific attitudes, the better we are able to use the basic tools of science. They reduce the likelihood that information will be based on unreliable personal beliefs, opinions, and emotions. As you go through this book, practice using these scientific attitudes. You also would do well to call on these attitudes whenever you hear people discussing "facts" and arguing about issues.

Using the Scientific Method

Theories and hypotheses play key roles in the scientific method, which is the second hallmark of the scientific approach. A **theory** is a broad idea or set of closely related ideas that attempt to explain certain observations. Theories try to explain why certain things have happened. They can also be used to predict future observations. If your friend's new car stops dead in the street, you might have a theory to explain why it happened. Your theory probably includes the idea that an engine somewhere inside the car is supposed to make it go. Your theory might also include the ideas that engines run on gasoline and that other parts of the car, such as the brakes, are designed to prevent the car from moving. This theory gives you a framework for trying to figure out why your friend's car isn't running.

In psychology, theories serve a similar purpose. They help to organize and connect observations and research (Leedy & Omrod, 2005). The overall meaning of the large numbers of psychological studies would be difficult to grasp if theories did not provide a structure for understanding them and putting them in a context with other studies. In addition, good theories generate interesting questions and further research that might answer those questions. In other words, theories might inspire hypotheses.

A **hypothesis** is a prediction that can be tested. For example, if your theory about the car includes the idea of gasoline, you can test the hypothesis that a lack of gasoline caused the car to stop. You would simply add gas to the tank. If you observe that the car runs again after you add the fuel, you might conclude that your hypothesis is correct. If the car still doesn't run, you might wonder not only whether your hypothesis is incorrect but also whether your theory needs revision: not all cars these days run on gasoline.

Testing hypotheses is at the heart of the scientific method. The **scientific method** is essentially a four-step process:

1. Conceptualize the problems.
2. Collect research information (data).
3. Analyze data.
4. Draw conclusions.

A good example of these steps and how they link theory and hypotheses is the work of James Pennebaker, a research psychologist at the University of Texas at Austin. He is interested in the connection between emotions and health, and his research has important implications for human adjustment (Pennebaker, 2001). His research proceeded through the four steps of the scientific method as follows.

Step 1: Conceptualize a Problem   Pennebaker's thinking about emotions and health began in a very personal way. He had gotten married just after finishing college, and a few years later his marriage was in trouble. After about a month of deep depression and emotional isolation, he began to write privately every day about his problems. After about a week of writing, he says, "I noticed my depression lifting. For the first time in years—perhaps ever—I had a sense of meaning and direction. I fundamentally understood my deep love for my wife and the degree to which I needed her" (Pennebaker, 1997).

Some years later, he looked back on that experience and wondered why his private writing had helped him. He became interested in a theory of catharsis that had been developed nearly 100 years earlier by Freud and other psychodynamic psychologists, who are discussed in chapters 2 and 15. The theory of catharsis proposes that by expressing pent-up emotions, a person can often eliminate those emotions, along with physical symptoms of stress and anxiety. This is the basis of psychotherapy—a

theory A broad idea or set of closely related ideas that attempt to explain certain observations.

hypothesis A prediction that can be tested.

scientific method A four-step process of conceptualizing a problem, collecting research information (data), analyzing data, and drawing conclusions.

process in which individuals experience relief by talking about their problems with a therapist.

Pennebaker's experience led him to ask whether this theory of catharsis should be modified. For example, to experience the benefits of emotional release, was it really necessary to talk to a psychotherapist? In fact, was it really necessary to speak to anyone at all? Could people with emotional troubles achieve the same relief by writing? And could people improve their physical health simply by writing about their problems? Pennebaker and a graduate student, Sandra Beall (1986), decided to test the following hypothesis:

If people write about their negative emotions and the situations that caused them, people will reduce their stress and be more healthy in the future.

Step 2: Collect Research Information (Data)

The second step of the scientific method is to collect research information (data). Researchers must decide (1) how to collect that data and (2) who will participate in the study as the source of the data. Pennebaker and Beall decided to conduct an experiment in which they would compare two groups: one group would write about an emotional experience and another group would write about other things.

Pennebaker and Beall's participants were a group of 46 students who volunteered to be in their study. The researchers decided to instruct their volunteer participants to write continuously for 15 minutes each day on 4 consecutive days. One group of participants (the experimental group) was told to write about an upsetting or traumatic experience and to express how they felt about the experience when it happened and how they felt about it while writing. The researchers asked a second group of participants (the control group) to write about a topic unrelated to an emotional event. To assess the health of the participants, Pennebaker and Beall decided to record the number of visits that their participants made to the student health center before, during, and after the study.

James Pennebaker (*right*) discussing the value of writing about emotional experiences with participants in one of his research studies.

Step 3: Analyze Data

Once psychologists have collected measurable data, they use mathematical (statistical) procedures to understand what the data mean (Moore, 2001). In this study, Pennebaker and Beall used a number of statistical procedures to determine whether students' health benefited from writing about emotional experiences. For example, they analyzed information about how often the students who wrote about their emotional experiences used the health center. As shown in figure 1.3, the two groups—the group that wrote about their emotional experiences and the group that did not—visited the health center about equally prior to the experiment. However, after the experimental group wrote about their emotional experiences, they visited the health center considerably less often than the control group.

Step 4: Draw Conclusions

Pennebaker and Beall concluded after they examined their results that the participants who wrote about their feelings made significantly fewer visits to the student health center afterward than those who did not write about their emotions. But scientific studies aim to allow conclusions that connect such findings back to a hypothesis and its underlying theory. In this case, the findings and conclusions were exciting. They confirmed the hypothesis and suggested that emotional "cathartic" writing actually causes improvements in a person's physical health. The results also suggested that the general theory of emotional catharsis should be modified to account for the fact that it can be achieved through writing, as well as talking, and does not require the presence of a therapist.

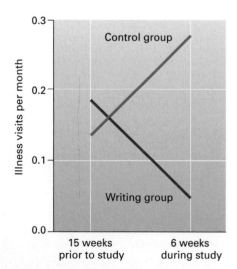

FIGURE 1.3 Health-Center Visits Before and After Writing About Emotional Experiences

Pennebaker and others performed later studies with further interesting results. One study redefined "health" in terms of certain measurements of participants' blood samples (Pennebaker, Kiecolt-Glaser, & Glaser, 1988). It found that the emotional writing led to improvements in the immune system. Another study involved a group of unemployed middle-aged engineers who were deeply angry after having been suddenly fired by a corporation for which some of them had worked for 30 years (Spera, Buhrfeind, & Pennebaker, 1994). This study found that emotional writing led many of the engineers to overcome their frustration and find new jobs, whereas engineers who did not do the writing remained angry and unemployed.

Adjustment Strategies
For Writing to Improve Your Health

James Pennebaker (1997, 2004) provided these recommendations for writing to improve your health:

1. ***What to write.*** You don't need to write about the most stressful thing in your life. Write about issues and concerns that currently preoccupy your thinking. Write about something that you may not be disclosing to others possibly because you feel you might be embarrassed or experience negative remarks. Write as accurately as possible about an experience that bothers you. Also reveal your emotions and describe your deepest feelings.
2. ***How to write it.*** Just start and continue to write. Don't worry about spelling or making good sentences. If you get stuck, go back and go over what you were writing before you got stuck.
3. ***When and where to write it.*** Emotional writing is not the same as keeping a journal of events and thoughts as they occur. Write when you feel like writing. Write when you feel prepared to become emotionally involved with the writing. Find a place where you won't be interrupted or distracted.
4. ***What to do with your writing.*** Keep the writing to yourself. Don't plan to show it to anyone. Don't write for an audience, which may cause you to hold back or justify yourself.
5. ***What to expect.*** Writing about your emotions won't solve all of your problems. It is not a substitute for coping with problems that may keep you angry, sad, or frustrated. If you are in the midst of turmoil over the death of a loved one or the end of a long-term relationship, your writing may not make you instantly feel better, but it probably will help you to see things in a better perspective. You may feel sad or depressed for a few hours or even a day after writing. However, most people feel relieved, happier, and more content soon after.

www.mhhe.com/santrockha

James Pennebaker's Ideas and Research

Experimental and Correlational Research

Pennebaker chose to conduct an experiment in order to test his hypothesis about the theory of catharsis, but experiments like his represent just one type of research. Many scientific studies are not experimental, but correlational. These two types of studies are very different, and they permit different types of conclusions.

Experimental Research   An **experiment** is a carefully regulated procedure in which one or more factors believed to influence the behavior being studied are manipulated while all other factors are held constant. If the behavior under study changes when a factor is manipulated, we say that the manipulated factor has caused the behavior to change. In other words, the experiment has demonstrated cause and effect. The cause is the factor that was manipulated, and the effect is the behavior that changed because of the manipulation.

experiment A carefully regulated procedure in which one or more factors believed to influence the behavior being studied are manipulated while all other factors are held constant.

Experiments have two types of changeable factors, or variables: independent and dependent. An **independent variable** is a manipulated, influential, experimental factor. It is a potential cause. The label *independent* is used because this variable can be manipulated independently of other factors to determine its effect. Researchers have a vast array of options open to them in selecting independent variables, and one experiment may include several independent variables (Kantowitz, Roediger, & Elmes, 2005; Shaughnessy, Zechmeister, & Zechmeister, 2003).

In Pennebaker and Beall's experiment, the independent variable was writing about emotions. They manipulated this variable by asking different participants to write about their problems in different ways. For example, they asked some participants to describe an experience and write about how they felt about it. They asked other participants to write about a topic that was unrelated to emotional events.

A **dependent variable** is a factor that can change in an experiment in response to changes in the independent variable. As researchers manipulate the independent variable, they measure the dependent variable for any resulting effect. In Pennebaker and Beall's experiment, the dependent variable was the number of visits that the student made to the health center during the several months after writing about an emotional experience. They found that the number of visits depended on the sort of writing that the student was asked to do.

Experiments can involve one or more experimental groups and one or more control groups. An **experimental group** is a group whose experience is manipulated. A **control group** is as much like the experimental group as possible and is treated in every way like the experimental group except for the manipulated factor. The control group thus serves as a baseline against which the effects of the manipulated condition can be compared. In Pennebaker and Beall's study, participants in the experimental group were asked to write about their emotions. The participants in the control group were asked to write about some other, nonemotional topic.

Random assignment is an important principle in deciding whether each participant will be placed in the experimental group or in the control group (Martin, 2004). **Random assignment** means that researchers assign participants to experimental and control groups by chance. It reduces the likelihood that the experiment's results will be due to any preexisting differences between groups. In Pennebaker and Beall's experiment, suppose the participants had not been randomly assigned but had been allowed to choose which group they would join—either the group that would write about emotions or the group that would write about something else. In that situation, people who were comfortable expressing their emotions might choose to join the first group, and people who were not comfortable expressing their emotions might choose to be in the second group. As a result, any difference between the groups in terms of health at the end of the experiment might owe nothing to the effects of writing but simply reflect the effects of a person's comfort in expressing emotions (see figure 1.4).

Pennebaker and Beall randomly assigned each participant to either the experimental group that wrote about emotional experiences or a control group that wrote about a nonemotional topic. The independent variable (which is always the manipulated variable) was the type of writing the students did (about the emotion situation or about something else). The dependent variable was the number of illness visits that students paid to the health center after the writing. The design of this experiment allowed Pennebaker and Beall to conclude that the emotional writing caused better health.

Correlational Research   Experiments are the type of research that provides the most compelling evidence that one factor causes another. Why, then, do researchers use any method other than experiments? Why don't they always conduct experiments? There are several reasons.

In some cases, the experiments that would be necessary to test hypotheses would be unethical. For example, it would be unethical to carry out an experiment in which expectant mothers are directed to smoke varying numbers of cigarettes to see how

Experimental and Correlational Research

independent variable The manipulated, influential, experimental factor in an experiment.

dependent variable The factor that can change in an experiment in response to changes in the independent variable.

experimental group The group whose experience is manipulated in an experiment.

control group The group that is as much like the experimental group as possible and is treated in every way like the experimental group except for the manipulated factor.

random assignment When researchers assign participants to experimental and control groups by chance.

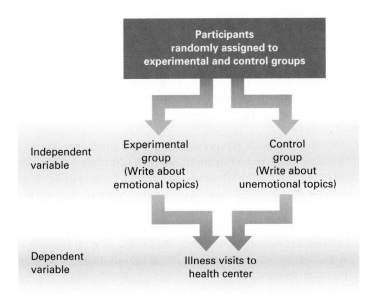

FIGURE 1.4 Random Assignment and Experimental Design

cigarette smoke affects birth weight. Sometimes an experiment cannot be carried out because the issue under investigation is post hoc (after the fact) or historical, such as studying the childhood backgrounds of people who are abusive parents. Consider again the case of Unabomber Ted Kaczynski. He claimed that his difficulties in life began because he grew up as a genius in a kid's body, who stuck out like a sore thumb as a child. Could his analysis be accurate? Suppose you wanted to test the broader hypothesis that being exceptional as a child causes an increased tendency toward violence in adulthood. How would you design an experiment to test that hypothesis? Sometimes factors simply cannot be manipulated experimentally, such as the effects of the September 11, 2001, attacks on New York City. Correlational research provides an alternative way of conducting research.

In **correlational research,** the goal is to describe the strength of the relationship between two or more events or characteristics. The more strongly the two events are correlated (or related or associated), the more effectively we can predict one event from the other (Babbie, 2005; Vernoy & Kyle, 2003). Earlier in the chapter, we described a number of factors that are related to happiness, including self-esteem, optimism, and self-control. The research on which this conclusion was based is correlational in nature. If this research is correlational, can we conclude that high self-esteem causes people to be happy? No, we cannot. The reverse might be true: being happy causes people to have high self-esteem. Further, one or more other factors might underlie the correlation between happiness and self-esteem, such as an easygoing temperament, biological inheritance, or positive relationships with parents.

In trying to make sense of the world, people often make a big mistake about correlation. Look at the terms in bold type in the following newspaper headlines:

Scientists Find **Connection** Between Ear Hair and Heart Attacks
Psychologists Discover **Relationship** Between Marital Status and Health
Researchers Identify **Association** Between Loneliness and Social Skills

Reading these headlines, many people jump to the conclusion that ear hair causes heart attacks, or that their marital status determines how often they get sick, and so on. But all of the words in bold type are synonymous only with correlation, not with causality. *Correlation does not equal causation.* Correlational research cannot establish cause and effect because it does not involve manipulating factors in a controlled way.

As you read about the findings of research, remember, correlation means only that two factors seem to occur together. Being able to predict one event based on the occurrence of another event does not necessarily tell us anything about the cause of either event (Mitchell & Jolley, 2004; Sprinthall, 2003).

Correlational methods permit research in situations that cannot be experimentally manipulated, such as disasters like the 2001 attack on the World Trade Center in New York. *What are some other examples of situations for which correlational methods might be well suited?*

correlational research Research in which the goal is to describe the strength of the relationship between two or more events or characteristics.

Being a Wise Consumer of Research Information

Television, radio, newspapers, and magazines all frequently report on research that is likely to be of interest to the general public. Much of the information has been published in professional journals or presented at national meetings. You should be aware, however, that not all psychological and adjustment information that is presented for public consumption comes from professionals with excellent credentials and reputations (Stanovich, 2004).

Because journalists, television reporters, and other media personnel are not usually trained in psychological and adjustment research, they often have trouble making sound decisions about the best information to present to the public. In addition, the media often focus on sensationalist findings to capture your attention. They tend to go beyond what the research really says. Even when the media present the results of excellent research, they have trouble adequately informing people about what has been found and the implications for people's lives. They often have only a few minutes or a few lines to summarize as best they can the complex findings of a study or a psychological or adjustment concept.

In the end, you have to take responsibility for evaluating the reports on psychological and adjustment research that you encounter. To put it another way, you have to consume psychological and adjustment information wisely.

Adjustment Strategies
For Understanding Adjustment Research

Five guidelines to help you be a wise consumer of information about psychological and adjustment research follow:

1. ***Distinguish between group results and individual needs.*** People who read about psychological research are likely to apply the results to their own lives. Yet most research focuses on groups, and individual variations in responses are seldom emphasized. In fact, researchers often fail to examine the overlap in the data on groups that they are comparing and look only for the differences in the groups.

   As a result, readers may get the wrong idea about the implications of the findings. For example, researchers interested in the effects of divorce on an adult's ability to cope with stress might conduct a study of 50 divorced women and 50 married women. They might conclude that the divorced women, as a group, cope more poorly with stress than the married women in the study do. In this particular study, however, some of the divorced women were likely to be coping better than some of the married women. Indeed, of the 100 women in the study, the 2 or 3 women who were coping the best with stress may have been divorced women. It would be accurate to report the findings as showing that divorced women (as a group) coped less effectively with stress than married women (as a group) did. But it would not be sensible to conclude, after reading a summary of the results of the study, that your divorced sister may not be coping with stress as well as she thinks and recommend that she see a therapist.

   Remember, if you read a report that states that the divorced women coped more poorly with stress than the married women did, you cannot conclude that all divorced women coped more poorly with stress. The only conclusion that you can reasonably draw is that more married women coped better than divorced women did.

2. ***Don't overgeneralize from a small sample.*** Media presentations often don't have the space or time to go into details about the participants in the study. If you can't learn anything else about the sample used in the study, at least pay attention to its size. Small or very small samples require caution in generalizing to a larger population of individuals. For example, a sample of only 10 or 20 divorced women may have some unique characteristics that would make the study's finding inapplicable to many women. The women in the sample might all have high incomes, be White, be childless, live in a small southern town, and be undergoing

psychotherapy. Divorced women who have moderate to low incomes, are from other ethnic backgrounds, have children, are living in different contexts, and are not undergoing psychotherapy might have given very different responses.

3. ***Look for answers beyond a single study.*** The media might identify an interesting finding and claim that it has far-reaching implications. Although pivotal studies do occur, they are rare. It is safer to assume that no single study will provide conclusive answers to an important question, especially answers that apply to all people. In fact, conflicting results are common. Answers to questions in research usually emerge after many scientists have conducted similar investigations that yield similar conclusions. For example, if one study reports that a particular therapy conducted by a particular therapist has been especially effective with divorced adults, you should not conclude that the therapy will work as effectively with all divorced adults and with other therapists until more studies are conducted. You should not take a report of one research study as the absolute, final answer to a problem.

4. ***Don't attribute causes where none have been found.*** Drawing causal conclusions from correlational studies is one of the most common mistakes made by the media. Remember that causal interpretations cannot be made when two or more factors are simply correlated. We cannot say that one causes the other.

    In the case of divorce, imagine that you read this headline: "Low income causes divorced women to have a high degree of stress." You can instantly conclude that the story is about a correlational study, not an experimental study. Why? Because for ethical and practical reasons, women participants cannot be randomly assigned to become divorced or stay married, and divorced women cannot be randomly assigned to be poor or rich. A more accurate heading would probably be "Low-income divorced women have a high degree of stress," meaning that the researchers found a correlation between being divorced, having a low income, and having a lot of stress. Be skeptical of words indicating causation until you know more about the research they are describing.

5. ***Evaluate the source of the information.*** Researchers usually must submit their findings to a journal for review by their colleagues, who decide whether to publish the paper or not depending on the care taken in conducting the research. Although the quality of research is not uniform among all psychological journals, most journals give research far greater scrutiny than the popular media do before publishing it. Among reports in the popular media, those in respected newspapers, such as the *New York Times* and *Washington Post,* as well as in credible magazines such as *Time* and *Newsweek,* are far more trustworthy than reports in tabloids, such as the *National Inquirer* and *Star.* But regardless of the source—serious publication, tabloid, or even academic journal—you are responsible for reading the details.

Review and Reflect

3 **Characterize the scientific foundations of the study of adjustment**

REVIEW

- What is psychology?
- What are the characteristics of scientific attitudes toward information?
- What is the scientific method? How can theory and hypothesis be defined?
- What characterizes experimental research? What characterizes correlational research?
- How can individuals become wise consumers of information about psychological and adjustment research?

REFLECT

- In the next few days, look through several newspapers and magazines for reports about psychological research. Also notice what you see and hear on television about psychology. Apply the guidelines for being a wise consumer of information about psychology and adjustment research to these media reports.

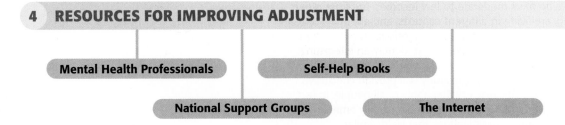

4 RESOURCES FOR IMPROVING ADJUSTMENT

Mental Health Professionals

National Support Groups

Self-Help Books

The Internet

An important goal of this textbook is to provide you with excellent resources for improving adjustment. Information is given about three types of resources: national support organizations, self-help books, and the Internet. However, in many cases, there is no substitute for talking with a competent mental health professional in person.

Mental Health Professionals

Various mental health professionals can help individuals adjust more effectively. These professionals include clinical psychologists, counselors, and psychiatrists. **Clinical and counseling psychology** is the specialization in psychology that involves evaluating and treating people who have psychological problems. Clinical psychologists and counselors do similar work, but counseling psychologists are more likely to work with people who have few serious problems. In some instances, counseling psychologists work with students, advising them about personal problems and career planning.

Counseling and clinical psychologists differ from psychiatrists. Typically, a clinical psychologist has earned a doctoral degree in psychology after four to six years in graduate school and has completed a one-year internship in a mental health facility. In contrast, **psychiatry** is a branch of medicine, and psychiatrists are physicians who have specialized in abnormal behavior and psychotherapy. Psychiatrists often prescribe drugs, whereas most clinical and counseling psychologists cannot, although several states have begun to allow clinical psychologists to prescribe drugs.

The counseling or health center at your college is a good place to go if you think you have a mental health problem; it is also a good place to recommend to other students if they ask you how they can get help for a problem. The center may have professionals who can help you with your problem, or the center may refer you to a mental health professional in the community. We will have much more to say about different types of mental health professionals in chapter 15, "Therapies."

National Support Groups

National support groups represent another important resource for improving adjustment. One study found that 5 percent of the U.S. adult population attended a branch of a national support group in the previous year (Eisenberg & others, 1998). These groups offer education and support for people with a particular problem. Participation is voluntary, members typically serve as leaders, and professionals rarely have an active role in the group.

The best-known national support group is Alcoholics Anonymous (AA), which seeks to help people reduce their addiction to alcohol. Other well-known support groups focus on eating or sexual problems. There are also national support groups that help people deal with death, divorce, fathering, Alzheimer disease, abusive partners, and many other problem areas. The effectiveness of a local chapter of a national support group depends largely on the local members and leaders. Thus, even though a national support group might have a good reputation, the quality of the group may vary considerably from one locale to another.

clinical and counseling psychology The specialization in psychology that involves evaluating and treating people who have psychological problems.

psychiatry A branch of medicine practiced by physicians who have specialized in abnormal behavior and psychotherapy.

We will further discuss national support groups in our examination of self-help groups in chapter 15, "Therapies." Also, at the end of most chapters (in the "Resources for Improving Adjustment" section), I provide information about national support groups related to the topics in the chapter, including contact information for groups' national offices (in many cases toll-free phone numbers as well as e-mail addresses and websites). By contacting the national office or going to a group's website, you can learn more about its mission and meetings and whether a branch of the group exists in your area.

Self-Help Books

Self-help books have become an important source of psychological advice for millions of Americans. Whether you aim to improve your marital life, control your anger, gain self-fulfillment, raise your self-esteem, become a better parent, lose weight, solve a sexual problem, cope with stress, recover from an addiction, or meet any of myriad other goals, you can probably find a self-help book on the topic.

Our preoccupation with self-help books is nothing new. Benjamin Franklin dispensed self-improvement advice in *Poor Richard's Almanac*—"Early to bed, early to rise, makes a man healthy, wealthy, and wise," for example. In the nineteenth century, homemakers read *Married Ladies' Companion* for help in managing their house and family. In the early twentieth century, Sigmund Freud wrote a self-help book on interpreting dreams, and in the 1930s, Dale Carnegie's *How to Win Friends and Influence People* made him the aspiring guru for entrepreneurs.

Interest in understanding the human psyche and how to improve it heated up in the 1960s and 1970s, and with the interest came an increase in self-help books. Today, self-help books appear at the rate of about 2,000 a year. Books are written on every conceivable topic, as witnessed by the titles *Dance Naked in Your Living Room* and *How to Juggle Women without Getting Killed* or *Going Broke*. Some self-help books have been

Self-help books are available on virtually every imaginable topic. *What makes a good self-help book?*

NOW IN PAPERBACK!

The Brave and Revealing Bestseller...

CATS WHO LOVE WOMEN WHO LOVE TOO MUCH

© Suzy Becker. Courtesy of Suzy Becker.

Authoritative Guide to Self-Help Resources
Self-Help Groups
Self-Help Group Clearinghouse

written by professionals with masterful insights. Others, as one concerned therapist commented, "are not worth the paper they are printed on."

You have probably heard or read about several of the following self-help books:

- *Feeling Good* by David Burns
- *Self-Matters* by Philip McGraw
- *Dianetics* by L. Ron Hubbard
- *The Dance of Intimacy* by Harriet Lerner
- *How to Win Friends and Influence People* by Dale Carnegie
- *You Just Don't Understand* by Deborah Tannen
- *Men Are from Mars, Women Are from Venus* by John Gray
- *The Seven Habits of Highly Effective People* by Steven Covey
- *10 Stupid Things People Do to Mess Up Their Relationship* by Laura Schlessinger
- *Your Perfect Right* by Robert Alberti and Michael Emmons

Each of these books was a national best-seller. But how can you know whether the advice offered in these books is worthwhile?

With John Norcross and other colleagues, I have conducted national studies of how clinical and counseling psychologists rate self-help books (Norcross, Santrock, & others, 2003; Santrock, Minnett, & Campbell, 1994). In all, we obtained ratings of self-help books from more than 2,500 psychologists. For the previous list of 10 books, the clinical and counseling psychologists gave positive ratings to only five: *Feeling Good* (a book about coping with depression), *The Dance of Intimacy* (a book about improving close relationships with a dating, life, or marital partner), *You Just Don't Understand* (a book about improving communication between women and men), *The Seven Habits of Highly Effective People* (a book about seven habits that can help you be a more competent person who has positive values, and *Your Perfect Right* (a book about how to become more assertive).

Bibliotherapy is the fancy term that has been given to using self-help books. In one thorough review, researchers found that bibliotherapy was as effective as therapist-administered treatments. Comparable findings have been reported on the effectiveness of high-quality self-help books involving specific problems, including sexual dysfunctions (van Lankveld, 1998), depression (Cuijpers, 1997), anxiety (Weekes, 1996), alcohol problems (Walters, 2000; Watson & Sher, 1998), and panic (Carlbring, Westling, & Andersson, 2000). In many cases, though, especially for individuals with serious mental health problems, self-help books should not be used as a substitute for professional help.

In each chapter's "Resources for Improving Your Adjustment" section, I profile the best self-help books related to the topics discussed in the chapter. The majority of these books were rated in the highest or next-to-highest category in our national surveys of self-help books.

bibliotherapy The fancy term for using self-help books.

Adjustment Strategies
For Selecting a Self-Help Book

Don't select a book because of its cover, its glitzy advertising, or because it is this year's so-called breakthrough book. Be an intelligent consumer of psychological advice by making your choices based on the following seven strategies.

1. ***Select a book that makes realistic recommendations, not grandiose claims.*** Unfortunately, books that make extravagant claims are the most alluring. But most problems do not arise overnight, and most can't be solved overnight. Avoid books that promise magical insights that can easily solve your problem. Coping effectively with a problem takes much more effort and work than many self-help books lead you to believe.

2. ***Examine the evidence reported in the book.*** Many self-help books are based not on reliable evidence, but rather on anecdotes drawn from the author's experiences and intuitions that are highly speculative. The best self-help books are supported by some form of reliable evidence.

3. ***Select a self-help book that recognizes that a problem is caused by a number of factors and has alternative solutions.*** It's not just your imagination—you are a complex human being, living in a complex world. Your problems are not so simple that they have a single cause and a single solution, yet the human mind is biased toward finding simple answers. After all, if there is one simple solution, then solving your problem is easier than if a number of factors have to be changed. The better books recognize that to solve a problem the best strategy is to change several factors in our lives, not just a single factor.

4. ***A self-help book that focuses on a particular problem is better than one that offers a general approach to solving all of your problems.*** The best self-help books focus on how to solve a particular problem rather than promising to cure all of life's ills. Books that try to solve all of life's problems are shallow and lack the specific, detailed solutions needed to solve a particular problem.

5. ***Don't be conned by psychobabble or slick writing.*** *Psychobabble* refers to vague but fashionable language about psychology (Rosen, 1977, 1993). Too often self-help book authors write in psychobabble like this: "You've got to get in touch with your feelings"; "Be the real you"; "You can do anything you want and it's o.k."; and on and on.

   Not all bad self-help books are infected with psychobabble. Some are smoothly written and disguise their inadequacies with slick writing that is so friendly you feel the authors are talking personally to you. All too often, however, slick books offer little more than one or two basic ideas, which could be communicated in two or three pages, plus hundreds of pages filled with polished writing and colorful examples. Such books lack detailed recommendations and sound strategies.

   Books characterized by psychobabble and slick writing frequently regress into cheerleading, which pumps you up to solve your problem. But too often, you just get motivated without ever learning precise strategies for solving your problem. After a few weeks or months, the motivation wears off because the author's recommendations lacked depth.

   It takes a lot more than slick language to help you cope with a problem. The best books are clearly written in a language that you can understand and include detailed recommendations for how to cope with a specific problem.

6. ***Check out the author's educational credentials.*** Just about anyone can write a self-help book if they can convince the publisher the book will make money. In most cases, the best self-help books are written by mental health professionals who have gone through rigorous training and spent many years helping people solve problems. Legitimate experts often come with one or more titles attached to their name. If self-help authors only have *Dr.* preceding their names, be suspicious. Some people purchase phony doctorates through the mail or obtain them from unaccredited "diploma mills" or even from religious cults. Although the presence of Ph.D., M.D., Ed.D., or Psy.D. after an author's name is no guarantee the author's advice will help you, the vast majority of good self-help books are written by individuals with such credentials.

7. ***Be wary of authors who complain about or reject the conventional knowledge of mental health experts.*** Some self-help book authors—especially those advocating New Age and Scientology ideas—tell you they are ahead of their time. These antiestablishment, antiscience mavericks attack the mental health professions as too conservative and too concerned with having scientific evidence to support claims for how to solve a problem. Consider such attacks as a red flag and avoid such authors. It is true that mental health professionals do not have the answers to all of life's problems and that new ideas are needed. But the ideas have to be supported by reliable evidence.

Dot.ComSense
Thinking Critically About Websites

The Internet

The Internet has opened up a new world for people seeking information about human adjustment (Norcross, Santrock, & others, 2003). Websites exist for every conceivable adjustment topic. Mental health topics are among the most frequently searched topics on the Internet (Davis & Miller, 1999).

Which websites offer good information to help you improve your adjustment? Researchers have found that almost half of mental health websites are inadequate in terms of accuracy and practicality (DiBlassio & others, 1999). Information is typically slanted toward the website's sponsor or owner (Lissman & Boehnlein, 2001). Unfortunately, the average person does not have the background to know how to sort through the maze of mental health sites and find the ones with the highest-quality information. For each chapter of the book, I have selected websites that provide good information about human adjustment. I have given these websites labels and noted the labels beneath a web icon in the margins of this book. If you go to the website for this text, http://www.mhhe.com/santrockha, and click on the same label as you see in the margin of the text, you will be taken to the website linked to the label.

Adjustment Strategies
For Finding the Best Information on the Internet Involving Human Adjustment

Here are some guidelines for selecting the best websites with information about human adjustment (American Psychological Association, 2003; Norcross, Santrock, & others, 2003):

1. *In many instances, the adjustment strategies for evaluating self-help books (see pages 26–27) also apply to websites.* For example, select websites that make realistic recommendations, not grandiose claims. Choose websites that recognize a problem is caused by several factors and has alternative solutions. Select websites that focus on a particular problem rather than offering a general approach to solving all of your problems. And be wary of websites that complain about or reject the knowledge of mental health experts.

2. *Evaluate the credibility of the website.* Does the site indicate a source for the information provided. Ask yourself, How credible is this information? For example, is it from a professional journal or other reputable publication? Is the information presented by a professional organization, university, or health-care institution? If the information cites an author, what is his or her professional background and experience? The best sites devoted to human adjustment are likely to be authored by a licensed mental health practitioner or experienced researcher in the field. If not, examine whether mental health professionals were consulted in the creation of the content on the website.

3. *Avoid websites that are purely commercial, such as those selling a particular book, seminar, drug, treatment center, or private clinical practice.* To learn about the site and its sponsors, look for a part of the site labeled "About" or "Our Company" or even "Investor Information," which states basic information about the website, its owners, financial supporters, and goals. Or go to the "site map"; it should also tell you where to find information about any commercial connections the site might have.

4. ***Be wary about information from blogs (journals), Listservs™, mailing lists, bulletin boards, and chat rooms.*** Anyone can post anything on these sites, including gossip, rumors, and superstition. In many cases, the people posting information use fictitious names or identities.

5. ***Protect your privacy.*** Some websites related to human adjustment will ask you to disclose personal information. Before submitting any private information to a website, make sure that the site has a privacy policy and read it. Look for a button labeled "Disclaimers" or "Privacy Policy" on any page that asks for personal information. Be cautious about sites that request personal information but do not post privacy policies. "The privacy policy should tell you if the information obtained on the site is traded or sold to other sites or organizations, or if it will be used to contact you in the future. If so, find out how you can opt out of this information exchange . . . " (American Psychological Association, 2003, p. 3). If you decide to join a chat room that asks you to provide your name and e-mail address, you may want to use a pseudonym.

6. ***Don't consider the Internet a substitute for professional help.*** Although the Internet can be a good source of information about human adjustment, it is not a substitute for professional help. If you have questions or concerns about the information on a website, you might want to talk with a mental health professional at your college's counseling or health center.

Review and Reflect

4   **Discuss some resources for improving adjustment and cautions in their use**

REVIEW

- Where can people can find mental health professionals to help them adjust more effectively?
- How are national support groups involved in human adjustment?
- What role do self-help books play in human adjustment? What are some cautions in their use?
- How extensively do individuals use the Internet to obtain information about human adjustment?
- What are some cautions in using the Internet for mental health information?

REFLECT

- Go to a book store or a library and select a self-help book. How does it fare in terms of the strategies described in this section for evaluating self-help books?

Reach Your Learning Goals

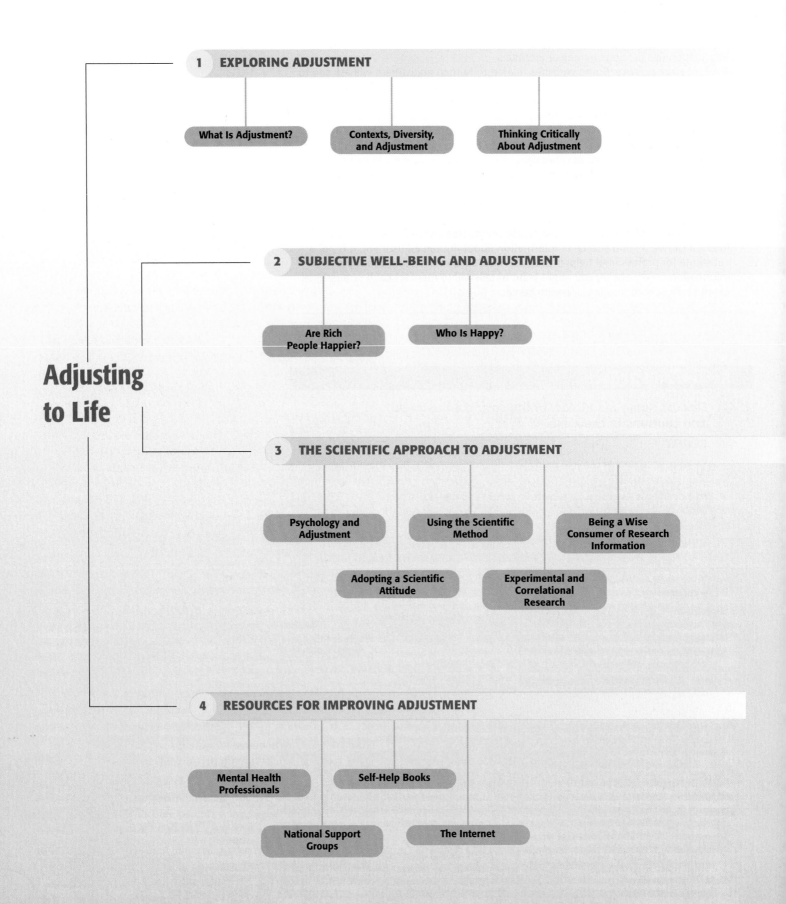

Adjusting to Life

1 **EXPLORING ADJUSTMENT**

- What Is Adjustment?
- Contexts, Diversity, and Adjustment
- Thinking Critically About Adjustment

2 **SUBJECTIVE WELL-BEING AND ADJUSTMENT**

- Are Rich People Happier?
- Who Is Happy?

3 **THE SCIENTIFIC APPROACH TO ADJUSTMENT**

- Psychology and Adjustment
- Adopting a Scientific Attitude
- Using the Scientific Method
- Experimental and Correlational Research
- Being a Wise Consumer of Research Information

4 **RESOURCES FOR IMPROVING ADJUSTMENT**

- Mental Health Professionals
- National Support Groups
- Self-Help Books
- The Internet

Summary

1   Identify some key concepts that provide a foundation for understanding adjustment

- Adjustment is the psychological process of adapting to, coping with, and managing the problems, challenges, and demands of everyday life.
- Contexts are the settings in which people live. Ecological theory is Bronfenbrenner's view that people's lives are influenced by five environmental systems: microsystem, mesosystem, exosystem, macrosystem, and chronosystem. Culture encompasses the behavior patterns, beliefs, and all other products of a particular group of people that are passed on from generation to generation. Cross-cultural studies involve a comparison of a culture with one or more other cultures. Ethnicity is rooted in cultural heritage, nationality characteristics, race, religion, and language. Gender involves the psychological and sociocultural dimensions of being female or male.
- Critical thinking involves thinking reflectively, productively, and evaluating the evidence. Being a critical thinker requires being open-minded, intellectually curious, intellectually careful, and skeptical. Critical thinkers examine the evidence for an idea or conclusion. Being a critical thinker about human adjustment involves describing and interpreting behavior carefully, identifying values and challenging assumptions about behavior, examining the influence of context and culture, evaluating the validity of claims about behavior, seeking multiple points of view and alternative explanations, appreciating individual and group differences, and engaging in self-reflection to enhance self-knowledge.

2   Define subjective well-being and describe the factors related to it

- Subjective well-being is the scientific term for how people evaluate their lives in terms of their happiness and life satisfaction. Extremely wealthy people are not happier than people who can purchase what they need. Those who strive the most for wealth tend to have lower subjective well-being than those who do not strive for wealth.
- Being happy and satisfied with one's life is linked to good social relationships; being mentally healthy and coping effectively with stress; having high levels of creativity, self-esteem, optimism, extraversion, and self-control; being a good citizen at work; having a spirituality and faith that embodies purpose, social support, and in some individuals, religious attendance; liking other people and others liking the individual, and being altruistic; and being satisfied with one's health. On average, most people are slightly happy, although everyone has their up and down moods. There is no single key to happiness, although the happiest people often say that they have good friends.

3   Characterize the scientific foundations of the study of adjustment

- Psychology is the scientific study of behavior and mental processes. Behavior is everything people do that can be directly observed. Inferences are conclusions that we draw from behavior. Mental processes encompass thoughts, feelings, and motives that each person experiences privately but that cannot be directly observed.
- Adopting a scientific attitude means thinking critically, being curious, being skeptical, and being objective.
- The scientific method is essentially a four-step process that involves conceptualizing a problem, collecting research information (data), analyzing data, and drawing conclusions. These steps link a theory, which is a broad idea or set of closely related ideas that attempt to explain certain observations, and a hypothesis, which is a prediction that can be tested.
- An experiment is a carefully regulated procedure in which one or more of the factors believed to influence the behavior being studied are manipulated while all other factors are held constant. Experiments have two types of changeable factors, or variables: independent and dependent. Experiments can involve one or more experimental groups and one or more control groups. Random assignment to these groups is an important principle in conducting an experiment. In correlational research, the goal is to describe the strength of the relationship between two or more events or characteristics. An important point is that correlation does not equal correlation.
- Individuals can become wise consumers of information about research by distinguishing between group results and individual needs, not overgeneralizing from a small sample, looking for answers beyond a simple study, not attributing causes where none have been found, and evaluating the source of the information.

4   Discuss some resources for improving adjustment and cautions in their use

- Professionals who can help individuals adjust more effectively include clinical psychologists, counseling psychologists, and psychiatrists. The counseling or health center at one's college is a good place to go to find help.
- National support groups are supportive, educational groups that address a single life problem or condition shared by its members. Participation is voluntary, members typically serve as leaders, and professionals rarely have an active role in the group's activities.

- Self-help books have become an important source of psychological advice for millions of Americans. High-quality self-help books can benefit individuals with problems in a number of areas. However, a number of cautions should be exercised in using these books: Don't select a book because of its cover, its title, its glitzy advertising, or because it is this year's so-called breakthrough book. Select a book that focuses on a specific problem, makes realistic recommendations, provides evidence, recognizes that a problem has multiple causes, is not characterized by psychobabble and slick writing, is authored by someone with excellent credentials, and is not authored by someone who rejects the knowledge of mental health experts.

- Mental health topics are among the most frequently searched topics on the Internet. Strategies for finding the best human adjustment information on the Internet include using many of the strategies for evaluating self-help books. Evaluate the credibility of the site and avoid sites that are purely commercial. Be careful with sites that involve blogs, Listservs™, mailing lists, bulletin boards, and chat rooms. Guard your privacy and block "cookies." Do not consider the Internet as a substitute for professional help.

Key Terms

adjustment 5	critical thinking 8	hypothesis 17	random assignment 20
contexts 6	subjective well-being 12	scientific method 17	correlational research 21
ecological theory 6	psychology 15	experiment 19	clinical and counseling
culture 6	behavior 15	independent variable 20	psychology 24
cross-cultural studies 7	inferences 15	dependent variable 20	psychiatry 24
ethnicity 7	mental processes 15	experimental group 20	bibliotherapy 26
gender 8	theory 17	control group 20	

Resources for Improving Your Adjustment

SELF-HELP BOOKS

The Authoritative Guide to Self-Help Resources

(2003) by John Norcross, John Santrock, Linda Campbell, Thomas Smith, Robert Sommer, and Edward Zuckerman. New York: Guilford.

This book presents the results of national surveys of more than 3,500 mental health professionals. Covering the full range of self-help topics, the mental health professionals evaluated books, movies, autobiographies, and Internet sites in 37 categories that included abuse, addiction, anger, anxiety, depression, divorce, love, self-improvement, sexuality, women's issues, and many others. Leading cognitive therapist Albert Ellis said this about the book, "An exceptional and truly authorita-tive guide for consumers seeking a range of resources and for professional referrals. . . . It is replete with remarkably comprehensive references for anyone interested in mental health."

Opening Up (1997) by James Pennebaker

New York: Guilford Press.

Earlier in the chapter, you read about Pennebaker's research on opening up one's emotions and how this process is linked with improved health. In *Opening Up*, Pennebaker provides many strategies for opening up and numerous case studies in which writing about one's emotions and stressful circumstances produced positive adjustment outcomes.

 **E-Learning Tools**

To help you master the material in this chapter, you will find a number of valuable study tools on the student CD-ROM that accompanies this book, and on the Online Learning Center, where you can find these valuable resources for Chapter 1, "Adjusting to Life."

SELF-ASSESSMENT

In Text

You can complete these self-assessments in the text:
- Self-Assessment 1.1: *My Beliefs About Psychic Phenomena*
- Self-Assessment 1.2: *My Subjective Well-Being*

Additional Self-Assessments

Complete this self-assessment on the Online Learning Center: *Opening Up.*

THINK CRITICALLY

To practice your critical thinking skills, complete these exercises on the Online Learning Center:

- *And the Winner Is* involves happiness and money.
- *Carrots and Sex* focuses on being a wise consumer of information in the media.
- *Where You've Been and Where You're Going* deals with your adjustment.

APPLY YOUR KNOWLEDGE

1. Your text discusses the characteristics of the experimental method. Choose something that you have always wondered about and "design" an experiment to test your hypothesis. Begin with the question that you want to answer, such as "is there a difference between x people and y people with regard to z?"

Once you have your question of interest, design an experiment that would allow you to test your hypothesis. Specify the independent variable (to be manipulated) and the dependent variable (the outcome.) How do you plan to measure the outcome? Do you need a control group—why or why not? From where would you recruit participants? Why?

Write out a one-page experiment that lists your hypothesis, your participants, your IVs and DVs, and your experimental design. Possible topic areas include health, stress, coping, and achievement.

2. Being a wise consumer of psychology.

Go to the library and search through back issues of newspapers or newsmagazines for a report of some scientific finding. Write a one-page report on the article, using the adjustment strategies as your base. Evaluate the article based on what you have learned about scientific reporting.

3. Being skeptical and thinking critically.

a. You have probably all heard someone say "if you dream that you are falling, and you hit the ground, you die in reality." This so-called "fact" is no doubt fueled by the person waking up out of fear. Upon closer examination, however, you will realize that there is no way to authenticate this statement. If it is true, then the person would be dead and you wouldn't be able to get any report on it! So, how do things that make no logical sense end up being accepted as fact?

Visit the Skeptic's Society at *www.skeptic.com* to find out more about examining things critically.

b. Many people have fallen victim to Internet scams or chain letters. Have you ever received an email telling you that certain things will happen if you forward a chain letter?

The reason why these scenarios are so appealing is that there appears to be something to gain with little or no risk involved. Did you ever forward one of these email messages to someone "just in case it's true?" Still other messages appeal to your altruistic tendencies to help find a missing child or send donations to a sick child.

All of these hoaxes have a number of characteristics in common. To learn the hallmarks of Internet hoaxes, go to *www.snopes.com* and type in "Disney" or "Microsoft" in the search box. You can also browse urban legends by subject area. You will be amazed to discover that some things that you thought were true were nothing more than fabrications.

VIDEO SEGMENT

Do the systems described by Bronfenbrenner really make a difference? What does adjustment look like in real life? For one case, watch the video "Adjustment in Context" in Chapter 1 of the CD-ROM.

Many of the findings discussed in coming chapters are based on correlational research. To learn more about this type of research, try the exercise "Correlations" in Chapter 1 of the CD-ROM.

Other findings reported in coming chapters come from experiments. Can these artificial situations really tell us anything about human adjustment? Designing situations in which facts about human behavior can be revealed while variables are controlled takes a lot of ingenuity. To see the situations devised for some famous experiments and get a better idea of how experiments are conducted, watch the videos for Chapters 2, 6, and 10 of the CD-ROM.

Personality

Images of Adjustment

Abraham Lincoln

Abraham Lincoln

I magine this. You have just become president of the United States, the most inexperienced person in history to be elected to this high office. You face the prospect of a long and bloody war that will claim almost 700,000 lives. You have to fire six generals before you finally find one who is effective. You will be vilified by political extremists. One of your children will die and as a result your wife will be overcome by grief and despair. You have a high level of anxiety and occasionally suffer bouts of depression.

The array of crises and problems just described belong to Abraham Lincoln, consistently rated as one of America's greatest presidents. Despite the overwhelming counts against him, Lincoln learned to manage his stress. Long before the age of positive thinking and cognitive therapy that we know today, Lincoln developed the ability to cope with his depression by not dwelling on his negative thoughts. He also used humor and relied on religion to cope with his problems. He once told his law partner that his storytelling and jokes served to protect him from his gloomy moods.

Might Lincoln have had certain personality traits that helped him become a great president and cope with problems? In a recent analysis, Steven Rubenzer and his colleagues (2000) asked more than 100 history experts to rate presidents on their personality traits five years before they became president. The history experts described Lincoln's personality as self-disciplined, open to experience, moderately extraverted, and conscientious, neurotic, and prone to bouts of depression.

Based on Lincoln's personality traits five years before he became president, would you have been able to predict his greatness as president? Even though we cannot predict exactly how a candidate will react to a crisis as president, we still think it is important to know something about a candidate's personality. We are not just a random collection of characteristics that change from one day to the next. Each of us has a more or less enduring style of thinking and acting, and that style influences how we adjust to challenges. That said, as Rubenzer and his colleagues (2000) recognized, an individual's personality traits do not predict how he or she will act in every situation. They did not ask the historians to assess a president's personality while in office because they believed that the pressure might affect his personality.

George W. Bush

John Kerry

In discussing Lincoln's personality, we described some of his enduring characteristics, but also mentioned that in some stressful situations they might change. In the first main section of the chapter, "What Is Personality?" you will see that psychologists agree that personality is a property of the individual, but that there is some disagreement about how consistent personality is across different situations. Then you will read about these main perspectives on personality: psychodynamic, behavioral and social cognitive, humanistic, and trait. Toward the end of the chapter, you will learn about the ways in which personality can be assessed.

1   WHAT IS PERSONALITY?

Personality is one of those concepts that is familiar to everyone but difficult to define. In this chapter, **personality** is defined as a pattern of enduring, distinctive thoughts, emotions, and behaviors that characterize the way an individual adapts to the world.

Why do individuals react to the same situation in different ways? For example, why is Sam so talkative and gregarious and Allie so shy and quiet when meeting someone for the first time? Why is Natasha so confident and Gretchen so insecure about upcoming job interviews? Some theorists believe that biological and genetic factors are responsible; others argue that life experiences are more important factors. Some theorists claim that the way we think about ourselves is the key to understanding personality, whereas others stress the way we behave toward each other.

This chapter presents four broad theoretical perspectives on personality—psychodynamic, behavioral and social cognitive, humanistic, and trait. They often give different answers to four important questions:

1. *What role do innate and learned characteristics play in personality?* Is personality due more to heredity and biological factors or more to learning and environmental experiences? For example, are individuals conceited and self-centered because they inherited the tendency to be conceited and self-centered from their parents, or did they learn to be that way through experiences with other conceited, self-centered individuals?
2. *To what extent is personality conscious or unconscious?* How aware are individuals that they are, say, conceited and self-centered? How aware are they of the reasons they became conceited and self-centered?
3. *How influential are internal or external factors in determining personality?* Is the way personality is expressed in any given situation due more to an inner disposition or to the situation itself? Are individuals conceited and self-centered because of something inside themselves, a characteristic they have and carry around with them, or are they conceited and self-centered because of the situations they are in and the way they are influenced by people around them?
4. *What characterizes a well-adjusted personality?* Is a person who is conceited and self-centered poorly adjusted? What combination of personality traits is linked to being well adjusted?

The diversity of theories makes understanding personality a challenging undertaking. Just when you think one theory has correctly explained personality, another theory will crop up and make you rethink that conclusion. Remember that personality is a complex topic and parts of the various theories are complementary rather than contradictory. Each theory has contributed an important piece or pieces to the personality puzzle. Together they let us see the total landscape of personality in all its richness (Burger, 2004; Derlega, Winstead & Jones, 2005; Ryckman, 2004).

www.mhhe.com/santrockha

Personality Theories
Personality Research
The Personality Project

personality A pattern of enduring, distinctive thoughts, emotions, and behaviors that characterize the way an individual adapts to the world.

Review and Reflect

1 Define personality and identify major issues in the study of personality

REVIEW

- What is personality and what are four issues addressed by the major personality perspectives?

REFLECT

- List the characteristics that you believe best describe your personality. Do you always describe all of these characteristics? Describe situations in which you have not displayed one of these characteristics. What external factors might account for this inconsistency?

2 PSYCHODYNAMIC PERSPECTIVES

Freud's Psychoanalytic Theory   Psychodynamic Revisionists   Evaluating Psychodynamic Perspectives

Sigmund Freud (1856–1939). The architect of psychoanalytic theory.

psychodynamic perspectives View personality as being primarily unconscious (that is, beyond awareness) and as developing in stages. Most psychodynamic perspectives emphasize that early experiences with parents play an important role in sculpting the individual's personality.

Psychodynamic perspectives view personality as being primarily unconscious (that is, beyond awareness) and as developing in stages. Most psychodynamic perspectives emphasize that early experiences with parents play an important role in sculpting the individual's personality. Psychodynamic theorists believe that behavior is merely a surface characteristic and that to truly understand someone's personality we have to explore the symbolic meanings of behavior and the deep inner workings of the mind (Feist & Feist, 2002). These ideas were sketched by the architect of psychoanalytic theory—Sigmund Freud.

Freud's Psychoanalytic Theory

Sigmund Freud (1917), one of the most influential thinkers of the twentieth century, was born in Austria in 1856 and spent most of his life in Vienna. He left Vienna near the end of his career to escape the Holocaust and died in London at the age of 83. As a child, Freud was regarded as a genius by his younger brothers and sisters. He was doted on by his beautiful mother, who was some 20 years younger than Freud's father. Freud became a medical doctor, specialized in neurology, and developed psychoanalytic theory through his work with psychiatric patients.

For Freud, the unconscious mind holds the key to understanding people. Our lives are filled with tension and conflict; to reduce them we keep troubling feelings and memories locked in our unconscious mind. Dreams, Freud believed, are unconscious representations of everyday conflicts and tensions that are too painful to handle consciously. Dreams disguise much of their content in symbols and require extensive analysis and probing to be understood, but Freud believed that dreams hold important clues to our behavior.

Even trivial behaviors, according to Freud, have special significance when the unconscious forces behind them are revealed. A twitch, a doodle, a joke, a smile, a slip of the tongue—each may have an unconscious reason for appearing. For example, Barbara is kissing and hugging Tom, whom she is to marry in several weeks. She says, "Oh, *Jeff,* I love you so much." Tom pushes her away and says, "Why did you call me Jeff? I thought you didn't think about him anymore. We need to have a talk!" Such a misstatement, or so-called *Freudian slip,* may reveal unconscious thoughts.

Personality Structures Freud likened personality to an iceberg, existing mostly below the level of awareness, just as the massive part of an iceberg is beneath the surface of the water. Figure 2.1 illustrates this analogy. Notice how extensive the unconscious is in Freud's view.

Notice, too, that figure 2.1 shows the iceberg divided into three segments. Freud (1917) believed that personality has three structures: the id, the ego, and the superego.

The **id** consists of instincts and is the reservoir of psychic energy. In Freud's view, the id is unconscious; it has no contact with reality. The id works according to the *pleasure principle*, which means that the id always seeks pleasure and avoids pain.

It would be a dangerous and scary world if our personalities were all id. Our sexual and aggressive impulses would be unrestrained. In fact, few of us are voracious gluttons, sexual wantons, or cold-blooded killers. As young children mature, they learn not to slug other children in the face. They come to accept that not all of their desires will be satisfied. Why, and how? As children experience the demands and constraints of reality, a new structure of personality is formed—the **ego**, the Freudian structure of personality that deals with the demands of reality. According to Freud, the ego abides by the *reality principle*. It checks the demands of the id for pleasure against what is possible in the real world. The ego helps us to test reality, to see how far we can go in satisfying our desires without getting into trouble and hurting ourselves.

Whereas the id is completely unconscious, the ego is partly conscious. It houses our higher mental functions—reasoning, problem solving, and decision making, for example. For this reason, the ego is referred to as the executive branch of the personality; like an executive in a company, it weighs competing demands and makes decisions to ensure survival and even success.

The id and ego have no morality. They do not consider whether something is right or wrong. The **superego** is the Freudian structure that is the moral branch of personality. It is what we often refer to as our "conscience." Like the id, the superego does not consider reality; it only considers whether the id's sexual and aggressive impulses can be satisfied in moral terms.

"Good morning beheaded—uh, I mean beloved."

id The Freudian structure of personality that consists of instincts and is the individual's reservoir of psychic energy.

ego The Freudian structure of personality that deals with the demands of reality.

superego The Freudian structure of personality that deals with morality.

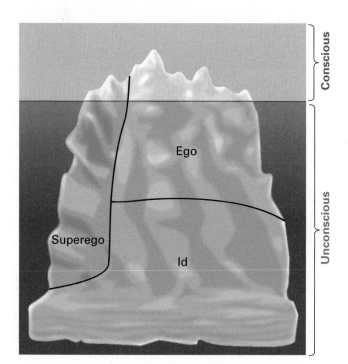

FIGURE 2.1 The Conscious and Unconscious Mind: The Iceberg Analogy The analogy of the conscious and unconscious mind to an iceberg is often used to illustrate how much of the mind is unconscious in Freud's theory. The conscious mind is the part of the iceberg above water, the unconscious mind, the part below water. Notice that the id is totally unconscious, while the ego and superego can operate at either the conscious or the unconscious level.

Both the id and the superego make life rough for the ego. Your ego might say, "I will have sex only occasionally and be sure to use an effective form of birth control." But your id is saying, "I want to be satisfied; sex feels so good." And your superego says, "I feel guilty about having sex at all." The ego must resolve conflicts among the desires of the id, the constraints of the superego, and the demands of reality.

Defense Mechanisms When the ego blocks the pleasurable pursuits of the id, a person feels anxiety, which the ego resolves by means of defense mechanisms. **Defense mechanisms** reduce anxiety by unconsciously distorting reality.

Repression is the most powerful and pervasive defense mechanism, according to Freud; it pushes unacceptable id impulses out of awareness and back into the unconscious mind. Freud said that our early childhood experiences, many of which he believed were sexually laden, are too threatening and stressful for us to deal with consciously; so we reduce the anxiety of childhood conflict through repression.

Repression is the foundation for all of the psychological defense mechanisms, the goal of which is to push, or *repress*, threatening impulses out of awareness. For example, through the defense mechanism of *sublimation*, the ego replaces an unacceptable impulse with an acceptable one. Figure 2.2 describes several of Freud's defense mechanisms and gives an example of each. All of them work to protect the ego and reduce anxiety.

Two points about defense mechanisms deserve emphasis. First, they are unconscious; we are not aware that we are calling on them. Second, when used in moderation or on a temporary basis, defense mechanisms are not necessarily unhealthy. For

defense mechanisms The ego's protective methods for reducing anxiety by unconsciously distorting reality.

FIGURE 2.2 Defense Mechanisms
Defense mechanisms reduce anxiety in various ways, in all instances by distorting reality.

Defense Mechanism	How It Works	Example
Repression	The master defense mechanism; the ego pushes unacceptable impulses out of awareness, back into the unconscious mind.	A young girl was sexually abused by her uncle. As an adult, she can't remember anything about the traumatic experience.
Rationalization	The ego replaces a less acceptable motive with a more acceptable one.	A college student does not get into the fraternity of his choice. He says that if he had tried harder he could have gotten in.
Displacement	The ego shifts feelings toward an unacceptable object to another, more acceptable object.	A woman can't take her anger out on her boss so she goes home and takes it out on her husband.
Sublimation	The ego replaces an unacceptable impulse with a socially acceptable one.	A man with strong sexual urges becomes an artist who paints nudes.
Projection	The ego attributes personal shortcomings, problems, and faults to others.	A man who has a strong desire to have an extramarital affair accuses his wife of flirting with other men.
Reaction Formation	The ego transforms an unacceptable motive into its opposite.	A woman who fears her sexual urges becomes a religious zealot.
Denial	The ego refuses to acknowledge anxiety-producing realities.	A man won't acknowledge that he has cancer even though a team of doctors has diagnosed his cancer.
Regression	The ego seeks the security of an earlier developmental period in the face of stress.	A woman returns home to mother every time she and her husband have a big argument.

example, the defense mechanism of *denial* can help a person cope with impending death. If defense mechanisms dominate our behavior, however, they prevent us from facing life's demands.

Personality Development   As Freud listened to, probed, and analyzed his patients, he became convinced that their personalities were the result of experiences early in life. Freud believed that we go through five stages of personality development and that at each stage of development we experience pleasure in one part of the body more than in others. Freud described the following five stages:

- *Oral stage* (first 18 months of age). The infant's pleasure centers on the mouth. Chewing, sucking, and biting are chief sources of pleasure.
- *Anal stage* (18 to 36 months of age). The child's greatest pleasure involves the anus or the eliminative functions associated with it.
- *Phallic stage* (3 to 6 years of age). During Freud's third stage, pleasure focuses on the genitals as the child discovers that self-stimulation is enjoyable. (The name of the stage comes from the Latin word *phallus,* which means "penis.") The phallic stage triggers the **Oedipus complex**, which is the young child's development of an intense desire to replace the parent of the same sex and enjoy the affections of the opposite-sex parent. (You might recall that in Greek mythology Oedipus unwittingly killed his father and married his mother.) At about 5 to 6 years of age, children recognize that their same-sex parent might punish them for their incestuous wishes. To reduce this conflict, the child identifies with the same-sex parent, striving to be like him or her.
- *Latency stage* (6 years of age to puberty). The child represses all interest in sexuality and develops social and intellectual skills. This activity channels much of the child's energy into emotionally safe areas and helps the child forget stressful conflicts of the phallic stage.
- *Genital stage* (adolescence and adulthood). This stage is the time of sexual reawakening; the source of sexual pleasure now becomes someone outside of the family. Unresolved conflicts with parents reemerge during adolescence. But once they are resolved, the individual becomes capable of developing a mature love relationship and functioning independently.

Freud claimed that at each of these stages, the demands of reality conflict with the source of pleasure (the mouth, the anus, or the genitals) and that our adult personality is determined by how we deal with the conflict. If the underlying conflict at a particular stage is not resolved and needs are either under- or overgratified, then the individual becomes *fixated*, or locked in that stage of development. For example, according to Freud, if a parent is too strict in toilet training, the child may become fixated at the anal stage; as a result, as the child grows up, he or she might strike back at authority figures by irresponsible or extravagant behavior—or become compulsively neat and frugal. Figure 2.3 illustrates some other possible links between adult personality characteristics and fixation at oral, anal, and phallic stages.

Oedipus complex In Freud's theory, the young child's development of an intense desire to replace the parent of the same sex and enjoy the affections of the opposite-sex parent.

FIGURE 2.3 Defense Mechanisms and Freudian Stages

Stage	Adult Extensions (Fixations)	Sublimations	Reaction Formations
Oral	Smoking, eating, kissing, oral hygiene, drinking, chewing gum	Seeking knowledge, humor, wit, sarcasm, being a food or wine expert	Speech purist, food faddist, prohibitionist, dislike of milk
Anal	Notable interest in one's bowel movements, love of bathroom humor, extreme messiness	Interest in painting or sculpture, being overly giving, great interest in statistics	Extreme disgust with feces, fear of dirt, prudishness, irritability
Phallic	Heavy reliance on masturbation, flirtatiousness, expressions of virility	Interest in poetry, love of love, interest in acting, striving for success	Puritanical attitude toward sex, excessive modesty

Psychodynamic Revisionists

Some psychoanalysts who followed Freud, embracing his core ideas about personality, soon took issue with some aspects of his theory. Dissenters questioned his ideas about sexuality, early experience, social factors, and the unconscious mind (Adler, 1927; Erikson, 1968; Fromm, 1947; Horney, 1945; Jung, 1917; Kohut, 1977; Rapaport, 1967; Sullivan, 1953). In particular, his critics stressed the following points:

- Sexuality is not the pervasive force behind personality that Freud believed it to be. Nor is the Oedipus complex as universal as Freud believed. Compared with contemporary society, Freud's society—turn of-the-century Vienna—was sexually repressed and paternalistic.
- The first 5 years of life are not as powerful in shaping adult personality as Freud thought; later experiences deserve more attention.
- The ego and conscious thought processes play more dominant roles in our personality than Freud gave them credit for; he claimed that we are forever in thrall to the instinctual, unconscious clutches of the id. Also, the ego has a separate line of development from the id, so achievement, thinking, and reasoning are not always tied to sexual impulses.
- Sociocultural factors are much more important than Freud believed. By stressing the id's dominance, Freud emphasized the biological basis of personality.

The theories of three revisionists—Horney, Jung, and Adler—have been especially influential in the development of psychodynamic theories, the successors to Freud's psychoanalytic theory.

Horney's Sociocultural Theory   Karen Horney (1885–1952) rejected the psychoanalytic concept that "anatomy is destiny" and cautioned that some of Freud's most popular ideas were only hypotheses. She insisted that these hypotheses be supported with observable data before being accepted as fact. Horney also argued that sociocultural influences on personality development should be considered.

Take Freud's concept of "penis envy": he attributed some of the behavior of his female patients to their repressed desire to have a penis. Horney pointed out that the people who had been describing women and the standards for suitable development were all men. She countered the notion of penis envy with the hypothesis that both sexes envy the attributes of the other, with men coveting women's reproductive capacities. She also argued that women who feel penis envy in fact desire only the superior status that men hold in most societies.

In Horney's view, the need for security, not for sex or aggression, is the prime motive in human existence. Horney reasoned that an individual whose needs for security are met should be able to develop his or her capacities to the fullest extent.

She also suggested that people usually develop one of three strategies in their effort to cope with anxiety. First, individuals might *move toward* people, seeking love and support. Second, individuals might *move away* from people, becoming more independent. And, third, individuals might *move against* people, becoming competitive and domineering. The secure individual uses these three ways of coping in moderation and balance, whereas the insecure individual often uses one or more of these strategies in an exaggerated fashion, becoming too dependent, too independent, or too aggressive.

Jung's Analytical Theory   Freud's contemporary Carl Jung (1875–1961) had a different complaint about psychoanalytic theory. Jung shared Freud's interest in the unconscious, but he believed that Freud underplayed the role of the unconscious in personality. Jung believed that because of their common past, all human beings share a **collective unconscious**, which is the impersonal, deepest layer of the unconscious. Thus, according to Jung, the roots of personality go back to the dawn of human

Karen Horney (1885–1952). Developed the first feminist criticism of Freud's theory. Horney's view emphasizes women's positive qualities and self-evaluation.

collective unconscious Jung's term for the impersonal, deepest layer of the unconscious mind, shared by all human beings because of their common ancestral past.

existence and the experiences of a common past have made a deep, permanent impression on the human mind (Mayer, 2002; Wilkinson, 2004).

The collective unconscious is expressed through what Jung called **archetypes**, emotionally laden ideas and images that have rich meaning for all people. Jung believed that archetypes emerge in art, religion, and dreams. He used archetypes to help people understand themselves (Jones, 2003; Knox, 2002; McDowell, 2001). For example, the mandala, a figure within a circle, is an archetype (see figure 2.4); it has been used so often in art that Jung concluded that it represents the self. Another archetype is the shadow, our darker self, which has been represented by fictional characters, such as Dracula, Mr. Hyde (of Jekyll and Hyde), and Darth Vader in the *Star Wars* films (Peterson, 1988).

Adler's Individual Psychology   Alfred Adler (1870–1937) was another of Freud's contemporaries. Adler emphasizes the importance of each individual's uniqueness. In Adler's **individual psychology,** people are motivated by purposes and goals. They are creators of their own lives. Unlike Freud, who believed in the overwhelming power of the unconscious mind, Adler argued that people have the ability to consciously monitor their lives. He also believed that social factors are more important than sexual motivation in shaping personality (Silverman & Corsini, 1984).

Adler thought that everyone strives for superiority, seeking to adapt, improve, and master the environment. Striving for superiority is our response to the uncomfortable feelings of inferiority that we all experience as infants and young children when we interact with people who are bigger and more powerful. *Compensation* is Adler's term for the individual's attempt to overcome imagined or real inferiorities or weaknesses by developing one's own abilities. Adler believed that compensation was normal, and he said that we often make up for a weakness in one ability by excelling in a different ability. For example, one person may be a mediocre student but compensate by excelling in athletics.

Overcompensation is Adler's term for the individual's attempt to deny a real situation or for the exaggerated effort to conceal a weakness. Adler described two patterns of overcompensation: *inferiority complex* is his term for exaggerated feelings of inadequacy; *superiority complex* is his term for exaggerated self-importance invoked to mask feelings of inferiority.

Carl Jung (1875–1961). Swiss psychoanalytic theorist Carl Jung developed the concepts of the collective unconscious and archetypes.

FIGURE 2.4 The Mandala as an Archetype of the Self
In his exploration of mythology, Carl Jung found that the self is often symbolized by a mandala, from the Sanskrit word for "circle." Jung believed that the mandala represents the self's unity.

Adjustment Strategies
Based on Psychodynamic Approaches

The concepts developed by Freud and his successors suggest several strategies that might help you understand yourself:

1. ***Think about your experiences as a child and how you act today.*** Although recent experiences are very important in your adjustment, your earlier experiences also may be influencing your behavior. It often is very difficult for adults to accurately examine their early experiences because they don't remember them well or distort them.
2. ***Recognize that you have unconscious feelings, drives, and desires that you may not easily identify.*** Most psychodynamic approaches emphasize that the unconscious aspects of your mind are so deep-seated that you won't be able to accurately identify these on your own and that you will need to see a therapist to unveil them. A psychodynamic therapist listens and interprets what a client says and does, bringing unconscious material into conscious awareness so the client can adjust more effectively.

archetypes The name Jung gave to the emotionally laden ideas and images in the collective unconscious that have rich meaning for all people.

individual psychology The term for Adler's approach, which views people as motivated by purposes and goals, being creators of their own lives.

continued

Carl Jung
Alfred Adler

3. *Examine your thoughts, feelings, and behaviors to determine the extent that you are using defense mechanisms.* Evaluate whether you tend to use defense mechanisms rather than face your problems. Look once again at figure 2.2 where we describe these defense mechanisms: repression, rationalization, displacement, sublimation, projection, reaction formation, denial, and regression. Try to come up with an example of when you have used each of these defense mechanisms in your life. Then be candid with yourself and reflect on whether you use these defense mechanisms too often in coping with problems and the possibility that your adjustment might benefit by facing your problems rather than repressing them.

4. *Evaluate the extent to which your security needs are being met.* If you feel insecure in your relationships, reflect on why you might feel this way and whether your feelings are exaggerated or realistic. Do you need to work through earlier relationships with your parents that might have produced the feelings of insecurity? Have you made some wrong choices in your friendship and romantic relationships that you could improve on in the future? Develop a plan to help you feel more secure in your relationships.

5. *Examine whether you have feelings of superiority or inferiority and discover areas of life in which you can excel.* If you have feelings of inferiority, think about ways that you can develop confidence in yourself. Examine the strengths in your life and build on your successes.

Evaluating Psychodynamic Perspectives

Although psychodynamic theories have offered revisions of Freud's psychoanalytic theory, they do share some core principles:

- Personality is determined both by current experiences and by experiences early in life.
- Personality develops through a series of stages that unfold with our physical, cognitive, and socioemotional development.
- We mentally transform our experiences, giving them meaning that shapes our personality.
- The mind is not all consciousness; unconscious motives lie behind some of our puzzling behavior.
- Our inner world often conflicts with the demands of external reality, creating anxiety that is not easy to resolve.

What constitutes effective adjustment for the psychodynamic perspectives? Individuals who are well adjusted likely have developed insight that allows them to bring unconscious conflicts into conscious awareness, understand how early experiences have influenced their behavior later in development, don't use defense mechanisms too extensively in coping with conflict and stress, and adapt effectively to reality.

One persistent criticism of the psychodynamic perspectives is that their main concepts have been difficult to test (Larsen & Buss, 2005). Researchers have not, for example, successfully tested such key concepts as repression in the laboratory. The evidence for psychodynamic concepts consists mainly of inference and interpretation. Support for psychodynamic perspectives has come largely from clinicians' subjective evaluations of their clients and from their clients' recollections of the distant past (especially early childhood). But clinicians can easily see evidence for the theories that they believe in and the accuracy of client's memories is unknown.

Others object that psychodynamic perspectives present a view of the person that is too negative and pessimistic. Their emphasis on early experiences within the family, claim critics, does not acknowledge that we retain the capacity for change throughout our lives. Some psychologists argue that Freud and Jung placed too much faith in the unconscious mind to control behavior. Others object that Freud overemphasized the importance of sexuality and biology in understanding personality. We are born into the world with more than a bundle of sexual and aggressive instincts, critics say, and the demands of reality do not always conflict with our biological needs. Furthermore, personality is not simply a matter of biology; social experiences and culture also shape personality. Psychologists are still revamping psychodynamic theory in the direction that Horney pioneered.

Finally, some critics have noted that many psychodynamic perspectives, especially Freud's, have a male, Western bias. Although Horney's theory helped to correct this bias, psychodynamic theory continues to be revised by psychologists who study female personality development, or personality development in various ethnic groups and cultures (Callan, 2001). Nancy Chodorow's (1978, 1989) theory, for example, emphasizes that many more women than men define themselves in terms of their relationships and that emotions tend to be more important in women's lives.

Review and Reflect

2 Summarize the psychodynamic perspectives

REVIEW

- What are the key concepts in Freud's theory?
- How do the key ideas of Jung, Adler, and Horney differ from Freud's theory?
- What are the strengths and weaknesses of the psychodynamic perspectives?

REFLECT

- What psychodynamic ideas may apply to all human beings? Which ones may not apply to everyone?

3 BEHAVIORAL AND SOCIAL COGNITIVE PERSPECTIVES

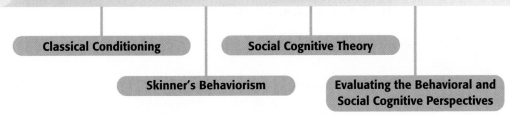

Classical Conditioning

Social Cognitive Theory

Skinner's Behaviorism

Evaluating the Behavioral and Social Cognitive Perspectives

Tom is engaged to marry Ann. Both have warm, friendly personalities, and they enjoy being with each other. Psychodynamic theorists would say that their personalities derive from long-standing relationships with their parents, especially from their early childhood experiences. They also would say that the reason for their attraction is unconscious, and that Tom and Ann are unaware of how their biological heritage and early life experiences have been carried forward to influence their adult personalities.

But if behaviorists and social cognitive theorists observed Tom and Ann, they would see something quite different. They would examine Tom and Ann's experiences, especially their most recent ones, to understand their attraction to each other. Instead of talking about the unconscious, they would examine how Tom might be rewarding Ann's behavior, and vice versa.

To understand personality, the behavioral and social cognitive perspectives focus on the environment, experience, and observable behavior. They analyze how people *learn* to behave in particular ways. How did Tom and Ann learn to be friendly rather than suspicious? How did they learn how to adjust to each other's eccentricities so that they continue to enjoy being with each other? Pioneers of the behavioral and social cognitive perspectives discovered three types of learning—classical conditioning, operant conditioning, and observational learning—that help us answer questions like these.

Classical Conditioning

Russian physiologist Ivan Pavlov discovered one important type of learning in the early twentieth century. Pavlov (1906) was trying to understand why dogs salivate to various sights and sounds before they eat. A dog automatically salivates if you put meat powder on its tongue. But Pavlov found that if a bell repeatedly rings just before the meat powder is given to the dog, the dog soon begins to salivate to the sound of the bell by itself. The dog has *learned* to respond to the bell. This is **classical conditioning**, a learning process in which a neutral stimulus becomes associated with a meaningful stimulus and acquires the capacity to elicit a response similar to the response to the meaningful stimulus. Pavlov revealed that classical conditioning consists of these components:

- *Unconditioned stimulus (UCS)*, a stimulus that produces a response without prior learning. Meat powder was the UCS in Pavlov's study.
- *Unconditioned response (UCR)*, an unlearned response that is automatically elicited by the UCS. In Pavlov's experiment, salivation in response to meat powder was the UCR.
- *Conditioned stimulus (CS)*, a previously neutral stimulus that is paired with the UCR. A ringing bell was the CS in Pavlov's experiment. Until Pavlov paired it with the meat powder, the ringing bell did not have a particular effect on the dog, except to perhaps wake the dog from a nap. The bell was a neutral stimulus.
- *Conditioned response (CR)*, the learned response to the conditioned stimulus that occurs after the CS-UCS pairing. After Pavlov rang the bell before giving meat powder to the dog, the dog began to salivate.

A summary of how classical conditioning works is shown in figure 2.5.

classical conditioning A learning process in which a neutral stimulus becomes associated with a meaningful stimulus and acquires the capacity to elicit a response similar to the response to the meaningful stimulus.

FIGURE 2.5 Pavlov's Classical Conditioning
In one experiment, Pavlov presented a neutral stimulus (bell) just before an unconditioned stimulus (food). The neutral stimulus became a conditioned stimulus by being paired with the unconditioned stimulus. Subsequently, the conditioned stimulus (bell) by itself was able to elicit the dog's salivation.

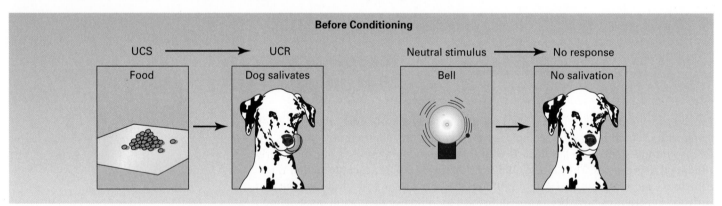

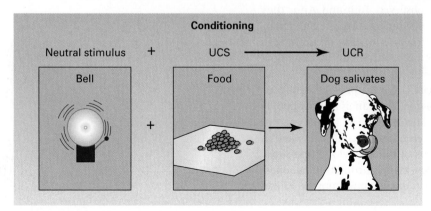

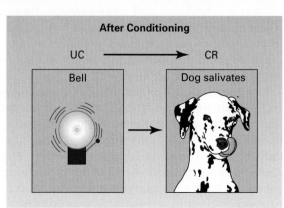

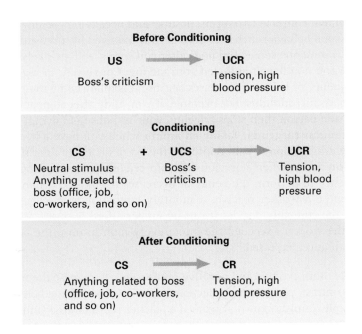

FIGURE 2.6 Classical Conditioning: Boss's Criticism and High Blood Pressure

Many behaviors may be learned through classical conditioning. For example, if a parent repeatedly says "No!" and yanks a little boy away from whatever he is about to touch, the boy may learn to stop whatever he is doing whenever he hears "No!" Through classical conditioning, children may learn to jerk their hands away from a flame before they are burned or not to eat certain things. Classical conditioning has a great deal of survival value for the individual.

Many of our fears are also learned through classical conditioning. We might develop a fear of the dentist after a painful extraction, fear of driving after having been in an automobile accident, and fear of dogs after having been bitten by one. Fears not only can be acquired through classical conditioning but also can be eliminated through conditioning procedures, which we will further discuss in chapter 15, "Therapies."

Classical conditioning may also play a role in some health problems and mental disorders. Asthma, headaches, ulcers, and high blood pressure—for example—can be partly the products of classical conditioning. We usually say that such health problems are caused by stress, but in many cases stimuli have become conditioned stimuli for physiological responses. Over time, as these responses become very frequent, they produce a health problem. For example, a boss's criticism may trigger muscle tension, headaches, or high blood pressure in an employee. Over time, as a result of persistent criticism, anything associated with the boss, such as work itself, may trigger these responses in the employee (see figure 2.6).

Skinner's Behaviorism

Classical conditioning influences our behavior, but other types of learning also determine how we act. Classical conditioning describes how we respond to the environment, but we also act on, or *operate* on, the environment, and those actions have consequences. The consequences, according to B. F. Skinner (1938), shape behavior. Skinner developed the concept of **operant conditioning** (or instrumental conditioning), which is a form of learning in which the consequences of a behavior change the probability of the behavior's occurrence.

Reinforcement and Extinction   **Reinforcement** is the process by which a stimulus or event that follows a behavior increases the probability that the behavior will occur again. A hug that follows a child's apology, for example, increases the probability that the child will apologize for a future transgression.

operant conditioning Also called instrumental conditioning, this learning process occurs when the consequences of the behavior change the probability of the behavior's occurrence.

reinforcement The learning process by which a stimulus or event that follows a behavior increases the probability that the behavior will occur again.

B.F. Skinner (1904–1990). Skinner's behavioral approach emphasizes operant conditioning.

Reinforcement comes in two forms: positive and negative. In *positive reinforcement,* the frequency of a behavior increases because it is followed by a rewarding stimulus. For example, if someone smiles and nods after you speak, you are likely to keep talking; the smile and nod have reinforced your talking. Conversely, in *negative reinforcement,* the frequency of behavior increases because it is followed by the removal of an aversive (unpleasant) stimulus. For example, if you study after someone nags at you to study, and the person then stops nagging, your response (studying) removed the unpleasant stimulus (nagging). Taking an aspirin when you have a headache works the same way. A reduction of pain reinforces the act of taking an aspirin.

Extinction occurs when a previously reinforced behavior is no longer reinforced and the tendency to perform the behavior decreases (Conklin & Tiffany, 2002). For example, suppose a worker receives a monthly bonus for producing more than a quota. Then, the company decides it can no longer afford bonuses. When bonuses were given, the worker exceeded the quota every month; once the bonus was removed, performance decreased.

extinction In operant conditioning, this process occurs when a previously reinforced behavior is no longer reinforced and the tendency to perform the behavior decreases.

punishment Refers to a consequence that decreases the likelihood that a behavior will occur.

Punishment   Both positive and negative reinforcement increase the frequency of a behavior. In contrast, **punishment** decreases the likelihood that a behavior will occur. For example, punishment is at work if a teacher reprimands a student for interrupting the teacher and the student then stops interrupting the teacher. Unlike reinforcement, punishment weakens a behavior. After punishment, the frequency of a response decreases.

The positive-negative distinction also can be applied to punishment. In *positive punishment,* a behavior decreases when it is followed by an unpleasant stimulus. In *negative punishment,* a behavior decreases when a positive stimulus is removed as a result of the behavior. *Time-out* is a form of negative punishment in which a child is removed from positive reinforcement. If a child is disrupting the classroom, the teacher might put the child in a corner of the room facing away from the class or take the child to a time-out room. Figure 2.7 compares positive reinforcement, negative reinforcement, positive punishment, and negative punishment.

Applying Skinner's Approach to Personality   What do operant conditioning and reinforcement have to do with personality? Skinner argued that personality is the

FIGURE 2.7 Positive Reinforcement, Negative Reinforcement, Positive Punishment, and Negative Punishment

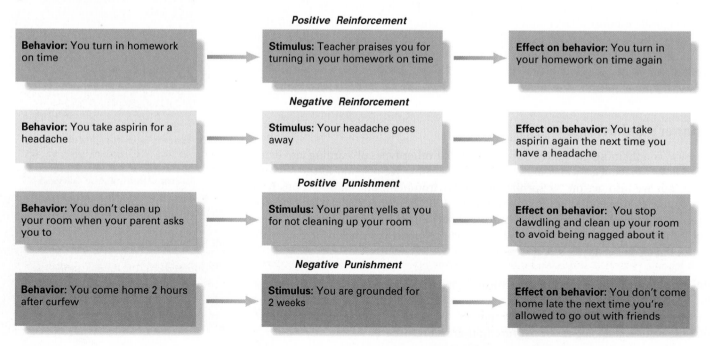

Positive Reinforcement

| **Behavior:** You turn in homework on time | **Stimulus:** Teacher praises you for turning in your homework on time | **Effect on behavior:** You turn in your homework on time again |

Negative Reinforcement

| **Behavior:** You take aspirin for a headache | **Stimulus:** Your headache goes away | **Effect on behavior:** You take aspirin again the next time you have a headache |

Positive Punishment

| **Behavior:** You don't clean up your room when your parent asks you to | **Stimulus:** Your parent yells at you for not cleaning up your room | **Effect on behavior:** You stop dawdling and clean up your room to avoid being nagged about it |

Negative Punishment

| **Behavior:** You come home 2 hours after curfew | **Stimulus:** You are grounded for 2 weeks | **Effect on behavior:** You don't come home late the next time you're allowed to go out with friends |

individual's external behavior, and that behavior is determined by the external environment. According to Skinner, we do not have to understand biological or cognitive processes to explain personality.

Some psychologists say that including Skinner among personality theorists is like inviting a wolf to a party of lambs because he took the "person" out of personality (Phares, 1984). Behaviorists counter that you cannot pinpoint where personality is or how it is determined; you can only observe what people do. For example, observations of Sam might reveal his shy, achievement-oriented, and caring behaviors. According to Skinner, these behaviors *are* his personality. Furthermore, Sam is this way because rewards and punishments in his environment shaped him into a shy, achievement-oriented, and caring person. Because of interactions with family members, friends, teachers, and others, Sam has *learned* to behave in this fashion.

Skinner stressed that our behavior always has the capacity for change if new experiences are encountered. Thus Sam's shy, achievement-oriented, and caring behavior may not be consistent and enduring. For example, Sam may be uninhibited on Saturday night with friends at a bar, unmotivated to excel in English class, and occasionally nasty to his sister. Skinnerians believe that consistency in behavior comes only from consistency in environmental experiences. If Sam's shy, achievement-oriented, and caring behavior is consistently rewarded, his pattern of behavior likely will be consistent.

Because behaviorists believe that personality is learned and often changes depending on experiences and situations, it follows that, by rearranging experiences and situations, the individual's personality can be changed (Miltenberger, 2004). For the behaviorist, shy behavior can be changed into outgoing behavior; aggressive behavior can be shaped into docile behavior; and lethargic, bored behavior can be shaped into enthusiastic, interested behavior.

Social Cognitive Theory

Some psychologists believe the behaviorists are right when they say that personality is learned and influenced strongly by environmental experiences. But they think Skinner went too far in declaring that characteristics of the person are irrelevant in understanding personality. **Social cognitive theory** states that behavior, environment, and cognitive factors—such as thoughts, memories, and expectations—are important in understanding personality. Like the behavioral approach of Skinner, the social cognitive view relies on empirical research in studying personality. But this research has focused not just on observable behavior but also on the cognitive factors that influence what we are like as people. Albert Bandura (1986, 1997, 2000, 2001, 2004) and Walter Mischel (1973, 1995, 2004) are the main architects of social cognitive theory's contemporary version, which initially was labeled *cognitive social learning theory* by Mischel (1973). Bandura, Mischel, and others are actively developing this perspective today.

Observational Learning   Bandura is perhaps best known for demonstrating that classical and operant conditioning are not the only ways that people learn. Suppose you think a particular instructor is a good teacher and you observe the way she teaches her class. Subsequently, when you are asked to give a talk in another class, you adopt her style of speaking and mannerisms. No one had given you any rewards in the past for imitating her. How did you learn her style and mannerisms? Bandura showed that by observing other people, we can learn; we can acquire knowledge, skills, rules, strategies, beliefs, and attitudes (Schunk, 2004).

Observational learning, also called imitation or modeling, is learning that occurs when a person observes and imitates someone else's behavior. Through observational learning we form ideas about the behavior of others and then possibly adopt this behavior ourselves.

Bandura (1986) described four main processes that are involved in observational learning: attention, retention, production, and reinforcement. For observational

Albert Bandura (*above*) and Walter Mischel are the architects of contemporary social cognitive theory.

social cognitive theory States that behavior, environment, and person/cognitive factors are important in understanding personality.

observational learning Also called imitation or modeling, the learning process that occurs when a person observes and imitates someone else's behavior.

learning to take place, the first process that has to occur is *attention*. You have to attend to what the model is saying or doing to reproduce the model's actions. Attention to a model is influenced by a host of characteristics. For example, warm, powerful, atypical people command more attention than do cold, weak, typical people.

Retention is the second process needed for observational learning to occur. You must code information about the model and keep it in memory so that it can be retrieved.

Production is the process of imitating the model's actions. People might pay attention to a model and retain what they have seen, but limitations in their motor skills might make it difficult for them to reproduce the model's actions.

Reinforcement is the final component of observational learning. On many occasions, we may attend to what a model says or does, retain the information in memory, and have the motor capabilities to perform the action, but not be motivated to do so. In Bandura's model, reinforcement may be needed to help motivate the person to imitate the model's behavior. In a classic study, Bandura (1965) demonstrated that children who had seen a model punished for aggression only reproduced the model's aggression when they were offered an incentive to do so.

Reciprocal Determinism   Bandura's demonstrations that people can learn through observational learning showed that cognitions can be important in learning. But what role do cognitions play in personality and how are they related to environmental factors, such as reinforcements? According to Bandura, behavior, the environment, and person (cognitive) factors interact to produce personality. To describe how these elements are related, Bandura coined the term **reciprocal determinism.** This term means that each factor influences and is influenced by the others, as figure 2.8 shows. Thus, the environment can determine a person's behavior, but a person's behavior can also change the environment. Furthermore, person/cognitive factors can influence behavior and can be influenced by behavior.

Let's consider how Bandura's concept of reciprocal determination might work in the case of a college student's achievement behavior. As the student diligently studies and gets good grades her behavior produces positive thoughts about her abilities. As part of her effort to maintain good grades, she plans and develops a number of strategies to make her studying more efficient. In these ways, her behavior has influenced her thought, and her thought has influenced her behavior. At the beginning of the term, her college made a special effort to involve students in a study skills program. She decided to join. Her success, along with that of other students who attended the program, has led the college to expand the program next term. In these ways, the environment influenced behavior, and behavior changed the environment. And the college administrators' expectations that the study skills program would work made it possible in the first place. The program's success has spurred expectations that this type of program could work in other colleges. In these ways, cognition changed the environment, and the environment changed cognition.

Personal Control   The concept of reciprocal determinism contrasts starkly with the behaviorist view that the environment rules us. Unlike Skinner, social cognitive theorists emphasize that we can regulate and control our own behavior, despite our changing environment (Mischel, 2004; Mischel & Shoda, 2001; Mischel, Shoda, & Mendoza-Denton, 2002). For example, imagine that someone tries to persuade you to join a particular social club on campus and makes you an enticing offer. You reflect on the offer, consider your interests and beliefs, and make the decision not to join. Your *cognitions* lead you to control your behavior and resist environmental influence in this instance.

Bandura (2001) and other social cognitive theorists and researchers emphasize that adjustment can be measured by people's beliefs in their capacity to exercise some control over their own functioning and over environmental events. Three aspects of personal control are delay of gratification, self-efficacy, and locus of control.

Behavior

Person and
Cognitive
factors   Environment

FIGURE 2.8 Bandura's Social Cognitive Theory
Bandura's social cognitive theory emphasizes reciprocal influences of behavior, environment, and person/cognitive factors.

reciprocal determinism Bandura's view that behavior, environment, and person/cognitive factors interact to create personality.

Delay of Gratification   One way you demonstrate personal control is by deferring immediate gratification in order to obtain a desirable future outcome. For example, in school you might resist the temptation to slack off and have a good time so that you can obtain a good grade at the end of the term. Walter Mischel (2004; Mischel, Cantor, & Feldman, 1996; Mischel & Moore, 1980) argues that the ability to delay gratification is an important characteristic in understanding an individual's personality.

Self-Efficacy   If you believe that no matter how hard you try you will not be able to perform well enough to obtain a decent grade in this course, are you likely to resist the temptation to skip class? Whether you delay gratification may be tied to your sense of self-efficacy.

Self-efficacy is the belief that one can master a situation and produce positive outcomes. Bandura (1997, 2000, 2001, 2004) and others have demonstrated that self-efficacy is related to a number of positive developments in people's lives, including solving problems, becoming more sociable, initiating a diet or exercise program and maintaining it, and quitting smoking (Fletcher & Banasik, 2001; Warnecke & others, 2001). Self-efficacy influences whether people even try to develop healthy habits, as well as how much effort they expend in coping with stress, how long they persist in the face of obstacles, and how much stress they experience (Clark & Dodge, 1999). Self-efficacy is related to whether people initiate psychotherapy to deal with their problems and whether it succeeds or not (Kavanaugh & Wilson, 1989; Longo, Lent, & Brown, 1992). Researchers also have found that self-efficacy is linked with successful job performance (Judge & Bono, 2001).

Self-efficacy helps people in unsatisfactory situations by encouraging them to believe that they can succeed (Schunk, 2004). Overweight individuals will likely have more success with their diets if they believe they have the self-control to restrict their eating. Smokers who believe they will not be able to break their habit probably won't even try to quit smoking, even though they know that smoking is likely to cause poor health and shorten their lives. To evaluate your self-efficacy, complete Self-Assessment 2.1.

Adjustment Strategies
For Increasing Your Self-Efficacy

How can you increase your self-efficacy? The following strategies can help (Watson & Tharp, 2002):

1. ***Select something you expect to be able to do, not something you expect to fail at accomplishing.*** Success breeds the belief that you can succeed. As you develop self-efficacy, you can tackle more daunting projects.
2. ***Distinguish between past performance and your present project.*** You might come to expect from past failures that you cannot do certain things. However, remind yourself that your past failures are in the past and that you now have a new sense of confidence and accomplishment.
3. ***Pay close attention to your successes.*** Some individuals have a tendency to remember their failures, but not their successes.
4. ***Keep written records so that you will be concretely aware of your successes.*** A student who sticks to a study schedule for four days and then fails to stick to it on the fifth day should not think, "I'm a failure. I can't do this." This statement ignores the fact that the student was successful 80 percent of the time (keeping to the schedule four out of five days).
5. ***List the specific kinds of situations in which you expect to have the most difficulty and the least difficulty.*** Begin with the easier tasks and cope with the harder ones after you have experienced some success.

self-efficacy The belief that one can master a situation and produce positive outcomes.

Evaluating My Self-Efficacy

Place a check mark in the column that best applies to you for each item: (1) not at all true, (2) barely true, (3) moderately true, and (4) exactly true.

	Self-Rating			
Items	**1**	**2**	**3**	**4**
1. I can always manage to solve difficult problems if I try hard enough.	____	____	____	____
2. If someone opposes me, I can find the means and ways to get what I want.	____	____	____	____
3. I am certain that I can accomplish my goals.				
4. I am confident that I could deal efficiently with unexpected events.	____	____	____	____
5. Thanks to my resourcefulness, I can handle unforeseen situations.	____	____	____	____
6. I can solve most problems if I invest the necessary effort.	____	____	____	____
7. I can remain calm when facing difficulties because I can rely on my coping abilities.	____	____	____	____
8. When I am confronted with a problem, I can find several solutions.	____	____	____	____
9. If I am in trouble, I can think of a solution.	____	____	____	____
10. I can handle whatever comes my way.				

Go to the appendix at the end of the book for scoring and interpretation of your responses.

Locus of Control People not only have expectations about their own ability to perform well, they also have expectations about how the world works. You might, for example, believe that you can perform very well at a job interview, but you might also expect that whether you obtain the job will depend mostly on whether you are lucky enough to have the interview when the interviewer is in a good mood. According to social cognitive theorists, how you adjust depends not only on your self-efficacy—your expectations about your own performance—but also on your locus of control.

Locus of control refers to whether individuals believe that the outcomes of their actions depend on what they do (internal locus) or on events outside of their personal control (external locus) (Rotter, 1966). People with an internal locus of control assume that their own behaviors and actions are responsible for the consequences that happen to them. In contrast, people with an external locus of control believe that, regardless of how they behave, they are subject to the whims of fate, luck, or other people.

Researchers have linked differences in locus of control to many characteristics, especially behaviors that influence physical and mental health. Compared with people who have an external locus of control, individuals with an internal locus know more about the conditions that lead to good physical and psychological health and are likelier to take positive steps to improve their health, such as quitting smoking, avoiding substance abuse, and exercising regularly (Lindquist & Aberg, 2002; Powell, 1992).

Individuals with an external locus of control are more likely than those with an internal locus to conform and not question authority (Singh, 1984). They often use defensive strategies in problem solving and coping instead of actively pursuing

locus of control Refers to whether individuals believe that the outcomes of their actions depend on what they do (internal control) or on events outside of their personal control (external control).

SELF-ASSESSMENT 2.2

Am I Internally or Externally Controlled?

Respond yes or no to the following items:

	Yes	No
1. Do you believe most problems will solve themselves if you just don't fool with them?	____	____
2. Do you believe that if somebody studies hard enough, he or she can pass any subject?	____	____
3. Are some people just born lucky?	____	____
4. Most of the time, do you feel that you can change what might happen tomorrow by what you do today?	____	____
5. Do you feel that most of the time it doesn't pay to try hard because things never turn out the right way?	____	____
6. Do you feel that when good things happen, they happen because of hard work?	____	____
7. Do you feel that when you do something wrong, there's very little you can do to make it right?	____	____
8. Do you believe that whether or not people like you depends on how you act?	____	____
9. Did you usually feel that it was almost useless to try in school because most other children were smarter than you?	____	____
10. Are you the kind of person who thinks that planning ahead makes things better?	____	____
11. Do you feel that when someone doesn't like you there's little you can do about it?	____	____
12. Do you think it is better to be smart than lucky?	____	____
13. Did you feel that one of the best ways to handle most problems is just not to think about them?	____	____
14. Do you feel that you have a lot of choice in deciding who your friends are going to be?	____	____

Go to the appendix at the end of the book for scoring and interpretation of your responses.

solutions; thus they more often fail (Lester, 1992). A wealth of research has documented that having an internal locus of control is associated with positive functioning and adjustment (Roden, 2004; Wu, Tang, & Kwok, 2004). To evaluate your locus of control, complete Self-Assessment 2.2.

Adjustments Strategies
Based on Behavioral and Social Cognitive Perspectives

What strategies can help a person become better adjusted according to the behavioral and social cognitive perspectives? The concepts proposed by these perspectives suggest adopting these strategies:

1. ***Recognize the extent to which reinforcement and punishment influence your behavior.*** Examine whether you are being controlled too much by reinforcement and punishment. If so, think about ways that you can gain personal control over your behavior. Look again at Adjustment Strategies for Increasing Your Self-Efficacy.

continued

2. ***Examine the extent to which you use reinforcement and punishment when interacting with others.*** When someone else does something you like, do you bother to reinforce their behavior with a smile, a compliment, or possibly even a gift?

3. ***Use your ability to learn through observation.*** Pay attention to one or more people you admire, observe their behavior, and engage in the behavior yourself to see if it will improve your adjustment.

4. ***If you don't have a mentor, consider obtaining one.*** A mentor is an adviser, coach, and confidant. A mentor can help you become successful and adjust to life's many challenges. He or she can advise you on ways to cope with problem situations and listen to what's on your mind. A mentor might be someone in the community you respect and trust or it might be a student at a more advanced level than you.

5. ***Evaluate the extent to which you are good at delaying gratification.*** Individuals who are well adjusted are characterized by the ability to delay gratification to reach important goals in life rather than impulsively seeking immediate gratification.

6. ***Examine whether you have an internal or an external locus of control.*** Well-adjusted individuals are more likely to have an internal locus of control than an external locus. For example, understand that your adjustment is due more to the effort you put forth than to luck.

Evaluating the Behavioral and Social Cognitive Perspectives

The behavioral and social cognitive perspectives have important implications for healthy adjustment (Hersen, 2005). Among the most important implications are the strategies just described, such as recognizing the extent to which reinforcement and punishment influence your behavior, thinking about ways that you can gain personal control over your behavior, examining the extent to which you use reinforcement and punishment when interacting with others, using your ability to learn through observation, obtaining a mentor, evaluating the extent to which you are good at delaying gratification, and examining whether you have an internal or external locus of control. These perspectives have highlighted the importance of analyzing an individual's environmental experiences for clues to his or her adjustment, and they have fostered a scientific climate for understanding adjustment. In addition, social cognitive theory emphasizes the importance of cognitive processes in explaining adjustment.

What are the weaknesses of these perspectives? Critics of both the behavioral and social cognitive perspectives take issue with one or more of these points:

- The behavioral view is criticized for ignoring the importance of cognition in adjustment and giving too much importance to the role of environmental experiences.
- Both approaches have been described as too concerned with change and situational influences on adjustment and not paying adequate tribute to the enduring qualities of personality.
- Both views are said to ignore the role biology plays in personality and adjustment.
- Both are labeled reductionistic, which means they try to explain the complexity of personality and adjustment in terms of one or two factors.
- Both the behavioral and social cognitive views are criticized for being too mechanical, missing the most exciting, richest dimensions of personality and adjustment.

This latter criticism—that the creative, spontaneous, human dimensions of personality and adjustment are missing from the behavioral and social cognitive perspectives—has been made on numerous occasions by humanists, whose perspective is considered next.

Review and Reflect

3 Explain the behavioral and social cognitive perspectives

REVIEW

- What is classical conditioning?
- What are the key ideas in Skinner's behaviorism?
- What is the social cognitive view of personality?
- What are the strengths and weaknesses of the behavioral and social cognitive perspectives?

REFLECT

How good are you at delaying gratification? How might delay of gratification be involved in college success?

4 HUMANISTIC PERSPECTIVES

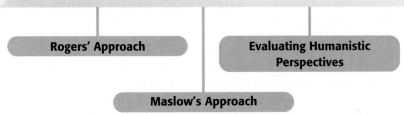

Rogers' Approach

Evaluating Humanistic Perspectives

Maslow's Approach

Remember the example of the engaged couple, Tom and Ann, who were described as having warm, friendly personalities? The psychodynamic and the behavioral and social cognitive perspectives suggest many factors that might explain their personalities and their relationship. These perspectives point to the possible roles of biological instincts, unconscious drives, childhood experiences, reinforcements, cognitions, and so on. But psychologists who take a humanistic perspective would argue that Tom's and Ann's warm, friendly personalities are a reflection of their inner selves. They would emphasize that a key to understanding the attraction between Tom and Ann is their positive perception of each other and that Tom and Ann have determined their own actions.

The **humanistic perspectives** stress a person's capacity for personal growth, freedom to choose one's own destiny, and positive human qualities. Humanistic psychologists believe that each of us has the ability to cope with stress, to control our lives, and to achieve what we desire (Cain, 2001; Smith, 2001; Spinelli, 2005). Each of us has the ability to break through and understand ourselves and our world; we can burst the cocoon and become a butterfly, say the humanists.

This optimistic view contrasts with the psychodynamic perspectives, which highlight the conflict and destructive drives in our lives and hold a pessimistic view of human nature. The humanistic perspectives also seem to contrast with the behavioral perspective, which emphasizes the power of rewards and punishments. It does have some similarities with the social cognitive perspective, though, especially with those theories that emphasize the role of personal control in personality. Carl Rogers and Abraham Maslow were the leading architects of the humanistic perspectives.

humanistic perspectives Stress a person's capacity for personal growth, freedom to choose one's own destiny, and positive human qualities.

Carl Rogers (1902–1987). Carl Rogers was a pioneer in the development of the humanistic perspective.

Carl Rogers
Abraham Maslow

Rogers' Approach

Like Freud, Carl Rogers (1902–1987) began his inquiry about human nature with people who were troubled. Rogers (1980) stressed the importance of becoming a fully functioning person—someone who takes a positive approach to life and believes in his or her capacity for personal growth, is open to experience, is not overly defensive, is aware of and sensitive to the self and the external world, and has harmonious relationships with others. Rogers believed that the tendency to reach this goal and actualize one's essential nature is inborn in every person. A person's basic tendencies, he thought, are to actualize, maintain, and enhance life. In the knotted, anxious, defensive talk of his clients, Rogers (1961) noted the obstacles that seemed to prevent them from reaching their full potential. His description of these obstacles focused on the development of the self and the *self-concept,* which in Rogers' theory refers to individuals' overall perceptions and assessments of their abilities, behavior, and personalities.

The Self   Through the individual's experiences with the world, a self emerges—the "I" or "me" of our existence. Rogers did not believe that all aspects of the self are conscious, but he did believe they are all accessible to consciousness. The self is a whole, consisting of one's self-perceptions (how attractive I am, how well I get along with others, how good an athlete I am) and the values we attach to these perceptions (good/bad, worthy/unworthy).

Rogers believed that as we grow up, we are conditioned to move away from our innately positive feelings toward ourselves, other people, and the world around us. Too often we hear our parents, siblings, teachers, and peers say things like, "Don't do that," "You didn't do that right," and "How can you be so stupid?" Parents may even threaten to withhold their love unless we conform to their standards.

These constraints and negative feedback continue in our adult lives. The result tends to be either that our relationships carry the dark cloud of conflict or that we conform to what others want. As we struggle to live up to society's standards, said Rogers, we distort and devalue our true selves. And we might even completely lose our sense of self by mirroring what others want. According to Rogers, the greater the discrepancy between the real self—which is the self resulting from our experiences—and the ideal self—which is the self we would like to be—the more maladjusted we will be. Furthermore, in Rogers' view, a person who has an inaccurate self-concept is likely to be maladjusted.

Unconditional Positive Regard, Empathy, and Genuineness   Rogers proposed three methods to help people develop a more positive self-concept: unconditional positive regard, empathy, and genuineness. **Unconditional positive regard** is his term for accepting, valuing, and being positive toward another person regardless of the person's behavior. Rogers strongly believed that unconditional positive regard elevates the person's self-worth. However, Rogers (1974) distinguished between unconditional positive regard directed at the individual as a person of worth and dignity and directed at the individual's behavior. For example, a therapist who adopts Rogers' view might say, "I don't like your behavior, but I accept you, value you, and care about you as a person."

Rogers also said that we can help other people develop a more positive self-concept if we are *empathic* and *genuine.* Being empathic means being a sensitive listener and understanding another's true feelings. Being genuine means being open with our feelings and dropping our pretenses and facades.

For Rogers, unconditional positive regard, empathy, and genuineness are three key ingredients of human relations. We can use these techniques to help other people feel good about themselves and to help us get along better with others (Bozarth, Zimring, & Tausch, 2001).

unconditional positive regard Rogers' term for accepting, valuing, and being positive toward another person regardless of the person's behavior.

Adjustment Strategies
For Becoming a Fully Functioning Person

Earlier we indicated that Rogers (1980) emphasized the importance of becoming a fully functioning person. For Rogers, being a fully functioning person meant that you are well adjusted. What strategies can you adopt to become fully functioning, and hence, well adjusted? Based on Rogers' view, here is what you can do:

1. ***Take a positive approach to life and believe in your capacity for positive growth.*** Rogers thought that individuals are highly resilient and capable of coping with stress and becoming well adjusted.
2. ***Be open to experience.*** Don't go into a shell and avoid the world. Recognize that through experiences, even tough ones, you will be able to learn how to adjust more effectively. Seek out new opportunities and view them as opportunities for personal growth rather than fear them.
3. ***Don't be overly defensive.*** Realize that you will make mistakes in life and be criticized for them. Don't let the criticism get you down. If the criticism is relevant, don't be defensive about it. Accept it and use it to your benefit.
4. ***Develop a more positive self-concept.*** Focus on positive perceptions of your self. If you notice that you are worrying about what others want, try to think of something else. Imagine positive experiences you might have and then develop a positive plan to make them possible.
5. ***Have harmonious relationships with others.*** Use unconditional positive regard when interacting with others. Be empathic, and learn to be a sensitive listener and understand another's true feelings. And be genuine. Don't be afraid to express your feelings. Drop your pretenses and facades.

Maslow's Approach

Are you motivated to fulfill your potential? Is that goal more important to you than finding a job you can be proud of? Is getting an A in this class more important than eating? According to Abraham Maslow (1908–1971), people must satisfy their basic needs before they try to satisfy higher needs. Maslow's (1954, 1971) **hierarchy of needs** states that individuals' main needs are satisfied in the following sequence: physiological, safety, love and belongingness, esteem, and **self-actualization,** which is the motivation to develop one's full potential as a human being (see figure 2.9). Thus, according to Maslow's hierarchy, your needs for food, shelter, and safety must be satisfied before you will be motivated to satisfy your need for love.

According to Maslow, self-actualization is possible only after the other needs in the hierarchy are met. As examples of self-actualized individuals, Maslow mentioned Pablo Casals (cellist), Albert Einstein (physicist), Ralph Waldo Emerson (writer), William James (psychologist), Thomas Jefferson (politician), Abraham Lincoln (politician), Eleanor Roosevelt (humanitarian, diplomat), and Albert Schweitzer (humanitarian). Maslow cautions that most people stop maturing after they have developed a high level of esteem and thus do not become self-actualized. To read further about the characteristics of self-actualized individuals, see figure 2.10.

The idea that human motives are hierarchically arranged is an appealing one. Maslow's theory stimulates us to think about the ordering of motives in our own lives. However, research has not confirmed that Maslow's hierarchy governs how people actually behave. The priority people give to their various needs appears to be subjective. For example, some people might put their needs for love and belongingness on hold while they seek greatness in a career in order to achieve self-esteem.

FIGURE 2.9 Maslow's Hierarchy of Needs
Abraham Maslow developed the hierarchy of human needs to show that we have to satisfy basic physiological needs before we can satisfy other, higher needs.

hierarchy of needs Maslow's concept that states that individuals' main needs follow this sequence: physiological, safety, love and belongingness, and self-actualization.

self-actualization The highest need in Maslow's hierarchy that involves the motivation to develop one's full potential as a human being.

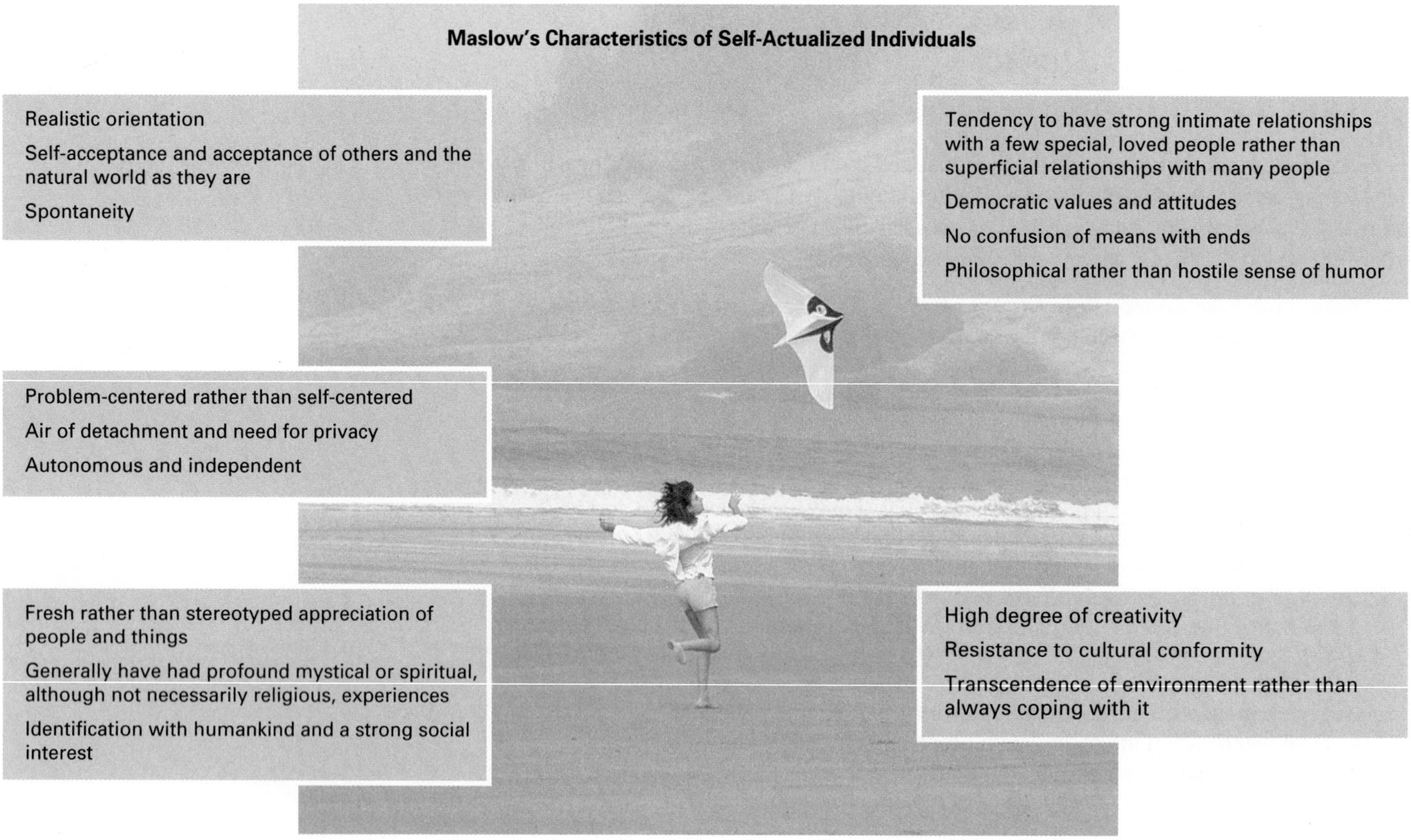

Maslow's Characteristics of Self-Actualized Individuals

Realistic orientation

Self-acceptance and acceptance of others and the natural world as they are

Spontaneity

Tendency to have strong intimate relationships with a few special, loved people rather than superficial relationships with many people

Democratic values and attitudes

No confusion of means with ends

Philosophical rather than hostile sense of humor

Problem-centered rather than self-centered

Air of detachment and need for privacy

Autonomous and independent

Fresh rather than stereotyped appreciation of people and things

Generally have had profound mystical or spiritual, although not necessarily religious, experiences

Identification with humankind and a strong social interest

High degree of creativity

Resistance to cultural conformity

Transcendence of environment rather than always coping with it

FIGURE 2.10 Maslow's Characteristics of Self-Actualized Individuals

Adjustment Strategies
For Becoming Self-Actualized

Is your life being stifled by unnecessary concern about your lower-level needs? Based on Maslow's writings, these strategies can help you to become more self-actualized:

1. ***Be motivated to change.*** Ask yourself how satisfied you are with your life. If you are not satisfied, commit to making some changes.
2. ***Be responsible.*** Be personally responsible for all aspects of your life. Recognize how important self-responsibility is for healthy adjustment. Assuming personal responsibility will help you to reduce the tendency to blame others or bad luck for your problems.
3. ***Evaluate your motives.*** Becoming self-actualized involves some risk. If most of your behavior seems to involve a need for safety or security, you might want to start exploring new avenues in your life. As you experience new choices and decisions, try to look at those as challenges and opportunities for growth rather than in terms of fear and anxiety.
4. ***Examine your positive emotional experiences.*** Think about which experiences in your life have produced feelings of awe, joy, fulfillment, amazement, and renewal. Consider how you might be able to repeat those experiences or find new ones that also might produce these positive emotions.
5. ***Have a mission in life.*** In Maslow's view, individuals who are self-actualizing have a mission or "calling in life." Their work is not just carried out to fulfill lower-level needs but to meet their need for such things as meaning and truth. Become personally

involved in a meaningful project and committed to making a difference in the world. You might want to create a *mission statement* of your desires, dreams, and destiny. This can involve thinking about what you would love to do, determining what matters most to you, pointing to your dreams for the future, figuring out what you want to contribute, and knowing what inspires you.

6. ***Monitor your progress.*** Maslow did not believe there is a final point at which someone becomes self-actualized. Thus, it is important to monitor and reevaluate your life on a regular basis. Each of us backslides from time to time. Continue to ask yourself whether you are taking responsibility for your adjustment, and if not, recommit to a path of self-actualization.

Evaluating Humanistic Perspectives

Maslow called the humanistic approach the "third force" in psychology—that is, an important alternative to the psychodynamic and behavioral forces. Psychodynamic theories, Maslow argued, place too much emphasis on disturbed individuals, and behaviorists ignore the person altogether. In contrast, the humanistic perspectives emphasize that the way we perceive ourselves and the world around us are key elements of personality (Spinelli, 2005). Humanistic psychologists also remind us that we need to consider the whole person and the positive bent of human nature (Bohart & Greening, 2001). Their emphasis on conscious experience has given us the view that people have a well of potential that can be developed to its fullest (Hill, 2000).

What do the humanistic perspectives have to say about what constitutes a well-adjusted person? They emphasize taking a positive approach and believe in one's capacity for positive growth, being open to experience, not being overly defensive, developing a positive self-concept, having harmonious relationships, and becoming self-actualized.

A weakness of the humanistic perspective is that it is difficult to test. How, for example, do you test the concept of self-actualization empirically? Self-actualization is not clearly defined, much less easy to observe. Complicating matters is the fact that some humanists scorn the experimental approach, preferring to depend on clinical interpretation as a database.

Some critics also believe that humanistic psychologists are too optimistic about human nature, overestimating the freedom and rationality of humans. And some critics say the humanists may encourage excessive self-love and narcissism by encouraging people to think so positively about themselves. However, to those interested in human adjustment, these weaknesses must be weighed against the fact that through Rogers' "fully functioning person" and Maslow's "self-actualized person," the humanistic perspectives offer rich portraits for healthy adaptation in life.

Review and Reflect

4 Describe the humanistic perspectives

REVIEW

- What are the key elements in Rogers' theory?
- How did Maslow explain human behavior?
- What are the strengths and weaknesses of the humanistic perspectives?

REFLECT

- With Maslow's description of self-actualization in mind (including the characteristics listed in figure 2.10), think of others you would add to Maslow's list of self-actualized persons. For starters, consider Mother Teresa (spiritual leader) and Martin Luther King (clergyman, civil rights activist).

Trait Theories

Traits, Situations, and Culture

Evaluating Trait Perspectives

So far, the perspectives on personality discussed have focused on trying to identify the factors that may determine personality and explain why one person is different from another. Every day, however, people take a more straightforward approach in their everyday lives. Even in the case of electing a president, as we saw in Images of Adjustment at the beginning of the chapter, people have described others in terms of their traits. Of course, we also describe ourselves in terms of traits.

A **trait** is an enduring characteristic that tends to lead to certain behaviors. You might say that you're outgoing and sociable and that, in contrast, one of your friends is shy and quiet. Similarly, many psychologists focus on traits as they attempt to understand personality.

Trait Theories

Trait theories state that personality consists of broad, enduring dispositions that tend to lead to characteristic responses. In other words, people can be described in terms of the basic ways they behave, such as whether they are outgoing and friendly or whether they are dominant and assertive. Gordon Allport (1937), the father of trait theory, believed that each individual has a unique set of personality traits. He argued that if we can determine a person's traits, we can predict how that person will behave in various circumstances. Although trait theorists disagree about which traits make up personality, they all agree that traits are the fundamental building blocks of personality.

Eysenck's Dimensions of Personality   Allport found more than 4,000 traits in an unabridged dictionary. Which traits are important? Do some traits always occur together as part of a "supertrait" or a basic dimension of personality?

Hans Eysenck (1967) tackled the task of determining the basic traits of personality. He gave personality tests to large numbers of people and analyzed the responses. Eysenck said that three main dimensions are needed to explain personality:

- *Introversion-extraversion.* An introverted person is quiet, unsociable, passive, and careful; an extraverted person is active, optimistic, sociable, and outgoing (Thorne, 2001).
- *Stable-unstable* (known as the *neuroticism* dimension). A stable person is calm, even-tempered, carefree, and capable of leadership; an unstable person is moody, anxious, restless, and touchy.
- *Psychoticism.* This dimension reflects the degree to which people are in contact with reality, control their impulses, and are cruel or caring toward others.

Eysenck believed that various combinations of these dimensions result in certain personality traits. For example, a person who is extraverted and unstable is likely to be impulsive. Figure 2.11 shows specific traits that arise from the interaction of the

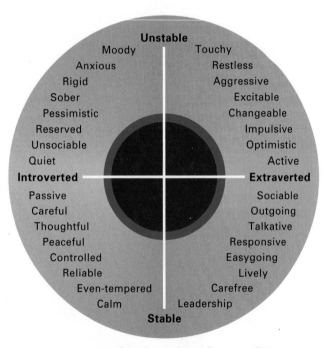

FIGURE 2.11 Eysenck's Dimensions of Personality
Eysenck believed that for people without a psychological disorder, personality consists of two basic dimensions: introversion-extraversion and stability-instability. He thought that a third dimension—psychoticism—was needed to describe the personality of individuals with a psychological disorder.

trait An enduring characteristic that tends to lead to certain behaviors.

trait theories State that personality consists of broad, enduring dispositions that lead to characteristic responses.

SELF-ASSESSMENT 2.3

How Introverted or Extraverted Am I?

To determine how extraverted or introverted you are, read each of the following 20 questions and answer either *yes* (if it is generally true for you) or *no* (if it is not generally true for you).

	Yes	No
1. Do you often long for excitement?	____	____
2. Are you usually carefree?	____	____
3. Do you stop and think things over before doing anything?	____	____
4. Would you do almost anything on a dare?	____	____
5. Do you often do things on the spur of the moment?	____	____
6. Generally, do you prefer reading to meeting people?	____	____
7. Do you prefer to have few but special friends?	____	____
8. When people shout at you, do you shout back?	____	____
9. Do other people think of you as very lively?	____	____
10. Are you mostly quiet when you are with people?	____	____
11. If there is something you want to know about, would you rather look it up in a book than talk to someone about it?	____	____
12. Do you like the kind of work that you need to pay close attention to?	____	____
13. Do you hate being with a crowd who plays jokes on one another?	____	____
14. Do you like doing things in which you have to act quickly?	____	____
15. Are you slow and unhurried in the way you move?	____	____
16. Do you like talking to people so much that you never miss a chance of talking to a stranger?	____	____
17. Would you be unhappy if you could not see lots of people most of the time?	____	____
18. Do you find it hard to enjoy yourself at a lively party?	____	____
19. Would you say that you were fairly self-confident?	____	____
20. Do you like playing pranks on others?	____	____

Go to the appendix at the end of the book for scoring and interpretation of your responses.

introversion/extraversion and stable/unstable dimensions. To evaluate the extent to which you are introverted or extraverted, complete Self-Assessment 2.3.

The Big Five Personality Factors Psychologists continue to try to identify the key dimensions of personality. Much recent research has focused on the hypothesis that five dimensions describe the foundations of personality (Costa & McCrae, 1995, 1998; McCrae & Costa, 2001, 2003). The **big five factors of personality,** the "supertraits," are openness, conscientiousness, extraversion, agreeableness, and neuroticism (or emotional stability). (Notice that if you create an acronym from these trait names, you get the word OCEAN.) Figure 2.12 describes each of these dimensions.

If the big five factors truly describe a person's fundamental traits, then these big five factors should be universal, stable, and predictive. Researchers are examining

> **big five factors of personality** The "supertraits" that consist of openness, conscientiousness, extraversion, agreeableness, and neuroticism (or emotional stability).

Openness	**C**onscientiousness	**E**xtraversion	**A**greeableness	**N**euroticism (emotional stability)
• Imaginative or practical	• Organized or disorganized	• Sociable or retiring	• Softhearted or ruthless	• Calm or anxious
• Interested in variety or routine	• Careful or careless	• Fun-loving or somber	• Trusting or suspicious	• Secure or insecure
• Independent or conforming	• Disciplined or impulsive	• Affectionate or reserved	• Helpful or uncooperative	• Self-satisfied or self-pitying

FIGURE 2.12 The Big Five Factors of Personality
Each of the broad supertraits that encompasses more narrow traits and characteristics. Use the acronym OCEAN to remember the big five personality factors (*Openness, Conscientiousness,* and so on).

Trait Theory
Five-Factor Model
Costa's Big Five Research
McCrae's Big Five Research

the extent to which the factors appear in personality profiles in different cultures, how stable the factors are over time, and the role the factors might play in predicting physical and mental health (Lingjaerde, Foreland, & Engvik, 2001; Pukrop, Sass, & Steinmeyer, 2000).

Do the big five show up in the assessment of personality in cultures around the world? There is increasing evidence that they do (Ozer & Riese, 1994; McCrae & Allik, 2002). Researchers have found that some version of the five factors appears in people in countries as diverse as Canada, Finland, Poland, China, and Japan (Paunonen & others, 1992).

Research has generally supported the concept of the big five factors, but some researchers believe they the big five might not end up being the final list of supertraits and that more specific traits are better predictors of behavior. Some support has been found for two additional personality dimensions: excellent-ordinary and evil-decent. The big five could become the big seven (Almagor, Tellegen, & Waller, 1995; Benet & Waller, 1995).

Traits, Situations, and Culture

Viewing people only in terms of their traits may provide only a partial view of personality. In his landmark book *Personality and Assessment,* Walter Mischel (1968) criticized the trait view of personality. Mischel reviewed an array of studies and concluded that many trait measures by themselves do a poor job of predicting actual behavior. For example, let's say Anne is described as an assertive person. But when we observe her, we find that she is assertive with her boyfriend but not assertive with her new boss. She is more or less assertive depending on the situation. Rather than consisting of broad, internal traits that are consistent across situations and time, Mischel argued, personality often changes with the situation. Mischel's view was called *situationism,* which means that personality often varies from one context to another.

Trait-Situation Interaction   Mischel's situationism helped to pave the way for viewing personality in terms of trait-situation interaction. According to this view, personality depends on both traits and situations.

Research is clarifying the link between traits and situations (Martin & Swartz-Kulstad, 2000; Mischel, 2004; Roberts & Robins, 2004; Walsh, 1995). For example, researchers have found the following:

- The narrower and more limited a trait is, the more likely it will predict behavior.
- Some people are consistent on some traits and other people are consistent on other traits.
- Personality traits exert a stronger influence on an individual's behavior when situational influences are less powerful.

Culture and Personality Is it only the specific setting that interacts with traits, or is the "situation" in trait-situation interactions something broader? Cross-cultural psychologists believe that both the immediate setting *and* the broader cultural context are important (Kitayama, 2002; Matsumoto, 2004; Triandis, 2001). For example, if they were investigating certain aspects of personality and religion, they might observe a person's behavior in a chapel (the immediate setting) and put it in the context of social conventions regarding who should be in church, when, and with whom and how the person is expected to behave (cultural characteristics).

One possibility is that the influence of the culture creates differences in the basic traits of whole nations. Recent cross-cultural research has focused on the traits of individualism and collectivism (Triandis, 2001). **Individualism** gives priority to personal goals rather than to group goals; it emphasizes values that serve the self, such as feeling good, personal achievement and distinction, and independence. **Collectivism** emphasizes values that serve the group by subordinating personal goals to preserve group integrity and relationships.

Cross-cultural psychologists describe the cultures in many Eastern countries such as China, Japan, and India as more collectivist than individualist, and they describe many Western countries such as the United States as more individualist than collectivist. Critics of Western culture say that an emphasis on individualism may undermine the basic need of the human species for relatedness (Kagitcibasi, 1995). Regardless of their cultural background, people need a positive sense of self *and* connectedness to others to develop fully as human beings and become well adjusted.

Adjustment Strategies
For Interacting with People from Individualist and Collectivist Cultures

If you come from a collectivist culture and you are about to interact with someone from an individualist culture, how can you communicate with the person more effectively? Some good strategies are as follows (Triandis, Brislin, & Hui, 1988):

1. ***Compliment the individual more than you are used to in your collectivist culture.*** A person from an individualist culture is likely to be very proud of his or her accomplishments.
2. ***Expect the person to be more competitive than people in your collectivist culture.*** Do not feel threatened if individualists act competitively.
3. ***Feel free to talk about your accomplishments.*** You do not have to be modest, but do not boast.
4. ***Expect that a person from an individualist culture will not be as attached to his or her family and extended family as you are.***
5. ***Do not expect the person to give a high priority to consensus.*** Efforts to change an individualist's views by avoiding confrontation and emphasizing cooperation are not as likely to work as they would in your collectivist culture.

If you come from an individualist culture and you are about to interact with someone from a collectivist culture, how can you communicate with the person more effectively? Effective strategies are (Triandis, Brislin, & Hui, 1988):

1. ***Pay attention to the person's group memberships.*** A person in a collectivist culture is likely to have stronger loyalty to these groups than you do. Spend time finding out about the groups that are the most important to the collectivist.

individualism Gives priority to personal goals rather than group goals; it emphasizes values that serve the self, such as feeling good, personal achievement and distinction, and independence.

collectivism Emphasizes values that serve the group by subordinating personal goals to preserve group integrity and relationships.

continued

2. ***Do not provoke competitive situations.*** A collectivist is likely to feel less comfortable in competitive situations than you do. Be sensitive about this.
3. ***If you have to criticize the collectivist, do so only in private, not in front of other people.***
4. ***Cultivate long-term relationships.*** Be patient. Collectivists value dealing with "old friends."

Critics of the individualism-collectivism dichotomy argue that describing entire nations of people as sharing a basic personality obscures the extensive variation that characterizes a nation's people. Also, certain values such as wisdom, mature love, and tolerance serve both collectivist and individualist interests (Schwartz, 1990).

Evaluating Trait Perspectives

Many trait psychologists are not willing to abandon the idea that people have consistent, enduring personality characteristics. Studying people in terms of their traits has practical value; identifying a person's traits does tell us something important about a person.

Researchers have linked traits to various aspects of adjustment, including health, the way people think, their success in a career, and how well they get along with others (Larson & Buss, 2002; McCrae & Costa, 2003). For example, as we saw in chapter 1, extraverts are more likely to be happy than introverts (Pavot & Diener, 2003). Also, individuals high in neuroticism tend to be prone to have irrational ideas, unable to effectively control their impulses, and poor at coping with stress (McCrae & Costa, 2003). People high in conscientiousness are more productive and have better marriages than their low-conscientiousness counterparts (Hogan & Ones, 1997).

Today, however, most psychologists in the field of personality are interactionists. They believe that both traits and situations need to be taken into account to understand personality (Mischel, 2004). They also agree that consistency in personality depends on the kind of persons, situations, and behaviors sampled (Mischel, 2004; Pervin, 2000; Swartz-Kulstad & Martin, 2000).

Suppose you want to assess the happiness of Bob, an introvert, and of Jane, an extravert. According to trait-situation interaction theory, you cannot predict who will be happier unless you know something about their situations. Imagine that you observe them in two situations, at a party and in a library. Do you think Bob or Jane will feel more comfortable at the party? Which one will be more content at the library? The extravert, Jane, is more likely to enjoy the party; and the introvert, Bob, is more likely to enjoy the library.

Review and Reflect

5   Discuss the trait perspectives

REVIEW

- What are the major trait theories?
- Are traits consistent across all situations?
- What are the strengths and weaknesses of the trait perspectives?

REFLECT

- To what extent do you believe the big five factors capture your personality? Look at the characteristics of the five factors listed in figure 2.12 and decide how you line up on each one. Then choose one of the factors, such as extraversion or openness to experience, and give an example of how a situation might influence expression of this trait in your life.

6 PERSONALITY ASSESSMENT

```
Types of Assessment          Self-Report Tests

        Projective Tests          Behavioral and Cognitive
                                         Assessment
```

"This line running this way indicates that you are a gregarious person. This division over here suggests that you are a risk taker; I bet you like to do things that are adventurous sometimes." These are words you might hear from a palmist. Palmistry purports to "read" an individual's personality by interpreting the irregularities and folds in the skin of the palm. Researchers debunk palmistry as quackery and point out that palmists give no reasonable explanation for their inferences about personality and point out that the palm's characteristics can change through age and even exercise.

Even so, palmists manage to stay in business. They do so, in part, because they are keen observers—they respond to such cues as voice, general demeanor, and dress, which are more relevant signs of personality than the lines and folds on a person's palm. Palmists also are experts at offering general, trivial statements such as "Although you usually are affectionate with others, sometimes you don't get along with people." If you make your predictions broad enough, any person can fit your description. Perhaps above all, palmists survive because many people are curious about themselves; they welcome help in figuring out who they really are.

Types of Assessment

Although going to a palmist is not likely to help you learn more about your personality or how to become better adjusted, an interest assessment can bring many benefits. As we discussed in chapter 1, self-assessment can give you insight about many aspects of your life that can help you to become better adjusted. Further, psychologists have developed many tests of personality. Clinical and school psychologists use personality tests to improve their diagnosis and treatment of the individual. Industrial psychologists and vocational counselors use personality tests to help the individual select a career. Most personality tests are designed to assess stable, enduring characteristics, free of situational influence (Ozer, 2001).

In contrast to palmists, psychologists use scientifically developed measures to assess personality (Gregory, 2004). In particular, they aim to develop tests that are both reliable and valid. Broadly speaking, a test is *reliable* if results of the test are consistent over time and in different situations; a test is *valid,* if it measures what it claims to measure. You can find many tests on the Internet that claim to assess your personality, but in many cases, their reliability and validity have not been assessed. Throughout this book and on the CD-ROM, you are given the opportunity to complete self-assessments related to many aspects of adjustment. In most cases, the reliability and validity of the self-assessments also have not been established and they are used for instructional purposes. In contrast, the reliability and validity of formal personality tests used by psychologists have usually been studied, although the reliability and validity of the tests can vary considerably. In clinical practice and in research, the three main types of personality assessments used by psychologists are projective tests, self-report tests, and behavioral and cognitive assessments.

Projective Tests

A **projective test** presents an ambiguous stimulus and asks you to describe it or tell a story about it—in other words, to *project* your own meaning onto the stimulus.

projective test Personality assessment tool that presents individuals with an ambiguous stimulus and then asks them to describe it or tell a story about it; based on the assumption that the ambiguity of the stimulus allows individuals to project their feelings, desires, needs, and attitudes onto it.

Projective tests are based on the assumption that the ambiguity of the stimulus allows individuals to invest it with their feelings, desires, needs, and attitudes (Hilsenroth, 2003; Leichtman, 2003). The tests are designed to elicit the individual's unconscious feelings and conflicts, providing an assessment that goes deeper than the surface of personality (Porcerelli & Hibbard, 2003). Thus, projective tests are theoretically aligned with the psychodynamic perspectives. They attempt to get inside of your mind to discover how you really feel and think, going beyond the way you present yourself.

Rorschach Inkblot Test The **Rorschach inkblot test,** developed in 1921 by the Swiss psychiatrist Hermann Rorschach, uses an individual's perception of the inkblots to assess his or her personality. The test consists of 10 cards, half in black and white and half in color, which are shown to the individual one at a time (see figure 2.13). The person taking the Rorschach test is asked to describe what he or she sees in each of the inkblots. For example, an individual may say, "That looks like two people fighting." After the individual has responded to all 10 inkblots, the examiner presents each of the inkblots again and asks about the individual's earlier response. For example, the examiner might ask, "*Where* did you see the two people fighting?" and "*What* about the inkblot made the two people look like they were fighting?" Besides recording the responses, the examiner notes the individual's mannerisms, gestures, and attitudes.

How useful is the Rorschach in assessing personality? The answer depends on one's perspective (Meyer, 2003). Researchers are skeptical about the Rorschach (Garb & others, 2001; Weiner, 2003). Their disenchantment stems from the failure of the Rorschach to meet the criteria of reliability and validity. If the Rorschach were reliable, two different scorers should agree on the personality characteristics of the individual being tested. If the Rorschach were valid, it should be able to predict behavior outside of the testing situation; that is, it should predict whether an individual will attempt

Rorschach inkblot test A widely used projective test; it uses an individual's perception of the inkblots to determine his or her personality.

FIGURE 2.13 Type of Stimulus Used in the Rorschach Inkblot Test

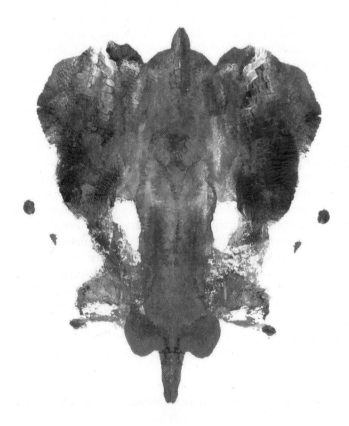

suicide, become severely depressed, cope successfully with stress, or get along well with others. Research suggests that the Rorschach does not meet these criteria of reliability and validity (Lilienfeld, Wood, & Garb, 2000).

Yet the Rorschach continues to enjoy widespread use in clinical circles. Some clinicians say it is better than any other measure at getting at the underlying core of an individual's personality (Ephraim, 2000; Meyer, 2001). They claim that the Rorschach is a valuable clinical tool, providing insights about the unconscious mind that no other personality test can provide (Hilsenroth, 2003).

The Rorschach controversy continues (Garb & others, 2001; Kaplan & Saccuzzo, 2005; Meyer, 2003). And it probably will not subside in the near future.

Other Projective Tests   Another popular projective test is the **Thematic Apperception Test (TAT),** which was developed in the 1930s and is designed to elicit stories that reveal something about an individual's personality. The TAT consists of a series of pictures like the one in figure 2.14, each on an individual card. The person taking the TAT is asked to tell a story about each of the pictures, including events leading up to the situation, the characters' thoughts and feelings, and the way the situation turns out. The tester assumes that the person projects unconscious feelings and thoughts into the story (Herzberg, 2000; Moretti & Rossini, 2003). In addition to being used in clinical practice, the TAT is used in research on people's need for achievement (Cramer, 1999; Cramer & Brilliant, 2001).

Many other projective tests are used in clinical assessment (Sherry, Dahlen, & Holaday, 2003). One test asks the individual to complete a sentence (for example, "I often feel . . . ," "I would like to . . ."); another test asks the individual to draw a person; and another test presents a word, such as *fear* or *happy,* and asks the individual to say the first thing that comes to mind. Like the Rorschach, these tests have been criticized for having low reliability and validity, but advocates argue that these projective tests reveal the underlying nature of the individual's personality better than other types of tests can (Lilienfeld & others, 2000; Sherry & others 2003).

Self-Report Tests

Unlike projective techniques, self-report tests do not attempt to assess an individual's unconscious personality. Rather, **self-report tests,** also called *objective tests* or *inventories,* directly ask people whether items describe them or not (Segal & Coolidge, 2003). For example, self-report personality tests include questions or statements such as "I am easily embarrassed," " I love to go to parties," and "I like to watch cartoons on TV." The respondent must choose from a limited number of answers, such as yes or no, true or false, agree or disagree.

Adherents of the trait perspectives argue that self-report tests have produced a better understanding of an individual's personality traits than can be derived from, for example, projective tests. However, some critics (especially psychodynamic theorists) believe that the self-report measures do not get at the underlying core of personality; other critics (especially behaviorists and social cognitive theorists) believe that the self-report measures do not adequately capture the way personality changes as the individual interacts with the environment.

Many of the early self-report tests were based on *face validity,* which is an assumption that the content of the test items is a good indicator of the individual's personality. For example, if I include the item "I enjoy being with people" to determine whether or not you are introverted and you answer "Yes," I accept your response as a straightforward indication that you are not introverted. Tests based on face validity assume that you are responding honestly and nondefensively, giving the examiner an accurate portrayal of your personality.

But not everyone is honest. And even if an individual is usually honest, he or she may give socially desirable answers. When motivated by *social desirability,*

"Roschach! What's to become of you?"
© Sidney Harris. Reprinted with permission.

FIGURE 2.14 Picture from the Thematic Apperception Test (TAT)

The Rorschach Inkblot Test

Thematic Apperception Test (TAT) A projective test designed to elicit stories that reveal something about an individual's personality.

self-report tests Also called *objective tests* or *inventories,* they directly ask people whether items describe them or not.

individuals say what they think the interviewer wants to hear or what they think will make them look better. For example, if I am a lazy person, I may try to present myself in a more positive way; therefore, I would respond "No" to: "I fritter away time too much."

Because of such responses, psychologists developed empirically keyed tests. An **empirically keyed test** relies on its items to predict some criterion. Unlike tests based on face validity, empirically keyed tests make no assumptions about the nature of the items (Segal & Coolidge, 2003). Imagine that we want to develop a test that will determine whether or not applicants for a position as police officer are likely to be competent at the job. We might ask a large number of questions of police officers, some of whom have excellent job records and others who have not performed as well. We would then use those questions that differentiate between competent and incompetent police officers. If the item "I enjoy reading poetry" predicts success as a police officer, then we would include it on the test even though it seems unrelated to police work.

Minnesota Multiphasic Personality Inventory (MMPI) The most widely used and researched empirically keyed self-report personality test is the **Minnesota Multiphasic Personality Inventory (MMPI)**. The MMPI was initially constructed in the 1940s to assess "abnormal" personality tendencies and to improve the diagnosis of individuals with mental disorders. One thousand statements were given to both mental patients and apparently normal people. How often individuals agreed with each item was calculated. Only the items that clearly differentiated the psychiatric patients from the normal individuals were retained. The items were grouped according to categories, or *scales,* such as depression, schizophrenia, and social introversion. For example, the statement "I sometimes tease animals" seems to have little to do with depression—that is, it has little face validity—but it might still be included on the depression scale of the MMPI if patients diagnosed with a depressive disorder agreed with the statement significantly more than did normal individuals (see figure 2.15).

empirically keyed test Relies on its items to predict some criterion.

Minnesota Multiphasic Personality Inventory (MMPI) The most widely used and researched empirically keyed self-report personality test.

FIGURE 2.15 Clinical Scales of the MMPI and Sample Items
The MMPI is the most widely used self-report personality test. This figure shows the 10 clinical scales and a sample item for each scale. Answering each sample item "true" would reflect the direction of the scales.

Clinical Scales	Sample Items
Hypochondriasis (Hs). (Abnormal concern with bodily functions)	"At times I get strong cramps in my intestines."
Depression (D). (Pessimism, hopelessness, slowing of action and thought)	"I am often very tense on the job."
Conversion Hysteria (Hy). (Unconscious use of physical and mental problems to avoid conflicts or responsibility)	"Sometimes there is a feeling like something is pressing in on my head."
Psychopathic Deviate (Pd). (Disregard of social custom, shallow emotions, inability to profit from experience)	"I wish I could do over some of the things I have done."
Masculinity-Femininity (Mf). (Items differentiating between men and women)	"I used to like to do the dances in gym class."
Paranoia (Pa). (Abnormal suspiciousness, delusions of grandeur or persecution)	"It distresses me that people have the wrong ideas about me."
Psychasthenia (Pt). (Obsessions, compulsiveness, fears, guilt, indecisiveness)	"The things that run through my head sometimes are horrible."
Schizophrenia (Sc). (Bizarre, unusual thoughts or behavior, withdrawal, hallucinations, delusions)	"There are those out there who want to get me."
Hypomania (Ma). (Emotional excitement, flight of ideas, overactivity)	"Sometimes I think so fast I can't keep up."
Social Introversion (Si). (Shyness, disinterest in others, insecurity)	"I give up too easily when discussing things with others."

The MMPI was streamlined to 550 items, each of which can be answered "true," "false," or "cannot say." The test was revised in 1989; the revision, called the MMPI-2, has 567 items. The items vary widely in content and include such statements as "I like to read magazines," "I never have trouble falling asleep," and "People are out to get me."

The items on the MMPI-2 are categorized into clinical scales not only for such serious disorders as schizophrenia but also for such problems as anger and inability to function in a job. In addition, the MMPI-2 includes four validity scales that are designed to indicate whether an individual is lying, careless, defensive, or evasive when answering the test items. For example, people who respond "false" repeatedly to items, such as "I get angry sometimes," might be trying to make themselves look better than they are.

The MMPI-2 continues to be widely used around the world to assess personality and predict outcomes (Archer & others, 2001; Butcher, 2003; Gotts & Knudsen, 2005). It has been so popular that it has been translated into more than 20 languages. It is used not only by clinical psychologists to assess a person's mental health, but also to predict which individuals will make the best job candidates or which career an individual should pursue.

Assessments of the Big Five Factors   Paul Costa and Robert McCrae (1992) constructed a test, the *Neuroticism Extraversion Openness Personality Inventory–Revised* (or *NEO-PI-R,* for short), to assess the big five factors: openness, conscientiousness, extraversion, agreeableness, and neuroticism (emotional stability). Costa and McCrae believe that the test can improve the diagnosis of personality disorders and help therapists understand how therapy might influence different types of clients. For instance, individuals who score high on the extraversion factor might prefer group over individual psychotherapy, whereas introverts might do better in individual psychotherapy.

Another measure that is used to assess the big five factors is the Hogan Personality Inventory (HPI) created by Robert Hogan (1986). Like the NEO-PI-R, one way in which the HPI is used is to attempt to predict job success. Researchers have found that the HPI predicts supervisor ratings and success in training courses (Wiggins & Trapnell, 1997).

Behavioral and Cognitive Assessment

Unlike either projective tests or self-report tests, behavioral assessment of personality does not aim to remove the influence of the situation on personality (Heiby & Haynes, 2004). Behavioral assessment is based on observing the individual's behavior directly (Hartmann, Barrios, & Wood, 2003).

Behavioral assessment of personality plays an important role in some treatments for psychological disorders. Often the first step in changing maladaptive behavior is to observe its frequency (Hartmann, & others, 2003). The therapist then modifies some aspect of the environment, such as getting the parents and the child's teacher to stop giving the child attention when he or she engages in aggressive behavior. After a specified time, the therapist will observe the child again to determine if the changes in the environment reduced the child's maladaptive behavior.

Direct observation of behavior, however, is not always possible (Barbour & Davison, 2003). When it is not, the psychologist might ask individuals to make their own assessments of behavior (Fernandez-Ballesteros, 2003).

Cognitive assessment of personality aims to discover what thoughts underlie behavior; that is, how do individuals think about their problems? What kinds of thoughts precede maladaptive behavior, occur during its manifestation, and follow it? Cognitive processes such as expectations, planning, and memory are assessed through interviews or questionnaires. For example, an interview or questionnaire might include questions that ask a person what his or her thoughts were after an upsetting event.

In this chapter we have examined a number of theoretical perspectives and assessment techniques. The choice of assessment technique often depends to a great extent on the psychologist's theoretical perspective (Frager & Fadiman, 2005). Figure 2.16 summarizes which methods are advocated by different theoretical perspectives. The figure also summarizes the positions of the four main personality perspectives on the four issues mentioned at the beginning of the chapter: whether personality is innate or learned, whether it is unconscious or conscious, whether it is determined internally or externally, and what characterizes a healthy personality.

FIGURE 2.16 Comparing Perspectives on Personality

PERSONALITY PERSPECTIVES

	Psychodynamic Perspectives	Behavioral and Social Cognitive Perspectives	Humanistic Perspectives	Trait Perspectives
Preferred Personality Assessment Techniques	Clinical interviews, unstructured personality tests, psychohistorical analysis of clients' lives	Observation, especially laboratory observation	Self-report tests, interviews. For many humanists, clinical judgment is more important than scientific measurement	Self-report tests, such as MMPI-2

Theoretical Issues

	Psychodynamic Perspectives	Behavioral and Social Cognitive Perspectives	Humanistic Perspectives	Trait Perspectives
Is personality innate or learned?	Freud strongly favored biological foundations. Horney, Jung, and Adler gave social experiences and culture more weight.	Skinner said personality is behavior, which is environmentally determined. Social cognitive theorists, such as Bandura, also emphasize environmental experiences.	Rogers, Maslow, and other humanistic psychologists believe personality is influenced by experience and can be changed.	Eysenck stresses personality's biological basis. Allport and other trait theorists consider both heredity and environment.
Is personality conscious or unconscious?	Psychodynamic theorists, especially Freud and Jung, place a strong emphasis on unconscious thought.	Skinner didn't think conscious or unconscious thought was important. Bandura and Mischel emphasize the cognitive process.	Humanistic psychologists stress the conscious aspects of personality, especially self-concept and self-perception.	Trait theorists pay little attention to this issue.
Is personality determined internally or externally?	Psychodynamic theorists emphasize internal determinants and internal personality structures.	Behaviorists emphasize external, situational determinants. Social cognitive theorists emphasize both internal and external determinants but especially self-control.	Humanistic theorists emphasize internal determinants such as self-concept and self-actualization.	Trait theorists stress internal, personal variables.

Review and Reflect

6 **Characterize the main methods of personality assessment**

REVIEW

- Why and how do people assess personality?
- What are projective tests?
- What are self-report tests?
- How do behavioral and cognitive assessments differ from projective and self-report tests?

REFLECT

- Which of the assessment tools that we discussed do you think would likely provide the most accurate picture of your personality?

Reach Your Learning Goals

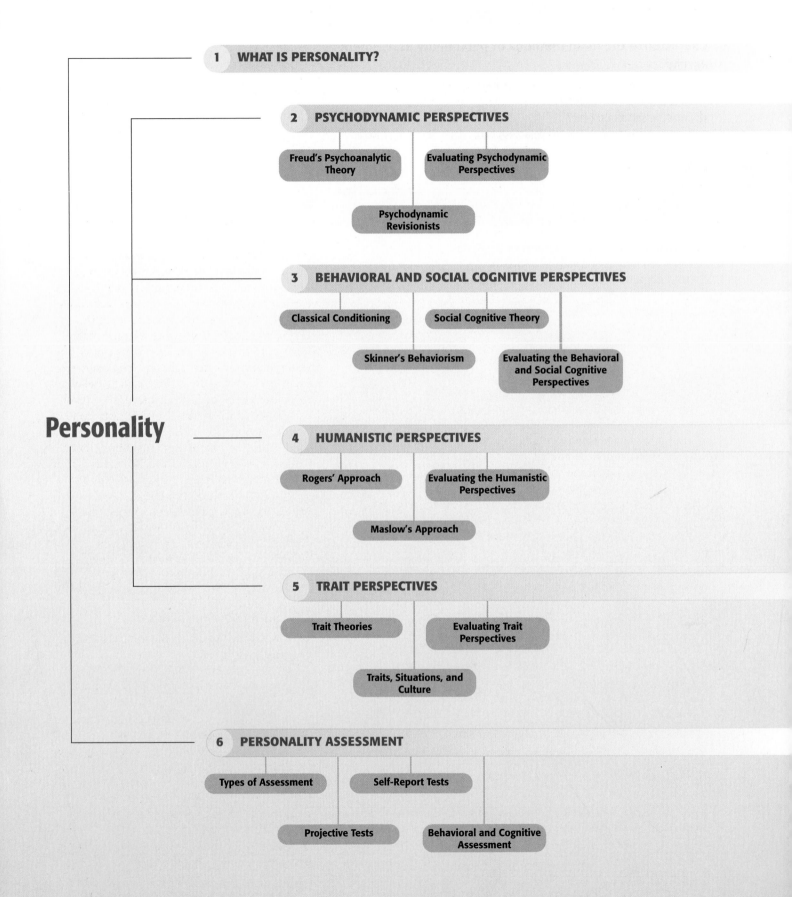

Personality

1   **WHAT IS PERSONALITY?**

2   **PSYCHODYNAMIC PERSPECTIVES**

Freud's Psychoanalytic Theory

Evaluating Psychodynamic Perspectives

Psychodynamic Revisionists

3   **BEHAVIORAL AND SOCIAL COGNITIVE PERSPECTIVES**

Classical Conditioning

Social Cognitive Theory

Skinner's Behaviorism

Evaluating the Behavioral and Social Cognitive Perspectives

4   **HUMANISTIC PERSPECTIVES**

Rogers' Approach

Evaluating the Humanistic Perspectives

Maslow's Approach

5   **TRAIT PERSPECTIVES**

Trait Theories

Evaluating Trait Perspectives

Traits, Situations, and Culture

6   **PERSONALITY ASSESSMENT**

Types of Assessment

Self-Report Tests

Projective Tests

Behavioral and Cognitive Assessment

Summary

1 Define personality and identify major issues in the study of personality

- Personality involves our enduring thoughts, emotions, and behaviors that characterize the way we adapt to the world. A key question is why different individuals respond to the same situation in different ways.

2 Summarize the psychodynamic perspectives

- Freud believed that most of the mind is unconscious, and his psychoanalytic theory stated that personality has three structures: id, ego, and superego. The conflicting demands of these personality structures produce anxiety. Defense mechanisms protect the ego and reduce this anxiety. Freud was convinced that problems develop because of early childhood experiences. He said that we go through five stages: oral, anal, phallic, latency, and genital. During the phallic stage, which occurs in early childhood, the Oedipus complex is a major source of conflict.

- A number of psychodynamic theorists criticized Freud for placing too much emphasis on sexuality and the first 5 years of life, and for giving too little emphasis to the ego, conscious thought, and sociocultural factors. Horney said that the need for security, not sex or aggression, is our most important need. Jung thought Freud underplayed the unconscious mind's role. He developed the concept of the collective unconscious and placed special emphasis on archetypes. Adler's theory, called individual psychology, stresses that people are striving toward a positive being and that they create their own goals. Adler placed more emphasis on social motivation than Freud did.

- The psychodynamic perspectives focused attention on many new ideas about personality. They share the view that personality is primarily unconscious and develops in stages. They also emphasize the role of the individual's past experiences, the mental representation and transformation of experience, and the influence of conflict on personality. Weaknesses of the psychodynamic perspectives include the difficulty of testing its concepts, too much emphasis on sexuality and the unconscious mind, a negative view of human nature, too much attention to early experience, and a male, Western bias.

3 Explain the behavioral and social cognitive perspectives

- Classical conditioning is a learning process discovered by Pavlov in which a neutral stimulus becomes associated with a meaningful stimulus and acquires the capacity to elicit a similar response. The four components of classical conditioning include: unconditioned stimulus (UCS), unconditioned response (UCR), conditioned stimulus (CS), and conditioned response (CR). Classical conditioning has a great deal of survival value for humans and has especially been applied to understanding fear.

- Skinner's behaviorism emphasizes that cognition is unimportant in personality; personality is observable behavior, which is influenced by rewards and punishments in the environment. Important concepts in Skinner's behavioral view include operant conditioning, reinforcement, extinction, and punishment. Reinforcement and punishment can include positive or negative forms. In the behavioral view, personality often varies according to the situation.

- Social cognitive theory, created by Albert Bandura and Walter Mischel, states that behavior, environment, and person/cognitive factors are important in understanding personality. In Bandura's view, these factors reciprocally interact. Two important concepts in social cognitive theory are observational learning and personal control. Delay of gratification, self-efficacy, and locus of control are key aspects of personal control. Numerous research studies reveal that individuals characterized by delay of gratification, self-efficacy, and internal locus of control generally show positive functioning and adjustment.

- Strengths of the behavioral and social cognitive perspectives include their emphases on environmental determinants and on a scientific climate for investigating personality. An additional strength of social cognitive theory is its focus on cognitive processes and self-control. The behavioral view has been criticized for taking the "person" out of personality and for ignoring cognition. These approaches also have not given adequate attention to enduring individual differences, to biological factors, and to personality as a whole.

4 Describe the humanistic perspectives

- Rogers stressed that each of us has the innate, inner capacity to become a fully functioning person. According to Rogers, each of us has a need for unconditional positive regard. The result is that the real self is not valued unless it meets the standards of other people. The self is the core of personality; it includes both the real and ideal selves. Rogers said that we can help others develop a more positive self-concept in three ways: through unconditional positive regard, empathy, and genuineness.

- Maslow argued that our behavior is motivated by a hierarchy of needs, with self-actualization being the highest human need.

- The humanistic movement offers what Maslow called a "third force" in psychology. The humanistic perspective stresses the person's capacity for personal growth and freedom. These perspectives brought new attention to the importance of our perceptions, of conscious experience, and of the positive aspects of human nature. Its weaknesses are a tendency to avoid empirical research, to be too optimistic, and to encourage excessive self-love.

5   *Discuss the trait perspectives*

- Trait theories emphasize that personality consists of traits, which are broad, enduring dispositions that lead to characteristic responses. Allport believed that each individual has a unique set of personality traits. Most trait theories hold that personality can be described in terms of a few supertraits or dimensions. Eysenck proposed that there are three dimensions of personality: introversion-extraversion, stability-instability (neuroticism), and psychoticism. Much current interest focuses on the big five factors in personality, which are openness to experience, conscientiousness, extraversion, agreeableness, and neuroticism (emotional stability).

- Mischel argued that personality varies across situations more than trait theorists acknowledged. His view helped stimulate research on how traits and situations interact. Cross-cultural research suggests that traits may vary across cultures. In particular, cultures around the world may be classified as individualist or collectivist.

- Studying people in terms of their traits has practical value. Understanding a person's traits also may help us better predict the person's health, thinking, job success, and interpersonal skills. Today, most personality psychologists are interactionists. They believe that personality is determined by a combination of traits, or person factors, and the situation, or environmental factors.

6   *Characterize the main methods of personality assessment*

- Many people assess their own personalities in order to be able to think critically about their lives and to improve their adjustment. Psychologists use assessments not only in research but also in their attempts to diagnose, treat, and counsel people. The measures used to assess personality vary from the quackery of palm readers to scientific measures that aim to be both reliable and valid. The major types of assessments used by psychologists are projective tests, self-report tests, and behavioral and cognitive assessments.

- Projective tests are designed to assess the unconscious aspects of personality. They present individuals with ambiguous stimuli and are based on the assumption that this ambiguity allows individuals to project their personalities onto the stimuli. The Rorschach inkblot test and The Thematic Apperception Test (TAT) are popular projective tests.

- Self-report tests assess personality traits by asking questions about preferences and behaviors. These tests may elicit deceptive responses when people try to answer in a socially desirable way. To overcome this problem, some tests are empirically keyed, which means that the items on the test have been included because they have been shown to predict some independent criterion. The Minnesota Multiphasic Personality Inventory (MMPI) is the most widely used and researched self-report personality test. The Neuroticism Extraversion Openness Personality Inventory (NEO-PI-R) and the Hogan Personality Inventory (HPI) are two popular self-report tests that assess the big five factors.

- Most personality assessments were designed to measure stable, enduring aspects of personality. Unlike projective and self-report tests, behavioral assessment does not try to remove the influence of the situation. Behavioral assessments consist of direct observations of behavior and its environmental ties. Cognitive assessment seeks information about an individual's cognitive processes through interviews and questionnaires.

Key Terms

personality 37
psychodynamic
  perspectives 38
id 39
ego 39
superego 39
defense mechanisms 40
Oedipus complex 41
collective unconscious 42
archetypes 43
individual psychology 43

classical conditioning 46
operant conditioning 47
reinforcement 47
extinction 48
punishment 48
social cognitive theory 49
observational learning 49
reciprocal determinism 50
self-efficacy 51
locus of control 52

humanistic perspectives 55
unconditional positive
  regard 56
hierarchy of needs 57
self-actualization 57
trait 60
trait theories 60
big five factors of
  personality 61
individualism 63

collectivism 63
projective test 65
Rorschach inkblot test 66
Thematic Apperception Test
  (TAT) 67
self-report tests 67
empirically keyed test 68
Minnesota Multiphasic
  Personality Inventory
  (MMPI) 68

E-Learning Tools

To help you master the material in this chapter, you will find a number of valuable tools on the student CD-ROM that accompanies this book, and on the Online Learning Center, where you can find these valuable resources for Chapter 2, "Personality."

SELF-ASSESSMENT

In Text

You can complete these self-assessments in the text:
- Self-Assessment 2.1: *Evaluating My Self-Efficacy*
- Self-Assessment 2.2: *Am I Internally or Externally Controlled?*
- Self-Assessment 2.3: *How Introverted or Extraverted Am I?*

Additional Self-Assessments

Complete these self-assessments on the Online Learning Center:
- *How Much Do I Have a Need to Be Unique?*
- *The Big Five Factors in My Personality*

THINK CRITICALLY

To practice your critical thinking skills, complete these exercises on the Online Learning Center:
- *Freud and Schwarzenegger* focuses on violence and sex in films.
- *What Am I Really Like?* involves your personality traits
- *What Makes a Healthy Personality?* focuses on the ego
- *What Causes Child Abuse?* deals with varied elements

APPLY YOUR KNOWLEDGE

1. What motivates you?

Have you ever had times when you didn't do as well as you would like to in school? Sometimes, there are compelling external reasons for not studying enough, such as being sick, or working full time. In most cases, however, people put off studying or writing term papers until it is too late to catch up. Some of these reasons could be due to emotional factors, and some to priorities.

First, consider the emotional factors that interfere with your achievement. A good place to start is by looking at defense mechanisms. According to Freud, we are unaware of our defense mechanisms at the time we are using them. But, looking back, are there times when the use of defense mechanisms hinders your progress? For each of the following defense mechanisms, list a time when either you or a friend used the defense mechanism to avoid studying: Repression, Rationalization, Displacement, Sublimation, Projection, Reaction formation, Denial, and Regression.

By examining these motivations, you might gain some insight into your own behavior and success. If you are doing well in school, congratulations! In this case, apply the principle to some other part of your life that is causing you concern.

Another factor in motivation is the issue of reinforcers. According to Skinner's operant conditioning theory, we are most likely to repeat behaviors that are reinforcing and decrease behaviors that are either punishing or not rewarding. Make two lists. Title one "reasons I study" and title the other "reasons I don't study." For each list, write out the positive reinforcers, the negative reinforcers, the positive punishers, and the negative punishers. Are there more reasons for "not studying" than for "studying"? Would changing your priorities change your reinforcers and your outcomes?

2. Are you "warm and fuzzy"?

Personality differs widely from person to person. Some people seem to naturally attract others, while other people have to work at good interpersonal relationships. Think of someone you know who is popular and who makes other people feel at ease. Then, think of someone who seems socially awkward or uncomfortable. Using concepts from the humanistic school of thought, evaluate each of these people based on the recommendations of humanistic theorists. Evaluate the two people on each dimension. When you are finished, give some thought to your own interpersonal habits. What things do you do well? What things could use improvement? Which of the things on these two lists correspond to what the humanists propose is essential for healthy functioning? Evaluate your two target people and yourself along the following dimensions: Self-concept, Self-esteem, Unconditional Positive Regard, Empathy, Genuineness, Fully Functioning, and Self-actualizing.

When you are finished, make a list of five small habits that you could change to improve your interpersonal interactions. You don't need to overhaul your entire personality; you just need to change a couple of habits. For help on ways that you can change, go to www.yahoo.com and type "active listening" into the search boxes.

3. Do projective tests work?

The Rorschach and the Thematic Apperception Test (TAT) are both projective tests; they use ambiguous images onto which a respondent "projects" an interpretation. It is assumed that in order to respond to a projective test, the person must put part of his or her own personality into the test.

You can make up your own TAT-like test and try it out on your friends. Go through various magazines and cut out 10 pictures. Try to select pictures that show two (and only two) people interacting in some way. Try to choose pictures that cannot be understood without reading a caption i.e. choose pictures as "ambiguous" as possible. Once you have your 10 pictures, Show the series, in the same order, to at least two friends. Be careful not to reveal to your friends what you are examining. For each card, ask the person to write a 5–10 sentence story about what is going on in the picture, and the nature of the relationship between the two people. Once you have all the responses, examine the story to see if there is an underlying theme. You may wish to use the TAT card shown in your textbook as picture #1.

VIDEO SEGMENT

How consistent is your personality from one situation to another? Are there situations in which you seem to take on a different personality? For a powerful demonstration of the influence that extreme situations can exert on us, watch the video for Chapter 2 on the CD-ROM.

Several concepts discussed in this chapter are illustrated by videos in other chapters on the CD-ROM. To learn more about the differences between individualist and collectivist cultures and their effects, watch the video "Culture and the Self" for Chapter 3 on the CD-ROM. For an example of how cognitions and the environment interact to affect our actions, see the video for Chapter 10.

The Self, Identity, and Values

Learning Goals

1 Discuss self-concept and self-esteem

2 Describe what identity is and how it is formed

3 Summarize some important aspects of value

4 Characterize the role of religion in people's lives

Images of Adjustment

Maxine Hong Kingston, Bridging Cultural Worlds

Maxine Hong Kingston

Maxine Hong Kingston's vivid portrayals of her Chinese ancestry and the struggles of Chinese immigrants have made her one of the world's leading Asian American writers. Kingston's parents were both Chinese immigrants. Born in California in 1940, she spent many hours working with her parents and five brothers and sisters in the family's laundry. As a youth, Kingston was profoundly influenced by her parents' struggle to adapt to American culture and descriptions of their Chinese heritage.

Growing up as she did, Kingston felt the pull of two very different cultures. She was especially intrigued by stories about Chinese women who were perceived as either privileged or degraded.

Her first book is titled *The Woman Warrior: Memoirs of a Girlhood among Ghosts*. According to a Chinese folk saying that Kingston (1976) recounts, "Better to raise geese than girls." In *The Woman Warrior*, Kingston also described her aunt, who gave birth to an illegitimate child. Because having a child outside of wedlock was taboo and perceived as a threat to the community's stability, the entire Chinese village condemned her, pushing her to kill herself and her child. From then on, even mentioning her name was forbidden.

In 1980, Kingston published *China Men*, which won the American Book Award for nonfiction and was runner-up for the Pulitzer Prize. Based on the experiences of her father and several generations of other male relatives, the book examines the lives of Chinese men who left their homeland to settle in the United States. It contains stories of loneliness and discrimination as well as determination and strength.

Kingston taught at the University of California at Berkeley. She says that she doesn't want to be viewed as an exotic writer but as someone who writes and teaches about Americans and what it means to be human. Kingston says she likes to guide people in how to find meaning in their lives, especially by exploring their cultural backgrounds.

Maxine Hong Kingston's life and writings reflect important aspects of each of our lives: our efforts to understand ourselves, to develop an identity that reflects our cultural heritage, and to adopt meaningful values. This chapter is about these topics: the self, identity, and values. As we examine these topics, reflect on how much you understand yourself, think deeply about the stamp of your identity, what your values are, and how they might influence your adjustment. Think also about the role of religion and spirituality in your life and how they might improve adjustment for some individuals.

1 THE SELF

Self-Concept   Self-Esteem

Who are you? Do you know why you succeed or fail, what makes you liked or disliked by others, why you find life good one day but not another? There are substantial individual variations in self-awareness and self-understanding, but most human beings have a sense of their own distinctiveness, and this sense of self helps shape their adjustment.

Self-Concept

How would you describe yourself? Do you start with your physical characteristics— how tall are you? how much do you weigh? Perhaps your description begins with your gender or ethnicity, your status in your family, or your goals and dreams. Contrast these two examples: a 20-year-old describes himself as a student, a male, a lead guitarist in a band, a hacker, and a hot-line volunteer; a 26-year-old describes herself as an executive in training for a corporation, a mother, an African American, a tennis player, and a mystery reader. These are two different self-concepts. **Self-concept** is an individual's perception of his or her abilities, personality, and other attributes; it consists of our overall thoughts and feelings about our characteristics.

As we grow up, our self-concept depends increasingly on our subjective experiences and personal reflections, but our concept is never completely cut off from the external world. Rather, the self-concept is influenced by the sociocultural contexts in which we live—our family experiences; our relationships with friends; our ethnic, cultural, and gender experiences; and so on (Leary, 2003). All of these influences help make the self-concept a very complex cognitive construction.

Maxine Hong Kingston, for example, was aware not only of how she perceived herself but also how her Chinese parents and her Anglo-American friends perceived her. In other words, the self-concept includes perceptions of a person's characteristics from different viewpoints. In addition, different domains are represented by the self-concept. For example, you may be aware of your perceptions not only of your actual characteristics but also of the characteristics you would like to possess and of the characteristics you think you ought to have.

Self-Congruence and Self-Discrepancy   Differences between the *real self*—the self that reflects our experiences—and the *ideal self*—the self we would like to be—play a key role in the course of our lives, according to humanistic theorist Carl Rogers (1961). As discussed in chapter 2, "Personality," Rogers argued that adjustment is more likely to go smoothly when these representations are *congruent*—when they fit together.

E. Tory Higgins (1987) expanded on Rogers' ideas by describing three domains: the *actual* self, the *ideal* self, and the *ought* self:

self-concept An individual's perception of his or her abilities, personality, and other attributes; it consists of our overall thoughts and feelings about our characteristics.

The Self
Rogers' View of Self-Concept
Higgins' Self Research

- The **actual self** is your representation of the attributes you believe you actually possess.
- The **ideal self** is your representation of the attributes you would like to ideally possess—that is, a representation of your hopes, aspirations, and wishes.
- The **ought self** is your representation of the attributes you believe you should possess—that is, a representation of your duties, obligations, and responsibilities.

Each of these three domains of the self can be seen from either the individual's view or the view of a significant other such as a parent, spouse, or friend.

What happens when these representations do not match? According to Higgins' (1987, 1999, 2000) **self-discrepancy theory,** problems occur when representations from different viewpoints or from different domains are inconsistent, or discrepant. Two types of discrepancies are especially problematic and create different emotions:

- Discrepancies between the actual and ideal selves lead people to experience dejection-related emotions, such as sadness, disappointment, and shame. They feel dejected because they believe they have failed to reach the goals that they set for themselves and that others set for them.
- Second, discrepancies between the actual self and the ought self can produce agitated emotions, such as anxiety, fear, and guilt. In these instances, people believe that they have failed to live up to standards (established by themselves or others) for good, dutiful, and responsible behavior. The agitated emotions emerge because people feel they are being punished (by themselves or by others) for not doing what they ought to do.

To test these predictions about the effects of discrepancies, college students were asked to list traits or attributes that described their actual, ideal, and ought selves (Higgins, 1984). Then matches and mismatches in traits across the three domains were coded. For example, as part of a self-description a person might evaluate the actual self as "friendly," "sincere," and "hot-tempered," and the ought self as "friendly," "sincere," and "calm." These evaluations include two matches (friendly and sincere) and one mismatch (hot-tempered and calm). In this study, researchers also measured the students' levels of depression (which involves dejection-related emotions) and anxiety (which involves agitated-related emotions). As predicted, discrepancies between the actual self and ideal self were associated with depression (but not anxiety); discrepancies between the actual self and ought self were associated with anxiety (but not depression) (see figure 3.1).

Not all discrepancies produce the predicted emotional states. Self-discrepancies are most likely to lead to the expected outcomes (1) when the expectancies are large, (2) when you are aware of the discrepancy, (3) when the discrepancy is important to you, and (4) when the discrepancy is real rather than imagined (Dweck, Higgins, & Grant-Pillow, 2003; Higgins, 1999).

Possible Selves Another way of analyzing self-concept involves our **possible selves,** which are conceptions of what we might become, including what we would like to become and what we are afraid of becoming (Markus & Nurius, 1986). Thus, our possible selves reflect both the outcomes that we hope for and the ones that we dread (Bybee & Wells, 2003). Some possible selves are more important to us than others. For example, a person's possible selves might include being a doctor, being fit, and being an excellent pianist, but being a doctor might be far more important to the person than the other possible selves.

Each possible self is a construction by the person, and the person may spell it out in considerable detail (McAdams, 2001). For example, if one of a person's possible selves is the *unemployed self,* the person might develop a painfully clear picture of this

actual self Your representation of the attributes you believe or you actually possess.

ideal self Your representation of the attributes you would like to ideally possess—that is, a representation of your hopes, aspirations, and wishes.

ought self Your representation of the attributes you believe you should possess—that is, a representation of your duties, obligations, and responsibilities.

self-discrepancy theory Higgins' theory that problems occur when representations from different viewpoints or from different domains are inconsistent or discrepant. Two types of discrepancies are especially problematic: between the actual and ideal selves (produces dejection-related emotions) and between the actual and ought selves (produces agitated emotions).

possible selves Individuals' conceptions of what they might become, including what they would like to become and what they are afraid of becoming.

self. The person might picture herself as being unable to make mortgage payments, struggling to get by on food stamps, living in an overpriced and undersized apartment in a seedy area of town, spending long hours with nothing much to do, applying for menial jobs, being humiliated in front of others, resenting peers who have good jobs, and gradually sinking into hopelessness and despair.

The presence of both dreaded and hoped-for selves is psychologically healthy, providing a balance (Harter, 1999). Positive possible selves can help direct efforts toward goals; negative possible selves define what is to be avoided. For example, if the unemployed self is an important *feared* possible self, then the person is likely to go to great lengths to avoid its realization.

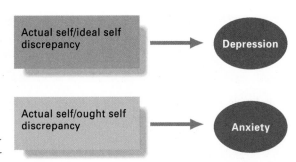

FIGURE 3.1 The Relation of Discrepancies in Actual, Ideal, and Ought Selves to Depression and Anxiety.

Possible selves also serve the important function of *self-evaluation.* They provide frameworks for evaluating how well or how poorly our lives are going. Thus, possible selves are powerful structures for determining the meaning of certain events. For example, suppose a college student who wants to become a doctor evaluates her current standing with regard to this possible self in very negative terms because she currently has a low grade-point average. This student's best friend also has low grades, but because her most cherished possible self involves being a housewife with a large family and she has just accepted a marriage proposal, her equally low grade-point average has less influence on her self-evaluation.

The student who wants to be a doctor but has a low grade-point average should make a critical evaluation and adjustments. She can make becoming a doctor a much less dominant possible self and choose a goal that does not require a high grade-point average. Or she can retain becoming a doctor as her dominant possible self and make changes that will help her to achieve this possible self. For example, to obtain better grades, she might enroll in a study skills program to improve her study strategies. She might use time management techniques to learn to use her time better.

Unfortunately, we sometimes engage in behaviors that keep us from becoming one or more of our hoped-for positive possible selves (Baumeister, 1991a). Some people persist in losing endeavors, with the result that they end up losing more. Some people seek immediate gratification rather than work toward future rewards. Many individuals do not adequately examine why they are the way they are; they do not strive to be aware of themselves. If we are not aware of what makes us win or lose, succeed or fail, be liked or disliked, and so on, adjustment can be a rocky road.

The Self in Sociocultural Context Although each possible self is a personalized construction, it also reflects culture. Hazel Markus and her colleagues (Markus & Kitayama, 1994; Markus, Mullally, & Kitayama, 1999) argue that all selves are culture-specific and emerge as individuals adapt to their cultural environments. Of course, all cultural groups are diverse, but Markus and her colleagues conclude that different ways of defining the self-concept and multiple selves dominate various cultures.

A key dividing line (as discussed in chapter 2, "Personality") occurs between individualist and collectivist cultures. Individualist and collectivist cultures view the self differently. Western, individualist cultures tend to favor possible selves that reflect the distinctiveness of the individual, individualism, and assertive self-management. In contrast, non-Western cultures revere possible selves that strengthen the groups to which they belong or aspire to belong. In Japan, for example, possible selves are often defined in terms of relatedness to others.

Self-Esteem

An important aspect of a person's self-conception is **self-esteem,** the overall evaluation of one's self-worth or self-image. High self-esteem refers to a highly favorable global self-evaluation, whereas low self-esteem is a global unfavorable self-evaluation

self-esteem The overall evaluation of one's self-worth or self-image.

SELF-ASSESSMENT 3.1

My Self-Esteem

Below is a list of statements that deal with your general feelings about yourself. Place a check mark in the appropriate column for each item based on whether you strongly agree with it (1), agree with it (2), disagree with it (3), or strongly disagree with it (4).

Item	Strongly Agree (1)	Agree (2)	Disagree (3)	Strongly Disagree (4)
1. On the whole, I am satisfied with myself.	_____	_____	_____	_____
2. At times, I think I'm no good at all.	_____	_____	_____	_____
3. I feel that I have a number of good qualities.	_____	_____	_____	_____
4. I am able to do things as well as most other people.	_____	_____	_____	_____
5. I feel I do not have much to be proud of.	_____	_____	_____	_____
6. I certainly feel useless at times.	_____	_____	_____	_____
7. I feel that I'm a person of worth, at least on an equal plane with others.	_____	_____	_____	_____
8. I wish I could have more respect for myself.	_____	_____	_____	_____
9. All in all, I am inclined to feel that I am a failure.	_____	_____	_____	_____
10. I take a positive attitude toward myself.	_____	_____	_____	_____

Go to the appendix at the end of the book for scoring and interpretation of your responses.

College of Positive Self-Image 7.

University of Low Self-Esteem 0.

(Dusek & McIntyre, 2003; Tesser, 2000). To evaluate your self-esteem, complete Self-Assessment 3.1.

Self-esteem reflects perceptions that do not always match reality (Baumeister, 1993; Baumeister & others, 2003). Your self-esteem might reflect a belief about whether you are intelligent and attractive, for example, but that belief is not necessarily accurate. Thus, high self-esteem may refer to accurate, justified perceptions of one's worth as a person and one's successes and accomplishments, but it can also refer to an arrogant, grandiose, unwarranted sense of superiority over others. In the same manner, low self-esteem may reflect either an accurate perception of one's shortcomings or a distorted, even pathological insecurity and inferiority.

Variations in Self-Esteem Is self-esteem something very general or does it consist of a number of specific, independent self-evaluations about different areas? Current thinking holds that people do have a general level of self-esteem but can still have fluctuating levels of self-esteem in particular domains of their lives (Harter, 1998; Vermeiren & others, 2004; Ward, 2004). For example, perhaps you have high self-esteem overall but low self-esteem regarding your athletic skills, and perhaps your self-esteem regarding academic competence has fluctuated from year to year.

Among the domains of self-esteem are academic competence, work competence, social or relationship competence, sexuality, athletic competence, and physical attractiveness. Within these categories are subdomains such as writing

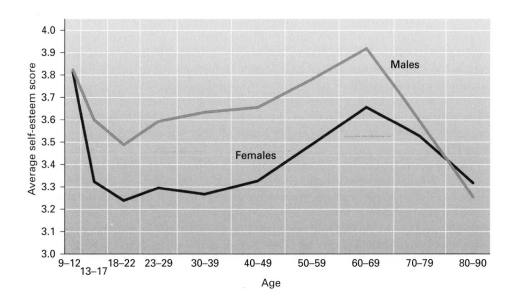

FIGURE 3.2 Self-Esteem Across the Life Span
One large-scale study asked more than 300,000 individuals to rate the extent to which they have high self-esteem on a 5-point scale, 5 being "Strongly Agree" and 1 being "Strongly Disagree." Self-esteem dropped in adolescence and late adulthood. Self-esteem of females was lower than self-esteem of males through most of the life span and was especially low for females during adolescence.

and math skills under academic competence and romantic relationships and friendships in the category of social or relationship competence.

Does self-esteem fluctuate from day to day or remain stable? Most research studies have found it to be stable at least across a month or so (Baumeister, 1991a). Self-esteem can change, however, especially in response to transitions in life, such as graduating from school and to events, such as getting or losing a job. One recent study found that self-esteem is high in childhood, declines in adolescence, and increases in adulthood until late adulthood, at which time it declines again (Robins & others, 2002) (see figure 3.2). In this study, the self-esteem of males was higher than that of females through most of the life span. During adolescence, the self-esteem of girls declined more than that of boys.

Some researchers argue that although there may be a decrease in self-esteem during adolescence, the drop is actually very slight (Harter, 2002; Kling & others, 1999). Also note in figure 3.2 that despite the drop in self-esteem among adolescent girls, their average self-esteem score (3.3) was still higher than the neutral point on the scale (3.0).

One explanation for the drop in self-esteem among females during early adolescence focuses on girls' more negative body images during pubertal change compared with boys' images. Another explanation emphasizes the greater interest that adolescent girls take in social relationships and society's failure to reward that interest.

The decrease in self-esteem among older adults might be expected given their declining physical status. However, some researchers actually have found no differences in the self-esteem of young adults, middle-aged adults, and older adults ((McGue, Hirsch, & Lykken, 1993). Given that older adults have more physical problems, why wouldn't they have lower self-esteem than young or middle-aged adults? One possible reason is that many older adults don't interpret their "losses" as negatively, and don't become as emotionally upset, as younger adults (Carstensen, Fung, & Charles, 2003; Charles & Carstensen, 2004). In sum, there is controversy about the extent to which self-esteem varies according age.

Variations in self-esteem have been linked with many aspects of adjustment; however, much of the research is *correlational* rather than *experimental*. Recall from chapter 1 that correlation does not equal causation. Thus, if a correlational study finds an association between low self-esteem and low academic achievement, low academic achievement could cause the low self-esteem as much as low self-esteem causes low academic achievement (Bowles, 1999).

Self-Esteem
Self-Esteem Strategies
Jennifer Crocker's Research

In fact, there are only "modest correlations between school performance and self-esteem, and these correlations do not indicate that high self-esteem leads to good performance" (Baumeister & others, 2003, p. 1). Attempts to increase students' self-esteem have not produced improved academic performance (Davies & Brember, 1999; Hansford & Hattie, 1982).

In some studies, adult job performance is linked to self-esteem, but the correlations vary greatly and the direction of the causation is not clear (Baumeister & others, 2003). Occupational success might lead to higher self-esteem, but the opposite might occur.

Self-esteem is strongly related to happiness and it seems likely that high self-esteem increases happiness (Baumeister & others, 2003). A large-scale international study of 13,000 college students from 49 universities in 31 countries found that high self-esteem was strongly related to happiness (Diener & Diener, 1995). The correlation was stronger in individualist countries than in collectivist countries. Other researchers have also found links between high self-esteem and happiness (DeNeve & Cooper, 1998; Lyubomirksy & Lepper, 2002).

A large number of studies have found that individuals with low self-esteem report that they feel more depressed than individuals with high self-esteem (Arndt & Goldenberg, 2002; Baumeister & others, 2003; Fox & others, 2004). Low self-esteem has also been linked to suicide attempts and to anorexia nervosa, an eating disorder involving a relentless pursuit of thinness through starvation (Fenzel, 1994; Osvath, Voros, & Fekete, 2004).

Adjustment Strategies
For Increasing Self-Esteem

Here are six strategies that can increase an individual's self-esteem:

1. ***Identify your sources of self-esteem and what is causing low self-esteem.*** A key first step in improving self-esteem is to determine what is contributing to low self-esteem. Is the source of low self-esteem academic performance? relationship problems? unrealistic insecurities? fear of losing your job? or possibly some combination of these or other problems?

2. ***Face a problem and try to cope with it.*** Self-esteem is often increased when individuals try to cope with a problem rather than avoiding it (Bednar, Wells, & Peterson, 1995). Facing problems realistically, honestly, and nondefensively leads to favorable thoughts about oneself, which lead to self-approval and higher self-esteem. In chapter 5, "Coping," we will describe a number of coping strategies that can benefit self-esteem.

3. ***Seek emotional support.*** Emotional support and social approval have a positive influence on self-esteem. However, some individuals experience little emotional support or social approval because their families are filled with conflict or their romantic relationships are marred by hostility. In some cases, alternative sources of emotional support can improve self-esteem. Quality friendships, counseling, or therapy can sometimes compensate for shortcomings in other sources of emotional support.

4. ***Take responsibility for your self-esteem.*** Assume that you have the ability to improve your self-esteem and take the initiative to do so (Crocker & Park, 2003).

5. ***Look for opportunities to achieve.*** Achievement can also improve self-esteem (Baumeister & others, 2003). Perhaps you can find a straightforward skill to master or a task to complete. If you know specific steps to take to

complete a goal, you are more likely to reach that goal and then to feel better about yourself as a result.

6. ***Explore resources to improve your self-understanding.*** Many individuals with low self-esteem don't know themselves very well. A number of resources can help you learn more about yourself and develop some good strategies for increasing your self-esteem. These include the self-help resources described at the end of the chapter, the Internet connections for this chapter on the book's Online Learning Center, and talking with a counselor or therapist.

The Dark Side of High Self-Esteem: Narcissism   Sometimes high self-esteem is undeserved; in fact, some people with high self-esteem are narcissistic and conceited (Baumeister & others, 2003; Kernis, 2003). **Narcissism** refers to a self-centered and self-concerned approach to others. Narcissus was a character in Greek mythology who so admired himself that a curse was placed on him. The gods caused him to fall in love with his own reflection. Absorbed by his own image in a pool, Narcissus reached into the pool to touch his reflection, fell in, and drowned.

Narcissists are excessively self-centered and self-congratulatory. They view their own needs and desires as paramount, and they rarely show empathy toward others. In fact, narcissistic individuals often devalue people around them to protect their own precarious self-esteem. They often respond with rage and shame when others do not admire them and treat them in accordance with their grandiose fantasies about themselves. Narcissistic persons are at their most grandiose when their self-esteem is threatened. They may fly into a frenzy if they have given an unsatisfactory performance.

Typically, narcissistic individuals are unaware of their actual selves and how others perceive them. They often make far-reaching claims about themselves without reflecting on how their behavior will be perceived by others. One narcissistic individual spoke of the special awards he received because his work was "greater than great." Another stated that he was perfect, then corrected this to: "No, not really perfect, but I could be."

Narcissists' extraordinary self-representations are a defensive transformation of their unconscious view of themselves as worthless. Even people who are reasonably well adjusted use similar defenses to ward off perceived threats to their self-esteem, but they do so in greater contact with reality than narcissists. To learn more about the characteristics of narcissism, turn to Self-Assessment 3.2.

www.mhhe.com/santrockha

Narcissism
Narcissistic Tendencies

Review and Reflect

1   **Discuss self-concept and self-esteem**

REVIEW

- What is self-concept? What are some important components of self-concept?
- What is self-esteem? What are some characteristics of self-esteem? What are some good strategies for enhancing self-esteem.

REFLECT

- Think about what your future selves might be. What do you envision will make you the happiest about the future selves you aspire to become? What prospective selves hold negative possibilities?

narcissism A self-centered and self-concerned approach in dealing with others.

SELF-ASSESSMENT 3.2

Do I Have Narcissistic Tendencies?

Instructions

The statements below describe characteristics of persons. Answer each statement Yes or No as it applies to you.

Leadership/Authority

	Yes	No
1. I see myself as a good leader.	_____	_____
2. I would prefer to be a leader.	_____	_____
3. I really like to be the center of attention.	_____	_____
4. I like having authority over other people.	_____	_____
5. I would be willing to describe myself as a strong personality.	_____	_____
6. I have a natural talent for influencing people.	_____	_____
7. I like to be the center of attention.	_____	_____
8. I am assertive.	_____	_____
9. People always seem to recognize my authority.	_____	_____

Self-Absorption/Self-Admiration

	Yes	No
10. I like to look at my body.	_____	_____
11. I like to look at myself in the mirror.	_____	_____
12. I am an extraordinary person.	_____	_____
13. I like to display my body.	_____	_____
14. I have good taste when it comes to beauty.	_____	_____
15. I think I am a special person.	_____	_____
16. I like to be complimented.	_____	_____
17. I am going to be a great person.	_____	_____
18. I know that I am good because everyone keeps telling me so.	_____	_____

Superiority/Arrogance

	Yes	No
19. Everybody likes to hear my stories.	_____	_____
20. I usually dominate any conversation.	_____	_____
21. I can make anybody believe anything.	_____	_____
22. I am a born leader.	_____	_____
23. I can read people like a book.	_____	_____
24. I am apt to show off if I get the chance.	_____	_____
25. People can learn a great deal from me.	_____	_____
26. I always know what I am doing.	_____	_____
27. I can usually talk my way out of anything.	_____	_____
28. Superiority is something you are born with.	_____	_____
29. I could do almost anything on a dare.	_____	_____

Explotiveness/Entitlement

	Yes	No
30. I expect a great deal from other people.	_____	_____
31. I am envious of other people's good fortune.	_____	_____
32. I insist upon getting the respect that is due me.	_____	_____
33. I will never be satisfied until I get all that I deserve.	_____	_____
34. I have a strong will to power.	_____	_____
35. I get upset when people don't notice how I look when I go out in public.	_____	_____
36. I find it easy to manipulate people.	_____	_____
37. I am more capable than other people.	_____	_____

Go to the appendix at the end of the book for an interpretation of your responses.

Reproduced with permission of authors and publisher from Raskin, R. N., & Hall, C. S. A narcissistic personality inventory. *Psychological Reports,* 1979, 45, 590. © Psychological Reports 1979.

2 IDENTITY

- Erikson's View
- Developmental Changes
- Gender and Identity
- The Four Statuses of Identity
- Ethnic Identity

Understanding self-concept and self-esteem helps us to understand how we think and feel about our characteristics, but our sense of self goes beyond these cognitive representations and emotions. You might be a fat adult with a skinny child, a churchgoing community leader who was once an agnostic rebel, but you would probably have the sense of somehow being "you." We have a subjective sense of ourselves continuing through time and existing within a social world.

Identity refers to having an integrated sense of self in which different parts come together in a unified whole. Indeed, identity is a self-portrait that is composed of many pieces—from the work path a person wants to follow (vocational/career identity) to a person's spiritual beliefs (religious identity), political attitudes, sexual orientation, cultural heritage, interests, values, and so on. By far the most comprehensive theory of how identity is formed was proposed by Erik Erikson.

Erikson's View

Who am I? What am I all about? What am I going to do with my life? What is different about me? How can I make it on my own? These questions about identity surface as a common, virtually universal concern during adolescence; they become especially important in the emerging adulthood years from about 18 to 25 years of age. These years constitute what Erikson (1950, 1968) called the **identity versus identity confusion stage,** the fifth of eight developmental stages he proposed that occurs during the adolescent and emerging adult years. During this time, individuals are faced with deciding who they are, what they are all about, and where they are going in life. (We will explore Erikson's theory and stages of life-span development in chapter 11, "Emerging Adulthood, Adult Development, and Aging.")

These questions about identity occur throughout life, but Erikson believed they are especially important for youth. Those who successfully cope with these questions emerge with a new sense of self that is both refreshing and acceptable. But youth who do not successfully resolve this *identity crisis* suffer what Erikson calls *identity confusion.* Either they withdraw, isolating themselves from peers and family, or they immerse themselves in the world of peers and lose their identity in the crowd.

The Role of Experimentation   The search for an identity during the adolescent and emerging adulthood years is aided by a **psychosocial moratorium,** which is Erikson's term for the gap between childhood security and adult autonomy. During this period adult commitments are delayed while society shows youth a "selective permissiveness" (Erikson, 1968, p. 156). They try out different roles and personalities. They might be argumentative one moment, cooperative the next. They might dress neatly one day and sloppily the next day. One week they might like a particular friend, the next week they might despise the friend. As youth gradually come to realize that they soon will be responsible for themselves and their lives, they experiment in an effort to find their place in the world.

Many parents and other adults may be bewildered or incensed by the wisecracks, rebelliousness, and rapid mood changes that accompany adolescence. But adolescents and emerging adults need the time and opportunity to explore different roles and personalities. Eventually, most adolescents and emerging adults discard undesirable roles.

There are literally hundreds of roles for adolescents and emerging adults to try out, and probably just as many ways to pursue each role. Erikson believed that during youth, vocational roles become central to identity development, especially in technological societies like that of the United States. Youth who have been well trained to enter a workforce that offers the potential of reasonably high self-esteem will experience the least stress during this phase of identity development.

Some youth may reject jobs offering good pay and high social status in order to do work that helps people directly, such as working in a mental health clinic or teaching school in a low-income neighborhood. Some youth may prefer unemployment to the prospect of work they feel they could not perform well or would make them feel useless. To Erikson, such choices reflect the desire to achieve a meaningful identity by being true to oneself instead of burying one's identity in the larger society.

One of Erik Erikson's strategies for explaining the nature of identity development was to analyze the lives of famous individuals. One such individual was Mahatma Gandhi (*center*), the spiritual leader of India in the mid-twentieth century, whom Erikson (1969) wrote about in *Gandhi's Truth.*

identity A sense of integration of self in which different parts come together in a unified whole.

identity versus identity confusion stage Erikson's fifth of eight developmental stages that occurs during the adolescent and emerging adult years at which time individuals are faced with deciding who they are, what they are all about, and where they are going in life.

psychological moratorium Erikson's terms for the gap between childhood security and adult autonomy.

Identity Over the Life Span   Identity development neither begins nor ends in adolescence or emerging adulthood (Kunnen & Klein Wassink, 2003; Layder, 2004). The process begins during infancy in the encounters between the infant and a caregiver. Childhood identities precede adolescent and emerging adult identities. What is important about identity development in adolescence and emerging adulthood is that physical, cognitive, and socioemotional development has advanced to the point at which the individual can sort through and synthesize childhood identities to construct a viable path toward adult maturity. Central questions such as "Who am I?" come up more frequently in the adolescent and emerging adult years than earlier, and identity development is characterized more strongly by the search for balance between the need for autonomy and the need for connectedness.

Identity formation does not happen neatly, nor is it usually cataclysmic. Identity development gets done in bits and pieces. At the bare minimum, it involves commitment to a vocational direction, an ideological stance, and a sexual orientation. Synthesizing the components of identity can be a long, drawn-out process, with many negations and affirmations of various roles (Moshman, 2005). Over the years, scores of decisions—whom to date; whether or not to have intercourse, to break up, to take drugs; whether to go to college or get a job, to study or play, to be politically active or not—begin to form the core of what an individual is all about.

The development of an identity during adolescence and emerging adulthood does not mean that identity will be stable through the remainder of one's life. Questions about identity come up throughout life. Decisions are not made once and for all but must be made again and again. An individual who develops a healthy identity is flexible, adaptive, and open to changes in society, in relationships, and careers. This openness assures numerous reorganizations of identity throughout the individual's life.

The Four Statuses of Identity

Have you gone through an identity crisis, exploring alternative roles and personalities? Have you made a commitment to an identity? According to James Marcia (1980, 1994), the answers to these questions indicate your identity status. That is, Marcia classifies individuals based on the existence or extent of their crisis and commitment. He defines the term *crisis* as a period of identity development during which the individual is choosing among meaningful alternatives. (Most researchers use the term *exploration.*) By *commitment*, he means a personal investment in an identity. Marcia believes that Erikson's theory of identity development implies four *identity statuses:* identity diffusion, identity foreclosure, identity moratorium, and identity achievement.

- **Identity diffusion** is Marcia's term for the status of individuals when they have not yet experienced an identity crisis (that is, have not yet explored meaningful alternatives) and have not made any commitments. Not only are individuals in this status undecided about occupational and ideological choices, they usually show little interest in such matters.
- **Identity foreclosure** is Marcia's term for the status of individuals when they have made a commitment but have not experienced an identity crisis. This status occurs most often when parents hand down commitments to their adolescents, usually in an authoritarian way, before they have explored different approaches, ideologies, and vocations on their own.
- **Identity moratorium** is Marcia's term for the status of individuals when they are in the midst of an identity crisis but have not made a clear commitment to an identity.
- **Identity achievement** is Marcia's term for the status of individuals who have undergone an identity crisis and made a commitment.

Figure 3.3 summarizes Marcia's four statuses of identity development. Here are some examples. A 13-year-old adolescent has neither begun to explore her identity in a meaningful way nor made an identity commitment; she is *identity diffused.* An

Erikson's View on Identity
Identity Research and Assessment

identity diffusion Marcia's term for the status of individuals when they have not yet experienced an identity crisis and have not made commitments.

identity foreclosure Marcia's term for the status of individuals when they have made a commitment but have not experienced an identity crisis.

identity moratorium Marcia's term for the status of individuals when they are in the midst of an identity crisis but have not made a clear commitment to an identity.

identity achievement Marcia's term for the status of individuals when they have undergone an identity crisis and made a commitment.

		Has the person made a commitment? Yes	No
Has the person explored meaningful alternatives regarding some identity question?	Yes	Identity Achievement	Identity Moratorium
	No	Identity Foreclosure	Identity Diffusion

FIGURE 3.3 Marcia's Four Statuses of Identity

18-year-old boy's parents want him to be a doctor, so he is planning on majoring in premedicine in college and has not adequately explored any other options; he is *identity foreclosed.* Nineteen-year-old Sasha is not quite sure what life path she wants to follow, but she recently went to the counseling center at her college to find out about different careers; she is in an *identity moratorium.* Twenty-one-year-old Marcelo extensively explored a number of different career options in college, eventually received his degree in science education, and is looking forward to his first year of teaching high school; he is *identity achieved.*

Although these examples of identity statuses focus on careers, remember that identity has multiple dimensions—such as achievement/intellectual identity (the extent to which a person is motivated to achieve and is intellectual), political identity (whether a person is politically conservative, middle-of-the-road, or liberal, and so on), sexual identity (whether an individual is heterosexual, homosexual, or bisexual), ethnic identity, and so on. To explore your identity status in a number of areas, complete Self-Assessment 3.3.

Developmental Changes

Some researchers believe that the most important identity changes take place in emerging adulthood rather than in adolescence. For example, Alan Waterman (1985, 1989, 1992, 1999) has found that from the years preceding high school through the last few years of college, the number of individuals who are identity achieved increases, while the number who are identity diffused decreases. College upperclassmen are more likely to be identity achieved than college freshmen or high school students. Many young adolescents, on the other hand, are identity diffused.

These developmental patterns are especially true for vocational choice. In terms of religious beliefs and political ideology, fewer college students reach the identity-achieved status; a substantial number are characterized by foreclosure and diffusion. Thus, the timing of identity development may depend on the particular dimension involved (Harter, 1998; Lewis, 2003).

Identity consolidation—the process of refining and enhancing the identity choices that are made in emerging adulthood—continues well into early adulthood and possibly the early part of middle adulthood (Pals, 1999). One research study found that women and men continued to show identity development from 27 through 36 years of age with the main changes in the direction of greater commitment (Pulkkinen & Kokko, 2000). In this study, adults more often moved into achieved and foreclosed identities than into moratorium or diffused identities. Further, as individuals move from early to middle adulthood they become more certain about their identity. For example, a longitudinal study of Smith college women found that identity certainty increased from the 30s through the 50s (Stewart, Ostrove, & Helson, 2001; Zucker, Ostrove, & Stewart, 2002).

SELF-ASSESSMENT 3.3

What Is My Identity?

Your identity is made up of many different dimensions. By completing this checklist, you should gain a better sense of your identity. Review Marcia's four identity statuses and then for each dimension, check your identity status as diffused, foreclosed, in a moratorium, or achieved.

	Identity Status			
Identity Dimension	Diffused	Foreclosed	Moratorium	Achieved
Vocational identity	_____	_____	_____	_____
Religious identity	_____	_____	_____	_____
Achievement/intellectual identity	_____	_____	_____	_____
Political identity	_____	_____	_____	_____
Sexual identity	_____	_____	_____	_____
Relationship/Lifestyle identity	_____	_____	_____	_____
Cultural and ethnic identity	_____	_____	_____	_____
Personality characteristics	_____	_____	_____	_____
Interests	_____	_____	_____	_____
Values	_____	_____	_____	_____

Go to the appendix at the end of the book for scoring and interpretation of your responses.

Michelle Chin, age 16: "Parents do not understand that teenagers need to find out who they are, which means a lot of experimenting, a lot of mood swings, a lot of emotions and awkwardness. Like any teenager, I am facing an identity crisis. I am still trying to figure out whether I am a Chinese American or an American with Asian eyes."

Some researchers believe that many individuals who develop positive identities follow the "MAMA" cycle: *moratorium–achievement–moratorium–achievement* (Archer, 1989). Individuals may repeat this cycle throughout their lives as personal, family, and societal changes require them to explore new alternatives and develop new commitments (Francis, Fraser, & Marcia, 1989). Indeed, Marcia (1996) believes that the first identity an individual commits to is just that—it is not the final product.

Ethnic Identity

"I feel that I have had to translate a whole Eastern culture and bring it to the West," Maxine Hong Kingston told one interviewer, "then bring the two cultures together seamlessly. . . " (Alegre & Welch, 2003). For Kingston, this melding is "how one makes sense of the Asian American culture." Her efforts illustrate one way of developing an **ethnic identity,** which is an enduring aspect of the self that includes a sense of membership in an ethnic group, along with the attitudes and feelings related to that membership (Phinney, 1996).

Erikson viewed identity as a driving force in the development of both individuals and civilizations. Throughout the world, he noted, ethnic minority groups have struggled to maintain their cultural identities while blending in with the dominant culture (Erikson, 1968). Erikson thought this struggle for an inclusive identity, or separate identity within the larger culture, has been the driving force in the founding of churches, empires, and revolutions throughout history.

Contexts and Variations in Ethnic Identity Many aspects of a person's context may influence ethnic identity (Davey & others, 2003; Farr, 2005; Keller, 2004; Wren

& Mendoza, 2004). Ethnic identity tends to be stronger among members of minority groups than among members of mainstream groups. For example, in one study, the exploration of ethnic identity was higher among ethnic minority college students than among White non-Latino college students (Phinney & Alipuria, 1990).

Time is another aspect of the context that influences ethnic identity. The indicators of identity often differ for each succeeding generation of immigrants (Phinney, 2003). First-generation immigrants are likely to be secure in their identities and unlikely to change much; they may or may not develop a new identity. The degree to which they begin to feel "American" appears to be related to whether or not they learn English, develop social networks beyond their ethnic group, and become culturally competent in their new country. Second-generation immigrants are more likely to think of themselves as "American" possibly because citizenship is granted at birth. Maxine Hong Kingston noted, "I have been in America all of my life; Chinese is a foreign culture to me" (Allegre & Welch, 2003). For second-generation immigrants, ethnic identity is likely to be linked to retention of their ethnic language and social networks. In the third and later generations, the issues become more complex. Broad social factors may affect the extent to which members of this generation retain their ethnic identities. For example, media images may either discourage or encourage members of an ethnic group from identifying with their group or retaining parts of its culture. Discrimination may force people to see themselves as cut off from the majority group and encourage them to seek the support of their own ethnic culture.

The immediate contexts in which ethnic minority youth live also influence their identity development (Cooper & others, 2005; Hecht, Jackson, & Ribeau, 2002; Spencer, 2000; Spencer & others, 2001). In the United States, many ethnic minority youth live in pockets of poverty; are exposed to drugs, gangs, and crime; and interact with youth and adults who have dropped out of school or are unemployed. Support for developing a positive identity is scarce. In such settings, programs for youth can make an important contribution to their identity development.

Shirley Heath and Milbrey McLaughlin (1993) studied 60 youth organizations that involved 24,000 adolescents over a period of five years. They found that these organizations were especially good at building a sense of ethnic pride in inner-city youth. Heath and McLaughlin believe that many inner-city youth have too much time on their hands, too little to do, and too few places to go. Organizations that perceive youth as fearful, vulnerable, and lonely but also as capable, worthy, and eager to have a healthy and productive life contribute in positive ways to the identity development of ethnic minority youth.

Ethnic Identity During Adolescence

In one study, minority students who had thought about and resolved issues involving their ethnicity had higher self-esteem than minority students who had not (Phinney & Alipuria, 1990). Researchers are increasingly finding that positive ratings of ethnic identity are related to more positive school engagement and fewer problem behaviors in African American and Latino adolescents (Fridrich & Flannery, 1995). For example, one recent study revealed that ethnic identity was linked with higher school engagement and lower aggression (Van Buren & Graham, 2003).

Helms' Model of Ethnic Identity Development

How do people develop an ethnic identity? Janet Helms (1990, 1996) has proposed that this process has four stages.

In *Stage 1, pre-encounter,* ethnic minority individuals prefer the dominant society's cultural values to those of their ethnic group. They draw their role models, lifestyles, and values from the dominant group, viewing the physical or cultural characteristics that single them out as ethnic minorities as a source of pain and stress. For example, African Americans in stage 1 may perceive their physical features as undesirable and their upbringing as an impediment to success.

www.mhhe.com/santrockha

Jean Phinney's Research

ethnic identity An enduring aspect of the self that includes a sense of membership in an ethnic group, along with the attitudes and feelings related to that membership.

The move to *stage 2, encounter,* is usually a gradual one. Individuals may reach this stage after an event that makes them realize they will never belong to the mainstream. The trigger might be a public event such as the assassination of Martin Luther King, Jr., or a personal "identity-shattering" event such as someone making blatantly racist remarks. In this stage, minority individuals begin to break through the denial of their ethnicity. For example, Latinos who feel ashamed of their upbringing may speak with Latinos who are proud of their heritage. Gradually, they become aware that not all values of the dominant group are beneficial to them. Conflicting attitudes about the self, the minority group, and the dominant culture characterize this stage. Helms proposes that minority individuals want to identify with their ethnic group but do not know how. The recognition that an ethnic identity must be developed rather than found leads to the third stage.

At the beginning of *stage 3, immersion/emersion,* ethnic minority individuals immerse themselves completely in the minority culture and reject the dominant society. Movement into this stage likely occurs when individuals begin to resolve some of the conflicts from the previous stage and develop a better understanding of societal forces such as racism and discrimination. They begin to ask themselves, "Why should I feel ashamed of who I am?" The answer, at this point, often elicits both guilt and anger— guilt at having "sold out" in the past, and anger at having been "brainwashed" by the dominant group.

Later, in the *emersion* portion of stage 3, individuals experience discontent and discomfort with the rigid attitudes they developed at the beginning of the stage. Gradually, they develop a sense of autonomy. They vent the anger developed at the beginning of stage 3 through cultural explorations, discussions of ethnic issues, and so on. Their emotions begin to level off, so that they can think more clearly and adaptively. No longer do they find it necessary to reject everything from the dominant culture and accept everything from their own culture. They now have the autonomy to evaluate the strengths and weaknesses of both their subculture and the mainstream culture, and to decide which parts of it will become part of their own identity.

In *stage 4, internalization/commitment,* individuals experience a sense of fulfillment that arises from the integration of their personal and cultural identities. They have resolved the conflicts and discomforts of the immersion/emersion stage and attained greater self-control and flexibility. They can also examine the cultural values of other ethnic groups, both minority and majority, more objectively. At this stage, individuals want to eliminate all forms of discrimination. The term *commitment* in the name for this stage refers to the enactment of the individual's newly realized identity. Individuals in this stage take action to eliminate discrimination, whether through large-scale political or social activism or through small, everyday activities that are consistent with their ethnic identities.

Individuals do not always follow the sequence of stages described in Helms' model. In fact, research studies to support the sequence of stages have not been conducted. However, the stages do provide a helpful way to think about some of the issues involved in developing an ethnic identity.

Gender and Identity

Erikson's (1968) classic presentation of identity development reflected the traditional division of labor between the sexes that was common at the time. Erikson wrote that males were mainly oriented toward career and ideological commitments, while females were mainly oriented toward marriage and childbearing. In the 1960s and 1970s researchers found support for this assertion of gender differences in identity. For example, they found that vocational concerns were more central to male identity, while affiliative concerns were more central to female identity (LaVoie, 1976). In the last several decades, however, as females have developed stronger vocational interests, these gender differences have begun to disappear (Madison & Foster-Clark, 1996; Waterman, 1985).

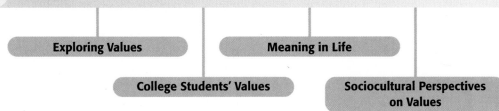

Review And Reflect

2 **Describe what identity is and how it is formed**

REVIEW

- What is Erikson's view of identity?
- What are the four statuses of identity?
- What are some developmental changes in identity?
- What is ethnic identity? What are some important aspects of ethnic identity?
- What role does gender play in identity?

REFLECT

- Describe one aspect of your identity you would like to change. Why? Can it be changed? What can you do to change it?

---

3 VALUES

- **Exploring Values**
- **College Students' Values**
- **Meaning in Life**
- **Sociocultural Perspectives on Values**

In our description of identity, we indicated that a person's values are one of identity's dimensions. Let's now further examine values, including some strategies for determining what your values are.

Exploring Values

Values are standards that we apply to determine the worth of things, ideas, or events. Our values reflect what matters most to us. We attach value to many things—education, money, sex, family, friends, work, cheating, self-respect, and so on.

Sometimes individuals might not be aware of their values until they are forced to take some action. For example, you might be surprised to find yourself reacting strongly if you see the student next to you cheating on an exam. You might experience a **value conflict,** a clash between values that encourage opposing actions (Wyer, 2004). Perhaps the value of integrity prompts you to turn in the cheater while the value you place on popularity or on tolerance encourages you to mind your own business.

For members of ethnic minority groups, clashes between their values and the values of the mainstream culture may force awareness of their own values. As Maxine Hong Kingston was growing up, for example, she saw her Chinese parents deal with conflicts between the values of the collectivist culture of their ancestors and the values of the individualist culture of their new land. For anyone who is not exposed to the values of other groups, however, the values of the mainstream group may be taken for granted. Their power may be difficult to recognize. Thus, we might not be conscious of our own values when they match those of the mainstream culture.

How well do you know what your values are? Without exploring and reflecting about your values, you may spend too much time on things that really aren't that important to you. Clarifying your values can help you understand which goals you want to pursue and where to direct your time. To explore your values, complete Self-Assessment 3.4.

"I've got the bowl, the bone, the big yard. I know I should be happy."

© The New Yorker Collection, 1992. Mike Twohy, from cartoonbank.com. All Rights Reserved.

values Standards that we apply to determine the worth of things, ideas, or events. Our values reflect what matters most to us.

value conflict A clash between values that encourage opposing actions.

SELF-ASSESSMENT 3.4

What Are My Values?

The 20-item list below describes a wide range of values. Place a check mark in the space next to the 10 values that are the most important to you.

_____ having good family relationships

_____ having high self-esteem

_____ being a loyal person

_____ experiencing sensory pleasure

_____ having peace of mind

_____ being independent

_____ being well-off financially

_____ having a good spiritual life

_____ being competent at my work

_____ being a moral person

_____ being well-educated

_____ being happy

_____ living a healthy lifestyle

_____ being intelligent

_____ helping others

_____ being a good citizen and showing loyalty to my country

_____ being physically fit

_____ being in control of my life

_____ getting recognition or becoming famous

_____ finding meaning in life

From the list of 10 items you checked, rank order the top 5. My 5 most important personal values are:

1. _____

2. _____

3. _____

4. _____

5. _____

Go to the appendix at the end of the book to explore further questions and clarification related to your responses.

Adjustment Strategies
For Clarifying Your Values

Here are some good strategies for clarifying your values (Covey, 1989; Covey, Merrill, & Merrill, 1994):

1. ***Imagine attending your own funeral.*** In his popular book, *The Seven Habits of Highly Successful People,* Covey (1989, pp. 96–97) asks readers to imagine

attending their own funeral and looking down at themselves in the casket. You then take a seat and four speakers (a family member, a friend, someone from work or school, and someone from your church or community organization) are about to describe their impression of you. How would they describe your values? What would you want them to say about you and the way you lived your life?

2. ***Take one minute and answer this question: If I had unlimited time and resources, what would I do?*** It is okay to dream and write down everything that comes into your mind for one minute (use your watch to time this exercise).

3. ***Go to Self-Assessment 3.4 and review the list of five values that are most important to you.*** Take several minutes to compare this list with the dream list you just created. You might be living with unconscious dreams that don't match with your values. If you don't get your dreams out in the open, you can spend years living with illusions. Spend some time reflecting about the two lists. Can you improve the match between your dreams and your values?

4. ***Take one minute to examine how your values relate to four basic areas of self-fulfillment: physical needs, social needs, mental needs, and spiritual needs.*** Do your values reflect these needs? Covey(1989) believes that you need to work on your list until they do.

College Students' Values

Since the early 1970s college students have shown an increased concern for personal well-being and a decreased concern for the well-being of others, especially for the disadvantaged (Sax & others, 2003). As shown in figure 3.4, today's college freshmen are more strongly motivated to be well-off financially and less motivated to develop a meaningful philosophy of life than were their counterparts of 30 years ago. Student commitment to becoming very well-off financially as a "very important" reason for attending college reached 74 percent in the 2003 survey, compared with 50 percent in 1971.

However, there are some signs that today's college students are shifting toward a stronger interest in the welfare of society. For example, the percentage of college freshmen who said they would very likely participate in volunteer or community service work in the coming year increased from 17 percent in 1990 to 25 percent in 2003 (Sax & others, 2003).

Service learning is a form of education that promotes social responsibility and service to the community, aiming to help adolescents and emerging adults to become

service learning A form of education that promotes social responsibility and service to the community, aiming to help adolescents and emerging adults to become less self-centered and more strongly motivated to help others.

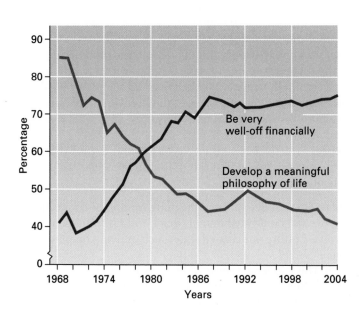

FIGURE 3.4 Changing Freshmen Life Goals, 1968–2002
In the last three decades, a significant change has occurred in freshmen students' life goals. A far greater percentage of today's college freshmen state that a "very important" life goal is to be well-off financially, and far fewer state that developing a meaningful philosophy of life is a "very important" life goal.

What are some of the personal benefits of volunteering?

College Students' Values

Viktor Frankl

less self-centered and more strongly motivated to help others. In service learning, adolescents and emerging adults engage in activities such as tutoring, helping older adults, working in a hospital, assisting at a child-care center, or cleaning up a vacant lot to make a play area. Thus, service learning takes education out into the community (Flanagan, 2004; Youniss & others, 2003).

A key feature of service learning is that it benefits both the student volunteers and the recipients of their help. For example, one college student worked as a reading tutor for students from low-income backgrounds with reading skills well below their grade levels. She commented that until she did the tutoring she did not realize how many students had not experienced the same opportunities that she had when she was growing up. An especially rewarding moment was when one young girl told her, "I want to learn to read like you so I can go to college when I grow up."

Volunteers tend to share certain characteristics, such as extraversion, a commitment to others, and a high degree of self-understanding (Eisenberg & Morris, 2004). Also, women are more likely to volunteer to engage in community service than men (Eisenberg & Morris, 2004).

Researchers have found that volunteering and community service benefit adolescents and emerging adults in a number of ways:

- Their grades improve, they become more motivated, and set more goals (Johnson & others, 1998; Search Institute, 1995).
- Their self-esteem improves (Hamburg, 1997; Johnson & others, 1998).
- They have an improved sense of being able to make a difference for others (Search Institute, 1995).
- They become less alienated (Calabrese & Schumer, 1986).
- They increasingly reflect on society's political organization and moral order (Yates, 1995).

Meaning in Life

For some people, helping others is a value in itself; for others, it is a way of finding meaning in life. This value was the topic of a book by Austrian psychiatrist Viktor Frankl. Frankl's mother, father, brother, and wife died in the concentration camps and gas chambers in Auschwitz, Poland. Frankl survived the concentration camp and went on to write *Man's Search for Meaning* (1984).

Frankl emphasizes each person's uniqueness and the finiteness of life. He believes that examining the finiteness of our existence and the certainty of death adds meaning to life. If life were not finite, says Frankl, we could spend our life doing just about whatever we please because time would continue forever. Frankl proposed that people need to ask themselves such questions as why they exist, what they want from life, and what the meaning of their life is.

Roy Baumeister (1991b; Baumeister & Vohs, 2002) argues that the quest for a meaningful life can be understood in terms of four main needs that guide how people try to make sense out of their lives:

- *Need for purpose.* Present events draw meaning from their connection with future events. Purposes can be divided into (1) goals and (2) fulfillments. Life can be oriented toward a future anticipated state, such as living happily ever after or being in love.
- *Need for values.* This can lend a sense of life's goodness and justify certain courses of action. Values help to determine whether certain acts are right or wrong. Frankl (1984) emphasized value as the main form of meaning that people need.

- *Need for a sense of efficacy.* Efficacy involves the belief that one can make a difference. A person who has purposes and values but no sense of efficacy might know what is desirable but feel unable to do anything with that knowledge. With a sense of efficacy, people believe that they can control their environment, which has positive physical and mental health benefits (Bandura, 2001, 2004).
- *Need for self-worth.* Most individuals want to be good, worthy persons. Self-worth can be pursued individually, such as finding out that one is good at doing something, or collectively, such as by identifying with the successes of one's ethnic group.

As you can see, Baumeister's description of the needs that can guide people in trying to make sense out of their lives reflect the main topics of this chapter: the self, identity, and values. Spend some reflecting on the extent to which your needs are being met in these areas.

Sociocultural Perspectives on Values

The values of Western culture are likely to encourage us to pursue needs for self-worth individually, by seeking to become our hoped-for possible selves and enhance our self-esteem. What are the consequences of emphasizing individuality over the collective good? Roy Baumeister (1991b) suggests that Americans are too concerned with self-fulfillment and personal identity, so much so that these have become burdens for many people. Because of the high priority Americans place on developing, maintaining, and enhancing a positive self-image, many of us are too self-critical, too motivated for change, and too stressed.

The pressures of seeking self-fulfillment can be overwhelming. Some people avoid these pressures by turning to activities that diminish self-preoccupation. Some turn on the television or read science fiction books. Others meditate or listen to classical music. Some people lose themselves in dance, others in a pitcher of beer. Society offers and endorses many ways to forget ourselves for a while. Unfortunately, many forms of escape have high costs. Some people develop substance-abuse problems, attempt suicide, or join radical cults. Escaping the burden of maintaining a personal identity can create even more serious challenges to the integrity of the self.

Non-Western Zen Buddhism offers a negative perspective on the Western preoccupation with individuality and worrying so much about failure. Zen Buddhism

Zen Buddhism being practiced. *What are some characteristics of Zen Buddhism?*

emphasizes living in the present moment by fully attending to the task at hand. Your goal should be to do what needs to be done, whether it is trivial or substantial, whether it is pleasant or not.

This approach—doing what needs to be done, rather than seeking pleasurable activity, and experiencing the task fully—is reflected in morita tasks. A therapy based on Zen Buddhism, **morita therapy** emphasizes accepting feelings, knowing one's purposes, and most important, doing what needs to be done. Morita exercises not only teach you to do constructive work with full attention but also decrease egocentrism and self-consciousness.

Review and Reflect

3 **Summarize some important aspects of values**

REVIEW

- What are values? Why is it important to clarify your values?
- What are college students' values? What is service learning and how does it influence people?
- What are some guidelines in searching for meaning in life?
- What are some sociocultural perspectives on values?

REFLECT

- What experiences have you had in volunteering and participating in community service? If you have had these experiences, what impact did they have on you? If you have not participated in volunteering and community service, what aspect interests you the most?

4 RELIGION

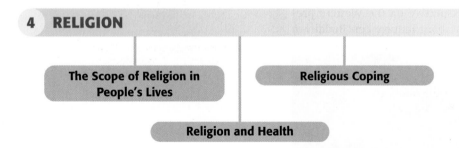

Religion is an important aspect of the self, identity, and values of many individuals. Recall from chapter 1 that happy people tend to have a meaningful religious faith (Diener, Lucas, & Oishi, 2002). Just how pervasive is religion in people's lives and how is it linked to their health? What is involved in religious coping.

The Scope of Religion in People's Lives

Religion plays an important role in the lives of many people around the world. For example, 98 percent of respondents in India, 88 percent in Italy, 72 percent in France, and 63 percent in Scandinavia say that they believe in God (Gallup, 1987).

In the McArthur Study of Midlife Development, more than 70 percent of U.S. middle-aged adults said they are religious and consider spirituality a major part of

morita therapy Emphasizes accepting feelings, knowing one's purposes, and most important, doing what needs to be done.

their lives (Brim, 1999). However, that does not mean they are committed to a single religion or house of worship. About one-half said they attend religious services less than once a month or never. In another study, about three-fourths of U.S. adults said that they pray (*Religion in America,* 1993). In a recent longitudinal study of individuals from their early 30s through their late 60s/early 70s, a significant increase in spirituality occurred between middle (mid-50s/early 60s) and late adulthood (late 60s/early 70s) (Wink & Dillon, 2002) (see figure 3.5).

Females have consistently shown a stronger interest in religion than males have (Bijur & others, 1993). Compared with men, they participate more in organized and personal forms of religion, are more likely to believe in a higher power or presence, and are more likely to feel that religion is an important dimension of their lives. In the recent longitudinal study just mentioned, the spirituality of women increased more than men in the second half of life (Wink & Dillon, 2002).

Americans are becoming less committed to particular religious denominations (such as Baptist or Catholic). They are more tolerant of other faiths and more focused on their own personal spiritual journeys (Paloutzian, 2000). This change may be partly generational, a consequence of postwar baby boomers' emphasis on experimentation and independent thinking that is reflected in a fluid religious orientation.

At the same time that Americans show a strong interest in religion and belief in God, they also are showing a declining faith in mainstream religious institutions, in religious leaders, and in the spiritual and moral stature of the nation (*Religion in America,* 1993; Sollod, 2000). To evaluate the role of spiritual well-being in your life, complete Self-Assessment 3.5.

FIGURE 3.5 Level of Spirituality

Religion and Health

Might religion have an effect on a person's physical health? Although people in some religious sects try to avoid using medical treatment or pain-relieving medications, individuals in the religious mainstream generally enjoy a positive link or neutral link between religion and physical health (Hill & Pargament, 2003; Paloutzian, 2000; Rayburn, 2004; Yates, 2004). Researchers have found that religious commitment helps to moderate blood pressure and hypertension (Levin & Vanderpool, 1989). Also, a number of studies have confirmed that religious participation is related to a longer life (Gartner, Larson, & Allen, 1991; Thoresen & Harris, 2002).

How might religion promote physical health? Part of the answer may be simply that some religious organizations provide some health-related services. Another possible explanation is that religious individuals have healthier life styles (for example, they use fewer drugs). Yet another explanation for the link between religion and good health is that religious organizations sponsor social connections. It is well documented that socially connected individuals have fewer health problems (Hill & Pargament, 2003). The social connections promoted by religious activity can forestall anxiety and depression and can help to prevent isolation and loneliness (Paloutzian, 2000).

Religious thoughts can play a role in maintaining hope and stimulating motivation for recovery from an illness or disease (Nairn & Merluzzi, 2003). Although the evidence is not clear, it also has been argued that prayer might be associated with positive health-related changes in the face of stress, such as decreased perception of pain and reduced muscle tension. A recent study found that some individuals with AIDS who lived much longer than expected had used religion as a coping strategy, participating in religious activities such as praying and attending church services (Ironson & others, 2001).

Exploring the Psychology of Religion
Psychology of Religion Journals
Mental Health, Religion, and Culture

SELF-ASSESSMENT 3.5

My Spiritual Well-Being

For each of the following statements, assign a score from 1 to 6 according to how strongly you agree or disagree with it.

	Strongly Agree					Strongly Disagree
1. I don't find much satisfaction in private prayer with God.	1	2	3	4	5	6
2. I don't know who I am, where I came from, or where I am going.	1	2	3	4	5	6
3. I believe that God loves me and cares about me.	1	2	3	4	5	6
4. I feel that life is a positive experience.	1	2	3	4	5	6
5. I believe that God is impersonal and not interested in my daily situations.	1	2	3	4	5	6
6. I feel unsettled about my future.	1	2	3	4	5	6
7. I have a personally meaningful relationship with God.	1	2	3	4	5	6
8. I feel very fulfilled and satisfied with life.	1	2	3	4	5	6
9. I don't get much personal strength and support from my God.	1	2	3	4	5	6
10. I feel a sense of well-being about the direction my life is headed in.	1	2	3	4	5	6
11. I believe that God is concerned about my problems.	1	2	3	4	5	6
12. I don't enjoy much about life.	1	2	3	4	5	6
13. I don't have a personally satisfying relationship with God.	1	2	3	4	5	6
14. I feel good about my future.	1	2	3	4	5	6
15. My relationship with God helps me not to feel lonely.	1	2	3	4	5	6
16. I feel that life is full of conflict and unhappiness.	1	2	3	4	5	6
17. I feel most fulfilled when I'm in close communion with God.	1	2	3	4	5	6
18. Life doesn't have much meaning.	1	2	3	4	5	6
19. My relationship with God contributes to my sense of well-being.	1	2	3	4	5	6
20. I believe there is some real purpose for my life.	1	2	3	4	5	6

Please turn to the appendix at the end of the book for scoring and interpretation.

Religious Coping

In general, various dimensions of religion can also help some people cope more effectively with the stress in their lives (Butter & Pargament, 2003). What aspects of religion are assessed when researchers seek to measure religious coping? A religious coping subscale in one coping assessment consists of four items (Carver, Scheier, & Weintraub, 1989): "I seek God's help," "I put my trust in God," "I try to find comfort in my religion," and "I pray." A more detailed religious coping assessment is designed to evaluate five religious coping functions (Pargament, Koenig, & Perez, 2000): finding meaning in the face of suffering and baffling life experiences, providing an avenue to achieve a sense of mastery and control, finding comfort and reducing apprehension by connecting with a force that goes beyond the individual, fostering social solidarity and identity, and assisting individuals in giving up old objects of value and finding new sources of significance. Yet another way of conceptualizing and assessing religious coping strategies is to categorize them as positive or negative. One effort in this regard was made by Kenneth Pargament and his colleagues (1998). Positive religious coping strategies were described as an expression of a sense of spirituality, a secure relationship with God, a belief that there is meaning to be found in life, and a sense of spiritual connectedness with others. Negative religious coping strategies included a less secure relationship with God, a tenuous and ominous view of the world, and a religious struggle in search of significance.

Review and Reflect

4   Characterize the role of religion in people's lives

REVIEW

- What is the scope of religion in people's lives?
- How is religion linked to health?
- What are some important aspects of religious coping?

REFLECT

- What role does religion or spirituality play in your life? Have you ever relied on religion or spirituality to help you cope with a problem or issue in your life? If so, describe the situation and how effectively religion or spirituality helped you to cope.

What are important dimensions of religious coping?

Reach Your Learning Goals

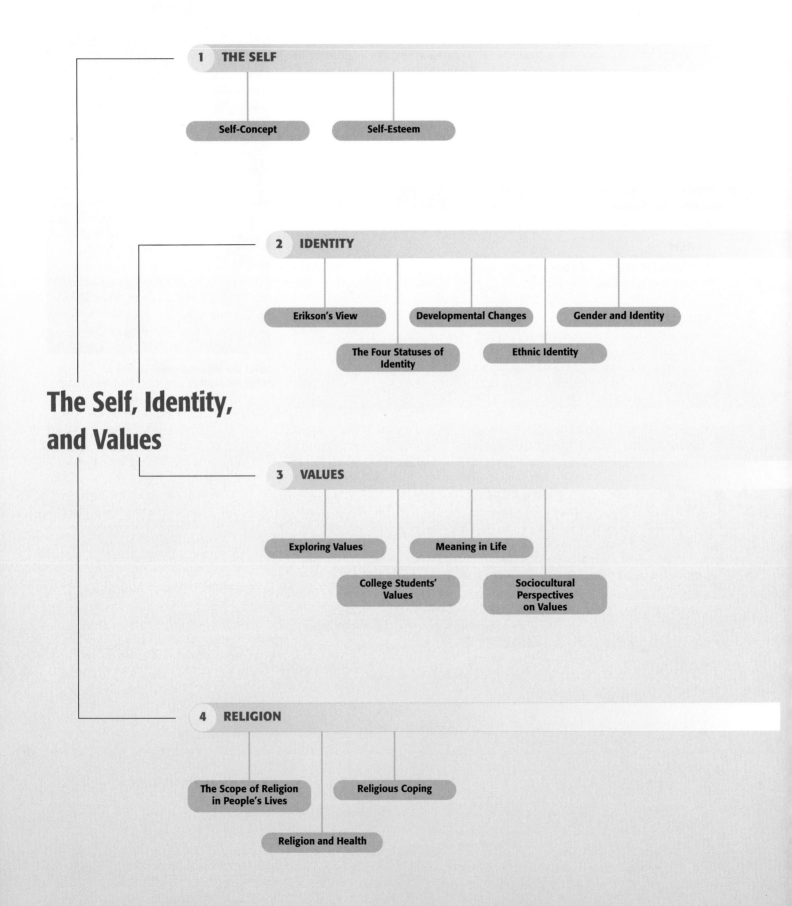

The Self, Identity, and Values

1 THE SELF

- Self-Concept
- Self-Esteem

2 IDENTITY

- Erikson's View
- The Four Statuses of Identity
- Developmental Changes
- Ethnic Identity
- Gender and Identity

3 VALUES

- Exploring Values
- College Students' Values
- Meaning in Life
- Sociocultural Perspectives on Values

4 RELIGION

- The Scope of Religion in People's Lives
- Religious Coping
- Religion and Health

Summary

1 *Discuss self-concept and self-esteem*

- Self-concept is an individual's perception of his or her abilities, personality, and other attributes; it consists of the overall thoughts and feelings about one's self. The self-concept includes representations of multiple selves—such as the real or actual self, the ideal self, the ought self, hoped-for possible selves, and dreaded possible selves—as well as representations of these selves from various viewpoints.

  Higgins' self-discrepancy theory argues that discrepancies between the actual and ideal selves tend to create dejection-relation emotions and discrepancies between the actual self and ought self tend to create agitated emotions.

- Self-esteem is a person's overall evaluation of his or her self-worth or self-image. This evaluation does not necessarily match reality. People have both a general level of self-esteem and fluctuating degrees of self-esteem related to specific domains of life. Self-esteem tends to be stable at least across a month or so. There is controversy about whether self-esteem varies according to the age of the individual. Researchers have found only moderate correlations between self-esteem and school performance and varying correlations between self-esteem and job performance. Self-esteem is strongly correlated with happiness. Some individuals who have high self-esteem are narcissistic. Strategies for enhancing self-esteem involve identifying sources of low self-esteem, facing a problem and coping with it, experiencing emotional support and social approval, taking responsibility for one's self-esteem, achieving, and exploring resources to improve self-understanding.

2 *Describe what identity is and how it is formed*

- Identity versus identity confusion is Erikson's fifth developmental stage, which individuals experience during adolescence and emerging adulthood. Youth enter a psychosocial moratorium during which they experiment with personalities and roles as they search for an identity. In technological societies like the United States, the vocational identity is especially important. Identity development is done in bits and pieces, and identity changes may occur throughout life.

- Marcia proposed four identity statuses: diffused, foreclosed, moratorium, and achieved. A combination of crisis (exploration) and commitment yields one of the statuses.

- Some experts believe that the main identity changes take place in late adolescence or emerging adulthood, rather than in early adolescence. College upperclassmen are more likely to be identity achieved than are freshmen or high school students, although many college students are still wrestling with ideological commitments. Individuals often follow "moratorium–achievement–moratorium–achievement" cycles.

- Throughout the world ethnic minority groups have struggled to maintain their cultural identities while blending into majority culture. Adolescence and emerging adulthood often represent a special juncture in the identity development of ethnic minority individuals because for the first time they consciously confront their ethnic identity. Many ethnic minority individuals have a bicultural identity. Helms proposed a model of ethnic identity development.

- Erikson believed that males have a stronger vocational identity, females a stronger social identity. However, researchers are finding that these gender differences are disappearing.

3 *Summarize some important aspects of values*

- Values are standards that we maintain about the things we prefer or ideas that capture our allegiance. Without deeply exploring and reflecting about your values, you may spend too much time on things that aren't really important to you. Clarifying your values can help you identify the goals you want to pursue and where to direct your motivation and time.

- Over the past two decades U.S. college students have shown an increased concern for personal well-being and a decreased concern for the well-being of others, especially the disadvantaged. However, an increasing number of students are showing an interest in volunteer or community service work. Service learning is a form of education that promotes social responsibility and service to the community; participating in service learning is related to higher grades, increased goal setting, and higher self-esteem.

- Frankl believes that examining the finiteness of our existence leads to exploration of meaning in life. Baumeister argues that a quest for a meaningful life involves four main needs: purpose, values, efficacy, and self-worth.

- Some critics argue that Americans are too concerned with self-fulfillment and personal identity. Non-Western Zen Buddhism offers a negative perspective on the Western preoccupation with individuality and worrying so much about failure. Zen Buddhism emphasizes living in the present moment by focusing on the task at hand. This approach is reflected in morita therapy.

4 *Characterize the role of religion in people's lives*

- Religion plays an important role in the lives of many people around the world. A majority of Americans say they are religious. Females have shown a stronger interest in religion than males have. Americans are becoming less committed to a particular religious denomination and show a declining faith in mainstream religious organizations.
- Although some people in some religious sects try to avoid using medical treatment or pain-relieving

medications, individuals in the religious mainstream generally enjoy a positive or neutral link between religion and physical health.
- Religion also helps some people cope more effectively with stress. Positive religious coping strategies include an expression of a sense of spirituality, a secure relationship with God, a belief that there is meaning to be found in life, and a sense of spiritual connectedness with others.

Key Terms

self-concept 81
actual self 82
ideal self 82
ought self 82
self-discrepancy theory 82
possible selves 82
self-esteem 83
narcissism 87
identity 89
identity versus identity confusion stage 89
psychological moratorium 89
identity diffusion 90
identity foreclosure 90
identity moratorium 90
identity achievement 90
ethnic identity 93
values 95
value conflict 95
service learning 97
morita therapy 100

Resources for Improving Your Adjustment

Self-Esteem

(2000) by Matthew McKay and Patrick Fanning. Oakland, CA: New Harbinger.

This book includes opportunities for you to evaluate your self-esteem and provides numerous strategies for increasing self-esteem. The authors especially emphasize the importance of countering negative self-statements.

Women & Self-Esteem

(1984) by Linda Sanford and Mary Donovan. New York: Anchor Doubleday.

Women & Self-Esteem explains why women often have low self-esteem and how they can improve the way they think about themselves. The authors provide readers with exercises that will help you engage in self-evaluation, reduce negative self-images, and decrease self-destructive behaviors. This is a good book for women with low self-esteem.

Man's Search for Meaning

(1984) by Viktor Frankl. New York: Pocket.

Frankl believes that the three most distinct human qualities are spirituality, freedom, and responsibility. The book will challenge you to think deeply about your values and the meaning of life.

Man's Search for Meaning was rated in the highest category (5 stars) in the national survey of self-help books (Norcross, Santrock, & others, 2003).

The Seven Habits of Highly Effective People

(1989) by Steven Covey. New York: Simon & Schuster.

Covey's best-selling book provides an in-depth examination of how people's perspectives and values determine how competent they are in their work and personal lives. This book was highly rated (5 stars) in the national survey of self-help books.

The Road Less Traveled

(1978) by M. Scott Peck. New York: Simon & Schuster.

The Road Less Traveled presents an approach to self-fulfillment based on spirituality and emotions. Peck begins by stating that life is difficult and that we all suffer pain and disappointment. He believes we should face up to life's difficulties, that people are thirsting for integrity in their lives, and that people need to move spirituality into all phases of their lives. Peck speaks of four important tools to use in life's journey: delaying gratification, accepting responsibility, dedication to the truth, and balancing. *The Road Less Traveled* received 4 of 5 stars in the national survey of self-help books (Norcross, Santrock, & others, 2003).

 # E-Learning Tools

To help you master the material in this chapter, you will find a number of valuable study tools on the student CD-ROM that accompanies this book. In addition, visit the Online Learning Center for *Human Adjustment,* where you can find these valuable resources for Chapter 3, "The Self, Identity, and Values."

SELF-ASSESSMENT

In Text

You can complete these self-assessments in the text:
- Self-Assessment 3.1: *My Self-Esteem*
- Self-Assessment 3.2: *Do I Have Narcissistic Tendencies?*
- Self-Assessment 3.3: *What Is My Identity?*
- Self-Assessment 3.4: *What Are My Values?*
- Self-Assessment 3.5: *My Spiritual Well-Being*

Additional Self-Assessments

Complete these self-assessments on the Online Learning Center:
- Self-Assessment: *Comparing My Attitudes and Values with Those of Other College Students*
- Self-Assessment: *What Is My Purpose in Life?*

THINK CRITICALLY

To practice your critical thinking skills, complete these exercises on the Online Learning Center:
- *Advertising and Self-Enhancement* relates to commercials and self-esteem
- *Major Decisions and Identity Formation* focuses on the decisions you make and how they affect your identity
- *Value Billboards* involves T-shirt decorations and values
- *Faith and Evidence* deals with gender differences in religion

APPLY YOUR KNOWLEDGE

1. Self-Esteem and the Average Person.

Is the idea of self-esteem discussed by psychologists the same as the everyday person's perception of self-esteem? To find out, select the items that researchers have found to be associated with or characteristic of good self-esteem in your textbook. Write out each one and put "true" and "false" next to the characteristic. Then, ask five people to indicate whether they think the item is more likely to be true or false. Three examples are listed to help get you started:

a. Self-esteem is more about one's belief than it is about one's actual abilities. (T)
b. People who have good self-esteem tend to have it in all areas of their lives. (F)
c. Researchers have found that making people feel good about themselves is a good strategy for improving self-esteem. (F)

For more information on improving self-esteem, go to www.google.com or www.yahoo.com and enter "improving self-esteem" into the search box. List ten ways that people can improve their self-esteem.

Are the suggestions you found consistent with what it says in your textbook? Why or why not? What reasons might there be for inconsistencies? Does your textbook address the issues raised by other sources?

2. How do you cope?

Do you use good coping skills, or are you more likely to use avoidance? For each of the following, indicate whether you use active coping or avoidance. For the items where your primary way of dealing with the issue is avoidance, list ways to overcome that avoidance. Also identify the pattern exhibited by someone who is using avoidance in that given situation.

a. You and your significant other are having a disagreement about something and this has created an uncomfortable atmosphere between you.
b. You dislike a particular class that you are taking.
c. You are in conflict with a co-worker.
d. You are having financial difficulties and are getting behind on your bills.
e. You are having trouble completing an assignment.
f. Someone has criticized you about a mistake you made at work.
g. Your neighbor has a dog that barks all the time, but you are otherwise on good terms with that neighbor.

3. Are you privileged?

The world is increasingly becoming a diverse place. Although discrimination is less evident than it used to be, there are still some people who have an advantage in society simply because of who they are rather than because of their abilities. In many cases, people who are privileged in one area may be less privileged in another area. In addition, we often fail to recognize areas where we are privileged because we have learned to take it for granted. Although people can recognize that some are "under-privileged" we often have difficulty seeing other things as "over-privileged."

a. Begin by listing all the ways in which you are privileged. Think hard, remembering that we often fail to recognize areas of privilege.

b. After you have made your list, compare it with the following list.

Possible answers: Generally people are in a position of privilege in the U.S. (and much of the rest of the world) if they are:

Male
White
Tall
Intelligent
Heterosexual
Attractive
Middle or upper class
English speaking
Speaking with a mid-western accent
Suburban dwellers

Did you fail to identify any areas of privilege? Do you now recognize your privilege, or do you deny that people in the groups listed get better treatment than those against whom they would be compared?

c. Try this exercise on at least three friends. Did you notice any trends?

Privilege is increasingly an area of interest with regard to self-concept. How do your areas of privilege affect your self-concept? How do they reflect your concept of people around you?

 VIDEO SEGMENT

Culture and the Self

If, as Hazel Markus argues, all selves are culture-specific, how does the sense of self fostered by individualist cultures differ from the self encouraged by collectivist cultures? The video for Chapter 3 on the CD-ROM describes these two types of selves.

Stress

Chapter Outline

Learning Goals

1 Explain what stress is and describe its main components

2 Discuss links between stress and illness

3 Identify key sources and buffers of stress

4 Characterize post-traumatic stress disorder

Images of Adjustment

Daphne Carlisle, La-Shawn Clark, Susan Kelly, and Mary Assanful: Stress and Coping in the Aftermath of September 11, 2001

On September 11, 2001, more than 3,000 people were killed when terrorists attacked the World Trade Center towers in New York City and the Pentagon in Washington, D.C. Port Authority worker Daphne Carlisle was one of those who managed to escape the World Trade Center. One year later, she said, "Before 9/11, I was a free-spirited outgoing person. A year later, I experience . . . bouts of depression and fears of loud noises, airplanes and tall buildings. . . . Thoughts of burning flesh haunt me daily" (Carlisle, 2002).

Beyond those like Carlisle who managed to escape the burning buildings, the terrorist attacks created many other victims of stress, including the families and friends of those who were killed. Kirsten Breitweiser was only 30 years old when her husband called her one morning to say he was fine and not to worry. He had seen a huge fireball outside his window, but it wasn't his building. She tuned into the *Today* show just in time to see the South Tower explode right where she knew he was sitting—on the 94th floor. For months thereafter, finding it impossible to sleep, Kirsten went back to the nightly ritual of her married life: She took out her husband's toothbrush and slowly, lovingly squeezed the toothpaste onto it. Then she would sit down and wait for him to come home (Sheey, 2003).

Individuals who survive a trauma may react in various ways, some better than others. By the summer of 2002, Kirsten, along with three other women who had lost their husbands on 9/11, was investigating the attack. The "Four Moms from New Jersey" read and rallied and lobbied until they helped to force the creation of an independent commission to investigate the 9/11 attacks. Here are some ways that three other survivors had coped two years after 9/11/01 (Shriver, 2003):

Mary Assanful (*front right*) along with former restaurant workers who lost their jobs as a result of the 9/11 terrorist attacks. They are trying to start their own restaurant as part of coping with the trauma and to give a focus to their lives.

- La-Shawn Clark's husband died in the collapse of the South Tower of the World Trade Center. She was a special education teacher at the time of her husband's death, which brought not only grief but also conflicts over 9/11 issues with her landlord, in-laws, pastor, the government, an insurance company, and even the Red Cross. Those she expected to support her let her down, she said, but one group, the Windows of Hope Family Relief Fund, gave her the financial and emotional support she needed. In spring 2003, she uprooted her family from Brooklyn and relocated to Pennsylvania to escape the conflicts and the reminders of the tragedy. Clark is writing down her thoughts and says that she has finally found some "peace of mind" and plans to remarry soon.

- Susan Kelly and her husband were rearing their five children in Long Island, New York, before he was killed in the World Trade Center attacks. She says that every day she gives herself a little pat on the back for coping with the trauma. Kelly was six weeks pregnant when her husband was killed. Her grief was compounded by the fear of how she was going to care for her children and maintain her home. She worried about what would happen to her children if something happened to her. Kelly's turning point came in fall 2002, when she abandoned a plan to move her family away from the site of so many memories and decided to refinance their home. Though investments had made her financially secure, she says that decision made her feel emotionally secure. Finally, Kelly says, "I was in control."

- Mary Assanful worked at Windows on the World restaurant located in the World Trade Center and lost her job when the terrorist attacks came. "I'm not myself," she says. "I still have nightmares." A Ghana native, Mary is still unemployed. She has joined several other workers who are planning to open a restaurant near Ground Zero. They hope the new restaurant will honor their co-workers who died and provide a focus for their still-unsettled lives. Mary says that since they have been working on this new project, her mind has calmed somewhat.

Although most people don't experience the intense trauma that these individuals did, stressful experiences are part of each of our lives. According to the American Academy of Family Physicians, two-thirds of office visits to family doctors today are for stress-related symptoms. Stress is believed to be a major contributor to coronary heart disease, cancer, lung problems, accidental injuries, cirrhosis of the liver, and suicide—six of the leading causes of death in the United States. In this chapter we examine what stress is, links between stress and illness, sources of stress, and post-traumatic stress disorder.

1 WHAT IS STRESS?

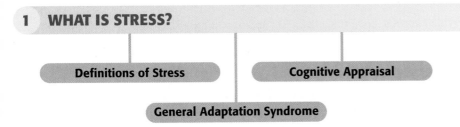

Stress is a sign of the times. Everywhere you look, people are trying to reduce the effects of excessive tension by jogging, going to health clubs, and following special diets. No one really knows whether we experience more stress than our parents or grandparents did, but it seems as if we do.

Definitions of Stress

Initially, the word *stress* was borrowed from physics. Physical objects such as metals resist moderate outside forces but lose their resiliency under greater pressure. Similarly, people adapt to pressures up to a point but then show diminished resistance. They might have difficulty concentrating, like Daphne Carlisle. They might lose their temper easily, feel fatigued and listless, or fall ill more easily than usual.

Unlike metals, however, human beings think and reason, and they experience a myriad of social and environmental circumstances that make defining stress more

SELF-ASSESSMENT 4.1

How Vulnerable Am I to Stress?

Rate each item from 1 (*always*) to 5 (*never*), according to how much of the time the statement is true of you. Be sure to mark each item, even if it does not apply to you—for example, if you don't smoke, circle 1 next to item six.

	Always		Sometimes		Never
1. I eat at least one hot, balanced meal a day.	1	2	3	4	5
2. I get seven to eight hours of sleep at least four nights a week.	1	2	3	4	5
3. I give and receive affection regularly.	1	2	3	4	5
4. I have at least one relative within 50 miles, on whom I can rely.	1	2	3	4	5
5. I exercise to the point of perspiration at least twice a week.	1	2	3	4	5
6. I limit myself to less than half a pack of cigarettes a day.	1	2	3	4	5
7. I take fewer than five alcohol drinks a week.	1	2	3	4	5
8. I am the appropriate weight for my height.	1	2	3	4	5
9. I have an income adequate to meet basic expenses.	1	2	3	4	5
10. I get strength from my religious beliefs.	1	2	3	4	5
11. I regularly attend club or social activities.	1	2	3	4	5
12. I have a network of friends and acquaintances.	1	2	3	4	5
13. I have one or more friends to confide in about personal matters.	1	2	3	4	5
14. I am in good health (including eyesight, hearing, teeth).	1	2	3	4	5
15. I am able to speak openly about my feelings when angry or worried.	1	2	3	4	5
16. I have regular conversations with the people I live with about domestic problems—for example, chores and money.	1	2	3	4	5
17. I do something for fun at least once a week.	1	2	3	4	5
18. I am able to organize my time effectively.	1	2	3	4	5
19. I drink fewer than three cups of coffee (or other caffeine-rich drinks) a day.	1	2	3	4	5
20. I take some quiet time for myself during the day.	1	2	3	4	5

Go to the appendix at the end of the book for scoring and interpretation of your responses.

stress The response of individuals to stressors.

stressors The circumstances and events that threaten individuals and tax their coping abilities.

complex in psychology than in physics (Hobfoll, 1989). Sometimes, the term *stress* is used to refer to the circumstances that threaten or put pressure on people. Here, we define **stress** as the response of individuals to **stressors,** which are circumstances and events that threaten them and tax their coping abilities.

A car accident, a failed job interview, a lost wallet, conflict with a friend—all of these might be stressors in your life. Some stressors are *acute;* in other words, they are sudden events or stimuli such as being cut by falling glass. Other stressors are *chronic,* or long-lasting, such as being malnourished or HIV-positive. These are physical stressors, but there are emotional and psychosocial stressors, such as the death of a loved one or being discriminated against. To evaluate how vulnerable you are to stress, complete Self-Assessment 4.1.

General Adaptation Syndrome

When faced with stressors, your body readies itself to handle the assault through a number of physiological changes. These changes were the main interest of Hans Selye (1974, 1983), the Austrian-born founder of stress research. He defined *stress* as the wear and tear on the body due to the demands placed on it. After observing patients with different problems—the death of someone close, loss of income, arrest for embezzlement—Selye concluded that any number of stressors will produce the same physical reactions and eventually similar symptoms: loss of appetite, muscular weakness, and decreased interest in the world.

General adaptation syndrome (GAS) is Selye's term for the common effects on the body when stressors persist. The GAS consists of three stages: alarm, resistance, and exhaustion (see figure 4.1).

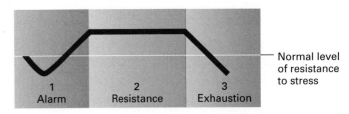

FIGURE 4.1 Selye's General Adaptation Syndrome
The general adaptation syndrome (GAS) describes an individual's general response to stress in terms of three stages: (1) alarm, in which the body mobilizes its resources; (2) resistance, in which resistance levels off; and (3) exhaustion, in which resistance becomes depleted.

Alarm During the *alarm stage,* the body quickly mobilizes resources to deal with whatever is threatening. One key player at this stage is the endocrine system, which consists of glands that secrete chemical messengers called *hormones* into the bloodstream. This stage is essentially the same as the *fight-or-flight response* described by Walter Cannon (1929). Cannon first observed this response when he studied the reaction of cats suddenly confronted by a dog. The cats showed changes such as more rapid blood circulation, muscular tension, and heavy breathing. Cannon called the entire reaction "fight or flight" because it prepared the animals either to fight or to flee when confronted with a threatening situation.

Cannon concluded that the fight-or-flight reaction prepares organisms to do what they need to do to survive. But threats to survival are not the only situations that generate this reaction, or what Selye called the alarm stage; virtually any threat might trigger it (Gilbert & Gilbert, 2003). The alarm stage passes rather quickly but you have probably experienced its dramatic effects. Faced with a near-accident, your heart races, your vigilance increases. You might gasp for breath or feel dizzy or queasy. These are side effects of your body's mobilization for action.

Scientists today are zeroing in on some more precise descriptions of the biological changes that take place during the alarm stage (Henderson & Baum, 2004). Many scientists now agree that these changes involve two main pathways: the neuroendocrine-immune pathway and the sympathetic nervous system pathway (Anderson, 1998, 2000; Anderson, Kiecolt-Glaser, & Glaser, 1994; Sternberg & Gold, 1996) (see figure 4.2).

The neuroendocrine-immune pathway (pathway 1 in figure 4.2) goes through two small structures in the brain—the hypothalamus and pituitary gland—to the adrenal glands, which release cortisol. *Cortisol* is a steroid that is good for the body over the short term because it causes glucose to move to muscles, giving them fuel for increased activity. High levels of cortisol also slow down the *immune system,* the body's defense system against invaders such as viruses and bacteria.

In the sympathetic nervous pathway (pathway 2 in figure 4.2), signals do not go through the pituitary gland. Instead, the route is through the hypothalamus and the *sympathetic nervous system,* which is the part of the nervous system responsible for the body's arousal. When a signal reaches the adrenal glands through this pathway, the hormones *epinephrine* and *norepinephrine* are released. This causes a number of physiological changes, including increased blood pressure, heart rate, and attention.

Resistance In the *resistance stage* of Selye's GAS, the body adapts to the continued presence of the stressor. Activity of the endocrine system and of the sympathetic nervous system is still elevated, but activity is not as high as during the alarm stage. In the resistance stage, a number of glands begin to manufacture different hormones that protect the individual in many ways. For example, hormones that reduce inflammation

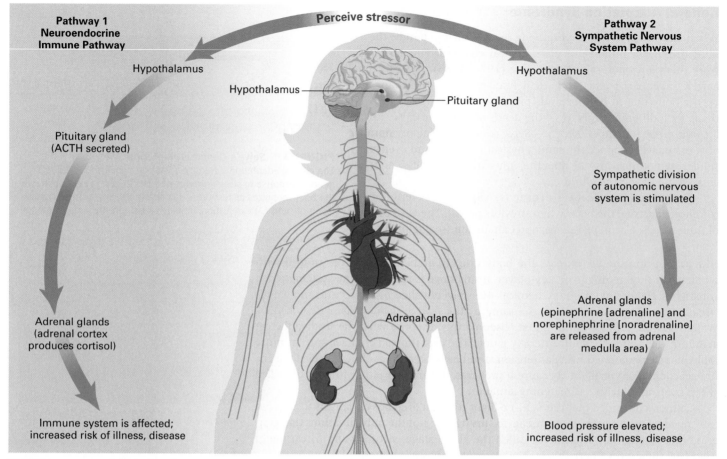

FIGURE 4.2 Two Biological Pathways in Stress

normally associated with injury circulate at high levels, and the immune system fights off infection.

Exhaustion If the threat and the body's all-out effort to combat it continues, the individual moves into the *exhaustion stage*. Responses that were helpful in the short term may now become damaging as they persist. For example, over the long term, high levels of cortisol suppress the immune system and strain the brain's cellular functioning. Also over time, elevated blood pressure can lead to increased risk of illness and disease, such as cardiovascular disease. The wear and tear on the body takes its toll—the person might collapse in a state of exhaustion, and vulnerability to disease increases. During the exhaustion phase, serious, possible irreversible damage to the body, or even death, may occur.

Cognitive Appraisal

Selye concluded that any number of events or stimuli will produce the same series of responses. However, human beings do not always react to stressors in the uniform way that Selye proposed (Seffge-Krenke, 1995). There is more to understanding stress in humans than knowing their physical reactions to it.

Although our bodies may have a similar response to stressors, not everyone perceives the same events as stressful. For example, one person may perceive an upcoming job interview as threatening, whereas another person may perceive it as challenging. One person may perceive a D on a paper as threatening; another person may perceive the same grade as an incentive to work harder.

To some degree, then, what is stressful depends on how people cognitively appraise and interpret events. This view has been most clearly presented by Richard Lazarus (1993, 2000). **Cognitive appraisal** is Lazarus' term for individuals' interpretation of the events in their lives as harmful, threatening, or challenging and their determination of whether they have the resources to effectively cope with the events. In Lazarus' view, events are appraised in two steps: primary appraisal and secondary appraisal (see figure 4.3).

In *primary appraisal,* individuals interpret whether an event involves *harm* or loss that has already occurred, a *threat* of some future danger, or a *challenge* to be overcome. Consider two students, each of whom has a failing grade in their psychology class at midterm. Student A is almost frozen by the stress of the low grade and looks at the rest of the term as a threatening circumstance. In contrast, student B does not become overwhelmed by the harm already done and the threat of future failures. She looks at the low grade as a challenge that she can address and overcome.

In *secondary appraisal,* individuals evaluate their resources and determine how effectively they can be used to cope with the event. This appraisal is *secondary* because it both comes after primary appraisal and depends on the degree to which the event was appraised as harmful, threatening, or challenging. For example, student A might have some helpful resources for coping with her low midterm grade, but she views the stressful circumstance as so harmful and threatening that she doesn't use her resources. Student B would instead evaluate the resources she can call on to improve her grade during the second half of the term. These include asking the instructor for suggestions about how to study better for the tests in the course, setting up a time management program to include more study hours, and asking several students who are doing well in the class about their strategies.

In many instances, viewing stress as a challenge during primary appraisal paves the way for finding effective coping resources during secondary appraisal. However, sometimes people do not have adequate resources for coping with an event they have defined as a challenge. For example, if student B is extremely shy, she might lack the courage and skills to talk to the instructor or to ask several students in the class about their strategies for doing well in the course.

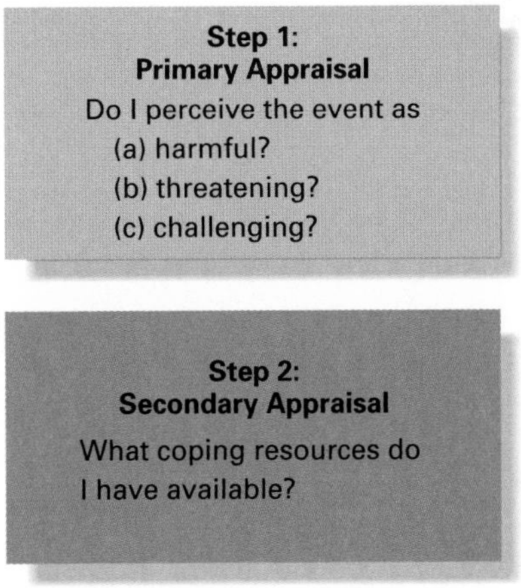

> **Step 1:**
> **Primary Appraisal**
> Do I perceive the event as
> (a) harmful?
> (b) threatening?
> (c) challenging?

> **Step 2:**
> **Secondary Appraisal**
> What coping resources do I have available?

FIGURE 4.3 Lazarus' Cognitive Appraisal View of Stress
Perceiving a stressor as harmful and/or threatening in step 1 and having few or no coping resources available in step 2 yields high stress. Perceiving a stressor as challenging in step 1 and having good coping resources available in step 2 reduces stress.

Review and Reflect

1 Explain what stress is and describe its main components

REVIEW

- What is stress?
- What is the general adaptation syndrome?
- How does cognitive appraisal influence the response to stress?

REFLECT

- How do your mind and body react when you face a stressful experience?

---

2 STRESS AND ILLNESS

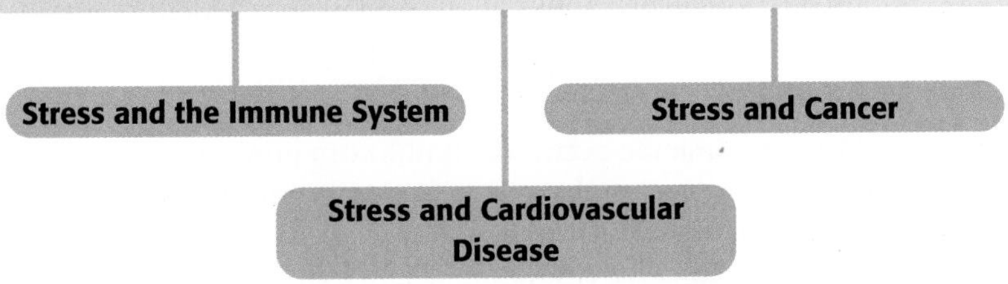

- Stress and the Immune System
- Stress and Cancer
- Stress and Cardiovascular Disease

cognitive appraisal Lazarus' term for individuals' interpretation of the events in their lives as harmful, threatening, or challenging and their determination of whether they have the resources to effectively cope with the events.

It has been mentioned several times that stress makes the body more vulnerable to illness. This section examines what research has revealed about links between stress and specific types of illness. In particular, stress has been identified as a factor in weakened immune systems, cardiovascular disease, and cancer (Steptoe & Ayers, 2004). The good news is that positive emotions help stave off illness.

Stress and the Immune System

Recall that when a person is in the alarm or exhaustion stage of GAS, the immune system functions poorly. During these stages, viruses and bacteria are more likely to multiply and cause disease. Currently, researchers have considerable interest in exploring such links between the immune system and stress (Heffner & others, 2004; Kiecolt-Glaser & others, 2002a, 2002b, 2003a; Ishihara & others, 2003). Their theory and research have spawned **psychoneuroimmunology,** a scientific field that explores connections among psychological factors (such as attitudes and emotions), the nervous system, and the immune system (Dantzer, 2004; Kop, 2003).

The immune system keeps us healthy by recognizing foreign materials such as bacteria, viruses, and tumors and then destroying them. Its machinery consists of billions of white blood cells located in the lymph system. These cells form, mature, and are released into the bloodstream from organs located throughout the body (spleen, lymph nodes, thymus, and bone marrow).

Although the immune system and the central nervous system at first glance appear to be very different, they have some important similarities. Both process "sensory" elements, which receive information from the environment and other parts of the body, and both possess "motor" elements, which carry out an appropriate response. Both systems also rely on chemical mediators for communication. A key hormone shared by the central nervous system and the immune system is *corticotrophin-releasing hormone (CRH),* which is produced in the hypothalamus and unites the stress and immune responses. It is the release of CRH from the hypothalamus that starts the chain of reactions that signals the adrenal gland to produce cortisol.

One example of research on psychoneuroimmunology comes from a study conducted by Sheldon Cohen and his colleagues (1998). They found that adults who faced interpersonal or work-related stress for at least one month were more likely than people who were less stressed to catch a cold after exposure to viruses. In the study, 276 adults were exposed to viruses, then quarantined for five days. The longer people had experienced major stress, the likelier they were to catch a cold. Individuals who reported high stress for the preceding two years tripled their risk of catching a cold. Those who experienced work-related stress for one month or longer were nearly five times likelier to develop colds than individuals without chronic stress. Those who experienced interpersonal stress for one month or more were twice as likely to catch a cold. Cohen concluded that stress-triggered changes in the immune system and hormones might create greater vulnerability to infection. The findings suggest that when we know we are under stress, we need to take better care of ourselves than usual, although often we do just the opposite (Cohen, 2002; Cohen, Miller, & Rabin, 2001). Cohen and his colleagues (1997) also found that positive social ties with friends and family provide a protective buffer that helps to prevent people from catching a cold when they are exposed to cold viruses.

More generally, three lines of research support the conclusion that the immune system and stress are linked (Anderson, 1998, 2000; Anderson, Golden-Kreutz, & DiLillo, 2001; Kiecolt-Glaser & others, 2002a; Reiche, Nunes, & Morimoto, 2004). This is what researchers have found:

- Acute stressors (sudden, onetime life events or stimuli) can produce changes in the immune system. For example, in relatively healthy HIV-infected individuals, as well as in individuals with cancer, acute stressors are associated with poorer immune system functioning (Roberts, Anderson, & Lubaroff, 1994).
- Chronic stressors (those that are long lasting) are associated with an increasing downturn in responsiveness of the immune system (Irwin, 2002; Kiecolt-Glaser &

Kiecolt-Glaser's Research

psychoneuroimmunology The scientific field that explores connections among psychological factors (such as attitudes and emotions), the nervous system, and the immune system.

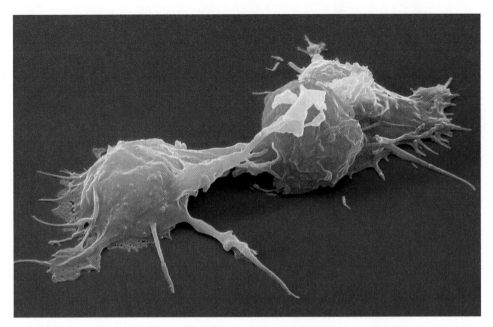

FIGURE 4.4 NK Cells and Cancer
Two natural killer (NK) cells (*yellow*) are shown attacking a leukemia cell (*red*). Notice the blisters that the leukemia cell developed to defend itself. Nonetheless, the NK cells are surrounding the leukemia cell and are about to destroy it.

others, 2002a, 2002b). This effect has been documented in people who live next to a damaged nuclear reactor, people who have experienced failures in close relationships (divorce, separation, and marital distress), and people who are taking care of a family member with progressive illness (Kiecolt-Glaser & others, 1991).

- Positive social circumstances and low stress are associated with increased ability to fight cancer. For example, having good social relationships and support is often linked with higher levels of the type of white blood cells called *NK-cells* (*NK* stands for "natural killer"), whereas a high degree of stress is often related to lower NK-cell levels (Levy & others, 1990). NK cells can attack tumor cells (Farag & others, 2003; Mailliard & others, 2003) (see figure 4.4).

Psychoneuroimmunology is relatively young. Much needs to be clarified, explained, and verified further. Researchers hope to clarify the precise links among psychological factors, the brain, and the immune system (Bosch & others, 2003; Redd, 1995; Vegas & others, 2004). Two preliminary hypotheses about additional interactions that cause vulnerability to disease include the following: (1) stress directly promotes disease-producing processes; and (2) stressful experiences may cause the activation of dormant viruses that diminish the individual's ability to cope with disease. These hypotheses may lead to clues for more successful treatments for some of the most baffling diseases—cancer and AIDS among them (Servaes & others, 1999).

Stress and Cardiovascular Disease

You may have heard someone say something like "It's no wonder she died of a heart attack with all of the stress he put her through." But is it true that emotional stress can cause a person to have a heart attack? A clear link has not been found, but apparently, the surge in epinephrine associated with the GAS causes the blood to clot more rapidly, and blood clotting is a major factor in heart attacks (Fogoros, 2001; Kario, McEwen, & Pickering, 2003).

There is evidence that chronic stress is associated with high blood pressure, heart disease, and early death (Kiecolt-Glaser & others, 2003a; Rosengren & others, 2004). Researchers have found that stress can affect the development and course of cardiovascular disease by altering underlying physiological processes (Claar & Blumenthal, 2003). In one recent study of 103 couples, each with one spouse who had mild hypertension (high blood pressure), a happy marriage was linked with lower blood pressure and an unhappy marriage was related to higher blood pressure (Baker, 2001).

FIGURE 4.6 Psychosocial Stressors and Disease
There are two pathways through which psychosocial stressors may contribute to the development and promotion of disease. First, stressors may contribute to behavioral risk factors, such as poor diet. These behavioral risk factors, in turn, lead to pathophysiological processes, such as atherosclerosis (blockages in the arteries of the heart) and vascular dysfunction. Second, stressors may directly promote pathophysiological processes. In either case, pathophysiological processes can lead to clinical events such as myocardial infarction (heart attack) and death.

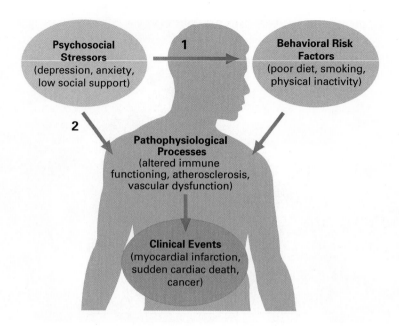

High Blood Pressure and Stress

Over the three years of the study, the blood pressure of the mildly hypertensive spouse in a happy marriage fell by 6 points on average, whereas the blood pressure of the mildly hypertensive spouse in an unhappy marriage rose by 6 points on average.

Stressors also influence the risk of cardiovascular disease indirectly, as shown in figure 4.5. When people live in chronically stressed conditions, they are more likely to smoke, overeat, and avoid exercise. All of these stress-related behaviors are linked with the development of cardiovascular disease (Schneiderman & others, 2001).

Stress and Cancer

In addition to finding that stress is linked to immune system weaknesses and cardiovascular disease, researchers have found links between stress and cancer (Heffner & others, 2003; Kiecolt-Glaser & others, 2003b). Barbara Andersen (2000; Andersen & others, 2001) believes that the link between stress and cancer can best be understood by examining three factors:

- *Quality of life.* A number of studies have documented acute stress at the time cancer is diagnosed (McKenna & others, 1999). Lengthy cancer treatments and the disruptions that the disease creates in the family, work, and social life can cause chronic stress. As has been shown, these stressors can suppress the body's ability to fight off many types of disease, including cancer.
- *Behavioral factors.* An increase in negative health behaviors or a decrease in positive health behaviors can accompany cancer. For instance, individuals with cancer may become depressed or anxious and more likely to medicate with alcohol and other drugs. Also, individuals who are stressed by cancer may not begin or may abandon their previous positive health behaviors, such as participating in regular exercise. These behaviors may in turn affect immunity. For example, substance abuse directly suppresses immunity and is associated with poor nutrition, which indirectly affects health (Anderson, 2000). Also, there is growing evidence that positive health behaviors such as exercise can have positive effects on both the immune and endocrine systems, even among individuals with chronic diseases (Phaneuf & Leeuwenburgh, 2001).
- *Biological pathways.* If the immune system is not compromised, it appears to help provide resistance to cancer and slow its progression (Anderson, 2000). But stressors set in motion biological changes that inhibit a number of cellular immune responses (Anderson & others, 2001). Cancer patients have diminished

NK-cell activity in the blood. Low NK-cell activity is linked with the development of further malignancies, and the length of survival for the cancer patient is related to NK-cell activity (McEwen, 1998).

Review and Reflect

2   **Discuss the links between stress and illness**

REVIEW

- What is psychoneuroimmunology, and what has it revealed about the immune system?
- How is stress linked with cardiovascular disease?
- What is the connection between stress and cancer?

REFLECT

- Think about the last several times you were sick. Did you experience any stressful circumstances prior to getting sick? Might they have contributed to your illness?

3   SOURCES AND MEDIATORS OF STRESS

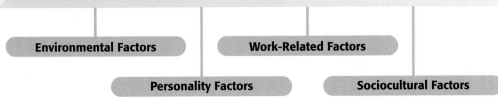

Environmental Factors

Work-Related Factors

Personality Factors

Sociocultural Factors

Are all stressors equal? If you had fled from a burning World Trade Center as Daphne Carlisle did, would you be fearful today? If you had lost a spouse in the burning tower as Kirsten Breitweiser did, would you have been able to pull your life back together as she did? To understand stress, we need to examine both the various sources of stress and the factors, in ourselves and in the contexts in which we live, that modify the effects of stressors. Let's look first at some of the environmental factors that can be sources of stress.

Environmental Factors

Many circumstances, large and small, can produce stress in our lives. In some instances, cataclysmic events, such as war, an automobile accident, a fire, or the death of a loved one, produce stress. More often, the everyday pounding of being overloaded with work, dealing with a difficult situation, or being frustrated in an unhappy relationship produces stress.

Life Events and Daily Hassles   Think about your own life. What events have created the most stress for you? Were they big problems like getting fired, a divorce, the death of someone you loved, a personal injury? Or were they the everyday circumstances of your life, such as not having enough time to study, arguing with your girlfriend or boyfriend, not getting enough credit for work you did at your job?

Some health psychologists have studied the effects of individual significant life events. People who have had major life changes (loss of spouse or other close relative, loss of job) have a higher incidence of cardiovascular disease and early death than those who do not (Taylor, 2003). Other psychologists have evaluated the effects of *clusters* of life events and their possible influence on illness. Thomas Holmes and

SELF-ASSESSMENT 4.2

Stressful Events in My Life

The events listed below commonly occur in the lives of college students. Check the space provided for the events that have occurred in your life during the last 12 months. When you have finished checking off all of the events that have happened in your life in the last 12 months, total the point values in parentheses for each checked item.

(100) _____ Death of a close family member

(80) _____ Jail term

(63) _____ Final year or first year in college

(60) _____ Pregnancy (yours or caused by you)

(53) ____/____ Severe personal illness or injury

(50) _____ Marriage

(45) ____/____ Any interpersonal problems

(40) ___//___ Financial difficulties

(40) _____ Death of a close friend

(40) _____ Arguments with your roommate (more than every other day)

(40) ____/____ Major disagreements with your family

(30) _____ Major change in personal habits

(30) _____ Change in living environment

(30) ____/____ Beginning or ending a job

(25) _____ Problems with your boss or professor

(25) _____ Outstanding personal achievement

(25) ____/____ Failure in some course

(20) ____/____ Final exams

(20) _____ Increased or decreased dating

(20) ____/____ Change in working conditions

(20) _____ Change in your major

(18) ____/____ Change in your sleeping habits

(15) ____/____ Several-day vacation

(15) ____/____ Change in eating habits

(15) _____ Family reunion

(15) ____/____ Change in recreational activities

(15) ____/____ Minor illness or injury

(11) _____ Minor violations of the law

351 _____ Total Life Events Score

Go to the appendix at the end of the book for scoring and interpretation of your responses.

Richard Rahe (1967) devised a scale to measure the possible cumulative effect of clusters of life events and their possible influence on illness. Their widely used Social Readjustment Rating Scale includes events ranging from the death of a spouse (100 stress points) to minor violations of the law (11 stress points). Self-Assessment 4.2

provides an opportunity for you to evaluate the stressfulness of life events you have experienced in the past year.

Researchers have found that when several stressors are simultaneously experienced, the effects may be compounded (Rutter & Garmezy, 1983). For example, one study found that people who felt besieged by two chronic life stressors were four times more likely to eventually need psychological services than those who had to cope with only one chronic stressor (Rutter, 1979). When people experience clusters of stressful life events, the chances are that they will become ill (Maddi, 1996).

However, the ability to predict illness from life events alone is modest. Total scores of life-events scales such as the Social Readjustment Rating Scale are frequently ineffective at predicting future health problems. A life-events checklist tells us nothing about a person's physiological makeup, constitutional strengths and weaknesses, ability to cope with stressful circumstances, support systems, or the nature of the social relationships involved. A divorce, for example, might be less stressful than a marriage filled with day-to-day tension. And the changes related to positive events in the Social Readjustment Scale, such as reconciling with a spouse and gaining a new family member, are not as difficult to cope with as the changes that result from negative events.

Because of these limitations, some health psychologists believe information about daily hassles and daily uplifts provide better clues to the effects of stressors than life events (Bottos & Dewey, 2004; Crowther & others, 2001; D'Angelo & Wierzbicki, 2003; Sher, 2004). Enduring a boring and tense job and living in poverty do not show up on scales of major life events. Yet the everyday tension involved in these living conditions creates a highly stressful life and, in some cases, psychological disorder or illness. In one study, people who experienced the most daily hassles had the most negative self-images (Tolan, Miller, & Thomas, 1988).

What are the biggest hassles for college students? One study showed that the most frequent daily hassles of college students were wasting time, being lonely, and worrying about meeting high achievement standards (Kanner & others, 1981). In fact, the fear of failing in our success-oriented world often plays a role in college students' depression. College students also found that the small things in life—having fun, laughing, going to movies, getting along well with friends, and completing a task—were their main sources of daily uplifts.

Critics of the daily-hassles approach argue that it suffers from some of the same weaknesses as life-events scales (Dohrenwend & Shrout, 1985). For example, knowing about a person's daily irritations and problems tells us nothing about her or his perceptions of stressors, physiological resilience to stress, or coping ability or strategies. Further, the daily-hassles and -uplifts scale has not been consistently related to objective measures of health and illness.

Yet another criticism is that daily hassles can be thought of as dependent measures rather than as causes. People who complain about things, who report being anxious and unhappy, and who see the bad side of everything are likely to see more problems in their daily lives than are people with an optimistic outlook. From this perspective, problems do not predict bad moods; bad moods predict problems. But supporters of the daily-hassles and -uplifts concept reply that information about daily events can be used in concert with information about a person's perceptions, physiological reactions, and coping to provide a more complete picture of the causes and consequences of stress.

Conflict   Another everyday experience that is stressful is conflict, which occurs when we must decide between two or more incompatible options. There are three major types of conflict, which were initially investigated by Neal Miller (1959):

- **Approach/approach conflict,** which is conflict in which the individual must choose between two attractive stimuli or circumstances. Should you go out with the attractive music lover or with the attractive sports lover? Do you buy a Corvette or a Porsche? The approach/approach conflict is the least stressful of the three types of conflict because either choice leads to a positive result.

approach/approach conflict A conflict in which the individual must choose between two attractive stimuli or circumstances.

- **Avoidance/avoidance conflict,** which is conflict in which the individual must choose between two unattractive stimuli or circumstances. Do you go through the stress of giving an oral presentation in class or not show up and get a zero? You want to avoid both, but you must choose one or the other. Obviously, this conflict is more stressful than having the luxury of having two enticing choices. In many instances, we delay our decision about the avoidance/avoidance conflict until the last possible moment.

- **Approach/avoidance conflict,** which is conflict involving a single stimulus or circumstance that has both positive and negative characteristics. Let's say you really like the person you are going with and are thinking about getting married. On the one hand, you are attracted by the steady affection and love that marriage might bring. On the other hand, marriage is a commitment you might not feel ready to make. On a more mundane level, you might look at a menu and face a dilemma—the double chocolate delight would be sumptuous, but is it worth the extra pound of weight? Our world is full of approach/avoidance conflicts, and they can be highly stressful. In these circumstances, we often vacillate before deciding.

Overload   Daily hassles can produce *overload,* which occurs when stimuli become so intense that we can no longer cope with them. For example, persistent high levels of noise overload our adaptability to other stimuli. Overload can occur with work as well. How often have you said to yourself, "There are not enough hours in the day to do all I have to do." Today we are especially faced with information overload. It is easy to develop the uncomfortable feeling that we don't know as much about a topic as we should, even if we are a so-called expert.

Overload can produce **burnout**—a state of physical and emotional exhaustion that includes a hopeless feeling, chronic fatigue, and low energy (Iacovides & others, 2003; Leiter & Maslach, 2001). Burnout usually occurs not because of one or two traumatic events but because of a gradual accumulation of everyday stresses (Demerouti & others, 2001; Roche, 2003). Burnout is most likely to occur among individuals who deal with others in highly emotional situations (such as nurses and social workers) but who have only limited control over the behavior of their clients or patients or the results of the cases they handle (DiGiacomo & Adamson, 2001).

Burnout affects a quarter of the students at some colleges. On a number of college campuses it is the most frequent reason students leave school before earning their degrees. Counselors may actually encourage some students who feel overwhelmed with stress to take a break from college, but most counselors first suggest that the student examine ways to reduce overload and explore possible coping strategies. Taking a reduced or better balanced course load sometimes works, for example. Most college counseling services have professionals who can effectively work with students to alleviate the sense of being overloaded and overwhelmed by life.

www.mhhe.com/santrockha

Burnout

avoidance/avoidance conflict A conflict in which the individual must choose between two unattractive stimuli or circumstances.

approach/avoidance conflict A conflict involving a single stimulus or circumstance that has both positive and negative characteristics.

burnout A state of physical and emotional exhaustion that includes a hopeless feeling, chronic fatigue, and low energy.

Adjustment Strategies
For Avoiding Burnout

Here are some good strategies for avoiding burnout (Stoppler, 2003):

1. ***Take inventory.*** Go someplace quiet, take a pen and paper, and list all of the things that are causing you to be so stressed. Identify all of your commitments and responsibilities in your present schedule. List your social obligations and anything you typically do that consumes time and energy. Identify those things most responsible for your current state and ask yourself which areas need to be changed.

2. ***Pare down.*** If you truly are burned out, accept that you are in a crisis. Cut back on some of your commitments and allow yourself to recover from your emotional and mental exhaustion. Decide on the areas that you can let go for a time.

3. ***Pamper yourself.*** Get plenty of sleep, rest, good nutrition, exercise, and support from friends or family. Do some things that you really enjoy, such as going to a movie you have been wanting to see, reading a good book, or getting a massage.
4. ***Recognize when to seek outside help.*** If nothing seems to be working to reduce your feeling of being burned out, see a mental health professional who can help you learn how to cope with the stress in your life.

Personality Factors

Do certain personality characteristics help people cope more effectively with stress and make them less vulnerable to illness? The answer to this question is yes. This section focuses on Type A/Type B behavior patterns, hardiness, and personal control.

Type A/Type B Behavior Patterns   In the late 1950s, a secretary for two California cardiologists, Meyer Friedman and Ray Rosenman, observed that the chairs in their waiting rooms were tattered and worn, but only on the front edges. The cardiologists had also noticed the impatience of their cardiac patients, who often arrived exactly on time for an appointment and were in a great hurry to leave. Intrigued by this consistency, they conducted a study of 3,000 healthy men between the ages of 35 and 59 over a period of eight years to find out whether people with certain behavioral characteristics might be prone to heart problems (Friedman & Rosenman, 1974). During the eight years, one group of men had twice as many heart attacks or other forms of heart disease as the other men. And autopsies of the men who died revealed that this same group had coronary arteries that were more obstructed than those of the other men.

Friedman and Rosenman described the common personality characteristics of the men who developed coronary disease as the **Type A behavior pattern.** They theorized that a cluster of characteristics—being excessively competitive, hard-driven, impatient, and hostile—is related to the incidence of heart disease. Rosenman and Friedman labeled the behavior of the healthier group, who were commonly relaxed and easygoing, the **Type B behavior pattern.**

Further research on the link between Type A behavior and coronary disease indicates that the association is not as strong as Friedman and Rosenman believed (Williams, 1995). However, researchers have found that certain components of Type A behavior are more precisely linked with coronary risk.

Hostile and Angry People   The Type A behavior component most consistently associated with coronary problems is hostility (Eaker & others, 2004; Matthews & others, 2004; Ouimette & others, 2004). People who are hostile outwardly or who turn anger inward are more likely to develop heart disease than their less angry counterparts (Allan & Scheidt, 1996). Such people have been called "hot reactors" because of their intense physiological reactions to stress: their hearts race, their breathing quickens, and their muscles tense up.

A hostile personality may also affect the course of such diseases as AIDS. One recent study of 140 HIV-positive individuals found that the immune systems of those with hostile personalities who confronted distressing events weakened more than the immune systems of their counterparts who did not have hostile personalities (Ironson, 2001). In another study, of 96 HIV-positive men who were assessed over a nine-year period, those who experienced a lot of stress, had high levels of anger, and felt less satisfied with support from others developed AIDS most quickly (Lesserman & others, 2001).

TYPE Z BEHAVIOR

Type A behavior pattern A cluster of characteristics—being excessively competitive, hard-driven, impatient, and hostile—is related to the incidence of heart disease.

Type B behavior pattern Relaxed and easygoing personality.

Anger can be caused by both external and internal factors (Stout & Farooque, 2003). You might be angry at a specific person, such as a co-worker or supervisor, or an event (such as a traffic jam). Your anger also might be caused by worrying or brooding about your personal problems. Memories of traumatic or enraging situations can also trigger anger. Even two years after the 9/11 attacks and despite moving away from New York, La-Shawn Clark, who was discussed in the chapter opening, observed, "A lot of things will burn forever inside me. I'll always have this anger and this deep hole that can't be filled because of what happened and the way it happened."

Some people really are more "hotheaded" than others are (Fitzgerald & others, 2003). They get angry more easily and more intensely than the average person does (Deffenbacher & others, 2003). Some people don't show their anger in loud and spectacular ways but are chronically irritable and mad about something. Easily angered people don't always curse and throw things. Sometimes they withdraw socially, sulk, or become physically ill. One study found that over a 17-year period, men's and women's suppressed anger was linked with subsequent death due to cardiovascular problems (Harburg & others, 2003).

Catharsis is the release of anger or aggressive energy by directly or vicariously engaging in anger or aggression; the *catharsis hypothesis* states that behaving angrily or watching others behave angrily reduces subsequent anger. Psychodynamic theory promotes catharsis as an important way to reduce anger, arguing that people have a natural, biological tendency to display anger. From this perspective, taking out your anger on a friend or a loved one should reduce your subsequent tendency to display anger; so should heavy doses of anger on television and the anger we see in professional sports and other aspects of our culture. Why? Because such experiences release pent-up anger.

Social cognitive theory argues strongly against this view. This theory states that by acting angrily, people often are rewarded for their anger, and that by watching others display anger, people learn how to be angry themselves. Which view is right?

Research on catharsis suggests that acting angrily does not have any long-term power to reduce anger. If the catharsis hypothesis were correct, war should have a cathartic effect in reducing anger and aggression, but a study of wars in 110 countries since 1900 showed that warfare actually stimulated domestic violence (Archer & Gartner, 1976; Archer & McDaniel, 1995). Compared with nations that remained at peace, postwar nations saw an increase in homicide rates. As psychologist Carol Tavris (1989) says in her book *Anger: The Misunderstood Emotion,* one of the main results of the ventilation approach to anger is to raise the noise level of our society, not to reduce anger or solve our problems. Individuals who are the most prone to anger get angrier, not less angry. Ventilating anger often follows a cycle of a precipitating event, an angry outburst, shouted recriminations, screaming or crying, a furious peak (sometimes accompanied by physical assault), exhaustion, and a sullen apology or just sullenness.

Redford Williams (1995, 2001, 2002), a leading researcher, believes that hot reactors can reduce their risk of heart disease by learning to control their anger and developing more trust in others. More strategies for reducing anger appear in the following.

www.mhhe.com/santrockha

Control Your Anger Self-Talk

catharsis The release of anger or aggressive energy by directly or vicariously engaging in anger or aggression; the catharsis hypothesis states that behaving angrily or watching others behave angrily reduces subsequent anger.

Adjustment Strategies
For Reducing Anger

Every person gets angry at one time or another. How can we control our anger so it does not become destructive? Mark Twain once remarked, "When angry, count four; when very angry, swear." Tavris would agree with Twain's first rule, if not the second. Tavris (1989) and the American Psychological Association (2003a) recommend the following strategies for controlling anger before it controls you:

1. *Wait.* When your anger starts to boil and your body is getting aroused, work on lowering the arousal by waiting. Emotional arousal will usually decrease if you just wait long enough.
2. *Relax.* Deep breathing and peaceful imagery can help reduce anger. We will have much more to say about relaxation in chapter 5, "Coping."
3. *Change the way you think.* Cope with the anger in ways that involve neither being chronically angry over every little annoyance nor passively sulking, "Remind yourself that getting angry is not going to fix anything, that it won't make you feel better (and may actually make you feel worse)" (American Psychological Association, 2003a, p. 3). Think logically because logic defeats anger. Realize that in most cases people are not trying to hurt you. We will further examine how to talk to yourself in stressful situations in chapter 5.
4. *Solve problems.* In some cases our anger is caused by problems we can't ignore. Make a plan to solve the problem and resolve to give it your very best effort.
5. *Help others.* Take action to help others, which can put your own miseries in perspective, as exemplified by the actions of the women who organized Mothers Against Drunk Driving or any number of people who work to change conditions so that others will not suffer as they did.
6. *Change your perspective.* Seek ways of breaking out of your usual perspective. Some people have been rehearsing their "story" for years, repeating over and over the reasons for their anger. Retelling the story from other participants' points of view often helps people to find routes to empathy.
7. *Join or form a self-help group.* Join or form a self-help group with others who have been through similar experiences with anger. The other people will likely know what you are feeling, and together you might come up with some good solutions to anger problems.
8. *Seek counseling.* If you feel that your anger is out of control, consider counseling to learn how to handle it better.

---

hardiness A personality style characterized by a sense of commitment (rather than alienation), control (rather than powerlessness), and a perception of problems as challenges (rather than threats).

Hardiness   Is there a type of personality that is protected from the harmful effects of stressors? Research suggests that a *hardy personality* may provide a buffer against stress. **Hardiness** is a personality style characterized by (1) a sense of commitment (rather than alienation), (2) a sense of control (rather than powerlessness) and, (3) a perception of problems as challenges (rather than threats).

The links between hardiness, stress, and illness were the focus of the Chicago Stress Project (Kobasa, Maddi, & Kahn, 1982; Maddi, 1998). It studied male business managers 32 to 65 years of age over a five-year period. During the five years, most of the managers experienced stressful events, such as divorce, job transfers, the death of a close friend, inferior performance evaluations at work, and working at a job with an unpleasant boss.

In one part of the Chicago study, managers who developed an illness (ranging from the flu to a heart attack) were compared with those who did not (Kobasa & others, 1982). Those who did not were likelier to have hardy personalities. In another aspect of the study, whether or not hardiness, along with exercise and social support, buffered stress and reduced illness in executives' lives was investigated (Kobasa & others, 1986). When all three factors were present in an executive's life, the level of illness dropped dramatically (see figure 4.6). Other researchers also have found support for the role of hardiness in illness and health (Lambert, Lambert, & Yamase, 2003; Steinhardt & others, 2003; Waysman, Schwarzwald, & Solomon, 2001).

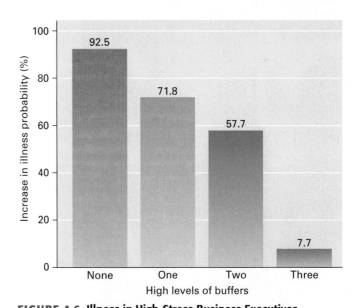

FIGURE 4.6 Illness in High-Stress Business Executives
In one study of high-stress business executives (all of whom were selected for this analysis because they were above the stress mean for the entire year of the study), a low level of all three buffers (hardiness, exercise, and social support) involved a high probability of at least one serious illness in that year. High levels of one, two, and all three buffers decreased the likelihood of at least one serious illness occurring in the year of the study.

Personal Control One component of the hardy personality is worth a closer look: the sense of control. As discussed in chapter 2, some people tend to believe that they can control both themselves and events around them. Recall that self-efficacy and internal locus of control are two aspects of personal control. *Self-efficacy* is the belief that you can master a situation and produce positive outcomes. *Internal locus of control* is the tendency to assume that your own behaviors are responsible for whatever happens to you.

Both the reality and the perception of being able to do something to control or reduce stressors has an important influence on their effects (Taylor, 2003; Wallston, 2001). Having a general sense of control reduces stress and can lead to the development of problem-solving strategies to cope with the stress. A person with a good sense of personal control might say, "If I stop smoking now, I will not develop lung cancer," or "If I exercise regularly, I won't develop cardiovascular disease."

A sense of control is important for people experiencing stressful events (Taylor, 2003). Consider a study of East German migrants to West Germany who found themselves unemployed (Mittag & Schwarzer, 1993). They often turned to heavy drinking for solace unless they had a sense of personal control (as measured by such survey items as, "When I'm in trouble, I can rely on my ability to deal with the problem effectively"). Across a wide range of studies, a sense of personal control over the stressful events that go on around people has been related to emotional well-being, successful coping with a stressful event, behavior change that can promote good health, and good health (Decruyenaere & others, 2000; Pickering, 2001; Sitzman, 2004; Taylor, 2003).

Work-Related Stress

The importance of control, or lack of it, shows up in the stress experienced by workers (Warr, 2004). Economic dips, downsizing, and outsourcing have made jobs less secure, increasing workers' stress levels (Probst, 2004). In addition, work-related stress usually increases when job demands are high and the individual has little choice in deciding how to meet the demands—in other words, under conditions of low autonomy and high external control. In one study of Swedish workers, men who held jobs that were demanding and low in autonomy reported high levels of exhaustion, depression, insomnia, tranquilizer and sleeping pill use, and sick leave (Karacek, 1979). In a more recent study, a combination of personal and job factors placed individuals at risk for getting sick (Schaubroeck, Jones, & Xie, 2001). Employees who perceived they had control over their job responsibilities but did not have confidence in their problem-solving abilities or who blamed themselves for bad outcomes were the likeliest to experience stress.

Overload is another source of workplace stress, and its effects are evident among American workers. American workers are working harder and longer than they have in past decades just to maintain their standard of living. In one generation, the number of hours Americans work each week has increased by 8 percent to a current average of 47. Twenty percent of Americans are working 49 hours or more per week (National Institute for Occupational Safety and Health [NIOSH], 2001). The predictable result is greater work-related stress and increased risk for psychological and physical health problems (Nelson, Quick, & Simmons, 2001). Researchers have found that one-fourth to one-third of American workers have high job stress and are emotionally drained at the end of a workday (NIOSH, 2001).

The stress level of workers also increases when their jobs do not meet their expectations (Chong, Killeen, & Clarke, 2004; Rabasca, 1999). When employees find their work personally rewarding, they are better able to handle the stress of the workplace. Americans want jobs that are secure, offer advancement, pro-

What creates stress for workers?

vide them with some control over the work they do, offer a sense of community among co-workers, and allow them to use their creative and problem-solving skills. However, many jobs do not match these expectations.

Work-related stress can carry over to influence well-being in other areas of a person's life, especially the family (Bellevia & Frone, 2004; Bowes, 2005; Gelfand & Knight, 2005; European Agency for Safety and Health at Work, 2000). In one survey, 56 percent of workers said that they felt "some" or "a great deal" of interference between their jobs and their home lives (Canadian Mental Health Association, 1984). The interference affected family routines and events, child-rearing and household responsibilities, leisure activities, and social life.

Sociocultural Factors

Sociocultural factors help to determine which stressors individuals are likely to encounter, whether they are likely to perceive events as stressful or not, and how they believe stressors should be confronted (Kawachi & Kennedy, 2001). As examples of sociocultural factors involved in stress, let's examine gender, conflict between cultures, and poverty.

Gender   Do males and females respond to stressors in the same way? Recently, Shelley Taylor (2002, 2004) proposed that females are less likely to respond to stressful and threatening situations with a fight-or-flight response than males are. They argue that females are likelier to "tend and befriend." That is, females often respond to stressful situations by protecting themselves and their young through nurturing behaviors (the *tend* part of the model) and forming alliances with a larger social group, especially one populated by other women (the *befriend* part of the model).

Is there evidence for this model? Taylor (2004) cites the following. Although females do show the same immediate hormonal and sympathetic nervous system response to acute stress that males do, other factors can intervene and make the fight-or-flight response less likely in females. In terms of the fight response, male aggression is regulated by androgen hormones, such as testosterone, and is linked to sympathetic nervous system reactivity and hostility. In contrast, female aggression appears to be more cerebral in nature, moderated more by social circumstances, learning, culture, and the situation.

Acculturative Stress   Moving to a new place is a stressful experience in the best of circumstances. It is even more stressful when a person from one culture moves into a different culture. **Acculturative stress** refers to the negative consequences that result from contact between two distinctive cultural groups. Many individuals who have immigrated to the United States have experienced acculturative stress (Fox & others, 2004; Vega & others, 2004).

South Florida middle school teacher Daniel Arnoux (1998) learned firsthand about acculturative stress when he called out a student's name in his class and asked her if she was Haitian. She was so embarrassed by his question that she slid under her seat and disappeared from his view. Later she told him, "You are not supposed to say you are Haitian around here!" That is when Arnoux realized how stressful school could be for many immigrant students, some of whom were beaten and harassed for being Haitian. He began developing lessons to help students gain empathy and tolerance for individuals from different ethnic and cultural backgrounds.

Canadian cross-cultural psychologist John Berry (1980) believes that when people like the young middle school girl experience cultural change, they can adapt in one of four main ways:

- *Assimilation* occurs when individuals relinquish their native cultural identity and adopt an identity that helps them blend into the larger society. If enough

acculturative stress The negative consequences that result from contact between two distinctive cultural groups.

This Chinese American family association has helped its members cope with acculturative stress. *What are some strategies for coping with acculturative stress?*

individuals follow this path, the nondominant group is absorbed into the established, mainstream society. Sometimes assimilation occurs when many groups merge to form a new society (what is often called a "melting pot").

- *Integration* implies that people move into the larger culture but maintain many aspects of their distinctive cultural identity. In this circumstance, a number of ethnic groups all cooperate within a large social system (a "mosaic").
- *Separation* refers to self-imposed withdrawal from the larger culture. If imposed by the larger society, however, separation becomes *segregation*. People might maintain their traditional way of life because they desire an independent existence (as in separatist movements), or the dominant culture may exercise its power to exclude the other culture (as in slavery and apartheid).
- *Marginalization* refers to the process by which nondominant groups lose cultural and social contact with both their traditional society and the larger, dominant society. The essential features of one's culture are lost, but they are not replaced by those of the larger society. Marginalization does not mean that a group has no culture, but its culture may be disorganized and unsupportive.

Although separation can have benefits, it may be especially stressful for individuals who seek separation while most members of their group seek assimilation. Because assimilation means some cultural loss, it may be more stressful than integration. Marginalization is likely to bring confusion, anxiety, feelings of alienation, and loss of identity. For the most part, acculturation may be least stressful for those persons who can pick and choose the most useful features of the two cultural systems.

Poverty Some groups faced with the stress of acculturation are also more likely than other Americans to be poor. A disproportionate percentage of ethnic minority families are poor, as are female-headed families. For example, Puerto Rican families headed by women are 15 times likelier to live in poverty than are families headed by White men, and families headed by African American women are 10 times likelier to

Vonnie McLoyd (*right*) has conducted a number of important investigations of the roles of poverty, ethnicity, and unemployment in children's and adolescents' development. She has found that economic stressors often diminish children's and adolescents' belief in the utility of education and their achievement strivings.

live in poverty than are families headed by White men (National Advisory Council on Economic Opportunity, 1980). Many people who become poor during their lives remain so for only one or two years. However, African Americans and female heads of household are especially at risk for persistent poverty.

Poverty can cause considerable stress for individuals and families (Cooper & others, 2005; Evans, 2004; Leyendecker & others, 2005; McLoyd, 2000, 2005). Chronic conditions such as inadequate housing, dangerous neighborhoods, burdensome responsibilities, and economic uncertainties are potent stressors in the lives of the poor (Evans, 2004). You are more likely to experience threatening and uncontrollable life events if you are poor than if you are well-off (Russo, 1990). For example, women living in poverty are more likely to experience crime and violence than are women with higher incomes. And poverty undermines sources of social support that help to buffer the effects of stress. Poverty is related to marital unhappiness and to having spouses who are unlikely to serve as confidants (Brown, Bhrolchain, & Harris, 1975). Further, poverty means having to depend on many overburdened and unresponsive bureaucratic systems for financial, housing, and health assistance, which may contribute to a poor person's perception of powerlessness—itself a factor in stress.

Review and Reflect

3   **Identify key sources and buffers of stress**

REVIEW

- What are some major environmental sources of stress?
- What role do personality characteristics play in stress?
- When is work most likely to be stressful?
- How do sociocultural factors influence stress?

REFLECT

- What are the main sources of stress in your life? Would you classify them as personality factors, environmental factors, or sociocultural factors?

4 POST-TRAUMATIC STRESS DISORDER

Symptoms and Developmental Course of PTSD

Stressful Events and PTSD

When the planes struck the World Trade Center on September 11, 2001, New York firefighters rushed to the scene and 343 of them were killed. For nine months following the attack, firefighters were among the volunteers who worked at Ground Zero to recover the victims. According to one psychiatrist who worked with the city's firefighters, the recovery effort induced severe trauma that for many was horrific and long-lasting. More than 5,000 firefighters and emergency workers contacted the fire department's counseling services for problems related to the terrorist attack and as of May 2003, 125 firefighters had been diagnosed with post-traumatic stress disorder.

Post-traumatic stress disorder (PTSD) is a psychological disorder that develops through exposure to a traumatic event, such as war; severely oppressive situations, such as the Holocaust; severe abuse, as in rape; natural disasters, such as floods and tornados; and unnatural disasters, such as plane crashes (Halligan & others, 2003; Kroll, 2003; Wilson, Friedman, & Lindy, 2001). Approximately 5.2 million Americans between the ages of 18 and 54, or about 3.6 percent of people in this age group, have PTSD in any given year (NIMH, 2001).

Symptoms and Developmental Course of PTSD

PTSD occurs when an individual's usual coping abilities are overloaded; not every individual exposed to the same event develops PTSD (Clark, 2001; Livanou & others, 2002; Yehnda, 2004). The symptoms of disorder vary but can include the following:

- Flashbacks, in which the individual relives the traumatic event and usually believes that it is happening all over again. A flashback might come in the form of images, sounds, smells, or feelings. The person may lose touch with reality and reenact the event for seconds, hours, or, very rarely, days.
- Constricted ability to feel emotions, often reported as feeling numb, resulting in an inability to experience happiness, sexual desire, or enjoyable interpersonal relationships.
- Excessive arousal, resulting in an exaggerated startle response, or inability to sleep.
- Difficulties with memory and concentration.
- Feelings of apprehension, including nervous tremors.
- Impulsive outbursts of behavior, such as aggressiveness, or sudden changes in lifestyle.

Most people who are exposed to a traumatic, stressful event experience some of the symptoms in the days and weeks following exposure (National Center for PTSD, 2003). For PTSD to be diagnosed, the symptoms must be severe. They can appear immediately after the trauma, or they may not appear until months or even years later (de Jong, Komproe, & Van Ommeren, 2003).

Overall, approximately 8 percent of men and 20 percent of women develop PTSD, and about 30 percent of these individuals develop a chronic form that persists through their lifetime. For example, Vietnam veterans who had some autonomy and decision-making authority during combat, such as Green Berets, were less likely to develop the disorder than soldiers who had no control over where they would be sent or when and who had no option but to follow orders. Preparation for a trauma also makes a difference in whether an individual will develop the disorder. For example, emergency workers who are trained to cope with traumatic circumstances usually do not develop PTSD.

The course of PTSD typically involves periods in which the symptoms increase, followed by remission or decrease. For some individuals, however, the symptoms may

post-traumatic stress disorder (PTSD) An anxiety disorder that develops through exposure to a traumatic event, severely oppressive situations, severe abuse, and natural and unnatural disasters.

be unremitting and severe. Ordinary events can serve as reminders of the trauma and trigger flashbacks or intrusive images.

Stressful Events and PTSD

A number of different highly stressful circumstances and events can trigger PTSD. Among these circumstances are combat and war-related traumas, abuse, and natural and unnatural disasters.

Trauma Metasite
Traumatic Stress
National Center for PTSD
Terrorism Fear

Combat and War-Related Traumas Much of what is known about PTSD comes from individuals who have developed the disorder because of combat and war-related traumas (Dobie & others, 2004; Fontana & Rosenheck, 2004; Freeman & Roca, 2001; Jones & others, 2003; Wild, 2003). The Holocaust created many victims of PTSD (Brodaty & others, 2004). In one study of 124 survivors of the Holocaust, almost half were still suffering from PTSD 40 years after experiencing this trauma (Kuch & Cox, 1992). In another study, 10 percent of Vietnamese, Hmong, Laotian, and Cambodian refugees who left their war-torn countries to live in California had PTSD (Gong-Guy, 1986). A study of Bosnian refugees just after they had come to the United States indicated that 65 percent had PTSD (Weine & others, 1995). This figure may be so high because many of these Bosnian refugees had experienced numerous atrocities, organized mass rapes, and murders of relatives and neighbors.

Rather than waiting for the stress of combat to take its toll, branches of the U.S. armed forces now use mental health professionals in preventive efforts in combat zones around the world (Rabasca, 2000). The mental health units typically include a psychologist, social worker, and several mental health technicians. Units also might have a psychiatrist, psychiatric nurses, and occupational therapists. The frontline teams take a rapid, short-term, on-site approach. Treatment begins as soon as possible after a service member shows symptoms such as tremors, nightmares, or headaches.

How effective is this new approach? The military believes that it is much more effective than the old practice of sending troubled individuals to the rear. Their data indicate that 70 to 90 percent of service members return to active duty within several days when they are treated at the front (Rabasca, 2000).

Abuse Abuse can come in many forms, including abuse of a spouse, the sexual abuse of rape or incest, and emotional abuse (as when parents harshly criticize and belittle their children (Campbell, Setl, & Ahrens, 2004; Chen & others, 2004; Guterman, 2004; Teicher & others, 2003). Some experts consider the victims of sexual abuse and sexual assault to be the single largest group of PTSD sufferers (Koss & Boeschen, 1998). Researchers have found that approximately 95 percent of rape survivors experience PTSD symptoms in the first two weeks following the traumatic event. About 50 percent still have symptoms three months later, and as many as 25 percent have symptoms four to five years after the rape (Foa & Riggs, 1995).

Natural and Unnatural Disasters Natural disasters such as tornados, hurricanes, earthquakes, and fires can trigger PTSD among the survivors (Goenjian & others, 2001; Kokai & others, 2004; Ozen & Sir, 2004; Schroeder & Polusny, 2004). One study of children who lived through Hurricane Andrew, in 1992, claimed 20 percent had PTSD one year later (La Greca & others, 1996). Another study found that 14 years after a flood destroyed the community of Buffalo Creek in West Virginia, 25 percent of the survivors were still suffering from PTSD (Green & others, 1992).

Unnatural disasters such as plane crashes and terrorist attacks can also trigger PTSD (Lamberg, 2003; Njenga & others, 2004; Thiel de Bocanegra & Brickman, 2004). In fact, the rates of PTSD are higher following deliberate events than after natural disasters (National Center for PTSD, 2003). The September 11, 2001, terrorist attacks on New York City and Washington, D.C., are expected to produce PTSD in many of the survivors (Norris & others, 2001). One estimate is that as many as 70,000 to 100,000 people in New York alone had the kind of exposure on September 11 that put them at risk for developing PTSD (Marmar, 2001).

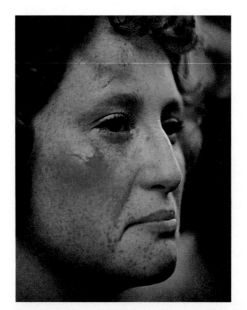

Post-traumatic stress disorder (PTSD) can be caused by a variety of traumatic events, including war (PTSD has been a common disorder in Vietnam veterans), abuse (such as spousal abuse or rape), unnatural disasters (such as terrorist attacks), and natural disasters (such as hurricanes).

After a terrorist attack, individuals who have experienced the trauma include: (1) survivors of past traumatic events, who may have a heightened sense of vulnerability, (2) individuals who personally witnessed or were victims of the terrorist attack, and (3) individuals who experience trauma because they learn of relatives, friends, and acquaintances who were subject to violence; or as a result of repeated media exposure of the trauma. What might people experience following a terrorist attack? They may have recurring thoughts of the event; become afraid of everything, not leave the house, or isolate themselves; stop their usual routines; feel a tremendous sense of loss; or be reluctant to express their feelings, losing a sense of control over their lives.

One recent study of 555 residents from Chinatown in New York City after the 9/11 attack found that more than half of the individuals persistently showed symptoms of emotional distress (Chen & others, 2003). Depression was prevalent in those who lost family members or friends. One study of the effects of the 9/11 terrorist attacks focused on university students in a midwestern city over which United Flight 93 circled before crashing in Pennsylvania (Cardenas & others, 2003). Approximately 6 percent of them showed the symptoms of PTSD.

Adjustment Strategies
The Road to Resilience

The American Psychological Association (2004) recommends these 10 ways to build resilience:

"1. **Make connections.** Good relationships with close family members, friends, or others are important. Accepting help and support from those who care about you and will listen to you strengthens resilience. . . . Assisting others in their time of need also can benefit the helper.

2. **Avoid seeing crises as insurmountable problems.** You can't change the fact that highly stressful events happen, but you can change how you interpret and respond to these events. Try looking beyond the present to how future circumstances may be a little better. . . .

3. **Accept that change is a part of living.** Certain goals may no longer be attainable as a result of adverse situations. Accepting circumstances that cannot be changed can help you focus on circumstances that you can alter.

4. **Move toward your goals.** Develop some realistic goals. Do something regularly—even if it seems like a small accomplishment—that enables you to move toward your goals. . . .

5. **Take decisive actions.** Act on adverse situations as much as you can. Take decisive actions, rather than detaching completely from problems and stresses and wishing they would just go away.

6. **Look for opportunities for self-discovery.** People often learn something about themselves and may find that they have grown in some respect as a result of their struggle with loss. . . .

7. **Nurture a positive view of yourself.** Developing confidence in your ability to solve problems and trusting your instincts helps build resilience.

8. **Keep things in perspective.** Even when facing very painful events, try to consider the stressful situation in a broader context and keep a long-term perspective. . . .

9. **Maintain a hopeful outlook.** An optimistic outlook enables you to expect that good things will happen in your life. Try visualizing what you want, rather than worrying about what you fear.

10. **Take care of yourself.** Pay attention to your own needs and feelings. Engage in activities that you enjoy and find relaxing. Exercise regularly. Taking care of yourself helps to keep your mind and body primed to deal with situations that require resilience."

What can you do if a friend, family member, or co-worker has been through a disaster, or trauma? The American Psychiatric Association (2003) recommends above all else being a supportive listener. You can listen patiently and nonjudgmentally while the person tells his or her story. Avoid offering direct advice other than encouraging the individual to find healthy ways—such as exercise—to cope with the stress involved. You also can discourage ineffective ways of coping such as excessive use of alcohol.

Review and Reflect

4 Characterize post-traumatic stress disorder

REVIEW

- What are the symptoms and typical course of PTSD?
- What types of stressful events can trigger PTSD?

REFLECT

- How did you react to the terrorist attack of 9/11/01? Now that you have read about some effective coping strategies with terrorist attacks, would you react differently to a terrorist attack in the future? Explain your answer.

Reach Your Learning Goals

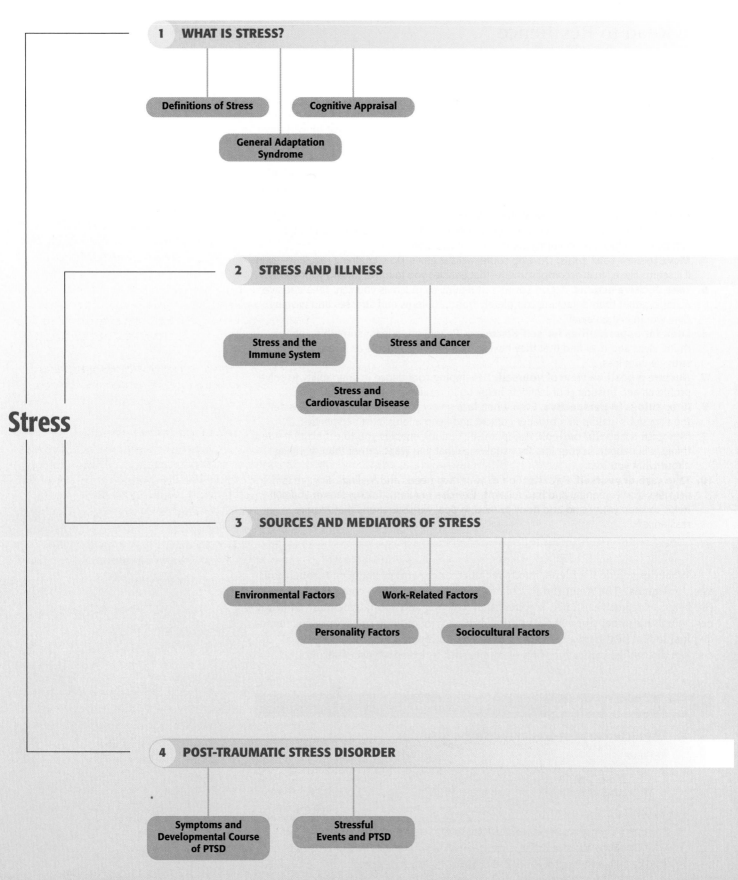

Stress

1 WHAT IS STRESS?

- Definitions of Stress
- Cognitive Appraisal
- General Adaptation Syndrome

2 STRESS AND ILLNESS

- Stress and the Immune System
- Stress and Cancer
- Stress and Cardiovascular Disease

3 SOURCES AND MEDIATORS OF STRESS

- Environmental Factors
- Work-Related Factors
- Personality Factors
- Sociocultural Factors

4 POST-TRAUMATIC STRESS DISORDER

- Symptoms and Developmental Course of PTSD
- Stressful Events and PTSD

Summary

1   *Explain what stress is and describe its main components*

- Stress is the response of individuals to stressors, which are circumstances and events that threaten them and tax their coping abilities.
- The general adaptation syndrome (GAS) is the model that Selye proposed to describe how the body responds when demands are placed on it. The GAS consists of three stages: alarm, resistance, and exhaustion. The alarm stage is much the same as the fight-or-flight response described by Cannon. During this stage, the body's resources are mobilized to prepare the organism to deal with threat. The body's reactions, however, can be harmful if they persist. Many scientists now agree that two main pathways are involved in the body's response to stressors: the neuroendocrine-immune pathway and the sympathetic nervous system pathway.
- Lazarus believed that how people respond to stress depends on the way in which they cognitively appraise events. Cognitive appraisal consists of primary appraisal (Is the stressful event harmful, threatening, or challenging?) and secondary appraisal (What resources do I have to cope with the stressful event?).

2   *Discuss links between stress and illness*

- Psychoneuroimmunology is the field that explores connections among psychological factors (such as attitudes and emotions), the nervous system, and the immune system. Acute stressors can produce immunological changes in healthy individuals. Chronic stressors are associated with a downturn in immune system functioning. Research with cancer patients shows that a good quality of life is associated with a healthier immune system.
- Emotional stress likely is an important factor contributing to cardiovascular disease. People who live in a chronically stressed condition are likelier to smoke, overeat, and not exercise. All of these stress-related behaviors are linked with cardiovascular disease.
- Stress and cancer are linked through their effects on quality of life, behavioral factors, and biological pathways. For example, by its effects on quality of life, cancer is likely to increase stress, which in turn can reduce the body's ability to fight cancer.

3   *Identify key sources and buffers of stress*

- Environmental factors that can be sources of stress include significant life events, such as major changes, daily hassles, conflict, and overload. People who experience clusters of life events tend to become ill; daily hassles, ongoing daily annoyances, can also produce health-sapping stress. Everyday conflicts can be stressful. The three types of conflict are approach/approach (least stressful), avoidance/avoidance, and approach/avoidance. Daily hassles can result in overload, which can lead to burnout.
- Certain personality factors can either increase the chances that a person will experience stress or provide a buffer against stressors. The Type A behavior pattern is a cluster of personality characteristics—being hostile, excessively competitive, impatient, and hard-driven—that seem to be related to cardiovascular disease. Of these characteristics, hostility is most consistently related to heart disease. Hostile and angry persons appear to have an increased risk of suffering the effects of stress. In contrast, hardiness—which involves a sense of commitment, a sense of control, and a perception of problems as challenges rather than threats—is a buffer against stressors and is related to reduced illness. By itself, the perception that one can control or reduce stressors is also a buffer. Across a wide range of studies, a sense of personal control over stressful events has been related to emotional well-being, successful coping with a stressful event, and behavior change that can promote good health.
- The stress level of workers increases when they have little control over their work, when job demands are high, and when their jobs do not meet their expectations.
- Sociocultural sources of stress include gender, acculturation, and poverty. In terms of gender, females are more likely to follow a tend-and-befriend strategy than males. Acculturative stress refers to the negative consequences that result from contact between two distinctive cultural groups. People can adapt to cultural change in one of four ways: assimilation, integration, separation, and marginalization. Poverty can cause considerable stress for individuals and families and is related to threatening and uncontrollable life events.

4   *Characterize post-traumatic stress disorder*

- Post-traumatic stress disorder (PTSD) is an anxiety disorder that develops through exposure to traumatic events, severely oppressive situations, abuse, and natural disasters and unnatural disasters. Only when symptoms are very severe is a diagnosis of PTSD made. Symptoms of PTSD include flashbacks, constricted ability to feel emotions, excessive arousal, difficulties with memory and concentration, feelings of apprehension, and impulsive outbursts of behavior. These symptoms may either immediately follow the trauma or be delayed by months or even years. The course of PTSD usually involves periods of symptom increase followed by remission or decrease, but for some individuals the symptoms may be unremitting and severe.

• Among the different types of events that can trigger PTSD are combat and war-related traumas, abuse (including abuse by a spouse, the sexual abuse of rape or incest, and emotional abuse), and natural (such as tornados, hurricanes, earthquakes, and fires) and unnatural disasters (such as terrorist attacks).

Key Terms

stress 114
stressors 114
general adaptation syndrome (GAS) 115
cognitive appraisal 117
psychoneuroimmunology 118
approach/approach conflict 123
avoidance/avoidance conflict 124
approach/avoidance conflict 124
burnout 124
Type A behavior pattern 125
Type B behavior pattern 125
catharsis 126
hardiness 127
acculturative stress 129
post-traumatic stress disorder (PTSD) 132

Resources for Improving Your Adjustment

SELF-HELP BOOKS

Why Zebras Don't Get Ulcers

(1998, revised ed.) by Robert Sapolsky. New York: Freeman.

This entertaining book examines links between emotion and physical well-being. Sapolsky explores the ways in which emotions can affect virtually every cell in the body. The connection between stress and diseases such as cardiovascular disease and depression is discussed. A final chapter describes how to manage stress. *Why Zebras Don't Get Ulcers* was given 4 out of 5 stars in the national study of self-help books (Norcross, Santrock, & others, 2003).

The Dance of Anger

(1997, reissued ed.) by Harriet Lerner. New York: Harper Perennial.

This book was written mainly for women about the anger in their lives, both their own anger and that of the people they live with, especially men. Lerner explains the difficulty many women have in expressing anger and describes how they can use their anger to gain a stronger, more independent sense of self. *The Dance of Anger* was rated in the highest category in the national study of self-help books, receiving 5 stars.

I Can't Get Over It

(1996) by Aphrodite Matsakis. Oakland, CA: New Harbinger.

Assessment and treatment options for PTSD are presented, the stages of trauma are examined, and a number of exercises and questionnaires help individuals to understand their trauma better. A 4-star book in the national study of self-help books.

NATIONAL SUPPORT GROUPS

Anxiety Disorders Association of America (ADAA)

http://www.adaa.org

National Organization for Victim Assistance (NOVA)

e-mail: nova@trynova.org
website: http://www.trynova.org

PTSD Support Services

http://ptsdsupport.net

E-Learning Tools

www.mhhe.com/santrockha

To help you master the material in this chapter, you will find a number of valuable study tools on the student CD-ROM that accompanies this book. In addition, visit the Online Learning Center for *Human Adjustment,* where you can find these valuable resources for Chapter 4, "Stress."

SELF-ASSESSMENT

In Text

You can complete these self-assessments in the text:
• Self-Assessment 4.1: *How Vulnerable Am I?*
• Self-Assessment 4.2: *Stressful Events in My Life*

Additional Self-Assessment

Complete this self-assessment on the Online Learning Center: *Am I Experiencing Burnout?*

THINK CRITICALLY

To practice your critical thinking skills, complete these exercises on the Online Learning Center:
• *Diagnosing Type-A Behavior* asks you to think about what behaviors might give you a clue as to whether a person has a Type-A personality.

- *Making (or Remaking) the Grade* focuses on a frustrating circumstance and how to cope with it.
- *Work-related Stress* focuses on the many items that can cause stress in the workplace.

APPLY YOUR KNOWLEDGE

1. What are your stressors?

Your textbook points out that some stressors are positive stressors, while others are negative stressors. Sometimes, people intentionally seek out stress, such as going on a scary roller coaster or going to a scary movie. Make a list of all the stressors in your life and identify whether each one is a positive stressor or a negative stressor.

List the stressors from each of the following areas of life: work, school, family, recreation, hobbies, living arrangements, goals, health practices, sexual practices, driving habits, social patterns.

List ways to reduce the negative stressors in your life. Then, list the reasons why you find the remaining stressors to be positive.

To help you with this task, go to a search engine such as www.google.com or www.yahoo.com and search for "stress reduction."

2. Changing your approach-avoidance conflicts.

Often, we express ambivalence toward a goal that has both negative and positive aspects. One of the most relevant conflicts for students is the conflict between wanting good grades and not wanting to study. How do you handle this conflict?

There are a number of ways to change the dynamics of this conflict:

a. increase the approach (e.g., make getting good grades more important, get closer to graduation faster, get a better job)
b. decrease the avoidance (organize your studying, study with a partner, or decide that the things you are learning aren't unpleasant after all)
c. both (a) and (b)

Often, we experience indecision or mixed feelings about choices that have both positive and negative aspects. Think of some relationship in your life that you have mixed feelings about. Under "approach," list everything that you LIKE about the relationship. Now, write down all the things you DON'T like about the relationship ("avoidance"). Take a close look at the items you have listed. Repeat the process of examining your priorities. Overall, is the relationship more good than bad? Or is it mostly bad? By evaluating the whole "package" rather than focusing on the components, you might feel less torn, whichever decision you ultimately make.

3. Reducing stress in college or university.

Many university students experience a great deal of stress from a variety of sources. Academic achievement, living arrangements, lifestyle changes, low income, and parental pressure can all contribute to stress. We have more control over some of these events than over others. One area where students can reduce stress is by changing their study habits.

Go to http://www.utexas.edu/student/utlc/handouts/1439.html and take the stress test. If you cannot reach this website, search for "reducing university stress" at www.yahoo.com. Read the tips for reducing stress and make a list of the things that you could do to reduce your stress. Be as specific as possible. Photocopy the list for each day. As you go through your list every day, check things off as you do them. It will provide you with a sense of accomplishment!

 VIDEO SEGMENT

Stressors are inevitable in life, but people can do a lot to determine their impact. Watch the videos "Sources of Stress" and "Post-traumatic Stress," which show people who are experiencing severe stress. What stressors are they facing, and how could their effects have been buffered?

Coping

Learning Goals

1 Describe what coping is, types of coping, and the role of contexts in coping

2 Discuss specific coping strategies

3 Summarize factors involved in coping with emotions

4 Explain stress management.

Images of Adjustment

The Remarkable Coping Skills of Rose Kennedy

What strategies did Rose Kennedy use to cope with stress?

Writer, activist, and matriarch of the Kennedy family, Rose Fitzgerald Kennedy (1890–1995) lived to be 104 years of age. She saw three of her sons gain election to high public office (including President John F. Kennedy), but she faced many highly stressful events.

As a young woman in Boston, Rose disobeyed her father (the mayor) and met secretly with Joseph Kennedy. Hoping to prevent their marriage, her father shipped Rose off to a convent school in Europe, but Rose and Joe married in 1914. Her married life would be marked by wealth and fame but also her husband's infidelity and her children's tragedies. Rose's oldest daughter, who was mentally retarded, was disabled by a botched brain lobotomy. Her first son, Joe, Jr., a distinguished navy pilot, was killed in 1944 when his plane exploded overseas. In 1948, another child, Kathleen, was killed in a plane crash. Her husband, suffered a debilitating stroke in 1961, less than one year after his son became the thirty-fifth U.S. president. He lingered for seven years before dying in 1968.

While coping with husband's incapacitation, Rose had to face the death of her two sons (John and Bobby) at the hands of assassins. She later wrote in a memoir, *Times to Remember*, "I wondered why it had happened to Jack. Everything—the culmination of all his efforts, abilities, dedication to good, and to the future—lay boundlessly before him. Everything was gone and I wondered why" (Maier, 2003). As America mourned the death of President John Kennedy, Rose coped with his death through her religion and faced the public with poise, dignity, and grace.

Reflecting on how she dealt with crisis after crisis, Rose said that she simply would not allow herself to succumb to tragedy. At her funeral, her son Senator Ted Kennedy had this to say about his mother, "She sustained us in the saddest of times—by her faith in God and by the strength of her character, which was a combination of the sweetest gentleness and the most tempered steel" (Maier, 2003).

This chapter describes how to cope with stress as well as how not to cope with stress. We will explore many types of coping that involve changes in the way you think and the way you behave. We will also examine how to cope effectively with emotions and the stress-management techniques of relaxation, meditation, and biofeedback. Throughout the chapter, you will read about many strategies that can help you to deal more effectively with the stress you are currently experiencing and to plan how to cope more effectively for stress in the future.

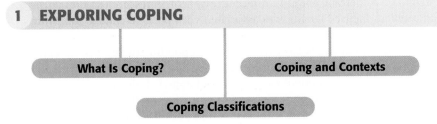

Not everyone responds the same way to stress. Some individuals throw in the towel when the slightest thing goes wrong in their lives. Others are motivated to work hard to find solutions to personal problems, and some successfully adjust even to extremely taxing circumstances. A stressful circumstance can be rendered considerably less stressful if you know how to cope with it.

What Is Coping?

Coping is the process of managing taxing circumstances, expending effort to solve life's problems, and seeking to master or reduce stress. What makes the difference between effective and ineffective efforts to cope?

Characteristics of the individual provide part of the answer. Success in coping has been linked with several characteristics, including a sense of personal control, positive emotions, and personal resources (Folkman & Moskowitz, 2004). Success in coping, however, also depends on the strategies used and on the context. People have many ways of coping—some more successful than others.

Coping Classifications

Two ways of classifying coping strategies have been especially influential among psychologists who study coping. One classification distinguishes problem-focused coping from emotion-focused coping. A second approach classifies coping into three categories: active-cognitive, active-behavioral, and avoidance coping. There also has been recent interest in a coping category called *meaning-making coping.*

Problem-Focused and Emotion-Focused Coping   Rose Kennedy's responses to stressors at different points in her life illustrate the first classification of coping strategies. Shortly before Rose married, her mother received an anonymous letter threatening to expose an affair between her husband and a "cigarette girl." Rose and her mother together confronted her father with the accusation. But a few years later Rose apparently turned a blind eye to her own husband's philandering. She would claim, "There was never any deceit on his part" (Maier, 2003, p. 260). When it seemed that all of the world knew about the affair between Joe Kennedy and actress Gloria Swanson and Swanson visited the family's summer home, Rose treated Swanson as a valued friend. Swanson later wrote that Rose never gave any indication of knowing about the affair, "Was she the fool . . . ," Swanson wrote, "or a saint? Or just a better

coping Involves managing taxing circumstances, expending effort to solve life's problems, and seeking to master or reduce stress.

actress than I was?" (Maier, 2003, p. 88). In the first case, Rose took action to deal with the problem; in the second case, she denied the problem existed.

The classification of coping strategies into problem-focused coping and emotion-focused coping was proposed by Richard Lazarus. Recall from our discussion of stress in chapter 4 Lazarus' (1993, 2000) emphasis on *cognitive appraisal*—interpreting events as harmful, threatening, or challenging, and determining whether one has the resources to effectively cope with the event.

Problem-focused coping is the strategy of squarely facing one's troubles and trying to solve them. For example, if you are having trouble with a class, you might go to the study skills center at your college or university and enter a training program to learn how to study more effectively. Having done so, you have faced your problem and attempted to do something about it. A recent review of 39 research studies documented that problem-focused coping was associated with positive change following trauma and adversity (Linley & Joseph, 2004).

Emotion-focused coping is Lazarus' term for responding to stress in an emotional manner, especially by using defensive mechanisms. Emotion-focused coping includes avoiding a problem, rationalizing what has happened, denying it is occurring, laughing it off, or calling on our religious faith for support. If you use emotion-focused coping, you might avoid going to a class that you find difficult. You might say the class doesn't matter, deny that you are having a problem, laugh and joke about it with your friends, or pray that you will do better. This is not necessarily a good way to face a problem. For example, in one study, depressed individuals tried to avoid facing problems more than individuals who were not depressed (Ebata & Moos, 1989).

Sometimes emotion-focused coping is adaptive. For example, denial is a protective mechanism for dealing with the flood of feelings that comes when the reality of death or dying becomes too great. Denial can protect against the destructive impact of shock by postponing the time when you have to deal with stress. In other circumstances, however, emotion-focused coping is maladaptive. Denying that the person you were dating doesn't love you anymore when that person has become engaged to someone else keeps you from getting on with your life.

Many individuals successfully use both problem-focused and emotion-focused coping to deal with a stressful circumstance. For example, in one study, individuals said they used both problem-focused and emotion-focused coping strategies in 98 percent of the stressful encounters they face (Folkman & Lazarus, 1980). Over the long term, though, problem-focused coping usually works better than emotion-focused coping (Heppner & Lee, 2001).

Meaning-Making Coping   Problem-focused and emotion-focused coping represent a good beginning for classifying coping strategies, but some psychologists argue that a third category, meaning-making coping, is needed (Folkman & Moskowitz, 2004). Consider Robert Kennedy's extemporaneous words to a crowd on the night in April 1968 when Martin Luther King was assassinated:

> For those of you who are Black and are tempted to be filled with hatred and distrust at the injustice of such an act . . . I can only say that I feel in my own heart the same kind of feeling. I had a member of my family killed. . . . But we have to make an effort. . . . My favorite poem was by Aeschylus. He wrote: 'In our sleep, pain which cannot forget falls drop by drop upon the heart until, in our own despair, against our will, comes wisdom through the awful grace of God.'
> (Quoted in Maier, 2003, pp. 497–498)

Meaning-making coping involves drawing on beliefs, values, and goals to change the meaning of a stressful situation, especially in cases of chronic stress that may resist problem-focused coping (Park & Folkman, 1997).

problem-focused coping Lazarus' term for the strategy of squarely facing one's troubles and trying to solve them.

emotion-focused coping Lazarus' term for responding to stress in an emotional manner, especially by using defense mechanisms.

meaning-making coping Involves drawing on beliefs, values, and goals to change the meaning of a stressful situation, especially in cases of chronic stress that may resist problem-focused efforts.

When stress is severe, integrating the stressor into one's beliefs about the world and self is central to coping (Janoff-Bulman, 1999). *Positive appraisal* is one example of this approach; it involves reinterpreting an event in a way that affirms one's values, beliefs, and goals. This affirmation in turn focuses your attention on what you value, which generates positive emotions and facilitates coping (Folkman & Moskowitz, 2004).

Active-Cognitive, Active-Behavioral, and Avoidance Coping Strategies For another look at a variety of techniques for dealing with stress, consider a second way of classifying strategies, which categorizes them as active-cognitive, active-behavioral, and avoidance (Billings & Moos, 1981):

- **Active-cognitive strategies** are coping responses in which individuals actively think about a situation in an effort to adjust more effectively. For example, if you have had a problem that involved breaking up with a girlfriend or a boyfriend, you may have coped by reasoning through why you are better off in the long run without her or him. Or you might analyze why the relationship did not work and use this information to help you develop better dating experiences in the future.
- **Active-behavioral strategies** are coping responses in which individuals take some type of action to improve their situation. To continue the example with dating, individuals who are having problems in dating may go to a counseling center, where they might be coached to improve their dating skills.

  Many of us are confronted with more than one stressor at the same time. As discussed in chapter 4, when several stressors occur simultaneously, the effects may be compounded (Rutter & Garmezy, 1983). An extremely valuable active-behavioral strategy is to try to remove at least one of the stressors. For example, a college student might be taking a very heavy course load, not have enough money to eat regularly, and have problems in a close relationship. The student facing this triple whammy probably would benefit from removing one of the stressors—for instance, by dropping one class and taking a normal course load.
- **Avoidance coping strategies** are responses to keep stressful circumstances out of awareness. If you adopted an avoidance strategy to a dating problem, you would never think about better ways to cope with dating problems and never take any actions either. Everything we know about coping suggests that avoidance strategies harm adjustment.

Active-cognitive and active-behavioral coping fall into Lazarus' category of problem-focused coping; avoidance coping falls under emotion-focused coping. Examples of active-coping, active-behavioral, and avoidance coping strategies are shown in figure 5.1.

COPING AND CONTEXTS

Coping is not a stand-alone process; it is influenced by the demands and resources of the environment. Consider the Vietnamese, who have suffered through numerous

Active-cognitive strategies

Pray for guidance and/or strength
Prepare for the worst
Try to see the positive side of the situation
Consider several alternatives for handling the problem
Draw on my past experiences
Take things one day at a time
Try to step back from the situation and be more objective
Go over the situation in my mind to try to understand it
Tell myself things that help me feel better
Promise myself that things will be different next time
Accept it; nothing can be done

Active-behavioral strategies

Try to find out more about the situation
Talk with spouse or other relative about the problem
Talk with friend about the problem
Talk with professional person (e.g., doctor, lawyer, clergy)
Get busy with other things to keep my mind off the problem
Make a plan of action and follow it
Try not to act too hastily or follow my first hunch
Get away from things for a while
Know what has to be done and try harder to make things work
Let my feelings out somehow
Seek help from persons or groups with similar experiences
Bargain or compromise to get something positive
    from the situation
Exercise more

Avoidance strategies

Take it out on other people when I feel angry or depressed
Keep my feelings to myself
Avoid being with people in general
Refuse to believe that it happened
Drink more to reduce tension
Eat more to reduce tension
Smoke more to reduce tension
Take more tranquilizing drugs to reduce tension

FIGURE 5.1 Examples of Active-Cognitive, Active-Behavioral, and Avoidance Coping Strategies in Response to Stress

active-cognitive strategies Coping responses in which individuals actively think about a situation in an effort to adjust more effectively.

active-behavioral strategies Coping responses in which individuals take some type of action to improve their problem situation.

avoidance coping strategies Responses to keep stressful circumstances out of awareness.

How might coping be influenced by the demands and resources of the environment?

wars, foreign invasions, and economic problems; 90 percent of Vietnamese live in poverty. Lesley Lambright (2003) recently interviewed a number of Vietnamese about how they coped with stress. One Vietnamese said, "Vietnamese are poor so they move ahead and look forward. There is no way to look back. It would be back to war." Lambright found that in addition to looking forward, a strong family system and traits of forgiveness, patience, and flexibility helped Vietnamese cope with the aftermath of war and poverty.

Strategies for coping need to be evaluated in the specific context in which they occur (Folkman & Moskowitz, 2004; Lazarus & Folkman, 1984). A particular strategy may be effective in one situation but not another depending on the extent to which the situation is controllable. For example, it is adaptive to engage in problem-focused coping before an exam and in mental disengagement while waiting for the results. In short, coping strategies in and of themselves are not necessarily good or bad. The contextual approach to coping points to the importance of *coping flexibility,* the ability to modify coping strategies to match the demands of the situation (Lester, Smart, & Baum, 1994).

Review and Reflect

1 **Describe what coping is, types of coping, and the role of contexts in coping**

REVIEW

- What is coping?
- What are major categories of coping strategies?
- How is coping linked with contexts?

REFLECT

- Which of the categories in the different classifications of coping strategies do you think best describes your coping style? Describe how you have used this coping style in recent months.

2 STRATEGIES FOR COPING

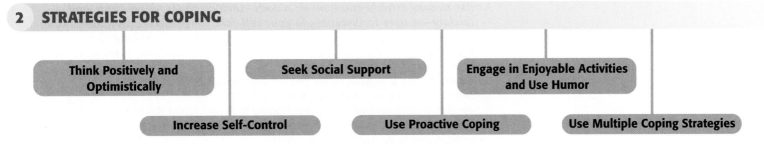

Think Positively and Optimistically   Seek Social Support   Engage in Enjoyable Activities and Use Humor

Increase Self-Control   Use Proactive Coping   Use Multiple Coping Strategies

Would Rose Kennedy have had a happier life if she had coped with her husband's infidelities by adopting an active-behavioral strategy and taken some action such as a divorce? Would she have had a more successful life if she had coped with the deaths of her children by abandoning her faith? Psychology has no answers to questions like these because psychology cannot tell us what the ultimate goals of our coping strategies should be. But psychologists have described and analyzed many specific techniques for coping with stress. Some involve attitude change. Others require taking some kind of action.

Think Positively and Optimistically

Thinking positively and avoiding negative thoughts is a good strategy when trying to handle stress in just about any circumstance. Why? A positive mood improves our ability to process information efficiently and enhances our self-esteem. In most cases, an optimistic attitude is superior to a pessimistic one. It gives us a sense that we are controlling our environment, much like what Albert Bandura (1997, 2001, 2004) talks about when he describes the importance of self-efficacy in coping.

Can you teach yourself to think positively? This section examines three specific techniques for doing so: positive self-talk, maintaining positive self-illusions, and developing an optimistic outlook.

Cognitive Restructuring and Positive Self-Talk   Thoughts, ideas, and beliefs often perpetuate our problems, but cognitive restructuring can help us modify them. **Cognitive restructuring** is the process of replacing the thoughts, ideas, and beliefs that maintain an individual's problems. It can be used to get people to think more positively and optimistically.

Self-talk (also called *self-statements*)—the soundless, mental speech we use when we think about something, plan, or solve problems—is often very helpful in cognitive restructuring. Positive self-talk can do a lot to give you the confidence that frees you to use your talents to the fullest.

Self-talk has a way of becoming a self-fulfilling prophecy. As a result, uncountered negative thinking can spell trouble. That's why it's so important to monitor your self-talk.

Adjustment Strategies
For Self-Talk

Several strategies can help you to monitor your self-talk.

1. ***Fine-tune your self-talk.*** First, at random times during the day, ask yourself, "What am I saying to myself right now?" Then, if you can, write down your thoughts along with a few notes about the situation you are in and how you're feeling. Before you begin, it is important to record your self-talk without any censorship.

continued

cognitive restructuring Process of replacing thoughts, ideas, and beliefs that maintain an individual's problems.

self-talk Also called self-statements, self-talk refers to the soundless, mental speech people use when they think about something, plan, or solve problems.

2. *Use uncomfortable emotions or moods—such as stress, depression, and anxiety—as cues for listening to your self-talk.* When this happens, identify the feeling as accurately as possible. Then ask yourself, "What was I saying to myself right before I started feeling this way?" or "What have I been saying to myself since I've been feeling this way?"

3. *Capitalize on situations that you anticipate might be difficult.* These are excellent times to assess your self-talk. Write down a description of the coming event. Then ask yourself, "What am I saying to myself about this event?" If your thoughts are negative, think how you can use your strengths to turn these disruptive feelings into more positive ones.

4. *Compare your self-talk predictions (what you thought would or should happen in a situation) with what actually took place.* If the reality conflicts with your predictions, pinpoint where your self-talk needs adjustments to fit reality.

5. *Enlist the help of a sympathetic friend, partner, or therapist.* Your thoughts might be biased so it might help to enlist the assistance of a sympathetic but objective friend, partner, or therapist who is willing to listen, discuss your self-assessment with you, and help you to identify ways your self-talk is distorted and might be improved.

6. *Find out which self-statements help you to cope more effectively.* Examples of positive self-statements that some individuals have found to be effective in replacing negative self-statements are presented in figure 5.2.

FIGURE 5.2 Replacing Negative Self-Statements with Positive Ones

Situation	Negative Self-Statements	Positive Self-Statements
Having a long, difficult assignment due the next day	"I'll never get this work done by tomorrow."	"If I work real hard I may be able to get it all done by tomorrow." "This is going to be tough but it is still possible to do it." "Finishing this assignment by tomorrow will be a real challenge." "If I don't get it finished, I'll just have to ask the teacher for an extension."
Losing one's job	"I'll never get another job."	"I'll just have to look harder for another job." "There will be rough times ahead, but I've dealt with rough times before." "Hey, maybe my next job will be a better deal altogether." "There are agencies that can probably help me get some kind of job."
Moving away from friends and family	"My whole life is left behind."	"I'll miss everyone, but it doesn't mean we can't stay in touch." "Just think of all the new people I'm going to meet." "I guess it will be kind of exciting moving to a new home." "Now I'll have two places to call home."
Breaking up with a person you love	"I have nothing to live for. He/she was all I had."	"I really thought our relationship would work, but it's not the end of the world." "Maybe we can try again in the future." "I'll just have to try to keep myself busy and not let it bother me." "If I met him (her), there is no reason why I won't meet someone else someday."
Not getting into graduate school	"I guess I'm really dumb. I don't know what I'll do."	"I'll just have to reapply next year." "There are things I can do with my life other than going to grad school." "I guess a lot of good students get turned down. It's just so unbelievably competitive." "Perhaps there are a few other programs that I could apply to."
Having to participate in a class discussion	"Everyone else knows more than I do, so what's the use of saying anything."	"I have as much to say as anyone else in the class." "My ideas may be different, but they're still valid." "It's OK to be a bit nervous; I'll relax when I start talking." "I may as well say something; how bad could it sound?"

Positive Self-Illusion For a number of years, mental health professionals believed that seeing reality as accurately as possible was the best path to health. Recently, though, researchers have found increasing evidence that maintaining some positive illusions about oneself and the world is healthy. Happy people often have falsely high opinions of themselves, give self-serving explanations for events, and have exaggerated beliefs about their ability to control the world around them (Taylor, 2003; Taylor & Brown, 1988).

In some instances, developing positive self-illusions has been shown to have dramatic effects on performance. For example, sport psychologist Jim Loehr (1989) pieced together videotaped segments of 17-year-old Michael Chang's most outstanding tennis points during the previous year. Chang periodically watched the videotape; he always saw himself winning, never saw himself make mistakes, and always saw himself in a positive mood. Several months later Chang became the youngest male to win the French Open tennis championship.

Having too grandiose an idea of yourself or thinking too negatively about yourself both have negative consequences. Rather, the ideal orientation may be to have either mildly inflated positive illusions or a reality orientation (Baumeister, 1989) (see figure 5.3).

Overstating the negative aspects of reality—what some people refer to as "just being realistic"—can be a problem. A negative outlook can increase our chances of getting angry, feeling guilty, and magnifying our mistakes. In fact, for some people, seeing things too accurately can lead to depression. Even if suffering is random and meaningless, seeing one's suffering as meaningless and random may not help a person cope and move forward. An absence of illusions may also thwart individuals from undertaking the risky and ambitious projects that sometimes yield the greatest rewards (Baumeister, 1993).

In some cases, though, defensive pessimism may actually work best in handling stress. Imagining negative outcomes can help people prepare for stressful circumstances (Norem & Cantor, 1986). Think about the honors student who is worried that she will flunk the next test or the nervous host who is afraid his lavish dinner party will fall apart. Thoughts of failure may not be paralyzing but instead may motivate you to do everything necessary to ensure that things go smoothly. By imagining potential problems, you may develop workable strategies for dealing with or preventing problems. One study found that negative thinking spurred several constructive responses: evaluating negative possibilities, wondering what the future would hold, psyching up for future experiences so they would be positive, and feeling good about being prepared to cope with the worst (Showers, 1986).

Developing an Optimistic Outlook An optimistic outlook on life might not be realistic for some people, but it often helps coping (Helgeson, Snyder, & Seltman, 2004; Matthews & others, 2004; Schmelling, 2004; Seligman & Pawelski, 2003). Interest in optimism has been fueled by Martin Seligman's (1990) theory and research. Seligman views optimism as a matter of how a person explains the causes of bad events. Optimists explain bad events as the result of external, unstable, and specific causes. Pessimists explain bad events as due to internal, stable, and global causes.

To illustrate the power of optimism, Seligman (1990) recalled the case of 45-year-old Bob Dell, who had a wife, two children, and a mortgage. After working 25 years in a meat-packing plant, he suddenly was fired from his job. With no immediate job prospects and only a high school education, his situation looked grim. He was approached by an insurance agent who wanted to sell him a policy. Bob informed the agent that he was unemployed and could not afford anything. The agent told Bob that his insurance company currently was hiring new sales representatives and suggested that he apply for a position. Bob had never sold anything, but, being an optimist, he decided to give it a try.

Seligman was a consultant for the insurance company at the time. He had persuaded the company to hire salespeople who did not meet all of their qualifications

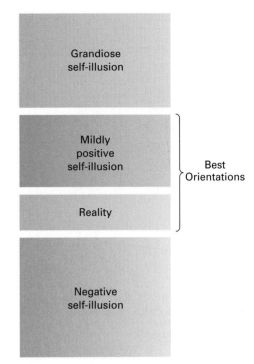

FIGURE 5.3 Reality and Self-Illusion
Individuals often have self-illusions that are slightly above average. However, having too grandiose an opinion or thinking negatively can have negative consequences. For some individuals, seeing things too accurately can be depressing. Overall, in most contexts, a reality orientation or a mildly inflated self-illusion might be most effective.

Optimism

but were high in optimism. Dell was one of 130 applicants who were identified as "optimists" on a measure Seligman had developed, which was included in the measures that job applicants had to complete.

In less than one year, Bob went from sausage-stuffer to super-salesman, earning twice what he had at the meat-packing plant. When Bob learned from a magazine article about the experimental program that he had participated in, with characteristic optimism, he called Seligman, introduced himself, and sold him a retirement policy!

Seligman's (1978) interest in optimism stemmed from his work on *learned helplessness*. He had conducted experiments in which animals became helpless (passive and unresponsive) after they experienced negative events such as shocks over which they had no control. In Seligman's view, pessimism is much like learned helplessness and belief in external locus of control. Optimism is much like self-efficacy and belief in an internal locus of control.

Other researchers have defined optimism as the expectancy that good things are more likely, and bad things less likely, to occur in the future (Carver & Scheier, 2002). This view focuses on how people pursue their goals and values. In the face of adversity, optimists continue to believe that their goals and values can be attained. Their optimism keeps them working to attain their goals, whereas pessimism encourages people to give up.

Numerous research studies reveal that optimists generally are physically healthier than pessimists. In one rather remarkable finding, people who were classified as optimistic at age 25 were healthier at ages 45 to 60 than those who had been classified as pessimistic (Peterson, Seligman, & Vaillant, 1986). In another study, pessimism was linked with less effective immune system functioning and poor health (Brennan & Charnetski, 2000). Optimists also have lower blood pressure than pessimists (Raikkonen & others, 1999).

Researchers also have found that optimists function more effectively and are mentally healthier than pessimists. In one study, optimism was better than self-efficacy in predicting a person's ability to avoid depression over time (Shnek & others, 2001). Optimism has also been linked to better mental health in cancer patients (Cohen, de Moor, & Amato, 2001), to less burnout in chronically stressed employees (Riolli & Savicki, 2003), and to better mental health and lower perceptions of pain in older adults (Achat & others, 2000).

Optimism is not always good, however. It can have costs if it is too unrealistic (Lazarus, 2003). But being optimistic is a good strategy when you have some chance of affecting the future through an optimistic outlook.

Adjustment Strategies
For Becoming More Optimistic

Here are some good strategies for becoming more optimistic (Seligman, 1990):

1. ***Identify the thoughts and feelings you have after something unpleasant happens.*** How did you interpret the event? Write down your interpretation and then reflect on it.
2. ***Become aware of your pattern of thinking when you experience unpleasant events.*** Write down your thoughts and feelings about other events that have happened in the last few months. These might involve an argument with a partner, roommate, or friend, a problem at school or work, and so on. Do you see a pattern in the way you interpret and react to events? Do you often think things like, "Nothing ever gets any better" "People are out to get me," or "My life is a failure"? If so, you likely have a pessimistic pattern. You can evaluate whether you have an optimistic or pessimistic style on the CD-ROM for this book. Becoming aware that

Thought Stopping   **Thought stopping** is a specific self-control strategy in which the individual says "Stop!" when an unwanted thought occurs and then replaces it immediately with a more pleasant thought. For example, if you imagine a circumstance in which you feel humiliated, say "Stop!" Say it clearly, and if not aloud, say it sharply in your mind. Then, as a second step, immediately substitute a pleasant, opposite thought by recalling or imagining a circumstance in which you feel successful and proud.

One woman used thought stopping to fall out of love with a man who was an exploiting liar. The woman initially made a list of the advantages of being out of love with this man, such as: "I will feel better about myself and won't feel so depressed and worthless," "I will be a better mother to my children," "I will enjoy spending more time with my friends," and "I will be able to become reinvolved in the community activities I gave up for him." She wrote them on a card that she carried with her and made a tape recording of the statements. She frequently read the list or listened to the tape. When she found herself thinking positively about this man, she would think, "Stop!" and substitute an item from her list. In addition, she kept herself busy doing other things so that her thoughts would focus on pleasant activities more than on this man. It took about two months for the thought-stopping strategy to accomplish her goals.

Empowerment   Scarce resources or especially stressful conditions may prevent some people from addressing their taxing circumstances on their own. In particular, people with low incomes have fewer resources for learning coping strategies—they are less likely to have counseling available for them, and they are less likely to have access to psychological ideas for change. At the same time, people with low incomes or people who are members of ethnic minority groups are likely to face above-average stressors in their daily lives (Ho, Rasheed, & Rasheed, 2004). Empowerment can help these people lead happier lives (Friedman, 2004).

Empowerment means assisting individuals to develop skills they need to control their own lives. One example of empowerment is the effort to increase community-based services by involving the community's natural caregivers. Mental health professionals consult with teachers, ministers, family physicians, and others who directly interact with community members to provide these caregivers with intervention skills. This approach allows services such as self-control programs to be delivered to more people in settings that they find more comfortable than a mental health center.

Mental health professionals are involved in the development of empowerment for many subgroups. In rural America, counselors have formed support groups for farmers who were losing their land during economic crises. Others have helped victims of rape and domestic violence to recover from their ordeal. Civil rights movements, women's movements, and gay liberation groups have used psychological education to improve the lives and self-esteem of their members.

Seek Social Support

Our crowded, polluted, noisy, and achievement-oriented world can make us feel overwhelmed and isolated. Now more than ever, we may need support systems such as family members, friends, and co-workers to buffer stress (Albrecht & Goldsmith, 2003; Levendosky & others, 2004; Park, Wilson, & Lee, 2004). **Social support** is information and feedback from others that one is loved and cared for, esteemed and valued, and included in a network of communication and mutual obligation.

Social support brings three types of benefits: tangible assistance, information, and emotional support (Taylor, 2003).

- *Tangible assistance.* Family and friends can provide actual goods and services in stressful circumstances. For example, gifts of food are often given after a death in the family occurs, so that bereaved family members won't have to cook for themselves and visiting relatives.

thought stopping A specific self-control strategy in which the individual says "Stop!" when an unwanted thought occurs and then immediately replaces it with a more pleasant thought.

empowerment The term used for assisting individuals to develop skills they need to control their own lives.

social support Information and feedback from others that one is loved and cared for, esteemed and valued, and included in a network of communication and mutual obligation.

ZIGGY © 1982 Ziggy and Friends, Inc. Reprinted with permission of Universal Press Syndicate. All Rights Reserved.

- *Information.* Individuals who provide support can also recommend specific actions and plans to help the person under stress cope more effectively. Friends may notice that a co-worker is overloaded with work and suggest ways for him or her to manage time more efficiently or delegate tasks more effectively.
- *Emotional support.* Friends and family can reassure the person under stress that he or she is a valuable individual who is loved by others. Knowing that others care allows a person to cope with stress with greater assurance.

Researchers consistently have found that social support helps individuals cope with stress (Arnold, 2004; Janisse & others, 2004; Minardi & Blanchard, 2004; Taylor, 2003). For example, in one study, depressed persons had fewer and less supportive relationships with family members, friends, and co-workers than people who were not depressed (Billings, Cronkite, & Moos, 1983). In another study, the prognosticators of cancer, mental disorders, and suicide were linked with distance from one's parents and a negative attitude toward one's family (Thomas, 1983). Yet another study found that individuals with chronic fatigue syndrome and fatigued employees had less social support than a healthy control group (Prins & others, 2004). And a study of displaced adults following the 1999 Taiwan earthquake revealed that those who had more social support from extended family members and neighbors had fewer depressive symptoms one year after the earthquake (Watanabe & others, 2004). Widows die at a rate that is 3 to 13 times higher than that of married women for every known cause of death.

Having diverse social ties may be especially important in coping with stress (Cohen & others, 2003). People who participate in more diverse social networks—for example, having a close relationship with a partner; interacting with family members, friends, neighbors, and fellow workers; and belonging to social and religious groups—live longer than people with fewer types of social relationships (Hill & Pargament, 2003). One study investigated the effects of diverse social ties on susceptibility to a common cold (Cohen & others, 1997). Individuals reported the extent of their participation in 12 types of social ties. Then they were given nasal drops containing a cold virus and monitored for the appearance of a cold. Individuals with more diverse social ties were less likely to get a cold than their counterparts with less diverse social networks (see figure 5.4).

Keep in mind that the studies of social support are correlational. What does that mean about interpreting their results?

Use Proactive Coping

So far we have examined strategies for coping with past or current stress; this is *reactive coping.* But people may also aim to cope with *potential stressors* such as a pending layoff or a scheduled medical procedure (Folkman & Moskowitz, 2004). Responses to potential stressors are called *proactive coping* (Aspinwall & Taylor, 1997; Taylor, 2003).

Proactive coping can eliminate, offset, or reduce the impact of stressful events before they occur. It may be either *anticipatory,* which means dealing with a stressor that is reasonably certain to occur in the near future, or *preventive,* which means dealing with an uncertain stressor in the distant future (Schwarzer & Knoll, 2003). Preparing for the stress of a midterm exam is anticipatory coping; beginning an exercise program to prevent heart disease is preventive coping.

Proactive coping differs from reactive coping in three ways (Greenglass, 2002). First, reactive coping strategies deal with events that have already occurred; proactive coping strategies are future oriented. Second, reactive coping manages risk; proactive coping manages goals. And third, reactive coping is motivated by an appraisal of risks; proactive coping is motivated by the perception of situations as challenging and stimulating.

FIGURE 5.4 Diversity of Social Roles and the Common Cold

In one study, the more social roles (diversity) involved in individuals' social networks, the less likely they were to develop a cold after being infected by a cold virus (Cohen & others, 1997). Note that low = 1 to 3 social roles; moderate = 4 to 5 social roles; and high = 6 or more social roles.

What do you do to cope proactively? Five strategies are (Aspinwall, 2001):

1. Build a reserve of resources (financial and social, for example) that can be used to prevent or offset future losses
2. Recognize possible stressors
3. Appraise potential stressors
4. Engage in preliminary coping efforts
5. Obtain and evaluate feedback about how successful your coping is going

Proactive Coping
Lisa Aspinwall's Research

Engage in Enjoyable Activities and Use Humor

When people encounter taxing circumstances and experience traumatic events, inhibition may affect their activities and their communications. Engaging in enjoyable activities and using humor can sometimes help individuals become less inhibited and cope more effectively.

Indeed, some people become immobilized and frozen as they become immersed in their sorrows and anxieties. For some people in stressful circumstances, it is easy to become a virtual hermit. Individuals who cope with stress in this way rarely engage in any enjoyable activities.

When stress comes your way, don't let it immobilize you. Don't let it encase you in a cocoon, untouched by anyone. Not only is it helpful to talk with others about your stressful experiences, but you can make your life less miserable by participating in activities that you enjoy. When you are feeling really down in the dumps and a friend suggests that the two of you go bowling, see a movie, eat at a restaurant, or take a weekend trip, go.

Engaging in enjoyable activities can bring many benefits. In one study, an increased frequency of desirable events was linked with an increased immune response on subsequent days (Stone & others, 1987). When enjoyable activities produce positive emotions, those emotions can aid coping in several ways, as discussed later in this chapter. And participating in enjoyable activities not only makes us feel good, it also sometimes makes us laugh.

Laughing releases pent-up emotions and aids redefinition of a stressful circumstance in a less threatening way. What does research say about using humor in coping? There is not enough research yet to be able to conclude that laugher is the "best medicine" (Martin, 2002). However, recent studies have revealed that positive humor (not hostile sarcasm) dampens stress and strengthens the immune system (Berk & others, 2001; Kimata, 2001). More specifically, the frequent use of humor as a coping strategy has been linked to increased levels of secretory immunoglobin A (S-IgA) (Dillon, Minchoff, & Baker, 1985/1986). S-IgA is an antibody believed to be the first line of defense against the common cold (Stone & others, 1987). In fact, as discussed later in the chapter, positive emotions generally have been linked with increased responses of the immune system.

A cautionary note about using humor. The best way to use humor is to release anxiety about a situation and to allow yourself to be "human rather than perfect." The use of sexist, racist, or ageist humor is not a recommended strategy.

How can you put more humor and laughter into your life? One way is to look for humor in everyday occurrences. Consider keeping an informal log of the ridiculous things that happen at home, school, or work. This five-minute daily activity allows you to regularly reflect on each day's events that can provide a laugh. You might want to include some of your own laughable mistakes in the informal log—learning to laugh at yourself is considered by some psychologists to be a reflection of self-acceptance.

Use Multiple Coping Strategies

Individuals who face stressful circumstances have many strategies from which to choose. Often it is wise to choose more than one because a single strategy may not

What are some multiple coping strategies that might be used in stressful times?

work in a particular context. For example, a person who has experienced a stressful life event or a cluster of such life events (such as the death of a parent, a divorce, or a significant loss of income) might seek social support, exercise regularly, reduce drinking, and practice relaxation. When used alone, no one of these strategies might be adequate but their combined effect may allow the person to cope successfully with stress.

Review And Reflect

2   Discuss specific coping strategies

REVIEW

- How are thinking positively and optimistically involved in coping effectively?
- What aspects of self-control are linked with effective coping?
- What role does social support play in coping?
- What is proactive coping?
- How is engaging in enjoyable activities and using humor involved in coping?
- How might engaging in multiple coping strategies benefit individuals?

REFLECT

- Think about a stressful circumstance that occurred in your life during the past year. How effectively did you cope with it? Would you have had better outcomes if you had used one or more of the coping strategies discussed in the preceding section? Explain.

3   COPING WITH EMOTIONS

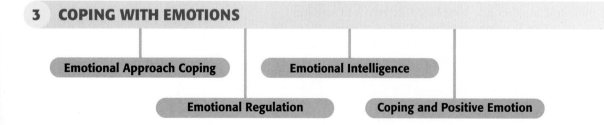

Emotional Approach Coping   Emotional Intelligence

Emotional Regulation   Coping and Positive Emotion

Emotions are an integral part of the coping process. In many instances, if coping with a stressful encounter has a successful resolution, positive emotions predominate. However, if the resolution is unclear or unfavorable, negative emotions predominate.

Emotional Approach Coping

For the most part, researchers have found that emotion-focused coping is linked with less effective outcomes than problem-focused coping over the long term (Folkman & Moskowitz, 2004). However, emotion-focused coping sometimes works in the short term, or a combination of problem-focused and emotion-focused coping might be effective.

Most studies of emotion-focused coping have considered different dimensions together when, in fact, the effects of the dimensions may be different (Folkman & Moskowitz, 2004). One effort to more precisely examine a particular dimension of emotion-focused coping centers on *emotional approach coping,* the strategy of actively processing emotion and expressing emotion (Stanton, Parsa, & Austenfeld, 2002). Actively processing emotion refers to a cognitive effort to approach and understand your emotions. For example, you might say to yourself, "I know my feelings are real and important." Expressing emotion refers to getting your emotions out in the open, such as talking about your fears. For example, you might say to yourself, "It's okay for me to let my emotions come out."

Research has documented mixed results for emotional approach coping. According to one study, combining emotional expression and emotional processing decreased women's depression and hostility, and increased their life satisfaction over a one-month period (Stanton & others, 1994). In another study of women with breast cancer, the use of emotional expression coping was related to improved perceptions of health, a lower level of distress, a reduction in medical visits, and increased energy at a three-month follow-up (Stanton & others, 2000). However, in this study, emotional processing was linked with an increase in distress over the three-month period.

Perhaps emotional processing is adaptive in the short term but over the long term it may turn into rumination (Folkman & Moskowitz, 2004). *Rumination* is the tendency to passively and repeatedly focus on negative emotions and their consequences. As discussed in chapter 14, "Psychological Disorders," Susan Nolen-Hoeksema and her colleagues (Nolen-Hoeksema, 2004; Nolen-Hoeksema, Larson, & Grayson, 1999) have found that ruminaton is related to increased incidences of depression.

Emotional Regulation

Being able to regulate emotional ups and downs, moodiness, and negative emotional responses such as sadness, anger, guilt, and anxiety is an important coping skill (Diamond & Aspinwall, 2003; Greenberg & Paivio, 2003; Sloan, 2004; Suveg & Zeman, 2004), and it is a skill that Rose Kennedy repeatedly demonstrated. When her oldest son was killed, she was at first "consumed in grief . . . But after days of prayer . . . rededicated herself to the daily activities of life and maintained an almost undaunted cheerfulness" (Maier, 2003, p. 183).

Emotion regulation is the process by which individuals control which emotions they experience, when they experience them, and how they experience and show them (Gross, 1998).

James Gross (2001) argues that emotion regulation strategies are more effective when they are used early rather than later in emotional experiences. He describes two widely used strategies for down-regulating emotion—reappraisal and suppression.

Reappraisal comes early in the emotional experience. It consists of changing how we think about a situation in order to dampen its emotional impact. For example, if you look at an event as challenging that you previously viewed as

emotion regulation The process by which individuals control which emotions they experience, when they experience them, and how they experience and show them.

threatening, you have engaged in reappraisal. The second strategy, *suppression,* comes later in the emotional experience. It involves inhibiting the outward signs of emotion. "Keeping a stiff upper lip" when you feel intense emotion is an example of suppression.

Researchers have found that reappraisal is more effective than suppression (Gross, 2001; Gross & John, 2003). Reappraisal decreases the experience and expression of emotion, whereas suppression decreases the expression of emotion but fails to decrease the experience.

We examined an important aspect of regulating emotion in chapter 4, "Stress," where we discussed anger and effective strategies for coping with it. We also will further explore emotion regulation in chapter 14, "Psychological Disorders," by studying anxiety and depression (which involves the emotion of sadness).

Emotional Intelligence

Regulating emotion is not simply a matter of will; the process depends in part on emotional intelligence, a concept initially developed by Peter Salovey and John Mayer (1990), They define **emotional intelligence** as the ability to perceive and express emotion (such as taking the perspective of others), understand emotion (such as understanding the roles that emotions play in friendship and marriage), and regulate emotion (such as being able to control one's anger).

Being emotionally intelligent can benefit your ability to cope with stress (Riley & Schutte, 2004; Trinidad & others, 2004). Emotionally intelligent individuals are self-aware. They regulate their emotions without being overwhelmed by anxiety, anger, and depression. Their empathy helps them to understand the emotions others are experiencing and helps them to be sensitive to the feelings involved in relationships. One recent study found that youths with higher emotional intelligence were less likely to have smoked cigarettes or to have used alcohol (Trinidad & Johnson, 2002).

Daniel Goleman (1995) popularized the concept of emotional intelligence in his book *Emotional Intelligence.* Goleman believes that being emotionally intelligent consists of

- *developing emotional awareness,* which includes the ability to separate feelings from actions;
- *managing emotions,* which includes being able to control your anger and anxiety;
- *reading emotions,* such as taking the perspective of others and being sensitive to when another individual is expressing an emotion; and
- *handling relationships,* such as being able to cope effectively with relationship problems.

To evaluate your emotional intelligence, complete Self-Assessment 5.1.

Coping and Positive Emotion

If you are anxious or sad, can you also experience joy? Positive and negative emotions are not mutually exclusive. An important recent development in the study of coping involves the growing awareness of the presence of positive emotion during stressful experiences (Folkman & Moskowitz, 2000, 2004). Positive emotion can emerge even in the most stressful circumstances and can occur when depression is present (Folkman, 1997). For example, in one study, although anxiety and depression were

www.mhhe.com/santrockha

Emotional Intelligence
Emotional Intelligence E-Journal

emotional intelligence The ability to perceive and express emotion, understand emotion, and regulate emotion.

SELF-ASSESSMENT 5.1

How Emotionally Intelligent Am I?

By responding to the following items, you can get a sense of your emotional intelligence. Score each of the items from 1 (very much unlike me) to 5 (very much like me):

	1	2	3	4	5

Emotional Self-Awareness

1. I am good at recognizing my emotions.

2. I am good at understanding the causes of my feelings.

3. I am good at separating my feelings from my actions.

Managing Emotions

4. I am good at tolerating frustration.

5. I am good at managing my anger.

6. I have positive feelings about myself.

7. I am good at coping with stress.

8. My emotions don't interfere with my ability to focus and accomplish my goals.

9. I have good self-control and am not impulsive.

Reading Emotions

10. I am good at taking the perspectives of others (such as students and parents).

11. I show empathy and sensitivity to others' feelings.

12. I am good at listening to what other people say.

Handling Relationships

13. I am good at analyzing and understanding relationships.

14. I am good at solving problems in relationships.

15. I am assertive (rather than passive, manipulative, or aggressive) in relationships.

16. I have one or more close friendships.

17. I am good at sharing and cooperating.

Go to the appendix at the end of the book for scoring and interpretation of your responses.

more frequent in a group of chronically ill men than in a control group of healthy men, enjoyment (a positive emotion) was more likely to be experienced by the sick men (Viney & others, 1989).

Individuals who have experienced a severe stressful event, such as a tornado or the death of a loved one, often say that something positive has come out of the event; they engage in *benefit-finding*, an effort to identify positive results of a stressful circumstance (Tennen & Affleck, 2002). The benefits might include closer relationships with family and friends, rethinking one's goals, and greater life satisfaction (Folkman & Moskowitz, 2000). In one study, when women with chronic pain periodically reminded themselves of the possible benefits of their illness, they were more likely to report being happy and cheerful, regardless of the severity of their pain (Tennen & Affleck, 2002).

Experiencing positive emotions in stressful experiences can facilitate coping in several ways. First, Barbara Frederickson (2001) believes that positive emotions improve the ability to deal with problems. In one study, individuals who experienced more positive emotions (such as happiness) used broader coping strategies than those who experienced more negative emotions (such as sadness) (Frederickson & Joiner, 2000). For example, compared with people who experienced negative emotions, individuals who experienced positive emotions were more likely to think about ways to deal with the problem, to step back from the situation, and to be objective.

Second, positive emotions and social support are reciprocally linked. That is, social support improves a person's emotional state, and a person's emotional state influences the likelihood that social support will be provided. Positive emotions are correlated with people having more family members and friends to count on in times of need (Cohen, 2002). And, as discussed earlier, social support helps us cope with stress.

Third, positive emotions appear to improve our ability to cope with the physical effects of stressors. Positive emotions have been linked with the release of S-IgA, which may defend us against the common cold (Stone & others, 1987). For example, in one study, S-IgA levels increased after healthy college women watched a funny, happy video but decreased after watching a sad video (Labott & Martin, 1990). Researchers also have found that when people can regain and maintain positive emotional states, they are less likely to get sick or to use medical services when faced with a stressful experience (Goldman, Kraemer, & Salovey, 1996). We will further discuss the role of positive emotions in health in chapter 16, "Health."

Review and Reflect

3 Summarize factors involved in coping with emotions

REVIEW

- What characterizes emotional approach coping?
- What is emotional regulation and how is it involved in coping?
- What is emotional intelligence?
- What role does positive emotion play in coping?

REFLECT

- How good are you at regulating your emotions? What strategies can you use that would benefit your ability to control intense emotions that you might experience in the future?

4 STRESS MANAGEMENT

Exploring Stress Management

Biofeedback

Meditation and Relaxation

Because many people have difficulty managing stress, psychologists have developed a variety of programs that teach stress-management techniques. Let's examine some of the techniques that are used in them.

Exploring Stress Management

Stress-management programs teach individuals how to appraise stressful events, how to develop skills for coping with stress, and how to put these skills into use in their everyday lives. Do these programs work? In one recent study, men and women with hypertension (blood pressure greater than 140/90) were randomly assigned to one of three groups. One group received 10 hours of individual stress-management training; a second group was placed in a wait-list control group and eventually received stress-management training; and a third group (a control group) received no stress-management training (Linden, Linz, & Con, 2001). The control group experienced no reduction in blood pressure. In the two groups that received stress-management training, blood pressure was significantly reduced. This reduction was linked to a reported reduction in psychological stress and improved ability to cope with anger.

A recent analysis of 153 stress-management programs revealed that most involve group sessions and average 8 to 10 sessions in length (Ong, Linden, & Young, 2004). Stress-management programs come in many forms. Some programs are broad in scope, teaching a variety of techniques; others may teach a specific technique, such as relaxation or assertiveness training (McGregor & others, 2004). Some programs are designed for individuals experiencing a particular problem—such as migraine headaches or chronically high blood pressure (Garcia-Vega & Fernandez-Rodriguez, 2004). Stress-management programs are often taught through workshops, which are being offered more often in the workplace (Taylor, 2003). Colleges also offer stress-management programs. If you are finding college life extremely stressful and are having difficulty coping with taxing circumstances in your life, you might consider enrolling in a stress-management program at your college or in your community.

To further explore stress management, we will examine three techniques that are often used in them: meditation, relaxation, and biofeedback.

Meditation and Relaxation

At one time, meditation was believed to have more in common with mysticism than with science. But it has been an important part of life in Asia for centuries and has become popular in the United States.

Meditation is a system of mental exercises that help the individual to attain bodily or mental control and well-being, as well as enlightenment (Astin, 2004; Shapiro & Walsh, 2003; Wolsko & others, 2004). The strategies of meditation vary but usually take one of two forms: either cleansing the mind for new experiences or increasing concentration.

Transcendental meditation (TM), the most popular form of meditation in the United States, is derived from an ancient Indian technique; it involves using a *mantra,* which is a resonant sound or phrase that is repeated mentally or aloud to focus

stress-management programs They teach individuals how to appraise stressful events, how to develop skills for coping with stress, and how to put these skills into use in one's everyday life.

meditation A system of mental exercises that help the individual to attain bodily or mental control and well-being, as well as enlightenment.

transcendental meditation (TM) The most popular form of meditation that is practiced in the United States that involves using a mantra, a resonant sound or phrase that is repeated mentally or aloud to focus attention.

Meditation has been an important dimension of Asian life for centuries.

Patients at Deaconess Hospital in Boston with hypertension learn meditation strategies to cope more effectively with stress.

attention. One widely used TM mantra is the phrase *Om mani padme hum*. By concentrating on this phrase, the individual replaces other thoughts with the syllables *Om mani padme hum*. In TM the individual learns to associate a mantra with a special meaning, such as beauty, peace, or tranquility (Canter & Ernst, 2004; Parati & Steptoe, 2004). Meditation groups that practice TM or other techniques meet on many campuses.

Mindfulness meditation (also called *awareness meditation*) is another form of meditation. It involves maintaining a floating state of consciousness that encourages individuals to focus on whatever comes to mind—a sensation, a thought—at that particular moment (Carlson & others, 2003; Davidson & others, 2003; Grossman & others, 2004; Hayes & Wilson, 2003; Travis & Areander, 2004). In one study, mindfulness meditation was effective in decreasing mood disturbance and stress symptoms in cancer patients (Speca & others, 2000). In another study, mindfulness meditation was associated with enhanced quality of life and decreased stress symptoms in breast and prostate cancer patients (Carlson & others, 2004).

Researchers have found that the practice of meditation activates the brain processes involved in attention and control of the autonomic nervous system, which carries information to and from the body's internal organs (Canter, 2003; Carlson & others, 2003, 2004). As a physiological state, meditation shows qualities of both sleep and wakefulness, yet it is distinct from either of them. It resembles a hypnagogic state, which is the transition from wakefulness to sleep, but at the very least it is prolongation of that state (Friedman, Myers, & Benson, 1998).

Early research on meditation's effects on the body found that it lowers oxygen consumption, slows heart rate, increases blood flow in the arms and forehead, and produces regular and rhythmic patterns of brain activity (Wallace & Benson, 1972). Some researchers have found support for the notion that meditation causes positive physiological changes and believe that meditation is superior to relaxation in reducing physical arousal and anxiety (Eppley, Abrams, & Shear, 1989); other researchers acknowledge meditation's positive physiological effects but believe that relaxation is just as effective (Holmes, 1988). One recent review of 60 studies found that meditation and relaxation procedures can help to reduce headaches, hypertension, anxiety, and insomnia (Stetter & Kupper, 2002).

Consider a group of patients with psoriasis, an incurable skin disease. It is often treated by asking patients to go to a hospital, put goggles on, and stand naked in a hot, loud ultraviolet light box. Apparently, many people find this experience to be stressful. So one researcher randomly taught half of a group of patients who had psoriasis to mediate in order to reduce stress when they were in the light box (Kabat-Zinn & others, 1998). The meditators' skin cleared up at four times the rate of the nonmeditators. In another study, a group of newly taught meditators and a group of nonmeditators were given flu shots. When the levels of antibodies in their blood were measured four weeks and eight weeks later, the meditators had more antibodies in their blood (Davidson & others, 2003).

Adjustment Strategies
For Practicing Meditation

Would you like to feel what a state of meditation is like? You can probably reach that state by following these simple instructions.

1. **Find a quiet place to sit.** Sit quietly and upright in a comfortable chair. Let your chin rest comfortably on your chest, your arms in your lap. Close your eyes.
2. **Pay attention to your breathing.** Every time you inhale and every time you exhale, pay attention to the sensations of air flowing through your body, the feeling of your lungs filling and emptying.
3. **Repeat a single word silently to yourself.** After you have focused on several breaths, begin to repeat silently to yourself a single word every time you breathe out. The word you choose does not have to mean anything: You can make a word up, you can use the word *one*, or you can try a word that is associated with the emotion you want to produce, such as *trust, love, patience,* or *happy.* Try several words to see which one works for you. At first, you will find that thoughts are intruding and that you are no longer paying attention to your breathing. Just return to your breathing and say the word each time you exhale.
4. **Practice meditation regularly.** Carry out this exercise for 10 to 15 minutes, twice a day for two weeks; then you will probably be ready for a shortened version. If you notice that you are experiencing stressful thoughts or circumstances, simply meditate on the spot for several minutes. If you are in public, you don't have to close your eyes; just fix your gaze on a nearby object, attend to your breathing, and say your word silently every time you exhale.

Biofeedback

For many years, physical conditions such as blood pressure, muscle tension, and pulse rate were thought to be outside the boundaries of operant conditioning. In the 1960s, though, psychologist Neal Miller (1969) and others demonstrated that people can learn to control physiological responses that are normally involuntary.

Biofeedback is the process in which individuals' muscular or visceral activities are monitored by instruments; then, the information from the instruments is given (fed back) to the individuals so that they can learn to voluntarily control their physiological activities.

How does biofeedback work? Suppose you want to reduce your muscle tension. Instruments are attached to you to monitor the tension, and information about the level of tension is fed back to you in the form of an audible tone. As muscle tension rises, the tone becomes louder; as it drops, the tone becomes softer. Thus, by changing muscle tension, you can control the tone. Raising and lowering the tone (or in some cases, seeing a dot move up or down on a screen) becomes the reinforcement for learning to control muscle tension (Egner & Gruzelier, 2004; Matuszek & Rycraft, 2003; Newman, 2004).

www.mhhe.com/santrockha

Guided Relaxation
Progressive Muscle Relaxation
Biofeedback

biofeedback The process by which individuals' muscular or visceral activities are monitored by instruments, then the information from the instruments is given (fed back) to the individuals so they can learn to voluntarily control their physiological activities.

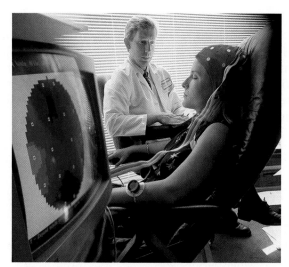

In biofeedback, instruments monitor physiological activities and give individuals information about them so they can learn to voluntarily control the activities.

Researchers have found that biofeedback can help people reduce the intensity of migraine headaches and chronic pain (Landy, 2004; Ramadan, 2004). But is biofeedback more effective than less expensive, simpler methods of relaxation? This issue has not been completely resolved, but several large-scale studies have found that biofeedback offers no distinct advantage over meditation and relaxation techniques (Labbé, 1998). Indeed, relaxation is believed to be a key aspect of how biofeedback works.

Throughout this chapter, we have described numerous ways that people can effectively cope with stress as well as some ineffective strategies. To evaluate your coping strategies, complete Self-Assessment 5.2.

Review and Reflect

4 Explain stress management

REVIEW

- What is stress management?
- What is involved in meditation and relaxation?
- What is biofeedback and what are its outcomes?

REFLECT

- Have you ever used meditation to help you cope with stress? If so, how effective was it? If you have not used meditation, are you now considering it as a way to help you cope with stress?

My Coping Strategies

Think about your life and experiences in the past year. In the left-hand column titled "Past Year" rate each of the coping strategies in terms of how extensively you used them in the past year with 1 = *never,* 2 = *a little,* 3 = *moderately,* 4 = *often,* and 5 = *very often.* Using the same 5-point scale, then rate each of the coping strategies in terms of how often you plan to use them in the coming year. If you don't remember much about a particular coping strategy, go back through the chapter and review the material related to the strategy before rating yourself.

Past Year	Coming Year	
_____	_____	Problem-focused
_____	_____	Emotion-focused
_____	_____	Meaning-making
_____	_____	Active-cognitive
_____	_____	Avoidance
_____	_____	Coping flexibility
_____	_____	Thinking positively
_____	_____	Cognitive restructuring
_____	_____	Positive self-talk
_____	_____	Positive self-illusion
_____	_____	Optimistic outlook
_____	_____	Self-control
_____	_____	Thought stopping
_____	_____	Empowerment
_____	_____	Social support
_____	_____	Religious
_____	_____	Proactive
_____	_____	Engage in enjoyable activities
_____	_____	Use humor
_____	_____	Emotional approach
_____	_____	Emotion regulation
_____	_____	Meditation
_____	_____	Relaxation
_____	_____	Biofeedback

Go to the appendix at the end of the book for scoring and interpretation of your responses.

Reach Your Learning Goals

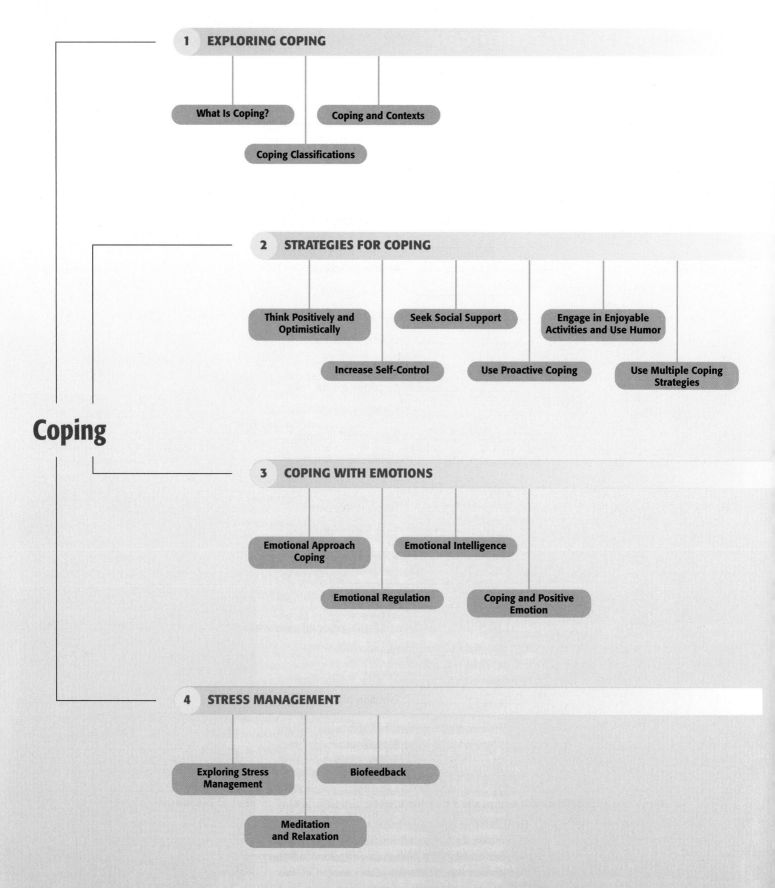

Coping

1 EXPLORING COPING

- What Is Coping?
- Coping and Contexts
- Coping Classifications

2 STRATEGIES FOR COPING

- Think Positively and Optimistically
- Seek Social Support
- Engage in Enjoyable Activities and Use Humor
- Increase Self-Control
- Use Proactive Coping
- Use Multiple Coping Strategies

3 COPING WITH EMOTIONS

- Emotional Approach Coping
- Emotional Intelligence
- Emotional Regulation
- Coping and Positive Emotion

4 STRESS MANAGEMENT

- Exploring Stress Management
- Biofeedback
- Meditation and Relaxation

Summary

1 ***Describe what coping is, types of coping, and the role of contexts in coping***

- Coping involves managing taxing circumstances, expending effort to solve problems, and seeking to master or reduce stress.
- One classification of coping proposed by Lazarus consists of problem-focused coping (the cognitive strategy of squarely facing one's troubles and trying to solve them) and emotion-focused coping (responding to stress in an emotional manner, especially by using defense mechanisms). Over the long term, problem-focusing coping is usually more effective than emotion-focused coping. In addition, another coping strategy is meaning-making coping, which involves drawing on beliefs, values, and goals to modify the meaning of a stressful situation. Another classification consists of active-cognitive strategies (actively thinking about a situation to adjust more effectively), active-behavioral strategies (taking some type of action to improve a problem situation), and avoidance strategies (keeping stressful circumstances out of awareness). Active-cognitive and active-behavioral strategies are more effective than avoidance strategies.
- Coping is not a stand-alone process but is influenced by the environment. A particular coping strategy may be effective in one context but not another, depending on the extent to which the situation is controllable. Thus, the ability to modify coping strategies to suit the context greatly enhances efforts to manage stress.

2 ***Discuss specific coping strategies***

- Thinking positively and optimistically facilitates our efforts to cope with stress. Cognitive restructuring, including modification of self-talk, can be used to help individuals to think more positively and optimistically. In most contexts, having either mildly inflated positive illusions or a reality orientation may benefit our efforts to cope with stress. Seligman has demonstrated that having an optimistic outlook is a wise coping strategy and in many cases optimists have better physical and mental health than pessimists.
- Engaging in self-control is an effective coping strategy. Components of self-control include an internal locus of control, high self-efficacy, and the ability to delay gratification. Thought stopping is a specific self-control and cognitive restructuring strategy in which the individual says "Stop!" when an unwanted thought occurs and then replaces it immediately with a more pleasant thought. Empowerment—assisting individuals in developing the skills they need to control their lives—is another helpful coping strategy.
- Researchers consistently find that having social support helps people cope with stress. Social support involves information and feedback from others that one is loved and cared for, esteemed and valued, and included in a network of communication and mutual obligation. Social support may provide us with tangible assistance, information, and emotional support.
- Proactive coping consists of coping in advance to prevent or mute the influence of events that are potential stressors in the future. Proactive coping includes building a reserve of resources, recognizing potential stressors, initial appraisal of stressors, preliminary coping efforts, and seeking and using feedback about the success of one's efforts.
- Engaging in enjoyable activities may bring us positive emotions and make us laugh. Laughing can release pent-up emotions and help us redefine stressful circumstances in a less threatening way. Humor can dampen stress and strengthen the immune system.
- Because a single strategy may not always work in a particular context, multiple strategies may be required for coping to be successful.

3 ***Summarize factors involved in coping with emotions***

- In many instances, emotion-focused coping is associated with higher distress. However, psychologists are now studying specific dimensions of emotion-focused coping, one of which is emotional approach coping. It consists of actively processing emotion and expressing emotion. Processing emotion might be adaptive in the short term but over time it may result in rumination, which is related to increased symptoms of depression.
- Emotion regulation is the process by which individuals influence which emotions they experience, when they experience them, and how they experience and express them. Emotion regulation strategies are more effective when they are used early in emotional experiences than when they are used later. Strategies of emotion regulation include appraisal, which consists of changing the way one thinks about a situation to dampen its emotional impact, and suppression, which consists of inhibiting the outward signs of emotion.
- Emotional intelligence is the ability to perceive and express emotion, understand emotion, and regulate emotion. Goleman believes that being emotionally intelligent includes developing emotional awareness, managing emotions, reading emotions, and handling relationships effectively.
- Positive emotion can occur with relatively high frequency even in the most stressful circumstances and can be present when depression and distress are elevated. Experiencing positive emotions in stressful circumstances can benefit coping.

4   *Explain stress management*

- Stress-management programs teach individuals how to appraise stressful events, how to develop skills for coping with stress, and how to apply these skills in everyday life. Some stress-management programs are broad in scope, teaching a variety of techniques, while others focus on a specific technique, such as meditation.
- Meditation is a system of mental exercises that help the individual to attain bodily or mental control and well-being, as well as enlightenment. Transcendental meditation (TM), the most popular style of meditation used in the United States, involves using a mantra. Mindfulness meditation is another form of meditation.

Researchers have found that meditation and relaxation bring physical and psychological benefits, but debate continues about whether meditation has superior effects to relaxation.

- Biofeedback is a process in which muscular or visceral activities are monitored by instruments; then the information from the instruments is given (fed back) to the individuals so that they can learn to voluntarily control their physiological activities. Researchers have found that biofeedback can reduce migraine headaches and chronic pain. Relaxation is believed to be a key aspect of how biofeedback works.

Key Terms

coping 143
problem-focused coping 144
emotion-focused coping 144
meaning-making coping 144
active-cognitive
   strategies 145

active-behavioral
   strategies 145
avoidance coping
   strategies 145
cognitive restructuring 147
self-talk 147

thought stopping 153
empowerment 153
social support 153
emotion regulation 157
emotional intelligence 158

stress-management
   programs 161
meditation 161
transcendental meditation
   (TM) 161
biofeedback 163

Resources For Improving Your Adjustment

SELF-HELP BOOKS

Learned Optimism

(1990) by Martin Seligman. New York: Pocket Books.

Seligman argues that optimism and pessimism are not fixed, in-born psychological traits, but rather are explanatory styles—habitual ways we explain things that happen to us. Pessimists, says Seligman, perceive defeat as permanent, catastrophic, and evidence of personal inadequacy; optimists, by contrast, perceive the same mishap as a temporary setback, something that can be controlled, and rooted in circumstances of luck. Seligman's positive message is that since pessimism is learned it can be unlearned. Included are self-tests to determine your levels of optimism, pessimism, and depression. *Learned Optimism* was rated in the highest category (5 stars) in the national study of self-help books (Norcross, Santrock, & others, 2003).

The Relaxation and Stress Reduction Workbook **(5th ed.)**

(2000) by Martha Davis, Elizabeth Eshelman, and Matthew McKay. Oakland, CA: New Harbinger.

This workbook provides easy-to-understand strategies for learning how to use a variety of stress-management techniques. It includes pictures of body positioning for specific techniques, such as meditation. *The Relaxation and Stress Reduction Workbook* was rated in the highest category (5 stars) in the national study of self-help books.

E-Learning Tools

To help you master the material in this chapter, you will find a number of valuable study tools on the CD-ROM that accompanies this book. In addition, visit the Online Learning Center for *Human Adjustment,* where you can find these valuable resources for Chapter 5, "Coping."

SELF-ASSESSMENT

In Text

You can complete these self-assessments in the text:
- Self-Assessment 5.1: *My Emotion Regulation*
- Self-Assessment 5.2: *How Emotionally Intelligent Am I?*
- Self-Assessment 5.3: *My Coping Strategies*

Additional Self-Assessments

Complete these self-assessments on the Online Learning Center:
- *Am I an Optimist or a Pessimist?*
- *My Proactive Coping Skills*

THINK CRITICALLY

To practice your critical thinking skills, complete these exercises on the Online Learning Center:
- *The Power of Positive Self-Talk* asks you to reflect on effective methods involving positive self-talk.
- *Enhancing Study Skills* focuses on applying five steps in developing self-control to improve your study skills.
- *Road Rage* explores rage and aggression.
- *Religion and Coping* focuses on relationship between religious participation and physical and mental health.

APPLY YOUR KNOWLEDGE

1. Make a list of the things that happen to you this week that cause you stress.

Record what stressed you, why it was stressful, and how you coped with the stress. At the end of the week, look back on your list. For each item, write out a response of how a person would deal with each stressor by using each of the following techniques. Review the various responses you have written and circle the one that most closely corresponds to the way you actually handled the situation. Is there a pattern emerging? Is that pattern an adaptive way of coping, according to your text? Which of your responses could be made more adaptable? How would you make those changes?

Categories: problem-focused, emotion-focused, viewing the event as a challenge, meaning-making, active-cognitive, active-behavioral, avoidance, and thinking positively.

2. Stress and college students.

How do college students in general manage stress? How do you manage stress at college? Does the coping strategy vary with the type of stressor To illustrate the difference between problem-focused and emotion-focused coping, visit some websites and decide whether the tips they give are mostly problem-focused, emotion-focused, or a combination of the two. Now look at how you deal with stress. Are your methods consistent with what is recommended? If not, which things might benefit from change?

To get you started, visit a search engine such as www.yahoo.com or www.google.com and search for "reducing college stress" or "managing student stress."

3. Identify your resources.

What resources do you have that you are currently using to cope? What resources might be available that you are not currently using but could be using? List your current and potential resources for each of the following: empowerment, social support, informational support, and proactive support. Think hard—there may be resources out there that you have never even considered. Look around your entire environment and all parts of your life to identify them.

VIDEO SEGMENT

For a closer look at one coping strategy, watch the videos for Chapter 5 on the CD-ROM. They examine how and why laughter can help us cope with stress.

CHAPTER

6

Social Thinking, Influence, and Intergroup Relations

Chapter Outline		*Learning Goals*
SOCIAL THINKING	**1**	Describe how people think about the social world
Making Attributions		
Forming Impressions		
Changing Attitudes		
SOCIAL INFLUENCE	**2**	Identify how people are influenced in social settings
Conformity		
Obedience		
Compliance		
INTERGROUP RELATIONS	**3**	Discuss intergroup relations
Groups and Their Functions		
Group Identity: Us Versus Them		
Prejudice and Discrimination		
Immigration		
Ways to Improve Interethnic Relations		

Images of Adjustment

Anna Bolado de Espina, an Immigrant with a Dream

Anna Bolado de Espina came to Dallas, Texas, from Mexico in 1980. When she arrived, she did not speak a word of English and she missed her friends and support systems in Mexico. But Anna had a dream: she wanted to become a medical doctor. Soon she made new friends in the United States and she worked hard at learning English. Despite the stress of adapting to a new country, she built a life. She worked as a maid, scrubbing floors and doing laundry for fifteen years to earn enough money to go to college. Divorced, she raised two children while attending college and working. Anna was a student in one of author John Santrock's undergraduate classes at the University of Texas at Dallas.

Anna began to fear that she would never make it to medical school. Her life hit a major roadblock when her 15-year-old daughter began to hang out with a gang, ran away from home, and became pregnant. Anna thought about dropping out of college to spend more time with her daughter but her daughter encouraged her to stay in college. Since then the daughter has begun to turn her life around.

Anna was 38 years old when she obtained her college degree with a GPA of almost 4.0. She worked as an AIDS outreach counselor for a year after she graduated from college. Recently, she was accepted into medical school. In her struggle to become a doctor, Anna faced prejudice and discrimination because she was an immigrant. Yet in her new culture, she adapted and learned how to interact in positive ways with people from different cultural groups.

In the fourth century B.C., *Greek philosopher Aristotle said that humans are by nature social animals. Imagine a typical day of your life. How much of it do you spend without any contact with other people and without thinking about anyone else or about your relationships to others? Understanding human adjustment means understanding our social lives. This chapter focuses on some aspects of social life that are critical to adjustment: how people think about other people, how people influence and are influenced by others, and how people interact with people from ethnic and cultural groups different from their own.*

1   SOCIAL THINKING

- Making Attributions
- Forming Impressions
- Changing Attitudes

Among the many aspects of social life that engage people, one of the most intriguing is how people think about the social world. This area of social psychology, which is called *social cognition,* involves how people select, interpret, remember, and use social information. Each person has a unique combination of expectations, memories, and attitudes. Nevertheless, certain common principles govern how people process information in a social situation. The most important of these principles apply to how people identify the causes of behavior, form impressions of other people, and form impressions of the social world.

Making Attributions

Human beings are curious, seeking answers to all sorts of questions. In our everyday lives, we often try to figure out why something has happened or is happening. We wonder why someone is yelling at another person, why someone is in love with a particular person, or why someone joined a certain organization. Our interactions with other people are shaped by what we think we know about why they do whatever they do.

Finding causal explanations for social behavior is a complex task. We can observe people's behavior and listen to what they say, but to determine the underlying cause of their behavior, we make inferences from these observations. For example, if you observe someone make a nasty remark to another person, do you infer that the person deserved to be talked to that way, or do you infer that the speaker has a hostile personality?

Attributions—thoughts about why people behave the way they do—are not always logical. As a result, actors and observers tend to have different ideas about what causes behavior; bias often accounts for these differences (Krull, 2001). Two of the most important tendencies in how people make attributions are known as the fundamental attribution error and the self-serving bias.

The Fundamental Attribution Error   If you had to speculate, what would you say led Anna Bolado de Espina to be a doctor? When we want to understand the causes of behavior, we look both at the person and at his or her situation. The **fundamental attribution error** is that observers tend to overestimate the importance of a person's traits and underestimate the importance of situations when they seek to explain someone else's behavior (see figure 6.1). The fundamental attribution error suggests

attributions Thoughts about why people behave the way they do.

fundamental attribution error The tendency for observers to overestimate the importance of a person's traits and underestimate the importance of situations when they seek to explain someone else's behavior.

FIGURE 6.1 The Fundamental Attribution Error
In this situation, the female supervisor is the observer and the male employee is the actor. *If the employee has made an error in his work, how are the employee and his supervisor likely to differ in their explanations of this behavior, based on your knowledge of actor/observer differences and the fundamental attribution error?*

Actor		Observer
Tends to give external, situational explanations of own behavior		Tends to give internal, trait explanations of actor's behavior
"I'm late with my report because other people keep asking me to help them with their projects."		"He's late with his report because he can't concentrate on his own responsibilities."

Social Psychology Metasite
Exploring Social Psychology

that when most people encounter examples of social behavior, they tend to explain the behavior in terms of the personalities of the people involved rather than the situation (Aronson, Wilson, & Akert, 2004).

For example, when we try to explain why people do repugnant or bizarre things, our tendency is to describe them as flawed human beings. In 1997, thirty-eight people in the Heaven's Gate cult took their own lives in response to the appearance of the Hale-Bopp comet. Their leader, Marshall Herff Applewhite, is known to have believed that this mass suicide would guarantee his followers a type of immortality, taking them to the "level above human." Delusion on such a scale is hard to fathom, and it was easy to conclude that all involved were "kooks." But Applewhite was highly charismatic and exerted enormous pressure on his acolytes to go along. Emphasizing the traits of his followers without considering how the social forces of the situation may have overpowered them reflects the fundamental attribution error.

Self-Serving Bias In contrast to how we explain other people's behavior, when we explain our own behavior, we are a bit more likely to attribute it to the situation. Another factor, however, also shapes the way we explain our own behavior. We tend to be self-enhancing, and we often exaggerate positive beliefs about ourselves (Nier, 2004; Sedikides & others, 1998). We often believe that we are more trustworthy, moral, and physically attractive than other people are. We also tend to believe that we are above-average teachers, managers, and leaders. We maintain exaggerated positive beliefs about ourselves through self-serving bias (Pittman, 1998).

Self-serving bias especially emerges when our self-esteem is threatened. We tend to attribute our successes to our own characteristics but to attribute our failures to external factors; that is, we tend to take credit for our successes and blame our failures on others or on the situation. If Anna Bolado de Espina is like most of us, she would have attributed her ability to go to college mostly to her own ambition, determination, and intelligence—but she would attribute her problems with her adolescent daughter mostly to her daughter's own traits or their difficult lives.

Forming Impressions

Usually, we not only want to think well of ourselves; we also want others to think the best of us. But how can we influence others to perceive us positively? How do people form impressions of others?

It is a cliché to say that first impressions form lasting impressions, but that is often the case. One reason first impressions endure is that we pay more attention to what we first learn about a person and less attention to subsequent information. Also, we tend to interpret later information in light of existing impressions.

Whatever information we gather about a person, we tend to unify it into a whole and fill in the missing piece. If you were introduced to Anna Bolado de Espina and were told that she is a doctor and a grandmother, you might come away with not only an impression of what she looks like but also the impression that she is intelligent and caring. You likely have unconsciously added those characteristics based on your ideas about doctors and grandmothers.

Stereotyping and Attitudes

What determines how you fill out incomplete information to form impressions of the people you meet? Human beings are limited in their capacity for careful and thorough thought (Allport, 1954). The social environment, however, is extremely complex. To meet the demands on our limited information-processing capacity, we simplify the social world by applying our existing categories and *schemas,* or frameworks (Fiske, 1998; Steele, 1996).

Often the result is that we apply stereotypes without being aware of it (Greenwald & Banaji, 1995). A **stereotype** is a generalization about a group's characteristics that does not account for variations from one individual to the next (Kite, 2001). Think about your image of a dedicated accountant. Most of us would probably describe such a person as quiet, boring, unsociable, and so on. Rarely would we come up with a mental image of this person as extraverted, the life of the party, or artistic. But characterizing all accountants as introverts is a clear example of a stereotype. Some accountants may be reserved, but at least some are likely to be sociable.

Emotions influence whether and how people apply stereotypes (Bodenhausen & others, 2001). Anger, for example, makes it more likely that you will use stereotypes and that the stereotypes will be negative ones.

Stereotypes often produce two very important problems. First, they lead us to inaccurate perceptions of people if we do not modify the stereotype when we deal with individuals, if we do not add specific information about the individual's characteristics. Second, stereotypes may lead us to develop negative attitudes toward whole groups of people (Klein & Snyder, 2003). **Attitudes** are evaluations of people, objects, and ideas. If we accept the stereotype that accountants are quiet and boring, we might develop the attitude that accountants make poor companions and leaders and are not really worth meeting. If we accept the stereotype that women are physically weak and emotional, we might develop the attitude that women make poor athletes, soldiers, managers, and leaders and do not deserve equal opportunities in those careers.

Impression Management

Impressions are a two-way street: while you are making impressions of someone, that person is probably trying to "make an impression." **Impression management,** or **self-presentation,** is the process of acting in a way that presents a desired image. In most instances, we try to present ourselves to look better than we are. We spend years and small fortunes rearranging our faces, bodies, minds, and social skills. We especially use impression management with people we are not familiar with and with people who interest us sexually (Leary & others, 1994).

Specific techniques of impression management that work in one cultural setting may not work in another. For example, Americans tend to believe that an open, friendly style makes a positive impression on others. But, in some places, people are more impressed by reserve. We will discuss such cultural differences in communication strategies in the next chapter, "Communicating Effectively."

If you want to make a good impression, what should you do? Nonverbal cues—facial expressions, patterns of eye contact, body posture, and gestures—are key

stereotype A generalization about a group's characteristics that does not account for variations from one individual to another.

attitudes Evaluations of people, objects, and ideas.

impression management (self-presentation) The process of acting in a way that presents a desired image.

"Hmmm... what shall I wear today...?"

© Mike Marland, 1991. Reprinted with permission.

elements of self-presentation. For example, to improve the chances that an interviewer will have a favorable impression of you, you should smile often, lean forward, maintain a high degree of eye contact, and frequently nod your head in agreement with the interviewer. In general, researchers have found that individuals who use these impression management techniques receive more favorable ratings than individuals who do not (Riggio, 1986). In one study, individuals who were selected for engineering apprenticeships were indeed the ones who had smiled more, maintained greater eye contact with the interviewer, and more often nodded their heads during interviews than rejected applicants did (Forbes & Jackson, 1980). Of course, impression management goes only so far: One study found that the frequent use of nonverbal cues had favorable outcomes in a job interview only when the applicants also had competent qualifications to do the job (Rasmussen, 1984).

Three other techniques of impression management are conforming to situational norms (for example, adopting the same form of dress and the same type of language and etiquette as other people in that setting), showing appreciation of others, and behavioral matching (engaging in behavior that the other person displays, such as clasping one's hands together).

Self-Monitoring   Some people are more concerned about and aware of the impressions they make than others are (Snyder & Stukas, 1999). **Self-monitoring** is paying attention to the impressions you make on others and fine-tuning your performance to optimize those impressions. Individuals who are very skilled at self-monitoring seek information about how to present themselves and invest considerable time in trying to "read" and understand others (Simpson, 1995).

Lawyers and actors are among the best self-monitors; salespeople, con artists, and politicians are not far behind. A former mayor of New York City, Fiorello LaGuardia, was so good at self-monitoring that, by watching silent films of his campaign speeches, it was possible to tell which ethnic group he was courting for votes. To get an idea of your skill at self-monitoring, complete Self-Assessment 6.1.

Changing Attitudes

Despite the power of stereotypes and attitudes to influence our impressions of the social world, they can be changed (McGuire, 2004). In fact, people are constantly trying to change our attitudes, as when politicians try to get our votes and advertisers try to persuade us that their product is the best. Professional persuaders use polished techniques based on extensive research on attitude change.

What makes people change an attitude? A full review of the factors involved in persuasion and attitude change could fill volumes. But here are a few findings, organized around the main elements of the communication process: who conveys the message (the source), what the message is (the communication), how the message is conveyed (the medium), and who receives the message (the target, or audience).

The Communicator (Source)   Suppose you are running for president of the student body. You tell your fellow students that you are going to make life at your college better. Would they believe you? That likely would depend on some of your characteristics as a communicator. Whether or not we believe someone depends in large part on their *expertise* or *credibility*. If you have held other elective offices, students would be likelier to believe you have the expertise to be their president. Trustworthiness, power, attractiveness, likability, and similarity are all credibility characteristics that help a communicator change people's attitudes or convince them to act.

The Message   What kind of a message is persuasive? One line of research has focused on whether an emotional or a rational strategy is more effective. Is it better to use feelings or facts? It depends.

self-monitoring Paying attention to the impressions you make on others and the degree to which you fine-tune your performances accordingly.

SELF-ASSESSMENT 6.1

Am I a High or Low Self-Monitorer?

These statements concern personal reactions to a number of situations. No two statements are exactly alike, so consider each statement carefully before answering. If a statement is true or mostly true as applied to you, check the T. If a statement is false or not usually true as applied to you, check the F.

	True	False
1. I find it hard to imitate the behavior of other people.	_____	_____
2. I guess I put on a show to impress or entertain people.	_____	_____
3. I would probably make a good actor.	_____	_____
4. I sometimes appear to others to be experiencing deeper emotions than I actually am.	_____	_____
5. In a group of people, I am rarely the center of attention.	_____	_____
6. In different situations and with different people, I often act like very different persons.	_____	_____
7. I can only argue for ideas I already believe.	_____	_____
8. In order to get along and be liked, I tend to be what people expect me to be.	_____	_____
9. I may deceive people by being friendly when I really dislike them.	_____	_____
10. I'm not always the person I appear to be.	_____	_____

Go to the appendix at the end of the book for scoring and interpretation of your responses.

Emotional appeals can be very powerful. Music is widely used to make us feel good about a message. Think about how few television commercials you have seen without some form of music either in the background or as a prominent part of the message. When we watch such commercials, we may associate the pleasant feelings of the music with the product, even though the music itself provides us with no information about the product.

All other things being equal, the more frightened we are, the more we will change our attitudes. Advertisers sometimes take advantage of our fears to stimulate attitude change. You may have seen the Michelin tire ad that shows a baby playing near tires or the life insurance company ad that shows a widow and her young children moving out of their home because they did not have enough insurance.

The less informed we are about the topic of the message, the likelier we are to respond to an emotional appeal. However, most people are persuaded only when rational and emotional appeals are used together. The emotional appeal arouses our interest, and the facts give us a logical reason for going along with the message. Consider an ad for a new cell phone. Our emotions might be aroused by images of people using the cell phone to call for help or to keep in touch with someone attractive. But then we are given the facts that make the cell phone an appealing purchase. Perhaps the cost is reasonable, it is engineered to reduce static and broken connections, or it combines in one device the capabilities of a phone and an Internet connection.

www.mhhe.com/santrockha

Attitudes

One model that has been proposed to explain the relation between emotional and rational appeals is the **elaboration likelihood model.** It proposes two ways to persuade: a central route and a peripheral route (Petty & Cacioppo, 1986; Petty, Wheeler, & Bizer, 2000; Wegener & others, 2004). The central route to persuasion works by engaging someone thoughtfully. The peripheral route involves nonmessage factors, such as the source's credibility and attractiveness or emotional appeals. The peripheral route is effective when people are not paying close attention to what the communicator is saying. As you might guess, television commercials often involve the peripheral route to persuasion on the assumption that during the commercials you are probably not paying full attention to the screen. However, the central route is more persuasive when people have the ability, and are motivated, to pay attention to the facts (Lammers, 2000).

The Medium Whether an attempt to change attitudes will be effective also depends on the medium that is used for the message. Consider the difference between watching a presidential debate on television and reading about it in the newspaper. Television lets us see how the candidates deliver their messages, what their appearance and mannerisms are like, and so on. Because it presents live images, television is often considered to be a more powerful medium for changing attitudes. In one study, the winners of various political primaries were predicted by the amount of media exposure they had (Grush, 1980).

The Target Age and attitude strength are two characteristics of the audience that determine whether a message will be effective. Younger people are more likely to change their attitudes than older ones. And people whose attitudes are weak are more likely to change than people who have strongly held attitudes.

From *It's a Mom's Life* by David Sipress. Copyright © 1988 by David Sipress. Used by permission of Dutton Signet, a division of Penguin Books (USA) Inc.

elaboration likelihood model A model that attempts to explain the relation between emotional and rational appeals through two routes: a central route and a peripheral route.

Review and Reflect

1 Describe how people think about the social world

REVIEW

- What is attribution? What are two ways in which our attributions tend to be biased?
- What determines our impressions of others?
- What factors influence whether people will change their attitudes?

REFLECT

- Which television ads do you like the best? Have they persuaded you to buy the products that are being advertised? What is it about the ads that is persuasive?

2 SOCIAL INFLUENCE

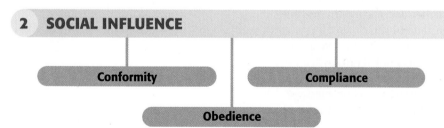

Why did Anna Bolado de Espina want to become a doctor, and why did her daughter begin to hang out with a gang? Part of the answer lies with other people—the influence of parents, teachers, friends, authority figures, the media, and the culture at large exerted on them. Because we are social animals, our behavior is influenced by other people and groups (Cialdini, 2001). The section on social thinking discussed how we present ourselves to others to influence their perceptions of us and how we can change other people's attitudes and behavior. This section explores three aspects of social influence: conformity, obedience, and compliance.

Research on conformity and obedience started in earnest after World War II. Psychologists began to seek answers to the disturbing question of how ordinary people could be influenced to commit the sort of atrocities inflicted on Jews, Gypsies, and other minorities during the Holocaust. How extensively will people change their behavior to coincide with what others are doing? How readily do people obey someone in authority? What factors influence whether people will resist such social influences? These questions are still relevant when we try to understand contemporary events such as vicious attacks on ethnic minorities or gays. They also are relevant in trying to understand everyday human behavior.

Conformity

Conformity is a change in a person's behavior to coincide more closely with a group standard. Conformity comes in many forms and affects many aspects of people's lives. Conformity is at work when a person takes up mountain biking because everyone else is doing it. Conformity also is at work when a teenager joins a gang because everyone else in the neighborhood who can join, does.

Although conformity has some unpleasant or unattractive aspects, it is not entirely a negative thing. People's conformity to rules and regulations allows society to run more smoothly. Consider how chaotic it would be if most people did not conform to social norms such as waiting in line at a cash register, going to school regularly, and not punching others in the face. However, some of the most dramatic and insightful work on conformity has examined how we sometimes act against our better judgment in order to conform.

Asch's Conformity Experiment   Put yourself in this situation: You are taken into a room in which you see five other people seated around a table. A person in a white lab coat enters the room and announces that you are about to participate in an experiment on perceptual accuracy. The group is shown two cards, the first having only a single vertical line on it, the second card three vertical lines of varying length. You are told that the task is to determine which of the three lines on the second card is the same length as the line on the first card. You look at the cards and think, "What a snap. It's so obvious which is the same" (see figure 6.2).

What you do not know is that the other people in the room are actually in league with the experimenter; they've been hired to perform in ways the experimenter dictates. On the first several trials, everyone agrees about which line matches the standard. Then, on the fourth trial, each of the others picks an incorrect line. As the last person to make a choice, you have the dilemma of responding as your eyes tell you or conforming to what the others before you said. How do you think you would answer?

Solomon Asch conducted this classic experiment on conformity in 1951. He believed few of his volunteer participants would yield to group pressure. To test his hypothesis, Asch instructed the hired accomplices to give incorrect responses on 12 of the 18 trials. To his surprise, Asch (1951) found that the volunteer participants conformed to the incorrect answers 35 percent of the time.

In a more recent test of group pressure and conformity, college students watched the third George H. W. Bush–Bill Clinton presidential debate and then rated the candidates' performances (Fern & others, 1993). Students were randomly assigned to one of three groups: (1) a 30-student group that included 10 confederates of the

conformity Involves a change in a person's behavior to coincide more closely with a group standard.

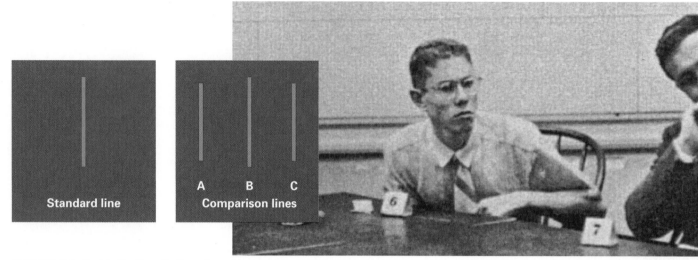

FIGURE 6.2 Asch's Conformity Experiment
The figures on the left shows the stimulus materials for the Asch conformity experiment on group influence. The photograph shows the puzzlement of one subject after five confederates of the experimenter chose the incorrect line.

experimenter who openly supported Bush and criticized Clinton, (2) a 30-student group that included 10 confederates who cheered Clinton and put down Bush, and (3) a 30-student group with no confederates of the experimenter. The effects of the group pressure exerted by the confederates were powerful; even Bush supporters rated Clinton's performance more favorably when their group included pro-Clinton confederates of the experimenter.

In sum, research has shown that the pressure to conform is strong (Pines & Maslach, 2002). Even when faced with clear-cut information such as the lines in the Asch experiment, we often conform to what others say and do. We do not want to be laughed at or make others angry at us.

Factors That Contribute to Conformity   Many factors influence whether an individual will conform or not (Cialdini & Trost, 1998). But in general people conform because of either normative social influence or informational social influence.

Normative social influence is the influence to conform that other people have on us because we seek their approval or seek to avoid their disapproval. So, if a group is important to us, we might wear a particular kind of clothing that people in the group wear, adopt a particular hairstyle, use the same slang words, and adopt a certain set of attitudes that characterize the group's members. This is true whether the group is an inner-city gang or members of a profession, such as the medical or legal profession.

Whereas normative social influence causes people to conform because they want to be liked, **informational social influence** causes people to conform because they want to be right (Taylor & others, 2003). The tendency to conform based on informational social influence depends especially on two factors: how confident we are in our own independent judgment and how well informed we perceive the group to be. Thus, if you don't know much about computers and three of your acquaintances who work in the computer industry tell you not to buy a particular brand of computer, you are likely to conform to their recommendation.

Researchers have found some other factors that are involved in conforming or not conforming:

- *Unanimity of the group.* When a group's opinion is divided, individuals feel less pressure to conform.

normative social influence The influence to conform that other people have on us because we seek their approval or seek to avoid their disapproval.

informational social influence The influence other people have on us because we want to be right.

- *Prior commitment.* If you do not have a prior commitment to an idea or action, you are more likely to be influenced by others. But if you have publicly committed to an idea or action, conformity to a different idea or action is less likely.
- *Personal characteristics.* People with low self-esteem and doubts about their abilities are likelier to conform (Campbell, Tesser, & Fairey, 1986).
- *Group members' characteristics.* You are more likely to conform if the group members are experts, attractive to you, or similar to you in any way.
- *Cultural values.* In experiments conducted in fourteen countries, conformity rates were lower in individualistic cultures (such as that of the United States), in which people tend to pursue their own interests, and higher in collectivistic cultures (such as that of China), in which people typically seek to contribute to the group's success (Bond & Smith, 1994).

Obedience

Obedience is behavior that complies with the explicit demands of the individual in authority. That is, we are obedient when an authority figure demands that we do something and we do it. How is obedience different from conformity? In conformity, people change their thinking or behavior without being told to do so.

Obedient behavior can be horrifically cruel. People were gassed in the concentration camps of Nazi Germany and in the Kurdish villages of Iraq because other people obeyed those in authority. Obedient people burned villages in Vietnam and shoved prisoners out of airplanes in Chile.

A classic experiment by Stanley Milgram (1965, 1974) provides insight into such obedience. Imagine that, as part of an experiment in psychology, you are asked to deliver a series of painful electric shocks to another person. You are told that the purpose of the study is to determine the effects of punishment on memory. Your role is to be the "teacher" and punish the mistakes made by the "learner." Each time the learner makes a mistake, you are to increase the intensity of the shock by a certain amount.

You are introduced to the learner, a nice 50-year-old man who mumbles something about having a heart condition. He is strapped to a chair in the next room; he communicates with you through an intercom. The apparatus in front of you has thirty switches, ranging from 15 volts (light) to 450 volts (marked as dangerous, "severe shock XXX"). Before this part of the experiment began, you had been given a 75-volt shock to see how it felt.

As the trials proceed, the learner quickly runs into trouble and is unable to give the correct answers. Should you shock him? As you increase the intensity of the shock, the learner says he's in pain. At 150 volts, he demands to have the experiment stopped. At 180 volts, he cries out that he can't stand it anymore. At 300 volts, he yells about his heart condition and pleads to be released. But if you hesitate in shocking the learner, the experimenter tells you that you have no choice; the experiment must continue.

By the way, the 50-year-old man is in league with the experimenter. He is not being shocked at all. Of course the teachers are completely unaware that the learner is pretending to be shocked.

As you might imagine, the teachers in this experiment were uneasy about shocking the learner. At 240 volts, one teacher responded, "240 volts delivered; aw, no. You mean I've got to keep going with that scale? No sir, I'm not going to kill that man— I'm not going to give him 450 volts!" (Milgram, 1965). At the very strong voltage, the learner quit responding. When the teacher asked the experimenter what to do, the experimenter simply instructed the teacher to continue the experiment and told him that it was his obligation to complete the job.

obedience Behavior that complies with the explicit demands of the individual in authority.

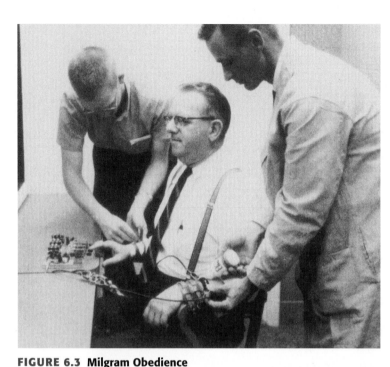

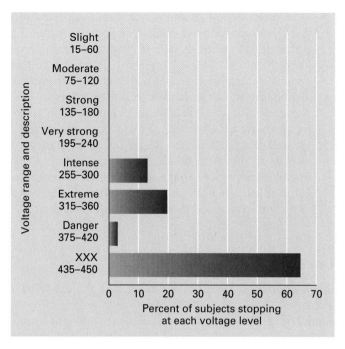

FIGURE 6.3 Milgram Obedience
A 50-year-old man, the "learner," is strapped into a chair. The experimenter makes it look as if a shock generator is being connected to his body through several electrodes. The chart at the right shows the percentage of "teachers" who stopped shocking the learner at each voltage level.

Forty psychiatrists were asked how they thought individuals would respond to this situation. The psychiatrists predicted that most teachers would go no further than 150 volts, that fewer than 1 in 25 would go as far as 300 volts, and that only 1 in 1,000 would deliver the full 450 volts. The psychiatrists, it turns out, were way off the mark. The majority of the teachers obeyed the experimenter. In fact, almost two-thirds delivered the full 450 volts. Figure 6.3 shows the results of the Milgram study.

In subsequent studies, Milgram set up a storefront in Bridgeport, Connecticut, and recruited volunteers through newspaper ads. Milgram wanted to create a more natural environment for the experiment and to use a wider cross section of volunteers. In these additional studies, close to two-thirds of the individuals still selected the highest level of shock for the learner.

In variations of the experiment, Milgram discovered that more people would disobey in certain circumstances. Disobedience was more common when participants could see others disobey, when the authority figure was not perceived to be legitimate and was not close by, and when the victim was made to seem more human.

Were Milgram experiments *ethical?* After all, the volunteer teachers in Milgram's experiment clearly felt anguish as they thought they were hurting the "learner." Milgram argued that his experiments taught us a great deal about human nature. The volunteers were told after the experiment was completed that they had not shocked anyone, and they were interviewed later. More than four-fifths said that they were glad they had participated in the study; none said that they were sorry they participated.

When Milgram conducted his studies on obedience, the ethical guidelines for research were not as stringent as they are today. According to current ethical guidelines of the American Psychological Association, researchers should obtain informed consent from their volunteers and deception should be used only for very important purposes. Individuals are supposed to feel as good about themselves when the experiment is over as they did when it began. Under today's guidelines, it is unlikely that the Milgram experiment would be conducted.

Adjustment Strategies
For Resisting an Unjust Request by a Person in a Position of Authority

If you believe that someone in a position of authority is making an unjust request or ordering you to do something wrong, what choice of action do you have? You can comply, but if you want to resist authority you can do the following:

1. Give the appearance of complying but secretly do otherwise.
2. Publicly dissent by showing doubts and disenchantment but still follow the request/order.
3. Openly disregard the order and refuse to comply.
4. Challenge or confront the authority.
5. Get higher authorities to intervene or organize a group of people who agree with you to show the strength of your view.

Resistance to authority can be difficult, but living with the knowledge that you compromised your own moral integrity may be more difficult in the long run.

Compliance

Most of the time, we are not obeying orders from someone in authority. More often, we face requests or efforts to persuade us to do something (Knowles & Linn, 2004). You've probably tried to persuade your friends to go to a movie or to play a game that you are interested in. You are seeking *compliance*—a change in behavior in response to a direct request.

Robert Cialdini (2001; Sagarin & Cialdini, 2004) is a social psychologist who has studied the tactics of compliance professionals—people such as sales representatives who make their living by gaining compliance with their requests. Cialdini has identified six basic principles of persuasion and compliance: (1) reciprocation, (2) commitment and consistency, (3) social proof, (4) liking, (5) authority, and (6) scarcity.

Reciprocation   The principle of *reciprocation* states that one person tries to repay, in kind, what another person has provided. If someone does you a favor, you feel that you owe a favor in return. Anna Belado de Espina's daughter might feel obliged to say yes to her mother's request to do her shopping for the week because Anna had just baby-sat for her.

Compliance professionals are counting on the tendency to reciprocate when they give something away before asking you to do what they wanted you to do all along.

CALVIN AND HOBBES   by Bill Waterson

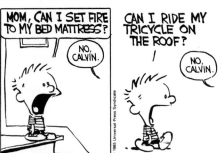

For example, restaurants and grocery stores give out free samples; they expect that the samples will make customers feel as if they owe them something in return—such as a purchase.

The **door-in-the-face-strategy** illustrates the principle of reciprocation. This strategy begins with an extreme request that is bound to be rejected; then the person retreats to a smaller request—the one that was desired all along. Because the smaller request seems like a concession, you might feel an obligation to reciprocate with a concession of your own—by going along with the smaller request. For example, the sales representative for a health spa might offer you the 1-year membership for $300, which you turn down, and then offer a "bargain" package of 4 weeks for $15.

Commitment and Consistency

Once people make a commitment, they are more likely to agree to requests that are in keeping with the prior commitment. Why? Most people prefer to be consistent in their behavior and see themselves as keeping their word. Thus, once you sign your name to volunteer to join a committee to find a way to clean up the neighborhood park, you might find it difficult to turn down a request to spend a few hours cleaning it up yourself. After all, by signing up you have declared yourself to be a civic-minded person who is interested in having the parks cleaned up. To turn down the new request might damage that self-image.

The commitment-and-consistency principle is applied in the **foot-in-the-door strategy,** which consists of obtaining compliance with a small request in order to obtain compliance later with a larger request. For example, a sales pitch from a health spa might offer you 4 weeks' use of their facility for $15 and hope that, after the 4 weeks, you will pay them $300 for a 1-year membership.

Social Proof

People examine what other people are doing in order to help them decide what to do; this is the principle of social proof. Because of this principle, bartenders place a few dollar bills in a tip jar at the beginning of an evening to simulate tips left by previous customers. The producers of charity telethons list viewers who have already pledged contributions.

Consider another situation involving social proof. A young woman named Kitty Genovese was brutally murdered. She was attacked at about 3 A.M. in a respectable area of New York City. The murderer left and returned three times; he finally put an end to Kitty's life as she crawled to her apartment and screamed for help. It took the slayer about 30 minutes to kill Kitty. Thirty-eight neighbors watched the gory scene and heard Kitty Genovese's screams. No one helped or even called the police. This incident illustrates what social psychologists later called the **bystander effect,** the tendency for an individual who observes an emergency to help less when other people are present than when the observer is alone (Darley & Latané, 1968). Most bystander studies reveal that when a person is alone he or she will help 75 percent of the time, but the figure drops to 50 percent when another bystander is present but not helping. Cialdini's (2001) concept of social proof may help to explain the bystander effect. In an emergency, people may not be sure whether it is an actual emergency so they look to the actions of others for clues about what to do. If others are present but not acting, bystanders conclude that it must not be an emergency.

Social proof is most likely to influence compliance under two conditions: First, when people are uncertain what to do, they often use the actions of others as a guide. Second, people are more likely to follow the lead of people they perceive as similar to themselves.

Liking

Individuals prefer to say yes to people they know and like. We tend to like people if they are physically attractive, if they are similar to us, or if they praise us. Praise can backfire, however, if it is seen as insincere manipulation. Increased familiarity

www.mhhe.com/santrockha

Social Influence Tactics
Mindless in America

door-in-the-face strategy Illustrates the principle of reciprocation; the strategy begins with an extreme request that is bound to be rejected, then the person retreats to a smaller request—the one that was desired all along.

foot-in-the-door strategy Obtaining compliance with a small request in order to obtain compliance later with a larger request.

bystander effect The tendency for an individual who observes an emergency to help less when other people are present than when the observer is alone.

through repeated contact in positive circumstances also increases the probability that a person will be liked.

Car, real estate, and insurance sales associates regularly send out holiday greeting cards, calendars, and other materials to former customers or potential customers. The hope is that these materials will increase the probability that the people who receive them will like the sales associate.

Authority   In the Milgram study that we discussed earlier, we saw how strong the pressure is to comply with the requests of an authority. Deference to authorities often occurs in an automatic, mindless manner. Mere symbols of authority, such as titles, clothing, and automobiles, can produce compliance.

Scarcity   People value opportunities more when they are less available. To create an impression of scarcity, sellers often announce that they have only a "limited number" of something for sale or they may set a "deadline" for an offer. The scarcity principle works best under two conditions: (1) when items are newly scarce, and (2) when we compete with others to obtain scarce items.

It is important to remember that our relation to the social world is reciprocal. Individuals may be trying to obtain our compliance, but we can control our actions and resist compliance strategies (Bandura, 2001).

From *The Penguin Leunig.* Copyright © 1983 by Michael Leunig. Published by Penguin Group Australia Ltd. Reprinted with permission.

Adjustment Strategies
For Resisting Persuasion and Compliance Tactics

Cialdini (2001) offers these strategies for resisting persuasion and compliance tactics:

1. ***Defend against the use of reciprocity pressures.*** You don't need to systematically reject the initial offers of others. Instead, accept them "in good faith, but be ready to redefine them as tricks should they later be proved as such. Once they are redefined in this way, we will no longer feel a need to respond with a favor or concession of our own," p. 50.
2. ***Recognize and resist the influence of commitment and consistency pressures.*** Be alert to tactics that pressure you to do what you do not want to do. If someone is urging you to follow up on an earlier commitment, ask yourself a key question, "Knowing what I know now, if I could go back in time, would I make the same commitment?" p. 96.
3. ***Reduce susceptibility to faulty social proof.*** Be sensitive to "counterfeit evidence of what similar others are doing...and recognize that the actions of similar others should not form the sole basis for our decisions," p. 141.
4. ***Reduce unwanted influence of liking.*** "Step back from the social interaction and mentally separate the requester from his or her offer, and make any compliance decision on the merits of the offer," p. 176.
5. ***Defend against the detrimental effects of authority.*** Ask yourself two important questions: "(1) Is this authority truly an expert? (2) How truthful can we expect this expert to be?" p. 201.
6. ***Combat scarcity pressures.*** This is not easy because scarcity tactics emotionally arouse us and make it difficult for us to think clearly. "Be alert to a rush of arousal in situations involving scarcity...take steps to calm the arousal and assess the merits of the opportunity in terms of why you want it," p. 231.

3 INTERGROUP RELATIONS

| Groups and Their Functions | Prejudice and Discrimination | Ways to Improve Interethnic Relations |

| Group Identity: Us Versus Them | Immigration |

Think again of Anna Bolado de Espina, the woman discussed at the beginning of the chapter. How would you describe her? As a mother? As a student? An immigrant? A Mexican American? All of these descriptions point to her membership in a particular group. Her identification with various groups, her relationships within each group, and each group's relationships with other groups are all important factors in understanding Anna's adjustment. Here, however, we can examine only a few characteristics of groups, beginning with their functions.

Groups and Their Functions

A student joining a campus organization, a jury making a decision about a criminal case, a president of a company delegating authority, a prejudiced remark against a minority group, conflict among nations, and attempts to reach peace—all of these circumstances reflect our lives as members of groups. Groups range in size from *dyads,* which consist of two people, to immense groups of people linked by national identity, religion, ethnicity, or gender. Some groups we choose, others we do not. We choose to belong to a club, but we are all born into a particular family, for example.

Regardless of their size, groups serve useful human purposes. They satisfy our personal needs, reward us, provide information, raise our self-esteem, and give us an identity. We might join a group because we think it will be enjoyable and exciting and satisfy our need for companionship. We might join a group because we will receive rewards, either material or psychological. For example, by taking a job with a company, we not only get paid to work as part of a group but we also reap a portion of the company's prestige and recognition. Groups are also an important source of information. For example, as we listen to other members talk in a Weight Watchers group we learn about their strategies for losing weight.

Many of the groups of which we are members—our family, college, religious group, or ethnic group—also provide identities. When asked who we are, we often answer in terms of which groups we belong to.

social identity Refers to the way you define yourself in terms of your group membership.

(*Left*) A Palestinian–Israeli clash in the Gaza Strip. (*Right*) An outbreak of violence in Northern Ireland.
How might a group's social identity be involved in such violence?

Conflicts between groups, especially ethnic groups, are rampant around the world (Chirot & Seligman, 2001). Groups such as al-Qaida attack countries such as the United States that they perceive to be enemies of Islam, and the United States retaliates. Israelis and Palestinians fight over territory, each claiming religious and historical rights to the disputed land. Clashes still break out between Catholics and Protestants in Northern Ireland and between Hindus and Moslems in India. Stereotyping, prejudice, and other concepts introduced by social psychologists can help us understand the intensity of these conflicts and how they might be reduced (Ellemers, Spears, & Doosje, 2002; Hewstone, Rubin, & Willis, 2002).

Group Identity: Us Versus Them

When someone asks you to identify yourself, how often do you respond by mentioning your membership in the group? Think about how you introduce yourself to a stranger. Are you more likely to say, "Hi, I'm an ambitious hardworking idealist" or "Hi, I'm a student at State U. and I'm a member of the debate team." Chances are you are more likely to tell people about the groups with which you identify. Your **social identity** is the way you define yourself in terms of your group membership (Deaux, 2001).

In contrast to personal identity, which emphasizes a unique combination of characteristics, social identity focuses on our commonalities with others (Bodenhausen, Macrae, & Hugenberg, 2004; Sidanius & others, 2004; Wren & Mendoza, 2004). To identify with a group does not mean that we know or interact with every other member of the group. However, it does mean that we believe that we share numerous features with other members of the group.

Many forms of social identity exist, reflecting the many ways in which people connect to groups and social categories. Social psychologist Kay Deaux (2001) identified five distinct types of social identity: ethnic and religious, political, vocations and avocations, personal relationships, and stigmatized groups (see figure 6.4).

Social Identity Theory   What difference does our social identity make? Social psychologist Henry Tajfel (1978) provides a compelling answer. Tajfel survived the

Ethnicity and Religion

Asian American
Jewish
Southern Baptist
West Indian

Political Affiliation

Feminist
Republican
Environmentalist

Vocations and Avocations

Psychologist
Artist
Athlete
Military veteran

Relationships

Mother
Parent
Teenager
Widow

Stigmatized Identities

Person with AIDS
Homeless person
Overweight person
Alcoholic

FIGURE 6.4 Types of Identity

Group members often show considerable pride in their group identity, as reflected in Mexican Americans' celebration of Cinco de Mayo, Native Americans' celebration of their heritage, Polish Americans' celebration of their cultural background, and African Americans' celebration of Martin Luther King Day.

social identity theory Tajfel's theory that we can improve our self-image by enhancing our social identity; this occurs by favoring our in-group and disparaging the out-group.

Holocaust, and he wanted to explain the extreme prejudice and violence Jews have experienced. According to Tajfel's **social identity theory,** we can improve our self-images by enhancing our social identity; this occurs either by favoring members of our own in-group or by disparaging members of the out-group. Thus, in Tajfel's view, individuals invariably think of their group as the in-group and favor its members against the out-group because they want to have a positive image.

In one experiment, Tajfel (1978) showed how easy it is to lead people to think and act in terms of an in-group, or "we," and out-group, or "they." First, participants were told to estimate the number of dots that were projected on a screen. Next, they were told in private whether they had overestimated or underestimated the number of dots. In fact, they had been randomly assigned to the "overestimator" or the "underestimator" group. Then the participants were asked to decide how to award money, confidentially, to the other participants, who were identified on a list only as overestimators or underestimators. Invariably, individuals awarded money to members of their own group—even though they knew nothing else about these people. If we favor our own group based on such trivial criteria, it is no wonder that we show intense in-group favoritism when differences are not so trivial (Abrams & Hogg, 2004; Jussim, Ashamore, & Wilder, 2001; Layder, 2004).

Imagine two fans of professional football teams, one a New England Patriots fan, the other a Carolina Panthers fan. As these two fans talk, they are less likely to discuss how much they both like football than to argue about the virtues of their teams. As they strive to promote their social identities, they soon lapse into self-congratulatory remarks about their own team and nasty comments about the opposing team. In short, the theme of the conversation becomes "My team is good and I am good. Your team is bad and you are bad." And so it goes with the sexes, ethnic groups, nations, socioeconomic groups, religions, sororities, fraternities, and countless other groups. We are continually comparing our groups (*in-groups*) with other groups (*out-groups*). These comparisons often lead to prejudice and conflict between groups.

Ethnocentrism   It is a natural tendency, called **ethnocentrism,** to favor one's own group and believe it is superior to other groups. Ethnocentrism fosters pride and fulfills the need for a positive self-image. Of course, the negative side of ethnocentrism is that it encourages in-group/out-group, we/they thinking (Cunningham, 2004; Matsumoto & Juang, 2004).

Members of many groups such as African Americans, Latinos, gays, and lesbians often assert in-group pride to counter the negative messages transmitted by society about their group. However, it is difficult to emphasize pride in one's own group without also stressing differences with other groups. Although members of ethnic groups often stress that they do not discriminate against other groups, most members of an ethnic group celebrate their own heritage and culture and set themselves apart from, and even above, others.

Ethnocentrism and the Social Sciences   Psychologists and other social scientists are not immune from the effects of ethnocentrism. For most of the twentieth century, the overwhelming majority of social scientists were White males, and most treated the differences between minority groups and the majority as *deficits* or inferior characteristics on the part of minorities. Research on minorities focused on their adjustment problems. For example, research on African American adolescent females invariably focused on such topics as poverty, dropping out of school, and unwed motherhood; research on positive characteristics of African American adolescent females was neglected.

Today, the emphasis has shifted. Social scientists have been stressing both the differences between groups and the strengths of minority groups (Cushner, McClelland, & Stafford, 2003). For example, the positive aspects of ethnic identity are now being emphasized (Phinney, 2003).

Understanding Prejudice
Exploring Prejudice

Prejudice and Discrimination

Antagonism between groups is both reflected in and perpetuated by prejudice and discrimination (Brammer, 2004; Fishbein, 2002; Tuffin, 2004). Like most people, you probably do not consider yourself as prejudiced, but each of us has prejudices. **Prejudice** is an unjustified negative attitude toward an individual based on the individual's membership in a group. The group may consist of people of a particular race, sex, age, religion, or nationality or people who share some other detectable difference from the prejudiced individual (Jones, 1997; Lambert, Chasteen, & Payne, 2004; Nelson, 2002; Plant, 2004).

Having a prejudice does not mean that you have to act on it. But if you do act on your prejudices, you may be guilty of **discrimination,** an unjustified negative or harmful action toward a member of a group simply because the person belongs to that group. Discrimination results when negative emotional reactions combine with prejudiced beliefs and are translated into behavior.

ethnocentrism The tendency to favor one's own group and believe it is superior to other groups.

prejudice An unjustified negative attitude toward an individual based on the individual's membership in a group.

discrimination An unjustified negative or harmful action toward a member of a group simply because the person belongs to that group.

Prejudice is a worldwide phenomenon that has fueled violence throughout human history (Baker, 2001). The Taliban were so prejudiced against women that they tried to make them invisible. Serbs were so prejudiced against Bosnians that they pursued a policy of "ethnic cleansing." Hutus in Rwanda were so prejudiced against Tutsis that they went on a murderous rampage, hacking off their arms and legs with machetes. European Americans were so prejudiced against Native Americans that they systematically robbed them of their property and self-respect, killed them, and herded the survivors like animals onto reservations.

The most blatant prejudice in U.S. history was White prejudice against African Americans. When Africans were brought to America as slaves, they were considered property and treated inhumanely. In the first half of the twentieth century, most African Americans still lived in the South and were still largely segregated from White society by law; restaurants, movie theaters, and buses had separate areas for Whites and African Americans. Even decades after legal segregation was abolished, much higher percentages of African Americans than Whites live in impoverished neighborhoods and lack access to good schools, jobs, and health care (Harrison-Hale, McLoyd, & Smedley, 2004).

African Americans and Native Americans are not the only ethnic minority groups that have been subjected to prejudice and discrimination in the United States. Historically, immigrants have struggled against the prejudice of those born in the United States. Ethnicity has often defined who will enjoy the privileges of citizenship and to what degree and in what ways (Jones, 1997). A person's ethnic background has often determined whether that individual will have the opportunity to live in housing with decent public services such as clean water, to go to good schools, or to work for a decent wage.

Lesbians and gays also have been subjected to considerable prejudice by the heterosexual majority. This prejudice has been so intense that most homosexuals stayed "in the closet" until recently, not revealing their sexual preferences for fear of jeopardizing other members of their community and losing their jobs or even their lives. In fact, virtually every social group has been the victim of prejudice at one time or another.

Sources of Prejudice Why do people develop prejudice? Among the reasons given by social psychologists are the following:

- *Individual personality.* Some years ago social psychologist Theodor Adorno and his colleagues (1950) described the *authoritarian personality:* its characteristics include strict adherence to conventional ways of behaving, aggression against people who violate conventional norms, rigid thinking, and exaggerated submission to authority. He believed that individuals with an authoritarian personality are likely to be prejudiced. However, not all individuals who harbor prejudice have an authoritarian personality.
- *Competition between groups over scarce resources.* Feelings of hostility and prejudice can develop when a society does not have enough jobs or land or power or status—or any of a number of other material and social resources—to go around. Given the historical distributions of resources in a particular society, certain groups may regularly compete with each other and thus be more likely to develop prejudice toward each other. For instance, immigrants often compete with established low-income citizens for jobs, leading to persistent conflict between the two groups.
- *Motivation to enhance self-esteem.* As Henry Tajfel (1978) stated, individuals derive a sense of self-esteem through their identification as members of a particular group and, to the extent that their group is viewed more favorably than other groups, their self-esteem will be further enhanced. In this view, prejudice against other groups leads to a positive social identity and higher self-esteem.

- *Cognitive processes that contribute to a tendency to apply stereotypes.* Once stereotypes are in place, prejudice is often not far behind. Researchers have found that we are less likely to detect variations among individuals who belong to "other" groups than among individuals who belong to "our" group. For example, studies of eyewitness identification have found that Whites tend to stereotype African Americans more than other Whites during eyewitness identification (Brigham, 1986). What might be occurring is the tendency to view members of one's own group as having heterogeneous and desirable qualities and to view the members of other groups as having homogeneous and undesirable qualities (Slattery, 2004).
- *Cultural learning.* Families, friends, traditional norms, and institutionalized patterns of discrimination provide plenty of opportunities for individuals to be exposed to the prejudice of others. In this manner, others' prejudiced belief systems can be incorporated into one's own system. Children often show prejudice before they even have the cognitive abilities or social opportunities to develop their own attitudes.

Modern Racism   Until recently, prejudice and discrimination in the United States were easy to identify. Old-fashioned racism (as well as old-fashioned sexism) was overt and relatively simple, asserting the inferiority of non-Whites. Old-fashioned racists tried to maintain self-esteem by using the power of being a member of the majority group to discriminate against others.

Overt discrimination is no longer acceptable in mainstream American society, however. Civil rights legislation and changing attitudes expressed widely in popular media have made it "politically incorrect" to present oneself as prejudiced. But more subtle forms of racism have appeared, described by such terms as *symbolic racism, aversive racism, ambivalent racism,* and *modern racism* (Blair, 2001). They involve negative feelings about minority groups, but not traditional stereotypes. For example, symbolic racism assumes that, because discrimination is no longer acceptable, it must not exist and that any difficulties encountered by individuals in minority groups must be their own fault. It encompasses the ideas that African Americans, for example, are making unfair demands, and are receiving undeserved special attention, such as favoritism in job hiring and college admissions (Taylor & others, 2003). This subtler form of racism brings discrimination that is covert rather than overt, unconscious rather than conscious, and denied rather than acknowledged (Monteith & Voils, 2001).

Immigration

The story of Anna Bolado de Espina that began this chapter is the story of more and more Americans. Relatively high rates of immigration are contributing to the growth in the proportion of ethnic minorities in the U.S. population (Chun & Akutsu, 2003; McLoyd, 2000; Phinney, 2003). Immigrants often experience stressors uncommon to or less prominent among longtime residents, such as language barriers, separations from support networks, and the dual struggle to preserve their ethnic identity and to acculturate (Davey & others, 2003; Goodkind, Hang, & Yang, 2004; Hubbard & Miller, 2004). Even today, many Latino, Vietnamese, and other immigrants face prejudice and discrimination that makes it difficult for them to obtain educational opportunities and good-paying jobs above the poverty line (Gonzales & others, 2004).

Most colleges have students from a wide range of countries who bring with them customs, values, and behaviors that may be quite different from U.S. students. If you are a U.S. student, consider getting to know one or more international students. The experience will expand your education.

If you are an international student, adapting to college in the United States can be challenging. You have to cope with many new customs and values and in some instances learn a new language.

If you are an international student, what can you do to become better adjusted on a U.S. college campus? If you are a student from the United States, what can you do to help international students feel more comfortable on your campus?

Adjustment Strategies
For International Students

Here are some adjustment strategies for international students:

1. ***Be patient.*** It takes time to adapt to a new culture and your life may be more difficult at the beginning than you envisioned. Over time, you are likely to feel more comfortable living in this new culture.
2. ***Develop a support system.*** You likely can meet other international students at an international student association at your college. In many instances, these organizations can provide support to help you adapt to your new setting.
3. ***Talk with U.S. students.*** Get to know some U.S. students and find out more about their culture.
4. ***Share your culture.*** Look for opportunities to provide information about your life experiences so others can learn about your culture.

Ways to Improve Interethnic Relations

Martin Luther King, Jr., once said, "I have a dream that my four little children will one day live in a nation where they will not be judged by the color of their skin but by the content of their character." How might we reach the world King envisioned, a world without prejudice and discrimination? Researchers have consistently found that contact itself—attending the same school or living next door to each other or working in the same company—does not necessarily improve relations among people from differing ethnic backgrounds (Brewer & Brown, 1998). More focused efforts, such as task-oriented cooperation and intimate contact, are needed to break down barriers based on prejudice (Pedersen, 2004).

Task-Oriented Cooperation When the schools in Austin, Texas, were desegregated through extensive busing, increased racial tension among African Americans, Mexican Americans, and Whites resulted in violence in the schools. The superintendent consulted Eliot Aronson, a prominent social psychologist, who was at the

University of Texas at Austin at the time. Aronson (1986) thought it was more important to prevent ethnic hostility than to control it. He observed a number of elementary school classrooms in Austin and saw fierce competition between children of unequal status.

Aronson stressed that the reward structure of the classrooms needed to be changed from a setting of unequal competition to one of cooperation among equals, without making any curriculum changes. To accomplish this, he put together the *jigsaw classroom*. A jigsaw classroom creates a situation in which all of the students have to pull together. Let's say we have a class of thirty students, some White, some African American, and some Latino. The academic goal is to learn about the life of Joseph Pulitzer. The class is broken up into five study groups of six students each, with the ethnic composition and academic achievement of the groups being as equal as possible. Learning about Pulitzer's life becomes a class project divided into six parts, with one part given to each member of the six-person group. The components might be paragraphs from Pulitzer's biography, such as how the Pulitzer family came to the United States, Pulitzer's childhood, his early work, and so on. The parts are like the pieces of a jigsaw puzzle: They have to be put together to form the complete puzzle.

Each student has an allotted time to study her or his part. Then the group meets, and each member tries to teach her or his part to the group. Each student must learn the entire lesson, so learning depends on the cooperation and effort of other members. After an hour or so, each student is tested on the life of Pulitzer. Aronson believes that cooperatively working to reach a common goal increases students' interdependence.

The strategy of emphasizing cooperation, rather than competition, and the jigsaw approach have been widely used in classrooms in the United States (Johnson & Johnson, 2003). According to a number of studies, this type of cooperative learning is linked with increased self-esteem, better academic performance, friendships among classmates, and improved perceptions of ethnic groups different from one's own (Slavin, 1989).

It is not easy to get groups who do not like each other to cooperate. The air of distrust and hostility is hard to overcome. Creating goals that require cooperation of both groups is one viable strategy, as shown in Aronson's work. Other strategies involve spreading positive information about the "other" and reducing the potential threat of each group.

Intimate Contact   I stated earlier that contact by itself does not improve interethnic relations. However, one form of contact—intimate contact—can (Brislin, 1993). Intimate contact in this context does not mean sexual relations; rather, it involves sharing one's personal worries, troubles, successes, failures, personal ambitions, and coping strategies. When people reveal personal information about themselves, they are more likely to be perceived as individuals than as members of a category. And the sharing of personal information often produces the discovery that others have many of the same feelings, hopes, and concerns that we have, which can help to break down barriers between groups. Intimate contact may be more effective, however, when the individuals have relatively equal status (Devine, Evett, & Vasquez-Suson, 1996).

One of the initial investigations of interethnic contact focused on African American and White residents in an integrated housing project (Deutsch & Collins, 1951). The residents lived in small apartments and shared facilities, such as laundry rooms and playgrounds for children. The residents discovered that it was more enjoyable to talk with each other than to stare at the walls while doing their laundry, and African American and White parents began to

Intimate personal contact that involves sharing doubts, hopes, problems, ambitions, and much more is one way to improve interethnic relations.

talk with each other as they watched their children play together. Initially the conversations focused on such nonintimate matters as the quality of the washing machines and the weather, but eventually they moved on to more personal matters. Whites and African Americans discovered that they shared concerns such as jobs and work, schools for their children, taxes, and so on. The revelation that both groups shared many concerns and problems helped to diminish in-group/out-group thoughts and feelings. Sharing intimate information and becoming friendly with someone from another ethnic group helped people become more tolerant and less prejudiced toward the other ethnic group.

Acknowledge Diversity Prejudice and discrimination depend on negative stereotyping, which overlooks at least one important dimension of ethnic minority individuals: their diversity (Bronstein & Quina, 2003). Often, misleadingly broad categories are used to describe ethnic groups. For example, Mexican, Cuban, and Puerto Rican immigrants are lumped together as Latinos, but they had different reasons for migrating, came from varying socioeconomic backgrounds in their native countries, and experience different rates of employment in the United States. The U.S. federal government now recognizes 511 different Native American tribes, each having a unique background, set of values, and other characteristics. Just as important, however, is the fact that even narrowly defined ethnic groups are not homogeneous. The individuals in them have different social, historical, and economic histories.

Nevertheless, individuals belonging to a particular group do tend to conform to its values, attitudes, and customs. Historical, economic, and social experiences produce real differences between ethnic groups. Recognizing and respecting differences is an important aspect of getting along with others in a diverse, multicultural world (Leong, 2000). Every person needs to take the perspective of individuals from groups that are different from theirs and think, "If I were in their shoes, what kind of experiences might I have had?" "How would I feel if I were a member of their group?" "How would I think and behave if I had grown up in their world?" Such perspective taking is a valuable way to increase our empathy and understanding of individuals from other groups.

Adjustment Strategies
For Improving Interethnic Relations

1. *Participate in cooperative tasks.* As we saw in Aronson's research, cooperating with others to reach a superordinate goal improves interethnic relations.
2. *Have intimate contact.* Interethnic relations improve when people talk with each other about their personal worries, successes, failures, coping strategies, interests, and so on.
3. *Pay attention to differences and diversity.* There are differences between people from different ethnic and cultural backgrounds. Showing respect for these differences can reduce interethnic conflict. Look for variations within an ethnic group. Understand how diverse an ethnic group is. Recognizing these variations reduces stereotyping.
4. *Engage in perspective taking.* Put yourself in the other person's shoes. Imagine what your life would be like if you were the other person. Think how you would perceive the world.
5. *Think reflectively.* Think deeply about interethnic relations. Instead of reacting automatically, delay judgment until you have more complete information.

6. ***Be emotionally intelligent.*** Develop your emotional self-awareness and learn to manage your emotions and read others' emotions more accurately. Become a better manager of your anger, and explore the cause of your feelings.
7. ***Be an effective communicator.*** In chapter 7, "Communicating Effectively," we will describe a number of strategies to help you explain your ideas more clearly and listen more attentively.

Review and Reflect

3 **Discuss intergroup relations**
   *   What functions do groups serve?
   *   How does social identity lead to "we/they" thinking?
   *   How are prejudice, stereotyping, and discrimination related?
   *   What are some of the special stresses faced by immigrants?
   *   What strategies for improving interethnic relations are effective?

REFLECT

   *   What personal experiences have you had with prejudice, stereotyping, and discrimination? Explain why you think these occurred.

Reach Your Learning Goals

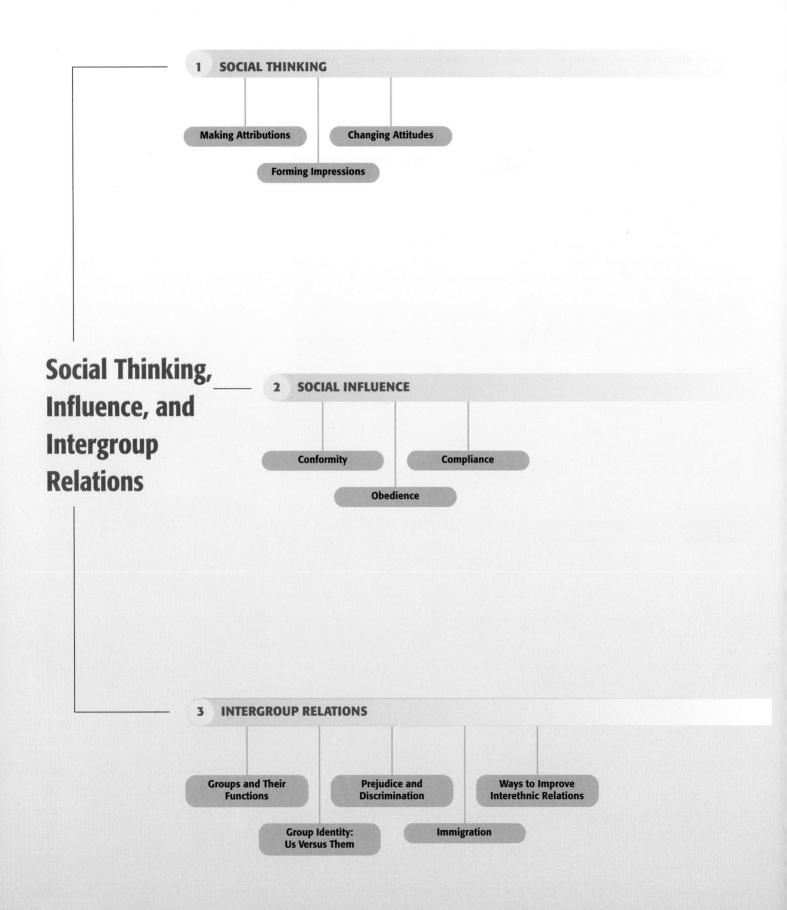

Social Thinking, Influence, and Intergroup Relations

1 SOCIAL THINKING

- Making Attributions
- Forming Impressions
- Changing Attitudes

2 SOCIAL INFLUENCE

- Conformity
- Obedience
- Compliance

3 INTERGROUP RELATIONS

- Groups and Their Functions
- Group Identity: Us Versus Them
- Prejudice and Discrimination
- Immigration
- Ways to Improve Interethnic Relations

Summary

1 Describe how people think about the social world

- Attributions are our thoughts about why people behave the way they do and about who or what is responsible for the outcome of events. The fundamental attribution error states that observers overestimate the importance of traits and underestimate the importance of situations when they seek explanations of an actor's behavior. When our self-esteem is threatened, we might depart from the fundamental attribution error and engage in a self-serving bias, attributing our successes to internal causes and our failures to external causes.
- In part, our impressions depend on their self-presentations. People tend to engage in impression management—trying to present a favorable image—and in varying degrees of self-monitoring to fine-tune the impressions they are making. Our impressions of people, however, also depend on the categories, stereotypes, and attitudes that we bring to the situation.
- Whether we change our attitudes may depend on characteristics of the communicator (source), the message, the medium, and ourselves.

2 Identify how people are influenced in social settings

- Conformity involves a change in a person's behavior to coincide with a group standard. Asch's classic study on judgments of line length illustrated the power of conformity. Many factors influence whether we will conform, including normative social influence and informational social influence.
- Obedience is behavior that complies with the explicit demands of an individual in authority. Milgram's classic experiment demonstrated the power of obedience. Participants obeyed the experimenter's directions even though they thought they were hurting someone.
- Cialdini believes there are six important principles of persuasion and compliance: (1) reciprocation (one person tries to repay, in kind, what another person has provided), (2) commitment and consistency (securing an initial commitment is a key strategy to obtain compliance), (3) social proof (people examine what other people are believing or doing especially under conditions of uncertainty and similarity), (4) liking

(individuals prefer to say yes to people they know and like, (5) authority (people feel a pressure to comply to people in authority positions), and (6) scarcity (people value opportunities more when they are less available).

3 Discuss intergroup relations

- Groups vary in size from two people to millions of people, and their possible functions vary as well. They may fulfill our need for companionship, provide material rewards, serve as sources of information, and provide an identity, which may enhance our self-esteem.
- Social identity is how we define ourselves in terms of our group memberships. According to Tajfel's social identity theory, by favoring our own group and disparaging other groups, we can enhance our self-esteem. As a result, when individuals are assigned to a group they invariably think of it as the in-group, or "we" and contrast it with the out-group, or "they."
- Prejudice is an unjustified negative attitude toward an individual based on the individual's membership in a group. It depends on stereotypes, which are generalizations about a group's characteristics that do not consider any variations from one individual to the next. Among the reasons people develop prejudice are an individual's personality (authoritarian), competition between groups over scarce resources, motivation to enhance one's self-esteem, and learning. When prejudice is translated into action, the result is discrimination, an unjustified harmful action toward a member of a group because he or she is a member of that group.
- Immigrants often experience stressors such as language barriers, separations from support networks, prejudice, discrimination, and the struggle both to preserve their ethnic identity and to adapt to the culture of their new country.
- Contact between ethnic groups, by itself, does not decrease conflict and improve relations. Effective strategies are to set up task-oriented cooperation, share intimate information, pay attention to differences and diversity, engage in perspective taking, think reflectively, be emotionally intelligent, and be an effective communicator.

Key Terms

attributions, 173
fundamental attribution
   error, 173
stereotype, 175
attitudes, 175
impression management
   (self-presentation), 175

self-monitoring, 176
elaboration likelihood
   model, 178
conformity, 179
normative social
   influence, 180

informational social
   influence, 180
obedience, 181
door-in-the-face strategy, 184
foot-in-the-door strategy, 184
bystander effect, 184

social identity, 186
social identity theory, 188
ethnocentrism, 189
prejudice, 189
discrimination, 189

Resources for Improving Your Adjustment

SELF-HELP BOOKS

Influence

(2001) by Robert Cialdini
Boston: Allyn & Bacon

The best book available to learn more about persuasion and compliance. Extensive descriptions and examples of the six

principles of persuasion and compliance discussed in this chapter are provided.

 E-Learning Tools

To help you master the material in this chapter, you will find a number of valuable study tools on the student CD-ROM that accompanies this book. In addition, visit the Online Learning Center for *Human Adjustment,* where you can find valuable resources for Chapter 6, "Social Thinking, Influence, and Group Relations."

SELF-ASSESSMENT

In Text

You can complete these self-assessments in the text:
- Self-Assessment 6.1: *Am I a High or Low Self-Monitorer?*

Additional Self-Assessments

Complete these self-assessments on the Online Learning Center:
- *Do I Have Unconscious Racial Tendencies?*
- *My Diversity Orientation and Cultural Awareness*

THINK CRITICALLY

To practice your critical thinking skills, complete these exercises on the Online Learning Center:
- *Fundamentals of Conflict* asks you to think reflectively about applying the fundamental attribution error to a classroom situation.

- *Milgram's Results and Standards of Humane Research* focuses on the ethics of Milgram's classic obedience study.
- *Persuasion and the Buddy System* involves thinking about the influence one of your friends might have on you.

APPLY YOUR KNOWLEDGE

1. Social psychology and police services.

What factors in social psychology could be applied to police training and community relations? To answer this question, first look at the social psychological factors that apply to police services. Review the subject heading for this chapter and make two lists—one showing how these factors positively affect police training and procedures and the other list showing the negatives. For example, what attributions do police make about themselves, their roles, the community, and criminals? When you have reviewed each area, generate a list of ideas that would help increase the positive and decrease the negative regarding the relations between the police and the community.

2. Stereotypes.

Some stereotypes are positive and some are negative. While most people can see the problems with negative stereotypes, it is more difficult to see the problems that positive stereotypes pose. Choose five groups and indicate two positive stereotypes for each of these groups. After each stereotype, write out the problem(s) that the stereotype creates. For example, the stereotype of the "model minority" applied to Asians can be used as a point of comparison to other groups who have high rates of poverty. Be sure to focus on the problems these stereotypes present in terms of the adjustment for the members of the group being stereotyped.

3. Interview techniques.

Your textbook indicates some of the factors that tend to produce positive results during a job interview. The text also states that the tips given are not a substitute for marketable skills. One way to present the skills you possess is by having a good résumé.

Go to the Internet and research both interview strategies and résumé writing strategies. Go to a search engine such as www.google.com or www.yahoo.com and search for "interview strategies" and "résumé writing" respectively.

Once you have done your research, evaluate your own résumé and interview skills. Make note of the things that you are doing well, and list things you could improve.

4. Promoting health behaviors.

Health professionals have tried various persuasive attempts to get people to change their health behaviors, including quitting smoking, eating better, getting enough sleep, and exercising. Make a list of your positive and negative health behaviors. When you are finished, make a list of the possible ways that you could improve some of your less healthy habits. To get some ideas, go to a search engine such as www.google.com or www.yahoo.com and search for "improving health."

 VIDEO SEGMENT

Asch's and Milgram's experiments on social influence rank among the best-known and most influential studies in social psychology. See a simulation of Asch's experiment on conformity and actual scenes from Milgram's experiment on obedience in the videos for Chapter 6 on the CD-ROM.

Another classic experiment on social influence is Philip Zimbardo's Stanford prison study. Watch the video for Chapter 2 on the CD-ROM to learn about this fascinating and disturbing study.

Do stereotypes harm you? Even if you are not a victim of discrimination, Claude Steele believes that stereotypes can prevent you from doing your best. For a discussion of Steele's concept of stereotype threat, watch the video for Chapter 10 on the CD-ROM.

Communicating Effectively

Learning Goals

1 Describe the basic aspects of interpersonal communication

2 Explain the keys to effective verbal interpersonal communication

3 Describe the elements of nonverbal interpersonal communication

Images of Adjustment

Misunderstanding in Communication

"Judy Scott is applying for a job as an officer manager at the headquarters of an ice-cream distributor—a position she's well qualified for. Her last job, although it was called 'administrative assistant,' actually involved running the whole office, and she did a great job. But at the interview, she never gets a chance to explain this. The interviewer does all the talking . . . Judy leaves feeling frustrated—and she doesn't get the job. . .

"Sandy and Matt have a good marriage. They love each other and are quite happy. But a recurring source of tension is that Sandy often feels that Matt doesn't really listen to her. He asks her a question, but before she can answer, he asks another—or starts to answer it himself. When they get together with Matt's friends, the conversation goes so fast, Sandy can't get a word in edgewise. Afterward, Matt complains that she was too quiet, though she certainly isn't quiet when she gets together with her friends. Matt thinks it's because she doesn't like his friends, but the only reason Sandy doesn't like them is that she feels they ignore her—she can't find a way to get into their conversations" (Tannen, 1986, pp. 18–19).

These descriptions from Deborah Tannen's (1986) book, *That's Not What I Meant*, illustrate the frequent misunderstandings that occur during the routine of everyday encounters. The most interesting aspect of these misunderstandings is that they are avoidable. Whatever our ability or personality, we can learn to communicate more effectively.

In this chapter, we focus on how we communicate with others. As our opening examples illustrate, this aspect of our lives influences everything from whether we obtain the job we want to whether our relationships flourish. It can make a difference in whether other people want to spend time with us or see us as someone to avoid, and whether they love us or even hate us. We begin by exploring the basic nature of communication and then turn to how we communicate verbally and nonverbally. At various junctures, we will examine how interpersonal communication is influenced by culture, ethnicity, and gender.

1 EXPLORING INTERPERSONAL COMMUNICATION

- Messages
  - The Transactional Aspect of Interpersonal Communication
- Context
  - Defining Interpersonal Communication

It would be hard to do much in this life for very long without communicating with someone. We communicate in every social context—in the heat of intense conflict, in the warmth of an intimate exchange, and even in the chill of a faded relationship. Interpersonal communication can be spontaneous or rehearsed, smooth or jagged, profound or negligible in its impact. In this section, we explore the building blocks and characteristics of interpersonal communication; this will lead to a definition of interpersonal communication.

Messages

A teacher tells a student, "You just aren't working hard enough." What are the components of interpersonal communication in this example?

The first component is the **message**—the information being delivered from the sender to the receiver. The **channel**—the mode of communication delivery—is the second component. For example, the teacher's message in this case was delivered verbally, but it could have been delivered in written form or nonverbally with a furrowed brow or a scowl. Scowling is a nonverbal channel for delivering an unfriendly message.

The building blocks of communication also include the processes of **encoding** (the act of producing messages) and **decoding** (the act of understanding messages). Speakers and writers are encoders; listeners and readers are decoders. For interpersonal communication to take place, messages must be both encoded and decoded (Wyer & Adaval, 2003). In the example that opened this chapter, Judy failed to communicate her message because she never encoded it. Our disappointed teacher might be unsuccessful in communicating her message if the student is daydreaming and thus never decodes it (DeVito, 2004).

Many elements may interfere with encoding and decoding (DeFleur & others, 2005). **Noise** is the label given to environmental, physiological, and psychological factors that decrease the likelihood a message will be accurately encoded or decoded. Environmental sources of noise include blaring stereos, the roar of nearby traffic, the yells of a crowd, and even the annoyances of air pollution—that make it difficult to concentrate on what someone is saying.

Physiological sources of noise include hearing problems, poor vision, and any other health condition that can inhibit how effectively a message is transmitted or received. Numerous psychological factors can also influence the accuracy of communication. For example, a depressed student might have such low self-esteem that even a positive message about her performance might not register as a compliment. Another student might be so anxious about the unwanted attention from the teacher

www.mhhe.com/santrockha

Communication Challenges
Interpersonal Communication Books

message The information being delivered from the sender to the receiver.

channel The mode of communication delivery.

encoding The act of producing messages.

decoding The act of understanding messages.

noise Environmental, physiological, and psychological factors that decrease the likelihood a message will be accurately encoded or decoded.

Why is the relationship component important in interpersonal communication?

that he jumps to his own defense before the teacher finishes her message.

Any communication includes both a content and a relationship dimension. In our example, the content is the sender's suggestion that someone needs to buckle down. From the vantage point of the relationship, the teacher's higher academic status and power are important in rendering her communication persuasive. She has the formal power over the student to make such judgments. However, imagine this statement being made by the student to the teacher—even if the content is on target, the message violates the power relationship between a student and a teacher.

Many of the problems people have communicating occur not because of what is said (the content) but because of the implications, especially the power implications, of the relationship (Kelly, Fincham, & Beach, 2003; Guerrero, Anderson, & Afifi, 2001; Rothwell, 2004). For example, if a student living in a dorm asks his roommate to pick up his socks, the student implies that he has the right to have the roommate do this (no matter how politely couched the request!). While the roommate might agree that the request is reasonable, he might fail to comply because he doesn't like the unstated implication that he is being given orders in this relationship. Similar situations occur in couple relationships, as when one member buys something, makes plans for the weekend, or invites a guest to dinner without first asking the other member.

The Transactional Aspect of Communication

In the example of Sandy and Matt that opened this chapter, who is doing the encoding and who is doing the decoding? The answer is not simple because interpersonal communication is **transactional.** This means that communication is an ongoing process between sender and receiver that unfolds over time, and that it is not unusual for information to be communicated almost simultaneously between the participants.

Much of interpersonal communication is not a onetime, brief interaction that lasts several seconds (Hybeis & Weaver, 2004). Rather, most interpersonal communication involves an ongoing volley or parley of verbal and nonverbal actions between the sender and the receiver. Initially person A may be the sender, person B the receiver; then after fifteen seconds, person A may become the receiver and person B the sender; and so on, back and forth, over a period of time. At the same time as person A is sending a message verbally, person B may be sending a message nonverbally.

Let's further consider an excerpt from Sandy and Matt's conversation to see how these transactional characteristics of interpersonal communication might work. Matt comes in from work and asks Sandy, "How come dinner isn't ready yet?" Sandy responds, "I got home late from work myself. It's going to be about an hour before it is ready." Already, in this brief social communication that has taken only about ten seconds, both individuals have served as senders and receivers of messages. When Matt got to the word *dinner* in his sentence, Sandy had begun to give him a blank stare, and by the time he spoke the word *yet,* the stare had a tone of anger as well. Further, by the time Sandy got to the words *an hour before it's ready,* Matt was displaying an angry grimace. Thus, in this interchange, Matt and Sandy were sending and receiving messages simultaneously.

Context

If Matt and Sandy were newly married instead of having been married for several years, their exchange about dinner almost certainly would have been different. Social

transactional Means that communication is an ongoing process between sender and receiver that unfolds over time, and that it is not unusual for information to be communicated almost simultaneously between the participants.

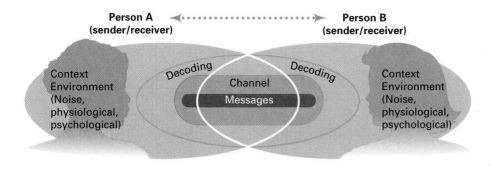

FIGURE 7.1 Some Important Components of Interpersonal Communication

communication always occurs in a *context*, the environment in which messages are sent and received. The context influences the form and content of social communication.

One aspect of the context is the relationship between the people who are communicating. In our earlier example, the content was the teacher's suggestion that someone needs to buckle down. The teacher's academic status and formal power over the student gave weight to this judgment. Imagine this statement being made by the student to the teacher: even if the content is on target, the message violates the power relationship between a student and a teacher.

The sociocultural dimensions of context are especially important for understanding interpersonal communication (Baney, 2004; Bonvillain, 2002; Gudykunst, 2004; Jandt, 2004). For example, when people from different cultural and ethnic groups interact, they might follow different rules of communication. This can produce confusion, unintentional insults, inaccurate perceptions, and other miscommunications (Martin & Nakayama, 2004).

The importance of paying attention to cultural context has sometimes escaped manufacturers trying to capture a world market (Petras & Petras, 1994). For example, the brand name *Coca-Cola* translates to the Chinese consumer as "Bite the wax tadpole." Japanese beverages have been marketed in the West with the names *Kolic, Ucc, Mucos,* and *Pocari Sweat.* Obviously, successful international marketing requires attention to the rich dimensions of language.

Defining Interpersonal Communication

Now that we have examined the main components and characteristics of interpersonal communication, we can define it. **Interpersonal communication** is an ongoing transactional process that involves at least two individuals, each of whom acts as both sender and receiver, encoding and decoding messages, sometimes simultaneously. These messages are sent through verbal or nonverbal channels. Noise can limit the accuracy of a communication. Communication always takes place in a context. See figure 7.1 for a visual depiction of these important components of communication.

Review and Reflect

1 **Describe the basic aspects of interpersonal communication**

REVIEW

- What are some key aspects of messages?
- Why is interpersonal communication described as transactional?
- How does context influence communication?
- How can interpersonal communication be defined?

REFLECT

- How effectively do you communicate with people from cultures different from yours? Give an example in which you feel that you did a good job at this and another example in which you didn't do as well.

interpersonal communication An ongoing transactional process that involves at least two individuals, each of whom acts as both sender and receiver, encoding and decoding messages, sometimes simultaneously. The messages can be sent through verbal or nonverbal channels with noise and context possibly influencing their accuracy.

2) VERBAL INTERPERSONAL COMMUNICATION

Speaking Skills

Listening Skills

Self-Disclosure

Conflict and Assertiveness

Gender and Verbal Communication

Barriers to Effective Verbal Communication

In discussing channels of communication, we indicated that messages are transmitted verbally or nonverbally. Let's explore verbal communication first.

Virtually every day of our lives we talk to other people, and they to us. How can we make all of these words effective? We need to develop speaking and listening skills and learn to deal with self-disclosure, conflict, and some common barriers to effective verbal communication.

Speaking Skills

When your speech is clear and accurate, your listener is more likely to understand what you mean. Of course, what is clear to one person may be confusing to another. Speakers often must establish context for the listener by providing an explicit introduction to the message that will follow. To communicate effectively, you need to consider the background, needs, abilities, and other characteristics of your listeners.

For one thing, your listeners influence which words are appropriate for your message. Keep in mind that words have denotative and connotative meanings. **Denotation** is the objective meaning of words; **connotation** is the subjective meaning. Consider the word *death* (DeVito, 2004). For a doctor, the meaning of *death* might be "the cessation of frontal brain activity," but its connotative meaning might be "the enemy." Some words—such as *parallel*—have few connotations; their meaning is mainly denotative. Other words—such as *commitment*—have many connotations. If the labels *good* and *bad* don't seem to apply to a word, then it has little connotative meaning for you—but it still might have connotative meaning for other people.

The connotative meaning of words may vary considerably from person to person. To communicate effectively, be sure to consider the connotative meanings of words for your listeners. Think back to the example that opened this chapter. To Judy's interviewer, the title "administrative assistant" had connotations of a relatively low-level person who took orders, had little authority, and would not be suitable for a managerial position.

The more concrete our word choices, the more people are likely to agree on their meaning. The more abstract the words we use, the greater the chances for varied interpretations. When we use abstract words too often and deliver too many connotative messages, communication becomes unclear. The result may be breakdowns in communication, misunderstanding, and difficulty in relationships.

Some people try to impress others by using technical terms or obscure words. Former secretary of state Alexander Haig set new records for obscurity with comments like "At the moment, we are subsumed in the vortex of criticality." The intelligent speaker uses words that are clear and whose meaning the listener can readily understand.

Good speakers also avoid hackneyed phrases. In his book *Strictly Speaking*, television commentator Edwin Newman (1974) gave these examples from sports announcers and coaches.

denotation The objective meaning of words.

connotation The subjective meaning of words.

- "We stopped them pretty good."
- "They read the papers pretty good for our remarks."
- "The loser might have been able to make up for their deficits except they were hurting pretty good."

Suffice it to say that there are a few too many "pretty goods" on the lips of sportscasters and coaches.

Messages are conveyed more effectively when spoken in a simple rather than a complex way, a concrete rather than an abstract way, and a specific rather than a general way. When you do want to convey ideas that are abstract, general, or complex, use appropriate examples to illustrate the ideas. Often the best examples are those that listeners can relate to their own personal experiences. For instance, if Margaret is trying to explain to some friends who do not know what feminism is what it is like to be a feminist, it will help if she gives examples of what she means by feminism—such as favoring equal opportunities regardless of gender—and then has her listeners think of other friends of theirs who are feminists.

Good speakers also make their verbal and nonverbal messages consistent. If you say one thing and nonverbally communicate the opposite, you are likely to create confusion and distrust. For example, if you are trying to explain why you didn't get a report in on time to your boss and you look down at the floor while you are talking to her rather than maintain eye contact, the boss might be less likely to believe you, even though you may have had a legitimate reason for being late with the report. Later in the chapter we discuss a variety of nonverbal behaviors that people use during interpersonal communication.

Listening Skills

Listening is an important aspect of interpersonal communication that we often overlook when seeking to become better communicators (Wood, 2004). By looking at figure 7.2, you can see that in one study, college students spent more than 50 percent of their communication time in listening (Barker & others, 1981). Most of us could use some help in this very important dimension of interpersonal communication.

How good a listener are you? **Hearing** is a physiological sensory process in which auditory sensations are received to the ears and transmitted by the brain. On the other hand, **listening** is the psychological process of interpreting and understanding what someone says. In other words, you can hear what another person is saying without really listening to the person. One teenager put it this way: "My friends listen to what I say, but my parents only hear me talk."

We spend a lot of time listening, but whether we listen as effectively as we could is another matter. In actual conversations, most of us probably aren't very good listeners. Given all the time we spend listening, working on our listening skills would seem well worth the effort.

Listening Skills
Be an Effective Listener

"If you can hear me, give me a sign."

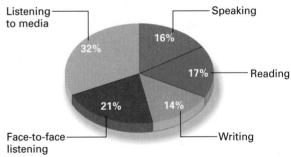

FIGURE 7.2 Percentage of Time Spent by College Students in Different Communication Activities

---

Adjustment Strategies
For Becoming a Better Listener

To become a better listener, try these basic strategies for good listening:

1. ***Don't hog the conversation.*** Simply talking less than you usually do can facilitate better listening. As Zeno of Citum said in 300 B.C., "The reason we have two ears and only one mouth is so we can listen more and talk less."

hearing A physiological sensory process in which auditory sensations are received by the ears and transmitted by the brain.

listening The psychological process of interpreting and understanding what someone says.

continued

2. *Pay careful attention to the person who is talking.* Paying attention shows the other person that you are interested in what she or he has to say. Adopt body language that shows respect to the speaker. For example, in Western cultures, better listeners face the speaker squarely, incline the body in a relaxed manner toward the speaker (rather than leaning back or slouching in a chair), and maintain eye contact with the speaker. More about these important aspects of nonverbal communication, including the influence of cultural contexts, appears later in this chapter.

3. *Use reflective skills.* **Reflective listening** is a strategy in which the listener restates the feelings or content of the speaker's message in a way that indicates acceptance and understanding. Reflective listening was especially emphasized by Carl Rogers (1980), who described *growth-promoting listeners* as individuals who are genuine in revealing their own feelings, accepting of others' feelings, and empathetic, sensitive, reflective listeners. One technique that can be used in reflective listening is **paraphrasing**, a concise restatement of the essence of the speaker's own words. Here is an example of paraphrasing:

Maria: "I just don't know. Maybe I should have a baby, maybe not. Bill isn't sure either. I like my work, but I think I would like to be a mother too. I keep feeling pulled back and forth on what to do."

Donata: "You seem like you feel some conflict about what to do—on the one hand you like your work a lot and don't want to quit that, but you also really want a baby too."

Maria: "That's right."

4. *Actively synthesize the themes and patterns you hear.* The conversational landscape can become strewn with bits and pieces of information that aren't tied together in meaningful ways. A good reflective listener periodically pulls together a *summative reflection* of the main themes and feelings the speaker has expressed over a reasonably long conversation or even several conversations that span several meetings. These sentence stems can help you get started in giving reflective summation:

- "One theme you seem to keep coming back to is . . . "
- "Let's go over the ground we've been covering so far . . . "
- "I've been thinking about what you have said. Let me see if the following is what you mean . . . "

5. *Give feedback in a competent manner.* Feedback involves sending a message back to the speaker regarding your reaction. Feedback gives the speaker an idea of how much progress he or she is making in getting an idea across. Good listeners give feedback to the speaker quickly, honestly, clearly, and informatively.

	Known to self	Not known to self
Known to others	Open self	Blind self
Not known to others	Hidden self	Unknown self

FIGURE 7.3 The Johari Window

reflective listening A strategy in which the listener restates the feelings or content of the speaker's message in a way that indicates acceptance and understanding.

paraphrasing A concise restatement of the essence of the speaker's own words.

self-disclosure The communication of intimate details about ourselves.

Johari Window A model of self-disclosure that helps us understand the proportion of information about ourselves that we and others are aware of.

Self-Disclosure

Just as some people talk too much in communicating with others, some people don't talk enough. Some people are especially reluctant to engage in **self-disclosure,** the communication of intimate details about ourselves. Self-disclosure involves revealing any of those things that are important to us but we are not willing to share with just anyone.

The Johari Window   Self-disclosure is not a simple behavior; the Johari Window captures its complexity (Pearson & others, 2003). The **Johari Window** is a model of self-disclosure that helps us understand the proportion of information about ourselves that we and others are aware of. It is divided into four basic areas, or quadrants: the open self, the hidden self, the blind self, and the unknown self (see figure 7.3):

- The *open self* reflects information about yourself known to you and to others. This might include your name, your sex, your religious affiliation, and where you live.
- The *hidden self* consists of information you are aware of but have not shared with others. This might include something you are ashamed about, such as cheating on a test or a private fantasy.
- The *blind self* is made up of information that others know about you but you do not. The blind self might include unpleasant aspects of yourself, such as being self-centered, bragging about your talents, or interrupting others.
- The *unknown self* includes information that no one—not you or anyone else—knows. For example, sometimes alcoholics have an unknown self involved in their addiction—they hide their alcoholism from others and are not willing to admit to themselves that they have a drinking problem.

What are some good adjustment strategies related to self-disclosure?

Self-Disclosure in Relationships Self-disclosure has a special power to deepen relationships. We usually don't engage in self-disclosure as much in the early part of relationships. As relationships deepen, one person will disclose something, then the other person will, and so on, back and forth, until friends and lovers eventually arrive at deeper intimacy.

A series of simple low-risk self-disclosures may be enough to stimulate a friendship or dating relationship, but deeper relationships usually demand risky self-disclosures, which leave you vulnerable (Baney, 2004). We engage in *risky self-disclosures* when we tell someone about a private thought, an embarrassing impulse, a romantic feeling, a dream for the future, or a truth we have previously concealed. An irony of close relationships is that such risky revelations not only give away power and leave us vulnerable, but also bring us strength and protection. Special confessions—confessions that are not necessarily about cardinal sins but rather unveil a person's inner life—sometimes connect hearts. Some of the possible risks of self-disclosure are listed in figure 7.4.

Self-disclosure is not easy for many people—males, in particular, often have a difficult time talking about their innermost feelings. In some instances, mental health problems develop because individuals are unwilling, too fearful, or do not have the ability to disclose psychologically painful facts to friends or family.

Disclosing psychologically painful information requires that we trust the listener. Privacy, a nonjudgmental ear, empathic understanding, and a common bond all increase the chances that an individual will engage in self-disclosure. For some people,

Indifference	In some situations when we disclose ourselves, others are indifferent to us and show no interest in getting to know us.
Rejection	When we reveal information about ourselves to others, they might reject us.
Loss of Control	Sometimes others use information we divulge about ourselves to control us.
Betrayal	When we self-disclose, we assume, or sometimes even explicitly request, that the information be treated confidentially. Sometimes our listeners betray our confidence and divulge what we've told them to someone else.

FIGURE 7.4 Some Self-Disclosure Risks

the feeling of psychological safety needed to disclose psychologically painful or embarrassing information never comes. These people might never be able to develop or maintain strong relationships with friends and lovers.

Might we self-disclose too much too soon in some cases, though? Too much self-disclosure or self-disclosure that comes too early in a relationship can damage the relationship. How do you know what is an appropriate disclosure? Individuals who are inexperienced in self-disclosing are most likely to overdisclose or underdisclose. Underdisclosers often bore others; overdisclosers scare people off. Look carefully for a reaction in others when you self-disclose; you hope that they will show interest and self-disclose in return. Researchers have found that a moderate amount of intimate disclosures often facilitates a relationship (Jourard, 1971).

Adjustment Strategies
For Increasing Self-Disclosure

If you want to disclose more about yourself to someone, how do you begin?

1. ***Proceed gradually.*** Don't rush out and unveil all of your darkest life moments to someone. Self-disclosure usually proceeds gradually, with one person turning a minimally threatening private thought into a revelation to a friend or lover, then the friend or lover reciprocates with a minor revelation. Eventually, each of you may reach a point at which you feel it is psychologically safe to reveal more painful or embarrassing truths.
2. ***Recognize that people have different levels of intimacy needs.*** Some people feel a lot more comfortable divulging private information about themselves than others do. There is no level of intimacy that is perfect for everyone.
3. ***Begin with facts.*** Learning how to self-disclose more effectively usually works best when you start with facts and later move on to thoughts, feelings, and needs (McKay, Davis, & Fanning, 1995). First, you might choose an acquaintance and tell him or her about your job, your last vacation, or an interesting experience. Stick to the facts.
4. ***When you are comfortable at disclosing facts, then include your thoughts, feelings, and needs.*** Refer to Self-Assessment 7.1 to find topics for this step. You might talk about your tastes in music, your work ambitions, and so on. In addition to the facts, say what you think about the matter, how you feel about it, and what needs you have regarding it.
5. ***Try here-and-now communication.*** After you feel comfortable disclosing facts, thoughts, and needs, consider moving on to the most difficult point in self-disclosure: here-and-now communications. Take the risk of sharing with the other person what you think, feel, and need right now. For example, you can talk about how you are feeling attracted to the other person, how his or her responses are affecting you, how you are holding something back, how relaxed or nervous you are feeling, and so on. Remember, though, don't jump into here-and-now communication too soon. Do it gradually.

Conflict and Assertiveness

Being competent at self-disclosure is an important aspect of verbal communication. So is dealing with conflict, which is inevitable in everyday communication. People deal with conflict in one of four basic ways—aggressively, manipulatively, passively, and assertively:

- *Aggressive Communication.* Aggressive individuals are often angry, abrasive, and try to make themselves look good at the expense of others. They often are insensitive to others' feelings.

SELF-ASSESSMENT 7.1

How Much Do I Self-Disclose?

Read each item on the left and then indicate how you have talked about it to your mother, father, mate, and best friends. If your parents are dead or you can't think of anyone to fill the friends or mates categories, leave those blank. Use this rating scale:

0 = Have told the other person *nothing* about this aspect of me.
1 = Have talked in *general terms* about this. The other person knows some of the facts, but not the complete message.
2 = Have told the other person about this *completely,* including my observations, thoughts, feelings, and needs.
X = Have *lied* or misrepresented myself regarding this aspect. The other person has a false picture of me.

	Mother	Father	Mate	Best Female Friend	Best Male Friend
Tastes and Interests					
My favorite foods and beverages and food dislikes.	_____	_____	_____	_____	_____
My likes and dislikes in music.	_____	_____	_____	_____	_____
My favorite reading matter.	_____	_____	_____	_____	_____
The kinds of movies and TV shows I like.	_____	_____	_____	_____	_____
The style of house, and kinds of furnishings I like best.	_____	_____	_____	_____	_____
The kind of party or social gathering I like best.	_____	_____	_____	_____	_____
Attitudes and Opinions					
What I think and feel about religion.	_____	_____	_____	_____	_____
My views on racial integration in schools.	_____	_____	_____	_____	_____
My personal views on drinking.	_____	_____	_____	_____	_____
My personal views on sexual morality.	_____	_____	_____	_____	_____
My personal standards of beauty and attractiveness in women.	_____	_____	_____	_____	_____
The things I regard as desirable for a man to be.	_____	_____	_____	_____	_____
Work (or Studies)					
What I enjoy most.	_____	_____	_____	_____	_____
What I enjoy least.	_____	_____	_____	_____	_____
What I feel are my shortcomings and handicaps.	_____	_____	_____	_____	_____
What I feel are my special strong points.	_____	_____	_____	_____	_____
How I feel my work is appreciated by others.	_____	_____	_____	_____	_____
My ambitions and goals in my work.	_____	_____	_____	_____	_____

continued

- *Manipulative Communication.* Manipulative individuals try to get what they want from others by making other people feel sorry for them or feel guilty.
- *Passive Communication.* Passive individuals act in submissive, inhibited, and nonassertive ways. They let others run over them without ever expressing their feelings or letting others know what they want.
- *Assertive Communication.* Assertive individuals act in their own best interests. They stand up for their legitimate rights, expressing their views directly and openly.

How Much Do I Self-Disclose? (concluded)

	Mother	Father	Mate	Best Female Friend	Best Male Friend
Money					
How much money I make at my work, or get as an allowance.	_____	_____	_____	_____	_____
Whether or not I owe money; if so, how much and to whom.	_____	_____	_____	_____	_____
Whether or not I have savings, and the amount.	_____	_____	_____	_____	_____
Whether or not others owe me money; the amount and who owes it to me.	_____	_____	_____	_____	_____
Whether or not I gamble, and how much.	_____	_____	_____	_____	_____
All of my present sources of income.	_____	_____	_____	_____	_____
Personality					
The aspects of my personality I dislike.	_____	_____	_____	_____	_____
The feelings I have trouble expressing or controlling.	_____	_____	_____	_____	_____
The facts of my present sex life.	_____	_____	_____	_____	_____
Whether or not I'm attractive to the opposite sex.	_____	_____	_____	_____	_____
Things in the past or present I feel guilty about.	_____	_____	_____	_____	_____
What I fear most.	_____	_____	_____	_____	_____
Body					
My feelings about the appearance of my face.	_____	_____	_____	_____	_____
How I wish I looked.	_____	_____	_____	_____	_____
My feelings about different parts of my body.	_____	_____	_____	_____	_____
Whether or not I have any health problems.	_____	_____	_____	_____	_____
My past record of illness and treatment.	_____	_____	_____	_____	_____
Whether or not I make a special effort to keep fit, healthy, and attractive.	_____	_____	_____	_____	_____

Go to the appendix at the end of the book for scoring and interpretation of your responses.

Which styles seem to characterize Judy, Sandy, and Matt, who were described at the beginning of this chapter? To evaluate which of the four communication styles for dealing with conflict characterizes you, complete Self-Assessment 7.2. Of the four communication styles for dealing with conflict, being assertive is clearly the best choice (Albert & Emmons, 1995).

In most cultures in the past, women were likely to be socialized to be too nonassertive and men to be too aggressive. As part of changing gender roles in the United States and other Western countries, more women are becoming assertive and more men are making the choice to move away from being aggressive to being assertive. Assertive men feel comfortable with themselves and don't have to put others down to enhance themselves. In contrast, aggressive men often try to demonstrate their manhood by being dominating, showing little concern for others' feelings. Our society would benefit by increasingly valuing assertiveness in both women and men.

SELF-ASSESSMENT 7.2

What Is My Communication Style?

Think about each of the following situations. Check which style you tend to use in each.

	Assertive	Aggressive	Manipulative	Passive
You're being kept on the phone by a salesperson trying to sell you something you don't want.				
You want to break off a relationship that no longer works for you.				
You're sitting in a movie and the people behind you are talking.				
Your doctor keeps you waiting more than 20 minutes.				
You're standing in line and someone moves in front of you.				
Your friend has owed you money for a long time and it's money you could use.				
You receive food at a restaurant that is over- or undercooked.				
You want to ask your friend, romantic partner, or roommate for a major favor.				
Your friend asks you to do something that you don't feel like doing.				
You're at a large lecture. The instructor is speaking too softly and you know other students are also having trouble hearing her.				
You want to start a conversation at a gathering, but you don't know anyone there.				
You're sitting next to someone who is smoking, and the smoke bothers you.				
You're talking to someone about something important to you, but they don't seem to be listening.				
You're speaking and someone interrupts you.				
You receive an unjust criticism from someone.				

Go to the appendix at the end of the book for scoring and interpretation of your responses.

Adjustment Strategies
For Becoming More Assertive

Some strategies for becoming more assertive include the following (Bourne, 1995):

1. ***Evaluate your rights.*** Examine your rights in the particular situation.
2. ***Designate a time for discussing what you want.*** You may need to be assertive on the spot, but if not, find a mutually convenient time to discuss the problem with the other person.
3. ***State the problem in terms of how it might affect you.*** Describe your view clearly to let the other person get a better sense of your position. Go over the problem as clearly as possible in a calm manner.

continued

4. *Describe the problem objectively.* Do not blame or judge the other person.
5. *Express your feelings about the situation.* Let the other person know how you feel without letting your feelings get out of hand.
6. *Ask for what you want.* An important aspect of being assertive is making your request in a frank, candid manner.

Gender and Verbal Communication

As we just noted, females have often been less assertive and males more aggressive in their communication. Indeed, gender plays a special role in interpersonal communication. In many cultures, gender roles dictate how people should talk to each other depending on whether the sender and receiver are both males, both females, or male and female (Ivy & Backlund, 2004; Wood, 2004).

John Gray's (1992) best-selling book *Men Are from Mars, Women Are from Venus* claims that the communication patterns of males and females are so dramatically different that it is as if they were from different planets. However, Gray's book is mainly based on speculation and informal observations (Matlin, 2004). In reality, there is far more variation in verbal communication patterns *within* each gender than Gray acknowledges (Aries, 1998). Recent studies, however, do find gender differences in communication. For example, one study of a sampling of students' e-mails found that people could guess the writer's gender two-thirds of the time (Thompson & Murachver, 2001). Another study revealed that women make 63 percent of phone calls and when talking to another woman stay on the phone longer (7.2 minutes) than men do when talking with other men (4.6 minutes) (Smoreda & Licoppe, 2000). Note, though, that this does not mean all women engage in these verbal patterns more than all men. There are substantial variations within each gender (Hyde, 2004). Let's explore some of the categories of verbal communication to see what gender differences do exist.

Rapport Talk   Deborah Tannen (1990) analyzed the talk of women and men. She reports that wives—like Sandy in the example at the beginning of the chapter—often complain about their husbands: "He doesn't listen to me anymore" and "He doesn't talk to me anymore." Lack of communication, though high on women's lists of reasons for divorce, is mentioned much less often by men. The problem might not be with individual men but with the difference in women's and men's styles of communication, and both men and women can make adjustments to improve communication.

To clarify gender differences in communication, Tannen distinguishes rapport talk from report talk. **Rapport talk** is conversation aimed at establishing connections and negotiating relationships. Women enjoy rapport talk more than men do, and men's lack of interest in rapport talk bothers many women. In contrast, **report talk** is talk that is designed to give information, which includes public speaking. Men prefer to engage in report talk. Men hold center stage through such verbal performances as telling stories and jokes. They learn to use talk as a way of getting and keeping attention.

Women's dissatisfaction with men's silence at home is captured in a typical cartoon setting: a husband and wife sitting at the breakfast table. He's opening a newspaper and asking his wife, "Is there anything you want to say to me before I begin reading the newspaper?" To him, talk is for information. So when his wife interrupts his reading, it must be to inform him of something he needs to know—so she might as well tell him what she thinks he needs to know before he starts reading. But for her, talk is for interaction. She believes that saying things is a way to show involvement; listening is a way to show caring and interest.

In sum, Tannen, concludes that females are more relationship oriented than males—and that this relationship orientation should be prized as a skill in our culture

"You have no idea how nice it is to have someone to talk to."

Copyright © 1964 Don Orehek. Reprinted with permission.

rapport talk   Conversation aimed at establishing connections and negotiating relationships.

report talk   Talk that is designed to give information, which includes public speaking.

more than it currently is. Note, however, that some researchers criticize Tannen's ideas as being overly simplified and that communication between males and females is more complex than Tannen indicates (Edwards & Hamilton, 2004). Further, some researchers have found in males' and females' relationship communication strategies. In one recent study, in their talk men and women described and responded to relationship problems in ways that were more similar than different (MacGeorge & others, 2004).

Self-Disclosure   Gender plays an important role in self-disclosure (Bruess & Pearson, 1996). Women tend to hone their self-disclosure skills and learn to trust the relationship-enhancing qualities of self-disclosure in their same-sex peer/friendship relationships. In peer/friendship relationships that emphasize competition and challenge, males often avoid revealing weaknesses and at times associate self-disclosure with loss of control and vulnerability. Thus, females and males not only reveal different preferences for and patterns of self-disclosure but also interpret the meaning and purpose of self-disclosure differently (Wood, 2004).

Interruptions   Do men interrupt more frequently than women? In many situations, they do. When an interrupter takes over a conversation, it is more likely to be a man than a woman (Matlin, 2004). Men also interrupt more than women do in conversations with relative strangers (Johnson, 1994).

Barriers to Effective Verbal Communication

Mike says, "Well, I messed up again. I took my wife and children to visit my parents last week. I told myself beforehand that I wouldn't fall into the trap of letting my parents get to me by criticizing the way I raise my children. I reminded myself I would bite my tongue when my mother told me I was too hard on them. We weren't there two hours when my mother started in on me. I told her she hadn't done such a great job with my sister and me. It emotionally exhausted me."

All too often, as in Mike's situation with his parents, we want to communicate better with others but we don't (DeVito, 2004; Wilmot & Hocker, 2001; Wood, 2004). What are some of the specific barriers to interpersonal communication? They fall into three main categories: judging, proposing solutions, and avoiding the other's concerns (Bolton, 1979).

Judging   Humanistic psychologist Carl Rogers (1961) once commented that the main roadblock to effective interpersonal communication is the tendency to make judgments—to approve or disapprove of the other person's statements. Judging is a barrier to effective communication that may take the form of criticizing, name-calling, labeling, and praising evaluatively.

Criticizing is one barrier to effective communication. Many of us think that if we don't criticize others, they will never get rid of their problems. Marital partners think they have to criticize their spouse's behaviors they don't like or she or he will never learn satisfying courses of action. One wife described her husband as being on a constant fault-finding mission. Among the husband's comments were "You are always leaving stuff out on the counter," "Why aren't you more responsible?" and "You never pick up your clothes." Such criticisms present a serious barrier to effective communication, because the person being judged stays chronically angry or loses self-esteem and withdraws.

Name-calling and *labeling* are other judgmental roadblocks to effective interpersonal communication. Calling

What are some barriers to effective communication?

someone a "loser," "immature," "sloppy," "dumb," "lazy," "boring," or a "jerk" introduces a negative atmosphere that can damage a relationship. One alternative to using negative labels is to describe specific behaviors that you object to. On the other hand, using positive labels—such *as bright, attractive, responsible, hardworking,* and *dedicated*—usually adds positive undertones to conversation.

However, though we often think that all praise is helpful, sometimes people use praise manipulatively. Some people say only nice things, especially about you, when they are talking with you. It is one thing to think positively and to say nice things to other people; it is quite another *always* to do this and to do it in a manipulative attempt to gain the other person's favor.

Proposing Solutions

Another set of barriers to effective communication involves proposing solutions for other people to adopt. Proposing solutions may take the form of advice, questioning, order, threat, and moralizing.

Advice can be constructive or destructive in relationships. What's wrong with giving advice? Advice too often implies a lack of confidence in the other person. Advice can come across as a message like this: "You have been making a big deal out of a problem whose solution is very apparent to me. How stupid you are." It is natural to fall into the trap of giving advice when you feel a need to help others, especially those you care about most. A safer strategy is first to ask if advice would be helpful. This shows greater respect for the person with the problem.

Orders have several possible outcomes, all harmful to effective communication. When ordered to do something, people often become angry or resentful, or they become passive, which is unhealthy in a relationship. People can also adopt a passive-aggressive response to orders, passively agreeing to comply with the orders but not following through. Ordering someone to do something suggests that the other person has made a poor decision.

Threats imply that punishment will result if the person does not go along. Like orders, threats suggest the other person has poor judgment.

Too many of us also try to *moralize* in the solutions we offer to others. Moralizing often includes words like *should* and *ought.* Other instances of moralizing include "You don't call me enough," "It's the wrong thing for you to do," "You are not a very moral person when you do that," and "You are a liar." Too often moralizing *demoralizes* by increasing anxiety and resentment.

Avoiding the Other's Concerns

A third set of barriers to effective communication involves avoiding the other person's concerns. This avoidance may be accomplished through diversion or logical argument.

The phrase *speaking of . . .* frequently signals the beginning of diverting. Consider the following example of diverting,

Person A: "I've been feeling a lot of stress lately."

Person B: "Speaking of stress, I was talking to someone yesterday and that's all she talked about. She was really stressed."

Person C: "Who was that?"

Person B: "Oh, that was Samantha. Her husband lost his job, you know. And they are having trouble making ends meet."

Person D: "Speaking of someone who lost a job, I know someone who lost her job six months ago and still doesn't have one."

Whatever happened to the stressful feelings of Person A? That person got lost in diversions created by the conversation's other participants.

One-upping is a particularly harmful form of diversion. Rather than respond to the speaker's concerns, the one-upper redirects the focus to her or his own concerns. A common one-up response is "You think that's bad, wait till you hear what happened to me!"

Another way of avoiding the other's concerns is to try to solve the communication problem with logical argument. We usually want to use the best logic possible when we solve problems. However, too often when one person tries to foist *logical solutions* to conflict on another person, the second person's feelings are ignored. Logic does not deal in feelings. In one couple's relationship, the husband likes to say, "Well, here is the way to think logically about this. Now listen carefully, and we will go through how to solve this disagreement logically." Of course, the logic is always according to his way of thinking about the disagreement and does not take into account his wife's feelings.

In sum, there are numerous ways we can spoil conversations. Further examples of these spoilers are presented in figure 7.5.

Arguments are characterized by many of the conversation spoilers because arguments express oppositional views rather than open dialogue. Everyone argues now and then, but some people may tend to argue more than others. To evaluate your own argumentativeness, complete Self-Assessment 7.3.

FIGURE 7.5 Eleven Conversation Spoilers That Can Undermine Effective Verbal Interpersonal Communication

	Communication spoiler	Its nature	Examples
Judging	Criticizing	Making a negative evaluation of the other person, his or her actions, or attitudes.	"You brought it on yourself—you've got no one else to blame for the mess you're in."
	Name-calling and labeling	"Putting down" or stereotyping the other person.	"What a dope!" "Just like a woman…" "Egghead." "You hardhats are all alike." "You are just another insensitive male."
	Praising evaluatively	Making a positive judgment of the other person, his or her actions, or attitudes with the intent to manipulate.	"You are always such a good girl. I know you will help me with the lawn."
Proposing solutions	Advising	Giving the other person the solution to his or her problem.	"If I were you, I'd sure turn him off." "That's an easy one to solve. First…"
	Excessive/ inappropriate questioning	Asking questions that often can be answered in just a few words, usually just "yes" or "no."	"Are you sorry you did it?" "Who is to blame…?"
	Ordering	Commanding the other person to do what you want to have done.	"Do your homework right now." "Why? Because I said so."
	Threatening	Trying to control the other person's actions by warning of negative consequences that you will instigate.	"You'll do it or else…" "Stop that noise right now or else…"
Avoiding others' concerns	Moralizing	Telling another person what he or she *should* do. "Preaching" at the other.	"You *shouldn't* get a divorce; think of what will happen to the children." "You *ought* to tell him you are sorry."
	Diverting	Pushing the other person's problems aside through distraction.	"Don't dwell on it. Let's talk about something more pleasant."
	One-upping	Displacing the other's problems with your own concerns.	"Something much worse happened to me."
	Logical argument	Attempting to convince the other with an appeal to facts or logic, usually without considering the emotional factors involved.	"Look at the facts; if you hadn't bought that new car, we could have made the down payment on the house."

SELF-ASSESSMENT 7.3

How Argumentative Am I?

Instructions

This questionnaire contains statements about arguing controversial issues. Indicate how often each statement is true for you personally by placing the appropriate number in the blank to the left of the statement:

1 = Almost never true   2 = Rarely true   3 = Occasionally true
4 = Often true   5 = Almost always true

Items

_____ 1. While in an argument, I worry that the person I am arguing with will form a negative impression of me.

_____ 2. Arguing over controversial issues improves my intelligence.

_____ 3. I enjoy avoiding arguments.

_____ 4. I am energetic and enthusiastic when I argue.

_____ 5. Once I finish an argument I promise myself that I will not get into another.

_____ 6. Arguing with a person creates more problems for me than it solves.

_____ 7. I have a pleasant, good feeling when I win a point in an argument.

_____ 8. When I finish arguing with someone I feel nervous and upset.

_____ 9. I enjoy a good argument over a controversial issue.

_____ 10. I get an unpleasant feeling when I realize I am about to get into an argument.

_____ 11. I enjoy defending my point of view on an issue.

_____ 12. I am happy when I keep an argument from happening.

_____ 13. I do not like to miss the opportunity to argue a controversial issue.

_____ 14. I prefer being with people who rarely disagree with me.

_____ 15. I consider an argument an exciting intellectual challenge.

_____ 16. I find myself unable to think of effective points during an argument.

_____ 17. I feel refreshed and satisfied after an argument on a controversial issue.

_____ 18. I have the ability to do well in an argument.

_____ 19. I try to avoid getting into arguments.

_____ 20. I feel excitement when I expect that a conversation I am in is leading to an argument.

Go to the appendix at the end of the book for scoring and interpretation of your responses.

Adjustment Strategies
For Effective Verbal Expression

Matthew McKay, Martha Davis, and Patrick Fanning (1995) recommend these strategies for effective verbal expression:

1. ***Make your message direct.*** Be aware of when you need to say something and "don't assume people know what you think or want . . . In fact, you should assume

that people are poor mind readers and haven't the faintest idea what goes on inside you," pp. 43–44. Also, don't tell third parties in the hope that the target person will eventually get the message. The original message often gets distorted in third-party communications.

2. ***Deliver your message immediately.*** If you are hurt or angry, delaying communication can often increase the intensity of feelings. "Your anger may smoulder and your frustrated need become a chronic irritant," p. 44. If you communicate immediately, people discover what you need and can adapt their behavior, and the communication may increase intimacy.

3. ***Make your message clear.*** A clear message is a complete and accurate reflection of your thoughts, feelings, needs, and observations. You don't leave things out. You don't fudge by being vague or abstract," p. 45.

4. ***Deliver a straight message.*** "A straight message is one in which the stated purpose is identical with the real purpose of the communication. Disguised intentions and hidden agendas destroy intimacy because they put you in a position of manipulating rather than relating to people," p. 47.

5. ***Make your message supportive.*** Being supportive means that you want the other person to understand what you are saying, not to hurt that person, or aggrandize yourself. To keep from hurting the other person, don't use negative global labels (such as *"stupid," "ugly," "selfish," "evil," "worthless,"* and *"lazy"*), don't be sarcastic, don't drag up the past (which hurts any chance of understanding how each of you feels), don't make negative comparisons (such as "Why don't you keep the grass mowed like other men in the neighborhood?"), don't use judgmental "you" messages (such as "You don't care about me"), and don't make threats. (Source: McKay, Davis, & Fanning, 1995, pp. 43–49)

Review and Reflect

2 **Explain the keys to effective verbal interpersonal communication**

REVIEW

- What are some important aspects of speaking skills?
- What are some important aspects of listening skills?
- What role does self-disclosure play in interpersonal communication?
- What are four ways of dealing with conflict in communication?
- Do men and women communicate differently?
- What are some barriers to effective verbal communication?

REFLECT

- Which of the barriers to verbal interpersonal communication stand out in your conversations? Which of the barriers do you use? What can you do to improve your verbal interpersonal communication skills?

3 NONVERBAL INTERPERSONAL COMMUNICATION

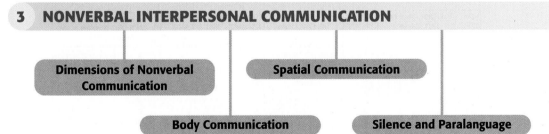

Dimensions of Nonverbal Communication

Spatial Communication

Body Communication

Silence and Paralanguage

Nonverbal communication refers to messages that are transmitted from one person to another by other than linguistic means. These other means include body communication (gestures, facial expressions, eye communication, and touch), spatial communication, and paralanguage (such as the tone of a person's voice) (Andersen, 1999; Pearson & others, 2003).

You might lift an eyebrow for disbelief, rub your nose for puzzlement, clasp your arms to isolate or to protect yourself, shrug your shoulders for indifference, wink one eye for intimacy, tap your fingers for impatience, and slap your forehead for forgetfulness. Some communication experts believe that a majority of our interpersonal communication is nonverbal—even a whopping 93 percent in one estimate (Mehrabian & Wiener, 1967). Let's examine some general characteristics of nonverbal communication and then explore more specifically how we use different parts of our body to communicate.

Dimensions of Nonverbal Communication

Nonverbal communication is complex (Burgoon & Bacue, 2003; Patterson, 2003). It often is spontaneous and ambiguous, but it always sends a message (Costanzo & Archer, 1995). Nonverbal communication tends to be coordinated in clusters, and it might send a different message than verbal communication is sending. Nonverbal communication is strongly influenced by cultural context.

Characteristics of Nonverbal Communication   Even if you are sitting in a corner silently reading a book, your nonverbal behavior is communicating something—perhaps that you want to be left alone or that you are intellectual. Staring out the window when the teacher is lecturing communicates something just as strongly as if you shouted, "I'm very bored!" You cannot *not* communicate, given the expressiveness of nonverbal behavior. It is difficult to mask or control our nonverbal messages, because nonverbal behavior is spontaneous. True feelings will usually express themselves, no matter how hard we try to conceal them (Hanna, 1995).

Nonverbal behavior can also be ambiguous and difficult to interpret. When a person sits quietly and doesn't say anything about what you have just said, how are you to interpret the silence? It is not easy. When a person smiles, is the smile communicating something positive or something sarcastic? Again, the message may be ambiguous. Because nonverbal behavior is often ambiguous, caution is warranted in interpreting it. Don't consider nonverbal behaviors in isolation. They must be seen in the context of verbal communication and the ongoing communication that takes place over hours, days, weeks, and even lifetimes.

People often pay more attention to what they are saying than to what they are doing with their bodies. Paul Ekman and Wallace Frieson (1974) argued that nonverbal leakage permeates our communication. **Nonverbal leakage** is the communication of true emotions through nonverbal channels even when the person tries to conceal the truth verbally. For example, a student might say that he is not nervous

nonverbal communication Messages that are transmitted from one person to another by other than linguistic means, including body communication, spatial communication, and paralanguage.

nonverbal leakage The communication of true emotions through nonverbal channels even when the person tries to conceal the truth verbally.

about an upcoming test, but as he speaks his voice becomes high-pitched and occasionally cracks, he blinks more than usual, and he bites his lower lip.

Detecting Deception   Can you tell if someone is being deceptive in their communication? Researchers have found that, compared with people telling the truth, liars do the following (DePaulo, 1994):

- Blink more and have more dilated pupils
- Show more self-manipulating gestures, such as rubbing and scratching
- Give shorter responses that are more negative, more irrelevant, and more generalized
- Speak in a more distancing way, as if they do not want to commit themselves to what they are saying
- Speak in a higher pitch
- Take more time to plan what they are about to say, but the resulting statements tend to be more internally discrepant and more marred by hesitations, repetitions, grammatical errors, and slips of the tongue

People are not very good at detecting deception unless they are trained to do so (DePaulo, 1994). In one study, Paul Ekman and Maureen O'Sullivan (1991) videotaped college students as they watched either an enjoyable film about nature or an emotion-laden gory film. Regardless of which film they saw, the students were asked to describe the film as pleasant and enjoyable. In more than four out of five cases, the researchers were able to detect correctly which students were lying and which were telling the truth by focusing on such cues as a raised voice. Ekman and O'Sullivan asked college students, psychiatrists, court judges, police officers, and polygraph experts if they could detect which students were lying and which were telling the truth. Each of these groups scored at about chance (50 percent). One additional group—secret service agents—did perform above chance, detecting the lies about two-thirds of the time.

Nonverbal Coordination   Nonverbal behaviors usually come in clusters. For example, if you are afraid, your muscles tense up, the pupils of your eyes dilate, your heart beats faster, your mouth becomes drier, and your sweat gland activity increases. When you become afraid, you might simultaneously open your mouth wider, grab hold of something in a tense way, clam up and become very quiet, or even begin shaking.

Sometimes nonverbal behavior and verbal expression conflict. For example, a husband's face becomes flushed, he clenches his fist, pounds the table, and shouts, "I am *not* angry!" His wife is likely to find her husband's nonverbal behavior more convincing than his verbal behavior. When there is a discrepancy between words and body language, both messages are usually important. People who shout loudly that they are not angry might not want to admit to themselves or others that they are angry.

Culture, Ethnicity, and Nonverbal Communication   Not only do many cultures have different languages, but they also often have different systems of nonverbal communication (Hajek & Giles, 2003; Hall, 2002; Martin & Nakayama, 2004; Samovar & Porter, 2004; Wood, 2004). Variations in how they use specific elements of nonverbal communication combine to give cultures, and even various groups within cultures, different styles of communication. For example, the nonverbal styles of non-Latino White Americans may differ from that of African Americans, Latinos, Asian Americans, and Native Americans. The generalizations that follow describe the predominant patterns of each group; of course, variations within each group are also likely (Lumdsen & Lumsden, 2003).

Communication style	Very little	Little	Medium	Much	Very much
Animation/ emotional expression	Asian American Native American	Latino	Non-Latino White		African American
Gestures	Asian American Native American		Non-Latino White	Latino	African American
Volume of speech	Asian American	Latino	Native American	Non-Latino White	African American
Directness of eye contact	Asian American Native American	Latino			Anglo American African American
Touching	Asian American Native American		Non-Latino White		African American Latino
Closeness when standing	Asian American Native American	Non-Latino White	African American		Latino

FIGURE 7.6 Predominant Communication Styles in Different Ethnic Groups

Intercultural Communication
Cross-Cultural Communication
Ethnicity and Communication

An important difference in the nonverbal communication styles of non-Latino White Americans and Latinos is that Latinos tend to stand close while communicating and to touch one another while communicating; non-Latino White Americans stand farther apart and tend not to touch one another while communicating.

African American and non-Latino White Americans often speak more loudly than Asian Americans. Non-Latino White Americans consider shifty eyes or an unwillingness to make eye contact as suspicious; however, looking someone in the eye is often perceived as a sign of disrespect or rudeness by many Asian Americans (Baruth & Manning, 1991).

Native Americans speak more softly and at a slower rate than non-Latino White Americans do. Native Americans also tend to avoid such direct interaction between speaker and listener expressed by signs such as head nods and "uh huh." Non-Latino White Americans view a firm handshake as a sign of strength and power. By contrast, Native Americans view a firm handshake as aggressive and disrespectful (Everett, Proctor, & Cartmell, 1989). Many Native Americans consider direct eye contact to be disrespectful. Non-Latino White Americans expect and maintain more eye contact and may interpret its absence as rude, disrespectful, and hostile as well as conveying disinterest.

A summary of communication styles in different ethnic groups is shown in figure 7.6 (Elliott, 1999). Keep in mind that the style for each ethnic group is the predominant style but that there are considerable individual variations within each ethnic group.

Adjustment Strategies
For Improving Intercultural Communication

Marcelle DuPraw and Marya Axner (2003) recommend these strategies for improving communication with someone from a different culture than yours:

1. ***Learn about predominant communication tendencies of people from other cultures.*** However, don't use these generalizations to stereotype or oversimplify your views of a person.
2. ***Recognize individual variation in communication styles within a culture.*** Remember that not everyone in a culture uses its predominant style. Watch for this individual variation.
3. ***Practice intercultural communication.*** Seek out people from different cultures to interact with. Only by doing so will you get better at intercultural communication.
4. ***Don't assume yours is the one right way to communicate.*** Question your views of the best way to communicate. Monitor your body language and how it might be interpreted differently in other cultures.
5. ***Listen carefully.*** Take the perspective of the other person.
6. ***Respect others' choices.*** Some people from other cultures may not want to communicate with you. Respect their right not to talk with you.

Gender and Nonverbal Communication   Gender is another important dimension of the sociocultural contexts that influence nonverbal communication. Researchers have consistently found that women are better than men at reading people's emotional cues (Algoe, Buswell, & DeLameter, 2000; Hall, 1987). Women are also more likely to smile than men (Hall, Carter, & Horgan, 2000) and to express empathy and to cry when they see someone in distress (Kring & Gordon, 1998). Women also look at their conversational partner more than men do (LaFrance & Henley, 1997).

Females are more likely to sit quietly, males are more likely to be active or even fidgety. Females are more likely to have good posture, males are more likely to have poor posture (Tannen, 1990). The next time you are in a group, observe how the males and females are sitting; females are more likely to sit erect with their legs close together, males are more likely to slouch or sprawl across a chair or sofa, with their legs spread wide apart, claiming a great deal of space.

Body Communication

We can communicate a nonverbal message through a gesture, a facial expression, a look, or a touch.

Gestures   A **gesture** is a motion of the limbs or body made to convey a message to someone else. As we talk with our mouths, we often make gestures with our hands—for example, shaking a fist to convey anger, holding our hands a particular distance apart as we describe how wide something is, waving our hands wildly as we talk about how confusing something is, and pointing a finger at someone as we are saying something nasty to them.

Gestures are not universal (Cohen & Borsoi, 1996). For instance, the sign shown in figure 7.7, which usually means "OK," can mean "coins" in Japan and "worthless" in France. In Greece, it is a hostile allusion to body parts.

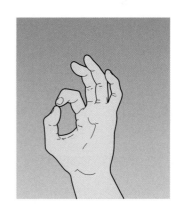

FIGURE 7.7 An Example of a Gesture and Its Meanings
In many cultures, the circle made with the thumb and forefinger means that everything is "OK."

gesture A motion of the limbs or body made to convey a message to someone else.

Facial Expressions Facial expressions can communicate important messages (Lee & Wagner, 2002). Our faces not only disclose specific emotions, but they can telegraph what really matters to us. In some situations, a person's face will take on a natural and lively intensity in the midst of a conversation that seems relatively unimportant.

Although some facial expressions appear to be universal, the meanings of facial expressions can also vary from culture to culture (Axtell, 1991). For example, shaking the head means no in our culture but means yes in Iran and Bulgaria and in India means that one is listening intently.

Eye Communication In the United States, eye contact generally serves four functions:

1. To monitor feedback (we often look at someone directly to see how they react to what we have just said)
2. To signal a turn in the conversation (as when someone speaks in a group and then looks at someone else in the group to convey that it is now his or her turn to speak)
3. To signal the nature of a relationship (when we like someone, we increase eye contact; we more often avoid eye contact when we dislike someone)
4. To compensate for physical distance (when we catch someone's eye at a party, even though we are some distance from them, we may be able to express psychological closeness to the person)

Pupil dilation sends a nonverbal message. In the fifteenth and sixteenth centuries, Italian women put drops of belladonna (which literally means "beautiful woman") into their eyes to dilate the pupils so they would be perceived as more attractive. Contemporary researchers have found that people are judged as more attractive when their pupils are dilated rather than contracted (DeVito, 2004).

Touch Communication We experience touch communication very early in our lives. Starting at birth, we are fondled, caressed, patted, and stroked by parents and other adults. All the world seems to want to touch the young infant. Touch is among our first pleasant experiences, not only the rewarding feelings of touch from others, but our own touching. Infants want to pick up just about everything, and their favorite objects (such as a teddy bear or a favorite blanket) often are chosen because of their tactile (touch) properties.

Touch continues to play a powerful role in nonverbal communication throughout life. Touch expresses sexuality, consolation, or dominance. Touch is a primary form of sexual interaction, from kissing to foreplay to sexual intercourse. Touch also plays an important role in consoling others, as when we put our arms around people, hold their head in our hands, hold their hands, or hug them. Higher-status people are more often allowed to touch lower-status people than vice versa—it is more permissible for teachers to touch students, doctors to touch patients, managers to touch workers, ministers to touch parishioners, and police officers to touch suspects than vice versa.

Who touches whom where? It depends to some extent on gender and culture. Generally, women touch more and are touched more than men (Hollender & Mercer, 1976). Touching patterns vary considerably from one culture to another. For example, in one study college students in the United States reported being touched twice as much as their counterparts in Japan did (Barnlund, 1975). There is a strong taboo against strangers' touching in Japan.

Spatial Communication

In the television show *The Simpsons,* Homer Simpson often gets upset if anyone sits near him when he is watching television. Most of us don't go into the tirades Homer does when our space is invaded, but most of us do communicate messages about

Category	Distance	Interaction activity
Intimate		
Close	0–6 inches	Love-making and wrestling
Far	6–18 inches	Intimate talk in public
Personal		
Close	1.5–2.5 feet	Peers, friends talk
Far	2.5–4 feet	Strangers, unequals talk
Social		
Close	4–7 feet	Impersonal business
Far	7–12 feet	Formal business
Public		
Close	12–25 feet	Formal presentation
Far	25 feet–outward	Famous person presents

FIGURE 7.8 Personal Space Categories, Distances, and Interactions

space. **Proxemics** is the study of the communicative function of space, especially how people unconsciously structure their space.

Anthropologist Edward Hall (1969) coined the term *proxemics* to specify the kind of space in which interactions are ordinarily and comfortably conducted. Hall identified four distinct zones in which we interact:

1. Intimate distance
2. Personal distance
3. Social distance
4. Public distance

For each of these zones, Hall specified what distances are "close" or "far" (see figure 7.8). For example, in the close intimate zone of 0–6 inches, lovemaking and wrestling are examples of activities, whereas in the far intimate zone of 6–18 inches, intimate talk in public is a representative activity.

Cultures have different standards for the appropriate distances for interactions. For example, individuals of Northern European heritage stand farther apart than their counterparts of Latin American and Middle Eastern heritage (Hall, 1969).

How people use space communicates information about power and status. People with higher status usually have more space and more privacy, those with lower status less space and less privacy. Executives of large corporations are often sheltered by an army of outer offices, secretaries, and guards, for example. We can't just barge into the executive's office, but we probably can come into direct contact with the owner of a small single-location business.

Silence and Paralanguage

We have seen that we can communicate with words and with nonverbal behaviors such as bodily signals and use of space. We also can communicate nonverbally through the use of silence.

proxemics The study of the communicative function of space, especially how people unconsciously structure their space.

Silence In our fast-paced modern world we often act as if there is something wrong with anyone who remains silent for more than a second or two after something is said to them. We often act as if silence is not golden (Goldin-Meadow, McNeill, & Singleton, 1996). According to communication skills expert Robert Bolton (1979), more than half the people who take communication skills training courses with him are initially uncomfortable with silence. Even a few seconds' pause in a conversation causes many of them to squirm.

By being silent, a good listener engages in certain activities, such as these:

1. Attending to the other person through body posture that indicates that he or she is really there for the other person
2. Observing the other by watching the speaker's eyes, facial expressions, posture, and gestures for communication
3. Thinking about what the other person is communicating, wondering what the other person is feeling, and considering the most appropriate response to make

Of course, silence can be overdone and sometimes is inappropriate. It is rarely appropriate to listen for an excessive length of time without making at least some verbal response. Interpersonal communication should not be a monologue, but rather a dialogue.

Communication expert Gerald Goodman (1988) believes that silences act like traffic signals. They establish and maintain order between talking people. Silences or lack of silences can change our sense of being allowed to say what we want or of being so rushed we can't get our points across.

Paralanguage **Paralanguage** refers to the nonlinguistic aspects of verbal expression, such as the rapidity of speech, the volume of speech, and the pitch of speech. The effective listener hears far more than the speaker's words. When a person says, "I quit my job," it may mean very different things depending on how it is said. The person may say it in a sad, angry, and fearful way in a low tone of voice that is quivering, or the person may say it in a brighter, bouncier way, suggesting possibly that better opportunities are available. A summary of some of the meanings and feelings that various paralanguage communications convey is shown in figure 7.9.

paralanguage The nonlinguistic aspects of verbal communication, such as the rapidity of speech, the volume of speech, and the pitch of speech.

Paralanguage	Probable meanings/ feelings
Monotone voice	Boredom
Slow speed, low pitch	Depression
High voice, emphatic pitch	Enthusiasm
Ascending tone	Astonishment
Abrupt speech	Defensiveness
Terse speech, loud tone	Anger
High pitch, drawn-out speech	Disbelief

FIGURE 7.9 Different Types of Paralanguage and Their Meanings/Feelings

Review and Reflect

3 **Describe the elements of nonverbal interpersonal communication**

REVIEW

- What are some important dimensions of nonverbal communication?
- What role does body communication play in nonverbal communication?
- How does spatial communication work?
- Why are silence and paralanguage important in communication?

REFLECT

- How good do you think you are at detecting nonverbal communication cues? Now that you have read about nonverbal interpersonal communication in this section, what aspects of it will you begin to pay more attention to in your relationships with people?

www.mhhe.com/santrockha

Paralanguage

Reach Your Learning Goals

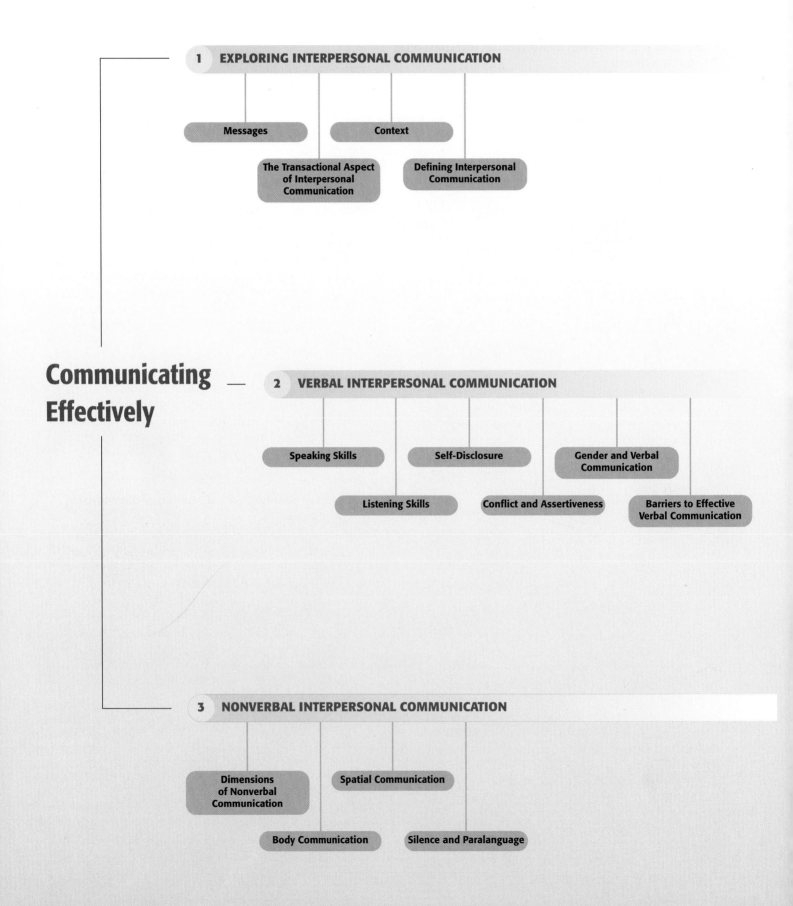

Communicating Effectively

1 EXPLORING INTERPERSONAL COMMUNICATION

- Messages
- The Transactional Aspect of Interpersonal Communication
- Context
- Defining Interpersonal Communication

2 VERBAL INTERPERSONAL COMMUNICATION

- Speaking Skills
- Listening Skills
- Self-Disclosure
- Conflict and Assertiveness
- Gender and Verbal Communication
- Barriers to Effective Verbal Communication

3 NONVERBAL INTERPERSONAL COMMUNICATION

- Dimensions of Nonverbal Communication
- Body Communication
- Spatial Communication
- Silence and Paralanguage

Summary

1   *Describe the basic aspects of interpersonal communication*

- The message is the information being delivered from the sender to the receiver. The channel is the mode of communication delivery. Communication involves encoding, the act of producing messages, and decoding, the act of understanding messages. Noise and context can influence the message.
- Interpersonal communication is transactional because it is an ongoing process between sender and receiver that unfolds over time, and it is not unusual for information to be communicated almost simultaneously.
- Social communication always occurs in context. The relationship between participants is an important part of this context, and it is often the source of communication problems. Sociocultural dimensions of context, such as ethnic variations in communication, can be especially important.
- Interpersonal communication can be defined as a transactional process that is ongoing over time. This process involves at least two people, each of whom acts as sender and receiver, encoding and decoding messages, sometimes simultaneously. These messages are sent through verbal and nonverbal channels. Noise can limit the accuracy of a message. Communication always takes place in a context.

2   *Explain the keys to effective verbal interpersonal communication*

- When your speech is clear and accurate, your listener is more likely to understand what you mean. To communicate effectively, you need to consider the background, needs, abilities, and other characteristics of your listeners. A distinction is made between denotation—the objective meaning of words—and connotation—the subjective meaning of words. To communicate effectively, it is important to consider the possible connotation of words for your listeners. Messages are usually better when we use concrete rather than abstract words and are spoken in simple rather than complex ways. Good speakers also make their verbal and nonverbal messages consistent.
- We spend more time in listening than any other communication activity. In actual conversations, however, most of us are not very good listeners. Although hearing is a physiological process, listening is a psychological process that involves interpreting and understanding the significance of what someone says. Most people can improve their listening skills by talking less and listening more; by paying careful attention to the person who is talking; by using reflective listening, including paraphrasing and summative reflection; and by giving feedback in a competent manner.

- Self-disclosure is the communication of intimate details about ourselves to someone else. Self-disclosure has a special power in deepening relationships. In some instances, mental health problems develop because individuals do not have the ability to disclose psychologically painful facts to friends or family. Self-disclosure usually proceeds gradually.
- Four ways of dealing with conflict in communication are being aggressive, manipulative, passive, or assertive. Being assertive is the best choice. In many cultures, women have been less assertive, men more aggressive.
- Gender plays an important role in interpersonal communication, but gender differences are often not as great as they are portrayed in popular books. Tanner argues that women are more likely to engage in rapport talk, men in report talk. However, critics stress that there are more gender similarities than differences in relationship communication. Women self-disclose more than men do, but men are more likely to interrupt and take over a conversation.
- Barriers to effective verbal communication include judging (criticizing, name-calling and labeling, and praising evaluatively), proposing solutions (advising, excessive/inappropriate questioning, ordering, threatening, and moralizing), and avoiding the other's concerns (diverting, using logical argument without considering feelings).

3   *Describe the elements of nonverbal interpersonal communication*

- Nonverbal communication refers to messages that are transmitted from one person to another by means other than linguistic. These other means include body communication (gestures, facial expressions, eye communication, and touch), space communication, silence, and paralanguage. Nonverbal communication may occur in clusters, always communicates, is culturally influenced, is often spontaneous and ambiguous, and may be discrepant from verbal communication. Nonverbal leakage often occurs in communication, especially when someone is trying to deceive another person.
- A gesture is a motion of the limbs or body to convey a message to someone else. The meaning of some gestures varies across cultures. Most psychologists believe that the facial expressions of basic emotions are universal across cultures. Eye contact serves a number of functions and pupil dilation also sends a nonverbal message—for example, people are perceived as more attractive when their pupils are dilated rather than contracted. Touch communication plays a powerful role in interpersonal communication. Its functions include

expressions of sexuality, consolation and support, and power and dominance.

- Proxemics is the study of the communicative function of space, especially how people unconsciously structure their space. Hall described four distinct zones in which we interact: intimate distance, personal distance, social distance, and public distance. How people use space communicates information about power and status.

- Being silent during parts of conversation does not mean being inactive during that time. While being silent, the good listener is attending to the other person, observing the other person's behavior, and thinking about what to say next. Paralanguage refers to the nonlinguistic aspects of verbal expression, such as the rapidity of speech, the volume of speech, and the pitch of speech. Different types of paralanguage often have different meanings; for instance, a high voice and emphatic pitch convey enthusiasm, and a monotone voice implies boredom.

Key Terms

message, 203
channel, 203
encoding, 203
decoding, 203
noise, 203
transactional, 204

interpersonal
    communication, 205
denotation, 206
connotation, 206
hearing, 207
listening, 207

reflective listening, 208
paraphrasing, 208
self-disclosure, 208
Johari Window, 208
rapport talk, 214
report talk, 214

nonverbal
    communication, 219
nonverbal leakage, 220
gesture, 223
proxemics, 224
paralanguage, 226

Resources for Improving Your Adjustment

SELF-HELP BOOKS

How to Communicate

(1997) by Matthew McKay, Martha Davis, and Patrick Fanning
New York: Fine

This book provides excellent recommendations for improving communication skills. Among the topics covered are communication skills in families, in conflicted situations, in social situations, and many others. Numerous strategies for improving listening skills, self-disclosure, and expressive skills are given. Information about body language, paralanguage, and hidden agendas is covered. *How to Communicate* was given 4 stars (out of 5) in the national study of self-help books (Norcross, Santrock, & others, 2003).

Your Perfect Right

(7th ed.) 1995 by Robert Alberti and Michael Emmons
San Luis Obispo, CA: Impact

This book emphasizes the importance of being assertive in communication that involves conflict. You learn how to be more assertive rather than passive, aggressive, or manipulative. Step-by-step procedures help you to start being more assertive and dealing with obstacles you might encounter. *Your Perfect Right* was rated in the highest category (5 stars) in the national survey of self-help books.

You Just Don't Understand!

(1990) by Deborah Tannen
New York: Ballentine

This book is about how women and men communicate—or all too often, miscommunicate—with each other. Tannen describes hundreds of situations in which this miscommunication occurs and recommends how men and women can improve their communication with each other. *You Just Don't Understand!* was given 4 (of 5) stars in the national study of self-help books (Norcross, Santrock, & others, 2003).

Getting to Yes: Negotiating Without Giving In

(1991, Rev. ed.) by Roger Fisher and William Ury
New York: Penguin

This brief book of about 150 pages provides a step-by-step strategy for reaching mutually acceptable agreements. The authors describe how to separate people from the problem, develop precise goals, work together to find options that will satisfy both parties, and negotiate successfully. This book was given 4 stars in the national study of self-help books.

E-Learning Tools

To help you master the material in this chapter, you will find a number of valuable study tools on the student CD-ROM that accompanies this book. In addition, visit the Online Learning Center for *Human Adjustment,* where you can find valuable resources for Chapter 7, "Communicating Effectively."

SELF-ASSESSMENT

In Text

You can complete these self-assessments in the text:
- Self-Assessment 7.1: *How Much Do I Self-Disclose?*
- Self-Assessment 7.2: *What Is My Communication Style?*
- Self-Assessment 7.3: *How Argumentative Am I?*

Additional Self-Assessments

Complete these self-assessments on the Online Learning Center:
- *How Good Are My Communication Skills?*
- *How Good Are My Listening Skills?*
- *My Self-Disclosure with a Partner*

THINK CRITICALLY

To practice your critical thinking skills, complete these exercises on the Online Learning Center:
- *The Limits of Self-Disclosure* explores just how much to self-disclose.
- *Civility in Context* examines the contexts in which assertiveness might be the best strategy.
- *My Own Barriers* helps you to explore obstacles to verbal communication you might encounter.
- *Civility in an Electronic Age* focuses on communication on the Internet and the importance of being civil with others.

APPLY YOUR KNOWLEDGE

1. What did you say?

In some cases, the ability to communicate effectively is enhanced by understanding how things appear from another persons point of view. Do different people "hear" things differently depending on who they are and who the speaker is? Think back on the interactions you had this week where there was some amount of miscommunication. What things about the other person might have affected the way he or she heard what you said? Does gender make a difference? In addition to the gender differences listed in your book, what other gender differences in communication exist.

Go to a search engine such as www.yahoo.com or www.google.com and search for "gender differences in communication." Make a list of other strategies that men and women use in conversation. Write an example of each that you have heard during normal conversations in the past week.

2. What's on TV?

Choose a TV program and analyze its content. For this exercise, you will need to tape the program so that you can code the content. You can ask a friend to help you with the following tasks:

a. Using a stop-watch or a watch with a second hand, record how much each character speaks. Who speaks more—men or women?
b. Pick out sections of dialogue and indicate whether they are aggressive, assertive, non-aggressive, or manipulative. Is there a tendency for male characters to use a different style than female characters?
c. Rewrite the aggressive, non-assertive arid manipulative statements and rewrite them in assertive style.
d. Categorize statements as either rapport talk or report talk and record whether they are being said by a male speaker or a female speaker.

3. Non-verbal communication and culture.

One of the greatest challenges in an increasingly diverse world is learn rig not only a second language, but also a second non-verbal language. For this exercise, describe in detail all the different hand signals that North Americans use in everyday speech. Be sure to include gestures that are used to communicate ideas, give commands, express emotional states or interact with others.

Alternately, sit in a public place and watch people in conversation. Record the meaning of every hand signal you see.

What would it be like to be an immigrant to North America? Conversely, what gestures would you have to change or be cautious about in dealing with businesspeople from other cultures, or if you moved to another country? Go to a search engine such as www.yahoo.com or www.google.com and search for either:
- Non-verbal communication in _____ (e.g. Japan, France, India, etc)
- Culture and non verbal communication

 VIDEO SEGMENT

Do people in different cultures really differ very much in how they communicate? Watch the video for Chapter 7 on the CD-ROM to see specific examples of cultural variations in the use of gestures.

Friendship and Love Relationships

Images of Adjustment

Gwenna and Greg: Her Pursuit and His Lack of Commitment

Gwenna has been dating Greg, who has unsuccessful first and second marriages, for two and a half years (Lerner, 1989). Gwenna wants to marry Greg, but he can't make up his mind about whether to marry her.

"Gwenna decides that she needs to have a talk with Greg about their relationship, calmly initiating the conversation in a low-keyed fashion. She shared her perspective on both the strengths and weaknesses of their relationship and what her hopes were for the future. She asked Greg to do the same. Unlike earlier conversations, this one was conducted without her pursuing him, pressuring him, or diagnosing his problems with women. At the same time, she asked Greg some clear questions, which exposed his vagueness.

'How will you know when you *are* ready to make a commitment? What specifically would you need to change or be different than it is today?'

'I don't know,' was Greg's response. When questioned further, the best he could come up with was that he'd just feel it.'

'How much more time do you need to make a decision one way or another?'

'I'm not sure,' Greg replied. 'Maybe a couple of years, but I really can't answer a question like that. I can't predict my feelings.'

And so it went.

Gwenna really loved this man, but two years (and maybe longer) was longer than she could comfortably wait. So, after much thought, she told Greg that she would wait till fall (about ten months), but that she would move on if he couldn't commit himself to marriage by then. She was open about her wish to marry and have a family with him, but she was equally clear that her first priority was a mutually committed relationship. If Greg was not at that point by fall, then she would end the relationship—painful though it would be.

During the waiting period, Gwenna was able to *not* pursue him and *not* get distant or otherwise reactive to his expressions of ambivalence and doubt. *In this way she gave Greg emotional space to struggle with his dilemma and the relationship had its best chance of succeeding.* Her bottom-line position ("a decision by fall") was not a threat or an attempt to rope Greg in, but rather" a clear statement of what was acceptable to her.

. . . "When fall arrived, Greg told Gwenna he needed another six months to make up his mind. Gwenna deliberated a while and decided she could live with that. But when the six months were up, Greg was uncertain and asked for more time. It was then that Gwenna took the painful but ultimately empowering step of ending their relationship." (Source: Lerner, 1989, pp. 44–45)

Our close relationships are among the most important aspects of our lives. In some cases, these relationships are extremely positive; in others, they can be highly conflicted. Perhaps worst of all is the lack of relationships, which creates the deeply unsettling feeling of loneliness. In this chapter, we explore many aspects of attraction, friendship, love, and the dark side of close relationships.

1 FORMING RELATIONSHIPS: ATTRACTION

- Familiarity and Similarity
- Personality Traits
- Physical Attractiveness

What attracts people like Gwenna and Greg to each other and motivates them to spend more time with each other? Does just being around someone increase the likelihood a relationship will develop? Or are we likely to seek out and associate with those who are similar to us? How important is physical attraction in the initial stages of a relationship? How much do the individuals' personality traits matter in forming a relationship?

Familiarity and Similarity

Familiarity breeds contempt, as the old saying goes, but social psychologists have found that familiarity is a necessary condition for a close relationship to develop. For the most part, friends and lovers are people who have been around each other for a long time; they may have grown up together, gone to high school or college together, worked together, or gone to the same social events (Brehm, 2002).

To test the importance of exposure and its effect on liking someone, researchers planted female students in a large college classroom (Moreland & Beach, 1992). The women did not interact with the professor or the other students. They just walked in and sat quietly in the first row where they were most likely to be seen. The females attended anywhere from 15 to 0 (the control group condition) classes. At the end of the term, the students were shown slides of the females and asked to rate the extent to which they liked them. As shown in figure 8.1, the more times they saw the women, the more they said they liked them.

Another old saying, "Birds of a feather flock together," also helps to explain attraction. One of the most powerful lessons generated by the study of close relationships is that we like to associate with people who are similar to us (Berscheid, 2000). Our friends and lovers are much more like us than unlike us. We have similar attitudes, behavior patterns, and personal characteristics, as well as similar taste in clothes, intelligence, personality, other friends, values, lifestyle, physical attractiveness, and so on. In some limited cases and on some isolated characteristics, opposites may attract. An introvert may wish to be with an extravert, or someone with little money may wish to associate with someone who has a lot of money, for example. But overall we are attracted to individuals with similar rather than opposite characteristics. One study, for example, found that depressed college students preferred to meet unhappy others, whereas nondepressed college students preferred to meet happy others (Wenzlaff & Prohaska, 1989).

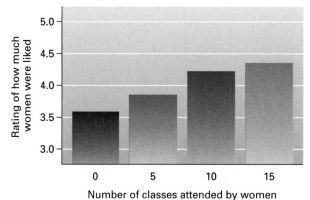

FIGURE 8.1 Exposure to Someone and the Extent to Which They Are Liked
The more frequently that students in a large college class saw women who had been planted there by researchers, the more they said they liked the women, even though they had not even interacted with them.

DILBERT reprinted by permission United Feature Syndicate, Inc.

Why are people attracted to others who are similar to them? **Consensual validation** is one reason. Our own attitudes and behavior are supported when someone else's attitudes and behavior are similar to ours—their attitudes and behavior validate ours. Another reason that similarity matters is that people tend to shy away from the unknown. We often prefer to be around people whose attitudes and behavior we can predict. And similarity implies that we will enjoy doing things with another person who likes the same things and has similar attitudes. In one study, this sort of similarity was shown to be especially important in successful marriages (Swann, De La Ronde, & Hixon, 1994).

Physical Attractiveness

You may be thinking at this point that something is missing from our discussion of attraction. As important as familiarity and similarity may be, they do not explain the spark that often ignites a romantic relationship: physical attractiveness. How important is physical attractiveness in relationships?

Many advertising agencies would have us believe that physical attractiveness is the most important factor in establishing and maintaining a relationship. Psychologists do not consider the link between physical beauty and attraction to be so clear-cut. For example, they have determined that heterosexual men and women differ on the importance of good looks when they seek an intimate partner. Women tend to rate as most important such traits as considerateness, honesty, dependability, kindness, and understanding; men prefer good looks, cooking skills, and frugality (Buss & Barnes, 1986).

Complicating research about the role of physical attraction is changing standards of what is deemed attractive. The criteria for beauty can differ, not just *across* cultures, but over time *within* cultures as well (Lamb & others, 1993). In the 1940s, the ideal of female beauty in the United States was typified by the well-rounded figure of Marilyn Monroe. Today, Monroe's 135-pound, 5-foot, 5-inch physique is regarded as overweight. The current ideal physique for both men and women is neither pleasingly plump nor extremely slender.

Social psychologists have found that the force of similarity also operates at a physical level. We usually seek out someone at our own level of attractiveness in both physical characteristics and social attributes. Research validates the **matching hypothesis**—which states that, although we may prefer a more attractive person in the abstract, in the real world we end up choosing someone who is close to our own level (Kalick & Hamilton, 1986).

What kind of tactics do U.S. men and women use? One study found that men more often used tactics that involve resource possession and display, while women were more likely to use tactics that altered their appearance (Buss, 1988). Men were more likely to brag about their resources, such as cars and money, display their strength in athleticism, and show off. By contrast, women were more likely to wear makeup, keep well groomed, wear stylish clothes, and wear jewelry.

Much of the research on physical attraction has focused on initial or short-term encounters; researchers have not often evaluated attraction over the course of months and years.

consensual validation Our own attitudes and behavior are supported when someone else's attitudes and behavior are similar to ours.

matching hypothesis Although people may prefer a more attractive person in the abstract, in the real world, they end up choosing someone close to their own level of attractiveness.

Maxine/Comix © Marian Henley. Reprinted by permission of the artist.

Highly likeable	Highly unlikeable
Sincere	Liar
Honest	Phony
Understanding	Mean
Loyal	Cruel
Truthful	Dishonest
Trustworthy	Untruthful
Intelligent	Obnoxious
Dependable	Malicious
Thoughtful	Dishonorable
Wise	Deceitful
Considerate	Untrustworthy
Good-natured	Unkind
Reliable	Insincere
Mature	Insulting
Warm	Spiteful
Earnest	Greedy
Kind	Conceited
Friendly	Rude
Kind-hearted	Thoughtless
Happy	Insolent

FIGURE 8.2 Personality Traits That People Like and Don't Like

Personality Traits

When you think of what attracts you to someone else, certain personality characteristics probably come to mind. Wouldn't you rather be around someone who is sincere, honest, understanding, loyal, truthful, trustworthy, intelligent, and dependable than someone who is mean, obnoxious, insulting, greedy, conceited, rude, and thoughtless? In one study, these and other personality traits were among those we like and do not like, respectively (Anderson, 1968) (figure 8.2).

Review and Reflect

1 Discuss the factors involved in attraction

REVIEW

- What roles do familiarity and similarity play in attraction?
- What is the link between physical attractiveness and attraction?
- How are personality traits related to attraction?

REFLECT

- Think about the people to whom you are attracted. What is it about them that attracts you?

2 FRIENDSHIP

The Benefits of Friendship   **Gender and Friendship**

Similarity is important not only in romantic relationships but also in **friendships,** close relationships that involve intimacy, trust, acceptance, mutual liking, and understanding. People not only tend to form friendships with people who are similar to themselves but also become more similar to their friends as the friendship develops (Aboud & Mendelson, 1996). This increase in similarity may serve to help maintain the friendship (Wood, 2000).

Who are our friends? We like to spend time with our friends, and we accept their friendship without trying to change them. We assume our friends will act in our best

friendships Close relationships that involve intimacy, trust, acceptance, mutual liking, and understanding.

How is adult friendship different among female friends, male friends, and cross-sex friends?

interest and believe that they make good judgments. We help and support our friends and they return the assistance. When we share experiences and deep personal matters with a friend, we believe that the friend will understand our perspective (Fehr, 2000). We feel free to be ourselves around our friends. One study of more than 40,000 individuals revealed that many of these characteristics are considered the qualities of a best friend (Parlee, 1979).

The Benefits of Friendship

Having one or more good friends has a number of benefits (Dainton, Zelley, & Langan, 2003). Friendship can reduce loneliness, be a source of self-esteem, and provide emotional support, especially in times of stress.

Harry Stack Sullivan (1953) was the most influential theorist to discuss the importance of friendships. In contrast to other psychoanalytic theorists' narrow emphasis on parent-child relationships, Sullivan contended that friends also play important roles in well-being and development. He argued that all people have a number of basic social needs, including the need for attachment, playful companionship, social acceptance, intimacy, and sexual relations. Whether or not these needs are fulfilled largely determines our emotional well-being. For example, if the need for playful companionship goes unmet, then we become bored and depressed; if the need for social acceptance is not met, we suffer a lowered sense of self-worth.

Gender and Friendship

Are the friendships of women and men different? To explore this question, we first focus on friendships between women and, second, friendships between men; we then examine friendships between women and men.

Friendships Between Women   Compared with men, women have more close friends and their friendships involve more self-disclosure and exchange of mutual support (Wood, 2000). Women are more likely to listen at length to what a friend has to say and be sympathetic (Gardner & Estep, 2001). Women have been labeled as "talking companions" because talk is so central to their relationship. Women's friendships tend to be characterized not only by depth but also by breadth: women share many aspects of their experiences, thoughts, and feelings (Wood, 2000).

Friendship Between Men   When female friends get together, they like to talk, but male friends are more likely to engage in activities, especially outdoors. Thus, the adult male pattern of friendship often involves keeping one's distance while sharing useful information. Men are less likely than women to talk about their weaknesses with their friends, and men want practical solutions to their problems rather than sympathy (Tannen, 1990). Also, adult male friendships are more competitive than those of women (Sharkey, 1993). For example, male friends disagree with each other more.

Friendship Between Women and Men   What about female-male friendship? Cross-gender friendships are more common among adults than among elementary school children, but not as common as same-gender friendships in adulthood (Fehr, 2000). Cross-gender friendships can provide both opportunities and problems. The opportunities involve learning more about common feelings and interests and shared characteristics, as well as acquiring knowledge and understanding of beliefs and activities that historically have been typical of one gender.

Problems can arise in cross-gender friendships because of different expectations. For example, a woman might expect sympathy from a male friend but might receive a proposed solution rather than a shoulder to cry on (Tannen, 1990). Another problem that can plague an adult cross-gender friendship is unclear sexual boundaries, which can produce tension and confusion (Swain, 1992).

Adjustment Strategies
For Getting and Keeping Friends

Regardless of whether you are a male or a female and are seeking a man or a woman as a friend, these strategies are likely to benefit your efforts to help you maintain the friendship (Wentzel & Erdley, 1993):

1. ***Be nice, kind, and considerate.*** Compliment others.
2. ***Be honest and trustworthy.*** Tell the truth, keep promises, share, and cooperate.
3. ***Respect others.*** Show good manners, be polite, be courteous. Listen to what others have to say. Have a positive attitude.
4. ***Provide emotional support.*** Be supportive, help, and show that you care. Engage in mutually enjoyable activities together.

The following strategies not only will harm your ability to make friends but they also can be friendship-ending:

1. ***Be disrespectful and inconsiderate.*** Have bad manners, be uncooperative. Ignore, don't share. Harm the other person's reputation. Gossip and spread rumors about the person. Embarrass the person or criticize them.
2. ***Present yourself negatively.*** Be self-centered, snobby, conceited, and jealous. Show off, be bossy. Be a grouch. Throw temper tantrums.
3. ***Be untrustworthy.*** Be dishonest, disloyal, tell lies, tell secrets, and break promises.

Review and Reflect

2   Describe friendship

REVIEW

- What is friendship? What are the benefits of friendship?
- What role does gender play in friendship?

REFLECT

- Think about the male and female friends that you have had or have now. How closely do your relationships with them fit the descriptions of gender and friendship you read about in the text?

---

3   LOVE

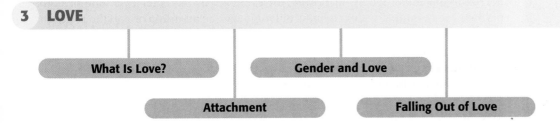

| What Is Love? | Gender and Love |
| Attachment | Falling Out of Love |

Some relationships never progress much beyond the attraction stage. But some relationships deepen to love in one of its guises (Harvey & Weber, 2002). What sets love apart from other ties? Do people differ in their ability to love? After we examine these questions about love, we will explore how gender is linked to love, and the factors involved in falling out of love.

Love scale
1. I feel that I can confide in _____ about virtually everything.
2. If I could never be with _____ , I would feel miserable.
3. One of my primary concerns is _____'s welfare.

Liking scale
1. I would highly recommend _____ for a responsible job.
2. Most people would react favorably to _____ after a brief acquaintance.
3. _____ is the sort of person I myself would like to be.

FIGURE 8.3 Sample Items from Rubin's Loving and Liking Scales
Subjects are asked to fill out the questionnaire in terms of their feelings for their boyfriend or girlfriend, and in terms of their feelings for a platonic friend of the opposite sex.

www.mhhe.com/santrockha

Exploring Love
Selecting a Partner
Love Topics

romantic love Also called *passionate love*, the type of love that has strong components of sexuality and infatuation, and often predominates in the early part of a love relationship.

affectionate love Also called *companionate love*, the type of love that occurs when individuals desire to have the other person near and have a deep, caring affection for the person.

consummate love In Sternberg's view, the strongest form of love that consists of passion, intimacy, and commitment.

What Is Love?

In Zick Rubin's (1970) view, *liking* involves our sense that someone else is similar to us; it includes a positive evaluation of the individual. *Loving*, he believes, involves being close to someone; it includes dependency, a more selfless orientation toward the individual, and qualities of absorption and exclusiveness (see figure 8.3).

Romantic Love   Think for a moment about songs that hit the top of the charts. Chances are they are about a particular kind of love—romantic love. Poets, playwrights, and musicians through the ages have lauded the fiery passion of romantic love—and lamented the searing pain when it fails. **Romantic love** is also called *passionate love.*

Romantic love has strong components of sexuality and infatuation, and it often predominates in the early part of a love relationship (Hendrick & Hendrick, 2000, 2004; Metts, 2004; Regan, 2004). Well-known love researcher Ellen Berscheid (1988) says that it is romantic love we mean when we say that we are "in love" with someone. It is romantic love she believes we need to understand if we are to learn what love is all about. Berscheid believes that sexual desire is the most important ingredient of romantic love.

Romantic relationships tend to be like friendships in a number of ways, but there are important differences (Pruchno & Rosenbaum, 2003). One study found that romantic lovers were more likely than friends to be the cause of depression (Berscheid & Fei, 1977). Relationships with spouses or lovers are more likely than friendships to involve fascination and exclusiveness, and relationships with friends are perceived as more stable than romantic relationships, especially more than among unmarried lovers (Davis, 1985). Romantic love includes a complex intermingling of emotions—fear, anger, sexual desire, joy, and jealousy, for example.

Affectionate Love   Love is more than just passion. **Affectionate love,** also called *companionate love,* is the type of love that occurs when someone desires to have the other person near and has a deep, caring affection for the person.

There is a growing belief that the early stages of love have more romantic ingredients but that as love matures, passion tends to give way to affection (Berscheid & Reis, 1998; Harvey & Weber, 2002). Phillip Shaver (1986) describes the initial phase of romantic love as a time that is fueled by a mixture of sexual attraction and gratification, a reduced sense of loneliness, uncertainty about the security of developing an attachment, and excitement from exploring the novelty of another human being. With time, he says, sexual attraction wanes, attachment anxieties either lessen or produce conflict and withdrawal, novelty is replaced with familiarity, and lovers either find themselves securely attached in a deeply caring relationship or distressed—feeling bored, disappointed, lonely, or hostile, for example. In the latter case, one or both partners may eventually seek to find a different close relationship or end the relationship as Gwenna did with Greg in the chapter opening story.

Consummate Love   So far we have discussed two forms of love: romantic (or passionate) and affectionate (or companionate). Robert J. Sternberg (1988) described a third form of love, **consummate love,** which he said is the strongest, fullest type of love. Sternberg proposed that love can be thought of as a triangle with three main dimensions—passion, intimacy, and commitment. Passion, as described earlier, is physical and sexual attraction to another. Intimacy is emotional feelings of warmth, closeness, and sharing in a relationship. Commitment is our cognitive appraisal of the relationship and our intent to maintain the relationship even in the face of problems (Rusbult & others, 2001). Passion and intimacy were present in Gwenna and Greg's relationship, but commitment was absent on Greg's part.

Sternberg's theory states that the ideal form of love—consummate love—involves all three dimensions (see figure 8.4). If passion is the only ingredient in a relationship (with intimacy and commitment low or absent), we are merely *infatuated.* An affair or a fling in which there is little intimacy and even less commitment would be an example. A relationship marked by intimacy and commitment but low or lacking in passion is *affectionate love,* a pattern often found among couples who have been married for many years. If passion and commitment are present but intimacy is not, Sternberg calls the relationship *fatuous love,* as when one person worships another from a distance. But if couples share all three dimensions—passion, intimacy, and commitment—they will experience consummate love. To evaluate the type of love you have, complete Self-Assessment 8.1.

Attachment

Can everybody fall in love? Are we all capable of Sternberg's consummate love? Researchers have found that the quality of our romantic relationships is linked with the quality of our attachment—or emotional bond—to caregivers such as our parents during infancy and childhood. What is the nature of attachment in adulthood? Like our parents, romantic partners can give us a secure base to which we can return and obtain comfort and security in stressful times (Collins & Feeney, 2004). According to attachment theory, we learn an attachment style as infants and then carry it forward as a working model, a sort of blueprint, for our relationships as adults (Atkinson & Goldberg, 2004; Egeland & Carlson, 2004). Let's examine these styles and the evidence for their influence.

Attachment Styles   Current ideas about attachment stem from the work of John Bowlby (1969, 1980) and Mary Ainsworth (1979), who argued that attachment to a caregiver, especially the mother, in the first year of life provides an important foundation for later development. Some babies have more positive attachment experiences than others. Ainsworth (1979) identified three attachment styles between infants and a caregiver, especially the mother.

- **Secure attachment style:** The caregiver is responsive to the infant's needs and shows positive emotions when interacting with the infant. Securely attached infants trust their caregiver, don't fear that they will be abandoned, and explore their world in positive ways.
- **Avoidant attachment style:** The caregiver is distant or rejecting, and fails to respond to the infant's bids to establish intimacy. Avoidant infants suppress their desire to be close to their caregiver.
- **Ambivalent attachment style:** The caregiver is inconsistently available and when present often overbearing with affection; as a result, the infants can't predict when and how their caregiver will respond. Ambivalent infants may cling anxiously to the caregiver and then fight against the closeness by pushing away.

To determine which of these attachment styles characterizes you, complete Self-Assessment 8.2. Studies of infants' behavior and the self-reports of adults indicate that about 70 percent have a secure attachment style, about 20 percent have an avoidant style, and about 10 percent have an ambivalent style (Jones & Cunningham, 1996; Mickelson & others, 1997).

Links Between Attachment in Childhood and Close Relationships in Adulthood

What evidence indicates that your attachment as a child is linked to your attachment style during adulthood? In a number of studies, Cindy Hazan and Phillip Shaver (1987; Shaver & Hazan, 1993) have examined the continuity between childhood attachment and romantic relationships. They interviewed adults about

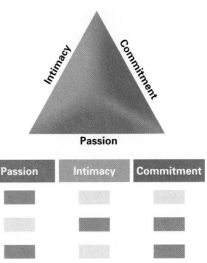

Types of Love	Passion	Intimacy	Commitment
Infatuation	Present	Absent or low	Absent or low
Affectionate love	Absent or low	Present	Present
Fatuous love	Present	Absent or low	Present
Consummate love	Present	Present	Present

Present   Absent or low

FIGURE 8.4 Sternberg's Triangle of Love
Sternberg identified three dimensions of love: passion, intimacy, and commitment. Various combinations of these types of love result in these patterns of love: infatuation, affectionate love, fatuous love, and consummate love.

secure attachment style The caregiver is responsive to the infant's needs and shows positive emotions when interacting with the infant. Securely attached infants trust their caregiver, don't fear that they will be abandoned, and explore their world in positive ways.

avoidant attachment style The caregiver is distant or rejecting, failing to respond to the infant's bids to establish intimacy. Although these infants want to be close to the caregiver, they suppress this desire.

ambivalent attachment style The caregiver is inconsistently available and when present often overbearing with affection. These infants are typically anxious because they can't predict when and how the caregiver will respond to their needs. They may cling anxiously to the caregiver and fight against the closeness by pushing away.

SELF-ASSESSMENT 8.1

What Type of Love Do I Have?

Imagine the blank spaces filled in with the name of one person you love or care about deeply. Then rate each of the items from 1 to 9 with 1 = not at all, 5 = moderately, and 9 = extremely.

_____ 1. I actively support _____'s well-being.

_____ 2. I have a warm relationship with _____ .

_____ 3. I can count on _____ in times of need.

_____ 4. _____ is able to count on me in times of need.

_____ 5. I am willing to share myself and my possessions with _____ .

_____ 6. I receive considerable emotional support from _____ .

_____ 7. I give considerable emotional support to _____ .

_____ 8. I communicate well with _____ .

_____ 9. I value _____ greatly in my life.

_____ 10. I feel close to _____ .

_____ 11. I have a comfortable relationship with _____ .

_____ 12. I feel that I really understand _____ .

_____ 13. I feel that _____ really understands me.

_____ 14. I feel that I can really trust _____ .

_____ 15. I share deeply personal information about myself with _____ .

_____ 16. Just seeing _____ excites me.

_____ 17. I find myself thinking about _____ frequently during the day.

_____ 18. My relationship with _____ is very romantic.

_____ 19. I find _____ to be very personally attractive.

_____ 20. I idealize _____ .

_____ 21. I cannot imagine another person making me as happy as _____ .

_____ 22. I would rather be with _____ than anyone.

_____ 23. There is nothing more important to me than my relationship with _____ .

_____ 24. I especially like physical contact with _____ .

_____ 25. There is something special about my relationship with _____ .

_____ 26. I adore _____ .

_____ 27. I cannot imagine my life without _____ .

_____ 28. My relationship with _____ is passionate.

_____ 29. When I see romantic movies and read romantic books I think of _____ .

_____ 30. I fantasize about _____ .

_____ 31. I know that I care about _____ .

_____ 32. I am committed to maintaining my relationship with _____ .

_____ 33. Because of my commitment to _____ , I would not let other people come between us.

_____ 34. I have confidence in the stability of my relationship with _____ .

_____ 35. I could not let anything get in the way of my commitment to _____ .

_____ 36. I expect my love for _____ to last for the rest of my life.

_____ 37. I will always feel a strong responsibility for _____ .

_____ 38. I view my commitment to _____ as a solid one.

_____ 39. I cannot imagine ending my relationship with _____ .

_____ 40. I am certain of my love for _____ .

_____ 41. I view my relationship with _____ as permanent.

_____ 42. I view my relationship with _____ as a good decision.

_____ 43. I feel a sense of responsibility toward _____ .

_____ 44. I plan to continue my relationship with _____ .

_____ 45. Even when _____ is hard to deal with, I remain committed to our relationship.

Go to the appendix at the end of the book for scoring and interpretation of your responses.

their relationship with their parents as they were growing up and about their current romantic relationship. They and other researchers have found that adults who report that they were securely attached to their parents as children are more likely to say that they have a secure attachment to their romantic partner than their adult counterparts who report having had an insecure attachment to their parents. In one

What Is My Attachment Style?

Which of the following paragraphs best describes your feelings about being emotionally close to other people? Place a checkmark next to the one paragraph that best describes you.

_____ I find it relatively easy to get close to others and am comfortable depending on them and having them depend on me. I don't often worry about being abandoned or about someone getting close to me.

_____ I am somewhat uncomfortable being close to others. I find it difficult to trust them completely, difficult to allow myself to depend on them. I am nervous when anyone gets too close, and often love partners want me to be more intimate than I feel comfortable being.

_____ I find that others are reluctant to get as close as I would like. I often worry that my partner doesn't really love me or won't stay with me. I want to merge completely with another person, and this desire sometimes scares people away.

Go to appendix at the end of the book for interpretation of your responses.

longitudinal study, individuals who were securely attached to caregivers at 1 year of age also were likely to have secure attachments to parents and romantic partners 20 years later (Waters & others, 2000).

Researchers have found other links between attachment in childhood and relationship patterns in adulthood (Atkinson & Goldberg, 2004; Bartholomew & Horowitz, 1991; Collins & Feeney, 2004; Edelstein & Shaver, 2004; Feeney, 1996; Fraley 2002):

- As adults, individuals who were securely attached to a caregiver in childhood find it easy to get close to others and don't worry much about becoming too dependent on someone or being abandoned.
- As adults, individuals who had an avoidant attachment style in childhood find it difficult to develop intimate relationships. Compared with securely attached adults, once in a relationship, they are more likely to quickly end it and more likely to engage in one-night stands without love. Gwenna, the woman described in the chapter opening story, had a father who was rarely involved in

Attachment Theory and Research
Adult Attachment
Measuring Adult Attachment

What are some ways that attachment to caregivers in childhood is linked to attachment styles and close relationships in adulthood?

her upbringing. The distant relationship with her father was likely related to her pattern of choosing distant males with poor track records in relationships (Lerner, 1989).

- As adults, individuals who had an ambivalent style are less trusting, which makes them more possessive and jealous, than securely attached adults. They may break up with the same individuals several times and when discussing conflicts they often become emotionally intense and angry.

Nonetheless, attachment styles are not cast in stone (Lewis, Feiring, & Rosenthal, 2000). For example, research indicates that links between earlier and later attachment styles are lessened by stressful and disruptive life experiences (such as the death of a parent and instability of caregiving) (Collins & Laursen, 2000). Also, some individuals revise their attachment styles as they experience relationships in their adult years (Baldwin & Fehr, 1995). For example, in one study, approximately 30 percent of young adults changed their attachment style over a four-year period (Kirkpatrick & Hazan, 1994).

Gender and Love

Do women and men hold different views of love? One recent study found that men conceptualize love in terms of passion, whereas women are likely to think of love more in terms of friendship (Fehr & Broughton, 2001). Both women and men include affection in their definition of love, but women usually rate it as more important than men do.

Gender differences in styles of communicating and interacting often complicate love relationships (Baumeister, 2004; Rogers & Escudero, 2004). Overall, women are more expressive and affectionate than men in marriage, and this difference bothers many women (Fox & Murray, 2000; Streil, 2001). As in the relationship of Gwenna and Greg, women consistently disclose more to their romantic partners than men do (Hendrick, 2002). And women tend to express more tenderness, fear, and sadness than their partners. Wives often complain that their husbands do not care about their emotional lives, that their husbands do not express their own feelings and thoughts, and that they have to literally pull things out of their husbands and push them to open up. Men frequently respond either that they are open or that they do not understand what their wives want from them. It is not unusual for men to protest that no matter how much they talk it is not enough for their wives. Women also say they want more warmth from their husbands. For example, women are more likely than men to give their partners a spontaneous kiss or hug when something positive happens.

Once the novelty, unpredictability, and urgency of sexual attraction in a love relationship have abated, women are more likely than men to detect deficiencies in caring that indicate the relationship has problems. Perhaps that sensitivity is why wives are almost twice as likely as husbands to initiate a divorce and why Gwenna finally ended her relationship with Greg (National Center for Health Statistics, 1989).

Love and Close Relationships
Love and Ethnic Diversity

Falling Out of Love

For Gwenna, as with most people, falling out of love was painful and highly emotional. The collapse of a close relationship may feel tragic. In the long run, however, as was the case for Gwenna, our happiness and personal development may benefit from getting over being in love and ending a close relationship.

In particular, falling out of love may be wise if you are obsessed with a person who repeatedly betrays your trust; if you are involved with someone who is draining you emotionally or financially; or if you are desperately in love with someone who does not return your feelings, which was occurring in Gwenna's relationship with Greg.

Being in love when love is not returned can lead to depression, obsessive thoughts, sexual dysfunction, inability to work effectively, difficulty in making new

SELF-ASSESSMENT 8.3

Am I Vulnerable in My Close Relationship?

Instructions

Read each question carefully while reflecting on your present or most recent close relationship. Check True or False as either relates to your situation.

Items	True	False
1. Is your partner often unavailable for phone calls at home or at work?	_____	_____
2. Does he/she ask about the amount of money you earn or your parents earn, or try to get involved with your financial planning?	_____	_____
3. Does your partner ever belittle your efforts and/or ideas?	_____	_____
4. Has your partner ever disappeared for any length of time (overnight, several days, a week) and not informed you of his/her whereabouts?	_____	_____
5. Does he/she live with you and contribute little or nothing to household maintenance?	_____	_____
6. Does your partner borrow money and seldom bother to repay it, or frequently ask you to buy him/her things, or always use your car?	_____	_____
7. Has he/she had one or more tragic misfortunes that needed your financial assistance?	_____	_____
8. Has your partner told you early in your relationship that he/she would like to be married and described a life of love and luxury for both of you, but made no definite steps in that direction?	_____	_____
9. Do you stop your present activity or postpone your plans when he/she calls to do something on the spur of the moment?	_____	_____
10. Is he/she the only person in your life?	_____	_____
11. Do you allow your partner to take the upper hand in your affairs?	_____	_____
12. Have you ever noticed any discrepancies concerning what your partner has told you in regard to his/her name, job, background, family, etc.?	_____	_____
13. When you are out does your partner avoid socializing with his/her or your family and friends?	_____	_____
14. Do you usually wait for others to introduce you to potential partners instead of taking the initiative to meet new people on your own?	_____	_____
15. When your partner describes his/her future goals, does it seem unclear as to where you fit into the future?	_____	_____
16. Do you feel that you should be married to be happy?	_____	_____

Go to the appendix at the end of the book for an interpretation of your responses.

friends, and self-condemnation. Thinking clearly in such relationships is often difficult, because they are so colored by arousing emotions.

Some people get taken advantage of in relationships. For example, without either person realizing it, a relationship can evolve in a way that creates dominant and submissive roles. Detecting this pattern is an important step toward learning either to reconstruct the relationship or to end it if the problems cannot be worked out. To evaluate your vulnerability in a close relationship, complete Self-Assessment 8.3.

Adjustment Strategies
For Breaking the Bonds of Love

What are some intelligent guidelines for breaking the bonds of love?

1. ***Identify the feelings that make it hard to surrender the relationship.*** Close friends can help us recognize the destructive aspects of the attachment. However, friends can help us only if we tell them openly and honestly what goes on in the relationship and our own conflicting feelings about the relationship.

2. ***Develop a stronger sense of self-esteem and independence.*** A main cause of getting into and staying in destructive relationships is feelings of being incomplete and inadequate by oneself. We must realize that we do not need the other person for our identity and self-esteem. Our friends can be invaluable in helping us to rebuild an identity as a competent, independent individual. They can provide support during the period of adjustment when we are breaking off a relationship.

   Ideally, a love relationship should reinforce self-esteem, but being rejected or involved in a destructive relationship may be devastating. One strategy for improving self-esteem is to record on individual index cards, every day, at least two positive things about ourselves, such as good characteristics or positive behaviors.

3. ***Recognize and stop the self-defeating thoughts that prevent us from taking effective actions to leave the relationship.*** When we find ourselves thinking negatively about ourselves, we should use thought stopping (discussed in chapter 5): Say "Stop" and immediately think a good thought about ourselves. We can also use thought stopping to think progressively less and less about the loved person. Letting a thought return again and again reinforces the thought, making it grow stronger and often more destructive.

4. ***Fall in love with someone else, but only when you are emotionally ready.*** Too often individuals engage in an immediate rebound romance, which is often as destructive as the relationship it replaced. There does come a time, though, when living in the memory of a past love is also destructive. At that point, we should get out and meet new people. This might lead to meeting someone with whom we can develop a healthy love relationship.

Review And Reflect

3 **Characterize the types of love and other factors involved in love**

REVIEW

- What forms do love take?
- Does our attachment to our parents in childhood shape our relationships as adults?
- How is gender linked to love?
- What factors are involved in falling out of love?

REFLECT

- What do you think is the most important aspect of love? Explain.

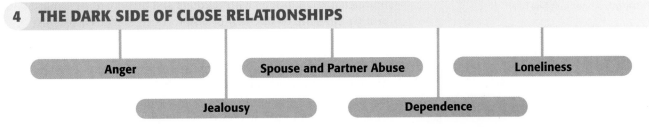

4   THE DARK SIDE OF CLOSE RELATIONSHIPS

| Anger | Spouse and Partner Abuse | Loneliness |

| Jealousy | Dependence |

Our close relationships bring us warm and cherished moments. They also have a chilling side, producing stress and pain (Cupach & Spitzberg, 2004). Let's now examine the dark side of close relationships by exploring anger, jealousy, dependence, and loneliness.

Anger

Anger is a powerful emotion and can sometimes become an extremely destructive element in close relationships (Nay, 2003). Anger in relationships may create a cycle with no beginning and no end. As figure 8.5 illustrates, three cyclic patterns of anger commonly occur in close relationships (Driscoll, 2002). In the "anger justifies itself" pattern, you make arguments to justify your anger and then allow your belief in those arguments and thoughts about your grievances to fuel further anger. In the "passivity and outburst" pattern, your resentment builds as a result of failure to confront problems. This pattern is common among individuals who fear any expression of anger or any conflict. In the "catharsis–perceived injustice" pattern, individuals are all too willing to express angry feelings (Tavris, 1989). Your partner's anger makes you angry, which makes your partner angry all over again.

How can couples make anger less destructive in their relationship and break out of these cycles? In *Anger: The Misunderstood Emotion,* Carol Tavris (1989) suggests that to break the destructive cycle of anger in close relationships, the first step is to drop the dream of rescuing or changing your partner. Often, when a couple has a problem, one partner becomes overfocused on the other, and the other is underfocused on himself or herself. Suppose the husband is out of work and won't look for a job. His naturally sympathetic wife becomes overfocused on his problem as she tries to help. She may say things like "I talked to my friend and she told me about a counselor you can see," or "I know a book you can read," and so on. The more he resists and the longer he sits and mopes around the house, the angrier she gets. The more she focuses on his problem, the less motivated he is to solve it. Overfocused individuals can be very self-righteous in their efforts to help and usually don't see how they are contributing to the continuation of the problem (Lerner, 1985). Ultimately the relationship becomes polarized between the competent helper and the incompetent helpee.

Venting your anger (catharsis) usually does not help you to manage it, as we discussed in chapter 4. Instead, managing anger depends on assuming responsibility for your emotions and actions by refusing the temptation to wallow in blaming, in fury, or in silent resentment. Civility, Tavris (1989) argues, is important. If you do not vent your anger but instead let it subside, more often than not it will be only momentary. After you have cooled down, you might decide that what bothered you an hour ago was trivial.

Jealousy

Jealousy can also become a destructive element in close relationships. **Jealousy** is fear of perceived possibility of losing someone's exclusive love. The possibility might or might not be real. Jealousy emerges when there is a challenge to a special relationship, or when we think there is (Anderson, 2003). When our sexual, affectionate, and

Jealousy

jealousy The fear of perceived possibility of losing someone else's exclusive love.

Pattern 1: Anger justifies itself

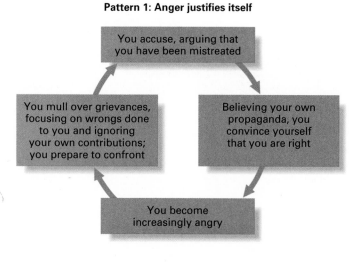

Pattern 2: Passivity and outburst

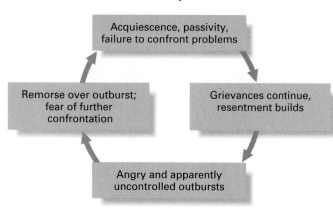

Pattern 3: Catharsis and perceived injustice

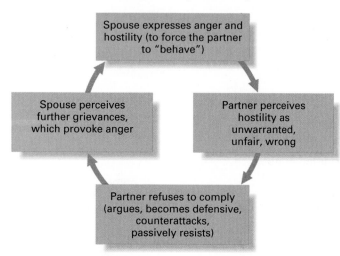

FIGURE 8.5 Three Destructive Patterns of Anger in Close Relationships

contractual relationships with partners and lovers are challenged through infidelity or threaten to disintegrate, an intense jealousy can arise (Buunk & Dijkstra, 2004; Marazziti & others, 2003).

Gender differences characterize jealousy (Guerrero, Spitzberg, & Yoshimura, 2004). Men especially show strong feelings of sexual jealousy and this can motivate them to be very concerned about their partner's faithfulness (Myers, 2002). While men tend to be especially upset about sexual infidelity, women are often more upset by their partner's emotional infidelity (Buss, 2004).

Jealousy is often stimulated by a specific event or situation. Situations likely to trigger jealous reactions in a relationship include the following (Salovey & Rodin, 1989):

- Finding out your lover is having an affair
- Discovering that someone is going out with the person you like
- Observing that someone is getting closer to a person to whom you are attracted
- Hearing your lover tell you how sexy an old girlfriend/boyfriend is
- Learning that your lover has visited a person she or he used to date
- Realizing that your partner would rather be with his or her friends than you

Some people are more likely to become jealous than others. Individuals with low self-esteem and feelings of insecurity are especially prone to becoming jealous, sometimes imagining threats to their exclusive love when no threat exists (Buunk & Dijkstra, 2004). Jealous individuals often perceive their partner as a highly desirable possession and doubt that their own attractiveness or sexual adequacy is enough to hold onto the other person. Jealous individuals tend to idealize their partner and underestimate their own self-worth.

Even the most secure people may occasionally feel some jealousy, but they don't let the feelings become so intense that they interfere with their productive functioning or threaten their relationship. Healthy relationships are not built on insecure feelings, and couples should work to develop trust in each other to increase feelings of security. In some cases, jealousy is irrational and the partner is doing nothing that will threaten the close relationship. The jealous person needs to examine how logical his or her thoughts and feelings of jealousy really are.

Overcoming jealous feelings involves reducing feelings of insecurity and thinking more rationally about the relationship (Guerrero, Spitzberg, & Yoshimura, 2004). People who feel good about themselves are less likely to be jealous than are those who feel bad about themselves. Developing stronger self-esteem can reduce your vulnerability in intimate relationships. Discussing your concerns and needs with a partner in subdued and non-accusing terms can clarify your intentions for your partner.

Spouse and Partner Abuse

Anger and jealousy can lead to spouse or partner abuse. Since the early 1970s, as people have begun to discuss and try to prevent spouse and partner abuse, the estimate of its prevalence has climbed from "not very common" to the current estimate that it affects at least one in four couples (Paludi, 2002). During the last three decades, growing knowledge of domestic violence has prompted communities to help protect victims by increasing shelters and counseling services, strengthening laws to help prosecute abusers, encouraging victims to leave their abusers and start new lives, and developing counseling programs to help batterers change their behavior (Fals-Stewart, Golden, & Schumacher, 2003; Loseke, Gelles, & Cavanaugh, 2004). Still, we are in the infancy of trying to amend this national and international problem (Arai, 2004; Ashy, 2004; Malley-Morrison, 2004).

Researchers have debunked a number of myths about domestic violence that include the following (Walker, 2001, p. 175):

What are some aspects of the dark side of close relationships?

"*Myth:* Batterers are just being men and they cannot control their violence, which is biologically caused.
Research: Battering behavior is learned behavior that can be unlearned and controlled by men and women.

Myth: Battering behavior is a man's response to provocation by the woman.
Research: Battering behavior is used by the man to intentionally demonstrate his power and control the woman.

Myth: The man only uses violence because he is drunk or high on drugs.
Research: Although there is an association between increased levels of violence with alcohol and other drugs, there are no data to suggest that alcohol causes the battering behavior.

Myth: Battered women stay in battering relationships, so therefore they must be masochistic or like being beaten up.
Research: Battered women stay in battering relationships because of many complex reasons including being terrified that they will get hurt worse or killed if they try to leave."

Lenore Walker (2000) described a three-phase cycle of domestic violence:

1. *Tension building.* Tension builds up and the battered person (usually but not always the woman) uses coping skills to avoid abusive situations.
2. *Acute battering incident.* Tension escalates until the batterer explodes into a violent episode.
3. *Loving-contrition.* Tension is reduced when the batterer is remorseful, loving, and generous, and the victim chooses to believe that the change is permanent. The tension soon starts to build again, however, and the cycle is repeated.

Batterers are contrite after the violent episode, so why don't they learn to make a permanent change? One obstacle is that batterers minimize and deny the amount of violence that has occurred—both because of loss of memory during the rage and because they use a pattern of blaming the victim for causing the violence (such as "She made me do it; she just wouldn't let up on me"). A second obstacle to permanent change is that men who batter are usually dependent on their spouse as the only source of intimacy, love, and support; in such an isolated, closed system, a natural outgrowth is the development of jealousy, which further poses a barrier to change and increases the amount of violence in a relationship. Often violent episodes are triggered from extreme suspiciousness and accusations of infidelity. To try to stem jealousy-driven rages, women in these relationships may give up all other friendships and outlets, which in the long run makes them very dependent within this violent relationship. Another obstacle to change is that batterers have low self-esteem; they even lack the skills and confidence to ask for what they want from their spouse in a nonthreatening manner. Finally, many batterers were socialized with violence—being physically or sexually abused themselves as children or witnessing violence between their parents (Barnett, Miller-Perrin, & Perrin, 2004). Their family scripts thus involve solving problems by physical force and psychological battering. Counseling programs try to change actual behavioral patterns and alter psychological obstacles to change (Loseke & others, 2004).

Dependence

A fourth destructive element in close relationships is excessive dependence. As children, we depended on our parents to satisfy most of our needs. As we grew up, we gradually assumed more independence and responsibility for our own well-being. Some individuals, though, never develop enough responsibility and depend excessively on others, especially their partners in close relationships.

An excessively dependent person is likely to be perceived as a burden by the partner. Two people in a close relationship normally enjoy doing things for each other, but there is a limit to the amount of time and energy most individuals are willing to devote even to someone they love very much. When the dependent person makes excessive demands, the partner often feels resentment and hostility. Even when the true cause of hostility (the overdependence, in this case) is not communicated to the dependent partner, the hostility will usually appear as frequent arguments, sexual problems, or the termination of the relationship.

Just as most jealous individuals have low self-esteem and feelings of insecurity, so do excessively dependent persons. Their feelings of dependence do nothing to improve their self-esteem, and they might become very jealous of their partner.

Adjustment Strategies
For Overcoming Excessive Dependence

Three basic steps are important in overcoming excessive dependence.

1. *Admit that the problem exists.* Usually, recognition of the problem is stimulated by a partner's complaints of feeling crowded or suffocated.
2. *Explore the reasons for such neediness.*
3. *Initiate some strategies that will lead to increased independence.* For example, a dependent person might seek to enrich friendships beyond the partnership in order to develop new interests and give the partner some emotional space. As adults, it is important for us not only to have strong, positive relationships but also to develop ourselves as persons in our own right.

Loneliness

People have a basic human desire to seek the company of others. Because of this strong human tendency, people who do not interact with others in close relationships on a regular basis may feel lonely. Lonely people may feel that no one knows them very well. They might feel isolated and sense that they do not have anyone to turn to in times of need and stress.

Each of us feels lonely at times, but for some people loneliness is a chronic condition (DiTommaso & others, 2003). More than just an unwelcome social situation, chronic loneliness is linked with impaired physical and mental health (Brehm, 2002; Hawkley & Cacioppo, 2003; McInnis & White, 2001). Chronic loneliness can even lead to an early death (Cuijpers, 2001; Valeri, 2003). In one recent study, lonely college students had higher levels of stress-related hormones and poorer sleep patterns than students who had relationships with others (Cacioppo & others, 2000).

SELF-ASSESSMENT 8.4

Am I Lonely?

Directions: Indicate how often you feel the way described in each of the following statements. Circle one number for each.

Statement	Never	Rarely	Sometimes	Often
1. I feel in tune with the people around me.	1	2	3	4
2. I lack companionship.	1	2	3	4
3. There is no one I can turn to.	1	2	3	4
4. I do not feel alone.	1	2	3	4
5. I feel part of a group of friends.	1	2	3	4
6. I have a lot in common with the people around me.	1	2	3	4
7. I am no longer close to anyone.	1	2	3	4
8. My interests and ideas are not shared by those around me.	1	2	3	4
9. I am an outgoing person.	1	2	3	4
10. There are people I feel close to.	1	2	3	4
11. I feel left out.	1	2	3	4
12. My social relationships are superficial.	1	2	3	4
13. No one really knows me well.	1	2	3	4
14. I feel isolated from others.	1	2	3	4
15. I can find companionship when I want it.	1	2	3	4
16. There are people who really understand me.	1	2	3	4
17. I am unhappy being so withdrawn.	1	2	3	4
18. People are around me but not with me.	1	2	3	4
19. There are people I can talk to.	1	2	3	4
20. There are people I can turn to.	1	2	3	4

Go to the appendix at the end of the book for scoring and interpretation of your responses.

Our society's emphasis on self-fulfillment and achievement, the importance we attach to commitment in relationships, and a decline in stable close relationships are among the reasons loneliness is common today (de Jong-Gierveld, 1987). Researchers have found that married individuals are less lonely than their nonmarried counterparts (never married, divorced, or widowed) in studies conducted in more than twenty countries (Perlman & Peplau, 1998).

Males and females attribute their loneliness to different sources, with men tending to blame themselves, women tending to blame external factors. Men are socialized to initiate relationships, whereas women are traditionally socialized to wait and then respond. Perhaps men blame themselves because they feel they should do something about their loneliness, whereas women wonder why no one calls.

How do you determine if you are lonely? One way is to complete Self-Assessment 8.4.

Loneliness and Life's Transitions Loneliness is interwoven with many life transitions, such as a move to a different part of the country, a divorce, or the death of a close friend or family member. The first year of college often creates loneliness. When students leave the familiar world of their hometown and family to enter college, they can feel especially lonely. Many college freshmen feel anxious about meeting new people, and developing a new social life can create considerable anxiety. As one student commented,

> My first year here at the university has been pretty lonely. I wasn't lonely at all in high school. I lived in a fairly small town—I knew everybody and everyone knew me. I was a member of several clubs and played on the basketball team. It's not that way at the university. It is a big place and I've felt like a stranger on so many occasions. I'm starting to get used to my life here and the last few months I've been making myself meet people and get to know them, but it has not been easy.

As this comment illustrates, freshmen rarely bring their popularity and social standing from high school into the college environment. There may be a dozen high school basketball stars, National Merit scholars, and former student council presidents in a single dormitory wing. Especially if students attend college away from home, they face the task of forming completely new social relationships.

One study found that two weeks after the school year began, 75 percent of 354 college freshmen felt lonely at least part of the time (Cutrona, 1982). More than 40 percent said their loneliness was moderate to severe. Students who were the most optimistic and had the highest self-esteem were the likeliest to overcome their loneliness by the end of their freshman year. Loneliness is not reserved for college freshmen, though. Upperclassmen are often lonely, as well. In one recent study of more than 2,600 undergraduates, lonely individuals were less likely to actively cope with stress than individuals who were able to make friends (Cacioppo & others, 2000).

Loneliness and Technology One of the factors that may be contributing to loneliness in contemporary society is technology. Although invention of the telephone more than a century ago seems to have decreased social isolation for many individuals and families, psychologists have found a link between TV viewing and loneliness. Correlation does not equal causation, but it does seem plausible that television can contribute to social disengagement.

Because most people isolate themselves at their computers when they use the Internet, the Internet also may increase disengagement. One study focused on 169 individuals during their first several years online (Kraut & others, 1998). In this study, greater use of the Internet was associated with declines in participants' communication with family members in the household and increases in depression and loneliness. However, some people use the Internet to form potentially strong new ties (Clay, 2000). Especially for socially anxious and lonely individuals, the Internet may provide a safe way to begin contacts that eventually lead to face-to-face meetings and possibly even intimate relationships (Wood & Smith, 2005). However, caution needs to be exercised in meeting and dating people through the Internet. If you decide to meet the person, go with one or more friends or find a place where there are many people, such as a restaurant. Don't depend on the other person's transportation so that you can leave at any time.

Loneliness Metasite
Coping with Loneliness

Loneliness in Single Adults
Shyness
Internet Romances

"What I'm trying to say, Mary, is that I want your site to be linked to my site."

© The New Yorker Collection 2000. Mick Stevens from cartoonbank.com. All Rights Reserved.

Adjustment Strategies
For Reducing Loneliness

If you are lonely, how can you become better connected with others? Here are some strategies:

1. ***Participate in activities that you can do with others.*** Join organizations or volunteer your time for a cause you believe in. You likely will get to know others whose views are similar to yours. Going to just one social gathering can help you develop social contacts. When you go, introduce yourself to others and start a conversation. Another strategy is to sit next to new people in your classes or find someone to study with.
2. ***Be aware of the early warning signs of loneliness.*** People often feel bored or alienated before loneliness becomes pervasive. Head off loneliness by becoming involved in new social activities.
3. ***Draw a diagram of your social network.*** Determine whether the people in the diagram meet your social needs. If not, pencil in the people you would like to get to know.
4. ***Engage in positive behaviors when you meet new people.*** You will improve your chances of developing enduring relationships if, when you meet new people, you are nice, considerate, honest, trustworthy, and cooperative. Have a positive attitude, be supportive of the other person, and make positive comments about him or her.
5. ***See a counselor or read a book on loneliness.*** If you can't get rid of your loneliness on your own, you might want to contact the counseling services at your college. The counselor can talk with you about strategies for reducing your loneliness. You also might want to read a good book on loneliness, such as *Intimate Connections* by David Burns (1985).

Review and Reflect

4   **Explain the dark side of close relationships**

REVIEW

- What are some characteristics of anger in close relationships?
- What are the sources of jealousy?
- What is the nature of spouse and partner abuse?
- What characterizes overdependence in a close relationship?
- What factors are involved in loneliness?

REFLECT

- What aspects of the dark side of relationships have you experienced?

Reach Your Learning Goals

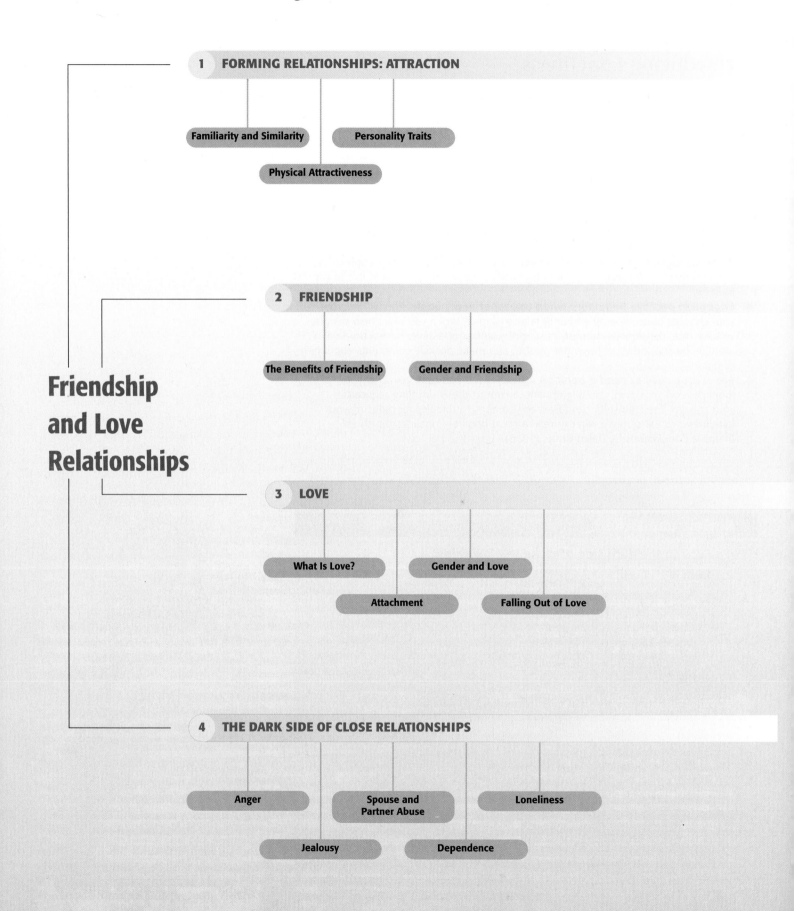

Friendship and Love Relationships

1 FORMING RELATIONSHIPS: ATTRACTION

- Familiarity and Similarity
- Physical Attractiveness
- Personality Traits

2 FRIENDSHIP

- The Benefits of Friendship
- Gender and Friendship

3 LOVE

- What Is Love?
- Attachment
- Gender and Love
- Falling Out of Love

4 THE DARK SIDE OF CLOSE RELATIONSHIPS

- Anger
- Jealousy
- Spouse and Partner Abuse
- Dependence
- Loneliness

Summary

1 Discuss the factors involved in attraction

- Familiarity precedes a close relationship. We also like to associate with people who are similar to us. The desire for consensual validation and a wariness of the unknown and unpredictable can explain the appeal of similarity.
- Physical attraction is usually more important in the early part of a relationship than it is later on. Criteria for physical attractiveness vary across cultures and over time. Furthermore, as the matching hypothesis predicts, although we may theoretically prefer more attractive people, we tend to form relationships with people who are close to our own level of attractiveness.
- Most people are attracted to individuals who have certain personality traits. We are especially attracted to people who are sincere, honest, understanding, loyal, and trustworthy. We are far less likely to be attracted to individuals who are mean, obnoxious, insulting, greedy, conceited, rude, and thoughtless.

2 Describe friendship

- Friendship is a close relationship that involves intimacy, trust, acceptance, mutual liking, and understanding. People not only tend to make friends with people similar to themselves but also tend to become more similar to their friends as the relationship develops. Friendship can reduce loneliness, be a source of self-esteem, and provide emotional support. Harry Stack Sullivan contended that friends play important roles in well-being and development.
- Women have more close friends than men do, and their friendships involve more self-disclosure and exchange of mutual support than men's friendships. Talk is central to women's friendships. Male friends are more likely to engage in activities, especially outdoors, than are female friends. Cross-gender friendships can produce both opportunities and problems.

3 Characterize the types of love and other factors involved in love

- Three types of love described by psychologists are romantic love, affectionate love, and consummate love. Romantic love (or passionate love) is involved when we say we are "in love." It includes passion, sexuality, and a mixture of emotions, not all of which are positive. Affectionate love (or companionate love) usually becomes more important as relationships mature. Sternberg proposed a triarchic model of love involving passion, intimacy, and commitment. Consummate love is the form of love in which all three elements are present.
- Attachment can be described as secure, avoidant, or ambivalent. There are links between an individual's attachment style in childhood and in close relationships in adulthood. Individuals who were securely attached in childhood tend to be securely attached as adults, although some individuals change their attachment styles as adults.
- Men tend to think of love in terms of passion whereas women are more likely to emphasize its similarities to friendship. Differences in how males and females communicate and interact often complicate relationships. Generally, women tend to be more expressive and affectionate.
- The collapse of a close relationship can be traumatic but for some individuals it results in happiness and personal development. For most individuals, falling out of love is painful and emotionally intense.

4 Explain the dark side of close relationships

- Anger is a powerful emotion that can sometimes become an extremely destructive aspect of close relationships. Anger often follows a destructive cycle in close relationships. Catharsis is usually not an effective way to handle anger. Managing anger involves assuming responsibility for one's emotions and actions and developing strategies for behavioral change.
- Jealousy is the fear of perceived possibility of losing someone's exclusive love. Gender differences characterize jealousy, with men showing stronger sexual jealousy and women displaying stronger emotional jealousy. Jealousy is often triggered by a specific event or situation such as finding out that one's lover is having an affair. Individuals with low self-esteem and feelings of insecurity are especially prone to becoming jealous.
- Spouse and partner abuse is a major concern. Many factors can conspire to isolate couples involved in spousal or partner abuse. Walker described a three-phase cycle of domestic violence: (1) tension builds and the battered person uses coping skills to avoid abusive situations, (2) tension escalates until the batterer explodes into a violent episode, and (3) tension is reduced when the batterer is remorseful, loving, and generous. However, later the tension builds again and the cycle is repeated.
- In some close relationships, one partner has an extreme degree of dependence, which may create resentment and hostility in the other partner. Excessively dependent individuals tend to have low self-esteem and feelings of insecurity.
- Men tend to blame themselves for their loneliness, whereas women tend to blame external sources.

Loneliness often emerges when people make life transitions, so it is not surprising that loneliness is common among college freshmen. Technology, such as the telephone, television, and the Internet, can affect loneliness. A number of strategies can help to reduce loneliness, including participating in activities that one can do with others and taking positive steps to meet new people.

Key Terms

consensual validation 236
matching hypothesis 236
friendships 237

romantic love 240
affectionate love 240
consummate love 240

secure attachment style 241
avoidant attachment
   style 241

ambivalent attachment
   style 241
jealousy 247

Resources for Improving Your Adjustment

SELF-HELP BOOKS

The Dance of Intimacy

(1990) by Harriet Lerner. New York: Harper Perennial

This book was written for women and is about women's intimate relationships. Lerner weaves together a portrait of a woman's self and relationships that she believes is derived from long-standing relationships with mothers, fathers, and siblings. She gives women insights about how to define themselves, how to understand their needs and limits, and how to positively change. *The Dance of Intimacy* was highly rated in the national study of self-help books, receiving 5 stars in one of the surveys and 4 stars in another (Norcross, Santrock, & others, 2003).

The Dance of Connection

(2002) by Harriet Lerner. New York: HarperCollins

In this book, Lerner describes the importance of connecting with people who matter most to them. She discusses stressful circumstances in relationships and provides strategies for improved communication. Recommendations for what do when individuals feel desperate and hurt by a relationship, as well as strategies for coping with betrayal, are provided. *The Dance of Connection* received 4 of 5 stars in the national survey of self-help books.

Getting the Love You Want

(1988) by Harville Hendrix. New York: Harper Perennial

This book is a guide for couples who want to improve their relationship. Hendrix instructs readers on how to conduct a 10-week course in couples therapy in the privacy of their home through a number of relationship exercises. This book was given 4 of 5 stars in the national survey of self-help books.

I Only Say This Because I Love You

(2001) by Deborah Tannen. New York: Random House

In this book, Tannen describes how individuals can improve their communication and circumstances in relationships that are quickly becoming destructive. Numerous strategies are given for communicating more effectively with someone you love. This book was given 4 of 5 stars in the national survey of self-help books.

The Relationship Cure

(2002) by John Gottman and Joan DeClaire. New York: Crown

This book focuses on how happiness is based on everyday communication that involves emotion. The authors set forth a five-step program to show readers how to become better at communicating in emotionally intense situations. Numerous case studies, sample dialogues, and self-assessments are included. *The Relationship Cure* was given 4 of 5 stars in the national self-help survey.

You Are Not Alone

(2000) by Linda Rouse. Holmes Beach, FL: Learning Publications

This book helps women understand a relationship in which they are abused by a spouse or partner and explains what to do about it. The profile of battering men is described as well as the causes of the violence. Adjustment strategies that are described include contacting a shelter, the importance of medical care, and how to get help from mental health professionals.

NATIONAL SUPPORT GROUPS

Batterers Anonymous
909-355-1100
(For men who want to control their anger and eliminate their violent abuse)

National Domestic Violence Hotline
http://www.ndvh.org
800-799-SAFE (7233)

E-Learning Tools

To help you master the material in this chapter, you will find a number of valuable study tools on the student CD-ROM that accompanies this book. In addition, visit the Online Learning Center for *Human Adjustment,* where you will find valuable resources for Chapter 8, "Friendships and Love Relationships."

SELF-ASSESSMENT

You can complete these self-assessments in the text:

- Self-Assessment 8.1: *What Type of Love Do I Have?*
- Self-Assessment 8.2: *What Is My Attachment Style?*
- Self-Assessment 8.3: *Am I Vulnerable in My Close Relationship?*
- Self-Assessment 8.4: *Am I Lonely?*

Additional Self-Assessment

Complete this self-assessment on the Online Learning Center: *My Friendship Compatibility*

THINK CRITICALLY

To practice your critical thinking skills, complete these exercises on the Online Learning Center:

- *How Do You Know When You Are in Love?* gets you to think about the symptoms of someone who is in love.
- *The Power of Love* asks you to think about a number of aspects of falling in and out of love.
- *Support and Suffocation* focuses on the difficulty some individuals have in developing mature intimate relationships.

APPLY YOUR KNOWLEDGE

1. Who's an ideal mate?

According to your text, men and women differ on what they consider important in a mate. Make a list of 20 physical or personality characteristics and make a dozen copies of them. Ask people to rate each characteristic on a scale of 1–10.

a. Give half of the copies to women and half to men. Tell your respondents to answer honestly. Is there a lot of consistency between the two sexes? Or are individual differences more important? –OR-

b. Choose one sex (either men or women) and give half the copies to younger people and the other half to middle-aged people, over 45.

c. If your professor is willing, you can combine your results with other members of the class.

Possible characteristics include: attractive, warm, sense of humor, dependable, kind, honest, intelligent, faithful, frugal, adventurous, healthy, good mental health, good hygiene, similar interests, outgoing, good income, family-oriented, athletic, and competent.

2. Loneliness or disappointment in love are challenges that face many people. Make a list of strategies that you use in dating. Then, compare your strategies to those suggested on the Internet. Keep in mind that not all information on the Internet is reliable. What new ideas did you find that might be worth trying? Which ones are not reliable suggestions? Based on what researchers know about human relationships, what makes a suggestion work or not work?

Select an Internet search engine such as www.yahoo.com or www.google.com and search for "dating strategies" or "successful dating."

3. Controlling anger and jealousy.

Everyone gets angry or jealous from time to time. What separates good adjustment from poor adjustment is how you handle these feelings. Think of times in your relationships (with friends, family, or romantic interests) when you became angry or jealous. Which things did you do that you would like to do differently? Using your textbook to get ideas, make a list of more constructive ways that you can manage your emotions. Then, go to the Internet and search for other suggestions that might help you handle anger or jealousy in your relationships. Select an Internet search engine such as www.yahoo.com or www.google.com and search for "jealousy" and "anger."

VIDEO SEGMENT

For a closer look at one coping strategy, watch the videos for Chapter 5 on the CD-ROM. They examine how and why laughter can help us cope with stress.

Adult Lifestyles

Chapter Outline

Learning Goals

1 Discuss the diversity of adult lifestyles and how they affect people's lives

2 Describe the family life cycle

3 Discuss parenting and how it affects children's adjustment

Images of Adjustment

Liddy's Adjustment to Postdivorce Life

Liddy Pennebaker had an unhappy marriage. She and her husband agreed about very little, and she was tired of her husband not spending time with their children. But the final straw came when she found out that he had a string of affairs. At the end of their marriage, they agreed about very little. The divorce was bitter.

Being divorced wasn't easy. Liddy's job as a sales clerk and her husband's child support payments were barely enough to make ends meet, but she decided to go back to school to obtain an MBA. To do so, she needed financial help from her mother, which she received; she moved in with her mother temporarily. The first several years as a divorced mother were painful for Liddy, but she ended up with a new career and better relationships.

Every divorce requires a great deal of adaptation and adjustment. Liddy Pennebaker was one of the participants in E. Mavis Hetherington's study of how divorce affects people's lives, and she is an example of someone who coped effectively (Hetherington & Kelly, 2002). Liddy developed a plan to cope with her financial problems. It included returning to school to obtain an MBA and obtaining financial support from her mother. Although the divorce and the first several years after it were a struggle for Liddy, the painful changes her divorce produced had a positive side. It opened the door to improved relationships and a new career.

Are you on your own or living with someone? Are you married, divorced, or single? The adjustments you make in life depend in part on your answers to these questions about your lifestyle. Adults can pursue a diversity of lifestyles and we explore these in the first section of the chapter. Then we examine how the family changes through the life span and the adjustments involved in these changes. Finally, we describe many aspects of parenting.

1 THE DIVERSITY OF ADULT LIFESTYLES

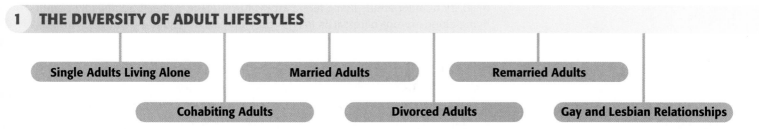

| Single Adults Living Alone | Married Adults | Remarried Adults |
| Cohabiting Adults | Divorced Adults | Gay and Lesbian Relationships |

One of the most striking social changes in the United States in recent decades is the increased acceptance of what were long considered unconventional lifestyles (Rubin, 2004; Scanzoni, 2004). Until about 1930, stable marriage was widely accepted as the endpoint in adult development. In the last 70 years, however, personal fulfillment has emerged as a competing goal. More adults are remaining single longer today, but eventually they are likely to marry at least once and for a little while. However, approximately 50 percent of marriages end in divorce.

Today, adults in the United States choose many lifestyles and form many types of families. They live alone, cohabit, marry, divorce, remarry, or live with someone of the same sex. Let's explore each of these lifestyles and the adjustment involved in each of them.

Single Adults Living Alone

There is no rehearsal. One day you don't live alone, the next day you do. College ends. Your wife walks out. Your husband dies. Suddenly, you face this increasingly common condition, living alone. Maybe you like it, maybe you don't. Maybe you thrive on the solitude, maybe you ache as if in exile. Either way, chances are you are only half prepared, if at all, to be sole proprietor of your bed, your toaster, and your time. Most of us were raised in the din and clutter of family life, jockeying for a place in the bathroom in the morning, fighting over the last piece of cake, and obliged to compromise on the simplest of choices—the volume of the stereo, the channel on the TV, for example.

There has been a dramatic rise in the percentage of single adults (see figure 9.1). Further, the percentage of single adults who live alone has multiplied. In 2000, 25 percent of adults in the United States who never had been married lived alone; this is more than three times the percentage in 1970 (8 percent) (National Center for Health Statistics, 2002).

Myths and stereotypes are associated with being single, ranging from the "swinging single" to the "desperately lonely, suicidal" single. Of course, most single adults are somewhere between these extremes. Common problems of single adults include forming intimate relationships with other adults, confronting loneliness, and finding a niche in a society that is marriage oriented.

Advantages of being single include time to make decisions about one's life course, time to develop personal resources to meet goals, freedom to make autonomous decisions and pursue one's own schedule and interests, opportunities to explore new places and try out new things, and privacy. One woman who never married commented, "I enjoy knowing that I can satisfy my own whims

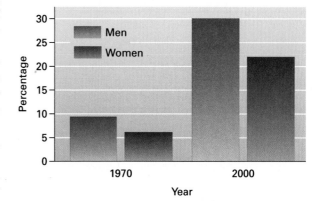

FIGURE 9.1 Percentage of U.S. Single Adults 30 to 34 Years of Age in 1970 and 2000
In three decades, the percentage of U.S. single adults 30 to 34 years of age more than tripled.

Singles and Couples

without someone else's interferences. If I want to wash my hair at two o'clock in the morning, no one complains. I can eat when I'm hungry and watch my favorite television shows without contradictions from anyone. I enjoy these freedoms."

Living alone when you are 20 years old is different from living alone when you are 30 or 50 or 70. Once adults reach the age of 30, there can be increasing pressure to settle down and get married. This is when many single adults make a conscious decision to marry or to remain single.

Once older adults age into their 70s, the greater are their odds of living alone. The majority of older adults living alone are widowed. Like younger adults, older adults living alone are not necessarily lonely; they may have regular exchanges with relatives, neighbors, and friends.

Cohabiting Adults

Cohabitation refers to living together in a sexual relationship without being married. Cohabitation has undergone considerable changes in recent years (Cherlin, 2004; Means & others, 2003; Oppenheimer, 2003; Seltzer, 2004) (see figure 9.2). The percentage of U.S. couples who cohabit before marriage has increased from approximately 11 percent in 1970 to almost 60 percent at the beginning of the twenty-first century (Bumpass & Lu, 2000). Cohabiting rates are even higher in some countries—in Sweden, cohabitation before marriage is virtually universal (Hoem, 1995).

How do cohabiting relationships differ from marriage? In the United States, cohabiting arrangements tend to be short-lived, with one-third lasting less than a year (Hyde & DeLamater, 2005). Less than 1 out of 10 lasts five years. Of course, it is easier to dissolve a cohabitation relationship than to divorce. Many couples view their cohabitation not as a precursor to marriage but as an ongoing lifestyle. These couples do not want the official aspects of marriage.

Do cohabiting relationships differ from marriage in other ways? Relationships between cohabiting men and women tend to be more equal than those between husbands and wives (Wineberg, 1994). For example, cohabiting couples are more likely to share household chores and tasks than married couples, in which wives do a majority of these.

Although cohabitation offers some advantages, it also can produce some problems (Solot & Miller, 2002). Disapproval by parents and other family members can place emotional strain on the cohabiting couple. Some cohabiting couples have difficulty owning property jointly. Legal rights are less certain than in a divorce.

Does cohabiting help or harm the chances that a couple will have a stable and happy marriage? Some researchers have found no differences in marital quality between individuals who earlier cohabited and those who did not (Newcomb & Bentler, 1980; Watson & DeMeo, 1987). Other researchers have found lower rates of marital satisfaction in couples who lived together before getting married (Booth & Johnson, 1988; Kline & others, 2004; Whitehead & Popenoe, 2003). For example, in one study of 13,000 individuals, married couples who cohabited prior to their marriage reported lower levels of happiness with and commitment to their marital relationship than their counterparts who had not previously cohabited (Nock, 1995). And in one recent study, after 10 years of marriage, 40 percent of couples who lived together before marriage had divorced, whereas 31 percent of those who had not cohabited first had divorced (Centers for Disease Control and Prevention, 2002).

In sum, researchers have found either that cohabitation leads to no differences or that cohabitation is not good for a marriage. Why would cohabiting be linked with divorce? The most frequently given explanation is that because cohabitation is a nontraditional lifestyle, it may attract less conventional individuals who are not great believers

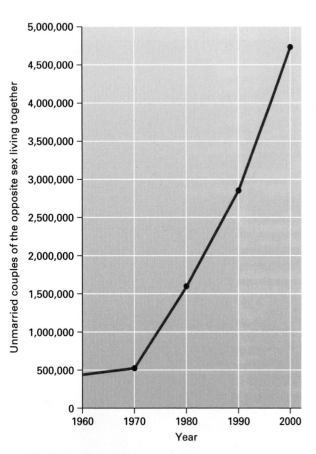

FIGURE 9.2 The Increase in Cohabitation in the United States
Since 1970 there has been a dramatic increase in the number of unmarried adults living together in the United States.

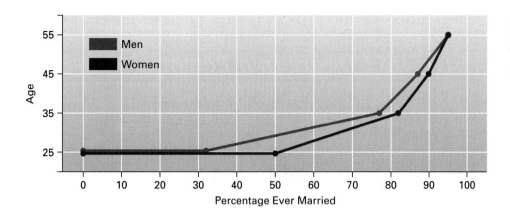

FIGURE 9.3 Percentage of U.S. Men and Women Who Have Ever Been Married By The Time They Have Reached a Particular Age

in marriage in the first place (Kline & others, 2004; Manning & Smock, 2002). An alternative explanation is that the experience of cohabiting changes people's attitudes and habits in ways that increase their likelihood of divorce (Solot & Miller, 2002).

Cohabitation is also increasing among older adults (Allen, Blieszner, & Roberto, 2000). By the 1990s, approximately 2.4 percent of older adults were cohabiting, compared with almost 0 percent in 1960 (Chevan, 1996). Older men are more likely to cohabit than older women. In some cases, older adults cohabit because of poverty.

Married Adults

Let's begin our examination of marriage by looking at some statistics.

- *The United States is still a marrying society.* In 2002, 95 percent of U.S. adults eventually had been married at least once and for a little while by the time they were 55 years of age, although this figure is likely to decline in the future as more young adults today choose not to marry (U.S. Bureau of the Census, 2003) (see figure 9.3). Currently, almost 60 percent of U.S. adults are married. By age 30, 65 percent of men and 71 percent of women have married.

- *Despite being a marrying society, marriages occur later, the percentage of adults married at any one point when surveyed has declined, and divorce is commonplace.* On average, brides and grooms in the United States are older than they used to be. In 2002, the average age for a first marriage climbed to almost 27 years for men and just over 25 years for women, up from 26 years for men and 24 years for women in 1990, and 23 years for men and 22 years for women in 1970 (U.S. Bureau of the Census, 2003). Further, the percentage of adults who are married at any one point when surveyed has steadily declined (see figure 9.4). And once married, approximately one-third of the couples become divorced before their tenth wedding anniversary. On average, a first marriage lasts for approximately eight years, a second marriage about seven years, before a divorce.

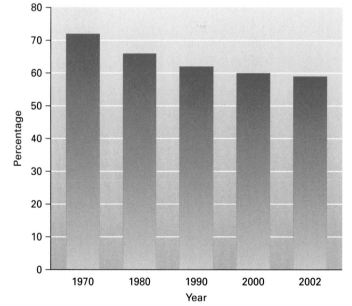

FIGURE 9.4 Percentage of U.S. Adults Who Are Married: 1970 to 2002

What adjustments do married couples face? That depends, not only on the individuals but also on their sociocultural context. The sociocultural context is a powerful influence on marriage, influencing everything from when people marry, what they look for in a partner, and how they relate to their partner. For example, as part of China's efforts to control population growth, a 1981 law sets the minimum age for marriage at 22 years for males, 20 for females. In the United States, increasing male-female equality in marriage has produced marital relationships that are more fragile and intense than they were decades ago (Bradbury, Finchum, & Beach, 2000).

SELF-ASSESSMENT 9.1

What Characteristics Do I Desire in a Potential Mate?

Rank order the following characteristics in terms of which characteristics you desire in a potential mate. Give a 1 to the characteristics you most desire and an 18 to the characteristic you least desire.

_____ Emotional stability and maturity

_____ Desire for home and children

_____ Similar religious background

_____ Education and intelligence

_____ Ambition and industriousness

_____ Dependable character

_____ Pleasing disposition

_____ Refinement, neatness

_____ Mutual attraction–love

_____ Favorable social status or rating

_____ Good cook and housekeeper

_____ Sociability

_____ Good looks

_____ Chastity (no prior sexual intercourse)

_____ Good financial prospect

_____ Similar education

_____ Good health

_____ Similar political background

Go to the appendix at the end of the book to see how your responses compared to people from a large number of cultures around the world.

How do individuals deal with the varied challenges of marriage? Let's first consider how people choose a spouse and then explore their expectations for marriage and their actual experiences.

Finding a Partner What do people look for in a spouse? The most desired traits vary around the world (Hamon & Ingoldsby, 2003; Sherif-Trask, 2003; Surra & others, 2004). In one large-scale study of 9,474 adults from 37 cultures on six continents and five islands, people varied most regarding how much they valued chastity—desiring a marital partner with no previous experience in sexual intercourse (Buss & others, 1990). Chastity was the most important characteristic in selecting a marital partner in China, India, Indonesia, Iran, Taiwan, and the Palestinian Arab culture. Adults from Ireland and Japan placed moderate importance on chastity. In contrast, adults in Sweden, Finland, Norway, the Netherlands, and Germany generally said that chastity was not important in selecting a marital partner.

Domesticity is also valued in some cultures and not in others. In this study, adults from the Zulu culture in South Africa, Estonia, and Colombia placed a high value on housekeeping skills in their marital preference. By contrast, adults in the United States, Canada, and all Western European countries except Spain said that housekeeping skill was not an important trait in their partner.

Religion plays an important role in marital preferences in many cultures (Ritblatt, 2003). For example, Islam stresses the honor of the male and the purity of the female. It also emphasizes the woman's role in childbearing, child rearing, educating children, and instilling the Islamic faith in their children.

For young adults in the United States, emotional depth and the ability to communicate are viewed as important characteristics of a spouse. These were the conclusions reached in a recent national survey in which an overwhelming number (94 percent) of never-married singles said that when you marry, you want your spouse to be your soul mate, first and foremost (Whitehead & Popenoe, 2003). More than 80 percent of women said that it is more important for them to have a husband who can communicate his deepest feelings than to have a husband who makes a good living. To evaluate the characteristics you desire in a potential mate, complete Self-Assessment 9.1.

SELF-ASSESSMENT 9.2

My Knowledge of Marital Myths and Realities

Answer each of the following items true or false.

	True	False
1. A husband's marital satisfaction is usually lower if his wife is employed full-time than if she is a full-time homemaker.	_____	_____
2. Today most young, single, never-married people will eventually get married.	_____	_____
3. In most marriages, having a child improves marital satisfaction for both spouses.	_____	_____
4. The best single predictor of overall marital satisfaction is the quality of a couple's sex life.	_____	_____
5. The divorce rate in America increased from 1960 to 1980.	_____	_____
6. A greater percentage of wives are in the workforce today than in 1970.	_____	_____
7. Marital satisfaction for a wife is usually lower if she is employed full-time than if she is a full-time homemaker.	_____	_____
8. If my spouse loves me, he/she should instinctively know what I want and need to be happy.	_____	_____
9. In a marriage in which the wife is employed full-time, the husband usually assumes an equal share of the housekeeping.	_____	_____
10. For most couples, marital satisfaction gradually increases from the first years of marriage through the childbearing years, the teen years, the empty nest period, and retirement.	_____	_____
11. No matter how I behave, my spouse should love me simply because he/she *is* my spouse.	_____	_____
12. One of the most frequent marital problems is poor communication.	_____	_____
13. Husbands usually make more lifestyle adjustments in marriage than wives.	_____	_____
14. Couples who cohabited before marriage usually report greater marital satisfaction than couples who did not.	_____	_____
15. I can change my spouse by pointing out his/her inadequacies, errors, etc.	_____	_____

To find out which of these statements are true and which are false, see the appendix at the end of the book.

Marital Expectations and Myths In some ways, the survey of young adults in the United States found very down-to-earth views (Whitehead & Popenoe, 2003). For example, a large majority of young adults indicated that it is unwise for women to rely on marriage for financial security; a high percentage (86 percent) reported that marriage is hard work and a full-time job. Still, we expect a spouse to simultaneously be a lover, a friend, a confidant, a counselor, a career person, and a parent.

Marriage therapists believe it is important to have realistic expectations about a marriage (Sharp & Ganong, 2000). Researchers have found that unrealistic expectations are linked with lower levels of marital satisfaction (Larson & Holman, 1994). If you have very romantic beliefs about marriage, you are likely to become disappointed as you realize that it is impossible to sustain your romantic ideal (Huston, Neihuis, & Smith, 1997).

Underlying unrealistic expectations about marriage are numerous myths—widely held beliefs unsupported by facts—about marriage (Markman, 2000). To test your beliefs about marriage against what research has found, complete Self-Assessment 9.2.

What are some of the myths about marriage? They include these (Gottman & Silver, 2000):

- *Affairs are the main reason people get divorced.* In most instances, it is the opposite. Marital problems produce stress in the relationship, and one or both partners seek an intimate relationship outside of the marriage. In many instances, these affairs are not about sex but about friendship, caring, and respect.
- *Men are not biologically made for marriage.* According to this myth, men are philanderers by nature, which makes them poorly suited for a monogamous marriage. From this perspective the male seeks to father as many offspring as possible and having only one mate restricts him from attaining this goal; in contrast, the female's main role is to care for her children, so she seeks a single mate who will provide for her and her children.(We discuss this idea again in chapter 12, "Gender.") However, as U.S. women have increasingly worked outside the home, their rate of extramarital affairs has increased.
- *Men are from "Mars" and women are from "Venus."* According to a best-selling book by John Gray (1992), men and women have serious relationship problems because he is from Mars and she is from Venus. Gender differences can contribute to marital problems, but they usually don't cause them. For example, the key factor in whether wives or husbands feel satisfied with the sex, romance, and passion in their marriage is the quality of the couple's friendship.

What Makes Marriages Work   John Gottman (1994; Driver & Gottman, 2004; Gottman & Notarius, 2000; Gottman & Silver, 2000; Gottman & others, 1998) has been studying married couples' lives since the early 1970s. He uses many methods to analyze what makes marriages work. Gottman interviews couples about the history of their marriage, their philosophy about marriage, and how they view their parents' marriages. He videotapes them talking to each other about how their day went and evaluates what they say about the good and bad times of their marriages. Gottman also uses physiological measures to measure their heart rate, blood flow, blood pressure, and immune functioning moment by moment. He also checks back in with the couples every year to see how their marriage is faring. Gottman's research represents the most extensive assessment of marital relationships available. Currently he and his colleagues are following 700 couples in seven studies. The Adjustment Strategies interlude that follows further explores Gottman's ideas.

Adjustment Strategies
For Making Marriages Work

Based on John Gottman's extensive research, the following seven principles are the ones that are most often linked with a successful marriage:

1. ***Establish love maps.*** Individuals in successful marriages have personal insights and detailed maps of each other's life and world. They aren't psychological strangers. In good marriages, partners are willing to share their feelings with each other. They use these "love maps" to express not only their understanding of each other but also their fondness and admiration.
2. ***Nurture fondness and admiration.*** In successful marriages, partners sing each other's praises. More than 90 percent of the time, when couples put a positive spin on their marriage's history, the marriage is likely to have a positive future.
3. ***Turn toward each other instead of away.*** In good marriages, spouses are adept at turning toward each other regularly. They respect each other, appreciate each other's point of view, and see each other as friends. This friendship doesn't keep arguments from occurring, but it can prevent differences from overwhelming the relationship.

4. ***Let your partner influence you.*** Bad marriages often involve one spouse who is unwilling to share power with the other. Although power-mongering is more common in husbands, some wives also show this trait. A willingness to share power and to respect the other person's view is a prerequisite to compromising.

5. ***Solve solvable conflicts.*** Two types of problems occur in marriage: (1) perpetual and (2) solvable. Perpetual problems include differences about whether to have children and how often to have sex. Solvable problems include not helping each other reduce daily stresses and not being verbally affectionate. Unfortunately, more than two-thirds of marital problems fall into the perpetual category—those that won't go away. Fortunately, marital therapists have found that couples often don't have to solve their perpetual problems for the marriage to work.

6. ***Overcome gridlock.*** One partner wants the other to attend church, the other is an atheist. One partner is a homebody, the other wants to go out and socialize a lot. Such problems often produce gridlock. Gottman believes the key to ending gridlock is not to solve the problem, but to move from gridlock to dialogue and be patient.

7. ***Create shared meaning.*** The more partners can speak candidly and respectfully with each other, the more likely it is that they will create shared meaning in their marriage. This also includes sharing goals with one's spouse and working together to achieve each other's goals.

Dealing with Conflict Work, stress, in-laws, money, sex, housework, a new baby: these are among the typical areas of marital conflict, even in happy marriages. When there is conflict in these areas, it usually means that a husband and wife have different ideas about the tasks involved, their importance, or how they should be accomplished. If the conflict is perpetual, no amount of problem-solving expertise will fix it. The tension will decrease only when both partners feel comfortable living with the ongoing difference. However, when the issue is solvable, the challenge is to find the right strategy for dealing with it (Sinclair & Monk, 2004).

The right strategy depends on the problem and the couple. Possible strategies include scheduling formal griping sessions about stressful issues and learning to talk about sex in a way that both partners feel comfortable with. In other cases, the couple might create lists of who does what to see how household labor is divided.

Gottman has found that resolving conflicts works best when couples start out solving the problem with a soft rather than a harsh approach, are motivated to repair the relationship, regulate their emotions, compromise, and are tolerant of each other's faults. Conflict resolution is not about one person making changes, it is about negotiating and accommodating each other.

What makes marriages work? What are the benefits of having a good marriage?

The Benefits of a Good Marriage A happy marriage does bring benefits. An unhappy marriage increases an individual's risk of getting sick by approximately one-third and can even shorten a person's life by an average of four years (Gove, Style, & Hughes, 1990). Individuals who are happily married live longer, healthier lives than either divorced individuals or those who are unhappily married (Cotten, 1999). One recent longitudinal study conducted over 13 years found that women who were in satisfying marriages were healthier than unmarried women or those in unsatisfying marriages (Gallo & others, 2003).

What are the reasons for these benefits of a happy marriage? People in happy marriages likely feel less physically and emotionally stressed, which puts less wear and tear on a person's body. Such wear and tear can lead to numerous physical ailments, such as high blood pressure and heart disease, as well as psychological problems such as anxiety, depression, and substance abuse.

FIGURE 9.5 Number of Divorces Per 1,000 U.S. Married Women Age 15 and Older: 1960 to 2000
Note the dramatic increase in divorce from the 1960s until about 1980, the smaller decline from 1980 through 2000.

Divorced Adults

Media reports often suggest that American society is becoming unglued and that soaring divorce rates are both a major cause and a major symptom of the crisis. In fact, the divorce rate in the United States dramatically increased from the 1960s through the mid-1980s but has been declining since then (see figure 9.5). Still, compared with most countries, the United States has a very high divorce rate (Amato, 2004). Currently, 10 percent of U.S. adults are divorced (U.S. Bureau of the Census, 2003). Low-income groups have a higher incidence of divorce than higher-income groups. Youthful marriage, premarital pregnancy, low educational level, and low income are associated with increases in divorce.

If we take a closer view and examine not society but individuals (like Liddy Pennebaker, who was described in the opening of the chapter), what does divorce look like? When are people likely to divorce, and how does it affect their lives?

The Timing of Divorce If a divorce is going to occur, it often takes place early in a marriage; the most likely time is in the fifth to tenth year of marriage (National Center for Health Statistics, 2000). It may be that people tend to divorce only after staying in a troubled marriage while trying to work things out. Although divorce has risen slightly among older adults recently, very few older adults divorce (National Center for Health Statistics, 2000). Older adults account for about 1 percent of all who divorce in any given year in the United States.

Are there differences between young adults who divorce and those who divorce in midlife? In a fourteen-year longitudinal study, John Gottman and Robert Levenson (2000) recently found that couples who divorce among younger adults (often in the first seven years of a marriage) are characterized by heated emotions that burn out the marriage. The young divorcing couples frequently were volatile and expressive, full of disappointments that they let each other know about. In contrast, Gottman and Levenson found that couples who divorce in midlife tend to be cool and distant with suppressed emotions. The midlife divorcing couples were alienated and avoidant. They were the kind of people you see in a restaurant who aren't talking with each other. It is a distant relationship with little or no laughter, love, or interest in each other. One of the divorcing midlife adults often feels that his or her life is "empty."

The Stresses of Divorce Even those adults who initiated their divorce experience challenges after a marriage dissolves (Amato, 2004; Hetherington, 2000). Both divorced women and divorced men complain of loneliness, diminished self-esteem, anxiety about the unknowns in their lives, and difficulty in forming satisfactory new intimate relationships (Lewis, Wallerstein, & Johnson-Reitz, 2004).

Divorce places both men and women at risk for psychological and physical difficulties (Hetherington & Stanley-Hagan, 2002; Segrin & Flora, 2005). Compared with married adults, separated and divorced women and men have higher rates of psychiatric disorders, admission to psychiatric hospitals, clinical depression, alcoholism, and psychosomatic problems, such as sleep disorders. And like other stressors discussed in chapter 4, marital separation can lead to reduced functioning of the immune system, rendering separated and divorced individuals vulnerable to disease and infection. In one study, women who had been separated for one year or less were more likely to show impaired immunological functioning than women whose separations had occurred one to six years earlier (Kiecolt-Glaser & Glaser, 1988).

The specific stressors associated with divorce depend in part on whether the divorced parent has custody of children. Custodial parents have concerns about child rearing and overload in their lives. Noncustodial parents register complaints about alienation from or lack of time with their children.

The stress of divorce also depends on its economic effects. Men show only modest declines in income following a divorce, but women face a significant decline, with estimates of the decline ranging from 20 to 35 percent. For divorced women, the financial decline means living in a less desirable neighborhood with fewer resources; if a divorced woman has custody of her children, this decline often means less effective schools and more deviant peer groups. However, the economic decline for women following a divorce has diminished as fewer women are full-time homemakers and more have experience in the workforce before divorce.

Coping with Divorce   How do people like Liddy Pennebaker deal so effectively with all of the stressors associated with divorce? Hetherington identified several factors that enable divorced adults to cope effectively: (1) social maturity, (2) autonomy, (3) internal locus of control, (4) religiosity, (5) work, (6) social support, and (7) a new intimate relationship (Hetherington & Kelly, 2002).

Social Maturity   In Hetherington's research, social maturity consisted of planfulness, self-regulation, adaptability, and social responsibility. Divorced adults who were planful had concrete rather than general goals and a reasonably good idea of how to reach these goals. Liddy, for example, didn't want just a "good job" five years after the divorce, she wanted a great job, and to reach this goal she went back to school to obtain an MBA.

Socially mature divorced adults also found ways to control the anxiety, depression, and fear associated with the failure of marriage so that these emotions did not interfere with their decisions. Because they were adaptable, socially mature divorced adults avoided turning solvable problems into unsolvable ones.

In terms of social responsibility, divorced adults who were giving received in turn when they needed help. Also, divorced adults who felt badly about themselves felt better when they helped others.

Autonomy   Divorced adults who were comfortable being alone found being single easier to cope with than those who were bothered by being alone. Some of the most independent women found that being free from joint decision making was a positive aspect of their postdivorce life.

Divorce
Flying Solo

Internal Locus of Control   Feeling helpless is common after divorce. Divorced adults with an internal locus of control or high self-efficacy (which we discussed in chapter 2) felt more in control of their lives than their counterparts with external locus of control or low self-efficacy. Divorced adults who believe they are in control of their lives and world adjust better than those who feel like one divorcee who said, "What's the use? Nothing I try works, anyhow" (Hetherington & Kelly, 2002, p. 75).

Religiosity   A religious affiliation often works as a buffer against stress and problems by providing access to a support network. Liddy Pennebaker, for example, met new friends and found a sense of rootedness and security when she attended a new religious group.

Work   For many people, work provides a sense of security in their life after divorce. Some men in Hetherington's study, having lost their home and families, poured themselves into their work in an effort to find continuity and stability.

Social Support   Hetherington found that transitional figures were especially important in helping divorced adults adjust to their postdivorce life. Transitional figures were part counselor and part comforter, lending support and giving advice during the divorce process and the transition to being a single adult. They also helped with practical matters such as finding a new place to live, selecting a good child care center, and finding new friends.

A New Intimate Relationship   In Hetherington's research, the most powerful factor in reducing postdivorce stress was a new intimate relationship, which often led to reduced depression and health problems, and an increase in self-esteem. This was true for both women and men.

Diversity of Postdivorce Pathways   After a divorce, people's lives can take diverse turns. Hetherington found six common pathways (Hetherington & Kelly, 2002, pp. 98–108):

- *The enhancers.* Accounting for 20 percent of the divorced group, most were females who "grew more competent, well adjusted, and self-fulfilled" following their divorce. They were competent in multiple areas of life, showed a remarkable ability to bounce back from stressful circumstances, and created something meaningful out of the problems.
- *The good enoughs.* The largest group of divorced individuals, they were described as average people coping with divorce. They showed some strengths and some weaknesses, some successes and some failures. When they experienced a problem, they tried to solve it. Many attended night classes, found new friends, developed active social lives, and were motivated to get higher-paying jobs. However, they were not as good at planning and were less persistent than the enhancers. Good enough women typically married men who educationally and economically were similar to their first husbands, often going into a new marriage that was not much of an improvement over the first one.
- *The seekers.* These individuals were motivated to find new mates as soon as possible. "At one year postdivorce, 40 percent of the men and 38 percent of the women had been classified as seekers. But as people found new partners or remarried, or became more secure or satisfied in their single life, this category shrunk and came to be predominated by men," p. 102.
- *The libertines.* They often spent more time in single bars and had more casual sex than their counterparts in the other divorce categories. However, by the end of the first year postdivorce, they often grew disillusioned with their sensation-seeking lifestyle and wanted a stable relationship.
- *The competent loners.* These individuals, which made up only about 10 percent of the divorced group, were "well adjusted, self-sufficient, and socially skilled." They had a successful career, an active social life, and a wide range of interests. However, "unlike enhancers, competent loners had little interest in sharing their lives with anyone," p. 105.
- *The defeated.* Some of these individuals had problems prior to their divorce, and these problems increased after the divorce when "the added stress of a failed marriage was more than they could handle. Others had difficulty coping because divorce cost them a spouse who had supported them, or in the case of a drinking problem, restricted them," p. 106.

Adjustment Strategies
For Divorced Adults

Hetherington recommends these strategies for divorced adults (Hetherington & Kelly, 2002, pp. 108–109):

1. ***"Look at divorce as an opportunity for personal growth and to build more fulfilling relationships."*** Liddy Pennebaker, for example, used her divorce as an opportunity for building a new career.
2. ***"Think carefully about your choices."*** The consequences of choices about work, lovers, and children may last a lifetime.

3. **Focus more on the future than the past.** "Set priorities and goals, and then work toward them."
4. **"Capitalize on your strengths and the resources available to you."**
5. **Don't expect to be successful and happy in everything you do.** "The road to a more satisfying life is bumpy and it will have many detours."
6. **"You are never trapped by one pathway."** Most of those who were categorized as defeated immediately after divorce gradually moved on to a better life, but moving onward usually requires some effort.

Remarried Adults

On average, divorced adults remarry within four years after their divorce, with men remarrying sooner than women. Stepfamilies come in many sizes and forms. The custodial and noncustodial parents and stepparents all might have been married and divorced, in some cases more than once. These parents might have residential children from prior marriages and a large network of grandparents and other relatives. Regardless of their form and size, the newly reconstituted families face some unique tasks. The couple must define and strengthen their marriage and at the same time renegotiate the biological parent-child relationships and establish stepparent-stepchild and stepsibling relationships (Coleman, Ganong, & Fine, 2000, 2004; Hetherington & Stanley-Hagan, 2002; Segrin & Flora, 2005).

The complex histories and multiple relationships make adjustment difficult in a stepfamily (Coleman, Ganong, & Weaver, 2001; Rice, 2001; Thomson & others, 2001). Only one-third of stepfamily couples stay remarried (Gerlach, 1998).

Why do remarried adults find it so difficult to stay remarried? For one thing, many remarry not for love but for financial reasons, for help in rearing children, and to reduce loneliness. They also might carry into the stepfamily negative patterns that produced failure in an earlier marriage. Remarried couples also experience more stress in rearing children than parents in never-divorced families (Ganong & Coleman, 1994).

What adjustments do remarried adults need to make?

Adjustment Strategies
For Remarried Adults

Among the strategies that help remarried couples cope with the stress of living in a stepfamily are these (Hetherington & Kelly, 2002; Visher & Visher, 1989):

1. **Have realistic expectations.** Allow time for loving relationships to develop, and look at the complexity of the stepfamily as a challenge to overcome.
2. **Develop new positive relationships within the family.** Create new traditions and ways of dealing with difficult circumstances.
3. **Allot time to be alone with each other.** Allocation of time can be especially important in a stepfamily because so many people may be involved.
4. **Learn from the first marriage.** Face your own shortcomings and don't make the same mistakes the second time around.
5. **"Don't expect instant love from stepchildren,"** Hetherington & Kelly, 2002, p. 201. Relationships in stepfamilies are built over time.

Stepfamilies

Gay and Lesbian Relationships

The legal and social context of marriage creates barriers to breaking up that do not usually exist for same-sex partners (Peplau & Beals, 2002, 2004). But in other ways

What are the research findings regarding the development and psychological well-being of children raised by gay and lesbian couples?

researchers have found that gay and lesbian relationships are similar—in their satisfactions, loves, joys, and conflicts—to heterosexual relationships (Hyde & DeLamater, 2005; Peplau & Beals, 2004). For example, like heterosexual couples, gay and lesbian couples need to find the balance of romantic love, affection, autonomy, and equality that is acceptable to both partners. Lesbian couples especially place a high priority on equality in their relationships (Peplau & Beals, 2004). In one study, gay and lesbian couples listed the areas of conflict in order of frequency: finances, driving style, affection and sex, being overly critical, and household tasks (Kurdek, 1995). The components of this list are likely to be familiar to heterosexual couples.

There are a number of misconceptions about homosexual couples. Contrary to stereotypes, one partner is masculine and the other feminine in only a small percentage of homosexual couples. Researchers have found that homosexuals prefer long-term, committed relationships (Peplau & Beals, 2004). However, about half of committed gay male couples have an open relationship—one that allows sex outside of the relationship but not affectionate love. Lesbian couples usually do not have this open relationship.

Increasingly, gay and lesbian couples are creating families that include children. Researchers have found that children growing up in gay or lesbian families are just as popular with their peers, and there are no differences in the adjustment and mental health of children living in these families when they are compared with children in heterosexual families (Anderssen, Amlie, & Ytteroy, 2002; Hyde & DeLamater, 2005). Also, the overwhelming majority of children growing up in a gay or lesbian family have a heterosexual orientation (Patterson, 1995, 2000, 2002).

Review and Reflect

1 Discuss the diversity of adult lifestyles and how they affect people's lives

REVIEW

- What characterizes single adults?
- What are the lives of cohabiting adults like?
- What are some key aspects of the lives of married adults?
- How is divorce linked with the adjustment of adults and children?
- What are the lives of remarried parents like?
- What characterizes the relationships of gay and lesbian couples?

REFLECT

- Which type of lifestyle are you living today? What do you think are its advantages and disadvantages for you? If you could have a different lifestyle, which one would it be? Why?

2 THE FAMILY LIFE CYCLE

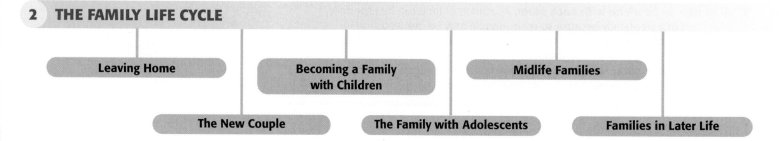

Leaving Home

The New Couple

Becoming a Family with Children

The Family with Adolescents

Midlife Families

Families in Later Life

No two families are the same; they vary as much as their individual members. Nevertheless, families do share some common features. In particular, they all change over time (Conger, Lorenz, & Wickrama, 2004). Liddy Pennebaker and husband as newlyweds were a far different family from the family of Liddy Pennebaker, husband, and two children years later.

Do families change in predictable ways with time? Six stages in the family life cycle have been proposed to reflect the changes that families experience through the years (Carter & McGoldrick, 1989) (see figure 9.6). Some critics argue that talking about stages of the family life cycle is misleading. They argue that clearly defined stages often do not develop, and the stages do not always occur in a sequential fashion (Elder, 1998). Further, they state that it is the variability associated with the stages that should be emphasized. For example, some people have children early during adolescence or their forties; some have children outside of marriage. Entry into these stages is increasingly independent from age. Further, many individuals have multiple families (such as children from a first marriage and children from a remarriage), and these families may develop at different points in the person's life course. Nonetheless, the stages provide a general framework for thinking about how many families change through the life span.

Leaving Home

Leaving home and becoming a single adult is the first stage in the family life cycle, and it involves **launching,** the process in which youth move into adulthood and exit their family of origin. Launching is a time to formulate life goals, to develop an identity, and to become more independent before joining with another person to form a new family. This is a time for young people to sort out what they will take along from the family of origin, what they will leave behind, and what they will create themselves.

In a successful launching, the young adult separates from the family of origin without cutting off ties completely or fleeing to some substitute emotional refuge. Young adults no longer feel compelled to comply with parental expectations and wishes. They shift to dealing with their parents adult-to-adult, which requires mutual respect and acceptance of their parents as they are. Complete cutoffs from parents rarely solve emotional problems.

The New Couple

The **new couple** is the second stage in the family life cycle. Marriage is usually described as the union of two individuals from separate families, but in reality it is the union of two entire family systems and the development of a new, third system. It also involves realignments as the families of origin and friends include the spouse. Changes in gender roles, marriage of partners from divergent cultural backgrounds, and physical distances between family members increase the burden on couples to define their relationships for themselves. Some experts on marriage and the family believe that marriage represents such a different phenomenon for women and men that we need to speak of "her" marriage and "his" marriage. In American society, women have anticipated marriage with greater enthusiasm and more positive expectations than men have.

Becoming a Family with Children

Becoming parents and a family with children is the third stage in the family life cycle. When they enter this stage, adults move up a generation and become caregivers to the younger generation. Moving through this lengthy stage successfully requires a commitment of time as a parent, an understanding of the parenting role, and a willingness to adapt to developmental changes in children (Cox & others, 2004; Stafford, 2004). Couples in this stage may face struggles with each other about their responsibilities as well as their ability to function as competent parents (Huston & Holmes, 2004).

Family Life-Cycle Stages	Emotional Process of Transition: Key Principles
1. Leaving home: single young adults	Accepting emotional and financial responsibility for self
2. The joining of families through marriage: the new couple	Commitment to new system
3. Becoming parents and families with children	Accepting new members into the system
4. The family with adolescents	Increasing flexibility of family boundaries to include children's independence and grandparents' frailties
5. The family at midlife	Accepting a multitude of exits and entries into the family system
6. The family in later life	Accepting the shifting of generational roles

FIGURE 9.6 The Family Life Cycle

leaving home and becoming a single adult The first stage in the family life cycle and it involves launching.

launching The process in which youth move into adulthood and exit their family of origin.

new couple Forming the new couple is the second stage in the family life cycle. Two individuals from separate families of origin unite to form a new family system.

becoming parents and a family with children The third stage in the family life cycle. Adults who enter this stage move up a generation and become caregivers to the younger generation.

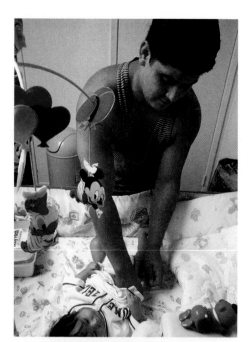

The postpartum period is a time of considerable adjustment and adaptation for both the mother and the father. *What are some of these adjustments?*

Journal of Family Psychology
Children and Families

family with adolescents The fourth stage of the family life cycle, in which adolescent children push for autonomy and seek to develop their own identities.

What is the transition to parenting like? A baby places new restrictions on partners; no longer will they be able to rush out to a movie on a moment's notice, and money may not be readily available for vacations and other luxuries. Dual-career parents ask, "Will it harm the baby to place her in child care? Will we be able to find responsible baby-sitters?" Whether people become parents through pregnancy, adoption, or stepparenting, they must adapt (Heinicke, 2002). Parents want to develop a strong attachment with their infant, but they still want to maintain strong attachments to their spouse and friends, and possibly continue their careers.

In short, parents face the difficult task of juggling their roles as parents, spouses, and self-actualizing adults. In a longitudinal investigation of couples from late pregnancy until three and a half years after the baby was born, marital relations were less positive after the baby was born (Cowan & Cowan, 2000). Still, almost one-third of the couples showed an increase in marital satisfaction after the baby was born. Some couples said that the baby had both brought them closer together *and* moved them farther apart. They commented that being parents enhanced their sense of themselves and gave them a new, more stable identity as a couple. Having a baby raised concerns for men about intimate relationships. The demands of juggling work and family roles stimulated women to manage family tasks more efficiently and pay attention to their own personal growth.

The Family with Adolescents

The *family with adolescents* represents the fourth stage of the family life cycle. Adolescence is a period in which individuals push for autonomy and seek to develop their own identity. This is a lengthy process, transpiring over at least ten to fifteen years. Compliant children may become noncompliant adolescents. In response, parents may either clamp down, pressuring the adolescent to conform to parental values, or become more permissive, giving the adolescent extensive freedom. Neither is a wise strategy. A flexible, adaptive approach is best.

For many years, the dominant view saw parent-adolescent conflict as intense and stressful throughout adolescence. Of course, a high degree of conflict does characterize some parent-adolescent relationships, and this prolonged, intense conflict is associated with adolescent problems such as juvenile delinquency, dropping out of school, pregnancy and early marriage, membership in cults, and drug abuse (Brook & others, 1990). According to current thinking, however, most parent-adolescent conflict is moderate rather than intense, and this moderate conflict can serve a positive function (Collins & Laursen, 2004; Santrock, 2005) (see figure 9.7).

Even the best parents at times may find their relationship with their adolescent strained. Adolescents acquire the ability to attain autonomy and gain control over their behavior through appropriate adult reactions to their desire for control (Laursen & Collins, 2004). At the onset of adolescence, the average individual does not have the maturity to make mature decisions in all areas of life. As the adolescent pushes for autonomy, the wise adult relinquishes control in those areas in which the adolescent can make reasonable decisions but guides the adolescent in areas in which the adolescent's knowledge is more limited. Gradually, adolescents acquire the ability to make mature decisions on their own (Zimmer-Gemback & Collins, 2003).

Although adolescents are moving toward independence, they still need to stay connected with families (Collins & Laursen, 2004; Santrock, 2005; Schellenbach, Leadbeater, & Moore, 2004). In the National Longitudinal Study on Adolescent Health of more than 12,000 adolescents, those who did not eat dinner with a parent five or more days a week had dramatically higher rates of smoking, drinking, marijuana use, getting into fights, and initiation of sexual activity (Council of Economic Advisors, 2000). In another recent study, parents who played an active role in monitoring and guiding their teens were more likely to have adolescents with positive peer relations and lower drug use than parents who took a less active role (Mounts, 2002).

Old Model		New Model
Autonomy, detachment from parents; parent and peer worlds are isolated		Attachment and autonomy; parents are important support systems and attachment figures; adolescent-parent and adolescent-peer worlds have some important connections
Intense, stressful conflict throughout adolescence; parent-adolescent relationships are filled with storm and stress on virtually a daily basis		Moderate parent-adolescent conflict common and can serve a positive developmental function; conflict greater in early adolescence, especially during the apex of puberty

FIGURE 9.7 Old and New Models of Parent-Adolescent Relationships

Adjustment Strategies
For Parenting Adolescents

Competent adolescent development is most likely when adolescents have parents who (Santrock, 2005; Small, 1990):

1. ***Show them warmth and respect, and avoid the tendency to be too controlling or too permissive.***
2. ***Demonstrate sustained interest in their lives.*** Parents need to spend time with their adolescents and monitor their lives.
3. ***Understand and adapt to their cognitive and socioemotional development.***
4. ***Communicate expectations for high standards of conduct and achievement.***
5. ***Display constructive ways of dealing with problems and conflict.*** Moderate conflict is a normal part of the adolescent's desire for independence and search for an identity.
6. ***Understand that adolescents don't become adults overnight.*** Adolescence is a long journey.

Midlife Families

The *family at midlife* is the fifth stage in the family life cycle. It is a time of launching children, linking generations, and adapting to midlife changes. Until about a generation ago, most families were involved in raising their children for much of their adult lives. Because of the lower birth rate and longer life of most adults, parents now launch their children about 20 years before retirement, which frees many midlife parents to pursue other activities.

The Empty Nest and Its Refilling   Launching a child into adult life is an important event in a family, forcing new adjustments (Fingerman, Nussbaum, & Birditt, 2004). Parents who live vicariously through their children might experience the **empty nest syndrome**—a decrease in marital satisfaction and an increase in feelings of emptiness brought on by the children's departure.

But most parents experience an increase, not a decrease, in marital satisfaction after their children have left home. With their children gone, marital partners have more time for each other and for their career interests.

family at midlife The fifth stage in the family life cycle, a time of launching children, linking generations, and adapting to midlife changes.

empty nest syndrome A decrease in marital satisfaction and increase in feelings of emptiness brought about by the children's departure.

Doonesbury

BY GARRY TRUDEAU

Traditionally, the middle generation has continued to support the younger generation even after it has left home—giving loans and gifts and emotional support. In today's uncertain economic climate, however, more parents are doing even more for their adult children. Some children don't leave home at all until their middle or late twenties because they cannot financially support themselves, and others are refilling the empty nest, returning to live at home after an unsuccessful career or a divorce.

As with most family living arrangements, there are both pluses and minuses when adult children live at home. Many parents expected that their adult children would support themselves, and adult children had expected that they would be on their own as young adults. Many adult children and parents complain about a loss of privacy. The adult children complain that their parents restrict their independence, cramp their sex lives, reduce their rock music listening, and treat them as children. Parents often complain that their quiet home has become noisy, that they stay up late worrying when their adult children will come home, that meals are difficult to plan because of conflicting schedules, that their relationship as a married couple has been invaded, and that they have to shoulder too much responsibility for their adult children. In sum, when adult children return home to live, both the parents and the adult children must make adjustments. This living arrangement usually works best when there is adequate space, when parents treat their adult children more like adults than children, and when there is trust and good communication.

Intergenerational Relationships With each new generation, personality characteristics, attitudes, and values of older family members are carried on in the next generation or changed. Both similarities and dissimilarities across generations are found (Palkovitz & others, 2003; Story & others, 2004). For example, similarity between parents and an adult child is most likely in religion and politics and least likely in gender roles, lifestyle, and work orientation.

For the most part, family members maintain considerable contact across generations (Bengtson, 2001). How do their relationships change over the years? As adult children become middle-aged they often develop more positive perceptions of their parents (Field, 1999). In one study, conflicts between mothers and daughters decreased across the life course in both the United States and Japan (Akiyama & Antonucci, 1999). In another study, the most common conflicts between parents and adult children concerned communication and interaction style (such as "He is always yelling" and "She is too critical"), habits and lifestyle choices (such as sexual activity, living arrangements), child-rearing practices and values (such as decisions about having children, being permissive or controlling), politics, religion, and ideology (such as lack of religious involvement) (Clarke & others, 1999). In this study, there were

What is the nature of intergenerational relationships?

generational differences in the perception of the main conflicts. Parents most often listed habits and lifestyle choices; adult children cited communication and interaction style.

Gender differences characterize intergenerational relationships (Bengtson, 2001; Brown & Roodin, 2003; Norris, Pratt, & Kuiack, 2003). In one study, mothers and their daughters had much closer relationships during their adult years than mothers and sons, fathers and daughters, and fathers and sons (Rossi, 1989). Also in this study, married men were more involved with their wives' kin than with their own. And maternal grandmothers and maternal aunts were cited twice as often as their counterparts on the paternal side of the family as the most important or loved relative.

Families in Later Life

The **family in later life** is the sixth and final stage in the family life cycle. Retirement and grandparenting are often key features of this stage. Retirement alters a couple's lifestyle, but the changes are likely to be greatest in traditional families, in which the husband works and the wife is a homemaker. The husband may not know what to do with his time, and the wife may feel uneasy having him around the house all of the time. The husband must adjust from being the good provider to being a helper around the house; the wife must become even more loving and understanding.

Many factors influence marital happiness among older adults, including each partner's ability to deal with personal conflicts, aging, illness, and eventual death (Cooney & Dunne, 2004; Dickson, Christian, & Remmo, 2004; Hoyer & Roodin, 2003). Marital satisfaction tends to be greater among women than among men, possibly because women place more emphasis on attaining satisfaction through marriage than men do. However, as more women develop careers, this gender difference may not continue.

Review and Reflect

2 Describe the family life cycle

REVIEW

- What is the first stage of the family life cycle?
- What is the stage of finding a partner like?
- How can the third stage be characterized?
- What is the fourth stage of the family life cycle?
- How can the fifth stage be described?
- What is the sixth stage of the family life cycle?

REFLECT

- Which stage of the family life cycle characterizes you at this time? What adjustment issues are you facing related to this stage?

family in later life The sixth and final stage in the family life cycle, involving retirement and, in many families, grandparenting.

3 PARENTING

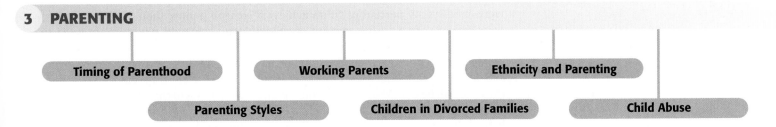

Timing of Parenthood | Parenting Styles | Working Parents | Children in Divorced Families | Ethnicity and Parenting | Child Abuse

Many adults plan when to become parents. For others, the discovery that they are about to become parents is a startling surprise. In either event, the prospective parents

Parenting and Marriage
Parenthood

may have mixed emotions and romantic illusions about having a child. The needs and expectations of parents have stimulated many myths about parenting:

- The birth of a child will save a failing marriage.
- As a possession or extension of the parent, the child will think, feel, and behave like the parents did in their childhood.
- Children will take care of parents in old age.
- Parents can expect respect and get obedience from their children.
- Having a child means that the parents will always have someone who loves them and is their best friend.
- Having a child gives the parents a "second chance" to achieve what they should have achieved.
- If parents learn the right techniques, they can mold their children into what they want.
- It's the parents' fault when children fail.
- Mothers are naturally better parents than fathers.
- Parenting is an instinct and requires no training.

All of the preceding statements are myths. What in fact do we know about parenting? Is there a best time to have children? Is there a best way to raise them? These are some of the questions we now consider.

Timing of Parenthood

As birth control has become common practice, many individuals choose when they will have children and how many children they will raise. Currently, there is a tendency in the United States to have fewer children; the number of one-child families is increasing. People are not only marrying later, but also having children later (Azar, 2003; Grolnick & Gurland, 2001). What are some of the advantages of having children early or late?

Some of the advantages of having children early (in the twenties) are these: The parents are likely to have more physical energy; for example, they can cope better with getting up in the middle of the night with infants and waiting up until adolescents come home at night. The mother is likely to have fewer medical problems with pregnancy and childbirth. And the parents may be less likely to build up expectations for their children, as do many couples who have waited many years to have children.

There are also advantages to having children later (in the thirties): The parents will have had more time to consider their goals in life, will be more mature, and will be able to benefit from their experiences to engage in more competent parenting. And the parents will be better established in their careers and have more income for child-rearing expenses.

Are U.S. women who have focused on their careers anxious about being childless? A recent book, *Creating a Life: Professional Women and the Quest for Children* (Hewlett, 2002), described the results of interviews with 1,186 high-achieving career women (that is, women whose income was in the top 10 percent of their age group) who were from 28 to 55 years of age. Forty-two percent who worked in corporations were childless; 49 percent of "ultra achievers" (earning more than $100,000 a year) were childless. Twenty-five percent of childless high achievers who were from 41 to 55 years of age would still like to have a child, and 31 percent of "ultra achievers" would still like to have a child. Many of the study's childless women in their forties and fifties recommended that younger women spend more time envisioning what their life will be like when they become middle-aged and whether they want their life to include a child. They argue that many high-achieving women will ultimately be happier if they have a child in their twenties or thirties. Critics respond that the optimal age for motherhood depends on the individual and that many women become mothers after they are 35 years of age.

Parenting Styles

Parenting requires interpersonal skills and makes emotional demands, yet there is little in the way of formal education for this task. Most parents learn parenting practices from their own parents; some they accept, some they discard. Husbands and wives may bring different views of parenting to the marriage. Unfortunately, when parenting methods are passed on from one generation to the next, both desirable and undesirable practices are perpetuated (Eliot & Thrash, 2004; Leifer & others, 2004).

Experts in development have long tried to identify desirable parenting practices. The work of Diana Baumrind (1971) has been especially influential. She believes parents should be neither punitive nor aloof. Rather, they should develop rules for their children and be affectionate with them. She identified four types of parenting styles:

- **Authoritarian parenting** is a restrictive, punitive style in which parents exhort the child to follow their directions and respect their effort. The authoritarian parent places firm limits on the child and allows little verbal exchange. For example, an authoritarian parent might say, "You do it my way or else." Authoritarian parents also might spank the child frequently, enforce rules rigidly but not explain them, and show rage. Children of authoritarian parents are often unhappy, fearful, and anxious about comparing themselves with others; they fail to initiate activity; and they have weak communication skills.

- **Authoritative parenting** encourages children to be independent but still places limits on their actions. Extensive verbal give-and-take is allowed, and parents are warm and nurturant toward the child. An authoritative parent might put his arm around the child in a comforting way and say, "You know you should not have done that. Let's talk about how you can handle the situation better next time." Authoritative parents support children's constructive behavior. They also expect mature, independent, and age-appropriate behavior of children. Children whose parents are authoritative are often cheerful, self-controlled, self-reliant, and achievement-oriented; they maintain friendly relations with peers, cooperate with adults, and cope well with stress.

- **Neglectful parenting** is a style in which the parent is very uninvolved in the child's life. Children whose parents are neglectful develop the sense that other aspects of the parents' lives are more important than they are. These children tend to be socially incompetent. Many have poor self-control and don't handle independence well. They frequently have low self-esteem, are immature, and may be alienated from the family. In adolescence, they may skip school and engage in delinquency.

- **Indulgent parenting** is a style of parenting in which parents are very involved with their children but place few demands or controls on them. These parents let their children do what they want. Children never learn to control their own

authoritarian parenting A restrictive, punitive parenting style in which the parent exhorts the child to follow their directions and respect their effort. Firm limits and controls are placed on the child, and little verbal exchange is allowed. This style is associated with children's socially incompetent behavior.

authoritative parenting A parenting style that encourages children to be independent but still places limits and controls on their actions. Extensive verbal give-and-take is allowed, and parents are warm and nurturant toward the child. This style is associated with children's socially competent behavior.

neglectful parenting A parenting style in which the parent is very uninvolved in the child's life. It is associated with children's social incompetence, especially a lack of self-control.

indulgent parenting A parenting style in which parents are highly involved with their children but place few demands or controls on them. This is associated with children's social incompetence, especially a lack of self-control.

CHEEVERWOOD   **by Michael Fry**

CHEEVERWOOD © 1986 Michael Fry. Used by permission of Michael Fry.

	Accepting, responsive	Rejecting, unresponsive
Demanding, controlling	Authoritative	Authoritarian
Undemanding, uncontrolling	Indulgent	Neglectful

FIGURE 9.8 Classification of Parenting Styles
The four types of parenting styles (authoritative, authoritarian, indulgent, and neglectful) involve the dimensions of acceptance and responsiveness, on the one hand, and demand and control on the other. For example, authoritative parenting involves being both accepting/responsive and demanding/controlling.

behavior and always expect to get their way. Some parents deliberately rear their children in this way because they believe that the combination of warm involvement and few restraints will produce a creative, confident child. However, children whose parents are indulgent rarely learn respect for others and have difficulty controlling their behavior. They might be domineering, egocentric, noncompliant, and have difficulty relating to their peers.

These four styles of parenting involve combinations of acceptance and responsiveness on the one hand and demand and control on the other. How these dimensions combine to produce authoritarian, authoritative, neglectful, and indulgent parenting is shown in figure 9.8.

Research studies document more positive links between authoritative parenting and the well-being of children and adolescents than for the other three types (Slicker & Thornberry, 2003). Why is authoritative parenting likely to be the most effective style? These reasons have been given (Steinberg & Silk, 2002): (1) Authoritative parents establish an appropriate balance between control and autonomy, giving children opportunities for self-initiative while providing the standards, limits, and guidance that children need (Reuter & Conger, 1995). (2) Authoritative parents are more likely to engage children in verbal give-and-take and allow children to express their views (Kuczynski & Lollis, 2002). This type of family discussion is likely to help children understand social relationships and what is required for social competence. (3) The warmth and parental involvement provided by authoritative parents make children more receptive to parental influence (Sim, 2000).

Do the benefits of authoritative parenting transcend the boundaries of ethnicity, socioeconomic status, and household composition? Although occasional exceptions have been found, researchers have documented evidence linking authoritative parenting with children's competence across a wide range of ethnic groups, social strata, cultures, and family structures (Steinberg & Silk, 2002).

Adjustment Strategies
For Effective Parenting

Five effective parenting strategies are as follows:

1. ***Use authoritative parenting.*** Be a warm, nurturant parent and engage in extensive verbal give-and-take with the child. Don't be too authoritarian or permissive but exercise control when necessary in a nonpunitive manner.
2. ***Understand that parenting takes time and effort.*** In today's society, there is an unfortunate theme that suggests that parenting can be done quickly and with little or no inconvenience (Sroufe, 2000). Two examples are playing Mozart CDs in the hope that they will enrich infants' and young children's brains and one-minute bedtime stories that are being marketed successfully for parents to read to their children (Walsh, 2000). What is wrong with these quick-fix approaches to parenting? Good parenting takes a lot of time and a lot of effort. You can't do it in a minute here and a minute there. You can't do it with CDs.
3. ***Be a good manager.*** Parents can play important roles as managers of children's opportunities, as monitors of children's social relationships, and as social initiators and arrangers (Parke, 2004; Parke & Buriel, 1998). Parents serve as regulators of opportunities for social contact with peers, friends, and adults. This is especially important as children move into the adolescent years.
4. ***Don't use physical punishment in disciplining children.*** Spanking children is not recommended by child psychologists because it presents an out-of-control model for

handling stressful situations; can instill rage, fear, and avoidance in children; tells them what not to do rather than what to do; and can be abusive (Gershoff, 2002). Most child psychologists recommend reasoning with the child, explaining how the child's behavior affects others (Duncan, 2005; Santrock, 2004). Time-outs, in which the child is removed from the setting where the child receives positive reinforcement, can also be effective. For example, when the child has misbehaved, a parent might take away TV viewing for a specified time.

Working Parents

As Lois Hoffman (1989) commented, maternal employment is a part of modern life. It is not an aberrant aspect of it but a response to other social changes. Some argue that when mothers work outside the home, their children suffer because they receive less attention. In fact, because technology has lessened the time needed for housework and because family size has decreased, it is not certain that U.S. children receive less attention than children in the past whose mothers were not employed. Parents might spend less time than in the past keeping the house clean or pursuing hobbies. Time once split among children might now be focused on one or two.

Is it good or bad for the child to have a mother who works outside the home? A number of researchers have found no detrimental effects of maternal employment on children's development (Gottfried, Gottfried, & Bathurst, 2002; Hoffman & Youngblade, 1999). Work can produce positive and negative effects on parenting. Work-related stress can spill over and harm parenting, but a sense of well-being produced by work can lead to more positive parenting.

However, when a child's mother works in the first year of life it can have a negative effect on the child's later development (Belsky & Eggebeen, 1991; Hill & others, 2001). For example, a recent major longitudinal study found that the 3-year-old children of mothers who went to work before the children were 9 months old had poorer cognitive outcomes than 3-year-old children whose mothers had stayed at home with them in the first nine months of the child's life (Brooks-Gunn, Han, & Waldfogel, 2002). The negative effects of going to work during the child's first nine months were less pronounced (1) when the mothers worked less than 30 hours a week, (2) when the mothers were more responsive and comforting in their caregiving, and (3) when the child care the children received outside the home was higher in quality.

Children in Divorced Families

Let's examine some important questions about children in divorced families.

Are children better adjusted in intact, never-divorced families than in divorced families? Most researchers agree that children from divorced families show poorer adjustment than their counterparts in nondivorced families (Amato, 2004; Harvey & Fine, 2004; Hetherington & Kelly, 2002; Hetherington & Stanley-Hagan, 2002) (see figure 9.9). Those who have experienced multiple divorces are at greater risk. Children in divorced families are more likely than children in nondivorced families to have academic problems, to show externalized problems (such as acting out and delinquency) and internalized problems (such as anxiety and depression), to be less socially responsible, to have less competent intimate relationships, to drop out of school, to become sexually active at an early age, to take drugs, to associate with antisocial peers, and to have low self-esteem (Conger & Chao, 1996; Lewis & others, 2004). Nonetheless, keep in mind that a majority of children in divorced families do not have significant adjustment problems (Buchanan, 2001).

Should parents stay together for the sake of the children? Whether parents should stay in an unhappy or conflicted marriage for the sake of their children is one of the most commonly asked questions about divorce (Hetherington, 2000). If the stresses and disruptions in family relationships associated with an unhappy, conflictual marriage that

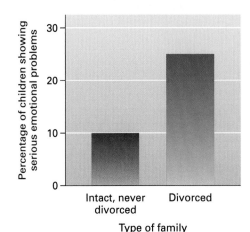

FIGURE 9.9 Divorce and Children's Emotional Problems
In Hetherington's research, 25 percent of children from divorced families showed serious emotional problems compared with only 10 percent of children from intact, never-divorced families. However, keep in mind that a substantial majority (75 percent) of the children from divorced families did not show serious emotional problems.

erode the well-being of children are reduced by the move to a divorced, single-parent family, divorce can be advantageous. However, if the diminished resources and increased risks associated with divorce also are accompanied by inept parenting and sustained or increased conflict, not only between the divorced couple but also between the parents, children, and siblings, the best choice for the children would be for an unhappy marriage to be retained (Hetherington & Stanley-Hagan, 2002). These are "ifs," and it is difficult to determine how these will play out when parents either remain together in an acrimonious marriage or become divorced.

How much do family processes matter in divorced families? Family processes matter a lot (Hetherington & Stanley-Hagan, 2002; Lamb & Lewis, 2005; Martin, Emery, & Peris, 2004). When divorced parents' relationship with each other is harmonious and when they use authoritative parenting, the adjustment of children improves (Hetherington, Bridges, & Insabella, 1998). A number of researchers have shown that a disequilibrium, which includes diminished parenting skills, occurs in the year following the divorce but that, by two years after the divorce, restabilization has occurred and parenting skills have improved (Hetherington, 1989).

What factors are involved in the child's individual risk and vulnerability in a divorced family? Among the factors involved in the child's risk and vulnerability are the child's adjustment prior to the divorce, as well as the child's personality and temperament, gender, and custody situation (Hetherington & Stanley-Hagan, 2002). Children whose parents later divorce show poorer adjustment before the breakup (Amato, 2004).

Personality and temperament also play a role in children's adjustment in divorced families. Children who are socially mature and responsible, who show few behavioral problems, and who have an easy temperament are better able to cope with their parents' divorce. Children with a difficult temperament often have problems in coping with their parents' divorce (Hetherington, 1989).

Earlier studies reported gender differences in response to divorce, with divorce being more negative for girls than boys in mother-custody families. However, more recent studies have shown that gender differences are less pronounced and consistent than was previously believed. Some of the inconsistency may be due to the increase in father custody, joint custody, and increased involvement of noncustodial fathers, especially in their sons' lives. One recent analysis of studies found that children in joint-custody families were better adjusted than children in sole-custody families (Bauserman, 2002). Some studies have shown that boys adjust better in father-custody families, girls in mother-custody families, while other studies have not (Maccoby & Mnookin, 1992; Santrock & Warshak, 1979).

www.mhhe.com/santrockha

Working Parents
Family Diversity

Adjustment Strategies
For Communicating with Children
About Divorce

Following are some guidelines for communicating with children about divorce (Galinsky & David, 1988):

1. ***Explain the separation in a sensitive way.*** As soon as the daily activities in the home make it obvious that one parent is leaving, tell the children. If possible, both parents should be present when the children are made aware of the separation to come. The reasons for the separation are very difficult for young children to understand. It is extremely important for parents to tell the children who is going to take care of them and to describe the specific arrangements for seeing the other parent.

2. ***Explain that the separation is not the child's fault.*** Children often believe that their parents' separation is their own fault. Thus, it is important tell children that they are not the cause of the separation. Parents need to repeat this a number of times.

3. ***Explain that it may take time to feel better.*** Tell children that it's normal to not feel good about what is happening and that many other children feel this way when their parents become separated. It is okay for divorcing parents to share some of their emotions with their children by saying something like, "I'm having a hard time with the separation just like you, but I know it is going to get better in a while." Such statements are best kept brief and should not criticize the other parent.

4. ***Keep the door open for further discussion.*** Tell your children to come to you anytime they want to talk about the separation. It is healthy for children to get out their pent-up emotions in discussions with their parents and to learn that parents are willing to listen about their feelings and fears.

5. ***Provide as much continuity as possible.*** The less children's worlds are disrupted by the separation, the easier their transition to a single-parent family will be. This means maintaining the rules already in place as much as possible. If the custodial parent moves to a new location, it is important to preserve as much of what is familiar to the child as possible. If children must leave friends behind, parents need to help the children stay in touch by phone, letter, or e-mail.

6. ***Provide support for your children.*** After a divorce or separation, parents are as important to children as before the divorce or separation. Divorced parents need to provide children with as much support as possible.

Ethnicity and Parenting

Families within different ethnic groups in the United States differ in many ways, such as their typical size, reliance on kinship networks, and levels of income and education (Coll & Pachter, 2002; Leyendecker & others, 2005; Parke, 2004). Large families and extended families are more common among minority groups than among the White majority (Schmeeckle & Sprecher, 2004). For example, 19 percent of Latino families have three or more children, compared with 14 percent of African American and 10 percent of White families. African American and Latino children interact more with grandparents, aunts, uncles, cousins, and more-distant relatives than do White children.

Certain stressors are more likely to challenge ethnic minority families than non-Latino White families (Cooper & others, 2005; Diggs & Socha, 2004). In particular,

- As discussed in chapter 6, parents and children in ethnic minority families may be at different stages of *acculturation,* the process of adapting to the majority culture (Fulgini & Yoshikawa, 2004). The result may be conflict over cultural values (Chun & Akutsu, 2003; Gonzales & others, 2004; Kwak, 2003; Unger, 2005).

- Single-parent families are more common among African Americans and Latinos than among White Americans (Weinraub, Horuath, & Gringlas, 2002). In comparison with two-parent households, single parents often have more limited resources of time, money, and energy (Gyamfi, Brooks-Gunn, & Jackson, 2001).

- Ethnic minority parents also are less educated and more likely to live in low-income circumstances than their White counterparts. Ethnic minority children experience a disproportionate share of the adverse effects of poverty and unemployment in America (Harrison-Hale, McLoyd, & Smedley, 2004; Stevens, 2005).

- Even when they are not poor, ethnic minority children face prejudice and discrimination (Harwood & others, 2002; McAdoo, 2002).

What are some characteristics of families within different ethnic groups?

Many ethnic minority children, therefore, experience a double disadvantage: (1) the stress of poverty and (2) prejudice and discrimination. Still, many impoverished ethnic minority families find ways to competently raise their children (Coll & Pachter, 2002). Families often help protect ethnic minority children from injustice. For example, the family may filter out destructive racist messages. The extended family also can serve as an important buffer to stress (McAdoo, 2002; McCubbin & McCubbin, 2005).

Child Abuse

In 2001, an estimated 903,000 U.S. children were victims of child abuse (U.S. Department of Health and Human Services, 2003). Eighty-four percent of these children were abused by a parent or parents. Laws in many states now require doctors and teachers to report suspected cases of child abuse, yet many cases go unreported, especially those of battered infants.

The four main types of child maltreatment are physical abuse, child neglect, sexual abuse, and emotional abuse (National Clearinghouse on Child Abuse and Neglect Information, 2004):

- *Physical abuse* is characterized by the infliction of physical injury as result of punching, beating, kicking, biting, burning, shaking, or otherwise harming a child. The parent or other person may not have intended to hurt the child; the injury may have resulted from excessive physical punishment.
- *Child neglect* is characterized by failure to provide for the child's basic needs. Neglect can be physical, educational, or emotional. *Physical neglect* includes refusing or delaying health care; abandonment; expulsion from the home or refusal to allow a runaway to return home; and inadequate supervision. *Educational neglect* involves allowing chronic truancy, failing to enroll a child of mandatory school age in school, and failing to attend to a special education need. *Emotional neglect* includes such actions as marked inattention to the child's needs for affection; failure to provide necessary psychological care; spouse abuse in the child's presence; and allowing the child to drink alcohol or use other drugs.
- *Sexual abuse* includes fondling a child's genitals, intercourse, incest, rape, sodomy, exhibitionism, and commercial exploitation through prostitution or the production of pornographic materials. Many experts believe that sexual abuse is the most underreported type of child maltreatment because of the secrecy or "conspiracy of silence" that so often characterizes sexual abuse cases.
- *Emotional abuse (including psychological or verbal abuse or mental injury)* includes acts or omissions by parents or other caregivers that have caused, or could cause, serious behavioral, cognitive, or emotional problems. Some cases of emotional abuse are serious enough to warrant intervention by child protective services. For example, parents or others may use unusual types of punishment, such as confining a child in a dark closet. Less severe acts, such as frequent belittling and rejection of the child, are often difficult to prove and make it difficult for child protective services to intervene.

Although any of these forms of child maltreatment may be found separately, they often occur in combination. Emotional abuse is almost always present when other forms occur.

The Cultural Context of Abuse
Many people have difficulty understanding parents who abuse or neglect their children. Our response is often outrage and anger at the parent. This outrage focuses attention on parents as bad, sick, monstrous, sadistic individuals who cause their children to suffer. Experts on child abuse believe that this view is too simple and deflects attention away from the social context of the abuse and the parents' coping skills. It is important to recognize that child abuse is a diverse condition, that it is usually mild to moderate in severity, and that it is only partially caused

by personality characteristics of the parent (Anderson, Umberson, & Elliott, 2004; Azar, 2002). Most often, the abuser is not a raging, uncontrolled physical abuser but an overwhelmed single mother in poverty who neglects the child. Many abusing parents report that they do not have sufficient resources or help from others.

Violence in American families reflects the extensive violence in American culture (Azar, 2002; Hines & Malley-Morrison, 2004). A regular diet of violence appears on television screens, and parents often resort to authoritarian parenting. Many parents who abuse their children come from families in which physical punishment was used; these parents often view physical punishment as a legitimate way of controlling the child's behavior. In China, where physical punishment is rarely used to discipline children, the incidence of child abuse is reported to be very low.

To understand abuse in the family, the interactions of all family members need to be considered, regardless of who performs the violent acts against the child (Margolin, 1994). For example, even though the father may be the one who physically abuses the child, contributions by the mother, the child, and siblings also should be evaluated.

Were parents who abuse children abused by their own parents? About one-third of parents who were abused themselves when they were young abuse their own children (Cicchetti & Toth, 1998). Thus, some, but not a majority, of parents are locked into an intergenerational transmission of abuse (Leifer & others, 2004). Mothers who break out of the intergenerational transmission of abuse often have at least one warm, caring adult in their background; have a close, positive marital relationship; and have received therapy (Egeland, Jacobvitz, & Sroufe, 1988).

Consequences of Abuse   The consequences of child maltreatment are wide-ranging, including problems in emotion regulation, in attachment, in peer relations, and in school, as well as other psychological problems (Azar, 2002; Pittman & Lee, 2004; Shonk & Cicchetti, 2001). Maltreated infants may show excessive anger or rarely smile. Children who have been maltreated are poorly equipped for successful peer relations, due to their aggressiveness, avoidance, and aberrant responses to peers (Bolger & Patterson, 2001; Mueller & Silverman, 1989). Physical abuse has been linked with children's anxiety, personality problems, depression, conduct disorder, delinquency, and language problems (Eigsti & others, 2004; Shonk & Cicchetti, 2001; Zielinski, Campa, & Eckenrode, 2003).

The scars of maltreatment may be carried into adulthood. Adults who were maltreated as children show increased violence toward other adults, dating partners, and marital partners; they also have increased rates of substance abuse problems, anxiety, and depression (Malinosky-Rummell & Hansen, 1993).

U.S. Domestic Violence
Child Abuse
Child Abuse Clearinghouse

Review and Reflect

 3   Discuss parenting and how it affects children's adjustment

REVIEW

- Is there an ideal time to have children?
- What are the main parenting styles and which is most effective?
- How are children affected by having working parents?
- What characterizes children in divorced families?
- How is ethnicity related to parenting children?
- What is the nature of child abuse?

REFLECT

- How would you characterize your parents' parenting style? How do you think their style influenced your development?

Reach Your Learning Goals

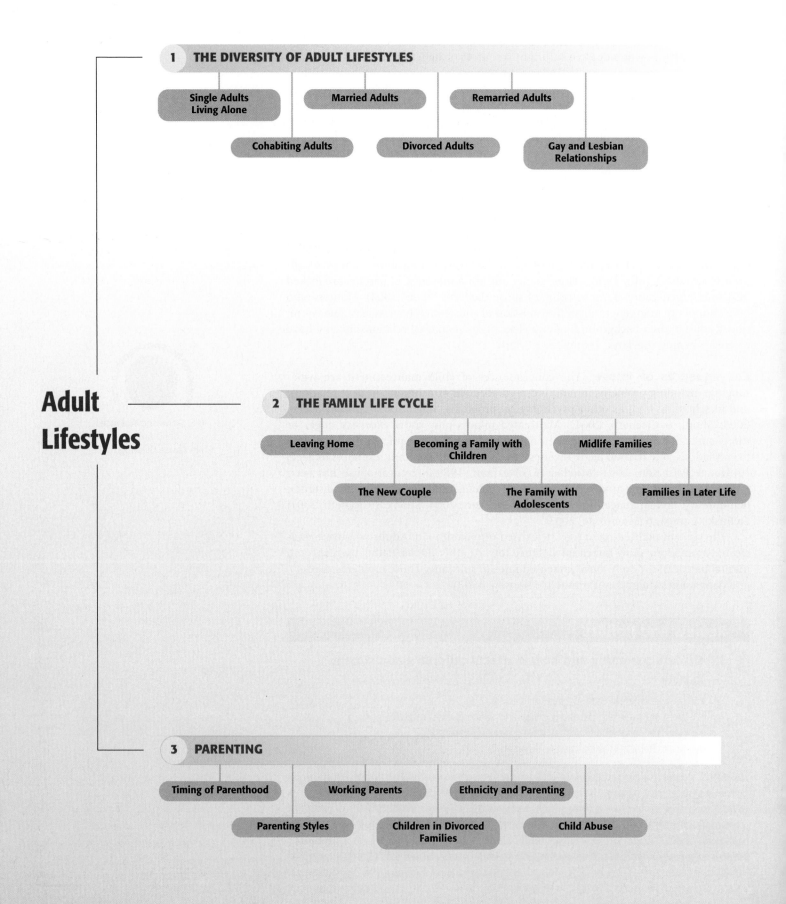

Adult Lifestyles

1 THE DIVERSITY OF ADULT LIFESTYLES

- Single Adults Living Alone
- Cohabiting Adults
- Married Adults
- Divorced Adults
- Remarried Adults
- Gay and Lesbian Relationships

2 THE FAMILY LIFE CYCLE

- Leaving Home
- The New Couple
- Becoming a Family with Children
- The Family with Adolescents
- Midlife Families
- Families in Later Life

3 PARENTING

- Timing of Parenthood
- Parenting Styles
- Working Parents
- Children in Divorced Families
- Ethnicity and Parenting
- Child Abuse

SUMMARY

1   *Discuss the diversity of adult lifestyles and how they affect people's lives*

- Being single has become an increasingly prominent lifestyle. Myths and stereotypes about singles abound, ranging from "swinging single" to "desperately lonely, suicidal single." There are advantages and disadvantages to being single, autonomy being one of the advantages. Intimacy, loneliness, and finding a positive identity in a marriage-oriented society are concerns of single adults.
- Cohabitation is an increasing lifestyle for many adults. Cohabitation offers some advantages as well as problems. Cohabitation does not lead to greater marital happiness but rather to no differences or differences suggesting that cohabitation is not good for a marriage.
- Even though adults are remaining single longer and the divorce rate is high, Americans still show a strong predilection for marriage. The age at which individuals marry, expectations about what the marriage will be like, and the developmental course of marriage vary over time not only within a culture but also across cultures. Gottman has conducted the most extensive research on what makes marriages work. In his research these principles characterize good marriages: establishing love maps, nurturing fondness and admiration, turning toward each other instead of away, letting your partner influence you, solving solvable conflicts, overcoming gridlock, and creating shared meaning. The benefits of marriage include better physical and mental health and a longer life.
- The divorce rate in the United States is high compared with the rate in most countries. The most likely time for divorce to occur is in the fifth to tenth year of marriage. The stresses of divorce put both men and women at risk for various physical and psychological difficulties. In Hetherington's research, the protective factors that helped divorced adults adjust better were social maturity, autonomy, internal locus of control, religiosity, work, social support, and a new intimate relationship. Hetherington also found that divorced adults follow a diversity of pathways.
- Stepfamilies are complex and adjustment is difficult. Only about one-third of remarried adults stay remarried.
- One of the most striking findings about gay and lesbian couples is how similar they are to heterosexual couples. The overwhelming number of children in gay and lesbian families grow up to be heterosexual.

2   *Describe the family life cycle*

- The family life cycle consists of six stages, although critics say that clearly defined stages often do not develop and that the stages do not always occur in sequential fashion. Leaving home and becoming a single adult is the first stage and it involves launching, the process in which youth move into adulthood and exit their family of origin. Complete cutoffs from parents rarely or never solve emotional problems.
- The new couple is the second stage in the family life cycle. Marriage is usually described as the union of two individuals but it also involves the union of two entire family systems.
- Becoming parents and a family with children is the third stage in the family life cycle, during which adults move up a generation and become caregivers to the next generation. The transition to parenting involves a great deal of adjustment.
- The family with adolescents is the fourth stage in the family life cycle. The new model of parent-adolescent relationships emphasizes that most parent-adolescent conflict is moderate rather than intense and that this moderate conflict can serve a positive function. Adolescents need both independence and attachment.
- The family at midlife is the fifth stage in the family life cycle and it is a time of launching children, linking generations, and adapting to midlife changes. Most parents do not experience the empty nest syndrome. An increasing number of young adults are returning home to live after college, career or financial difficulties, or a divorce. In many families, there are substantial connections across generations; women tend to play a stronger role in these links than men do.
- The family in later life is the sixth and final stage in the family life cycle and for many older adults this stage involves adjustment to retirement.

3   *Discuss parenting and how it affects children's adjustment*

- Many U.S. adults are marrying later and having children later. There are different advantages to having children younger or later. There is controversy over when the best age is for women to have children.
- Authoritarian, authoritative, neglectful, and indulgent are four main parenting styles. Authoritative parenting is the style most often associated with children's social competence. Physical punishment is widely used by U.S. parents, but there are a number of reasons why it is not a good choice. Good parenting takes extensive time and effort.
- Overall, there is no indication that both parents working full-time outside the home has negative long-term effects on children, although some negative effects have been found in specific circumstances when mothers work outside the home during the infant's first nine months of life.
- About 25 percent of children in divorced families have adjustment problems compared with about 10 percent in never-divorced families. However, this means that the

majority of children in divorced families do not have serious adjustment problems. Many factors, including quality of parenting and economic factors, influence the adjustment of children in divorced families.

- African American and Latino children are more likely than White American children to live in single-parent families and larger families and to have extended family connections. Parents and children may be at different levels of acculturation, which can result in conflict over

cultural values. Poverty and prejudice contribute to the stressful life experiences of many ethnic minority children.

- The four main types of child abuse are physical abuse, child neglect, sexual abuse, and emotional abuse. An understanding of child abuse requires information about cultural, familial, and community influences. Child abuse places the child at risk for a number of developmental problems.

Key Terms

leaving home and becoming a single adult 273
launching 273
new couple 273

becoming parents and a family with children 273
family with adolescents 274
family at midlife 275

empty nest syndrome 275
family in later life 277
authoritarian parenting 279
authoritative parenting 279

neglectful parenting 279
indulgent parenting 279

Resources for Improving Your Adjustment

SELF-HELP BOOKS

The Seven Principles for Making Marriages Work

(2000) by John Gottman and Nan Silver. New York: Crown.

This outstanding self-help book was rated in the highest category (5 stars) in the national survey of self-help books (Norcross, Santrock, & others, 2003). Excellent strategies for helping couples to understand their problems and make their relationship work are provided.

For Better or for Worse: Divorce Reconsidered

(2002) by E. Mavis Hetherington and John Kelly. New York: Norton.

This is an outstanding book on the nature of divorce and the best and worst ways to adjust to it. Written by leading divorce researcher Hetherington and writer Kelly, this book provides a very up-to-date account of divorce that includes many descriptions of actual divorce situations.

To Listen to a Child

(1984) by T. Berry Brazelton. Reading, MA: Addison-Wesley.

To Listen to a Child addresses parenting throughout the childhood years. The focus is primarily on problematic events that arise in children's lives. Fears, feeding, sleep problems, stomachaches, and asthma are among the normal problems of growing up that Brazelton covers. He assures parents that it is only when

parents let their own anxieties interfere that these problems (such as bedwetting) become chronic and guilt-laden. Each chapter closes with practical guidelines for parents. Brazelton deals with common issues parents face, such as discipline, children's search for limits, and the child's emotional well-being. *To Listen to a Child* was rated in the highest category (5 stars) in the national study of self-help books (Norcross, Santrock, & others, 2003).

NATIONAL SUPPORT GROUPS

Association for Couples in Marriage Enrichment
http://www.bettermarriages.com

No Kidding!
http://www.nokidding.net
(Support and social activities for married and single adults who have chosen not to have children, are postponing parenthood, or cannot have children)

Child Help USA
http://www.childhelpusa.org
(Some crisis counseling provided and referrals to local agency for child abuse reporting provided)

National Child Abuse Hotline
800-422-4453

E-Learning Tools

To help you master the material in this chapter, you will find a number of valuable study tools on the student CD-ROM that accompanies this book. In addition, visit the Online Learning Center for *Human Adjustment,* where you can find these valuable resources for Chapter 9, "Adult Lifestyles."

SELF-ASSESSMENT

In Text

You can complete these self-assessments in the text:
- Self-Assessment 9.1: *What Characteristics Do I Desire in a Mate?*
- Self-Assessment 9.2: *My Knowledge of Marital Myths*

Additional Self-Assessments

Complete these self-assessments on the Online Learning Center:
- *How Realistic Am I About Cohabitation?*
- *Am I Ready for a Committed Relationship?*

THINK CRITICALLY

To practice your critical thinking skills, complete these exercises on the Online Learning Center:
- *The Family Script* gives you an opportunity to evaluate how your family has influenced the way you relate to people.
- *Keeping the Watch* examines your knowledge of how to detect family violence when it occurs.
- *Should I Get Married?* looks at the advantages and disadvantages of being single.
- *Would I Ever Get Divorced?* explores the reasons for divorce.

APPLY YOUR KNOWLEDGE

1. Who does the work?

Married women, especially those who are employed outside the home, often complain that they do more than their share of household and childcare tasks than their husbands do. Sometimes, their husbands don't see a large difference. If you are married, you can use your own marriage to determine who does the work. If you are not married, find a married couple where both partners work full-time. You can do one of two things:

a. Have each partner write down every task that he or she has done over the past week. A good way to do this is to mentally walk through the day's events.

b. Have each partner keep a diary for the week. Every time each person does a family or household chore, record it.

At the end of the week, have the two people (or yourselves) switch lists and perform all the tasks on the partner's list the following week. Are the household tasks evenly divided? Does the partner who is doing less of the work realize how much the other person does? If the work is roughly equal, what strategies are used to fairly allocate tasks?

2. How prevalent is heterosexism?

Heterosexism is the existence of advantages and rewards on heterosexuals solely as a result of their sexual orientation. Many of the things that heterosexuals take for granted may be unavailable to gay or bisexual people. If you are "straight," what advantages do you enjoy that gay people are less likely to enjoy? Think hard—many of the things that heterosexuals take for granted are not equally available to everyone. Examples include displaying a picture of one's loved one without fear of retaliation or ridicule, not having to hide parts of one's life from family, friends, and coworkers, or having the loved one be legally recognized as the next-of-kin.

When you have made your list, go to www.yahoo.com or www.google.com and type "heterosexism" into the search box. What items could be added to your list as a result of your search? Why do you think you didn't see them earlier?

3. What is battering really about?

A common stereotype is that people who batter others typically "lose their tempers." Most research on battery suggests that battery is actually an extreme form of control, and that "losing one's temper" is an excuse, not a cause.

Go to www.yahoo.com or www.google.com and type "battering" into the search box. Then, type in "tactics used by batterers."

VIDEO SEGMENT

Any lifestyle has certain drawbacks and challenges. Imagine being in high school and living with your parents—along with your spouse and a young baby. Could you be happy? What strategies might you use to adjust to your situation? Compare your ideas with the approach described by Andrea and Joel in the video for Chapter 9 on the CD-ROM.

Achievement, Careers, and Work

Learning Goals

1 Discuss achievement and related adjustment strategies

2 Describe some important aspects of careers and jobs

3 Summarize some key aspects of work

Images of Adjustment

David Eggers, Pursuing a Career in the Face of Stress

David Eggers, talented and insightful author

He was a senior in college when both of his parents died of cancer within five weeks of each other. What would he do? He and his 8-year-old brother left Chicago to live in California, where his older sister was entering law school. David would take care of his younger brother, but he needed a job. That first summer, he took a class in furniture painting; then he worked for a geological surveying company, re-creating maps on a computer. Soon, though, he did something very different: with friends from high school, David Eggers started *Might,* a satirical magazine for twentysomethings. It was an edgy, highly acclaimed publication, but not a moneymaker. After a few years, Eggers had to shut down the magazine, and he abandoned California for New York.

This does not sound like a promising start for a career. But within a decade after his parents' death, Eggers had not only raised his young brother but had also founded a quarterly journal and website, *McSweeney's,* and had written a bestseller, *A Heartbreaking Work of Staggering Genius,* which received the National Book Critics Circle Award and was nominated for a Pultizer Prize. It is a slightly fictionalized account of Eggers' life as he helped care for his dying mother, raised his brother, and searched for his own place in the world.

Despite the pain of his loss and the responsibility for his brother, Eggers quickly built a record of achievement. Would his achievement have been greater or less without these stressors? We don't know, but psychologists have discovered a great deal about how people achieve and how they adjust to obstacles to achievement.

Achievement is an important aspect of life for most individuals. As a college student, you currently are involved in the process of achieving by striving for success in your courses and building a foundation of knowledge and skills that will enable you to pursue a meaningful career. Getting a good job in that career is also likely an important goal for you. In this chapter, we explore the intertwined topics of achievement, careers, work, and jobs, and adjustment strategies related to them.

1 ACHIEVEMENT

Intrinsic and Extrinsic Motivation		Time Management
	Goal Setting, Planning, and Monitoring	Some Obstacles to Achievement

A number of processes—including intrinsic and extrinsic motivation, goal setting, and time management—may be involved in achievement. We explore these processes as well as some obstacles to achievement and strategies for reducing or eliminating them.

Intrinsic and Extrinsic Motivation

How hard will you work in order to achieve? If you are the only person who will know whether you succeed at a task, does it still matter to you whether you succeed or fail? Will you be more motivated to succeed if you are paid or praised for your effort?

The effects of rewards such as money and praise have been studied in detail by the behaviorists discussed in chapter 2, "Personality." Their operant conditioning experiments demonstrated the power of extrinsic incentives such as rewards to motivate and shape behavior. However, **extrinsic motivation**—the influence of external rewards and punishments—is not the only driving force in our lives. Researchers have found, for instance, that motivation and interest in school tasks increases when students have some choices about their work and opportunities for their own learning (Alderman, 2004; Brophy, 2004; Stipek, 2001). Some students study hard because they want to make good grades or avoid parental disapproval (extrinsic motivation), but students may also study because they are curious or want to meet their own high standards. These are examples of **intrinsic motivation,** which is the influence of internal factors such as self-determination and curiosity.

Many psychologists believe intrinsic motivation has more positive outcomes than extrinsic motivation (Deci & Ryan, 1994). They argue that intrinsic motivation is more likely to produce competent behavior and mastery. Indeed, research comparisons often reveal that people whose motivation is intrinsic show more interest, excitement, and confidence in what they are doing than those whose motivation is extrinsic. Intrinsic motivation often results in improved performance, persistence, creativity, and self-esteem (Ryan & Deci, 2000, 2001).

Highly successful individuals are often both intrinsically motivated (have a high personal standard of achievement and emphasize personal effort) and extrinsically motivated (are highly competitive). The six-time Tour de France winner, cyclist Lance Armstrong, is a good example. Armstrong was diagnosed with testicular cancer in 1996 and was thought to have less than a 50 percent chance of recovering. He had an incredible amount of intrinsic motivation to come back from testicular cancer to win

extrinsic motivation Involves external incentives such as rewards and punishments.

intrinsic motivation Is based on internal factors such as self-determination, curiosity, challenge, and effort.

Goal Setting

the Tour de France. However, the extrinsic motivation of winning the Tour de France trophy and the millions of dollars in endorsement contracts also likely played a role in his motivation. For the most part, though, psychologists believe that intrinsic motivation is the key to achievement. Lance Armstrong, like many other athletic champions, decided early on that he was training and racing for himself, not for his parents, coaches, or the medals.

Goal Setting, Planning, and Monitoring

What possessed young David Eggers to start a magazine? In *A Heartbreaking Work of Staggering Genius,* he recounts this conversation with a friend on the beach:

> I tell her how funny it is we're talking about all this because as it so happens I'm already working to change all this, am currently in the middle of putting something together something that will . . . inspire millions to greatness . . . help us all to throw off the shackles of our supposed obligations, our fruitless career tracks, how we will force, at least urge, millions to live more exceptional lives, to . . . do extraordinary things, to travel the world, to help people and start things and end things and build things . . . "A Magazine." (Eggers, 2001, pp. 107–108)

Eggers clearly had some goals. Goal setting, planning, and self-monitoring are critical aspects of achievement (Pintrich, 2003; Schunk, 2004). Goals help individuals to reach their dreams, increase their self-discipline, and maintain interest.

People generate many goals for themselves (Eccles, 2004). You may have *personal projects*—such as letting a bad haircut grow out or becoming a good parent—or *personal strivings*—such as trying to do well in school this year. You probably also have *life tasks*, such as graduating from college, getting married, or entering an occupation. Life tasks usually focus on transitions in life. Many college students say that their life tasks revolve around academic achievement and social concerns (Cantor & Langston, 1989).

Researchers have found that achievement improves when they set goals that are specific, short term, and challenging (Bandura, 1997; Schunk, 2004). A fuzzy, nonspecific goal might be "I want to inspire millions to greatness, to live more exceptional lives." A more concrete, specific goal might be "I want to start a magazine" or "I want to have a 3.5 average at the end of the semester." One study revealed that individuals who cast their goals in concrete terms were 50 percent more confident in their ability to reach the goals and 32 percent more likely to feel in control of their lives than those who constructed abstract goals (Howatt, 1999).

You can set both long-term and short-term goals (Dembo, 2004). If you set long-term goals, such as "I want to be a clinical psychologist," make sure that you also create short-term goals as steps along the way, such as "I want to get an A on the next psychology test" or "I will do all of my studying for this class by 4 P.M. Sunday." David McNally (1990), author of *Even Eagles Need a Push,* advises that when individuals set goals and plan how to reach them, they should remind themselves to live their lives one day at a time. Make commitments in small chunks.

Another good strategy is to set challenging goals. A challenging goal is a commitment to self-improvement. Strong interest and involvement in work and activities are sparked by challenges. Goals that are easy to reach generate little interest or effort. However, unrealistically high goals can bring failure and reduce confidence.

Planning how to reach a goal and monitoring progress toward the goal are critical aspects of achievement (Alderman, 2004; Eccles, Wigfield, & Schiefele, 1998). Researchers have found that high-achieving individuals monitor themselves; they systematically evaluate their progress toward their goals more than low-achieving individuals do (Zimmerman & Schunk, 2004).

Adjustment Strategies
For Setting Goals

Here are some good strategies for setting goals:

1. ***Set goals that are challenging, reasonable, and specific.***
2. ***Set completion dates for your goals and work out schedules to meet them.*** If you want to obtain a college degree, write down the date you want to achieve this goal.
3. ***Create subgoals.*** Think in terms of creating intermediate steps or subgoals on the way to achieving a goal. U.S. Olympic speed-skating champion Bonnie Blair commented that no matter what the competition is, she tries to find a goal that day and better that goal. The more you can order steps or subgoals into a series, the more easily you can accomplish each.
4. ***Make a commitment.*** Commit yourself to setting goals and reaching them. Some people have dreams and the best intentions but lack the commitment to make their dreams a reality.
5. ***Monitor your progress.*** Monitoring your progress toward a goal is a critical process in reaching it. If after a week or a month, your monitoring indicates that you are falling behind your schedule to reach a goal, you may need to devote more time to the tasks involved.

Time Management

Reaching important life goals often takes considerable time—even years or decades. Your life will benefit enormously if you are a competent manager of time. For example, if you waste too much time, you might find yourself poorly prepared the night before an important exam. If you manage your time effectively, you will have time to relax between exams and other deadlines. Time management will help you be more productive and less stressed, providing you with a balance between work and play.

Plan and Set Priorities   Break down your time by the year (or academic term), month, week, and day. As you create plans within these time frames, set priorities. Management expert Steven Covey (1989) created a time matrix of four quadrants, shown in figure 10.1, based on the urgency of planned activities. *Important* activities are those that are linked to your values and goals. *Urgent* activities are those that require immediate attention. Covey (1989) gives these tips on how to use the time matrix:

*   Spend time on important nonurgent activities (Quadrant 2) before they become urgent.
*   Don't let your life be ruled by urgency. Don't avoid important work because of tasks that are just urgent.

Time Management Skills
Personal Time Management Guide

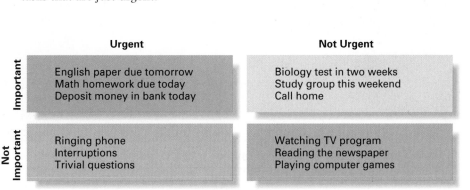

	Urgent	Not Urgent
Important	English paper due tomorrow Math homework due today Deposit money in bank today	Biology test in two weeks Study group this weekend Call home
Not Important	Ringing phone Interruptions Trivial questions	Watching TV program Reading the newspaper Playing computer games

FIGURE 10.1 Covey's Four Quadrants of Time Management
Shown here is one student's time management schedule based on Covey's four-quadrant system.

- Do important activities early. If you wait until they are urgent, you will just increase your stress level.
- Set priorities for your tasks and complete them in that order.

To Do

The Most Vital:

1. Study for Math Test

Next Two Most Important:

2. Go to Human Adjustment and Math Classes
3. Deposit Money in Bank

Task	Time	Done
Study for math test	Early morn, night	
Go to adjust class	Morn	
Go to Math class	Morn	
Exercise	Noon	
Deposit money	Aft	
Buy test booklet	Aft	
Call Aretha for date	Eve	

FIGURE 10.2 Example of a To-Do List
Shown here is one student's to-do list. It is best to get as many important tasks done in the morning. Once completed, you can check off the task in the "Done" column.

Create and Monitor Time Plans Competent time managers determine what the most important activities are for each day and allocate adequate time for them. To stay focused on what is important for you to do each day, create a *to-do list,* which involves listing and setting priorities for daily tasks and activities. Make a to-do list in the evening for the next day or early the next morning for the same day. Figure 10.2 shows one college student's to-do list.

It is also important to monitor how well you are doing with your time plans on a yearly (or term), monthly, weekly, and daily basis. Many people find it helpful to create a plan for a week's tasks and activities, then at the end of each day and at the end of the week evaluate the extent to which they used their time in the manner they planned. This provides you with a sense of what you might have spent too much and too little time on.

Some Obstacles to Achievement

Achievement problems can surface when you don't set goals, don't plan how to reach them, and don't monitor your progress toward the goals. They also can arise when you don't manage your time effectively, procrastinate, insist on perfection, or try to protect self-worth by avoiding failure.

Procrastination Why do individuals procrastinate? The reasons include (University of Buffalo Counseling Services, 2003): poor time management, difficulty concentrating, fear and anxiety (being overwhelmed by the task and afraid of getting a bad grade, for example), negative beliefs ("I can never succeed at anything," for example), personal problems (financial problems, problems with a boyfriend or girlfriend, and so on), boredom, unrealistic expectations and perfectionism (believing you must read everything written on a subject before you begin to write a paper, for example), and fear of failure (thinking that if you don't get an "A," you are a failure, for example).

Two main types of time management planning tools are paper-and-pencil planners (*left*) and electronic planners (*right*). If you are not currently using one of the types of time management planners, start doing it now.

Procrastination can take many forms, including these (University of Illinois Counseling Center, 1996):

- Ignoring the task with the hope that it will go away.
- Underestimating the work involved in the task or overestimating your abilities and resources.
- Spending endless hours on computer games and surfing the Internet.
- Deceiving yourself that an average or poor performance is acceptable.
- Substituting a worthy but lower-priority activity. For example, you might clean your room instead of studying for a test.
- Believing that repeated minor delays won't hurt you.
- Dramatizing a commitment to a task rather than doing it. For example, you might take your books along for a weekend trip but never open them.
- Persevering on only part of the task. For example, you might write and rewrite the first paragraph of a paper but you never get to the body of it.
- Becoming paralyzed when having to choose between two alternatives. For example, you agonize over doing your biology homework or your English homework first with the outcome that you don't do either.

Adjustment Strategies
For Conquering Procrastination

Here are some good strategies for reducing or eliminating procrastination:

1. ***Acknowledge that procrastination is a problem.*** Too often, procrastinators don't face up to their problem. When individuals admit that they procrastinate, this can sometimes get them to begin thinking about how to solve the problem.
2. ***Identify your values and goals.*** Think about how procrastination can undermine your values and goals.
3. ***Work on your time management.*** Make yearly (or term), monthly, weekly, and daily plans. Then monitor how you are using your time to find out ways to use it more wisely.
4. ***Divide the task into smaller parts.*** Sometimes individuals procrastinate because they view the task as so large and overwhelming that they will never be able to finish it. When this is the case, divide the task into smaller units and set subgoals for completing one unit at a time. This strategy can often make what seems to be a completely unmanageable task manageable.
5. ***Use behavioral strategies.*** Identify the diversions that might be keeping you from focusing on the most important tasks and activities. Note when and where you engage in these diversions. Plan how to diminish and control their use. Another behavioral strategy is to make a contract with yourself or someone you see regularly related to your procrastination problem. And yet another behavioral strategy is to build in a reward for yourself, which gives you an incentive to complete all or part of the task. For example, if you get all of your math problems completed, treat yourself to a movie when you finish them.
6. ***Use cognitive strategies.*** Watch for mental self-seductions that can lead to behavioral diversions, such as, "I'll do it tomorrow," "What's the problem with watching an hour of TV now?" and "I can't do it." Dispute mental diversions. For example, tell yourself, "I really don't have much time left and other things are sure to come up later," "If I get this done, I'll be able to better enjoy my time," or "Maybe if I just go ahead and get going on this, it won't be so bad."

Perfectionism   As was already mentioned, perfectionism is sometimes the underlying reason for procrastinating. Perfectionists think that mistakes are never acceptable and that the highest standards of performance always have to be achieved. As

SELF-ASSESSMENT 10.1

Am I a Perfectionist?

For each item, place a check mark in the column that most applies to you.

	Never	Rarely	Sometimes	Often
1. If I don't set the very highest standards for myself, and meet them, I will end up a second-rate person.	_____	_____	_____	_____
2. People will think less of me if I make a mistake.	_____	_____	_____	_____
3. If I cannot do something really well, there is no point in doing it at all.	_____	_____	_____	_____
4. I should be very upset with myself if I make a mistake.	_____	_____	_____	_____
5. If I try hard enough, I can excel at anything I attempt.	_____	_____	_____	_____
6. It is very shameful for me to display weaknesses.	_____	_____	_____	_____
7. I should never make the same mistake twice.	_____	_____	_____	_____
8. An average performance is unacceptable for me regardless of what type of activity it is.	_____	_____	_____	_____
9. Not doing well at something means I'm less of a person.	_____	_____	_____	_____
10. Scolding myself for failing to live up to my expectations will help me to do better in the future.	_____	_____	_____	_____

Go to the appendix at the end of the book for scoring and interpretation of your responses.

indicated in figure 10.3, healthy achievement and perfectionism differ in a number of ways. Perfectionists are vulnerable to decreased productivity, impaired health, relationship problems, and low self-esteem (Bottos, 2004; Haring, Hewitt, & Flett, 2003). Depression, anxiety, and eating disorders are common outcomes of perfectionism (Sherry & others, 2003, 2004; Young, 2004). To evaluate whether you are a perfectionist, complete Self-Assessment 10.1.

FIGURE 10.3 Differences Between Perfectionists and Healthy Strivers

Perfectionist	Healthy striver
Sets standards beyond reach and reason	Sets high standards, but just beyond reach
Is never satisfied by anything less than perfection	Enjoys process as well as outcome
Becomes dysfuntionally depressed when experiences failure and disappointment	Bounces back from failure and disappointment quickly and with energy
Is preoccupied with fear of failure and disapproval—this can deplete energy levels	Keeps normal anxiety and fear of failure and disapproval within bounds—uses them to create energy
Sees mistakes as evidence of unworthiness	Sees mistakes as opportunities for growth and learning
Becomes overly defensive when criticized	Reacts positively to helpful criticism

Adjustment Strategies
For Coping with Perfectionism

Here are some good strategies for reducing or eliminating perfectionist tendencies (University of Texas at Austin Counseling and Mental Health Center, 1999, pp. 4–5):

"**1.** ***Make a list of the advantages and disadvantages of trying to be perfect.***
When you make your own lists of costs and benefits, you may find that the costs are too great. You may discover that problems with relationships, excessive workaholism, eating and substance abuse problems, . . . and so on actually outweigh whatever advantages perfectionism holds for you.

2. ***Increase your awareness of the self-critical nature of your all-or-nothing thoughts, and how they extend to other people in your life.*** Learn to substitute more realistic, reasonable thoughts for your habitually critical ones. When you find yourself berating a less-than-perfect performance, whether your own or someone else's, force yourself to look at and acknowledge the good parts of that performance. Then ask yourself questions like these: Is it really as bad as I feel it is? How do other people see it? . . .

3. ***Be realistic about what you can do.*** By setting more realistic goals, you will gradually see that 'imperfect' results do not lead to punitive consequences you expect and fear . . .

4. ***Set strict time limits on each of your projects. When the time is up, move on (and) attend to another activity.*** This technique reduces the procrastination that typically results from perfectionism. Suppose you must find references for a term paper and also study for exam. Set time limits . . .

5. ***Learn how to deal with criticism.*** Perfectionists often view criticism as a personal attack responding to it defensively. Concentrate on being more objective about the criticism, and about yourself. If someone criticizes you for making a mistake, acknowledge the mistake and assert your right to make mistakes."

www.mhhe.com/santrockha

Procrastination
Perfectionism

Protecting Self-Worth by Avoiding Failure   Some individuals are so interested in protecting their self-worth and avoiding failure that they become distracted from pursuing goals and engage in ineffective strategies. These strategies include (Covington, 1992; Covington & Dray, 2002):

- *Nonperformance.* The most obvious strategy for avoiding failure is to not try. In the classroom, nonperformance tactics include appearing eager to answer a teacher's question but hoping the teacher will call on another student, sliding down in the seat to avoid being seen by the teacher, and avoiding eye contact. These can seem like minor deceptions, but they might portend other, more chronic forms of noninvolvement such as dropping out and excessive absences.

- *Sham effort.* To avoid being criticized for not trying, some individuals appear to participate but do so more to avoid punishment than to succeed. Examples include asking a question even though you know the answer; adopting a pensive, quizzical expression; and feigning attention during a class discussion.

- *Procrastination.* Individuals who postpone studying for a test until the last minute can blame failure on poor time management, thus deflecting attention away from the possibility that they are incompetent. A variation on this theme is to take on so many responsibilities that you have an excuse for not doing any one of them in a highly competent manner.

- *Setting unreachable goals.* By setting goals so high that success is virtually impossible, individuals can avoid the implication that they are incompetent, because virtually anyone would fail to reach this goal.

- *The academic wooden leg.* This strategy involves admitting to a minor personal weakness in order to avoid acknowledging the greater, feared weakness of being incompetent. One example is to blame a failing test score on anxiety. Having test anxiety is not as devastating to a personal sense of self-worth as lack of ability.

Efforts to avoid failure often involve **self-handicapping strategies** (Ryska, 2004; Urdan & Midgley, 2001). That is, some individuals deliberately handicap themselves by not making an effort, by putting off a project until the last minute, by fooling around the night before a test, and so on, so that if their subsequent performance is at a low level, these circumstances, rather than lack of ability, will be seen as the cause.

Here are a few strategies to reduce preoccupation with protecting self-worth and avoiding failure (Covington, 2002):

- Set challenging but realistic goals.
- Strengthen the link between your effort and self-worth. Take pride in your effort and minimize social comparison.
- Have positive beliefs about your abilities.

Review and Reflect

1 Discuss achievement and related adjustment strategies

REVIEW

- What motivates people to achieve?
- How are goals related to achievement?
- What are some important aspects of time management?
- What are some obstacles to achievement and ways to deal with them?

REFLECT

- Based on what you have read about achievement, do you think you have a healthy perspective on achievement and engage in achievement processes that benefit you? Explain.

2 CAREERS AND JOBS

Career Development Across the Life Span

Knowledge, Goals, and Careers

Skills and Personality Traits

Getting a Job

If you are typical reader of this book, you are still exploring, planning, or making decisions about your career path. The process might be easier if we were as talented as David Eggers, who was described at the opening of this chapter. But even Eggers' career path has had its twists, turns, and potholes. In *A Heartbreaking Work of Staggering Genius,* he wrote:

> In the month or so since that first issue, *Might* has become something different. We're much less inspired than we were then, and going through with another one seems, on a certain level, more dutiful than impassioned. After all, we want from this, or at least the last thing I want from this, is some kind of job. (Eggers, 2001, p. 204)

self-handicapping strategies Involve efforts by individuals to avoid failure.

What is it that you expect from a career or a job? Let's first explore how people think about careers at different points in the life span and then examine some key factors in your ability to find the career and job that is best for you.

Career Development Across the Life Span

Have your thoughts about a career changed as you developed? Probably so—otherwise the earth would have a tremendous surplus of cowboys, astronauts, dancers, teachers, and firefighters. Eli Ginzberg (1972) and Donald Super (1976) believe that individuals go through stages in their career development. Ginzberg proposes three stages: fantasy (birth through age 11), tentative (ages 11 through 17), and realistic (ages 18 to 25). Super describes five stages in career development: growth (birth to 14 years of age), exploration (15 through 24), establishment (25 through 44), maintenance (from 45 through 64), and decline (beginning at 65). Let's examine some changes in career development that typically take place across the life span.

Childhood   How far back do you have to go to a time at which you did not even think about possible careers? Even as a preschooler you probably began to fantasize about some careers, and you likely continued this fantasy career orientation through most of your childhood years. When asked what they want to be when they grow up, children in what Ginzberg calls the **fantasy stage** commonly say they want to be a doctor, an astronaut, a superhero, a teacher, a movie star, a sports hero, and so forth, and many of their aspirations are not very realistic.

The **growth stage** is Super's label for the period from birth through early adolescence. According to Super, children move from having no interest in vocations (birth to 3 years) to having, first, extensive fantasies about careers (4 to 10 years), and then (at 10 to 12 years of age) to career interests based on likes and dislikes (10 to 12).

What role do parents play in this process? Anne Roe (1956) believes that parents are an important influence on the selection of an occupation. For example, she says that individuals who have warm and accepting parents are likely to choose careers that involve work with people, such as sales positions and public relations jobs. By contrast, she says, individuals who have neglecting or rejecting parents are more likely to choose careers that do not require a good "personality" or strong social skills, such as accounting.

Adolescence   During the adolescent years, interest in career exploration increases (Helwig, 2004). During early adolescence, at about 10 to 15 years of age, individuals tone down their wildest, most unrealistic dreams about careers. Super includes these years in his first growth stage and says that when they are about 13 and 14 years old, young adolescents start to consider their abilities when thinking about career choices, but most are not completely realistic.

The **tentative stage** is Ginzberg's label for the adolescent period of 11 to 17 years of age, when individuals are in transition between the fantasy stage of childhood and the more realistic stage that comes later.

Although Ginzberg and Super divide the years of adolescence and early adulthood differently in their analyses, both depict adolescents and young adults as beginning to explore the world of work in a more realistic way. According to Ginzberg, when they are about 18 to 25 years of age, individuals are in the **realistic stage** and discard their fantasies about careers and make pragmatic decisions. Super calls the period from 15 to 24 years the **exploration stage.** According to Super, during this stage individuals become more likely to take their needs, interests, capacities, values, and opportunities into account when considering career choices. People often make initial vocational commitment and might begin a first trial job in the latter part of this stage.

fantasy stage Ginzberg's stage for the childhood years during which careers are perceived in an unrealistic manner.

growth stage Super's label for the period in which physical and cognitive growth takes place from birth through adolescence.

tentative stage Ginzberg's stage for the adolescent period of 11 to 17 when individuals are between the fantasy stage of childhood and the more realistic stage that will come later.

realistic stage Ginzberg's stage for the age period of 18 to 25 when individuals rid themselves of their fantasies about careers and make pragmatic decisions.

exploration stage Super's stage (15 to 24 years of age) when individuals become more likely to take their needs, interests, capacities, values, and opportunities into account when considering career choices.

Exploration of many career options is widely recommended by career counselors. Too often, though, individuals receive little direction or guidance as they explore careers. In one study of individuals after they left high school, over half the position changes made between leaving high school and the age of 25 involved floundering and unplanned changes (Super, Kowalski, & Gotkin, 1967).

Too much guidance also creates problems. Some parents push their children toward a particular career and become overinvested in the children's decisions. The mother who did not get into medical school and the father who did not make it as a professional athlete might pressure their children to achieve a career status that is beyond the children's talents. Other parents may push their children to avoid other tasks. One 35-year-old female looks back and describes how her family discouraged her from exploring careers. Her parents expected that she would graduate from high school, but they emphasized that she needed to get a job to help them pay the family's bills. She was never told that she could not go to college, but both parents encouraged her to find someone to marry who could support her financially. This bright woman is now divorced and feels intellectually cheated by her parents, who socialized her in the direction of marriage and away from a college education.

One place where adolescents can get advice about career choices is school. Current trends, however, are limiting high school students' access to meaningful career advice. First, the back-to-basics movement leaves little time for instruction on career exploration and development. Second, as budgets of secondary schools tighten, the number of guidance counselors tends to decrease. In many schools, students take no career development classes and never come in contact with a career counselor. Many adolescents do not know what information to seek about careers or how to seek it. Later in the chapter we examine some specific steps in exploring, planning, and making decisions about careers.

Early Adulthood   Should young adults in college study a wide range of subjects, or should they focus on a specific discipline in order to obtain what amounts to vocational training to increase their chances of obtaining a job? Career counselors disagree on the answer. Many students change majors in college, discover that their employment after college is not related to their college major, and change careers during the course of adulthood.

Entering an occupation brings new roles and responsibilities. The employer's expectations and demands are likely to be higher than the individual experienced as a temporary or part-time worker during high school or college. The young adult might not anticipate how real the pressures are in this first job, nor understand how important relationships with other employees are, nor expect such extreme demands on their time.

The **establishment stage** is Super's label for the period from 25 to 45 years of age, when individuals pursue a permanent career and attain a stable pattern of work in a particular career. In the first part of this stage, considerable adjustment is still required to adapt to the career path the individual has chosen. Clinical psychologist Daniel Levinson (1978) believes that this is a time when individuals need to develop a distinct occupational identity and establish themselves in the occupational world. Along the way, they might fail, drop out, or begin a new path. They might stay on a single narrow track or try several new directions before settling firmly on one.

Many of us think of our adult work life as a series of discrete steps, much like the rungs on a ladder. In a factory, a person might move from laborer, to foreman, to superintendent, to production manager, and so on up the ladder. In a business, an individual might move from salesperson, to sales manager, to regional sales manager, to national sales manager, to vice president of the company, and then even possibly to president of the company. Not all occupations have such clearly defined

establishment stage Super's term for the period from 25 to 45 years of age when individuals pursue a permanent career and attain a stable pattern of work in a particular career.

Reprinted with special permission of King Features Syndicate.

steps, but most jobs involve a hierarchy in which low-level workers and high-level workers are clearly distinguished (Herr, 2004a). How can an individual move up the career ladder?

Having a college education helps. A college degree is associated with earlier and greater career advancement (Golan, 1986). Furthermore, persons who are promoted early tend to move farther up the career ladder than those who are promoted later. Indeed, most career advancement occurs early in our adult lives. By their early forties, many individuals have gone as far as they will go up the career ladder. In one study of a large corporation, this pattern occurred regardless of whether the positions were nonmanagement, lower management, or foreman (Rosenbaum, 1984).

Middle Adulthood   In the United States, approximately 80 percent of individuals 40 to 59 years of age are employed, and the percentage of those 55 and older is expected to increase (Schwerha & McMullin, 2002). By the time they are 40 to 45, as indicated earlier, most people have gone as far as they will up the career ladder, and most middle-aged adults remain in the same career. Super calls this stage of career development the **maintenance stage,** a period from about 45 to 64 years of age during which individuals maintain their career status.

For many adults, though, this stage involves far more than maintenance. Realizing that they are unlikely to advance much further in their career, many middle-aged adults reflect about what they have done with their career years and what they expect from their future years in their career. They face issues such as the limitation of their career progress, decisions about whether to change careers and rebalance family and work, and plans for retirement (Sterns & Huyck, 2001). Many middle-aged adults show an increased concern for figuring out the meaning of life and determining how their career needs and success fit into the larger picture of their life.

Levinson (1978) believes that the midlife career experience is a significant turning point in life. Most people have to adjust idealistic hopes to realistic possibilities in light of how much time they have left in an occupation. Focus often turns to how much time remains before retirement and the pace with which occupational goals are being reached (Pines & Aronson, 1988). If people perceive that they are behind schedule or that their goals have been unrealistic, they might reassess and readjust these goals. Levinson (1978) believes this readjustment can result in a sadness or grieving over unfulfilled dreams. In his research, he found that many middle-aged men felt constrained by their bosses, their wives, and their children. Such feelings, he says, can produce rebellion, which can take several forms—extramarital affairs, divorce, alcoholism, suicide, or career change. Although Levinson only studied men's lives in this research, some researchers believe that women experience parallel feelings.

www.mhhe.com/santrockha

Midlife Baby Boomers

maintenance stage In Super's view, a period from about 45 to 64 years of age during which individuals continue their career and maintain their career status.

Growth stage Birth–14 years of age	General physical and cognitive growth	In this stage, children move from a time when they have no interest in careers (0–3 years), to having extensive fantasies about careers (4–10 years), to career interests based on likes and dislikes (10–12 years), to beginning to take ability into account in their career choices (13–14 years).
Exploration stage 15–24 years of age	General exploration of the world of work	In the early part of this stage, individuals begin to take needs, interests, capacities, values, and opportunities into account when career choices are considered. In the latter part of the stage, they often make an initial vocational commitment and may begin a first trial job.
Establishment stage 25–44 years of age	Entrance into a permanent career and emergence of a stable work pattern	In the first part of this stage, considerable adjustment is still required to adapt to the career path that has been chosen. As individuals move through the stage, they establish a distinct occupational identity and a pattern of consistent work.
Maintenance stage 45–64 years of age	Continuation in a career and maintenance of career status	A large majority of middle-aged adults remain in the same career; only about 10% change careers in middle age.
Decline stage 65+ years of age	Career activity declines and retirement takes place	While some individuals maintain a productive life through even the late adulthood years, most people do show a decline in career activity and retire at some point in late adulthood.

FIGURE 10.4 Super's Stages of Career Development

Middle-aged workers may also be forced to reassess their careers by conditions in today's workplace (Avolio & Sosik, 1999). Rapid changes in computer technology compel middle-aged adults to become increasingly computer literate (Csaja, 2001). Economic trends such as globalization, outsourcing, and the downsizing of workforces push some adults out of their jobs. Some companies shrink the workforce by offering incentives to middle-aged employees to retire early—in their fifties or even their forties.

About 10 percent of middle-aged Americans do change jobs. Some midlife career changes are the result of losing a job; others are self-motivated (Moen & Wethington, 1999). Some individuals in middle age decide that they don't want to do the same work for the rest of their lives (Hoyer & Roodin, 2003). Perhaps they want to redefine their identity through a career change, or perhaps they have lost their passion for their current job and feel stuck. If they perceive that they are far behind schedule in achieving career goals or that their goals are unrealistic, that they don't like the work they are doing, or that their job has become too stressful, they may be motivated to change jobs. Many older adults return to the college classroom to begin a new direction in their careers. Although middle-aged adults can feel thrown off balance by a career shift, most feel rejuvenated by a change.

Late Adulthood When most of us think of careers during late adulthood, the two words most likely to come to mind are *decline* and *retirement*. Indeed, the **decline stage** is Super's label for the period when people are 65 years and older and career activity declines and retirement takes place. (Figure 10.4 provides a summary of Super's five stages of career development.)

In fact, some individuals maintain their productivity throughout their adult lives, and some older workers work as many or more hours than younger workers (Barnes-Farrell, 2004). Older workers actually have a 20 percent better attendance record than younger workers. And older workers have fewer accidents and increased job satisfaction compared with their younger workers (Warr, 1994). Cognitive ability is one of the best predictors of job performance in older adults

decline stage Super's label for the period of 65 years and older when individuals' career activity declines and retirement takes place.

(Brown & Park, 2003). Individuals with higher cognitive ability are more likely to continue work as older adults, and when they work in substantively complex jobs, this likely enhances their intellectual functioning (Schooler, 2001).

Who is most likely to keep working after they are 65? According to the National Longitudinal Survey of Older Men, good health, a strong psychological commitment to work, and a distaste for retirement were the most important characteristics related to continued employment into old age (seventies and eighties) (Parnes & Sommers, 1994). The probability of employment also was positively correlated with educational attainment and being married to a working wife. Among creative persons, scientists, and writers, many are productive well into their elderly years, with some of their best works produced later in life.

Today, the percentage of men over the age of 65 who work full-time is much lower than it was at the beginning of the twentieth century, but the percentage of older adults who work part-time has steadily increased since the 1960s. Aging and work expert James House (1998) believes that many middle-aged workers would like to do less paid work, whereas many older adults would like to do more. We say more about retirement later in the chapter.

Skills and Personality Traits

Is there an intelligent way to choose a career? To discover a career that you are likely to enjoy and in which you will have success it is important to examine your strengths and weaknesses. Realistically evaluating your academic and personal skills is a key to finding the best career for you.

The U.S. Department of Labor (2005) publishes information about career skills under the title of Secretary's Commission on Achieving Necessary Skills (SCANS). SCANS emphasizes three types of skills (basic, thinking, and people) plus personal qualities. To evaluate your strengths and weaknesses, complete Self-Assessment 10.2.

Your personality traits also influence which careers will suit you (Herr, 2004b). Vocational theorist John Holland argues that it is important for your personality type to fit your career. When individuals find careers that fit their personality, Holland (1973, 1996) believes that they are more likely to enjoy the work and stay in their jobs than if they work at jobs not suited for their personality. It is difficult to imagine David Eggers, who was described at the opening of the chapter, working happily or successfully as a surgeon or an air traffic controller.

Holland's **personality type theory** outlines six career-related personality styles (see figure 10.5):

- *Realistic.* Individuals who are a realistic type are physically robust, practical, and tend to be nonintellectual or even anti-intellectual. They like the outdoors and enjoy manual activities. They tend to be less social than most other types, have difficulty in demanding situations, and prefer to work alone or with other realistic persons. The jobs that fit well with the realistic type are mostly blue-collar positions, such as labor, farming, truck driving, and construction, along with a few technical jobs such as engineers and pilots (Lowman, 1991). The realistic type has the lowest prestige level of the six occupational interest types (Lowman, 1987).
- *Investigative.* The investigative type is interested in ideas more than people, is rather indifferent to social relationships, is troubled by very emotional situations, and may be perceived by others as being somewhat aloof and very intelligent. The investigative type has the highest educational level and the highest prestige level of the six types (Gottfredson, 1980). Most of the scientific, intellectually oriented professions fall into this category.

personality type theory Holland's view that it is important to develop a match or fit between an individual's personality type and the selection of a particular career.

SELF-ASSESSMENT 10.2

What Are My Academic and Personal Skills Strengths and Weaknesses?

Place a check mark in the column that best describes your skills in a particular with 1 = Very much unlike me, 2 = Somewhat unlike me, 3 = Somewhat like me, and 4 = Very much like me.

	Very Much Unlike Me	Somewhat Unlike Me	Somewhat Like Me	Very Much Like Me
BASIC SKILLS				
Reading (Identify basic facts, locate information in books/manuals, find meanings of unknown words, judge accuracy of reports, and use computers to find information)	_____	_____	_____	_____
Writing (Write ideas completely and accurately in letters and reports with proper grammar, spelling, and punctuation, and use computers to communicate information)	_____	_____	_____	_____
Mathematics (Use numbers, fractions, and percentages to solve problems, use tables, graphs, and charts, and use computers to enter, retrieve, change, and compute numerical information)	_____	_____	_____	_____
Speaking (Speak clearly, and select language, tone of voice, and gestures appropriate to an audience)	_____	_____	_____	_____
Listening (Listen clearly to what a person says, noting tone of voice and body language, and respond in a way that indicates an understanding of what is said)	_____	_____	_____	_____
THINKING SKILLS				
Creative Thinking (Use imagination freely, combining information in innovative ways, and make connections between ideas that seem unrelated)	_____	_____	_____	_____
Decision Making (Identify goals, generate alternatives and gather information about them, weigh pros and cons, choose the best alternatives, and plan how to carry out a choice)	_____	_____	_____	_____
Visualization (Imagine building an object or system by studying a blueprint or a drawing)	_____	_____	_____	_____
PERSONAL QUALITIES				
Self-Esteem (Understand how beliefs affect how a person feels and acts, listen and identify irrational or harmful beliefs that you may have, and know how to change these negative beliefs when they occur)	_____	_____	_____	_____
Self-Management (Assess one's own knowledge and skills accurately, set specific and realistic personal goals, and monitor progress toward goals)	_____	_____	_____	_____
Responsibility (Work hard to reach goals, even if a task is unpleasant, do quality work, and have a high standard of attendance, honesty, energy, and optimism)	_____	_____	_____	_____

continued

What Are My Academic and Personal Skills Strengths and Weaknesses?

	Very Much Unlike Me	Somewhat Unlike Me	Somewhat Like Me	Very Much Like Me
PEOPLE SKILLS				
Social (Show understanding, friendliness, and respect for others' feelings, be assertive when appropriate, and take an interest in what people say and why they think and behave the way they do)	_____	_____	_____	_____
Negotiation (Identify common goals among different people, clearly present one's position, understand your group's position and the other group's position, examine possible options, and make reasonable compromises)	_____	_____	_____	_____
Leadership (Communicate thoughts and feelings to justify a position, encourage or convince, make positive use of rules and values, and demonstrate the ability to get others to believe in and trust because of your competence and honesty)	_____	_____	_____	_____

Go to the appendix at the end of the book for scoring and interpretation of your responses.

- *Artistic.* Individuals who are the artistic type have a creative orientation and enjoy working with ideas and materials to express themselves in new ways. They have a distaste for conformity, value freedom and ambiguity, and sometimes have difficulty in interpersonal relations. They tend to have high educational levels and experience moderate to high prestige. Relatively few jobs match up with the artistic type. As a result, some artistic types may choose careers in other categories and express their artistic tendencies in hobbies and other leisure activities.
- *Social.* Oriented toward working through and with other people, social types tend to enjoy helping others, perhaps working to assist people in need, especially the less advantaged. They have a much greater interest in people than in intellectual pursuits and often have excellent interpersonal skills. They are likely to be best equipped for professions such as teaching, social work, and counseling. The social type also has a high prestige rating.
- *Enterprising.* Another type that is more oriented toward people than toward either things or ideas is the enterprising type. These individuals seek to dominate others, especially when they want to reach specific goals. They are good at coordinating the work of others and at persuading other people to do something and to adopt their own attitudes and choices. Ranking fourth of the six types in education and prestige, they match up best with careers in fields such as sales, management, and politics.
- *Conventional.* The conventional type usually functions best in well-structured circumstances and is skilled at working with details. Conventional individuals prefer to work with numbers and perform clerical tasks rather than working with ideas or people. They usually do not aspire to high-level positions. They are best suited for structured jobs such as bank tellers, secretaries, and file clerks. Of the six types, they are fifth in education and prestige.

FIGURE 10.5 Holland's Model of Personality Types and Career Choices

If all individuals (and careers) fell conveniently into Holland's personality types, career counselors would have an easy job. However, individuals are rarely pure types, and most people reflect a combination of two or three types (Holland, 1987, 1996). Still, the idea of matching the abilities and attitudes of individuals to particular careers is an important contribution to the career development field (Tay, Ward, & Hill, 1993).

The influence of Holland's ideas is found in tests that are widely used by career counselors. Holland has developed a career interest inventory called the *Self-Directed Search,* and Holland's personality types are incorporated in the Strong-Campbell Interest Inventory (Dik & Hansen, 2004). Another test often used by career counselors is the Myers-Briggs Type Indicator (MBTI). If you are interested in taking one of these tests, contact the career counseling center at your college.

Now that we have examined three major theories of career development (Ginzberg's, Super's, and Holland's), a few final thoughts about career theories is in order. The changing nature of work (for example, organizational downsizing, the pervasive use of advanced technology to increase productivity, the increasing use of part-time workers, and international competition) and of career paths is providing new challenges to career theory in the twenty-first century (Herr, 2004a). Theories have focused on career development that was linear and predictable within stable organizations. These conditions are rapidly changing as workplaces use new strategies to stay competitive. The result is a widening diversity of career patterns and experiences, more frequent career transitions, and increased expectations that workers must become their own career managers. Later in the chapter, we will revisit some of these changes in work.

Successful Career Planning
Career Interests
Career Self-Evaluation
National Career Development Association
Occupational Outlook Handbook

Knowledge, Goals, and Careers

Knowing your skills and personality traits is not all that is involved in career exploration. Two other important aspects of exploring careers are (1) becoming knowledgeable about careers and (2) setting career goals.

Become Knowledgeable About Careers   As you explore the type of work you are likely to enjoy and in which you can succeed, it is important to be knowledgeable about different fields and companies. Occupations may have many job openings one year but few in another year as economic conditions change. Thus, it is critical to keep up with the occupational outlook in various fields. An excellent source for doing this is the *Occupational Outlook Handbook,* which is revised every two years. Based on the 2004–2005 handbook, service industries are expected to provide the most new jobs, with professional and related occupations projected to increase the most. Figure 10.6 shows the percentage change in employment in occupations projected to grow the fastest from 2002 through 2012 (*Occupational Outlook Handbook,* 2004–2005). Approximately three-fourths of the job growth will come from three groups of professional occupations: computer and mathematical occupations; health practitioners and technical occupations; and education, training, and library occupations.

Projected job growth varies widely by education requirements. Jobs that require a college degree are expected to grow the fastest. Education is essential to getting a high-paying job. All but one of the fifty highest-paying occupations require a college degree (*Occupational Outlook Handbook,* 2004–2005).

To become more knowledgeable about careers, network with people you know, such as your family, friends, people in the community, and alumni. They might be able to answer your questions themselves or put you in touch with someone who can. Many college career centers have the names of alumni who are willing to talk with students about careers and their line of work. You might also make an appointment to

"Your son has made a career choice, Mildred. He's going to win the lottery and travel a lot."

© 2004. Reprinted courtesy of Bunny Hoest and Parade Magazine.

see a career counselor at your college. This professional is trained to help you evaluate your strengths and weaknesses and guide you in the direction of careers that will best meet your needs and goals.

The incredible growth of the Internet has spawned many websites with information about careers. Most companies and government agencies have sites that provide information about the types of careers and jobs they have available. Figure 10.7 describes some of the most widely used computer-aided occupation searches.

Set Career Goals Most people don't find it easy to articulate their goals. If setting goals is difficult for you, begin with general goals, such as wanting to be happy (which is on everyone's list), and then work toward more specific ones (such as, "I want to retire the December after I am 60 years old"). Think about goals in multiple categories, such as health and fitness, intellectual, social, special relationships, careers, and so on.

For some individuals, living in a specific geographical location is as important or more important than finding a job in a certain type of career. Ardent surfers drive taxis just to be in Honolulu, and aspiring actors wait tables just to live in Hollywood. Some people refuse to live in a large city, others find heaven in Manhattan.

One person, already a systems analyst, didn't have location on his list of goals, but he did have these: (1) losing 15 pounds and getting in good shape, (2) taking some management courses, (3) spending less time with the people he cared little about and more time with those he loved, and (4) becoming a manager in a computer-oriented department or company. To explore your own career goals, complete Self-Assessment 10.3.

Getting a Job

What are some things to know about landing a great job? They include being aware of what employers want, finding out about jobs, creating a résumé and writing letters, and being able to have a great job interview.

Be Aware of What Employers Want An employer looks for evidence of your accomplishments and experiences, which might include leadership positions; participation in campus organizations or extracurricular activities; relevant experiences in co-ops, internships, or part-time work; and good grades. In a national survey of employers of college students, the communication skills of prospective employees were especially important (Collins, 1996) (see figure 10.8).

Do a Thorough Job Search
You can conduct a job search in a number of ways. Check out ads in newspapers and use websites. Two widely used job search websites are *The Riley Guide* (www.dbm.com/jobguide), which takes you through a series of steps on how to use the Internet for a job search, and *The Job Hunter's Bible* (www.jobhuntersbible.com). Networking is also helpful in finding out about job openings. You might want to talk with instructors, guest speakers, friends, alumni of your high school and college, members of community organizations, and so on.

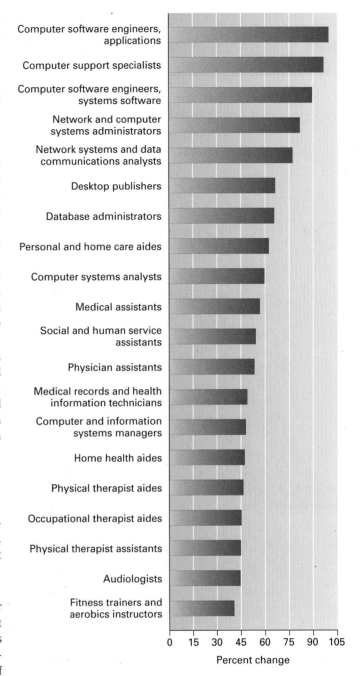

FIGURE 10.6 Percentage Change in Employment in Occupations Projected to Grow Fastest, 2000–2012

Exploring Careers and Jobs
Job-Hunting Strategies

SELF-ASSESSMENT 10.3

My Career Goals

Following are some of the most important dimensions to include when creating your career goals (Office of Career Services [OCS], 2002). Write down your thoughts about your career goals related to each of these areas.

Major Career Field Target(s): _____

_____

Preferred Type of Work (Include the ideas and or issues you would like to pursue) _____

_____

_____

Income Requirements _____

_____

Geographical Requirements (city, rural, mobility, near home, climate, and so on) _____

_____

_____

Special Needs (training, management development, advancement opportunities, career flexibility, entrepreneurial opportunities, and so on) _____

_____

_____

_____

Industry Preferences (manufacturing, government, communications, nonprofit, high tech, products, services, and so on) _____

_____

_____

FIGURE 10.7 Computer-Guided Career Systems

System	Publisher
Career Information System	Career Information System National Office, Eugene, OR
Career Visions	Wisconsin Career Information System, Madison, WI
Career Ways	Wisconsin Career Information System, Madison, WI
Choices	Careerware: ISM Systems Corp., Ottawa, Ontario (Canada)
Modular C-Lect	Chronicle Press, Moravia, NY
COIN	COIN Educational Products, Toledo, OH
Discover	American College Testing, Hunt Valley, MD
Guidance Information System	Riverside Publishing, Chicago, IL
SIGI Plus	Educational Testing Service, Princeton, NJ

Note: To learn more about any of these systems, type in the title of the system or the publisher on an Internet search engine like Google and you will be able to learn about the systems.

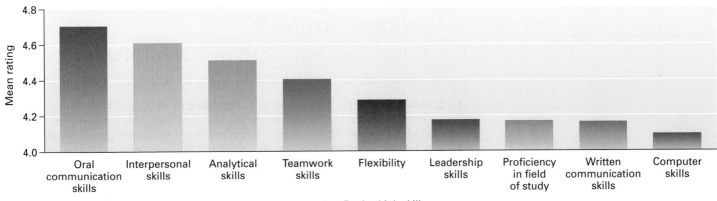

FIGURE 10.8 Desired Skills of an Ideal Job Candidate Rated by Employers
In a national survey of employers, desired characteristics of job applicants were rated on a scale of
1 = extremely unimportant to 5 = extremely important. Note how important communication skills
were to the employers. Three of the four highest-rated skills were communication skills (oral,
interpersonal, and teamwork).

Create a Résumé To obtain a good job you will need a high-quality résumé. A résumé is a clear and concise description of your interests, skills, experiences, and responsibilities in work, service, extracurricular, and academic settings. Three types of
résumés are most often used (OCS, 2002, p. 1):

1. *Chronological,* the most common type in which you describe your experiences in
   reverse chronological order, beginning with your most recent experiences.
2. *Functional,* which focuses on your marketable skills by organizing your
   accomplishments by skill or career area. This type may be best when you have
   little experience related to the job you are seeking.
3. *Achievement,* which highlights prior work or academic accomplishments. This
   type can be used as an alternative to the chronological or functional formats
   when your accomplishments emphasize a particular skill or experience.

Be sure to use white paper, a 10- to 12-point font size, and black type. The résumé
should be an accurate reflection of your job history and accomplishments, and it
should have no typos or other errors.

Learn How to Have a Great Job Interview How well you handle a job interview is a critical factor in obtaining a job. You can take control of the interview
process. Before the interview, research the company so that you are aware of its
needs, goals, and problems. Then consider videotaping practice interviews to determine how you will actually present yourself. This will help you to detect any nervous habits or weak spots in your presentation. Interview experts recommend
spending a minimum of 10 hours practicing and fine-tuning your presentation
before the interview.

During the interview, avoid asking questions about salary and benefits or anything else that is self-serving. There will be ample time to obtain this type of information in later negotiations.

Preparation and research will give you a competitive edge in the interview,
giving you the confidence to meet any challenging circumstances that might arise.
Some other strategies for successful interviewing follow.

*"Uh-huh. Uh-huh. And for precisely how long
were you a hunter-gatherer at I.B.M.?"*

Adjustment Strategies
For Knocking 'Em Dead in a Job Interview

Here are some good strategies for having a great job interview (Yate, 2005):

1. ***Create an excellent résumé.*** Résumés are used by employers to decide whether they want to interview you in the first place. Organize your résumé, write it clearly, don't use a lot of jargon, and follow the other advice outlined earlier.

2. ***Don't wing an interview.*** Do your homework. Find out as much about your prospective employer as possible. What does the company/organization do? How successful is it? Employers are impressed by job candidates who have taken the time to learn about their organization whether you are interviewing for a part-time job at your college library or for a full-time job in a large corporation.

3. ***Be prepared to give positive examples of your past work experience.*** Interviewers anticipate that your past work behavior is a good predictor of how well you do in this new job, so the examples you give from past jobs may seal your fate.

4. ***Anticipate the questions that you will be asked in the interview.*** Do some practice interviews. Some typical interview questions include: What is your greatest strength? What interests you the most about this job? Why should I hire you? Also be prepared for questions designed to catch you off guard and to determine how you handle yourself in a stressful situation. For example, consider how you would respond to these requests: Tell me something you are not very proud of. Describe a situation in which your idea was criticized.

5. ***Ask appropriate job-related questions yourself.*** Review the job requirements with the interviewer.

6. ***Keep your cool.*** Always leave in the same polite way you entered.

7. ***As the interview closes, decide whether you want the job.*** If so, ask for it. If the job is not offered on the spot, ask when the two of you can talk again.

8. ***Immediately after the interview, type a follow-up letter.*** Keep it short, less than one page. Mail the letter within 24 hours after the interview. If you do not hear anything within five days, call the organization and ask about the status of the job.

Review and Reflect

2 Describe some important aspects of careers and jobs

REVIEW

- How do our thoughts about careers typically develop through the life span?
- How do our skills and traits influence our careers?
- What are some key factors involved in obtaining a good job?

REFLECT

- What job experiences have you had so far? Are they linked to the career(s) you want to pursue? If so, how?

3 WORK

The Role of Work in People's Lives	Work and Retirement

Work During College	Leisure

Work provides us more than a means of earning a living; it can give us a sense of purpose and self-fulfillment, but it also can bring stress and conflict. Even if you are your own boss, even if you start and run your own business, as David Eggers did, the motivation for a job might fade. As Eggers wrote,

> But the grind had begun. The windows don't open. . . . We've reached the end of pure inspiration, and are now somewhere else, something implying routine, or doing something because other people expect us to do it, going somewhere each day because we went there the day before, . . . and this seems like the work of a different sort of animal, contrary to our plan, and this is very bad. (Eggers, 2001, p. 287)

How does a job fit into life? In this section we explore how people balance their work with the rest of their lives, retirement and the best ways to adjust to it, and the importance of leisure in adjustment.

The Role of Work in People's Lives

Do you work to live or live to work? Most individuals spend about one-third of their lives at work. In one survey, 35 percent of Americans worked 40 hours a week, but 18 percent even worked 51 hours or more per week (Center for Survey Research at the University of Connecticut, 2000). Only 10 percent worked less than 30 hours a week.

Work defines people in fundamental ways (Osipow, 2000). It is an important influence on their financial standing, housing, the way they spend their time, where they live, their friendships, and their health. Some people define their identity through their work. Work also creates a structure and rhythm to life that is often missed when individuals do not work for an extended period. When unable to work, many individuals experience emotional distress and low self-esteem.

Of course, work also creates stress (Barling, Kelloway, & Frone, 2004; Boswell, Olson-Buchanan, & LePine, 2004; Dewe, 2004). Four characteristics of work settings are linked with employee stress and health problems (Moos, 1986): (1) high job demands such as having a heavy workload and time pressure, (2) inadequate opportunities to participate in decision making, (3) a high level of supervisor control, and (4) a lack of clarity about the criteria for competent performance.

Even people who find their jobs very satisfying may have difficulty balancing the demands of work with other demands on their time and energy (Peterson & Wilson, 2004). Let's examine two examples: workaholics and dual-career couples.

www.mhhe.com/santrockha

Journal of Vocational Behavior

Workaholics   Have you known people who seemed to be at work every time you saw them, regardless of the time of day or day of the week? They most likely go to work early, stay late, take work home with them, and may even work during a flight and while on vacation. They probably have few if any hobbies or interests outside of work. Such a *workaholic* seems to be addicted to work (McMillan, Driscoll, & Brady, 2004).

What are some characteristics of work settings linked with employees' stress?

Workaholics do not necessarily experience their work as stressful. In fact, they may enjoy their work as much as other people enjoy their hobbies or other forms of recreation. Workaholics are likely to identify strongly with their careers, to find them to be a source of pride and personal fulfillment, and to be very satisfied with their jobs.

It is important not to confuse a workaholic with a Type A personality. You might recall from chapter 4 that Type A personalities tend to be aggressive and impatient. They may have an obsession with work, but unlike the workaholic, people with the Type A personality are likely to experience stress and pressure related to their work. In contrast, workaholics are likely to have a calm, collected obsession with their work and productivity.

How can a workaholic find satisfaction in other areas of their lives, such as their relationships? They might involve others in their work, share aspects of their jobs with others, or try to find at least some time for others. Still, a part of being a workaholic is that little else will likely fit into a schedule.

Dual-Career Couples   Like workaholics, dual-career couples may have particular problems finding a balance between work and the rest of life (Desmarais & Alksnis, 2004; Greenhaus, Collins, & Shaw, 2003; Parker & Arthur, 2004). If both partners are working, who cleans up the house or calls the repairman or takes care of the other endless details involved in maintaining a home? If the couple has children, who is responsible for being sure that the children get to school or to piano practice, who writes the notes to approve field trips or meets the teacher or makes the dental appointments?

Although single-earner married families still make up a sizable minority of families, the two-earner couple has increased considerably in the last three decades (Barnett, 2001) (see figure 10.9). As more U.S. women worked outside the home, the division responsibility for work and family changed. Recent research suggests that (Barnett, 2001; Barnett & others, 2001):

- *U.S. husbands are taking increased responsibility for maintaining the home.* Men in dual-career families do about 45 percent of the housework.
- *U.S. women are taking increased responsibility for breadwinning.* In about one-third of two-earner couples, wives earn as much or more than their husbands.
- *U.S. men are showing greater interest in their families and parenting.* Young adult men are reporting that family is at least as important to them as work. Among men with egalitarian attitudes toward gender roles, fatherhood is linked with a

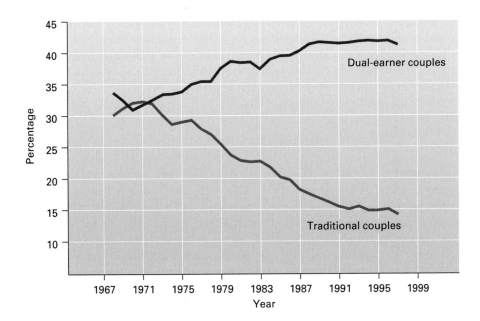

FIGURE 10.9 Changes in the Percentage of U.S. Traditional and Dual-Career Couples Notice the dramatic increase in dual-earner couples in the last three decades. Traditional couples are those in which the husband is the sole breadwinner.

decrease of nine hours per week at work; among men with more traditional views about gender roles, fatherhood is associated with an increase of almost eleven hours per week.

Diversity in the Workplace The workplace is becoming increasingly diverse. Whereas at one time few women were employed outside the home, in developed countries women have increasingly entered the labor force (Lakes & Carter, 2004; Lips, 2003). In 2001, 74 percent of U.S. men were in the labor force compared with 60 percent of U.S. women (U.S. Bureau of Labor Statistics, 2003). Only in Scandinavian countries such as Sweden did women participate in the labor force at the same rate as American women.

Gender diversity increasingly characterizes many occupations (Desmarais & Alksnis, 2004). In the United States, more than one-fourth of all lawyers, physicians, computer scientists, and chemists today are females. However, some occupations continue to be sex-segregated. For example, in the United States more than nine of ten registered nurses are females while more than nine of ten males are firefighters. Even in these occupations, gender barriers are coming down, with twice as many men now entering the nursing profession and twice as many women becoming firefighters as two decades ago.

Ethnic diversity is also increasing in the workplace in every developed country except France. In the United States, between 1980 and 2002, the percentage of Latinos and Asian Americans more than doubled, a trend that is expected to continue (U.S. Bureau of Labor Statistics, 2003). Latinos are projected to constitute a larger percentage of the labor force than African Americans by 2012, growing from 12 percent to 15 percent (*Occupational Outlook Handbook,* 2004–2005). Asian Americans will continue to be the fastest growing of the labor force groups. The increasing diversity in the workplace requires a sensitivity to cultural differences, and the cultural values that workers bring to a job need to be recognized and appreciated (Powell, 2004).

How has the diversity of the workplace changed in recent years?

Carly Fiorina, chairman and chief executive officer of Hewlett-Packard, a leading global technology company. She is one of a minority of women who have been able to break through the glass ceiling.

The increasing diversity in the workplace has resulted in women and ethnic minorities experiencing difficulty in breaking through the **glass ceiling.** This invisible barrier to career advancement prevents women and ethnic minorities from holding managerial or executive jobs regardless of their accomplishments and merits. Females' share of executive management positions dropped from 32 percent in 1990 to 19 percent in 2000 (U.S. Bureau of Labor Statistics, 2003). However, over the same period, the percentage of ethnic minorities in management jobs increased from 13 percent in 1990 to 17 percent in 2000.

Unemployment   Unemployment produces stress regardless of whether the job loss is temporary, cyclical, or permanent (Hoyer & Roodin, 2003). Researchers have found that unemployment is related to physical problems (such as heart attack and stroke), mental problems (such as depression and anxiety), marital and family problems, homicide, and other crimes (Laporte, 2004; Merva & Fowles, 1992; Papalia & others, 2002). A recent 15-year longitudinal study of more than 24,000 adults found that life satisfaction dropped considerably following unemployment and increased after becoming reemployed but did not completely return to the life satisfaction level previous to being unemployed (Lucas & others, 2004).

Stress comes not only from a loss of income and the resulting financial hardships but also from decreased self-esteem (Voydanoff, 1990). Women are as likely to be upset over losing their job as men are. In a study of former employees of a plant that closed, both unemployed women and men reported increases in headaches, stomach problems, and blood pressure, and a decrease in control over their lives (Perrucci, Perrucci, & Targ, 1988). In a study of 190 unemployed workers, those who believed they had some control over their circumstances were less depressed and had fewer physical problems than those who believed that they had little control over their lives (Cvetanovski & Jex, 1994). Workers laid off in middle age often find unemployment more stressful than younger workers because they have more financial responsibilities and they typically are out of work longer (Papalia & others, 2002).

Individuals who cope best with unemployment have financial resources to rely on, often savings or the earnings of other family members. The support of understanding, adaptable family members also helps individuals cope with unemployment. Job counseling and self-help groups can provide practical advice on job searching, résumés, and interviewing skills and also give emotional support.

Working During College

Eighty percent of U.S. undergraduate students worked during the 1999–2000 academic year (National Center for Education Statistics, 2002). Forty-eight percent of undergraduates identified themselves mainly as students working to meet school expenses and 32 percent as employees who decided to enroll in school. Undergraduate students who identified themselves as working to meet expenses worked an average of 26 hours per week; those who considered themselves to be employees worked an average of 40 hours per week.

Working can pay or help offset some costs of schooling, but working can also restrict students' opportunities to learn. For those who identified themselves primarily as students, one recent national study found that as the number of hours worked per week increased, their grades suffered (National Center for Education Statistics, 2002) (see figure 10.10). Other research has found that as the number of hours college students work increases, the more likely they are to drop out of college (National Center for Education Statistics, 2002). Thus, college students need to carefully examine whether the number of hours they work is having a negative impact on their college success.

Of course, jobs can also contribute to your education. More than 1,000 colleges in the United States offer *cooperative (co-op) programs,* which are paid apprenticeships in a field that you are interested in pursuing. (You may not be permitted to participate in

glass ceiling The invisible barrier to career advancement that prevents women and ethnic minorities from holding managerial or executive jobs regardless of their accomplishments and merits.

a co-op program until your junior year.) Other useful opportunities for working while going to college include internships and part-time or summer jobs relevant to your field of study. In a national survey of employers, almost 60 percent said their entry-level college hires had co-op or internship experience (Collins, 1996). Participating in these work experiences can be a key factor in whether you land the job you want when you graduate.

Work and Retirement

The mid to late twentieth century saw two key gains for older U.S. workers. First, retirement became a widespread option after the Social Security system, which guarantees benefits to retirees, was implemented in 1935. Second, a series of federal laws protected many workers against being forced to retire because of their age. In 1967, the Age Discrimination Act prohibited the firing of employees because of their age before they reach the mandatory retirement age. In 1978, the federal government raised the mandatory retirement age from 65 to 70. In 1986, it banned mandatory retirement in all but a few occupations, such as police officer, firefighter, and airline pilot, where safety is an issue. Federal law now prohibits employers from firing older workers (who have seniority and higher salaries) just to save money. Thus, more often than in the past, U.S. workers choose when to retire.

Competing forces are working to raise and to lower the typical retirement age. On the one hand, some urge that the retirement age for receiving full Social Security benefits in the United States should be raised in order to save money. And the Netherlands recently tried to recruit persons to reenter the workforce because of a shortage of workers. On the other hand, to shrink payrolls without firing people, companies and governments sometimes offer programs to encourage workers to retire early. Germany, Sweden, Great Britain, Italy, France, Czechoslovakia, Hungary, and Russia are among the nations that are moving toward earlier retirement.

Retiring Part-Time Many retirees only partially retire, moving to part-time employment (Han & Moen, 1999). Self-employed men are especially likely to continue paid employment, either on the same job or on a new job. Nearly one-third of the men who take on a part-time job do not do so until two years after their retirement (Burkhauser & Quinn, 1989).

In one survey, 80 percent of baby boomers said that they expect to work during their retirement years (Roper Starch Worldwide, 2000). They cited the following as their main reasons for continuing to work: (1) part-time work for interest or enjoyment (35 percent), (2) income (23 percent), (3) the desire to start a business (17 percent), and (4) the desire to try a different field of work (5 percent). In another survey, nearly 70 percent of current employees said that they expect to work for pay once they retire, mainly because they enjoy working and want to stay active and involved (Anthony Greenwald & Associates, 2000).

Adjusting to Retirement On average, today's workers will spend 10 to 15 percent of their lives in retirement. In thinking about adjustment to retirement, it is important to conceptualize retirement as a process rather than an event (Kim & Moen, 2001). One recent study found that men who had been retired for more than two years had lower morale than men who had been retired within the last two years (Kim & Moen, 2002). Let's examine some other factors that may be linked to well-being in retirement.

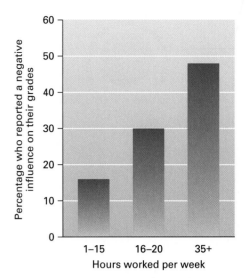

FIGURE 10.10 The Relation of Hours Worked per Week in College to Grades Among students working to pay for school expenses, 16 percent of those working 1 to 15 hours per week reported that working negatively influenced their grades. Thirty percent of college students who worked 16 to 20 hours a week said the same, as did 48 percent who worked 35 hours or more per week.

Ninety-two-year-old Russell "Bob" Harrell (*right*) puts in 12-hour days at Sieco Consulting Engineers in Columbus, Indiana. A highway and bridge engineer, he designs and plans roads. James Rice (age 48), a vice president of client services at Sieco, says that "Bob" wants to learn something new every day and that he has learned many life lessons from being around him. Harrell says he is not planning on retiring. *What are some variations in work and retirement in older adults?*

Work and Careers in Older Adults
AARP
Factors Influencing Retirement

Older adults who adjust best to retirement are healthy, have adequate income, are active, are better educated, have an extended social network including both friends and family, and usually were satisfied with their lives before they retired (Gall, Evans, & Howard, 1997; Moen & Quick, 1998; Palmore & others, 1985; Schlossberg, 2004). Older adults who have inadequate income and poor health and who must adjust to other stress at the same time as retirement, such as the death of a spouse, have the most difficult time adjusting to retirement (Stull & Hatch, 1984).

Flexibility is also a key factor in whether individuals adjust well to retirement. When people retire, they no longer have the structured environment they had when they were working, so they need to be flexible and discover and pursue their own interests (Eisdorfer, 1996). Cultivating interests and friends unrelated to work improves adaptation to retirement (Zarit & Knight, 1996). Many older adults participate in unpaid work—as a volunteer or an active participant in a voluntary association. These options afford older adults opportunities for productive activity, social interaction, and a positive identity.

Individuals who view retirement planning only in terms of finances don't adapt as well to retirement as those who have a more balanced retirement plan (Birren, 1996). It is important not only to plan financially for retirement, but to consider other areas of your life as well (Choi, 2001; Solomon, Acock & Walker, 2004). What are you going to do with your time? What are you going to do to stay active? What are you going to do socially? What are you going to do to keep your mind active?

Leisure

As adults, we must learn not only how to work well but also how to relax and enjoy leisure (Strain & others, 2002; van Eijck & Mommaas, 2004). **Leisure** refers to the times after work when individuals are free to pursue activities and interests of their own choosing—hobbies, sports, or reading, for example. Even Aristotle recognized leisure's importance in life, describing it as better than work.

Leisure can be an especially important aspect of middle adulthood (Mannell, 2000; McGuire, 2000). Many middle-aged adults find that they have more money, more free time, and more paid vacations than at any time in their lives. In short, they have expanded opportunities for leisure. For many individuals, middle adulthood is the first time in their lives when they have the opportunity to diversify their interests.

The American work ethic does not encourage us to value leisure; in fact, many Americans find it boring and unnecessary. Some adults pass on taking a vacation—perhaps because they do not trust anyone to fill in while they are gone or fear that they will fall behind in their work or that someone will replace them. These are behaviors that have been described as part of the Type A behavioral pattern, and they tend to promote heart disease. In one study, 12,338 men 35 to 57 years of age were assessed each year for five years regarding whether they took vacations or not (Gump & Matthews, 2000). Then, the researchers examined the medical and death records over nine years for men who lived for at least a year after the last vacation survey. Compared with those who never took vacations, men who went on annual vacations were 21 percent less likely to die over the nine years and 32 percent less likely to die of coronary heart disease.

Sigmund Freud once commented that the two things adults need to do well to adapt to society's demands are to work and to love. To his list we add "to play." In our fast-paced society, it is all too easy to get caught up in the frenzied, hectic pace of our achievement-oriented work world and ignore leisure and play. *Imagine your life as a middle-aged adult. What would be the ideal mix of work and leisure? What leisure activities do you want to enjoy as a middle-aged adult?*

leisure The pleasant times after work when individuals are free to pursue activities and interests of their own choosing such as hobbies, sports, or reading.

Adults at midlife need to begin preparing psychologically for retirement. Constructive and fulfilling leisure activities in middle adulthood are an important part of this preparation (Kelly, 1996). If an adult develops leisure activities that can be continued into retirement, the transition from work to retirement can be less stressful.

Review and Reflect

3 Summarize some key aspects of work

REVIEW

- What role does work play in people's lives?
- What are things to know about working while going to college?
- What characterizes work and retirement in older adults?
- What is leisure and what role does it play in people's lives?

REFLECT

- When would you like to retire, if at all? How difficult do you think it will be for you to adjust to retirement? Explain.

Reach Your Learning Goals

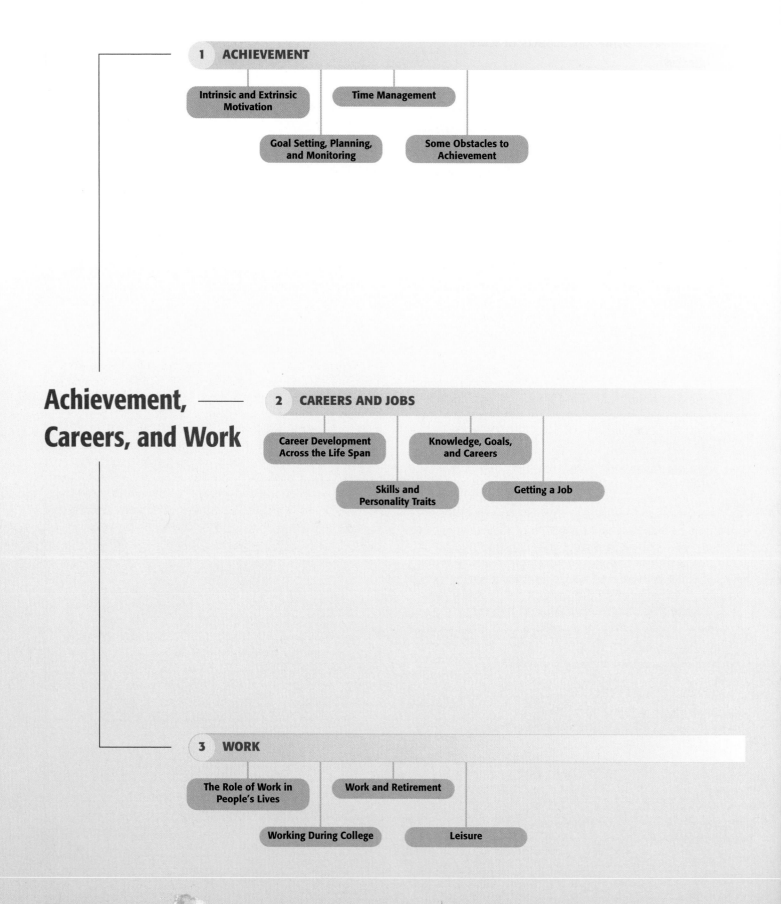

Achievement, Careers, and Work

1 ACHIEVEMENT

- Intrinsic and Extrinsic Motivation
- Goal Setting, Planning, and Monitoring
- Time Management
- Some Obstacles to Achievement

2 CAREERS AND JOBS

- Career Development Across the Life Span
- Skills and Personality Traits
- Knowledge, Goals, and Careers
- Getting a Job

3 WORK

- The Role of Work in People's Lives
- Working During College
- Work and Retirement
- Leisure

Summary

1 Discuss achievement and related adjustment strategies

- Both intrinsic motivation (based on internal factors such as self-determination, curiosity, challenge, and effort) and extrinsic motivation (based on external incentives such as rewards and punishments) may play a role in achievement. Many psychologists argue that intrinsic motivation is more likely than extrinsic motivation to produce competence and even mastery, but some of the most successful individuals have both types of motivation.
- Setting goals, planning, and monitoring efforts to achieve goals are central aspects of achievement. Achievement improves when people set specific, short-term, and challenging goals.
- Time management is a key aspect of achievement and success. Good time managers plan and set priorities, create a daily plan, and monitor their time plans.
- Some achievement problems include procrastination, perfectionism, and protecting self-worth by avoiding failure. The effort to avoid failure may involve self-handicapping strategies, such as deliberately not trying in school or putting off studying until the last minute.

2 Describe some important aspects of careers and jobs

- Ginzberg proposed that the fantasy stage characterizes birth through 11 years of age. Super thinks that individuals experience the growth stage from birth through early adolescence. Parents often have an important influence on their children's and adolescents' career interests. During adolescence, career exploration increases. The tentative stage characterizes career exploration from 11 to 17 and the realistic stage describes individuals from about 18 to 25, according to Ginzberg. The exploration stage describes individuals from 15 to 24 years of age, according to Super. The establishment stage is Super's term for the 25- to 45-year age period when individuals pursue a permanent career and attain a stable pattern of work in a particular career. The maintenance stage is Super's label for 45- to 64-year-olds. Super's fifth and final stage is retirement, beginning at about 65 years of age.
- Realistically evaluating academic and personal skills is important in choosing a career. Basic, thinking, and social skills, as well as personal qualities, are important. According to Holland's personality type theory, certain careers fit certain personality types, and it is important to find a career that fits your personality.
- Two other important aspects of exploring careers are becoming knowledgeable about careers (through such strategies as using the *Occupational Outlook Handbook* as a resource, networking, seeing a career counselor, and using the Internet to learn more about companies and jobs) and setting career goals.
- Getting a good job involves being aware of what employers want, finding out more information about particular jobs, creating an excellent résumé, and learning how to have a great job interview.

3 Summarize some key aspects of work

- Work is an important influence on people's financial standing, housing, the way they spend their time, where they live, their friendships, and their health. Some people define their identity in terms of their work. Most individuals spend about one-third of their lives at work. Among the aspects of work that can create stress are high job demands, inadequate decision-making opportunities, a high level of supervisor control, and a lack of clarity about the criteria for competent performance. Some people are workaholics, individuals who are seemingly addicted to work. Dual-career couples may face special challenges in balancing work and family responsibilities. The workplace is becoming increasingly diverse. Women and ethnic minorities make up a much greater percentage of the U.S. labor force today than in the past. A special concern is the glass ceiling, an invisible barrier to career advancement that prevents women and ethnic minorities from holding managerial or executive jobs regardless of their accomplishments and merits. Unemployment produces stress regardless of whether the job loss is temporary, cyclical, or permanent. Unemployment is related to physical problems, mental problems, and other difficulties.
- Eighty percent of U.S. college students work while going to college. Working during college can have negative outcomes, especially when students work long hours, or positive outcomes, especially when students participate in co-op programs, internships, or part-time or summer work relevant to their field of study.
- Having the option to retire is a late-twentieth-century phenomenon in the United States. An important change in older adults' work patterns is the increase in part-time work. Individuals who are healthy, have adequate income, are active, are better educated, have an extended social network of friends and family, and are satisfied with their lives before they retire adjust best to retirement.
- We not only need to learn to work well, but we also need to learn to enjoy leisure. Leisure may be especially important during midlife. Learning to enjoy leisure time helps prepare people for retirement.

Key Terms

Resources for Improving Your Adjustment

SELF-HELP BOOKS

What Color Is Your Parachute?

(2005) by Richard Bolles. Berkeley, CA: Ten Speed Press.

What Color Is Your Parachute? is an extremely popular book on job hunting. Since 1975 an annual edition has appeared. This book has become the career seeker's bible. Bolles tries to answer concerns about the job-hunting process and refers readers to many sources that provide valuable information. Bolles describes many myths about job hunting and successfully combats them. He also provides invaluable advice about where jobs are, what to do to get yourself hired, and how to cut through all of the red tape and confusing hierarchies of the business world to meet with the key people who are most likely to make the decision about whether to hire you or not. *What Color Is Your Parachute?* was rated in the top category (5 stars) in the national survey of self-help books (Norcross, Santrock, & others, 2003).

The 7 Habits of Highly Effective People

(1989) by Stephen Covey. New York: Simon & Schuster.

The 7 Habits of Highly Effective People tells you how to harness your potential to achieve your goals. Covey argues that to become a quality leader in an organization, you must first become a quality-oriented individual. He also believes there are seven basic habits that are fundamental to anyone's success and competence. The first three are private victories and the next three are public victories. The seven habits include: Be proactive instead of reactive; begin with the end in mind; put first things first; think win/win; seek first to understand, then to be understood; synergize; sharpen the saw (renewal). This book was given 5 stars (highest category) in the national survey of self-help books.

Retire Smart, Retire Happy

(2004) by Nancy Schlossberg. Washington, DC: American Psychological Association.

This book explores how retirement alters our roles, relationships, and routines in life. Schlossberg describes a number of resources to help people make the transition to retirement effectively. A self-quiz, *Your Retirement,* is helpful.

E-Learning Tools

To help you master the material in this chapter, you will find a number of valuable study tools on the student CD-ROM that accompanies this book. In addition, visit the Online Learning Center for *Human Adjustment,* where you can find helpful resources for chapter 10, "Achievement, Careers, and Work."

SELF-ASSESSMENT

In Text

You can complete these self-assessments in the text:
- Self-Assessment 10.1: *Am I a Perfectionist?*
- Self-Assessment 10.2: *What Are My Academic and Personal Skills Strengths and Weaknesses?*
- Self-Assessment 10.3: *My Career Goals*

Additional Self-Assessments

Complete these self-assessments on the Online Learning Center:
- *My Weekly Plan*
- *Matching My Personality Type to Careers*
- *Exploring My Career Options*

THINK CRITICALLY

To practice your critical thinking skills, complete these exercises on the Online Learning Center:
- *What Do You Want to Be When You Grow Up?* gives you an opportunity to think about your development as a child and an adolescent, and how your career interests might have changed.
- *The Superhuman Perspective* focuses on the strain from having too many things to do at once.
- *Who Is Responsible?* explores employers and the extent to which they are socially responsible for their workers.

APPLY YOUR KNOWLEDGE

1. Balancing work and school

Many students feel a conflict between working to pay for school and getting good grades. In some cases, students work full-time while attempting to complete school quickly. This often results in poor grades and burnout. Other students go into debt in order to focus on school. In some cases, options may be available that are not immediately known. To explore your options for paying for school, select a search engine such as www.yahoo.com or www.google.come and search for "paying for college."

2. Planning for retirement

An interesting paradox has evolved over the past 50 years. On the one hand, people are living longer and healthier lives and 65 (traditional retirement age) is no longer considered to be "elderly." At the same time, more and more workers are opting for early retirement. Do you want to retire early? Why or why not? What are you willing to give up in order to retire early? Regardless of the age at which you want to retire, starting now to plan for retirement is a good idea. The earlier you start, the less money per year you need to put away in order to have enough money to retire. To see how much you need to be able to retire, and to plan accordingly, visit a search engine such as www.yahoo.com or www.google.come and search for "planning for retirement" or "saving for retirement."

3. Volunteering

People volunteer for many reasons: to share skills with the community, to provide balance to working lives, to form network and friendships, or to fill retirement with interesting activities. One of the challenges that faces workers when they retire is the void in their lives caused by unlimited free time. Getting into the habit of volunteering now makes the transition to retirement easier, helps round-out people's lives, and provides a sense of pride from helping others. Make a list of the talents that you have that might be useful to others, or that you would like to use more often than you do. Then look in your local yellow page section of the phone book under "social service" or phone your local United Way office. You can also phone women's shelters, humane societies, and fund-raising clubs. Volunteer activities cover a wide variety of interests, and range from low or sporadic time commitment to a weekly commitment. Volunteering is also a valuable item to have on your résumé.

VIDEO SEGMENT

Sometimes, obstacles to achievement are far from obvious. Watch the video for Chapter 10 on the CD-ROM to learn about one test of the idea that the fear of confirming a negative stereotype about your group might keep you from doing your best.

Emerging Adulthood, Adult Development, and Aging

Images of Adjustment

Sister Mary and Anthony Pirelli

JONATHAN SWIFT said, "No wise man ever wished to be younger." Without a doubt, a 70-year-old body does not work as well as it once did. It is also true that an individual's fear of aging is often greater than need be. As more individuals live to a ripe *and* active old age, our image of aging is changing. Although on the average a 75-year-old's joints should be stiffening, people can practice not to be average. For example, a 75-year-old man might *choose* to train for and run a marathon.

Consider Sister Mary who was born in 1892 in Philadelphia. She died in 1993 at 101 years of age. Mary was a remarkable woman who had high cognitive test scores even after she reached 100 years of age (Snowdon, 1997). What is more remarkable is that she maintained this high level of cognitive competence despite having extensive tangles and plaques, which are classic neurological characteristics of Alzheimer disease.

Sister Mary taught full-time until she was 77 years old. Then for several years more she worked part-time as a math teacher and teacher's aide. She finally retired at 84, although she once commented that she never really retired: "I only retire at night."

Only 4 feet, 6 inches tall, and weighing only about 85 pounds, Sister Mary spent the last years of her life in the convent she had entered when she was a young girl. In her so-called retirement, she continued to give talks about various life and religious issues and to be active in the community. She was also an avid reader, often seen poring over newspapers and books with her magnifying glass.

Sister Mary was known for her great attitude. She had a wide smile and a warm, hearty laugh. When she asked her doctor if he was secretly giving her medicine to keep her alive and healthy, he replied that it was her wonderful attitude that was doing the trick.

Anthony Pirelli suffered a serious heart attack when he was 63, but at 70 he was happy, working part-time, and playing tennis (Vaillant, 2002). Pirelli seemed to set his own rules for development. His father drank too much and beat Anthony's brothers; his mother had bipolar disorder; both could barely speak English. Anthony grew up in a crowded tenement building with eight siblings, unassertive and fearful at 13. These and other characteristics made him a child "at risk" for many problems in life. Yet by the time he was 50, Pirelli was a prosperous, happily married suburban father who had become a very successful businessman. Our lives take many different paths.

The stories of Sister Mary and Anthony Pirelli raise some fascinating questions. How do we develop from the time we make the transition to adulthood through the time when we become older adults and eventually die? What, if anything, can we do to slow down the aging process? Examining the course of our development helps us to understand it better. We begin the chapter by exploring what development is and our adjustment as we become adults. Then we will examine three main strands of development—physical, cognitive, and socioemotional—through three periods of adulthood. We conclude the chapter by discussing adjustment in facing our own death and the death of someone else.

1 BECOMING AN ADULT

The Nature of Development   **Emerging Adulthood**

How did Anthony Pirelli develop from a fearful adolescent living in poverty into a confident middle-aged man? Just what is development? More specifically, what is our development like as we make the transition from adolescence to adulthood?

The Nature of Development

Development refers to the pattern of change in human capabilities that begins at conception and continues throughout the life span. Development involves growth but also decline; for example, as we age, we are likely to process information less quickly. The pattern of development is complex because it is the product of several processes:

- *Physical processes* involve changes in an individual's biological nature. The inheritance of genes from parents, the hormonal changes of puberty and menopause, and changes throughout life in the brain, height and weight, and motor skills all reflect the developmental role of biological processes. Psychologists refer to such biological growth processes as *maturation.*
- *Cognitive processes* involve changes in an individual's thinking, intelligence, and language. Observing a colorful mobile as it swings above a crib, constructing a sentence about the future, imagining oneself as a movie star, memorizing a new telephone number—all these activities reflect the role of cognitive processes in development.
- *Socioemotional processes* involve changes in an individual's relationships with other people, changes in emotions, and changes in personality. An infant's smile in response to her mother's touch, a girl's development of assertiveness, an adolescent's joy at the senior prom, a young man's aggressiveness in sport, and an older couple's affection for each other all reflect socioemotional processes.

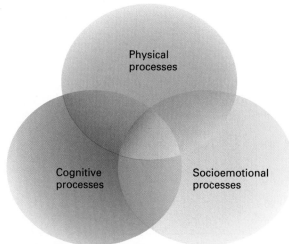

FIGURE 11.1 Developmental Changes Are the Result of Physical, Cognitive, and Socioemotional Processes These processes interact as individuals develop.

All of these processes are intricately interwoven, as figure 11.1 shows. For example, socioemotional processes shape cognitive processes, cognitive processes promote or restrict socioemotional processes, physical processes influence cognitive processes, and so on.

Adult Periods of Development   To analyze how we develop through the life span, it helps to organize the years into a few distinct periods, such as childhood, adolescence, and adulthood. Adulthood is often further divided into early, middle, and late periods.

Early adulthood is the developmental period that begins in the late teens or early twenties and lasts through the thirties. It is a time of establishing personal and

development The pattern of change in human capabilities that begins at conception and continues through the life span.

early adulthood The developmental period that begins in the late teens or early twenties and lasts through the thirties.

25 to 34 Years	35 to 54 Years	55 to 65 Years	70 to 84 Years	85 to 105 Years
Work	Family	Family	Family	Health
Friends	Work	Health	Health	Family
Family	Friends	Friends	Cognitive fitness	Thinking about life
Independence	Cognitive fitness	Cognitive fitness	Friends	Cognitive fitness

FIGURE 11.2 Degree of Personal Life Investment at Different Points in Life
Shown here are the top four domains of personal life investment at different points in life. The highest degree of investment is listed at the top (for example, work was the highest personal investment from 25 to 34 years of age, family from 35 to 84, and health from 85 to 105).

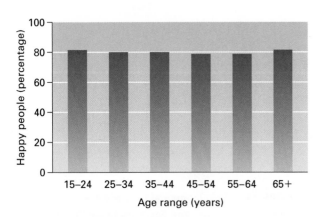

FIGURE 11.3 Age and Happiness
Analysis of surveys of nearly 170,000 people in sixteen countries found no age differences in happiness from adolescence into the late adulthood years.

middle adulthood The developmental period from approximately 40 years of age to about 60.

late adulthood The developmental period that begins in the sixties and lasts until death.

economic independence, developing a career, and, for many, selecting a mate, learning to live with someone in an intimate way, starting a family, and rearing children.

Middle adulthood is the developmental period from approximately 40 years of age to about 60. It is a time of expanding personal and social involvement and responsibility; of assisting the next generation in becoming competent, mature individuals; and of reaching and maintaining satisfaction in a career.

Late adulthood is the developmental period that begins in the sixties and lasts until death. It is a time of adjusting to retirement, to decreasing strength and health, and to new social roles, as well as a time for reviewing one's life.

A person's goals and priorities are likely to change over the course of these periods (Cantor & Blanton, 1996). One cross-sectional study assessed the life investments of 25- to 105-year olds (Staudinger, 1996; Staudinger & Fleeson, 1996) (see figure 11.2). From 25 to 34 years of age, participants said that they personally invested more time in work, friends, family, and independence, in that order. From 35 to 54 and 55 to 65 years of age, family became more important than friends in terms of their personal investment. Little changed in the priorities for 70 to 84 years old, but for those 85 to 105 years old, health became the most important personal investment. Thinking about life showed up for the first time on the list of priorities for 85- to 105-year-olds. Other researchers have found similar ratings of life domains across the life span (Heckhausen, 2002).

Are adults happier in one of these periods more than the others? When individuals report how happy they are and how satisfied they are with their lives, no particular age group says they are happier or more satisfied than any other age group (Diener, Lucas, & Oishi, 2002). When nearly 170,000 people in sixteen countries were surveyed, no differences in their happiness from adolescence into the late adulthood years were found (Inglehart, 1990) (see figure 11.3). About the same percentage of people in each age group—slightly less than 20 percent—reported that they were very happy.

Every period of the life span has its stresses, pluses and minuses, hills and valleys. Although adolescents must cope with developing an identity, insecurity, mood swings, and peer pressure, the majority of adolescents develop positive perceptions of themselves, feelings of competence, positive relationships with friends and family, and an optimistic view of their future. And although older adults face a life of reduced income, less energy, declining physical skills, and concerns about death, they are also less pressured to achieve, have more time for leisurely pursuits, and have accumulated many years of experience that help them adapt to their lives with a wisdom they may not have had in their younger years. Because growing older is a certain outcome of living, we can derive considerable pleasure from knowing that we are likely to be just as happy as older adults as when we were younger.

Emerging Adulthood

An important transition occurs from adolescence to adulthood (Eccles, 2004; King & Chassin, 2004; Lefkowitz & others, 2004). It has been said that adolescence begins in biology and ends in culture. That is, the transition from childhood to adolescence begins with the onset of pubertal maturation, while the transition from adolescence to adulthood is determined by cultural standards and experiences.

The transition can be a long one. Around the world, youth are increasingly expected to delay their entry into adulthood, in large part because contemporary society requires adults who are more educated and skilled than previous generations (Brown, Larson, & Saraswathi, 2002; Larson & Wilson, 2004). Thus, the transition between adolescence and adulthood can be a long one. **Emerging adulthood** is the term now given to the transition from adolescence to adulthood (Arnett, 2000, 2004). The age range for emerging adulthood is approximately 18 to 25 years of age.

Experimentation and exploration characterize the emerging adult. At this point in their development, many individuals are still exploring which career path they want to follow, what they want their identity to be, and which lifestyle they want to adopt (for example, single, cohabiting, or married) (Reifman, Arnett, & Colwell, 2003). To evaluate your characteristics in terms of what is experienced during emerging adulthood, complete Self-Assessment 11.1.

Who Is an Adult? Determining just when an individual becomes an adult is difficult. In developing countries, marriage is often a more significant marker for entry into adulthood than in the United States, and it usually occurs much earlier than in the United States (Arnett, 2000, 2004). Our discussion here mainly addresses individuals in industrialized societies, especially the United States.

The most widely recognized marker of entry into adulthood is holding a more or less permanent, full-time job, which usually happens when an individual finishes school—high school for some, college for others, graduate or professional school for still others. However, other criteria are far from clear.

Economic independence is one marker of adult status but achieving it is often a long process. Increasingly, college graduates are returning to live with their parents as they seek to get their feet on the ground financially. About 40 percent of individuals in their late teens to early twenties move back into their parents' home at least once (Goldscheider & Goldscheider, 1999).

Self-responsibility and independent decision making are other possible markers of adulthood. Indeed, in one study, adolescents cited taking responsibility for themselves and making independent decisions as the markers of entry into adulthood (Scheer & Unger, 1994). In another study, more than 70 percent of college students said that being an adult means accepting responsibility for the consequences of one's actions; deciding on one's own beliefs and values; and establishing a relationship equal with one's parents (Arnett, 1995).

Is there a specific age at which individuals become adults? One study examined emerging adults' perception of whether they were adults (Arnett, 2000). The majority of the 18- to 25-year-olds responded neither "yes" nor "no," but "in some respects yes, in some respects no" (see figure 11.4). In this study, not until the late twenties and

Aging Megasite
Resources for Older Adults
Gerontological Society of America

Emerging Adulthood Resources
Exploring Emerging Adulthood

emerging adulthood The term for the transition from adolescence to adulthood, about 18 to 25 years of age, that is characterized by experimentation and exploration.

SELF-ASSESSMENT 11.1

My View of Life

Think about this time in your life—the present time plus the last few years that have gone by and the next few years to come, as you see them. In short, you should think about a roughly five-year period, with the present time right in the middle. For each phrase below, place a check mark in one of the four columns to indicate the degree to which you agree or disagree that the phrase describes this time in your life. Be sure to put only one check mark per line.

Is this period of your life a . . .	Strongly Disagree (1)	Somewhat Disagree (2)	Somewhat Agree (3)	Strongly Agree (4)
1. time of many possibilities?	_____	_____	_____	_____
2. time of exploration?	_____	_____	_____	_____
3. time of confusion?	_____	_____	_____	_____
4. time of experimentation?	_____	_____	_____	_____
5. time of personal freedom?	_____	_____	_____	_____
6. time of feeling restricted?	_____	_____	_____	_____
7. time of responsibility for yourself?	_____	_____	_____	_____
8. time of feeling stressed out?	_____	_____	_____	_____
9. time of instability?	_____	_____	_____	_____
10. time of optimism?	_____	_____	_____	_____
11. time of high pressure?	_____	_____	_____	_____
12. time of finding out who you are?	_____	_____	_____	_____
13. time of settling down?	_____	_____	_____	_____
14. time of responsibility for others?	_____	_____	_____	_____
15. time of independence?	_____	_____	_____	_____
16. time of open choices?	_____	_____	_____	_____
17. time of unpredictability?	_____	_____	_____	_____
18. time of commitments to others?	_____	_____	_____	_____
19. time of self-sufficiency?	_____	_____	_____	_____
20. time of many worries?	_____	_____	_____	_____
21. time of trying out new things?	_____	_____	_____	_____
22. time of focusing on yourself?	_____	_____	_____	_____
23. time of separating from parents?	_____	_____	_____	_____
24. time of defining yourself?	_____	_____	_____	_____
25. time of planning for the future?	_____	_____	_____	_____
26. time of seeking a sense of meaning?	_____	_____	_____	_____
27. time of deciding on your own beliefs and values?	_____	_____	_____	_____
28. time of learning to think for yourself?	_____	_____	_____	_____
29. time of feeling adult in some ways but not others?	_____	_____	_____	_____
30. time of gradually becoming an adult?	_____	_____	_____	_____
31. time of being not sure whether you have reached full adulthood?	_____	_____	_____	_____

Go to the appendix at the end of the book for scoring and interpretation of your responses.

early thirties did a clear majority of respondents agree that they had reached adulthood. Thus, these emerging adults saw themselves as neither adolescents nor full-fledged adults.

In another study, however, 21-year-olds said that they had reached adult status when they were 18 to 19 years old (Scheer, 1996). In this study, both social status factors (financial status and graduation/education) and cognitive factors (being responsible and making independent decisions) were cited as markers for reaching adulthood. Clearly, reaching adulthood involves more than just attaining a specific chronological age.

At some point in the late teens through the early twenties, then, individuals reach adulthood. In becoming an adult, they accept responsibility for themselves, become capable of making independent decisions, and gain financial independence from their parents (Arnett, 2000, 2004).

Personal and Social Assets   For Anthony Pirelli, the transition from adolescence to adulthood was an eventful time. He graduated from trade school, enlisted in the air force, and then became a skilled laborer. At 19 he married. By age 25 he owned his own home, had earned a degree in accounting, and was described as hard driving and mature. How had he fared so well?

Certain personal and social assets are linked to well-being in adolescence and emerging adulthood. In Pirelli's case, intelligence, a sense of joy and gratitude, a nurturing sister, and a lucky marriage may all have been keys to his well-being (Vaillant, 2002). Jacqueline Eccles and her colleagues (Eccles & Goodman, 2002; Eccles & others, 2002) recently examined research and concluded that three types of assets are especially important: intellectual (academic success, planfulness, and good decision-making skills); psychological (mental health, mastery motivation, confidence in one's competence, identity, values, and community contributions); and social (connectedness to others through friendship and positive peer relations).

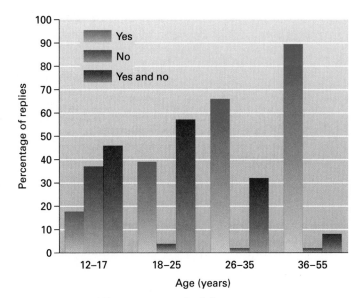

FIGURE 11.4 Self-Perceptions of Adult Status
In one study, individuals were asked "Do you feel that you have reached adult status?" and were given a choice of answering "yes," "no," or "in some respects yes, in some respects no" (Arnett, 2000). As indicated in the graph, the majority of the emerging adults (18 to 25) responded "in some respects yes, in some respects no."

Adjustment Strategies
For Emerging Adulthood

Here are some adjustment strategies for making the transition to adulthood effectively:

1. ***Experiment and explore responsibly.*** Be aware of what the transition from adolescence to adulthood involves. It is a time of experimentation and exploration that can last as long as seven or eight years. During this time it is important for you to explore what career path you want to follow, what you want your identity to be, and which lifestyle you want to adopt. Responsibly handle the new freedoms and responsibilities that emerging adulthood brings.
2. ***Develop intellectual assets.*** Work on improving your life skills, academic success, planfulness, and decision-making skills. The strategies for setting goals and conquering procrastination described in chapter 10, "Achievement, Careers, and Work," might benefit your ability to develop your intellectual assets.
3. ***Create psychological assets.*** Develop an optimistic style of thinking and coping, and be in control of your life. To develop an optimistic style, you might want to review the adjustment strategies recommended in chapter 5, "Coping." These include identifying the thoughts and feelings you have after something pleasant happens, becoming aware of your pattern of thinking when you experience unpleasant events, and distracting yourself from pessimistic thoughts. You might also benefit from reviewing the adjustment strategies for increasing your self-efficacy in chapter 2, "Personality."

continued

4. ***Establish social assets.*** Be connected and integrated in a social world of friends and acquaintances. Avoid becoming socially isolated and lonely. Develop your communication skills as part of your effort to get along well with people and enjoy social relationships. Manage your emotions so that they benefit your relationships with others rather than harming them. Take the perspective of others and consider others' feelings. The strategies for getting and keeping friends, and for reducing loneliness, discussed in chapter 8, "Friendship and Love Relationships," might benefit your ability to establish social assets.

Change and Continuity   The new freedoms and responsibilities of emerging adulthood represent major changes in individuals' lives. Although change characterizes the transition from adolescence to adulthood, considerable continuity still links these periods together. For example, one recent longitudinal study found that religious views and behaviors were especially stable in emerging adults, and to a lesser degree, attitudes toward drugs were stable as well (Bachman & others, 2002).

Consider also the data collected in a longitudinal study of more than 2,000 males from the time they were in the tenth grade until five years after high school (Bachman, O'Malley, & Johnston, 1978). Some of the males dropped out, others graduated from high school. Some took jobs after graduating from high school, others went to college. Some were employed, others were unemployed. The dominant picture of the males as they went through this eight-year period was stability rather than change. For example, the tenth-graders who had the highest self-esteem were virtually the same individuals who had the highest self-esteem five years after high school. Similarly, those who were the most achievement oriented in the tenth grade remained the most achievement oriented eight years later. Some environmental changes produced differences in this transition period. For example, marriage reduced drug use, unemployment increased it. Success in college and career increased achievement orientation; less education and poor occupational performance diminished achievement orientation.

Adapting to College   Going from being a senior in high school to being a freshman in college brings many changes. Instead of being part of the oldest, most powerful group of students to the youngest and least powerful group of students in high school (the seniors), college freshmen find themselves part of the youngest, least powerful group. The

What are some effective adjustment strategies in emerging adulthood?

transition from high school to college involves movement to a larger, more impersonal structure; interaction with peers from more diverse geographical and sometimes more diverse ethnic backgrounds; and increased focus on achievement and its assessment. But the transition may also involve positive features. College students are likely to have more time to spend with peers; have more opportunities to explore different academic subjects, lifestyles, and values; enjoy greater independence from their parents; and be challenged intellectually by academic work (Santrock & Halonen, 2004).

Today's college students experience more stress and are more depressed than in the past, according to a national study of more than 300,000 freshmen at more than 500 colleges and universities (Sax & others, 2003). In 2003, 27 percent said they frequently "felt overwhelmed with what I have to do" (up from 16 percent in 1985). And college freshmen in 2003 indicated that they felt more depressed than their counterparts from the 1980s had indicated. The pressure to succeed in college, get a great job, and make lots of money were pervasive concerns of these students. To find out college students' main reasons for seeking counseling on one campus, see figure 11.5.

What makes college students happy? One recent study of 222 undergraduates found that the upper 10 percent of college students who were very happy were highly social, more extraverted, and had stronger romantic and social relationships than the less happy college students (Diener & Seligman, 2002).

How well adjusted are you to college? To evaluate this aspect of your life, complete Self-Assessment 11.2.

Special challenges may face college students who are *returning students*—that is, students who either did not go to college right out of high school or went to college, dropped out, and now have returned. More than one of every five full-time college students today is a returning student, and about two-thirds of part-time college students are (Sax & others, 2003). Many returning students have to balance their course work with commitments to a partner, children, job, and community responsibilities. Despite the many challenges that returning students face, they bring many strengths to campus, such as life experiences that can be applied to a wide range of issues and topics.

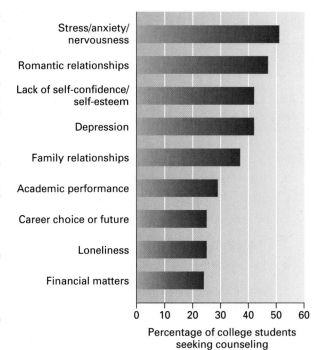

FIGURE 11.5 College Students' Main Reasons for Seeking Counseling

Adjustment Strategies
For Returning Students

Here are some strategies that returning students can use for effectively adjusting to college:

1. ***Develop strategies to cope with your new environment.*** You likely will encounter a number of challenges as you make the transition to being a student once again. Review the coping strategies discussed in chapter 5 to determine which ones might help you the most as a returning student.
2. ***Connect with your campus.*** Spend some time finding out about various campus organizations, groups, and activities. Consider joining a campus group.
3. ***Get to know other students.*** Talk with students of different ages, including some traditional-age college students and some older returning students.
4. ***Take advantage of support services.*** Your college has a number of services it provides students. Learn about those services and how they might help you succeed in college. Many returning students find that putting some effort into improving their study skills benefits their grades. If you think this might help you, contact the study skills specialists at your college. A counselor also can advise you about personal problems and issues.

SELF-ASSESSMENT 11.2

My College Adjustment

Read each of the items below and reflect on them. Then place a check mark in one of the four columns to the extent the item is like you or not like you.

	Very Much Unlike Me	Somewhat Unlike Me	Somewhat Like Me	Very Much Like Me
1. I have developed meaningful values.	_____	_____	_____	_____
2. I set goals, plan how to reach them, and regularly monitor my progress toward these goals.	_____	_____	_____	_____
3. I manage my time effectively.	_____	_____	_____	_____
4. I am a good thinker and learner.	_____	_____	_____	_____
5. I am highly motivated and take responsibility for my behavior.	_____	_____	_____	_____
6. I am well connected to campus and use its resources effectively.	_____	_____	_____	_____
7. I have mapped out an academic plan that I like.	_____	_____	_____	_____
8. I am aware of the types of jobs during college that could benefit my career in the future.	_____	_____	_____	_____
9. My academic major connects with the type of job and career I want to pursue after college.	_____	_____	_____	_____
10. I have good social relationships.	_____	_____	_____	_____
11. I engage in health-enhancing behaviors (regular exercise, good eating habits, and so on) rather than health-harming behaviors (such as smoking, binge drinking, and so on).	_____	_____	_____	_____
12. My life is reasonably well balanced and I don't put all of my energy into just one area.	_____	_____	_____	_____

Go to the appendix at the end of the book for interpretation of your responses.

Review and Reflect

1 **Describe the nature of development and becoming an adult**

REVIEW
- How can development be characterized?
- What is emerging adulthood?

REFLECT
- What do you think are the most important aspects of being well adjusted during emerging adulthood?

2 PHYSICAL DEVELOPMENT IN ADULTHOOD

- Early Adulthood
- Late Adulthood
- Middle Adulthood

Singer-actress Bette Midler said that after 30 a body has a mind of its own. Comedian Bob Hope once remarked that middle age is when your age starts to show around your middle. How do we age physically as we go through the adult years?

Early Adulthood

Most adults reach their peak physical development and are the healthiest during their twenties (Payne & Isaacs, 2005). For athletes—not only at the Olympic level but also the average athlete—performance peaks in the twenties, especially for strength and speed events such as weight lifting and the 100-meter dash (Schultz & Curnow, 1988). The main exceptions are female gymnasts and swimmers, who often peak in adolescence, and marathon runners, who tend to peak in their late thirties. Unfortunately, early adulthood also is when many skills begin to decline. The decline in strength and speed often is noticeable in the thirties.

Perhaps because of their robust physical skills and overall health, young adults rarely recognize that bad eating habits, heavy drinking, and smoking in early adulthood can impair their health as they age (Bachman & others, 2002). People also increase their use of alcohol, marijuana, amphetamines, barbiturates, and hallucinogens.

Middle Adulthood

Physical changes in middle adulthood include changes in appearance. By the forties or fifties, the skin begins to wrinkle and sag because of a loss of fat and collagen in underlying tissues. Small, localized areas of pigmentation in the skin produce age spots, especially in areas exposed to sunlight, such as the hands and face. Hair becomes thinner and grayer due to a lower replacement rate and a decline in melanin production. In an effort to look young, many middle-aged adults dye their hair, and an increasing number have cosmetic surgery.

Individuals actually begin to lose height in middle age, and many gain weight. Adults lose about one-half inch of height per decade beginning in their forties (Memmler & others, 1995). Fat generally accounts for about 10 percent of body weight in adolescence but for 20 percent or more in middle age.

Perhaps because the signs of aging are all too visible, people tend to become more acutely concerned about their health in their forties. In fact, we do experience a general decline in physical fitness throughout middle adulthood and some deterioration in health. The three greatest health concerns at this age are heart disease, cancer, and weight. Cancer related to smoking often surfaces in middle adulthood.

For women, entering middle age also means that menopause will soon occur. Usually in the late forties or early fifties, the production of estrogen by the ovaries declines dramatically, and a woman's menstrual periods cease completely. The average age at

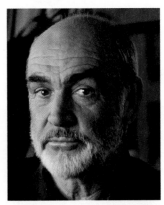

Famous actor Sean Connery as a young adult in his 20s (left) and as a middle-aged adult in his 50s (right). *What are some of the most outwardly noticeable signs of aging in the middle adulthood years?*

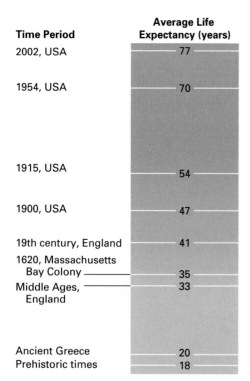

Time Period	Average Life Expectancy (years)
2002, USA	77
1954, USA	70
1915, USA	54
1900, USA	47
19th century, England	41
1620, Massachusetts Bay Colony	35
Middle Ages, England	33
Ancient Greece	20
Prehistoric times	18

FIGURE 11.6 Human Life Expectancy at Birth from Prehistoric to Contemporary Times

Centenarian Study

life span The upper boundary of a species' life, the maximum number of years any member of the species has been documented to live.

life expectancy The number of years that will probably be lived by the average person born in a particular year.

which women have their last period is 52, but 10 percent of women undergo menopause before age 40. The loss of fertility is an important marker for women, and its approach means that they must make final decisions about having children (Sommer, 2001).

For some women, estrogen decline produces uncomfortable symptoms, such as hot flashes (sudden brief flushing of the skin and a feeling of elevated body temperature), nausea, fatigue, and rapid heartbeat. Some women report depression and irritability, but in some instances these feelings are related to other circumstances in the women's lives, such as becoming divorced, losing a job, or caring for a sick parent (Dickson, 1990; Steiner, Dunn, & Born, 2003). For most women, menopause does not produce psychological or physical problems (McKinlay & McKinlay, 1984).

Do men go through anything like menopause? Men do experience sex-related hormone declines in their fifties and sixties, but they are usually not as precipitous as the estrogen decline in women (Hyde & DeLamater, 2005).

Late Adulthood

For Sister Mary, described at the opening of this chapter, even the years after middle age constituted a long and active period. People like her led to the concept of a period called "late adulthood," which is a recent idea: Until the twentieth century, most individuals died before they were 65. From 1950 to 1990, however, the world's population of individuals 65 and older doubled; the fastest growing segment of the population today is 85 years and older. The average age of people in many societies around the world has risen, so we need a better understanding of the later years of life (Bee & Bjorkland, 2004; Birren, 2000; Post & Binstock, 2004).

Life Span and Life Expectancy   The maximum number of years human beings can live—our **life span**—is about 120 to 125. The human life span does not seem to have increased since the beginning of recorded history, but life expectancy can and has increased. **Life expectancy** refers to the number of years that will probably be lived by the average person born in a particular year. Improvements in medicine, nutrition, exercise, and lifestyle have increased our life expectancy an average of 30 years since 1900 (see figure 11.6). The life expectancy of individuals born today in the United States is 77 years (80 for women, 73 for men). One in three women born today is expected to live to be 100 or more. To evaluate whether you might live to be 100, complete Self-Assessment 11.3.

In 2000, there were 77,000 centenarians (individuals 100 years and older) in the United States, and it is projected that this number will be 834,000 in 2050. Today's centenarians are healthier than you might expect. One recent study found that 15 percent of more than 400 centenarians had never been diagnosed with common age-associated diseases such as heart disease, cancer, and stroke (Evert & others, 2003).

Is an easy life or freedom from stressors necessary for living to be 100? Not at all. In the New England Centenarian study, a majority of the centenarians have had difficult lives, such as surviving the Holocaust and living in extreme poverty as an immigrant to the United States (Perls, Lauerman, & Silver, 1999). What has contributed to their survival is their ability to cope successfully with stress.

Individuals live longer on the Japanese island of Okinawa than anywhere else in the world. What is responsible for their longevity? Some possible explanations (Willcox, Willcox, & Suzuki, 2002) are diet (they eat healthy food, heavy on grains, fish, and vegetables, light on meat, eggs, and dairy products), low-stress lifestyle, caring community (Okinawans look out for one another and do not isolate or ignore older adults), activity (many older Okinawans are active, engaging in such activities as

Can I Live to Be 100?

Decide how each item applies to you and add or subtract the appropriate number of years from your basic life expectancy.

1. Family history

___ Add five years if two or more of your grandparents lived to 80 or beyond.

___ Subtract four years if any parent, grandparent, sister, or brother died of a heart attack or stroke before 50.

___ Subtract two years if anyone died from these diseases before 60.

___ Subtract three years for each case of diabetes, thyroid disorder, breast cancer, cancer of the digestive system, asthma, or chronic bronchitis among parents or grandparents.

2. Marital status

___ If you are married, add four years.

___ If you are over 25 and not married, subtract one year for every unmarried decade.

3. Economic status

___ Add two years if your family income is over $60,000 per year.

___ Subtract three years if you have been poor for the greater part of your life.

4. Physique

___ Subtract one year for every 10 pounds you are overweight.

___ For each inch your girth measurement exceeds your chest measurement deduct two years.

___ Add three years if you are over 40 and not overweight.

5. Exercise

___ Add three years if you exercise regularly and moderately (jogging three times a week).

___ Add five years if you exercise regularly and vigorously (long-distance running three times a week).

___ Subtract three years if your job is sedentary.

___ Add three years if your job is active.

6. Alcohol

___ Add two years if you are a light drinker (one to three drinks a day).

___ Subtract five to ten years if you are a heavy drinker (more than four drinks per day).

___ Subtract one year if you are a teetotaler.

7. Smoking

___ Subtract eight years if you smoke two or more packs of cigarettes per day.

___ Subtract two years if you smoke one to two packs per day.

___ Subtract two years if you smoke less than one pack.

___ Subtract two years if you regularly smoke a pipe or cigars.

8. Disposition

___ Add two years if you are a reasoned, practical person.

___ Subtract two years if you are aggressive, intense, and competitive.

___ Add one to five years if you are basically happy and content with life.

___ Subtract one to five years if you are often unhappy, worried, and often feel guilty.

9. Education

___ Subtract two years if you have less than a high school education.

___ Add one year if you attended four years of school beyond high school.

___ Add three years if you attended five or more years beyond high school.

10. Environment

___ Add four years if you have lived most of your life in a rural environment.

___ Subtract two years if you have lived most of your life in an urban environment.

11. Sleep

___ Subtract five years if you sleep more than nine hours a day.

12. Temperature

___ Add two years if your home's thermostat is set at no more than 68°F.

13. Health care

___ Add three years if you have regular medical checkups and regular dental care.

___ Subtract two years if you are frequently ill.

Go to the appendix at the end of the book for scoring.

Toskiko Taira, 80, weaves cloth from the fibers of banana trees on a loom in Okinawa.
What are some possible explanations for the longevity of Okinawans?

taking walks, gardening, and continuing their career work), and spirituality (many older Okinawans find a sense of purpose in spiritual matters).

Hormonal Stress Theory One of the factors believed to be at work in the longevity of Okinawans is low levels of stress. **Hormonal stress theory** states that aging in the body's hormonal system can lower resilience to stress and increase the likelihood of disease (Finch & Seeman, 1999). As discussed in chapter 4, "Stress," the neuroendocrine-immune pathway is one of the body's main regulatory systems for responding to stress. According to hormonal stress theory, as we age, the hormones that flow through the neuroendocrine-immune pathway remain elevated longer than when we were younger. These prolonged, elevated levels of stress-related hormones are associated with increased risks for many diseases, including cardiovascular disease, cancer, diabetes, and hypertension (Blonna, 2005; Harmon, 2004; Hawkley & Cacioppo, 2004).

Physical Changes and Health Changes in physical appearance become more pronounced in older adults, including wrinkles and aging spots. Whereas weight often increases in middle age, it frequently declines after 60 because of muscle loss. Blood pressure often rises in older adults but can be treated by exercise and drugs.

Normal aging also brings some loss of bone tissue. When the loss is severe, the result is *osteoporosis,* a disease that makes bones easy to fracture and slow to heal (Dolan & others, 2004; Hauselmann & Rizzoli, 2003; Mirza & Prestonwood, 2004). Almost two-thirds of women over 60 are affected to some degree by osteoporosis. A program of weight lifting can help (Nelson & others, 1994).

Chronic diseases—characterized by a slow onset and long duration—are rare in early adulthood, increase in middle adulthood, and become more common in late adulthood. The most common chronic disorder in late adulthood is arthritis; the second most common is hypertension (high blood pressure).

This list of physical deteriorations may sound rather dismal. However, a substantial portion of individuals even over the age of 85 are still robust and active.

hormonal stress theory States that aging in the body's hormonal system can lower resilience to stress and increase the likelihood of disease.

Eighty-five-year-old Sadie Halperin doubled her strength in exercise after just 11 months. Before developing an exercise routine, she felt wobbly and often had to hold on to a wall when she walked. Now she walks down the middle of hallways and says she feels wonderful.

Consider 85-year-old Sadie Halperin, who has been working out for 11 months at a rehabilitation center for the aged in Boston. She lifts weights and rides a stationary bicycle. She says that before she started working out, almost everything she did—shopping, cooking, walking—was a major struggle. She felt wobbly and had to hold on to a wall when she walked. Now she walks down the center of the hallways and reports that she feels great. Sadie's exercise routine has increased her muscle strength and helped her to battle osteoporosis by slowing the calcium loss in her bones (Ubell, 1992). Researchers continue to document how effective exercise is in slowing the aging process and helping older adults function in society (Dejong & Franklin, 2004; Holahan & Suzuki, 2004; Schutzer & Graves, 2004).

Another important factor in the health of older adults is their sense of control over their lives (Robins, Power & Burgess, 2005; Shaw & others, 2004). In a classic experimental study, Judith Rodin and Ellen Langer (1977) found that the sense of control was linked not only with the health of nursing home residents but even with their survival. The researchers encouraged one group of elderly nursing home residents to make day-to-day choices and thus to feel more responsible and have more control over their lives. They were allowed to decide on such matters as what they ate, when visitors could come, what movies to see, and who could come to their rooms. A similar group in the same nursing home was told by the administrator how caring the nursing home was and how much the staff wanted to help. However, they were given no opportunities to be responsible and make their own decisions. Eighteen months later, the nursing home residents who were given responsibility and control were more alert, active, and happier, and they were likelier to still be alive than residents who were encouraged to be dependent on the nursing staff. Perceived control and responsibility for oneself, then, may be literally a matter of life or death. Researchers continue to document the importance of perceived control over one's world in the health and well-being of older adults (Clark-Plaskie & Lachman, 1999; DeVellis & DeVellis, 2001; Lachman, 2004; Shaw & others, 2004).

Dementias Among the most debilitating of mental disorders in older adults are the dementias (Brown & Ott, 2004). **Dementia** is a global term for any neurological disorder in which the primary symptoms involve a deterioration of mental

Alzheimer Disease

dementia A global term for any neurological disorder in which the primary symptoms involve a deterioration of mental functioning.

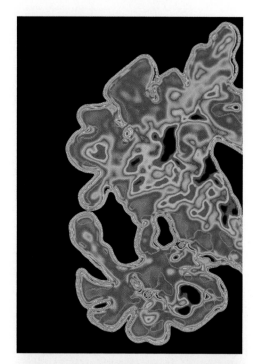

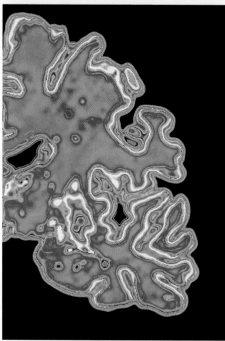

FIGURE 11.7 Two Brains: Normal Aging and Alzheimer Disease
The brain image at the top is from a brain ravaged by Alzheimer disease. The brain image at the bottom is from a brain of a normal aging individual. Notice the deterioration and shrinking in the Alzheimer brain.

Alzheimer disease A progressive, irreversible brain disorder characterized by a gradual deterioration of memory, reasoning, language, and, eventually, physical function.

functioning. Individuals with dementia often lose the ability to care for themselves and can lose the ability to recognize familiar surroundings and people (including family members) (Seshadri & others, 2004). It is estimated that 20 percent of individuals over the age of 80 years of age have dementia.

More than seventy types or causes of dementia have been identified (Skoog, Blennow, & Marcusson, 1996). Approximately 10 to 20 percent of dementias stem from vascular disease (Fitzpatrick & others, 2004). The most common form of dementia is **Alzheimer disease,** a progressive, irreversible disorder that is characterized by gradual deterioration of memory, reasoning, language, and eventually physical functioning. More than 50 percent of dementias involve Alzheimer disease.

Approximately 4 million adults in the United States have Alzheimer disease. Cases are classified as *early-onset* (initially occurring in individuals younger than 65 years of age) or *late-onset* (which has its initial onset in individuals 65 years of age and older). Early-onset Alzheimer disease is rare (about 10 percent of all cases) and generally affects people 30 to 60 years of age. It has been predicted that Alzheimer disease could triple in the next 50 years, as increasing numbers of people live to older ages. Researchers have stepped up their efforts to discover its causes and to find ways to treat it (Lee & others, 2004; Levey, 2004; Li & others, 2004; Meyer, 2004).

As Alzheimer disease progresses, the brain deteriorates and shrinks. Figure 11.7 provides a comparison of the normally aging brain of a healthy individual and the brain of an individual with Alzheimer disease. The deterioration of the brain in Alzheimer disease is characterized by the formation of *amyloid plaques* (dense deposits of protein that accumulate in blood vessels) and *neurofibrillary tangles* (twisted fibers that build up in neurons (Blumenthal, 2004; Leuba & others, 2004). Researchers are especially seeking ways to interrupt the progression of amyloid plaques in Alzheimer patients (Frenkel, Dori, & Solomon, 2004; Lopez-Toledano & Shelanksi, 2004). Recall that Sister Mary, described in the opening of this chapter, was functioning quite well despite having tangles and plaques in her brain. The formation of tangles and plaques is a normal part of aging but these are much more pervasive in Alzheimer disease.

A special concern is caring for Alzheimer patients (Matzo, 2004; Schneider & others, 2003; Sounder & Beck, 2004). Families provide important support for Alzheimer patients, but the extensive care that patients with Alzheimer disease require can drain families emotionally and physically (McCarty & Drebing, 2003; Vitaliano, Young, & Zhang, 2004). For example, depression has been reported in 50 percent of family caregivers for Alzheimer patients (Redinbaugh, MacCallum, & Kiecolt-Glaser, 1995). Respite care has been developed to help people who have to meet the day-to-day needs of Alzheimer patients. This type of care provides an important break away from the burden of providing chronic care.

The Brain   Just as the aging body has a greater capacity for renewal than previously believed, so has the aging brain (Taub, 2001). For decades, scientists believed that no new brain cells are generated after the early childhood years. However, researchers recently discovered that adults can grow new brain cells throughout their lives (Gould & others, 1999; Nelson, 2003; Manev & Manev, 2005; Schaffer & Guge, 2004). In one study, the growth of dendrites (the receiving, branching part of the neuron or nerve cell) continued through the seventies, although no new dendritic growth was discovered in people in their nineties (Coleman, 1986).

Even in late adulthood, the brain has remarkable repair capability. Stanley Rapaport (1994), chief of the neurosciences laboratory at the National Institute of Aging, compared the brains of younger and older adults when they were engaged in the same tasks. If neurons in one part of the brain were not up to the task, neighboring neurons helped to pick up the slack. Rapaport concluded that as brains age, they can shift responsibilities for a given task from one region to another.

Research on the aging brain does give cause for hope. One intriguing ongoing investigation of the brain involves nearly 700 nuns, many of whom are from a convent in Mankato, Minnesota (Kemper & others, 2001; Mortimer, Snowdon, & Markesbery, 2003; Mortimer & others, 2004; Riley, Snowdon & Markesbery, 2002; Snowdon, 1995, 1997, 2002, 2003). The nuns, one of whom was Sister Mary described at the opening of the chapter, are the largest group of brain donors in the world. The Sisters of Notre Dame in Mankato lead an intellectually challenging life and brain researchers believe this contributes to their quality of life as older adults and possibly to their longevity. Findings from the Nun Study so far include:

- Sisters who had taught for most of their lives showed more moderate declines in intellectual skills than those who had spent most of their lives in service-based tasks, which supports the notion that stimulating the brain with intellectual activity keeps neurons healthy and alive (Snowdon, 2002).
- Sisters with high levels of folic acid showed little evidence of Alzheimer-like damage to their brain after death (Snowdon & others, 2000). Possibly the substantial folic acid in the blood means less chance of having a stroke and helps to protect the brain from decline.

This and other research provides hope that scientists will discover ways to tap into the brain's capacity to adapt in order to prevent and treat brain diseases (Murayama & Saito, 2004; Troen, 2003). For example, scientists might learn more effective ways to help older adults recover from strokes. Even when areas of the brain are permanently damaged by stroke, new message routes can be created to get around the blockage or to resume the function of that area.

Top: **Sister Marcella Zachman (*left*) finally stopped teaching at age 97. Now, at 99, she helps ailing nuns exercise their brains by quizzing them on vocabulary or playing a card game called Skip-Bo, at which she deliberately loses. Sister Mary Esther Boor (*right*), also 99 years of age at the time of this photo, was a former teacher who stayed alert by doing puzzles and volunteering to work the front desk. *Below:* A technician holds the brain of a deceased Mankato nun. The nuns donate their brains for research that explores the effects of stimulation on brain growth.**

Review and Reflect

2 Explain physical changes in adulthood

REVIEW

- What physical changes characterize early adulthood?
- What physical changes occur in middle adulthood?
- What physical changes take place in late adulthood?

REFLECT

- How long would you like to live? Why? Describe the oldest person you know. What is he or she like?

3 COGNITIVE DEVELOPMENT IN ADULTHOOD

> **Early Adulthood**   **Late Adulthood**
>
>   **Middle Adulthood**

www.mhhe.com/santrockha

The Nun Study

Despite an aging brain, Sister Mary continued to be alert and mentally competent into her old age, perhaps in part because she had long been intellectually active. Can we expect to be as fortunate? What kind of cognitive changes occur in adults? Are younger adults more intelligent than older adults? Are older adults wiser?

Early Adulthood

The work of Swiss psychologist Jean Piaget (1896–1980) offers one way to address these questions. Piaget (1952) argued that we actively construct our understanding of the world and that as we develop, we go through distinctive stages of cognitive development. At each stage of development, according to Piaget, people come to think in a qualitatively different way.

Do adults think differently than adolescents? Not according to Piaget. Piaget believed that the highest stage of thinking is the **formal operational stage,** which appears between the ages of 11 and 15. In this stage, individuals begin to think in abstract and more logical terms. They develop images of ideal circumstances, such as what an ideal parent is like. In solving problems, formal operational thinkers develop hypotheses about why something is happening the way it is and then test these hypotheses. According to Piaget, formal operational thought is the final level of thinking; no qualitative changes in cognition take place in adulthood. Adults might gain more knowledge, but their ways of thinking are the same as those of an adolescent who has reached the formal operational stage of cognitive development.

Piaget was right about some adolescents and some adults—but not about all of them. Some people never reach the formal operational stage of development. Some experts in cognitive development believe that Piaget's view of adult thinking was wrong in another way: they argue that there are qualitative changes in thinking in adulthood. For example, according to some experts, thinking in early adulthood becomes more realistic and pragmatic (Labouvie-Vief, 1986). According to William Perry (1970), adolescents often view the world in terms of polarities—right/wrong, we/they, or good/bad. In Perry's view, they become aware of diverse opinions and multiple perspectives, and the absolutist, dualistic thinking of adolescence gives way to the reflective, relativistic thinking of adulthood.

Some theorists have pieced together these descriptions of adult thinking and proposed that young adults move into a new stage of cognitive development, postformal thought (Sinnott, 2003). **Postformal thought** is:

- *Reflective, relativistic, and contextual.* As young adults engage in solving problems, they might think deeply about many aspects of work, politics, relationships, and other areas of life (Labouvie-Vief, 1986). They find that what might be the best solution to a problem at work (with a boss or co-worker) might not be the best solution at home (with a romantic partner). Thus, postformal thought holds that the correct answer to a problem requires reflective thinking and may vary from one situation to another.
- *Provisional.* Many young adults also become more skeptical about the truth and unwilling to accept an answer as final. Thus, they come to see the search for truth as an ongoing and perhaps never-ending process.
- *Realistic.* Young adults understand that thinking can't always be abstract. In many instances it must be realistic and pragmatic.
- *Open to emotions and subjective.* Many young adults accept that emotion and subjective factors can influence thinking (Kitchener & King, 1981; Kramer, Kahlbaugh, & Goldston, 1992). For example, as young adults, they understand that a person thinks more clearly in a calm rather than an angry state.

Whether or not we go through any qualitative changes in how we think during adulthood, our cognitive skills are likely to change. There is some evidence, for example, that the ability to make simple, accurate discriminations among visual stimuli slows down during early adulthood but that other skills—such as verbal memory and the ability to perform simple mathematical computations—tends to improve (Schaie

formal operational stage Piaget's fourth and final stage of cognitive development, which he believed emerges between 11 and 15 years of age. It involves an increase in abstract and logical thinking.

postformal thought Thought that is reflective, relativistic, and contextual; provisional; realistic; and open to emotions and subjective.

& Willis, 2001; Willis & Schaie, 1999). In sum, for the most part, intellectual skills are strong in early adulthood.

Middle Adulthood

Do cognitive skills decline in middle age? The answer seems to depend on which skills you are talking about and how you study them (Li & Li, 2004). John Horn's view is that some intellectual abilities begin to decline in middle age, whereas others increase (Horn & Donaldson, 1980). He believes that **crystallized intelligence,** an individual's accumulated information and verbal skills, increases in middle adulthood. By contrast, **fluid intelligence,** one's ability to reason abstractly, begins to decline in middle adulthood.

Horn's view is based on data he collected in a *cross-sectional study*, which assesses a number of people all at one point in time. A cross-sectional study, for example, might assess the intelligence of six hundred 40-, 50-, and 60-year-olds in a single evaluation in September 2004. In a cross-sectional study, differences on intelligence tests might be due to *cohort effects*, the effects of living through a certain historical time in a certain culture, rather than to age. The 40-year-olds and the 60-year-olds were born in different eras, which offered different economic, educational, and health opportunities. For example, as the 60-year-olds grew up, they likely had fewer educational opportunities than the 40-year-olds had, which may influence their performance on intelligence tests.

A different method of studying cognitive skills in middle adulthood may yield different results. In contrast to a cross-sectional study, a *longitudinal study* assesses the same participants over a lengthy period. A longitudinal study of intelligence in middle adulthood might consist of giving the same intelligence test to the same individuals over a twenty-year time span, when they are 40, 50, and 60 years of age.

K. Warner Schaie (1993, 1996) is conducting an extensive longitudinal study of intellectual abilities in adulthood. Five hundred individuals initially were tested in 1956. New waves of participants are added periodically. The main abilities tested by Schaie are as follows:

- Vocabulary (ability to encode and understand ideas expressed in words)
- Verbal memory (ability to encode and recall meaningful language units, such as a list of words)
- Number (ability to perform simple mathematical computations such as addition, subtraction, and multiplication)
- Spatial orientation (ability to visualize and mentally rotate stimuli in two- and three-dimensional space)
- Inductive reasoning (ability to recognize and understand patterns and relationships in a problem and use this understanding to solve other instances of the problem)
- Perceptual speed (ability to quickly and accurately make simple discriminations in visual stimuli)

As shown in figure 11.8, only two of the six abilities—numerical ability and perceptual speed—declined in middle age. Four of the six intellectual abilities—vocabulary, verbal memory, inductive reasoning, and spatial orientation—improved after early adulthood (Schaie & Willis, 2001; Willis & Schaie, 1999).

Those are encouraging results, but they are not the final word. When Schaie (1994) assessed intellectual skills both cross-sectionally and longitudinally, he found more decline in middle age in the cross-sectional assessment. For example, when he assessed inductive reasoning longitudinally, it increased until the end of middle adulthood, at which point it began a slight decline. By contrast, when he assessed it cross-sectionally, inductive reasoning already was declining at the beginning of middle adulthood.

www.mhhe.com/santrockha

Midlife Research
Cognitive Aging Research

crystallized intelligence An individual's accumulated information and verbal skills.

fluid intelligence A person's ability to reason abstractly.

FIGURE 11.8 Longitudinal Changes in Six Intellectual Abilities from Age 25 to Age 67

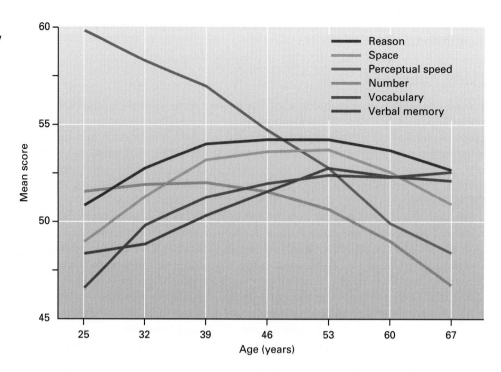

Interestingly, Schaie found middle adulthood to be a time of peak performance for some aspects of both crystallized intelligence (vocabulary) and fluid intelligence (spatial orientation and inductive reasoning). John Horn, as you may recall, found that fluid intelligence peaks in early adulthood and crystallized intelligence in middle age. Schaie concluded, based on the longitudinal data he has collected so far, that middle adulthood, not early adulthood, is when many people reach their peak for many intellectual skills.

Late Adulthood

At age 70, medical researcher John Rock introduced the birth control pill. At age 76, Anna Mary Robertson, better known as Grandma Moses, took up painting and became internationally famous. When Pablo Casals reached 95 years of age, a reporter called him the greatest cellist who ever lived but wondered why he still practiced six hours a day. Casals replied, "Because I feel like I am making progress." Although some cognitive skills may decline in late adulthood (as in middle adulthood), others are maintained or may even improve (Dixon & Cohen, 2003; Hoyer & Roodin, 2003).

Older adults might not be as quick with their thoughts or behavior as younger people, but wisdom may be an entirely different matter. This older woman shares the wisdom of her experience with a classroom of children. *How is wisdom described by life-span developmentalists?*

One of the most consistent findings is that, when speed of processing information is involved, older adults do more poorly than their younger counterparts (Baudovin, Vanneste, & Isingrini, 2004; Craik & Salthouse, 2000; Joy, Kaplan, & Fein, 2004). This decline in speed of processing is apparent in middle-aged adults and becomes more pronounced in older adults.

Older adults also tend to do more poorly than younger adults in most areas of memory (Anstey & Low, 2004; Light, 2000). Older adults do not remember the "where" and "when" of life's happenings as well as younger adults (Tulving, 2000). For example, older adults don't remember their high school classmates or the names of their teachers as well as younger adults do. In the area of memory involving knowledge of the world (for instance, the capital of Peru or the chemical formula for water), older adults usually take longer than younger adults to retrieve the information, but they often are able to retrieve it. And in the important area of memory in which individuals manipulate and assemble information to solve problems and make decisions, decline occurs in older adults (Light, 2000).

However, some aspects of cognition might actually improve with age. One candidate is **wisdom,** expert knowledge about the practical aspects of life. Wisdom may increase with age because of the buildup of life experiences we have (Staudinger, 2004). However, not every older person has wisdom (Baltes, 2003). Individual variations characterize all aspects of our cognitive lives (Belsky, 1999).

For those aspects of cognitive abilities that decline with age, such as memory, educating and training can make a difference (Hoyer & Touron, 2003; Kramer & Willis, 2002). For example, researchers have demonstrated that training older adults to use certain strategies can even improve their memories (Baltes, 1993; Schaie & Willis, 2001). However, many experts on aging believe that older adults are less able to change and adapt than younger adults and thus are limited in how much they can improve their cognitive skills (Baltes & Smith, 2003).

Review and Reflect

3   Characterize cognitive changes in adulthood

REVIEW

- What cognitive changes take place in early adulthood?
- What cognitive changes occur in middle adulthood?
- What cognitive changes take place in late adulthood?

REFLECT

- What do you think are the most important cognitive changes that take place in young adults?

4   SOCIOEMOTIONAL DEVELOPMENT IN ADULTHOOD

| Early Adulthood | Late Adulthood |
| Middle Adulthood | |

Love and work, according to both Sigmund Freud and the nineteenth-century Russian novelist Leo Tolstoy, are adulthood's most important themes. The study of socioemotional development during the adult years largely bears them out. As a framework for understanding these years, we will look again at Erik Erikson's theory of life-span development, which we introduced in chapter 3, "The Self, Identity, and Values."

Early Adulthood

In **Erikson's theory,** eight stages of development unfold as we go through the life span (see figure 11.9). Each stage consists of a unique developmental task that confronts individuals with a crisis—a turning point marked by both increased vulnerability and enhanced potential. For example, as discussed in chapter 3, during adolescence the crucial task is the development of an identity. The more successfully an individual resolves the crisis of each stage, the healthier development will be (Hopkins, 2000). During early adulthood, according to Erikson, individuals enter the sixth stage of development, in which the crisis is **intimacy versus isolation.**

What is the developmental task that young adults face during the intimacy-versus-isolation stage? According to Erikson (1986), they either form intimate relationships with others or become socially isolated. Intimacy, as Erikson uses the word,

wisdom Expert knowledge about the practical aspects of life.

Erikson's theory Proposes that eight stages of development unfold as people go through the life span with each stage consisting of a unique developmental task that confronts individuals with a crisis that must be resolved.

intimacy versus isolation Erikson's sixth stage that he believed occurs in early adulthood in which individuals face the developmental task of forming intimate relationships with others or becoming socially isolated.

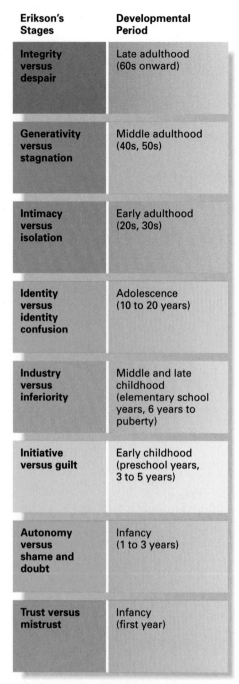

Erikson's Stages	Developmental Period
Integrity versus despair	Late adulthood (60s onward)
Generativity versus stagnation	Middle adulthood (40s, 50s)
Intimacy versus isolation	Early adulthood (20s, 30s)
Identity versus identity confusion	Adolescence (10 to 20 years)
Industry versus inferiority	Middle and late childhood (elementary school years, 6 years to puberty)
Initiative versus guilt	Early childhood (preschool years, 3 to 5 years)
Autonomy versus shame and doubt	Infancy (1 to 3 years)
Trust versus mistrust	Infancy (first year)

FIGURE 11.9 Erikson's Eight Life-Span Stages

requires a commitment to another person, and that commitment is only possible when a person is willing to let go of his or her own ego. The commitment may involve a close friendship or a sexual relationship or some other form of solidarity, but at its core it involves finding oneself as one loses oneself in another. Intimacy requires the willingness to choose a joint identity. A failure to form intimate relations leads to a sense of isolation.

The search for intimacy during early adulthood is likely to lead to very concrete questions, such as Should I get married? If I wait any longer, will it be too late? Should I stay single or is that too lonely a life? If I get married, do I want to have children? How will children affect my marriage?

In some cultures, these questions scarcely exist; rather than choosing a lifestyle for themselves, young adults are expected to follow a traditional way of life. In fact, until 1930, a stable marriage was accepted as the standard goal of adult development in the United States. During the past seventy years, however, personal fulfillment—both inside and outside a marriage—has become a goal for many people in the United States.

Unfortunately, the quest for personal fulfillment may destabilize a marriage (Markman, 2000). We expect our spouse to simultaneously be a lover, a friend, a confidant, a counselor, a career person, and a parent. These cultural changes may help to account for two facts about American life: as discussed in chapter 9, U.S. adults are remaining single longer today than a few decades ago, and the average duration of a marriage in the United States is just over nine years.

Young adults in the United States today feel varying pressures and hear varying messages from their culture about marriage and commitment. Some may feel pressured to "settle down." As one 30-year-old male recently commented, "It's real. You are supposed to get married by 30—that is a standard. It is part of getting on with your life that you are supposed to do. You have career and who-am-I concerns in your twenties. In your thirties, you have to get on with your life, keep on track, and make headway—financially and family-wise." But, to another 30-year-old, getting married is less important than buying a house and some property. A training manager for a computer company, Jane, says, "I'm competent in making relationships and being committed, so I don't feel a big rush to get married. When it happens, it happens."

Careers and Work   A few people seem to have known what they wanted to be ever since childhood. For the rest of us, choosing an occupation involves exploring a number of options during college and even beyond. Establishing oneself in a job and then a career is one of the central concerns of people in their twenties and thirties. The choice of a career and a job may have a broad and deep impact. Work defines individuals in fundamental ways (Osipow, 2000). People identify with their work, and the work shapes many aspects of their lives, from their financial standing to their health. Work also eats up big chunks of people's time—for the majority of Americans, 40 hours a week or more (Center for Survey Research, 2000).

This devotion to the job may create conflicts at home. Most parents, women and men alike, are working. Although many men have taken on more home responsibilities, including child care, women in this type of family still bear the majority of the load at home (Barnett, 2001). In chapter 10, "Achievement, Careers, and Work," you read about these and other aspects of work and careers.

Middle Adulthood

At some time around the fortieth birthday, we are likely to feel that we have entered a new phase of life—middle age. A participant in a longitudinal study described the change this way, "From twenty to thirty, I learned how to get along with my wife. From thirty to forty, I learned how to be a success at my job, and at forty to fifty, I worried less about myself and more about my children" (Vaillant, 2002, p. 114). Generativity, the consciousness of being in the middle of one's life, and questions about the meaning of life are themes of middle adulthood.

Love and work are key themes of adult development. *What are some challenges adults face in these important aspects of their lives?*

Generativity Erikson (1968) believes that middle-aged adults face the issue of **generativity versus stagnation,** which is the name Erikson gave to the seventh stage in his life-span theory. Generativity encompasses adults' desire to leave a legacy of themselves to the next generation (Peterson, 2002). Through generativity, the adult achieves a kind of immortality. By contrast, stagnation (sometimes called "self-absorption") develops when individuals sense that they have done little or nothing for the next generation.

Middle-aged adults can develop generativity in a number of ways (Kotre, 1984). Through biological generativity, adults conceive and give birth to an infant. Through parental generativity, adults provide nurturance and guidance to children. Through work generativity, adults develop skills that are passed down to others. And through cultural generativity, adults create, renovate, or conserve some aspect of culture that ultimately survives. Sister Mary could find generativity through her work as a teacher; Anthony Pirelli, through his children.

In short, through generativity, adults promote and guide the next generation by parenting, teaching, leading, and doing things that benefit the community (Lachman, 2004; Pratt & others, 2001; Westermeyer, 2004). Generative adults commit themselves to the continuation and improvement of society as a whole through their connection to the next generation. Generative adults develop a positive legacy of the self and then offer it as a gift to the next generation.

What are some ways that middle-aged adults can develop generativity?

Is there evidence that generativity is important in middle age? A longitudinal study of women from Smith College examined generativity among women at various ages and found that it increased from the thirties through the fifties (Cole & Stewart, 1996; Roberts & Helson, 1997; Stewart, Ostrove, & Helson, 2001; Zucker, Ostrove, & Stewart, 2002). In George Vaillant's (2002) longitudinal studies of aging, generativity (defined in these studies as "taking care of the next generation") at age 50 was the best predictor of whether individuals would have an enduring and happy marriage at 75 to 80 years of age.

generativity versus stagnation Erikson's seventh stage that he believed occurs in middle adulthood in which individuals leave a legacy of themselves to the next generation (generativity) or do little or nothing for the next generation (stagnation).

Midlife Crises How do people react to the fact that they are no longer young? In *The Seasons of a Man's Life,* Daniel Levinson (1978) described the results of extensive interviews with middle-aged men in a variety of occupations: hourly workers, biologists, business executives, and novelists. Levinson argued that, by age 40, people reach a stable point in their careers, outgrow their earlier, more tenuous status as adults; and they begin to define the kind of lives they will lead in middle age. They enter a transition period during which they experience a crisis that lasts about five years. During this transition, according to Levinson, they must come to grips with four major conflicts that have existed since adolescence:

- Being young versus being old
- Being destructive versus being constructive
- Being masculine versus being feminine
- Being attached to others versus being separated from them

Although Levinson's original participants were all men, he subsequently reported that the midlife issues he uncovered affect women as well (Levinson, 1996).

Levinson's portrait of a midlife crisis is interesting, but research on middle-aged adults reveals that few experience midlife in the tumultuous way he described. Individuals vary extensively in how they cope with and perceive midlife (Vaillant, 1977). However, in a recent large-scale study of 3,032 Americans 25 to 74 years of age, the portrait of midlife was mainly positive (Brim, 1999). Only about 10 percent of individuals described themselves as experiencing a midlife crisis. In fact, middle-aged individuals (40–65 years old) had lower anxiety levels and worried less than people under 40. The middle-aged individuals did report more negative life events than people under 40, but they showed considerable resiliency and good coping skills in facing these stressors.

More accurate than the phrase "midlife crisis" might be the phrase "midlife consciousness" (Santrock, 2004). That is, during middle age, people do become aware of the gap between being young and being old and the shrinking time left in their lives. They do think about their role in contributing to the next generation. They do contemplate the meaning of life. But for most people, midlife consciousness does not become tumultuous and take on crisis proportions (Lachman, 2004).

Meaning of Life and Life Themes Even if your midlife years are relatively tranquil, this period may trigger new questions about your life, for two reasons. First, during middle adulthood, you are likely to experience the death of people who are close to you, especially the deaths of parents and older relatives. When Anthony Pirelli was 47, for example, both a brother and his closest friend died unexpectedly. Second, midlife consciousness involves recognition of the shrinking time left to you on this earth. In short, middle adulthood is likely to make the finiteness of life real to you.

Examining your life's finiteness, according to Austrian psychiatrist Victor Frankl, adds meaning to life. As discussed in chapter 3, during World War II, Frankl's mother, father, brother, and wife died in the concentration camps and gas chambers in Auschwitz, Germany. Frankl survived the camp and went on to write *Man's Search for Meaning* (1984), in which he proposed that people need to ask themselves such questions as why they exist, what they want from life, and what the meaning of life is. During middle adulthood, the recognition of life's finiteness leads many individuals to think more deeply about what life is all about and what they want the rest of their lives to be like.

The search for meaning emphasized by Frankl fits with the concept of *life themes.* Life themes involve people's efforts to cultivate meaningful, optimal experiences (Csikszentmihalyi & Rathunde, 1998; Massimini & Delle Fave, 2000; Sugarman, 2004). Thus some people who have spent much of their lives trying to make a lot of money turn their attention in middle age to more selfless pursuits, such as helping others by volunteering.

Late Adulthood

Even vibrant, active people are likely to find that late adulthood brings changes beyond their control. Anthony Pirelli had a severe heart attack and turned his businesses over to others; even Sister Mary eventually retired when she was 84. But neither faded away; both took pleasure in other activities and in the people around them. Do their successes point to broad lessons about aging? What are some important ways for older adults to effectively adjust to the socioemotional aspects of their aging?

Integrity Versus Despair   Late adulthood, according to Erikson, is the **integrity versus despair** stage of life; the task of this stage is to look back and evaluate what we have done with our lives. If the older adult has resolved many of the earlier stages negatively, looking back likely will produce doubt or gloom—the *despair* Erikson speaks of. But if the older adult has successfully negotiated most or all of the previous stages of development, the looking back will reveal a picture of a life well spent, and the person will feel a sense of satisfaction. *Integrity* will be attained.

A prominent feature in this final stage is *life review*, which involves looking back at one's life experiences, evaluating them, interpreting them, and often reinterpreting them. Distinguished aging researcher Robert Butler (1975, 1996) believes the life review is set in motion by looking forward to death. Sometimes the life review proceeds quietly, at other times it is intense. At first, the life review may consist of stray and insignificant thoughts about oneself and one's life history. Over time, these thoughts may continue to be intermittent or they might become essentially continuous. One 76-year-old man commented, "My life is in the back of my mind. It can't be any other way. Thoughts of the past play on me. Sometimes I play with them, encouraging and savoring them; at other times I dismiss them."

As the life review proceeds, the older adult may reveal to a spouse, children, or other close associates characteristics and experiences that had been undisclosed. Hidden themes of great meaning may emerge, changing the nature of the older adult's sense of self. Successful aging, though, doesn't mean thinking about the past all of the time. In one study, older adults who were obsessed about the past were less well adjusted than older adults who integrated their past and present (Wong & Watt, 1991).

Stereotypes would lead us to expect that the emotional landscape for older adults is bleak, that most live sad, lonely lives. Researchers have found a different picture (Lockenhoff & Carstensen, 2004). One study of a very large U.S. sample examined emotions at different ages (Mroczek & Kolarz, 1998). Older adults reported experiencing more positive emotion and less negative emotion than younger adults, and positive emotion increased with age in adults at an accelerating rate (see figure 11.10).

Researchers have found that across diverse samples—Norwegians, Catholic nuns, African Americans, Chinese Americans, and European Americans—older adults report better control of their emotions than younger adults (Carstensen, Gottman, & Levenson, 1995; Carstensen & others, 2003; Lawton & others, 1992; Mroczek, 2001). Compared with younger adults, the feelings of older adults mellow. Emotional life is on a more even keel, with fewer highs and lows. It may be that although older adults have less extreme joy, they have more contentment, especially when they are connected in positive ways with friends and family (Carstensen & Charles, 2003; Carstensen & others, 2003; Mroczek, 2001).

Social Networks   Connections with family, friends, and others can improve the physical and mental health of older adults in many ways (Oxman & Hall, 2001; Pruchno & Rosenbaum, 2003). Social support is linked with a reduction in symptoms of disease and with an increased ability to meet one's own health-care needs, as well as with a decreased probability that an older adult will be institutionalized (Antonucci, 1990, 2001) and decreased incidence of depression (Joiner, 2000; Taylor & Lynch, 2004). Being lonely and socially isolated is a significant health risk factor in older adults (Rowe & Kahn, 1997; McReynolds & Rossen, 2004).

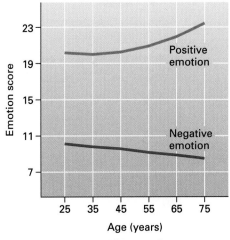

FIGURE 11.10 Negative Emotion Across the Adult Years
Positive and negative scores had a possible range of 6 to 30 with higher scores reflecting positive emotion and lower scores negative emotion. Positive emotion increased in the middle adulthood and late adulthood years while negative emotion declined.

integrity versus despair Erikson's eighth stage that he believed occurs in late adulthood in which individuals engage in a life review that is either positive (integrity) or negative (despair).

Laura Carstensen (*right*), in a caring relationship with an older woman. Her theory of socioemotional selectivity is gaining recognition as an important theory.

Activities for Older Adults
Laura Carstensen's Research

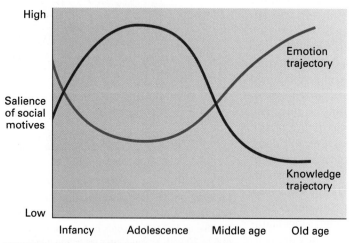

FIGURE 11.11 Idealized Model of Socioemotional Selectivity Through the Life Span
In Carstensen's theory of socioemotional selectivity, the motivation to reach knowledge-related and emotion-related goals changes across the life span.

socioemotional selectivity theory States that older adults become more selective about their social networks and because they place a high value on emotional satisfaction, they often spend more time with familiar individuals with whom they have had rewarding relationships.

Older adults tend to have far smaller networks than younger adults (Lee & Markides, 1990), but a smaller social world is not necessarily a poorer one. In one study of individuals 69 to 104 years of age, the oldest participants had fewer peripheral social contacts than the relatively younger participants—but they had about the same number of emotional relationships (Lang & Carstensen, 1994). According to a theory developed by Laura Carstensen (1991, 1993, 1995, 1998; Carstensen & others, 2003), small social networks may reflect the changing goals of older adults and their own choices. Carstensen's **socioemotional selectivity theory** states that older adults emphasize goals related to emotion, and they become more selective about their social networks.

According to this theory, motivation for knowledge-related goals starts relatively high in the early years of life, peaks in adolescence and early adulthood, then declines in middle and late adulthood (see figure 11.11). In contrast, motivation for emotion-related goals is high during infancy and early childhood, declines from middle childhood through early adulthood, and increases in middle and late adulthood. As older adults perceive that they have less time left in their lives, they are motivated to spend more time seeking emotion-related goals (Carstensen & Charles, 2003; Carstensen & others, 2003).

Because they place a high value on emotional satisfaction, older adults often spend more time with familiar individuals with whom they have had rewarding relationships. This theory argues that older adults deliberately withdraw from social contact with individuals peripheral to their lives while they maintain or increase contact with close friends and family members with whom they have had enjoyable relationships. This selective narrowing of social interaction maximizes positive emotional experiences and minimizes emotional risks as individuals become older. According to this theory, older adults systematically hone their social networks so that available social partners satisfy their emotional needs.

Self-Regulation As we age, the regulation of our capacities and activities is a key aspect of adjustment. This self-regulation allows us to deal with the losses that are part of aging (Wahl & others, 2004). One theory that addresses this issue was proposed by Paul Baltes and his colleagues (Baltes, 1993; Baltes & Smith, 2003). According to **selective optimization with compensation theory,** successful self-regulation in aging involves three processes—selection, optimization, and compensation:

- *Selection* is a reduction in performance in most life domains. Reduced capacity and loss make selection necessary. For example, when Sister Mary could no longer work as a full-time teacher, she continued to give talks about religious issues.

- *Optimization* is the maintenance of standards of performance in some areas through continued practice and the use of new technologies.

- *Compensation* becomes relevant when tasks require a level of capacity beyond the current potential. For example, older adults need to compensate when circumstances demand that they react quickly when driving a car or memorize new material quickly.

When the late Arthur Rubinstein was interviewed at 80 years of age, he said that three factors were responsible for his ability to maintain his status as an admired concert pianist. First, he mastered the weakness of old age by reducing the scope of his performances and playing fewer pieces (which reflects *selection*). Second, he spent more time at practice than earlier in his life (which reflects *optimization*). Third, he used special strategies such as slowing down before fast segments, thus creating the image of faster playing (which reflects *compensation*). Selective optimization with compensation is likely to be effective whenever loss is prominent in a person's life.

Religion   For many people, religion can help people cope with loss. Religion can provide some important psychological needs in older adults, helping them face impending death, find and maintain a sense of meaningfulness and significance in life, and accept the inevitable losses of old age (Fry, 1999; Koenig & Larson, 1998; Krause, 2003, 2004). In one recent study, although church attendance decreased in older adults in their last year of life, their feelings of religiousness and the strength or comfort they received from religion were either stable or increased (Idler, Kasl, & Hays, 2001). Socially, the religious community can provide a number of functions for older adults, such as social activities, social support, and the opportunity to assume teaching and leadership roles. Older adults can become deacons, elders, or religion teachers, assuming leadership roles they might have been unable to take on before they retired (Cox & Hammonds, 1988).

When the significance of religion in people's lives has been assessed, individuals over 65 years of age are more likely than younger people to say that religious faith is the most significant influence in their lives, that they try to put religious faith into practice, and that they attend religious services (Gallup & Bezilla, 1992). In another survey, compared with younger adults, adults in old age were more likely to have a strong interest in spirituality and to pray (Gallup & Jones, 1989).

Is religion related to a sense of well-being and life satisfaction in old age? In one recent study it was. Interviews were conducted with 1,500 U.S. White and African American individuals 66 years of age and older (Krause, 2003). Older adults who derived a sense of meaning in life from religion had higher levels of life satisfaction, self-esteem, and optimism. Also, older African American adults were more likely to find meaning in religion than their White counterparts. In another study, religious practices—such as prayer and scripture reading—and religious feelings were associated with a sense of well-being, especially for women and individuals over 75 years of age (Koenig, Smiley, & Gonzales, 1988).

Might praying or meditating actually be associated with longevity? In one recent study, they were (McCullough & others, 2000). Nearly 4,000 women and men 65 years and older, mostly Christians, were asked about their health and whether they prayed or meditated. Those who said they rarely or never prayed had about a 50 percent greater risk of dying during the six-year study compared with those who prayed or meditated at least once a month. In this study, the researchers controlled for many factors known to place people at risk for dying, such as smoking, drinking, and social isolation. It is possible that prayer and meditation lower the incidence of death in older adults because they reduce stress and dampen the body's production of stress hormones such as adrenaline. A decrease in stress hormones is linked with a number of health benefits, including a stronger immune system (McCullough & others, 2000).

Socioeconomic Status and Ethnicity   The majority of older adults face a life of reduced income. The average income of retired Americans is only about half of what they earned when they were fully employed. Middle-aged Americans who will retire in 20 to 25 years will need an income equal to 75 percent of their current annual expenditures (adjusted for inflation) to maintain their current middle-aged lifestyle.

Older adults who live in poverty are a special concern (Adams & White, 2004; Mishra & others, 2004; Seeman & others, 2004). Although the overall number of older people living in poverty has declined since the 1960s, the percentage of older persons living in poverty has remained in the 10 to 12 percent range since the early 1980s (U.S. Bureau of the Census, 2003). Furthermore, poverty rates soar

During late adulthood, many individual increasingly engage in prayer. *How might this be linked with longevity?*

Spirituality in Older Adults

selective optimization with compensation theory States that successful self-regulation involves three factors: selectivity, optimization, and compensation. As individuals get older, they face losses so they are likely to adjust best when they reduce performance in areas in which they are not competent (selectivity), perform in areas in which they can still function effectively (optimization), and compensate in circumstances with high mental or physical demands (compensation).

What challenges do ethnic minority older adults face? What are some ways they cope with these challenges?

among some groups of older Americans. More than 25 percent of older women who live alone live in poverty. Poverty rates among ethnic minorities are two to three times higher than the rate for Whites. Combining sex and ethnicity, 60 percent of older African American women and 50 percent of older Latino women who live alone live in poverty.

Ethnic minority adults face possible double jeopardy. They confront problems related to *both* ageism and racism (Jackson, Chatters, & Taylor, 1993). Both the wealth and the health of ethnic minority older adults decrease more rapidly than for non-Latino White older adults (Edmonds, 1993). Ethnic minority older adults are more likely to become ill but less likely to receive treatment. They are also more likely to have a history of less education, unemployment, worse housing conditions, and shorter life expectancies than their non-Latino White older adult counterparts (Himes, Hogan, & Eggebeen, 1996). And many ethnic minority workers never enjoy the Social Security and Medicare benefits to which their earnings contribute, because they die before reaching the age of eligibility for benefits.

Despite the stress and discrimination faced by older adult ethnic minority individuals, many of these older adults have developed successful coping mechanisms that allow them to survive in the dominant non-Latino White world (Barnes & others, 2004; Markides & Rudkin, 1996). Extensions of family networks, ethnic neighborhoods, and churches provide avenues for meaningful social participation, feelings of power, satisfaction, a sense of belonging and being loved. Thus, it always is important to consider individual variations in the lives of aging minorities.

Mental Health and Aging   Although a substantial portion of the population can now look forward to a longer life, that life may unfortunately be hampered by a mental disorder in old age. Older adults do not have a higher incidence of mental disorders than younger adults (Busse & Blazer, 1996); what they do suffer is a lack of mental health services. Older U.S. adults receive disproportionately fewer mental health services than people of other ages (Smith, 2003). One estimate is that only 2.7 percent of all clinical services provided by psychologists go to older adults, although individuals aged 65 and over make up more than 11 percent of the population.

Consider **major depression,** a mood disorder in which the individual is deeply unhappy, demoralized, self-derogatory, and bored (we will examine this and other psychological disorders in chapter 14).

Depression is a treatable condition, not only in young adults but in older adults as well (Mecocci & others, 2004; Nolen-Hoeksema, 2004). Unfortunately, as many as 80 percent of older adults with depressive symptoms receive no treatment at all. Combinations of medications and psychotherapy produce significant improvement in almost four out of five elderly adults with depression (Koenig & Blazer, 1996).

Major depression can result in suicidal tendencies (O'Connell & others, 2004). Nearly 25 percent of individuals who commit suicide in the United States are 65 years of age or older (Church, Siegel, & Fowler, 1988). The older adult most likely to commit suicide is a male who lives alone, has lost his spouse, and is experiencing failing health.

How can we better meet the mental health needs of older adults? First, psychologists must be encouraged to include more older adults in their client lists, and older adults must be convinced that they can benefit from therapy (Knight, 2004). Second, we must make mental health care affordable: Medicare currently pays lower percentages for mental health care than for physical health care, for example. Some common mechanisms of change that improve the mental health of older adults are (Gatz, 1989): (1) fostering a sense of control, self-efficacy, and hope; (2) establishing a relationship with a helper; (3) providing or elucidating a sense of meaning; and (4) promoting educative activities and the development of skills.

Positive Psychology and Aging   Until fairly recently, older adults were perceived as enduring a long decline in physical, cognitive, and socioemotional functioning, and the positive dimensions of aging were ignored (Antonucci, 2001; Holstein & Minkler,

major depression   A mood disorder in which the individual is deeply unhappy, demoralized, self-derogatory, and bored. The person does not feel well, loses stamina easily, has poor appetite, and is listless and unmotivated. Major depression is so widespread that it has been called the "common cold" of mental disorders.

2003; Phelan & others, 2004; Rowe & Kahn, 1997). Once developmentalists began focusing on the positive aspects of aging, they discovered that far more robust, healthy older adults existed than they previously thought. Although we are in the evening of our lives during late adulthood, we need not live out those years lonely and unhappy.

The more active and involved older adults are, the more satisfied they are, and the more likely they are to stay healthy (Antonucci, 2001). Older people who go to church, attend meetings, take trips, and exercise are happier than those who simply sit at home (George, 2001). A longitudinal study found that poor social connections, infrequent participation in social activities, and social disengagement predicted cognitive decline in older adults (Zunzenegui & others, 2003). And in another longitudinal study, both women and men with more organizational memberships lived longer than their counterparts with low participation in organizations (Tucker & others, 1999).

Are there other characteristics linked with successful aging? In the Nun Study discussed earlier, positive emotions early in adulthood were related to the nuns' longevity (Danner, Snowdon, & Friesen, 2001). Handwritten autobiographies from 180 nuns, composed when they were 22 years old, were scored for emotional content. The nuns whose early writings had higher scores for positive emotional content were more likely to still be alive at 75 to 95 years of age than their counterparts whose earlier writings were characterized by negative emotional content.

Habits during middle age also influence aging. One impressive longitudinal study assessed individuals when they were 50 years old and then again at 75 to 80 years of age (Vaillant, 2002). As shown in figure 11.12, when individuals at 50 years of age were not heavy smokers, did not abuse alcohol, had a stable marriage, engaged in exercise, maintained a normal weight, and had good coping skills, they were more likely to be alive and happy at 75 to 80 years of age.

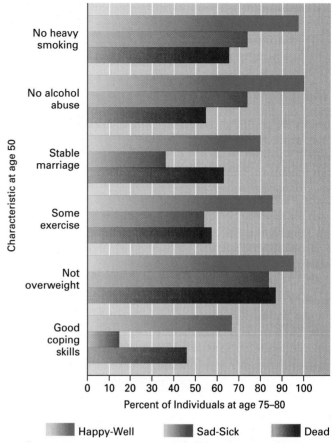

FIGURE 11.12 Links Between Characteristics at Age 50 and Health and Happiness at Age 75 to 80
In a longitudinal study, the characteristics shown above at age 50 were related to whether individuals were happy-well, sad-sick, or dead at age 75 to 80 (Vaillant, 2002).

Adjustment Strategies
For Successful Aging

Here are some effective adjustment strategies for aging successfully:

1. ***Don't abuse alcohol and don't smoke.*** In Vaillant's study, alcohol abuse and smoking were the two best predictors at age 50 of which older adults would be dead at 75 to 80 years of age.
2. ***Exercise regularly and avoid being overweight.*** A large number of studies have documented the powerful role that exercise plays in being a healthy adult. Also, researchers have found that overweight individuals are more likely to die earlier than average weight or thin individuals.
3. ***Be well educated.*** If you go to college for five years or more, you are expected to live three years longer than if you had only finished high school.
4. ***Use your intellectual skills.*** "Use it or lose it" applies to successful cognitive aging. It is important to stay intellectually active throughout your life.
5. ***Develop coping skills.*** These include perceiving that you are in control of your life and other coping skills that we discussed in chapter 5, "Coping."
6. ***Have good friends and/or a loving partner.*** The adjustment strategies described in chapter 9, "Friendship and Love Relationships," can benefit you in this area of your life.

Review and Reflect

4 **Summarize socioemotional changes in adulthood**

REVIEW

- What socioemotional changes characterize early adulthood?
- What socioemotional changes occur in middle adulthood?
- What socioemotional changes take place in late adulthood?

REFLECT

- Suppose that you wanted to construct a test for wisdom that would be fair to adults of all ages. Write down two or three questions or items that you would want to include in your test.

5   DEATH AND GRIEVING

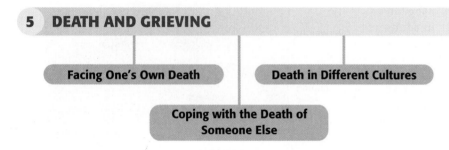

Facing One's Own Death

Death in Different Cultures

Coping with the Death of Someone Else

Our life ultimately ends. How do people face their own death? How do people cope with the death of someone else? How do different cultures deal with death?

Facing One's Own Death

Knowledge of death's inevitability permits us to establish priorities and structure our time accordingly. As we age, these priorities and structurings change in recognition of diminishing future time. Values concerning the most important uses of time also change. For example, when asked how they would spend six remaining months of life, younger adults described such activities as traveling and accomplishing things they previously had not done; older adults described more inner-focused activities—contemplation and meditation, for example (Kalish & Reynolds, 1976).

Most dying individuals want an opportunity to make some decisions regarding their own life and death (Kastenbaum, 2004). Some individuals want to complete unfinished business; they want time to resolve problems and conflicts and to put their affairs in order. Might there be a sequence of stages we go through as we face death?

Elisabeth Kübler-Ross (1969) divided the behavior and thinking of dying persons into five stages. **Kübler-Ross' stages of dying** are denial and isolation, anger, bargaining, depression, and acceptance.

Denial and isolation is Kübler-Ross' first stage of dying, in which the person denies that death is really going to take place. The person may say, "No, it can't be me. It's not possible." This is a common reaction to terminal illness. However, denial is usually only a temporary defense and is eventually replaced with increased awareness when the person is confronted with such matters as financial considerations, unfinished business, and worry about surviving family members.

Anger is Kübler-Ross' second stage of dying, in which the dying person recognizes that denial can no longer be maintained. Denial often gives way to anger, resentment, rage, and envy. The dying person's question is, "Why me?" At this point, the person becomes increasingly difficult to care for as anger may become displaced and projected

Kübler-Ross' stages of dying Consists of these five stages: denial and isolation, anger, bargaining, depression, and acceptance.

onto physicians, nurses, family members, and even God. The realization of loss is great, and those who symbolize life, energy, and competent functioning are especially salient targets of the dying person's resentment and jealousy.

Bargaining is Kübler-Ross' third stage of dying, in which the person develops the hope that death can somehow be postponed or delayed. Some persons enter into a bargaining or negotiation—often with God—as they try to delay their death. Psychologically, the person is saying, "Yes, me, but . . . " In exchange for a few more days, weeks, or months of life, the person promises to lead a reformed life dedicated to God or to the service of others.

Depression is Kübler-Ross' fourth stage of dying, in which the dying person comes to accept the certainty of death. At this point, a period of depression or preparatory grief may appear. The dying person may become silent, refuse visitors, and spend much of the time crying or grieving. This behavior is normal and is an effort to disconnect the self from love objects. Attempts to cheer up the dying person at this stage should be discouraged, says Kübler-Ross, because the dying person has a need to contemplate impending death.

Acceptance is Kübler-Ross' fifth stage of dying, in which the person develops a sense of peace, an acceptance of fate, and in many cases, a desire to be left alone. In this stage, feelings and physical pain may be virtually absent. Kübler-Ross describes this fifth stage as the end of the dying struggle, the final resting stage before death. A summary of Kübler-Ross' dying stages is presented in figure 11.13.

What is the current evaluation of Kübler-Ross' approach? Kübler-Ross' pioneering efforts were important in calling attention to those who are attempting to cope with life-threatening illnesses. She did much to encourage attention to the quality of life for dying persons and their families. However, Robert Kastenbaum (2004) points out the following problems with Kübler-Ross' approach:

- The existence of the five-stage sequence has not been demonstrated by either Kübler-Ross or independent research.
- The stage interpretation neglected the patients' situations, including support from relationships, the specific effects of their illnesses, their family obligations, and the institutional climate in which they were interviewed.

Because of the criticisms of Kübler-Ross' stages of dying, some psychologists prefer to describe them not as stages but as potential reactions to dying. At any one moment, a number of emotions may wax and wane. Hope, disbelief, bewilderment, anger, and acceptance may come and go as individuals try to make sense of what is happening to them.

In facing their own death, some individuals struggle until the end, desperately trying to hang on to their lives. Acceptance of death never comes for them. Some psychologists believe that the harder individuals fight to avoid the inevitable death they face and the more they deny it, the more difficulty they will have in dying peacefully and in a dignified way; other psychologists argue that not confronting death until the end may be adaptive for some individuals (Lifton, 1977).

The extent to which people have found meaning and purpose in their lives is linked with how they approach death. A recent study of 160 individuals with less than three months to live revealed that those who had found purpose and meaning in their lives felt the least despair in the final weeks, while dying individuals who saw no reason for living were the most distressed and wanted to hasten death (McClain, Rosenfeld, & Breitbart, 2003). In this and other studies, spirituality helped to buffer dying individuals from severe depression (DeSpelder & Strickland, 2005).

Coping with the Death of Someone Else

Loss can come in many forms in our lives—divorce, a pet's death, loss of a job—but no loss is greater than that which comes through the death of someone we love and care

www.mhhe.com/santrockha

Death and Dying
Kübler-Ross
Death and Dying Topics

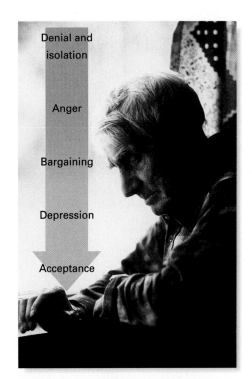

FIGURE 11.13 Kübler-Ross' Stages of Dying
According to Elisabeth Kübler-Ross, we go through five stages of dying: denial and isolation, anger, bargaining, depression, and acceptance. *Does everyone go through these stages, or go through them in the same order? Explain.*

for—a parent, sibling, spouse, relative, or friend. Ratings of life's stresses rank the death of a spouse as the one that requires the most adjustment. How should we communicate with a dying individual? How do we cope with the death of someone we love?

Communicating with a Dying Person   Most psychologists believe that it is best for dying individuals to know that they are dying and that significant others know they are dying so they can interact and communicate with each other on the basis of this mutual knowledge. What are some of the advantages of this shared awareness for the dying individual? There are at least four advantages. First, dying individuals can close their lives in accord with their own ideas about proper dying. Second, they may be able to complete some plans and projects, can make arrangements for survivors, and can participate in decisions about a funeral and burial. Third, this gives dying individuals the opportunity to reminisce, to converse with others who have been important to them, and to end life conscious of what life has been like. And fourth, this awareness increases the chances that dying individuals will understand what is happening within their bodies and what the medical staff is doing to them (Kalish, 1981).

In addition to keeping communication open, what are some suggestions for conversing with a dying individual? Some experts believe that conversation should not focus on preparation for death but should focus on strengths of the individual and preparation for the remainder of life. Since external accomplishments are not possible, communication should emphasize internal growth.

Adjustment Strategies
For Communicating with a Dying Person

Effective strategies for communicating with a dying person include these:

1. ***Establish your presence.*** Be at the same eye level; don't be afraid to touch the dying person—dying individuals are often starved for human touch.
2. ***Eliminate distraction.*** For example, ask if it is okay to turn off the TV. Realize that excessive small talk can be a distraction.
3. ***Be sensitive to how long you should stay.*** Dying individuals who are very frail often have little energy. If the dying person you are visiting is very frail, you may not want to visit for very long.
4. ***Don't insist that the dying person feel acceptance of death.*** If the dying person wants to deny the reality of the situation, accept their attitude; on the other hand, don't insist on denial if the dying individual indicates acceptance.
5. ***Encourage the expression of feelings.*** Allow the dying person to express guilt or anger, for example.
6. ***Don't be afraid to ask the person what the expected outcome for their illness is.*** Discuss unfinished business.
7. ***Ask the dying person if there is anyone he or she would like to see that you can contact.*** Sometimes dying individuals don't have access to other people.
8. ***Encourage the dying person to reminisce.*** Especially do this if you have memories in common.
9. ***Talk with the individual when she or he wishes to talk.*** If this is impossible, make an appointment and keep it.
10. ***Express your regard for the dying person.*** Don't be afraid to express love, and don't be afraid to say good-bye.

---

grief The emotional numbness, disbelief, separation anxiety, despair, sadness, and loneliness that accompany the loss of someone we love.

Grieving   Grief is the emotional numbness, disbelief, separation anxiety, despair, sadness, and loneliness that accompany the loss of someone we love. Grief is not a simple emotional state but rather a complex, evolving process with multiple dimensions (Harvey, 2004; Robak, 2004). Pining for the lost person is one important dimension. Pining or yearning reflects an intermittent, recurrent wish or need to recover the lost person. Another important dimension of grief is separation anxiety, which not only includes pining and preoccupation with thoughts of the deceased person but also focuses on places and things associated with the deceased, as well as crying or sighing. Grief may also involve despair and sadness, which include a sense of hopelessness and defeat, depressive symptoms, apathy, loss of meaning for activities that used to involve the person who is gone, and growing desolation (Dunne, 2004; Giddens & Giddens, 2000; Ringdal & others, 2001; Turner & others, 2004).

Grief counseling can help many individuals cope with the loss of a loved one. Here Sarah Wheeler (*right*), a grief counselor, is providing support, empathy, information, and guidance.

These feelings do not represent a clear-cut stage but occur repeatedly shortly after a loss. Nonetheless, as time passes, pining and protest over the loss tend to diminish, although episodes of depression and apathy may remain or increase. The sense of separation anxiety and loss may continue to the end of one's life, but most of us emerge from grief's tears, turning our attention once again to productive tasks and regaining a more positive view of life (Powers & Wampold, 1994).

The grieving process is more like a roller-coaster ride than an orderly progression of stages (Lund, 1996). The ups and downs of grief often involve rapidly changing emotions, meeting the challenges of learning new skills, detecting personal weaknesses and limitations, creating new patterns of behavior, and forming new friendships and relationships (Bruce, 2002; Mitchell & Catron, 2002). For most individuals, grief becomes more manageable over time, with fewer abrupt highs and lows. But many grieving spouses report that even though time has brought some healing, they have never gotten over their loss (Ungar & Florian, 2004). They have just learned to live with it.

Long-term grief is sometimes masked and can predispose individuals to become depressed and even suicidal (Davis, 2001; Kastenbaum, 2004). Good family communication can help reduce the incidence of depression and suicidal thoughts. For example, in one study, family members who communicated poorly with each other had more negative grief reactions six months later than those who communicated effectively with each other just after the loss of a family member (Schoka & Hayslip, 1999).

Death in Different Cultures

To live a full life and die with glory was the prevailing goal of the ancient Greeks. Individuals are more conscious of death in times of war, famine, and plague. Whereas Americans are conditioned from early in life to live as though they were immortal, in much of the world this fiction cannot be maintained. Death crowds the streets of Calcutta in daily overdisplay, as it does the scrubby villages of Africa's Sahel. Children live with the ultimate toll of malnutrition and disease, mothers lose as many babies as survive into adulthood, and it is rare that a family remains intact for many years. Even in peasant areas where life is better, and health and maturity may be reasonable expectations, the presence of dying people in the house, the large attendance at funerals, and the daily contact with aging adults prepare the young for death and provide them with guidelines on how to die. By contrast, in the United States it is not uncommon to reach adulthood without having seen anyone die.

Most societies throughout history have had philosophical or religious beliefs about death, and most societies have a ritual that deals with death. Death may be seen as a punishment for one's sins, an act of atonement, or a judgment of a just God. For some, death means loneliness; for others, death is a quest for happiness. For still others, death represents redemption, a relief from the trials and tribulations of the earthly

Family memorial day at the national cemetery in Seoul, Korea. *How does dealing with death vary across cultures?*

world. Some embrace death and welcome it; others abhor and fear it. For those who welcome it, death may be seen as the fitting end to a fulfilled life. From this perspective, how we depart from earth is influenced by how we have lived.

In most societies, death is not viewed as the end of existence—though the biological body has died, the spiritual body is believed to live on. This religious perspective is favored by most Americans as well. Cultural variations in attitudes toward death include belief in reincarnation, which is an important aspect of the Hindu and Buddhist religions (Truitner & Truitner, 1993). In the Gond culture of India, death is believed to be caused by magic and demons. The members of the Gond culture react angrily to death. In the Tanala culture of Madagascar, death is believed to be caused by natural forces. The members of the Tanala culture show a much more peaceful reaction to death than their counterparts in the Gond culture.

In many ways, we in the United States are death avoiders and death deniers. This denial can take many forms:

- The tendency of the funeral industry to gloss over death and fashion lifelike qualities in the dead
- The adoption of euphemistic language for death—for example, *exiting, passing on, never say die,* and *good for life,* which implies forever
- The persistent search for a fountain of youth
- The rejection and isolation of the aged, who may remind us of death
- The adoption of the concept of a pleasant and rewarding afterlife, suggesting that we are immortal
- The medical community's emphasis on prolonging biological life rather than on diminishing human suffering

Review and Reflect

5   **Discuss death and grieving**

REVIEW

- How do people face their own death?
- How do people cope with the death of someone else?
- How is death viewed in different cultures?

REFLECT

- Is there a best or a worst way to grieve? Explain.

Reach Your Learning Goals

Chapter 11

Emerging Adulthood, Adult Development, and Aging

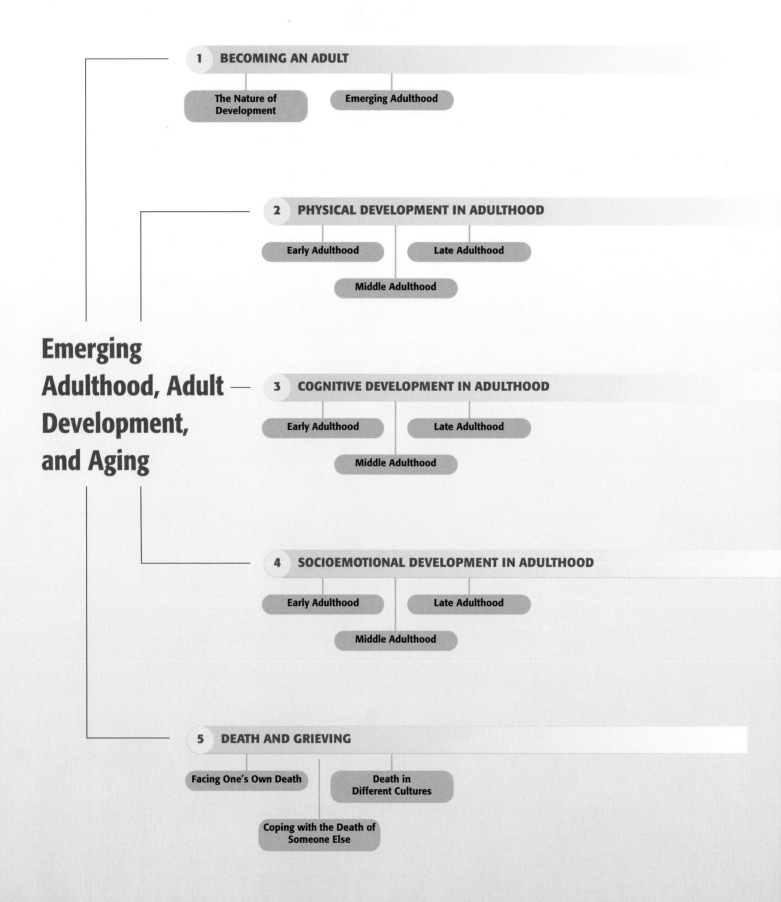

1 BECOMING AN ADULT

- The Nature of Development
- Emerging Adulthood

2 PHYSICAL DEVELOPMENT IN ADULTHOOD

- Early Adulthood
- Late Adulthood
- Middle Adulthood

3 COGNITIVE DEVELOPMENT IN ADULTHOOD

- Early Adulthood
- Late Adulthood
- Middle Adulthood

4 SOCIOEMOTIONAL DEVELOPMENT IN ADULTHOOD

- Early Adulthood
- Late Adulthood
- Middle Adulthood

5 DEATH AND GRIEVING

- Facing One's Own Death
- Death in Different Cultures
- Coping with the Death of Someone Else

SUMMARY

1 *Describe the nature of development and becoming an adult*

- Development refers to the pattern of change in human capabilities that begins at conception and continues through the life span. The pattern of development is the product of several processes, especially physical processes, cognitive processes, and socioemotional processes. There are three main periods of adult development: early adulthood (beginning in the late teens/early twenties and lasting through the thirties), middle adulthood (beginning at approximately 40 years of age and lasting to about 60), and late adulthood (beginning in the sixties and lasting until death). There is not evidence that people are happier in one of these age periods than others.

- Emerging adulthood is the term now given to the transition from adolescence to adulthood. Its age range is about 18 to 25 years of age and it is characterized by experimentation and exploration. These personal and social assets are linked to well-being in adolescence and emerging adulthood: intellectual (academic success, good decision making), psychological (positive mental health, optimism), and social (connectedness, integration). Going to college involves considerable adaptation.

2 *Explain physical changes in adulthood*

- Most adults reach their peak physical performance during their twenties and also are the healthiest then. However, physical skills begin to decline during the thirties.

- Changes in physical appearance are among the most visible signs of aging in middle adulthood. Menopause also takes place during middle adulthood.

- A distinction is made between life span and life expectancy. Individuals live longer on the Japanese island of Okinawa than any other place in the world likely because of their diet, low stress, caring, activity, and spirituality. Hormonal stress theory provides one possible explanation for the biological aspects of aging. Chronic disease increases in middle adulthood and becomes even more common in late adulthood. An important factor in the health of older adults is perceived control over their lives. Dementia is a global term for any neurological disorder in which the primary symptoms involve a deterioration of mental functioning. Alzheimer disease is by far the most common dementia. This progressive, irreversible disorder is characterized by gradual deterioration of memory, reasoning, language, and eventually physical functioning. An important concern is caring for Alzheimer patients and the burdens this places on caregivers. Even in late adulthood, the brain has remarkable repair capacity and plasticity. The

Mankato nuns lead intellectually challenging lives and researchers believe this contributes to the quality of their lives and to their longevity.

3 *Characterize cognitive changes in adulthood*

- Piaget proposed that the formal operational stage—characterized by abstract and logical thinking—is the highest cognitive stage and is entered at about 11 to 15 years of age. He argued that no new cognitive changes occur in adulthood. However, some psychologists have proposed that the idealistic thinking of adolescents is replaced by the more realistic, pragmatic thinking of young adults. Postformal thought is reflective, realistic, and contextual; provisional; realistic; and open to emotions and subjective.

- Horn argued that crystallized intelligence increases in middle age, whereas fluid intelligence declines. Schaie conducted a longitudinal study of intelligence and found that many cognitive skills reach their peak in middle age.

- Overall, older adults do not do as well on memory and other cognitive tasks and are slower to process information than younger adults. But older adults may have greater wisdom than younger adults.

4 *Summarize socioemotional changes in adulthood*

- In Erikson's theory, eight stages of development unfold as people go through the life span. Each stage consists of a unique developmental task that confronts the individual with a crisis that must be resolved. The more successfully an individual resolves the crisis, the healthier development will be. Erikson believed that intimacy versus isolation is the stage that characterizes early adulthood, a time when people either form intimate relationships with others or become socially isolated. At this stage, decisions about whether to marry or to make other commitments are important for most people. Career and work become central themes in the life of young adults.

- Erikson said that the stage of generativity versus stagnation characterizes middle adulthood. Generativity encompasses adults' desire to leave a legacy of themselves to the next generation versus stagnation, the sense of having done little or nothing for the next generation. Although only a small percentage of middle-aged adults experience a midlife crisis, for many adults this period of life is marked by midlife consciousness and increased contemplation of the meaning of life.

- Erikson proposed that late adulthood is characterized by the stage of integrity versus despair. This involves engaging in a life review, which is either positive (integrity) or negative (despair). Older adults report better control of their emotions and experience more positive and less negative emotions than younger adults. Older adults also often reduce their general social affiliations. Instead, they are motivated to spend more time with close friends and family members (social selectivity theory). Social support can improve the physical and mental health of older adults. Social integration also plays an important role in the lives of many older adults. The need to accommodate to losses is an important aspect of self-regulation in aging. According to selective optimization with compensation theory, successful self-regulation involves three main factors—selection, optimization, and compensation. Religion plays an important role in the lives of many older adults. Poverty and ethnicity are special concerns in late adulthood. Older adults receive disproportionately less mental health treatment. Many adults can sustain or even improve their functioning as they age. Remaining active and maintaining social connection increase the likelihood that older adults will be happy and healthy.

5 Discuss death and grieving

- Kübler-Ross proposed five stages that characterize the behavior and thinking of a dying person: denial and isolation; anger; bargaining; depression; and acceptance. Criticisms of her stage view have been made and some psychologists prefer to talk about her view as potential reactions to dying rather than a sequence of stages.
- Coping with the death of someone else involves effectively communicating with the dying person and grieving, which is the emotional numbness, disbelief, separation anxiety, despair, sadness, and loneliness that accompany the loss of someone we love.
- How death is dealt with varies across cultures. Most societies have philosophical or religious beliefs about death, as well as rituals that deal with death. In most societies, death is not viewed as the end of existence, with the spiritual body but not the physical body, believed to live on. In many ways the United States is a death-avoiding and death-denying culture.

Key Terms

development 327
early adulthood 327
middle adulthood 328
late adulthood 328
emerging adulthood 329
life span 336
life expectancy 336
hormonal stress theory 338

dementia 339
Alzheimer disease 340
formal operational stage 342
postformal thought 342
crystallized intelligence 343
fluid intelligence 343
wisdom 345

Erikson's theory 345
intimacy versus isolation 345
generativity versus stagnation 347
integrity versus despair 349
socioemotional selectivity theory 350

selective optimization with compensation theory 350
major depression 352
Kübler-Ross' stages of dying 354
grief 356

Resources for Improving Your Adjustment

SELF-HELP BOOKS

Your Guide to College Success (3rd ed.)

(2004) by John Santrock and Jane Halonen. Belmont, CA: Wadsworth.

This is a book I wrote with co-author Jane Halonen that provides extensive strategies for effectively adjusting to college life. The book provides information about both academic skills and life skills that can benefit you while you are in college.

Aging Well

(2002) by George Vaillant. Boston: Little Brown.

Vaillant describes the results from his longitudinal studies of aging and provides inspirational messages about how aging adults can lead happier and more fulfilling lives. Numerous case studies reveal how a number of people have aged successfully.

How to Survive the Loss of Love (2nd ed.)

(1991) by Melba Cosgrove, Harold Bloomfield, and Peter McWilliams. Los Angeles: Prelude.

This book gives recommendations for coping with the loss of a loved one. Poetry, common sense, and psychological advice are interwoven throughout more than 100 brief topics organized according to these categories: understanding loss, surviving, healing, and growing. *How to Survive the Loss of Love* was rated in the highest category (5 stars) in the national study of self-help resources (Norcross, Santrock, & others, 2003).

AUTOBIOGRAPHIES

Tuesdays with Morrie

(1997) by Mitch Albom. New York: Doubleday.

Sportswriter Mitch Albom was a student of sociology professor Morrie Schwartz and became reunited with him after he found out Morrie was dying of Lou Gehrig's disease. The book describes fourteen Tuesday visits Albom made to his dying mentor and the nature of their discussions. *Tuesdays with Morrie* was rated in the highest category (5 stars) in the national survey of mental health resources (Norcross, Santrock, & others, 2003).

NATIONAL SUPPORT GROUPS

American Association of Retired Persons (AARP)
601 East St. NW
Washington, DC 20049
1-800-424-3410
http://www.aarp.org

National Council on Aging
409 3rd Street SW, Suite 200
Washington, DC 20024
800-424-9046
http://www.ncoa.org

Alzheimer's Association
919 North Michigan Ave Suite 1100
Chicago IL 60611-1676
1-800-272-3900
http://www.alz.org

E-Learning Tools

To help you master the material in this chapter, you will find a number of valuable study tools on the student CD-ROM and the Online Learning Center.

SELF-ASSESSMENT

In Text

You can complete these self-assessments in the text:
- Self-Assessment 11.1: *My View of Life*
- Self-Assessment 11.2: *My College Adjustment*
- Self-Assessment 11.3: *Can I Live to Be 100?*

THINK CRITICALLY

To practice your critical thinking skills, complete these exercises on the Online Learning Center:
- *How Long Would You Like to Live?* explores some aspects of longevity.
- *Seasons of a Woman's Life* examines whether Levinson's view applies to women as well as to men.
- *Engaging in a Life Review* guides you through a review of your life.

APPLY YOUR KNOWLEDGE

1. Write your own obituary.

As children, we were asked "what do you want to be when you grow up?" Now that you are an adult a more appropriate question might be "WHO do you want to be?" To help put your priorities into perspective, you may find it an enlightening experience to write your own obituary and/or your eulogy. Look over the information in the textbook about what challenges you will face as you continue through the life span.

2. Preventing Alzheimer disease.

Your textbook points out that a "use it or lose it" strategy is helpful in warding off various kinds of dementia. To a large degree, keeping active after retirement is one way to improve your odds. But the ability to keep active after retirement may depend in part on the abilities and habits that you begin to develop now. Go to a search engine such as www.yahoo.com or www.google.com and search for "warding off dementia" or "preventing dementia."

3. Myths of aging.

Many people assume that seniors inevitably experience memory loss and no longer engage in the same activities as younger people, including having sex. Think of a typical nursing home. What kind of policies are likely to be in place, and which of those policies are based on these myths? First, make a list of how you think most nursing homes are run. Then, go to a search engine such as www.yahoo.com or www.google.com and search for "myths of aging." Based on the information that you have gathered, write out at least three ways that nursing homes could better serve their residents, based on a debunking of these myths.

 VIDEO SEGMENT

"Use it or lose it" is one of the strategies for successful aging discussed in the text. Does it work? To learn more about this idea and about how aging is studied, watch the video "Aging Well" in Chapter 11 on the CD-ROM.

Gender

Learning Goals

1 Define gender and explain evolutionary, social, and cognitive theories of gender

2 Discuss gender comparisons and classifications

3 Characterize women's and men's lives

Images of Adjustment

Tita de la Garza: Bound by Tradition

The setting for Laura Esquival's (1989) novel, *Like Water for Chocolate*, is a ranch in Mexico. Two days after Tita, the youngest daughter in the De La Garza family was born, her father died. Their family tradition dictated that the youngest daughter has to care for her mother until her death. This tradition produced a great deal of conflict when she grew up. She and Pedro Muzquiz fell deeply in love and wanted to get married but because of their family tradition (the youngest daughter being required to help her mother) she was not allowed to marry him. Instead, her mother (Mama Elena) told Pedro he could marry Tita's oldest sister, Rosaura. Pedro goes ahead and marries Rosaura so he can be close to Tita.

Esquival describes a scene involving young Tita and her mother. Tita had told her mother that Pedro intended to come and speak with her, and her mother emotionally responded:

> "If he intends to ask for your hand, tell him not to bother. He'll be wasting his time and mine, too. You know perfectly well that being the youngest daughter means you have to take care of me until the day I die."
>
> With that Mama Elena got slowly to her feet, put her glasses on her apron, and said in a tone of final command:
>
> "That's it for today."
>
> Tita knew that discussion was not one of the forms of communication permitted in Mama Elena's household, but even so, for the first time in her life, she intended to protest her mother's ruling.
>
> "But in my opinion . . ."
>
> "You don't have an opinion, and that's all I want to hear about it. For generations, not a single person in my family has ever questioned this tradition, and no daughter of mine is going to be the one to start."

Laura Esquivel's descriptions reveal how culture can be a context in which gender and destiny are intertwined. Traditionally, in Mexico, the youngest daughter is expected to become the care provider for her aging parents. Tita's reflections and questions reveal much about gender roles. In some cultures, privilege, responsibility, sacrifice, and restriction are clearly delineated along gender lines. In this chapter, we discuss these topics regarding how gender influences adjustment: What is gender, and what are the roots of gender? How do men and women differ? How does the fact that you are a man or a woman influence your life and adjustment?

1   PERSPECTIVES ON GENDER

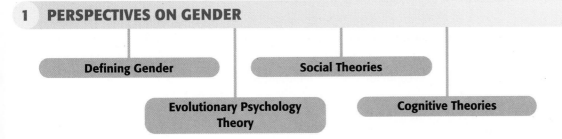

To American college men and women, Mama Elena's comments to Tita are likely to sound extreme and even cruel. But the constraints on Tita's world would not seem unusual to many women around the world. In this section, we examine explanations for differences in expectations about how men and women should live.

Defining Gender

Until not long ago, Americans believed that boys should grow up to be masculine and that girls should grow up to be feminine; boys were said to be made of "frogs and snails and puppy dogs' tails," and girls of "sugar and spice and everything nice." In children's literature, boys were depicted as active and exploring, girls as passive admirers. The well-adjusted adult male was expected to be independent, aggressive, and power oriented. The well-adjusted adult female was expected to be dependent, nurturant, and uninterested in power. Further, masculine characteristics were considered to be healthy and good by society; female characteristics were deemed undesirable.

Over the last four decades, these once-firm lines between what is considered appropriate for a man and what is appropriate for a woman blurred. Instead of simply cheering on their school's sports teams, millions of American girls began to compete on teams of their own. Instead of devoting their lives solely to taking care of husband, home, and children, millions of women in the United States and other Western countries joined the paid workforce, forging their own careers. Women became firefighters and police officers, construction workers and pilots, legislators, governors, and CEOs— jobs long considered suitable only for men.

Changes in the roles of men and women in Western society demonstrate the difference between sex and gender. *Sex* refers to biological characteristics; **gender** is the psychological and social dimension of being female or male. The biology of men and women has not altered, but our social construction of what it means to be a man or a woman has changed. Thus, recent decades have seen dramatic revisions in **gender roles,** which are sets of expectations that prescribe how female and males should think, act, and feel (Lenton & Blair, 2004; Lippa, 2005). Restrictions on women have declined as a belief in equality for men and women has increased. To evaluate the extent to which you endorse gender equality, complete Self-Assessment 12.1.

Despite the dramatic changes in gender roles in Western countries, the roots of differences between men and women are strong and deep. In many cultures, well-defined and well-practiced gender roles even today take the ambiguity out of how

Gender and Society
Gender Resources and Links

gender   The psychological and social dimension of being female or male.

gender roles   Sets of expectations that prescribe how females or males should think, act, or feel.

SELF-ASSESSMENT 12.1

My Beliefs About Gender Equality

For each of the ten items, place a check mark in the appropriate column to reflect whether you agree or disagree with the statement.

	Agree	Disagree
1. Boys and girls should be encouraged to do the same things.	_____	_____
2. The responsibility for taking care of infants should be equally divided between parents, irrespective of their gender.	_____	_____
3. The husband and wife should share equally in housework such as cooking, washing dishes, and housecleaning.	_____	_____
4. The husband and wife should have equal responsibility in contributing to the family income by working.	_____	_____
5. High schools should spend as much money on girls' sports as boys' sports.	_____	_____
6. Fathers and mothers should be treated equally by the law in child custody cases.	_____	_____
7. Families should spend as much money on the education of daughters as on the education of sons.	_____	_____
8. In relationships, disloyalty should be equally censured for men and women.	_____	_____
9. Both parents should have an equal say in the decision to have a child.	_____	_____
10. There should be no differential dress codes for men and women at workplaces, such as codes that women must wear skirts.	_____	_____

Go to the appendix at the end of the book for scoring and interpretation of your responses.

women and men relate to each other. However, even where such definitive roles exist, there is likely to be some strain (Zhou & others, 2004). It is likely that not all members of a culture are content with the gender roles practiced in their culture.

Evolutionary Psychology Theory

Why do men and women have different roles? How did gender differences emerge? One suggested answer comes from **evolutionary psychology theory,** which argues that adaptation during the evolution of humans produced psychological differences between males and females (Buss, 2000, 2004).

Evolutionary psychologists argue that primarily because of their differing roles in reproduction, males and females faced different pressures in primeval environments when the human species was evolving (Jackson, 2004; Weisfeld & Woodward, 2004). In particular, because having multiple sexual liaisons improves the likelihood that males will pass on their genes, natural selection favored males who adopted short-term mating strategies. These males competed with other males to acquire more resources in order to access females. Therefore, say evolutionary psychologists, males evolved dispositions that favor violence, competition, and risk taking (Bassett & Moss, 2004).

In contrast, according to evolutionary psychologists, females' contributions to the gene pool was improved by securing resources for their offspring, which was promoted by obtaining long-term mates who could support a family. As a consequence, natural selection favored females who devoted effort to parenting and chose mates who could provide their offspring with resources and protection. Females developed preferences for successful, ambitious men who could provide these resources.

evolutionary psychology theory
Emphasizes that adaptation during the evolution of humans produced psychological differences between males and females. In this theory, primarily because of their differing roles in reproduction, males and females faced different pressures as they were evolving.

This evolutionary unfolding, according to some evolutionary psychologists, explains key gender differences in sexual attitudes and sexual behavior. For example, in one study, men said that ideally they would like to have more than eighteen sexual partners in their lifetime, whereas women stated that ideally they would like to have only four or five (Buss & Schmitt, 1993). In another study, 75 percent of the men but none of the women approached by an attractive stranger of the opposite sex consented to a request for sex (Clark & Hatfield, 1989).

Such gender differences, says David Buss (2000, 2004), are exactly the type predicted by evolutionary psychology. Buss argues that men and women differ psychologically in those domains in which they have faced different adaptive problems during evolutionary history. In all other domains, predicts Buss, the sexes will be psychologically similar.

Critics of evolutionary psychology argue that its hypotheses are backed by speculations about prehistory, not evidence. Critics also claim that the evolutionary view pays little attention to cultural and individual variations in gender differences. In any event, people are not locked into behavior that was adaptive in the evolutionary past.

Social Theories

Unlike evolutionary theorists, many social scientists do not locate the cause of psychological gender differences in biological dispositions. Rather, they argue that these differences are due to social experiences. Three theories have been influential in this regard.

Alice Eagly (2000, 2001) proposed **social role theory,** which states that gender differences result from the contrasting roles of women and men. In most cultures around the world, women have less power and status than men have and they control fewer resources (Wood & Eagly, 2002). Compared with men, women perform more domestic work, spend fewer hours in paid employment, receive lower pay, and are more thinly represented in the highest levels of organizations. In Eagly's view, as women adapted to roles with less power and less status in society, they showed more cooperative, less dominant profiles than men. Thus, the social hierarchy and division of labor are important causes of gender differences in power, assertiveness, and nurture (Eagly & Diekman, 2003).

The **psychoanalytic theory of gender** stems from Freud's view that the preschool child develops a sexual attraction to the opposite-sex parent. At 5 or 6 years of age, the child renounces this attraction because of anxiety. Subsequently, the child identifies with the same-sex parent, unconsciously adopting the same-sex parent's characteristics. However, research indicates that gender development does not proceed as Freud proposed (Callan, 2001). Children become gender typed much earlier than 5 or 6 years of age, and they become masculine or feminine even when the same-sex parent is not present in the family.

The social cognitive approach discussed in chapter 1 provides an alternative explanation of how children develop gender-typed behavior (see figure 12.1). According to the **social cognitive theory of gender,** children's gender development occurs

Evolutionary Psychology
Alice Eagly's Research

social role theory Eagly's theory that psychological gender differences are caused by the contrasting social roles of women and men.

psychoanalytic theory of gender Stems from Freud's view that preschool children develop a sexual attraction to the opposite-sex parent, then, at 5 to 6 years of age, renounce the attraction because of anxious feelings, subsequently identifying with the same-sex parent and unconsciously adopting the same-sex parent's characteristics.

social cognitive theory of gender The idea that children's gender development occurs through observation and imitation, and through rewards and punishment for gender-appropriate and –inappropriate behavior.

Theory	Processes	Outcome
Psychoanalytic theory	Sexual attraction to opposite-sex parent at 3 to 5 years of age; anxiety about sexual attraction and subsequent identification with same-sex parent at 5 to 6 years of age	Gender behavior similar to that of same-sex parent
Social cognitive theory	Rewards and punishments of gender-appropriate and -inappropriate behavior by adults and peers; observation and initiation of models' masculine and feminine behavior	Gender behavior

FIGURE 12.1 Parents Influence Their Children's Gender Development by Action and Example

through observation and imitation, and through rewards and punishments for gender-appropriate and -inappropriate behavior (Bussey & Bandura, 1999). Children learn about gender from observing other adults in the neighborhood and on television (Fagot, Rodgers, & Leinbach, 2000). They also learn when parents use rewards and punishments to teach their daughters to be feminine ("Karen, you are being a good girl when you play gently with your doll") and their sons to be masculine ("Keith, a boy as big as you is not supposed to cry"). As children get older, peers become increasingly important. Peers extensively reward and punish behavior depending on whether it is considered masculine or feminine (Lott & Maluso, 2001). For example, when children play in ways that the culture says are gender appropriate, their peers tend to reward them. Those who engage in activities that are considered inappropriate tend to be criticized or abandoned by their peers.

From 4 to about 12 years of age, children spend a large majority of their free play time exclusively with others of their own sex (Maccoby, 2002). What kind of socialization takes place in these same-sex play groups? In one study, researchers observed preschoolers over six months (Martin & Fabes, 2001). The more time boys spent interacting with other boys, the more their activity level, rough-and-tumble play, and sex-typed choice of toys and games increased, and the less time boys spent near adults. By contrast, the more time the preschool girls spent interacting with other girls, the more their activity level and aggression decreased, and the more their girl-type play activities and time spent near adults increased. After watching elementary school children repeatedly play in same-sex groups, two researchers characterized the playground as "gender school" (Luria & Herzog, 1985).

Cognitive Theories

Observation, imitation, rewards, and punishment—these are the mechanisms by which gender develops according to social cognitive theory. Interactions between the child and the social environment are the main keys to gender development in this view. Some critics argue that this explanation pays too little attention to the child's own mind and understanding and portrays the child as passively acquiring gender roles (Martin, Ruble, & Szkrybalo, 2002). Two cognitive theories—cognitive developmental theory and gender schema theory—stress that individuals actively construct their gender world:

- The **cognitive developmental theory of gender** states that children's gender typing occurs *after* children think of themselves as boys and girls. Once they consistently conceive of themselves as male or female, children prefer activities, objects, and attitudes consistent with this label.
- **Gender schema theory** states that gender typing emerges as children gradually develop schemas of what is gender appropriate and gender inappropriate in their culture. Children are internally motivated to perceive the world and to act in accordance with their developing schemas.

Initially proposed by Lawrence Kohlberg (1966), the cognitive developmental theory of gender holds that gender development depends on cognition. As young children develop, they construct a concept of gender. What's more, they come to see that they will always be male or female. As a result, they begin to select models of their own sex to imitate. The little girl acts as if she is thinking, "I'm a girl, so I want to do girl things. Therefore, the opportunity to do girl things is rewarding."

Notice that in this view gender-typed behavior occurs only after children develop *gender constancy*, which is the understanding that sex remains the same, even though activities, clothing, and hairstyle might change (Ruble, 2000). However, researchers have found that children do not develop gender constancy until they are about 6 or 7 years old. Before this time, most little girls already prefer girlish toys and clothes and

cognitive developmental theory of gender The theory that children's gender typing occurs after they think of themselves as boys and girls. Once they consistently conceive of themselves as male or female, children prefer activities, objects, and attitudes that are consistent with this label.

gender schema theory The theory that gender typing emerges as children gradually develop gender schemas of what is gender appropriate and gender inappropriate in their culture.

Theory	Processes	Emphasis
Cognitive developmental theory	Development of gender constancy, especially around 6 to 7 years of age, when conservation skills develop; after children develop ability to consistently conceive of themselves as male or female, children often organize their world on the basis of gender, such as selecting same-sex models to imitate	Cognitive readiness facilitates gender identity
Gender schema theory	Sociocultural emphasis on gender-based standards and stereotypes; children's attention and behavior are guided by an internal motivation to conform to these gender-based standards and stereotypes, allowing children to interpret the world through a network of gender-organized thoughts	Gender schemas reinforce gender behavior

FIGURE 12.2 The Development of Gender-Typed Behavior According to the Cognitive Developmental and Gender Schema Theories of Gender Development

games, and most little boys prefer boyish toys and games. Thus, contrary to Kohlberg's description of cognitive developmental theory, gender typing does not appear to depend on gender constancy.

Unlike cognitive developmental theory, gender schema theory does not require children to perceive gender constancy before they begin gender typing (see figure 12.2). Instead, gender schema theory states that gender typing occurs when children are ready to encode and organize information along the lines of what is considered appropriate for females and males in their society (Martin & Dinella, 2001; Ampbell, Shirley & Candy, 2004; Martin & Ruble, 2004). Bit by bit, children pick up what is gender appropriate and gender inappropriate in their culture, and they develop gender schemas that shape how they perceive the world and what they remember. A *gender schema* is a cognitive structure, a network of associations, that organizes the world in terms of female and male and guides a person's perceptions, thinking, and behavior. Children are motivated to act in ways that conform with these gender schemas. Thus, gender schemas fuel gender typing.

In sum, cognitive factors contribute to the way children think and act as males and females. Through biological, social, and cognitive processes, children develop their gender attitudes and behaviors.

Review and Reflect

1 Define gender and explain evolutionary, social, and cognitive theories of gender

REVIEW

- How can these two terms be defined: gender and gender roles?
- What is the evolutionary psychology theory of gender differences?
- What are three social theories of gender?
- What are two cognitive views of gender?

REFLECT

- Does any theory of gender development explain everything you know about differences between men and women? What might a theory of gender development be like that takes parts of each of the theories—what is called an *eclectic theory?*

2   GENDER COMPARISONS

Gender Stereotypes

Masculinity, Femininity, and Androgyny

Gender Similarities and Differences

Biology, culture and the social structure of society, social learning, and cognitive processes act to make men and women different. But why have so many cultures assigned the job of providing care to females, like Tita, who was described at the opening of this chapter? What do people believe about the differences between males and females, and to what extent are these beliefs accurate?

Gender Stereotypes

Gender stereotypes are general beliefs about females and males. For example, men are powerful; women are weak. Men make good mechanics; women make good nurses. Men are good with numbers; women are good with words. Women are emotional; men are not. All of these are stereotypes. They are generalizations that reflect widely held beliefs (Abrams, 2003; Bandura & Bussey, 2004). As we discussed in chapter 6, people may apply stereotypes even without being aware of them.

Traditional Masculinity and Femininity   What beliefs actually make up the stereotypes about men and women? A classic study in the early 1970s assessed which traits and behaviors college students believed were characteristic of females and which they believed were characteristic of males (Broverman & others, 1972). The traits associated with males were labeled *instrumental:* they included characteristics such as being independent, aggressive, and power oriented. The traits associated with females were labeled *expressive*: they included characteristics such as being warm and sensitive.

Thus, the instrumental traits associated with males suited them for the traditional masculine role of going out into the world as the breadwinner. The expressive traits associated with females paralleled the traditional feminine role of being the sensitive, nurturing caregiver in the home.

gender stereotypes General beliefs about females and males.

CATHY © 1986 Cathy Guisewhite. Reprinted with permission of Universal Press Syndicate. All Rights Reserved.

These roles and traits, however, are not just different; they also are unequal in terms of social status and power (Agars, 2004). The traditional feminine characteristics are childlike, suitable for someone who is dependent and subordinate to others. The traditional masculine characteristics suit one to deal competently with the wider world and to wield authority. However, men's strong adherence to rigid gender stereotyping is associated with alcohol-related problems and interpersonal violence (Graham-Bermann, Eastin, & Bermann, 2001).

Stereotyping and Culture How widespread is gender stereotyping? In a far-ranging study of college students in thirty countries, stereotyping of females and males was pervasive (Williams & Best, 1982). Males were widely believed to be dominant, independent, aggressive, achievement oriented, and enduring. Females were widely believed to be nurturant, affiliative, less esteemed, and more helpful in times of distress.

Of course, in the decades since this study was conducted, traditional gender stereotypes and gender roles have been challenged in many societies, and social inequalities between men and women have diminished. Do gender stereotypes change when the relationship between men and women changes? In a subsequent study, women and men who lived in relatively wealthy, industrialized countries perceived themselves as more similar than did women and men who lived in less developed countries (Williams & Best, 1989). In the more developed countries, the women were more likely to attend college and be gainfully employed. Thus, as sexual equality increases, gender stereotypes may diminish. However, recent research continues to find that gender stereotyping is pervasive (Best, 2001; Kite, 2001).

Gender Stereotypes and Ethnicity If you meet a grandmother, is your reaction the same as when you meet a 20-year-old woman? If you meet an African American woman, is your reaction the same as when you meet a Mexican American woman? We have stereotypes not only of men and women but also of grandfathers and grandmothers, teenage boys and teenage girls, rich men and rich women, and so on. In other words, we form subtypes or subcategories, and these are reflected in stereotypes.

Yoland Niemann and her colleagues (1994) asked a diverse group of college students to list ten adjectives that they believed best described women or men from four ethnic groups: non-Latino White, African American, Mexican American, and Asian American. As indicated in figure 12.3, people link certain characteristics with men and women from different ethnic groups. Thus, people not only may have a stereotype that represents all men or all women, they also may stereotype people on the basis of gender and ethnicity (Lott & Saxon, 2002; Matlin, 2004).

Sexism As discussed in chapter 6, negative stereotypes provide the foundation for prejudice and discrimination (Dipboye & Colella, 2005; Foster & others, 2004). **Sexism** is prejudice and discrimination against an individual because of his or her sex. A person who believes that women cannot be competent lawyers is expressing sexism; so is a person who says that men cannot be competent nursery school teachers. Prejudice and discrimination against women have a long history, and they continue.

Sexism can be obvious, as when a chemistry professor tells a female premed student that women belong in the home (Matlin, 2004). Sexism can also be more subtle, as when the word *girl* is used to refer to a mature woman. To evaluate your attitudes toward women, complete Self-Assessment 12.2.

Non-Latino white males	**Non-Latino white females**
Intelligent	Attractive
Egotistical	Intelligent
Upper-class	Egotistical

African American males	**African American females**
Athletic	Speak loudly
Antagonistic	Dark skin
Dark skin	Antagonistic

Mexican American males	**Mexican American females**
Lower-class	Black/brown/dark hair
Hard workers	Attractive
Antagonistic	Pleasant/friendly

Asian American males	**Asian American females**
Intelligent	Intelligent
Short	Speak softly
Achievement-oriented	Pleasant/friendly

FIGURE 12.3 Most Frequently Described

sexism Prejudice and discrimination against an individual because of his or her sex.

Attitudes Toward Women

Instructions

The statements listed below describe attitudes toward the role of women in society that different people have. There are no right or wrong answers, only opinions. Express your feeling about each statement by indicating whether you (A) agree strongly, (B) agree mildly, (C) disagree mildly, or (D) disagree strongly.

Items	Agree Strongly	Agree Mildly	Disagree Mildly	Disagree Strongly
1. Swearing and obscenity are more repulsive in the speech of a woman than of a man.	A	B	C	D
2. Women should take increasing responsibility for leadership in solving the intellectual and social problems of the day.	A	B	C	D
3. Both husband and wife should be allowed the same grounds for divorce.	A	B	C	D
4. Telling dirty jokes should be mostly a masculine prerogative.	A	B	C	D
5. Intoxication among women is worse than intoxication among men.	A	B	C	D
6. Under modern economic conditions with women being active outside the home, men should share in household tasks such as washing dishes and doing the laundry.	A	B	C	D
7. It is insulting to women to have the "obey" clause remain in the marriage service.	A	B	C	D
8. There should be a strict merit system in job appointment and promotion without regard to sex.	A	B	C	D
9. A woman should be as free as a man to propose marriage.	A	B	C	D
10. Women should worry less about their rights and more about becoming good wives and mothers.	A	B	C	D
11. Women earning as much as their dates should bear equally the expense when they go out together.	A	B	C	D
12. Women should assume their rightful place in business and all the professions along with men.	A	B	C	D
13. A woman should not expect to go to exactly the same places or to have quite the same freedom of action as a man.	A	B	C	D
14. Sons in a family should be given more encouragement to go to college than daughters.	A	B	C	D
15. It is ridiculous for a woman to run a locomotive and for a man to darn socks.	A	B	C	D
16. In general, the father should have greater authority than the mother in the bringing up of children.	A	B	C	D

continued

SELF-ASSESSMENT 12.2
Attitudes Toward Women

Items	Agree Strongly	Agree Mildly	Disagree Mildly	Disagree Strongly
17. Women should be encouraged not to become sexually intimate with anyone before marriage, even their fiancés.	A	B	C	D
18. The husband should not be favored by law over the wife in the disposal of family property or income.	A	B	C	D
19. Women should be concerned with their duties of childbearing and house tending, rather than with desires for professional and business careers.	A	B	C	D
20. The intellectual leadership of a community should be largely in the hands of men.	A	B	C	D
21. Economic and social freedom is worth far more to women than acceptance of the ideal of femininity that has been set up by men.	A	B	C	D
22. On the average, women should be regarded as less capable of contributing to economic production than men.	A	B	C	D
23. There are many jobs in which men should be given preference over women in being hired or promoted.	A	B	C	D
24. Women should be given equal opportunity with men for apprenticeship in the various trades.	A	B	C	D
25. The modern girl is entitled to the same freedom from regulation and control that is given to the modern boy.	A	B	C	D

Go to the appendix at the back of the book for scoring and interpretation of your responses.

Gender Similarities and Differences

What is the reality behind gender stereotypes? To what extent do they summarize real differences between men and women? Interpreting research on gender differences is difficult for several reasons. In particular,

- The differences are averages and do apply to all females or all males.
- Even when gender differences occur, there often is considerable overlap between males and females.
- The differences may be due primarily to biological factors, sociocultural factors, or both.

With these cautions in mind, let's explore some of the differences between the sexes. First, we examine physical differences, and then we turn to cognitive and socioemotional differences.

Physical Similarities and Differences We could devote pages to describing physical differences between the average man and woman. For example, women have about twice the body fat of men, most concentrated around breasts and hips. In males, fat is more likely to go to the abdomen. On the average, males grow to be 10 percent taller than females. Androgens (the "male" hormones) promote the growth of long bones; estrogens (the "female" hormones) stop such growth at puberty.

Many physical differences between men and women are tied to health. From conception on, females have a longer life expectancy than males, and females are less likely than males to develop physical or mental disorders. Females are more resistant to infection, and their blood vessels are more elastic than males'. Males have higher levels of stress hormones, which cause faster clotting and higher blood pressure.

Does gender matter when it comes to brain structure and activity? Human brains are much alike, whether the brain belongs to a male or a female (Halpern, 2001). However, researchers have found some differences (Goldstein & others, 2001; Kimura, 2000):

- One part of the hypothalamus involved in sexual behavior tends to be larger in men than women (Swaab & others, 2001).
- Portions of the corpus callosum—the band of tissues through which the brains' two hemispheres communicate—tend to be larger in females than males (Le Vay, 1991).
- An area of the parietal lobe that functions in visuospatial skills tends to be larger in males than females (Frederikse & others, 2000).
- The areas of the brain involved in emotional expression tend to show more metabolic activity in females than males (Gur & others, 1995).

Similarities and differences in the brains of males and females could be due to evolution and heredity, as well as social experiences. That is, the brain changes physically as a result of experience. Thus, even if research documents ways in which the brains of most men differ from the brains of most women, those differences might not reflect inborn differences, and they might be changeable.

Cognitive Similarities and Differences   Many years ago, after reviewing many studies, Eleanor Maccoby and Carol Jacklin (1974) concluded that males have better math and visuospatial skills (the kinds of skills an architect needs to design a building's angles and dimensions) than females whereas females have better verbal abilities than males. Subsequently, Maccoby (1987) concluded that the verbal differences between females and males had virtually disappeared but that the math and visuospatial differences persisted.

"So according to the stereotype, you can put two and two together, but I can read the handwriting on the wall."

What is the situation today? In school and on standardized tests, some differences between U.S. boys and girls persist. In a national study by the U.S. Department of Education (2000), boys did slightly better than girls at math and science. Overall, though, girls were far superior students, and they were significantly better than boys in reading. In another recent national study, females had higher reading achievement and better writing skills than males in grades 4, 8, and 12; the gap widened as students progressed through school (Coley, 2001).

Some experts in gender, such as Janet Shibley Hyde (2004; Hyde & Mezulis, 2001), argue that the cognitive differences between females and males have been exaggerated. After all, there is considerable overlap in the distributions of female and male scores on math and visuospatial tasks (see figure 12.4). Also, measures of achievement in school or scores on standardized tests may reflect many factors besides cognitive ability. They may in part reflect attempts to conform to gender roles and differences in motivation, self-regulation, or other socioemotional characteristics. For example, Joey's father may praise him for making the first team in baseball but ignore his report card.

Socioemotional Similarities and Differences Perhaps the gender differences that most fascinate people are those in how males and females relate to each other as people. For just about every imaginable socioemotional characteristic, researchers have examined whether there are differences between males and females. For example, in chapter 7, "Communicating Effectively," we described females' stronger interest in relationship talk and greater self-disclosure than males. In chapter 8, "Friendship and Love Relationships," we indicated that women have more close friends, engage in more self-disclosure, and provide more social support in friendship than males. We also concluded that men tend to think of love more in terms of passion, whereas women are more likely to emphasize its similarities to friendship. Here we examine just two gender differences that have been very closely studied: aggression and self-regulation.

One of the most consistent gender differences is that boys are more physically aggressive than girls. The difference occurs in all cultures and appears very early in children's development (White, 2001). The difference in physical aggression is especially pronounced when children are provoked. Although boys are consistently more physically aggressive than girls, might girls be just as aggressive or even more aggressive than boys in other ways? The answer appears to be yes when two other types of aggression are considered. First, when researchers examine verbal aggression, such as yelling, females are often as aggressive or even more aggressive than males (Eagly & Steffen, 1986). Second, girls are more likely than boys to engage in *relational aggression*, which involves such behaviors as spreading malicious rumors in order to get others to dislike a child or ignoring someone (Crick & others, 2001; Underwood, 2004).

Males usually show less self-regulation of emotions and behavior than females, and this low self-control can translate into behavioral problems (Eisenberg, Martin, & Fabes, 1996; Eisenberg & others, 2002). In one study, children's low self-regulation was linked with greater aggression, teasing, overreaction to frustration, low cooperation, and inability to delay gratification (Block & Block, 1980).

Interpreting Gender Differences Are psychological differences between males and females large or small? Traditionally, differences between males and females were interpreted as biologically based *deficiencies* in females. Feminists have therefore feared that research documenting gender differences will be used to promote old stereotypes that women are inferior to men (Crawford & Unger, 2004). Alice Eagly (2001) argues that this fear has biased the interpretation of research. According to Eagly, research reveals that behavior varies with gender and the differences are

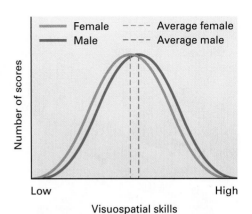

FIGURE 12.4 Visuospatial Skills of Males and Females
Notice that, although an average male's visuospatial skills are better than the average female's, scores for the two sexes almost entirely overlap. Not all males have better visuospatial skills than all females—the overlap indicates that, although the average male score is higher, many females outperform most males on such tasks.

In China, females and males are usually socialized to behave, feel, and think differently. The old patriarchal traditions of male supremacy have not been completely uprooted. Chinese women still make considerably less money than Chinese men do, and, in rural China (such as here in the Lixian Village of Sichuan) male supremacy still governs many women's lives.

socially induced. A belief that the differences are small arose from a feminist commitment to similarity between the sexes as a route to political equality, she says, and from inadequate interpretations of research. Controversy continues over whether sex differences are rare and small or common and large, in part because gender is a political issue.

Gender in Context   In thinking about gender, it is important to look at the context of behavior (Eun Jung Suh & others, 2004; MacGeorge, 2003; Ryan & David, 2003). Consider helping behavior. Males are more likely than females to help in contexts in which a perceived danger is present and they feel competent to help (Eagly & Crowley, 1986). For example, men are more likely than women to help a person who is stranded by the roadside with a flat tire; automobile problems are an area about which many males feel competent. In contrast, when the context involves volunteering time to help a child with a personal problem, women are more likely to help than men are, because there is little danger present and women feel more competent at nurturing. In many cultures, girls show more caregiving behavior than boys do. However, in the few cultures where they both care for younger siblings on a regular basis, girls and boys display similar tendencies to nurture (Whiting & Edwards, 1998).

Context is also relevant to gender differences in the display of emotions (Shields, 1991, 1998). Consider anger. Males are more likely to show anger toward strangers, especially other males, when they think they have been challenged. Males also are more likely than females to turn their anger into aggressive action, especially when the culture endorses such action (Tavris & Wade, 1984).

Of course, the culture is part of the context that influences gender differences in behavior (Nadien & Denmark, 1999). Sociocultural contexts determine what is considered to be gender appropriate and gender inappropriate in socioemotional behavior. In many cultures around the world, traditional gender roles guide the behavior of males and females. In China and Iran, for instance, it is still widely expected that males will engage in dominant behavior and females will act in subordinate ways. Many Western cultures, such as the United States, have become more flexible about gender behavior. One recent study found that societal changes are leading females to have more instrumental traits (Spence & Buckner, 2000).

Today, controversy swirls around the question of what roles are appropriate for women and men. The turmoil offers opportunity for both genders (Bronstein & Quina, 2003; Matlin, 2004). A girl's mother might promote femininity, the girl might be close friends with a tomboy, and the girls' teachers at school might encourage her assertiveness. Boys might experience fewer restrictions in the goals they set for themselves. For example, Wall Street star Peter Lynch, who headed Fidelity Investment's leading mutual fund, resigned to have more time with his family and pursue humanitarian projects. As you might guess, some people are not pleased with the expanded opportunities for women, because they believe this expansion requires undesirable and unwarranted sacrifices by men.

Masculinity, Femininity, and Androgyny

androgyny The presence of a high degree of feminine and masculine characteristics in the same individual.

In the 1970s, as both males and females became dissatisfied with the burdens imposed by their stereotyped roles, alternatives to "masculinity" and "femininity" were explored. Instead of thinking of masculinity and femininity as a continuum, with more of one meaning less of the other, it was proposed that individuals could show both expressive and instrumental traits. This thinking led to the development of the concept of **androgyny,** the presence of a high degree of masculine and feminine

The following items are from the Bem Sex-Role Inventory, (BSRI). When taking the BSRI, a person is asked to indicate on a 7-point scale how well each of the 60 characteristics describes herself or himself. The scale ranges from 1 (never or almost never true) to 7 (always or almost always true).

Examples of masculine items	Examples of feminine items
Defends open beliefs	Does not use harsh language
Forceful	Affectionate
Willing to take risks	Loves children
Dominant	Understanding
Aggressive	Gentle

Scoring: The items are scored on independent dimensions of masculinity and femininity as well as androgyny and undifferentiate classifications.

characteristics in the same individual (Bem, 1977; Spence & Helmreich, 1978). The androgynous individual might be a male who is assertive (masculine) and sensitive to others' feelings (feminine), or a female who is dominant (masculine) and caring (feminine).

Measures have been developed to assess androgyny. One of the most widely used measures, the *Bem Sex-Role Inventory,* was constructed by a leading proponent of androgyny, Sandra Bem (1974). Based on their responses to items in the Bem Sex-Role Inventory, individuals are classified as having one of four gender-role orientations: masculine, feminine, androgynous, or undifferentiated (see figure 12.5):

- The androgynous individual is a female or a male who has a high degree of both feminine (expressive) and masculine (instrumental) traits.
- A feminine individual is high on feminine (expressive) traits and low on masculine (instrumental) traits.
- A masculine individual is high on instrumental traits and low on expressive traits.
- An undifferentiated person is low on both feminine and masculine traits.

To determine your gender-role classification, complete Self-Assessment 12.3.

Androgynous women and men, according to Bem, are more flexible and more mentally healthy than either masculine or feminine individuals; undifferentiated individuals are the least competent. In support of Bem's view, one recent study found that androgynous individuals were more emotionally intelligent than masculine or feminine individuals (Guastello & Guastello, 2003). To some degree, though, *context* influences which gender role is most adaptive. For example, in close relationships, a feminine or androgynous gender role may be more desirable than a masculine orientation because of the expressive nature of close relationships. However, a masculine or androgynous gender role may be more desirable in work settings because they demand action and assertiveness.

Some critics of androgyny say enough is enough: there is too much talk about gender, and it encourages stereotyping. They advocate **gender-role transcendence,** which means thinking about ourselves and others as people, not as masculine, feminine, or androgynous (Pleck, 1983). Parents should rear their children to be competent individuals, not masculine, feminine, or androgynous, say the gender-role critics.

Even if you believe that gender-role transcendence is desirable, is it a realistic alternative? In the next section, we examine how our lives today are still influenced by gender roles.

www.mhhe.com/santrockha

Androgyny

gender-role transcendence Thinking about ourselves and others as people, not as masculine, feminine, or androgynous.

SELF-ASSESSMENT 12.3

My Gender-Role Classification

The items below inquire about what kind of person you think you are. Place a check mark in the column that best describes you for each item: 1 = Not like me at all, 2 = Somewhat unlike me, 3 = Somewhat like me, and 4 = Very much like me.

ITEM	1	2	3	4
1. I'm independent.	___	___	___	___
2. My emotional life is important to me.	___	___	___	___
3. I provide social support to others.	___	___	___	___
4. I'm competitive.	___	___	___	___
5. I'm a kind person.	___	___	___	___
6. I'm sensitive to others' feelings.	___	___	___	___
7. I'm self-confident.	___	___	___	___
8. I'm self-reflective.	___	___	___	___
9. I'm patient.	___	___	___	___
10. I'm self-assertive.	___	___	___	___
11. I'm aggressive.	___	___	___	___
12. I'm willing to take risks.	___	___	___	___
13. I like to tell secrets to my friends.	___	___	___	___
14. I like to feel powerful.	___	___	___	___

Go to the appendix at the end of the book for scoring and interpretation of your responses.

Review and Reflect

2 **Discuss gender comparisons and classifications**

REVIEW

- What is gender stereotyping and how extensive is it?
- What are some physical, cognitive, and socioemotional differences in gender?
- What are some alternatives to classifying behavior and traits as masculine or feminine?

REFLECT

- Several decades ago, the word *dependency* was used to describe the relational orientation of femininity. Dependency took on a negative connotation for females—for instance, that females can't take care of themselves while males can. Today, the term *dependency* is being replaced by the term *relational abilities*, which has more positive connotations (Caplan & Caplan, 1999). Rather than being thought of as dependent, women are now more often described as skilled in forming and maintaining relationships. Make up a list of words that you associate with masculinity and femininity. Do these words have any negative connotations for males and females? For the words that do have negative connotations, are there words that could replace them?

3 WOMEN'S AND MEN'S LIVES

Women's Lives	Men's Lives

In the world of Tita, described at the opening of this chapter, the influence of gender and culture were impossible to ignore. As women's equality has become an accepted ideal in Western cultures, the influence of gender is less obvious, but it is still far-reaching. How do gender stereotypes and gender roles shape the lives of men and women today, and what adjustment challenges are likely to be faced because women are women and because men are men?

Women's Lives

There are many indications that traditional gender roles have eroded and that women have won new opportunities. But conflicting currents shape women's lives. For example, as we described in chapter 10, "Achievement, Careers, and Work," many women sill find themselves confronted by invisible ceilings that limit access to the most powerful positions. At the same time, women who choose traditional roles sometimes are criticized by other women for "selling out." Furthermore, the roles and positions of women vary greatly from one country to another and even within the United States. Let's examine some of these variations, as well as some of the particular stressors facing many women.

Women's Status Around the World In much of the world, people's lives are governed by traditional gender roles that assign a subordinate status to women. This status creates troubling political, economic, educational, and psychological and social conditions for women in many countries (Culbertson, 1991; UNESCO, 2004; UNICEF, 2004). Let's examine these conditions.

Politics In politics, too often women are treated as burdens rather than assets. Especially in developing countries, women marry early and quickly have many children. These women have little access to education, work, health care, and family planning. Women would likely have a better chance of their needs being met if they were more strongly represented at the decision-making and managerial levels of governments and international organizations. Although most countries in the world now grant to both women and men the right to vote and be elected, women continue to experience difficulties in exercising this right. In 2003, globally the proportion of seats held by women in national governments stood at 15 percent, an increase of only 2 percent since 1990 (UNESCO, 2004).

Work Women's work around the world is more limiting and narrow than men's. Domestic workers in North, Central, and South America are mainly women. Around the world, jobs defined as women's work are more likely to have low pay, low status, and little security compared with jobs defined as men's work.

Education Canada, the United States, and Russia have the highest percentages of educated women. The countries with the fewest women being educated are in Africa, where in some areas women are given no education at all. In sub-Saharan Africa, the ratio of girls' to boys' enrollments in elementary and secondary school has barely changed since 1990 and recently stood at only 82 percent (UNESCO, 2004).

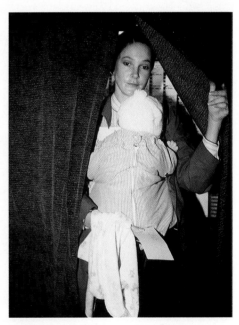

Around the world women too often are treated as burdens rather than assets in the political process. Few women have leadership positions in government. Some experts on women's issues believe that if women are to gain more access to work, education, health care, and family planning, they need to be more strongly represented at the decision-making and managerial levels of government and business.

Ethnic Minority Women in the United States What about conditions for women in the United States? The picture varies with ethnicity. Women from other ethnic minority groups have experienced the double jeopardy of racism and sexism. In addition, women from ethnic minority groups may be especially likely to find themselves caught in a conflict about gender roles (Shorter-Gooden, 2004).

For example, for Asian American women, the attitudes toward gender roles found in the mainstream culture clash with the traditions of their ancestors (Chun & Akutsa, 2003). Asian females are often expected to carry out domestic duties, to marry, to become obedient helpers of their mothers-in-law, and to bear children, especially sons (Nishio & Bilmes, 1993). In China, the mother's responsibility for the emotional nurturance and well-being of the family, and for raising children, derives from Confucian ethics (Huang & Ying, 1989). However, as China has become modernized, these roles have become less rigid. Similarly, in acculturated Chinese families in the United States, only derivatives of these rigidly defined roles remain. For example, Chinese American females are not entirely relegated to subservient roles. Author Amy Tan, in works like *The Joy Luck Club* (1989), has eloquently described how Chinese Americans manage bicultural gender expectations, as has Maxine Hong Kingston, whose life and work you read about at the opening of chapter 3, "The Self, Identity, and Values."

What are some themes in the lives of women from different ethnic groups?

The role of spirituality is central to many ethnic minority women's coping. For example, the church has played a key role in the life of African American families. Researchers have shown that African American women take a more pensive approach to problems than non-Latino White women by pondering their options before taking action, praying, or biding their time by waiting patiently for alternatives to develop (Graham-Bermann & others, 2001).

In traditional Mexican families, women assume the expressive role of homemaker and caretaker of children. This continues to be the norm, although less so than in the past (Comas-Díaz, 2001; Denner & Dunbar, 2004; Leong, 1996). Historically, the Mexican female's role has been one of self-denial. Her needs were subordinated to those of other family members. Joint decision making and greater equality of males' and females' roles are becoming more characteristic of Mexican American families. Of special significance is the increased frequency of Mexican American women's employment outside the home, which in many instances has enhanced a wife's status in the family and in decision making (Marin & Gamba, 2003). Recall our description of Anna Bolado de Espino in the opening of chapter 6, "Social Thinking, Influence, and Intergroup Relations," who juggled caring for her children, work, and going to college, and eventually gained entrance to medical school. However, in one recent study of Latino college students, females reported that they had far less access to privileges than males (Raffaelli & Ontai, 2004).

For Native Americans, roles and family configurations involving women and men depend on the tribe (LaFromboise, 1993). For example, in the traditional matriarchal Navajo family, an older woman might live with her husband, her unmarried children, her married daughter, and the daughter's husband and children. In patriarchal tribes, women function as the central "core" of the family, maintaining primary responsibility for the welfare of children. Grandmothers and aunts often provide child care. As with other ethnic minority females, Native American females who have moved to urban areas experience the cultural conflict of traditional ethnic values and the values of mainstream American society (LaFromboise & Trimble, 1996).

Psychological Health   Whatever their ethnicity, U.S. women face some special stressors because they are women. Far too many women are victims of domestic violence (examined in chapter 8) or of rape (to be discussed in chapter 13). A number of studies have shown that women who experience frequent sexism have more symptoms of depression, anxiety, and body complaints than men in similar circumstances or than women who have not experienced sexism (Graham-Bermann & others, 2001).

Also, gender differences continue to exist in work roles (Apparala, Reifman, & Munsch, 2003; Bridges, Etaugh, & Barnes-Farrell, 2002). Although men have increased their responsibility in family roles, women overall still bear the largest share of the burden for housework and child care and for maintaining the social and emotional health of their families. Researchers have found that women rate their family roles to be more stressful than men do (Graham-Bermann & others, 2001).

The quest for beauty may be the root of other stressors. Beginning in elementary school, girls are more dissatisfied with their weight and shape than boys are (Smolak & Striegel-Moore, 2001). Body dissatisfaction increases among girls as they move into adolescence and early adulthood, and this gender difference continues through the adult years (Forbes & others, 2004; Polivy & others, 2003). Further, the size of this gender difference seems to have increased in the last 30 years (Smolak & Striegel-Moore, 2001).

This dissatisfaction with their bodies may contribute to many problems among women. Dissatisfaction with their bodies translates into dieting and other weight-control practices among girls and women and into cosmetic surgery, which women are far more likely to undergo than men (Evans, 2003; Gapinski, Brownell, & LaFrance, 2003; Gorney, 2002). Results vary as to whether cosmetic surgery substantially affects a woman's satisfaction with her body (Figueroa, 2003; Sarwer, Crerand, & Didie, 2003). More seriously, body dissatisfaction is related to such eating disorders as anorexia nervosa and bulimia nervosa, which we will discuss in chapter 16, "Health" (Presnell & Stice, 2003). There also is a link between body dissatisfaction and depression in adolescent girls (Stice & Whitenton, 2002).

In fact, the frequency of many mental disorders varies with gender. In general, women are more likely to be diagnosed with mood and anxiety disorders (Nolen-Hoeksema, 2004).

Women's Studies Resources
Women's Issues
Wellesley Centers for Women
Psychology of Women
National Organization of Women

Coping with Stress   What strategies do women use to cope with stress? Many studies have shown that women's but not men's physical problems following stress are reduced when they receive social support (Rook, 2001). And women tend to engage in nurturing and protective behaviors that seek alliances with others when faced with stressful situations (Taylor, 2003).

Gender differences also have been identified in how men and women exposed to the same everyday stressful events perceive or evaluate those events (Graham-Bermann & others, 2001). For example, women are more likely to think about or to ruminate over stressful events than men (Nolen-Hoeksema, 2004). In studies of women who have been physically abused, some women report deciding to bide their time or to wait to do something until they have acquired enough resources to move out (Graham-Bermann & Edleson, 2001).

Conclusions   Is there a theme behind the strengths and stressors of women's lives? Jean Baker Miller (1986) concluded that when researchers examine what women have been doing in their lives, a large part of it is active participation in the development of other people. In Miller's view, women often try to interact with others in ways that will foster the other person's development—emotionally, intellectually, and socially. These efforts bring gains to the women themselves, to those they help, and to society at large—but they also bring special vulnerabilities to women. A focus on other

Gender and Diversity

people may help women develop their relationship skills but also leave them dependent on others to maintain their self-esteem.

Most experts believe it is important for women to maintain their competency in relationships but also to be self-motivated (Donelson, 1998). In other words, women benefit from helping others and engaging in behavior that benefits their own well-being. Miller believes that by coupling their relationship skills with increased self-determination, women will gain greater power in American culture. And as Harriet Lerner (1989) concluded in her book *The Dance of Intimacy,* it is important for women to bring to their relationships a strong, assertive, independent, and authentic self. She believes competent relationships are those in which the separate "I-ness" of both persons can be appreciated and enhanced while still staying emotionally connected to each other.

Adjustment Strategies
For Women

Adjustment strategies for women include:

1. ***Recognize your competencies.*** Women are certainly not inferior to men. In evaluating your competencies, be sure to include important female competencies, such as relationship skills.
2. ***Pay attention to developing your self as well as your relationships.*** Competent women can stay connected to others while improving themselves. Harriet Lerner (1989) calls this developing your "I-ness" (self) and "You-ness" (relationships with others). Focus on becoming more aware of your own needs and how to meet them. Go beyond the idea that this is selfish. Be more self-assertive.
3. ***Don't put up with sexism.*** Sexist remarks and behavior that insult and degrade women should not tolerated. If this happens at your college, report it to your college's administration.

What are some themes in lives of males in different ethnic groups in the United States?

Men's Lives

The male of the species—what is he really like? What are his concerns? For men, as well as for women, the answer varies to some extent with ethnicity (Guttman & Viveros, 2004).

Ethnic Minority Males Just as ethnic minority females have experienced considerable discrimination and have had to develop coping strategies in the face of adversity, so have ethnic minority males (Jones, 2002; Matsumoto, 2004). As with ethnic minority females, our order of discussion focuses on African American males, Asian American males, Latino males, and Native American males.

Statistics indicate the difficulties many African American males have faced (National Center for Health Statistics, 2003). African American males of all ages are three times as likely as non-Latino White males to live in poverty. Of males aged 20 to 44, African Americans are twice as likely to die as non-Latino Whites. African American male heads of households earn 70 percent of the income of their non-Latino White male counterparts. Although they make up only 6.3 percent of the U.S. population, African American males constitute 42 percent of jail inmates and more than 50 percent of men executed for any reason in the last 50 years.

Asian cultural values are reflected in traditional patriarchal Chinese and Japanese families (Sue & Sue, 1993). The father's behavior in relation to other family members is generally dignified, authoritative, remote, and aloof. Sons are generally valued over daughters. Firstborn sons have an especially high status. As with Asian American females, the acculturation experienced by Asian American males has eroded some of the rigid gender roles that characterized Asian families in the past. Fathers still are often the figurative heads of families, especially when dealing with the public, but in private they have relinquished some of their decision-making powers to their wives.

In Mexican families, men traditionally assume the instrumental role of provider and protector of the family (Marin & Gamba, 2003). The concept of machismo continues to influence the role of the male and the patriarchal orientation of Mexican families, though less than in the past. Traditionally, this orientation required men to be forceful and strong, and also to withhold affectionate emotions. Ideally, it involved a strong sense of personal honor, family, loyalty, and care for children. However, it also has involved exaggerated masculinity and aggression. The concepts of machismo and absolute patriarchy are currently diminishing in influence, but adolescent males are still given much more freedom than adolescent females in Mexican American families.

Some Native American tribes are also patriarchal, with the male being the head of the family and primary decision maker. In some tribes, though, child care is shared by men. For example, Mescalero Apache men take responsibility for children when not working away from the family. Autonomy is highly valued among the male children in many Native American tribes, with the males operating semi-independently at an early age. As with Native American females, increased movement to urban areas has led to modifications in the values and traditions of some Native American males.

Men's Resources
Men and Masculinity
National Organization of Men

Role Strain   Although traditional gender roles give men significant power and freedom, they bring some disadvantages as well (Smiler, 2004). For example, men's groups have complained that because of gender stereotypes, men are far less likely than women to be granted custody of their children. And men report being stressed by the expectation that they should make most of the money for the family, which translates into longer work hours and less time spent with children.

How are boys and men adjusting to the increased flexibility of gender roles in the United States? Some observers believe that conflict and confusion characterize the current situation. The old rules for males—for example, be self-reliant, dominant, and assertive—have not disappeared, but they are contradicted by new rules—such as to show affection and other emotions, to be cooperative, and to accept the equality of women.

In fact, William Pollack (1999) says that the way boys are being brought up is a "national crisis of boyhood." Pollack says that little has been done to change what he calls the "boy code." Boy code tells boys they should not show their feelings and act tough, says Pollack. Boys learn the boy code in many contexts—sandboxes, playgrounds, schoolrooms, camps, hangouts—and are taught the code by parents, peers, coaches, teachers, and other adults. Pollack, as well as many others, believes that boys would benefit from being socialized to express their anxieties and concerns and to better regulate their aggression.

Meanwhile, according to Joseph Pleck (1983, 1995), men face *role strain* because male roles are contradictory and inconsistent. Men not only experience stress when they violate traditional male roles, they also are harmed when they act in accord with those roles (Levant, 2001). Some of the areas in which men's roles can cause

Tom Cruise (*left*) played Jerry Maguire in the movie *Jerry Maguire* with 6-year-old Ray, son of Jerry's love interest. The image of nurturing and nurtured males was woven throughout the movie. Jerry's relationship with Ray was a significant theme in the movie. It is through the caring relationship with Ray that Jerry makes his first genuine movement toward emotional maturity. The boy is guide to the man (Shields, 1998) Many experts on gender believe that men and boys would benefit from engaging in more nurturant behaviors.

considerable strain follow (Brooks, 2003; Levant & Brooks, 1997; Levant & Habben, 2003; Petersen, 2003):

- *Health.* Men's life expectancy is eight to ten years less than women's. Men have higher rates of stress-related disorders, alcoholism, car accidents, and suicide. Men are more likely than women to be the victims of homicide. Men are less likely than women to seek health care. In sum, the male role is hazardous to men's health (McCreary, 2003).
- *Male-female relationships.* Too often, the male's role involves expectations that men should be dominant, powerful, and aggressive, should control women, should think of women in terms of their bodies rather than their minds and feelings, and should not consider them equal to men. Too often these dimensions of the male role have produced men who have disparaged women, been violent toward women, and been unwilling to have equal relationships with women (Thomas, 2003).
- *Male-male relationships.* Too many men have had too little interaction with their fathers, especially fathers who are positive role models. Nurturing and being sensitive to others have been considered aspects of the female role, and not the male role. And the male role emphasizes competition rather than cooperation. All of these aspects of the male role have left men with inadequate positive emotional connections with other males.

Adjustment Strategies
For Men

Following are some adjustment strategies for men:

1. ***Understand yourself and your emotions.*** Explore yourself. Ask yourself what kind of person you want to be and think more about how you want others to perceive you. If you are aggressive and hostile, tone down your anger. Be self-assertive but not overly aggressive.
2. ***Improve your social relationships.*** Pay attention to your close relationships with friends, a partner, and family. Give more consideration to the feelings of others. Make relationships a higher priority in your life.
3. ***Lower your health risks.*** Engage in less-risky behaviors that can undermine your health.

Review and Reflect

3   Characterize women's and men's lives

REVIEW

- What are some key characteristics of women's lives?
- What are some key characteristics of men's lives?

REFLECT

- Examine the strategies described for improving women's and men's lives. What other recommendations would you make in this regard?

Reach Your Learning Goals

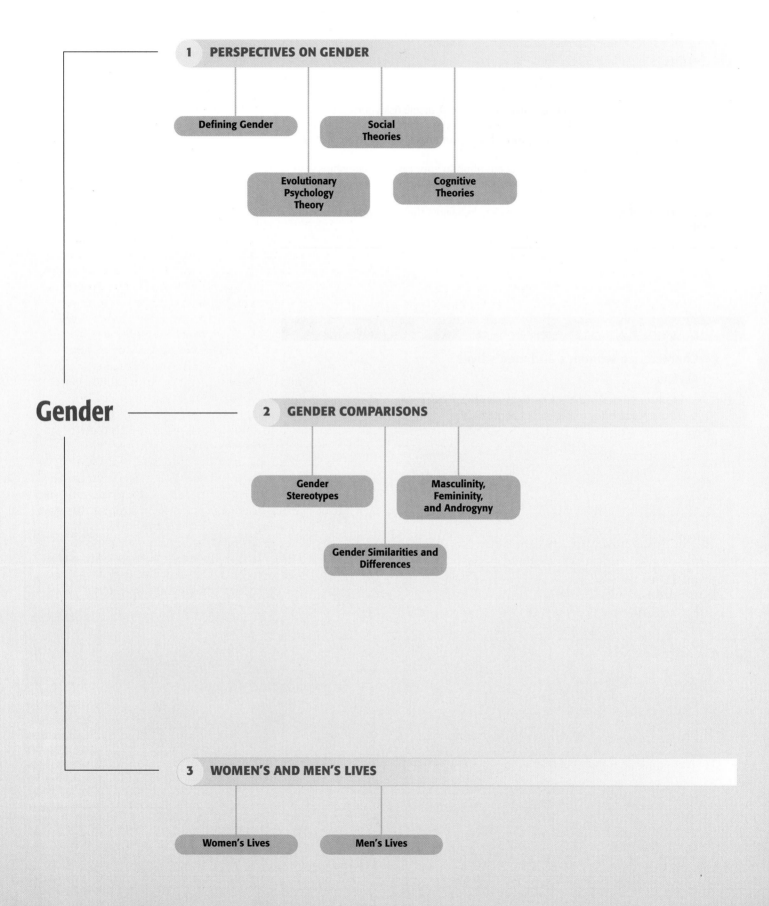

Gender

1 PERSPECTIVES ON GENDER

- Defining Gender
- Social Theories
- Evolutionary Psychology Theory
- Cognitive Theories

2 GENDER COMPARISONS

- Gender Stereotypes
- Masculinity, Femininity, and Androgyny
- Gender Similarities and Differences

3 WOMEN'S AND MEN'S LIVES

- Women's Lives
- Men's Lives

Summary

1   *Define gender and explain evolutionary, social, and cognitive theories of gender*

- Gender refers to the psychological and social aspects of being female or male. Gender roles are sets of expectations that prescribe how females and males should act, feel, and think.
- Evolutionary psychology argues that adaptation during the evolution of humans produced psychological differences between males and females. Evolutionary psychologists assert that primarily because of their differing roles in reproduction, males and females faced different evolutionary pressures as they were evolving.
- Three theories have been influential in arguing that psychological differences in gender are due to social factors. Social role theory states that gender differences result from the contrasting roles of women and men. The psychoanalytic theory of gender stems from Freud's view that the preschool child develops a sexual attraction to the opposite-sex parent. The social cognitive theory of gender states that children learn about gender through observation, imitation, reward, and punishment.
- Two cognitive theories stress that individuals cognitively construct their gender world. The cognitive developmental theory of gender states that children's gender typing occurs *after* they think of themselves as boys and girls. Gender schema theory states that gender typing emerges as children gradually develop gender schemas of what is gender appropriate and inappropriate in their culture.

2   *Discuss gender comparisons and classifications*

- Gender stereotypes are general impressions and beliefs about males and females. Gender stereotypes are widespread.
- There are many physical differences between males and females (including those involving strength and the brain), small or nonexistent cognitive differences, and some socioemotional differences. For example, males are more physically aggressive and active, but engage in less self-regulation; females show a stronger interest in relationships. Gender differences in behavior depend in part on the context.
- Androgyny is the presence of a high degree of masculine and feminine characteristics in the same individual. Gender-role transcendence is an alternative.

3   *Characterize women's and men's lives*

- Around the world, many women face political, economic, and educational inequalities due to their gender. Ethnic minority females experience the double jeopardy of racism and sexism. Women especially show a strong interest in the development of other people. Women tend to engage in nurturing and protective behaviors and seek alliances with others when faced with stressful situations. Women are also more likely than men to think about or ruminate over stressful events than men. Both Jean Baker Miller and Harriet Lerner believe women need to develop both their self and their relationships. Adjustment strategies for women include recognizing their competencies, paying attention to developing their self as well as their relationships, and not putting up with sexism.
- Just as ethnic minority females have experienced discrimination and had to develop coping strategies in the face of adversity, so have many ethnic minority males. Joseph Pleck's role-strain view suggests that male roles are contradictory and inconsistent. Among the areas where men's roles can cause strain are health, male-female relationships, and male-male relationships. Adjustment strategies for men include understanding one's self and emotions, improving social relationships, and lowering health risks.

Key Terms

gender 367
gender roles 367
evolutionary psychology
   theory 368
social role theory 369

psychoanalytic theory of
   gender 369
social cognitive theory of
   gender 369

cognitive developmental
   theory of gender 370
gender schema theory 370
gender stereotypes 372

sexism 373
androgyny 378
gender-role
   transcendence 379

Resources for Improving Your Adjustment

SELF-HELP BOOKS

The Mismeasure of Woman

(1992) by Carol Tavris. New York: Touchstone.

The Mismeasure of Woman explores the stereotyping of women and similarities and differences between women and men. Tavris believes that no matter how hard women try, they can't measure up. They are criticized for being too female or not female enough, but they are always judged and mismeasured by how well they fit into a male world. *The Mismeasure of Woman* contains a thorough review of research studies that document how women are ignored, misrepresented, and even harmed by the still-male-dominated health professions. *The Mismeasure of Woman* received 4 stars in the national study of self-help books (Norcross, Santrock, & others, 2003).

The New Male

(1990) by Herb Goldberg. New York: Signet.

This book is subtitled *From Macho to Sensitive but Still Male.* Goldberg's purpose in writing *The New Male* was to explore what the world of the traditional male has been like in the past, including his relationship with females; what the male's world is like in today's era of changing gender roles; and what the future could hold for males if they examine, reshape, and expand their gender-role behavior and self-awareness. Goldberg argues that the way the traditional male role has been defined has made it virtually impossible for males to explore their inner selves, examine their feelings, and show sensitivity toward others.

NATIONAL SUPPORT GROUPS

National Organization for Women (NOW)

http://www.now.org/
NOW's website has information about many different aspects
   of women's lives. NOW has chapters in almost all states
   and you can find out about these chapters on the
   organization's website.

The National Center for Men

P.O. Box 555
Old Bethpage, NY 11804
516-942-2020
e-mail: menscenter@aol.com
Provides nationwide phone counseling on men's issues.

National Organization of Men

30 Vesey Street Room 1400
New York, NY 10007
212-766-4030
http://www.tnom.com
Information for men seeking equal rights divorce and issues
   related to custody.

 **E-Learning Tools**

To help you master the material in this chapter, you will find a number of valuable study tools on the student CD-ROM and the Online Learning Center.

SELF-ASSESSMENT

In Text

You can complete these self-assessments in the text:
- Self-Assessment 12.1: *My Beliefs About Gender Equality*
- Self-Assessment 12.2: *Attitudes Toward Women*
- Self-Assessment 12.3: *My Gender-Role Classification*

Additional Self-Assessments

Complete these self-assessments on the Online Learning Center: *Evaluating My Gender Bias*

THINK CRITICALLY

To practice your critical thinking skills, complete these exercises on the Online Learning Center:
- *Gender Roles and the Future* encourages you to reflect on what gender roles will be like in the future.
- *Rethinking the Words We Use in Gender Worlds* explores whether there might be bias in the words used to describe females and males.
- *Gender Inequality and Imbalance* guides you through a number of circumstances and asks you to think about how women and men might experience the world differently.

APPLY YOUR KNOWLEDGE

1. Developing gender roles.

Most children grow up learning the traditional fairy tales of the culture. Although not all children's stories are limited to the traditional, most children learn about Cinderella, Hansel and Gretel, Rumplestiltskin, Snow White, Sleeping Beauty, and Jack-in-the-Beanstalk. Review these stories. How are the women presented? How are the men presented? What is the "moral" of these stories?

Animated films are another source of children's socialization. List the characters in recent children's films (e.g., *The Lion King, Aladdin, The Little Mermaid*, etc.). How many of the characters are male and how many are female? Who is most involved in the film's activities? Which gender gets more total screen time? What are the characteristics of these films with which children identify? What messages do these films send to young children?

2. Watch your language!

According to many psychologists, the words we use influence the way we think about ourselves and others. People routinely refer to adult females as "girls" but the term "boys" is rarely used when referring to adult males. People are often unaware of the words they use and frequently deny that they have a significant psychological impact. Begin by going to a search engine such as www.yahoo.com or www.google.com and search for "sexism in language." Once you have reviewed examples of sexist language and remedies for sexist language, search for examples of sexist language in books and magazines and on radio and TV. You might also listen to other people speaking. When you have found 10 quotes, rewrite them using grammatically correct and nonsexist language.

3. Gender roles and health care.

Your textbook states that men are less likely to seek health care than women. This is one of the ways that gender roles hurt men. Interview five men of different ages and ask them to answer 10 questions on health care from strongly disagree to strongly agree (5-point scale). Items may include such things as "I go to the doctor when I have health symptoms that worry me" or "I go for yearly health checkups," etc. When you are finished, ask the men "why not" for items that suggest low levels of health-seeking behavior. If you wish to include some items for specific diseases (e.g., prostate or testicular cancer) you may find some ideas by searching www.yahoo.com or www.google.com for "men's health."

When you have collected your information, it can be pooled with other students in a class discussion about why men are less likely to seek out health care and what might be done to change counterproductive attitudes.

VIDEO SEGMENT

One interesting difference between males and females occurs in the selection of mates. Across many cultures, researchers have found that men and women emphasize different characteristics when they select a romantic partner. Why? The explanations offered by evolutionary psychology and social role theory are described in the video for Chapter 12 on the CD-ROM.

Sexuality

Learning Goals

1 Describe the key factors that influence sexual motivation and behavior

2 Discuss the relation between sexuality and adjustment

3 Explain aspects of sexuality that can be harmful

Images of Adjustment

Variations in Sexual Behavior: Magic Johnson and Alberto

Magic Johnson

Alberto with his girlfriend

In 1991, Los Angeles Laker basketball star Magic Johnson announced that he had tested positive for HIV, the virus that causes AIDS, and was retiring from professional basketball. He learned that he had HIV after a routine blood test and his forthright disclosure was viewed as a turning point in AIDS awareness. He was the first major celebrity to contract HIV through heterosexual sex. Johnson admitted that he had led a promiscuous and careless lifestyle and urged others to learn from his mistakes.

Johnson said that he planned to use his celebrity status to educate people about HIV and AIDS and looked forward to a long life. Since then Johnson has built a successful business that opens movie theaters in low-income inner-city areas, runs the nonprofit Magic Johnson Foundation to help inner cities, and has raised millions of dollars for AIDS research and prevention. Contracting HIV was once viewed as tantamount to a death sentence, but Johnson has remained healthy through the use of new HIV treatments and vigorous exercise.

Magic Johnson's case is at least as exceptional as his basketball skills. Most people around the world who contract HIV do not receive effective drugs, and most die a terrible, painful death within years. Johnson's sexual history is also unusual: most American males are not as promiscuous.

Consider Aberto, a 16-year-old from the Bronx. Alberto's maternal grandmother was a heroin addict who died of cancer at age 40. His father, who was only 17 when Alberto was born, had been in prison most of Alberto's life. His mother and stepfather are not married but have lived together for a dozen years and have four other children. Alberto's stepbrother dropped out of school when he was 17, fathered a child, and is now unemployed. But Alberto has different plans for his own future. He wants to be a dentist, he said, "like the kind of woman who fixed his teeth at Bronx-Lebanon Hospital Center clinic when he was a child" (Bernstein, 2004, p. A22). And Alberto, along with his girlfriend, Jasmine, wants to remain a virgin until he is married.

The contrasting sexual choices made by Magic and Alberto offer a sampling of the extensive variations in sexual behavior. To give a full explanation of these sexual variations we need to understand not only the characteristics of the individuals involved but also their social contexts. In this chapter, we explore some of the key factors that influence sexual motivation and behavior, major issues involved in sexual adjustment, and ways in which people can be harmed by sexual behaviors.

1 SEXUAL MOTIVATION AND BEHAVIOR

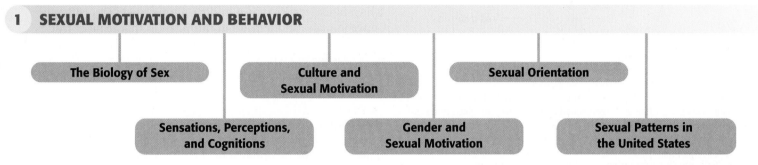

The Biology of Sex

Culture and Sexual Motivation

Sexual Orientation

Sensations, Perceptions, and Cognitions

Gender and Sexual Motivation

Sexual Patterns in the United States

What is it about people and their partners that motivates them to have sex? Their biology, their cognitions, and their culture are all part of the answer.

The Biology of Sex

What actually happens to our bodies during sexual activity? To answer this question, gynecologist William Masters and his colleague Virginia Johnson (1966) carefully observed and measured the physiological responses of 382 female and 312 male volunteers as they masturbated or had sexual intercourse. The **human sexual response pattern** consists of four phases—excitement, plateau, orgasm, and resolution—as identified by Masters and Johnson (see figure 13.1).

The *excitement phase* begins erotic responsiveness; it lasts from several minutes to several hours depending on the nature of the sex play involved. Engorgement of blood vessels and increased blood flow in genital areas and muscle tension characterize the excitement phase. The most obvious signs of response in this phase are lubrication of the vagina and partial erection of the penis.

The second phase of the human sexual response, called the *plateau phase*, is a continuation and heightening of the arousal begun in the excitement phase. The increases in breathing, pulse rate, and blood pressure that occurred during the excitement phase become more intense, penile erection and vaginal lubrication are more complete, and orgasm is closer.

The third phase of the human sexual response cycle is *orgasm*. How long does orgasm last? Some individuals sense that time is standing still when it takes place, but

human sexual response pattern Masters and Johnson developed this concept to describe four phases of physiological responses as individuals masturbated or had sexual intercourse: excitement, plateau, orgasm, and resolution.

FIGURE 13.1 Male and Female Sexual Response Patterns Identified by Masters and Johnson

(*a*) The excitement, plateau, orgasm, and resolution phases of the human male sexual response pattern. Notice that males enter a refractory period, which lasts from several minutes up to a day, in which they cannot have another orgasm. (*b*) The excitement, plateau, orgasm, and resolution phases of the human female sexual response pattern. Notice that female sexual responses follow one of three basic patterns: Pattern A somewhat resembles the male pattern, except it includes the possibility of multiple orgasm (the second peak in pattern A) without falling below the plateau level. Pattern B represents nonorgasmic arousal. Pattern C represents intense female orgasm, which resembles the male pattern in its intensity and rapid resolution.

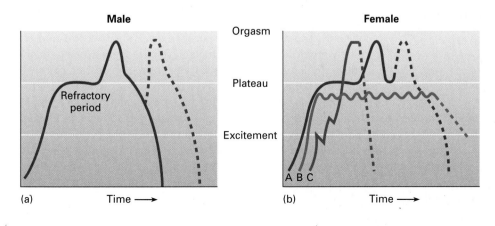

Male

Female

Orgasm

Plateau

Excitement

Refractory period

A B C

(a) Time ⟶

(b) Time ⟶

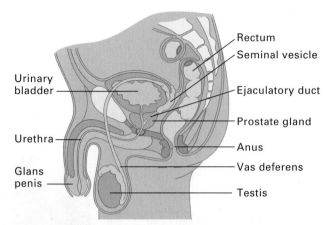

FIGURE 13.2 Male Reproductive Organs
The testes are the male gonads that produce sperm cells and manufacture the male androgen called testosterone. The glans penis is the head of the penis. The vas deferens is the duct through which stored sperm is passed. It is the vas deferens that is cut or blocked in a vasectomy. The seminal vesicles are the two sacs of the male internal genitalia, which secret nutrients to help sperm become motile. The prostate gland is a structure of the internal male genitalia that secretes a fluid into the semen prior to ejaculation to aid sperm motility and elongate sperm life. The urethra is the tube through which the bladder empties urine outside the body and through which the male sperm exits.

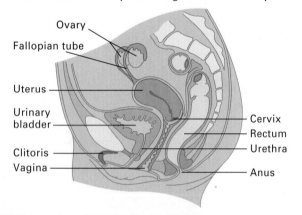

FIGURE 13.3 Female Reproductive Organs
The uterus is a pear-shaped, hollow structure of the female genitalia, in which the embryo and fetus develop prior to birth. The thick, muscular wall of the uterus expands and contracts during pregnancy. The cervix is the mouth of the uterus, through which the vagina extends. The vagina is the hollow, tunneled structure of the female internal genitalia; its reproductive functions are to receive the penis and its ejaculate, to be a route of exit for the newborn, and to provide an exit for menstrual flow. The clitoris is a part of the female genitalia that is very sensitive to stimulation. The ovaries, adjacent to both sides of the uterus, house ova prior to their maturation and discharge; they also produce estrogen. The fallopian tubes are the routes through which eggs leave the ovaries on their way to the uterus. Fertilization usually takes place in the fallopian tubes.

estrogens The class of hormones that predominate in females and are produced by the ovaries.

androgens The class of hormones that predominate in males and are produced by the testes in males and by the adrenal glands in both males and females.

orgasm lasts for only about 3 to 15 seconds. Orgasm involves an explosive discharge of neuromuscular tension and an intense pleasurable feeling. However, orgasms are not all alike. For example, females show three different patterns in the orgasm phase: multiple orgasms; no orgasm; and excitement rapidly leading to orgasm, bypassing the plateau phase (this pattern most clearly corresponds to the male pattern in intensity and resolution; see figure 13.1).

Following orgasm, the individual enters the *resolution phase,* in which blood vessels return to their normal state. One difference between males and females in this phase is that females may be stimulated to orgasm again without delay. Males enter a *refractory period,* lasting anywhere from several minutes to a day, in which they cannot have another orgasm. The length of the refractory period increases as men age.

Hormones What gets the sexual response pattern started? In many animals, a sexual response occurs only during specific times, which are determined by their hormones. Sexual behavior is so individualized in humans, though, that it is difficult to specify the effects of hormones. Their role in motivating human sexual behavior, especially in females, is not clear (Crooks & Bauer, 2005).

Nevertheless, it is clear that estrogens and androgens can influence sexual behavior in both sexes. **Estrogens,** the class of sex hormones that predominate in females, are produced mainly by the ovaries. **Androgens,** the class of sex hormones that predominate in males, are produced by the testes in males and by the adrenal glands in both males and females. Testosterone is an androgen.

For human males, higher androgen levels are associated with sexual motivation and orgasm frequency (Booth, Johnson, & Granger, 1999; Booth & others, 2003). At puberty, males experience a dramatic increase in testosterone level along with an increase in sexual thoughts and fantasies, masturbation, and nocturnal emissions (Susman & Rogol, 2004). Indeed, in male adolescents, the higher the blood levels of testosterone, the more the adolescent is preoccupied with sexual thoughts and engages in sexual activities. Throughout the year, the male's testes secrete androgens in fairly consistent amounts (see figure 13.2 for a diagram of the male reproductive system, including the testes). As a man ages, his testosterone level gradually declines; this is usually accompanied by a decline in sexual interest and activity.

At puberty, females' ovaries begin to produce the female sex hormones called estrogen (see figure 13.3 for a diagram of the female reproductive system). Unlike androgen, estrogen is not constantly produced. Rather, estrogen levels vary over an approximately monthlong cycle. Estrogen levels are highest when the female is ovulating (releasing an egg from one of her ovaries), which is midway through the menstrual cycle (Liu & others, 2004). It is at this time that a female is most likely to become pregnant. But unlike many nonhuman animals, which are receptive to mating only during this high-estrogen period, human females may be interested in sexual activity at any time during the menstrual cycle.

Although postmenopausal women have a significant drop in estrogen, they are still sexually active. If given estrogen, however, they experience an increased interest in sex and report sexual activity that is more pleasurable (Alexander & others, 2004; Kelly, 2004).

In short, as we move from the lower to the higher animals, hormonal control over behavior is less dominant, although still important, in sexual arousal. For humans, both sociocultural and cognitive factors play more important roles.

Sensations, Perceptions, and Cognitions

Even in nonhuman animals, hormones alone do not explain sexual behavior. Animals have all sorts of ways of attracting mates. Peacocks display their feathers, mockingbirds fly in loops, male bullfrogs call loudly through the night. Signs and sounds and specific behaviors are important preludes to mating (Strong & others, 2005).

For people, the sensory system of touch usually predominates during sexual intimacy, but vision also plays a prominent role for some individuals (Beres, Herold, & Maitland, 2004; Brown, Steele, & Walsh-Childers, 2002). In general, women are more aroused by touch, men by what they see. This might explain why erotic magazines and movies are directed more toward males than toward females (Money, 1986). Women are more aroused by tender, loving touches that are coupled with verbal expressions of love than men are. Moreover, men are likely to become sexually aroused quickly, whereas women's sexual arousal tends to build gradually.

Is the sense of smell also involved in sexual interest between women and men? In other animals it is. **Pheromones** are scented substances that are powerful sexual attractants in some animals (Beckman, 2002; Keverne, 2004). For example, pheromones in the urine of ovulating female guinea pigs attract male guinea pigs. All the male cats in a neighborhood know that a female cat is in heat when they pick up the scent of pheromones. Whether pheromones operate in humans in a way that triggers sexual attractions continues to be debated (Carroll, 2005; Wysocki & Preti, 2004).

Various foods and other substances have been promoted as dramatically increasing sexual arousal. *Aphrodisiacs* are substances that supposedly arouse sexual desire and increase the capacity for sexual activity (Pertovaara & others, 2004). Some foods, such as oysters, bananas, celery, tomatoes, and potatoes, are touted as aphrodisiacs. Be wary of such claims. These foods do not influence sexual behavior. A substance referred to as "Spanish fly" also has been promoted as a powerful aphrodisiac. Spanish fly is not only an ineffective sexual stimulant, it can also cause genital inflammation, tissue damage, and even death.

The producer of the greatest "aphrodisiac" is probably your own mind. From experience, we know that our cognitive world plays an important role in sexuality (Hyde & DeLamater, 2005). Sometimes, cognitions generate sexual activity. For example, some individuals become sexually aroused by generating erotic images and even reach orgasm while they are having fantasy images of sex (Whipple, Ogden, & Komisaruk, 1992). Of course, sometimes our thoughts deter us from sexual activity. For example, we might be sexually attracted to someone but inhibit our sexual urges until the relationship has developed and we know the person better.

More broadly, our cognitions about sexual activity, about potential sexual partners, about actual partners, and about ourselves influence our decisions about having sex, our experience of sex, and our interpretations of our experience (Zurbriggen & Yost, 2004). We like to ask ourselves endless questions about our partners. Is he loyal to me? What is our future relationship going to be like? How important is sex to her? What if she gets pregnant? Amid the wash of hormones in sexual activity we retain the cognitive ability to control, reason about, and try to make sense of sexual activity.

Culture and Sexual Motivation

For Alberto, as described in the chapter opening, one cognition about sex is the idea that he should remain a virgin until he is married. His girlfriend, Jasmine, agrees, for several reasons. She wants to wait to lose her virginity "to whoever I'm going to be with forever. That's what I want, but it's hard. . . . If I do have sex before I'm married, then the honeymoon won't be all exciting like you see on TV—so romantic and like a

pheromones Scented substances that are powerful sexual attractants in some animals.

Sexual behavior has it magnificent moments throughout the animal kingdom. Insects mate in midair, peacocks display their plumage, and male elephant seals have prolific sex lives. Experience plays a more important role in human sexual behavior. We can talk about sex with each other, read about it in magazines, and watch it on television and the movie screen.

big deal" (Bernstein, 2004, p. A22). These young people are reflecting some of the many values related to sex in the American culture.

The range of sexual values across cultures is substantial (Nieto, 2004). Some cultures consider sexual pleasures "weird" or "abnormal." Consider the people who live on the small island of Ines Beag off the coast of Ireland. They are some of the most sexually repressed people in the world. They know nothing about tongue kissing or hand stimulation of the penis, and they detest nudity. For both females and males, premarital sex is out of the question. Men avoid most sexual experiences because they believe that sexual intercourse reduces their energy level and is bad for their health. Under these repressive conditions, sexual intercourse occurs only at night and takes place as quickly as possible as the husband opens his nightclothes under the covers and the wife raises her nightgown. As you might suspect, female orgasm is rare in this culture (Messinger, 1971).

In contrast, consider the Mangaian culture in the South Pacific. In Mangaia, young boys are taught about masturbation and are encouraged to engage in it as much as they like. At age 13, the boys undergo a ritual that initiates them into sexual manhood. First, their elders instruct them about sexual strategies, including how to help their female partner have orgasms. Then, two weeks later, the boy has intercourse with an experienced woman who helps him hold back ejaculation until she can achieve orgasm with him. By the end of adolescence, Mangaians have sex virtually every day. Mangaian women report a high frequency of orgasms.

In the very different behavior of the people of Ines Beag and of the Mangaian culture, we can see the influence of **sexual scripts.** These are stereotyped patterns of expectancies for how people should behave sexually (Emmers-Sommer & Allen, 2005). Two well-known sexual scripts in the U.S. culture are the traditional religious script and the romantic script. In the **traditional religious script,** sex is accepted only within marriage. Extramarital sex is taboo, especially for women. Sex means

sexual scripts Stereotyped patterns of expectancies for how people should behave sexually.

traditional religious script Sex is accepted only within marriage.

reproduction and sometimes affection. In the **romantic script,** sex is synonymous with love. If we develop a relationship with someone and fall in love, it is acceptable to have sex with the person whether we are married or not.

Gender and Sexual Motivation

Differences in female and male sexual scripts can cause problems for individuals (King, 2005). Females learn to link sexual intercourse with love more than males do (Hyde & DeLamater, 2005). Therefore females are more likely than males to justify their sexual behavior by telling themselves that they were swept away by love. A number of investigators have found that females, more than males, cite being in love as the main reason for being sexually active. Far more females than males have intercourse only with partners they love and would like to marry. In contrast, the male sexual script emphasizes sexual conquest; higher status tends to accrue to males who can claim substantial sexual activity. For males, sex and love might not be as intertwined as they are for females.

Despite the movement toward equality between women and men, many people still hold a **double standard,** a belief that many sexual activities are acceptable for males but not for females. The double standard can be problematic. It encourages males to dismiss or devalue their female partner's values and feelings, and it puts considerable pressure on males to be as sexually active as possible. It encourages women to deny their sexuality and do minimal planning to ensure that their sexual encounters are safe. It can also lead females to think that males are more sexual than females, that males are less in control of their sexual behaviors.

Are men more sexually motivated than women? According to a 1994 survey of American sexual partners, men do think about sex far more than women do—54 percent of the men said they think about it every day or several times a day, whereas 67 percent of the women said they think about it only a few times a week or a few times a month (Michael & others, 1994). A recent review of research also concluded that men report more frequent feelings of sexual arousal, have more frequent sexual fantasies, and rate the strength of their own sex drive higher than women (Baumeister, Catanese, & Vohs, 2001). Men also have more permissive attitudes about casual premarital sex (Oliver & Hyde, 1993; Peplau, 2003).

Researchers have documented many of these gender differences in homosexual as well as heterosexual relationships (Peplau, 2002, 2003; Peplau, Fingerhut, & Beals, 2004):

- Lesbians' sexual fantasies are more likely than gay men's to be personal and romantic.
- Lesbians have fewer sex partners than gay men.
- Lesbians have less permissive attitudes about casual sex and sex outside a primary relationship than gay men.

Thus, whether they have a heterosexual or homosexual orientation, for many women, sexuality is strongly linked to a close relationship with the best context for enjoyable sex being a committed relationship; this is less so for men (Peplau & others, 2004).

Sexual Orientation

The similarities between lesbians and heterosexual women counteract some old stereotypes. In recent years, many Americans have managed to let go of many stereotypes about homosexual men and women. For example, people had long believed that an individual was either heterosexual or homosexual. Today's view of sexual orientation is more complicated.

Sexual orientation refers to an enduring attraction toward members of one's own sex (homosexual orientation) or members of the other sex (heterosexual orientation). It is accepted today that sexual orientation is a continuum from exclusive

Sexuality Megasite
Scientific Study of Sexuality
Positive Sexuality
The Kinsey Institute

romantic script Sex is synonymous with love. If a person develops a relationship and falls in love, it is acceptable to have sex whether married or not.

double standard A belief that many sexual activities are acceptable for males but not females.

sexual orientation An enduring attraction toward members of one's own sex (homosexual orientation) or members of the other sex (heterosexual orientation).

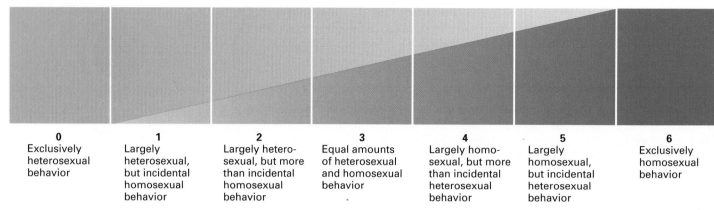

0	1	2	3	4	5	6
Exclusively heterosexual behavior	Largely heterosexual, but incidental homosexual behavior	Largely heterosexual, but more than incidental homosexual behavior	Equal amounts of heterosexual and homosexual behavior	Largely homosexual, but more than incidental heterosexual behavior	Largely homosexual, but incidental heterosexual behavior	Exclusively homosexual behavior

FIGURE 13.4 The Continuum of Sexual Orientation
The continuum ranges from exclusive heterosexuality, which Kinsey and associates (1948) labeled 0, to exclusive homosexuality, 6. People who are about equally attracted to both sexes, 2 to 4, are bisexual.

heterosexuality to exclusive homosexuality rather than as an either/or proposition (see figure 13.4). Some individuals are **bisexual,** being sexually attracted to people of both sexes.

What Causes Sexual Orientation?

Why are some individuals homosexual and others heterosexual? Speculation about this question has been extensive. Homosexuals and heterosexuals have similar physiological responses during sexual arousal and they seem to be aroused by the same types of tactile stimulation. Investigators find no differences between homosexuals and heterosexuals in a wide range of attitudes, behaviors, and adjustments (Bell, Weinberg, & Mammersmith, 1981).

Researchers have tried to find a biological basis for homosexuality (Gladue, 1994; Kinnunen & others, 2004). One theory that is still being explored holds that if a fetus during the second to fifth months after conception is exposed to hormone levels characteristic of females, then the fetus will eventually grow up to find males attractive (Ellis & Ames, 1987). Other biological theories have tried to find differences between the brains of heterosexuals and homosexuals.

Simon LeVay (1991) did find that an area of the hypothalamus was twice as large (about the size of a grain of sand) in heterosexual males as in homosexual males, but critics of this research point out that LeVay looked at very few brains and many of the homosexuals in the study had AIDS, which may have altered their brains. To date, no specific biological "cause" of homosexuality has been found.

Most likely an individual's sexual orientation is determined by a combination of genetic, hormonal, cognitive, and environmental factors (Baldwin & Baldwin, 1998). Most experts believe that no one factor alone causes sexual orientation and that the relative weight of each factor varies from one individual to the next. No one knows exactly why some individuals are homosexual and others bisexual or heterosexual (Herek, 2000).

Scientists have a clearer picture of what does not cause homosexuality. For example, children raised by gay or lesbian parents or couples are no more likely to be homosexual than children raised by heterosexual parents (Patterson, 2000). There also is no evidence that male homosexuality is caused by a dominant mother or a weak father, or that female homosexuality is caused by girls choosing male role models. Homosexuality once was classified as a mental disorder, but both the American Psychiatric Association and the American Psychological Association discontinued this classification as a mental disorder in the 1970s.

Developmental Pathways

One stereotype of gay and lesbian individuals holds that they quietly struggle with same-sex attractions in childhood, do not engage in

What likely determines an individual's sexual preference?

bisexual A person who is sexually attracted to people of both sexes.

interruption of sexual activity. Most experts on sexuality recommend not to rely on spermicides alone for contraception because their rate of effectiveness is low.

- *IUD.* The intrauterine device (IUD) is a small, plastic device that is inserted into the vagina. The IUD's advantages include uninterrupted sexual activity and ease of use. A possible disadvantage is pelvic inflammation (Steen & Shapiro, 2004).
- *Norplant.* This consists of six thin capsules filled with a synthetic hormone that are implanted under the skin of a woman's upper arm. The capsules gradually release the hormone into the bloodstream over a five-year period to prevent conception. Norplant is a highly effective contraceptive. A disadvantage includes potential bleeding (d'Arcangues & others, 2004).
- *Depo-Provera.* This is an injectable contraceptive that lasts three months and works by suspending a woman's menstrual periods. Users have to get a shot every 12 weeks. Depo-Provera is a very effective contraceptive but can cause menstrual irregularities and weight gain (Freeman, 2004).
- *Ortho Evra.* This is a 2-inch patch applied to the abdomen, buttocks, or upper arm for seven-day intervals over three weeks, with one week off. One downside is that it may cause a rash. Women who forget to change the patch every seven days may still get up to three days additional protection.
- *Preven and Plan B.* These are pills that must be taken within 72 hours of unprotected intercourse. They can reduce pregnancy risk by almost 80 percent but may cause nausea, vomiting, and abdominal pain (Weismiller, 2004).
- *Tubal ligation.* This is the most common sterilization procedure for women. It involves severing or tying the fallopian tubes.
- *Vasectomy.* This is a male sterilization procedure that involves cutting the sperm-carrying ducts.

Figure 13.6 describes the degree of effectiveness of many of these contraceptive methods and lists some other ineffective choices.

Psychosexual Dysfunctions and Disorders

Individuals can develop a number of psychosexual problems. Here we focus on three types: psychosexual dysfunctions, paraphilias, and gender identity disorder.

Psychosexual Dysfunctions   Both men and women can experience psychological problems that interfere with the attainment of sexual pleasure. **Psychosexual dysfunctions** are disorders that involve impairments in the sexual response pattern, either in the desire for gratification or in the inability to achieve it.

- In disorders associated with the desire phase, both men and women show little or no sexual drive or interest.
- In disorders associated with the excitement phase, men may not be able to maintain an erection.
- In disorders associated with the orgasmic phase, both women and men reach orgasm either too quickly or not at all. Premature ejaculation in men occurs when the time between the beginning of sexual stimulation and ejaculation is unsatisfactorily brief. Many women do not routinely experience orgasm in sexual intercourse. Inhibited male orgasm does occur, but it is much less common than inhibited female orgasm.

Figure 13.7 shows the prevalence of sexual problems in U.S. men and women in a nonclinical sample.

Treatment for Psychosexual Dysfunctions   The treatment of psychosexual dysfunctions has undergone a revolution in recent years. Most cases of psychosexual dysfunction now yield to techniques tailored to improve sexual functioning (Bhugra & de Silva, 1998; Hyde & DeLamater, 2005).

The following are birth control methods and their failure rates in one year of average use.

Method	Unintended-pregnancy rate*
No method (chance)	85.0
Spermicides	30.0
Withdrawal	24.0
Periodic abstinence	19.0
Cervical cap	18.0
Diaphragm	18.0
Condom	16.0
Pill	6.0
IUD	4.0
Tubal ligation	0.5
Depo-Provera	0.4
Vasectomy	0.2
Norplant	0.05

*Figures are based on women of reproductive age, 15 to 44. Rates vary with age. Failure rates with perfect use are lower, but people rarely use methods perfectly.

FIGURE 13.6 Failure Rates of Birth Control Methods

psychosexual dysfunctions Disorders that involve impairments in the sexual response pattern, either in the desire for gratification or the inability to achieve it.

FIGURE 13.7 Prevalence of Sexual Problems in U.S. Men and Women
Note that men are more likely to have erection difficulties and premature ejaculation, while women are more likely to experience lack of sexual desire, difficulty lubricating, and pain during intercourse.

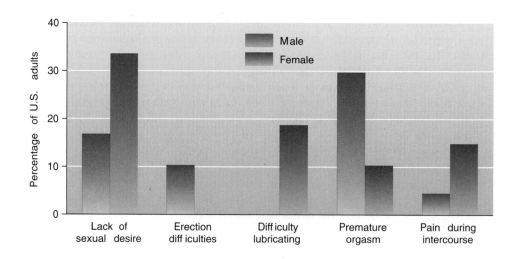

Psychosexual Dysfunctions
Psychosexual Dysfunctions in Men and Women

paraphilias Psychosexual disorders in which the source of an individual's satisfaction is an unusual object, ritual, or situation.

fetishism A psychosexual disorder in which an individual relies on inanimate objects or a specific body part for sexual gratification.

transvestism A psychosexual disorder in which an individual obtains sexual gratification by dressing up as a member of the opposite sex.

Traditional forms of psychotherapy have not been very successful, but new treatments that focus directly on each sexual dysfunction have reached success rates of 90 percent or more (McConaghy, 1993). For example, the success rate of a treatment that encourages women to enjoy their bodies and engage in self-stimulation to orgasm, with a vibrator if necessary, approaches 100 percent (Anderson, 1983). Some of these women subsequently transfer their newly developed sexual responsiveness to interactions with partners.

Recently, the most attention in helping individuals with a sexual dysfunction has focused on Viagra, a drug designed to conquer impotence. Viagra works by allowing increased blood flow into the penis, which produces an erection. Its success rate is in the range of 60 to 80 percent (Carson, 2003; Flower, 2004; Montorsi & Althof, 2004). The possible downside of Viagra involves headaches in one of ten men, or men seeing blue (about 3 percent of users develop temporary vision problems ranging from blurred vision to a blue or green halo effect). Viagra should not be taken by men using nitroglycerin for the treatment of cardiovascular disease because the combination can significantly lower blood pressure and lead to fainting or even death in some men (Cheitlin, 2003; Israilov & others, 2004). Also, the long-term effects of taking the drug are not known, although in short-term trials it appears to be a relatively safe drug. Recently, two alternatives to Viagra (Levitra and Cialis) for improving erectile dysfunction have been approved, and early studies indicate they are as successful as Viagra in treating erectile dysfunction and also have few side effects (Crowe & Streetman, 2004; Meuleman, 2004).

Paraphilias Paraphilias are psychosexual disorders in which the source of an individual's satisfaction is an unusual object, ritual, or situation. Many sexual patterns deviate from what we consider to be "normal." These abnormal patterns of sexual arousal from unusual sources include fetishism, transvestism, exhibitionism, voyeurism, sadism, masochism, and pedophilia.

Fetishism is a psychosexual disorder in which an individual relies on inanimate objects or a specific body part for sexual gratification. Some fetishists become obsessed with certain objects—fur, women's underpants, stockings—that arouse them. The objects take on greater importance than the arousing qualities of any one partner. Most fetishists are male.

Transvestism is a psychosexual disorder in which an individual obtains sexual gratification by dressing up as a member of the opposite sex. Most transvestites view themselves as heterosexual and lead quiet, conventional lives, cross-dressing only in the privacy of their homes. One pattern of transvestites is to cross-dress only during sexual relations with their partners.

Exhibitionism and voyeurism are the two sex practices that most often come to the attention of the police. **Exhibitionism** is a psychosexual disorder in which individuals expose their sexual anatomy to others to obtain sexual gratification. **Voyeurism** is a psychosexual disorder in which individuals derive sexual gratification from observing the sex organs or sex acts of others, often from a secret vantage point. Both exhibitionism and voyeurism provide substitute gratification and a sense of power to otherwise sexually anxious individuals, especially males. In many instances, voyeurs are sexually inhibited.

Sadism is a psychosexual disorder in which individuals derive sexual gratification from inflicting pain on others. The word *sadism* comes from the novels of the Marquis de Sade (1740–1814), who wrote about erotic scenes in which women were whipped. **Masochism** is a psychosexual disorder in which individuals derive sexual gratification from being subjected to physical pain inflicted by others or themselves. The word *masochism* comes from the novels of Austrian writer Leopold von Sacher-Masoch (1836–1895), whose male characters became sexually excited and gratified when they were physically abused by women. It is not unusual for a sadist and a masochist to pair up to satisfy each other's sexual wishes; such relationships are called sadomasochistic. However, it is rare for a sadist and masochist to match each other's needs and have a stable and lasting relationship.

Pedophilia is a psychosexual disorder in which the sex object is a child, and the intimacy involves manipulation of the child's genitals (Renshaw, 2003). A pedophile covertly or overtly masturbates while talking to children, manipulates the child's sex organs, or engages the child in sexual behavior. Most pedophiles are men, usually in their thirties or forties. Like exhibitionists, pedophiles often have puritanical ideas about sex and see sex with children as being purer, safer, or less embarrassing. Often the target of a male pedophile is a child he knows, such as a child of a relative, neighbor, or family friend (Frost, 2004).

Gender Identity Disorder   **Transsexualism** is a disorder of gender identity in which an individual has an overwhelming desire to become a member of the opposite sex. The individual's gender identity is at odds with his or her genetic makeup and anatomical features (Feldman & Bockting, 2003; Neumann & Welzel, 2004). A transsexual might eventually decide to undergo surgery to change sex. Transsexuals often say that, as far back as they can remember, they have felt uncomfortable in their own bodies. They believe that they were born in a body of the wrong sex. Psychologists are uncertain why people are transsexual.

Can transsexuals lead full sex lives? In the female-to-male transsexual transformation, the surgically constructed male sex organs are cosmetic and the clitoris retains its orgasmic sensations; male sex hormones are given to intensify orgasm. Male-to-female transsexuals describe their sexual sensations as diffuse and intense. They report that they enjoy functioning as females, especially in terms of physical closeness, skin responsiveness, and breast sensations.

Paraphilias
Gender Identity Disorder

exhibitionism A psychosexual disorder in which individuals expose their sexual anatomy to others to obtain sexual gratification.

voyeurism A psychosexual disorder in which individuals derive sexual gratification from observing the sex organs or sex acts of others, often from a secret vantage point.

sadism A psychosexual disorder in which individuals derive sexual gratification from inflicting pain on others.

masochism A psychosexual disorder in which individuals derive sexual gratification from being subjected to physical pain inflicted by others or themselves.

pedophilia A psychosexual disorder in which the sex object is a child and the intimacy involves manipulating the child's genitals.

transsexualism A gender identity disorder in which an individual has an overwhelming desire to become a member of the opposite sex.

Review and Reflect

2   Discuss the relation between sexuality and adjustment

REVIEW

- What are some key aspects of effective sexual communication?
- What are some widespread myths about sexuality?
- What is the range of contraceptives that are available?
- What are psychosexual dysfunctions, paraphilias, and gender identity disorder?

REFLECT

- Why might a person be reluctant and anxious about seeking help for a psychosexual function or disorder?

3 **SEXUALITY AND HARM**

| Sexually Transmitted Infections | Sexual Harassment | Pornography and Violence Against Women |

| Rape | Incest |

People often compare sex to a game. For Magic Johnson and millions of other people, however, it was a life-threatening game. Sexuality can be a context in which the participants are harmed. We next examine some harsh realities associated with sex, from the physical and emotional harm that results from sexually transmitted infections, rape, and incest to the psychological harm that results from sexual harassment. We also explore the effects of pornography on sexual behavior.

Sexually Transmitted Infections

Sexually transmitted infections (STIs) are diseases that are contracted primarily through sexual contact. This contact includes oral-genital and anal-genital contact as well as vaginal intercourse. STIs are an increasing health problem. The main STIs are three caused by bacterial infections—gonorrhea, syphilis, and chlamydia—and three STIs caused by viruses—genital herpes, HPV (human papillomavirus), and AIDS (acquired immune deficiency syndrome).

Gonorrhea   Gonorrhea is an STI that is commonly called the "drip" or the "clap." It is one of the most common STIs in the United States and is caused by a bacterium from the gonococcus family, which thrives in the mucous membranes lining the mouth, throat, vagina, cervix, urethra, and anal tract. The bacterium is spread by contact between the infected moist membranes of one individual and the membranes of another.

Gonorrhea can be successfully treated in its early stages with penicillin or other antibiotics. Untreated, gonorrhea can lead to infections that can move to various organs and can cause infertility. More than 650,000 cases are reported in the United States annually (Centers for Disease Control and Prevention, 2004).

Syphilis   Syphilis is an STI caused by the bacterium *Treponema palladium,* a member of the spirochete family. The spirochete needs a warm, moist environment to survive, and it is transmitted by penile-vaginal, oral-genital, or anal contact. It can also be transmitted from a pregnant woman to her fetus after the fourth month of pregnancy. If the mother is treated with penicillin, the syphilis will not be transmitted to the fetus.

In its early stages, syphilis can be effectively treated with penicillin (Zeger & Holt, 2003). In its advanced stages, syphilis can cause paralysis or even death. Approximately 40,000 cases of syphilis are reported in the United States each year.

Chlamydia   Chlamydia, the most common of all STIs in the United States, is named for *Chlamydia trachomitis,* a bacterium that spreads by sexual contact and infects the genital organs of both sexes. Although fewer individuals have heard of chlamydia than have heard of gonorrhea and syphilis, its incidence is much higher (Centers for Disease Control and Prevention, 2004). About 4 million Americans are infected with chlamydia each year. About 10 percent of all college students have chlamydia. This STI is highly infectious, and women run a 70 percent risk of contracting it in a single sexual encounter. The male risk is estimated at between 25 and 50 percent (Krause & Bohring, 2003).

Males with chlamydia often get treatment because of noticeable symptoms in the genital region; however, females are asymptomatic. Therefore, many females go untreated and the chlamydia spreads to the upper reproductive tract, where it can cause pelvic inflammatory disease (PID). PID, in turn, can result in ectopic pregnancies (a

sexually transmitted infections (STIs) Diseases that are contracted primarily through sexual intercourse—vaginally as well as through oral-genital and anal-genital contact.

gonorrhea A sexually transmitted infection that is commonly called the "drip" or the "clap" and is caused by a bacterium from the gonococcus family.

syphilis A sexually transmitted infection caused by the bacterium *Treponema palladium.*

chlamydia A sexually transmitted infection caused by the bacterium *Chlamydia trachomitis.*

pregnancy in which the fertilized egg is implanted outside the uterus) or infertility. One-quarter of females who have PID become infertile; multiple cases of PID increase the rate of infertility to half. Some researchers suggest that chlamydia is the number one preventable cause of female infertility.

Genital Herpes   **Genital herpes** is an STI caused by a large family of viruses with many different strains. These strains produce other, non-sexually-transmitted infections such as chicken pox and mononucleosis. Three to five days after contact, itching and tingling can occur, followed by an eruption of sores and blisters. The attacks can last up to three weeks and may recur in a few weeks or a few years (Brentjens & others, 2003).

Although drugs such as acyclovir alleviate symptoms, there is no known cure for herpes (Patel, 2004). The virus can be transmitted through nonlatex condoms and foams, making infected individuals reluctant to have sex, angry about the unpredictability of their lives, and fearful that they won't be able to cope with the pain and stress of the next attack (Fortenberry, 2004; Nasraty, 2003). For these reasons, support groups for individuals with herpes have been established.

HPV   **HPV** is a virus (human papillomavirus) that causes genital warts on people. The warts can be as large as nickels or so small that they cannot be seen. There are more than a million new cases of HPV each year in the United States. The most common way to contract HPV is by having sex with or touching the genitals of someone who already has the virus.

Women with HPV face an increased risk for cervical cancer (Ah Lee & others, 2003). Genital warts can be removed by physicians. Sometimes the warts are frozen off; at other times a laser is used to remove them. Although the warts can be removed, it generally is believed that once the virus is acquired, HPV does not go away.

AIDS   No single STI has had a greater impact on sexual behavior, or created more public fear, in the last several decades than AIDS. **AIDS** is a sexually transmitted infection that is caused by the *human immunodeficiency virus (HIV)*, which destroys the body's immune system. A person who has contracted HIV is vulnerable to infections that a normal immune system could destroy (Carey & Vanable, 2003).

Of the AIDS cases reported as of January 1, 2003, in the United States, more than 80 percent were men and almost half were intravenous (IV) drug users (Centers for Disease Control and Prevention, 2004). Overall, slightly less than half of the AIDS cases were gay men.

Because of education and the development of more effective drug treatments, deaths due to AIDS have begun to decline in the United States (Carey & Vanable, 2003). Multidrug combinations can suppress the HIV virus to low levels for an extended time (Harwell & others, 2003; Kelly, 2004). However, the number of people with HIV continues to rise.

Furthermore, in many locations around the world AIDS is increasing. For example, in Africa more than 4 million people had AIDS in 2000. To put this in perspective, a total of 886,575 cases of AIDS had been reported to the Centers for Disease Control and Prevention as of January 1, 2003, in the United States.

Experts say that AIDS can be transmitted only by (Kalichman, 1996)

- sexual contact,
- sharing hypodermic needles,
- blood transfusion (which in the last few years has been tightly monitored), or
- other direct contact with blood or sexual fluids of an infected person.

Remember that it is not who you are, but what you do, that puts you at risk for getting HIV. Anyone who is sexually active or uses intravenous drugs is at risk. *No one is immune.* Once an individual is infected, the prognosis is likely illness and possibly death. The only safe behavior is abstinence from sex, which most individuals do not perceive as an option. Beyond abstinence, there is only "safer" behavior, such as sexual behavior without exchange of semen, vaginal fluids, or blood, and sexual intercourse with a condom.

www.mhhe.com/santrockha

Sexual Health
Sexual Health Topics
National Prevention of HIV/AIDS
AIDS Prevention Studies

genital herpes A sexually transmitted infection caused by a large family of viruses with different strains.

HPV A virus (human papillomavirus) that causes genital warts.

AIDS A sexually transmitted infection that is caused by the *human immunodeficiency virus (HIV)*, which destroys the body's immune system.

Just asking a date about his or her sexual behavior does not guarantee protection from AIDS and other sexually transmitted diseases. For example, in one investigation, 655 college students were asked to answer questions about lying and sexual behavior (Cochran & Mays, 1990). Of the 422 respondents who said they were sexually active, 34 percent of the men and 10 percent of the women said they had lied so that their partner would be more inclined to have sex with them. Much higher percentages—47 percent of the men and 60 percent of the women—said they had been lied to by a potential sexual partner. When asked what aspects of their past they would be most likely to lie about, more than 40 percent of the men and women said they would understate the number of their sexual partners. Twenty percent of the men, but only 4 percent of the women, said they would lie about results from an HIV blood test.

Adjustment Strategies
For Protecting Against STIs

What are some good strategies for protecting against AIDS and other sexually transmitted infections? They include these:

1. ***Know your and your partner's risk status.*** Anyone who has had previous sexual activity with another person might have contracted an STI without being aware of it. Get to know a prospective partner before you have sex. Use this time to inform the other person of your STI status and inquire about your partner's. Remember that many people lie about their STI status.
2. ***Obtain medical examinations.*** Many experts recommend that couples who want to begin a sexual relationship should have a medical checkup to rule out STIs before they engage in sex. If cost is an issue, contact your campus health service or a public health clinic.
3. ***Have protected, not unprotected, sex.*** When correctly used, latex condoms help to prevent many STIs from being transmitted. Condoms are more effective in preventing gonorrhea, syphilis, chlamydia, and HIV than herpes.
4. ***Don't have sex with multiple partners.*** One of the best predictors of getting an STI is having sex with multiple partners. Having more than one sex partner elevates the likelihood that you will encounter an infected partner.

Rape

Rape is forcible sexual intercourse with a person who does not give consent. Legal definitions of rape differ from state to state; for example, in some states, husbands are not prohibited from forcing their wives to have intercourse. Because victims may be reluctant to suffer the consequences of reporting rape, the actual incidence is not easily determined (Danielson & Holmes, 2004; Kilpatrick, 2004). It appears that rape occurs most often in large cities, where it has been reported that 8 of every 10,000 women 12 years and older are raped each year. Nearly 200,000 rapes are reported each year in the United States.

Although most victims of rape are women, male rape does occur (Ellis, 2002). Men in prisons are especially vulnerable to rape, usually by heterosexual males who use rape as a means of establishing their dominance and power. Though it might seem impossible for a man to be raped by a woman, a man's erection is not completely under his voluntary control, and some cases of male rape by women have been reported (Sarrel & Masters, 1982). Male victims account for fewer than 5 percent of all rapes.

Why does rape occur so often in the United States? One proposed explanation points to how U.S. males are socialized, arguing that they are encouraged to be sexually aggressive, to regard women as inferior beings, and to view their own pleasure as the most important objective (Adams-Curtis & Forbes, 2004). Researchers have found that male rapists share the following characteristics: aggression enhances their sense of power or masculinity; they are angry at women in general; and they want to hurt and humiliate the victim (Giotakos & others, 2003; Yodanis, 2004).

rape Forcible sexual intercourse with a person who does not give consent.

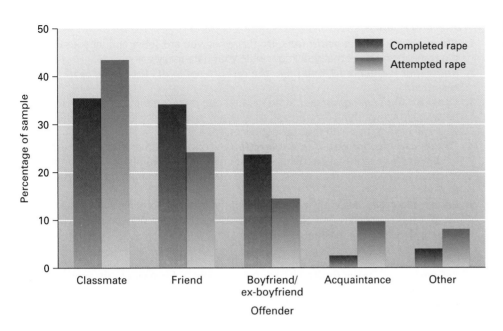

FIGURE 13.8 Completed Rape and Attempted Rape of College Women According to Victim-Offender Relationship

Rape is a traumatic experience for the victims and those close to them (Christopher & Sprecher, 2000; Erlick Robinson, 2003). Victims initially feel shock and numbness and are often acutely disorganized. Some show their distress through words and tears; others internalize their suffering. As victims strive to get their lives back to normal, they may experience depression, fear, and anxiety for months or years (Thompson & others, 2003). Sexual dysfunctions, such as reduced sexual desire and an inability to reach orgasm, occur in 50 percent of female rape victims (Sprei & Courtois, 1988). Many victims make changes in their lives—such as moving to a new apartment or refusing to go out at night. Recovery depends on a victim's coping abilities, psychological adjustments prior to the assault, and social support. Parents, boyfriend or husband, and others close to a victim are important factors in recovery, as is the availability of professional counseling (Faravelli & others, 2004; Mein & others, 2003).

An increasing concern is **date or acquaintance rape,** which is coercive sexual activity by someone with whom the victim is at least casually acquainted (Adams-Curtis & Forbes, 2004; Smith, White, & Holland, 2003). A major study that focused on campus sexual assault involved a phone survey of 4,446 women attending two- or four-year colleges (Fisher, Cullen, & Turner, 2000). In this study, slightly less than 3 percent said that they either had experienced a rape or an attempted rate during the academic year. About one of ten college women said that they had experienced rape in their lifetime. Unwanted or uninvited sexual contacts were widespread with more than one-third of the college women reporting these incidents. As shown in figure 13.8, in this study, most women (about nine of ten) knew the person who sexually victimized them. Most of the women attempted to take protective actions against their assailants but were then reluctant to report the victimization to the police. Several factors were associated with sexual victimization: living on campus, being unmarried, getting drunk frequently, and experiencing prior sexual victimization.

Adjustment Strategies
Involving Acquaintance Rape

Use the following strategies developed by the Northern Michigan University counseling staff (2004, pp. 3–7):

date or acquaintance rape Coercive sexual activity directed at someone with whom the victim is at least casually acquainted.

continued

For Men and Women

1. ***Clearly state your expectations.*** Do this when you are sober and let your date do the same. Don't think that you know what your date really wants.
2. ***Know that women and men have the right to set limits that need to be respected.***
3. ***Consider the consequences.*** "Both women and men sometimes feel pressure to be sexually active. Think for yourself; as with any serious decision, you are the one who will have to live with the consequences," p. 4.
4. ***"If you use alcohol, use it in moderation.*** Alcohol and other drugs decrease inhibitions, lead to impulsive behavior, and interfere with rational thought. In most reported acquaintance rape cases, both the man and the woman have been drinking," p. 4.
5. ***Report the rape.*** Talk with someone about the incident. Virtually every college campus has counseling and administrative services that can help you in deciding what to do about the incident.

For Women

1. ***Set and reset sexual limits.*** Nobody has the right to force you to do anything you don't want to do.
2. ***Think about where you go with a man.*** Be careful about inviting a man to your room, apartment, or house. Some men see this as an invitation to have sex.
3. ***Get to know the person well first.*** Until you get to know the person well, try to set up double dates or recommend the first few dates occur in public places such as at a movie, a sporting event, or a concert.
4. ***Be careful about sending conflicting messages.*** "Heavy petting or removing some of your clothing may confuse your date about what you are willing to do sexually. When you send conflicting messages, the situation becomes more difficult for you and your date/partner to control," p. 7.
5. ***"Educate yourself about men and sex.*** Many women have been taught by men to believe that a man cannot control himself sexually once he reaches a 'certain point.' This is simply not true," p. 6.

For Men

1. ***"Trust that 'no' always means 'no.'*** It is NEVER permissible to force yourself on a partner, even if you believe he/she is leading you on," p. 4.
2. ***Your partner can change her mind at any time.*** Even if you have had sex with her previously, she has the right to not have sex with you at a subsequent time or at any time during the sexual situation.
3. ***Be aware of cultural expectations.*** Many men in the United States have been taught that the goal of a date is to have sex and that they have somehow not been successful if they don't have sex. Avoid this culture script and behave in a sexually responsible way.
4. ***Know that a woman who wears provocative clothing is not asking to have sex with you.***
5. ***Spending money on a date does not give you the right to have sex.***
6. ***Be aware of the consequences of your sexual conduct.*** You could go to prison for many years, be expelled from your college, and have difficulty finding a job throughout your life if you commit acquaintance rape.

www.mhhe.com/santrockha

College Sexual Problems
Sexual Assault Links
Date Rape Resources
Acquaintance Rape Issues
Sexual Victimization

Sexual Harassment

Sexual harassment takes many forms—from sexist remarks and physical contact (patting, brushing against an individual's body) to blatant propositions and sexual assaults (Bronner, Peretz, & Ehrenfeld, 2003; Cortina, 2004). Millions of women experience sexual harassment each year in work and educational settings (Gregg, 2004; Hoffmann, 2004). Sexual harassment of men by women also occurs but to a far lesser extent than sexual harassment of women by men.

Sexual harassment can result in serious psychological consequences for the victim (Erlick Robinson, 2003). Sexual harassment is a manifestation of power of one person over another. The elimination of such exploitation requires the development of work and academic environments that provide equal opportunities to develop a career and obtain education in a climate free of sexual harassment.

Incest

Incest is sex between people who are close relatives. By far the most common form of incest in the United States is brother-sister incest; father-daughter incest is the second most common. Incest is psychologically harmful, not only for immediate family relationships, but also for the future relationships of a child involved in incest. Another misfortune associated with incest is that any resulting offspring have higher-than-average risks for genetic disorders and mental retardation.

Taboos against incest have developed in virtually all human societies, although a few exceptions have been noted, such as the Incan society and the societies of ancient Iran and ancient Egypt (Murdock, 1949). Possibly the taboos arose because of the harmful physical, psychological, and social effects of incest.

Pornography and Violence Against Women

Contemporary campaigns against pornography began in the late 1970s. Initial feminist arguments against pornography were of two main sorts: (1) pornography demeans women (for instance, by depicting them as sex slaves in male fantasies); and (2) much of pornography glorifies violence against women, perpetuating the cultural myth that women who say no to sex really want to be overpowered and raped.

Reviews of research indicate that pornography does have a small connection to male sexual aggression, but it is only one of several factors that may lead to sexual violence against women (Malamuth, 2003). Also, the nature of the pornographic material, the characteristics of the men viewing the pornography, and the surrounding culture need to be taken into account. In other words, no single factor, such as pornography in general, is likely to cause men's violence against women.

Pornography means all sexually explicit materials, but of course, there are different types of pornography. Some pornography shows nudity and explicit consensual sex while other pornography depicts sexual violence toward women. Researchers have found that pornography showing sexual violence toward women is more likely to increase violence toward women by male viewers than pornography that displays consensual sex with no violence (Donnerstein, 2001).

Most men are not prone to be violent toward women. However, when men who are attracted to sexual aggression, have a hostile masculine personality, and have low intelligence are exposed to pornography, they are even more likely to be violent toward women (Donnerstein, 2001). Also, pornography increases violence toward women in men who come from family and cultural backgrounds in which gender equality is de-emphasized and their education about sexuality is limited (Malamuth, 2003).

Sexual Harassment
Sexual Harassment Myths and Realities

Review and Reflect

3 **Explain aspects of sexuality that can be harmful**

REVIEW

- What are the main sexually transmitted infections?
- What are some key things to know about rape?
- What is incest?
- What link exists between pornography and violence against women?

REFLECT

- Have you ever participated in unwelcome sexual advances, either as the person engaging in those advances or the recipient of them? How did you handle the situation? After reading about forcible sexual behavior in this chapter, would you do anything differently now if something similar occurred?

incest Sex between people who are close relatives. Incest is virtually a universal taboo.

Reach Your Learning Goals

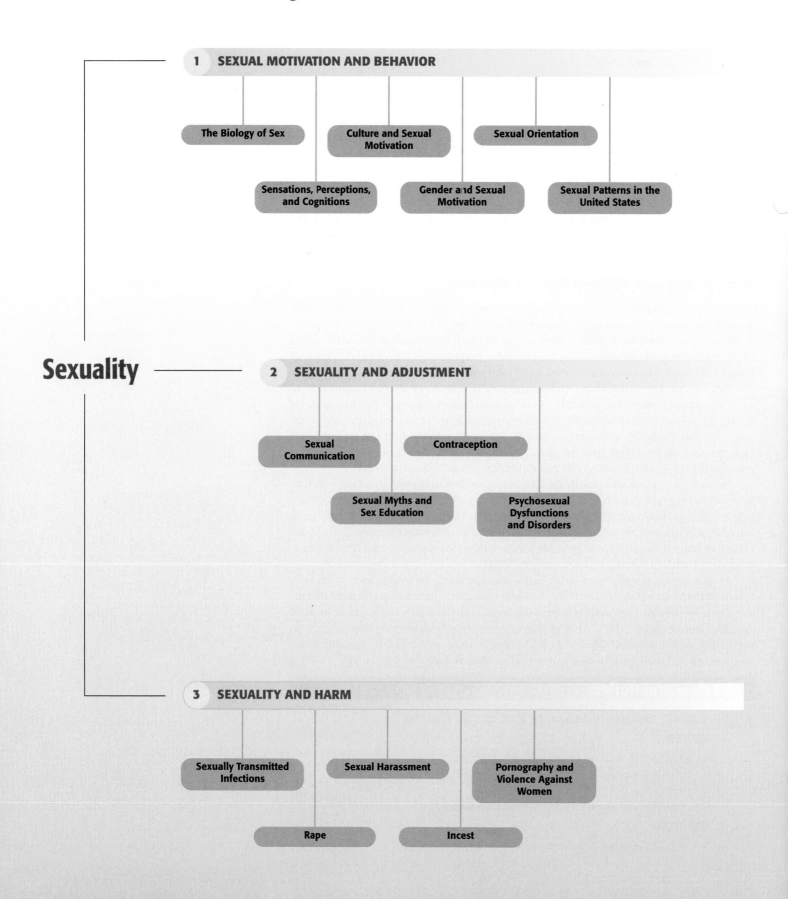

Sexuality

1 SEXUAL MOTIVATION AND BEHAVIOR

- The Biology of Sex
- Sensations, Perceptions, and Cognitions
- Culture and Sexual Motivation
- Gender and Sexual Motivation
- Sexual Orientation
- Sexual Patterns in the United States

2 SEXUALITY AND ADJUSTMENT

- Sexual Communication
- Sexual Myths and Sex Education
- Contraception
- Psychosexual Dysfunctions and Disorders

3 SEXUALITY AND HARM

- Sexually Transmitted Infections
- Rape
- Sexual Harassment
- Incest
- Pornography and Violence Against Women

Summary

1. Describe the key factors that influence sexual motivation and behavior

- Regarding biological factors, the role of sex hormones in sexual behavior, especially for women, is not clear. Masters and Johnson mapped out the human sexual response pattern, which consists of four physiological phases: excitement, plateau, orgasm, and resolution.
- Thoughts and images are central to the sexual lives of humans. Pheromones are sexual attractants for many nonhuman animals, but there is no clear evidence that what we eat, drink, or inject has aphrodisiac qualities.
- Sexual values vary across cultures and these values exert a strong influence on sexual attitudes and behavior. Sexual scripts, such as the traditional religious script and the romantic script, are involved in sexual motivation. Americans' views of sex are also heavily influenced by the media.
- Females tend to be more sexually aroused by touch, males by visual stimulation. Men report more frequent feelings of sexual arousal, have more frequent sexual fantasies, and rate the strength of their sex drive higher than women. Men also are more likely to masturbate, have more permissive attitudes about casual premarital sex, and have a more difficult time adhering to their vows of celibacy when they become married. Despite movement toward equality between men and women, many people still hold a double standard, a belief that many sexual activities are acceptable for males but not for females.
- Sexual orientation refers to an enduring attraction toward members of one's own sex (homosexual orientation) or members of the other sex (heterosexual orientation). An individual's homosexual orientation most likely is determined by a combination of genetic, hormonal, cognitive, and environmental factors. Youth follow different developmental pathways to same-sex attraction.
- The 1994 *Sex in America* survey was a major improvement over earlier surveys by Kinsey and Hunt. The 1994 survey revealed that Americans' sex lives are more conservative than indicated by earlier surveys. U.S. males report their first sexual intercourse experience occurs at 17.4 years of age while U.S. females report a slightly earlier age—16.9 years.

2. Discuss the relation between sexuality and adjustment

- Sexual communication consists of verbal and nonverbal communication. In terms of verbal communication, it is important to take responsibility for your own sexual needs and discover your partner's needs, criticize your partner constructively and handle criticism from your partner effectively, and say no when you do not want to

engage in some aspect of sexual behavior. In terms of nonverbal communication, touch has an especially powerful role.
- Some experts believe that the United States is a nation whose population is not very sexually knowledgeable and that Americans believe in a number of sexual myths, which are especially fueled by the media. The myths include that a man needs a large penis to satisfy a women, that orgasm is necessary for sexual satisfaction, that intercourse is the only real sexual act, and that good sex has to be spontaneous. In terms of sex education, U.S. youth get very little information from their parents. An overwhelming majority of American adults now support the teaching of sex education in schools.
- Inadequate knowledge about contraception, coupled with inconsistent use of effective contraceptive methods, has resulted in the United States having one of the industrialized world's highest adolescent pregnancy rates. The main contraceptive choices are oral contraceptives, condoms, diaphragms, spermicides, IUDs, Norplant, Depo-Provera, Ortho Evra, Preven and Plan B, tubal ligation, and vasectomy. The degree of effectiveness of these contraceptive methods varies.
- Psychosexual dysfunctions are disorders that involve impairments in the sexual response pattern, either in the desire for gratification or the inability to achieve it. New treatments that focus on each type of sexual dysfunction have very high success rates—far better than traditional psychotherapy. Viagra has been especially effective in helping men overcome impotence problems. Paraphilias are psychosexual disorders in which the source of an individual's satisfaction is an unusual object, ritual, or situation. Paraphilias include fetishism, transvestism, exhibitionism, voyeurism, sadism, masochism, and pedophilia. Gender identity disorder is the formal term for transsexualism, in which an individual has an overwhelming desire to become a member of the opposite sex.

3. Explain aspects of sexuality that can be harmful

- Sexually transmitted infections (STIs) are diseases that are primarily contracted through sexual contact, which includes oral-genital and anal-genital contact as well as vaginal intercourse. Gonorrhea is a sexually transmitted disease that is commonly called the "drip" or the "clap," and it is caused by a bacterium from the gonococcus family. It can be successfully treated with penicillin or other antibiotics in its early stages. Syphilis is an STI caused by the bacterium *Treponema palladium*, and in its early stages it can be treated with penicillin. Chlamydia, the most common of all STIs in the U.S., is caused by the bacterium *Chlamydia trachomitus* and is highly infectious. This STI can cause pelvic inflammatory disease (PID) in females, which can cause infertility. Treatment of chlamydia is usually successful, but a problem in females is that females are asymptomatic and many go untreated. Genital herpes is an STI caused by a family of viruses with different strains. Although drugs such as acyclovir alleviate symptoms, there is no known cure for herpes. HPV is a virus (human papillomavirus) that causes genital warts. Women with HPV face an increased risk of cervical cancer. Genital warts can be removed by a physician. AIDS is an STI caused by the human immunodeficiency virus (HIV), which destroys the body's immune system. Because of education and the development of more effective drug treatments, deaths due to AIDS have begun to decline in the United States, although in many locations around the world, especially in Africa, AIDS is increasing.

- Rape is forcible sexual intercourse with a person who does not give consent. Rape is a traumatic experience for the victim and the people close to them. An increasing concern is date or acquaintance rape, which is coercive sexual activity directed at someone with whom the victim is at least casually acquainted.

- Sexual harassment can take many forms—from sexist remarks and physical contact to blatant propositions and sexual assaults. Sexual harassment can result in serious consequences for the victim.

- Incest is sex between people who are close relatives and it is virtually universally taboo.

- Pornography has a small connection to male sexual aggression, but it is only one of several factors that may lead to sexual violence against women. Most men are not prone to violence against women. However, a small percentage are, and for those who are, pornography (especially pornography involving violence toward women) increases the likelihood that they will enact their aggressive tendencies.

Key Terms

human sexual response pattern 395	double standard 399	voyeurism 411	chlamydia 412
estrogens 396	sexual orientation 399	sadism 411	genital herpes 413
androgens 396	bisexual 400	masochism 411	HPV 413
pheromones 397	psychosexual dysfunctions 409	pedophilia 411	AIDS 413
sexual scripts 398	paraphilias 410	transsexualism 411	rape 414
traditional religious script 398	fetishism 410	sexually transmitted infections (STIs) 412	date or acquaintance rape 415
romantic script 399	transvestism 410	gonorrhea 412	incest 417
	exhibitionism 411	syphilis 412	

Resources for Improving Your Adjustment

SELF-HELP BOOKS

Becoming Orgasmic

(1998 Rev. ed.). New York: Prentice-Hall.

This book provides women encouragement and specific exercises for becoming more sexually fulfilled. The topics include looking at oneself, vaginal exercises, erotic literature, fantasizing, using a vibrator, and intercourse. *Becoming Orgasmic* was given 4 (out of 5) stars in the national survey of self-help books (Norcross, Santrock, & others, 2003).

The New Male Sexuality

(1992) by Bernie Zilbergeld. New York: Bantam.

The New Male Sexuality is a very comprehensive book about male sexuality. An introductory section in *The New Male Sexuality* tackles male sexual myths and unrealistic expectations, and then the author turns to sexual reality and gives men a brief course in sexual knowledge. The next section explores better sex through topics such as how to be a good lover with your partner, how to be a better listener, touching, arousal, and how to keep the spark alive in long-standing relationships. A final section is devoted to resolving problems and includes discussion of ejaculatory control, erection difficulties, problems of sexual desire, and even advice for fathers on how to communicate more effectively about sex with their sons.

Illustrated Manual of Sexual Therapy

(1987) by Helen Kaplan. Brunner/Mazel.

A number of exercises are provided to improve sexual functioning. Specific techniques are given for specific dysfunctions, such as orgasmic difficulties and premature ejaculation. Numerous drawings are included. This book received 4 (of 5) stars in the national survey of self-help books.

Permanent Partners

(1988) by Betty Berzon. New York: Plume.

Permanent Partners describes how gay and lesbian couples can make their relationship work and last. Berzon examines the obstacles that same-sex couples face as they try to create a new life together. This book provides good information for gays and lesbians who are thinking about becoming coupled or are perplexed about their current relationship, and for anyone who wants to improve their understanding of gay and lesbian couples. Two other good books on gay and lesbian relationships are *The New Loving Someone Gay,* by Don Clark, and *Lesbian Couples,* by D. Merilee Clunis and G. Dorsey Green.

NATIONAL SUPPORT GROUPS

CDC National STI Hotline
1-800-227-8922

National AIDS Hotline
1-800-342-AIDS

National Herpes Hotline
1-888-843-4564

National Gay and Lesbian Hotline
1-888-843-4564
Provides free over-the-phone counseling.

PFLAG (Parents and Friends of Lesbians and Gays)
1726 M Street, Suite 400
Washington, DC 20036
http://www.pflag.org

National Rape, Abuse, and Neglect Hotline
1-880-656-HOPE

E-Learning Tools

To help you master the material in this chapter, you will find a number of valuable study tools on the student CD-ROM and the Online Learning Center.

SELF-ASSESSMENT

In Text

You can complete these self-assessments in the text:
- Self-Assessment 13.1: *What Are My Sexual Attitudes?*
- Self-Assessment 13.2: *Sexual Satisfaction for My Partner and Myself*
- Self-Assessment 13.3: *My Awareness of Sexual Myths*

Additional Self-Assessments

Complete the self-assessment on the Online Learning Center: *Am I a Giver or a Taker in a Romantic Relationship?*

THINK CRITICALLY

To practice your critical thinking skills, complete these exercises on the Online Learning Center:
- *The Value of Sexual Skepticism* guides you in thinking about sexual myths.
- *Apply Psychological Concepts to Your Own Sexual History* encourages you to think about how you learned about sex and how accurate the information was.
- *Understanding Rape as a Complex Phenomenon* helps you understand the circumstances that might be involved in a rape.

APPLY YOUR KNOWLEDGE

1. What's your sexual knowledge?

Although people like to think they are knowledgeable about sex, they may fall victim to misinformation or lack of awareness. Go to a search engine such as www.yahoo.com or www.google.com and search for a *serious* "Sexual knowledge quiz."

You may also wish to explore your knowledge in other areas, including: "seniors and sex," "sexual myths," "sexually transmitted diseases," "contraception quiz," and "sexual assault quiz"

2. How available is abortion?

The topic of abortion is very controversial and personal. Some people believe that it should be illegal. Others believe that it is a woman's unalienable right. Still others believe that abortion should be legal, but don't believe that it would be the decision that they would make for themselves. At present, abortion is legal, but is it available? What are some of the factors that limit its availability? To find out how available abortion is by state and what laws limit abortion availability, visit the website for the Alan Guttmacher Institute. The Guttmacher Institute is a sexuality research center. You may also wish to visit the website of the National Organization of Women (NOW) and do a search for abortion.

Whether or not you think that limiting abortion availability is a good thing or a bad thing, the statistics might surprise you.

3. How widespread is AIDS?

Your textbook states that the Centers for Disease Control have recorded 774,467 cases of AIDS in the United States through the end of 2000. How fast is AIDS spreading in the rest of the world? One important consideration in tracking AIDS rates is the *per capita* rate. How does the rate per 100,000 people in the United States compare to other parts of the world? What countries have lower per capita rates? Why do you think that might be? What are some of the conditions in other parts of the world that increase the rate of AIDS? To answer these questions, go to a search engine such as www.yahoo.com or www.google.com and search for "AIDS rates" or "AIDS worldwide."

VIDEO SEGMENT

How do people come to see themselves as gay or lesbian? Watch the video for Chapter 13 on the CD-ROM to see how two young people, Sara and Daniel, describe coming out.

Psychological Disorders

Chapter Outline	*Learning Goals*

UNDERSTANDING ABNORMAL BEHAVIOR **1**

Defining Abnormal Behavior

Theoretical Approaches to Psychological Disorders

Classifying Abnormal Behavior

> Discuss the characteristics and classification of abnormal behavior

ANXIETY DISORDERS **2**

Generalized Anxiety Disorder

Panic Disorder

Phobic Disorders

Obsessive-Compulsive Disorder

> Distinguish among the various anxiety disorders

DISSOCIATIVE DISORDERS **3**

Dissociative Amnesia and Fugue

Dissociative Identity Disorder

> Describe the dissociative disorders

MOOD DISORDERS **4**

Depressive Disorders

Bipolar Disorder

Causes of Mood Disorders

Suicide

> Compare the mood disorders and specify risk factors for depression and suicide

SCHIZOPHRENIA **5**

Types of Schizophrenia

Causes of Schizophrenia

> Identify characteristics and possible causes of schizophrenia

PERSONALITY DISORDERS **6**

Odd or Eccentric Cluster

Dramatic or Emotionally Problematic Cluster

Anxious or Fearfulness Cluster

> Identify the behavior patterns typical of personality disorders

Images of Adjustment

Kay Redfield Jamison

Kay Redfield Jamison, a psychologist who has waged her own personal battle with bipolar disorder.

Kay Redfield Jamison is a psychologist and a leading expert on serious mood disorders. As a child, she was, she says, "intensely emotional"; as a young girl, "mercurial." Within three months of becoming a professor at UCLA, she was "mad beyond recognition." She had a serious psychological disorder: bipolar disorder, in which moods alternate between mania (an overexcited, unrealistically optimistic state) and depression.

For years, Jamison kept her psychological disorder hidden. In her memoir, Jamison (1995) tells of her battle with the disorder, of the joy of manic highs and the terrifying depressions that led her to want to die:

> "There is a particular kind of pain, elation, loneliness, and terror involved in this kind of madness. When you're high it's tremendous. The ideas and feelings are fast and frequent like shooting stars, and you follow them until you find better and brighter ones. Shyness goes, the right words and gestures are suddenly there, the power to captivate others a felt certainty. There are interests found in uninteresting people. Sensuality is pervasive and the desire to seduce and be seduced irresistible. Feelings of ease, intensity, power, well-being, financial omnipotence, and euphoria pervade one's marrow. But, somewhere this changes. The fast ideas are too fast, and there are far too many, overwhelming confusion replaces clarity. Memory goes. Everything previously moving with the grain is now against you. . . . You are irritable, angry, frightened, uncontrollable, and submerged totally in the blackest caves of the mind." (p. 67)

Jamison eventually, through strong support from friends and colleagues, excellent mental health care, medication, and her own acceptance of the disorder, reached a point at which her mood swings were dampened. Today, she continues to be a leading expert on psychological disorders as a professor of psychology at Johns Hopkins University.

Psychological disorders impair adjustment and know no social and economic boundaries. They find their way into the lives of the rich and famous and poor and unknown. In this chapter, we study a number of psychological disorders, including the mood disorder that enveloped Kay Redfield Jamison's life. We begin by exploring some basic questions about the nature of abnormal behavior, then turn our attention to several types of psychological disorders.

1   UNDERSTANDING ABNORMAL BEHAVIOR

> **Defining Abnormal Behavior**
>
> **Classifying Abnormal Behavior**
>
> **Theoretical Approaches to Psychological Disorders**

An estimated 44 million Americans each year suffer from some kind of psychological disorder (National Institute of Mental Health [NIMH], 2001). In one study, nearly 20,000 randomly selected individuals from five different regions of the United States were asked whether they had experienced any item on a list of psychological disorders in their lifetimes and whether they currently were suffering from one (Robins & Regier, 1991). Almost one-third (32 percent) of the respondents said that they had experienced one or more psychological disorders in their lifetimes, and 20 percent said they currently had a disorder.

You might be surprised that so many individuals acknowledge having a psychological disorder. However, the figures from the study include both individuals in institutions and in the community. They also include individuals with a substance abuse disorder (alcohol or other drugs, 17 percent). Surprisingly, only one-third of the individuals in this study who said they currently had a psychological disorder had received treatment for it in the previous six months.

Defining Abnormal Behavior

To understand psychological disorders, we need to examine what is meant by abnormal behavior. Consider the following three individuals:

- "Bernice engaged in a variety of rituals that took up almost all of her waking hours. In the morning she spent three or four hours in the bathroom, washing and rewashing herself. Between baths she scraped away the outside layer of her bar of soap so that it would be totally free of germs. Mealtimes lasted for hours, as Bernice performed her rituals—eating three bites of food at a time, chewing each mouthful 300 times," Davison & Neale, 2001, p. 146.
- Lavella is a 33-year-old computer sales representation who recently became divorced and is unhappy in her work, where she feels that she is not appreciated and was passed over in a recent promotion. She has become more depressed in recent weeks and increasingly pessimistic about her life.
- Twenty-seven-year-old Jim is an unemployed, single man who "told the psychiatrist that what really bothered him was that he had a special power. Specifically, he could influence other people, even endanger them, with the way he breathed. Now he has to go to great lengths to avoid contact with others, so as to avoid putting anyone in jeopardy," Gorenstein, 1997, p. 285.

Mental Health Resources
NIMH
National Mental Health Association

On January 16, 1996, multimillionaire John Dupont (*above*), a 58-year-old heir to the Dupont chemical fortune, pulled out a gun and killed Olympic Gold Medal wrestler David Schultz, who lived in a home on Dupont's estate and was one of several wrestlers training at Dupont's state-of-the art wrestling facility. No one disputes that Dupont killed Schultz, but Dupont's lawyers, using the so-called insanity defense, argued that he was too incapacitated by schizophrenia that he could not be held accountable for the murder. Prosecutors claimed he was an eccentric man driven by envy and anger who knew exactly what he was doing. After a week's deliberation, the jury concluded that Dupont had a psychological disorder but found him guilty of third-degree murder.

Would you agree that the behavior of all three of these individuals is abnormal? How would you define abnormal behavior? There are a number of myths about it. Here are two of the most common:

Myth: Abnormal behavior is always bizarre.
Fact: The behavior of many people who are diagnosed as having a mental disorder often cannot be distinguished from that of normal people. In Jim's case, belief in the power of his breath is bizarre. However, Janet's behavior would not be considered bizarre.
Myth: Normal and abnormal behavior are different in kind.
Fact: Few, if any, types of behavior displayed by people with a mental disorder are unique to them. Abnormal behavior consists of a poor fit between the behavior and the situation in which it is enacted.

Abnormal behavior is one of those concepts that is not easy to define (Oltmanns & Emery, 2004). The line between what is normal and what is abnormal is not always clear-cut. We can use three criteria to help distinguish normal from abnormal behavior. **Abnormal behavior** is behavior that is deviant, maladaptive, or personally distressful. Only one of the three criteria listed needs to be met for the behavior to be classified as abnormal, but two or all three may be present. Let's take a closer look at each of these criteria.

First, abnormal behavior is *deviant*. One way that abnormal behavior has been described is as being *atypical*. It is atypical behavior that deviates from what is acceptable in a culture. Bernice's compulsive behavior deviates from acceptable norms; people do not normally wash their hands three to four hours a day and chew each mouthful of food 300 times. Not all atypical behavior is considered deviant. For example, Albert Einstein and Barbara Walters are atypical because of their special talents, but we do not usually categorize them as deviant or abnormal.

Second, abnormal behavior is *maladaptive*. Maladaptive behavior interferes with a person's ability to function effectively in the world. Jim's belief that his breath has powerful, even harmful, effects on others keeps him isolated from society and prevents him from functioning in the everyday world.

Third, abnormal behavior involves *personal distress*. Bernice is distressed about how driven she is to stay clean and keep her immediate environment clean. Lavella also is distressed about her life and sees her future as extremely bleak.

Theoretical Approaches to Psychological Disorders

What is the *etiology* of psychological disorders? In other words, what causes people to develop a psychological disorder—to behave in deviant, maladaptive, and personally distressful ways? We can look to biological, psychological, and sociocultural factors for possible causes and consider the possibility that a combination of factors might contribute to an individual's maladaptive behavior.

The Biological Approach   The biological approach to psychological disorders attributes them to organic, internal causes (Howland, 2005). This approach is evident in the **medical model,** which describes psychological disorders as medical diseases with a biological origin. From the perspective of the medical model, abnormalities are called mental *illnesses*, the individuals afflicted are *patients*, and they are treated by *doctors*, often with drugs.

Biological factors that may contribute to psychological disorders fall into three main categories (Nolen-Hoeksema, 2004):

- Abnormalities in the brain's structure.
- Imbalances in neurotransmitters or hormones. Recall from chapter 4, "Stress," that neurotransmitters are chemicals that carry information from one neuron

abnormal behavior Behavior that is deviant, maladaptive, or personally distressful.

medical model A biological approach that describes psychological disorders as medical diseases with a biological origin.

(nerve cell) to the next and that hormones are chemical messengers manufactured by the endocrine glands.

- Disordered genes.

The Psychological Approach Most psychologists do not believe that biological factors by themselves can explain most psychological disorders (Hankin & Abela, 2005). The psychodynamic, behavioral and social cognitive, and humanistic perspectives on personality discussed in chapter 2, "Personality," serve as a foundation for understanding the psychological factors involved in psychological disorders:

- According to the psychodynamic perspective, psychological disorders arise from unconscious conflicts that produce anxiety and result in maladaptive behavior. Ineffective early relationships with parents are believed to be the origin of psychological disorders. Recall that these ideas stem from Freud's psychoanalytic theory but that some contemporary proponents of this approach place less emphasis on unconscious thought and sexuality.
- In the behavioral perspective, the focus is on rewards and punishments in the environment that shape abnormal behavior.
- The social cognitive perspective accepts that environmental experiences are important determinants of psychological disorders but adds that a number of social cognitive factors also are involved. In this way, observational learning, expectancies, self-efficacy, self-control, beliefs about oneself and the world, and many other cognitive processes may be key factors in psychological disorders.

The Sociocultural Approach The psychological approach mainly attributes psychological problems to unconscious conflicts, negative cognitions, low self-concept, and other factors within the individual (Nolen-Hoeksema, 2004). The sociocultural approach places more emphasis on the larger social contexts in which a person lives—including the individual's marriage or family, neighborhood, socioeconomic status, ethnicity, gender, or culture (Winstead & Sanchez, 2005). For example, marital conflict might be the cause of mental disorder in one individual. In this view, when a member of a family has a psychological problem, it may not be due to something within the individual but rather to ineffective family functioning (Atwood, 2001). Any number of psychological problems can develop because of power struggles in a family: sibling conflicts, one child being favored over another, marital conflict, and so on.

Most experts on abnormal behavior agree that many psychological disorders are universal (Al-Issa, 1982). However, the frequency and intensity of psychological disorders varies across cultures and depends on social, economic, technological, and religious aspects of cultures (Higgins, 2004; Lopez & Guarnaccia, 2000, 2005; Marsella, 2004; Tanaka-Matsumi, 2001). Some culture-related disorders are shown in figure 14.1.

Disorder	Culture	Description/Characteristics
Amok	Malaysia, Philippines, Africa	This disorder involves sudden, uncontrolled outbursts of anger in which the person may injure or kill someone. Amok is often found in males who are emotionally withdrawn before the onset of the disorder. After the attack on someone, the individual feels exhausted and depressed and does not remember the rage and attack.
Anorexia Nervosa	Western cultures, especially the United States	This eating disorder involves a relentless pursuit of thinness through starvation and can eventually lead to death.
Windigo	Algonquin Indian hunters	This disorder involves a fear of being bewitched. The hunter becomes anxious and agitated, worrying he will be turned into a cannibal with a craving for human flesh.

FIGURE 14.1 Some Culture-Related Disorders

Individuals from low-income, minority neighborhoods have the highest rates of mental disorders. In studies of the role of socioeconomic status and ethnicity in psychological disorders, socioeconomic status plays a much stronger role than does ethnicity: the living conditions of poverty create stressful circumstances that can contribute to the development of a mental disorder (Almeida-Filho & others, 2004; Elliott, Beattie, & Kaitfors, 2001; Schultz & others, 2000).

Gender, another sociocultural factor, is associated with the presence of certain psychological disorders (Hyde, 2004; Nolen-Hoeksema, 2004; Wood, 2001). Women tend to be diagnosed as having internalized disorders. In particular, women are likelier than men to suffer from anxiety disorders and depression, which have symptoms that are turned inward (internalized). Conversely, men are socialized to direct their energy toward the external world (to externalize their feelings) and they more often have externalized disorders that involve aggression and substance abuse.

An Interactionist Approach: Biopsychosocial Does genetics account for Bernice's compulsion to clean? Is the key to her problem in her relationship with her parents, or perhaps her gender? Each of these factors (and Bernice's problem) will be discussed later in the chapter, but no single factor is likely to account for Bernice's abnormal behavior.

Normal and abnormal behavior alike may involve biological, psychological, and sociocultural factors alone or in combination with other factors. Abnormal behavior can be influenced by biological factors (such as brain processes and heredity), psychological factors (such as distorted thoughts or low self-esteem), and sociocultural factors (such as ineffective family functioning or poverty). These factors can interact to produce abnormal behavior. Sometimes this interactionist approach is called *biopsychosocial*.

Classifying Abnormal Behavior

Ever since human history began, people have suffered from diseases, sadness, and bizarre behavior. And, for almost as long, healers have tried to treat and cure them. The classification of psychological disorders goes back to the ancient Egyptians and Greeks and has roots in biology and medicine. To this day, the classification of mental disorders follows a medical model.

The DSM-IV-TR Classification System In 1952, the American Psychiatric Association published the first major classification of psychological disorders in the United States in the *Diagnostic and Statistical Manual of Mental Disorders*. Over the years, continuing changes in the *DSM* have reflected advances in knowledge (First & Pincus, 2002; Widiger, 2000). On the basis of research and clinical experience, categories of disorders have been dropped, added, or revised as new editions of the *DSM* have been published. **DSM-IV-TR** (*Diagnostic and Statistical Manual of Mental Disorders*, Fourth Edition, Text Revision) is the current edition of the American Psychiatric Association's guidelines; it describes 17 major classifications and more than 200 specific disorders (American Psychiatric Association, 2000).

A key feature of the *DSM-IV-TR* is its *multiaxial system*, which classifies individuals on the basis of five dimensions, or axes. The system ensures that the individual is not merely assigned to a category but instead is evaluated in terms of a number of factors, including the individual's history and highest level of functioning in the previous year. Axes I and II comprise the classification of psychological disorders (Davison & Neale, 2004). Figure 14.2 describes the major categories of these psychological disorders. The five axes of *DSM-IV-TR* are as follows:

Axis I: All diagnostic categories except personality disorders and mental retardation

Axis II: Personality disorders and mental retardation

DSM-IV-TR *Diagnostic and Statistical Manual of Mental Disorders,* Fourth Edition, Text Revision; the American Psychiatric Association's major classification of psychological disorders.

Major Categories of Psychological Disorders	Description
Axis I Disorders	
Disorders usually first diagnosed in infancy, childhood, or adolescence and communication disorders	Include disorders that appear before adolescence, such as attention-deficit hyperactivity disorder, autism, learning disorders (stuttering, for example).
Anxiety disorders	Characterized by motor tension, hyperactivity, and apprehensive expectations/thoughts. Includes generalized anxiety disorder, panic disorder, phobic disorder, obsessive-compulsive disorder, and post-traumatic stress disorder.
Somatoform disorders	Occur when psychological symptoms take a physical form even though no physical causes can be found. Includes hypochondriasis and conversion disorder.
Factitious disorders	The person deliberately fabricates symptoms of a medical or mental disorder, but not for external gain (such as a disability claim).
Dissociative disorders	Involve a sudden loss of memory or change of identity. Includes the disorders of dissociative amnesia, dissociative fugue, and dissociative identity disorder.
Delirium, dementia, amnestic, and other cognitive disorders	Consist of mental disorders involving problems in consciousness and cognition, such as substance-induced delirium or dementia involving Alzheimer's disease.
Mood disorders	Disorders in which there is a primary disturbance in mood; includes depressive disorders and bipolar disorder (which involves wide mood swings from deep depression to extreme euphoria and agitation).
Schizophrenia and other psychotic disorders	Disorders characterized by distorted thoughts and perceptions, odd communication, inappropriate emotion, and other unusual behaviors.
Substance-related disorders	Include alcohol-related disorders, cocaine-related disorders, hallucinogen-related disorders, and other drug-related disorders.
Sexual and gender identity disorders	Consist of three main types of disorders: gender-identity disorders (person is not comfortable with identity as a female or male), (person has a preference for unusual sexual acts to stimulate sexual arousal), and sexual dysfunctions (impairments in sexual functioning; see chapter 13).
Eating disorders	Include anorexia nervosa and bulimia nervosa, (see chapter 16).
Sleep disorders	Consist of primary sleep disorders, such as insomnia and narcolepsy and sleep disorder due to a general medical condition.
Impulse control disorders not elsewhere classified	Include kleptomania, pyromania, and compulsive gambling.
Adjustment disorders	Characterized by distressing emotional or behavioral symptoms in response to an identifiable stressor.
Axis II Disorders	
Mental retardation	Low intellectual functioning and an inability to adapt to everyday life.
Personality disorders	Develop when personality traits become inflexible and maladaptive.
Other conditions that may be a focus of clinical attention.	Include relational problems (with a partner, sibling, and so on), problems related to abuse or neglect (physical abuse of a child, for example), or additional conditions (such as bereavement, academic problems, religious or spiritual problems).

FIGURE 14.2 Main Categories of Psychological Disorders in *DSM-IV*

Axis III: General medical conditions, such as hypertension or leukemia

Axis IV: Psychosocial and environmental problems, such as death of a friend or homelessness

Axis V: Current level of functioning, which is assigned a number from 0 to 100

Axes III through V may not be needed to diagnose a psychological disorder, but they are included so that the person's overall situation is considered. For example, a person might have a heart condition (Axis III), which has important implications for treatment because some antidepressant drugs can worsen heart conditions. Axis IV includes occupational problems, economic problems, and family problems. On Axis V, the clinician makes a diagnosis about the highest level of functioning that the person has reached in the preceding year in social, occupational, or school activities.

Notice that the *DSM* reflects the medical model of psychological disorders. It classifies individuals based on their symptoms, and it uses medical terminology, describing mental disorders in terms of illness or disease (Nathan & Langenbucher, 2003). This strategy implies the disorders have an internal cause that is more or less independent of environmental factors—even though researchers have begun to shed light on how the complex interaction of biological, psychological, and sociocultural factors influences abnormal as well as normal behavior (Sarbin & Keen, 1998; Widiger, 2005).

The Issue of Labeling   The *DSM* classification of psychological disorders is controversial for several reasons. For one, it labels as psychological disorders what are often thought of as everyday problems. For example, the *DSM-IV-TR* includes reading disorder, mathematics disorder, disorders of written expression, and caffeine-induced disorders. We don't usually think of these everyday problems as mental disorders. One practical reason for including everyday problems in living in the *DSM* is to help individuals receive reimbursement from their insurance companies to pay for professional help. Most health insurance companies reimburse their clients only for disorders listed in the *DSM* system.

Another criticism of the *DSM*, and indeed of this type of classification system in general, is that the system focuses strictly on pathology, with a bias toward finding something wrong with anyone who becomes the object of diagnostic study. Because labels can become self-fulfilling prophecies, emphasizing strengths as well as weaknesses might help to destigmatize labels such as *paranoid schizophrenic* or *ex-mental patient*. It would also help to provide clues to treatments that promote mental competence rather than working only to reduce mental distress.

The *DSM*, like other classification systems, is also criticized because it puts labels on people, and labels can be damaging. They draw attention to one aspect of a person and ignore others (Sarason & Sarason, 2004). If the label has negative connotations—such as incompetent, dangerous, and socially unacceptable—it can reduce a person's self-esteem and lead to discrimination. Also, when people feel they might be stigmatized, they may be reluctant to seek help because they don't want to be labeled "mentally ill" or "crazy." Further, even when a person who has had a psychological disorder improves, the label may stay with the person.

Despite its problems, the *DSM-IV-TR* is the most comprehensive classification system available. Furthermore, any classification of psychological disorders will provoke criticism, but most mental health professionals believe the benefits of a classification system outweigh its disadvantages. For one, a classification system gives mental health professionals a common basis for communicating with one another (Canino & others, 2004; Lowe & others, 2004). For example, if one psychologist says that her client has a panic disorder and another psychologist says that his client has schizophrenia, the two psychologists understand that the clients have exhibited certain behavior that led to their diagnoses. In addition, a classification system can help clinicians make predictions about disorders; it provides information about the likelihood that a disorder will occur, about which individuals are most susceptible to the disorder, about the progress of the disorder once it has appeared, and about the prognosis for effective treatment (Blumentritt, Angle, & Brown, 2004; Meehl, 1986, 2004).

With this information about the basic nature of psychological disorders in hand, it is now time to examine the main categories of disorders and some specific disorders. We begin with the anxiety disorders.

Review and Reflect

1 **Discuss the characteristics and classification of abnormal behavior**

REVIEW

- What is abnormal behavior?
- What factors might be involved in the etiology of psychological disorders?
- How does the *Diagnostic and Statistical Manual of Mental Disorders* classify psychological disorders, and what are its advantages and disadvantages?

REFLECT

- Ed Gein, a serial killer from Wisconsin, admitted to murdering two women in the 1950s and to robbing bodies from graves. He made corpse parts into ornaments and clothes that he wore to replicate the image of his dead mother. Gein was acquitted by reason of insanity and committed to a mental institution. He was the inspiration for *Psycho* and *Silence of the Lambs.* Do you think Gein should have been acquitted? What do you think about the insanity defense?

2 ANXIETY DISORDERS

- **Generalized Anxiety Disorder**
- **Phobic Disorders**
- **Panic Disorder**
- **Obsessive-Compulsive Disorder**

Unless you are very unusual, at some time or another you have felt anxiety, which is a diffuse, vague, unpleasant feeling of fear and apprehension. People with high levels of anxiety worry a lot, but their anxiety does not necessarily impair their ability to function in the world. However, for a person to be diagnosed as having an anxiety disorder the individual must feel marked distress or suffer significant impairment of functioning (Anthony, 2004; Williams, 2005). **Anxiety disorders** are psychological disorders that feature motor tension (jumpiness, trembling, inability to relax); hyperactivity (dizziness, a racing heart, or possibly perspiration); and apprehensive expectations and thoughts. Approximately 19.1 million American adults from 18 to 54 years of age, or about 13.3 percent of people in this age group, are diagnosed with an anxiety disorder in any given year (NIMH, 2004a). The five types of anxiety disorders are generalized anxiety disorder, panic disorder, phobic disorders, obsessive-compulsive disorder, and post-traumatic stress disorder. We discussed post-traumatic stress disorder in chapter 4, "Stress," and examine the other four disorders here.

Generalized Anxiety Disorder

Generalized anxiety disorder consists of persistent anxiety for at least one month; the individual with generalized anxiety disorder is unable to specify the reasons for the anxiety (Wetherell & others, 2004). People with generalized anxiety disorder are nervous most of the time. They may worry about their work, their relationships, their health. They also may worry about minor things in life, such as whether their

anxiety disorders Psychological disorders that include these features: motor tension, hyperactivity, and apprehensive expectations and thoughts.

generalized anxiety disorder An anxiety disorder that consists of persistent anxiety over at least one month; the individual with this disorder cannot specify the reasons for the anxiety.

clothes fit just right. Their anxiety often shifts from one aspect of life to another. Approximately 4 million Americans from 18 to 54 years of age, or about 2.8 percent of people in this age group, have generalized anxiety disorder in any given year (NIMH, 2004a).

What is the etiology of generalized anxiety disorder? Among the biological factors involved in generalized anxiety disorder are a genetic predisposition and a deficiency in the neurotransmitter GABA (Nutt, 2001). Psychological and sociocultural factors include harsh standards that are almost impossible to achieve, parents who were overly strict and critical (which can produce low self-esteem and excessive self-criticism), automatic negative thoughts in the face of stress, and a history of uncontrollable stressors, such as having an abusive parent.

Panic Disorder

Panic disorder is an anxiety disorder marked by the recurrent sudden onset of intense apprehension or terror. The individual often has a feeling of impending doom but may not feel anxious all the time. Panic attacks often strike without warning and produce severe palpitations, extreme shortness of breath, chest pains, trembling, sweating, dizziness, and a feeling of helplessness (Anderson & Hetta, 2004; Meuret, Wilhelm, & Roth, 2004). Victims are seized by fear that they will die, go crazy, or do something they cannot control. Approximately 2.4 million Americans from 18 to 54 years of age, or about 1.7 percent of the people in this age group, have panic disorder in any given year (NIMH, 2004a).

In *DSM-IV-TR*, panic disorder may be diagnosed with or without **agoraphobia,** a cluster of fears centered on public places and an inability to escape or find help should one become incapacitated (Fava & others, 2001; Miller & others, 2005). Crowded public places; traveling away from home, especially by public transportation; feeling confined or trapped; and being separated from a place or person all can produce agoraphobia, which causes some people to remain housebound. Agoraphobia usually first appears in early adulthood, with 2.5 percent of individuals in the United States classified as having the disorder.

What is the etiology of panic disorder? Several biological contributors have been proposed (Amrhein & others, 2005). For example, a panic attack is associated with an overreaction to lactic acid (which is produced by the body when it is under stress). There may be a genetic predisposition for panic disorder; it runs in families and occurs more often in identical than fraternal twins (Goldstein & others, 1997). One possibility is that individuals who experience panic disorder may have an autonomic nervous system that is predisposed to be overly active (Barlow & Durand, 2005). Also, panic disorder may be caused by problems involving either or both of the neurotransmitters norepinephrine and GABA (Goddard & others, 2004).

Psychological factors may be important in the etiology of panic disorder (Marcaurelle & others, 2005). In many instances, a stressful life event has occurred in the six months prior to the onset of panic disorder, most often a threatened or actual separation from a loved one or a change in job. One view of panic disorder with agoraphobia, the *fear-of-fear hypothesis,* suggests that agoraphobia may not represent a fear of public places per se but rather a fear of having a panic attack in public places.

Sociocultural factors have also been linked with panic disorder. In particular, U.S. women are twice as likely as men to have panic attacks with or without agoraphobia (Fodor & Epstein, 2001). However, in India, men are far more likely to have panic disorders than women; women rarely leave home alone (McNally, 1994). Reasons for U.S. women having a higher incidence than men of panic disorder with or without agoraphobia include gender socialization (boys are encouraged to be more independent, girls are protected more) and traumatic experiences (rape and child sexual abuse occur more often in the backgrounds of women than men) (Fodor & Epstein, 2001).

www.mhhe.com/santrockha

Anxiety Disorders
Anxiety Disorders Association
Anxiety and Panic
Panic & Anxiety Hub

panic disorder An anxiety disorder marked by the recurrent sudden onset of intense apprehension or terror.

agoraphobia A cluster of fears centered around public places and being unable to escape or to find help should one become incapacitated.

phobic disorder Commonly called *phobia,* an anxiety disorder in which the individual has an irrational, overwhelming, persistent fear of a particular object or situation.

Adjustment Strategies
For Coping with Panic

An expert on anxiety disorders, Edmund Bourne (2001) recommends these strategies to cope with oncoming symptoms of panic:

1. ***Retreat.*** If panic symptoms begin to intensify when you are approaching or dealing with a phobic situation (such as driving on the freeway, going into a grocery store, or staying at home alone), simply leave the situation until your panic subsides.
2. ***Divert your attention.*** If panic symptoms come on spontaneously, apart from any phobic situation, it may help to distract yourself. You can divert your attention from the panic through such strategies as talking to someone, doing simple repetitive tasks (such as counting change or timing a stoplight), engaging in a physical activity, doing something enjoyable (such as getting a massage, eating a snack), or practicing thought stopping (discussed in chapter 5, "Coping").
3. ***Engage in deep breathing relaxation and positive self-talk.*** For many individuals, these are powerful strategies for counteracting panic; they are described in chapter 5, "Coping." Relaxation and positive self-talk can be used separately or in combination.

Acrophobia	Fear of high places
Aerophobia	Fear of flying
Ailurophobia	Fear of cats
Algophobia	Fear of pain
Amaxophobia	Fear of vehicles, driving
Arachnophobia	Fear of spiders
Astrapophobia	Fear of lightning
Cynophobia	Fear of dogs
Gamophobia	Fear of marriage
Hydrophobia	Fear of water
Melissophobia	Fear of bees
Mysophobia	Fear of dirt
Nyctophobia	Fear of darkness
Ophidiophobia	Fear of nonpoisonous snakes
Thanatophobia	Fear of death
Xenophobia	Fear of strangers

FIGURE 14.3 Phobias
This is only a partial listing.

Phobic Disorders

A **phobic disorder,** commonly called *phobia,* is an anxiety disorder in which the individual has an irrational, overwhelming, persistent fear of a particular object or situation. Individuals with generalized anxiety disorder cannot pinpoint the cause of their nervous feelings; individuals with phobias can (Barlow, 2001). A fear becomes a phobia when a situation is so dreaded that an individual goes to almost any length to avoid it. Some phobias are more debilitating than others. An individual with a fear of automobiles has a more difficult time functioning in our society than a person with a fear of snakes, for example. Approximately 6.3 million Americans from 18 to 54 years of age, or about 4.4 percent of the people in this age group, have a phobic disorder in any given year (NIMH, 2004a).

Phobias come in many forms. Some of the most common phobias involve social situations, dogs, height, dirt, flying, and snakes. Figure 14.3 labels and describes a number of phobias.

Another phobia is *social phobia,* which is an intense fear of being humiliated or embarrassed in social situations. Individuals with this phobia are afraid that they will say or do the wrong thing. As a consequence, they might avoid speaking up in a conversation, giving a speech, going out to eat, or attending a party. Their intense fear of such contexts can severely restrict their social life and increase their loneliness (Curtis, Kimball, & Stroup, 2004; Erwin & others, 2002). Figure 14.4 shows the percentage of people in the United States who say they have experienced a social phobia in their lifetimes (Kessler, Steini, & Bergland, 1998).

What is the etiology of phobic disorders? In terms of biological factors, individuals who are more closely related are more likely to have a phobic disorder than those who are less closely related (Kessler, Olfson, & Bergland, 1998). A neural circuit has been proposed for social phobia that includes the thalamus, amygdala, and cerebral cortex (Li, Chokka, & Tibbo, 2001). Several neurotransmitters may be involved in social phobia, especially serotonin (Furmock & others, 2004).

In terms of psychological factors, different theoretical perspectives provide different explanations (Abbott & Rapee, 2004; Stravynski, Bond, & Amado, 2004).

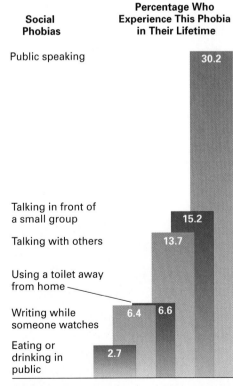

FIGURE 14.4

Social Phobias in the United States
In a national survey, the most common social phobia was public speaking.

Popular professional football announcer John Madden has a fear of flying. Because of this phobia, Madden crisscrosses the United States from week to week during football season in his "Madden-cruiser" bus.

"He always times '60 Minutes.'"

© The New Yorker Collection 1983 Mischa Richter from cartoonbank.com. All Rights Reserved.

Jack Nicholson portrayed an individual with obsessive-compulsive disorder in the movie, *As Good As It Gets.*

Psychodynamic theorists, for example, say phobias develop as defense mechanisms to ward off threatening or unacceptable impulses. Learning theorists, however, explain phobias differently; they say phobias are learned fears.

Obsessive-Compulsive Disorder

Earlier, you read about 30-year-old Bernice, who has an obsessive-compulsive disorder. **Obsessive-compulsive disorder (OCD)** is an anxiety disorder in which the individual has anxiety-provoking thoughts that will not go away (obsession) or urges to perform repetitive, ritualistic behaviors to prevent or produce some future situation (compulsion). Individuals with OCD repeat and rehearse normal doubts and daily routines, sometimes hundreds of times a day (Frost & Steketee, 1998). Approximately 3.3 million Americans from 18 to 54 years of age, or about 2.3 percent of the people in this age group, have obsessive-compulsive disorder in any given year (NIMH, 2004a).

The most common compulsions are excessive checking, cleansing, and counting. For example, a young man feels he has to check his apartment for gas leaks and make sure the windows are locked. His behavior is not compulsive if he does this once, but if he goes back to check five or six times and then constantly worries that he might not have checked carefully enough once he has left the house, his behavior is compulsive. Most individuals do not enjoy their ritualistic behavior but feel anxious when they do not carry it out.

What is the etiology of obsessive-compulsive disorder? In terms of biological factors, there seems to be a genetic component, because OCD runs in families (Bellodi & others, 2001). Also, imaging of the brain suggests that people who suffer from OCD have distinct neurological patterns (Anderson & Savage, 2004; Kuelz, Hohagen, & Voderholzer, 2004). One interpretation is that some regions of the brain become so active that neural impulses generate obsessive thoughts or compulsive actions (Rappaport, 1989). Depletion of the neurotransmitter serotonin likely is involved in the neural circuitry linked with OCD (Dougherty, Rauch, & Jenike, 2005; Jenike, 2001).

Research also links psychological factors to the onset of OCD. This disorder often occurs during a period of life stress, such as childbirth, a change in occupational status, or a change in marital status. Onset of the disorder frequently occurs in late adolescence or early adulthood, although it can also emerge in young children (Masi & others, 2004). According to the cognitive perspective, what differentiates individuals with OCD from those who do not have it is the ability to turn off negative, intrusive thoughts by ignoring or dismissing them (Bouvard, Milliery, & Cottraux, 2004; Purdon, Rowa, & Antony, 2005; Woods, Tolin, & Abramowitz, 2004).

Adjustment Strategies
For Coping with an Anxiety Disorder

The National Institute of Mental Health (2004a) and the Anxiety Disorders Association of America (2004) recommends these strategies if you think you might have an anxiety disorder:

1. ***Understand that effective treatments, developed through research, are available for each of the anxiety disorders.*** The choice of either drug therapy (antianxiety medication), psychotherapy, or both will depend on your and the therapist's preference, and on the particular anxiety disorder. In the next chapter, we will examine these treatments in greater depth.
2. ***Ask the therapist or physician what training and experience he or she has in treating anxiety disorders.*** If the mental health professional does not have experience in this area, ask for the name of a therapist who does. Also ask what the therapist's approach to treating anxiety disorders is.
3. ***Expect the therapist to conduct a thorough diagnostic evaluation.*** Before treatment begins the therapist will conduct a thorough diagnostic evaluation to determine whether your symptoms are due to an anxiety disorder, which anxiety disorder(s) you might have, and what coexisting conditions might be present. Sometimes alcoholism, depression, or another coexisting condition has such a strong impact that it is necessary to treat it at the same time or before treating the anxiety disorder.
4. ***Recognize that the length of treatment required varies with the individual.*** Some individuals respond to treatment after several months, while others may take a year or more.
5. ***Know that if one treatment doesn't work, chances are that another one will.*** And new treatments are continually being developed through research.

Review and Reflect

2 Distinguish among the various anxiety disorders

REVIEW
- What are anxiety disorders, and what is generalized anxiety disorder?
- What are the key features of panic disorder?
- How is a phobic disorder different from a normal fear, and what might cause it?
- What is obsessive-compulsive disorder?

REFLECT
- Family members and friends of individuals with obsessive-compulsive disorder frequently tell them to stop their obsessions and compulsions. However, just telling someone to stop these obsessions and compulsions usually does not work. If you had a friend with this disorder, what would you try to do about it?

obsessive-compulsive disorder (OCD) An anxiety disorder; the individual has anxiety-provoking thoughts that will not go away (obsession) and/or urges to perform repetitive, ritualistic behaviors to prevent or produce some future situation (compulsion).

3   DISSOCIATIVE DISORDERS

Dissociative Amnesia and Fugue

Dissociative Identity Disorder

Dissociative disorders are psychological disorders that involve a sudden loss of memory or change in identity. Under extreme stress or shock, the individual's conscious awareness becomes dissociated (separated or split) from previous memories and thoughts (Simeon & others, 2002). Three kinds of dissociative disorders are dissociative amnesia, dissociative fugue, and dissociative identity.

Dissociative Amnesia and Fugue

Amnesia is the inability to recall important events and it may be caused by a blow to the head (LaBar & others, 2002). But **dissociative amnesia** is a dissociative disorder characterized by extreme memory loss that is caused by extensive psychological stress. For example, an individual showed up at a hospital and said he did not know who he was. After several days in the hospital, he awoke one morning and demanded to be released. Eventually he remembered that he had been involved in an automobile accident in which a pedestrian had been killed. The extreme stress of the accident and the fear that he might be held responsible triggered the amnesia.

Dissociative fugue (*fugue* means "flight") is a dissociative disorder in which the individual not only develops amnesia but also unexpectedly travels away from home and assumes a new identity. Consider the case of Barbara, a 31-year-old woman who one day simply vanished (Goldstein & Palmer, 1975). When she was found in a nearby city two weeks later, she was wearing bobby socks and had her hair in a ponytail. She had taken a bus to the town where she grew up, walked the streets, and gone to a motel, where she entertained a series of men. When she was found, looking more like a teenager than an adult, she could not remember the last two weeks and did not recognize her husband.

Dissociative Identity Disorder

Dissociative identity disorder (DID), formerly called *multiple personality disorder,* is the most dramatic but least common dissociative disorder; individuals suffering from this disorder have two or more distinct personalities or selves, like the fictional Dr. Jekyll and Mr. Hyde of Robert Louis Stevenson's short story. Each personality has its own memories, behaviors, and relationships; one personality dominates the individual at one time, and another personality will take over at another time. Some research suggests that a person's different personalities have different EEG patterns (Allen & Movius, 2000). The shift from one personality to the other usually occurs under distress (Dell, 2002).

One of the most famous cases of dissociative identity disorder involves the "three faces of Eve" (see figure 14.5) (Thigpen & Cleckley, 1957):

> Eve White was the original dominant personality. She had no knowledge of her second personality, Eve Black, although Eve Black had been alternating with Eve White for a number of years. Eve White was bland, quiet, and serious—a rather dull personality. By contrast, Eve Black was carefree, mischievous, and uninhibited. She would "come out" at the most inappropriate times, leaving Eve White with hangovers, bills, and a reputation in local bars that she could not explain. During treatment, a third personality, Jane, emerged. More mature than the other two, Jane seemed to have developed as a result of therapy.

The vast majority of individuals diagnosed with dissociative identity disorder are adult females. Males diagnosed with the disorder show more aggression than females with the disorder (Ross & Norton, 1989).

dissociative disorders Psychological disorders that involve a sudden loss of memory or change in identity.

dissociative amnesia A dissociative disorder involving extreme memory loss caused by extensive psychological stress.

dissociative fugue A dissociative disorder in which the individual not only develops amnesia but also unexpectedly travels away from home and establishes a new identity.

dissociative identity disorder (DID) Formerly called *multiple personality disorder,* this is the most dramatic but least common dissociative disorder; individuals suffering from this disorder have two or more distinct personalities.

FIGURE 14.5 The Three Faces of Eve
Chris Sizemore, the subject of *The Three Faces of Eve,* is shown here with a work she painted, titled *Three Faces in One.*

Research on dissociative identity disorder suggests that the disorder is characterized by an inordinately high rate of sexual or physical abuse during early childhood (McAllister, 2000; Stafford &Lynn, 2002). Sexual abuse occurs in more than 50 percent of reported cases of the disorder. Note, though, that the majority of individuals who have been sexually abused do not develop dissociative identity disorder. Mothers of individuals who develop this disorder tend to be rejecting and depressed; fathers distant, alcoholic, and abusive. A genetic predisposition might exist (Dell & Eisenhower, 1990).

Until the 1980s, only about 300 cases had ever been reported (Suinn, 1984). In the past decade, hundreds more have been diagnosed with "dissociative identity disorder." Some psychologists argue this increase represents a fad; others believe that the disorder has been frequently misdiagnosed as schizophrenia; yet others claim it isn't a real condition. In some cases, therapists have been blamed for creating a second or third personality. (At one point, Eve said that her therapist had created one of her personalities.)

Review and Reflect

3   Describe the dissociative disorders

REVIEW

- What are the characteristics of the dissociative disorders, dissociative amnesia, and fugue?
- What is dissociative identity disorder?

REFLECT

- Imagine that you are on a jury in which an individual who has been accused of killing someone claims that he suffers from dissociative identity disorder and doesn't remember committing the murder. How difficult would it be for you and the other jury members to determine if he really has this disorder? What questions would you want answered before making your decision about the individual?

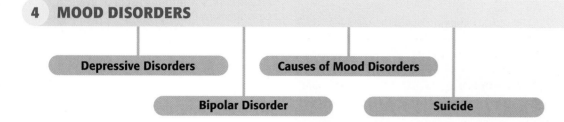

4 MOOD DISORDERS

Depressive Disorders

Bipolar Disorder

Causes of Mood Disorders

Suicide

Neither anxiety disorders nor dissociative disorders bring the manic highs and terrifying depressions suffered in Kay Redfield Jamison's (described at the opening of the chapter) mood disorder. The **mood disorders** are psychological disorders in which the dominant feature is a disturbance of mood (prolonged emotion that colors the individual's entire emotional state). The disturbance of mood can involve cognitive, behavioral, and physical symptoms, as well as interpersonal difficulties (Coyne, 2000).

Two main types of mood disorders are the depressive disorders and bipolar disorder. Depression can occur alone, without mania (an overexcited, unrealistically optimistic state) as in the **depressive disorders,** or depression can alternate with mania, as in bipolar disorder (Ingram & Trenary, 2005). Approximately 18.8 million Americans between the ages of 18 and 54, or about 9.5 percent of the people in this age group, have a mood disorder in any given year (NIMH, 2004b).

Depressive Disorders

Everyone feels "blue" sometimes, and people use the term *depression* to describe brief bouts of normal sadness or discontent. Perhaps you haven't done well in a class or things aren't working out in your love life. You feel down in the dumps and say you are depressed. In most instances, though, after a few hours, days, or weeks, you snap out of your gloomy state and begin to cope more effectively with your problems. In contrast, consider a person with a depressive disorder:

> "My brain is like on time out. I just can't get anything done. I feel virtually exhausted all of the time. I try to study but I read the same pages over and over again and can't remember a thing I've read. I feel like the bottom is falling out of my life. It's so empty." Nothing cheered Peter up. His depression began when the girl he wanted to marry decided that marriage was not for her, at least not marriage to Peter. Peter's emotional state deteriorated to the point at which he didn't leave his room for days at a time, he kept his shades down and the room dark, and he could hardly get out of bed in the morning. When he managed to leave the room, he had trouble maintaining a conversation.

Peter was diagnosed with **major depressive disorder (MDD),** a depressive disorder in which the individual experiences a major depressive episode, which means that at least five of the following symptoms are present for at least two weeks:

1. Depressed mood most of the day
2. Reduced interest or pleasure in all or most activities
3. Significant weight loss or gain, or significant decrease or interest in appetite
4. Trouble sleeping or sleeping too much
5. Psychomotor agitation or retardation
6. Fatigue or loss of energy
7. Feeling worthless or guilty in an excessive or inappropriate manner
8. Problems in thinking, concentrating, or making decisions
9. Recurrent thoughts of death and suicide

In addition, to be diagnosed with MDD a person must experience significant distress or impairment of daily functioning as a result of the symptoms.

A recent national study found that 16.2 percent of U.S. adults (about 34 million) had experienced MDD in their lifetime and 6.2 percent had MDD in the previous

This painting by Vincent Van Gogh, *Portrait of Dr. Gachet,* reflects the extreme melancholy that characterizes the depressive disorders.

mood disorders Psychological disorders in which there is a disturbance in mood (prolonged emotion that colors the individual's entire emotional state). Two main types are the depressive disorders and bipolar disorder.

depressive disorders Mood disorders in which the individual suffers depression without ever experiencing mania.

major depressive disorder (MDD) A depressive disorder in which the individual experiences a major depressive episode with the symptoms lasting at least two weeks.

twelve months (Kessler & others, 2003). The individuals with MDD were on average unable to work or do normal activities for five weeks out of a year. In this study, only 20 percent of the individuals with MDD were getting effective treatment, although most can be successfully treated, as we will discuss in chapter 15.

A second type of depressive disorder does not involve a major depressive episode. **Dysthymic disorder** is generally more chronic and has fewer symptoms than major depressive disorder. The individual is in a depressed mood for most days for at least two years as an adult or at least one year as a child or adolescent. The two-year period of depression must not have been broken by a normal mood lasting more than two months. Two or more of the six symptoms must be present: poor appetite or overeating, sleep problems, low energy or fatigue, low self-esteem, poor concentration or difficulty making decisions, and feelings of hopelessness (Munoz, 1998). Approximately 5.4 percent of the population will have dysthymic disorder in their lifetimes (NIMH, 2004b).

Depression is so widespread that it has been called the "common cold" of psychological disorders; more than 250,000 individuals in the United States are hospitalized each year for the disorder. Students, professors, corporate executives, laborers—no one is immune to depression, not even F. Scott Fitzgerald, Ernest Hemingway, Virginia Woolf, Abraham Lincoln, or Winston Churchill—each of whom experienced depression.

Individuals who go untreated suffer needlessly. To evaluate whether you might be depressed, complete Self-Assessment 14.1.

Adjustment Strategies
For Coping with Depression

The National Institute of Mental Health (2000) provides these recommendations for coping with depression:

For the Depressed Individual

1. ***Recognize that feeling exhausted, worthless, helpless, and hopeless are part of the depression.*** These feelings make some people want to give up, but it is important to realize that these negative feelings do not reflect actual circumstances. They fade as treatment begins to take effect.
2. ***See a therapist.*** Most individuals with depression show substantial improvement through psychotherapy, drug therapy (antidepressant medications), or a combination of the two. In the next chapter, we will thoroughly examine these treatments and which ones are the most effective. In the meantime, do the following (National Institute of Mental Health, 2000, p. 7):
   - "Set realistic goals in light of the depression and assume a reasonable amount of responsibility.
   - Break large tasks into small ones, set some priorities, and do what you can as you can.
   - Try to be with other people and to confide in someone; it is usually better than being alone and secretive.
   - Participate in activities that may make you feel better.
   - Mild exercise, going to a movie, a ballgame, or participating in religious, social, or other activities may help.
   - Expect your mood to improve gradually, not immediately. Feeling better takes time.
   - It is advisable to postpone important decisions until the depression has lifted. Before deciding to make a significant transition—change jobs, get married or divorced—discuss it with others who know you well and have a more objective view of your situation.
   - People rarely "snap out of" a depression. But they can feel a little better day-by-day.
   - *Remember*, positive thinking will replace the negative thinking that is part of the depression and will disappear as your depression responds to treatment.
   - Let your family and friends help you."

dysthymic disorder A depressive disorder that is generally more chronic and has fewer symptoms than major depressive disorder.

continued

SELF-ASSESSMENT 14.1

Am I Depressed?

Below is a list of the ways that you might have felt or behaved in the past week. Indicate what you felt by putting an X in the appropriate box for each item.

During the past week	Rarely or None of the Time (Less Than 1 Day)	Some or a Little of the Time (1–2 Days)	Occasionally or a Moderate Amount of the Time (3–4 Days)	Most or All of the Time (5–7 Days)
1. I was bothered by things that usually don't bother me.				
2. I did not feel like eating; my appetite was poor.				
3. I felt that I could not shake off the blues even with help from my family and friends.				
4. I felt that I was just as good as other people.				
5. I had trouble keeping my mind on what I was doing.				
6. I felt depressed.				
7. I felt that everything I did was an effort.				
8. I felt hopeful about the future.				
9. I thought my life had been a failure.				
10. I felt fearful.				
11. My sleep was restless.				
12. I was happy.				
13. I talked less than usual.				
14. I felt lonely.				
15. People were unfriendly.				
16. I enjoyed life.				
17. I had crying spells.				
18. I felt sad.				
19. I felt that people disliked me.				
20. I could not get going.				

Go to the appendix at the end of the book for scoring and interpretation of your responses.

For Family and Friends

1. ***Help the individual get competent diagnosis and treatment.*** The most important thing that anyone can do for the depressed person is to help him or her get competent diagnosis and treatment. This may involve encouraging the individual to stay with treatment until symptoms begin to abate (several weeks) or to seek different treatment if no improvement occurs. On occasion, you may need to make an appointment and accompany the depressed person to the therapist.

You also may need to monitor whether the depressed individual is taking medication, if it is prescribed.

2. ***Offer emotional support.*** This involves understanding, patience, affection, and encouragement. Engage the depressed individual in conversation and practice the listening skills we described in chapter 7, "Communicating Effectively." Do not disparage feelings expressed by the depressed individual but point out realities and hope. Do not ignore remarks about suicide. Report them to the depressed person's therapist.

3. ***Invite the depressed person for walks, outings, the movies, and other activities.*** Be gently insistent if your invitation is turned down.

4. ***Encourage the depressed individual to participate in activities that he or she once enjoyed.*** Hobbies, sports, religious, or cultural activities are examples. Do not push the depressed person to undertake too much too soon. The depressed individual needs diversion and companionship, but too many demands can increase feelings of failure.

5. ***Don't accuse the depressed person of faking illness or laziness, or expect him or her to "snap out of it."*** Eventually, with treatment, most individuals do get considerably better. Keep that in mind, and keep reassuring the depressed person that, with time and help, he or she will feel better.

Bipolar Disorder

Extreme elation can be as irrational and terrifying as depression. Imagine finding yourself flung from one to the other, as did Kay Jamison, discussed in the opening of this chapter. In her words (Jamison, 1995),

> "The vividness that mania infuses into one's experiences of life creates strong keenly recollected states—much as war must, and love and early memories surely do . . . the glorious moods of dancing all night and into the morning, the gliding through star fields and dancing among the rings of Saturn, the zany manic enthusiasms. . . . My high moods and hopes having ridden briefly in the top car of the ferris wheel, will as suddenly as they came, plummet into a black and grey and tired heap."

Bipolar Disorder
BPD

Jamison offers vivid descriptions of her experiences of **bipolar disorder,** a mood disorder that is characterized by extreme mood swings that include one or more episodes of mania (an overexcited, unrealistically optimistic state). *Bipolar* means that the person may experience both depression and mania. Most bipolar individuals experience multiple cycles of depression interspersed with mania. Less than 10 percent of bipolar individuals tend to experience manic-type episodes without depression.

A manic episode is like the flip side of a depressive episode (Jamison, 2004; Miklowitz, 2002, 2004). Instead of feeling depressed, the person feels euphoric and on top of the world. Instead of feeling fatigued, as many depressed individuals do, the person has tremendous energy and might sleep very little. When individuals are in a manic state, they may be very impulsive, which can get them in trouble. For example, they might spend their life savings on a foolish business venture. As the manic episode unfolds, the person can experience panic and eventually depression.

By definition in the *DSM* classification, manic episodes must last one week. They average eight to sixteen weeks. Individuals with bipolar disorder can have manic and depressive episodes that occur four or more times a year, but they usually are separated by six months to a year.

Bipolar disorder is much less common than depressive disorders (Mackinnon & others, 2002), but unlike depressive disorders (which are more likely to occur in females), bipolar disorder is equally common in females and males. Approximately 2.3 million Americans, or about 1.2 percent of the U.S. population 18 years and older, have bipolar disorder in any given year (NIMH, 2004b).

bipolar disorder A mood disorder characterized by extreme mood swings that include one or more episodes of mania.

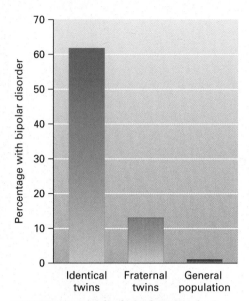

FIGURE 14.6 **Risk of Bipolar Disorder in Identical Twins, Fraternal Twins, and the General Population**
Notice how much stronger the incidence of bipolar disorder is in identical twins compared with fraternal twins and the general population; these statistics suggest a strong genetic role in the disorder.

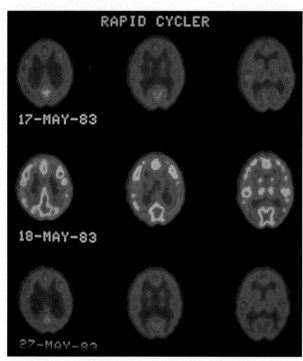

FIGURE 14.7 **Brain Metabolism in Mania and Depression**
PET scans of an individual with bipolar disorder, who is described as a rapid-cycler because of how quickly severe mood changes occurred in the individual. (*Top, bottom*) The person's brain in a depressed state. (*Middle*) A manic state. The PET scans reveal how the brain's energy consumption falls in depression and rises in mania. The red areas in the middle row reflect rapid consumption of glucose.

Causes of Mood Disorders

Mood disorders, such as Peter's depression and Kay Jamison's bipolar disorder, can involve biological, psychological, and sociocultural factors. I distinguish between depressive disorders and bipolar disorder as appropriate in discussing the causes of mood disorders.

Biological Factors Biological explanations of mood disorders include heredity, neurophysiological abnormalities, neurotransmitter deregulation, and hormonal factors (Nolen-Hoeksema, 2004). The links between biology and mood disorders are well established.

Heredity Depressive and bipolar disorders tend to run in families (Benazzi, 2004), although the family link is stronger for bipolar disorder than for depressive disorders (see figure 14.6). One of the greatest risks for developing a mood disorder is having a biological parent who suffers from a mood disorder (MacKinnon, Jamison, & DePaulo, 1997).

Neurobiological Abnormalities One of the most consistent findings of neurobiological abnormalities in individuals with mood disorders is altered brain-wave activity during sleep. Depressed individuals experience less slow-wave sleep (which contributes to a feeling of being rested and restored) and go into rapid-eye-movement (REM) sleep earlier in the night than nondepressed individuals (Lauer & others, 2004). These neurobiological abnormalities correspond to the reports of depressed individuals that they have difficulty going to sleep at night or remaining asleep, that they often wake up early in the morning and can't get back to sleep, and that they do not feel rested after they sleep (Cosgrave & others, 2000).

Other abnormalities in brain activity have also been linked to mood disorders. Figure 14.7 shows the metabolic activity of an individual cycling through depressive and manic phases of bipolar disorder. Notice the decrease in metabolic activity in the brain during depression and the increase during mania (Baxter & others, 1995). Decreased metabolic activity in the cerebral cortex has been linked to severe major depressive disorder (Kanner, 2004).

Most areas of the brains of depressed individuals are underactive, including part of the prefrontal cortex, which is involved in generating actions. However, certain brain areas are overactive, including the amygdala (Van Elst, Ebert, & Trimble, 2001). The amygdala helps us to store and recall emotionally charged memories and sends information to the prefrontal cortex at the sight of something fearful. In turn, the prefrontal cortex should signal the amygdala to slow down when the source of the fear is gone. But, in depression, the prefrontal cortex may fail to send the all-clear signal. Thus the amygdala may continue sending signals that keep triggering extended rumination about sad events (Haldane & Frangou, 2004).

Another neurobiological abnormality in depressive disorders is neuron death or disability (Duman, 2004; Manji, 2001). Individuals with depression seem to have fewer neurons in some parts of their brain, including the prefrontal cortex, which should be sending the slowdown signals to the amygdala (Drevets, 2001).

Abnormalities in a class of neurotransmitters known as the *monoamine neurotransmitters*—such as norepinephrine, serotonin, and dopamine—have also been linked to mood disorders (Dean, 2004). An imbalance in the monoamine neurotransmitters in one direction is thought to be involved in depression, an imbalance in the other direction in mania. Researchers have found abnormalities related to monoamine neurotransmitters in individuals with mood disorders, such as a low number of receptors for serotonin and norepinephrine (Wong & others, 2000). In fact, deregulation of several neurotransmitters, including a neurotransmitter called substance P, is likely involved in depression (Lieb & others, 2004). Recent studies also have revealed that changes in the neurotransmitter glutamate occur in bipolar disorder (Benes & others, 2000; Ronnback & Hansson, 2004; Sari, 2004).

Hormones Depressed individuals show chronic hyperactivity in the neuroendocrine glandular system and an inability to return to normal functioning following a stressful experience (Young & Korzun, 1998). In turn, the excess hormones produced by the neuroendocrine glands (such as the pituitary gland and adrenal cortex) may be linked to the deregulation of the monoamine neurotransmitters just discussed.

It has been argued that women's increased vulnerability to depression is linked to their ovarian hormones, estrogen and progesterone. However, the evidence that women's moods are tied to their hormones is mixed at best (Nolen-Hoeksema, 2004).

Psychological Factors   Psychodynamic, behavioral, and cognitive theories have all proposed explanations for depression. These ideas are significant for their influence on treatment of disorders, as discussed in chapter 15.

Psychodynamic   Freud (1917) argued that depression is a turning inward of aggressive instincts. Freud theorized that a child's early attachment to a love object (usually the mother) contains a mixture of love and hate. When the child loses the love object or when his or her dependency needs are frustrated, feelings of loss coexist with anger. Because the child cannot openly accept such angry feelings toward the individual he or she loves, the hostility is turned inward and experienced as depression. The unresolved mixture of anger and love is carried forward to adolescence and adulthood, when loss can bring back these early feelings of abandonment.

Modern psychodynamic theories emphasizes that depression stems from childhood experiences that prevented the person from developing a strong, positive sense of self (Nolen-Hoeksema, 2004). In this view, depressed individuals become overly dependent on the evaluations and approval of others for their self-esteem, mainly because of inadequate nurturing by parents. One study of college students found that those with an anxious insecure attachment style were more likely to have depressive symptoms than their counterparts with a secure attachment style (Roberts, Gottlib, & Kassel, 1996).

Behavioral Explanations   Peter Lewinsohn and his colleagues (Lewinsohn, 2004; Lewinsohn & Gottlib, 1995; Lewinsohn, Joiner, & Rohde, 2001) proposed that life's stresses can lead to depression by reducing the positive reinforcers in a person's life. The sequence goes like this: When people experience considerable stress in their lives, they may withdraw from the stress. The withdrawal produces a further reduction in positive reinforcers, which can lead to more withdrawal, which leads to even fewer positive reinforcers.

Another behavioral view of depression focuses on **learned helplessness,** which occurs when individuals are exposed to aversive stimulation, such as prolonged stress, over which they have no control. The inability to avoid such aversive stimulation produces an apathetic state of helplessness (Peterson, 2004). Martin Seligman (1975) proposed that learned helplessness is one reason that some individuals become depressed. When individuals cannot control the stress they encounter, they eventually feel helpless and depressed.

Research on learned helplessness led Susan Nolen-Hoeksema (1995, 2000) to examine the ways that people cope when they are depressed. She found that some depressed individuals use a *ruminative coping style,* in which they focus intently on how they feel (their sadness and hopelessness) but do not try to do anything about the feelings; they just ruminate about their depression. In a series of research studies, Nolen-Hoeksema and her colleagues (Nolen-Hoeksema, Larson, & Grayson, 1999; Nolen-Hoeksema, Parker, & Larson, 1994; Nolen-Hoeksema & Morrow, 1991) have found that individuals with depression remain depressed longer when they use a ruminative

learned helplessness Occurs when individuals are exposed to aversive stimulation, such as prolonged stress, over which they have no control. The inability to avoid such aversive stimulation can produce an apathetic state of helplessness.

FIGURE 14.8 Learned Helplessness and Attributional Reformulation of Learned Helplessness

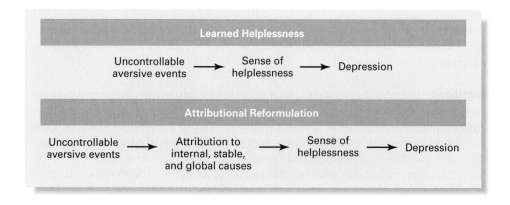

coping style rather than an action-oriented coping style. Women are more likely to ruminate when they are depressed than men are (Nolen-Hoeksema & others, 1999).

Cognitive Explanations The cognitive approach provides another perspective on mood disorders (Craighead & Craighead, 2004; Hammen, 2003; Joorman & Siemer, 2004). Individuals who are depressed rarely think positive thoughts. They interpret their lives in self-defeating ways and have negative expectations about the future (Gilbert, 2001). Psychologist Aaron Beck (1967) believes that such negative thoughts reflect schemas that shape the depressed individual's experiences. These habitual negative thoughts magnify and expand a depressed person's negative experiences. The depressed person might overgeneralize about a minor occurrence and think that he is worthless because a work assignment was turned in late, his son was arrested for shoplifting, or a friend made a negative comment about his hair. An individual might be given a work evaluation that shows a deficiency in one area and then magnify the significance of the evaluation. *Catastrophic thinking,* such as expecting to be fired and not being able to find another job, might ensue. The accumulation of such cognitive distortions can lead to depression.

Another cognitive view of depression involves a cognitive reformulation of the hopelessness involved in learned helplessness (Joiner & others, 2001). It focuses on people's *attributions,* which were discussed in chapter 6, "Social Thinking, Influence, and Intergroup Relations." When people make attributions, they attempt to explain what caused something to happen. In this attributional view of depression, individuals who regularly explain negative events as being caused by internal ("It is my fault I failed the exam"), stable ("I'm going to fail again and again"), and global ("Failing this exam shows how I won't do well in any of my courses") causes blame themselves for these negative events, expect the negative events to recur in their lives in the future, and tend to experience negative events in many areas of their lives (Abramson, Seligman, & Teasdale, 1978) (see figure 14.8).

Closely related to the attributional view of learned helplessness is a distinction between optimistic and pessimistic cognitive styles. Recall from chapter 5 that being either optimistic or pessimistic can have profound effects on a person's well-being, with optimistic individuals showing better physical and mental health. In one study, researchers interviewed first-year college students at two universities and distinguished those with an optimistic style from those with a pessimistic style (Alloy, Abramson, & Francis, 1999). They interviewed the students on a regular basis over the next two and a half years. In this time frame, among students with no prior history of depression, 17 percent of the students with a pessimistic style developed major depression, whereas only 1 percent of those with an optimistic style did. Also, among students with a prior history of depression, 27 percent of those who had a pessimistic style relapsed into depression over the two and a half years, but only 6 percent of those with the optimistic style did.

Another cognitive explanation of depression focuses on what is called *depressive realism* (McKendree-Smith & Scogin, 2000). Some people who are depressed may be

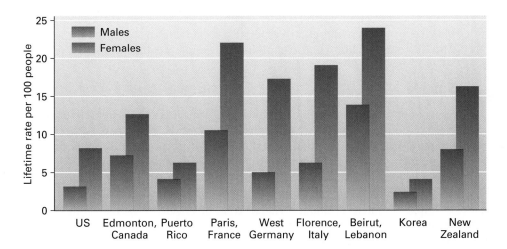

seeing their world accurately and realistically. That is, there really are negative things going on in their lives that make them depressed. Researchers have found that when depressed individuals are asked to make judgments about how much control they have over situations that actually cannot be controlled, they are accurate in saying that they do not have control (Alloy & Abramson, 1979). In contrast, nondepressed individuals overestimate the amount of control they have in such situations. Thus nondepressed individuals often have an illusion of control over their world that depressed individuals do not. In this view, it may not be accurate, realistic thinking that prevents individuals from becoming depressed but optimism and a perceived sense of illusory control over one's world.

Sociocultural Factors   Among the sociocultural factors involved in depression are cultural, socioeconomic, and ethnic variations, as well as gender.

Cultural Variations   Depressive disorders are found in virtually all cultures in the world, but their incidence, intensity, and components vary across cultures. The incidence of depressive disorders is lower in less industrialized, less modernized countries than in more industrialized, modernized countries (Cross-National Collaborative Group, 1992). Martin Seligman (1989) believes that the reason so many young American adults are prone to depression is our society's emphasis on self, independence, and individualism, coupled with an erosion of connectedness to others, family, and religion. This phenomenon, Seligman says, has spawned a widespread sense of hopelessness.

Socioeconomic and Ethnic Factors   Individuals with a low socioeconomic status (SES), especially those living in poverty, are more likely to develop depression than their higher SES counterparts (Dearing, Taylor, & McCartney, 2004). In addition, in one study, Latinos in the United States had a higher incidence of depression than Whites (Blazer & others, 1994). The higher rate of depression among Latinos may be due to their higher incidence of poverty. Very high rates of depression also have been found in Native Americans, among whom poverty is widespread (Manson & others, 1990).

Gender   Bipolar disorder occurs about equally among women and men, but women are about twice as likely as men to develop depression. This gender difference occurs in many countries (Weissman & Olfson, 1995) (see figure 14.9).

   A closer look at rates of depression among U.S. women might provide clues about the reasons for the gender difference in depression. Rates of depression are especially high among single women who are the heads of households and among young married women who work at unsatisfying, dead-end jobs (Bernstein, 2001). In unhappy marriages, women are three times as likely as men to be depressed; marriage often

Suicide tends to run in families. Five suicides occurred in different generations of the Hemingway family, including famous author Ernest (*top*) and his granddaughter Margaux (*bottom*).

confers a greater protective buffer against stress for men than for women. Mothers of young children are especially vulnerable to stress and depression. Also, the more children in the household, the more depression women report.

Suicide

Severe depression and other psychological disorders can cause individuals to want to end their lives, as bipolar disorder did to Kay Jamison. Although attempting suicide is abnormal behavior, it is not uncommon for individuals to contemplate suicide at some point in their lives (Holmes & Holmes, 2005). For example, as many as two of every three college students have thought about suicide on at least one occasion.

Approximately 31,000 individuals commit suicide every year in the United States, and the number of attempted suicides is estimated at 600,000 (NIMH, 2004c). The number of actual suicides reflects a threefold increase since 1950.

After about age 15, the suicide rate begins to rise rapidly. Suicide is the third-leading cause (after automobile accidents and homicides) of death today in U.S. adolescents age 13 through 19 years of age (National Center for Health Statistics, 2004).

Females are more likely than males to attempt suicide, but males are more likely to actually commit suicide. This difference may be due to the fact that males tend to use lethal means, such as guns, whereas females tend to cut their wrists or take overdoses of sleeping pills, both less likely to cause death.

Biological Factors   Genetic factors appear to play a role in suicide, which tends to run in families (Fu & others, 2002). One famous family that has been plagued by suicide is the Hemingway family. Five members of the family, spread across generations, committed suicide. The best known of the five Hemingways are the author Ernest Hemingway and his granddaughter Margaux (who committed suicide on the thirty-fifth anniversary of her grandfather's suicide).

A number of studies have linked suicide with low levels of the neurotransmitter serotonin (Courtet & others, 2004; Shen, 2004). Postmortem analyses of the brains of individuals who have committed suicide show abnormally low levels of this neurotransmitter. Poor physical health, especially when it is long-standing and chronic, is another risk factor for suicide (Smyth & Maclachlan, 2004). For example, Ernest Hemingway had been in failing health for a number of years when he committed suicide.

Psychological Factors   Psychological factors that can contribute to suicide include psychological disorders and traumas such as sexual abuse (Evans, 2004). Approximately 90 percent of individuals who commit suicide are estimated to have a diagnosable psychological disorder (NIMH, 2004c). The most common psychological disorder among individuals who commit suicide is depression (Jarbin & von Knorring, 2004).

Immediate and highly stressful circumstances, such as the loss of a job, flunking out of school, or an unwanted pregnancy can lead people to threaten or commit suicide (Nishimura & others, 2004; Rudd, Joiner, & Rajab, 2001). Also, substance abuse is linked with suicide today more than it was in the past (Kaslow & others, 2004).

Sociocultural Factors   The loss of a loved one through death, divorce, or separation can lead to a suicide attempt (Kaslow & Jackson, 2004). There also is a link between suicide and a long-standing history of family instability and unhappiness. And chronic economic hardship can be a factor in suicide (O'Donnell & others, 2004). In one study, 8.5 percent of people living below the poverty line, compared with 5.4 percent living above the line, said that they had contemplated suicide (Crobsy, Cheltenham, & Sacks, 1999).

In the United States, Native Americans have the highest suicide rate of all demographic groups, followed by non-Latino Whites. Across cultures, Hungary, Germany, Austria, Denmark, and Japan have the highest suicide rates, and Egypt, Mexico, Greece, and Spain have the lowest rates (National Center for Health Statistics, 1994). Suicide rates for the United States and Canada fall between the rates of these countries. Among the reasons for the variations is the degree to which there are cultural and religious norms against suicide.

Adjustment Strategies
For Communicating with Someone Threatening Suicide

Here are some strategies for what to do and what not to do when someone is threatening suicide.

What To Do

1. ***Ask direct, straightforward questions in a calm manner.*** For example, "Are you thinking about hurting yourself?"
2. ***Be a good listener and be supportive.*** Emphasize that unbearable pain can be survived.
3. ***Take the suicide threat very seriously.*** Ask questions about the person's feelings, relationships, and thoughts about the type of method to be used. Stay with the person until help arrives.
4. ***Encourage the person to get professional help and assist him or her in getting help.*** You might take the person to a mental health facility or hospital.

What Not To Do

1. ***Don't ignore the warning signs.***
2. ***Don't refuse to talk about suicide if the person wants to talk about it.***
3. ***Don't react with horror, disapproval, or repulsion.***
4. ***Don't offer false reassurances or make judgments.*** For example, don't say, "Everything will be all right," or "You should be thankful for . . . "
5. ***Don't abandon the person after this crisis seems to have passed or after professional counseling has begun.***

Review and Reflect

4 **Compare the mood disorders and specify risk factors for depression**

REVIEW

- What are mood disorders? How can the depressive disorders be characterized?
- What are the main features of bipolar disorder?
- What causes mood disorders?
- What is the nature of suicide?

REFLECT

- Do any of the theories about the causes of depression seem better at accounting for depression in college students? Explain.

5 SCHIZOPHRENIA

Types of Schizophrenia   **Causes of Schizophrenia**

"One day, while I was in the principal's office, suddenly the room became enormous, illuminated by a dreadful electric light that cast false shadows. Everything was exact, smooth, artificial, extremely tense; the chairs and tables seemed models placed here and there. Pupils and teachers were puppets revolving without cause, without objective. I recognized nothing, nobody. It was as though reality, attenuated, had slipped away from all these things and these people. Profound dread overwhelmed me, and as though lost, I looked around desperately for help. I heard people talking, but I did not grasp the meaning of their words. The voices were metallic, without warmth or color. From time to time, a word detached itself from the rest. It repeated itself over and over in my head, absurd, as though cut off by a knife." (Sechehaye, 1951, p. 22)

This passage was written by a person with **schizophrenia,** a severe psychological disorder that is characterized by highly disordered thought processes. Individuals with schizophrenia may show odd communication, inappropriate emotion, abnormal motor behavior, and social withdrawal (Heinrichs, 2001; Walker & others, 2005). The term *schizophrenia* comes from the Latin words *schizo*, meaning "split," and *phrenia*, meaning "mind." It signifies that the individual's mind is split from reality and that personality disintegrates. Schizophrenia is not the same as multiple personality, which sometimes is called "split personality." Schizophrenia involves the split of an individual's personality from reality, not the coexistence of several personalities within one individual. Approximately 2.2 million adults in the United States, or about 1.1 percent of the population 18 years and older, have schizophrenia in any given year (NIMH, 2004d).

Schizophrenia is a serious, debilitating mental disorder (Fowles, 2003). About one-half of the patients in mental hospitals are individuals with schizophrenia. More often now than in the past, individuals with schizophrenia live in society and return to mental hospitals periodically for treatment. Drug therapy is primarily responsible for fewer individuals with schizophrenia being hospitalized. The "rule of fourths" characterizes outcomes for individuals with schizophrenia: one-fourth get well and stay well; one-fourth go on medication, do relatively well, and are able to live independently; another one-fourth are well enough to live in a group home; and one-fourth do poorly and are usually institutionalized.

Schizophrenia produces a bizarre set of symptoms and wreaks havoc on the individual's personality. At the core of these symptoms are highly disordered thought processes. For example, individuals with schizophrenia have *delusions*, or false beliefs. One individual might think he is Jesus Christ, another Napoléon. The delusions are utterly implausible. One individual might think her thoughts are being broadcast over the radio, another might think that a double agent is controlling her every move. Individuals with schizophrenia also might hear, see, feel, smell, and taste things that are not there. These *hallucinations* often take the form of voices. An individual with schizophrenia might think that he hears two people talking about him. Or, on another occasion, he might say, "Hear that rumbling noise in the pipe. That is one of my men watching out for me."

Often individuals with schizophrenia do not make sense when they talk or write. For example, one individual with schizophrenia might say, "Well, Rocky, babe, help is out, happening, but where, when, up, top, side, over, you know, out of the way, that's it. Sign off." These incoherent, loose word associations are called *word salad*.

The motor behavior of the individual with schizophrenia can be bizarre, sometimes taking the form of an odd appearance, pacing, statuelike postures, or strange

schizophrenia A severe psychological disorder that is characterized by highly disordered thought processes.

mannerisms. Some individuals with schizophrenia withdraw from their social world, totally absorbed in their own thoughts.

Types of Schizophrenia

There are four main types of schizophrenia: disorganized, catatonic, paranoid, and undifferentiated. Their outward behavior patterns vary, but they share the characteristics of disordered thought processes.

Disorganized Schizophrenia

In **disorganized schizophrenia,** an individual has delusions and hallucinations that have little or no recognizable meaning—hence, the label "disorganized." An individual with disorganized schizophrenia may withdraw from human contact and may regress to silly, childlike gestures and behavior. Many of these individuals were isolated or maladjusted during adolescence.

Catatonic Schizophrenia

Catatonic schizophrenia is characterized by bizarre motor behavior, which sometimes takes the form of a completely immobile stupor (see figure 14.10). Even in this stupor, individuals with catatonic schizophrenia are completely conscious of what is happening around them. In a catatonic state, the individual sometimes shows *waxy flexibility*; for example, if the person's arm is raised and then allowed to fall, the arm stays in the new position.

Paranoid Schizophrenia

Paranoid schizophrenia is characterized by delusions of reference, grandeur, and persecution. The delusions usually form a complex, elaborate system based on a complete misinterpretation of actual events. It is not unusual for individuals with paranoid schizophrenia to develop all three delusions in the following order. First, they sense that they are special and have been singled out for attention (delusions of reference). Individuals with delusions of reference misinterpret chance events as being directly relevant to their own lives—a thunderstorm, for example, might be perceived as a personal message from God. Second, they believe that this special attention is the result of their admirable and special characteristics (delusions of grandeur). Individuals with delusions of grandeur think of themselves as exalted beings—the pope or the president, for example. Third, they think that others are so jealous and threatened by these characteristics that they spy and plot against them (delusions of persecution).

Undifferentiated Schizophrenia

Undifferentiated schizophrenia is characterized by disorganized behavior, hallucinations, delusions, and incoherence. This diagnosis is used when an individual's symptoms either do not meet the criteria for one of the other types or meet the criteria for more than one of the other types.

Causes of Schizophrenia

Like the mood disorders, schizophrenia may have biological, psychological, and sociocultural causes. Much of recent research has focused on biological factors (Walker & others, 2004).

Biological Factors

There is strong research support for biological explanations of schizophrenia. Particularly compelling is the evidence for a genetic predisposition. Abnormalities in brain structure and neurotransmitters also seem to be linked to this devastating disorder.

FIGURE 14.10 A Person with Catatonic Schizophrenia
Unusual motor behaviors are prominent symptoms in catatonic schizophrenia. Individuals may cease to move altogether, sometimes holding bizarre postures.

www.mhhe.com/santrockha
Schizophrenia.com
Schizophrenia

disorganized schizophrenia A type of schizophrenia in which an individual has delusions and hallucinations that have little or no recognizable meaning.

catatonic schizophrenia A type of schizophrenia that is characterized by bizarre motor behavior, which sometimes takes the form of a completely immobile stupor.

paranoid schizophrenia A type of schizophrenia that is characterized by delusions of reference, grandeur, and persecution.

undifferentiated schizophrenia A type of schizophrenia that is characterized by disorganized behavior, hallucinations, delusions, and incoherence.

Heredity   If you have a relative with schizophrenia, what are the chances you will develop schizophrenia? It depends on how closely you are related. As genetic similarity increases, so does a person's risk of becoming schizophrenic (Elkin, Kalidindi, & McGuffin, 2004). Data like those strongly suggest that genetic factors are involved in schizophrenia.

Brain Abnormalities   An early biological explanation for schizophrenia stated that individuals with schizophrenia produce higher than normal levels of the neurotransmitter dopamine and that the excess dopamine causes schizophrenia (Awad, 2004; Takano & others, 2004). That theory is probably too simple, but there is good evidence that dopamine does play a role in schizophrenia (Bressan & others, 2001; Kalivas, 2004; Vogel & others, 2004).

Two structural abnormalities have been found in the brains of some individuals with schizophrenia. First, images of their brains show enlarged *ventricles*, which are fluid-filled spaces in the brain (Puri & others, 2001). Enlargement of the ventricles indicates atrophy and deterioration in other brain tissue. Second, individuals with schizophrenia have a small frontal cortex (the area in which thinking, planning, and decision making take place) and show less activity in this area than is seen in individuals who do not have schizophrenia (Allen, Goldstein, & Weiner, 2001).

Among the questions raised by these findings are, Do these abnormalities cause schizophrenia? Or are they simply symptoms of a disorder with other origins?

Psychological Factors   Although contemporary theorists do not propose psychological factors as stand-alone causes of schizophrenia, stress may be a contributing factor. The **diathesis-stress model** argues that a combination of biological disposition and stress causes schizophrenia (Meehl, 1962). (The term *diathesis* means physical vulnerability or predisposition.) Thus, according to this model, a defective gene makeup might produce schizophrenia only when the individual lives in a stressful environment.

Sociocultural Factors   Disorders of thought and emotion are common to schizophrenia in all cultures, but the type and incidence of schizophrenic disorders may vary from culture to culture.

Individuals living in poverty are more likely to have schizophrenia than people at higher socioeconomic levels. The link between schizophrenia and poverty is correlational, and contemporary theorists do not believe that poverty causes schizophrenia (Schiffman & Walker, 1998).

diathesis-stress model A model of schizophrenia that proposes a combination of biogenetic disposition and stress as the cause of the disorder.

Review and Reflect

5   Identify characteristics and possible causes of schizophrenia

REVIEW

- What are the different types of schizophrenia?
- What factors appear to play a role in the etiology of schizophrenia?

REFLECT

- Imagine that you are a clinical psychologist who has been given the opportunity to interview the Genain quadruplets. What questions would you want to ask them in an effort to sort through why the paths of their schizophrenia varied through their adult years?

6   PERSONALITY DISORDERS

- **Odd or Eccentric Cluster**
- **Anxious or Fearfulness Cluster**
- **Dramatic or Emotionally Problematic Cluster**

Personality disorders are chronic, maladaptive cognitive-behavioral patterns that are thoroughly integrated into the individual's personality and that are troublesome to others or whose pleasure sources are either harmful or illegal (Bagge & others, 2004; Coker & Widiger, 2005; Trull & Widiger, 2003). The patterns are often recognizable by adolescence or earlier. Personality disorders usually are not as bizarre as schizophrenia, and they do not have the intense, diffuse feelings of fear and apprehension that characterize the anxiety disorders (Evans & others, 2002). Most HMOs will not authorize treatment of the personality disorders. (Managed care issues are discussed in the next chapter.)

The *DSM* groups the personality disorders into three clusters: odd or eccentric, dramatic or emotionally problematic, and anxious or fearful.

Odd or Eccentric Cluster

The odd or eccentric cluster includes the paranoid, schizoid, and schizotypal disorders:

- *Paranoid*. These individuals have a lack of trust in others and are suspicious. They see themselves as morally correct yet vulnerable and envied.
- *Schizoid*. They do not form adequate social relationships. They show shy, withdrawn behavior and have difficulty expressing anger. Most are considered to be "cold" people.
- *Schizotypal*. They show odd thinking patterns that reflect eccentric beliefs, overt suspicion, and overt hostility. However, individuals with schizotypal disorder are not as clearly bizarre in their thinking and behavior as individuals with schizophrenia.

Individuals with paranoid personality disorder show chronic and pervasive mistrust and suspicion of other people that is not warranted.

Dramatic or Emotionally Problematic Cluster

The dramatic or emotionally problematic cluster consists of the histrionic, narcissistic, borderline, and antisocial personality disorders.

- *Histrionic*. These individuals seek a lot of attention and tend to overreact. They respond more dramatically and intensely than is required by the situation. The disorder is more common in women than men.
- *Narcissistic*. They have an unrealistic sense of self-importance, can't take criticism, manipulate people, and lack empathy. These characteristics lead to substantial problems in relationships.
- *Borderline*. These individuals are often emotionally unstable, impulsive, unpredictable, irritable, and anxious. They also are prone to boredom. Their behavior is similar to that of individuals with schizotypal personality disorder, but they are not as consistently withdrawn and bizarre.
- *Antisocial*. They are guiltless, law-breaking, exploitive, self-indulgent, irresponsible, and intrusive. They often resort to a life of crime and violence. This disorder is far more common in men than in women.

www.mhhe.com/santrockha

Personality Disorders
Narcissistic Personality Disorder
Borderline Personality Disorder

personality disorders Chronic, maladaptive cognitive-behavioral patterns that are thoroughly integrated into the individual's personality.

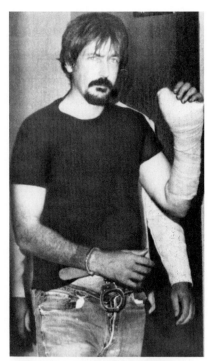

Gary Gilmore was a classic case of antisocial personality disorder. As a young adolescent, Gilmore had low grades, was often truant, and stole from classmates. At 14, he was placed in a juvenile detention center for stealing a car. He was arrested on numerous occasions in high school and at 20 was sent to the state penitentiary for burglary and robbery. Several years later, Gilmore was released, but it didn't take long for him to be put back in the penitentiary for other armed robberies. Released again, he moved in with a woman, but his drinking carousing, and fighting caused her to kick him out. Later that year, he pulled into a gas station in Utah and ordered the attendant to hand over his cash, which the attendant did. Gilmore shot him twice in the head, anyway, killing him. The next morning, Gilmore walked into a hotel and shot the manager. Gilmore was caught and convicted of the two murders. He was executed in 1977.

In the national study of the prevalence of psychological disorders, 2.6 percent of individuals reported that they had at some point experienced an antisocial personality disorder (Robins & Regier, 1991). People with antisocial personality disorder used to be called psychopaths or sociopaths. They regularly violate other people's rights. The disorder begins before the age of 15 and continues into adulthood. These individuals represent a small percentage of the population but commit a disproportionately large percentage of violent and property crimes (Meyer, Wolverton, & Deitsch, 1998). The disorder is very difficult to treat.

Explanations for the causes of antisocial personality disorder include biological, psychological, and sociocultural factors. In terms of biological factors, a genetic predisposition for the disorder may be present (Black, 2004; Goldstein, Prescott, & Kendler, 2001). For example, the disorder is more likely to appear in identical twins than in fraternal twins (Gottesman & Goldsmith, 1994). In terms of psychological factors, the impulsive and aggressive behavior that characterizes individuals with antisocial personality disorders suggests that they have not adequately learned how to delay gratification. In terms of sociocultural factors, inadequate socialization regularly appears in the history of individuals who develop antisocial personality disorder (Sutker & Allain, 1993). Parents of these children may be neglectful or inconsistent and punitive in their discipline. Individuals with this disorder are more likely to have at least one parent with antisocial personality traits than are their counterparts without the disorder. Thus children growing up in these families presumably have many opportunities to observe and imitate parents who behave in exploitive, immoral ways.

Anxious or Fearfulness Cluster

The anxious or fearfulness cluster includes the avoidant, dependent, and obsessive-compulsive personality disorders:

- *Avoidant.* These individuals are shy and inhibited yet desire interpersonal relationships, which distinguishes them from the schizoid and schizotypal disorders. They often have low self-esteem and are extremely sensitive to rejection. This disorder is close to being an anxiety disorder but is not characterized by as much personal distress.
- *Dependent.* These individuals lack self-confidence and do not express their own personalities. They have a pervasive need to cling to stronger personalities, whom they allow to make decisions for them. The disorder is far more common in women than in men.
- *Obsessive-Compulsive.* These individuals are obsessed with rules, are emotionally insensitive, and are oriented toward a lifestyle of productivity and efficiency.

6 Identify the behavior patterns typical of personality disorders

REVIEW

- What are personality disorders?
- What is the odd or eccentric cluster?
- What is the dramatic or emotionally problematic cluster?
- What is the anxious or fearfulness cluster?

REFLECT

- We described a possible psychological cause for antisocial personality disorder. Go down the list of other personality disorders and try to come up with psychological causes for them.

Reach Your Learning Goals

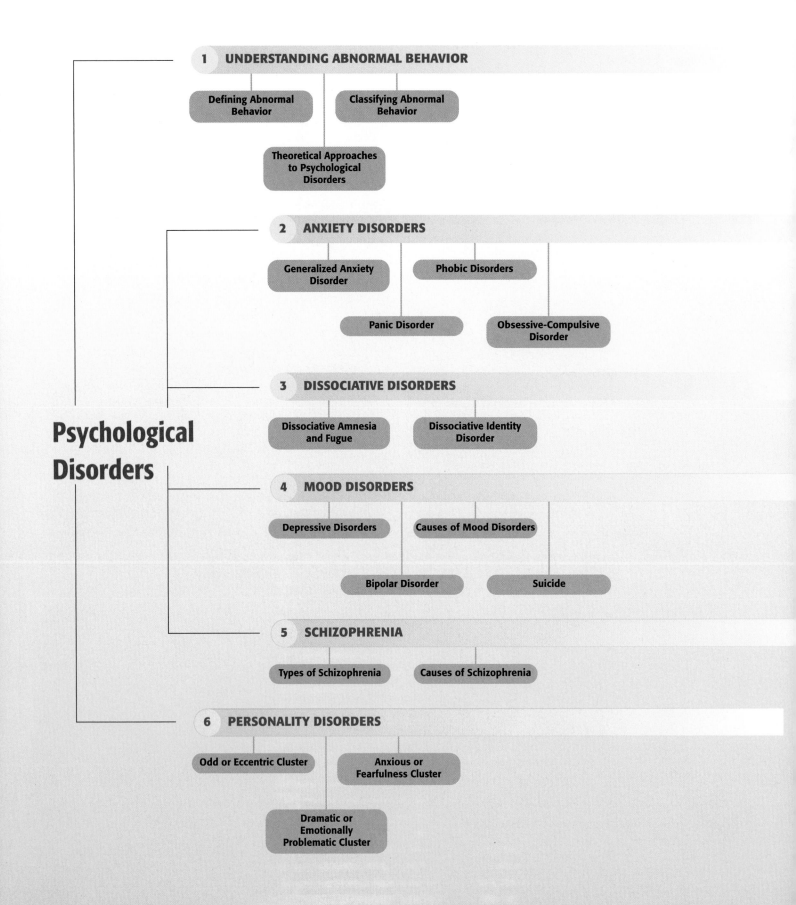

Psychological Disorders

1 UNDERSTANDING ABNORMAL BEHAVIOR

- Defining Abnormal Behavior
- Classifying Abnormal Behavior
- Theoretical Approaches to Psychological Disorders

2 ANXIETY DISORDERS

- Generalized Anxiety Disorder
- Phobic Disorders
- Panic Disorder
- Obsessive-Compulsive Disorder

3 DISSOCIATIVE DISORDERS

- Dissociative Amnesia and Fugue
- Dissociative Identity Disorder

4 MOOD DISORDERS

- Depressive Disorders
- Causes of Mood Disorders
- Bipolar Disorder
- Suicide

5 SCHIZOPHRENIA

- Types of Schizophrenia
- Causes of Schizophrenia

6 PERSONALITY DISORDERS

- Odd or Eccentric Cluster
- Anxious or Fearfulness Cluster
- Dramatic or Emotionally Problematic Cluster

Summary

1 Discuss the characteristics and classification of abnormal behavior

- Psychologists define abnormal behavior as behavior that is deviant, maladaptive, or personally distressful. Only one of these criteria is necessary for the classification of abnormal behavior, but two or three can be present. There are a number of myths about abnormal behavior, and a thin line often exists between normal and abnormal behavior.
- Theoretical perspectives on the causes of psychological disorders include biological, psychological, and sociocultural approaches. The medical model describes psychological disorders as diseases with a biological origin. The biological origin may involve problems related to the structure of the brain, neurotransmitters, hormones, or genetics. The psychodynamic, behavioral, and social cognitive perspectives point to numerous psychological factors that may contribute to psychological disorders. The sociocultural approach places more emphasis on the larger social context in which a person lives than on psychological factors. Sociocultural contexts include the individual's marriage or family, neighborhood, socioeconomic status, ethnicity, gender, and culture. The biopsychosocial approach is an interactionist approach to understanding psychological disorders.
- The classification of mental disorders gives mental health professionals a shorthand to use in their communications and allows clinicians to make predictions about disorders and determine what kind of treatment is appropriate. The *Diagnostic and Statistical Manual of Mental Disorders (DSM)*, published by the American Psychiatric Association, is the classification system used by clinicians to diagnose and treat psychological disorders. The *DSM-IV-TR* features a multiaxial diagnostic system that enables clinicians to characterize an individual on the basis of five dimensions. Some psychologists contend that *DSM-IV-TR* perpetuates the medical model of psychological disorders and labels some everyday problems that are not considered deviant or maladaptive as psychological disorders.

2 Distinguish among the various anxiety disorders

- Anxiety is a diffuse, vague, highly unpleasant feeling of fear and apprehension. The main features of anxiety disorders are motor tension, hyperactivity, and apprehensive expectations and thoughts. Generalized anxiety disorder is defined as anxiety that persists for at least one month with no specific reason for the anxiety. Biological, psychological, and sociocultural factors may be involved.

- Recurrent panic attacks marked by the sudden onset of intense apprehension or terror characterize panic disorder. Panic disorder can occur with or without agoraphobia. Biological and psychological factors may contribute to the development of panic disorder.
- Phobic disorders involve an irrational, overwhelming fear of a particular object, such as snakes, or a situation, such as flying. Biological and psychological factors have been proposed as causes of phobias.
- Obsessive-compulsive disorder (OCD) is an anxiety disorder in which the individual has anxiety-provoking thoughts that will not go away (obsession) and/or urges to perform repetitive, ritualistic behaviors to prevent or produce some future situation (compulsion). Biological and psychological factors are likely involved in OCD.

3 Describe the dissociative disorders

- Dissociative disorders are characterized by a sudden loss of memory or change in identity. Under extreme stress, conscious awareness becomes dissociated (separated or split) from previous memories and thoughts. Dissociative amnesia involves memory loss caused by extensive psychological stress. Dissociative fugue also involves a loss of memory, but individuals with this disorder also unexpectedly travel away from home or work, assume a new identity, and do not remember the old one.
- Dissociative identity disorder, formerly called multiple personality disorder, involves the presence of two or more distinct personalities in the same individual. This disorder is rare.

4 Compare the mood disorders and specify risk factors for depression and suicide

- The depressive disorders are a type of mood disorder, which is a psychological disorder in which the dominant feature is disturbance of mood; the mood disturbance can be characterized by cognitive, behavioral, or physical symptoms, as well as interpersonal difficulties. The depressive disorders are mood disorders in which the individual suffers depression without experiencing mania. In major depressive disorder, the individual experiences a major depressive episode and depressed characteristics, such as lethargy and hopelessness, for two weeks or longer. Dysthymic disorder is generally more chronic and does not involve a major depressive episode.
- Bipolar disorder is characterized by extreme mood swings that include one or more episodes of mania (an overexcited, unrealistic, optimistic state). *Bipolar* means that the person may experience both depression and mania. Less than 10 percent of bipolar individuals experience mania without depression.

- Biological explanations of mood disorders focus on heredity, neurophysiological abnormalities, neurotransmitter deregulation, and hormonal factors. Psychological explanations include psychoanalytic, behavioral, and cognitive perspectives. Cultural variations, socioeconomic and ethnic factors, and gender are sociocultural factors that may influence the development of depression.
- Severe depression and other psychological disorders can cause individuals to want to end their lives. Biological, psychological, and sociocultural explanations of suicide have been proposed.

5 *Identify characteristics and possible causes of schizophrenia*

- Schizophrenia is a severe psychological disorder that is characterized by highly disordered thought processes. Individuals with schizophrenia may show odd communication, inappropriate emotion, abnormal motor behavior, and social withdrawal. There are four main types of schizophrenia: disorganized, catatonic, paranoid, and undifferentiated. In disorganized schizophrenia, an individual has delusions and hallucinations that have little or no recognizable meaning. Catatonic schizophrenia is characterized by bizarre motor behavior, which may take the form of a completely immobile stupor. Paranoid schizophrenia is characterized by delusions of reference, grandeur, and persecution. Undifferentiated schizophrenia is characterized by disorganized behavior, hallucinations, delusions, and incoherence.
- Biological factors (heredity, structural brain abnormalities, and neurotransmitter deregulation), psychological factors (diathesis-stress view), and sociocultural factors may be involved in schizophrenia. Psychological and sociocultural factors are not viewed as stand-alone causes of schizophrenia.

6 *Identify the behavior patterns typical of personality disorders*

- Personality disorders are chronic, maladaptive cognitive-behavioral patterns that are thoroughly integrated into the individual's personality. The three main clusters of personality disorders are odd or eccentric, dramatic or emotionally problematic, and anxious or fearfulness cluster.
- The odd or eccentric cluster includes the paranoid, schizoid, and schizotypal personality disorders.
- The dramatic or emotionally problematic cluster consists of the histrionic, narcissistic, borderline, and antisocial personality disorders. Biological, psychological, and sociocultural explanations of antisocial personality disorder have been proposed.
- The anxious or fearfulness cluster includes the avoidant, dependent, and obsessive-compulsive personality disorders.

Key Terms

abnormal behavior 426
medical model 426
DSM-IV-TR 428
anxiety disorders 431
generalized anxiety disorder 431
panic disorder 432
agoraphobia 432

phobic disorder 433
obsessive-compulsive disorder (OCD) 434
dissociative disorders 436
dissociative amnesia 436
dissociative fugue 436
dissociative identity disorder (DID) 436

mood disorders 438
depressive disorders 438
major depressive disorder 438
dysthymic disorder 439
bipolar disorder 441
learned helplessness 443
schizophrenia 448

disorganized schizophrenia 449
catatonic schizophrenia 449
paranoid schizophrenia 449
undifferentiated schizophrenia 449
diathesis-stress model 450
personality disorders 451

Resources for Improving Your Adjustment

SELF-HELP BOOKS

The Anxiety and Phobia Workbook (3rd ed.)

(2001) by Edmund Bourne. Oakland, CA: New Harbinger.

A 5-star (highest rating) self-help book in the national survey of self-help books (Norcross, Santrock, & others, 2003). Bourne describes specific skills needed to overcome problems with panic, anxiety, and phobias, and gives step-by-step instructions for mastering these skills.

The Shyness and Social Anxiety Workbook

(2002) by Martin Anthony and Richard Swinson. Oakland, CA: New Harbinger.

A 4-star (next to highest rating) self-help book in the national survey (Norcross, Santrock, & others, 2003). Worksheets and exercises help individuals to learn how to be more comfortable around people.

S.T.O.P. Obsessing: How to Overcome Your Obsessions and Compulsions

(1991) by Edna Foa and Reid Wilson. New York: Bantam.

Two experts describe a cognitive approach to reducing obsessions and compulsions. This book was given 5 stars in the national study of self-help books (Norcross, Santrock, & others, 2003).

Mind Over Mood

(1995) by Dennis Greenberger and Christine Padesky. New York: Guilford Press.

A 5-star book in the national survey that provides a cognitive therapy approach to coping with depression. The book helps individuals identify and make necessary changes in their thoughts, emotions, and behaviors. Each chapter includes practical exercises. Note: In chapter 15, "Therapies," we will recommend other excellent books on coping with depression.

The Bipolar Survival Guide: What You and Your Family Need to Know

(2002) by David Miklowitz. New York: Guilford Press.

This book provides information about recognizing the early warning signs of bipolar disorder and how to obtain the best treatment and medication. It was the most highly rated book in the recent national survey (3 stars).

Surviving Schizophrenia (4th ed.)

(2001) by E. Fuller Torrey. New York: Harper Perennial.

An expert on schizophrenia, Torrey is a psychiatrist whose brother was diagnosed with schizophrenia. The book is an excellent resource for families with an individual who has been diagnosed with schizophrenia and is widely recognized as the best self-help book on the subject (receiving 5 stars in the recent national study).

NATIONAL SUPPORT GROUPS

National self-help support groups related to the psychological disorders in this chapter include (Norcross, Santrock, & others, 2003):

Anxiety Disorders
Anxiety Disorders Association of America (ADAA)
http://www.adaa.org

Agorophobics Building Independent Lives (ABIL)
E-mail: answers@anxietysupport.org
http://www.anxietysupport.org/b001menu.htm

Mood Disorders
Depression and Related Affective Disorders Association
E-mail: drada@jhmi.edu
http://www.drada.org

National Depressive and Manic Depressive Association
http://www.ndmda.org

Schizophrenia
National Mental Health Association (NMHA)
http://www.nmha.org

E-Learning Tools

To help you master the material in this chapter, you will find a number of valuable study tools on the student CD-ROM and the Online Learning Center.

SELF-ASSESSMENT

In Text

You can complete the self-assessment in the text:

- Self-Assessment 14.1: *Am I Depressed?*

Additional Self-Assessments

Complete these self-assessments on the Online Learning Center:

- *How Much Anxiety Do I Have?*
- *Do I Have the Symptoms of Panic Disorder?*
- *What Are My Fears?*
- *Do I Have the Characteristics of Social Phobia?*
- *Do I Have the Characteristics of Obsessive-Compulsive Disorder?*
- *Do I Have the Characteristics of Any Personality Disorders?*

THINK CRITICALLY

To practice your critical thinking skills, complete these exercises on the Online Learning Center:

- *Judging Abnormality in Context* asks you to evaluate whether certain contexts in the United States involve abnormal behavior.
- *Asking Questions to Create a Complete Picture of Mental Distress* asks you to apply your knowledge of different perspectives to a particular case.
- *The Contexts of Public Speaking* asks you to examine situations in which you might fear public speaking and contexts in which you might not.

APPLY YOUR KNOWLEDGE

1. What makes a person insane?

A mainstay of TV crime shows is the insanity defense. But in reality, the insanity defense is rarely used and is seldom successful. First, go to the American Psychiatric Association webpage (http://www.psych.org/public_info/insanity.cfm) and read about the insanity defense. Next, review the criteria for mental illness. When you are finished, go to www.yahoo.com or www.google.com and search for "famous insanity defense cases."

What were the characteristics of these cases that made them examples of "insane" behavior and not just despicable acts? How do these characteristics relate back to the criteria of mental illness, as outlined in your text? Most people who are mentally ill are not insane; which characteristics put someone "over the line?"

2. Myths about mental illnesses

Your textbook lists three common myths about mental illness. What additional myths are there? Begin by making two lists – one list that you know are myths and one list about mental illness that you believe is true. When you are finished, go to www.yahoo.com or www.google.com and search for "myths of mental illness.

Which of the myths that you found might interfere with people getting the help they need, and why? Do you apply any of these myths to yourself? Would you go for help if you needed it, or would you "buy into" the same myths that exist in much of society?

3. Famous people with mental illnesses

People often think of schizophrenia as a disorder that is always profoundly debilitating. But many schizophrenics are able to either recover or manage their illness. The story of economist John Nash was recently made into the movie "A Beautiful Mind." Who are some other famous schizophrenics or people with other forms of mental illness? Go to www.yahoo.com or www.google.com and search for "famous schizophrenics" or "famous people with mental illness."

 **VIDEO SEGMENT**

Major depressive disorder is one of the most common psychological disorders. But what do people diagnosed with this mood disorder actually experience? A woman who has suffered episodes of major depression for the last 15 years describes her experience in the video for Chapter 14 on the CD-ROM. (To learn about her experience with therapy, watch the video "Electroconvulsive Therapy" in Chapter 15 on the CD-ROM.)

Therapies

Images of Adjustment

Steve M., Benefiting from Therapy

Steve M. has paranoid schizophrenia, which you read about in chapter 14. He hears voices all the time, telling him he has done something wrong, and feels that he is being constantly monitored by people he doesn't know. He is convinced that a transmitter has been placed in his head and that someone is transmitting messages to it.

Medication has significantly reduced the frequency of the voices Steve hears. Several times he has stopped taking the medication, and each time he has had to be hospitalized for treatment. In between hospitalizations, he goes to a day treatment program and has taken some college classes.

In the clinic at the day program Steve has developed a long-term relationship with the psychologist he sees once a week. These sessions supplement periodic visits with a psychiatrist, who monitors his medication. The psychologist is helping Steve to set some short-term goals and improve his outlook on life. These sessions, and other elements of the day treatment program, are providing him with practice in coping with stress, interacting more effectively with people, and living an independent life.

Steve still struggles with what is real and not real in his life. However, through psychotherapy, he has learned to trust certain people, especially his stepmother, brother, and father. Steve says that he now understands the importance of taking the medication to ward off the intruding voices and the fear of being monitored. His mother and stepfather have joined a support group, which is helping them to understand Steve's psychological disorder and what needs to be done to help him. Clearly, Steve M. has not been "cured," but his treatment is helping him to cope with his psychological disorder and adjust to daily living (adapted from Bernheim, 1997, pp. 126–130).

What happens in the therapies that Steve M. is receiving, and what treatment do people with other types of disorders receive? This chapter addresses those and other questions. The discussion of personality and psychological disorders in chapters 2 and 14 provide a foundation for understanding the modes of treatment that are used to help people with psychological problems. For example, chapter 14 explored the biological, psychological, and sociocultural factors involved in anxiety disorders, mood disorders, schizophrenia, and personality disorders. This chapter examines biological, psychological, and sociocultural approaches for helping people with psychological disorders. Later, the chapter addresses questions about the effectiveness of therapy, the wide range of mental health professionals who provide therapy, and how to be a wise consumer of mental health services.

1 BIOLOGICAL THERAPIES

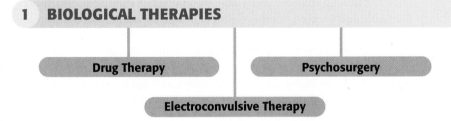

The medications that helped Steve M. are one example of the **biological therapies,** which are treatments to reduce or eliminate the symptoms of psychological disorders by altering the way an individual's body functions. Drug therapy is the most common form of biological therapy. Much less widely used biological therapies are electroconvulsive therapy and psychosurgery. Recall from chapter 1 that psychiatrists, who are medical doctors, can administer drugs as part of therapy. However, in most states, psychologists, who are not trained as medical doctors, cannot administer drugs as part of therapy. Psychologists and other mental health professionals may provide **psychotherapy** to help individuals recognize and overcome their problems in conjunction with the biological therapy administered by psychiatrists and other medical doctors. Indeed, in many instances, a combination of psychotherapy and medication is a desirable course of treatment (Abbass & Gardner, 2004; Kay, 2002; Ostow, 2004).

Drug Therapy

Although medicine and herbs have long been used to alleviate emotional distress, it was not until the twentieth century that drug treatments began to revolutionize mental health care. Drugs are used mainly to treat three types of disorders: anxiety disorders, mood disorders, and schizophrenia. Let's begin with drugs used to treat anxiety.

Antianxiety Drugs **Antianxiety drugs** are commonly known as *tranquilizers.* These drugs reduce anxiety by making individuals calmer and less excitable. Benzodiazepines are the antianxiety drugs that most often offer the greatest relief for anxiety symptoms. They are relatively fast-acting medications, taking effect within hours. Benzodiazepines work by binding to the receptor sites of neurotransmitters that become overactive during anxiety. The most frequently prescribed benzodiazepines include Xanax, Valium, and Librium.

Like all drugs, benzodiazepines have some side effects (Chouinard, 2004; Davies & others, 2004). They can be addicting. Also, drowsiness, loss of coordination, fatigue, and mental slowing can accompany their use. These effects can be hazardous when driving or operating some types of machinery, especially when the person first starts taking benzodiazepines. Benzodiazepines also have been linked to abnormalities in babies born to mothers who took them during pregnancy (Perault & others, 2000).

biological therapies Treatments to reduce or eliminate the symptoms of psychological disorders by altering the way an individual's body functions.

psychotherapy The process used by mental health professionals to help individuals recognize, define, and overcome their psychological and interpersonal difficulties.

antianxiety drugs Commonly known as *tranquilizers.* These drugs reduce anxiety by making individuals calmer and less excitable.

Combined with alcohol, anesthetics, antihistamines, sedatives, muscle relaxants, and some prescription pain medications, benzodiazepines can lead to depression (Cassano & others, 2004). A nonbenzodiazepine—buspirone, or BuSpar—is commonly used to treat generalized anxiety disorder. (See chapter 14 to review the characteristics of this and other psychological disorders.) Buspirone must be taken daily for two to three weeks before it takes effect.

Antianxiety drugs are very widely used because many individuals experience stress or anxiety. Family physicians and psychiatrists prescribe these drugs to improve people's ability to cope with their problems effectively. Antianxiety medications are best used only temporarily for symptomatic relief. Too often they are overused and, as mentioned earlier, can become addictive.

Antidepressant Drugs Linda has a good marriage and her second child, a healthy boy, was just born. You might think that everything would be great in her life, but she feels as if her life were an unbearable weight on her shoulders. Usually energetic and focused, Linda considers it a major accomplishment to get through the day. These feelings continue for several months and finally she decides to see a psychiatrist, who prescribes an antidepressant drug for treating her depression, along with psychotherapy. After several weeks of being on the medication and participating in psychotherapy, Linda begins to feel better. The dreary Midwest winter and the responsibility involved in caring for her young children no longer overwhelm her (Nathan, Gorman, & Salkind, 1999).

Linda's experience matches that of many people who take **antidepressant drugs,** which regulate mood. The three main classes of antidepressant drugs are tricyclics, such as Elavil; MAO inhibitors, such as Nardil; and SSRI drugs, such as Prozac.

The *tricyclics,* so called because of their three-ringed molecular structure, are believed to work by increasing the level of certain neurotransmitters, especially norepinephrine and serotonin (Roose & Pesce, 2004). The tricyclics reduce the symptoms of depression in approximately 60 to 70 percent of cases. The tricyclics usually take two to four weeks to improve mood. They sometimes have adverse side effects, such as restlessness, faintness, trembling, sleepiness, and difficulty remembering.

The MAO (monoamine oxidase) inhibitors are not as widely used as the tricyclics because they are more toxic. However, some individuals who do not respond to the tricyclics do respond to the MAO inhibitors. The MAO inhibitors may be especially risky because of their potential interactions with certain foods and drugs. Cheese and other fermented foods, as well as some alcoholic beverages such as red wine, can interact with the MAOs to increase blood pressure and eventually cause a stroke.

A third class of antidepressants, selective serotonin reuptake inhibitors (SSRIs), includes the drugs most familiar to the general public: Prozac (fluoxetine), Paxil (paroxetine), and Zoloft (sertraline). SSRIs work mainly by interfering with the reabsorption of serotonin in the brain (Bandelow & others, 2004; Cohen & others, 2004). Figure 15.1 shows how this process works.

The popularity of SSRIs is based on their effectiveness in reducing the symptoms of depression with fewer side effects than the other antidepressant drugs (Green, 2003; Nemeroff & Schatzberg, 2002). Nonetheless, SSRIs can have negative effects, including insomnia, anxiety, headache, and diarrhea. They also can impair sexual functioning and produce severe withdrawal symptoms if their use is ended too abruptly (Clayton & others, 2001).

Although antidepressant drugs, especially the SSRI drugs, have been effective in treating many cases of depression, at least 25 percent of individuals with major depressive disorder do not respond to any antidepressant drug (Shelton & Hollon,

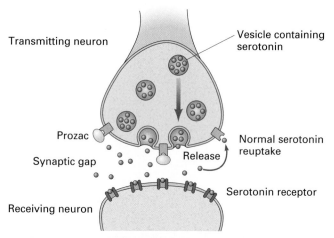

FIGURE 15.1 How the Antidepressant Prozac Works
Serotonin is secreted by a transmitting neuron, moves across the synaptic gap, and then binds to receptors in a receiving neuron. Excess serotonin in the synaptic gap is normally reabsorbed by the transmitting neuron. However, Prozac blocks the reuptake of serotonin to the transmitting neuron, which leaves excess serotonin in the synaptic gap. The excess serotonin will be transmitted to the receiving neuron and circulated through the brain, thus reducing the serotonin deficit found in depressed individuals.

www.mhhe.com/santrockha

Mental Health Resources
Psychopharmacology Links
Psychopharmacology Resources

antidepressant drugs Drugs that regulate mood.

2000). Factors related to nonresponse include the presence of a personality disorder or psychotic symptoms. Antidepressant drugs are also often effective for a number of anxiety disorders, including generalized anxiety disorder, panic disorder, obsessive-compulsive disorder, social phobia, agoraphobia, and post-traumatic stress disorder (Shelton & Hollon, 2000). In addition, eating disorders, especially bulimia nervosa (discussed in chapter 16), may be amenable to treatment with antidepressant drugs (Devlin & others, 2000).

Additional antidepressant drugs are being developed that target an amino acid, substance P. Preliminary studies reveal that drugs that affect substance P may reduce depression with few serious side effects (Herpher & Lieb, 2003; Lieb & others, 2004).

Lithium   For bipolar disorder, **lithium** is the most widely prescribed drug, helping to reduce mood swings. This is the drug that Kay Redfield Jamison, whose story opened chapter 14, credits with saving her life. Without lithium, she wrote, "I would be constantly beholden to the crushing movements of a mental sea. I would be dead or insane." The amount of lithium that circulates in the bloodstream must be carefully monitored because the effective dosage is precariously close to toxic levels. Kidney and thyroid gland complications can arise as a consequence of lithium therapy (Keck, McElroy, & Arnold, 2001).

Antipsychotic Drugs   Another type of medication—**antipsychotic drugs**—has given Peter M. (who was described at the opening of this chapter) the chance for life outside of a hospital. These are powerful drugs that diminish agitated behavior, reduce tension, decrease hallucinations, improve social behavior, and produce better sleep patterns in individuals who have a severe psychological disorder, especially schizophrenia. Before antipsychotic drugs were developed in the 1950s, few, if any, interventions brought relief from the torment of psychotic symptoms.

The *neuroleptics* are the most widely used class of antipsychotic drugs (Bradford, Stroup, & Lieberman, 2002). The most widely accepted explanation for the effectiveness of the neuroleptics is their ability to block the dopamine system's action in the brain. When used in sufficient doses, the neuroleptics reduce a variety of schizophrenic symptoms, at least in the short term (Friedman, Temporini, & Davis, 1999). The neuroleptics do not cure schizophrenia; they only treat the symptom, not its causes. If an individual with schizophrenia stops taking the drug, the symptoms return. Also, the neuroleptics can have severe side effects.

Tardive dyskinesia is a major side effect of neuroleptics; it is a neurological disorder characterized by grotesque, involuntary movements of the facial muscles and mouth, as well as extensive twitching of the neck, arms, and legs. As many as 20 percent of individuals with schizophrenia who take neuroleptics develop this disorder. Older women are especially vulnerable. Long-term neuroleptic therapy also is associated with increased depression and anxiety. Nonetheless, for the majority of schizophrenics, the benefits of neuroleptic treatment outweigh its risks and discomforts.

Another group of medications, the *atypical antipsychotic medications,* was introduced in the 1990s. Like the SSRI drugs, atypical antipsychotic medications block the reuptake of the neurotransmitter serotonin. The two most widely used atypical antipsychotic medications are clozapine (trade name Clozaril) and risperidone (Risperdal); these drugs show promise for reducing schizophrenia's symptoms without the side effects of neuroleptics (Awad & Voruganti, 2004; Buckley & others, 2001; O'Brien, 2004). Figure 15.2 shows the substantial reduction in negative symptoms when schizophrenics take risperidone (Marder, Davis, & Chouinard, 1997).

Neuroleptic drugs have substantially reduced the length of hospital stays for individuals with schizophrenia. However, although these individuals are able to return to the community because drug therapy keeps their symptoms from reappearing, most have difficulty coping with the demands of society, and most are chronically

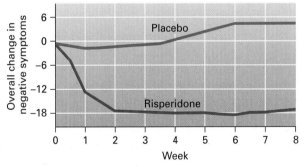

FIGURE 15.2 Effects of Risperidone (Risperdal) on Schizophrenics' Negative Symptoms
In one study, researchers found that by just 1 week after starting treatment with risperidone, negative symptoms (such as disorganized thought and uncontrolled hostility/excitement) were substantially reduced in schizophrenics. Negative symptoms in the placebo group actually increased slightly over the 8 weeks of the study.

lithium A drug that is widely used to treat bipolar disorder.

antipsychotic drugs Powerful drugs that diminish agitated behavior, reduce tension, decrease hallucinations, improve social behavior, and produce better sleep patterns in individuals who have a severe psychological disorder, especially schizophrenia.

Psychological Disorder	Drug	Effectiveness	Side Effects
Everyday Anxiety and Anxiety Disorders			
Everyday anxiety	Antianxiety drugs; antidepressant drugs	Substantial improvement short-term	Antianxiety drugs: less powerful the longer people take them; may be addictive Antidepressant drugs: see below under depressive disorders
Generalized anxiety disorder	Antianxiety drugs	Not very effective	Less powerful the longer people take them; may be addictive
Panic disorder	Antianxiety drugs	About half show improvement	Less powerful the longer people take them; may be addictive
Agoraphobia	Tricyclic drugs and MAO inhibitors	Majority show improvement	Tricyclics: restlessness, fainting, and trembling MAO inhibitors: toxicity
Specific phobias	Antianxiety drugs	Not very effective	Less powerful the longer people take them; may be addictive
Mood Disorders			
Depressive disorders	Tricyclic drugs, MAO inhibitors, and SSRI drugs	Majority show moderate improvement	Tricylics: cardiac problems, mania, confusion, memory loss, fatigue MAO inhibitors: toxicity SSRI drugs: nausea, nervousness, insomnia, and in a few cases possible suicidal thoughts
Bipolar disorder	Lithium	Large majority show substantial improvement	Toxicity
Schizophrenic Disorders			
Schizophrenia	Neuroleptics; atypical antipsychotic medications	Majority show partial improvement	Neuroleptics: irregular heartbeat, low blood pressure, uncontrolled fidgeting, tardive dyskinesia, and immobility of face Atypical antipsychotic medications: Less extensive side effects than with neuroleptics, but can have a toxic effect on white blood cells.

FIGURE 15.3 Drug Therapy for Psychological Disorders

unemployed. This suggests that drugs alone will not allow most of them to be contributing members of society. They also need training in vocational, family, and social skills. To increase the effectiveness of treatment, antipsychotic medication may be combined with psychotherapy (Bandelow & Ruther, 2004; Pampallona & others, 2004; Rouillon, 2004.

A summary of the drugs used to treat various psychological disorders, the disorders for which they are used, their effectiveness, and their side effects are shown in figure 15.3.

Electroconvulsive Therapy

Electroconvulsive therapy (ECT), commonly called *shock therapy,* is used mainly to treat severely depressed individuals. The goal of ECT is to cause a seizure in the brain much like what happens spontaneously in some forms of epilepsy. A small electric current lasting for one second or less passes through two electrodes placed on the individual's head. The current excites neural tissue, stimulating a seizure that lasts for approximately one minute.

ECT has been used for more than 40 years. In earlier years it often was used indiscriminately, sometimes even to punish patients. ECT is still used with as many as 60,000 individuals a year, mainly to treat major depressive disorder. Today ECT is given mainly to individuals who have not responded to drug therapy or psychotherapy. You

electroconvulsive therapy (ECT)
Commonly called *shock therapy,* this treatment is used mainly to treat severely depressed individuals. It causes a seizure in the brain.

may think that ECT would entail intolerable pain, but the manner in which it is administered today involves little discomfort. The patient is given anesthesia and muscle relaxants before the current is applied; this allows the individual to sleep through the procedure, minimizes convulsions, and reduces the risk of physical injury. The individual awakens shortly afterward with no conscious memory of the treatment.

How effective is electroconvulsive therapy? In one analysis of studies of the use of electroconvulsive therapy, its effectiveness in treating depression was compared with that of cognitive therapy (which is described later in the chapter) and antidepressant drugs (Seligman, 1994). ECT was as effective as cognitive therapy or drug therapy, with about four of five individuals showing marked improvement in all three therapies. However, as with the other therapies, the relapse rate for ECT is moderate to high.

There are several factors to consider in evaluating ECT (Dew & McCall, 2004; Mehta & others, 2004; Pagnin & others, 2004). Adverse side effects of ECT include memory loss and other cognitive impairments. These side effects are more severe than the side effects of antidepressants. Cognitive therapy shows no side effects. A positive aspect of ECT is that its beneficial effects appear in a matter of days, whereas the beneficial effects of antidepressant drugs can take weeks, and those of cognitive therapy months, to appear (Dannon & others, 2002; McCall, Dunn, & Rosenquist, 2004).

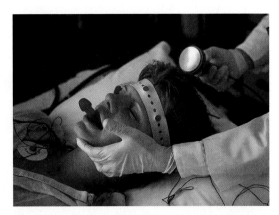

Electroconvulsive therapy (ECT), commonly called *shock therapy,* **causes a seizure in the brain. ECT is still given to as many as 60,000 people a year, mainly to treat major depressive disorder.**

Psychosurgery

Psychosurgery is a biological therapy that involves removal or destruction of brain tissue to improve the individual's adjustment; the effects are irreversible. A landmark in psychosurgery occurred in the 1930s, when Portuguese physician Egas Moniz developed a procedure known as a *prefrontal lobotomy.* In this procedure, a surgical instrument is inserted into the brain and rotated, severing fibers that connect the frontal lobe, which is important in higher thought processes, and the thalamus, important in emotion. Moniz theorized that by severing the connections between these brain structures, the symptoms of severe mental disorders could be alleviated. Prefrontal lobotomies were conducted on thousands of patients from the 1930s through the 1950s. Moniz was awarded the Nobel Prize for his work. However, although some patients may have benefited from the lobotomies, many were left in a vegetable-like state because of the massive assaults on their brains.

These crude lobotomies are no longer performed. Since the 1960s psychosurgery has become more precise (Balon, 2004). When psychosurgery is now performed, a small lesion is made in the amygdala or another part of the limbic system. Today, only several hundred patients who have severely debilitating conditions undergo psychosurgery each year. It is used only as a last resort and with extreme caution.

Review and Reflect

1 Describe the biological therapies

REVIEW

- What types of drugs are most often used to treat anxiety disorders, mood disorders, and schizophrenia, and what are their effects?
- What is electroconvulsive therapy and when is it used?
- What is psychosurgery?

REFLECT

- Before prescribing drug therapy for an individual, what might be some important factors for a psychiatrist or other medical doctor (such as a general practitioner) to consider?

psychosurgery A biological therapy that involves removal or destruction of brain tissue to improve the individual's adjustment.

2 PSYCHOTHERAPIES

| Psychodynamic Therapies | | Behavior Therapies | | Integrative Therapy |
| Humanistic Therapies | | Cognitive Therapies | |

For Steve M., medication was just one part of his therapy. As described at the opening of the chapter, Steve also met with a psychologist once a week and attended a day treatment program. He was the beneficiary of *psychotherapy,* which we defined earlier as the process by which mental health professionals help individuals recognize, define, and overcome psychological and interpersonal difficulties and improve their adjustment. Psychotherapists use many strategies to accomplish these goals: talking, interpreting, listening, rewarding, and modeling, for example. This section examines four approaches to psychotherapy: psychodynamic, humanistic, behavioral, and cognitive.

Psychodynamic Therapies

The **psychodynamic therapies** stress the importance of the unconscious mind, extensive interpretation by the therapist, and the role of early childhood experiences in the development of an individual's problems. The psychodynamic therapies aim to help individuals recognize the maladaptive ways and the sources of their unconscious conflicts (Nolen-Hoeskema, 2004). Most contemporary psychodynamic therapies trace their roots to the work of Sigmund Freud. Many psychodynamic approaches grew out of Freud's theory of personality.

Freud's Psychoanalysis   Freud once said that if you give psychoanalysis your little finger, it will soon have your whole hand. Freud (1917) believed that the therapist acts like a psychological detective, sometimes taking the smallest clue and using it as a springboard for understanding the individual's major problems. Current problems, Freud argued, can be traced to childhood experiences, many of which involve conflicts

www.mhhe.com/santrockha

Psychotherapies
About Psychotherapy
American Psychoanalytic Association
Psychoanalytic Techniques
Contemporary Psychoanalysis

psychodynamic therapies Stress the importance of the unconscious mind, extensive interpretation by the therapist, and the role of the early childhood years. The goal of the psychodynamic therapies is to help individuals recognize their maladaptive ways of coping and the sources of their unconscious conflicts.

psychoanalysis Freud's psychotherapeutic technique for analyzing an individual's unconscious thoughts. Freud believed that clients' current problems could be traced to childhood experiences, involving conflicts about sexuality.

free association The psychoanalytic technique of having individuals say aloud whatever comes to mind.

To encourage his patients to relax, Freud had them recline on this couch while he sat in the chair on the left, out of their view.

about sexuality, as discussed in chapter 2. These early experiences are not readily available to the conscious mind. To put the pieces of the person's personality together and help the individual become aware of how these early experiences affect present behavior, the unconscious mind must be probed and revealed.

Psychoanalysis is Freud's therapeutic technique for analyzing an individual's unconscious thoughts. *Interpretation* plays an important role in this process. The person's statements and behavior are not taken at face value. To understand what is truly causing the person's conflicts, the therapist constantly searchers for symbolic, hidden meanings in what the individual says and does. From time to time the therapist suggests possible meanings of the person's statements and behavior (McWilliams, 2004; Milton, 2004). To reach the shadowy world of the unconscious, psychoanalytic therapists often use the following techniques: free association, catharsis, dream analysis, analysis of resistance, and analysis of transference.

Free association consists of encouraging individuals to say aloud whatever comes to mind no matter how trivial or embarrassing (Busch, 2004; Kris, 2002). When Freud detected a person resisting the spontaneous flow of thoughts, he probed further. He believed that the crux of the person's emotional problem probably lurked below this point of resistance. Encouraging people to talk freely, Freud thought, would help emotions to emerge. **Catharsis** is the psychoanalytic term for the release of emotional tension a person experiences when reliving an emotionally charged and conflict-filled experience.

Dream analysis is the psychoanalytic technique used to interpret a person's dream. Psychoanalysts believe dreams contain information about the individual's unconscious thoughts and conflicts. Freud distinguished between the dream's manifest and latent content. *Manifest content* is the psychoanalytic term for the conscious, remembered aspects of a dream. *Latent content* is the psychoanalytic term for the unconscious, unremembered, symbolic aspects of a dream. The psychoanalyst interprets the dream by analyzing the manifest content for disguised unconscious wishes and needs, especially those that are sexual and aggressive. For some examples of the sexual symbols psychoanalysts use to interpret dreams, see figure 15.4. But even Freud cautioned against overinterpreting. As he once quipped, "Sometimes a cigar is just a cigar."

Resistance is the psychoanalytic term for the person's unconscious defense strategies that prevent the analyst from understanding the person's problems. Resistance occurs because it is painful to bring conflicts into conscious awareness. By resisting therapy, individuals do not have to face their problems. Showing up late or missing sessions, arguing with the psychoanalyst, or faking free associations are examples of resistance. Some people go on endlessly about a trivial matter to avoid facing their conflicts. A major goal of the analyst is to break through this resistance (Shill, 2004).

An inevitable and essential aspect of psychoanalysis, according to Freud, is **transference.** It is process through which the person relates to the analyst in ways that reproduce or relive important relationships in the individual's life. A person might interact with an analyst as if the analyst were a parent or lover, for example. Thus, transference can reveal how individuals relate to important people in their lives (Marcus, 2002; Waldron & others, 2004).

As an example of psychoanalysis, consider the case of a very successful 50-year-old executive. Because he feels depressed and anxious, weak and incompetent, he goes to a psychoanalyst. Here is a description of the therapy he received:

Through many sessions, the psychoanalyst had begun to suspect that the man's feelings of failure stemmed from his childhood experiences with a critical and punitive father. The father never seemed satisfied with the son's efforts. Following is an exchange between the analyst and the businessman that occurred one year into therapy:
Client: "I don't really feel like talking today."

Sexual Theme	Objects or Activities in Dreams That Symbolize Sexual Themes
Male genitals, especially penis	Umbrellas, knives, poles, swords, airplanes, guns, serpents, neckties, tree trunks, hoses
Female genitals, especially vagina	Boxes, caves, pockets, pouches, the mouth, jewel cases, ovens, closets
Sexual intercourse	Climbing, swimming, flying, riding (a horse, an elevator, a roller coaster)
Parents	Kings, queens, emperors, empresses
Siblings	Little animals

FIGURE 15.4 Freudian Interpretation of Sexual Symbolism in Dreams

catharsis The psychoanalytic term for the release of emotional tension a person experiences when reliving an emotionally charged and conflicting experience.

dream analysis The psychotherapeutic technique used by psychoanalysts to interpret a person's dream. Psychoanalysts believe dreams contain information about the individual's unconscious thoughts and conflicts.

resistance The psychoanalytic term for the person's unconscious defense strategies that prevent the analyst from understanding the person's problems.

transference The psychoanalytic term for the person's relating to the analyst in ways that reproduce or relive important relationships in the individual's life.

"Looking good!"

© The New Yorker Collection 1994. Gahan Wilson from cartoonbank.com All Rights Reserved.

Analyst: Remains silent for several minutes, then says, "Perhaps you would like to talk today about why you don't feel like talking."

Client: "There you go again, making demands on me, insisting I do what I just don't feel like doing." (Pause) "Do I always have to talk here, when I don't feel like it?" (Voice becomes angry and petulant.) "Can't you just get off my back? You don't really care how I feel."

Analyst: "I wonder why you feel I don't care."

Client: "Because you're always pressuring me to do what I feel I can't do."

This exchange was interpreted by the analyst as an expression of resentment by the client of the father's pressures that were put on him and had little to do with the analyst himself. The transfer of the client's feelings from the father to the analyst was regarded as significant by the analyst and was used in subsequent sessions to help the client overcome his fear of expressing anger toward his father. (Source: Davison & Neale, 2001, p. 33)

A psychoanalyst may see an individual frequently, and the analysis may go on for many years. Freud saw clients as often as three to five times a week for a number of years. Today, however, only a small percentage of therapists rigorously practice Freudian psychoanalysis. Freud's ideas have been adapted and put to use in contemporary psychodynamic therapies.

Contemporary Psychodynamic Therapies Today individuals in psychodynamic therapy rarely lie on a couch or see their therapist several times a week. Instead, people sit in a comfortable chair facing the therapist. Weekly appointments are typical, and the therapy sometimes lasts only a few months (Binder, 2004). Behind these changes in the format of psychodynamic therapy are changes in the ideas that guide it. Many contemporary psychodynamic therapists still probe a person's early childhood to obtain clues to the person's current problems (Marcus, 2002). Many contemporary psychodynamic therapists also try to help individuals gain insight into their emotionally laden, repressed conflicts (Godbout, 2004; Sonnenberg & Ursano, 2002). They also accord more power to the conscious mind and to a person's current relationships (Orfanos, 2002). Further, they may emphasize the development of the self in social contexts (Erikson, 1968; Horowitz, 1998; Kohut, 1977).

The work of Heinz Kohut provides one prominent example of the contemporary psychodynamic approach. In Kohut's view, early relationships with attachment figures, such as one's parents, are critical. As we develop we do not relinquish these attachments; we continue to need them. Kohut's prescription for therapy involves helping the person to identify and seek out appropriate relationships with others. He also wants individuals to develop realistic appraisals of relationships. Kohut (1977) believes therapists need to interact with individuals in ways that are empathic and understanding. Empathy and understanding are also the cornerstones for humanistic therapies.

Adjustment Strategies
Based on Psychodynamic Therapies

1. ***Recognize that the reasons for your good or poor adjustment are likely beyond your conscious awareness.*** A psychodynamic therapist can help you to bring unconscious material into conscious awareness, which is an important step in being able to cope more effectively.

2. ***Examine your childhood experiences in your family.*** Psychodynamic therapists believe that many psychological problems can be traced to experiences individuals have in their interactions with family members as they were growing up.

3. ***Explore whether you are relying too heavily on defense mechanisms to cope with stress.*** Recall from chapter 2 that defense mechanisms, such as repression, projection, rationalization, and others, are used to reduce anxiety by distorting reality.

Used moderately or on a temporary basis, defense mechanisms are not necessarily unhealthy, but when they are used more than problem-focused coping to cope with stress, they can become maladaptive.

4. ***Realize that different psychodynamic therapies offer different approaches to adjustment.*** The adjustment strategies mentioned reflect the views of psychodynamic therapies in general. However, psychodynamic therapies vary. One therapist might base his or her approach on Freud's ideas, another on Karen Horney's emphasis on the need for security and gender, and yet another on Heinz Kohut's self-development. Thus, an individual who is attracted to psychodynamic therapy should explore which of these psychodynamic therapies might be the best match for his or her psychological problem.

Humanistic Therapies

Like the psychodynamic therapies, humanistic therapies are a form of **insight therapy** because they encourage insight and awareness. But in contrast to the psychodynamic therapies, the humanistic therapies emphasize conscious rather than unconscious thoughts, the present rather than the past, and growth and self-fulfillment rather than illness. The underlying philosophy of humanistic therapies is captured by the metaphor of an acorn: if provided with appropriate conditions, it will grow naturally toward its actualization as an oak (Schneider, 2002). In the **humanistic therapies,** people are encouraged to understand themselves and to grow personally. The humanistic therapies are unique in their emphasis on the person's self-healing capacities (Bohart, 1995; Bohart & Greening, 2001).

Client-Centered Therapy   **Client-centered therapy** is a form of humanistic therapy developed by Carl Rogers (1961, 1980), in which the therapist provides a warm, supportive atmosphere to improve the client's self-concept and encourage the client to gain insight about problems. Compared with psychodynamic therapies, which emphasize analysis and interpretation by the therapist, client-centered therapy places far more emphasis on the client's self-reflection (Hill, 2000).

The relationship between the therapist and the person is an important aspect of Rogers' therapy. The therapist must enter into an intensely personal relationship with the client, not as a physician diagnosing a disease but as one human being to another. Notice that Rogers referred to the "client" and then the "person" rather than the "patient."

Rogers believed each of us grows up in a world filled with *conditional positive regard;* in other words, the sense of worth we receive from others has strings attached. We usually do not receive love and praise unless we conform to the standards and demands of others. This causes us to be unhappy and have low self-esteem. Rarely do we feel that we measure up to such standards or that we are as good as others expect us to be.

To free a person from worry about society's demands, the therapist engages in *unconditional positive regard,* in which the therapist creates a warm and caring environment, never disapproving of the client (although the therapist does not always approve of the person's behavior). Rogers believed this unconditional positive regard improves the person's self-esteem. The therapist's role is *nondirective;* that is, he or she does not lead the client to any particular revelation. The therapist is there to listen sympathetically to the client's problems and to encourage positive self-regard, independent self-appraisal, and decision making.

In addition to unconditional positive regard, Rogers advocated the use of these two techniques in client-centered therapy:

- *Genuineness* (also called *congruence*), which involves letting a client know the therapist's feelings and not hiding behind a facade.

insight therapy Encourages insight and self-awareness; includes both psychodynamic and humanistic therapies, because they encourage insight and self-awareness.

humanistic therapies Encourage people to understand themselves and to grow personally. The humanistic therapies are unique in their emphasis on self-healing capacities.

client-centered therapy Rogers' humanistic therapy in which the therapist provides a warm, supportive atmosphere to improve the client's self-concept and encourage the client to gain insight about problems.

- *Active listening,* which consists of giving total attention to what the person says and means. One way therapists improve active listening is to restate and support what the client has said and done.

In chapter 2, "Personality," we described five adjustment strategies for becoming a fully functioning person based on Rogers' ideas. These include: Take a positive approach to life and believe in your capacity for positive growth; be open to experience; don't be overly defensive; develop a more positive self-concept; and have harmonious relationships with others. You might want to review the details of these adjustment strategies in chapter 2.

Gestalt Therapy   Compared with a client-centered therapist, a Gestalt therapist is much more directive, providing more interpretation and feedback (Glass, 2004; Zahm & Gold, 2002). **Gestalt therapy** is a humanistic therapy developed by Fritz Perls (1893–1970), in which the therapist challenges clients to help them become more aware of their feelings and face their problems.

Perls was trained in Europe as a Freudian psychoanalyst, but he developed his own ideas. Perls (1969) agreed with Freud that psychological problems originate in unresolved past conflicts and that these conflicts need to be acknowledged and worked through. Also like Freud, Perls stressed that interpretation of dreams is an important aspect of therapy. But, in other ways, Perls and Freud were miles apart. Perls believed that unresolved conflicts should be brought to bear on the here and now of the individual's life. The therapist *pushes* clients into deciding whether they will continue to allow the past to control their future or whether they will choose right now what they want to be in the future. To this end, Perls both confronted individuals and encouraged them to actively control their lives and to be open about their feelings.

Like client-centered therapists, Gestalt therapists encourage individuals to be open about their feelings, to develop self-awareness, to be themselves, to develop a sense of freedom, and to look at what they are doing with their lives. But the techniques used by Gestalt therapists differ greatly from those used by client-centered therapists. The Gestalt therapist sets examples and encourages congruence between verbal and nonverbal behavior. To stimulate change, the therapist often openly confronts the client. To demonstrate an important point to a client, the Gestalt therapist might exaggerate a client's characteristics. Another technique used in Gestalt therapy is role playing, either by the client, the therapist, or both. For example, if an individual is bothered by conflict with her mother, the therapist might play the role of the mother and reopen the quarrel. The therapist might encourage the individual to act out her hostile feelings toward her mother by yelling, swearing, or kicking the couch, for example. In this way, Gestalt therapists hope to help individuals better manage their feelings instead of letting their feelings control them.

**Frederick (Fritz) Perls (1893–1970).
The founder of Gestalt therapy.**

www.mhhe.com/santrockha

Person-Centered Therapy
Gestalt Therapy

Gestalt therapy Perls' humanistic therapy in which the therapist challenges clients to help them become more aware of their feelings and face their problems.

behavior therapies Use principles of learning to reduce or eliminate maladaptive behavior.

Behavior Therapies

According to psychodynamic and humanistic therapies, insight and self-awareness are keys to helping individuals. Not so, say behavior therapists. Behavior therapists do not search for unconscious conflicts, as psychodynamic therapists do, or encourage individuals to develop accurate perceptions of their feelings as humanistic therapists do. **Behavior therapies** use principles of learning to reduce or eliminate maladaptive behavior. Behavior therapies offer action-oriented strategies to help people change what they are doing (Herson, 2005).

According to behavior therapists, the maladaptive symptoms displayed by people with psychological disorders *are* the problem. Individuals can become aware of why they are depressed and still be depressed, say the behavior therapists. The behavior therapist tries to eliminate the depressed symptoms or behaviors themselves rather than trying to get individuals to gain insight or awareness of why they are depressed (Forsyth & Savsevitz, 2002).

1. A month before an examination
2. Two weeks before an examination
3. A week before an examination
4. Five days before an examination
5. Four days before an examination
6. Three days before an examination
7. Two days before an examination
8. One day before an examination
9. The night before an examination
10. On the way to the university on the day of an examination
11. Before the unopened doors of the examination room
12. Awaiting distribution of examination papers
13. The examination paper lies facedown before her
14. In the process of answering the exam questions

FIGURE 15.5 A Desensitization Hierarchy Involving Test Anxiety
In the above hierarchy, the individual begins with their least feared circumstance (a month before the exam) and moves through each of the circumstances until reaching their most feared circumstance (being in the process of answering the exam questions). At each step of the way, the person replaces fear with deep relaxation and successful visualizations.

The behavior therapies were initially based almost exclusively on the learning principles of classical and operant conditioning, but behavior therapies soon became more diverse (McKay & Tryon, 2002; Morley, 2004). As social cognitive theory grew in popularity, behavior therapists incorporated techniques based on observational learning, cognitive factors, and self-instruction. Let's look first at some techniques based on classical and operant conditioning.

Applications of Classical Conditioning Some behaviors, especially fears, are learned through *classical conditioning,* which was discussed in chapter 2, "Personality." Behavior therapists apply the principle that if fears can be learned, they also can be unlearned (Lazarus & Ambrumovitz, 2004; Taylor, 2002). If an individual has learned to fear snakes or heights through classical conditioning, perhaps the individual can unlearn the fear through counterconditioning. Two types of counterconditioning involve systematic desensitization and aversive conditioning.

Systematic Desensitization **Systematic desensitization** is a method of behavior therapy based on classical conditioning that treats anxiety by teaching the person to associate deep relaxation with increasingly intense anxiety-producing situations (Powell, 2004; Wolpe, 1963). Consider the fear of taking an exam. Using systematic desensitization, the behavior therapist first asks the person which aspects of the feared situation—in this case, taking an exam—are the most and least frightening. Then the behavior therapist arranges these circumstances in order from most to least frightening. An example of this type of desensitization hierarchy is shown in figure 15.5.

The next step is to teach individuals to relax. Clients are taught to recognize the presence of muscular contractions or tensions in various parts of their bodies and then how to contract and relax different muscles. Once individuals are relaxed, the therapist asks them to imagine the least feared stimulus in the hierarchy. Subsequently, the therapist moves up the list of items, from least to most feared, while clients remain relaxed. Eventually, individuals are able to imagine the most fearsome circumstance without being afraid—in our example, being in the process of answering exam questions. In this manner, individuals learn to relax while thinking about the exam instead of feeling anxious.

Aversive Conditioning The other behavior therapy technique involving classical conditioning is **aversive conditioning,** which consists of repeated pairings of the

Systematic desensitization has a new format. Virtual reality technology is being used by some therapists to expose individuals to more vivid situations than their imagination might generate. Here, an individual with a fear of spiders is wearing a virtual reality headset and has become immersed in a vivid, three-dimensional world in which spiders appear very real.

systematic desensitization A method of behavior therapy based on classical conditioning that treats anxiety by getting the person to associate deep relaxation with increasingly intense anxiety-producing situations.

aversive conditioning A classical conditioning treatment that consists of repeated pairings of the undesirable behavior with aversive stimuli to decrease the behavior's rewards.

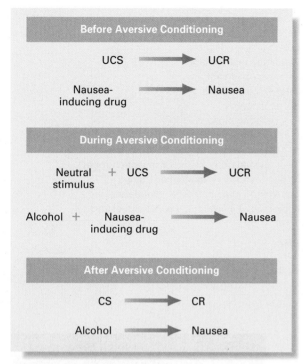

FIGURE 15.6 Classical Conditioning: The Backbone of Aversive Conditioning
The above illustrates how classical conditioning can provide a conditional aversion to alcohol. After the association of the drug with alcohol, the alcohol becomes a conditioned stimulus for nausea. Recall these abbreviations: UCS (unconditioned stimulus), UCR (unconditioned response), CS (conditioned stimulus), and CR (conditioned response).

behavior modification The application of operant conditioning principles to change human behaviors, especially to replace unacceptable, maladaptive behaviors with acceptable, adaptive behaviors.

undesirable behavior with aversive stimuli. Aversive conditioning is used to teach people to avoid such behaviors as smoking, eating, and drinking. Electric shocks, nausea-inducing substances, and verbal insults are some of the noxious stimuli used in aversive conditioning. How could aversive conditioning be used to reduce a person's alcohol consumption? Every time a person drank an alcoholic beverage, he or she also would consume a mixture that induced nausea. As result of pairing alcohol with a nausea-inducing agent, alcohol becomes associated not with something pleasant but with something extremely unpleasant. Figure 15.6 illustrates how classical conditioning is the backbone of aversive conditioning.

Applications of Operant Conditioning Operant conditioning, which was introduced in chapter 2, "Personality," also provides the basis for helping people to unlearn maladaptive behavior. Recall that in operant conditioning the consequences of behavior alter the frequency of behavior. Behavior therapists believe that many emotional and behavioral problems are caused by a history of inappropriate consequences. In the technique known as **behavior modification,** therapists aim to replace maladaptive behaviors with adaptive ones by ensuring that acceptable actions are reinforced and unacceptable ones are not (Kearney & Vecchio, 2002). Advocates of behavior modification believe that many emotional and behavioral problems are caused by inadequate (or inappropriate) response consequences.

A first step in behavior modification is to analyze the person's environment in order to determine what should be modified to help the individual replace maladaptive responses with more adaptive ones. Consider the case in which behavior modification was used to help a 36-year-old lawyer, Henry Greene, reduce his depression (Rosenfeld, 1985). Green had lost his appetite and 15 pounds, as well as his interest in sex. His sleep often ended at 3 A.M. He had become convinced that he was a third-rate lawyer, husband, lover, and father. To treat Greene, the therapist gave Greene the assignment of monitoring his moods. This task forced him to pay attention to his daily mood changes, and the information was used to determine which events were associated with which events. Relaxation training followed because relaxation skills can improve an individual's sense of well-being.

The next step for Henry Greene was to evaluate how his moods were associated with pleasant and unpleasant events in his life. Henry was asked to fill out a "Pleasant Events Schedule" and an "Unpleasant Events Schedule." Each week, Henry completed a graph showing the number of pleasant and unpleasant events, as well as his mood, for each day. Henry was able to see a close relation between pleasant events and pleasant moods and between unpleasant events and unpleasant moods. The therapist then encouraged Henry to increase the amount of time he spends in pleasant activities with the hope that more positive moods would follow. The positive outcome was that Henry was able to gain control over his moods.

The final stage for Henry was maintenance planning. Henry was asked to identify the components of behavior therapy that were the most successful in changing his maladaptive behavior. Once Henry identified these, he was encouraged to continue their use.

Greene's treatment was based on the "Coping with Depression" course developed by Peter Lewinsohn and his colleagues (1984). This course is built on the idea that feelings are caused by behaviors. By teaching individuals to increase the ratio of positive life events to negative life events, therapists aim to improve their mood.

A better-known application of behavior modification is the *token economy,* which is a system in which desired behaviors are reinforced with tokens (such as poker chips) that later can be exchanged for desired rewards (such as candy, money, or going to a movie). Token economies have been established in classrooms, institutions for the mentally retarded, homes for delinquents, and mental hospitals (Field & others,

2004). The system does not always work. One person may become so wedded to the tokens that when they are no longer given, the positive behavior associated with them may disappear. Furthermore, some critics object that token economies impose an unethical degree of control over the individual. However, token economies can increase the frequency of adaptive behaviors.

Cognitive Therapies

D., a 21-year-old, single, undergraduate student, perceives himself as a failure in school and a failure to his parents. He is preoccupied with negative thoughts, dwells on his problems, and exaggerates his faults. Such thinking is common among depressed individuals. Would changing how D. thinks end or ease his depression? That is the approach taken by cognitive therapies.

Cognitive therapies are based on the idea that cognitions, or thoughts, are the main source of psychological problems, and they attempt to change the individual's feelings and behaviors by changing cognitions. Compared with psychodynamic therapies, cognitive therapies focus more on overt symptoms than on unconscious thoughts, provide more structure to the individual's thoughts, and are less concerned about the origin of the problem (Thorn, 2004). Unlike humanistic therapies, cognitive therapies provide more structure and more analysis. Cognitive therapists aim for *cognitive restructuring,* which means changing a pattern of thought (Leahy, 2004).

How do cognitive therapists achieve cognitive restructuring? First, they guide individuals to identify their irrational and self-defeating thoughts; then they use various techniques to help clients challenge these thoughts and consider different, more positive ways of thinking. These techniques often are implemented by asking questions to help clients understand their negative thinking. This section examines two main forms of cognitive therapy—Albert Ellis' rational-emotive behavior therapy and Aaron Beck's cognitive therapy—as well as cognitive-behavior therapy, which uses a combination of cognitive and behavioral techniques.

Ellis' Rational-Emotive Behavior Therapy
Beck's Cognitive Therapy

Rational-Emotive Behavior Therapy   Rational-emotive behavior therapy **(REBT)** is based on Albert Ellis' assertion that individuals develop a psychological disorder because of their beliefs, especially irrational and self-defeating beliefs. Ellis (1962, 1996, 2002, 2004) says that we usually talk to ourselves when we experience stress; too often the statements are irrational, making them more harmful than helpful. To evaluate whether you have irrational beliefs, complete Self-Assessment 15.1.

Ellis (2000, 2002) believes that many individuals construct three basic demands: (1) I *absolutely must* perform well and win the approval of other people; (2) Other people *have to* treat me kindly and fairly; and (3) My life conditions *should not* be frustrating but rather *should be* enjoyable. Once people convert their important desires into demands, they often create dysfunctional, exaggerated beliefs, such as "Because I'm not performing well, as I *absolutely must,* I'm an inadequate person."

The goal of REBT is to get the person to eliminate self-defeating beliefs by rationally examining them (Dryden, 2004). Clients are shown how to dispute their dysfunctional beliefs—especially their absolute musts—and change them to realistic and logical thoughts. Homework assignments provide them opportunities to engage in the new self-talk and experience the positive results of not viewing life in such a catastrophic way.

Beck's Cognitive Therapy   Like Ellis, Aaron Beck (1976, 1993; Beck & others, 1979, 2003) believes that therapy should help people discard self-defeating cognitions, but Beck developed a somewhat different form of cognitive therapy to treat psychological problems, especially depression. Ellis' REBT is very directive, persuasive, and confrontational. In contrast, Beck's cognitive therapy resembles an open-ended dialogue in which the therapist helps individuals to reflect on personal issues, to discover

cognitive therapies Emphasize that individuals' cognitions or thoughts are the main source of abnormal behavior and psychological problems.

rational-emotive behavior therapy (REBT) Based on Albert Ellis' assertion that individuals develop a psychological disorder because of their beliefs, especially those that are irrational and self-defeating; the goal of REBT is to get the person to eliminate self-defeating beliefs by rationally examining them.

Do I Have Irrational Beliefs?

People have different beliefs and opinions. We are interested in knowing your beliefs concerning the following issues. There are no right or wrong answers for the items; we are interested in opinions only. Please indicate your own opinion by circling a number from one to nine on the scale provided for each statement. In case of doubt, circle the number that comes closest to representing your true opinion.

1. It is essential that one be loved or approved by virtually everyone in one's community.

Completely disagree   *Completely agree*

　　1　　　2　　　3　　　4　　　5　　　6　　　7　　　8　　　9

2. One must be perfectly competent, adequate, and achieving to consider oneself worthwhile.

Completely disagree   *Completely agree*

　　1　　　2　　　3　　　4　　　5　　　6　　　7　　　8　　　9

3. Some people are bad, wicked, or villainous and therefore should be blamed and punished.

Completely disagree   *Completely agree*

　　1　　　2　　　3　　　4　　　5　　　6　　　7　　　8　　　9

4. It is a terrible catastrophe when things are not as one wants them to be.

Completely disagree   *Completely agree*

　　1　　　2　　　3　　　4　　　5　　　6　　　7　　　8　　　9

5. Unhappiness is caused by outside circumstances and the individual has no control over it.

Completely disagree   *Completely agree*

　　1　　　2　　　3　　　4　　　5　　　6　　　7　　　8　　　9

6. Dangerous or fearsome things are causes for great concern, and their possibility must be continually dwelt upon.

Completely disagree   *Completely agree*

　　1　　　2　　　3　　　4　　　5　　　6　　　7　　　8　　　9

7. One should be dependent on others and must have someone stronger on whom to rely.

Completely disagree   *Completely agree*

　　1　　　2　　　3　　　4　　　5　　　6　　　7　　　8　　　9

8. One should be quite upset over people's problems and disturbances.

Completely disagree   *Completely agree*

　　1　　　2　　　3　　　4　　　5　　　6　　　7　　　8　　　9

9. There is always a right or perfect solution to every problem, and it must be found or the results will be catastrophic.

Completely disagree   *Completely agree*

　　1　　　2　　　3　　　4　　　5　　　6　　　7　　　8　　　9

Go to the appendix at the end of the book for scoring and interpretation of your responses.

their own misconceptions, to try out unbiased experiments that reveal the inaccuracies of their beliefs.

Beck assumes that psychological problems such as depression result when people think illogically about themselves, the world they live in, and the future (Fox & Newman, 2004). Illogical thinking can lead an individual to the following errors (Butcher, Mineka, & Hooley, 2004):

- Perceiving the world as harmful while ignoring evidence to the contrary; for example, still feeling worthless even though a friend has just told you how much other people like you
- Overgeneralizing on the basis of limited examples, such as seeing yourself as worthless because one individual stopped dating you
- Magnifying the importance of undesirable events, such as seeing the loss of your dating partner as the end of the world
- Engaging in absolutist thinking, such as exaggerating the importance of someone's mildly critical comment and perceiving it as proof of total inadequacy

In the initial phases of Beck's cognitive therapy, individuals are taught to make connections between their patterns of thinking and their emotional responses. The therapist helps them to identify their own automatic thoughts and to keep records of their thought content and emotional reactions. With the therapist's assistance, they learn about logical errors in their thinking and learn to challenge the accuracy of these automatic thoughts. In the following example, a cognitive therapist guides a depressed 26-year-old graduate student to understand the connection between how she interprets her experiences and the way she feels and to begin seeing the inaccuracy of her interpretations (Beck & others, 1979, pp. 145–146):

> **Student:** I agree with the description of me but I guess I don't agree that the way I think makes me depressed.
>
> **Therapist:** How do you understand it?
>
> **Student:** I get depressed when things go wrong. Like when I fail a test.
>
> **Therapist:** How can failing a test make you depressed.
>
> **Student:** Well, if I fail I'll never get into law school.
>
> **Therapist:** So failing the test means a lot to you. But if failing a test could drive people into clinical depression, wouldn't you expect everyone who failed the test to have depression? Did everyone who failed the test get depressed enough to require treatment?
>
> **Student:** No, but it depends on how important the test was to the person.
>
> **Therapist:** Right, and who decides the importance?
>
> **Student:** I do.
>
> **Therapist:** And so, what we have to examine is your way of viewing the test or the way that you think about the test and how it affects your chances of getting into law school. Do you agree?
>
> **Student:** Right …
>
> **Therapist:** Now what did failing mean?
>
> **Student:** (Tearful) That I couldn't get into law school.
>
> **Therapist:** And what does that mean to you?
>
> **Student:** That I'm just not smart enough.
>
> **Therapist:** Anything else?
>
> **Student:** That I can never be happy.
>
> **Therapist:** And how do these thoughts make you feel?
>
> **Student:** Very unhappy.
>
> **Therapist:** So it is the meaning of failing a test that makes you very unhappy. In fact, believing that you can never be happy is a powerful factor in producing unhappiness. So, you get yourself into a trap—by definition, failure to get into law school equals, "I can never be happy."

Adjustment Strategies
Based on Beck's Cognitive Therapy

Here are some adjustment strategies based on Aaron Beck's cognitive therapy (Freeman & Reinecke, 1995):

1. ***Keep records of your thought content and emotional reactions.*** This helps you to identify your automatic thoughts and logical errors in your thinking. David Burns' (1999) book, *Feeling Good,* is a good source for learning how to keep these records.
2. ***Engage in thought stopping.*** Thought stopping involves stopping a cascade of negative thoughts. You might picture a stop sign or hear a bell when anxious thoughts begin to snowball.
3. ***Examine options and alternatives.*** Generate adaptive alternatives to maladaptive ones. If you consider quitting college, explore whether tutoring or going to school part-time might be positive alternatives.
4. ***Question the evidence.*** Systematically examine the evidence for your beliefs and assertions. If you think you can't live without a spouse or partner, ask yourself how you were able to do this before living with the individual.
5. ***Become positively distracted.*** Find positive distractions to draw attention away from negative thoughts or feelings temporarily. You might count to 200 by 13s when you feel yourself becoming highly anxious.
6. ***Decatastrophize.*** Think clearly and evaluate whether you are overestimating the negative aspects of a situation. For example, if you get a "C" in one course and think that you must give up the dream of going to graduate school, question whether this is a necessary conclusion.
7. ***Fantasize consequences.*** Explore fantasies about a feared situation. If unrealistic, recognize this; if realistic, work on effective coping strategies.
8. ***Turn adversity into advantage.*** Think about ways that you can transform stressful circumstances into opportunities. For example, if you become laid off from a job, evaluate whether this can be an opportunity to take more courses and finish your education sooner.

www.mhhe.com/santrockha

Cognitive-Behavior Therapy

cognitive-behavior therapy Consists of a combination of cognitive therapy and behavior therapy; self-efficacy is an important goal of cognitive-behavior therapy.

Cognitive-Behavior Therapy Techniques from cognitive therapy, with its emphasis on reducing self-defeating thoughts, and from behavior therapy, with its emphasis on changing behavior, can be combined in **cognitive-behavior therapy.** *Self-instructional methods* aimed at teaching individuals to modify their own behavior are often used in cognitive-behavior therapy (Dowd, 2002; Grant, 2004; Meichenbaum, 1977). For example, the therapist helps clients to change what they say to themselves by giving them examples of constructive statements, known as *reinforcing self-statements.* For example, an individual might be instructed to say, "Way to go. You did it." The therapist also encourages the client to practice the statements through role playing and strengthens the client's newly acquired skills through reinforcement (Cartwright-Hatton & others, 2004; Fava & others, 2004).

An important aspect of cognitive-behavior therapy is *self-efficacy,* the belief that one can master a situation and produce positive outcomes. Albert Bandura (1997, 2001) believes that self-efficacy is the key to successful therapy. At each step of therapy, people need to bolster their confidence by telling themselves, "I'm going to master my problem," "I can do it," "I'm improving," "I'm getting better," and so on. As people gain confidence and engage in adaptive behavior, the successes become intrinsically motivating. Before long, individuals persist with considerable effort in their attempts to solve personal problems because of the positive outcomes that were set in motion by self-efficacy.

Adjustment Strategies
For Self-Instructional Methods

Here is a series of examples of self-instructional methods that individuals can use to cope with stressful situations (Meichenbaum, Turk, & Burstein, 1975):

1. ***Preparing for Stress or Anxiety:***
   What do I have to do?
   I'm going to map out a plan to deal with it.
   I'll just think about what I have to do.
   I won't worry. Worry doesn't help anything.
   I have a lot of different strategies I can call on.
2. ***Confronting and Handling the Anxiety or Stress:***
   I can meet the challenge.
   I'll keep on taking one step at a time.
   I can handle it. I'll just relax, breathe deeply, and use one of the strategies.
   I won't think about the pain. I will think about what I have to do.
3. ***Coping with Feelings at Critical Moments:***
   What is it I have to do?
   I was supposed to expect the pain to increase. I just have to keep myself in control.
   When the pain comes, I will just pause and keep focusing on what I have to do.
4. ***Reinforcing Self-Statements:***
   Good, I did it.
   I handled it well.
   I knew I could do it.
   Wait until I tell other people how I did it!

Integrative Therapy

In the single-therapy approach, the therapist believes that one particular kind of therapy works best. However, approximately 30 to 50 percent of practicing therapists do not identify themselves as adhering to one particular approach but rather refer to themselves as "integrative" or "eclectic" (Castonguay & others, 2003; Gold, 2002; Norcross & Kobayshi, 2000; Norcross & Prochaska,1988). **Integrative therapy** is a combination of techniques from different therapies based on the therapist's judgment of which particular techniques will provide the greatest benefit for the client.

Integrative therapy is characterized by an openness to various ways of integrating diverse therapies (Castonguay & others, 2003; Greben, 2004). For example, a therapist might use a behavioral approach to treat an individual with panic disorder and a cognitive therapy approach to treat an individual with major depressive disorder. There is no single well-defined integrative therapy that ties all of the therapy approaches together. For that reason, the term *therapy integrations* probably best captures what is taking place in this field.

In the past two decades, therapy integration has grown dramatically (Arkowitz, 1997). What has fostered the movement toward integrative therapy? The motivating factors include the proliferation of therapies, the inadequacy of a single therapy to be relevant to all clients and all problems, a lack of evidence that one therapy is better than others, and recognition that therapy commonalities play an important role in therapy outcomes (Norcross & Newman, 1992).

At their best, integrative therapies are effective, systematic uses of a variety of therapy approaches (Corey, 1996). However, one worry about integrative therapies is that their increased use will result in an unsystematic, haphazard eclecticism, which some therapists say would be no better than a narrow, dogmatic approach to therapy (Lazarus, Beutler, & Norcross, 1992).

integrative therapy A combination of techniques from different therapies based on the therapist's judgment of which particular techniques will provide the greatest benefit for the client.

With the increased diversity of client problems and populations, future therapy integration is likely to include more attention to ethnic and cultural factors in treating clients (Sue, 2000). This increased ethnic and cultural diversity also will require therapists to integrate spiritual concerns into their therapy approach (Pate & Bondi, 1992).

Integrative therapy also is at work when individuals are treated with both psychotherapy and drug therapy. For example, combined drug therapy and cognitive therapy have been effective in treating anxiety and depressive disorders (Dunner, 2001; Kuzma & Black, 2004). And combined drug therapy and cognitive therapy hold promise in treating schizophrenia (Rector & Beck, 2001). This integrative therapy might be conducted by a mental health team that included a psychiatrist and a clinical psychologist.

Therapy integrations are conceptually compatible with the bio-psycho-social model of abnormal behavior described in chapter 14. That is, many therapists believe that abnormal behavior involves biological, psychological, and social factors. Many single-therapy approaches focus on one aspect of the person more than others; for instance, drug therapies focus on biological factors, and cognitive therapies focus on psychological factors. Therapy integrations often taken a broader look at individuals' problems.

Review and Reflect

2 Characterize four types of psychotherapies

REVIEW

- What is psychodynamic therapy?
- How do the humanistic therapies of Rogers and Perls differ?
- How are classical conditioning and operant conditioning applied in behavioral therapies?
- What are the key characteristics of RMBT, Beck's cognitive therapy, and cognitive-behavior therapy?
- What is integrative therapy?

REFLECT

- Imagine that you are a psychotherapist and that you diagnose an individual as having a depressive disorder. Which of the psychotherapies would you use to treat the individual? Explain your choice.

3 SOCIOCULTURAL APPROACHES AND ISSUES IN TREATMENT

| Group Therapy | Self-Help Support Groups | Cultural Perspectives |

| Family and Couples Therapy | Community Mental Health |

In the treatment of psychological disorders, biological therapies change the person's body, behavioral therapies modify the person's behavior, and cognitive therapies alter the person's thinking. Does it matter if the person involved is American or Egyptian or Japanese? Does it matter if the person is married or single, male or female? Sociocultural approaches to the treatment of psychological disorders answer that these and other characteristics of the contexts of a person's life matter a great deal. These approaches view the individual as part of a social system of relationships, influenced by various social and cultural factors, and believe that these sociocultural aspects must be dealt with in the treatment of psychological disorders (Nolen-Hoeksema, 2004).

The sociocultural approaches and issues include group therapy, family and couples therapy, self-help support groups, community mental health, and cultural perspectives on therapy.

Group Therapy

Nine people make their way into a room, each looking tentatively at the others. Although each person has met the therapist during a diagnostic interview, no one knows any of the other clients. Some of the people seem reluctant, others enthusiastic. All are willing to follow the therapist's recommendation that group therapy might help each of them learn to cope better with their problems. As they sit down and wait for the session to begin, one thinks, "Will they really understand me?" Another thinks, "Do the others have problems like mine?" Yet another thinks, "How can I stick my neck out with these people?" This is the beginning of a session of group therapy. Psychodynamic, humanistic, behavior, and cognitive therapy are all used in group therapy, in addition to approaches that are not based on the major therapeutic perspectives.

Why would people choose to provide or to receive group therapy rather than individual therapy? Individual therapy is often expensive and time consuming; by seeing clients in a group, therapists can make treatment more affordable for more people (Burlingame & Ridge, 2004; MacKenzie, 2002). Also, advocates of group therapy stress that individual therapy is limited because the client is seen outside the normal context of relationships, relationships that may hold the key to successful therapy (Kline, 2003; Malekoff, 2004; Yalom, 2004). Many psychological problems develop in the context of interpersonal relationships—within one's family, marriage, or peer group, for example. By taking into account the context of these important groups, therapy may be more successful (Capuzzi, 2003).

Six features make group therapy an attractive treatment format (Yalom, 1975, 1995):

1. *Information.* Individuals receive information about their problem from either the group leader or other group members.
2. *Universality.* In the group, individuals observe that their frightening impulses are not unique and that others feel anguish and suffering.

Because many psychological problems develop in the context of interpersonal relationships and group experiences—within family, marriage, work or social group—group therapy can be an important context for learning how to cope more effectively with these problems.

3. *Altruism.* Group members support one another with advice and sympathy and learn that they have something to offer others.

4. *Corrective recapitulation of the family group.* A therapy group often resembles a family (in family therapy, the group *is* a family), with the leaders representing parents and the other members siblings. In this "new" family, old wounds may be healed and new, more positive "family" ties made.

5. *Development of social skills.* Group members may receive feedback from peers that helps them correct flaws in their interpersonal behavior. Self-centered individuals may see that they are self-centered if five other group members tell them about their self-centeredness; in individual therapy, people might not believe the therapist.

6. *Interpersonal learning.* The group can serve as a training ground for practicing new behaviors and relationships. A hostile woman may learn that she can get along better with others by behaving less aggressively, for example.

Family and Couples Therapy

"A friend loves you for your intelligence, a mistress for your charm, but your family's love is unreasoning; you were born into it and are of its flesh and blood. Nevertheless, it can irritate you more than any group of people in the world," commented the French biographer André Maurois. As his statement suggests, the family may be the source of an individual's problems.

Family therapy is group therapy with family members. **Couples therapy** is group therapy with married or unmarried couples whose major problem is their relationship. These approaches stress that, although one person may have some abnormal symptoms, the symptoms are a function of the family or couple (Kaslow, 2004; Nichols & Schwartz, 2004; Sharpe, 2004). Psychodynamic, humanistic, and behavior therapies may be used in family and couples therapy.

Family therapy has become increasingly popular in recent years. In family therapy, the assumption is that psychological adjustment is related to patterns of interaction within the family unit.

family therapy Group therapy with family members.

couples therapy Therapy with married or unmarried couples whose major problem is their relationship.

Adjustment Strategies
Based on Family Therapy

Four of the most widely used family therapy techniques are:

1. ***Validation.*** The therapist expresses an understanding and acceptance of each family member's feelings and beliefs and thus validates the person. When the therapist talks with each family member, she finds something positive to say.

2. ***Reframing.*** The therapist helps families reframe problems as family problems, not an individual's problems. A delinquent adolescent boy's problems are reframed in terms of how each family member contributed to the situation. The father's lack of attention to his son and marital conflict may be involved, for example.

3. ***Structural Change.*** The family systems therapist tries to restructure the coalitions in a family. In a mother-son coalition, the therapist might suggest that the father take a stronger disciplinarian role to relieve some of the burden from the mother. Restructuring might be as simple as suggesting that parents explore satisfying ways to be together; the therapist may recommend that once a week the parents go out for a quiet dinner together, for example.

4. ***Detriangulation.*** In some families, one member is the scapegoat for two other members who are in conflict but pretend not to be. For example, in the triangle of two parents and one child, the parents may insist that their marriage is fine but find themselves in subtle conflict over how to handle the child. The therapist tries to disentangle, or detriangulate, this situation by shifting attention away from the child to the conflict between the parents.

Couples therapy proceeds in much the same way as family therapy. Conflict in marriages and in relationships between unmarried individuals frequently involves poor communication. In some instances, communication has broken down entirely. The therapist tries to improve the communication between the partners. In some cases, she will focus on the roles partners play: one may be "strong," the other "weak"; one may be "responsible," the other "spoiled," for example. Couples therapy addresses diverse problems such as jealousy, sexual messages, delayed childbearing, infidelity, gender roles, two-career families, divorce, and remarriage (Heitler, 2004; Lebow, 2004; Sullivan & Christensen, 1998).

Self-Help Support Groups

Couples therapy and other types of group therapy involve only a fraction of the number of people who (like Steve M.'s parents) join a self-help group. Self-help groups are voluntary organizations of individuals who get together on a regular basis to discuss topics of common interest (Norcross & others, 2003; Reidy & Norcross, 2004). The groups are not conducted by a professional therapist but rather by a paraprofessional or a member of the common interest group. A paraprofessional is someone who has been taught by a professional to provide some mental health services but who does not have formal mental health training.

Self-help support groups provide members with a sympathetic audience for confession and emotional release (Burlingame & Davies, 2002). The social support, role modeling, and concrete strategies for solving problems. A woman who has been raped might not believe a male therapist who tells her that, with time, she will be able to put the pieces of her shattered life back together. But the same message from another rape survivor—someone who has had to work through the same feelings of rage, fear, and violation—might be more believable.

Alcoholics Anonymous (AA), founded in 1935 by a reformed alcoholic and a physician, is one of the best-known self-help groups (Perkinson, 2004). Mental health professionals often recommend AA for their alcoholic clients. Another self-help organization is Compeer, which matches volunteers with children and adults receiving mental health treatment. In some cases, both partners in a Compeer relationship may have psychological disorders. There are myriad self-help groups, such as Parents Without Partners, lesbian and gay support groups, cocaine abuse support groups, Weight Watchers and TOPS (Take Off Pounds Sensibly), child abuse support groups, and many medical (heart disease, cancer) support groups.

Self-Help Group Resources

Self-help support groups play an important role in our nation's mental health. Approximately 26 million people in the United States have participated in self-help groups, and about 11 million are currently attending them (Klaw & Humphreys, 2004; Humphreys, 2003). These groups are relatively inexpensive, and they serve people who are less likely to receive help otherwise, such as less educated adults, individuals living in low-income circumstances, and homemakers. An increasing number of people are turning to online groups on the Internet for support. Self-help group researcher Keith Humphreys (2003) recently concluded that we don't know how effective these online groups are because they have not been carefully studied yet.

Self-help support groups have broad, though not universal, appeal (Gottlieb, 1998). For people who tend to cope by seeking information and affiliation with peers, these groups can reduce stress and promote adjustment. However, as with any group therapy, there is the possibility that negative emotions will spread through the group, especially if the members face circumstances that deteriorate over time, such as terminal cancer. Group leaders who are sensitive to the spread of negative emotions can minimize such effects.

Adjustment Strategies
For Benefiting from Self-Help Support Groups

1. *The effectiveness of self-help support groups largely depends on the local members and leaders so it is difficult to make general claims about the overall quality of any national support group* (Norcross, Santrock, & others, 2003).
2. *Learn more about how self-help support groups work.* One resource for doing this is the American Self-Help Group Clearinghouse (http://mentalhelp.net/self-help/).
3. *Find out the self-help support groups that are available in your community.* The Clearinghouse just mentioned is one source for this information.
4. *If a self-help support group that deals with the topic in which you are interested is not available in your community, consider starting one yourself.* The American Self-Help Group Clearinghouse provides information on how to do this.

Community Mental Health

Self-help groups represent just one way in which people can be helped outside of traditional therapies. Through the community mental health movement, mental health professionals themselves have tried to extend the reach of therapeutic efforts (Van Citters & Bartels, 2004; Wells & others, 2004). This movement was born in the 1960s. First, it became apparent that the mental health care system was not reaching the poor. Second, large numbers of individuals with psychological disorders were released from mental institutions to community-based facilities. This transfer (called *deinstitutionalization*) came about largely because of the development of new drugs for treating individuals with psychological disorders, especially schizophrenia. The theory was that after release these people would receive help at community-based facilities.

The community mental health approach includes training teachers, ministers, family physicians, and others who interact with community members to offer lay counseling and workshops on such topics as coping with stress, reducing drug use, and using assertiveness training techniques. In the community mental health approach, it is believed that the best way to treat a psychological disorder is to prevent it from developing in the first place. Prevention takes one of three courses: primary, secondary, or tertiary.

In *primary prevention,* efforts are made to reduce the number of new cases of psychological disorders. In some instances, high-risk populations are targeted for prevention, such as children of alcoholics, children with chronic illnesses, and children in poverty.

In *secondary prevention,* screening for early detection of problems and early intervention may take place. For example, school children might be screened to find those who show early signs of problems and provide them with psychological services. Secondary prevention programs seek to reach large numbers of people. One way they do this is by educating paraprofessionals about preventing psychological problems and by having them work with psychologists.

In *tertiary prevention,* an effort is made to treat psychological disorders that were not prevented or arrested early in the course of the disorders (Greenfield, 2004). An example of a tertiary intervention is *halfway houses* (community residences for individuals who no longer require institutionalization but who still need support in readjusting to the community) for formerly hospitalized schizophrenics.

An explicit goal of community mental health is to help people who are disenfranchised from society, such as those living in poverty, to lead happier, more productive lives. A key concept in this effort is *empowerment*, which consists of assisting individuals to develop the skills they need to control their own lives (Dyregrov, 2004).

Cultural Perspectives

The psychotherapies that were discussed earlier in the chapter—psychodynamic, humanistic, behavioral, and cognitive—focus on the individual. This approach is compatible with the needs of many people in Western cultures, such as the United States, where the focus is on the individual rather than the group—family, community, ethnic group. However, these psychotherapies may not be as effective with people who live in cultures that place more importance on the group—called *collectivist* cultures (Draguns, 2004). Some psychologists argue that family therapy is likely to be more effective with people in cultures that place a high value on the family, such as Latino and Asian cultures (Tharp, 1991).

Ethnicity   Many ethnic-minority individuals prefer discussing problems with parents, friends, and relatives rather than mental health professionals (Pedersen, 2004; Sue, 2002). Might therapy progress best when the therapist and the client are from the same ethnic background? Researchers have found that when there is an ethnic match between the therapist and the client and when ethnic-specific services are provided, clients are less likely to drop out of therapy early and in many cases have better treatment outcomes. Ethnic-specific services include culturally appropriate greetings and arrangements (for example, serving tea rather than coffee to Chinese American clients), providing flexible hours for treatment, and employing a bicultural/bilingual staff.

Nonetheless, therapy can be effective when the therapist and client are from different ethnic backgrounds if the therapist has excellent clinical skills and is culturally sensitive (Gibson & Mitchell, 2003; Pedersen & Carey, 2003). Culturally skilled psychotherapists have good knowledge of the cultural groups they work with, understand sociopolitical influences, and have skills in working with culturally diverse groups (Atkinson & Hackett, 2004; Jenkins, 2002; Kim, 2004; Thompson & Isaac, 2004).

Gender   One by-product of changing gender roles for women and men is evaluation of the goals of psychotherapy (Nolen-Hoeksema, 2004; Vatcher & Bogo, 2001). Traditionally, the goal of psychotherapy has been autonomy or self-determination for the client. However, autonomy and self-determination are often more central to the lives of men than those of women, whose lives generally are more characterized by connection with others. Thus some psychologists believe that therapy goals should involve more emphasis on relatedness, especially for women, or an emphasis on both self-determination and connection to others (Notman & Nadelson, 2002).

Because traditional therapy often has not adequately addressed the specific concerns of women in a sexist society, several nontraditional approaches have arisen. These nontraditional therapies emphasize the importance of helping people break free from traditional gender roles and stereotypes. Feminist therapists believe that traditional psychotherapy continues to carry considerable gender bias and that women clients cannot realize their full potential without becoming aware of society's sexism.

The goals of feminist therapists are no different from other therapists' goals, and feminist therapists make no effort to turn clients into feminists. However, they do want the female client to be fully aware of how the nature of the female role in American society can contribute to the development of a psychological disorder. Feminist therapists believe that women must become aware of the bias and discrimination in their own lives to achieve their mental health goals (Brown & Mueller, 2004).

Stanley Sue is a professor of clinical psychology at UCLA and the director of the National Research Center on Asian American Health. Unlike psychologists who specialize in a technique or a theory, he specializes in a population. Much of his work focuses on Asian American clients with special needs, especially if they are immigrants. When he was thinking about a career, Sue told his father, who was a Chinese immigrant to the United States, that he wanted to be a clinical psychologist. His father told him that he didn't understand what a psychologist does and didn't think he could make a living at it. But Sue persisted and obtained a Ph.D. in clinical psychology. His three brothers are psychologists and one even married a psychologist! In his research, Sue has found that Asian Americans underutilize mental health services and that those who do use them often have very serious psychological problems. This means that many Asian Americans with more moderate psychological problems are not getting adequate therapy.

Review and Reflect

3 **Explain sociocultural approaches and issues in treatment**

REVIEW

- What is group therapy?
- What characterizes family and couples therapy?
- What are some important features of self-help support groups?
- How can the community mental health approach be described?
- How might ethnicity and gender affect the success of psychotherapy?

REFLECT

- Which therapy setting do you think you would benefit from the most—individual or group? Why?

4 EVALUATING THERAPY

- **Is Therapy Effective?**
- **Common Themes in Psychotherapy**
- **Funding Therapy**
- **Selecting a Therapist**

All of the forms of treatment that we have discussed have compelling ideas behind them. But how do they work in the real world? For people like Steve M. and his parents, therapy is a very practical as well as a very serious matter. They need answers to questions such as the following: Do individuals who go through therapy get better? Are there any characteristics that distinguish successful therapy? How is treatment funded, and how should you go about finding a therapist?

Is Therapy Effective?

Five decades ago, Hans Eysenck (1952) came to the shocking conclusion that psychotherapy is ineffective. Eysenck analyzed 24 studies of psychotherapy and found that approximately two-thirds of the individuals with neurotic symptoms improved. Sounds impressive so far. But Eysenck also found that a similar percentage of neurotic individuals on waiting lists to see a psychotherapist also showed marked improvement, even though they were not given any psychotherapy at all.

Eysenck's pronouncement prompted a flurry of research on psychotherapy's effectiveness (Chambless, 2004; Lambert, 2001; Orlinsky & Howard, 2000). How should we evaluate its effectiveness? Should we take the client's word? The therapist's word? What would be our criteria for effectiveness? Would it be "feeling good," "adaptive behavior," "improved interpersonal relationships," "autonomous decision making," or "more positive self-concept," for example? During the past several decades an extensive amount of thought and research has addressed these questions (Austed, 2004; Castonguay, Constantino, & Schut, 2004; Crits-Christoph, 2004; Moras, 2002). Hundreds of studies on the outcome of psychotherapy have now been conducted.

One strategy for analyzing these diverse studies is called **meta-analysis,** in which the researcher statistically combines the results of many different studies (Lam & Kennedy, 2004; Rosenthal & DiMatteo, 2001). But how are the individual studies conducted?

meta-analysis Statistical analysis that combines the results of many different studies.

Research that evaluates the effectiveness of a psychotherapy usually includes a comparison group—either a control group of individuals who do not experience the therapy or a group that receives a different type of psychotherapy (Alloy, Jacobson, & Acocella, 1999). When a control group is included, it often consists of individuals waiting to see a psychotherapist but who as yet have not been given therapy (this is called a *wait-list control group*). Why is it so important for psychotherapy research to include a control or comparison group? Because it gives us some idea of how many people in the study who experienced the targeted psychotherapy (such as cognitive therapy for depression) would have gotten better without the psychotherapy.

For example, the National Institute of Mental Health conducted an evaluation of three types of treatment for depression: cognitive therapy; interpersonal therapy, which emphasized improving the individual's social relationships; and drug therapy (Mervis, 1996). Two hundred and forty individuals who were depressed were randomly assigned to one of the three psychotherapy conditions or to a control group who received a placebo medication along with supportive advice. After sixteen weeks in treatment, just over 50 percent of the individuals in each of the three psychotherapy groups were no longer depressed. How did the people in the control group fare? After 16 weeks, 29 percent of them no longer were depressed, a significantly lower percentage than in the psychotherapy groups.

Figure 15.7 provides a summary of numerous studies and reviews of research in which clients were randomly assigned to a no-treatment control group, a placebo control group, or a psychotherapy treatment (Lambert, 2001; Lambert & Ogles, 2002). As can be seen, individuals who did not get treatment improved, probably because they sought help from friends, family, the clergy, or others. Individuals who were in a placebo control group fared better than nontreated individuals, probably because of having contact with a therapist, expectations of being helped, or the reassurance and support that they were given during the study. However, by far the best outcomes were for individuals who were given psychotherapy.

People who are thinking about seeing a psychotherapist want to know not only whether psychotherapy in general is effective but also especially which form of psychotherapy is most effective for their particular problem. Some therapies have been found to be more effective than others in treating some disorders:

- Cognitive therapies and behavior therapies have been successful in treating anxiety disorders (Barlow, 2001; Bowers & Clum, 1988; Lam & Kennedy, 2004).
- Cognitive therapies and behavior therapies have been successful in treating depressive disorders (Butler & others, 1991; Clark & others, 1994; Craighead & Craighead, 2001).
- Relaxation therapy (discussed in chapter 5, "Coping") also has been successful in treating anxiety disorders (Hidalgo & Davidson, 2001).

Individuals who see a therapist also want to know how long it will take them to get better. In one study, individuals showed substantial improvement in therapy over the course of the first six months, with diminishing returns after that (Howard & others, 1996). In a recent study, individuals rated their symptoms, interpersonal relations, and quality of life on a weekly basis before each treatment session (Anderson & Lambert, 2001). Figure 15.8 shows that one-third of the individuals had improved outcomes by the

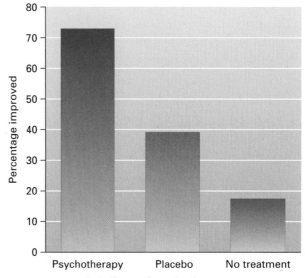

FIGURE 15.7 The Effects of Psychotherapy
In a recent review of studies, more than 70 percent of individuals who saw a therapist improved, whereas less than 40 percent who received a placebo and less than 20 percent who received no treatment improved.

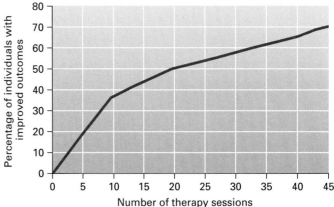

FIGURE 15.8 Number of Therapy Sessions and Improvement
In one recent study, a large number of people undergoing therapy rated their well-being (based on symptoms, interpersonal relations, and quality of life) before each treatment session (Anderson & Lambert, 2001). The percentage of people who showed improved outcomes after each additional session of treatment indicated that about one-third of the individuals recovered by the 10th session, 50 percent by the 20th session, and 70 percent by the 45th session.

10th session, 50 percent by the 20th session, and 70 percent by the 45th session. In sum, therapy benefits most individuals with psychological problems at least through the first six months of therapy and possibly longer.

Common Themes in Effective Psychotherapy

After carefully studying psychotherapy for more than 25 years, Jerome Frank (1982) concluded that effective psychotherapies share three elements: positive expectations, mastery, and emotional arousal.

- *Effective psychotherapies inspire positive expectations.* By creating expectations of help, the therapist motivates the client to continue coming to therapy (Jennings & Skovholt, 1999). These expectations are powerful morale builders and symptom relievers in themselves (Arnkoff, Glass, & Shapiro, 2002).
- *Effective psychotherapies increase the client's sense of mastery and competence.* For example, clients begin to feel that they can cope effectively with their world.
- *Effective psychotherapies arouse the individual's emotions.* This is an essential motivator for behavior change, according to Frank.

The therapeutic relationship is another important element of successful psychotherapy (Frank, 2004; Norcross, 2002; Norcross & Hill, 2004; Strupp, 1995). A relationship in which the client has confidence and trust in the therapist is essential to effective psychotherapy. In one study, the most common ingredient in the success of different psychotherapies was the therapist's supportiveness of the client (Wallerstein, 1989). The client and therapist engage in a "healing ritual," which requires the active participation of both the client and the therapist. As part of this ritual, the client gains hope and becomes less alienated.

Funding Therapy

Therapy can be expensive. Even though public hospitals and community mental health centers may offer reduced fees and, in some cases, free services, many people who most need treatment for psychological disorders do not get it. Psychotherapists have been criticized for limiting their work to *y*oung, *a*ttractive, *v*erbal, *i*ntelligent, and *s*uccessful clients (*YAVIS*es) rather than *q*uiet, *u*gly, *o*ld, *i*nstitutionalized, and *d*ifferent clients (*QUOID*s). Mental health professionals have become increasingly sensitive to this problem, but it still has not been solved (Nielson, Johnson, & Ellis, 2001).

If you need treatment for a psychological problem, is your insurance company or HMO or local government likely to pay or at least help you pay for services? That depends. The delivery of health care, including mental health care, has undergone a revolution in the United States since the early 1980s, when managed care systems emerged (Hoge, 1998). *Managed care* injects an organization between the client and providers of health services as part of an effort to control costs and ensure accountability for treatment success (Busch, Frank, & Lehman, 2004). Managed care providers attempt to offer services at lower cost by limiting traditional services, using stringent review procedures, and shortening the length of treatment.

Criticisms of managed care abound. Regarding the treatment of psychological problems, the criticisms include the following (Giles & Marafiote, 1998; Roback & others, 1999):

- Managed care organizations are reluctant to provide for more than a few therapy sessions for a given patient.
- Long-term psychotherapy has been eliminated except for a relatively few wealthy clients who can pay their own way.
- Some managed care organizations are employing less well-trained therapists who work at lower fees.

Professional Type	Degree	Education Beyond Bachelor's Degree	Nature of Training
Clinical psychologist	Ph.D. or Psy.D	5–7 years	Requires both clinical and research training. Includes a 1-year internship in a psychiatric hospital or mental health facility. Some universities have developed Psy.D. programs, which have a stronger clinical than research emphasis. The Psy.D. training program takes as long as the clinical psychology Ph.D. program and also requires the equivalent of a 1-year internship.
Psychiatrist	M.D.	7–9 years	Four years of medical school, plus an internship and residency in psychiatry are required. A psychiatry residency involves supervision in therapies, including psychotherapy and biomedical therapy.
Counseling psychologist	M.A., Ph.D., Psy.D., or Ed.D.	3–7 years	Similar to clinical psychologist but with emphasis on counseling and therapy. Some counseling psychologists specialize in vocational counseling. Some counselors complete master's degree training, others Ph.D. or Ed.D training, in graduate schools of psychology or education.
School psychologist	M.A., Ph.D., Psy.D., or Ed.D.	3–7 years	Training in graduate programs of education or psychology. Emphasis on psychological assessment and counseling practices involving students' school-related problems. Training is at the master's or doctoral level.
Social worker	M.S.W./D.S.W. or Ph.D.	2–5 years	Graduate work in a school of social work that includes specialized clinical training in mental health facilities.
Psychiatric nurse	R.N., M.A., or Ph.D.	0–5 years	Graduate work in a school of nursing with special emphasis on care of mentally disturbed individuals in hospital settings and mental health facilities.
Occupational therapist	B.S., M.A., or Ph.D.	0–5 years	Emphasis on occupational training with focus on physically or psychologically handicapped individuals. Stresses getting individuals back into the mainstream of work.
Pastoral counselor	None to Ph.D. or D.D. (Doctor of Divinity)	0–5 years	Requires ministerial background and training in psychology. An internship in a mental health facility as a chaplain is recommended.
Counselor	M.A. or M.Ed.	2 years	Graduate work in a department of psychology or department of education with specialized training in counseling techniques.

FIGURE 15.9 Main Types of Mental Health Professionals

Selecting a Therapist

Psychotherapy is practiced by a variety of mental health professionals, including clinical psychologists, psychiatrists, and counselors. Recall that psychiatrists have a medical degree. Clinical psychologists, in contrast, are trained in graduate programs in psychology. Figure 15.9 lists the main types of mental health professionals, their degrees, the years of education required, and the nature of their training.

Although all types of mental health professionals may be competent, they differ in their approach to therapy based on differences in training. Psychologists tend to focus on the person's thoughts, emotions, and behaviors. Psychiatrists are trained as medical doctors, so their perspective is likely to involve the physical aspects of psychological problems. Social workers are trained to take a person's family and social situation into account.

Regardless of their specific profession or approach, therapists should have some minimal credentials. Licensing and certification are two ways in which society retains control over individuals who practice psychotherapy (Harmatz, 1997). Laws at the state level are used to license or certify such professionals. These laws vary in toughness

Do I Need to See a Therapist?

There are no hard-and-fast rules about when people should go to a psychotherapist for help with their personal problems. However, to get a sense of whether you should see a psychotherapist, evaluate whether you have recently experienced the following by checking either the "Yes" or "No" box for each item:

	Yes	No
I feel sad or blue a lot.	_____	_____
My self-esteem is really low.	_____	_____
I feel like other people are always out to get me.	_____	_____
I feel so anxious that it is hard for me to function.	_____	_____
I have trouble concentrating on my academic work.	_____	_____
I don't do anything social and spend much of my spare time alone.	_____	_____
I have a tendency to alienate people when I don't really want to.	_____	_____
I'm frightened by things that I know should not be fear-provoking.	_____	_____
I hear voices that tell me what I should do.	_____	_____
I know I have problems, but I just don't feel I can talk with anyone about them.	_____	_____

Go to the appendix at the end of the book for interpretation of your responses.

from one state to another, but invariably they specify the training the mental health professional must have and provide for some assessment of the applicant's skill through formal examination. Licensing boards exist to protect the public from unscrupulous individuals who might use the title *psychologist* to offer treatment, and collect payment, without sufficient training to do so.

Licensing and certification require mental health practitioners to engage in ethical practices. Laws typically address the importance of doing no harm to clients, protecting the privacy of clients, and avoiding inappropriate relationships with clients. Violations of ethical codes can result in a loss of the license to practice psychotherapy.

To evaluate whether you might benefit from seeing a mental health professional, complete Self-Assessment 15.2. And for some guidelines in seeking and benefiting from professional help, read the adjustment strategies that follow.

Adjustment Strategies
For Seeking Professional Help

Here are some general suggestions when looking for a therapist:
1. ***Become informed about the services offered by therapists.*** The more informed you are about the services provided, the better decision you can make about whether or not the services are right for you. Call around and ask specific questions about approaches and specializations offered by therapists.

2. ***Consider which characteristics of a therapist are important to you.*** Will you be comfortable with a therapist of your or the opposite sex? Is it important to you that the therapist share your ethnic or economic background? Is it important that the therapist have experience with your particular difficulty? Does his or her theoretical orientation to therapy as described in this chapter matter? Ask questions about these kinds of characteristics during your first visit. Most professionals are quite comfortable talking about their background and training. Your confidence and trust in the professional is an important part of how well therapy will work for you.

3. ***Identify the professional's credentials.*** A therapist should be licensed or certified by a state to practice. In addition, in some cases it may be important for a professional to have some advanced, specialized training in a certain area. For example, if a person is seeking help with a specific problem, such as drug abuse, alcohol abuse, or a sexual problem, the therapist should have some training in that area. You should ask about the professional's credentials either before or during a first visit.

4. ***Give therapy some time.*** Making changes is very difficult. Expecting too much too soon can result in premature dissatisfaction and disappointment. Because a large part of therapy involves the development of a relationship with the therapist, it may take several meetings to really know if things are going well. One suggestion is to give it between four and six weekly meetings. If it does not seem as if things are going the way you would like, it is a good idea to discuss your progress with the therapist and ask what you should expect with regard to making progress. Setting specific goals with specific time expectations can be helpful.

5. ***If your goals are not being met, consider finding a new therapist.*** Remember that therapy is like other services: When dissatisfied, look for another therapist. Don't think that just because one therapist has not been helpful, none will be. All therapists and therapeutic relationships are different. Finding the right therapist is one of the most important factors in therapy success.

6. ***Continually evaluate your progress throughout therapy.*** If you are dissatisfied with how therapy is going, discuss this feeling with your therapist.

Review and Reflect

4 **Evaluate the effectiveness of therapy**

REVIEW
- How effective is therapy?
- What are some common themes in psychotherapy?
- What kinds of health professionals are qualified to provide mental health treatment? What role is managed care playing in mental health treatment?

REFLECT
- Explain why a control group is important in research on psychotherapy effectiveness.

Reach Your Learning Goals

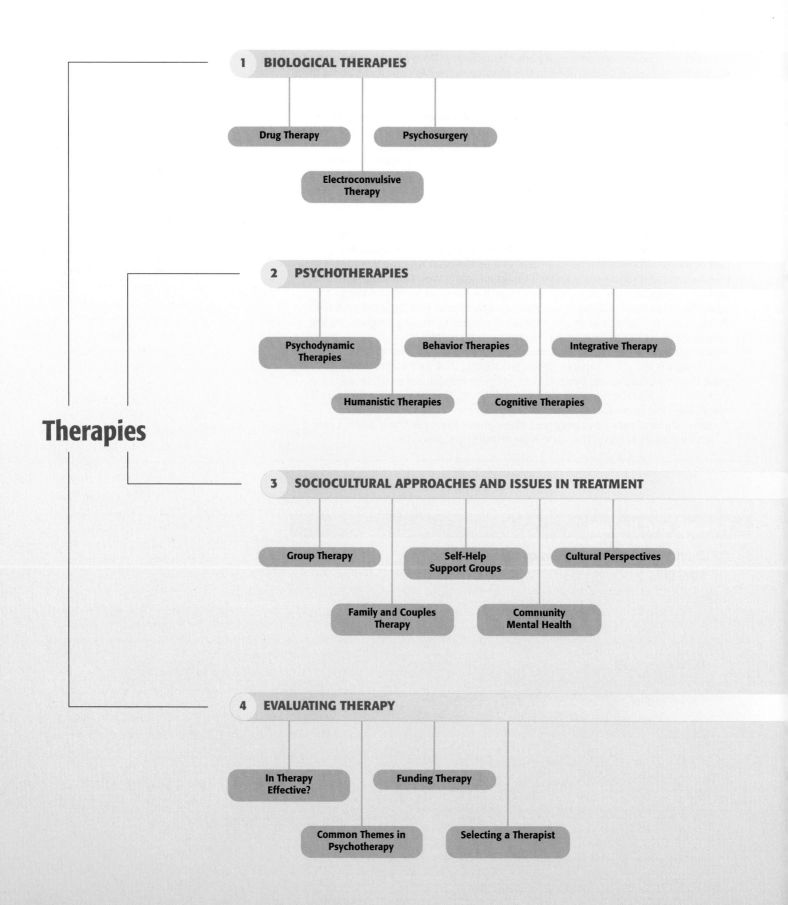

Therapies

1 BIOLOGICAL THERAPIES

- Drug Therapy
- Psychosurgery
- Electroconvulsive Therapy

2 PSYCHOTHERAPIES

- Psychodynamic Therapies
- Behavior Therapies
- Integrative Therapy
- Humanistic Therapies
- Cognitive Therapies

3 SOCIOCULTURAL APPROACHES AND ISSUES IN TREATMENT

- Group Therapy
- Self-Help Support Groups
- Cultural Perspectives
- Family and Couples Therapy
- Community Mental Health

4 EVALUATING THERAPY

- In Therapy Effective?
- Funding Therapy
- Common Themes in Psychotherapy
- Selecting a Therapist

Summary

1 Describe the biological therapies

- Psychotherapeutic drugs that are used to treat psychological disorders fall into three main categories: antianxiety drugs, antidepressant drugs, and antipsychotic drugs. Antianxiety drugs are commonly known as tranquilizers. Benzodiazepines are the most commonly used antianxiety drugs. Antidepressant drugs regulate mood; the three main classes are tricyclics, MAO inhibitors, and SSRI drugs. Lithium often is successful in treating bipolar disorder. The antidepressant drugs are increasingly being used to treat some anxiety disorders as well. Antipsychotic drugs are powerful drugs that are used to treat people with severe psychological disorders, especially schizophrenia. Psychotherapeutic drugs have varying effectiveness and side effects.
- Electroconvulsive therapy, commonly called *shock therapy,* is used to treat severe depression when other strategies have not worked.
- Psychosurgery is an irreversible procedure in which brain tissue is destroyed in an attempt to improve adjustment. Today, psychosurgery is rarely used but is more precise than the early prefrontal lobotomies.

2 Characterize four types of psychotherapy

- Psychotherapy is the process used by mental health professionals to help individuals recognize, define, and overcome their psychological and interpersonal difficulties and improve their adjustment. Psychodynamic therapies stress the importance of the unconscious mind, early family experiences, and extensive interpretation by therapists. In Freudian psychoanalysis, the therapist's interpretation of free association, dreams, transference, and resistance provide tools for understanding the client's unconscious conflicts. Many contemporary psychodynamic therapists still probe the unconscious mind and early family experiences but they give increased emphasis to the conscious mind and current relationships. Kohut's focus on the development of the self in social contexts illustrates a contemporary approach.
- In humanistic therapy, clients are encouraged to understand themselves and to grow personally. The humanistic therapies emphasize conscious thoughts, the present, and growth and fulfillment. In client-centered therapy, developed by Carl Rogers, the therapist provides a warm, supportive atmosphere to improve the client's self-concept and to encourage the client to gain insight into problems. Client-centered techniques include unconditional positive regard, genuineness, empathy, and active listening to raise the client's self-esteem. The techniques of Gestalt therapy, developed by Fritz Perls, are more directive. Gestalt psychologists challenge clients to help them become more aware of their feelings and face their problems.
- Behavior therapies use principles of learning to reduce or eliminate maladaptive behavior. Behavior therapies seek to eliminate the symptoms of behaviors rather than to help individuals to gain insight into their problems. The two main therapy techniques based on classical conditioning are systematic desensitization and aversive conditioning. In systematic desensitization, anxiety is treated by getting the individual to associate deep relaxation with increasingly intense anxiety-producing situations. In aversive conditioning, the undesirable behavior is associated with aversive stimuli. In operant conditioning approaches to therapy, a careful analysis of the person's environment is conducted to determine which factors need to be modified. In behavior modification, the consequences of the behavior are changed in order to replace maladaptive behaviors with adaptive ones. A token economy is a behavior modification system in which behaviors are reinforced with tokens that later can be exchanged for desired rewards.
- Cognitive therapies attempt to change the person's feelings and behaviors by changing cognitions. Three main forms of cognitive therapy are Ellis' rationale-motive behavior therapy, Beck's cognitive therapy, and cognitive-behavior therapy. Ellis' approach is based on the assertion that individuals develop psychological disorders because of their beliefs, especially those that are irrational and self-defeating. Beck's cognitive therapy has been especially effective in treating depression. In Beck's therapy, the therapist assists the client in learning about logical errors in thinking and then guides the client in challenging these thinking errors. Ellis' approach is more directive, persuasive, and confrontational than Beck's. Cognitive-behavior therapy combines cognitive therapy and behavior therapy techniques. Self-efficacy and self-instructional methods are used in this approach.
- Approximately 30 to 50 percent of practicing therapists refer to themselves as "integrative" or "eclectic." Integrative therapy combines techniques from different therapies based on the therapist's judgment of which particular techniques will provide the greatest benefit for the client.

3 Explain sociocultural approaches and issues in treatment

- Group therapies emphasize that relationships can hold the key to successful therapy. Psychodynamic, humanistic, behavior, and cognitive therapies, as well as unique group approaches, are used in group therapy.

- Family therapy is group therapy with family members. Four widely used family therapy techniques are validation, reframing, structural change, and detriangulation. Couples therapy is group therapy with married or unmarried couples whose major problem is within their relationship.
- Self-help support groups are voluntary organizations of individuals who get together on a regular basis to discuss topics of common interest. They are conducted without a professional therapist.
- The community mental health movement was born out of the belief that the mental health care system was not adequately reaching people in poverty or people who had been deinstitutionalized. Community mental health emphasizes primary, secondary, and tertiary prevention. Empowerment is often a goal of community mental health.
- Psychotherapies have mainly focused on the individual, which may work well in individualized cultures such as in the United States but may not work as well in collectivist cultures. Many ethnic-minority individuals prefer to discuss problems with parents, friends, and relatives rather than with mental health professionals. Therapy is often more effective when there is an ethnic match between the therapist and the client, although culturally sensitive therapy can be provided by a therapist who is from a different ethnic background. The emphasis on autonomy in psychotherapies may

be inappropriate for many women. Some feminist-based therapies have emerged.

4 Evaluate the effectiveness of therapy

- Psychotherapy is generally effective. Researchers have found, using meta-analysis, that the cognitive and behavior therapies are successful in treating anxiety and depressive disorders. Relaxation therapy also has been effective in treating anxiety disorders.
- Successful psychotherapy commonly includes positive expectations of help, increasing the client's sense of mastery, arousing the client's emotions, and developing the client's confidence and trust in the therapist.
- Psychotherapy is not always available to those who need it. Managed care has led to substantial changes in the delivery of mental health care and has been criticized for eliminating long-term treatment for all but the wealthy and for using less well-trained therapists who accept low fees.
- Mental health professionals include clinical and counseling psychologists, psychiatrists, school psychologists, social workers, psychiatric nurses, occupational therapists, pastoral counselors, and counselors. These mental health professionals have different degrees, education, and training. Society retains control over individuals who practice psychotherapy through licensing and certification.

Key Terms

biological therapies 463
psychotherapy 463
antianxiety drugs 463
antidepressant drugs 464
lithium 465
antipsychotic drugs 465
electroconvulsive therapy (ECT) 466
psychosurgery 467

psychodynamic therapies 468
psychoanalysis 469
free association 469
catharsis 469
dream analysis 469
resistance 469
transference 469
insight therapy 471
humanistic therapies 471

client-centered therapy 471
Gestalt therapy 472
behavior therapies 472
systematic desensitization 473
aversive conditioning 473
behavior modification 474
cognitive therapies 475

rational-emotive behavior therapy (REBT) 475
cognitive-behavior therapy 478
integrative therapy 479
family therapy 482
couples therapy 482
meta-analysis 486

Resources for Improving Your Adjustment

SELF-HELP BOOKS

Feeling Good

(1999, Revised ed.) by David Burns. New York: Avon.

Burns provides a cognitive therapy approach to treating depression. He outlines strategies people can use to change their faulty thinking. Burns' book has been shown to be effective in research studies (Ackerson & others, 1998; Cuijpers, 1997). It has extensive self-assessments and charts. *Feeling Good* was one of the highest rated of all books in the national survey of self-help books (Norcross, Santrock, & others, 2003). Burns also has written *The Feeling Good Handbook* (Revised ed., 1999), which in-

cludes a number of daily logs to fill in and covers anxiety and relationships as well as depression.

The Consumer's Guide to Psychotherapy

(1992) by Jack Engler and Daniel Goleman. New York: Simon & Schuster.

This a comprehensive manual on psychotherapy for consumers. Among the topics examined are how to decide if you need therapy, which therapy approach is best for you, what questions you should ask in the first session, how to tell if the therapy is working, and how to know when to end the therapy.

Five Therapies and One Client

(1991) by Raymond Corsini and Contributors. Itasca, IL: Peacock.

Therapists with five distinctive approaches to helping clients describe their strategies and demonstrate how they would work with the same fictitious client. Adler's individual therapy, Rogers' person-centered therapy, Ellis' rational-emotive behavior therapy, behavior therapy, and eclectic therapy are compared.

Am I Crazy or Is It My Shrink?

(1998) by Larry Reutler, Bruce Bonger, and Joel Shurkin. New York: Oxford University Press.

Good advice is given on how to choose a therapist, what questions to ask the therapist, how to determine when the therapy isn't working, and others. The authors also describe which therapies work best with which problems.

E-Learning Tools

www.mhhe.com/santrockha

To help you master the material in this chapter, you will find a number of valuable study tools on the Student CD-ROM and the Online Learning Center.

SELF-ASSESSMENT

In Text

You can complete these self-assessments in the text:
- Self-Assessment 15.1: *Do I Have Irrational Beliefs?*
- Self-Assessment 15.2: *Do I Need to See a Therapist?*

THINK CRITICALLY

To practice your critical thinking skills, complete these exercises on the Online Learning Center:
- *The Designer Brain and Enhancing Abilities* gets you to think about the use of drugs to treat psychological disorders.
- *The Match Game* involves examining whether it is critical to have the therapist's and the client's backgrounds and characteristics be similar for therapy to be effective.
- *Are drugs for me?* explores the issue of mental illness and medication.
- *Who is the right therapist for you?* What characteristics do you look for in a therapist?

APPLY YOUR KNOWLEDGE

1. How confidential is therapy?

If you were a therapist and your client threatened to harm self or another, would you break confidentiality? If your client admitted to you that he or she had committed a felony, would you report it? Is confidentiality absolute? If not, under what conditions is a therapist permitted to violate confidentiality? Select a search engine such as www.yahoo.com or www.google.com and search for "confidentiality in psychotherapy."

2. Gender differences in depression.

It is well known that women suffer from depression at a much higher rate than men. Make a list of factors that are different in men's and women's lives that could account for this difference.

Be sure to consider biology, gender roles, socialization, coping style, and sexism. When you have finished, select a search engine such as www.yahoo.com or www.google.com and search for "gender differences in depression" or "gender differences in coping with depression."

What explanations did you find that would account for these differences? Do women cope differently with depression than men do? Should therapy for depression for women be different than for men? If so, which things should be addressed in therapy with women? Should therapists try to help women adapt to the world the way it is? Or should therapy try to empower women in a world that is often sexist?

3. Self-help groups.

Self-help groups can take many forms. Some are traditional (like Alcoholics Anonymous) where people relate to each other face-to-face. In addition, there are many Internet self-help groups. What are the advantages and disadvantages of these two types of self-help groups? Would you ever join an Internet support group? What in-person self-help groups are available in your community? Select a search engine such as www.yahoo.com or www.google.com and search for "self-help groups." Alternatively, you may want to search for self-help groups by topic (e.g., "self-help groups for depression)."

In addition, do a search on the Internet for one or more self help groups of your choice. It may be particularly useful to join one that has a chat room. Are the chat rooms mostly about helping each other, or are they largely people with a shared problem chatting about things in general?

VIDEO SEGMENT

Advances in biological therapies have revolutionized the treatment of psychological disorders, but sometimes these therapies fail. For firsthand accounts of the limitations as well as the benefits of drug therapy and ECT, watch the videos for Chapter 15 on the CD-ROM.

Health

Learning Goals

1 Describe some key factors in health and illness

2 Discuss nutrition, eating behavior, and eating problems

3 Summarize the role of exercise in health

4 Explain drug use and addiction

5 Characterize some important aspects of the patient and the health-care setting

Images of Adjustment

Lance Armstrong, Coping with Cancer

What coping strategies did Lance Armstrong show in his bout with cancer?

The three-week 2,000-mile-plus Tour de France, the world's premier bicycle race, is one of the great tests of human motivation in sports. American Lance Armstrong won the Tour de France six years in a row from 1999 through 2004, a remarkable accomplishment, especially in light of Armstrong developing testicular cancer in 1996. Chances of his recovery were estimated at less than 50 percent when he began chemotherapy.

Before being diagnosed with cancer, Armstrong was a specimen of positive health. As a teenager, every day after school he ran six miles and then would get on his bike and ride 30 miles. In his twenties, his physical training became more rigorous, and he carefully monitored his eating habits to improve his cycling performance.

When he found out that he had cancer, Lance recalled, "Initially, I was very fearful and without much hope, but as I sat there and absorbed the full extent of my illness, I refused to let this fear completely blot out my optimism. Something told me that fear should never fully rule the heart, and I decided not to be afraid," (Armstrong, 2000, pp. 98–99).

Lance says that if you get a life-threatening disease like cancer you have to fight it and believe that you will be able to conquer it. By fighting he means arming yourself with all of the information, getting second opinions, third opinions, and fourth opinions. Learn what is invading your body and what the possible cures are. Lance believes that the more informed and empowered patient has a better chance of long-term survival.

Lance's experiences with cancer motivated him to think about his priorities in life. He says that the experience made him a happier and better person. For example, he became a spokesperson for cancer and established the Lance Armstrong Foundation, which supports cancer awareness and research. He married and became a father, although in 2003 he and his wife divorced.

Lance Armstrong engaged in health-enhancing behaviors before getting cancer and showed remarkable adjustment strategies as he underwent medical treatment for the disease. Unlike Armstrong, too often individuals have lifestyles that are characterized by health-harming behaviors. An important theme of this chapter is that a person's lifestyle is a key factor in the individual's health. We begin the chapter by examining the bio-psycho-social health model and then turn to some key aspects of health behavior: nutrition and eating, exercise, and drugs. We conclude the chapter by exploring various aspects of the patient and health-care setting that are health enhancing or health harming.

1 EXPLAINING HEALTH AND ILLNESS

- **The Bio-Psycho-Social Model**
- **Social Factors in Health and Illness**
- **Psychological Factors in Health and Illness**

Asian physicians, around 2600 B.C., and later Greek physicians, around 500 B.C., recognized that good habits are essential for good health. They did not blame the gods for illness and think that magic would cure illness. They realized that people had control over their health.

Today, we are returning to this ancient view that the ultimate responsibility for influencing health rests with individuals themselves (Marks, Sykes, & McKinley, 2003; Payne, Hahn, & Mauer, 2005; Smith, & Suls, 2004). Your lifestyle plays a critical role in your health. *Lifestyle* is your way of living—your attitudes, habits, choices, and behaviors. To see if you have a healthy lifestyle, complete Self-Assessment 16.1.

The Bio-Psycho-Social Model

How does your lifestyle influence your health? What factors determine whether one person is healthy most of the time and another is constantly sick?

Except in ancient Asia and Greece, throughout most of history physical illness has been viewed purely in biological terms—that is, as involving only bodily factors, not environmental factors. In the biological approach, health problems are caused by the functions of the individual's body (Henderson, Baum, & Sutton, 2005). For example, some people have a genetic predisposition for developing high cholesterol, which is a risk factor for cardiovascular disease. In the biological approach, drug therapy is frequently used to treat health problems. For example, if a person has high cholesterol, a cholesterol-lowering drug is typically prescribed.

Today, changing patterns of illness in developed countries have fueled the increased interest in psychological and social aspects of the bio-psycho-social model of health. Just a century ago, the leading causes of death were infectious diseases such as influenza, tuberculosis, polio, typhoid fever, rubella, and smallpox. Today, none of these diseases are among the major causes of death in developed countries. Rather, seven of the ten leading causes of death in the United States today are related to personal habits and lifestyles. The major causes of death now are heart disease (36 percent), cancer (22 percent), and stroke (17 percent). Other chronic diseases such as diabetes are also major contributors to disability and death.

The contemporary view is that body *and* mind can exert important influences on health. Indeed, health psychologists endorse the **bio-psycho-social health model,** which states that health is best understood in terms of a combination of biological,

bio-psycho-social health model States that health is best understood in terms of a combination of biological, psychological, and social factors.

Is My Lifestyle Good for My Health?

There are many aspects to your lifestyle, including the manner in which you work, communicate, and engage in other activities. This assessment is designed to evaluate your lifestyle choices and determine if they are affecting your health positively or negatively. Your responses should help you to understand the influence of your lifestyle on your health.

Directions:
Respond to each of the statements as follows: 5 = definitely like me, 4 = mostly like me, 3 = not sure, 2 = mostly unlike me, and 1 = definitely not like me.

_____ I am doing well in school.

_____ I am enjoying myself, not feeling bored or angry.

_____ I have satisfying relationships with other people.

_____ I express my emotions when I want to.

_____ I use my leisure time well and enjoy it.

_____ I am satisfied with my sexual relationships.

_____ I am satisfied with what I accomplish during the day.

_____ I am having fun.

_____ I am making use of the talents I have.

_____ I feel physically well and full of vitality.

_____ I am developing my skills and abilities.

_____ I am contributing to society.

_____ I am helpful to other people.

_____ I have a sense of freedom and adventure in my life.

_____ I feel joy or pleasure on most days.

_____ I feel that my body is fit enough to meet the demands made upon it.

_____ I feel rested and full of energy.

_____ I am able to relax most of the day.

_____ I enjoy a good night's sleep most nights.

_____ I usually go to bed feeling happy and satisfied about the day.

Go to the appendix at the end of the book for scoring and interpretation of your responses.

psychological, and social factors (Rugulies, Aust, & Syme, 2005; Stowell & others, 2003; Suls & Rothman, 2004; Sutton, Baum, & Johnston, 2005).

Psychological Factors in Health and Illness

Among the psychological factors that have been proposed as causes of health problems are lack of self-control, emotional turmoil, and negative thinking (Contrada & Goyal, 2005). Lance Armstrong (2000) says that he doesn't know the extent to which science or psychological factors were responsible for his cancer survival. However, he clearly became highly self-motivated to cope with his cancer and do everything within his power to overcome the disease.

Psychological factors may be involved not only in surviving diseases such as cancer, but also in many illnesses (Leventhal & others, 2005; Montogomery, 2004; Steptoe & Ayers, 2005). Consider cardiovascular disease:

- As we saw in chapter 4, "Stress," individuals who develop coronary problems are more likely to be outwardly hostile or turn anger inward (Pickering, 2001). People can reduce their risk of coronary problems by learning to control their anger (Williams, 2001).
- Chronic emotional stress is linked with cardiovascular disease (O'Callahan, Andrews, & Krantz, 2003; Fogoros, 2001). Apparently, the surge in adrenaline caused by emotional stress causes the blood to clot more rapidly and blood clotting is a key contributor to heart attacks.

In addition, although the data concerning the effects of negative states are more extensive, positive emotional states are associated with health patterns of physiological functioning in both the cardiovascular system and the immune system (Booth-Kewley & Friedman, 1987; Herbert & Cohen, 1993; Mann, 2003). In one study, older men and older women who expressed a positive outlook toward life were less likely to suffer heart attacks than those who expressed a negative outlook (Danner, Snowdon, & Friesen, 2001).

In regard to immune system, positive emotions are linked with the release of secretory immunoglobin A (S-IgA), the antibody that is believed to be the first line of defense against the common cold (Stone & others, 1994). One recent study further documented the role of positive emotion in preventing people from getting a cold. Sheldon Cohen and his colleagues (2003) interviewed 334 healthy volunteers about their emotional styles on seven occasions over weeks. Information about positive emotional style focused on three areas—vigor, well-being, and calm. Then they administered a shot of a rhinovirus, the germ that causes colds, into each participant's nose. Afterward, participants were observed for five days to see if they became sick. Individuals with a low positive emotional style were three times more likely to get a cold than those with a high positive emotional style.

Moods can also influence people's beliefs regarding their ability to carry out health-promoting behaviors. For example, in one study, happy individuals were more likely than sad individuals to engage in health-promoting behaviors and had more confidence that these behaviors would relieve their illness (Salovey & Birnbaum, 1989).

Social Factors in Health and Illness

Most health problems are found in most cultures, but the frequency and intensity of problems vary across cultures (Gielen, Fish, & Draguns, 2004; Murphy & Bennett, 2005). The variations are linked to social, economic, technological, and religious aspects of cultures (Contrada & others, 2004; Tanaka-Matsumi, 2001; Whifield & others, 2003).

Social factors that influence health problems include socioeconomic status and poverty. People living in poverty encounter more health problems, such as cardiovascular disease, and have less access to health-care professionals than their higher-income counterparts (Tovian, 2004).

Prejudice and discrimination are the historical underpinnings for the fact that African Americans and Latinos are more likely to have low socioeconomic status and live in poverty than White non-Latino individuals. These conditions contribute to their health problems. In general, African Americans have a higher mortality rate than White non-Latino individuals for 13 of the 15 leading causes of death (National Center for Health Statistics, 2004). Of all ethnic minority women, African American women are the most vulnerable to health problems. For example, African American women, compared with White non-Latino women, are three times more likely to have high blood pressure, are twice as likely to die from cardiovascular disease, have a 35 percent higher death rate for diabetes, and are four more times likely to be a victim of homicide. There is increasing evidence that diabetes occurs at an above-average rate in Latinos, making this disease a health problem that parallels the above-average rate of high blood pressure in African Americans (Melnik & others, 2004).

Keep in mind that differences occur within ethnic groups as well as between them. For example, Asian Americans have a broad diversity of national backgrounds and lifestyles. They include Japanese Americans and Cambodian Americans, highly acculturated and recent immigrants, highly educated people who may have excellent access to health care and people who have few economic resources and may be in poor health. The spectrum of living conditions and lifestyles within an ethnic group are influenced by socioeconomic status, immigrant status, social and language skills, occupational opportunities, and social resources such as the availability of meaningful social resources (Yali & Revenson, 2004). All of these can play a role in an ethnic minority member's health.

How might these social factors influence health? In part, the answer is likely to involve the frequency of stressors in daily lives. And in part the answer can probably be traced to unhealthy lifestyles—to habits related to eating, exercise, smoking, use of alcohol, and other drugs—and to poor health care, which are topics we discuss in the remainder of the chapter.

Review and Reflect

1 Describe some key factors in health and illness

REVIEW

- How is the bio-psycho-social model of health defined?
- What are some psychological influences on health?
- What are some social influences on health?

REFLECT

- What did you find out from your assessment of your lifestyle in Self-Assessment 16.1. Are your lifestyle choices promoting good health or are they placing you at risk for developing serious health problems?

---

2 NUTRITION AND EATING

Nutrition and Eating Behavior

Eating Problems

When Lance Armstrong is racing, his meals are "gargantuan" (Specter, 2002). According to one visitor, before one race, three men were needed to carry the food for Armstrong's breakfast. Later, a few hours before the race, Armstrong ate "two heaping plates of pasta and a power bar." Obviously, this is not likely to be a healthy pattern for most of us, but few of us burn up as many calories as Armstrong does in his bicycle races and training. What constitutes a balanced, healthy meal? What eating problems can individuals develop?

Nutrition and Eating Behavior

To explore nutrition and eating behavior we next examine the Food Guide Pyramid and proposed changes in it, nutrition in aging individuals and whether eating less is linked with increased longevity, and cultural variations in eating behavior.

The Food Guide Pyramid Since 1992 the current pyramid has served as a guide for use by dieters and nutritionists, is taught to schoolchildren, and is included on various food packages, such as bread. The Food Guide Pyramid consists of recommended daily servings of food with an emphasis on consuming more bread, cereals, rice, pasta, vegetables, and fruits than milk, meats, fats, oils, and sweets. Figure 16.1 shows the current Food Guide Pyramid and Americans' actual food consumption. The U.S. Department of Agriculture is planning some changes in the current pyramid that are anticipated to be published in 2005. What is now a one-size-fits-all Food Guide Pyramid is likely to become considerably more complex (Wardlaw, Hampl, & DiSilvestro, 2004). Proposed changes are designed to help people eat better and reduce the U.S. weight epidemic with as many as 65 percent of adults either overweight or obese. A new version might be a revised pyramid or a different image altogether (see figure 16.2 for one proposal). Listing quantities in cups and ounces instead of servings,

Nutrition Navigator

which often vary in size, is a likely change. Also, more detailed serving information for 12 different calorie levels has been proposed. These would range from 1,000 calories to 3,200 a day and would be available on websites and in brochures. Individuals could determine how much to eat based on their age and activity level. For example, sedentary men ages 35 to 50 might be advised to eat about 2,200 calories a day and consume about 1½ cups of fruit (3 servings); 2 cups of vegetables (4 servings); 6 ounces of meat; 2 to 3 cups of milk or other dairy products; and 4½ cups of grains (9 servings).

Adjustment Strategies
For Eating Right

Here are good strategies for eating in healthier ways (U.S. Department of Health and Human Services, 2004):

1. **Study the Food Guide Pyramid and monitor proposed changes in it.** Spend some time learning more about the Food Guide Pyramid and the planned changes in it. For more information about the pyramid and proposed changes in it, go to http://www.cnpp.usda.gov.
2. **Follow a diet low in fat, saturated fat, and cholesterol.** Unfortunately, many of the best-tasting foods are the worst for you. Fat appears in fried foods (fried chicken, doughnuts), rich foods (ice cream, pastries), greasy foods (spare ribs, bacon), and many spreads (butter, mayonnaise). In contrast, yogurt is low in saturated fat. Cholesterol, a key contributor to heart disease, is found only in animal products.
3. **Substitute plenty of vegetables, fruits, and grain products for unhealthy foods.** Replace fatty foods with more healthy sources of starch and fiber, such as grain products, legumes (dried beans, peas), fruits, and vegetables not cooked in fat.
4. **Use sugar only in moderation.** Common sources of sugar are table sugar and sugar products such as syrups, honey, jams, ice cream, cookies, cakes, and most other desserts. If you eat dessert, try eating fresh fruits instead of foods with added sugar. Replace soft drinks with water.
5. **Use sodium in moderation.** Some individuals are sensitive to sodium and are at risk for hypertension (persistent high blood pressure). To reduce the sodium in your diet, eat less salt. Flavor your foods with lemon, spices, herbs, or pepper.

continued

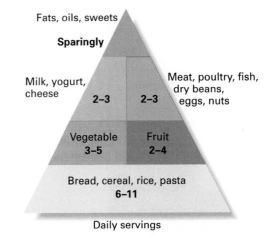

Current Food Guide

FIGURE 16.1 Current Food Guide Pyramid and Americans' Actual Food Consumption Research

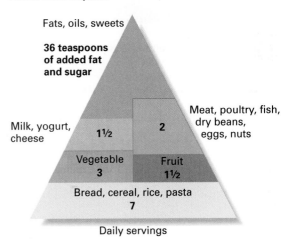

Actual Consumption

FIGURE 16.2 One Proposed Revision of the Food Guide

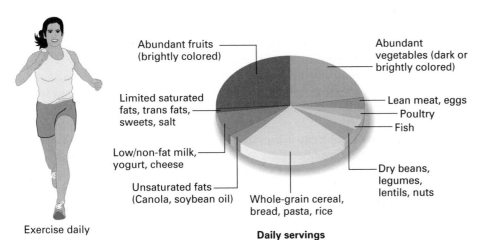

Exercise daily

Daily servings

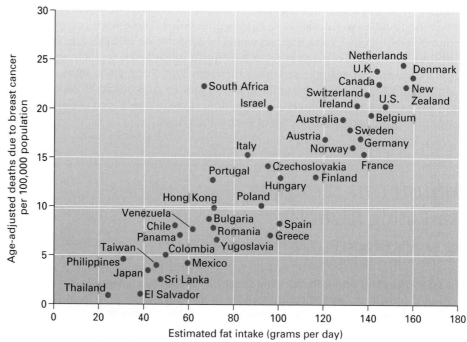

FIGURE 16.3 Cross-Cultural Comparisons of Diet and Breast Cancer Rates
In countries in which individuals have a low daily intake of fat, the rate of breast cancer is low (in Thailand, for example). In countries in which individuals have a high daily intake of fat, the rate of breast cancer is high (the Netherlands, for example).

6. *Drink plenty of water.* Aim for about eight 8-ounce glasses of water each day.
7. *Eat breakfast every day.* Individuals who eat breakfast are less likely to overeat later in the day.

Cultural Variations   Evidence for the negative effects of poor nutritional choices comes from both animal and cross-cultural research. For example, mice fed a high-fat diet are likelier to develop breast cancer than are mice fed a low-fat diet. And a cross-cultural study of women found a strong positive correlation between fat consumption and death rates from breast cancer (Cohen, 1987). (See figure 16.3.)

One of the most telling comparisons to link fat intake and cancer is between the United States and Japan. These countries have similar levels of industrialization and education, as well as similarly high medical standards. Although the overall cancer rates of the two countries are similar, cancers of the breast, colon, and prostate are common in the United States but rare in Japan. Yet, within two generations, descendants of Japanese immigrants to Hawaii and California have developed breast cancer rates that are significantly higher than those in Japan and that approach those of Americans. Many researchers believe that the high fat intake of Americans and the low fat intake of the Japanese are implicated in the countries' different cancer rates.

Eating and Longevity   Recently, considerable interest has developed in two ideas about how people might lengthen their lives by changing their eating habits. The first is caloric restriction, the second is vitamins.

Caloric Restriction   Scientists have accumulated considerable evidence that food restriction in laboratory animals (in most cases, rats) can increase the animals' life span (Goto & others, 2002; Hadley & others, 2001; Kirk, 2001). Animals fed diets restricted in calories—although adequate in protein, vitamins, and minerals—live as much as 40 percent longer than animals given unlimited access to food. And chronic problems such as kidney disease appear only at a later age. Diet restriction also delays biochemical alterations such as the age-related rise in cholesterol observed in both humans and animals (Bauer, Hamm, & Pankratz, 2004; Mattson & others, 2002).

Might a decrease in the intake of food increase your longevity or even extend your life span? In some instances, the animals in these studies ate 40 percent less than normal. Whether similar very low-calorie diets can stretch the human life span is not known (Roth & others, 2002). Most nutritional experts do not recommend very low-calorie diets for older adults; rather, they recommend a well-balanced, low-fat diet that includes the nutritional factors needed to maintain good health.

No one knows for certain how calorie restriction works to increase the life span of animals. Some scientists believe it might lower the level of free radicals or potentially toxic particles created by the breakdown of food. Others believe caloric restriction might trigger a state of emergency called *survival mode* in which the body eliminates all unnecessary functions to focus only on staying alive. Encouraged by the research on animals, the National Institute of Health is planning caloric restriction studies on humans (Johannes, 2002). Caloric restriction of 30 percent in humans would translate into about 1,120 calories a day for the average woman and 1,540 for the average man.

Leaner men do live longer, healthier lives (Williams, 2005). In one study of 19,297 Harvard alumni, those weighing the least were less likely to die over the past three decades (Lee & others, 1993). The men were divided into five categories according to body mass index (a complex formula that takes into account weight and height). As body mass increased, so did risk of death. The most overweight men had a 67 percent higher risk of dying than the thinnest men. For example, the heaviest men (such as 181 pounds or more for a 5-foot-10-inch man) also had two and a half times the risk of death from cardiovascular disease. Currently, these researchers are studying the relation of body mass index to longevity in women.

The Vitamin-and-Aging Controversy

The Vitamin-and-Aging Controversy   For years, most experts on aging and health argued that a balanced diet is all that is needed for successful aging; vitamin supplements were not recommended. However, recent research suggests the possibility that some vitamin supplements—mainly antioxidants, which include vitamin C, vitamin E, and beta-carotene—help slow the aging process and improve the health of older adults.

The theory is that antioxidants counteract the cell damage caused by free radicals, which are produced both by the body's own metabolism and by environmental factors such as smoking, pollution, and bad chemicals in the diet. When free radicals cause damage (oxidation) in one cell, a chain reaction of damage follows. Antioxidants act much like a fire extinguisher, helping to neutralize free-radical activity.

One leading expert on nutrition and aging at the National Institute of Aging, Hubert Warner (2002), recently concluded that most scientists agree that oxidative damage has something to do with aging. As people get older, their bodies aren't as good at mopping up free radicals. However, the degree to which oxidative damage plays a role in aging and whether antioxidant vitamins can slow the aging process have not yet been determined. Studies are mixed on whether vitamin E and vitamin C can prevent heart disease (Huang & others, 2002; Iannuzi & others, 2002). Vitamin C and vitamin E might provide some protection against Alzheimer's disease (Engelhart & others, 2002). A recent review of studies concluded that vitamin E may increase the risk of early death in individuals with chronic diseases (Miller & others, 2005, in press).

Researchers are continuing to study whether vitamins can slow aging. Perhaps certain combinations of vitamins are beneficial and the form of the vitamin may make a difference. For example, a diet rich in foods that naturally contain antioxidants may protect better against disease than pill supplements.

www.mhhe.com/santrockha

Caloric Restriction

Weight (pounds)

Height	120	130	140	150	160	170	180	190	200	210	220	230	240	250
4'6"	29	31	34	36	39	41	43	46	48	51	53	56	58	60
4'8"	27	29	31	34	36	38	40	43	45	47	49	52	54	56
4'10"	25	27	29	31	34	36	38	40	42	44	46	48	50	52
5'0"	23	25	27	29	31	33	35	37	39	41	43	45	47	49
5'2"	22	24	26	27	29	31	33	35	37	38	40	42	44	46
5'4"	21	22	24	26	28	29	31	33	34	36	38	40	41	43
5'6"	19	21	23	24	26	27	29	31	32	34	36	37	39	40
5'8"	18	20	21	23	24	26	27	29	30	32	34	35	37	38
5'10"	17	19	20	22	23	24	26	27	29	30	32	33	35	36
6'0"	16	18	19	20	22	23	24	26	27	28	30	31	33	34
6'2"	15	17	18	19	21	22	23	24	26	27	28	30	31	32
6'4"	15	16	17	18	20	21	22	23	24	26	27	28	29	30
6'6"	14	15	16	17	19	20	21	22	23	24	25	27	28	29
6'8"	13	14	15	17	18	19	20	21	22	23	24	25	26	28

■ Underweight ■ Healthy weight ■ Overweight ■ Obese

FIGURE 16.4 Figuring Your Body Mass Index
Body mass index is a measure of weight in relation to height. Anyone with a BMI of 25 or more is considered overweight. People who have a body mass index of 30 or more (a BMI of 30 is roughly 30 pounds over a healthy weight) are considered obese. BMI has some limitations: It can overestimate body fat in people who are very muscular, and it can underestimate body fat in people who have lost muscle mass, such as the elderly.

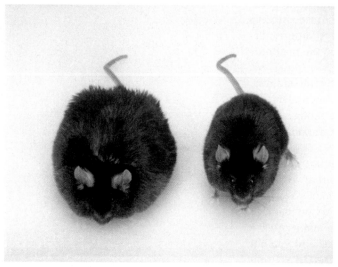

FIGURE 16.5 Leptin and Obesity
The *ob* mouse on the left is untreated; the one on the right has been given injections of leptin.

leptin A protein that is involved in satiety (the condition of being full to satisfaction) and released by fat cells resulting in decreased food intake and increased energy expenditure.

Eating Problems

In one large-scale study of middle-aged individuals, seven of ten said they were overweight (Brim, 1999). Some eating problems involve eating too much. Others involve eating too little or binging and purging.

Obesity   Obesity is a serious and pervasive health problem for many individuals (Corsica & Perri, 2003; International Obesity Task Force, 2004; Steiger, Bruce, & Israel, 2003). The prevalence of obesity in U.S. adults increased from 19 percent to 25 percent in 2002. More than 60 percent of U.S. adults are either overweight or obese (National Center for Health Statistics, 2004). Obesity is linked to increased risk of hypertension, diabetes, and cardiovascular disease (Stunkard, 2000). For individuals who are 30 percent overweight, the probability of dying in middle adulthood increases by about 40 percent. *Body mass index*, a measure of weight in relation to height, is used to determine whether an individual is underweight, a healthy weight, overweight, or obese (see figure 16.4).

What factors are involved in obesity? The possible culprits are heredity, leptin, set point and metabolism, environmental factors, ethnicity, and gender.

Heredity   Until recently, the genetic component of obesity had been underestimated by scientists. Some individuals do inherit a tendency to be overweight. Researchers have documented that animals can be inbred to have a propensity for obesity (Blundell, 1984). Further, identical human twins have similar weights, even when they are reared apart (Collaku & others, 2004). Estimates of the variance in body mass that can be explained by heredity range from 25 to 70 percent.

Leptin   Leptin (from the Greek word *leptos,* which means "thin") is a protein that is involved in satiety (the condition of being full to satisfaction) and is released by fat cells, resulting in decreased food intake and increased energy expenditure (Oberauer & others, 2001). Leptin acts as an antiobesity hormone (Misra & others, 2001).

Initial research focused on a strain of mice called the *ob mouse.* Because of a genetic mutation, the fat cells of ob mice cannot produce leptin. The ob mice also have a low metabolism, overeat, and get extremely fat. A particular gene called *ob* normally produces leptin. But when ob mice are given daily injections of leptin, their metabolic rate increases, they become more active, and they eat less. Consequently, their weight falls to normal. Figure 16.5 shows an untreated ob mouse and an ob mouse that has received injections of leptin. In humans, leptin concentrations have been linked with weight, percentage of body fat, weight loss in a single diet episode, and cumulative percentage of weight loss in all diet episodes (Benini & others, 2001; De Graaf & others, 2004; Erturk & others, 2004). Today, scientists are interested in the possibility that leptin might help obese individuals lose weight.

Set Point and Metabolism   The amount of stored fat in your body is an important factor in your *set point,* the weight maintained when no effort is made to gain or lose weight. Fat is stored in what are called adipose cells. When these cells are filled, you do not get hungry. When people gain weight—because of genetic predisposition, childhood eating patterns, or adult overeating—the number of their fat cells increases, and they might not be able to get rid of them. A normal-weight individual has 30 to 40 billion fat cells. An obese individual has 80 to 120 billion fat cells. Some scientists have proposed that these fat cells can shrink but might not go away.

Another factor in weight is **basal metabolism rate (BMR),** the minimal amount of energy an individual uses in a resting state. BMR varies with age and sex. Rates decline precipitously during adolescence and then more gradually in adulthood; they also are slightly higher for males than females. Many people gradually increase their weight over many years (Wing & Polley, 2001). To some degree the weight gain can be due to a declining basal metabolism rate.

Environmental Factors The human gustatory system and taste preferences developed at a time when reliable food sources were scarce. Our earliest ancestors probably developed a preference for sweets because ripe fruit, which is a concentrated source of sugar (and calories), was so accessible. Today many people still have a "sweet tooth," but unlike our ancestors' ripe fruit that contained sugar *plus* vitamins and minerals, the soft drinks and candy bars we snack on today often fill us with empty calories.

Strong evidence of the environment's influence on weight is the doubling of the rate of obesity in the United States since 1900. This dramatic increase in obesity likely is due to greater availability of food (especially food high in fat), energy-saving devices, and declining physical activity. One recent study found that in 2000, U.S. women ate 335 calories more a day and men 168 more a day than they did in the early 1970s (National Center for Health Statistics, 2004).

Sociocultural factors are involved in obesity, which is six times more prevalent among women with low incomes than among women with high incomes. Americans also are more obese than Europeans and people in many other areas of the world.

Ethnicity and Gender A recent study found that African American and Latino women in their twenties and thirties become obese faster than their White counterparts, and Latino men become obese faster than White and African American men (McTigue, Garrett, & Popkin, 2002). Two possibilities might explain these findings (Brownell, 2002). There may be some biological vulnerability that makes some ethnicgender groups more susceptible to obesity. Also, some individuals may be at risk for obesity because of their environment, as when their exposure to junk food and fast food is high and their opportunities to be active are minimal.

Dieting Ironically, while obesity is on the rise, dieting has become an obsession with many Americans. The topic of dieting is of great interest to many diverse groups in the United States, including the public, health professionals, policymakers, the media, and the powerful diet and food industries. On one side are the societal norms that promote a very lean, aesthetic body. This ideal is supported by $30 billion a year in sales of diet books, programs, videos, foods, and pills. On the other side are health professionals and a growing minority of the press. Although they recognize the alarmingly high rate of obesity, they are frustrated by high relapse rates and the obsession with excessive thinness that can lead to chronic dieting and serious health risks (Brownell, 2000; Brownell & Rodin, 1994).

Many people live their lives as one big long diet, interrupted by occasional hot fudge sundaes or chocolate chip cookies. They are **restrained eaters,** individuals who chronically restrict their food intake to control their weight. Restrained eaters are often on diets, are very conscious of what they eat, and tend to feel guilty after splurging on sweets (Wallis & Hetherington, 2004). An interesting characteristic of restrained eaters is that when they stop dieting, they tend to binge eat—that is, eat large quantities of food in a short time (Lowe & Timko, 2004; McFarlane, Polivy, & Herman, 1998).

Although many Americans regularly embark on a diet, few are successful in keeping weight off for the long term. Some critics argue that all diets fail (Wooley &

www.mhhe.com/santrockha

Healthy Weight Network
Obesity
Weight.Com
Overcoming Overeating
Calorie Control
TOPS

basal metabolism rate (BMR) The minimal amount of energy an individual uses in a resting state.

restrained eaters Individuals who chronically restrict their food intake to control their weight.

Garner, 1991). However, studies show that some individuals do lose weight and maintain the loss (Brownell & Cohen, 1995). How often this occurs and whether some diet programs work better than others are still open questions.

The current hot diet trend is a low-carbohydrate diet promoted by Robert Atkins (1997) in his book *Dr. Atkins' NEW Diet Revolution.* The diet restricts carbohydrates to less than 10 percent of total calories eaten, whereas people in the United States typically get more than 50 percent of their total calories from carbohydrates such as bread, processed foods, starch in vegetables, and sugar in fruits. On the Atkins diet, individuals eat as much protein and fat as they want. Short-term studies show that individuals who follow the Atkins diet do lose weight (Noakes & Clifton, 2004; Stern & others, 2004). However, critics argue that long-term studies have yet to be carried out and that the Atkins diet may pose health risks, especially for the heart, over the long term (Astrup, Meinhert, Larson, & Harper, 2004; Gau, 2004). It is well documented that foods promoted in the low-carbohydrate diets—for example, foods high in saturated fats such as meat, butter, or cream—increase the risk of heart disease in some types of cancer. And foods restricted on these diets—such as whole grains, vegetables, and fruits—have vitamins, minerals, and other nutrients that reduce the risk of heart disease, cancer, and other diseases.

What we do know about losing weight is that the most effective programs include exercise (Bray & Champagne, 2004; Kemper, Stasse-Wolthuis, & Bosman, 2004). Exercise not only burns up calories but also continues to elevate the person's metabolic rate for several hours *after* the exercise (Janssen & others, 2004). Also, exercise lowers a person's set point for weight, which makes it easier to maintain a lower weight (Bennett & Gurin, 1982).

Even when diets do produce weight loss, they can place the dieter at risk for other health problems. One main concern focuses on weight cycling—yo-yo dieting—in which the person is in a recurring cycle of dieting and weight gain (Marchesini & others, 2004; Wadden & others, 1996). Researchers have found a link between frequent changes in weight and chronic disease (Brownell & Rodin, 1994). Also, liquid diets and other very-low calorie strategies are linked with gall bladder damage.

When overweight people do lose weight and maintain their weight loss, however, they gain many benefits. They become less depressed and reduce their risk for a number of health-impairing disorders (Christensen, 1996).

Adjustment Strategies
For Losing Weight

Here are some strategies for losing weight, most of which are based on recommendations by the National Institute of Diabetes and Digestive and Kidney Diseases (2003, p. 7):

1. *Exercise regularly.*
2. *"Keep a food diary."*
3. *"Shop from a list and don't shop when you are hungry."*
4. *Minimize your exposure to food cues.* Keep tempting foods out of sight.
5. *"Use a smaller plate with smaller servings."*
6. *"Eat at the table with the TV off."*
7. *"At restaurants, eat only half your meal and take the rest home."*
8. *Don't starve yourself all day and then eat one big meal in the evening.* This is a common tactic of overweight individuals that slows metabolism.
9. *"Seek support from family and friends."*
10. *"Be realistic about weight loss goals.* Aim for a slow, modest weight loss." Avoid extreme, crash diets that might work in the short term but cannot be maintained over the long term.

What Are My Eating Attitudes and Behaviors Like?

Check off the items that apply to you.

☐ I constantly think about eating, weight, and body size.

☐ I get anxious before eating.

☐ I'm terrified of gaining weight.

☐ I don't know when I'm physically hungry.

☐ I feel that no matter what I do, it will never be good enough.

☐ I go on eating binges and can't stop until I feel sick.

☐ I often feel bloated or uncomfortable after meals.

☐ I spend a lot of time daydreaming about food.

☐ I weigh myself several times a day.

☐ I lie or make excuses about what I have eaten.

☐ I exercise too much or get very rigid about my exercise plan.

☐ I take laxatives and/or throw up after eating to prevent weight gain.

☐ I restrict my eating when I get upset.

☐ I feel guilty or angry with myself after overeating.

☐ I eat when I am anxious, lonely, or depressed.

☐ I don't think I look good in clothes.

☐ Because of my weight, I feel uncomfortable around people I find attractive.

☐ I know the calorie and/or fat content in the foods that I eat.

☐ For women—I have not had a menstrual cycle for three months or more.

☐ I feel out of control when I eat.

☐ I feel powerful and in control when I restrict myself from eating.

☐ I think I'm fat even though other people tell me I'm not.

☐ I exercise to burn calories, not to stay fit.

☐ I get angry with people who question my eating habits.

☐ I avoid social events when I know there will be food present.

☐ I think my life would be better if I were thinner.

☐ Family members and/or friends have expressed concern about my weight and eating habits.

☐ I think I might have an eating disorder.

☐ I have one or more of the following: intolerance to cold, heart races or skips beats, fainting/dizziness/headaches, blood in vomit or stool, swollen cheeks, change in texture of skin, hair, and nails, dental problems (enamel erosion), constipation.

Go to the appendix at the end of the book for scoring and interpretation of your responses.

Dieting is a pervasive concern of many Americans, but many people who are on diets should not be. A 10 percent reduction in body weight might produce striking benefits for an older, obese, hypertensive man but be unhealthy for a female college student who is not overweight. The pressure to be thin, and thus diet, is greatest among young women, yet they do not have the highest risk of obesity. To evaluate your eating attitudes and behaviors, complete Self-Assessment 16.2.

Anorexia nervosa has become an increasing problem for adolescent girls and young adult women. *What are some possible causes of anorexia nervosa?*

National Eating Disorders Association
Eating Disorders

anorexia nervosa An eating disorder that involves the relentless pursuit of thinness through starvation.

bulimia nervosa An eating disorder in which the individual consistently follows a binge-and-purge eating pattern.

Anorexia Nervosa Although most U.S. American girls have been on a diet at some point, slightly less than 1 percent ever develop anorexia nervosa (Walters & Kendler, 1994). **Anorexia nervosa** is an eating disorder that involves the relentless pursuit of thinness through starvation. Anorexia nervosa is a serious disorder that can lead to death. Three main characteristics of anorexia nervosa are as follows (Davison & Neale, 2001, p. 223):

- Weighing less than 85 percent of what is considered normal for their age and height.
- Having an intense fear of gaining weight. The fear does not decrease as the individual loses weight.
- Having a distorted image of their body (Polivy & others, 2003; Stice, Presnell, & Spangler, 2002). Even when they are extremely thin, they see themselves as fat. They never think they are thin enough, especially in the abdomen, buttocks, and thighs. They usually weigh themselves frequently, often take their body measurements, and critically evaluate themselves in mirrors.

Anorexia nervosa typically begins in the early to middle teenage years, often following an episode of dieting and some type of life stress. It is about 10 times more likely to characterize females than males. When anorexia nervosa does occur in males, the symptoms and other characteristics (such as family conflict) are usually similar to those reported by females who have the disorder (Olivardia & others, 1995).

Most anorexics are White adolescent or young adult females from well-educated, middle- and upper-income families that are competitive and high achieving (Schmidt, 2003). They set high standards, become stressed about not being able to reach the standards, and are intensely concerned about how others perceive them (Striegel-Moore, Silberstein, & Rodin, 1993). Unable to meet these high expectations, they turn to something they can control: their weight.

The fashion image in the American culture that emphasizes that "thin is beautiful" contributes to the incidence of anorexia nervosa (Hsu, 2004; Polivy & others, 2003). This image is reflected in the saying, "You never can be too rich or too thin." The media portrays thin as beautiful in their choice of fashion models, which many adolescent girls want to emulate.

Bulimia Nervosa While anorexics control their eating by restricting it, most bulimics cannot (Mitchell & Mazzeo, 2004). **Bulimia nervosa** is an eating disorder in which the individual consistently follows a binge-and-purge pattern. The bulimic goes on an eating binge and then purges by self-inducing vomiting or using a laxative. Although many people binge and purge occasionally and some experiment with it, a person is considered to have a serious bulimic disorder only if the episodes occur at least twice a week for three months

As with anorexics, most bulimics are preoccupied with food, have a strong fear of becoming overweight, and are depressed or anxious (Davison & Neale, 2004; Garcia-Alba, 2004; Quadflieg & Fichter, 2003). Unlike anorexics, people who binge and purge typically fall within a normal weight range, which makes bulimia more difficult to detect (Orbanic, 2001).

Approximately 1 to 2 percent of U.S. women are estimated to develop bulimia nervosa (Gotesdam & Agras, 1995), and about 90 percent of the cases are women. Bulimia nervosa typically begins in late adolescence or early adulthood. About 90 percent of the cases are women. Many women who develop bulimia nervosa were somewhat overweight before the onset of the disorder and the binge eating often began during an episode of dieting. One recent study of adolescent girls found that increased dieting, pressure to be thin, exaggerated emphasis on appearance, body dissatisfaction, depression symptoms, low self-esteem, and low social support predicted binge eating two years later (Stice & others, 2002). As with anorexia nervosa, about 70 percent of individuals who develop bulimia nervosa eventually recover from the disorder (Keel & others, 1999).

2   Discuss nutrition, eating behavior, and eating problems

REVIEW

- What is the Food Guide Pyramid and how is it changing? What are some cultural variations in eating behavior? What are some links between nutrition and longevity?
- What characterizes obesity and dieting? What are anorexia nervosa and bulimia nervosa?

REFLECT

- How good are you at eating nutritiously and healthily? Has your lifestyle and behavior in this area affected your health? Might they affect your health in the future?

3   EXERCISE

The Benefits of Exercise   **Exercise and Longevity**

In 1961 President John F. Kennedy offered the following message: "We are under-exercised as a nation. We look instead of play. We ride instead of walk. Our existence deprives us of the minimum of physical activity essential for healthy living."

Without question, people are jogging, cycling, and aerobically exercising more today than in 1961, but far too many of us are still couch potatoes, spending most of our leisure time in front of the TV or a computer screen. In one large-scale U.S. study, nearly half of the individuals over 45 years of age said they were less fit than they were five years ago (Brim, 1999). Most of us will never come close to a regimen like that of Lance Armstrong, who spends 20 to 30 hours a week on his bicycle when he is training. But almost all of us could benefit greatly from exercising more.

The Benefits of Exercise

Different types of exercise bring varying specific benefits. Although exercise designed to strengthen muscles and bones or to improve flexibility is important to fitness, many health experts stress aerobic exercise. **Aerobic exercise** is sustained exercise—jogging, swimming, or cycling, for example—that stimulates heart and lung activity.

One of the main reasons that health experts want people to exercise is that it helps to prevent heart disease (Williams, 2001). Elaborate studies of 17,000 male alumni of Harvard University found that those who exercised strenuously on a regular basis had a lower risk of heart disease and were more likely to be alive in their middle adulthood years than their more sedentary counterparts (Lee, Hsieh, & Paffenbarger, 1995; Paffenbarger & others, 1993). Longshoremen—who are on their feet all day and lift, push, and carry heavy cargo—have about half the risk of fatal heart attacks as co-workers like crane drivers and clerks, who have physically less demanding jobs.

Some experts conclude that, regardless of other risk factors (smoking, high blood pressure, overweight, heredity), if you exercise enough to burn more than 2,000 calories a week, you can cut your risk of heart attack by an impressive two-thirds. Burning up 2,000 calories a week through exercise requires a lot of effort, far more than most of us are willing to expend. To burn 300 calories a day, through exercise, you would

The Jogging Hog Experiment. Jogging hogs reveal the dramatic effects of exercise on health. In one investigation, a group of hogs was trained to run approximately 100 miles per week (Bloor & White, 1983). Then, the researchers narrowed the arteries that supplied blood to the hogs' hearts. The hearts of the jogging hogs developed extensive alternate pathways for blood supply, and 42 percent of the threatened heart tissue was salvaged compared to only 17 percent in a control group of nonjogging hogs.

aerobic exercise Sustained exercise—jogging, swimming, or cycling, for example—that stimulates heart and lung activity.

have to do one of the following: swim or run for about 25 minutes, walk for 45 minutes at about 4 miles an hour, or participate in aerobic dancing for 30 minutes.

As a more realistic goal, health experts recommend that adults engage in 30 minutes or more of moderate-intensity physical activity on most, preferably all, days of the week (Blair, LaMonte, & Nichaman, 2004). Examples of physical activities that qualify as moderate are included in figure 16.6. Most experts recommend that you should try to raise your heart rate to at least 60 percent of your maximum heart rate. However, only about one-fifth of adults meet these recommended levels of physical activity.

Researchers have found that exercise benefits not only physical health, but mental health as well (Phillips, Kiernan, & King, 2001). In particular, exercise improves self-concept and reduces anxiety and depression (Moses & others, 1989).

Both moderate and intense activities produce important physical and psychological gains (Thayer & others, 1996). Some people enjoy rigorous, intense exercise. Others enjoy more moderate exercise routines. The enjoyment and pleasure we derive from exercise added to its aerobic benefits make exercise one of life's most important activities.

Exercise and Longevity

Regular exercise can lead to a healthier life as a middle-aged and older adult, and increase longevity (Fahey, Insel, & Roth, 2005). In one study, exercise meant a difference in life or death for middle-aged and older adults (Blair & others, 1989). More than 10,000 men and women were divided into categories of low fitness, medium fitness, and high fitness. Then they were studied over a period of eight years. As shown in figure 16.7, sedentary participants (low fitness) were more than twice as likely to die during the eight-year time span of the study than those who were moderately fit and more than three times as likely to die as those who were highly fit. The positive effects of being physically fit occurred for both men and women in this study. In another study, beginning moderately vigorous sports activity from the forties through the eighties was associated with a 23 percent lower risk of death, quitting cigarette smoking with a 41 percent lower death risk (Paffenbarger & others, 1993).

Gerontologists recommend strength training in addition to aerobic activity and stretching for older adults (Penninx & others, 2002; Rubenstein & others, 2000). The average person's lean body mass declines with age—about 6.6 pounds of lean muscle

FIGURE 16.6 Moderate and Vigorous Physical Activities

Moderate	Vigorous
Walking, briskly (3 to 4 mph)	Walking, briskly uphill or with a load
Cycling, for pleasure or transportation (≤10 mph)	Cycling, fast or racing (>10 mph)
Swimming, moderate effort	Swimming, fast treading crawl
Conditioning exercise, general calisthenics	Conditioning exercise, stair ergometer or ski machine
Racket sports, table tennis	Racket sports, singles tennis or racquetball
Golf, pulling cart or carrying clubs	Golf, practice at driving range
Canoeing, leisurely (2.0 to 3.9 mph)	Canoeing, rapidly (≥4 mph)
Home care, general cleaning	Moving furniture
Mowing lawn, with power mower	Mowing lawn, with hand mower
Home repair, painting	Home repair, fix-up projects

are lost each decade during the adult years. The rate of loss accelerates after age 45. Also, the average percentage ratio of muscle to fat for a 60- to 70-year-old woman is 44 percent fat. In a 20-year-old woman the ratio is 23 to 24 percent. Weight lifting can preserve and possibly increase muscle mass in older adults (Slade & others, 2002).

In short, exercise can contribute to health and well-being and minimize physiological changes associated with aging such as declines in motor coordination and attention span (Dejong & Franklin, 2004). A recent review of research on exercise and aging reached these conclusions (Singh, 2002):

- *Exercise can influence physiological changes in brain tissue associated with aging.* In one recent study using magnetic resonance imaging, aerobic exercise was linked with less loss of brain tissue in the frontal, parietal, and temporal lobes (Colcombe & others, 2003).
- *Exercise can optimize body composition as aging occurs.* Exercise can increase muscle mass and bone mass, as well as decrease bone fragility (Slade & others, 2002).
- *Exercise is related to prevention of common chronic diseases.* Exercise can reduce the risk of cardiovascular disease, type 2 diabetes, osteoporosis, stroke, and breast cancer (McReynolds & Rossen, 2004; Miller & others, 2000).
- *Exercise is associated with improvement in the treatment of many diseases.* When exercise is used as part of the treatment, individuals with these diseases show improvement in symptoms: arthritis, pulmonary disease, congestive heart failure, coronary artery disease, hypertension, type 2 diabetes, and obesity (Jadelis & others, 2001; Wallace, Mills, & Browning, 1997).
- *Exercise is related to the prevention of disability and can be used effectively in the treatment of disability.* One study of more than 5,000 individuals found that physical activity was associated with slower progression of functional limitations and disability (Miller & others, 2000). Specifically, older adults who walked a mile at least once per week were less likely than their sedentary counterparts to face functional limitations over the six years of the study.
- *Exercise can be used to counteract the side effects of standard medical care and thus improve disease outcomes and quality of life.* For example, depression is sometimes an unintended side effect of drugs used to treat hypertension and exercise may reduce the depression (Singh, 2002). In one study, weight lifting reduced depression in older adults (Singh, Clements, & Fiatarone, 1997).
- *Exercise is linked to increased longevity.* Energy expenditure during exercise of at least 1,000 kcal/week reduces mortality by about 30 percent, while 2,000 kcal/week reduces mortality by about 50 percent (Lee & Skerrett, 2001).

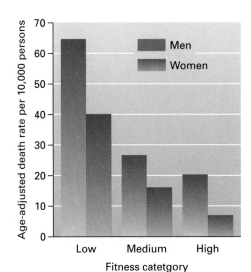

FIGURE 16.7 Physical Fitness and Mortality
In this study of middle-aged and older adults, being moderately fit or highly fit meant that individuals were less likely to die over a period of eight years than their low-fitness (sedentary) counterparts (Blair & others, 1989).

What have researchers found about links between exercise and aging?

www.mhhe.com/santrockha
Exercise and Aging

Adjustment Strategies
For Exercising Regularly

Here are some helpful strategies for building exercise into your life:

1. **Consult with your doctor and get a physical examination.** It is important to have a physical examination before beginning an exercise program. This is especially true if you have a sedentary lifestyle or have a medical condition.
2. **Make exercise a high priority in your life.** Ask yourself whether you are too busy to take care of your own health. What will your life be like if you lose your health?

continued

3. ***Reduce TV time.*** Heavy TV viewing by college students is linked to their poor health (Astin, 1993). Replace some of your TV time with exercise time.
4. ***Chart your progress.*** Systematically recording your exercise workouts will help you to chart your progress. This strategy is especially helpful in maintaining an exercise program over an extended period.
5. ***Get rid of excuses.*** People make up all kinds of excuses for not exercising. A typical excuse is "I just don't have enough time." You probably do have the time to make exercise a priority.
6. ***Learn more about exercise.*** The more you know about exercise, the more you are likely to start an exercise program and continue it. Explore the resources at the end of the chapter and on the Online Learning Center for this book, including recommended Internet sites.

Review and Reflect

3 Summarize the role of exercise in health

REVIEW

- What is aerobic exercise? What are the benefits of exercise?
- What is the connection between exercise and longevity?

REFLECT

- Describe your exercise habits? How satisfied are you with them?

---

4 DRUGS AND ADDICTION

Besides eating healthily and exercising regularly, another important healthy practice is to avoid abusing alcohol or using other **psychoactive drugs,** which are substances that act on the nervous system to alter states of consciousness, modify perceptions, and change moods. For example, in one longitudinal study, individuals who exercised when they were 50 years of age were more likely to be alive and healthy when they were 75 to 80 years old than their counterparts who did not exercise (Vaillant, 2002). In this same study, not abusing alcohol at age 50 was also linked with still being alive and healthy at 75 to 80 years of age.

Psychoactive Drugs

Psychoactive drugs have been classified into three main categories: depressants, stimulants, and hallucinogens:

- **Depressants** are drugs that slow down the central nervous system, body functions, and behavior. Among the most widely used depressants are alcohol, barbiturates, and tranquilizers.
- **Stimulants** are drugs that increase the activity of the nervous system. The most widely used stimulants are caffeine, nicotine, amphetamines, and cocaine.
- **Hallucinogens** are drugs that modify an individual's perceptual experiences and produce hallucinations. LSD, marijuana, and ecstasy are hallucinogens.

psychoactive drugs Substances that act on the nervous system to alter states of consciousness, modify perceptions, and change moods.

depressants Drugs that slow down the nervous system, body functions, and behaviors; alcohol, barbiturates, and tranquilizers are examples.

stimulants Drugs that increase the activity of the nervous system; caffeine, nicotine, amphetamines, and cocaine are examples.

hallucinogens Drugs that modify an individual's perceptual experiences and produce hallucinations; LSD, marijuana, and ecstasy are examples.

People are attracted to psychoactive substances because they help them adapt to an ever-changing environment. Drinking, smoking, and taking drugs reduce tension, relieve boredom and fatigue, and in some cases help people to escape from the harsh realities of the world. Some people take drugs because they are curious about their effects. Others may take drugs for social reasons; for example, to feel more at ease and happier when interacting with others.

Addiction

The use of psychoactive drugs for personal gratification and temporary adaptation can carry a high price tag: drug dependence, personal disarray, and a predisposition to serious, sometimes fatal, diseases. What was initially intended to be pleasurable and adaptive can eventually turn to sorrow and maladaptation. For example, drinking alcohol may help people relax and forget about their own worries. But if they turn more and more to alcohol to escape reality, they may develop a dependence that can destroy relationships, careers, and their bodies. In one study, first-year college students who met the criteria for alcohol dependence were more likely to have failing grades than their counterparts who did not meet the criteria (Aertgeerts & Buntinx, 2002).

Beyond the risks to physical health and safety, using psychoactive drugs can distort a person's experience of life and opportunities by creating psychological dependence, physical dependence, or both (Fields, 2004; Ray & Ksir, 2004). **Psychological dependence** exists when a person is preoccupied with obtaining a drug for emotional reasons, such as the reduction of stress. **Physical dependence** exists when discontinuing use of a drug creates unpleasant, significant changes in physical functioning and behavior. These changes are called *withdrawal symptoms*. Depending on the drug, withdrawal symptoms include insomnia, tremors, nausea, vomiting, cramps, elevation of heart rate and blood pressure, convulsions, anxiety, and depression.

Controversy continues about whether addictions are diseases (Ray & Ksir, 2004). The **disease model of addiction** describes addictions as biologically based, lifelong diseases that involve a loss of control over behavior and require medical and/or spiritual treatment for recovery. In the disease model, addiction is either inherited or bred into a person early in life. Current or recent problems or relationships are not believed to be causes of the disease. Once involved in the disease, you can never completely rid yourself of it, according to this model. The disease model has been strongly promoted and supported by the medical profession and Alcoholics Anonymous (AA) (Humphreys, 2000).

In contrast to the disease model of addiction, which focuses on biological mechanisms, some psychologists believe that understanding addiction requires that it be placed in context as part of people's lives, their personalities, their relationships, their environments, and their perspectives. In this **life-process model of addiction,** addiction is not a disease but rather a habitual response and a source of gratification or security that can be understood best in the context of social relationships and experiences. Each of these views of addiction—the disease model and the nondisease, life-process model—has its supporters.

An overview of the medical uses, short-term effects, overdose, health risks, and risk of physical/psychological dependence is presented in figure 16.8. To evaluate whether you abuse drugs, complete Self-Assessment 16.3. In our further discussion of psychoactive drugs, we focus primarily on alcohol and cigarettes because their use is so widespread. They pose serious dangers to health and development.

Alcohol

We don't always think of alcohol as a drug, but it is a very powerful one. Alcohol primarily acts on the body as a depressant and slows down the brain's activities. This might seem surprising, as people who normally tend to be inhibited may begin to talk,

National Institute of Drug Abuse

Web of Addictions
AA
Rational Recovery

psychological dependence Exists when a person is preoccupied with a drug for emotional reasons, such as the reduction of stress.

physical dependence Exists when discontinuing the use of a drug creates unpleasant, significant changes in physical functioning and behavior.

disease model of addiction Describes addictions as biologically based, lifelong diseases that involve a loss of control over behavior and require medical and/or spiritual treatment for recovery.

life-process model of addiction Describes addiction not as a disease but as a habitual response and a source of gratification or security that can be understood best in the context of social relationships and experiences.

Drug Classification	Medical Uses	Short-Term Effects	Overdose	Health Risks	Risk of Physical/ Psychological Dependence
Depressants					
Alcohol	Pain relief	Relaxation, depressed brain activity, slowed behavior, reduced inhibitions	Disorientation, loss of consciousness, even death at high blood-alcohol levels	Accidents, brain damage, liver disease, heart disease, ulcers, birth defects	Physical: moderate Psychological: moderate
Barbiturates	Sleeping pill	Relaxation, sleep	Breathing difficulty, coma, possible death	Accidents, coma, possible death	Physical and psychological: moderate to high
Tranquilizers	Anxiety reduction	Relaxation, slowed behavior	Breathing difficulty, coma, possible death	Accidents, coma, possible death	Physical: low to moderate Psychological: moderate to high
Opiates (narcotics)	Pain relief	Euphoric feelings, drowsiness, nausea	Convulsions, coma, possible death	Accidents, infectious diseases such as AIDS (when the drug is injected)	Physical: high Psychological: moderate to high
Stimulants					
Amphetamines	Weight control	Increased alertness, excitability; decreased fatigue, irritability	Extreme irritability, feelings of persecution, convulsions	Insomnia, hypertension, malnutrition, possible death	Physical: possible Psychological: moderate to high
Cocaine	Local anesthetic	Increased alertness, excitability, euphoric feelings; decreased fatigue, irritability	Extreme irritability, feelings of persecution, convulsions, cardiac arrest, possible death	Insomnia, hypertension, malnutrition, possible death	Physical: possible Psychological: moderate (oral) to very high (injected or smoked)
Hallucinogens					
LSD	None	Strong hallucinations, distorted time perception	Severe mental disturbance, loss of contact with reality	Accidents	Physical: none Psychological: low
Marijuana	Treatment of the eye disorder glaucoma	Euphoric feelings, relaxation, mild hallucinations, time distortion, attention and memory impairment	Fatigue, disoriented behavior	Accidents, respiratory disease	Physical: very low Psychological: moderate

FIGURE 16.8 Psychoactive Drugs: Depressants, Stimulants, and Hallucinogens

dance, and socialize after a few drinks. However, people "loosen up" after a few drinks because the areas of the brain involved in inhibition and judgment slow down. As people drink more, their inhibitions decrease even more and their judgment becomes further impaired. Activities that require decision making and motor skills, such as driving, become increasingly impaired as more alcohol is consumed. Eventually, the drinker becomes drowsy and falls asleep. With extreme intoxication, a person may lapse into a coma and die. Each of these effects varies with the way the person's body metabolizes alcohol, body weight, the amount of alcohol consumed, and whether previous drinking has led to tolerance (the need to take increasing amounts of a drug to get the same effect) (Fields, 2004; Gotz & others, 2001).

The costs of alcohol abuse are high. Approximately 1.4 million people in the United States are alcoholics (Brink, 2001). Alcoholism is the third-leading killer in the United States. Approximately 20,000 people are killed and 1.5 million injured by drunk drivers each year. More than 60 percent of homicides involve the use of alcohol by either the offender or the victim, and 65 percent of aggressive attacks on women involve the use of alcohol by the offender.

SELF-ASSESSMENT 16.3

Do I Abuse Drugs?

Check yes or no in terms of whether the statement applies to you or not.

	Yes	No
I have gotten into financial problems because of using drugs.	_____	_____
Using alcohol or other drugs has made my college life unhappy at times.	_____	_____
Drinking alcohol or taking other drugs has been a factor in my losing a job.	_____	_____
Drinking alcohol or taking other drugs has interfered with my preparation for exams.	_____	_____
Drinking alcohol or taking drugs is jeopardizing my academic performance.	_____	_____
My ambition is not as strong since I started drinking a lot or taking drugs.	_____	_____
Drinking or taking other drugs has caused me to have difficulty sleeping.	_____	_____
I have felt remorse after drinking or using other drugs.	_____	_____
I crave a drink or other drugs at a definite time of the day.	_____	_____
I want a drink or another drug the next morning.	_____	_____
I have had a complete or partial loss of memory as a result of drinking or using other drugs.	_____	_____
Drinking or using other drugs is affecting my reputation.	_____	_____
I have been in a hospital or institution because of drinking or taking other drugs.	_____	_____

Go to the appendix at the end of the book for scoring and interpretation of your responses.

The RCSAST is to be used only as part of a complete assessment battery since more research needs to be done with this instrument. Reprinted with permission from *Journal of Studies on Alcohol,* Vol. 54, pp. 522–527, 1993. Copyright by Alcohol Research Documentation, Inc., Rutgers Center of Alcohol Studies, Piscataway, NJ 08854.

Drinking in College Students and Young Adults Binge drinking often increases in college, and it can take its toll on students (Schulenberg, 1999). In a national survey of drinking patterns on 140 campuses, almost half of the binge drinkers reported problems that included missing classes, physical injuries, and trouble with the police (Wechsler & others, 1994). Binge-drinking college students were 11 times more likely to drive after drinking, and twice as likely to have unprotected sex, than college students who did not binge drink.

More than 40,000 full-time U.S. college students were asked about their drinking habits in 1993, 1997, 1999, and 2001 (Wechsler & others, 2002). In this case, binge drinkers were defined as men who drank five or more drinks in a row and women who drank four or more drinks at least once in the two weeks prior to the questionnaire. Rates of binge drinking remained remarkably consistent—at about 44 percent—over the eight years. Further, almost 75 percent of underage students living in fraternities or sororities were binge drinkers and 70 percent of traditional-age college students who lived away from home were binge drinkers. The lowest rate of binge drinking—25 percent—occurred for students living at home with their parents. Chronic binge drinking is more common among college men than women (Schulenberg, 1999), but one study found a 125 percent increase in binge drinking at all-women colleges from 1993 through 2001 (Wechsler & others, 2002).

Fortunately, by the time individuals reach their mid-twenties, many have reduced their use of alcohol. That is the conclusion reached by Jerald Bachman and his

What kinds of problems are associated with binge drinking in college?

FIGURE 16.9 Binge Drinking in the Adolescence-Early Adulthood Transition
Note that the percentage of individuals engaging in binge drinking peaked at 21 or 22 years of age and then began to gradually decline through the remainder of the twenties. Binge drinking was defined as having five or more alcoholic drinks in a row in the past two weeks.

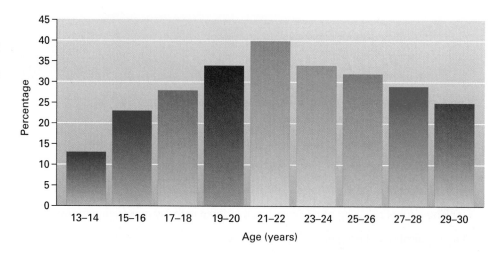

colleagues (2002) in a longitudinal analysis that evaluated more than 38,000 individuals from the time they were high school seniors through their twenties (see figure 16.9). The study found that college students drank more than youth who end their education after high school and that drinking was heaviest among singles and divorced individuals. Becoming engaged, married, or even remarried quickly reduced alcohol use.

Cultural Variations Around the world, there are differences in alcohol use by gender and religion (Koenig, 2001; Melinder & Andersson, 2001). Males drink alcohol more than females. Use of alcohol is forbidden by some religions, such as Islam. In contrast, Catholics, Reform Jews, and liberal Protestants all consume alcohol at a fairly high level.

Europeans, especially the French, drink alcohol at high rates. Estimates are that about 30 percent of French adults have impaired health related to alcohol consumption. Alcohol use is also high in Russia, but its use in China is low.

Alcoholism **Alcoholism** is a disorder that involves long-term, repeated, uncontrolled, compulsive, and excessive use of alcoholic beverages and that impairs the drinker's health and social relationships. One in nine individuals who drink continues the path to alcoholism.

Studies reveal that both genetic and environmental factors play a role in alcoholism (Ehlers & others, 2004; Heath & Nelson, 2002; Palomo & others, 2004). Indeed, researchers have estimated that heredity likely plays a role in 50 to 60 percent of the cases of alcoholism, although the precise hereditary mechanism has not been found (Crabbe, 2002; Wall & others, 2001). Family studies consistently find a high frequency of alcoholism in the first-degree relatives of alcoholics (Gamm, Nussbaum, & Bowles Biesecker, 2004; Pastor & Evans, 2003), but family studies also indicate that many alcoholics do not have close relatives who are alcoholics (Matin & Sher, 1994).

About one-third of alcoholics recover whether they are in a treatment program or not. This figure was found in a long-term study of 700 individuals over 50 years and has consistently been found by other researchers as well (Vaillant, 1992). There is a "one-third rule" for alcoholism: by age 65, one-third are dead or in terrible shape, one-third are abstinent or drinking socially, and one-third are still trying to beat their addiction. Recovery from alcoholism is predicted by certain factors:

1. A strong negative experience related to drinking, such as a serious medical emergency or condition
2. Finding a substitute dependency to compete with alcohol abuse, such as meditation, exercise, or overeating (which of course has its own negative health consequences)

www.mhhe.com/santrockha

Alcohol Abuse and Alcoholism

alcoholism A disorder that involves long-term, repeated, uncontrolled, compulsive, and excessive use of alcoholic beverages and that impairs the drinker's health and social relationships.

3. Having new social supports (such as a concerned, helpful employer or a new marriage)
4. Joining an inspirational group, such as a religious organization or AA

Adjustment Strategies
For Curbing Alcohol Use

Here are some strategies for reducing alcohol use:

1. ***Admit that you have a problem.*** This is not an easy task. Many individuals who have an alcohol abuse problem deny they have the problem. Admitting that you have a drinking problem is a major first step in helping yourself cope with the problem.

2. ***Write down your reasons for cutting down or eliminating your drinking.*** Ask yourself why you want to drink less? Your list might include improving your health, sleeping better, getting higher grades, or getting along better with your friends and family.

3. ***Set a drinking goal and keep a drinking diary.*** State your drinking goal: My drinking goal is _____ . I will not drink more than _____ drinks in one day. I will not drink more than _____ drinks in one week. Or I will stop drinking alcohol. Then to help you reach your goal(s), keep a diary of your drinking. For example, write down every time you have a drink for one week. Try keeping your diary for a month and it will show you how much you drink and when.

4. ***Don't ignore what others are saying to you.*** Chances are that your roommate, a friend, someone you've dated, or a spouse/life partner has told you that you have a drinking problem. You likely denied it. They are trying to help you. Listen to them.

5. ***Don't go out with people who make you feel uncomfortable if you are not drinking.*** Make alternative plans with friends and acquaintances who are less inclined to drink.

6. ***Don't keep beer, wine, or hard liquor at home.*** It is easier to resist the temptation to drink if it is not there.

7. ***Seek help for your problem.*** There are numerous resources for individuals who have a drinking problem, such as Alcoholics Anonymous and the counseling/health services at your college.

8. ***Use the resources at the end of this chapter and on the book's Online Learning Center.*** These resources include phone numbers and information about organizations that can help you to conquer a drinking problem.

Smoking

Converging evidence from a number of studies underscores the dangers of smoking or being around those who do (Pomerleau, 2000). For example, smoking is linked to 30 percent of cancer deaths, 21 percent of heart disease deaths, and 82 percent of chronic pulmonary disease deaths. Secondhand smoke is implicated in as many as 9,000 lung cancer deaths a year. Children of smokers are at special risk for respiratory and middle-ear diseases.

Fewer people in the United States smoke today than in the past, and almost half of all living adults in the United States who ever smoked have quit. The prevalence of smoking in men has dropped from over 50 percent in 1965 to about 28 percent today (National Center for Health Statistics, 2004). However, more than 50 million Americans still smoke cigarettes today. And cigar smoking and tobacco chewing, with risks similar to those of cigarette smoking, have increased.

www.mhhe.com/santrockha

Smoking and Cancer
Quit Smoking

"there's no shooting—we just make you keep smoking."

Most adult smokers would like to quit, but their addiction to nicotine often makes quitting a challenge. Nicotine, the active drug in cigarettes, is a stimulant that increases the smoker's energy and alertness, a pleasurable and reinforcing experience. Nicotine also stimulates neurotransmitters that have a calming or pain-reducing effect.

Studies indicate that when people do stop smoking their risk of cancer is reduced (Centers for Disease Control and Prevention, 2004). Five years after people stop smoking their health risk is noticeably lower than for people who continue to smoke (U.S. Surgeon General's Report, 1990).

Adjustment Strategies
For Quitting Smoking

1. ***Develop a strong self-motivation to quit.*** Self-motivation is vital to quitting smoking or reducing any bad habit. You need to develop a "deep down" commitment and desire to quit for your own health and happiness. Once you make a strong commitment to quit smoking, you can choose from five main methods to help you quit, each of which is described below.

2. ***Use a substitute source of nicotine.*** Nicotine gum, the nicotine patch, the nicotine inhaler, and nicotine spray work on the principle of supplying small amounts of nicotine to diminish the intensity of withdrawal. Recent research shows that the percentage of individuals who are still not smoking after five months range from 18 percent for the nicotine patch to 30 percent for the nicotine spray (Centers for Disease Control and Prevention, 2004).

3. ***Take the antidepressant Bupropion ST.*** This drug is sold as Zyban and it helps smokers control their cravings while they ease off nicotine. Recent research indicates that smokers using Zyban to quit have had a 30 percent average success rate for five months after they started taking the drug (Centers for Disease Control and Prevention, 2004).

4. ***Control stimuli associated with smoking.*** For example, you might be accustomed to having a cigarette with a morning cup of coffee or a social drink; smoking has become associated with these activities. Stimulus control strategies help the smoker to avoid these cues or learn to substitute other behaviors for smoking.

5. ***Undergo aversive conditioning.*** The behavior therapy technique of **aversive conditioning** involves repeated pairings of an undesirable behavior with aversive stimuli to decrease the behavior's rewards. Imagine smoking as many cigarettes as possible until the ashtray overflows, the smell of stale cigarettes seems permanently embedded in your fingertips, your throat is dry and scratchy, and you feel nauseated. Smoking might become so unpleasant that you won't want to smoke again. Sometimes this technique works, sometimes it doesn't.

6. ***Go "cold turkey."*** Some people succeed by simply stopping smoking without making any major changes in their lifestyle. They decide they are going to quit and they do. Lighter smokers usually have more success with this approach than heavier smokers.

7. ***Stay smoke-free.*** In addition to choosing one of the five methods for quitting smoking, an important goal is maintenance—being able to quit smoking for weeks, months, years, and the rest of your life. Once you quit, stay strong. Never allow yourself to think that "just one cigarette won't hurt." Make this concession and you will likely have another and another, making quitting more difficult. Occasionally, you will crave a cigarette. When this happens think of the meaningful reasons you quit smoking—for example, to become more healthy, feel better, save money, and live long enough to see your grandchildren. Also exercise. Researchers have found that individuals with higher success rates over time regularly exercise (Bock & others, 1999). And watch out for unexpected situational triggers, such as an especially stressful event that occurs in the first three months after quitting. Being aware of such triggers can keep you on guard and help you resist the urge to smoke.

aversive conditioning A behavior therapy technique that consists of repeated pairings of an undesirable behavior with aversive stimuli to decrease the behavior's rewards.

Review and Reflect

4 **Explain drug use and addiction**

REVIEW

- What are psychoactive drugs? What are the three main classifications of psychoactive drugs?
- What is addiction? What are two models of addiction?
- What is the effect of alcohol use, and how extensive is it? What is alcoholism?
- What are the effects of smoking cigarettes, and how extensive is cigarette smoking in the United States? How effective are strategies for quitting smoking?

REFLECT

- To discourage smoking, many governments now levy heavy taxes on cigarettes because of their negative health effects. Would you recommend that the U.S. government levy similar heavy taxes on fatty foods because of their negative health effects? Explain.

5 THE PATIENT AND THE HEALTH-CARE SETTING

Recognizing and Interpreting Symptoms

The Patient's Role

Socioeconomic Status and Ethnicity

Seeking Treatment

Adherence to Medical Advice and Treatment

Gender

Even if you manage stress effectively and practice good health habits, you cannot always prevent illness. Even athletes with the most superb physical conditioning, such as Lance Armstrong, fall sick. How do we recognize, interpret, and seek treatment for the symptoms of an illness? What is a patient's role? How good are people at adhering to medical advice and treatment? What roles do socioeconomic status, ethnicity, and gender play in health care?

Recognizing and Interpreting Symptoms

How do you know if you are sick? Each of us diagnoses how we feel and interprets the meaning of symptoms to decide whether we have a cold, the flu, a sexually transmitted disease, an ulcer, heart disease, and so on. However, many of us are not very accurate at recognizing the symptoms of an illness. For example, most people believe that they can tell when their blood pressure is elevated. The facts say otherwise. Most heart attack victims have never sought medical attention for cardiac problems. Many of us do not go to the doctor when the early warning signs of cancers, such as a lump or cyst, appear. Also, we are better at recognizing the symptoms of illnesses we are more familiar with, such as a cold or the flu, than of illnesses we are less familiar with, such as diabetes.

We use schemas, organized ways of looking at things that influence our expectations, to interpret information about ourselves in our world (Taylor, 2003). Our prior experiences with a particular symptom may lead us to interpret it based on the schema we have for that symptom. For example, an individual with a long record of sprained ankles might dismiss a swollen ankle as simply another sprain, not recognizing that she has a more serious injury—a fracture. By contrast, an individual who has

How much do you know about the services provided by your college's health center?

never had a sprained ankle might perceive the swelling as serious and pursue medical intervention.

Seeking Treatment

Whether or not you seek treatment for symptoms depends on your perception of their severity and of the likelihood that medical treatment will relieve or eliminate them. If your ankle is fractured so badly you cannot walk without assistance, you are more likely to seek treatment than if the fracture produces only a slight limp. Also, you may not seek treatment for a viral infection if you believe that no drug is available to combat it effectively. By contrast, you are more likely to seek treatment if you believe that a fungus infection on your foot can be remedied by antibiotics.

When people direct their attention outward, they are less likely to notice symptoms than when they direct their attention inward. For example, a woman whose life is extremely busy and full of distracting activities is less likely to notice a lump on her breast than is a woman who has a much less active life. People who have boring jobs, who are socially inactive, and who live alone are more likely to report symptoms than people who have interesting jobs, who have active social lives, and who live with others (Pennebaker, 1983). Perhaps people who lead more active lives have more distractions and focus their attention less on themselves than do people with quieter lives. Even for people who have active lives, situational factors influence whether they will be attentive to symptoms. In one experiment, joggers were more likely to experience fatigue and be aware of their running-related aches and pains when they ran on a boring course than when they ran on a more interesting and varied course (Pennebaker & Lightner, 1980). The boring course likely increased the joggers' tendency to turn their attention inward and, thus, recognize their fatigue and pain.

Belief systems are also a factor in responding to symptoms (Robbins, Powers, & Burgess, 2005). For example, Western people generally maintain a very positive, confident attitude about their health care. That attitude has only strengthened with advances in technological interventions. This belief in modern medicine may bring drawbacks, however. Many critics suggest that overconfidence in technological prowess may encourage excessive use of medical intervention. In addition, physicians in the United States are trained to regard illness and death as enemies to be fought. Our "medicalization" of many of life's processes may prevent us from seeing them as natural parts of the cycle of life.

The Patient's Role

Health psychology researcher Shelley Taylor (1979) identified two general types of patient roles. According to her analysis, some hospitalized individuals take on a "good patient" role, others a "bad patient" role:

- The **"good patient" role** describes a patient who is passive and unquestioning, and behaves properly. The positive consequences of this role include being well liked by the hospital staff, who in turn respond quickly to the "good patient's" emergencies. Like many roles, however, the "good patient" is somewhat superficial, and Taylor believes that, behind the facade, the patient may feel helpless, powerless, anxious, and depressed.
- The **"bad patient" role** describes an individual who complains to the staff, demands attention, disobeys staff orders, and generally misbehaves. The refusal to become helpless, and the accompanying anger, might have some positive consequences, because "bad patients" take an active role in their own health care. The negative side of "bad patient" behavior, however, is that it might aggravate such conditions as hypertension and angina, and it might stimulate staff members to ignore, overmedicate, or prematurely discharge the "bad patient."

How can the stress of hospitalization be relieved? Realistic expectations about the experience, predictable events, and social support reduce the stress of hospitalization. When doctors communicate clearly to their patients about the nature of the treatment procedures and what to expect when they are hospitalized, patients' confidence in the medical treatment also increases. In addition, as we learned in the discussion of stress and coping in chapters 4 and 5, the social network of individuals who deeply care about us goes a long way toward reducing stress. Visits, phone calls, cards, and flowers from family members and friends lift patients' spirits and improve their recovery from illness.

Adherence to Medical Advice and Treatment

An estimated one-third of patients fail to follow recommended treatments. Adherence depends on the disorder and the recommendation. Only about 15 percent of patients do not follow doctors' orders for tablets and ointments, but more than 90 percent of patients do not heed lifestyle advice, such as to stop smoking, to lose weight, or to stop drinking (DiNicola & DiMatteo, 1984).

Why do we pay money to doctors and then not follow their advice? We might not adhere to a doctor's recommendations because we are not satisfied with the quality of the care we are receiving and because we have our own theories about our health and do not completely trust the doctor's advice. This mistrust is exacerbated when doctors use very technical descriptions to inform patients about a treatment. Sometimes doctors do not give patients clear information or fully explain the risks of ignoring their orders (Ray, 2005). Sometimes patients might not communicate their concerns as clearly as they could, leaving doctors with an incomplete profile of the patient's concerns. To be motivated to stop smoking, to eat more nutritionally, or to stop drinking, patients need a clear understanding of the dangers involved in failure to adhere to the doctor's recommendation. Success or failure in treatment may depend on whether the doctor can convince patients that a valid, believable danger exists and can offer an effective, concrete strategy for coping with the problem (Ray, 2004).

Socioeconomic Status and Ethnicity

Individuals from low socioeconomic status backgrounds use medical services less than individuals from middle and high socioeconomic status backgrounds, in part because

"good patient" role Describes a patient who is passive and unquestioning and behaves properly.

"bad patient" role Describes an individual who complains to the staff, demands attention, disobeys staff orders, and generally misbehaves.

the low socioeconomic status individuals have less money to spend on health services (Taylor, 2003). Through Medicare, which is primarily for older adults, and Medicaid, which is primarily for individuals in poverty, the U.S. government aims to ensure that low-income individuals can obtain at least some health services.

Low income is not the only reason that low socioeconomic status individuals do not use health services as much as their higher-status counterparts. There are not as many medical services for the poor as for more well-to-do individuals and the services that are available to the poor are often inadequate and understaffed. Thus, many individuals living in poverty do not receive regular medical care and see physicians only on an emergency basis.

Cultural barriers to adequate health care include a lack of financial resources and poor language skills. Language is often a barrier for unacculturated Latinos in doctor-patient communications. In addition, members of ethnic minority groups are often unfamiliar with how the medical system operates, confused about the need to see numerous people, and uncertain about why they have to wait so long for service (Snowdon & Cheung, 1990).

Other barriers may be specific to certain cultures, reflecting differing ideas regarding what causes disease and how it should be treated. For example, there are Chinese herbalists and folk healers in every Chinatown in the United States. Depending on their degree of acculturation to Western society, Chinese Americans might go to either a folk healer or a Western doctor first, but generally they will consult a folk healer for follow-up care. Chinese medicines are usually used for home care. These include ginseng tea, boiled centipede soup for cancer, and eucalyptus oil for dizziness resulting from hypertension.

Native Americans sometimes view Western medicine as a source of crisis intervention, quick fixes for broken legs, or cures for other symptoms; but they might not rely on Western medicine as a source for treating the causes of disease or for preventing disease. They also are reluctant to become involved in care that requires long-term hospitalization or surgery.

Both Navajo Indians and Mexican Americans rely on family members to make decisions about treatment. Doctors who expect such patients to decide on the spot whether or not to undergo treatment will likely embarrass the patient or force the patient to give an answer that may lead to canceled appointments. Mexican Americans also believe that some illnesses are due to natural causes whereas others are due to supernatural causes. Depending on their level of acculturation, Mexican Americans may be disappointed and confused by doctors who do not show an awareness of how to treat diseases with supposed supernatural origins.

Health-care professionals can increase their effectiveness with ethnic minority patients by improving their knowledge of patients' attitudes, beliefs, and folk practices regarding health and disease. Recent research found that Chinese Americans and Vietnamese Americans wanted to discuss the use of non-Western medical practices with their providers but encountered considerable barriers (Ngo-Metzger & others, 2003). By integrating such information into Western medical treatments, health-care professionals can avoid alienating patients.

Gender

Women and men experience health and the health-care system differently (Murphy & Bennett, 2005; Paludi, 2002; Pin, 2003). Special concerns about women's health today focus on unintended and unwanted childbirth, abuse and violence, AIDS, the role of poverty in women's health, eating disorders, drug abuse, breast diseases, reproductive health, and the discrimination of the medical establishment against women.

During the 1960s and 1970s, the women's health movement in the United States worked to ensure that women would have more control over their health care. In consciousness-raising and self-help groups throughout the country, women educated themselves about their bodies, reproductive rights, nutrition, and health care. One possible outcome of the women's health movement is that recent research shows that female patients, especially young women, are more demanding in interactions with health-care professionals than male patients are (Foss & Sundby, 2003).

Despite a growing number of female physicians, medicine continues to be a male-dominated profession. All too often in this male-dominated world, women's physical complaints are devalued, interpreted as "emotional" rather than physical in origin, and dismissed as trivial. In one study, physicians described their men and women patients differently. The men were characterized as very direct, very logical, good decision makers, and rarely emotional. In contrast, the women were characterized as very excitable in minor crises, more easily influenced, less adventurous, less independent, very illogical, and even very sneaky (Broverman & others, 1972).

Gender bias has also affected medical research (Geller, Graf, & Dyson-Washington, 2003; Rabinowitz & Sechzur, 1994). Most medical research has been conducted with men, and frequently the results are generalized to women without apparent justification. For example, in a large-scale study involving 22,000 physicians that demonstrated the beneficial effect of an aspirin every other day on coronary heart disease, not a single woman was included in the study. Women's health advocates continue to press for greater inclusion of women in medical studies to reduce the bias that has characterized research on health. They also hope that the medical establishment will give increased attention to women's health concerns and treat women in less prejudiced and biased ways (Strickland, 1988).

There are also concerns about the failure of many men to adequately use the health-care system. For example, male college students are less likely than female college students to consult a physician or health-care provider when they have unfamiliar physical symptoms, and less likely to go to scheduled health checkups (Courtenay, McCreary, & Merighi, 2002). In many instances, this gender difference continues through the adult years, with males being less likely to go to a medical doctor when they have an illness.

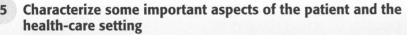

Review and Reflect

5 Characterize some important aspects of the patient and the health-care setting

REVIEW

- How good are individuals at recognizing and interpreting symptoms?
- What factors influence whether individuals seek treatment?
- What are "good patient" and "bad patient" roles?
- To what extent do individuals adhere to medical advice and treatment?
- What roles do socioeconomic status and ethnicity play in health care?
- How is gender involved in the health-care system?

REFLECT

- How good are you at recognizing and interpreting illness symptoms? Are you a "good patient" or a "bad patient"? Explain. To what extent do you adhere to medical advice and treatment?

Reach Your Learning Goals

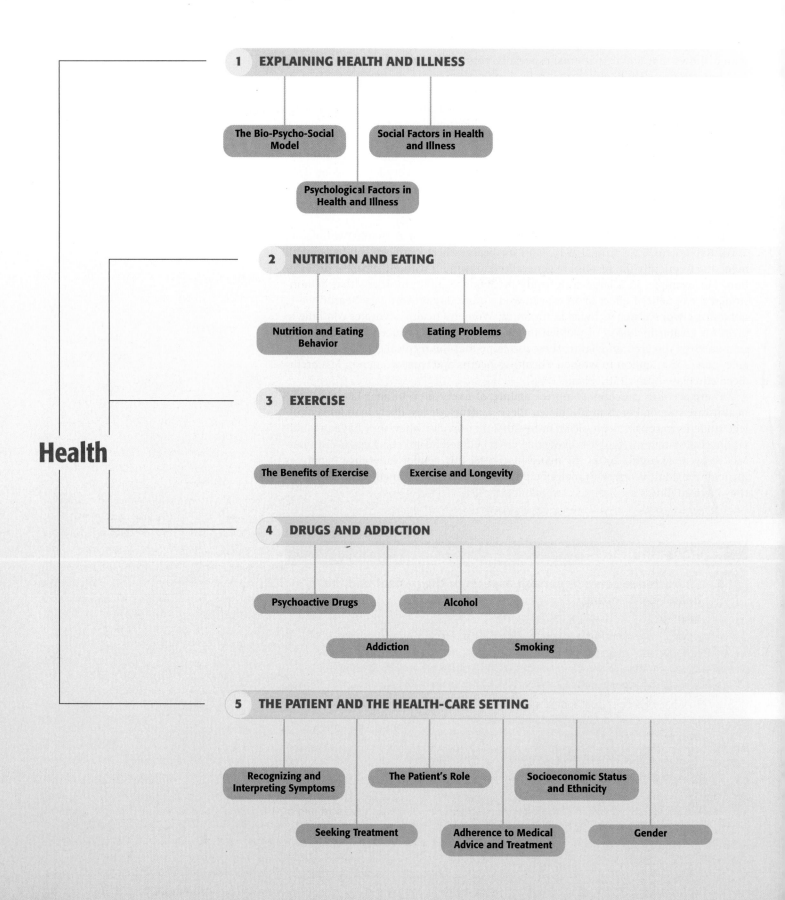

Health

1 EXPLAINING HEALTH AND ILLNESS

- The Bio-Psycho-Social Model
- Social Factors in Health and Illness
- Psychological Factors in Health and Illness

2 NUTRITION AND EATING

- Nutrition and Eating Behavior
- Eating Problems

3 EXERCISE

- The Benefits of Exercise
- Exercise and Longevity

4 DRUGS AND ADDICTION

- Psychoactive Drugs
- Alcohol
- Addiction
- Smoking

5 THE PATIENT AND THE HEALTH-CARE SETTING

- Recognizing and Interpreting Symptoms
- The Patient's Role
- Socioeconomic Status and Ethnicity
- Seeking Treatment
- Adherence to Medical Advice and Treatment
- Gender

Summary

1 **_Describe some key factors in health and illness_**

- Health is best understood as a combination of biological, psychological, and social factors. In the biological approach, health problems are caused by the function of the individual's body.
- Among the psychological factors that have been proposed as causes of health problems are a lack of self-control, emotional turmoil, and negative thinking.
- Social factors include cross-cultural variations, socioeconomic factors, and poverty. African American and Latinos often are more vulnerable to health problems than non-Latino Whites, in many instances because they are more likely to live in low-income circumstances.

2 **_Discuss nutrition, eating behavior, and eating problems_**

- The Food Guide Pyramid, which consists of recommended daily servings of food with an emphasis on consuming more bread, cereals, rice, pasta, vegetables, and fruits than milk, meats, fats, oils, and sweets, has been the guide used by dieters and nutritionists since 1992. Proposed revisions include less emphasis on a one-size-fits-all model with tailored information for individuals of different ages and activity levels. Cultural variations in eating behavior include lower fat intake by Japanese than Americans, which is correlated with greater incidence of breast, colon, and prostate cancer in Americans. Food restriction is associated with longevity, but a balanced diet is usually recommended for older adults. Controversy surrounds whether antioxidant vitamins can reduce the risk of disease.
- Obesity is a serious and pervasive problem for many individuals with more than 60 percent of U.S. adults classified as either overweight or obese. Factors involved in obesity include heredity, leptin, set point and metabolism, environmental factors, and ethnicity and gender. Ironically, while obesity has been increasing in the United States, dieting has become an obsession. Issues in dieting include restrained eaters, as well as the use and misuse of diets. Anorexia nervosa is an eating disorder that involves the relentless pursuit of thinness through starvation. Bulimia nervosa is an eating disorder in which the individual consistently follows a binge-and-purge eating pattern. Both anorexia nervosa and bulimia nervosa are far more common in females than males.

3 **_Summarize the role of exercise in health_**

- Aerobic exercise is sustained exercise—jogging, swimming, or cycling, for example—that stimulates heart and lung activity. Exercise produces both physical and psychological advantages, such as lowered risk of heart disease and lower anxiety.
- Regular exercise can lead to a healthier life as a middle-aged and older adult, and increase longevity.

4 **_Explain drug use and addiction_**

- Psychoactive drugs are substances that act on the nervous system to alter states of consciousness, modify perceptions, and change moods. Psychoactive drugs can provide temporary adaptation but also carry a high price tag that can involve drug dependence, personal disarray, and a predisposition for serious, sometimes fatal diseases. The three main classifications of psychoactive drugs are depressants, stimulants, and hallucinogens.
- Addiction may involve psychological dependence or physical dependence or both. Psychological dependence exists when a person is preoccupied with a drug for emotional reasons, such as stress. Physical dependence exists when discontinuing use of a drug creates unpleasant, significant changes in physical functioning and behavior. Two models of addiction are the disease model and the life-process model.
- Alcohol is a drug that slows down the brain's activities. Around the world and within the United States, use of alcohol varies with religion, gender, and other social characteristics. Binge drinking often increases in college and it is linked with a number of problems, including missing classes, injuries, troubles with police, and having unprotected sex. Alcoholism is a disorder that involves long-term, repeated, uncontrolled, compulsive, and excessive use of alcoholic beverages and that impairs the drinker's health and social relationships.
- Smoking cigarettes has been linked to an increased risk for many diseases, including cancer and heart disease. The percentage of U.S. adults who smoke has declined dramatically since the 1960s. Strategies to quit smoking vary in effectiveness, ranging from a 30 percent success rate for nicotine spray and the antidepressant Bupropion ST to much less success for going "cold turkey."

5 **_Characterize some important aspects of the patient and the health-care setting_**

- Many people are not very accurate at diagnosing the symptoms of illness. When our attention is directed outward, we are less likely to detect symptoms than when it is directed inward.
- Seeking treatment depends on our perception of the severity of the symptoms and the likelihood that medical treatment will reduce or eliminate the symptoms.
- Some hospitalized patients take on the "good patient" role (passive and unquestioning, and behaves properly) and the "bad patient" role (demands attention, disobeys

staff orders, and generally misbehaves). There may be some positive consequences in the "bad patient" role.

- Approximately one-third of patients do not follow treatment recommendations. Compliance varies with the disorder and the treatment recommendation, whether we are satisfied with the quality of care we are receiving, and our own theories about why we are sick and how we can get well. Clearer doctor-patient communication is required for improved compliance.
- Individuals from lower socioeconomic status backgrounds use medical services less than individuals from middle and high socioeconomic status backgrounds. There are not as many medical services for the poor as for more well-to-do individuals. There also are cultural barriers to health care for some cultural groups, such as Asian Americans and Native Americans.
- Women and men experience the health-care system differently. Special concerns about women's health focus on such matters as the role of poverty and discrimination of the medical establishment against women. There also are concerns about men, especially their lower use of medical care than women.

Key Terms

bio-psycho-social health model 499
leptin 506
basal metabolism rate (BMR) 507
restrained eaters 507
anorexia nervosa 510
bulimia nervosa 510
aerobic exercise 511
psychoactive drugs 514
depressants 514
stimulants 514
hallucinogens 514
psychological dependence 515
physical dependence 515
disease model of addiction 515
life-process model of addiction 515
alcoholism 518
aversive conditioning 520
"good patient" role 523
"bad patient" role 523

Resources for Improving Your Adjustment

SELF-HELP BOOKS

The New Fit or Fat

(1991) by Covert Bailey. Boston: Houghton Mifflin.

This book describes ways to become healthy by developing better diet and exercise routines. Bailey argues that the basic problem for many people is not losing weight but gaining weight. Information is provided about strategies for getting started on a weight loss program and a sensible low-fat diet.

Dying to Be Thin (updated edition)

(2001) by Ira Sacker and Marc Zimmer. New York: Warner Books.

This book is about anorexia nervosa and bulimia nervosa. It provides information for an individual with anorexia or bulimia and their families and friends, as well as sections on personal histories and resources. This book was given 4 (of 5) stars in the national survey of self-help books (Norcross, Santrock, & others, 2003).

The Aerobics Program for Total Well-Being

(1985) by Kenneth Cooper New York: Bantam.

Kenneth Cooper created the concept of aerobic exercise, and in this book he describes a number of different types of exercise that will enable you to reap the physical and psychological benefits of aerobic exercise.

Alcoholics Anonymous (4th ed.)

(2001). New York: Alcoholics Anonymous World Services.

This book is the basic text for Alcoholics Anonymous (AA) self-help groups. Information is provided about what AA self-help groups are like, and extensive personal testimonies by AA members from many different walks of life are included. This book was given 4 of 5 stars in the national survey of self-help books.

NATIONAL SUPPORT ORGANIZATIONS

Healthy Weight Network
420 South 14th St.
Hettinger, ND 58639
701-567-2646
http://www.healthyweight.net

Overeaters Anonymous
P.O. Box 44020
Rio Rancho, NM 87174-4020
505-891-2664
http://www.overeatersanonymous.org

Take Off Pounds Sensibly (TOPS)
P.O. Box 07360
4575 South Fifth Street
Milwaukee, WI 53207-02360
800-932-8677
http://www.tops.org

National Association of Anorexia Nervosa and Associated Disorders
P.O. Box 7
Highland Park, IL 60035
847-831-3438
http://www.anad.org

National Eating Disorders Association
603 Stewart Street Suite 803
Seattle, WA 98101
800-931-2237
http://nationaleatingdisorders.org

Alcoholics Anonymous
Box 459 Grand Central Station
New York, NY: 10163
212-870-3400
http://www.AA.org

Cocaine Anonymous
3740 Overland Ave., Suite C
Los Angeles, CA 90034-6337
For local chapters: 800-347-8988
http://www.ca.org

 **E-Learning Tools**

To help you master the material in this chapter, you will find a number of valuable study tools on the Student CD-ROM and the Online Learning Center.

SELF-ASSESSMENT

In Text

You can complete these self-assessments in the text:
- Self-Assessment 16.1: *Is My Lifestyle Good for My Health?*
- Self-Assessment 16.2: *What Are My Eating Attitudes and Behaviors Like?*
- Self-Assessment 16.3: *Do I Abuse Drugs?*

Additional Self-Assessments

Complete these self-assessments on the Online Learning Center:
- *My Eating Log*
- *My Exercise Log*
- *My Drinking Diary*

THINK CRITICALLY

To practice your critical thinking skills, complete these exercises on the Online Learning Center:
- *An Alcohol Detour* gets you to think about your values and drinking.
- *The George Burns Paradox* focuses on why George Burns was able to live to be 100 years of age.
- *The Addicted Society* explores what the term "addiction" means.

APPLY YOUR KNOWLEDGE

1. Which foods are high in antioxidants?

Your textbook states that researchers believe that foods that are high in antioxidants may ward off the effects of aging. Which foods do you think these might be? After you have made your list of "best guesses" do an Internet search for "antioxidant foods." The findings might surprise you!

2. Your text states that exercise wards off depression and helps weight loss by lowering a person's set point. Which exercises burn the most calories? Go to www.yahoo.com or www.google.com and search for "exercise and calories."

Compare the calorie use per hour against the number of calories burned in sedentary activities—like sitting at the computer.

3. Who's got an eating disorder?

Which famous people have had eating disorders? Go to www.yahoo.com or www.google.com and search for "eating disorders famous people."

What are the demands of the roles that these people experience? Are they similar to or different from the social messages to which we are all exposed? Do you think that the "be thin" message applies to female celebrities and male celebrities equally? If not, how are they different?

 VIDEO SEGMENT

Addiction exacts a high cost, physically and psychologically, but it can be overcome. Watch the video "Alcohol Addiction" to learn more about alcoholism and its treatment.

Appendix *Self-Assessment Scoring and Interpretation*

Chapter 1

SELF-ASSESSMENT 1.1: *My Beliefs About Psychic Phenomena*

Interpretation

If you believe in any of these phenomena, psychologists urge you to be more skeptical. Remember that thinking like a scientist means that you demand to see the evidence for such phenomena as channeling, crystal power, and plant consciousness. There is no scientific evidence for the existence of any of the listed phenomena, only personal anecdotes and coincidences—and those do not meet science's criteria of objectivity and public verifiability.

SELF-ASSESSMENT 1.2: *My Subjective Well-Being*

Scoring

31 to 35 points: Extremely satisfied with my life

26 to 30 points: Satisfied with my life

21 to 25 points: Slightly satisfied with my life

20 points: Neutral

15 to 19 points: Slightly dissatisfied with my life

10 to 14 points: Dissatisfied with my life

5 to 9 points: Extremely dissatisfied with my life

Interpretation

If you scored 25 points or lower, spend some time reflecting on why you are not happier and more satisfied with your life. A good starting point is to examine the numerous factors that we described earlier in the chapter that are linked with happiness and life satisfaction. These included having good social relationships, especially one or more good friends and a positive romantic relationship; being mentally healthy and coping effectively with stress; having high levels of certain psychological and personality characteristics, such as creativity, self-esteem, optimism, extraversion, and self-control; a spirituality and faith that embodies social support, purpose, and possibly religious attendance; liking other people, having other people like you, and being altruistic; being satisfied with your health; and having enough money to buy life's necessities. No single one of these factors can ensure your happiness and in most cases the happiest people aren't going to have all of them. However, happy people often have a combination of some of these factors and if you want to be happier you likely will benefit from developing a plan to change your life in the direction of having more of these characteristics.

Chapter 2

SELF-ASSESSMENT 2.1: *Evaluating My Self-Efficacy*

Scoring

Total your score for the 10 items. Total scores can range from 10 to 40. The higher your score, the more general self-efficacy you are likely to have.

Interpretation

The items in this scale are designed to assess your general self-efficacy—your belief that you can master your world and have positive outcomes in your life. The items are not tied to any specific situation. The higher your score, the more general self-efficacy you are likely to have. If you scored 31 or higher, you likely have a reasonably strong sense of self-efficacy. If you scored 20 or lower, think of ways that you can improve your self-efficacy.

This measure has been used internationally for more than two decades. Researchers have found that it is linked to adaptation after life changes and is an indicator of quality of life at any point in time (Scholz & others, 2002).

SELF-ASSESSMENT 2.2: *Am I Internally or Externally Controlled?*

Scoring

For each odd-numbered item that you answered no and each even-numbered item that you answered yes, give yourself one point. Thus, your locus of control score can range from 0 to 14.

Interpretation

The higher your score, the more likely you are to be internally controlled and take charge of what happens to you. The lower your score, the more likely you are externally controlled and let your environment or luck control your life. You are more likely to be better adjusted if you are internally controlled. If you scored 7 or lower, think critically about yourself and how you can gain more control over your life.

SELF-ASSESSMENT 2.3: *How Introverted or Extraverted Am I?*

Scoring

To arrive at your score for extraversion, give one point for each of the following items answered yes: #1, 2, 4, 5, 8, 9, 14, 16, 17, 19, and 20. Then, give yourself one point for each of the following items answered no: #3, 6, 7, 10, 11, 12, 13, 15, 18. Add up all the points to arrive at a total score.

Interpretation

Your total score should be between 0 and 20 inclusive. The higher your score, the higher your extraversion (and, of course, the lower your introversion). Therefore, high scores suggest extraversion and low scores suggest introversion.

Chapter 3

SELF-ASSESSMENT 3.1: *My Self-Esteem*

Scoring

Add up your scores for items 1, 2, 4, 6, and 7 = _____

Now reverse your scores on items 3, 5, 8, 9, and 10 (that is, if you had a 1—strongly agree; give yourself a 4 instead—if you had a 2 on item 1, give yourself a 3, and so on) = _____

Next, total your scores for the two sets of items to get your overall self-esteem score: _____

Interpretation

Your score can range from 10 to 40. If you scored 35 to 40 points, you likely have very high self-esteem. If you scored 30 to 34 points you likely have high self-esteem. If you scored 20 to 29 points, you likely have low self-esteem. And if you scored 10 to 19 points, you likely have very low self-esteem.

If your total self-esteem score was below 30 points, think about ways that you can improve your self-esteem. Go back and review the strategies described in chapter 3 for improving self-esteem. Also, if you feel that you have low self-esteem, consider talking with a counselor at your college about your self-esteem.

SELF-ASSESSMENT 3.2: *Do I Have Narcissistic Tendencies?*

Scoring

1. Give yourself one point for every true statement in items 1–9. This is your score on the leadership/authority section.
2. Give yourself one point for every true statement in items 10–18. This is your score on the self-absorption/self-admiration section.
3. Give yourself one point for every true statement in items 19–29. This is your score on the superiority/arrogance section.

4. Give yourself one point for every true statement in items 30–37. This is your score on the exploitiveness/entitlement section.
5. Total your score from (1) through (4) above; this is your score on the narcissistic personality inventory.

Interpretation

Narcissistic personality disorder/pathological narcissism occurs only with extreme manifestations of the previous beliefs and behaviors. If you endorsed many of the statements, your narcissistic characteristics reflect a personality style that is characterized by self-absorption, self-serving bias, egocentricism, high sense of self-importance and uniqueness, exhibitionism, entitlement, and preoccupation with grandiose fantasies. Most students will endorse at least a few of these statements. Some of the results of narcissistic beliefs are the denial of personal blame for failed outcomes; increases in racism, sexism, nationalism, or political and religious beliefs; more selfish marital interactions; and self-absorption. Levels of self-esteem may be healthy or pathological.

SELF-ASSESSMENT 3.3: *What Is My Identity?*

Scoring and Interpretation

If you checked "diffused" or "foreclosed" for any areas, take some time to reflect about what you need to do to move into a "moratorium" identity status in those areas. Likewise, if you checked "moratorium" for any areas, what aspects of this dimension of identity are you exploring? Are there other aspects of the dimension you need to explore? A good exercise is to write about your identity statuses for each of the dimensions and reflect on how satisfied you are with the statuses and the extent to which you need to engage in further exploration. Also describe how much your identity has changed in recent years for each of the dimensions and what brought about the change.

SELF-ASSESSMENT 3.4: *What Are My Values?*

Scoring and Interpretation

Review which values you checked as characteristic of you. How did you get these values? Did you learn them from your parents, friends, teachers, or other individuals? Have your values changed since you began going to college? If so, how? Also think about the extent to which your behavior supports your values. Are you living up to your values? Do they reflect who you really are?

SELF-ASSESSMENT 3.5: *Spiritual Well-Being*

Scoring and Interpretation

The spiritual well-being scales measure two main areas: (1) religious well-being and (2) existential well-being. The religious scale refers to religion and one's relationship with God, the existential scale to meaning in life and questions about the nature of one's existence. To obtain your spiritual well-being score, add up your responses to items 1, 5, 9, and 13; reverse the scores for items 3, 7, 11, 15, 17, and 19 (that is change the 1 to a 6, the 2 to a 5, the 3 to a 4, and so on). Combine these two subtotals to get your overall spiritual well-being score.

To obtain your existential well-being score, add up your responses to items 2, 6, 12, 16, and 18; reverse the scores for items 4, 8, 10, 14, and 20. Combine these two subtotals to obtain your overall existential well-being score.

Your overall scores on each of these two scales can range from 10 to 60. On each of the scales, a score of 40 or higher reflects well-being (religious or existential).

Chapter 4

SELF-ASSESSMENT 4.1: *How Vulnerable Am I to Stress?*

Scoring

To get your score, add up the figures and subtract 20.

Interpretation

A score below 10 indicates excellent resistance to stress. A score of 10 to 29 suggests moderate resistance to stress. A score over 30 indicates some vulnerability to stress; you are seriously vulnerable if your score is over 50. You can make yourself less vulnerable by reviewing the items on which you scored three or higher and trying to modify them. Notice that nearly all of them describe situations and behaviors over which you have a great deal of control. Concentrate first on those that are easiest to change—for example, eating a hot, balanced meal daily and having fun at least once a week—before tackling those that seem difficult.

SELF-ASSESSMENT 4.2: *Stressful Events in My Life*

Scoring and Interpretation

The total number that you added up may predict the frequency of serious illness you will experience in the coming year. If your life events score totals 300 points or more, you have an 80 percent chance of having a significant illness in the coming year. If your total score is 299 to 150, you have a 50 percent chance of having a major illness. If your total score is 149 or less, your risk of significant illness decreases to 30 percent.

Keep in mind, in interpreting your life events total score, that such event checklists don't take into account how you cope with such events. Some people who experience stressful life events cope and adjust well to them, others do not.

Chapter 5

SELF-ASSESSMENT 5.1: *Am I Emotionally Intelligent?*

Scoring and Interpretation

Add up your scores for all 17 items. My Total Emotional Intelligence Score is: _____ . If you scored 75–85, you probably

are very emotionally intelligent, someone who is emotionally self-aware, manages emotions effectively, knows how to read emotions, and has positive relationships with others. If you scored 65–74, you probably have good emotional intelligence, but there probably are some areas that you still need to work on. Look at the items on which you scored 3 or below to see where you need to improve. If you scored 45–64, you likely have average emotional intelligence. Give some serious thought to working on your emotional life. Examine your emotional weaknesses and strive to improve them. If you scored 44 or below, you likely have below-average emotional intelligence. If your scores are in the average or below-average range, examine the resources available for improving your emotional intelligence. You might contact the counseling service at your college for some recommendations. It is a sign of strength, not a weakness, when you recognize the importance of calling on resources for improving your life skills.

SELF-ASSESSMENT 5.2: *My Coping Skills*

Interpretation

Examine the coping strategies that you rated 4 and 5 for the past year. Are these the coping strategies that you think served you best in handling stress? Now look at the coping strategies you rated 4 and 5 that you plan to use the most in the coming year. Are these the same ones you used last year the most or do you plan to use some coping strategies more frequently?

Write out a coping strategy plan for the coming year and include in the plan those coping strategies that you want to use more often in your life as you experience stressful circumstances.

Chapter 6

SELF-ASSESSMENT 6.1: *Am I a High or Low Self-Monitorer?*

Scoring

Give yourself one point for each of questions 1, 5, and 7 that you answered F. Give yourself one point for each of the remaining questions that you answered T. Add up your points.

Interpretation

If you are a good judge of yourself and scored 7 or above, you are probably a high-self-monitoring individual; 3 or below, you are probably a low-self-monitoring individual.

Chapter 7

SELF-ASSESSMENT 7.1: *How Much Do I Self-Disclose?*

Scoring and Interpretation

Notice which areas seem easier for you to talk about—the ones with the 1s and 2s. Notice which items you consistently remain quiet or lie about. How much energy are you devoting to keep these things hidden?

Notice to whom you talk and from who you are hiding. Are there any obvious patterns along family lines? Along gender lines?

SELF-ASSESSMENT 7.2: *What Is My Communication Style?*

Scoring

Total up the number of your aggressive, manipulative, passive, and assertive marks. Whichever style has the most marks is your dominant personal style of interacting with others in conflicts. If you did not mark the assertive category 10 or more times, you would benefit from working on your assertiveness.

Interpretation

The middle score equals 60. Scores below 60 represent lower levels of assertiveness and scores over 60 represent higher levels of assertiveness. Use your responses to individual items to determine areas in which you could profit from being more assertive.

SELF-ASSESSMENT 7.3: *How Argumentative Am I?*

The Argumentativeness scale has two separate sections: one that measures a tendency to approach arguments and one that measures the tendency to avoid them.

Scoring

Score each of the two sections separately. Approaching arguments can be scored by adding your answers to questions 2, 4, 7, 9, 11, 13, 15, 17, 18, and 20. Avoiding arguments is scored by adding your answers to questions 1, 3, 5, 6, 8, 10, 12, 14, 16, and 19.

Interpretation

If your score on the approaching section is higher than the avoidance section, you may tend to move toward arguments more than avoid arguments.

Chapter 8

SELF-ASSESSMENT 8.1: *What Type of Love Do I Have?*

Scoring

Add up your score for each of the three areas of love: 1–15 (intimacy), 16–30 (passion), and 31–45 (commitment).

Interpretation

Following are the average scores of a group of women and men (average age = 31) who either were married or in a close relationship:

Intimacy	Passion	Commitment	Percentile
93	73	85	15
102	85	96	30
111	98	108	50
120	110	120	70
129	123	131	85

The fourth column (percentile) shows the percentage of adults who scored at that level or above. Thus, if your intimacy score is 122, your intimacy is greater than 70 percent of the adults whose scores are averaged here.

SELF-ASSESSMENT 8.2: *What Is My Attachment Style?*

Interpretation

Checking the first item indicates that you likely have a secure attachment style.

Checking the second item suggests that you likely have an avoidant attachment style.

Checking the third item indicates that you have an ambivalent attachment style.

Researchers have found that a secure attachment style is often linked with positive aspects of romantic and social relationships. If you feel you have an avoidant or an ambivalent attachment style, consider talking with a counselor or psychologist at your college university's counseling office to explore ways to change your attachment style to more of a secure attachment style.

SELF-ASSESSMENT 8.3: *Am I Vulnerable in My Close Relationship?*

Scoring

Give yourself one point for each true response to the questions.

Interpretation

13–16: You are very vulnerable to being in a lopsided relationship, which may result in hurt feelings in the future. You should seriously examine the contour and direction of your relationship with your partner. For you to continue with your present situation is almost certain to be a waste of time and energy.

9–12: You are vulnerable to being taken advantage of. Stop and ask yourself if you are getting out of this relationship what you are putting into it.

5–8: You are somewhat vulnerable to being hurt. Your relationship probably has potential but needs to be evaluated. You and your partner should discuss your future to determine what type of lifestyle you both desire.

1–4: You do not seem vulnerable to being dominated in your relationship. Keep the statements to which you responded *true* in mind and openly discuss them with your partner.

SELF-ASSESSMENT 8.4: *Am I Lonely?*

Scoring

First, reverse the scores you circled for items 1, 4, 5, 6, 9, 10, 15, 16, 19, and 20. That is, each of these items should be reversed before adding up your scores (1 becomes 4, 2 becomes 3, 3 becomes 2, and 4 becomes 1). Then, total your score for all 20 items.

Interpretation

If you scored 70 or above, you likely have good social connections and experience little loneliness. If you scored 60–69, you likely experience quite a bit of loneliness. If you scored 59 or below, you likely experience a lot of loneliness. If you are a lonely individual, a counselor at your college can likely help you develop some good strategies for reducing your loneliness and becoming more socially connected. Also review the strategies for reducing loneliness described in this chapter.

Chapter 9

SELF-ASSESSMENT 9.1: *What Characteristics Do I Desire in a Potential Mate?*

Scoring

Following is how a large sample of males and females from a number of different cultures rated the importance of 18 characteristics in a potential mate. How do the characteristics you most and least desire in a potential mate compare with the ordering of the characteristics in the cross-cultural study? A rank of 1 is the most important and 18 is the least important.

Characteristic	Rank	
	Males	Females
Mutual attraction-love	1	1
Emotional stability and maturity	2	2
Dependable character	3	3
Pleasing disposition	4	4
Education and intelligence	5	5
Good health	6	9
Good looks	7	13
Sociability	8	8
Desire for home and children	9	7
Refinement, neatness	10	12
Ambition and industriousness	11	6
Similar education	12	10
Good cook and housekeeper	13	16

continued

Characteristic	Rank	
	Males	Females
Favorable social status or rating	14	14
Similar religious background	15	15
Good financial prospect	16	11
Chastity (no prior sexual intercourse)	17	18
Similar political background	18	17

SELF-ASSESSMENT 9.2: *My Knowledge of Marital Myths and Realities*

Scoring

1. False	5. True	9. False	13. False
2. True	6. True	10. False	14. False
3. False	7. False	11. False	15. False
4. False	8. False	12. True	

SELF-ASSESSMENT 9.3: *How Well Do I Know My Partner?*

Scoring

Total the number of times you checked the yes boxes.

Interpretation

15 or more yes answers: You have a lot of strength in your relationship. Congratulations!

8 to 14: This is a pivotal time in your relationship. There are many strengths you can build upon but there are also some weaknesses that need your attention.

7 or fewer: Your relationship may be in serious trouble. If this concerns you, you probably still value the relationship enough to try to get help.

Chapter 10

SELF-ASSESSMENT 10.1: *Am I a Perfectionist?*

Scoring

Add up your scores with 1 = Never, 2 = Rarely, 3 = Sometimes, and 4 = Often. My total perfectionism score: _____ .

Interpretation

If your total score is 10 to 20 points, you likely are not a perfectionist; 21 to 30 points, you likely have average perfectionist tendencies; and 31 to 40 points, you likely are a perfectionist. If you scored in the high range (31 to 40 points), go back and analyze each statement. To which ones did you respond *often.* Those statements are irrational beliefs, which you need to challenge.

SELF-ASSESSMENT 10.2: *Career Goal-Setting*

Needs no additional scoring. Use the exercise as a guide for your career goals. Another activity related to goal-setting is to set goals for 20 years from now, 10 years from now, and 5 years from now, being as concrete as possible.

SELF-ASSESSMENT 10.3: *What Are My Academic and Personal Skills Strengths and Weaknesses?*

Scoring

Add up your totals for each of the four skills areas with 1 = Very Much Unlike Me, 2 = Somewhat Unlike Me, 3 = Somewhat Like Me, and 4 = Very Much Like Me:

Basic Skills Score: _____

Thinking Skills Score: _____

Personal Qualities Skills Score: _____

People Skills Score: _____

Interpretation

Your Basic Skills score can range from 5 to 20. You likely have good basic skills if your score is from 17 to 20, average basic skills if your score is from 12 to 16, and weak basic skills if your score is below 12.

Your Thinking Skills score can range from 4 to 16. You likely have good thinking skills if your score is from 13 to 16, average thinking skills if your score is from 9 to 12, and weak thinking skills if your score is below 9.

Your Personal Qualities Skills score can range from 3 to 12. You likely have good personal qualities skills if your score is from 10 to 12, average personal qualities skills if your score is 7 to 9, and weak personal qualities if your score is 6 or below.

Your People Skills score can range from 3 to 12. You likely have good people skills if your score is from 10 to 12, average people skills if your score is 7 to 9, and weak people skills if your score is 6 or below.

For those areas in which you scored in the average or weak categories, think about the extent these are skills that you will need to be successful in the career(s) you want to pursue. If you think they are relevant to your career plans, think about how you can improve them. A good strategy is to talk with a study skills and/or career counselor at your college about this. Also look at the descriptions for each of the categories, each of which includes multiple skills. You likely are better at some of these skills than others. For example, in the Self-Management category of Personal Qualities you might be better at assessing your own knowledge and skills accurately than you are at setting specific and reasonable personal goals. This type of detailed analysis can further help you to detect which skills are your strengths and weaknesses.

Chapter 11

SELF-ASSESSMENT 11.1: *My View of Life*

Scoring and Interpretation

Look at the pattern of your scores for each of the following aspects of life:

Aspect of Life	Items
Experimentation/Possibilities	1, 2, 4, 16, 21
Identity Exploration	12, 23, 24, 25, 26, 27, 28
Feeling "In-Between"	29, 30, 31
Self-Focused	5, 7, 10, 15, 19, 22
Other-Focused	13, 14, 18
Negativity/Instability	3, 6, 8, 9, 11, 17, 20

If most of your check parks were in the strongly agree (4) and somewhat agree (3) categories for a particular aspect of life (such as experimentation/possibilities), you likely have that particular characteristic. This survey was especially developed to assess the characteristics of emerging adulthood, which occurs from 18 to 25 years of age. Thus, if you are in the 18 to 25 year range, you likely have many of the characteristics in the survey. However, if you are not in the 18 to 25 age range and you place check marks in the strongly agree and somewhat agree categories, don't consider that to be a sign of poor adjustment. These characteristics can describe people at any point in their development as an adult, although for many individuals they are most pronounced during the emerging adulthood period of 18 to 25 years of age.

SELF-ASSESSMENT 11.2: *My College Adjustment*

Interpretation

Look at your responses to each of the items in Self-Assessment 11.2. For any items that you checked somewhat unlike you or very much unlike you, spend some time reflecting and analyzing what you can do to improve your college adjustment in those areas. You don't always have to do this by yourself. The personal counseling and academic study skills services at your college are likely to be excellent resources for helping your college adjustment.

SELF-ASSESSMENT 11.3: *Can I Live to Be 100?*

Scoring

This self-assessment gives you a rough guide for predicting your longevity. The basic life expectancy for males is 73 and for females it is 80. Write down your basic life expectancy: _____ . If you are in your 50s or 60s, add 10 years to this figure because you have already proved to be a durable individual: _____ . If you are over 60 and active, you can even add two more years: _____ . Now total your score from the self-assessment in terms of the years you added or subtracted for various items. Add or subtract this number to the previous figure to obtain your total life expectancy: _____ .

Chapter 12

SELF-ASSESSMENT 12.1: *My Beliefs About Gender Equality*

Scoring and Interpretation

Look at the pattern of your responses. The more statements you agreed with, the more you are likely to believe in equality between men and women. For example, if you agreed with 8 to 10 of the statements, you likely have strong feelings about the importance of gender equality. The more statements you disagreed with, the more likely you believe in the inequality of men and women. If you disagreed with 8 to 10 of the statements, you likely have strong feelings that males and females are not equal.

SELF-ASSESSMENT 12.2: *My Attitudes Toward Women*

Scoring

Score the following questions using the scale A = 0, B = 1, C = 2, and D = 3: 1, 4, 5, 10, 13, 14, 15, 16, 17, 19, 20, 22, and 23. For questions 2, 3, 6, 7, 8, 9, 11, 12, 18, 21, 24, and 25, use the scale A = 3, B = 2, C = 1, D = 0. Add your answers to get your score.

Interpretation

Higher scores indicate more liberal attitudes, and lower scores indicate more traditional views. Scores range between 0 and 75. Scores lower than 36 suggest relatively traditional views, with most women scoring more liberal than most men.

SELF-ASSESSMENT 12.3: *My Gender-Role Classification*

Scoring and Interpretation

Items 1, 4, 7, 10, 11, 12, and 14 are masculine items. Items 2, 3, 5, 6, 8, 9, and 13 are feminine items. Look at the pattern of your responses. If you mainly checked 3 and 4 for the masculine items and mainly 1 and 2 for the feminine items, you likely are characterized by masculinity. If you mainly checked 3 and 4 for the feminine items and 1 and 2 for the masculine items, you likely are characterized by femininity. If you mainly checked 3 and 4 for both the masculine items and the feminine items, you likely are characterized by androgyny. If you mainly checked 1 and 2 for both the masculine and feminine items, your gender-role classification is likely undifferentiated.

Chapter 13

SELF-ASSESSMENT 13.1: *What Are My Sexual Attitudes?*

Scoring

Total your scores for items 2, 7, and 13 to arrive at your communication score. Total your scores for items 1, 11, 12, and 14 to obtain your premarital relations score. Total your scores for items 3, 6, and 10 for your oral sex score. Total your scores for items 5, 9, and 15 for your masturbation score. And total your scores for items 4, 8, and 16 for your homosexual attitudes score.

Interpretation

The following chart gives you an idea of how liberal, undecided, or conservative you are in these five aspects of sexual attitudes:

	Liberal	Undecided	Conservative
Sexual communication	12–15	7–11	3–6
Premarital sex	16–20	9–15	4–8
Oral sex	12–15	7–11	3–6
Masturbation	12–15	7–11	3–6
Homosexual attitudes	12–15	7–11	3–6

SELF-ASSESSMENT 13.2: *Satisfaction for My Partner and Myself*

Scoring

First, be sure you have responded to all the items.

Second, you have to rescore some of the items because they are worded in a different direction than the others. Change the scores for items 1, 2, 3, 9, 10, 12, 17, 19, 21, 22, 23 as follows:

An answer of 5 is changed to a 1

4 is changed to a 2

3 remains a 3

2 is changed to a 4

1 is changed to a 5

Third, after rescoring, add these scores for all 24 items and from the total subtract 20. This is your **total score:** _____ .

Interpretation

Fourth, the possible range of scores is from 0 to 100. This exercise, of course, is not absolute but only an indication of the magnitude of sexual satisfaction in a two-person relationship. A low score would indicate a very small or no sexual problem existing in your relationship with this person and a high score would indicate the presence of a sexual problem to some degree. Keep in mind that a "sexual problem" will be relative to the personality dynamics of the individuals involved in the relationship. It could be helpful to go back over your responses and look for ways to improve the sexual aspect of your relationship with your partner.

SELF-ASSESSMENT 13.3: *My Awareness of Sexual Myths*

Scoring and Interpretation

Most people think that one or more of the items are true, but all 12 of the items are myths. For those items that you missed, go to the related resources and websites that accompany this chapter to read about the topics.

Chapter 14

SELF-ASSESSMENT 14.1: *Am I Depressed?*

Scoring

For items 4, 8, 12, and 16, give yourself a 3 each time you checked Rarely or None, 2 each time you checked Some or a

Little, 1 each time you checked Occasionally or Moderate, and a 0 each time you checked Most or All of the Time. For the remaining items, give yourself a 0 each time you checked Rarely or None, 1 each time you checked Some or a Little, 2 each time you checked Occasionally or Moderate, and 3 each time you checked Most or All of the time. Total up your score for all 20 items.

Interpretation

If your score is around 7, then you are like the average male in terms of how much depression you have experienced in the past week. If your score is around 8 or 9, your score is similar to the average female's. Scores less than the average for either males or females indicate that depression probably has not been a problem for you during the past week. If your score is 16 or more and you are bothered by your feelings, you might benefit from professional help.

Keep in mind, though, that self-diagnosis is not always accurate and to adequately diagnose anyone, the professional judgment of a qualified clinician is required.

Chapter 15

SELF-ASSESSMENT 15.1: *Do I Have Irrational Beliefs?*

Scoring

This test is scored by adding up your answers. Scores range from 9 to 81.

Interpretation

Higher scores indicate a greater degree of irrational belief systems. The middle range on the test is in the mid 40s.

SELF-ASSESSMENT 15.2: *Do I Need to See a Therapist?*

As indicated in the Self-Assessment, there are no hard and fast rules about when an individual should go to a psychotherapist for help with their problems. However, if you checked yes to any of the 10 items, you might benefit from going to a psychotherapist.

Chapter 16

SELF-ASSESSMENT 16.1: *Is My Lifestyle Good for My Health?*

Scoring and Interpretation

Add up the numbers in your answers. Total Lifestyle score: _____ . If you scored 90 to 100, you likely are making lifestyle choices that enhance your health. If you scored 80 to 89, you are doing well in many areas. Look at the statements you marked 1, 2, or 3 for areas in which you likely could improve. If you scored 61 to 79, there likely are many aspects of your lifestyle you could improve, and your lifestyle likely is negatively affecting your health. Examine the items you marked 1, 2, or 3 for areas in which you likely could improve. If you scored 60 or below, your lifestyle likely is placing you at high risk for health problems. Carefully review your responses, focusing on the statements you marked 1 or 2 and make a commitment to improve your lifestyle in those areas.

SELF-ASSESSMENT 16.2: *What Are My Eating Attitudes and Behaviors Like?*

Scoring and Interpretation

This self-assessment is used by the psychological counseling services at the College of New Jersey as a screening device to determine if a student has an eating disorder. According to the counseling services, if you checked three or more of the statements in Self-Assessment 16.2, it could be a sign that you have an eating disorder or the beginning of one. If you do, you may want to talk with a health counselor at your college about your responses on this self-assessment.

SELF-ASSESSMENT 16.3: *Do I Abuse Drugs?*

Scoring and Interpretation

Researchers have found that college students who respond yes to the items in Self-Assessment 16.3 are more likely to have substance abuse problems than those who answer no. If you responded yes to even 1 of the 13 items on this drug-screening test, you likely are a substance abuser and should go to your college health or counseling center for help with your problem.

Glossary

abnormal behavior Behavior that is deviant, maladaptive, or personally distressful. 426

acculturative stress The negative consequences that result from contact between two distinctive cultural groups. 129

active-behavioral strategies Coping responses in which individuals take some type of action to improve their problem situation. 145

active-cognitive strategies Coping responses in which individuals actively think about a situation in an effort to adjust more effectively. 145

actual self Your representation of the attributes you believe or you actually possess. 82

adjustment The psychological process of adapting to, coping with, and managing the challenges of everyday life. 5

aerobic exercise Sustained exercise—jogging, swimming, or cycling, for example—that stimulates heart and lung activity. 511

affectionate love Also called *companionate love*, the type of love that occurs when individuals desire to have the other person near and have a deep, caring affection for the person. 240

agoraphobia A cluster of fears centered around public places and being unable to escape or to find help should one become incapacitated. 432

AIDS A sexually transmitted infection that is caused by the *human immunodeficiency virus (HIV)*, which destroys the body's immune system. 413

alcoholism A disorder that involves long-term, repeated, uncontrolled, compulsive, and excessive use of alcoholic beverages and that impairs the drinker's health and social relationships. 518

Alzheimer disease A progressive, irreversible brain disorder characterized by a gradual deterioration of memory, reasoning, language, and, eventually, physical function. 340

ambivalent attachment style The caregiver is inconsistently available and when present often overbearing with affection. These infants are typically anxious because they can't predict when and how the caregiver will respond to their needs. They may cling anxiously to the caregiver and fight against the closeness by pushing away. 241

androgens The class of hormones that predominate in males and are produced by the testes in males and by the adrenal glands in both males and females. 396

androgyny The presence of a high degree of feminine and masculine characteristics in the same individual. 378

anorexia nervosa An eating disorder that involves the relentless pursuit of thinness through starvation. 510

antianxiety drugs Commonly known as *tranquilizers*. These drugs reduce anxiety by making individuals calmer and less excitable. 463

antidepressant drugs Drugs that regulate mood. 464

antipsychotic drugs Powerful drugs that diminish agitated behavior, reduce tension, decrease hallucinations, improve social behavior, and produce better sleep patterns in individuals who have a severe psychological disorder, especially schizophrenia. 465

anxiety disorders Psychological disorders that include these features: motor tension, hyperactivity, and apprehensive expectations and thoughts. 431

approach/approach conflict A conflict in which the individual must choose between two attractive stimuli or circumstances. 123

approach/avoidance conflict A conflict involving a single stimulus or circumstance that has both positive and negative characteristics. 124

archetypes The name Jung gave to the emotionally laden ideas and images in the collective unconscious that have rich meaning for all people. 43

attitudes Evaluations of people, objects, and ideas. 175

attributions Thoughts about why people behave the way they do. 173

authoritarian parenting A restrictive, punitive parenting style in which the parent exhorts the child to follow the parent's directions and to respect work and effort. Firm limits and controls are placed on the child, and little verbal exchange is allowed. This style is associated with children's socially incompetent behavior. 279

authoritative parenting A parenting style that encourages children to be independent but still places limits and controls on their actions. Extensive verbal give-and-take is allowed, and parents are warm and nurturant toward the child. This style is associated with children's socially competent behavior. 279

aversive conditioning A behavior therapy technique that consists of repeated pairings of an undesirable behavior with aversive stimuli to decrease the behavior's rewards. 520

aversive conditioning A classical conditioning treatment that consists of repeated pairings of the undesirable behavior with aversive stimuli to decrease the behavior's rewards. 473

avoidance coping strategies Responses to keep stressful circumstances out of their awareness. 145

avoidance/avoidance conflict A conflict in which the individual must choose between two unattractive stimuli or circumstances. 124

avoidant attachment style The caregiver is distant or rejecting, failing to respond to the infant's bids to establish intimacy. Although these infants want to be close to the caregiver, they suppress this desire. 241

B

"bad patient" role Describes an individual who complains to the staff, demands attention, disobeys staff orders, and generally misbehaves. 523

basal metabolism rate (BMR) The minimal amount of energy an individual uses in a resting state. 507

becoming parents and a family with children The third stage in the family life cycle. Adults who enter this stage move up a generation and become caregivers to the younger generation. 273

behavior Everything that people do that can be directly observed. 15

behavior modification The application of operant conditioning principles to change human behaviors, especially to replace unacceptable, maladaptive behaviors with acceptable, adaptive behaviors. 474

behavior therapies Use principles of learning to reduce or eliminate maladaptive behavior. 472

bibliotherapy The fancy term for using self-help books. 26

big five factors of personality The "supertraits" that consist of openness, conscientiousness, extraversion, agreeableness, and neuroticism (or emotional stability). 61

bio-psycho-social health model States that health is best understood in terms of a combination of biological, psychological, and social factors. 499

biofeedback The process by which individuals' muscular or visceral activities are monitored by instruments, then the information from the instruments is given (fed back) to the individuals so they can learn to voluntarily control their physiological activities. 163

biological therapies Treatments to reduce or eliminate the symptoms of psychological disorders by altering the way an individual's body functions. 463

bipolar disorder A mood disorder characterized by extreme mood swings that include one or more episodes of mania. 441

bisexual A person who is sexually attracted to people of both sexes. 400

bulimia nervosa An eating disorder in which the individual consistently follows a binge-and-purge eating pattern. 510

burnout A state of physical and emotional exhaustion that includes a hopeless feeling, chronic fatigue, and low energy. 124

bystander effect The tendency for an individual who observes an emergency to help less when other people are present than when the observer is alone. 184

C

catatonic schizophrenia A type of schizophrenia that is characterized by bizarre motor behavior, which sometimes takes the form of a completely immobile stupor. 449

catharsis The psychoanalytic term for the release of emotional tension a person experiences when reliving an emotionally charged and conflicting experience. 469

catharsis The release of anger or aggressive energy by directly or vicariously engaging in anger or aggression; the catharsis hypothesis states that behaving angrily or watching others behave angrily reduces subsequent anger. 126

channel The mode of communication delivery. 203

chlamydia A sexually transmitted infection caused by the bacterium *Chlamydia trachomitis*. 412

classical conditioning A learning process in which a neutral stimulus becomes associated with a meaningful stimulus and acquires the capacity to elicit a response similar to the response to the meaningful stimulus. 46

client-centered therapy Rogers' humanistic therapy in which the therapist provides a warm, supportive atmosphere to improve the client's self-concept and encourage the client to gain insight about problems. 471

clinical and counseling psychology The specialization in psychology that involves evaluating and treating people who have psychological problems. 24

cognitive appraisal Lazarus' term for individuals' interpretation of the events in their lives as harmful, threatening, or challenging and their determination of whether they have the resources to effectively cope with the events. 117

cognitive developmental theory of gender The theory that children's gender typing occurs after they think of themselves as boys and girls. Once they consistently conceive of themselves as male or female, children prefer activities, objects, and attitudes that are consistent with this label. 370

cognitive restructuring Process of replacing thoughts, ideas, and beliefs that maintain an individual's problems. 147

cognitive therapies Emphasize that individuals' cognitions or thoughts are the main source of abnormal behavior and psychological problems. 475

cognitive-behavior therapy Consists of a combination of cognitive therapy and behavior therapy; self-efficacy is an important goal of cognitive-behavior therapy. 478

collective unconscious Jung's term for the impersonal, deepest layer of the unconscious mind, shared by all human beings because of their common ancestral past. 42

collectivism Emphasizes values that serve the group by subordinating personal goals to preserve group integrity and relationships. 63

conformity Involves a change in a person's behavior to coincide more closely with a group standard. 179

connotation The subjective meaning of words. 206

consensual validation Our own attitudes and behavior are supported when someone else's attitudes and behavior are similar to ours. 236

consummate love In Sternberg's view, the strongest form of love that consists of passion, intimacy, and commitment. 240

contexts The historical, economonic, social, and cultural factors and settings that influence us. 6

control group The group that is as much like the experimental group as possible and is treated in every way like the experimental group except for the manipulated factor. 20

coping Involves managing taxing circumstances, expending effort to solve life's problems, and seeking to master or reduce stress. 143

correlational research Research in which the goal is to describe the strength of the relationship between two or more events or characteristics. 21

couples therapy Therapy with married or unmarried couples whose major problem is their relationship. 482

critical thinking The process of thinking reflectively, productively, and evaluating the evidence. 8

cross-cultural studies Involve a comparison of a culture with one or more other cultures. 7

crystallized intelligence An individual's accumulated information and verbal skills. 343

culture Refers to the behavior patterns, beliefs, and all other products of a group of people that are passed on from generation to generation. 6

D

date or acquaintance rape Coercive sexual activity directed at someone with whom the victim is at least casually acquainted. 415

decline stage Super's label for the period of 65 years and older when individuals' career activity declines and retirement takes place. 304

decoding The act of understanding messages. 203

defense mechanisms The ego's protective methods for reducing anxiety by unconsciously distorting reality. 40

dementia A global term for any neurological disorder in which the primary symptoms involve a deterioration of mental functioning. 339

denotation The objective meaning of words. 206

dependent variable The factor that can change in an experiment in response to changes in the independent variable. 20

depressants Drugs that slow down the nervous system, body functions, and behaviors; alcohol, barbiturates, and tranquilizers are examples. 514

depressive disorders Mood disorders in which the individual suffers depression without ever experiencing mania. 438

development The pattern of change in human capabilities that begins at conception and continues through the life span. 327

diathesis-stress model A model of schizophrenia that proposes a combination of biogenetic disposition and stress as the cause of the disorder. 450

discrimination An unjustified negative or harmful action toward a member of a group simply because the person belongs to that group. 189

disease model of addiction Describes addictions as biologically based, lifelong diseases that involve a loss of control over behavior and require medical and/or spiritual treatment for recovery. 515

disorganized schizophrenia A type of schizophrenia in which an individual has delusions and hallucinations that have little or no recognizable meaning. 449

dissociative amnesia A dissociative disorder involving extreme memory loss caused by extensive psychological stress. 436

dissociative disorders Psychological disorders that involve a sudden loss of memory or change in identity. 436

dissociative fugue A dissociative disorder in which the individual not only develops amnesia but also unexpectedly travels away from home and establishes a new identity. 436

dissociative identity disorder (DID) Formerly called *multiple personality disorder,* this is the most dramatic but least common dissociative disorder; individuals suffering from this disorder have two or more distinct personalities. 436

door-in-the-face strategy Illustrates the principle of reciprocation; the strategy begins with an extreme request that is bound to be rejected, then the person retreats to a smaller request—the one that was desired all along. 184

double standard A belief that many sexual activities are acceptable for males but not females. 399

dream analysis The psychotherapeutic technique used by psychoanalysts to interpret a person's dream. Psychoanalysts believe dreams contain information about the individual's unconscious thoughts and conflicts. 469

DSM-IV-TR *Diagnostic and Statistical Manual of Mental Disorders,* Fourth Edition, Text Revision; the American Psychiatric Association's major classification of psychological disorders. 428

dysthymic disorder A depressive disorder that is generally more chronic and has fewer symptoms than major depressive disorder. 439

E

early adulthood The developmental period that begins in the late teens or early twenties and lasts through the thirties. 327

ecological theory Bronfenbrenner's theory that people's lives are influenced by five environmental systems: microsystem, mesosystem, exosystem, macrosystem, and chronosystem. 6

ego The Freudian structure of personality that deals with the demands of reality. 39

elaboration likelihood model A model that attempts to explain the relation between emotional and rational appeals through two routes: a central route and a peripheral route. 178

electroconvulsive therapy (ECT) Commonly called *shock therapy,* this treatment is used mainly to treat severely depressed individuals. It causes a seizure in the brain. 466

emerging adulthood The term for the transition from adolescence to adulthood, about 18 to 25 years of age, that is characterized by experimentation and exploration. 329

emotion regulation The process by which individuals control which emotions they experience, when they experience them, and how they experience and show them. 157

emotion-focused coping Lazarus' term for responding to stress in an emotional manner, especially by using defense mechanisms. 144

emotional intelligence The ability to perceive and express emotion, understand emotion, and regulate emotion. 158

empirically keyed test Relies on its items to predict some criterion. 68

empowerment The term used for assisting individuals to develop skills they need to control their own lives. 153

empty nest syndrome A decrease in marital satisfaction and increase in feelings of emptiness brought about by the children's departure. 275

encoding The act of producing messages. 203

Erikson's theory Proposes that eight stages of development unfold as people go through the life span with each stage consisting of a unique developmental task that confronts individuals with a crisis that must be resolved. 345

establishment stage Super's term for the period from 25 to 45 years of age when individuals pursue a permanent career and attain a stable pattern of work in a particular career. 303

estrogens The class of hormones that predominate in females and are produced by the ovaries. 396

ethnic identity An enduring aspect of the self that includes a sense of membership in an ethnic group, along with the attitudes and feelings related to that membership. 93

ethnicity Is rooted in cultural heritage, nationality characteristics, race, religion, and language. 7

ethnocentrism The tendency to favor one's own group and believe it is superior to other groups. 189

evolutionary psychology theory Emphasizes that adaptation during the evolution of humans produced psychological differences between males and females. In this theory, primarily because of their differing roles in reproduction, males and females faced different pressures as they were evolving. 368

exhibitionism A psychosexual disorder in which individuals expose their sexual anatomy to others to obtain sexual gratification. 411

experiment A carefully regulated procedure in which one or more factors believed to influence the behavior being studied are manipulated while all other factors are held constant. 19

experimental group The group whose experience is manipulated in an experiment. 20

exploration stage Super's stage (15 to 24 years of age) when individuals become more likely to take their needs, interests, capacities, values, and opportunities into account when considering career choices. 302

extinction In operant conditioning, this process occurs when a previously reinforced behavior is no longer reinforced and the tendency to perform the behavior decreases. 48

extrinsic motivation Involves external incentives such as rewards and punishments. 293

family at midlife The fifth stage in the family life cycle, a time of launching children, linking generations, and adapting to midlife changes. 275

family in later life The sixth and final stage in the family life cycle, involving retirement and, in many families, grandparenting. 277

family therapy Group therapy with family members. 482

family with adolescents The fourth stage of the family life cycle, in which adolescent children push for autonomy and seek to develop their own identities. 274

fantasy stage Ginzberg's stage for the childhood years during which careers are perceived in an unrealistic manner. 302

fetishism A psychosexual disorder in which an individual relies on inanimate objects or a specific body part for sexual gratification. 410

fluid intelligence A person's ability to reason abstractly. 343

foot-in-the-door strategy Obtaining compliance with a small request in order to obtain compliance later with a larger request. 184

formal operational stage Piaget's fourth and final stage of cognitive development, which he believed emerges between 11 and 15 years of age. It involves an increase in abstract and logical thinking. 342

free association The psychoanalytic technique of having individuals say aloud whatever comes to mind. 469

friendships Close relationships that involve intimacy, trust, acceptance, mutual liking, and understanding. 237

fundamental attribution error The tendency for observers to overestimate the importance of a person's traits and underestimate the importance of situations when they seek to explain someone else's behavior. 173

gender Involves the psychological and sociocultural dimensions of being female or male. 8

gender The psychological and social dimension of being female or male. 367

gender roles Sets of expectations that prescribe how females or males should think, act, or feel. 367

gender schema theory The theory that gender typing emerges as children gradually develop gender schemas of what is gender appropriate and gender inappropriate in their culture. 370

gender stereotypes General beliefs about females and males. 372

gender-role transcendence Thinking about ourselves and others as people, not as masculine, feminine, or androgynous. 379

general adaptation syndrome (GAS) Selye's term for the common effects on the body when stressors persist. The GAS consists of three stages: alarm, resistance, and exhaustion. 115

generalized anxiety disorder An anxiety disorder that consists of persistent anxiety over at least one month; the individual with this disorder cannot specify the reasons for the anxiety. 431

generativity versus stagnation Erikson's seventh stage that he believed occurs in middle adulthood in which individuals leave a legacy of themselves to the next generation (generativity) or do little or nothing for the next generation (stagnation). 347

genital herpes A sexually transmitted infection caused by a large family of viruses with different strains. 413

Gestalt therapy Perls' humanistic therapy in which the therapist challenges clients to help them become more aware of their feelings and face their problems. 472

gesture A motion of the limbs or body made to convey a message to someone else. 223

glass ceiling The invisible barrier to career advancement that prevents women and ethnic minorities from holding managerial or executive jobs regardless of their accomplishments and merits. 316

"good patient" role Describes a patient who is passive and unquestioning and behaves properly. 523

gonorrhea A sexually transmitted infection that is commonly called the "drip" or the "clap" and is caused by a bacterium from the gonococcus family. 412

grief The emotional numbness, disbelief, separation anxiety, despair, sadness, and loneliness that accompany the loss of someone we love. 356

growth stage Super's label for the period in which physical and cognitive growth takes place from birth through adolescence. 302

hallucinogens Drugs that modify an individual's perceptual experiences and produce hallucinations; LSD, marijuana, and ecstasy are examples. 514

hardiness A personality style characterized by a sense of commitment (rather than alienation), control (rather than powerlessness), and a perception of problems as challenges (rather than threats). 127

hearing A physiological sensory process in which auditory sensations are received by the ears and transmitted by the brain. 207

hierarchy of needs Maslow's concept that states that individuals' main needs follow this sequence: physiological, safety, love and belongingness, and self-actualization. 57

hormonal stress theory States that aging in the body's hormonal system can lower resilience to stress and increase the likelihood of disease. 338

HPV A virus (human papillomavirus) that causes genital warts. 413

human sexual response pattern Masters and Johnson developed this concept to describe four phases of physiological responses as individuals masturbated or had sexual intercourse: excitement, plateau, orgasm, and resolution. 395

humanistic perspectives Stress a person's capacity for personal growth, freedom to choose one's own destiny, and positive human qualities. 55

humanistic therapies Encourage people to understand themselves and to grow personally. The humanistic therapies are unique in their emphasis on self-healing capacities. 471

hypothesis A prediction that can be tested. 17

id The Freudian structure of personality that consists of instincts and is the individual's reservoir of psychic energy. 39

ideal self Your representation of the attributes you would like to ideally possess—that is, a representation of your hopes, aspirations, and wishes. 82

identity A sense of integration of self in which different parts come together in a unified whole. 89

identity achievement Marcia's term for the status of individuals when they have undergone an identity crisis and made a commitment. 90

identity diffusion Marcia's term for the status of individuals when they have not yet experienced an identity crisis and have not made commitments. 90

identity foreclosure Marcia's term for the status of individuals when they have made a

commitment but have not experienced an identity crisis. 90

identity moratorium Marcia's term for the status of individuals when they are in the midst of an identity crisis but have not made a clear commitment to an identity. 90

identity versus identity confusion stage Erikson's fifth of eight developmental stages that occurs during the adolescent and emerging adult years at which time individuals are faced with deciding who they are, what they are all about, and where they are going in life. 89

impression management (self-presentation) The process of acting in a way that presents a desired image. 175

incest Sex between people who are close relatives. Incest is virtually a universal taboo. 417

independent variable The manipulated, influential, experimental factor in an experiment. 20

individual psychology The term for Adler's approach, which views people as motivated by purposes and goals, being creators of their own lives. 43

individualism Gives priority to personal goals rather than group goals; it emphasizes values that serve the self, such as feeling good, personal achievement and distinction, and independence. 63

indulgent parenting A parenting style in which parents are highly involved with their children but place few demands or controls on them. This is associated with children's social incompetence, especially a lack of self-control. 279

inferences Conclusions that people draw from behavior. 15

informational social influence The influence other people have on us because we want to be right. 180

insight therapy Encourages insight and self-awareness; includes both psychodynamic and humanistic therapies, because they encourage insight and self-awareness. 471

integrative therapy A combination of techniques from different therapies based on the therapist's judgment of which particular techniques will provide the greatest benefit for the client. 479

integrity versus despair Erikson's eighth stage that he believed occurs in late adulthood in which individuals engage in a life review that is either positive (integrity) or negative (despair). 349

interpersonal communication An ongoing transactional process that involves at least two individuals, each of whom acts as both sender and receiver, encoding and decoding messages, sometimes simultaneously. The messages can be sent through verbal or nonverbal channels with noise and context possibly influencing their accuracy. 205

intimacy versus isolation Erikson's sixth stage that he believed occurs in early adulthood in which individuals face the developmental task of forming intimate relationships with others or becoming socially isolated. 345

intrinsic motivation Is based on internal factors such as self-determination, curiosity, challenge, and effort. 293

jealousy The fear of perceived possibility of losing someone else's exclusive love. 247

Johari Window A model of self-disclosure that helps us understand the proportion of information about ourselves that we and others are aware of. 208

Kübler-Ross' stages of dying Consists of these five stages: denial and isolation, anger, bargaining, depression, and acceptance. 351

late adulthood The developmental period that begins in the sixties and lasts until death. 328

launching The process in which youth move into adulthood and exit their family of origin. 273

learned helplessness Occurs when individuals are exposed to aversive stimulation, such as prolonged stress, over which they have no control. The inability to avoid such aversive stimulation can produce an apathetic state of helplessness. 443

leaving home and becoming a single adult The first stage in the family life cycle and that involves launching. 273

leisure The pleasant times after work when individuals are free to pursue activities and interests of their own choosing such as hobbies, sports, or reading. 318

leptin A protein that is involved in satiety (the condition of being full to satisfaction) and released by fat cells resulting in decreased food intake and increased energy expenditure. 506

life expectancy The number of years that will probably be lived by the average person born in a particular year. 336

life span The upper boundary of a species' life, the maximum number of years any member of the species has been documented to live. 336

life-process model of addiction Describes addiction not as a disease but as a habitual response and a source of gratification or security that can be understood best in the context of social relationships and experiences. 515

listening The psychological process of interpreting and understanding what someone says. 207

lithium A drug that is widely used to treat bipolar disorder. 465

locus of control Refers to whether individuals believe that the outcomes of their actions depend on what they do (internal control) or on events outside of their personal control (external control). 52

maintenance stage In Super's view, a period from about 45 to 64 years of age during which individuals continue their career and maintain their career status. 303

major depression A mood disorder in which the individual is deeply unhappy, demoralized, self-derogatory, and bored. The person does not feel well, loses stamina easily, has poor appetite, and is listless and unmotivated. Major depression is so widespread that it has been called the "common cold" of mental disorders. 352

major depressive disorder (MDD) A depressive disorder in which the individual experiences a major depressive episode with the symptoms lasting at least two weeks. 438

masochism A psychosexual disorder in which individuals derive sexual gratification from being subjected to physical pain inflicted by others or themselves. 411

matching hypothesis Although people may prefer a more attractive person in the

abstract, in the real world, they end up choosing someone close to their own level of attractiveness. 236

meaning-making coping Involves drawing on beliefs, values, and goals to change the meaning of a stressful situation, especially in cases of chronic stress that may resist problem-focused efforts. 144

medical model A biological approach that describes psychological disorders as medical diseases with a biological origin. 426

meditation A system of mental exercises that help the individual to attain bodily mental control and well-being, as well as enlightenment. 161

mental processes Consist of thoughts, feelings, and motives that each person experiences privately but cannot be observed directly. 15

message The information being delivered from the sender to the receiver. 203

meta-analysis Statistical analysis that combines the results of many different studies. 486

middle adulthood The developmental period from approximately 40 years of age to about 60. 328

Minnesota Multiphasic Personality Inventory (MMPI) The most widely used and researched empirically keyed self-report personality test. 68

mood disorders Psychological disorders in which there is a disturbance in mood (prolonged emotion that colors the individual's entire emotional state). Two main types are the depressive disorders and bipolar disorder. 438

morita therapy Emphasizes accepting feelings, knowing one's purposes, and most important, doing what needs to be done. 100

narcissism A self-centered and self-concerned approach in dealing with others. 87

neglectful parenting A parenting style in which the parent is very uninvolved in the child's life. It is associated with children's social incompetence, especially a lack of self-control. 279

new couple Forming the new couple is the second stage in the family life cycle. Two individuals from separate families of origin unite to form a new family system. 273

noise Environmental, physiological, and psychological factors that decrease the likelihood a message will be accurately encoded or decoded. 203

nonverbal communication Messages that are transmitted from one person to another by other than linguistic means, including body communication, spatial communication, and paralanguage. 219

nonverbal leakage The communication of true emotions through nonverbal channels even when the person tries to conceal the truth verbally. 220

normative social influence The influence to conform that other people have on us because we seek their approval or seek to avoid their disapproval. 180

obedience Behavior that complies with the explicit demands of the individual in authority. 181

observational learning Also called imitation or modeling, the learning process that occurs when a person observes and imitates someone else's behavior. 49

obsessive-compulsive disorder (OCD) An anxiety disorder; the individual has anxiety-provoking thoughts that will not go away (obsession) and/or urges to perform repetitive, ritualistic behaviors to prevent or produce some future situation (compulsion). 434

Oedipus complex In Freud's theory, the young child's development of an intense desire to replace the parent of the same sex and enjoy the affections of the opposite-sex parent. 41

operant conditioning Also called instrumental conditioning, this learning process occurs when the consequences of the behavior change the probability of the behavior's occurrence. 47

ought self Your representation of the attributes you believe you should possess—that is, a representation of your duties, obligations, and responsibilities. 82

P

panic disorder An anxiety disorder marked by the recurrent sudden onset of intense apprehension or terror. 432

paralanguage The nonlinguistic aspects of verbal communication, such as the rapidity of speech, the volume of speech, and the pitch of speech. 226

paranoid schizophrenia A type of schizophrenia that is characterized by delusions of reference, grandeur, and persecution. 449

paraphilias Psychosexual disorders in which the source of an individual's satisfaction is an unusual object, ritual, or situation. 410

paraphrasing A concise restatement of the essence of the speaker's own words. 208

pedophilia A psychosexual disorder in which the sex object is a child and the intimacy involves manipulating the child's genitals. 411

personality A pattern of enduring, distinctive thoughts, emotions, and behaviors that characterize the way an individual adapts to the world. 37

personality disorders Chronic, maladaptive cognitive-behavioral patterns that are thoroughly integrated into the individual's personality. 451

personality type theory Holland's view that it is important to develop a match or fit between an individual's personality type and the selection of a particular career. 307

pheromones Scented substances that are powerful sexual attractants in some animals. 397

phobic disorder Commonly called *phobia*, an anxiety disorder in which the individual has an irrational, overwhelming, persistent fear of a particular object or situation. 433

physical dependence Exists when discontinuing the use of a drug creates unpleasant, significant changes in physical functioning and behavior. 515

possible selves Individuals' conceptions of what they might become, including what they would like to become and what they are afraid of becoming. 82

post-traumatic stress disorder (PTSD) An anxiety disorder that develops through exposure to a traumatic event, severely oppressive situations, severe abuse, and natural and unnatural disasters. 132

postformal thought Thought that is reflective, relativistic, and contextual; provisional; realistic; and open to emotions and subjective. 342

prejudice An unjustified negative attitude toward an individual based on the individual's membership in a group. 189

problem-focused coping Lazarus' term for the strategy of squarely facing one's troubles and trying to solve them. 144

projective test Personality assessment tool that presents individuals with an ambiguous stimulus and then asks them to describe it or tell a story about it; based on the assumption that the ambiguity of the stimulus allows individuals to project their feelings, desires, needs, and attitudes onto it. 65

proxemics The study of the communicative function of space, especially how people unconsciously structure their space. 224

psychiatry A branch of medicine practiced by physicians who have specialized in abnormal behavior and psychotherapy. 24

psychoactive drugs Substances that act on the nervous system to alter states of consciousness, modify perceptions, and change moods. 514

psychoanalysis Freud's psychotherapeutic technique for analyzing an individual's unconscious thoughts. Freud believed that clients' current problems could be traced to childhood experiences, involving conflicts about sexuality. 469

psychoanalytic theory of gender Stems from Freud's view that preschool children develop a sexual attraction to the opposite-sex parent, then, at 5 to 6 years of age, renounce the attraction because of anxious feelings, subsequently identifying with the same-sex parent and unconsciously adopting the same-sex parent's characteristics. 369

psychodynamic perspectives View personality as being primarily unconscious (that is, beyond awareness) and as developing in stages. Most psychodynamic perspectives emphasize that early experiences with parents play an important role in sculpting the individual's personality. 38

psychodynamic therapies Stress the importance of the unconscious mind, extensive interpretation by the therapist, and the role of the early childhood years. The goal of the psychodynamic therapies is to help individuals recognize their maladaptive ways of coping and the sources of their unconscious conflicts. 468

psychological dependence Exists when a person is preoccupied with a drug for emotional reasons, such as the reduction of stress. 515

psychological moratorium Erikson's terms for the gap between childhood security and adult autonomy. 89

psychology The scientific study of behavior and mental processes. 15

psychoneuroimmunology The scientific field that explores connections among psychological factors (such as attitudes and emotions), the nervous system, and the immune system. 118

psychosexual dysfunctions Disorders that involve impairments in the sexual response pattern, either in the desire for gratification or the inability to achieve it. 409

psychosurgery A biological therapy that involves removal or destruction of brain tissue to improve the individual's adjustment. 467

psychotherapy The process used by mental health professionals to help individuals recognize, define, and overcome their psychological and interpersonal difficulties. 463

punishment Refers to a consequence that decreases the likelihood that a behavior will occur. 48

R

random assignment When researchers assign participants to experimental and control groups by chance. 20

rape Forcible sexual intercourse with a person who does not give consent. 414

rapport talk Conversation aimed at establishing connections and negotiating relationships. 214

rational-emotive behavior therapy (REBT) Based on Albert Ellis' assertion that individuals develop a psychological disorder because of their beliefs, especially those that are irrational and self-defeating; the goal of REBT is to get the person to eliminate self-defeating beliefs by rationally examining them. 475

realistic stage Ginzberg's stage for the age period of 18 to 25 when individuals rid themselves of their fantasies about careers and make pragmatic decisions. 302

reciprocal determinism Bandura's view that behavior, environment, and person/cognitive factors interact to create personality. 50

reflective listening A strategy in which the listener restates the feelings or content of the speaker's message in a way that indicates acceptance and understanding. 208

reinforcement The learning process by which a stimulus or event that follows a behavior increases the probability that the behavior will occur again. 47

report talk Talk that is designed to give information, which includes public speaking. 214

resistance The psychoanalytic term for the person's unconscious defense strategies that prevent the analyst from understanding the person's problems. 469

restrained eaters Individuals who chronically restrict their food intake to control their weight. 507

romantic love Also called *passionate love,* the type of love that has strong components of sexuality and infatuation, and often predominates in the early part of a love relationship. 240

romantic script Sex is synonymous with love. If a person develops a relationship and falls in love, it is acceptable to have sex whether married or not. 399

Rorschach inkblot test A widely used projective test; it uses an individual's perception of the inkblots to determine his or her personality. 66

S

sadism A psychosexual disorder in which individuals derive sexual gratification from inflicting pain on others. 411

schizophrenia A severe psychological disorder that is characterized by highly disordered thought processes. 448

scientific method A four-step process of conceptualizing a problem, collecting research information (data), analyzing data, and drawing conclusions. 17

secure attachment style The caregiver is responsive to the infant's needs and shows positive emotions when interacting with the infant. Securely attached infants trust their caregiver, don't fear that they will be abandoned, and explore their world in positive ways. 241

selective optimization with compensation theory States that successful self-regulation involves three factors: selectivity, optimization, and compensation. As individuals get older, they face losses so they are likely to adjust best when they reduce performance in areas in which they are not competent (selectivity), perform in areas in which they can still

function effectively (optimization), and compensate in circumstances with high mental or physical demands (compensation). 350

self-actualization The highest need in Maslow's hierarchy that involves the motivation to develop one's full potential as a human being. 57

self-concept An individual's perception of his or her abilities, personality, and other attributes; it consists of our overall thoughts and feelings about our characteristics. 81

self-disclosure The communication of intimate details about ourselves. 208

self-discrepancy theory Higgins' theory that problems occur when representations from different viewpoints or from different domains are inconsistent or discrepant. Two types of discrepancies are especially problematic: between the actual and ideal selves (produces dejection-related emotions) and between the actual and ought selves (produces agitated emotions). 82

self-efficacy The belief that one can master a situation and produce positive outcomes. 51

self-esteem The overall evaluation of one's self-worth or self-image. 83

self-handicapping strategies Involve efforts by individuals to avoid failure. 300

self-monitoring Paying attention to the impressions you make on others and the degree to which you fine-tune your performances accordingly. 176

self-report tests Also called *objective tests* or *inventories,* they directly ask people whether items describe them or not. 67

self-talk Also called self-statements, self-talk refers to the soundless, mental speech people use when they think about something, plan, or solve problems. 147

service learning A form of education that promotes social responsibility and service to the community, aiming to help adolescents and emerging adults to become less self-centered and more strongly motivated to help others. 97

sexism Prejudice and discrimination against an individual because of his or her sex. 373

sexual orientation An enduring attraction toward members of one's own sex (homosexual orientation) or members of the other sex (heterosexual orientation). 399

sexual scripts Stereotyped patterns of expectancies for how people should behave sexually. 398

sexually transmitted infections (STIs) Diseases that are contracted primarily through sexual intercourse—vaginally as well as through oral-genital and anal-genital contact. 412

social cognitive theory States that behavior, environment, and person/cognitive factors are important in understanding personality. 49

social cognitive theory of gender The idea that children's gender development occurs through observation and imitation, and through rewards and punishment for gender-appropriate and -inappropriate behavior. 369

social identity Refers to the way you define yourself in terms of your group membership. 186

social identity theory Tajfel's theory that we can improve our self-image by enhancing our social identity; this occurs by favoring our in-group and disparaging the out-group. 188

social role theory Eagly's theory that psychological gender differences are caused by the contrasting social roles of women and men. 369

social support Information and feedback from others that one is loved and cared for, esteemed and valued, and included in a network of communication and mutual obligation. 153

socioemotional selectivity theory States that older adults become more selective about their social networks and because they place a high value on emotional satisfaction, they often spend more time with familiar individuals with whom they have had rewarding relationships. 350

stereotype A generalization about a group's characteristics that does not account for variations from one individual to another. 175

stimulants Drugs that increase the activity of the nervous system; caffeine, nicotine, amphetamines, and cocaine are examples. 514

stress The response of individuals to stressors. 114

stress-management programs They teach individuals how to appraise stressful events, how to develop skills for coping with stress, and how to put these skills into use in one's everyday life. 161

stressors The circumstances and events that threaten individuals and tax their coping abilities. 114

subjective well-being The scientific term for how people evaluate their lives in terms of their happiness and life satisfaction. 12

superego The Freudian structure of personality that deals with morality. 39

syphilis A sexually transmitted infection caused by the bacterium *Treponema palladium*. 412

systematic desensitization A method of behavior therapy based on classical conditioning that treats anxiety by getting the person to associate deep relaxation with increasingly intense anxiety-producing situations. 473

tentative stage Ginzberg's stage for the adolescent period of 11 to 17 when individuals are between the fantasy stage of childhood and the more realistic stage that will come later. 302

Thematic Apperception Test (TAT) A projective test designed to elicit stories that reveal something about an individual's personality. 67

theory A broad idea or set of closely related ideas that attempt to explain certain observations. 17

thought stopping A specific self-control strategy in which the individual says "Stop!" when an unwanted thought occurs and then immediately replaces it with a more pleasant thought. 153

traditional religious script Sex is accepted only within marriage. 398

trait An enduring characteristic that tends to lead to certain behaviors. 60

trait theories State that personality consists of broad, enduring dispositions that lead to characteristic responses. 60

transactional Means that communication is an ongoing process between sender and receiver that unfolds over time, and that it is not unusual for information to be communicated almost simultaneously between the participants. 204

transcendental meditation (TM) The most popular form of meditation that is practiced in the United States that involves using a mantra, a resonant sound or phrase that is repeated mentally or aloud to focus attention. 161

transference The psychoanalytic term for the person's relating to the analyst in ways that reproduce or relive important relationships in the individual's life. 469

transsexualism A gender identity disorder in which an individual has an overwhelming desire to become a member of the opposite sex. 411

transvestism A psychosexual disorder in which an individual obtains sexual gratification by dressing up as a member of the opposite sex. 410

Type A behavior pattern A cluster of characteristics—being excessively competitive, hard-driven, impatient, and hostile—is related to the incidence of heart disease. 125

Type B behavior pattern Relaxed and easygoing personality. 125

unconditional positive regard Rogers' term for accepting, valuing, and being positive toward another person regardless of the person's behavior. 56

undifferentiated schizophrenia A type of schizophrenia that is characterized by disorganized behavior, hallucinations, delusions, and incoherence. 449

value conflict A clash between values that encourage opposing actions. 95

values Standards that we apply to determine the worth of things, ideas, or events. Our values reflect what matters most to us. 95

voyeurism A psychosexual disorder in which individuals derive sexual gratification from observing the sex organs or sex acts of others, often from a secret vantage point. 411

wisdom Expert knowledge about the practical aspects of life. 345

References

A

Abbass, A., & Gardner, D. M. (2004). Psychotherapy and medication options for depression. *American Family Physician, 69,* 2071–2072.

Abbott, M. J., & Rapee, R. M. (2004). Post-event rumination and negative self-appraisal in social phobia before and after treatment. *Journal of Abnormal Psychology, 113,* 136–144.

Aboud, F. E., & Mendelson, M. J. (1996). Determinants of friendship selection and quality: Developmental perspectives. In W. M. Bukowski, A. F. Newcomb, & W. W. Hartup (Eds.), *The company they keep: Friendship in childhood and adolescence.* Cambridge, UK: Cambridge University Press.

Abrams, D., & Hogg, M. A. (2004). Metatheory: Lessons from social identity research. In A. W. Kruglanski & E. Tory Higgins (Eds.), *Theory construction in social-personality psychology.* Mahwah, NJ: Erlbaum.

Abrams, L. S. (2003). Contextual variations in young women's gender identity negotiations. *Psychology of Women Quarterly, 27,* (1), 64–74.

Abramson, L. Y., Seligman, M. E. P., & Teasdale, J. (1978). Learned helplessness in humans: Critique and reformulation. *Journal of Abnormal Psychology, 87,* 49–74.

Achat, H., Kawachi, I., Spiro, A., DeMolles, D. A., & Sparrow, D. (2000). Optimism and depression as predictors of physical and mental health functioning: The Normative Aging Study. *Annals of Behavioral Medicine, 22,* 127–130.

Ackerson, J., Scogin, F., McKendree-Smith, N., & Lyman, R. D. (1998). Cognitive bibliotherapy for mild and moderate adolescent depressive symptomatology. *Journal of Consulting and Clinical Psychology, 66,* 685–690.

Adams, J. M., & White, M. (2004). Biological aging: a fundamental, biological link between socioeconomic status and health? *European Journal of Public Health, 14,* 331–334.

Adams-Curtis, L. E., & Forbes, G. B. (2004). College women's experiences of sexual coercion: A review of cultural, perpetrator, victim, and situational variables. *Trauma, Violence, and Abuse, 5,* 91–122.

Adler, A. (1927). *The theory and practice of individual psychology.* Fort Worth: Harcourt Brace.

Adorno, T. W., Frenkel-Brunswick, E., Levinson, D. J., & Sanford, R. N. (1950). *The authoritarian personality.* New York: Harper & Row.

Aertgeerts, B., & Buntinx, F. (2002). The relation between alcohol abuse or dependence and academic performance in first-year college students. *Journal of Adolescent Health, 31,* 223–225.

Agars, M. D. (2004). Reconsidering the impact of gender stereotypes on the advancement of women in organizations. *Psychology of Women Quarterly, 28,* 103–101.

Ah Lee, S., & others. (2003). Multiple HPV infection in cervical cancer screened by HPVDNAChip. *Cancer Letters, 198,* 187–192.

Ainsworth, M. D. S. (1979). Infant-mother attachment. *American Psychologist, 34,* 932–937.

Akiyama, H., & Antonucci, T. C. (1999, November). *Mother-daughter dynamics over the life course.* Paper presented at the meeting of the Gerontological Association of America, San Francisco.

Al-Issa, I. (1982). Does culture make a difference in psychopathology? In I. Al-Issa (Ed.), *Culture and psychopathology.* Baltimore: University Park Press.

Alan Guttmacher Institute (1995). *National survey of adolescent men and family growth.* New York: Author.

Alan Guttmacher Institute. (2002). *In their own right: Addressing the sexual and reproductive health needs of American men.* New York: Author.

Albert, R., & Emmons, M. (1995). *Your perfect right* (7th ed.). San Luis Obispo, CA: Impact.

Albrecht, T. L., & Goldsmith, D. J. (2003). Social support, social networks, and health. In T. L. Thompson & A. M. Dorsey (Eds.), *Handbook of health communication.* Mahwah, NJ: Erlbaum.

Alderman, M. K. (2004). *Motivation for achievement.* Mahwah, NJ: Erlbaum.

Alegre, M., & Welch, D. (2003). *Maxine Hong Kingston after the fire.* www.powers.com/authors.

Alexander, J. L., Kotz, K., Dennerstein, L., Kutner, S. J., Wallen, K., & Notelovitz, M. (2004). The effects of postmenopausal hormone therapies on female sexual functioning: a review of double-blind, randomized control trials. *Menopause, 11,* 749–765.

Algoe, S. B., Buswell, B. N., & DeLamater, J. D. (2000). Gender and job status as contextual cues for the interpretation of facial expression of emotion. *Sex Roles, 42,* 183–208.

Allan, R., & Scheidt, S. (Eds.). (1996). *Heart and mind.* Washington, DC: American Psychological Association.

Allen, D. N., Goldstein, G., & Weiner, C. (2001). Differential neuropsychological patterns of frontal- and temporal-lobe dysfunction in patients with schizophrenia. *Schizophrenia Research, 48,* 7–15.

Allen, J. J., & Movius, H. L. (2000). The objective assessment of amnesia in dissociative identity disorder using event-related potentials. *International Journal of Psychophysiology, 38,* 21–41.

Allen, K. R., Blieszner, R., & Roberto, K. A. (2000). Families in middle and later years: A review and critique of research in the 1990s. *Journal of Marriage and the Family, 62,* 911–926.

Alloy, L. B., & Abramson, L. Y. (1979). Judgment of contingency in depressed and nondepressed students: Sadder but wiser? *Journal of Experimental Psychology: General, 108,* 441–485.

Alloy, L. B., Abramson, L. Y., & Francis, E. L. (1999). Do negative cognitive styles confer vulnerability to depression? *Current Directions in Psychological Science, 8,* 128–132.

Alloy, L. B., Jacobson, N. S., & Acocella, J. (1999). *Abnormal psychology* (8th ed.). New York: McGraw-Hill.

Allport, G. (1954). *The nature of prejudice.* Reading, MA: Addison-Wesley.

Allport, G. W. (1937). *Personality: A psychological interpretation.* New York: Holt.

Almagor, M., Tellegen, A., & Waller, N. G. (1995). The big seven model: A cross-cultural replication and further exploration of the basic dimensions of natural language trait descriptors.

Almeida-Filho, N., Lessa, I., Magalhaes, L., Araujo, M. J., Aquino, E., James, S. A., & Kawachi, I. (2004). Social inequality and depressive disorders in Bahia, Brazil: interactions of gender, ethnicity, and social class. *Social Science Medicine, 59,* 1339–1353.

Amato, P. (2004). To have and have not: Marriage and divorce in the United States. In M. Coleman & L. Ganong (Eds.), *Handbook of contemporary families.* Thousand Oaks, CA: Sage.

American Psychiatric Association. (2000). *Diagnostic and statistical manual of mental disorders* (4th ed., Text revision). Washington, DC: American Psychiatric Press.

American Psychiatric Association. (2003). *Disaster psychiatry.* Washington, DC: American Psychiatric Association.

American Psychological Association. (2003). *DotCOMSENSE.* Washington, DC: American Psychological Association.

American Psychological Association (2003a). *Controlling anger—Before it controls you.* Washington, DC: APA.

American Psychological Association. (2004). *The Road to Resilience.* Washington, DC: APA.

Amrhein, C., Pauli, P., Dengler, W., & Wiedemann, G. (2005). Covariation bias and its physiological correlates in panic disorder patients. *Journal of Anxiety Disorders, 19,* 177–191.

Andersen, B. L. (1983). Primary orgasmic dysfunction: Diagnostic considerations and a review of treatment. *Psychological Bulletin, 93,* 105–136.

Andersen, B. L. (1998). Cancer. In H. S. Friedman (Ed.), *Encyclopedia of mental health* (Vol. 1). San Diego: Academic Press.

Andersen, B. L. (2000). Cancer. In A. Kazdin (Ed.), *Encyclopedia of psychology.* Washington, DC, & New York: American Psychological Association and Oxford University Press.

Andersen, B. L., Golden-Kreutz, D. M., & DiLillo, V. (2001). Cancer. In A. Baum, T. A. Revenson, & J. E. Singer (Eds.), *Handbook of health psychology.* Mahwah, NJ: Erlbaum.

Andersen, B. L., Kiecolt-Glaser, J. K., & Glaser, R. (1994). A biobehavioral model of cancer stress and disease course. *American Psychologist, 49,* 389–404.

Andersen, P. (1999). *Nonverbal communication.* New York: McGraw-Hill.

Anderson, E. M., & Lambert, M. J. (2001). A survival analysis of clinically significant change in outpatient psychotherapy. *Journal of Clinical Psychology, 57,* 875–888.

Anderson, K. E., & Savage, C. R. (2004). Cognitive and neurobiological findings in obsessive-compulsive disorder. *Psychiatric Clinics of North America, 27,* 37–47.

Anderson, K. L., Umberson, D., & Elliott, S. (2004). Violence and abuse in families. In A. L. Vangelisti (Ed.), Handbook of family communication. Mahwah, NJ: Erlbaum.

Anderson, N. H. (1968). Likableness ratings of 55 personality trait words. *Journal of Personality and Social Psychology, 9,* 272–279.

Anderson, R. E. (2003). Envy and jealousy. *American Journal of Psychotherapy, 56,* 455–479.

Anderson, S., & Hetta, J. (2004). A 15–year follow-up study of patients with panic disorder. *European Psychiatry, 18,* 401–418.

Anderssen, N., Amlie, C., & Ytteroy, E. A. (2002). Outcomes for children with lesbian or gay parents. A review of studies from 1978 to 2000. *Scandinavian Journal of Psychology, 43,* 335–351.

Anstey, K. J., & Low, L. F. (2004). Normal cognitive changes in aging. *Australian Family Physician, 33,* 783–787.

Anthony Greenwald & Associates. (2000). *Current views toward retirement: A poll.* New York: Author.

Anthony, M. M. (2004). Anxiety disorders. In W. E. Craighead & C. B. Nemeroff (Eds.), *The concise Corsini encyclopedia of psychology and behavioral science.* New York: Wiley.

Antonucci, T. C. (1990). Social supports and social relationships. In R. H. Binstock & L. K. George (Eds.), *Handbook of aging and the social sciences* (3rd ed.). San Diego: Academic Press.

Antonucci, T. C. (2001). Social relations. In J. E. Birren & K. W. Schaie (Eds.). *Handbook of the psychology of aging* (5th ed.). San Diego: Academic Press.

Anxiety Disorders Association of America. (2004). *Anxiety disorders.* Silver Springs, MD: Author.

Apker, J., & Ray, E. B. (2003). Stress and social support in health care organizations. In T. L. Thompson & A. M. Dorsey (Eds.), *Handbook of health communication.* Mahwah, NJ: Erlbaum.

Apparala, M. L., Reifman, A., & Munsch, J. (2003). Cross-national comparisons of attitudes toward fathers' and mothers' participation in household tasks and childcare. *Sex Roles, 48,* 189–203.

Arai, M. (2004). Japan. In K. Malley-Morrison (Ed.), *International perspectives on family violence and abuse.* Mahwah, NJ: Erlbaum.

Archer, D., & Gartner, R. (1976). Violent acts and violent times: A comparative approach in postwar homicide. *American Sociological Review, 41,* 937–963.

Archer, D., & McDaniel, P. (1995). Violence and gender: Differences and similarities across societies. In R. B. Ruback & N. A. Weiner (Eds.), *Interpersonal violent behaviors: Social and cultural aspects.* New York: Springer.

Archer, R. P., Handel, R. W., Greene, R. L., Baer, R. A., & Elkins, D. E. (2001). An evaluation of the usefulness of the MMPI-2 F (p) sale. *Journal of Personality Assessment, 76,* 282–285.

Archer, S. L. (1989). The status of identity: Reflections on the need for intervention. *Journal of Adolescence, 12,* 345–359.

Aries, E. (1998). Gender differences in interaction. In D. J. Canary & K. Dindia (Eds.), *Sex differences and similarities in communication.* Mahwah, NJ: Erlbaum.

Arkowitz, H. (1997). Integrative theories of therapy. In P. L. Wachtel & S. B. Messer (Eds.), *Theories of psychotherapy.* Washington, DC: American Psychological Association.

Armstrong, L. (2000). *It's not about the bike.* New York: Putnam.

Arndt, J., & Goldenberg, J. L. (2002). From threat to sweat: The role of psysiological arousal in the motivation to maintain self-esteem. In A. Tesser, D. A. Stapel, & J. V. Wood (Eds.), *Self and motivation: Emerging psychological perspectives.* Washington, DC: American Psychological Association.

Arnett, J. J. (1995, March). *Are college students adults?* Paper presented at the meeting of the Society for Research in Child Development, Indianapolis.

Arnett, J. J. (2000). Emerging adulthood. *American Psychologist, 55,* 469–480.

Arnett, J. J. (2004). *Emerging adulthood.* New York: Oxford University Press.

Arnkoff, D. B., Glass, C. R., & Shapiro, S. J. (2002). Expectations and preferences. In J. C. Norcross (Ed.), *Psychotherapy relationships that work.* New York: Oxford University Press.

Arnold, E. M. (2004). Factors that influence consideration of hastening death among people with life-threatening illnesses. *Health and Social Work, 29,* 17–26.

Arnoux, D. (1998, September). Description of teaching experiences prepared for John Santrock's text, *Educational Psychology.* New York: McGraw-Hill.

Aronson, E. (1986, August). *Teaching students things they think they already know all about: The case of prejudice and desegregation.* Paper presented at the meeting of the American Psychological Association, Washington, DC.

Aronson, E., Wilson, T. D., & Akert, R. M. (2004). *Social psychology* (4th ed.). Upper Saddle River, NJ: Prentice Hall.

Asch, S. E. (1951). Effects of group pressure on the modification and distortion of judgments. In H. S. Guetzkow (Ed.), *Groups, leadership, and men.* Pittsburgh: Carnegie University Press.

Ashy, M. A. (2004). Saudi Arabia. In K. Malley-Morrison (Ed.), *International perspectives on family violence and abuse.* Mahwah, NJ: Erlbaum.

Aspinwall, L. G. (2001). Proactive coping, well-being, and health. In N. J. Smelser & P. B. Baltes (Eds.), *The international encyclopedia of the social and behavioral sciences.* Oxford: Elsevier.

Aspinwall, L. G., & Taylor, S. E. (1997). A stitch in time: Self-regulation and proactive coping. *Psychological Bulletin, 121,* 417–436.

Astin, A. (1993). *What matters in college: Four critical years revisited.* San Francisco: Jossey-Bass.

Astin, J. (2004). Mind-body therapies for the management of pain. *Clinical Journal of Pain, 20,* 27–32.

Astrup, A., Meinert Larson, T., & Harper, A. (2004). Atkins and other low-carbohydrate diets: hoax or an effective tool for weight loss? *Lancet, 364,* 897–899.

Atkins, R. C. (1997). *Dr. Atkins' New Diet Revolution.* New York: Avon.

Atkinson, D. R., & Hackett, G. (2004). *Counseling diverse populations* (3rd Ed.). New York: McGraw-Hill.

Atkinson, L., & Goldberg, S. (Eds.) (2004). *Attachment issues in psychopathology and intervention.* Mahwah, NJ: Erlbaum.

Atwood, J. D. (Ed.). (2001). *Family systems/family therapy.* Binghamton, NY: Haworth Press.

Austed, C. S. (2004). Psychotherapy effectiveness. In W. E. Craighead & C. B. Nemeroff (Eds.), *The concise Corsini encyclopedia of psychology and behavioral science.* New York: Wiley.

Avolilo, B. J., & Sosik, J. J. (1999). A lifespan framework for assessing the impact of work on white-collar workers. In S. L. Willis & J. D. Reid (Eds.), *Life in the middle: Psychological and social development in middle age.* San Diego: Academic Press.

Awad, A. G. (2004). Antipsychotic medications. *Current Opinion in Psychiatry, 17,* 75–80.

Awad, A. G., & Voruganti, L. N. (2004). Impact of atypical antipsychotics on quality of life in patients with schizophrenia. *CNS Drugs, 18,* 877–893.

Axtell, R. (1991). *Gestures!: The do's and taboos of body language around the world.* New York: Wiley.

Axtell, R. (1992). *Gestures! The do's and taboos of body language around the world.* New York: Wiley.

Azar, S. T. (2002). Parenting and child maltreatment. In M. H. Bornstein (Ed.), *Handbook of parenting* (2nd ed., Vol. 4). Mahwah, NJ: Erlbaum.

Azar, S. T. (2003). Adult development and parenting. In J. Demick & C. Andreoletti (Eds.), *Handbook of adult development.* New York: Kluwer.

B

Babbie, E. R. (2005). *The basics of social research* (3rd ed.). Belmont, CA: Wadsworth.

Bachman, J., O'Malley, P., & Johnston, L. (1978). *Youth in transition: Vol. 6. Adolescence to adulthood—Change and stability of the lives of young men.* Ann Arbor: University of Michigan, Institute of Social Research.

Bachman, J. G., O'Malley, P. M., Schulenberg, J., Johnston, L. D., Bryant, A. L., & Merline, A. C. (2002). *The decline of substance abuse in young adulthood.* Mahwah, NJ: Erlbaum.

Bagge, C., Nickell, A., Stepp, S., Durrett, C., Jackson, K., & Trull, T. J. (2004). Borderline personality disorder features predict negative outcomes 2 years later. *Journal of Abnormal Psychology, 113,* 279–288.

Baker, B. (2001, March). *Marital interaction in mild hypertension.* Paper presented at the meeting of the American Psychosomatic Association, Monterey, CA.

Baker, N. L. (2001). Prejudice. In J. Worell (Ed.), *Encyclopedia of gender and women.* San Diego: Academic Press.

Baldwin, J. D., & Baldwin, J. I. (1998). Sexual behavior. In H. S. Friedman (Ed.), *Encyclopedia of mental health* (Vol. 3). San Diego: Academic Press.

Baldwin, M., & Fehr, B. (1995). On the instability of attachment ratings. *Personal Relationships 2,* 247–261.

Balon, R. (2004). Developments in the treatment of anxiety disorders: Psychotherapy, pharmacotherapy, and psychosurgery. *Depression and Anxiety, 19,* 63–76.

Baltes, P. B. (1993). The aging mind: Potentials and limits. *Gerontologist, 33,* 580–594.

Baltes, P. B. (2003). On the incomplete architecture of human ontogeny: Selection, optimization, and compensation as foundation for developmental theory. In U. M. Staudinger & U. Lindenberger (Eds.), *Understanding human development.* Boston: Kluwer.

Baltes, P. B., & Smith, J. (2003). New frontiers in the future of aging: From successful aging of the young old to the dilemmas of the fourth age. *Gerontology, 49,* 123–135.

Bandelow, B., Behnke, K., Lenoir, S., Hendriks, G. J., Aikin, T., Goebel, C., & Clary, C. M. (2004). Sertraline versus paroxetine in the treatment of panic disorder. *Journal of Clinical Psychiatry, 65,* 405–413.

Bandelow, B., & Ruther, E. (2004). Treatment-resistant panic disorder. *CNS Spectrum 9,* 725–739.

Bandura, A. (1965). Influences of models' reinforcement contingencies on the acquisition of imitative responses. *Journal of Personality and Social Psychology, 1,* 589–596.

Bandura, A. (1986). *Social foundations of thought and action: A social cognitive theory.* Englewood Cliffs, NJ: Prentice Hall.

Bandura, A. (1997). *Self-efficacy.* New York: W. H. Freeman.

Bandura, A. (2000). Social cognitive theory. In A. Kazdin (Ed.), *Encyclopedia of psychology.* Washington, DC, and New York: American Psychological Association and Oxford University Press.

Bandura, A. (2004, May). *Toward a psychology of human agency.* Paper presented at the meeting of the American Psychological Society, Chicago.

Bandura, A., & Bussey, K. (2004). On broadening the cognitive, motivational, and sociostructural scope of theorizing about gender development and functioning: Comment on Martin, Ruble, and Szkrybalo (2002). *Psychological Bulletin, 130,* 691–701.

Baney, J. (2004). *Guide to interpersonal communication.* Upper Saddle River, NJ: Prentice Hall.

Barbour, K. A., & Davison, G. C. (2003). Clinical interviewing. In M. Hersen (Ed.), *Comprehensive handbook of psychological assessment* (Vol. 3). New York: Wiley.

Barker, L., Edwards, R., Gaines, C., Gladney, K., & Holley, F. (1981). An investigation of proportional time spent in various communication activities by college students. *Journal of Applied Communication Research, 8,* 101–109.

Barling, J., Kelloway, E. K., & Frone, M. R. (Eds.). (2004). *Handbook of work and stress.* Thousand Oaks, CA: Sage.

Barlow, D. H. (2001). *Anxiety and its disorders* (2nd ed.). New York: Guilford.

Barlow, D. H., & Durand, V. M. (2005). *Abnormal psychology* (4th ed.). Belmont, CA: Wadsworth.

Barnert, O., Miller-Perrin, C. L., & Perrin, R. D. (2004). *Family violence across the life span* (2nd ed.). Thousand Oaks, CA: Sage.

Barnes, L. L., Mendes De Leon, C. F., Wilson, R. S., Bienias, J. L., Bennett, D. A., & Evans, D. A. (2004). Racial differences in perceived discrimination in a community population of older blacks and whites. *Journal of Aging and Health, 16,* 315–337.

Barnes-Farrell, J. L. (2004). Older workers. In J. Barling, E. K. Kelloway, & M. R. Frone (Eds.), *Handbook of work and stress.* Thousand Oaks, CA: Sage.

Barnett, R. C. (2001). Work-family balance. In J. Worell (Ed.), *Encyclopedia of women and gender.* San Diego: Academic Press.

Barnett, R. C., Gareis, K. C., James, J. B., & Steele, J. (2001, August). *Planning ahead: College seniors' concerns about work-family conflict.* Paper presented at the meeting of the American Psychological Association, San Francisco.

Barnlund, D. C. (1975). Communicative styles in two cultures: Japan and the United States. In A. Kendon, R. M. Harris, & M. R. Key (Eds.), *Organization of behavior in face-to-face interaction.* The Hague: Mouton.

Bartholomew K., & Horowitz L. (1991). Attachment styles among young adults: A test of four-category model. *Journal of Personality and Social Psychology, 61,* 226–244.

Baruth, L. G., & Manning, M. L. (1991). *Multicultural counseling and psychotherapy: A lifespan perspective.* New York: Macmillan.

Bassett, J. F., & Moss, B. (2004). Men and women prefer risk takers as romantic and nonromantic partners. *Current Research in Social Psychology, 9,* 1–10.

Battaglia, M. (2002). Beyond the usual suspects: A cholingeric route for panic attacks. *Molecular Psychiatry, 7,* 239–246.

Baudouin, A., Vanneste, S., & Isingrini, M. (2004). Age-related cognitive slowing: the role of spontaneous tempo and processing speed. *Experimental Aging Research, 30,* 225–239.

Bauer, M., Hamm, A., & Pankratz, M. J. (2004). Linking nutrition to genomics. *Biological Chemistry, 385,* 593–596.

Baumeister, R. F. (1989). The optimal margin of illusion. *Journal of Social and Clinical Psychology, 8,* 176–189.

Baumeister, R. F. (1991a). The self against the self: Escape or defeat. In R. C. Curtis (Ed.), *The relational self.* New York: Guilford.

Baumeister, R. F. (1991b). *Meaning of life.* New York: Guilford.

Baumeister, R. F. (1993). *Self-esteem: The puzzle of low self-regard.* New York: Plenum Press.

Baumeister, R. F. (2004). Sex in "his" and "her" relationships. In J. H. Harvey, A. Wenzel, & S. Sprecher (Eds.), *The handbook of sexuality in close relationships.* Mahwah, NJ: Erlbaum.

Baumeister, R. F., Campbell, J. D., Krueger, J. I., & Vohs, K. D. (2003). Does high self-esteem cause better performance, interpersonal success, happiness, or healthier lifestyles? *Psychological Science in the Public Interest, 4* (1), 1–44.

Baumeister, R. F., Catanese, K. R., & Vohs, K. D. (2001). Is there a gender difference in strength of sex drive? *Personality and Social Psychology Review, 5,* 242–273.

Baumeister, R. F., & Vohs, K. D. (2002). The pursuit of meaningfulness in life. In C. R. Snyder & S. J. Lopez (Eds.), *Handbook of positive psychology.* New York: Oxford University Press.

Baumrind, D. (1971). Current patterns of parental authority. *Developmental Psychology Monographs, 4* (1, Pt. 2).

Bauserman, R. (2002). Child adjustment in joint-custody versus sole-custody arrangements: A meta-analytic review. *Journal of Family Psychology, 16,* 91–102.

Baxter, L. R., Jr., Phelps, M. E., Mazziotta, J. C., Schwartz, J. M., Gerner, R. H., Selin, C. E., & Sumida, R. M. (1995). Cerebral metabolic rates for glucose in mood disorders: Studies with positron emission tomography and fluorodeoxyglucose F 18. *Archives of General Psychiatry, 42,* 441–447.

Beck, A. T. (1967). *Depression.* New York: Harper & Row.

Beck, A. T. (1976). *Cognitive therapies and the emotional disorders.* New York: International Universities Press.

Beck, A. T. (1993). Cognitive therapy: Past, present, and future. *Journal of Consulting and Clinical Psychology, 61,* 194–198.

Beck, A. T., Freeman, A., Davis, D., & Associates. (2003). *Cognitive therapy of personality disorders* (2nd ed.). New York: Guilford.

Beck, A. T., Rush, A. J., Shaw, B. F., & Emery, G. (1979). *Cognitive therapy of depression.* New York: Guilford.

Beckman, M. (2002). Pheromone reception: When in doubt, mice mate rather than hate. *Science, 295,* 782.

Bednar, R. L., Wells, M. G., & Peterson, S. R. (1995). *Self-esteem* (2nd ed.). Washington, DC: American Psychological Association.

Bee, H. L., & Bjorkland, B. R. (2004). *The journey of adulthood.* (5th ed.). Upper Saddle River, NJ: Prentice Hall.

Beins, B. (2004). *Research methods.* Boston: Allyn & Bacon.

Bell, A. P., Weinberg, M. S., & Mammersmith, S. K. (1981). *Sexual preference.* New York: Simon & Schuster.

Bellevia, G., & Frone, J. R. (2004). Work-family conflict. In J. Baring, E. K. Kelloway, & M. R. Frone (Eds.), *Handbook of work stress.* Thousand Oaks, CA: Sage.

Bellodi, L., Cavallini, M. C., Bertelli, S., Chiapparino, D., Riboldi, C., & Smeraldi, E. (2001). Morbidity risk for obsessive-compulsive spectrum disorders in first-degree relatives of patients with eating disorders. *American Journal of Psychiatry, 158,* 563–569.

Belsky, J., & Eggebeen, D. (1991). Early and extensive maternal employment/child care and 4–6-year-olds socioemotional development: Children of the National Longitudinal Survey of Youth. *Journal of Marriage and the Family, 53,* 1083–1099.

Belsky, J. K. (1999). *The psychology of aging* (3rd ed.). Belmont, CA: Wadsworth.

Bem, S. L. (1974). The measurement of psychological androgyny. *Journal of Consulting and Clinical Psychology, 42,* 155–162.

Bem, S. L. (1977). On the utility of alternative procedures for assessing psychological androgyny. *Journal of Consulting and Clinical Psychology, 45,* 196–205.

Benazzi, F. (2004). Bipolar II disorder family history using the Family History Screen. *Comprehensive Psychiatry, 45,* 77–82.

Benca, R. M. (2001). Consequences of insomnia and its therapies. *Journal of Clinical Psychiatry, 62* (Suppl. 10), 33–38.

Benes, F. M., Todtenkopf, M. S., Logiotatos, P., & Williams, M. (2000). Glutamite decarboxylase (65)-immunoreactive terminals in cingulate and prefrontal cortices of schizophrenic and bipolar brains. *Journal of Chemistry and Neuroanatomy, 20,* 259–269.

Benet, V., & Waller, N. G. (1995). The big seven model of personality description: Evidence for its cross-cultural generality in a Spanish sample. *Journal of Personality and Social Psychology, 69,* 701–718.

Bengtson, V. L. (2001). Beyond the nuclear family: The increasing importance of multigenerational bonds. *Journal of Marriage and the Family, 63,* 1–16.

Benini, A. L., Camilloni, M. A., Scordato, C., Lezzi, G., Savia, G., Oriani, G., Bertoli, S., Balzola, F., Liuzzi, A., & Petroni, M. L. (2001). Contribution of weight cycling to serum leptin in human obesity. *International Journal of Obesity and Related Metabolic Disorders, 25,* 721–726.

Bennett, W. I., & Gurin, J. (1982). *The dieter's dilemma: Eating less and weighing more.* New York: Basic Books.

Beres, M. A., Herold, E., & Maitland, S. B. (2004). Sexual consent behaviors in same-sex relationships. *Archives of Sexual Behavior, 33,* 475–486.

Berk, L. S., Felten, D. L., Tan, S. A., Bittman, B. B., & Westengard, J. (2001). Modulation of neuroimmune parameters during the eustress of humor-associated mirthful laughter. *Alternative Therapies, 7,* 62–76.

Bernheim, K. F. (1997). *The Lanahan cases and readings in abnormal behavior.* Baltimore, MD: Lanahan.

Bernstein, A. B. (2001). Motherhood, health status, and health care. *Women's Health Issues, 11,* 173–184.

Bernstein, N. (2004, March). Behind fall in pregnancy, a new teenage culture of restraint. *New York Times,* pp. A1, A22.

Berry, J. W. (1980). Acculturation as varieties of adaptation. In A. Padilla (Ed.), *Acculturation: Theory, model, and some new findings.* Washington, DC: American Association for the Advancement of Science.

Berscheid, E. (1988). Some comments on love's anatomy. Or whatever happened to an old-fashioned lust? In R. J. Sternberg & M. L. Barnes (Eds.), *Anatomy of love.* New Haven, CT: Yale University Press.

Berscheid, E. (2000). Attraction. In A. Kazdin (Ed.). *Encyclopedia of psychology.* Washington, DC, & New York: American Psychological Association and Oxford University Press.

Berscheid, E., & Fei, J. (1977). Sexual jealousy and romantic love. In G. Clinton & G. Smith (Eds.), *Sexual jealousy.* Englewood Cliffs, NJ: Prentice-Hall.

Berscheid, E., & Reis, H. T. (1998). Attraction and close relationships. In D. T. Gilbert, S. T. Fiske, & G. Lindzey (Eds.), *Handbook of social psychology* (4th ed., Vol. 2). New York: McGraw-Hill.

Best, D. (2001). Cross-cultural gender roles. In J. Worell (Ed.), *Encyclopedia of women and gender.* San Diego: Academic Press.

Bhugra, D., & de Silva, P. (1998). Sexual dysfunction therapy. In H. S. Friedman (Ed.), *Encyclopedia of mental health* (Vol. 3). San Diego: Academic Press.

Bijur, P. E., Wallston, K. A., Smith, C. A., Lifrak, S., & Friedman, S. B. (1993, August). *Gender differences in turning to religion for coping.* Paper presented at the meeting of the American Psychological Association, Toronto.

Billings, A. G., Cronkite, R. C., & Moos, R. H. (1983). Social-environmental factors in unipolar depression. *Journal of Abnormal Psychology, 92,* 119–133.

Billings, A. G., & Moos, R. H. (1981). The role of coping responses and social resources in attenuating the stress of life events. *Journal of Behavioral Medicine, 4,* 157–189.

Binder, J. L. (2004). *Key competencies in brief dynamic psychotherapy.* New York: Guilford.

Birren, J. E. (Ed.). (1996). *Encyclopedia of gerontology.* San Diego: Academic Press.

Black, D. W. (2004). Antisocial personality disorder. In W. E. Craighead & C. B. Nemeroff (Eds.), *The concise Corsini encyclopedia of psychology and behavioral science.* New York: Wiley.

Blair, L. V. (2001). Implicit stereotypes and prejudice. In G. B. Moscowitz (Ed.), *Cognitive social psychology.* Mahwah, NJ: Erlbaum.

Blair, S. N., Kohl, H. W., Paffenbarger, R. S., Clark, D. G., Cooper, K. H., & Gibbons, L. W. (1989). Physical fitness and all-cause mortality: A prospective study of healthy men and women. *Journal of the American Medical Association, 262,* 2395–2401.

Blair, S. N., LaMonte, M. J., & Nichaman, M. Z. (2004). The evolution of physical activity recommendations: How much is enough? *American Journal of Clinical Nutrition, 79,* 913S–920S.

Blazer, D. G., Kessler, R. C., McGonagle, K. A., & Swartz, M. S. (1994). The prevalence and distribution of major depression in a national community sample: The National Comorbidity Study. *American Journal of Psychiatry, 151,* 979–986.

Block, J. H., & Block, J. (1980). The role of ego-control and ego-resiliency in the organization of behavior. In W. A. Collins (Ed.), *Minnesota symposium on child psychology* (Vol. 13). Minneapolis: University of Minnesota Press.

Blonna, R. (2005). *Coping with stress in a changing world* (3rd ed.). New York: McGraw-Hill.

Bloor, C., & White, F. (1983). *Unpublished manuscript.* University of California at San Diego, LaJolla, CA.

Blumenthal, H. T. (2004). Amyloidosis: A universal disease of aging? *Journals of Gerontology A: Biological and Medical Sciences, 59,* M361–M369.

Blumentritt, T. L., Angle, R. L., & Brown, J. M. (2004). MACI personality patterns and DSM-IV symptomotology in a sample of troubled Mexican-American adolescents. *Journal of Child and Family Studies, 13,* 163–178.

Blundell, J. E. (1984). Systems and interactions: An approach to the pharmacology of feeding. In A. J. Stunkdard & E. Stellar (Eds.), *Eating and its disorders.* New York: Raven Press.

Bock, B. C., Marcus, B. H., King, T. E., Borrelli, B., & Roberts, M. R. (1999). Exercise effects on withdrawal and mood among women attempting smoking cessation. *Addictive Behavior, 24,* 399–410.

Bodenhausen, G. V., Macrae, K., & Hugenberg, K. (2004). Activating and inhibiting social identities. In G. V. Bodenhausen & A. J. Lambert (Eds.), *Foundations of social cognition.* Mahwah, NJ: Erlbaum.

Bodenhausen, G. V., Mussweiler, T., Gabriel S., & Moreno, K. N. (2001). Affective influences on stereotyping and intergroup relations. In J. P. Forgas (Ed.), *Handbook of affect and cognition.* Mahwah, NJ: Erlbaum.

Bohart, A. C. (1995). The person-centered psychotherapies. In A. S. Gurman (Ed.), *Essential psychotherapies: Theory and practice.* New York: Guilford Press.

Bohart, A. C., & Greening, T. (2001). Humanistic psychology and positive psychology. *American Psychologist, 56,* 81–82.

Bolger, K. E., & Patterson, C. J. (2001). Developmental pathways from child maltreatment to peer rejection. *Child Development, 72,* 339–351.

Bolton, R. (1979). *People skills.* New York: Touchstone.

Bond, R., & Smith, P. B. (1994). Culture and conformity: A meta-analysis of studies using the Asch-type perceptual judgment task. *British Psychological Society 1994 Proceedings, 9,* 297–308.

Bonvillain, N. (2002). *Language, culture, and communication: The mean messages* (4th ed.). Upper Saddle River, NJ: Prentice Hall.

Booth, A., & Johnson, D. (1988). Premarital cohabitation and marital success. *Journal of Family Issues, 9,* 255–272.

Booth, A., Johnson, D. R., & Granger, D. A. (1999). Testosterone and men's health. *Journal of Behavioral Medicine, 22,* 1–12.

Booth, A., Johnson, D. R., Granger, D. A., Crouter, A. C., & McHale, S. (2003). Testosterone and child and adolescent adjustment: The moderating role of parent-child relationships. *Developmental Psychology, 39,* 85–98.

Booth-Kewley, S., & Friedman, H. S. (1987). Psychological predictors of heart disease: A quantitative review. *Psychological Bulletin, 101,* 343–362.

Bosch, J. A., Bernston, G. G., Cacioppo, J. T., Dhabhar, F. S., & Marucha, P. T. (2003). Acute stress evokes selective mobilization of T cells that differ in chemokine receptor expression. *Brain, Behavior, and Immunology, 17,* 251–259.

Boswell, W. R., Olson-Buchanan, J. B., & LePine, M. A. (2004). Relations between stress and work outcomes. *Journal of Vocational Behavior, 64,* 165–181.

Bottos, S. (2004). Perfectionists' appraisal of daily hassles and chronic Headache. *Headache, 44,* 772–779.

Bottos, S., & Dewey, D. (2004). Perfectionists' appraisal of daily hassles and chronic headache. *Headache, 44,* 772–779.

Bourne, E. J. (1995). *The anxiety and phobia workbook* (2nd ed.). Oakland, CA: New Harbinger Publications.

Bourne, E. J. (2001). *The anxiety and phobia workbook* (3rd ed.). Oakland, CA: New Harbinger.

Bouvard, M. A., Milliery, M., & Cottraux, J. (2004). Management of obsessive-compulsive disorder. *Psychotherapy and Psychosomatics, 73,* 149–157.

Bowers, T. G., & Clum, G. A. (1988). Relative contribution of specific and nonspecific treatment effects: Meta-analysis of placebo-controlled behavior therapy research. *Psychological Bulletin, 103,* 315–323.

Bowes, J. (2005). Emphasizing the family in work-family research. In S. A. Poelmans (Ed.), *Work and family.* Mahwah, NJ: Erlbaum.

Bowlby, J. (1969). *Attachment and loss:* (Vol. 1). London: Hogarth Press.

Bowlby, J. (1980). *Attachment and loss: Loss, sadness, and depression.* (Vol. 3). New York: Basic Books.

Bowles, T. (1999). Focusing on time orientation to explain adolescent self-concept and academic achievement: Part II.

Testing a model. *Journal of Applied Health Behaviour, 1,* 1–8.

Bozarth, J. D., Zimring, F. M., & Tausch, R. (2001). Client-centered therapy: The evolution of a revolution. In D. J. Cain & J. Seeman (Eds.), *Humanistic psychotherapies.* Washington, DC: American Psychological Association.

Bradbury, F. D., Finchum, F. D., & Beach, S. R. H. (2000). Research on the nature and determinants of marital satisfaction: A decade in review. *Journal of Marriage and the Family, 62,* 964–980.

Bradford, D., Stroup, S., & Lieberman, J. (2002). Pharmacological treatments for schizophrenia. In P. Nathan & J. M. Gorman (Eds.), *A guide to treatments that work* (2nd ed.). New York: Oxford University Press.

Brammer, R. (2004). *Counseling diverse populations.* Belmont, CA: Brooks/Cole.

Brass, L. M. (2004). Estrogens and stroke: use of oral contraceptives and postmenopausal use of estrogen: current recommendations. *Current Treatment Options in Neurology, 6,* 459–467.

Bray, G. A., & Champagne, C. M. (2004). Obesity and the metabolic syndrome. *Journal of the American Diet Association, 104,* 86–89.

Brehm, S. S. (2002). *Intimate relationships* (3rd ed.). New York: McGraw-Hill.

Brennan, F. X., & Charnetski, C. J. (2000). Explanatory style and Immunoglobulin A (IgA). *Integration in Physiological and Behavioral Sciences, 35,* 251–255.

Brentjens, M., Yeung-Yue, K., Lee, P., & Tyring, S. (2003). Recurrent genital herpes treatments and their impact on quality of life. *Pharmacoeconomics, 21,* 853–863.

Bressan, R. A., Jones, H. M., Ell, P. J., & Pilowsky, L. S. (2001). Dopamine d (2) receptor blockade in schizophrenia. *American Journal of Psychiatry, 158,* 971–972.

Brewer, M. B., & Gaertner, S. L. (2001). Toward reduction of prejudice: Intergroup contact and social categorization. In R. Brown & S. L. Gaertner (Eds.), *Handbook of social psychology: Intergroup processes.* Maiden, MA: Blackwell.

Bridges, J. S., Etaugh, C., & Barnes-Farrell, J. (2002). Trait judgements of stay-at-home and employed parents: A function of social role and/or shifting standards? *Psychology of Women Quarterly, 26* (2), 140–142.

Brigham, J. C. (1986). Race and eyewitness identifications. In S. Worschel & W. G. Austin (Eds.), *Psychology of intergroup relations.* Chicago: Nelson-Hall.

Brim, O. (1999). *The MacArthur Foundation study of midlife development.* Vero Beach, FL: MacArthur Foundation.

Brink, S. (2001, May 7). Your brain on alcohol. *U.S. News & World Report, 130* (18), 50–57.

Brislin, R. (1993). *Understanding culture's influence on behavior.* Fort Worth, TX: Harcourt Brace.

Brodaty, H., Joffe, C., Luscombe, C., & Thompson, C. (2004). Vulnerability to post-traumatic stress disorder and psychological morbidity in aged holocaust survivors. *International Journal of Geriatric Psychiatry, 19,* 968.

Bronfenbrenner, U. (1986). Ecology of the family as a context for human development: Research perspectives. *Developmental Psychology, 22,* 723–742.

Bronfenbrenner, U. (1995, March). *The role research has played in Head Start.* Paper presented at the meeting of the Society for Research in Child Development, Indianapolis.

Bronfenbrenner, U. (2000). Ecological theory. In A. Kazdin (Ed.), *Encyclopedia of psychology.* Washington, DC, & New York: American Psychological Association and Oxford University Press.

Bronfenbrenner, U. (2004). *Making human beings human.* Thousand Oaks, CA: Sage.

Bronner, G., Peretz, C., & Ehrenfeld, M. (2003). Sexual harassment of nurses and nursing students. *Journal of Advanced Nursing, 42,* 637–644.

Bronstein, P., & Quina, K. (Eds.). (2003). *Teaching gender and cultural awareness.* Washington, DC: American Psychological Association.

Brook, J. S., Brook, D. W., Gordon, A. S., Whiteman, M., & Cohen, P. (1990). The psychological etiology of adolescent drug use: A family interactional approach. *Genetic Psychology Monographs, 116,* no. 2.

Brooks, G. R. (2003). Helping men embrace equality. In L. B. Silverstein & T. J. Goodrich (Eds.), *Empowerment in social context.* Washington, DC: American Psychological Association.

Brooks, J. G., & Brooks, M. G. (2001). *The case for constructivist classrooms* (2nd ed.). Upper Saddle River, NJ: Erlbaum.

Brooks-Gunn, J., Han W. J., & Waldfogel, J. (2002). Maternal employment and child cognitive outcomes in the first three years of life: The NICHD Study of Early Child Care. *Child Development, 73,* 1052–1072.

Brophy, J. (2004). *Motivating students to learn* (2nd ed.). Mahwah, NJ: Erlbaum.

Broverman, I., Vogel, S., Boverman, D., Clarkson, F., & Rosenkranz, P. (1972).

Sex-role stereotypes: A current appraisal. *Journal of Social Issues, 28,* 59–78.

Brown, B. B., Larson, R. W., & Saraswathi, T. S. (Eds.) (2002). *The world's youth.* New York: Cambridge University Press.

Brown, G., Bhrolchain, M., & Harris, T. (1975). Social class and psychiatric disturbance among women in an urban population. *Sociology, 9,* 225–254.

Brown, J. D., Steele, J. R., & Walsh-Childers, K. (Eds.). (2002). *Sexual teens, sexual media.* Mahwah, NJ: Erlbaum.

Brown, L., & Mueller, F. A. (2004). Guidelines for treating women in therapy. In G. P. Koocher, J. C. Norcross, & S. S. Hill (Eds.), *Psychologists' desk reference* (2nd Ed.). New York: Oxford University Press.

Brown, L. B., & Ott, B. R. (2004). Driving and dementia: A review of the literature. *Journal of Geriatric Psychiatry and Neurology, 17,* 232–240.

Brown, L. H., & Roodin, P. A. (2003). Grandparent-grandchild relationships and the life course perspective. In J. Dement & C. Andreoletti (Eds.), *Handbook of adult development.* New York: Kluwer.

Brown, L. S. (1989). New voices, new visions: Toward a lesbian/gay paradigm for psychology. *Psychology of Women Quarterly, 13,* 445–458.

Brown, S. C., & Park, D. C. (2003). Theoretical models of cognitive aging and implications for translational research in medicine. *The Gerontologist, 43* (Special Issue 1), 57–67.

Browne, A., & Williams, R. R. (1993). Gender, intimacy, and lethal violence: Trends from 1976 through 1987. *Gender and Society, 7,* 78–98.

Brownell, K. D. (2000). Dieting. In A. Kazdin (Ed.), *Encyclopedia of psychology.* Washington, DC, & New York: American Psychological Association and Oxford University Press.

Brownell, K. D. (2002, June 18). Commentary. *USA Today,* p. 8D.

Brownell, K. D., & Cohen, I. R. (1995). Adherence to dietary regimens. *Behavioral Medicine, 20,* 226–242.

Brownell, K. D., & Rodin, J. (1994). The dieting maelstrom: Is it possible to lose weight? *American Psychologist, 9,* 781–791.

Bruce, C. A. (2002). The grief process for patient, family, and physician. *Journal of the American Osteopathic Association, 102* (9, Supplement 3), S28–S32.

Bruess, C. J., & Pearson, J. C. (1996). Gendered patterns in family communication. In J. T. Wood (Ed.), *Gendered relationships.* Mountain View, CA: Mayfield.

Buchanan, C. M. (2001, August). *Understanding the variability in children's adjustment after divorce.* Paper presented at the meeting of the American Psychological Association, San Francisco.

Buchsbaum, M. S., Someya, T., Wu, J. C., Tang, C. Y., & Bunney, W. E. (1997). Neuroimaging bipolar illness with positron emission tomography and magnetic resonance imaging. *Psychiatric Annals, 27,* 489–495.

Buckley, P. F., Miller, D. D., Singer, B., & Donenwirth, K. (2001). The evolving clinical profile of a atypical antipsychotic medications. *Canadian Journal of Psychiatry, 46,* 285.

Buki, L. P., Ma, T., Strom, R. D., & Strom, S. K. (2003). Chinese immigrant mothers of adolescents: Self-perceptions of acculturation effects on parenting. *Cultural Diversity and Ethnic Minority Parenting, 9,* 127–140.

Bumpass, L. L., & Lu, H. H. (2002). Trends in cohabitation and implications for children's family contexts in the United States. *Population Studies, 54,* 29–41.

Burger, J. M. (2004). *Personality* (6th ed.). Belmont, CA: Wadsworth.

Burgoon, J. K., & Bacue, A. E. (2003). Nonverbal communication skills. In J. O. Greene & B. R. Burleson (Eds.), *Handbook of communication and social interactional skills.* Mahwah, NJ: Erlbaum.

Burke, G. L., Arnold, A. M., Bild, D., Cushman, M., Fried, O., Newman, A., & Robbins, C. (2001). Factors associated with healthy aging. *Journal of the American Geriatric Society, 49,* 254–262.

Burkhauser, R. V., & Quinn, J. F. (1989). American patterns of work and retirement. In W. Schmall (Ed.), *Redefining the process of retirement.* Berlin: Springer.

Burlingame, G., & Davies, R. (2002). Self-help groups. In M. Hersen & W. H. Sledge (Eds.), *Encyclopedia of psychotherapy.* San Diego: Academic Press.

Burlingame, G. M., & Ridge, N. W. (2004). Psychoeducational group treatment. In G. P. Koocher, J. C. Norcross, & S. S. Hill (Eds.), *Psychologists' desk reference* (2nd Ed.). New York: Oxford University Press.

Burns, D. (1985). *Intimate connections.* New York: Morrow.

Burns, D. (1999). *Feeling good* (Rev. ed.). New York: Avon.

Busch, A. B., Frank, R. G., & Lehman, A. F. (2004). The effect of managed behavioral health carve-out on quality of care for Medicaid patients diagnosed as having schizophrenia. *Archives of General Psychiatry, 61,* 442–448.

Buss, D. M. (1988). The evolution of human intrasexual competition: Tactics of male attraction. *Journal of Personality and Social Psychology, 54,* 616–628.

Buss, D. M. (2000). Evolutionary psychology. In A. Kazdin (Ed.), *Encyclopedia of psychology.* Washington, DC, & New York: American Psychological Association and Oxford University Press.

Buss, D. M. (2004). *Evolutionary psychology.* (2nd ed.). Boston: Allyn & Bacon.

Buss, D. M., & Barnes, M. (1986). Preferences in human mate selection. *Journal of Personality and Social Psychology, 50,* 559–570.

Buss, D. M., & Others. (1990). International preferences in selecting mates: A study of 37 cultures. *Journal of Cross-Cultural Psychology, 21,* 5–47.

Buss, D. M., & Schmitt, D. P. (1993). Sexual strategies theory: An evolutionary perspective on human mating. *Psychological Review, 100,* 200–232.

Busse, E. W., & Blazer, D. G. (1996). *The American Psychiatric Press textbook of geriatric psychiatry* (2nd ed.). Washington, DC: American Psychiatric Press.

Bussey, K., & Bandura, A. (1999). Social cognitive theory of gender development and differentiation. *Psychological Review, 106,* 676–713.

Butcher, J. N. (2003). The Minnesota Multiphasic Personality Inventory (MMPI-2). In M. Hersen (Ed.), *Comprehensive handbook of psychological assessment* (Vol. 2). New York: Wiley.

Butcher, J. N., Mineka, S., & Mooley, J. M. (2004). *Abnormal psychology and life* (12th ed.). New York: HarperCollins.

Butler, G., Fennell, M., Robson, P., & Gelder, M. (1991). Comparison of behavior therapy and cognitive behavior therapy in the treatment of generalized anxiety disorder. *Journal of Consulting and Clinical Psychology, 59,* 167–175.

Butler, R. N. (1975). *Why survive? Being old in America.* New York: Harper & Row.

Butler, R. N. (1996). Global aging: Challenges and opportunities of the next century. *Ageing International, 21,* 12–32.

Butter, E. M., & Pargament, K. I. (2003). Development of a model for assessing religious coping: Initial validation of the process evaluation model. *Mental Health, Religion, and Culture, 6,* 175–194.

Buunk, B. P., & Dijkstra, P. (2004). Men, women, and infidelity. In J. Duncombe, K. Harrison, G. Allan, & D. Marsden (Eds.), *The state of affairs.* Mahwah, NJ: Erlbaum.

Bybee, J. A., & Wells, Y. V. (2003). The development of possible selves during adulthood. In J. Demick & C. Andreoletti

(Eds.), *Handbook of adult development.* New York: Kluwer.

C

Cacioppo, J. T., Ernst, J. M., Burleson, M. H., McClintock, M. K., Malarkey, W. B., Hawkley, L. C., Kowalewski, R. B., Paulsen. A., Hobson, J. A., Hugdahl, K., Spiegel, D., & Berntson, G. G. (2000). Lonely traits and concomitant physiological processes: The MacArthur Social Neuroscience Studies. *International Journal of Psychophysiology, 35,* 143–154.

Cain, D. J. (2001). Defining characteristics, history, and evolution of humanistic psychotherapies. In D. J. Cain & J. Seeman (Eds.), *Humanistic psychotherapies.* Washington, DC: American Psychological Association.

Calabrese, R. L., & Schumer, H. (1986). The effects of service activities on adolescent alienation. *Adolescence, 21,* 675–687.

Callan, J. E. (2001). Gender development: Psychoanalytic perspectives. In J. Worell (Ed.), *Encyclopedia of women and gender.* San Diego: Academic Press.

Campbell, A., Shirley, L., & Candy, J. (2004). A longitudinal study of gender-related cognition and behavior. *Developmental Science, 7,* 1–9.

Campbell, J. D., Teaser, A., & Fairey, P. J. (1986). Conformity and attention to the stimulus: Some temporal and contextual dynamics. *Journal of Personality and Social Psychology, 51,* 315–324.

Campbell, R., Setl, T., & Ahrens, C. E. (2004). The impact of rape on women's sexual health risk behaviors. *Health Psychology, 23,* 67–74.

Canadian Mental Health Association. (1984). *Links between work and home.* Toronto: Canadian Mental Health Association.

Canino, G., & others. (2004). The DSM-IV rates of child and adolescent disorders in Puerto Rico. *Archives of General Psychiatry, 61,* 85–93.

Cannon, W. B. (1929). *Bodily changes in pain, hunger, fear, and rage* (2nd ed.). New York: Appleton-Century-Crofts.

Canter, P. H. (2003). The therapeutic effects of meditation. *British Medical Journal, 326,* 1049–1050.

Canter, P. H., & Ernst, E. (2004). Insufficient evidence to conclude whether transcendental meditation decreases blood pressure. *Journal of Hypertension, 22,* 2049–2054.

Cantor, N., & Blanton, H. (1996). Effortful pursuit of personal goals in daily life. In P. M. Gollwitzer & J. A. Bargh (Eds.), *The psychology of the action: Linking cognition and motivation to behavior.* New York: Guilford Press.

Cantor, N., & Langston, C. A. (1989). Ups and downs of life tasks in a life transition. In L. A. Pervin (Ed.), *Good concepts in personality and social psychology.* Mahwah, NJ: Erlbaum.

Caplan, P. J., & Caplan, J. B. (1999). *Thinking critically about research on sex and gender* (2nd ed.). New York: Longman.

Capuzzi, D. (2003). *Approaches to group counseling.* Upper Saddle River, NJ: Prentice-Hall.

Cardenas, J., Williams, K., Wilson, J. P., Fanouraki, G., & Singh, A. (2003). PTSD, major depressive symptoms, and substance abuse following September 11, 2001, in a midwestern university population. *International Journal of Emergency Mental Health, 5,* 15–28.

Carey, M. P., & Vanable, P. A. (2003). AIDS/HIV. In I. B. Weiner (Ed.), *Handbook of psychology* (Vol. 9). New York: Wiley.

Carlbring, P., Westling, B. E., & Andersson, G. (2000). A review of published self-help books for panic disorder. *Scandinavian Journal of Behaviour Therapy, 29,* 5–13.

Carlisle, D. (2002, September 11). For survivors, wounds remain fresh. *USA Today,* p. A12, letters.

Carlson, L. E., Speca, M., Patel, K. D., & Goddey, E. (2003). Mindfulness-based stress reduction in relation to quality of life, symptoms of stress, and immune parameters in breast and prostate cancer outpatients. *Psychosomatic Medicine, 65,* 571–581.

Carlson, L. E., Speca, M., Patel, K. D., & Goodey, E. (2004). Mindfulness-based stress reduction in relation to quality of life, mood, symptoms of stress and levels of cortisol, DHEAS, and melatonin in breast and prostate cancer outpatients. *Psychoneuroendocrinology, 29,* 448–474.

Carroll, J. L. (2005). *Sexuality now.* Belmont, CA: Wadsworth.

Carson, C. C. (2003). Sildenafil: A 4–year update in the treatment of 20 million erectile dysfunction patients. *Current Urology Reports, 4,* 488–496.

Carstensen, L. L. (1991). Selectivity theory: Social activity in life-span context. *Annual Review of Gerontology and Geriatrics, 11,* 195–217.

Carstensen, L. L. (1993). Motivation for social contact across the life span: A theory of socioemotional selectivity. In J. E. Jacobs (Ed.), *Nebraska symposium on motivation.* Lincoln: University of Nebraska Press.

Carstensen, L. L. (1995). Evidence for life-span theory of socioemotional selectivity. *Current Directions in Psychological Science, 4,* 151–156.

Carstensen, L. L. (1998). A life-span approach to social motivation. In J. Heckhausen & C. Dweck (Eds.), *Motivation and self-regulation across the life span.* New York: Cambridge University Press.

Carstensen, L. L., & Charles, S. T. (2003). Human aging: Why is even good news taken as bad? In L. A. Aspinell & U. M. Staudinger (Eds.), *A psychology of human strengths.* Washington, DC: American Psychological Association.

Carstensen, L. L., Charles, S. T., Isaacowitz, D., & Kennedy, Q. (2003). Life-span development and emotion. In R. J. Davidson, K. Scherer, & H. H. Goldsmith (Eds.), *Handbook of affective sciences.* New York: Oxford University Press.

Carstensen, L. L., Fung, H., & Charles, S. (2003). Socioemotional selectivity theory and the regulation of emotion in the second half of life. *Motivation and Emotion, 27*(2), 103–123.

Carstensen, L. L., Gottman, J. M., & Levenson, R. W. (1995). Emotional behavior in long-term marriage. *Psychology and Aging, 10,* 140–149.

Carter, B., & McGoldrick, M. (1989). Overview: The changing family life cycle—A framework for family therapy. In B. Carter & M. McGoldrick (Eds.), *The changing family life cycle* (2nd ed.). Boston: Allyn & Bacon.

Cartwright-Hatton, S., Roberts, C., Chitsabesan, P., Fothergill, C., & Harrington, R. (2004). Systematic review of the efficacy of cognitive behavior therapies for childhood and adolescent anxiety disorders. *British Journal of Clinical Psychology, 43,* 421–436.

Carver, C. S., & Scheier, M. F. (2002). Optimism. In C. R. Snyder & S. J. Lopez (Eds.), *Handbook of positive psychology.* New York: Oxford University Press.

Carver, C. S., Scheier, M. F., & Weintraub, J. K. (1989). Assessing coping strategies: A theoretically based approach. *Journal of Personality and Social Psychology, 56,* 267–283.

Cassano, P., Lattanzi, L., Soldani, F., Navari, S., Battistini, G., Gemingnani, A., & Cassano, G. B. (2004). Pramipexole in treatment-resistant depression: an extended follow-up. *Depression and Anxiety, 20,* 131–138.

Castonguay, L. G., Constantino, M. J., & Schut, A. J. (2004). Psychotherapy research. In W. E. Craighead & C. B. Nemeroff (Eds.), *The concise Corsini* *encyclopedia of psychology and behavioral science.* New York: Wiley.

Castonguay, L. G., Gottfried, M. R., Halperin, G. S., & Reid, J. J. (2003). Psychotherapy integration. In I. B. Weiner (Ed.), *Handbook of psychology* (Vol. 8). New York: Wiley.

Cayley, W. E. (2004). Effectiveness of condoms in reducing heterosexual transmission of HIV. *American Family Physician, 70,* 1268–1269.

Center for Survey Research at the University of Connecticut. (2000). *Hours on the job.* Storrs: University of Connecticut, Center for Survey Research.

Centers for Disease Control and Prevention. (2002). *America's families and living arrangements.* Atlanta: Author.

Centers for Disease Control and Prevention (2002). *Cohabitation.* Atlanta, GA: Author.

Centers for Disease Control and Prevention. (2004). *Sexually transmitted diseases.* Atlanta: Author.

Centers for Disease Control and Prevention. (2004). *Strategies for stopping smoking.* Atlanta, GA: Author.

Chambless, D. L. (2004). Compendium of empirically supported treatments. In Koocher, G. P., Norcross, J. C., & Hill. S. S. (2004). *Psychologists' desk reference* (2nd Ed.). New York: Oxford University Press.

Charles, S. T., & Carstensen, L. L. (2004). A life-span view of emotional functioning in adulthood and old age. In P. Costa (Ed.), *Advances in Cell Aging and Gerontology Series.* New York: Elsevier.

Cheitlin, M. D. (2003). Sexual activity and cardiovascular disease. *American Journal of Cardiology, 92,* 3M-9M.

Chen, H., Chung, H., Chen, T., Fang, L., & Chen, J. P. (2003). The emotional distress in a community after the terrorist attack on the World Trade Center. *Community Mental Health Journal, 39,* 157–165.

Chen, X., Tyler, K. A., Whitbeck, L. B., & Hoyt, D. R. (2004). Early sexual abuse, street adversity, and drug use among female homeless and runaway adolescents in the Midwest. *Journal of Drug Issues, 34,* 1–20.

Cherlin, A. J. (2004). The deinstitutionalization of American marriages. *Journal of Marriage and the Family, 66,* 848–861.

Chevan, A. (1996). As cheaply as one: Cohabitation in the older population. *Journal of Marriage and the Family, 58,* 656–667.

Chirot, D., & Seligman M. E. P. (Eds.). (2001). *Ethnopolitical warfare.* Washington, DC: American Psychological Association.

Chodorow, N. (1978). *The reproduction of mothering.* Berkeley: University of California Press.

Chodorow, N. (1989). *Femininism and psychoanalytic theory.* New Haven, CT: Yale University Press.

Choi, N. G. (2001). Relationship between life, satisfaction and postretirement employment among older women. *International Journal of Aging and Human Development, 52,* 45–70.

Chong, A., Killeen, O., & Clarke, T. (2004). Work-related stress among pediatric non-consultant hospital doctors. *Irish Medical Journal, 97,* 203–205.

Chouinard, G. (2004). Issues in the clinical use of benzodiazepines. *Journal of Clinical Psychiatry, 65* (Supplement 5), 7–12.

Christensen, L. (1996). *Diet-behavior relationships.* Washington, DC: American Psychological Association.

Christensen, L. B. (2004). *Experimental methodology* (9th ed.). Boston: Allyn & Bacon.

Christopher, F. S., & Sprecher, S. (2000). Sexuality in marriage, dating, and other relationships: Decade review. *Journal of Marriage and Family, 62,* 999–1017.

Chun, K. M., & Akutsu, P. D. (2003). Acculturation among ethnic minority families. In K. M. Chun, P. B. Organista, & G. Marin (Eds.), *Acculturation.* Washington, DC: American Psychological Association.

Church, D. K., Siegel, M. A., & Fowler, C. D. (1988). *Growing old in America.* Wylie, TX: Information Aids.

Cialdini, R. B. (2001). *Influence* (4th ed.). Boston: Allyn & Bacon.

Cialdini, R. B., & Trost, M. R. (1998). Social influence: Social norms, conformity, and compliance. In D. T. Gilbert, S. T. Fiske, & G. Lindzey (Eds.), *Handbook of social psychology* (4th ed., Vol. 2). New York: McGraw-Hill.

Cicchetti, D., & Toth, S. L. (1998). Perspectives on research and practice in developmental psychology. In W. Damon (Ed.), *Handbook of child psychology* (Vol. 4). New York: Wiley.

Claar, R. L., & Blumenthal, J. A. (2003). The value of stress-management interventions in life-threatening medical conditions. *Current Directions in Psychological Science, 12,* 133–137.

Clark, D. M., Salkovskis, P. M., Hackmann, A., Middleton, H., Anastasiades, P., & Gelder, M. (1994). A comparison of cognitive therapy, applied relaxation, and imipramine in the treatment of panic disorder. *British Journal of Psychiatry, 164,* 759–769.

Clark, N. M., & Dodge, J. A. (1999). Exploring self-efficacy as a predictor of disease management. *Health Education & Behavior, 26,* 72–89.

Clark, R. D., & Hatfield, E. (1989). Gender differences in receptivity to sexual offers. *Journal of Psychology and Human Sexuality, 2,* 39–55.

Clark, T. (2001). Post-traumatic stress disorder: Baby should not be thrown out with the bath water. *British Journal of Medicine, 322,* 1303–1304.

Clark-Plaskie, M., & Lachman, M. E. (1999). The sense of control in midlife. In S. L. Willis & J. D. Reid (Eds.), *Life in the middle.* San Diego: Academic Press.

Clarke, E. J., Preston, M., Raksin, J., & Bengston, V. L. (1999). Types of conflicts and tensions between older adults and adult children. *Gerontologist, 39,* 261–270.

Clay, R. A. (2000, April). Linking up online: Is the Internet enhancing interpersonal connections or leading to greater isolation? *Monitor on Psychology,* 20–23.

Clayton, A. H., McGarvey, E. L., Abouesh, A. L., & Pinkerton, R. C. (2001). Substitution of an SSRI with bupropion sustained release following SSRI-induced sexual dysfunction. *Journal of Clinical Psychiatry, 62,* 185–190.

Cochran, S. D., & Mays, V. M. (1990). Sex, lies, and HIV. *New England Journal of Medicine, 322,* 774–775.

Cohen, D., Gerardin, P., Maxet, P., Purper-Ouakil, D., & Flament, M. E. (2004). Pharmacological treatment of adolescent major depression. *Journal of Child and Adolescent Psychopharmacology, 14,* 19–31.

Cohen, L. A. (1987, November). Diet and cancer. *Scientific American,* pp. 128–137.

Cohen, L. A., de Moor, C., & Amato, R. J. (2001). The association between treatment-specific optimism and depressive symptomatology in patients enrolled in a phase I cancer trial. *Cancer, 91,* 1949–1955.

Cohen, R. L., & Borsoi, D. (1996). The role of gestures in description-communication: A cross-sectional study of aging. *Journal of Nonverbal Behavior, 20,* 45–64.

Cohen, S. (2002). Psychosocial stress, social networks, and susceptibility to infection. In H. G. Koenig & H. J. Cohen (Eds.), *The link between religion and health.* New York: Oxford University Press.

Cohen, S., Doyle, W. J., Skoner, D. P., Rabin, B. S., & Gawaltney, J. M. (1997). Social ties and susceptibility to the common cold. *Journal of the American Medical Association, 277,* 1940–1944.

Cohen, S., Doyle, W. J., Turner, R. B., Alper, C. M., & Skoner, D. P. (2003). Emotional style and susceptibility to the common cold. *Psychosomatic Medicine, 65,* 652–657.

Cohen, S., Doyle, W. J., Turner, R. B., Alper, C. M., & Skoner, D. P. (2003). Sociability and the common cold. *Psychological Science, 14,* 389–395.

Cohen, S., Line, S., Manuck, S. B., Rabin, B. S., Heise, E. R., & Kaplan, J. R. (1997). Chronic social stress, social status, and susceptibility to upper respiratory infections in nonhuman primates. *Psychosomatic Medicine, 59,* 213–221.

Cohen, S., Miller, G. E., & Rabin, B. S. (2001). Psychological stress and antibody response to immunization. *Psychosomatic Medicine, 63,* 7–18.

Coker, L. A., & Widiger, T. A. (2005). *Personality disorders.* In J. E. Maddux & B. A. Winstead (Eds.), *Psychopathology.* Mahwah, NJ: Erlbaum.

Colcombe, S. J., Erickson, K. I., Raz, N., Webb, A. G., Cohen, N. J., McAuley, E., & Kramer, A. F. (2003). Aerobic fitness reduces brain tissue loss in aging humans. *Journal of Gerontology: Biological Sciences and Medical Sciences, 58,* M176–M180.

Cole, E. R., & Stewart, A. J. (1996). Black and White women's political activism: Personality development, political identity and social responsibility. *Journal of Personality and Social Psychology, 71,* 130–140.

Coleman, M., Ganong, L., & Fine, M. (2000). Reinvestigating remarriage: Another decade of progress. *Journal of Marriage and the Family, 62,* 1288–1307.

Coleman, M., Ganong, L., & Fine, M. (2004). Communication in stepfamilies. In A. L. Vangelisti (Ed.), *Handbook of family communication.* Mahwah, NJ: Erlbaum.

Coleman, M., Ganong, L., & Weaver, S. E. (2001). Relationship maintenance and enhancement in remarried families. In. J. H. Harvey & A. Wenzel (Eds.), *Close romantic relationships.* Mahwah, NJ: Erlbaum.

Coleman, P. D. (1986, August). *Regulation of dendritic extent: Human aging brain and Alzheimer's disease.* Paper presented at the meeting of the American Psychological Association, Washington, DC.

Coley, R. (2001). *Differences in the gender gap: Comparisons across racial/ethnic groups in the United States.* Princeton, NJ: Educational Testing Service.

Coll, C. T. G., & Pachter, L. M. (2002). Ethnic and minority parenting. In M. H. Bornstein (Ed.), *Handbook of parenting* (2nd ed.). Mahwah, NJ: Erlbaum.

Collaku, A., Rankinen, T., Rice, T., Leon, A. S., Rao, D. C., Skinner, J. S., Wilmore, J. H., & Bouchard, C. (2004). A genome-wide linkage scan for dietary energy and nutrient intakes. *American Journal of Clinical Nutrition, 79,* 881–886.

Collins, M. (1996, Winter). The job outlook for '96 grads. *Journal of Career Planning,* 51–54.

Collins, N. L., & Feeney, B. C. (2004). An attachment theory perspective on closeness and intimacy. In D. J. Mashek & A. P. Aron (Eds.), *Handbook of closeness and intimacy.* Mahwah, NJ: Erlbaum.

Collins, W. A., & Laursen, B. (2000). Adolescent relationships: The art of fugue. In C. Hendrick & S. S. Hendrick (Eds.), *Close relationships: A sourcebook.* Thousand Oaks, CA: Sage.

Comas-Díaz, L. (2001). Hispanics, Latinos, or Americanos: The evolution of identity. *Cultural Diversity and Ethnic Minority Psychology, 7,* 115–120.

Conger, R. D., & Chao, W. (1996). Adolescent depressed mood. In R. L. Simons (Ed.), *Understanding differences between divorced and intact families: Stress, interaction, and child outcome.* Thousand Oaks, CA: Sage.

Conger, R. D., Lorenz, F. O., & Wickrama, K. A. S. (Eds.). (2004). *Continuity and change in family relations.* Mahwah, NJ: Erlbaum.

Conklin, C. A., & Tiffany, S. T. (2002). Applying extinction research and theory to cue-exposure addiction treatments. *Addiction, 97,* 155–167.

Contrada, R. J., & Goyal, M. (2005). Individual differences, health, and illness. In S. Sutton, A. Baum, & M. Johnston (Eds.), *The SAGE handbook of health psychology.* Thousand Oaks, CA: Sage.

Contrada, R. J., Goyal, T. M., Cahter, C., Rafalson, L., Idler, E. L., & Krause, T. J. (2004). Psychosocial factors in outcomes of heart surgery: The impact of religious involvement and depressive symptoms. *Health Psychology, 23,* 227–238.

Conway, K. P., Swendsen, J. D., & Merikangas, K. R. (2003). Alcohol expectancies, alcohol consumption, and problem drinking: The moderating role of family history. *Addictive Behavior, 28,* 823–836.

Cooney, T., & Dunne, K. (2004). Intimate relationships in later life. In M. Coleman & L. Ganong (Eds.), *Handbook of contemporary families.* Thousand Oaks, CA: Sage.

Cooper, A., Galbreath, N., & Becker, M. A. (2004). Sex on the internet: furthering our understanding of men with online sexual problems. *Psychology of Addictive Behaviors, 18,* 223–230.

Cooper, C. R., Garcia Coll, C. T., Bartko, W. T., Davis, H. M., & Chatman, C. (Eds.), (2005). *Developmental pathways through middle childhood.* Mahwah, NJ: Erlbaum.

Corey, G. (1996). *Theory and practice of counseling and psychotherapy* (5th ed.). Pacific Grove, CA: Brooks/Cole.

Corsica, J. A., & Perri, M. G. (2003). Obesity. In I. B. Weiner (Ed.), *Handbook of psychology* (Vol. 9). New York: Wiley.

Corsini, R. J. (1999). *The dictionary of psychology.* Philadelphia: Brunner/Mazel.

Cortina, L. M. (2004). Hispanic perspectives on sexual harassment and social support. *Personality and Social Psychology Bulletin, 30,* 574–584.

Cosgrave, E., McGorry, P., Allen, N., & Jackson, H. (2000). Depression in young people: A growing challenge for primary care. *Australian Family Physician, 29,* 123–127.

Costa, P. T., & McCrae, R. R. (1992). *Revised NEO personality inventory.* Odessa, FL: Psychological Assessment Resources.

Costa, P. T., & McCrae, R. R. (1995). Solid ground on the wetlands of personality: A reply to Black. *Psychological Bulletin, 177,* 216–220.

Costa, P. T., & McCrae, R. R. (1998) Personality assessment. In H. S. Friedman (Ed.), *Encyclopedia of mental health* (Vol. 3). San Diego: Academic Press.

Costanzo, M., & Archer, D. (1995). A method for teaching about verbal and nonverbal communication. In M. E. Ware & D. E. Johnson (Eds.), *Demonstrations and activities in teaching of psychology* (Vol. 3). Hillsdale, NJ: Erlbaum.

Cotten, S. R. (1999). Marital status and mental health revisited: Examining the importance of risk factors and resources. *Family Relations, 48,* 225–233.

Council of Economic Advisors. (2000). *Teens and their parents in the 21st century: An examination of trends in teen behavior and the role of parent involvement.* Washington, DC: Author.

Courtenay, W. H., McCreary, D. R., & Merighi, J. R. (2002). Gender and ethnic differences in health beliefs and behaviors. *Journal of Health Psychology, 7,* 219–231.

Courtet, P., & others. (2004). Serotonin transporter gene may be involved in short-term risk of subsequent suicide attempts. *Biological Psychiatry, 55,* 46–51.

Covey, S. R. (1989). *The seven habits of highly effective people.* New York: Simon & Schuster.

Covey, S. R., Merrill, A. R., & Merrill, R. R. (1994). *First things first.* New York: Simon & Schuster.

Covington, M. V. (1992). *Making the grade: A self-worth perspective on motivation and school reform.* New York: Cambridge University Press.

Covington, M. V. (2002). Patterns of adaptive learning study: Where do we go from here? In C. Midgley (Ed.), *Goals, goal structures, and patterns of adaptive learning.* Mahwah, NJ: Erlbaum.

Covington, M. V., & Dray, E. (2002). The development course of achievement motivation: A need-based approach. In A. Wigfield & J. S. Eccles (Eds.), *Development of achievement motivation.* San Diego: Academic Press.

Cowan, C. P., & Cowan, P. A. (2000). *When partners become parents.* Mahwah, NJ: Erlbaum.

Cox, H., & Hammonds, A. (1998). Religiosity, aging, and life satisfaction. *Journal of Religion and Aging, 5,* 1–21.

Cox, M. J., Burchinal, M., Taylor, L. C., Frosch, C., Goldman, B., & Kanoy, K. (2004). The transition to parenting: Continuity and change in early parenting behavior and attitudes. In R. D. Conger, F. O. Lorenz, & K. A. S. Wickrama (Eds.), *Continuity and change in family relations.* Mahwah, NJ: Erlbaum.

Coyne, J. C. (2000). Mood disorders. In A. Kazdin (Ed.), *Encyclopedia of psychology.* Washington, DC, & New York: American Psychological Association and Oxford University Press.

Crabbe, J. C. (2002). Alcohol and genetics: New Models. *American Journal of Genetics, 114,* 969–974.

Craighead, W. E., & Craighead, B. H. (2004). Depression. In W. E. Craighead & C. B. Nemeroff (Eds.), *The concise Corsini encyclopedia of psychology and behavioral science.* New York: Wiley.

Craighead, W. E., & Craighead, L. W. (2001). The role of psychotherapy in treating psychiatric disorders. *Medical Clinics of North America, 85,* 617–629.

Craik, F. I. M., & Salthouse, T. A. (Eds.) (2000). *The handbook of aging and cognition.* Mahwah, NJ: Erlbaum.

Cramer, P. (1999). Future directions for the Thematic Apperception Test. *Journal of Personality Assessment, 72,* 74–92.

Cramer, P., & Brilliant, M. A. (2001). Defense use and defense understanding in children. *Journal of Personality, 69,* 297–322.

Crawford, M., & Unger, R. (2004). *Women and gender* (4th ed.). New York: McGraw-Hill.

Crick, N. R., Nelson, D. A., Morales, J. R., Cullerton-Sen, C., Casas, J. F., & Hickman, S. (2001). Relational victimization in childhood and adolescence: I hurt you through the grapevine. In J. Juvonen & S. Graham (Eds.), *Peer harassment in school: The plight of the vulnerable and victimized.* New York: Guilford.

Crits-Christoph, P. (2004). Psychotherapy. In W. E. Craighead & C. B. Nemeroff (Eds.), *The concise Corsini encyclopedia of psychology and behavioral science.* New York: Wiley.

Crocker, J., & Park, L. E. (2003). Seeking self-esteem: Construction, maintenance, and protection of self-worth. In M. Leary & J. Tangney (Eds.), *Handbook of self and identity* (pp. 291–313). New York: Guilford.

Crooks, R., & Bauer, K. (2005). *Our sexuality* (9th ed.). Belmont, CA: Wadsworth.

Crosby, A. E., Cheltenham, M. P., & Sacks, J. J. (1999). Incidence of suicidal ideation and behavior in the United States, 1994. *Suicide and Life-Threatening Behavior, 29,* 131–140.

Cross-National Collaborative Group (1992). The changing rate of major depression. *Journal of the American Medical Association, 268,* 3098–3105.

Crowe, S. M., & Wimett, L. (2004). Varenafil treatment for erectile dysfunction. *Annals of Pharmacotherapy, 38,* 77–85.

Crowther, J. H., Sanftner, J., Bonifazi, D. Z., & Shepherd, K. L. (2001). The role of daily hassles in binge eating. *International Journal of Eating Disorders, 29,* 449–454.

Csaja, S. J. (2001). Technological change and the older worker. In J. E. Birren & K. W. Schaie (Eds.), *Handbook of the psychology of aging* (5th ed.). San Diego: Academic Press.

Csikszentmihalyi, M., & Rathunde, K. (1998). The development of the person: An experiential perspective on the ontogenesis of psychological complexity. In W. Damon (Ed.), *Handbook of child psychology* (5th ed., Vol. 1). New York: Wiley.

Cuijpers, P. (1997). Bibliotherapy in unipolar depression: A meta-analysis. *Journal of Behavior Therapy and Experimental Psychiatry, 28,* 139–147.

Cuijpers, P. (2001). Mortality and depressive symptoms in inhabitants of residential homes. *International Journal of Geriatric Psychiatry, 16,* 131–138.

Culbertson, F. M. (1991, August). *Mental health of women: An international journey.* Paper presented at the meeting of the American Psychological Association, San Francisco.

Cunnignham, W. A. (2004). Implicit and explicit ethnocentrism: revisiting the ideologies of prejudice. *Personality and Social Psychology Bulletin, 30,* 133–1346.

Cupach, W. R., & Spitzberg, B. H. (2004). *The dark side of relationship pursuit.* Mahwah, NJ: Erlbaum.

Curtis, R. C., Kimball, A., & Stroup, E. L. (2004). Understanding and treating social phobia. *Journal of Counseling and Development, 82,* 3–9.

Cushner, K. H. (2003). *Human diversity in action: Developing multicultural competencies for the classroom.* New York: McGraw-Hill.

Cushner, K. H., McClelland, A., & Stafford, P. (2003). *Human diversity in action: An integrative approach* (4th ed.). New York: McGraw-Hill.

Cutrona, C. E. (1982). Transition to college: Loneliness and the process of social adjustment. In L. A. Peplau & D. Perlman (Eds.), *Loneliness.* New York: Wiley.

Cvetanovski, J., & Jex, S. (1994). Locus of control of unemployed people and its relationship to psychological and physical well-being. *Work and Stress, 8* (1), 60–67.

D

D'Angelo, B., & Wierzbicki, M. (2003). Relations of daily hassles with both anxious and depressed mood in students. *Psychological Reports, 92,* 416–418.

D'Arcangues, C., Piaggio, G., Brache, V., Aissa, R. B., Hazelden, C., Massai, R., Pinol, A., Subakir, S. B., & Su-Juan, G. (2004). Effectiveness and acceptability of vitamin E and low dose aspirin, alone or in combination, on Norplant-induced prolonged bleeding. *Contraception, 70,* 451–462.

Dainton, M., Zelley, E., & Langan, E. (2003). Maintaining friendships throughout the lifespan. In D. J. Canary & M. Dainton (Eds.), *Maintaining relationships through communication.* Mahwah, NJ: Erlbaum.

Danielson, C. K., & Holmes, M. M. (2004). Adolescent sexual assault: an update of the literature. *Current Opinions in Obstetrics and Gynecology, 16,* 383–388.

Danner, D., Snowdon, D., & Friesen, W. (2001). Positive emotions in early life and longevity: Findings from the Nun Study. *Journal of Personality and Social Psychology, 80* (5), 813–814.

Dannon, P. N., Dolberg, O. T., Schrieber, S., & Grunhaus, L. (2002). Three and six-month outcome following courses of either ECT or rTMS in a population of severely depressed individuals—preliminary report. *Biological Psychiatry, 51,* 687–690.

Dantzer, R. (2004). Innate immunity at the forefront of psychoneuroimmunology. *Brain, Behavior, and Immunity, 18,* 1–6.

Darley, J. M., & Latané, B. (1968). Bystander intervention in emergencies:

Diffusion of responsibility. *Journal of Personality and Social Psychology, 8,* 377–383.

Davey, M., Goettler Eaker, D., Stone Fish, L., & Klock, K. (2003). Ethnic identity in an American white minority group. *Identity, 3,* 143–158.

Davidson, R. J., Kabat-Zinn, J., Schumacher, J., Rosenkranz, M., Muller, D., Santorelli, S. F., Urbanowski, F., Harrington, A., Bonus, K., & Sheridan, J. F. (2003). Alterations in brain and immune function produced by mindfulness meditation. *Psychosomatic Medicine, 65,* 564–570.

Davies, J., & Brember, I. (1999). Reading and mathematics attainments and self-esteem in years 2 and 6—an eight-year cross-sectional study. *Educational Studies, 25,* 145–157.

Davies, S. J., Jackson, P. R., Potokar, J., & Nutt, D. J. (2004). Treatment of anxiety and depressive disorders in patients with cardiovascular disease. *British Medical Journal, 328,* 939–943.

Davis, G. F. (2001). Loss and duration of grief. *Journal of the American Medical Association, 285,* 1152–1153.

Davis, K. E. (1985, February). Neat and dear: Friendship and love compared. *Psychology Today,* pp. 22–29.

Davis, R., & Miller, L. (1999, July 15). Millions comb the web for medical information. *USA Today,* p. 1D.

Davison, G. C., & Neale, J. M. (2001). *Abnormal psychology* (8th ed.). New York: Wiley.

Davison, G. C., & Neale, J. M. (2004). *Abnormal psychology* (9th ed.). New York: Wiley.

De Graaf, C., Blom, W. A., Smeets, P. A., Stafleu, A., & Hendriks, H. F. (2004). Biomarkers of satiation and satiety. *American Journal of Clinical Nutrition, 79,* 946–961.

de Jong-Gierveld, J. (1987). Developing and testing a model of loneliness. *Journal of Personality and Social Psychology, 53,* 119–128.

Dean, B. (2004). The neurobiology of bipolar disorder. *Australian and New Zealand Journal of Psychiatry, 38,* 135–140.

Dearing, E., Taylor, B. A., & McCartney, K. (2004). Implications of family income dynamics for women's depressive symptoms during the first three years after childbirth. *American Journal of Public Health, 94,* 1372–1377.

Deaux, K. (2001). Social identity. In J. Worell (Ed.), *Encyclopedia of gender and women.* San Diego: Academic Press.

Deci, E., & Ryan, R. (1994). Promoting self-determined education. *Scandinavian Journal of Educational Research, 38,* 3–14.

Decruyenaere, M., Evers-Kiebooms, G., Welkenhuysen, M., Denayer, L., & Claes, E. (2000). Cognitive representations of breast cancer, emotional distress, and preventive health behavior: A theoretical perspective. *Psychooncology, 9,* 528–536.

Deffenbacher, J. L., Deffenbacher, D. M., Lynch, R. S., & Richards, T. L. (2003). Anger, aggression, and risky behavior: A comparison of high and low anger drivers. *Behavior Research and Therapy, 41,* 701–708.

DeFleur, M. L., Kearney, P., Plax, T., & DeFleur, M. H. (2005). *Fundamentals of human communication* (3rd ed.). New York: McGraw-Hill.

Dejong, A., & Franklin, B. A. (2004). Prescribing exercise for the elderly: current research and recommendations. *Current Sports Medicine Reports, 3,* 337–343.

deJong, J. T., Komproe, I. H., & Van Ommeren, M. (2003). Common mental disorders in postconflict settings. *Lancet, 361,* 2128–2130.

Dell, P. F. (2002). Dissociative phenomena of dissociative identity disorder. *Journal of Nervous and Mental Disorders, 190,* 10–15.

Dell, P. F., & Eisenhower, J. W. (1990). Adolescent multiple personality disorder: A preliminary study of eleven cases. *Journal of the American Academy of Child & Adolescent Psychiatry, 29,* 359–366.

Dembo, M. H., (2004). *Motivation and learning strategies for college success (2nd Ed.).* Mahwah, NJ: Erlbaum.

Demerouti, E., Bakker, A. B., Nachreiner, F., & Schaufeli, W. B. (2001). The job demands-resources model of burnout. *Journal of Applied Psychology, 86,* 499–512.

DeNeve, K. M., & Cooper, H. (1998). The happy personality: A meta-analysis of 137 personality traits and subjective well-being. *Psychological Bulletin, 124,* 197–229.

Denner, J., & Dunbar, N. (2004). Negotiating femininity: Power and strategies of Mexican American girls. *Sex roles, 50,* 301–314.

DePaulo, B. M. (1994). Spotting lies: Can humans learn to do better? *Current Directions in Psychological Science, 3,* 83–86.

Derlega, V. J., Winstead, B. A., & Jones, W. H. (2005). *Personality* (3rd ed.). Belmont, CA: Wadsworth.

Desmarais, S., & C. Alksnis. (2004). Gender issues. In J. Barling, E. K. Kelloway, & M. R. Frone (Eds.), *Handbook of work and stress.* Thousand Oaks, CA: Sage.

DeSpelder, L. A., & Strickland, A. L. (2005). *The last dance: Encountering death and dying* (6th ed.). Mountain View, CA: Mayfield.

Deutsch, M., & Collins, M. (1951). *Interracial housing: A psychological evaluation of a social experiment.* Minneapolis: University of Minnesota Press.

DeVellis, B. M., & DeVellis, R. F. (2001). Self-efficacy and health. In A. Baum, T. A. Revenson, & J. E. Singer (Eds.), *Handbook of health psychology.* Mahwah, NJ: Erlbaum.

Devine, P. G., Evett, S. R., & Vasquez-Suson, K. A. (1996). Exploring the interpersonal dynamics of intergroup contact. In R. M. Sorrentino & E. T. Higgins (Eds.), *Handbook of motivation and cognition: The interpersonal context* (Vol. 3). New York: Guilford Press.

DeVito, J. (2004). *Interpersonal communication workbook* (10th ed.). Upper Saddle River, NJ: Prentice Hall.

Devlin, M. J., Golfein, J. A., Crino, J. S., & Wolk, S. L. (2000). Open treatment of overweight binge eaters with phentermine and fluoxetine as an adjunct to cognitive-behavioral therapy. *International Journal of Eating Disorders, 28,* 325–332.

Dew, R., & McCall, W. V. (2004). Efficency of outpatient ECT. *Journal of Electroconvulsive Therapy, 20,* 24–25.

Dewe, P. (2004). Work stress and coping: theory, research, and practice. *British Journal of Guidance and Counseling, 32,* 139–142.

Diamond, L. M. (2003). Love matters: Romantic relationships among sexual-minority adolescents. In P. Florsheim (Ed.), *Adolescent romantic relations and sexual behavior.* Mahwah, NJ: Erlbaum.

Diamond, L. M., & Aspinwall, L. G. (2003). Emotion regulation across the life span: An integrative process emphasizing self-regulation, positive affect, and dyadic processes. *Motivation and Emotion, 27,* 125–156.

DiBlassio, J., Simonin, D., DeCarolis, A., Morse, L., Jean, J., Vassalotti, L., Franks, K., & Chambliss, C. (1999, April). *Assessing the quality of psychological healthcare sites available on the Internet.* Paper presented at the meeting of the Eastern Psychological Association, Providence, RI.

Dickson, F. C., Christian, A., & Remmo, C. J. (2004). An exploration of marital and family issues of the later-life adult. In A. L. Vangelisti (Ed.), *Handbook of family communication.* Mahwah, NJ: Erlbaum.

Dickson, G. L. (1990). A feminist poststructuralist analysis of the knowledge of menopause. *Advances in Nursing Science, 12,* 15–31.

Diener, E. (2000). Positive leadership: Moving into the future. *The Psychologist-Manager Journal, 4,* 233–236.

Diener, E. (2003). *Frequently asked questions (FAQs) about subjective well-being (happiness and life satisfaction).* Champaign, IL: Department of Psychology, University of Illinois.

Diener, E., & Biswas-Diener, R. (2002). Will money increase subjective well-being? A literature review and guide to needed research. *Social Indicators Research, 57,* 119–169.

Diener, E., & Diener, M. (1995). Cross-cultural correlates of life satisfaction and self-esteem. *Journal of Personality and Social Psychology, 68,* 653–663.

Diener, E., Emmons, R. A., Larsen, R. J., & Griffin, S. (1985). The Satisfaction with Life Scale. *Journal of Personality Assessment, 49,* 71–75.

Diener, E., Lucas, R. E., & Oishi, S. (2002). Subjective well-being: The science of happiness and satisfaction. In C. R. Snyder & S. J. Lopez (Eds.), *Handbook of positive psychology.* New York: Oxford University Press.

Diener, E., & Oishi, S. (2000). Money and happiness: Income and subjective well-being across nations. In E. Diener & E. M. Suh (Eds.), *Subjective well-being across cultures.* Cambridge, MA: MIT Press.

Diener, E., & Seligman, M. E. P. (2002). Very happy people. *Psychological Science, 13,* 80–84.

Diener, E., Wolsic, B., & Fujita, F. (1995). Physical attractiveness and subjective well-being. *Journal of Personality and Social Psychology, 69,* 120–129.

Diggs, R. C., & Socha, T. (2004). Communication, families, and exploring the boundaries of cultural diversity. In A. L. Vangelisti (Ed.), *Handbook of family communication.* Mahwah, NJ: Erlbaum.

DiGiacomo, M., & Adamson, B. (2001). Coping with stress in the workplace: Implications for new health professionals. *Journal of Allied Health, 30,* 106–111.

Dik, B. J., & Hansen, J. C. (2004). Development and validation of discriminant functions for the Strong Interest Inventory. *Journal of Vocational Behavior, 64,* 182–197.

DiNicola, D. D., & DiMatteo, M. R. (1984). Practitioners, patients, and compliance with medical regimens: A social psychological perspective. In A. Baum, S. E. Taylor, & J. E. Singer (Eds.), *Handbook of psychology and health* (Vol. 4). Mahwah, NJ: Erlbaum.

Dipboye, R., & Colella, A. (Eds.) (2005). *Discrimination at work.* Mahwah, NJ: Erlbaum.

DiTommaso, B., McNulty, B., Ross, L., & Burgess, M. (2003). Attachment styles, social skills, and loneliness in young adults. *Personality and Individual Differences, 35,* 303–312.

Dixon, R. A., & Cohen, A. (2003). Cognitive development in adulthood. In I. B. Weiner (Ed.), *Handbook of psychology* (Vol. 6). New York: Wiley.

Dobie, D. J., Kivahan, D. R., Maynard, C., Bush, K. R., Davis, T. M., & Bradley, K. A. (2004). Posttraumatic stress disorder in female veterans: Association with self-reported health problems and functional impairment. *Archives of Internal Medicine, 164,* 394–400.

Dohrenwend, B. S., & Shrout, P. E. (1985). "Hassles" in the conceptualization and measurement of life event stress variables. *American Psychologist, 40,* 780–785.

Dolan, A. L., Koshy, E., Waker, M., & Goble, C. M. (2004). Access to bone densitometry increases general practitioners' prescribing for osteoporosis in steroid treated patients. *Annals of Rheumatoid Diseases, 63,* 183–186.

Donelson, F. E. (1998). *Women's experiences.* Mountain View, CA: Mayfield.

Donnerstein, E. (2001). Media violence. In J. Worell (Ed.), *Encyclopedia of gender and women.* San Diego: Academic Press.

Dougherty, D. D., Rauch, S. L., & Jenike, M. A. (2004). Pharmacotherapy for obsessive-compulsive disorder. *Journal of Clinical Psychology, 60,* 1195–1202.

Dowd, E. T. (2002). Self-statement modification. In M. Hersen & W. H. Sledge (Eds.), *Encyclopedia of psychotherapy.* San Diego: Academic Press.

Draguns, J. G. (2004). Culture and psychotherapy. In W. E. Craighead & C. B. Nemeroff (Eds.), *The concise Corsini encyclopedia of psychology and behavioral science.* New York: Wiley.

Drevets, W. C. (2001). Neuroimaging and neuropathological studies of depression: Implications for the cognitive-emotional features of mood disorders. *Current Opinions in Neurobiology, 11,* 240–249.

Driscoll, R. (2002). Personal shielding to deflect hostility. Los Angeles: Westside Publishing.

Driver, J. L., & Gottman, J. M. (2004). Daily marital interactions and positive affect during marital conflict among newlywed couples. *Family Process, 43,* 301–304.

Dryden, W. (2004). *Rational emotive behavioral therapy* (3rd ed.). Thousand Oaks, CA: Sage.

Duman, R. S. (2004). Depression: A case of neuronal life and death? *Biological Psychiatry, 56,* 140–145.

Duncan, S. F. (2005). *Family life education.* Thousand Oaks, CA: Sage.

Dunne, K. (2004). Grief and its manifestations. *Nursing Standards, 18,* 45–51.

Dunne, M. (2002). Sampling considerations. In M. W. Wiederman & B. E. Whitley (Eds.), *Handbook for conducting research on human sexuality.* Mahwah, NJ: Erlbaum.

Dunner, D. L. (2001). Acute and maintenance treatment of chronic depression. *Journal of Clinical Psychiatry, 62* (Suppl. 6), 10–16.

DuPraw, M., & Axner, M. (2003). *Toward a more perfect union in an age of diversity.* Available on the World Wide Web at http://www.wwcd.org/action/ampu/crosscult.html

Dusek, J. B., & McIntyre, J. G. (2003). Self-concept and self-esteem development. In G. Adams & M. Berzonsky (Eds.), *Blackwell handbook of adolescence.* Malden, MA: Blackwell.

Dweck, C. S., Higgins, E. T., & Grant-Pillow, H. (2003). Self-systems give unique meaning to self variables. In M. R. Leary (Ed.), *Handbook of self and identity.* New York: Guilford.

Dyregrov, K. (2004). Strategies of professional assistance after traumatic deaths: empowerment or disempowerment? *Scandinavian Journal of Psychology, 45,* 181–189.

Eagly, A. H. (2000). Gender roles. In A. Kazdin (Ed.), *Encyclopedia of psychology.* Washington, DC, & New York: American Psychological Association and Oxford University Press.

Eagly, A. H. (2001). Social role theory of sex differences and similarities. In J. Worrell (Ed.), *Encyclopedia of women and gender.* San Diego: Academic Press.

Eagly, A. H., & Crowley, M. (1986). Gender and helping behavior: A meta-analytic review of the social psychological literature. *Psychological Bulletin, 100,* 283–308.

Eagly, A. H., & Diekman, A. B. (2003). The malleability of sex differences in response to social roles. In L. G. Aspinwall & V. M. Staudinger (Eds.), *A psychology of human strengths.* Washington, DC: American Psychological Association.

Eagly, A. H., & Steffen, V. J. (1986). Gender and aggressive behavior: A meta-analytic review of the social psychological literature. *Psychological Bulletin, 100,* 309–330.

Eaker, E. D., Sullivan, L. M., Kelly-Hayes, M., D'Agostino, R. B., & Benjamin, E. J. (2004). Anger and hostility predict the development of atrial fibrillation in men in the Framington Offspring Study. *Circulation, 109,* 1267–1271.

Ebata, A. T., & Moos, R. H. (1989, April). *Coping and adjustment in four groups of adolescents.* Paper presented at the biennial meeting of the Society for Research in Child Development, Kansas City.

Eccles, J. (2004). Schools, academic motivation, and stage-environment fit. In R. Lerner & L. Steinberg (Eds.), *Handbook of adolescent psychology* (2nd Ed.). New York: Wiley.

Eccles, J., Barber, B., Stone, M., & Templeton, J. (2002). In C. Keyes (Ed.), *Well-being: Positive development across the life-span.* Mahwah, NJ: Erlbaum.

Eccles, J. S., & Goodman, J. (Eds.). (2002). *Community programs to promote youth development.* Washington, DC: National Academy Press.

Eccles, J. S., Wigfield, A., & Schiefele, U. (1998). Motivation to succeed. In W. Damon (Ed.), *Handbook of child psychology* (Vol. 3). New York: Wiley.

Edelstein, R. S., & Shaver P. R. (2004). Avoidant attachment: Exploration of an oxymoron. In D. J. Mashek & A. P. Aron (Eds.), *Handbook of closeness and intimacy.* Mahwah, NJ: Erlbaum.

Edmonds, M. M. (1993). Physical health. In J. S. Jackson, L. M. Chatters, & R. J. Taylor (Eds.), *Aging in Black America.* Newbury Park, CA: Sage.

Edwards, R., & Hamilton, M. A. (2004). You need to understand my gender role: An empirical test of Tannen's model of gender and communication. *Sex Roles, 50,* 491–504.

Egeland, B., & Carlson, B. (2004). Attachment and psychopathology. In L. Atkinson & S. Goldberg (Eds.), *Attachment issues in psychopathology and intervention.* Mahwah, NJ: Erlbaum.

Egeland, B., Jacobvitz, D., & Sroufe, L. A. (1988). Breaking the cycle of abuse. *New Directions for Child Development, 11,* 77–92.

Eggers, D. (2001). *Heartbreaking work of staggering genius.* New York: Picador.

Egner, T., & Gruzelier, J. H. (2004). EEG biofeedback of low beta band components. *Clinical Neurophysiology, 115,* 131–139.

Ehlers, C. L., Gilder, D. A., Wall, T. L., Phillips, E., Feilder, H., & Wilhelmsen, K. C. (2004). Genomic screen for loci associated with alcohol dependence in Mission Indians. *American Journal of Medical Genetics, 129B,* 110–115.

Eigsti, I. M., & Cicchetti, D. (2004). The impact of child maltreatment on expressive syntax at 60 months. *Developmental Science, 7,* 88–102.

Eisdorfer, C. (1996, December). Interview. *APA Monitor, 35.*

Eisenberg, D. M., Davis, R. B., Ettner, S. L., Appel, S., Wilkey, S., Rompay, M. V., & Kessler, R. C. (1998). Trends in alternative medicine use in the United States, 1990–1997. *Journal of the American Medical Association, 280,* 1575–1589.

Eisenberg, M. E., Bearinger, L. H., Sieving, R. E., Swain, C., & Resnick, M. D. (2004). Parents' beliefs about condoms and oral contraceptives. *Perspectives on Sexual and Reproductive Behavior, 36*(2), 50–57.

Eisenberg, N., Fabes, R. A., Guthrie, I. K., & Reiser, M. (2002). The role of emotionality and regulation in children's social competence and adjustment. In L. Pulkkinen & A. Caspi (Eds.), *Paths to successful development.* New York: Cambridge University Press.

Eisenberg, N., Martin, C. L., & Fabes, R. A. (1996). Gender development and gender effects. In D. C. Berliner & R. C. Calfee (Eds.), *Handbook of educational psychology.* New York: Macmillan.

Eisenberg, N., & Morris, A. S. (2004). Moral cognitions and prosocial responding in adolescence. In R. Lerner & L. Steinberg (Eds.), *Handbook of adolescent psychology* (2nd Ed.). New York: Wiley.

Ekman, P., & Friesen, W. (1974). Detecting deception from the body or face. *Journal of Personality and Social Psychology, 29,* 288–298.

Ekman, P., & O'Sullivan, M. (1991). Who can catch a liar? *American Psychologist, 46,* 913–920.

Elder, G. H. (1998). The life course and human development. In W. Damon (Ed.), *Handbook of child development* (5th ed.). New York: Wiley.

Elkin, A., Kalidindi, S., & McGuffin, P. (2004). Have schizophrenia genes been found? *Current Opinion in Psychiatry, 17,* 107–113.

Ellemers, N., Spears, R., & Doosje, B. (2002). Self and social identity. *Annual Review of Psychology* (Vol. 53). Palo Alto, CA: Annual Reviews.

Elliot, A. J., & Thrash, T. M. (2004). The intergenerational transmission of child abuse. *Personality and Social Psychology Bulletin, 30,* 957–971.

Elliott, B. A., Beattie, M. K., & Kaitfors, S. E. (2001). Health needs of people living below the poverty level. *Family Medicine, 33,* 361–366.

Elliott, C. E. (1999). *Cross-cultural communication styles.* Portland, OR: Diversity Training Associates.

Ellis, A. (1962). *Reason and emotion in psychotherapy.* New York: Lyle Stuart.

Ellis, A. (1996). A rational-emotive behavior therapist's perspective on Ruth. In G. Corey (Ed.), *Case approach to counseling and psychotherapy.* Pacific Grove, CA: Brooks/Cole.

Ellis, A. (2000). Rational emotive behavior therapy. In A. Kazdin (Ed.), *Encyclopedia of Psychology.* Washington, DC, and New York: American Psychological Association and Oxford University Press.

Ellis, A. (2002). Rational emotive behavior therapy. In M. Hersen & W. H. Sledge (Eds.), *Encyclopedia of psychotherapy.* San Diego: Academic Press.

Ellis, A. (2004). Current psychotherapies. In W. E. Craighead & C. B. Nemeroff (Eds.), *The concise Corsini encyclopedia of psychology and behavioral science.* New York: Wiley.

Ellis, C. D. (2002). Male rape. *Collegian, 9,* 34–39.

Ellis, L., & Ames, M. A. (1987). Neurohormonal functioning and sexual orientation. *Psychological Bulletin, 101,* 233–258.

Emmers-Sommer, T. M., & Allen, M. (2005). *Safer sex in personal relationships: The role of sexual scripts in HIV infection and prevention.* Mahwah, NJ: Erlbaum.

Engelhart, M. J., Geerlings, M. I., Ruitenberg, A., van Swieten, J. C., Hofman, A., Witteman, J. C. M., & Breteler, M. B. (2002). Dietary intake of antioxidants and risk of Alzheimer's disease. *Journal of the American Medical Association, 287,* 3223–3229.

Ephraim, D. (2000). Culturally relevant research and practice with the Rorschach comprehensive system in Iberomerica. In R. H. Dana (Ed.), *Handbook of cross-cultural and multicultural personality assessment.* Mahwah, NJ: Erlbaum.

Eppley, K. R., Abrams, A. I., & Shear, J. (1989). Differential effects of relaxation effects on trait anxiety. *Journal of Clinical Psychology, 45,* 957–974.

Erikson, E. H. (1950). *Childhood and society.* New York: W. W. Norton.

Erikson, E. H. (1968). *Identity: Youth and crisis.* New York: W. W. Norton.

Erikson, E. H. (1969). *Gandhi's truth.* New York: W. W. Norton.

Erlick Robinson, G. (2003). Violence against women in North America. *Archives of Women's Health, 6,* 185–191.

Ertruck, E., Kuru, N., Savei, V., Tuncel, E., Ersoy, C., & Imamoglu, S. (2004). Serum leptin levels correlate with obesity parameters but not with hyperinsulinism in women with polycystic ovary syndrome. *Fertility and Sterility, 82,* 1364–1368.

Erwin, B. A., Heimberg, R. G., Juster, H., & Mindlin, M. (2002). Comorbid anxiety and mood disorders among persons with social anxiety disorder. *Behavior Therapy and Research, 40,* 19–35.

Esquivel, L. (1989). *Like water for chocolate.* New York: Random House.

Esquivel, L. (1994). *Like water for chocolate.* New York: Doubleday.

Eun Jung Suh, A., Moskowitz, D. S., Fuornier, M.A., Zuroff, D. C. (2004). Gender and relationships: influence on agentic and communal behaviors. *Personal Relationships, 11,* 41–60.

European Agency for Safety and Health at Work. (2000). *Research on work-related stress.* Retrieved November 15, 2001, from http://agency.osha.eu.int/

Evans, D. L., Herbert, J. D., Nelson-Gray, R. O., & Gaudiano, B. A. (2002). Determinants of diagnostic prototypicality judgments of the personality disorders. *Journal of Personality Disorders, 16,* 95–106.

Evans, E. (2004). Factors associated with suicidal phenomena in adolescents: A systematic review of population-based studies. *Clinical Psychology Review, 24,* 957–979.

Evans, G. W. (2004). The environment of childhood poverty. *American Psychologist, 59,* 77–92.

Evans, P. C. (2003). "If only I were thin like her, maybe I could be happy like her": The self-implications of associating a thin female ideal with life success. *Psychology of Women Quarterly, 27* (3), 209–215.

Everett, F., Proctor, N., & Cartmell, B. (1989). Providing psychological services to American Indian children and families. In D. R. Atkinson, G. Morten, & D. W. Sue (Eds.), *Counseling American minorities.* Dubuque, IA: Wm. C. Brown.

Evert, J., Lawler, E., Bogan, H., & Perls, T. (2003). Morbidity profiles of centenarians: Survivors, delayers, and escapers. *Journal of Gerontology: Biological sciences and medical sciences, 58,* M232–M237.

Eysenck, H. J. (1952). The efforts of psychotherapy: An evaluation. *Journal of Consulting Psychology, 16,* 319–324.

Eysenck, H. J. (1967). *The biological basis of personality.* Springfield, IL: Thomas.

Fagot, B. I., Rodgers, C. S., & Leinbach, M. D. (2000). Theories of gender socialization. In T. Eckes & H. M. Trautner (Eds.), *The developmental social psychology of gender.* Mahwah, NJ: Erlbaum.

Fahey. T. D., Insel, P. M., & Roth, W. T. (2005). *Fit & well* (6th Ed.). New York: McGraw-Hill.

Fairfield, K. M., & Fletcher, R. H. (2002). Vitamins for chronic disease prevention in adults. *Journal of the American Medical Association, 287,* 3116–3126.

Fals-Stewart, W., Golden, J., & Schumacher, J. A. (2003). Intimate partner violence and substance abuse: A longitudinal day-to-day examination. *Addictive Behavior, 28,* 1555–1574.

Farag, S. S., VanDesuen, J. B., Fehniger, T. A., & Caliguiri, M. A. (2003). Biology and clinical impact of human natural killer cells. *International Journal of Hematology, 78,* 7–17.

Faravelli, C., Giugni, A., Salvarori, S., & Ricca, V. (2004). Psychopathology after rape. *American Journal of Psychiatry, 161,* 1483–1485.

Farr, M. (Ed.) (2005). *Latino language and literacy in ethnolinguistic Chicago.* Mahwah, NJ: Erlbaum.

Fava, G. A., Rafanelli, C., Ottolini, F., Ruini, C., Cazzaro, M., & Grandi, S. (2001). Psychological well-being and residual symptoms in remitted patients with panic disorder and agoraphobia. *Journal of Affective Disorders, 65,* 185–190.

Fava, G. A., Ruini, C., Rafanelli, C., Finos, L., Conti, S., & Grandi, S. (2004). Six-year outcome of cognitive behavior therapy for prevention of recurrent depression. *American Journal of Psychiatry, 161,* 1872–1876.

Feeney, R. A. (1996). Attachment, caregiving, and marital satisfaction. *Personal Relationships, 3,* 401–416.

Fehr, B. (2000). The life cycle of friendships. In C. Hendrick & S. S. Hendrick (Eds.), *Close relationships.* Thousand Oaks, CA: Sage.

Fehr, B., & Broughton, R. (2001) Gender and personality differences in conceptions of love: An interpersonal theory analysis. *Personal Relationships, 8,* 115–136.

Feldman, J., & Bockting, W. (2003). Transgender health. *Minnesota Medicine, 86,* 25–32.

Fenzel, L. M. (1994, February). *A prospective study of the effects of chronic strains on early adolescent self-worth and school adjustment.* Paper presented at the meeting of the Society for Research on Adolescence, San Diego.

Fern, S., Goethals, G. R., Kassin, S. M., & Cross, J. (1993, August). *Social influence and presidential debates.* Paper presented at the meeting of the American Psychological Association, Toronto.

Fernandez-Ballesteros, R. (2003). Self-report questionnaires. In M. Hersen (Ed.), *Comprehensive handbook of psychological assessment* (Vol. 3). New York: Wiley.

Field, C. E., Nash, H. M., Handwerk, M. L., & Friman, P. C. (2004). A modification of the token economy for nonresponsive youth in family-style residential care. *Behavior Modification, 28,* 438–457.

Field, D. (1999). A cross-cultural perspective on continuity and change in social relations in old age: Introduction to a special issue. *International Journal of Aging and Human Development, 48,* 257–262.

Fields, R. (2004). *Drugs* (5th Ed.). New York: McGraw-Hill.

Figueroa, C. (2003). Self-esteem and cosmetic surgery: Is there a relationship between the two? *Plastic Surgery Nursing, 23,* 21–24.

Finch, C. E., & Seeman, T. E. (1999). Stress theories of aging. In V. L. Bengston & K. W. Schaie (Eds.). *Handbook of theories of aging.* New York: Springer.

Fine, M. (1988). Sexuality, schooling, and adolescent females: The missing discourse of desire. *Harvard Educational Review, 58*(1), 29–53.

Fingerman, K. L., Nussbaum, J., & Birditt, K. S. (2004). Keeping all five balls in the air: Juggling family communication at midlife. In A. L. Vangelisti (Ed.), *Handbook of family communication.* Mahwah, NJ: Erlbaum.

First, M. B., & Pincus, H. A. (2002). The DSM-IV text revision: Rationale and potential impact on clinical practice. *Psychiatric Services, 53,* 288–292.

Fisher, B. S., Cullen, F. T., & Turner, M. G. (2000). *The sexual victimization of college women.* Washington, DC: National Institute of Justice.

Fiske, S. T. (1998). Stereotyping, prejudice, and discrimination. In D. T. Gilbert, S. T. Fiske, & G. Lindzey (Eds.), *The handbook of social psychology* (4th ed., Vol. 2). New York: McGraw-Hill.

Fitzgerald, S. T., Haythornthwaite, J. A., Suchday, S., & Ewart, C. K. (2003). Anger in young black and white workers: Effects of job control, dissatisfaction, and support.

Journal of Behavioral Medicine, 26, 283–296.

Fitzpatrick, A. L., Kuller, L. H., Ives, D. G., Lopez, O. L., Jagust, W., Breitner, J. C., Jones, B., Lyketsos, C., & Dulberg, C. (2004). Incidence and prevalence of dementia in the cardiovascular health study. *Journal of the American Geriatric Society, 52,* 195–204.

Flanagan, C. A. (2004). Volunteerism, leadership, political socialization, and civic engagement. In R. Lerner & L. Steinberg (Eds.), *Handbook of adolescent psychology.* New York: Wiley.

Fletcher, J. S., & Banasik, J. L. (2001). Exercise self-efficacy. *Clinical Excellence in Nursing Practice, 5,* 134–143.

Flower, R. (2004). Lifestyle drugs: Pharmacology and the social agenda. *Trends in Pharmacological Science, 25,* 182–185.

Foa, E. D., & Riggs, D. S. (1995). Posttraumatic stress disorder following assault: Theoretical considerations and empirical findings. *Current Directions in Psychological Science, 4,* 61–65.

Fodor, I., & Epstein, J. (2001). Agoraphobia, panic disorder, and gender. In J. Worell (Ed.), *Encyclopedia of women and gender.* San Diego: Academic Press.

Fogoros, R. N. (2001). *Does stress really cause heart disease?* Retrieved October 10, 2001, from http://www.about.com.

Folkman, S. (1997). Positive psychological states and coping with severe stress. *Social Science and Medicine, 45,* 1207–1221.

Folkman, S., & Lazarus, R. S. (1980). An analysis of coping in a middle-aged community sample. *Journal of Health and Social Behavior, 21,* 219–239.

Folkman, S., & Moskowitz, J. T. (2000). Positive affect and the other side of coping. *American Psychologist, 55,* 647–654.

Folkman, S., & Moskowitz, J. T. (2004). Coping: Pitfalls and promises. *Annual Review of Psychology,* Vol. 55. Palo Alto, CA: Annual Reviews.

Fontana, A., & Rosenheck, R. (2004). Trauma, change in strength of religious faith, and mental health service use among veterans treated for PTSD. *Journal of Nervous and Mental Disorders, 192* 579–584.

Forbes, G. B., Adams-Curtis, L. E., White, K. B., & Holmgren, K. M. (2003). The role of hostile and benevolent sexism in women's and men's perceptions of menstruating women. *Psychology of Women Quarterly, 27* (1), 58–63.

Forbes, G. B., Doroszewicz, K., Card, K., & Adams-Curtis, L. (2004). Association of the thin body ideal, ambivalent sexism, and self-esteem with body acceptance and the preferred body size of college women in Poland and the United States. *Sex Roles, 50,* 331–345.

Forbes, R. J., & Jackson, P. R. **(1980). Nonverbal behavior and the outcome of selection interviews.** *Journal of Occupational Psychology, 53,* 65–72.

Forsyth, J. P., & Savsevitz, J. (2002). Behavior therapy: Historical perspective and overview. In M. Hersen & W. H. Sledge (Eds.), *Encyclopedia of psychotherapy.* San Diego: Academic Press.

Fortenberry, J. D. (2004). The effects of stigma on genital herpes care-seeking behaviors. *Herpes, 11,* 8–11.

Foss, C., & Sundby, J. (2003). The construction of the gendered patient: Hospital staff's attitudes to female and male patients. *Patient Education and Counseling, 49,* 45–52.

Foster, M. D., Jackson, L. C., Hartmann, R., & Woulfe, S. (2004). Minimizing the pervasiveness of women's personal experiences of gender discrimination. *Psychology of Women Quarterly, 28,* 224–232.

Fowles, D. (2003). Schizophrenia spectrum disorders. In I. B. Weiner (Ed.). *Handbook of psychology* (Vol. 8). New York: Wiley.

Fox, G. L., & Murray, V. M. (2000). Gender and families: Feminist perspectives and family research. *Journal of Marriage and the Family, 62,* 1160–1172.

Fox, M. G., & Newman, C. F. (2004). Cognitive therapy. In W. E. Craighead & B. G. Nemeroff (Eds.), *The concise Corsini encyclopedia of psychology and behavioral science.* New York: Wiley.

Fox, P. G., Burns, K. R., Popovich, J. M., Belknap, R. A., & Frank-Stromborg, M. (2004). Southeast Asian refugee children: self-esteem as a predictor of depression and scholastic achievement in the U.S. *International Journal of Psychiatric Nursing Research, 9,* 1063–1072.

Frager, R., & Fadiman, J. (2005). *Personality and personal growth* (6th ed.). Upper Saddle River, NJ: Prentice-Hall.

Fraley, R. C. (2002). Attachment stability from infancy to adulthood: Meta-analysis and dynamic modeling of developmental mechanisms. *Personality and Social Psychology Review, 6,* 123–151.

Francis, J., Fraser, G., & Marcia, J. E. (1989). *Cognitive and experimental factors in moratorium-achievement (MAMA) cycles.* Unpublished manuscript, Department of Psychology, Simon Frasier University, Burnaby, British Columbia.

Frank, J. D. (1982). Therapeutic components shared by all psychotherapies. In J. H. Harvey & M. M. Parks (Eds.), *Psychotherapy research and behavior change.* Washington, DC: American Psychological Association.

Frank, J. D. (2004). Effective components of psychotherapy research. In W. E. Craighead & C. B. Nemeroff (Eds.), *The concise Corsini encyclopedia of psychology and behavioral science.* New York: Wiley.

Frankl, V. (1984). *Man's search for meaning.* New York: Basic Books.

Frederickson, B. L. (2001). The role of positive emotions in positive psychology. *American Psychologist, 56,* 218–226.

Frederickson, B. L., & Joiner, T. (2000). *Positive emotions trigger upward spirals toward emotional well-being.* Unpublished manuscript. University of Michigan, Ann Arbor, Department of Psychology.

Frederikse, M., Lu, A., Aylward, E., Barta, P., Sharma, T., & Pearlson, G. (2000). Sex differences in inferior lobule volume in schizophrenia. *American Journal of Psychiatry, 157,* 422–427.

Freeman, A., & Reinecke, M. A. (1995). Cognitive therapy. In A. S. Gurman (Ed.), *Essential psychotherapies.* New York: Guilford Press.

Freeman, S. (2004). Nondaily hormonal contraception: considerations in contraceptive choice and patient counseling. *Journal of the American Academy of Nurse Practitioners, 16,* 226–238.

Freeman, T. W., & Roca, V. (2001). Gun use, attitudes toward violence, and aggression among combat veterans with chronic post-traumatic stress disorder. *Journal of Nervous and Mental Disorders, 189,* 317–320.

Frenkel, D., Dori, M., & Solomon, B. (2004). Generation of anti-beta-amyloid antibodies via phage display technology. *Vaccine, 22,* 2505–2508.

Freud, S. (1917). *A general introduction to psychoanalysis.* New York: Washington Square Press.

Fridrich, A. H., & Flannery, D. J. (1995). The effects of ethnicity and acculturation on early adolescent delinquency. *Journal of Child and Family Studies, 4*(1), 69–87.

Friedman, J. I., Temporini, H., & Davis, K. L. (1999). Pharmacologic strategies for augmenting cognitive performance in schizophrenia. *Biological Psychiatry, 45,* 1–16.

Friedman, M., & Rosenman, R. (1974). *Type A behavior and your heart.* New York: Knopf.

Friedman, R., Myers, P., & Benson, H. (1998). Meditation and the relaxation response. In H. S. Friedman (Ed.), *Encyclopedia of mental health.* San Diego: Academic Press.

Friedman, S. (Ed.). (2004). *Culturally competent practice with immigrant and refugee children and families.* New York: Guilford.

Fromm, E. (1947). *Man for himself.* New York: Holt, Rinehart & Winston.

Frost, A. (2004). Therapeutic engagement styles of child sexual offenders in a group treatment program: a grounded theory study. *Sexual Abuse, 16,* 191–208.

Frost, R. O., & Steketee, G. (1998). Obsessive-compulsive disorder. In H. S. Friedman (Ed.), *Encyclopedia of mental health* (Vol. 3). San Diego: Academic Press.

Fry, P. S. (1999, November). *Significance of religiosity and spirituality to psychological well-being of older adults.* Paper presented at the meeting of the Gerontological Society of America, San Francisco.

Fu, Q., Heath, A. C., Bucholz, K. K., Nelson, E. C., Glowinski, A. L., Goldberg, J., Lyons, M. J., Tsuang, M. T., Jacob, T., True, M. R., & Eisen, M. A. (2002). A twin study of genetic and environmental influences of suicidality in men. *Psychological Medicine, 32,* 11–24.

Fulgini, H., & Yoshikawa, H. (2004). Investments in children among immigrant families. In A. Kalil & T. DeLeire (Eds.), *Family investments in children's potential.* Mahwah, NJ: Erlbaum.

Furmark, T., Tillfors, M., Garpenstrand, H., Marteinsdottir, I., Langstrom, B., Oreland, L., & Fredrikson, M. (2004). *Neuroscience Letters, 362,* 189–192.

G

Galician, M. L. (2004). *Sex, love, and romance in the mass media.* Mahwah, NJ: Erlbaum.

Galinsky, E., & David, J. (1988).*The preschool years: Family strategies that work—from experts and parents.* New York: Times Books.

Gall, T. L., Evans, D. R., & Howard, J. (1997). The retirement adjustment process: Changes in well-being of male retirees across time. *Journal of Gerontology, 52B,* 110–117.

Gallo, L. C., Troxel, W. M., Matthews, K. A., & Kuller, L. H. (2003). Marital status and quality in middle-aged women: Associations with levels and trajectories of cardiovascular risk factors. *Health Psychology, 22,* 453–463.

Gallup, G. H. (1987). *The Gallup poll: Public opinion 1986.* Wilmington, DE: Scholarly Resources.

Gallup, G. H., & Bezilla, R. (1992). *The religious life of young Americans.* Princeton, NJ: Gallup Institute.

Gallup, G. H., & Jones, S. (1989). *One hundred questions and answers: Religion in America.* Princeton, NJ: Gallup Institute.

Gamm, J. L., Nussbaum, R. I., & Bowles Biesecker, B. (2004). Genetics an alcoholism in at-risk relatives II: interest and concerns about hypothetical genetic testing for alcoholism risk. *American Journal of Medical Genetics, 128A,* 151–155.

Gangestad, S. W., & Thornhill, R. (1998). Menstrual cycle variation in women's preferences for the scent of symmetrical men. *Proceedings of the Royal Society of London, 265,* 927–933.

Ganong, L. H., & Coleman, M. (1994). *Remarried family relationships.* Thousand Oaks, CA: Sage.

Gapinski, K. D., Brownell, K. D., & LaFrance, M. (2003). Body objectification and "fat talk": Effects of emotion, motivation, and cognitive performance. *Sex Roles, 48,* 377–388.

Garafalo, R., Wolf, R. C., Wissow, L. S., Woods, E. R., & Goodman, E. (1999). Sexual orientation and risk of suicide attempts among a representative sample of youth. *Archives of Pediatrics and Adolescent Medicine, 153,* 487–493.

Garb, H. N., Wood, J. M., Nezworski, M. T., Grove, W. M., & Stejskal, W. J. (2001). Toward a resolution of the Rorschach controversy. *Psychological Assessment, 13,* 433–448.

Garcia-Alba, C. (2004). Anorexia and depression. *Spanish Journal of Psychology, 7,* 40–52.

Garcia-Vega, E., & Fernandez-Rodriguez, C. (2004). A stress management program for Crohn's disease. *Behavior Research and Therapy, 42,* 367–383.

Gardner, J., & Oswald, A. (2001). Does money buy happiness? A longitudinal study using data on windfalls. Working paper, Department of Economics, Cambridge University.

Gartner, J., Larson, D. B., & Allen, G. D. (1991). Religious commitment and mental health: A review of the empirical literature. *Journal of Psychology and Theology, 19,* 6–25.

Gatz, M. (1989). Clinical psychology and aging. In M. Storandt & G. R. VandenBos (Eds.), *The adult years: Continuity and change.* Washington, DC: American Psychological Association.

Gau, G. T. (2004). The hunt for the perfect heart diet. *Asian Pacific Journal of Clinical Nutrition, 13* (Supplement), S4.

Gelfand, M., & Knight, A. P. (2005). Cross-cultural perspectives on work-family conflict. In S. A. Poelmans (Ed.), *Work and family.* Mahwah, NJ: Erlbaum.

Geller, P. A., Graf, M. C., & Dyson-Washington, F. (2003). Women's health psychology. In I. B. Weiner (Ed.), *Handbook of psychology* (Vol. 9). New York: Wiley.

George, L. K. (2001). The social psychology of health. In R. H. Binstock & L. K. George (Eds.), *Handbook of the psychology of aging* (5th ed.). San Diego: Academic Press.

Gerlach, P. (1998). *Stepfamily in formation.* Chicago: Stepfamily Association of Illinois.

Gershoff, E. T. (2002). Corporal punishment by parents and associated child behaviors and experiences: A meta-analysis and theoretical review. *Psychological Bulletin, 128,* 539–579.

Gibson, R., & Mitchell, M. (2003). *Introduction to counseling and guidance* (6th ed.). Upper Saddle River, NJ: Prentice-Hall.

Giddens, S., & Giddens, O. (2000). *Coping with grieving and loss.* New York: Rosen.

Gielen, U. P., Fish, J. M., & Draguns, J. G. (Eds.). (2004). *Handbook of culture, therapy, and healing.* Mahwah, NJ: Erlbaum.

Gilbert, P. (2001). *Overcoming depression.* New York: Oxford University Press.

Gilbert, P., & Gilbert, J. (2003). Entrapment and arrested fight and flight in depression: An exploration using focus groups. *Psychology and Psychotherapy, 76,* 173–188.

Giles, T. R., & Marafliote, R. A. (1998). Managed care and the practitioner. *Clinical Psychology and Practice, 5,* 41–50.

Ginzberg, E. (1972). Toward a theory of occupational choice: A restatement. *Vocational Guidance Quarterly, 20,* 169–176.

Giotakos, O., Markianos, M., Vaidakis, N., & Christodoulou, G. N. (2003). Aggression, impulsivity, plasma sex hormones, and biogenic amine turnover in a forensic population of rapists. *Journal of Sex and Marital Therapy, 29,* 215–225.

Gladue, B. A. (1994). The biopsychology of sexual orientation. *Current Directions in Psychological Science, 3,* 150–154.

Glass, T. A. (2004). Gestalt therapy. In W. E. Craighead & C. B. Nemeroff (Eds.), *The concise Corsini encyclopedia of psychology and behavioral science.* New York: Wiley.

Glidden—Traccy, C. (2005). *Counseling and therapy with clients who abuse alcohol or other drugs.* Mahwah, NJ: Erlbaum.

Godbout, C. (2004). Reflections on Bion's elements of psychoanalysis: experience, thought, and growth. *International Journal of Psychoanalysis, 85,* 1123–1136.

Goddard, A. W., Mason, G. F., Rothman, D. L., Behar, K. L., Petroff, O. A., & Krystal, J. H. (2004). Family psychopathology and magnitude of reductions in occipital cortex GABA levels in panic disorder. *Neuropsychopharmacology, 29,* 639–640.

Goenjian, A. K., Molina, L., Steinberg, A. M., Fairbanks, L. A., Alvarez, M. L., Goenjian, H. A., & Pynoos, R. S. (2001). Post-traumatic stress and depression reactions among Nicaraguan adolescents after Hurricane Mitch. *American Journal of Psychiatry, 158,* 788–794.

Golan, N. (1986). *The perilous bridge.* New York: Free Press.

Gold, B. (2002). Integrative approaches to psychotherapy. In M. Hersen & W. H. Sledge (Eds.), *Encyclopedia of psychotherapy.* San Diego: Academic Press.

Goldin-Meadow, S., McNeill, D., & Singleton, J. (1996). Silence liberating: Removing the handcuffs on grammatical expression in the manual modality. *Psychological Review, 103,* 34–55.

Goldman, S. L., Kraemer, D. T., & Salovey, P. (1996). Beliefs about mood moderate the relationship of stress to illness and symptom reporting. *Journal of Psychosomatic Research, 41,* 115–128.

Goldscheider, F., & Goldscheider, C. (1999). *The changing transition to adulthood: Leaving and returning home.* Thousand Oaks, CA: Sage.

Goldstein, J. M., Seidman, L. J., Horton, N. J., Makris, N., Kennedy, D. N., Caviness, V. S., Faraone, S. V., & Tsuang, M. T. (2001). Normal sexual dimorphism of the adult human brain assessed by in vivo magnetic resonance imaging. *Cerebral Cortex, 11,* 490–497.

Goldstein, M. J., & Palmer, J. O. (1975). *The experience of anxiety.* New York: Oxford University Press.

Goldstein, R. B., Prescott, C. A., & Kendler, K. S. (2001). Genetic and environmental factors in conduct problems and adult antisocial behavior among adult female twins. *Journal of Nervous and Mental Disorders, 189,* 201–209.

Goldstein, R. B., Wickramaratne, P. J., Horwath, E., & Weissman, M. M. (1997). Familial aggregation and phenomenology of "early"-onset (at or before age 20 years) panic disorder. *Archives of General Psychiatry, 54,* 271–278.

Gong-Guy, E. (1986). *Depression in students of Chinese and Japanese ancestry: An acculturation, vulnerability and stress model.* Unpublished dissertation, University of California, Los Angeles.

Gonzales, N. A., Knight, G. P., Birman, D., & Sirolli, A. A. (2004). Acculturation and enculturation among Latino youths. In K. L. Maton, C. J. Schellenbach, B. J. Leadbetter, & A. L. Solarz (Eds.), *Investing in children, families, and communities.* Washington, DC: American Psychological Association.

Goodkind, J., Hang, P., & Yang, M. (2004). Hmong refugees in the United States. In K. E. Miller & L. M. Rasco (Eds.), *The mental health of refugees.* Mahwah, NJ: Erlbaum.

Goodman, G. (1988). Silences. In C. Goodman & C. Esterly (Eds.), *The talk book.* New York: Ballantine.

Gorenstein, E. E. (1997). *Case studies in abnormal psychology.* New York: Longman.

Gorney, M. (2002). Cosmetic surgery in males. *Plastic and Reconstructive Surgery, 110,* 719.

Gotesdam, K. G., & Agras, W. S. (1995). General population-based epidemiological survey of eating disorders in Norway. *International Journal of Eating Disorders, 18,* 119–126.

Goto, S., Takashasi, R., Araki, S., & Nakamoto, H. (2002). Dietary restriction initiated in late adulthood can reverse age-related alterations of protein and protein metabolism. *Annals of the New York Academy of Science, 959,* 50–60.

Gottesman, I. I., & Goldsmith, H. H. (1994). Developmental psychopathology of antisocial behavior. In C. A. Nelson (Ed.), *Threats to optimal development.* Mahwah, NJ: Erlbaum.

Gottfredson, L. (1980). Construct validity of Holland's occupational typology in terms of prestige, census, Department of Labor, and other classification systems. *Journal of Applied Psychology, 651,* 697–714.

Gottfried, A. E., Gottfried, A. W., & Bathurst, K. (2002). Maternal and dual-earner employment status and parenting. In M. H. Bornstein (Ed.), *Handbook of parenting* (2nd ed., Vol. 2). Mahwah, NJ: Erlbaum.

Gottlieb, B. H. (1998). Support groups. In H. S. Friedman (Eds.), *Encyclopedia of mental health* (Vol. 3). San Diego: Academic Press.

Gottman, J. M. (1994). *Why marriages succeed or fail.* New York: Simon & Schuster.

Gottman, J. M., Coan, J., Carrere, S., & Swanson, C. (1998). Predicting marital happiness and stability from newlywed interactions. *Journal of Marriage and the Family, 60,* 5–22.

Gottman, J. M., & Levenson, R. W. (2000). The timing of divorce: Predicting when a couple will divorce over a 14–year period. *Journal of Marriage and the Family, 62,* 737–745.

Gottman, J. M., & Notarius, C. I. (2000). Decade review: Observing marital interaction. *Journal of Marriage and the Family, 62,* 927–947.

Gottman, J. M., & Silver, N. (2000). *The seven principles for making marriages work.* New York: Crown.

Gotts, E. E., & Knudsen, T. E. (2005). *The clinical interpretation of the MMPI-2.* Mahwah, NJ: Erlbaum.

Gotz, M. E., Janetzky, B., Pohli, S., Gottschalk, S., Gsell, A., Tatshchner, T., Ransmyar, G., Leblhuber, F., Gerlach, M., Reichmann, H., Riederer, P., & Boning, J. (2001). Chronic alcohol consumption and cerebral indices of oxidative stress: Is there a link? *Alcoholism: Clinical and Experimental Research, 25,* 717–725.

Gould, E., Reeves, A. J., Graziano, M. S., & Gross, C. G. (1999). Neurogenesis in the neocortex of adult primates. *Science, 286* (1), 548–552.

Gove, W. R., Style, C. B., & Hughes, M. (1990). The effect of marriage on the well-being of adults: A theoretical analysis. *Journal of Health and Social Behavior, 24,* 122–131.

Graham-Bermann, S., Eastin, J. A., & Bermann, E. A. (2001). Stress and coping. In J. Worell (Ed.), *Encyclopedia of women and gender.* San Diego: Academic Press.

Graham-Bermann, S. A., & Edleson, J. L. (Eds.). (2001). *Domestic violence in the lives of children.* Washington, DC: American Psychological Association.

Grant, A. (2004). *Cognitive behavioral therapy in mental health care.* New York: Guilford.

Gray, J. (1992). *Men are from Mars, women are from Venus.* New York: HarperCollins.

Greben, D. H. (2004). Integrative dimensions of psychotherapy training. *Canadian Journal of Psychiatry, 49,* 238–248.

Green, B. (2003). Focus on paroxetine. *Current Medical Research Opinions, 19,* 13–21.

Green, B. L., Lindy, J. D., Grace, M. C., & Leonard, A. C. (1992). Chronic posttraumatic stress disorder and diagnostic comorbidity in a disaster sample. *Journal of Nervous & Mental Disease, 180,* 760–766.

Greenberg, B. S., & Busselle, R. W. (1996). Soap operas and sexual activity: A decade later. *Journal of Communication, 46,* 153–160.

Greenberg, L. S., & Paivio, S. C. (2003). *Working with emotions in psychotherapy.* New York: Guilford.

Greenfield, S. F. (2004). Tertiary prevention. In W. E. Craighead & C. B. Nemeroff (Eds.), *The concise Corsini encyclopedia of psychology and behavioral science.* New York: Wiley.

Greenglass, E. R. (2002). Proactive coping and quality of life management. In E. Frydenberg (Ed.), *Beyond coping.* New York: Oxford University Press.

Greenhaus, J. H., Collins, K. M. & Shaw, J. D. (2003). The relation between work-family balance and quality of life. *Journal of Vocational Behavior, 63,* 510–531.

Greenwald, A. G., & Banaji, M. R. (1995). Implicit social cognition: Attitudes, self-esteem, and stereotypes. *Psychological Review, 102,* 4–27.

Greenwood, D., & Isbell, L. M. (2002). Ambivalent sexism and the dumb blond joke: Men's and women's reactions to sexist jokes. *Psychology of Women Quarterly, 26* (4), 10–11.

Gregg, R. E. (2004). Restrictions on workplace romance and consensual relationship policies. *Journal of Medical Practice Management, 19,* 314–316.

Gregory, R. L. (2004). *Psychological testing* (4th ed.). Boston: Allyn & Bacon.

Grolnick, W. S., & Gurland, S. T. (2001). Mothering: Retrospect and prospect. In J. P. McHale & W. S. Grolnick (Eds.), *Retrospect and prospect in the psychological study of families.* Mahwah, NJ: Erlbaum.

Gross, J. J. (1998). The emerging field of emotion regulation: An integrative review. *Review of General Psychology, 2,* 271–299.

Gross, J. J. (2001). Emotion regulation in adulthood: Timing is everything. *Current Directions in Psychological Science, 10,* 214–219.

Gross, J. J., & John, O. P. (2003). Individual differences in two emotion regulation processes: Implications for affect, relationships, and well-being. *Journal of Personality and Social Psychology, 85,* 348–362.

Grossman, P., Niemann, L., Schmidt, S., & Walach, H. (2004). Mindfulness-based stress reduction and health benefits: a meta-analysis. *Journal of Psychosomatic Research, 57,* 35–43.

Grush, J. E. (1980). Impact of candidate expenditures, regionality, and prior outcomes on the 1976 Democratic presidential primaries. *Journal of Personality and Social Psychology, 38,* 337–347.

Guastello, D. D., & Guastello, S. J. (2003). Androgyny, gender role behavior, and emotional intelligence among college students and their parents. *Sex Roles, 49,* 663–673.

Gudykunst, W. B. (2004). *Bridging differences* (4th ed.). Thousand Oaks, CA: Sage.

Guerrero, L. K., Anderson, P., & Afifi, W. (2001). *Close encounters: Communicating in relationships.* New York: McGraw-Hill.

Guerrero, L. K., Spitzberg, B. H., & Yoshimura, S. M. (2004). Sexual and emotional jealousy. In J. H. Harvey, A. Wenzel, & S. Sprecher (Eds.), *The handbook of sexuality in close relationships.* Mahwah, NJ: Erlbaum.

Gump, B., & Matthews, K. (2000 March). *Annual vacations, health, and death.* Paper presented at the meeting of American Psychosomatic Society, Savannah, GA.

Gur, R. C., Mozley, L. H., Mozley, P. D., Resnick, S. M., Karp, J. S., Alavi, A., Arnold, S. E., & Gur, R. E. (1995). Sex differences in regional cerebral glucose metabolism during a resting state. *Science, 267,* 528–531.

Guterman, N. B. (2004). Advancing prevention research on child abuse, youth violence, and domestic violence: emerging strategies and issues. *Journal of Interpersonal Violence, 19,* 299–321.

Gutierrez-Lobos, K., Frohlich, S., Quiner, S., Haring, C., & Barnas, C. (2001). Prescription patterns and quality of information provided for consumers of benzodiazepines. *Acta Medica Austrica, 28,* 56–59.

Gutman, L. M. (2002, April). *The role of stage-environment fit from early adolescence to young adulthood.* Paper presented at the meeting of the Society for Research on Adolescence, New Orleans.

Gutmann, M., & Viveros, M. (2004). Masculinities in Latin America. In M. S. Kimmel, J. Hearn, & Ro. W. Connell (Eds.), *Handbook of studies on men and masculinities.* Thousand Oaks, CA: Sage.

Gyamfi, P., Brooks-Gunn, J., & Jackson, A. P. (2001). Associations between employment and financial and parental stress in low-income single Black mothers. In M. C. Lennon (Ed.), *Welfare, work, and well-being.* New York: Haworth.

H

Hadley, E. C., Dutta, C., Finkelstein, J., Harris, T., Lane, M., Oth, G., Sherman, S., & Starke-Reed, P. (2001). Human implications of caloric restriction's effects on aging in laboratory animals. *Journal of Gerontology, 56A,* Supplement, 5–7.

Hajek, C., & Giles, H. (2003). New directions in intercultural communication. In J. O. Greene & B. R. Burleson (Eds.), *Handbook of communication and interactional skills.* Mahwah, NJ: Erlbaum.

Haldane, M., & Frangou, S. (2004). New insights help define the pathophysiology of bipolar affective disorder: neuroimaging and neuropathology findings. *Progress in Neuropharmacology and Biological Psychiatry, 28,* 943–960.

Hall, B. J. (2002). *Among cultures—Communication and challenges.* Belmont, CA: Wadsworth.

Hall, E. (1969). *The hidden dimension.* Garden City, NY: Anchor.

Hall, J. A. (1987). On explaining gender differences: The case of nonverbal communication. In P. Shaver & C. Hendrick (Eds.), *Review of Personality and Social Psychology, 7,* 177–200.

Hall, J. A., Carter, J. D., & Horgan, T. G. (2000). Gender differences in nonverbal communication of emotion. In A. H. Fischer (Ed.), *Gender and emotion: Social psychological perspectives* (pp. 97–117). New York: Cambridge University Press.

Halligan, S. L., Michael, T., Clark, D. M., & Ehlers, A. (2003). Posttraumatic stress disorder following assault: The role of cognitive processing, trauma memory, and appraisals. *Journal of Consulting and Clinical Psychology, 71,* 419–431.

Halpern, D. F. (1998). Teaching critical thinking for transfer across domains: Dispositions, skills, structure training, and metacognitive monitoring. *American Psychologist, 53,* 449–455.

Halpern, D. F. (2001). Sex difference research: Cognitive abilities. In J. Worell (Ed.), *Encyclopedia of women and gender.* San Diego: Academic Press.

Halpern, D. F. (2003). *Thought and knowledge: An introduction to critical thinking* (4th ed.). Mahwah, NJ: Erlbaum.

Halpern, D. F., & Riggio, H. (2003). *Thinking critically about critical thinking* (4th ed.). Mahwah, NJ: Erlbaum.

Hamburg, D. A. (1997). Meeting the essential requirements for healthy adolescent development in a transforming world. In R. Takanishi & D. Hamburg (Eds.), *Preparing adolescents for the 21st century.* New York: Cambridge University Press.

Hammen, C. (2003). Mood disorders. In I. B. Weiner (Ed.), *Handbook of psychology* (Vol. 8). New York: Wiley.

Hamon, R. R., & Ingoldsby, B. B. (Eds.), 2003). *Mate selection across cultures.* Thousand Oaks. CA: Sage.

Han, S. K., & Moen, P. (1999). *Clocking out: Multiplex time use in retirement.* Bronfenbrenner Life Course Center Working Paper Series No. 98–03m. Ithaca, NY: Cornell University.

Handel, R. W., & Ben-Porath, Y. S. (2000). Multicultural assessment with the MMPI-2. In R. H. Dana (Ed.), *Handbook of cross-cultural and multicultural personality assessment.* Mahwah, NJ: Erlbaum.

Hankin, B. L., & Abela, J. R. Z. (2005). *Development of psychopathology.* Thousand Oaks, CA: Sage.

Hanna, S. L. (1995). *Person to person* (2nd ed.). Upper Saddle River, NJ: Prentice Hall.

Hansford, B. C., & Hattie, J. A. (1982). The relationship between self and achievement/performance measures. *Review of Educational Research, 52,* 123–142.

Harburg, E., Julius, M., Kaciroti, N., Geibeman, L., & Schork, M. A. (2003). Expressive/suppressive anger-coping responses, gender, and types of mortality: A 17–year follow-up. *Psychosomatic Medicine, 65,* 588–597.

Haring, M., Hewitt, P. L., & Flett, G. L. (2003). Perfectionism and quality of intimate relationships. *Journal of Marriage and the Family, 65,* 143–158.

Harman, S. M. (2004). What do hormones have to do with aging? What does aging have to do with hormones? *Annals of the New York Academy of Science, 1019,* 299–308.

Harmatz, M. (1997). Introduction to clinical psychology. In J. W. Santrock, *Psychology* (5th ed.). New York: McGraw-Hill.

Harrison-Hale, A. O., McLoyd, V. C., & Smedley, B. (2004). Racial and ethnic status: Risk and protective processes among African-American families. In K. L. Maton, C. J. Schellenbach, B. J. Leadbetter, & A. L. Solarz (Eds.), *Investing in children, families, and communities.* Washington, DC: American Psychological Association.

Harter, S. (1998). The development of self-representation. In W. Damon (Ed.), *Handbook of child psychology* (5th ed., Vol. 3). New York: Wiley.

Harter, S. (1999). *The construction of the self.* New York: Guilford.

Harter, S. (2002). Review of Santrock, *Child Development,* 10th ed. New York: McGraw-Hill.

Hartmann, D. P., Barrios, B. A., & Wood, D. D. (2003). Principles of behavioral observation. In M. Hersen (Ed.), *Comprehensive handbook of psychological assessment* (Vol. 3). New York: Wiley.

Harvey, J. H. (2004). Death, loss, and trauma. In W. E. Craighead & C. B. Nemeroff (Eds.), *The concise Corsini encyclopedia of psychology and behavioral science* (3rd ed.). New York: Wiley.

Harvey, J. H., & Fine, M. A. (2004). *Children of divorce.* Mahwah, NJ: Erlbaum.

Harvey, J. H., & Weber, A. L. (2002). *The odyssey of the heart* (2nd ed.). Mahwah, NJ: Erlbaum.

Harvey, J. H., & Wenzel, A. (Eds.). (2004). *The handbook of sexuality in close relationships.* Mahwah, NJ: Erlbaum.

Harwell, J. I., Flanigan, T. P., Mitty, J. A., Macalino, G. E., Caliendo, A. M., Ingersoll, J., Stenzel, M. S., Carpenter, C. C., & Cu-Vin, S. (2003). Directly observed antiretroviral therapy to reduce genital tract and plasma HIV-1 RNA in women with poor adherence. *AIDS, 17,* 1990–1993.

Harwood, R. Leyendecker, B., Carlson, V., Asencio, M., & Miller, A. (2002). Parenting among Latino families in the U.S. In M. H. Bornstein (Ed.), *Handbook of parenting* (2nd ed.). Mahwah, NJ: Erlbaum.

Hatcher, R., & others. (1988). *Contraceptive technology, 1988–1989* (14th ed.). New York: Irvington.

Hauselmann, H. J., & Rizzoli, R. (2003). A comprehensive review of treatments for postmenopausal osteoporosis. *Osteoporosis International, 14,* 2–12.

Hawkley, L. C., & Cacioppo, J. T. (2003). Loneliness and pathways to disease. *Brain, Behavior, and Immunity, 17* (Supplement 1), S98–S105.

Hawkley, L. C., & Cacioppo, J. T. (2004). Stress and the aging immune system. *Brain, Behavior, and Immunity, 18,* 114–119.

Hayes, S. C., & Wilson, K. G. (2003). Mindfulness: Method and process. *Clinical Psychology: Science and Practice, 10,* 157–160.

Hazan, C., & Shaver, P. R. (1987). Romantic love conceptualized as an attachment process. *Journal of Personality and Social Psychology, 52,* 522–524.

Heath, A. C., & Nelson, E. C. (2002). Effects of the interaction between genotype and environment. *Alcohol Research and Health, 26,* 193–206.

Heath, S. B., & McLaughlin, M. W. (Eds.), (1993). *Identity and inner-city youth: Beyond ethnicity and gender.* New York: Teachers College Press.

Hecht, M. L., Jackson, R. L., & Ribeau, S. A. (2002). *African American communication* (2nd ed.). Mahwah: NJ: Erlbaum.

Heckhausen, J. (2002). Developmental regulation of life-course transitions: A control theory approach. In L. Pulkkinen & A. Caspi (Eds.), *Paths to successful development: Personality in the life course.* New York: Cambridge University Press.

Heffner, K. L., Kiecolt-Glaser, J. K., Loving, T. J., Glaser, R., & Malarkey, W. B. (2004). Spousal conflict satisfaction as a modifier of physiological responses to marital conflict in younger and older couples. *Journal of Behavioral Medicine, 27,* 233–254.

Heffner, K. L., Loving, T. J., Robles, T. F., & Kiecolt-Glaser, J. K. (2003). Examining psychosocial factors related to cancer incidence and progression: In search of a silver lining. *Brain, Behavior, and Immunity, 17* (Supplement 1), 109–111.

Heiby, E. M., & Haynes, S. (2004). Introduction to behavioral assessment. In M. Hersen (Ed.), *Comprehensive handbook of psychological assessment* (Vol. 3). New York: Wiley.

Heinicke, C. M. (2002). The transition to parenting. In M. H. Bornstein (Ed.), *Handbook of parenting* (2nd ed.). Mahwah, NJ: Erlbaum.

Heinrichs, R. W. (2001). *In search of madness.* New York: Oxford University Press.

Heitler, S. (2004). Treating high-conflict couples. In G. P. Koocher, J. C. Norcross, & S. S. Hill (Eds.), *Psychologists' desk reference* (2nd Ed.). New York: Oxford University Press.

Helgeson, V. S., Snyder, P., & Seltman, H. (2004). Psychological and physical adjustment to breast cancer over 4 years: Identifying distinct trajectories of change. *Health Psychology, 23,* 3–15.

Helms, J. E. (Ed.), (1990). *Black and white racial identity: Theory, research, and practice.* Westport, CT: Greenwood Press.

Helms, J. E. (1996). *Where do we go from here? Affirmative action: Who benefits?* Washington, DC: American Psychological Association.

Helwig, A. A. (2004). A ten-year longitudinal study of the career development of students: Summary findings. *Journal of Counseling and Development, 82,* 49–57.

Henderson, B. N., & Baum, A. B. (2004). Biological mechanisms of health and disease. In S. Sutton, A. Baum, & M. Johnston (Eds.), *The Sage handbook of health psychology.* Thousand Oaks, CA: Sage.

Henderson, B. N., Baum, A., & Sutton, S. (2005). Biological mechanisms of health and disease. In S. Sutton, A. Baum, & M. Johnston (Eds.), *The SAGE handbook of health psychology.* Thousand Oaks, CA: Sage.

Hendrick, C., & Hendrick, S. S. (2004). Sex and romantic love. In J. H. Harvey, A. Wenzel, & S. Sprecher (Eds.), *The handbook of sexuality in close relationships.* Mahwah, NJ: Erlbaum.

Hendrick, C., & Hendrick, S. S. (Eds.). (2004). *Close relationships.* Thousand Oaks, CA: Sage.

Hendrick, S. (2001). Intimacy and love. In J. Worell (Ed.), *Encyclopedia of women and gender.* San Diego: Academic Press.

Heppner, P., & Lee, D. (2001). Problem-solving appraisal and psychological adjustment. In C. R. Snyder & S. J. Lopez

(Eds.), *Handbook of positive psychology.* New York: Oxford University Press.

Herbert, T. B., & Cohen, S. (1993). Depression and immunity: A meta-analytic review. *Psychological Bulletin, 113,* 472–486.

Herek, G. (2000). Homosexuality. In A. Kazdin (Ed.), *Encyclopedia of psychology.* Washington, DC, & New York: American Psychological Association and Oxford University Press.

Herpher, I., & Lieb, K. (2003). Substance p and substance p receptor antagonists in the pathogenesis and treatment of affective disorders. *World Journal of Biological Psychiatry, 4,* 56–63.

Herr, E. L. (2004a). Career development. In W. E. Craighead & C. B. Nemeroff (Eds.), *The concise Corsini encyclopedia of psychology and behavioral science.* New York: Wiley.

Herr, E. L. (2004b). Career counseling. In W. E. Craighead & C. B. Nemeroff (Eds.), *The concise Corsini encyclopedia of psychology and behavioral science.* New York: Wiley.

Hersen, M. (Ed.) (2005). *Encyclopedia of behavior modification and cognitive behavior therapy.* Thousand Oaks, CA: Sage.

Herzberg, E. (2000). Use of TAT in multicultural societies: Brazil and the United States. In R. H. Dana (Ed.), *Handbook of cross-cultural and multicultural personality assessment.* Mahwah, NJ: Erlbaum.

Hetherington, E. M. (1989). Coping with family transitions: Winners, losers, and survivors. *Child Development, 60,* 1–14.

Hetherington, E. M. (2000). Divorce. In A. Kazdin (Ed.), *Encyclopedia of psychology.* Washington, DC, & New York: American Psychological Association and Oxford University Press.

Hetherington, E. M., Bridges, M., & Insabella, G. M. (1998). What matters? What does not? Five perspectives on the association between marital transitions and children's adjustment. *American Psychologist, 53,* 167–184.

Hetherington, E. M., & Kelly, J. (2002). *For better or for worse: Divorce reconsidered.* New York: Norton.

Hetherington, E. M., & Stanley-Hagan, M. (2002). Parenting in divorced and remarried families. In M. Bornstein (Ed.), *Handbook of parenting.* Mahwah, NJ: Erlbaum.

Hewlett, S. A. (2002). *Creating a life: Professional women and the quest for children.* New York: Talk Miramax Books.

Hewstone, M., Rubin, M., & Willis, H. (2002). Intergroup bias. *Annual Review of Psychology* (Vol. 53). Palo Alto, CA: Annual Reviews.

Hidalgo, R. B., & Davidson, J. R. (2001). Generalized anxiety disorder: An important

clinical concern. *Medical Clinics of North America, 85,* 691–710.

Higgins, E. T. (1984). *Self-discrepancy: A theory relating self and affect.* Unpublished manuscript, New York University.

Higgins, E. T. (1987). Self-discrepancy: A theory relating self and affect. *Psychological Review, 94,* 319–340.

Higgins, E. T. (1999). Self-discrepancy: A theory relating self and affect. In R. F. Baumeister (Ed.), *The self in social psychology, Key readings in social psychology.* Philadelphia, PA: Psychology Press/Taylor & Francis.

Higgins, E. T. (2000). Social cognition: Learning about what matters in the social world. *European Journal of Social Psychology, 30,* 3–39.

Higgins, L. T. (2004). Cultural effects on the expression of some fears by Chinese and British female students. *Journal of Genetic Psychology, 165,* 37–49.

Hill, C. E. (2000). Client-centered therapy. In A. Kazdin (Ed.), *Encyclopedia of psychology.* Washington, DC, & New York: American Psychological Association and Oxford University Press.

Hill, J., Waldfogel, J., Brooks-Gunn, J., & Han, W. (2001, November). *Towards a better estimate of causal links in child policy: The case of maternal employment and child outcomes.* Paper presented at the Association for Public Policy Analysis and Management Fall research Conference, Washington, DC.

Hill, P. C., & Pargament, K. I. (2003). Advances in the conceptualization and measurement of religion and spirituality: Implications for physical and mental health research. *American Psychologist, 58,* 64–74.

Hiller, W., Leibbrand, R., Rief, W., & Fichter, M. M. (2005). Differentiating hypochondriasis from panic disorder. *Journal of Anxiety Disorders, 19,* 29–49.

Hilsenroth, M. J. (2003). Projective assessment of personality and psychopathology: A review. In M. Hersen (Ed.), *Comprehensive handbook of psychological assessment* (Vol. 2). New York: Wiley.

Himes, C. L., Hogan, D. P., & Eggebeen, D. J. (1996). Living arrangements of minority elders. *Journal of Gerontology, 51A,* S42–S48.

Hines, D. A., & Malley-Morrison, K. (2004). *Family violence in the United States.* Thousand Oaks, CA: Sage.

Ho, M. K., Rasheed, J. M., & Rasheed, M. N. (2004). *Family therapy with ethnic minorities* (2nd ed.). Thousand Oaks, CA: Sage.

Hobfoll, S. E. (1989). Conservation of resources: A new attempt at conceptualizing stress. *American Psychologist, 44,* 513–524.

Hoem, B. (1995). Sweden. In H.P. Blossfeld (Ed.), *The new role of women: Family formation in modern societies.* Boulder, CO: Westview Press.

Hofferth, S. L. (1990). Trends in adolescent sexual activity, contraception, and pregnancy in the United States. In J. Bancroft & J. M. Reinisch (Eds.), *Adolescence and puberty.* New York: Oxford University Press.

Hoffman, L. W. (1989). Effects of maternal employment in two-parent families. *American Psychologist, 44,* 283–293.

Hoffman, L. W., & Youngblade, L. M. (1999). *Mothers at work: Effects on children's well-being.* New York: Cambridge.

Hoffmann, E. A. (2004). Selective sexual harassment: Differential treatment of similar groups of women. *Law and Human Behavior, 28,* 29–45.

Hogan, J. (1986). *Hogan Personality Inventory manual.* Minneapolis National Computer Systems.

Hogan, J., & Ones, D. S. (1997). Conscientiousness and integrity at work. In R. Hogan, J. Johnson, & S. Briggs (Eds.), *Handbook of personality psychology.* San Diego: Academic Press.

Hoge, M. A. (1998). Managed care. In J. S. Friedman (Ed.), *Encyclopedia of mental health* (Vol. 2). San Diego: Academic Press.

Holahan, C. K., & Suzuki, R. (2004). Adulthood predictors of health promoting behavior in later aging. *International Journal of Aging and Human Development, 58,* 289–313.

Holland, J. L. (1973). *Making vocational choices: A theory of careers.* Englewood Cliffs, NJ: Prentice Hall.

Holland, J. L. (1987). Current status of Holland's theory of careers: Another perspective. *Career Development Quarterly, 36,* 24–30.

Holland, J. L. (1996). Exploring careers with a typology: What we have learned and some new directions. *American Psychologist, 51,* 397–406.

Hollender, M., & Mercer, A. (1976). Wish to be held and wish to hold in men and women. *Archives of General Psychiatry, 33,* 49–51.

Holmes, D. S. (1988). The influence of meditation versus rest on physiological considerations. In M. West (Ed.), *The psychology of meditation.* New York: Oxford University Press.

Holmes, R. M., & Holmes, S. T. (2005). *Suicide in the U.S.* Thousand Oaks, CA: Sage.

Holmes, T. H., & Rahe, R. H. (1967). The social readjustment rating scale. *Journal of Psychosomatic Research, 11,* 213–218.

Holstein, M. B., & Minkler, M. (2003). Self, society, and the "new gerontology." *Gerontologist, 43*, 787–796.

Hopkins, J. R. (2000). Erickson, E. H. (2000). In A. Kazdin (Ed.), *Encyclopedia of psychology*. Washington, DC, & New York: American Psychological Association and Oxford University Press.

Horn, J. L., & Donaldson, G. (1980). Cognitive development II: Adulthood development of human abilities. In O. G. Brim & J. Kagan (Eds.), *Constancy and change in human development*. Cambridge, MA: Harvard University Press.

Horney, K. (1945). *Our inner conflicts*. New York: Norton.

Horowitz, M. J. (1998). Psychoanalysis. In H. S. Friedman (Ed.), *Encyclopedia of mental health* (Vol. 3). San Diego: Academic Press.

House, J. S. (1998). Commentary: Age, work, and well-being. In K. W. Schaie & C. Schooler (Eds.), *The impact of work on older adults*. New York: Springer.

Hovey, J. D. (2000). Psychosocial predictors of acculturative stress in Mexican immigrants. *Journal of Psychology, 134*, 490–502.

Howatt, W. A. (1999). Journaling to self-evaluation: A tool for adult learners. *International Journal of Reality Therapy, 18*, 32–34.

Howland, R. H. (2005). Biological basis of psychopathology. In J. E. Maddux & B. A. Winstead (Eds.), *Psychopathology*. Mahwah, NJ: Erlbaum.

Hoyer, W. J., & Roodin, P. A. (2003). *Adult development and aging* (5th ed.). New York: McGraw-Hill.

Hoyer, W. J., & Touron, D. R. (2003). Learning in adulthood. In J. Demick & C. Andreoletti (Eds.), *Handbook of adult development*. New York: Kluwer.

Hsu, L. K. (2004). Eating disorders: Practical interventions. *Journal of the American Medical Women's Association, 59*, 113–124.

Huang, H., Appel, L. J., Croft, K. D., Miller, E. R., Mori, T. A., & Puddey, I. B. (2002). Effects of vitamin C and vitamin E on in vivo lipid peroxidation: Results of a randomized clinical trial. *The American Journal of Clinical Nutrition, 76*, 549–555.

Huang, L. N., & Ying, Y. (1989). Chinese American children and adolescents. In J. T. Gibbs & L. N. Huang (Eds.), *Children of color*. San Francisco: Jossey-Bass.

Hubbard, J., & Miller, K. E. (2004). Evaluating ecological mental health interventions in refugee communities. In K. E. Miller & L. M. Rasco (Eds.), *The mental health of refugees*. Mahwah, NJ: Erlbaum.

Humphreys, K. N. (2000). Alcoholics Anonymous. In A. Kazdin (Ed.), *Encyclopedia of psychology*. Washington, DC, & New York: American Psychological Association and Oxford University Press.

Humphreys, K. N. (2003, August). *Self-help groups for addiction, mental illness, and other human problems*. Paper presented at the meeting of the American Psychological Association, Toronto.

Hunt, M. (1974). *Sexual behavior in the 1970s*. Chicago: Playboy.

Huston, T. L., & Holmes, E. K. (2004). Becoming parents. In A. L. Vangelisti (Ed.), *Handbook of family communication*. Mahwah, NJ: Erlbaum.

Huston, T. L., Neihuis, S., & Smith, S. (1997, November). *Divergent experiential and behavioral pathways leading to marital distress and divorce*. Paper presented at the meeting of the National Council on Family Relations, Washington, DC.

Hybeis, S., & Weaver, R. L. (2004). *Communicating effectively* (7th ed.). New York: McGraw-Hill.

Hyde, J. S. (2004). *Half the human experience* (5th ed.). Boston: Houghton Mifflin.

Hyde, J. S., & DeLamater, J. D. (2005). *Human sexuality* (8th ed., revised update). New York: McGraw-Hill.

Hyde, J. S., & Mezulis, A. H. (2001). Gender difference research: Issues and critique. In J. Worell (Ed.), *Encyclopedia of women and gender*. San Diego: Academic Press.

I

Iacovides, A., Fountoulakis, K. N., Kaprinis, S., & Kaprinis, G. (2003). The relationship between job stress, burnout, and clinical depression. *Journal of Affective Disorders, 75*, 209–221.

Iannuzi, A., Celentano, P., Galasso, R., Covetti, G., Sacchetti, L., Zarrilli, F., De Michele, M., & Rubbu, P. (2002). Dietary and circulating antioxidant vitamins in relation to carotid plaques in middle-aged women. *The American Journal of Clinical Nutrition, 76*, 582–587.

Idler, E. L., Kasl, S. V., & Hays, J. C. (2001). Patterns of religious practice and belief in the last year of life. *Journal of Gerontology: Social Sciences, 56B*, S326–S334.

Inglehart, R. (1990). *Culture shift in advanced industrial society*. Princeton, NJ: Princeton University Press.

Ingram, R., & Ternary, L. (2005). Mood disorders. In J. E. Maddux & B. A. Winstead (Eds.), *Psychopathology*. Mahwah, NJ: Erlbaum.

International Obesity Task Force. (2004). The obesity epidemic, metabolic syndrome, and future prevention strategies. *European Journal of Cardiovascular Prevention and Rehabilitation, 11*, 3–8.

Ironson, G. (2001, March). *Hostile personality and AIDS*. Paper presented at the meeting of the American Psychosomatic Society, Monterey, CA.

Ironson, G., Solomon, G., Balbin, E., O'Cleirigh, C., George, A., Schneiderman, N., & Woods, T. (2001, March). *Religious behavior, religious coping, and compassionate view of others is associated with long-term survival with AIDS*. Paper presented at the meeting of the American Psychosomatic Society, Monterey, CA.

Irwin, M. (2002). Psychoneuroimmunology of depression: Clinical implications. *Brain, Behavior, and Immunity, 16*, 1–16.

Ishihara, S., Makita, S., Imai, M., Hashimoto, T., & Nohara, R. (2003). Relationship between natural killer activity and anger expression in patients with coronary heart disease. *Heart Vessels, 18*, 85–92.

Israilov, S., Bamel, J., Shmueli, J., Niv, E., Engelstein, D., Segenreich, E., & Livne, P. M. (2004). Treatment program for erectile dysfunction in patients with cardiovascular disease. *American Journal of Cardiology, 93*, 689–693.

Ivy, D. K., & Backlund, P. (2004). *Genderspeak* (3rd ed.). New York: McGraw-Hill.

J

Jackson, J. S., Chatters, L. M., & Taylor, R. J. (Eds.). (1993). *Aging in Black America*. Newbury Park, CA: Sage.

Jackson, R. (2004). Evolutionary psychology. In W. E. Craighead & C. B. Nemeroff (Eds.), *The concise Corsini encyclopedia of psychology and behavioral science*. New York: Wiley.

Jadelis, K., Miller, M., Ettinger, W., & Messier, S. (2001). Strength, balance, and the modifying effects of obesity and knee pain: Results from the Observational Arthritis Study in Seniors (OASIS). *Journal of the American Geriatric Society, 49*, 884–891.

Jakupeak, M., Salters, K., Gratz, K. L., & Roemer, L. (2003). Masculinity and emotionality: An investigation of men's primary and secondary emotional responding. *Sex Roles, 49*, 111–120.

Jamison, K. R. (1995). *An unquiet mind.* New York: Random House.

Jamison, K. R. (2004). *Exuberance: the passion of live.* New York: Knopf.

Jandt, F. E. (2004). *An introduction to intercultural communication.* Thousand Oaks, CA: Sage.

Janisse, H. C., Nedd, D., Escamilla, S., & Nies, M. A. (2004). Physical activity, social support, and family structure as determinants of mood among European-American and African-American women. *Women and Health, 39,* 101–116.

Janoff-Bulman, R. (1999). Rebuilding shattered assumptions after traumatic life events: Coping processes and outcomes. In C. R. Snyder (Ed.), *Coping, The psychology of what works.* New York: Oxford.

Janssen, I., Katzmarzyk, P. T., Ross, R., Leon, A. S., Skinner, J. S., Rao, D. C., Wilmore, J. H., Rankinen, T., & Bouchard, C. (2004). Fitness alters the associations of BMI and waist circumference with total and abdominal fat. *Obesity Research, 12,* 525–537.

Jarbin, H., & von Knorring, A-L. (2004). Suicide and suicide attempts in adolescent-onset psychotic disorders. *Nordic Journal of Psychiatry, 58,* 115–123.

Jenike, M. A. (2001). An update on obsessive-compulsive disorder. *Bulletin of the Menninger Clinic, 65,* 4–25.

Jenkins, S. (2002). Race and human diversity. In M. Hersen & W. H. Sledge (Eds.), *Encyclopedia of psychotherapy.* San Diego: Academic Press.

Jennings, L., & Skovholt, T. M. (1999). The cognitive, emotional, and relational characteristics of master therapists. *Journal of Counseling Psychology, 46,* 3–11.

Johannes, L. (2002, June 3). The surprising rise of radical diet: "Calorie restriction." *Wall Street Journal,* pp. A1, A10.

Johnson, C. (1994). Gender, legitimate authority, and leader-subordinate conversations. *American Sociological Review, 59,* 122–135.

Johnson, D. W., & Johnson, F. P. (2003). *Joining together: Group theory and group skills.* (8th ed.). Boston: Allyn & Bacon.

Johnson, M. K., Beebe, T., Mortimer, J. T., & Snyder, M. (1998). Volunteerism in adolescence: A process perspective. *Journal of Research on Adolescence, 8,* 309–332.

Joiner, T. E. (2000). Depression: Current developments and controversies. In S. H. Qualls & N. Abeles (Eds.), *Psychology and the aging revolution.* Washington DC: American Psychological Association.

Joiner, T. E., Steer, R. A., Abramson, L. Y., Mealsky, G. I., & Schmidt, N. B. (2001). Hopelessness depression as a distinct dimension of depressive symptoms among clinical and non-clinical samples. *Behavior Research and Therapy, 39,* 523–536.

Jones, E., Vermaas, R. H., Beech, C., Palmer, I., Hyams, K., & Wessely, S. (2003). Mortality and postcombat disorders. *Military Medicine, 168,* 414–418.

Jones, J. H. (1997). *Prejudice and racism* (2nd ed.). New York: McGraw-Hill.

Jones, J. M. (2002). Toward a cultural psychology of African Americans. In W. J. Lonner, D. L. Dinner, S. A. Hayes, & D. N. Sattler (Eds.), *Online readings in psychology and culture* (http://www.wwu.edu/culture). Bellingham, WA: Center for Cross-Cultural Research, Western Washington University.

Jones, J. T., & Cunningham, J. D. (1996). Attachment styles and other predictors of relationship satisfaction in dating couples. *Personal Relationships, 3,* 387–399.

Jones, R. A. (2003). Jung's view of myths and post-modern psychology. *Journal of Analytical Psychology, 48,* 619–628.

Joormann, J., & Siemer, M. (2004). Memory accessibility, mood regulation, and dysphoria: Difficulties in repairing sad mood with happy memories? *Journal of Abnormal Psychology, 113,* 179–188.

Jourard, S. M. (1971). *The transparent self.* New York: Van Nostrand Reinhold.

Joy, S., Kaplan, E., & Fein, D. (2004). Speed and memory in the WAIS-III digit symbol-coding subtest. *Archieves of Clinical Neuropsychology, 19,* 759–767.

Judge, T. A., & Bono, J. E. (2001). Relationship of core self-evaluation traits— self-esteem, generalized self-efficacy, locus of control, and emotional stability—with job satisfaction and job performance: A meta-analysis. *Journal of Applied Psychology, 20,* 411–436.

Jung, C. (1917). *Analytic psychology.* New York: Moffat, Yard.

Jussim, L., Ashmore R., & Wilder, D. (2001). Introduction: Social identity and intergroup conflict. In R. D. Ashmore, L. Jussim, & D. Wilder (Eds.), *Social identity, intergroup conflict, and conflict resolution.* New York: Oxford University Press.

K

Kabat-Zinn, J., Wheeler, E., Light, T., Skillings, A., Scharf, M. J., Cropley, T. G., Hosmer, D., & Bernard, J. D. (1998). Influence of mindfulness meditation-based stress reduction intervention on rates of skin clearing in patients with moderate to severe psoriasis undergoing phototherapy (UVB) and photochemotherapy (PUVA). *Psychosomatic Medicine, 60,* 625–632.

Kagitcibasi, C. (1995). Is psychology relevant to global human development issues? Experience from Turkey. *American Psychologist, 50,* 293–300.

Kalichman, S. (1996). *Answering your questions about AIDS.* Washington, DC: American Psychological Association.

Kalick, S. M., & Hamilton T. E. (1986). The matching hypothesis reexamined. *Journal of Personality and Social Psychology, 51,* 673–682.

Kalish, R. A. (1981). *Death, grief, and caring relationships.* Monterey, CA: Brooks/Cole.

Kalish, R. A., & Reynolds, D. K. (1976). *An overview of death and ethnicity.* Farmingdale, NY: Baywood.

Kalivas, P. W. (2004). Dopamine systems. In W. E. Craighead & C. B. Nemeroff (Eds.), *The concise Corsini encyclopedia of psychology and behavioral science.* New York: Wiley.

Kanner, A. D., Coyne, J. C., Schaeter, C., & Lazarus, R. S. (1981). Comparisons of two modes of stress measurement: Daily hassles and uplifts versus major life events. *Journal of Behavioral Medicine, 4,* 1–39.

Kanner, A. M. (2004). Is major depression a neurologic disorder with psychiatric symptoms? *Epilepsy Behavior, 5,* 636–644.

Kantowitz, B. H., Roediger, H. L., & Elmes, D. G. (2005). *Experimental psychology* (8th ed.). Belmont, CA: Wadsworth.

Kaplan, R. M., & Saccuzzo, D. P. (2005). *Psychological testing* (6th ed.). Belmont, CA: Wadsworth.

Karacek, R. (1979). Job demands, job decision latitude, and mental strain: Implications for job redesign. *Administrative Science Quarterly, 24,* 285–307.

Kario, K., McEwen, B. S., & Pickering, T. G. (2003). Disasters and the heart: A review of the effects of earthquake-induced stress on cardiovascular disease. *Hypertension Research, 26,* 355–367.

Kaslow, F. W. (2004). Family therapy. In W. E. Craighead & C. G. Nemeroff (Eds.), *The concise Corsini encyclopedia of psychology and behavioral science.* New York: Wiley.

Kaslow, N. J., & Jackson, E. B. (2004). Suicidal behavior among youth. In W. E. Craighead & C. B. Nemeroff (Eds.), *The concise Corsini encyclopedia of psychology and behavioral science.* New York: Wiley.

Kaslow, N. J., & others. (2004). Person factors associated with suicidal behavior among African American women and men. *Cultural Diversity and Ethnic Minority Psychology, 10,* 5–22.

Kasser, T. (2002). *The high price of materialism.* Cambridge, MA: MIT Press.

Kastenbaum, R. (2004). *Death, society, and the human experience* (8th ed.). Boston: Allyn & Bacon.

Kavanaugh, D. J., & Wilson, P. H. (1989). Prediction of outcome with a group version of cognitive therapy for depression. *Behaviour Research and Therapy, 27,* 333–347.

Kawachi, I., & Kennedy, B. P. (2001). How income inequality affects health: Evidence from research in the United States. In J. A. Auerbach & B. K. Krimgold (Eds.), *Income, socioeconomic status, and health.* Washington, DC: National Policy Association.

Kay, J. (2002). Psychopharmacology: Combined treatment. In M. Hersen & W. H. Sledge (Eds.), *Encyclopedia of psychotherapy.* San Diego: Academic Press.

Kearney, C. A., & Vecchio, J. (2002). Contingency management. In M. Hersen & W. H. Sledge (Eds.), *Encyclopedia of psychotherapy.* San Diego: Academic Press.

Keck, P. E., McElroy, S. L., & Arnold, I. M. (2001). Bipolar disorder. *Medical Clinics of North America, 85,* 645–661.

Keel, P. K., Mitchell, J. E., Miller, K. B., Davis, T. L., & Crowe, S. J. (1999). Long-term outcome of bulimia nervosa. *Archives of General Psychiatry, 56,* 63–69.

Keller, M. (2004). Self in relationship. In D. Lapsley & D. Narvaez (Eds.), *Moral development, self, and identity.* Mahwah, NJ: Erlbaum.

Kelly, A. B., Fincham, F. K., & Beach, S. R. H. (2003). Communication skills in couples. In J. O. Greene & B. R. Burleson (Eds.), *Handbook of communication and social interactional skills.* Mahwah, NJ: Erlbaum.

Kelly, G. F. (2004). *Sexuality today* (7th ed., updated). New York: McGraw-Hill.

Kelly, J. R. (1996). Leisure. In J. E. Birren (Ed.), *Encyclopedia of gerontology* (Vol. 2). San Diego: Academic Press.

Kemper, H. C., Stasse-Walthuis, M., & Bosman, W. (2004). The prevention and treatment of overweight and obesity. *Netherlands Journal of Medicine, 62,* 10–17.

Kendler, K. S., Myers, J., & Prescott, C. A. (2002). The etiology of phobias: An evaluation of the diathesis-stress model. *Archives of General Psychiatry, 59,* 242–248.

Kernis, M. H. (2003). Toward a conceptualization of optimal self-esteem. *Psychological Inquiry, 14,* 1–25.

Kessler, R. C., Berglund, P., Demler, O., Jin, R., Koretz, D., Merikangas, K. R., Rush, J., Walters, E. E., & Wang, P. S. (2003). The epidemiology of major depressive disorder. *Journal of the American Medical Association, 289,* 3095–3105.

Kessler, R. C., Olfson, M., & Bergland, P. A. (1998). Patterns and predictors of treatment contact after first onset of psychiatric disorders. *American Journal of Psychiatry, 155,* 62–69.

Kessler, R. C., Stein, M. B., & Berglund, P. (1998). Social phobia subtypes in the National Comorbidity Survey. *American Journal of Psychiatry, 155,* 613–619.

Keverne, E. B. (2004). Importance of olfactory and vomeronasal systems for male sexual function. *Physiology of Behavior, 83,* 177–187.

Kiecolt-Glaser, J. K., Dura, J. R., Specher, C. E., Trask, O. J., & Glaser, R. (1991). Spousal caregivers of dementia victims. *Psychosomatic Medicine, 53,* 345–362.

Kiecolt-Glaser, J. K., & Glaser, R. (1988). Behavioral influences on immune function. In T. Field, P. McCabe, & N. Schneiderman (Eds.), *Stress and coping across development.* Hillsdale, NJ: Erlbaum.

Kiecolt-Glaser, J. K., McGuire, L., Robies, T. F., & Glaser, R. (2002a). Psychoneuroimmunology and psychosomatic medicine: Back to the future. *Psychosomatic Medicine, 64,* 15–28.

Kiecolt-Glaser, J. K., McGuire, L., Robles, T. F., & Glaser, R. (2002b). Emotions, morbidity, and mortality: New perspectives from psychoneuroimmunology. *Annual Review of Psychology, 53.* Palo Alto, CA: Annual Reviews.

Kiecolt-Glaser, J. K., Preacher, K. J., MacCallum, R. C., Atkinson, C., Malarkey, W. B., & Glaser, R. (2003a). Chronic stress and age-related increases in the proinflammatory cytokine IL-6. *Proceedings of the National Academy of Science, USA, 100,* 9090–9095.

Kiecolt-Glaser, J. K., Robles, T. F., Heffner, K. L., Loving, T. J., & Glaser, R. (2003b). Psycho-oncology and cancer: Psychoneuroimmunology and cancer. *Annals of Oncology, 13* (Supplement 4), 166–169.

Kilpatrick, D. G. (2004). What is violence against women: defining and measuring the problem. *Journal of Interpersonal Violence, 19,* 1209–1234.

Kim B. S. K. (2004). Treatment issues with Asian American clients. In D. R. Atkinson (Ed.), *Counseling American minorities* (6th Ed.). New York: McGraw-Hill.

Kim, J. E., & Moen, P. (2001). Is retirement good or bad for subjective well-being? *Current Directions in Psychological Science, 3,* 83–87.

Kim, J. E., & Moen, P. (2002). Retirement transitions, gender, psychological well-being: A life-course, ecological model. *Journal of Gerontology: Psychological Sciences, 57B,* P212–P222.

Kimata, H. (2001). Effect of humor on allergen-induced wheal reactions. *Journal of the American Medical Association, 285,* 737.

Kimura, D. (2000). *Sex and cognition.* Cambridge, MA: MIT Press.

King, B. M. (2005). *Human sexuality today* (5th ed.). Upper Saddle River, NJ: Prentice Hall.

King, K. M., & Chassin, L. (2004). Mediating and moderated effects of adolescent behavioral undercontrol and parenting in the prediction of drug use disorders. *Psychology of Addictive Behaviors, 18,* 239–249.

Kingston, M. K. (1976). *The woman warrior: Memoirs of a girlhood among ghosts.* New York: Vintage Books.

Kingston, M. K. (1980). *China men.* New York: Knopf.

Kinnunen, L. H., Moltz, H., Metz, J., & Cooper, M. (2004). Differential brain activation in homosexual and heterosexual men produced by the selective serotonin reuptake inhibitor, fluoxetine, *Brain Research, 1024,* 251–254.

Kinsey, A. C., Pomeroy, W. B., & Martin, E. E. (1948). *Sexual behavior in the human male.* Philadelphia: W. B. Saunders.

Kirk, K. L. (2001). Dietary restriction and aging. *Journal of Gerontology, 56A* (2), B123–B129.

Kirkpatrick, L. A., & Hazan, C. (1994). Attachment styles and close relationships: A four-year prospective study. *Personal Relationships, 1,* 123–142.

Kitayama, S. (2002). Culture and basic psychological processes—Toward a system view of culture: Comment on Oyserman et al. (2002). *Psychological Bulletin, 128,* 89–96.

Kitchener, K. S., & King, P. M. (1981). Reflective judgment: Concepts of justification and their relationship to age and education. *Journal of Applied Developmental Psychology, 2,* 89–111.

Kite, M. (2001). Gender stereotypes. In J. Worell (Ed.), *Encyclopedia of women and gender.* San Diego: Academic Press.

Klaw, E., & Humphreys, K. (2004). Facilitating client involvement in self-help groups. In G. P. Koocher, J. C. Norcross, & S. S. Hill (Eds.), *Psychologists' desk reference* (2nd Ed.). New York: Oxford University Press.

Klein, O., & Snyder, M. (2003). Stereotypes and behavioral confirmation: From interpersonal to intergroup perspectives. In M. P. Zanna (Ed.), *Advances in experimental social psychology* (Vol. 35). San Diego: Academic Press.

Kline, G. H., Stanley, S. M., Markman, H. J., Olmos-Gallo, P. A., St. Peters, M., Whitton, S. W., & Prado, L. M. (2004). Timing is everything: Pre-engagement cohabitation and increased risk for poor marital outcomes. *Journal of Family Psychology, 18,* 311–318.

Kline, W. B. (2003). *Interactive group work.* Upper Saddle River, NJ: Prentice-Hall.

Kling, K. C., Hyde, J. S., Showers, C. J., & Buswell, B. N. (1999). Gender differences in self-esteem: A meta-analysis. *Psychological Bulletin, 125,* 470–500.

Knight, B. G. (2004). *Psychotherapy with older adults* (3rd ed.). Thousand Oaks, CA: Sage.

Knowles, E. S., & Linn, J. A. (Eds.). (2004). *Resistance and persuasion.* Mahwah, NJ: Erlbaum.

Knox, J. M. (2002). Memories, fantasies, archetypes: An exploration of some connections between cognitive science and analytical psychology. *Journal of Analytical Psychology, 46,* 613–635.

Kobasa, S. C., Maddi, S. R., & Kahn, S. (1982). Hardiness and health: A prospective study. *Journal of Personality and Social Psychology, 42,* 168–177.

Kobasa, S. C., Maddi, S. R., Puccetti, M. C., & Zola, M. (1986). Relative effectiveness of hardiness, exercise, and social support as resources against illness. *Journal of Psychosomatic Research, 29,* 525–533.

Koenig, H. G. (2001). Religion and medicine II: Religion, mental health, and related behaviors. *International Journal of Psychiatry, 31,* 97–109.

Koenig, H. G., & Blazer, D. G. (1996). Depression. In J. E. Birren (Ed.), *Encyclopedia of gerontology* (Vol. 1). San Diego: Academic Press.

Koenig, H. G., Larson, D. B. (1998). Religion and mental health. In H. S. Friedman (Ed.), *Encyclopedia of mental health* (Vol. 3). San Diego: Academic Press.

Koenig, H. G., Smiley, M., & Gonzales, J. A. T. (1988). *Religion, health, and aging.* New York: Greenwood Press.

Kohlberg, L. (1966). A cognitive-developmental analysis of children's sex-role concepts and attitudes. In E. E. Maccoby (Ed.), *The development of sex differences.* Palo Alto, CA: Stanford University Press.

Kohut, H. (1977). *Restoration of the self.* New York: International Universities Press.

Kokai, M., Fujii, S., Shinfuku, N., & Edwards, G. (2004). Natural disaster and mental health in Asia. *Psychiatry and Clinical Neuroscience, 58,* 110–116.

Kop, W. J. (2003). The integration of cardiovascular behavioral medicine and

psychoneuroimmunology: New developments based on converging research fields. *Brain, Behavior, and Immunology, 17,* 233–237.

Koppelman, K., & Goodhart, L. (2005). *Understanding human differences.* Boston: Allyn & Bacon.

Koss, M., & Boeschen, L. (1998). Rape. In H. S. Friedman (Ed.), *Encyclopedia of mental health* (Vol. 3). San Diego: Academic Press.

Kotre, J. (1984). *Outliving the self: Generativity and the interpretation of lives.* Baltimore: Johns Hopkins University Press.

Kramer, A. F., & Willis, S. L. (2002). Enhancing the cognitive vitality of older adults. *Current Directions in Psychological Research, 11,* 173–177.

Kramer, D. A., Kahlbaugh, P. E., & Goldston, R. B. (1992). A measure of paradigm beliefs about the social world. *Journal of Gerontology, 47,* 180–189.

Krause, N. (2003). Religious meaning and subjective well-being in late life. *Journals of Gerontology B: Psychological Social Sciences, 58,* S160–S170.

Krause, N. (2004). Common facets of religion, unique facets of religion, and life satisfaction among older adults. *Journal of Gerontology B: Psychological and Social Sciences, 59,* S109–S117.

Krause, W., & Bohring, C. (2003). Male infertility and genital chlamydial infection: Victim or perpetrator? *Andrologia, 35,* 209–216.

Kraut, K., Patterson, M., Lundmark, V., Kiesler S., Mukopadhyay, T., & Scherlis, W. (1998). Internet paradox. *American Psychologist, 53,* 1017–1031.

Kring, A. M., & Gordon, A. H. (1998). Sex differences in emotion: Expression, experience, and physiology. *Journal of Personality and Social Psychology, 74,* 686–703.

Kris, A. O. (2002). Free association. In M. Hersen & W. H. Sledge (Eds.), *Encyclopedia of psychotherapy.* San Diego: Academic Press.

Kroll, J. (2003). Posttraumatic symptoms and the complexity of responses to trauma. *Journal of the American Medical Association, 290,* 667–670.

Krull, D. S. (2001). On partitioning the fundamental attribution error. In G. B. Moskowitz (Ed.), *Cognitive social psychology.* Mahwah, NJ: Erlbaum.

Kübler-Ross, E. (1969). *On death and dying.* New York: Macmillan.

Kuch, K., & Cox, B. J. (1992). Symptoms of PTSD in 124 survivors of the Holocaust. *American Journal of Psychiatry, 149,* 339–340.

Kuczynski, L., & Lollis, S. (2002). Four foundations for a dynamic model of parenting. In J. R. M. Gerris (Ed.),

Kuczunski, L., & Lollis, S. (Eds.), *Dynamics of parenting.* Hillsdale, NJ: Erlbaum.

Kuelz, A. K., Hohagen, F., & Voderholzer, U. (2004). Neuropsychological performance in obsessive-compulsive disorder: A critical review. *Biological Psychiatry, 65,* 183–236.

Kunnen, E. S., & Klein Wassink, M. E. (2003). An analysis of identity change in adulthood. *Identity, 3,* 347–366.

Kurdek, O. A. (1995). Developmental changes in relationship quality in gay and lesbian cohabiting couples. *Developmental Psychology, 31,* 86–94.

Kuzman, J. M., & Black, D. W. (2004). Integrating pharmacotherapy and psychotherapy in the management of anxiety disorders. *Current Psychiatry Reports, 6,* 268–273.

Kwak, K. (2003). Adolescents and their parents: A review of intergenerational family relations for immigrant and non-immigrant families. *Human Development, 46,* 15–136.

L

La Greca, A., Silverman, W. K., Vernberg, E. M., & Prinstein, M. J. (1996). Symptoms of post-traumatic stress in children after Hurricane Andrew: A prospective study. *Journal of Consulting and Clinical Psychology, 64,* 712–723.

LaBar, K. S., Gitelman, D. R., Parrish, T. B., & Mesulam, M. M. (2002). Functional changes in temporal lobe activity during transient global amnesia. *Neurology, 58,* 638–641.

Labbé, E. E. (1998). Biofeedback. In H. S. Friedman (Ed.), *Encyclopedia of mental health.* San Diego: Academic Press.

Labott, S. M., & Martin, R. B. (1990). Emotional coping, age, and physical disorder. *Behavioral Medicine, 16,* 53–61.

Labouvie, Vief, G. (1986, August). *Modes of knowing and life-span cognition.* Paper presented at the meeting of the American Psychological Association, Washington DC.

Lachman, M. (2004). Development in midlife. *Annual review of psychology (Vol. 55).* Palo Alto, CA: Annual Reviews.

LaFrance, M., & Henley, N. M. (1997). On oppressing hypotheses: Or, differences in nonverbal sensitivity revisited. In M. R. Walsh (Ed.), *Women, men, and gender: Ongoing debates* (pp. 104–119). New Haven, CT: Yale University Press.

LaFromboise, T. D. (1993). American-Indian mental health policy. In D. R. Atkinson, G. Morten, & D. W. Sue (Eds.),

Counseling American minorities. Madison, WI: Brown & Benchmark.

LaFromboise, T. D., & Trimble, J. (1996). Multicultural counseling theory and American-Indian populations. In D. W. Sue (Ed.), *Theory of multicultural counseling and therapy.* Pacific Grove, CA: Brooks/Cole.

Lakes, R. D., & Carter, P. A. (2004). Globalization, vocational education, and gender equity: A review. In R. D. Lakes & P. A. Carter (Eds.), *Globalizing education for work.* Mahwah, NJ: Erlbaum.

Lam, R. W., & Kennedy, S. H. (2004). Evidence-based strategies for achieving and sustaining full remission in depression: Focus on metaanalyses. *Canadian Journal of Psychiatry, 49* (3, Supplement 1), 17S-26S.

Lamb, C. S., Jackson, L. A., Cassiday, P. B., & Priest, D. J. (1993). Body figure preferences of men and women: A comparison of two generations. *Sex Roles, 28,* 345–358.

Lamb, M. E., & Lewis, C. (2005). The role of parent-child relationships in child development. In M. H. Bornstein & M. E. Lamb (Eds.), *Developmental psychology* (5th Ed.). Mahwah, NJ: Erlbaum.

Lamberg, L. (2003). In the wake of tragedy studies track psychological responses to mass violence. *Journal of the American Medical Association, 290,* 587–589.

Lambert, A. J., Chasteen, A., & Payne, B. K. (2004). Finding prejudice in all the wrong places. In G. V. Bodenhausen & A. J. Lambert (Eds.), *Foundations of social cognition.* Mahwah, NJ: Erlbaum

Lambert, M. J. (2001). The effectiveness of psychotherapy: What a century of research tells us about the effects of treatment. *Psychotherapeutically speaking—Updates from the Division of Psychotherapy (29).* Washington, DC: American Psychological Association.

Lambert, M. J., & Ogles, B. M. (2002). The efficacy and effectiveness of psychotherapy. In M. J. Lambert (Ed.), *Handbook of psychotherapy and behavior change* (5th ed.). New York: Wiley.

Lambert, V. A., Lambert, C. E., & Yamase, H. (2003). Psychological hardiness, workplace stress, and related stress reduction. *Nursing and Health Science, 5,* 181–184.

Lambright, L. L. (2003). *Lessons from Vietnam.* Unpublished manuscript, Macomb Community College, Warren, MI.

Lammers, H. B. (2000). Effects of deceptive packaging and product involvement on purchase intention: An elaboration likelihood model perspective. *Psychological Reports, 86,* 546–550.

Lammers, W. J. & Badia, P. (2005). *Fundamentals of behavioral research.* Belmont, CA: Wadsworth.

Landrine, H., & Klonoff, E. A. (2001). Cultural diversity and health psychology. In A. Baum, T. A. Revenson, & J. E. Singer (Eds.), *Handbook of health psychology.* Mahwah, NJ: Erlbaum.

Landy, S. (2004). Migraine through the life cycle: Treatment through the ages. *Neurology, 62* (Supplement 2), S2–28.

Lang, F. R., & Carstensen, L. L. (1994). Close emotional relationships in late life: Further support for proactive aging in the social domain. *Psychology and Aging, 9,* 315–324.

Laporte, A. (2004). Do economic cycles have a permanent effect on population health? Revisiting the Brenner hypothesis, *Health Economics, 13,* 767–779.

Larsen, R. J. & Buss, D. M. (2005). *Personality psychology* (2nd ed.). New York: McGraw-Hill.

Larson, J. H., & Holman, T. B. (1994). Premarital predictors of marital quality and stability. *Family Relations, 43,* 228–237.

Larson, R., & Wilson, S. (2004). Adolescence across place and time. In R. Lerner & L. Steinberg (Eds.), *Handbook of adolescent psychology* (2nd Ed.). New York: Wiley.

Larson, R. J., & Buss, D. M. (2002). *Personality psychology.* New York: McGraw-Hill.

Lauer, C. J., Modell, S., Schreiber, W., Krieg, J. C., & Holsboer, F. (2004). Prediction of the development of a first major depressive episode with a rapid eye movement sleep induction test using the cholinergic agonist RS 86. *Journal of Clinical Psychopharmacology, 24,* 356–357.

Laurin, D., Verreault, R., Lindsay, J., MacPherson, K., & Rockwood, K. (2001). Physical activity and risk of cognitive impairment and dementia in elderly persons. *Archives of Neurology, 58,* 498–504.

Laursen, B., & Collins, W. A. (2004). Parent-child communication during adolescence. In A. Vangelisti (Ed.), *Handbook of family communication.* Mahwah, NJ: Erlbaum.

LaVoie, J. (1976). Ego identity formation in middle adolescence. *Journal of Youth and Adolescence, 5,* 371–385.

Layder, D. (2004). *Social and personal identity.* Thousand Oaks, CA: Sage.

Lazarus, A. A., & Abramovitz, A. (2004). A multimodal behavioral approach to anxiety. *Journal of Clinical Psychology, 60,* 831–840.

Lazarus, A. A., Beutler, L. E., & Norcross, J. C. (1992). The future of technical eclecticism. *Psychotherapy, 29,* 11–20.

Lazarus, R. S. (1993). Coping theory and research: Past, present, and future. *Psychosomatic Medicine, 55,* 234–247.

Lazarus, R. S. (1993). From psychological stress to the emotions: A history of a changing outlook. *Annual Review of Psychology, 44,* 1–21.

Lazarus, R. S. (2000). Toward better research on stress and coping. *American Psychologist, 55*(6), 665–673.

Lazarus, R. S. (2003). The Lazarus manifesto to positive psychology and psychology in general. *Psychological Inquiry, 14,* 173–189.

Lazarus, R. S., & Folkman, S. (1984). *Stress, appraisal, and coping.* New York: Springer.

Leahy, R. L. (2004). *Contemporary cognitive therapy.* New York: Guilford.

Leary, M. R. (2003). Interpersonal aspects of optimal self-esteem and the authentic self. *Psychological Inquiry, 14,* 52–54.

Leary, M. R., Nezlek, J. B., Downs, D., Radford-Davenport, J., Martin, J., & McMullen, A. (1994). Self-presentation in everyday interactions. *Journal of Personality and Social Psychology, 67,* 664–673.

Lebow, J. L. (2004). Guidelines for conducting couple and family therapy. In G. P. Koocher, J. C. Norcross, & S. S. Hill (Eds.), *Psychologists' desk reference* (2nd Ed.). New York: Oxford University Press.

Lee, D. J., & Markides, K. S. (1990). Activity and mortality among aged persons over an eight-year period. *Journals of Gerontology: Social Sciences, 45,* S39–S42.

Lee, H. G., Moreira, P. I., Zhu, X., Smith, M. A., & Perry, G. (2004). Staying connected: synapses in Alzheimer's disease. *American Journal of Pathology, 165,* 1461–1464.

Lee, I. M., Hsieh, C., & Paffenbarger, O. (1995). Exercise intensity and longevity in men. *Journal of the American Medical Association, 273,* 1179–1184.

Lee, I. M., Manson, J. E., Hennekens, C. H., & Paffenbarger, R. S. (1993). Bodyweight and mortality: A 27–year-follow-up. *Journal of the American Medical Association, 270,* 2823–2828.

Lee, I. M., & Skerrett, P. J. (2001). Physical activity and all-cause mortality: What is the dose-response relation? *Medical Science and Sports Exercise, 33* (6 Supplement C), S459–S471.

Lee, V., & Wagner, H. (2002). The effect of social presence on the facial and verbal expression of emotion and the interrelationships among emotion components. *Journal of Nonverbal Behavior, 26*, 3–25.

Leedy, P., & Omrod, J. E. (2005). *Practice research* (8th ed.). Upper Saddle River, NJ: Prentice-Hall.

Leftkowitz, E. S., Boone, T. L., & Shearer, C. L. (2004). Developmental trajectories of cigarette smoking and their correlates from early adolesence to early adulthood. *Journal of Consulting and Clinical Psychology, 72*, 400–410.

Leichtman, M. (2003). Projective tests: The nature of the task. In M. Hersen (Ed.), *Comprehensive handbook of psychological assessment* (Vol. 2). New York: Wiley.

Leifer, M., Kilbane, T., Jacobsen, T., & Grossman, G. (2004). A three-generation study of transmission of risk for sexual abuse. *Journal of Clinical Child and Adolescent Psychology, 33*, 662–672.

Leiter, M. P., & Maslach, C. (2001). Burnout and health. In A. Baum, T. A. Revenson, & J. E. Singer (Eds.), *Handbook of health psychology.* Mahwah, NJ: Erlbaum.

Lenton, A. P., & Blair, I. V. (2004). Gender roles. In W. E. Craighead & C. B. Nemeroff (Eds.), *The concise Corsini encyclopedia of psychology and behavioral science.* New York: Wiley.

Leong, F. (1996). Multicultural counseling theory and Asian-American populations. In D. W. Sue (Ed.), *Theory of multicultural counseling and therapy.* Pacific Grove, CA: Brooks/Cole.

Leong, F. T. L. (2000). Cultural pluralism. In A. Kazdin (Ed.), *Encyclopedia of psychology.* Washington, DC, & New York: American Psychological Association and Oxford University Press.

Lerner, H. G. (1985). *The danger of anger.* New York: Harper & Row.

Lerner, H. G. (1989). *The dance of intimacy.* New York: Harper & Row.

Lesserman, J., Golden, R. N., Petitto, J. M., Gaynes, B. N., Gu, H., Folds, J. D., & Evans, D. L. (2001, March). *Progression to AIDS: The effects of stress, social support, coping, cortisol, and viral load.* Paper presented at the meeting of the American Psychosomatic Society. Monterey, CA.

Lester, D. (1992). Cooperative/competitive strategies and locus of control. *Psychological Reports, 71*(2), 594.

Lester, N., Smart, L., & Baum, A. (1994). Measuring coping flexibility. *Psychology & Health, 9*(6), 409–424.

Leuba, G., Vernay, A., Va D., Waltzer, C., Belloir, B., Kraftsik, R., Bouras, C., & Savioz, A. (2004). Differential expression of LMO4 protein in Alzheimer's disease.

Neuropathology and Applied Neurobiology, 30, 57–69.

Levant, R. F. (2001). Men and masculinity. In J. Worell (Ed.), *Encyclopedia of women and gender.* San Diego: Academic Press.

Levant, R. F., & Brooks, G. R. (1997). *Men and sex: New psychological perspectives.* New York: Wiley.

Levant, R. F., & Habben, C. (2003). The new psychology of men: Application to rural men. In S. B. Hudnall (Ed.), *Rural behavior health care.* Washington, DC: American Psychological Association.

Le Vay, S. (1991). A difference in the hypothalamic structure between heterosexual and homosexual men. *Science, 253*, 1034–1037.

Levendosky, A. A., Bogat, G. A., Theran, S. A., Trotter, J. S., von Eye, A., & Davidson, W. S. (2004). The social networks of women experiencing domestic violence. *American Journal of Community Psychology, 34*, 95–109.

Leventhal, H., Halm, E., Horowitz, C., Leventhal, E. A., & Ozakinci, G. (2005). Living with chronic illness: A contextualized, self-regulation approach. In S. Sutton, A. Baum, & M. Johnston (Eds.), *The SAGE handbook of health psychology.* Thousand Oaks, CA: Sage.

Levey, A. (2004). Alzheimer's disease. In W. E. Craighead & C. B. Nemeroff (Eds.), *The concise Corsini encyclopedia of psychology and behavioral science* (3rd ed.). New York: Wiley.

Levin, J. S., & Vanderpool, H. Y. (1989). Is religion therapeutically significant for hypertension? *Social Science and Medicine, 29*, 69–78.

Levinson, D. J. (1978). *The seasons of a man's life.* New York: Knopf.

Levinson, D. J. (1996). *Seasons of a woman's life.* New York: Alfred Knopf.

Levy, S. M., Herberman, R. B., Lee, J., Whiteside, T., Kirchwood, J., & McFreeley, S. (1990). Estrogen receptor concentration and social factors at predictors of natural killer cell activity in early-stage breast cancer patients. *Natural Immunity and Cell Growth Regulation, 9*, 313–324.

Lewinsohn, P. M. (2004). Lewinsohn's model of depression. In W. E. Craighead & C. B. Nemeroff (Eds.), *The concise Corsini encyclopedia of psychology and behavioral science.* New York: Wiley.

Lewinsohn, P. M., Antonuccio, D. O., Steinmetz, J., & Teri, L. (1984). *The coping with depression course: A psychoeducational intervention for unipolar depression.* Eugene, OR: Castalia.

Lewinsohn, P. M., & Gottlib, I. H. (1995). Behavioral therapy and treatment of

depression. In E. E. Beckham & W. R. Leber (Eds.), *Handbook of depression* (2nd ed., pp. 352–375). New York: Guilford.

Lewinsohn, P. M., Joiner, T. E., & Rohde, P. (2001). Evaluation of cognitive diathesis-stress models in predicting major depressive disorder in adolescence. *Journal of Abnormal Psychology, 110*, 203–215.

Lewis, H. L. (2003). Differences in ego identity among college students across age, ethnicity, and gender. *Identity, 3*, 159–190.

Lewis, J. M., Wallerstein, J. S., & Johnson-Reitz, L. (2004). Communication in divorced and single parent families. In A. L. Vangelisti (Ed.), *Handbook of family communication.* Mahwah, NJ: Erlbaum.

Lewis, M., Feiring, C., & Rosenthal, S. (2000). Attachment over time. *Child Development, 71*, 707–720.

Leyendecker, R. L., Harwood, R. L., Comparini, L., & Yalcinkay, A. (2005). Socioeconomic status, ethnicity, and parenting. In T. Luster & L. Okaghi (Eds.), *Parenting: An ecological perspective* (2nd Ed.). Mahwah, NJ: Erlbaum.

Li, D., Chokka, P., & Tibbo, P. (2001). Toward an integrative understanding of social phobia. *Journal of Psychiatry and Neuroscience, 26*, 190–202.

Li, G., & others (2004). Statin therapy and risk of dementia in the elderly: A community-based cohort study. *Neurology, 63*, 1624–1628.

Lieb, K., Walden, J., Grunze, H., Fiebich, B. L., Berger, M., & Normann, C. (2004). Serum levels of substance P and response to antidepressant pharmacotherapy. *Pharmacopsychiatry, 37*, 238–239.

Lifton, R. J. (1977). The sense of immortality: On death and the continuity of life. In H. Feifel (Ed.), *New meanings of death.* New York: McGraw-Hill.

Light, L. L. (2000). Memory changes in adulthood. In S. H. Qualls & N. Abeles (Eds.), *Psychology and the aging revolution.* Washington, DC, & New York: American Psychological Association and Oxford University Press.

Lilienfeld, S. O., Wood, J. M., & Garb, H. N. (2000, November). The scientific status of projective techniques. *Psychological Science in the Public Interest, 1* (2).

Linden, W., Linz, J. W., & Con, A. H. (2001). Individualized stress management for primary hypertension. *Archives of Internal Medicine, 161*, 1071–1080.

Lindqvist, R., & Aberg, H. (2002). Locus of control in relation to smoking cessation during pregnancy. *Scandinavian Journal of Public Health, 30*, 30–35.

Lingjaerde, O., Foreland, A. R., & Engvik, H. (2001). Personality structure in patients with winter depression, assessed in a depression-free state according to the five-factor model of personality. *Journal of Affective Disorders, 62,* 165–174.

Linley, P. A., & Joseph, S. (2004). Positive change following trauma and adversity: A review. *Journal of Traumatic Stress, 17,* 11–21.

Lippa, R. A. (2005). *Gender, nature, and nurture* (2nd ed.). Mahwah, NJ: Erlbaum.

Lips, H. M. (2003). The gender pay cap: Concrete indicator of women's progress toward equality. *Analyses of Social Issues and Policy, 3,* 87–109.

Lissman, T. L., & Boehnlein, J. K. (2001). A critical review of Internet information about depression. *Psychiatric Services, 52,* 1046–1050.

Lister, P. (1992, July). A skeptic's guide to psychics. *Redbook,* pp. 103–105, 112–113.

Liu, Y., Gold, E. B., Lasley, B. L., & Johnson, W. O. (2004). Factors affecting menstrual cycle characteristics. *American Journal of Epidemiology, 160,* 131–140.

Livanou, M., Basoglu, M., Marks, I. M., De, S. P., Noshirvani, H., & Lovell, K. (2002). Beliefs, sense of control, and treatment outcome in post-traumatic stress disorder. *Psychological Medicine, 32,* 157–165.

Lockenhoff, C. E., & Carstensen, L. L. (2004). Socioemotional selectivity theory, aging, and health: the increasingly delicate balance between regulating emotions and making tough choices. *Journal of Personality, 72,* 1395–1424.

Loehr, J. (1989, May). (Personal Communication). United States Tennis Association Training Camp, Saddlebrook, FL.

Longo, D. A., Lent, R. W., & Brown, S. D. (1992). Social cognitive variables in the prediction of client motivation and attribution. *Journal of Counseling Psychology, 39,* 447–452.

López, P. J., & Guarnaccia, P. J. (2005). Cultural dimensions of psychopathology. In J. E. Maddux & B. A. Winstead (Eds.), *Psychopathology.* Mahwah, NJ: Erlbaum.

Lopez, S. R., & Guarnaccia, P. J. (2000). Cultural psychopathology: Uncovering the social world of mental illness. *Annual Review of Psychology, 51.* Palo Alto, CA: Annual Reviews.

Lopez, S. R., & Guarnaccia, P. J. (2005). Cultural dimensions of psychopatholgy. In J. E. Maddux & B. A. Winstead (Eds.), *Psychopathology.* Mahwah, NJ: Erlbaum.

Lopez-Toledano, M. A., & Shelanski, M. L. (2004). Neurogenic effect of beta-amyloid peptide in the development of neural stem cells. *Journal of Neuroscience, 24,* 5439–5444.

Loseke, D. R., Gelles, R. J., & Cavanaugh, M. M. (2004). *Current controversies in family violence* (2nd ed.). Thousand Oaks, CA: Sage.

Lott, B., & Maluso, D. (2001). Gender development: Social learning. In J. Worell (Ed.), *Encyclopedia of women and gender.* San Diego: Academic Press.

Lott, B., & Saxon, S. (2002). The influence of ethnicity, social class, and context on judgements about U.S. women. *Journal of Social Psychology, 142,* 481–499.

Lowe, B., Spitzer, R. L., Grafe, K., Kroenke, K., Quneter, A., Zipfel, S., Buchholtz, C., Witte, S., & Herzog, W. (2004). Comparative validity of three screening questionnaires for DSM-IV depressive disorders and physicians' diagnoses. *Journal of Affective Disorders, 78,* 131–140.

Lowe, M. R., & Timko, C. A. (2004). What a difference a diet makes: Towards an understanding of differences between retrained dieters and restrained nondieters. *Eating Behavior, 5,* 199–208.

Lowman, R. L. (1987). Occupational choice as a moderator of psychotherapeutic choice. *Psychotherapy, 24,* 801–808.

Lowman, R. L. (1991). *The clinical practice of career assessment.* Washington, DC: American Psychological Association.

Lucas, R. E., & Diener, E. (2000). Personality and subjective well-being across the life span. In D. L. Molfese & V. J. Molfese (Eds.), *Temperament and personality development across the life span.* Mahwah, NJ: Erlbaum.

Lucas, R. E., Clark, A. E., Yannis, G., & Diener, E. (2004). Unemployment alters the setpoint for life satisfaction. *Psychological Science, 15,* 8–13.

Lumsden, G., & Lumsden, D. (2003). *Communicating with credibility and confidence— diverse people, diverse settings.* Belmont, CA Wadsworth.

Lund, D. A. (1996). Bereavement and loss. In J. E. Birren (Ed.), *Encyclopedia of gerontology* (Vol. 1). San Diego: Academic Press.

Luria, A., & Herzog, E. (1985, April). *Gender segregation across and within settings.* Paper presented at the biennial meeting of the Society for Research in Child Development, Toronto.

Luster, T., & Okaghi, L. (Eds.) (2005). *Parenting: An ecological perspective* (2nd ed.). Mahwah, NJ: Erlbaum.

Lyubomirsky, S., & Lepper, H. S. (2002). *What are the differences between happiness and self-esteem?* Unpublished manuscript, University of California, Riverside.

M

Maccoby, E. E. (1987, November). Interview with Elizabeth Hall: All in the family. *Psychology Today,* pp. 54–60.

Maccoby, E. E. (2002). Gender and group process: A developmental perspective. *Current Directions in Psychological Science, 11,* 54–57.

Maccoby, E. E., & Jacklin, C. N. (1974). *The psychology of sex differences.* Palo Alto, CA: Stanford University Press.

Maccoby, E. E., & Mnookin, R. H. (1992). *Dividing the child: Social and legal dilemmas of custody.* Cambridge, MA: Harvard University Press.

MacGeorge, E. L. (2003). Gender differences in attributions and emotions in helping contexts. *Sex Roles, 48,* 175–182.

MacGeorge, E. L. (2004). The myth of gender cultures: Similarities outweigh differences in men's and women's provisions of and responses to supportive communication. *Sex Roles, 50,* 143–175.

MacKenzie, R. (2002). Group psychotherapy. In M. Hersen & W. H. Sledge (Eds.), *Encyclopedia of psychotherapy.* San Diego: Academic Press.

MacKinnon, D., Jamison, K. R., & DePaulo, J. R. (1997). Genetics of manic depressive illness. *Annual Review of Neuroscience, 20,* 355–373.

MacKinnon, D. F., Zandi, P. P., Cooper, J., Potash, J. B., Simpson, S. G., & Gershon, E. (2002). Comorbid bipolar and panic disorder in families with a high prevalence of bipolar disorder. *American Journal of Psychiatry, 159,* 30–35.

Madden, D. J. (2001). Speed and timing of behavioral processes. In J. E. Birren & K. W. Schaie (Eds.), *Handbook of the psychology of aging* (5th ed.). San Diego: Academic Press.

Maddi, S. (1996). *Personality theories* (6th ed.). Pacific Grove, CA: Brooks/Cole.

Maddi, S. (1998). Hardiness. In H. S. Friedman (Ed.), *Encyclopedia of mental health* (Vol. 3). San Diego: Academic Press.

Maddux, J. E. (2002). Self-efficacy. In C. R. Snyder & S. J. Lopez (Eds.), *Handbook of positive psychology.* New York: Oxford University Press.

Maddux, J. E. & Winstead, B. A. (Eds.) (2005). Psychopathology. Mahwah, NJ: Erlbaum.

Madison. B. E., & Foster-Clark, F. S. (1996, March). *Pathways to identity and* *intimacy: Effects of gender and personality.* Paper presented at the meeting of the Society for Research on Adolescence, Boston.

Maier, T. (2003). *The Kennedys: America's Emerald Kings.* New York: Basic Books.

Mailliard, R. B., Son, Y. I., Redlinger, R., Coates, P. T., Giermasz, A., Morel, P. A., Storkus, W. J., & Kalinski, P. (2003). Dendritic cells mediate NK cell help for Th1 and CTL responses. *Journal of Immunology, 171,* 2366–2373.

Malamuth, N. M. (2003). Criminal and noncriminal sexual aggression. *Annals of the New York Academy of Science, 989,* 33–58.

Malekoff, A. (2004). *Group work with adolescents.* New York: Guilford.

Malinosky-Rummell, R., & Hansen, D. J. (1993). Long-term consequences of childhood physical abuse. *Psychological Bulletin, 114,* 68–79.

Malley-Morrison, K. (Ed.). (2004). *International perspectives on family violence and abuse.* Mahwah, NJ: Erlbaum.

Manev, R., & Manvev, H. (2005). The meaning of mammalian adult neurogenesis and the function of newly added neurons: the "small-world" network. *Medical Hypotheses, 64,* 114–117.

Manji, H. K. (2001). Strategies for gene and protein expression studies in neuro-psychopharmacology and biological psychiatry. *International Journal of Neuropsycho-pharmacology, 4,* 45.

Mann, S. (2003). Coping and social support. In I. B. Weiner (Ed.), *Handbook of psychology* (Vol. 9). New York: Wiley.

Mannell, R. C. (2000). Older adults, leisure, and wellness. *Journal of Leisurability, 26,* 3–10.

Manning, W. D., & Smock, J. (2002). First comes cohabitation and then comes marriage. *Journal of Family Issues, 23,* 1065–1087.

Manson, S. M., Ackerson, L. M., Dick, R. W., & Baron, A. E. (1990). Depressive symptoms among American Indian adolescents: Psychometric characteristics of the Center for Epidemiologic Studies Depression Scale (CES-D). *Psychological Assessment, 2,* 231–237.

Marazziti, D., Di-Nasso, E., Masla, I., Baroni, S., Aelli, M., Mengali, F., Mungal, F., & Rucci, P. (2003). Normal and obessial jealousy: A study of a population of young adults. *European Psychiatry, 18,* 106–111.

Marcaurelle, R., Belanger, C., Marchand, A., Katerelos, T. E., & Mainguy, N. (2005). Marital predictors of symptom severity in panic disorder with agoraphobia. *Journal of Anxiety Disorders, 19,* 211–232.

Marchesini, G., Cuzzolaro, M., Mannucci, E., Dalle Grave, R., Gennaro, M., Tmasi, F., Barantani, E. G., Melchionda, N., & the QUOVADIS Study Group. (2004). Weight cycling in treatment-seeking obese persons: data from the QUOVADIS study. *International Journal of Obesity and Related Metabolic Disorders, 28,* 1456–1462.

Marcia, J. E. (1980). Ego identity development. In J. Adelson (Ed.), *Handbook of adolescent psychology.* New York: Wiley.

Marcia, J. E. (1996). The empirical study of ego identity. In H. A. Bosman, T. L. G. Graafsma, H. D. Grotevant, & D. J. De Levita (Eds.), *Identity and development.* Newbury Park, CA: Sage.

Marcus, E. (2002). Psychoanalytic psychotherapy and psychoanalysis: An overview. In M. Hersen & W. H. Sledge (Eds.), *Encyclopedia of psychotherapy.* San Diego: Academic Press.

Marder, S. R., Davis, J. M., & Chouinard, G. (1997). The effects of risperidone on the five dimensions of schizophrenia derived by factor analysis: Combined results of the North American trials. *Journal of Clinical Psychiatry, 58,* 538–546.

Margolin, L. (1994). Child sexual abuse by uncles. *Child Abuse and Neglect, 18,* 215–224.

Marin, G., & Gamba, R. J. (2003). Acculturation and changes in cultural values. In K. M. Chun, P. B. Organista, & G. Marin (Eds.), *Acculturation.* Washington, DC: American Psychological Association.

Markides, K. S., & Rudkin, L. (1996). Race and ethnic diversity. In J. E. Birren (Ed.), *Encyclopedia of gerontology* (Vol. 2). San Diego: Academic Press.

Markman, H. J. (2000). Marriage. In A. Kazdin (Ed.), *Encyclopedia of psychology.* Washington, DC, & New York: American Psychological Association and Oxford University Press.

Markovitz, J. H., Jonas, B. S., & Davidson, K. (2001). Psychological factors as precursors to hypertension. *Current Hypertension Reports, 3,* 25–32.

Marks, D. F., Sykes, C. M., & McKinley, J. M. (2003). Health psychology: Overview and professional issues. In I. B. Weiner (Ed.), *Handbook of psychology* (Vol. 9). New York: Wiley.

Markus, H. R., & Kitayama, S. (1994). The cultural construction of self and emotions: Implications for social behavior. In S. Kitayama & H. R. Markus (Eds.), *Emotion and culture.* Washington, DC: American Psychological Association.

Markus, H. R., & Nurius, P. (1986). Possible selves. *American Psychologist, 41,* 954–969.

Markus, H. R., Mullally, P. R., & Kitayama, S. (1999) *Selfways: Diversity in modes of cultural participation.* Unpublished manuscript, Department of Psychology, University of Michigan.

Marsella, A. J. (2004). Culture-bound disorders. In W. E. Craighead & C. B. Nemeroff (Eds.), *The concise Corsini encyclopedia of psychology and behavioral science.* New York: Wiley.

Martin, C. L., & Dinella, L. (2001). Gender development: Gender schema theory. In J. Worell (Ed.), *Encyclopedia of women and gender.* San Diego: Academic Press.

Martin, C. L., & Fabes, R. A. (2001). The stability and consequences of young children's segregated social play. *Developmental Psychology, 37,* 431–446.

Martin, C. L., & Halverson, C. F., Jr. (1981). A schematic processing model of sex typing and stereotyping in children. *Child Development, 52,* 1119–1134.

Martin, C. L., & Ruble, D. (2004). Children's search for gender cues. *Current Directions in Psychological Science, 13,* 67–70.

Martin, C. L., Ruble, D. N., & Szkrybalo, J. (2002). Cognitive theories of early gender development. *Psychological Bulletin, 128,* 903–933.

Martin, D. W. (2004). *Doing psychology experiments* (6th ed.). Belmont, CA: Wadsworth.

Martin, G. L., & Pear, J. (2003). *Behavior modification* (7th ed.). Upper Saddle River, NJ: Prentice Hall.

Martin, J. N., & Nakayama, T. K. (2004). *Intercultural communication in contexts* (3rd ed.). Upper Saddle River, NJ: Prentice Hall.

Martin, M. T., Emery, R., & Peris, T. S. (2004). Children and parents in single-parent families. In M. Coleman, & L. Ganong (Eds.), *Handbook of contemporary families.* Thousand Oaks, CA: Sage.

Martin, R. A. (2002). Is laughter the best medicine? Humor, laughter, and physical health. *Current Directions in Psychological Science, 11,* 216–220.

Martin, W. E., & Swartz-Kulstad, J. L. (Eds.). (2000). Person-environment psychology and mental health. Mahwah, NJ: Erlbaum.

Masi, G., Pergui, G., Toni, C., Milleiedi, S., Mucci, M., Bertini, N., & Akiskai, H. S. (2004). Obsessive-compulsive disorder in comorbidity: Focus on children and adolescents. *Journal of Affective Disorders, 78,* 175–183.

Maslow, A. H. (1954). *Motivation and personality.* New York: Harper & Row.

Maslow, A. H. (1971). *The farther reaches of human nature.* New York: Viking.

Massimini, F., & Delle Fave, A. (2000). Individual development in bio-cultural perspective. *American Psychologist, 55,* 24–33.

Masters, W. H., & Johnson, V. E. (1966). *Human sexual response.* Boston: Little, Brown.

Matlin, M. W. (2004). *The psychology of women* (5th ed.). Belmont, CA: Wadsworth.

Matsumoto, D. (2004). *Culture and modern life.* Belmont, CA: Wadsworth.

Matsumoto, D., & Juang, L. (2004). *Culture and psychology* (3rd ed.). Belmont, CA: Wadsworth.

Matthews, K. A., Gump, B. B., Harris, K. F., Haney, T. L., & Barefoot, J. C. (2004). Hostile behaviors predict cardiovascular mortality among men enrolled in the multiple risk factor intervention trial. *Circulation, 109,* 66–70.

Matthews, K. A., Raikkonen, K., Sutton-Tyrrell, K., & Kuller, L. H. (2004). Optimistic attitudes protect against progression of carotid atherosclerosis in healthy middle-aged women. *Psychosomatic Medicine, 66,* 640–644.

Mattson, M. P., Duan, W., Chan, S. L., Cheng, A., Haughey, N., Gary, D. S., Guo, Z., Lee, J., & Furukawa, K. (2002). Neuroprotective and neurorestorative signal tranduction mechanisms in brain aging: Modification by genes, diet, and behavior. *Neurobiology of Aging, 23,* 707.

Matuszek, T., & Rycraft, J. R. (2003). Using biofeedback to enhance interventions in schools. *Journal of Technology in Human Services, 21,* 31–56.

Matzo, M. L. (2004). Pallative care. *American Journal of Nursing, 104,* 40–49.

Mayer, E. L. (2002). Freud and Jung: The boundaried mind and the radically connected mind. *Journal of Analytical Psychology, 47,* 91–99.

McAdams, D. P. (2001). *The person.* New York: Wiley.

McAdoo, H. P. (2002). African-American parenting. In M. H. Bornstein (Ed.), *Handbook of parenting* (2nd ed., Vol. 4). Mahwah, NJ: Erlbaum.

McAllister, M. M. (2000). Dissociative identity disorder: A literature review. *Journal of Psychiatric and Mental Health Nursing, 7,* 25–33.

McCall, W. V., Dunn, A., & Rosenquist, P. B. (2004). Quality of life and function after electroconvulsive therapy. *British Journal of Psychiatry, 185,* 405–409.

McCarty, E. F., & Drebing, C. (2003). Exploring professional caregivers' perceptions: Balancing self-care with care for patients with Alzheimer's disease. *Journal of Gerontological Nursing, 29,* 42–48.

McClain, C. S., Rosenfeld, B., & Breitbart, W. S. (2003, March). *The influence of spirituality on end-of-life despair in cancer patients close to death.* Paper presented at the meeting of American Psychosomatic Society, Phoenix.

McConaghy, N. (1993). *Sexual behavior: Problems and management.* New York: Plenum Press.

McCrae, R. R., & Allik, J. (Eds.). (2002). The five-factor model across cultures. New York: Kluwer.

McCrae, R. R., & Costa, P. T. (2001). A five-factor theory of personality. In L. A. Pervin and O. P. John (Eds.), *Handbook of personality.* New York: Guilford Press.

McCrae, R. R., & Costa, P. T. (2003). *Personality in adulthood* (3rd ed.). New York: Guilford Press.

McCreary, D. R. (2003). The psychology of men's health. *Psychology and Health, 18,* 417–418.

McCubbin, L., & McCubbin, H. (2005). Culture and ethnic identity in family resilience. In M. Ungar (Ed.), *Handbook for working with children and youth.* Thousand Oaks, CA: Sage.

McCullough, M. E., Hoyt, W. T., Larson, D. B., Koenig, H. G., & Thoresen, C. (2000). Religious involvement and mortality: A meta-analytic review. *Health Psychology, 19,* 211–222.

McDowell, M. J. (2001). Principle of organization: A dynamic-systems view of the archetype-as-such. *Journal of Analytical Psychology, 46,* 637–654.

McEwen, B. S. (1998). Protective and damaging effects of stress mediators. *New England Journal of Medicine, 338,* 171–179.

McFarlane, T., Polivy, J., & Herman, C. P. (1998). Dieting. In H. S. Friedman (Ed.), *Encyclopedia of mental health* (Vol. 1). San Diego: Academic Press.

McGregor, B. A., Antoni, M. H., Boyers, A., Alferi, S. M., Blomberg, B. B., & Carver, C. S. (2004). Cognitive-behavioral stress management increases benefit finding and immune function among women with early-stage breast cancer. *Journal of Psychosomatic Research, 56,* 1–8.

McGuire, F. (2000). What do we know? Not much. The state of leisure and aging research. *Journal of Leisurability, 26,* 97–100.

McGuire, W. J. (2004). The morphing of attitude-change into social-cognition. In G. V. Bodenhausen & A. J. Lambert (Eds.), *Foundations of social cognition.* Mahwah, NJ: Erlbaum.

McKay, D., & Tryon, W. W. (2002). Behavior therapy: Theoretical bases. In M. Hersen & W. H. Sledge (Eds.), *Encyclopedia of psychotherapy.* San Diego: Academic Press.

McKay, M., Davis, M., & Fanning, P. (1995). *Messages* (2nd ed.). Oakland, CA: New Harbinger.

McKenna, M. C., Zevon, M. A., Corn, B., & Rounds, J. (1999). Psychsocial factors and the development of breast cancer: A meta-analysis. *Health Psychology, 18,* 520–531.

McKinlay, S. M., & McKinlay, J. B. (1984). *Health status and health care utilization by menopausal women.* Unpublished manuscript, Cambridge Research Center, American Institutes for Research, Cambridge, MA.

Mclnnis, G. J., & White, J. H. (2001). A phenomenological exploration of loneliness in the older adult. *Archives of Psychiatric Nursing, 15,* 128–139.

McLoyd, V. C. (2000). Poverty. In A. Kazdin (Ed.), *Encyclopedia of psychology.* Washington, DC, and New York: American Psychological Association and Oxford University Press.

McLoyd, V. C. (2005). Pathways to academic achievement among children from immigrant families: A commentary. In C. R. Cooper, C. T. Garcia Coll, W. T. Bartko, H. M. Davis, & C. Chatman (Eds.), *Developmental pathways through middle childhood.* Mahwah, NJ: Erlbaum.

McMillan, J. H. (2004). *Educational research* (4th ed.). Boston: Allyn & Bacon.

McMillan, J. H., & Wergin, J. F. (2002). *Understanding and evaluating educational research* (2nd ed.). Upper Saddle River, NJ: Prentice Hall.

McMillan, L. H. W., O'Driscoll, M. P., & Brady, E. C. (2004). The impact of workalcoholism on personal relationships. *British Journal of Guidance and Counseling, 32,* 171–186.

McNally, D. (1990). *Even eagles need a push.* New York: Dell.

McNally, R. (1994). *Panic Disorder: A critical analysis.* New York: Guilford.

McNeil, E. B. (1967). *The quiet furies.* Englewood Cliffs, NJ: Prentice-Hall.

McReynolds, J. L., & Rossen, E. K. (2004). Importance of physical activity, nutrition, and social support for optimal aging. *Clinical Nurse Specialist, 18,* 200–206.

McTigue, K. M., Garrett, J. M., & Popkin, B. M. (2002). The natural history of the development of obesity in a cohort of young U.S. adults between 1981 and 1998. *Annals of Internal Medicine, 136,* 857–864.

McWilliams, N. (2004). *Psychoanalytic psychotherapy.* New York: Guilford.

Means, C., Adrienne, J., Snyder, D. K., & Negy, C. (2003). Assessing nontraditional couples. *Journal of Marital and Family Therapy, 29,* 69–83.

Mecocci, P., Cherubini, A., Mariani, E., Ruggiero, C., & Senin, U. (2004). Depression in the elderly: new concepts and theoretical approaches. *Aging: Clinical and Experimental Research, 16,* 176–189.

Meehl, P. E. (1962). Schizotonia, schizotypy, schizophrenia. *American Psychologist, 17,* 827–838.

Meehl, P. E. (1986). Diagnostic taxa as open concepts. In T. Millon & G. I. Klerman (Eds.), *Contemporary directions in psychopathology.* New York: Guilford.

Meehl, P. E. (2004). What's in a taxon? *Journal of Abnormal Psychology, 113,* 39–43.

Mehrabian, A., & Wiener, M. (1967). Decoding of inconsistent communications *Journal of Personality and Social Psychology, 6,* 109–114.

Mehta, V., Mueller, P. S., Gonzalez-Arriaza, H. L., Pankratz, V. S., & Runumans, T. A. (2004). Safety of electroconvulsive therapy in patients receiving long-term warfarin therapy. *Mayo Clinic Proceedings, 79,* 1396–1401.

Meichenbaum, D. (1977). *Cognitive-behavior modification: An integrative approach.* New York: Plenum Press.

Meichenbaum, D., Turk, D., & Burstein, S. (1975). The nature of coping with stress. In I. Sarason & C. Spielberger (Eds.), *Stress and anxiety.* Washington, DC: Hemisphere.

Mein, J. K., Palmer, C. M., Shand, M. C., Templeton, D. J., Parekh, V., Mobbs, M., Haig, K., Huffman, S. E., & Young, L. (2003). Management of acute sexual assault. *Medical Journal of Australia, 178,* 226–230.

Melinder, K. A., & Andersson, R. (2001). The impact of structural factors on the injury rate in different European countries. *European Journal of Public Health, 11,* 301–308.

Melnik, T. A., Hosler, A. S., Sekhobo, J. P., Duffy, T. P., Tierney, E. F., Engelgau, M. M., & Geiss, L. S. (2004). Diabetes prevalence among Puerto Rican adults in New York City, NY, 2000. *American Journal of Public Health, 94,* 434–437.

Memmler, R. L., Cohen, B. J., Wood, D. L., & Schweglr, J. (1995). *The human body in health and disease* (8th ed.). Philadelphia: Lippincott Williams & Wilkins.

Merva, M., & Fowles, R. (1992). *Effects of diminished economic opportunities on social stress: Heart attacks, strokes, and crime* [Briefing paper]. Washington, DC: Economic Policy Institute.

Mervis, J. (1996, July). NIMH data point way to effective treatment. *APA Monitor,* pp. 1, 13.

Messer, W. S., & Griggs, R. A. (1989). Student belief and involvement in the paranormal and performance in introductory psychology. *Teaching of Psychology, 16,* 187–191.

Messinger, J. C. (1971). Sex and repression in an Irish folk community. In D. S. Marshall & R. C. Suggs (Eds.), *Human sexual behavior.* New York: Basic Books.

Metts, S. (2004). First sexual involvement in romantic relationships. In J. H. Harvey, A. Wenzel, & S. Sprecher (Eds.), *The handbook of sexuality in close relationships.* Mahwah, NJ: Erlbaum.

Meuleman, E. J. (2004). Review of tadalafil in the treatment of erectile dysfunction. *Expert Opinions on Pharmacotherapy, 4,* 2049–2056.

Meuret, A. E., Wilhelm, F. H., & Roth, W. T. (2004). Respiratory feedback for treating panic disorder. *Journal of Clinical Psychology, 60,* 197–207.

Meyer, G. J. (2001). Introduction to the special section in the special series on the utility of the Rorschach for clinical assessment. *Psychological Assessment, 13,* 419–422.

Meyer, G. J. (2003). The reliability and validity of the Rorschach and TAT compared to other psychological and medical procedures: An analysis of systematically gathered evidence. In M. Hersen (Ed.), *Comprehensive handbook of psychological assessment* (Vol. 2). New York: Wiley.

Meyer, M. A. (2004). Drug therapy in Alzheimer's disease. *New England Journal of Medicine, 351,* 1911–1913.

Meyer, R. G., Wolverton, D., & Deitsch, S. E. (1998). Antisocial personality disorder. In H. S. Friedman (Ed.), *Encyclopedia of mental health* (Vol. 2). San Diego: Academic Press.

Michael, R. T., Gagnon, J. H., Laumann, E. O., & Kolata, G. (1994). *Sex in America.* Boston: Little, Brown.

Mickelson, K. D., Kessler, R. C., & Shaver, P. R. (1997). Adult attachment in a nationally representative sample. *Journal of Personality and Social Psychology, 73,* 1092–1106.

Miklowitz, D. J. (2002). *The bipolar disorder survival guide.* New York: Guilford.

Miklowitz, D. J. (2004). Bipolar affective disorder. In W. E. Craighead & C. B. Nemeroff (Eds.), *The concise Corsini encyclopedia of psychology and behavioral science.* New York: Wiley.

Milgram, S. (1965). Some conditions of obedience and disobedience to authority. *Human Relations, 18,* 56–76.

Milgram, S. (1974). *Obedience to authority.* New York: Harper & Row.

Miller, E. R., Pastor-Barriuso, R., Dalal, D., Riemersama, R. A., Appel, L. J., & Guallar, E. (2005, in press). Meta-analysis: High-dosage vitamin E supplementation may increase all-cause mortality. *Annals of Internal Medicine.*

Miller, J. B. (1986). *Toward a new psychology of women* (2nd ed.). Boston: Beacon Press.

Miller, M., Rejeski, W., Reboussin, B., Ten Have, T., & Ettinger, W. (2000). Physical activity, functional limitations, and disability in older adults. *Journal of the American Geriatric Society, 48,* 1264–1272.

Miller, N. E. (1959). Liberalization of basic S-R concepts: Extension to conflict behavior, motivation, and social learning. In S. Koch (Ed.), *Psychology: A study of science.* New York: McGraw-Hill.

Miller, N. E. (1969). Learning of visceral glandular responses. *Science, 163,* 434–445.

Miltenberger, R. G. (2004). *Behavior modification* (3rd ed.). Belmont, CA: Wadsworth.

Milton, J. (2004). *A short introduction to psychoanalysis.* Thousand Oaks, CA: Sage.

Minardi, H. A., & Blanchard, M. (2004). Older people with depression: Pilot study. *Journal of Advanced Nursing, 46,* 23–32.

Mirza, F. S., & Prestwood, K. M. (2004). Bone health and aging: implications for menopause. *Endocrinology and Metabolism Clinics of North America, 33,* 741–759.

Mischel, W. (1968). *Personality and assessment.* New York: Wiley.

Mischel, W. (1973). Toward a cognitive social learning theory reformulation of personality. *Psychological Review, 80,* 252–283.

Mischel, W. (1995, August). *Cognitive-affective theory of person-environment psychology.* Paper presented at the meeting of the American Psychological Association, New York City.

Mischel, W. (2004). Toward an integrative science of the person. *Annual Review of Psychology, 55.* Palo Alto, CA: Annual Reviews.

Mischel, W. & Moore, B. S. (1980). The role of ideation in voluntary delay for symbolically presented rewards. *Cognitive Therapy and Research, 4,* 211–221.

Mischel, W., & Shoda, Y. (2001). Integrating dispositions and processing dynamics within a unified theory of personality: The cognitive affective personality system. In L. A. Pervin &

O. P. John (Eds.), *Handbook of personality.* New York: Guilford Press.

Mischel, W., Cantor, N., & Feldman, S. (1996). Principles of self-regulation: The nature of will power and self-control. In E. T. Higgins & A. W. Kruglanski (Eds.), *Social psychology: Handbook of basic principles.* New York: Guilford Press.

Mischel, W., Shoda, Y., & Mendoza-Denton, R. (2002). Situation-behavior profiles as a locus of consistency in personality. *Current Directions in Psychological Science, 11,* 50–53.

Mishra, G. G., Ball, K., Dobson, A. J., & Byles, H. (2004). Do socioeconomic gradients in women's health widen over time and with age? *Social Science Medicine, 58,* 1585–1595.

Misra, A., Arora, N., Mondal, S., Pandey, R. M., Jailkhani, B., Peshin, S., Chaudhary, D., Saluja, T., Singh, P., Chandra, S., Luithra, K., & Vikram, N. K. (2001). Relation between plasma leptin and anthropometric and metabolic covarites in lean and obese diabetic and hyperlipdaemic Asian Northern Indian subjects. *Diabetes, Nutrition, and Metabolism, 14,* 18–26.

Mitchell, K. S., & Mazzeo, S. E. (2004). Binge eating and psychological distress in ethnically diverse undergraduate men and women. *Eating Behavior, 5,* 157–169.

Mitchell, M., & Catron, G. (2002). Teaching grief and bereavement: Involving support groups in educating student midwives. *The Practicing Midwife, 5,* 26–27.

Mitchell, M. L., & Jolley, H. M. (2004). *Research design* (5th ed.). Belmont, CA: Wadsworth.

Mittag, W., & Schwarzer, R. (1993). Interaction of employment status and self-efficacy on alcohol consumption: A two-wave study on stressful life transitions. *Psychology and Health, 8,* 77–87.

Moen, P., & Quick, H. E. (1998). Retirement. In H. S. Friedman, (Ed.), *Encyclopedia of mental health* (Vol. 3). San Diego: Academic Press.

Moen, P., & Wethington, E. (1999). Midlife development in a life course context. In S. L. Willis & J. D. Reid (Eds.), *Life in the middle: Psychological and social development in middle age.* San Diego: Academic Press.

Money, J. (1986). *Lovemaps: Clinical concepts of sexual/erotic health and pathology, paraphilia, and gender transposition in childhood, adolescence, and maturity.* New York: Irvington.

Montgomery, G. H. (2004). Cognitive factors in health psychology and behavioral medicine. *Journal of Clinical Psychology, 60,* 405–413.

Montgomery, M. J., & Cote, J. E. (2003). College as a transition to adulthood. In G. Adams & M. Berzonsky (Eds.), *Blackwell handbook of adolescence.* Malden, MA: Blackwell.

Montorsi, F., & Althof, S. E. (2004). Partner responses to sildenafil citrate (Viagra) treatment of erectile dysfunction. *Urology, 63,* 762–767.

Moos, E. H. (1986). Work as a human context. In M. S. Pallack & R. Perloff (Eds.), *Psychology and work: Productivity, change, and employment.* Washington, DC: American Psychological Association.

Moore, D. S. (2001). *Statistics* (5th ed.). New York: Worth.

Moras, K. (2002). Research on psychotherapy. In M. Hersen & W. H. Sledge (Eds.), *Encyclopedia of psychotherapy.* San Diego: Academic Press.

Moreland, R. L., & Beach, R. (1992). Exposure effects in the classroom: The development of affinity among students. *Journal of Experimental Social Psychology, 28,* 255–276.

Moretti, R. J., & Rossini, E. D. (2003). Thematic apperception technique (TAT): A new look at an old friend. In M. Hersen (Ed.), *Comprehensive handbook of psychological assessment* (Vol. 2). New York: Wiley.

Morley, S. (2004). Process and change in behavior therapy for chronic pain. *Pain, 109,* 205–206.

Mortimer, J. A., Gosche, K. M., Riley, K. P., Markesbery, W. R., & Snowdon, D. A. (2004). Delayed recall, hippocampal volume, and Alzheimer neuropathology: Findings from the Nun Study. *Neurology, 62,* 428–432.

Mortimer, J. A., Snowdon, D. A., & Markesbery, W. R. (2003). Head circumference, education, and risk of dementia: Findings from the Nun Study. *Journal of Clinical and Experimental Neuropsychology, 25,* 671–679.

Moshman, D. (2005). *Adolescent psychological development,* (2nd ed.). Mahwah, NJ: Erlbaum.

Mounts, N. S. (2002). Parental management of adolescent peer relationships in context: The role of parenting style. *Journal of Family Psychology, 16,* 58–69.

Mroczek, D. K. (2001). Age and emotion in adulthood. *Current Directions in Psychological Science, 10,* 87–90.

Mroczek, D. K., & Kolarz, C. M. (1998). The effect of age on positive and negative affect: A developmental perspective on happiness. *Journal of Personality and Social Psychology, 75,* 1333–1349.

Mueller, N., & Silverman, N. (1989). Peer relations in maltreated children. In D.

Cicchetti & V. Carlson (Eds.), *Child maltreatment.* New York: Cambridge University Press.

Munoz, R. F. (1998). Depression—applied aspects. In H. S. Friedman (Ed.), *Encyclopedia of mental health* (Vol. 1). San Diego: Academic Press.

Murayama, S., & Saito, Y. (2004). Neuropathological diagnostic criteria for Alzheimer's disease. *Neuropathology, 24,* 254–260.

Murdock, G. P. (1949). *Social Structure.* New York: Macmillan.

Murphy, S., & Bennett, P. (2005). Lifespan, gender, and cross-cultural perspectives in health psychology. In S. Sutton, A. Baum, & J. Johnston (Eds.), *The SAGE handbook of health psychology.* Thousand Oaks, CA: Sage.

Myers, D. G. (2000). *The American paradox.* New Haven, CT: Yale University Press.

Myers, D. G. (2002). *Social psychology* (7th ed.). New York: McGraw-Hill.

Myers, D. G. (2004). *Social psychology* (7th ed., updated). New York: McGraw-Hill.

N

Nadien, M. B., & Denmark, F. L. (Eds.). (1999). *Females and autonomy.* Boston: Allyn & Bacon.

Nairn, R. C., & Merluzzi, T. V. (2003). The role of religious coping in adjustment to cancer. *Psycho-Oncology, 12,* 428–441.

Nasraty, S. (2003). Infections of the female genital tract. *Primary Care, 30,* 193–203.

Nathan, P. E., Gorman, J. M., & Salkind, N. J. (1999). *Treating mental disorders.* New York: Oxford University Press.

Nathan, P. E., & Langenbucher, J. (2003). Diagnosis and classification. In I. B. Weiner (Ed.), *Handbook of psychology* (Vol. 8). New York: Wiley.

National Advisory Council on Economic Opportunity. (1980). *Critical choices for the 80s.* Washington, DC: U.S. Government Printing Office.

National Center for Education Statistics. (2002). *Work during college.* Washington, DC: U.S. Office of Education.

National Center for Health Statistics. (1989, June). *Statistics on marriage and divorce.* Washington, DC: U.S. Government Printing Office.

National Center for Health Statistics. (1994). Advance report of final mortality statistics, 1991. *Monthly Vital Statistics Report, 42.*

National Center for Health Statistics. (2000). *Health United States, 1999.* Atlanta: Centers for Disease Control and Prevention.

National Center for Health Statistics. (2002). *America's families and living arrangements.* Atlanta: Centers for Disease Control and Prevention.

National Center for Health Statistics. (2003). *Health United States.* Atlanta: Centers for Disease Control and Prevention.

National Center for Health Statistics. (2004). *Suicide.* Atlanta, GA: Centers for disease control and prevention.

National Center for Health Statistics. (2004). *Health, United States.* Atlanta: Centers for Disease Control and Prevention.

National Center for PTSD (2003). *What is post-traumatic stress disorder?* Washington, DC: Author.

National Clearinghouse on Child Abuse and Neglect. (2004). *What is child abuse and neglect?* Washington, DC: Administration for Children & Families.

National Institute for Occupational Safety and Health. (2001). *Job stress in American workers.* Washington, DC: Centers for Disease Control and Prevention.

National Institute of Diabetes & Digestive & Kidney Diseases. (2003). *Better health and you.* Washington, DC: Author.

National Institute of Mental Health (NIMH). (2000). *Depression.* Bethesda, MD: Author.

National Institute of Mental Health (NIMH). (2001). *The numbers count.* Bethesda, MD: Author.

National Institute of Mental Health (NIMH). (2004a). *Anxiety Disorders.* Bethesda, MD: Author.

National Institute of Mental Health (NIMH). (2004b). *Depressive disorders.* Bethesda, MD: Author.

National Institute of Mental Health (NIMH). (2004c). *Suicide.* Bethesda, MD: Author.

National Institute of Mental Health (NIMH). (2004d). *Schizophrenia.* Bethesda, MD: Author.

Nay, W. R. (2003) *Taking charge of anger.* New York: Guilford.

Nelson, C. A. (2003). Neural development and lifelong plasticity. In R. M. Lerner, F. Jacobs, & D. Wertlieb (Eds.), *Handbook of applied developmental science* (Vol. 1). Thousand Oaks, CA: Sage.

Nelson, D. L., Quick, J. C., & Simmons, B. L. (2001). Preventive management of work stress: Current themes and future challenges. In A. Baum, T. A. Revenson, & J. E. Singer (Eds.), *Handbook of health psychology.* Mahwah, NJ: Erlbaum.

Nelson, M. E., Flatarone, M. A., Moranti, C. M., Trice, I., Greenberg, R. A., & Evans, W. J. (1994). Effects of high-intensity strength training on multiple risk factors for osteoporotic fractures: A randomized controlled trial. *Journal of the American Medical Association, 272,* 1909–1914.

Nemeroff, C. B., & Schatzberg, A. F. (2002). Pharmacological treatments for unipolar depression. In P. Nathan & J. M. Gorman (Eds.), *A guide to treatments that work* (2nd ed.). New York: Oxford University Press.

Neumann, K., & Welzel, C. (2004). The importance of voice in male-to-female transsexualism. *Journal of Voice, 18,* 153–167.

Newcomb, M., & Bentler, P. (1980). Assessment of personality and demographic aspects of cohabitation and marital success. *Journal of Personality Development, 4,* 11–24.

Newman, E. (1974). *Strictly speaking.* Indianapolis: Bobbs-Merrill.

Newman, M. G. (2004). Technology in psychotherapy: An introduction. *Journal of Clinical Psychology, 60,* 141–145.

Nichols, M. P., & Schwartz, R. C. (2004). *Family Therapy* (6th ed.). Boston: Allyn & Bacon.

Nichols, S. L., & Good, T. L. (2004). *America's teenagers—myths and realities.* Mahwah, NJ: Erlbaum.

Nielson, S. L., Johnson, W. B., & Ellis, A. (2001). *Counseling and psychotherapy with religious persons.* Mahwah, NJ: Erlbaum.

Niemann, Y. F., Jennings, L., Rozelle, R. M., Baxter, J. C., & Sullivan, E. (1994). Use of free responses and cluster analysis to determine stereotypes of eight groups. *Personality and Social Psychology Bulletin, 20,* 379–390.

Nier, J. (2004). Why does the "above average effect" exit? Demonstrating idiosyncratic trait definition. *Teaching of Psychology, 31,* 53–54.

Nieto, J. A. (2004). Children and adolescents as sexual beings: cross-cultural perspectives. *Child and Adolescent Psychiatric Clinics of North America, 13,* 461–477.

NIMH (National Institute of Mental Health). (2001). *Post=traumatic stress disorder.* Washington, DC: Author.

Nishimura, M., Terao, T., Soeda, S., Nakamura, J., Iwata, N., & Sakamoto, K. (2004). Suicide and occupation: Further supportive evidence for their relevance. *Progress in Neuropharmacology and Biological Psychiatry, 28,* 83–87.

Nishio, K., & Bilmes, M. (1993). Psychotherapy with Southeast Asian clients. In D. R. Atkinson, G. Morten, & D. W. Sue (Eds.), *Counseling American minorities.* Madison, WI: Brown & Benchmark.

Njenga, F. G., Nicholls, P. J., Nyamai, C., Kiganmwa, P., & Davidson, J. R. (2004). Post-traumatic stress after a terrorist attack: psychological reactions following the U.S. embassy bombing in Nairobi. *British Journal of Psychiatry, 185,* 328–333.

Noakes, M., & Clifton, P. (2004). Weight loss, diet composition, and cardiovascular risk. *Current Opinions in Lipidology, 15,* 31–35.

Nock, S. (1995). A comparison of marriages and cohabiting relationships. *Journal of Family Issues, 16,* 53–76.

Noel, J. G., Forsyth, D. R., & Kelley, K. N. (1987). Improving the performance of failing students by overcoming their self-serving attributional biases. *Basic and Applied Social Psychology, 8,* 151–162.

Nolen-Hoeksema, S. (1995). Gender differences in coping with depression across the lifespan. *Depression, 3,* 81–90.

Nolen-Hoeksema, S. (2000). The role of rumination in depressive disorders and mixed anxiety/depressive symptoms. *Journal of Abnormal Psychology, 109,* 504–511.

Nolen-Hoeksema, S. (2004). *Abnormal Psychology* (3rd ed.). New York: McGraw-Hill.

Nolen-Hoeksema, S., Larson, J., & Grayson, C. (1999). Explaining the gender difference in depressive symptoms. *Journal of Personality & Social Psychology, 77,* 1061–1072.

Nolen-Hoeksema, S., & Morrow, J. (1991). A prospective study of depression and distress following a natural disaster: The 1989 Loma Prieta earthquake. *Journal of Personality & Social Psychology, 61,* 105–121.

Nolen-Hoeksema, S., Parker, L. E., & Larson, J. (1994). Ruminative coping with depressed mood following loss. *Journal of Personality & Social Psychology, 67,* 92–104.

Norcross, J. C. (Ed.). (2002). *Psychotherapy relationships that work.* New York: Oxford University Press.

Norcross, J. C., & Hill, C. E. (2004). Compendium of empirically supported relationships. In G. P. Koocher, J. C. Norcross, & S. S. Hill (Eds.), *Psychologists' desk reference* (2nd Ed.). New York: Oxford University Press.

Norcross, J. C., & Kobayshi, M. (2000). Psychotherapy: Clinical practice. In A. Kazdin (Ed.), *Encyclopedia of psychology.* Washington, DC, & New York: American Psychological Association and Oxford University Press.

Norcross, J. C., & Newman, C. F. (1992). Psychotherapy integration: Setting the context. In J. C. Norcross & M. R. Gottfried (Eds.), *Handbook of psychotherapy integration.* New York: Basic Books.

Norcross, J. C., & Prochaska, J. O. (1988). A study of eclectic (and integrative) views revisited. *Professional Psychology: Research and Practice, 19,* 170–174.

Norcross, J. C., Santrock, J. W., Campbell, L. F., Smith, T. P., Sommer, R., & Zuckerman, E. L. (2003). *Authoritative guide to self-help resources in mental health* (Revised ed.). New York: Guilford.

Norem, J. K., & Cantor, N. (1986). Anticipatory and post-hoc cushioning strategies: Optimism and defensive pessimism in a "risky" situation. *Cognitive Therapy Research, 10,* 347–362.

Norris, F. N., Byrne, C. M., Diaz, E., & Kaniasty, K. (2001). *The range, magnitude, and duration of effects of natural and human-caused disasters: A review of the empirical literature.* Washington, DC: National Center for PTSD.

Norris, J. E., Pratt, M. W., & Kuiak, S. L. (2003). Parent-child relations in adulthood: An intergenerational family systems perspective. In L. Kuczynski (Ed.), *Handbook of dynamics in parent-child relations.* Newbury Park, CA: Sage.

Northern Michigan University Counseling Staff. (2004). *Acquaintance rape.* Marquette, MI: Northern Michigan University.

Notman, M. T., & Nadelson, C. C. (2002). Women's issues. In M. Hersen & W. H. Sledge (Eds.), *Encyclopedia of psychotherapy.* San Diego: Academic Press.

Nutt, D. J. (2001). Neurobiological mechanisms in generalized anxiety disorder. *Journal of Clinical Psychology, 62* (Suppl. 11), 22–27.

O'Brien, A. (2004). Starting clozpanine in the community: A UK perspective. *CNS Drugs, 18,* 845–852.

O'Callahan, M., Andrews, A. M., & Krantz, D. S. (2003). Coronary heart disease and hypertension. In I. B. Weiner (Ed.), *Handbook of psychology* (Vol. 9). New York: Wiley.

O'Connell, H., Chin, A. V., Cunningham, C., & Lawlor, B. A. (2004). Recent developments: suicide in older people. *British Medical Journal, 329,* 895–899.

O'Donnell, L., O'Donnell, C., Wardlaw, D. M., & Stueve, A. (2004). Risk and resiliency factors influencing suicidality among urban African American and Latino youth. *American Journal of Community Psychology, 33,* 37–49.

O'Hara, M., & Taylor, E. (2000). Humanistic psychology. In A. Kazdin (Ed.), *Encyclopedia of psychology.* Washington, DC, & New York: American Psychological Association and Oxford University Press.

Oberauer, K., Demmrich, A., Mayr, U., & Kliegl, R. (2001). Dissociating retention and access in working memory. *Memory and cognition, 29,* 18–33.

Occupational Outlook Handbook. (2004–2005). Washington, DC: U.S. Department of Labor.

Office of Career Services. (2002). *Job search basics.* Cambridge, MA: Office of Career Services, Harvard University.

Olivardia, R., Pope, H. G., Mangweth, B., & Hudson, J. I. (1995). Eating disorders in college men. *American Journal of Psychiatry, 152,* 1279–1284.

Oliver, M. B., & Hyde, J. S. (1993). Gender differences in sexuality: A meta-analysis. *Psychological Bulletin, 114,* 29–51.

Oltmanns, T. F., & Emery, R. E. (2004). *Abnormal psychology* (4th ed.). Upper Saddle River, NJ: Prentice-Hall.

Ong, L., Linden, W., & Young, S. (2004). Stress management: What is it? *Journal of Psychosomatic Research, 56,* 133–137.

Oppenheimer, V. K. (2003). Cohabiting and marriage during young men's career-development process. *Demography, 40,* 127–149.

Orbanic, S. (2001). Understanding bulimia. *American Journal of Nursing, 101,* 35–41.

Orfanos, S. D. (2002). Relational psychoanalysis. In M. Hersen & W. H. Sledge (Eds.), *Encyclopedia of psychotherapy.* San Diego: Academic Press.

Orlinsky, D. E., & Howard, K. L. (2000). Psychotherapy: Research. In A. Kazdin (Ed.), *Encyclopedia of psychology.* Washington, DC, & New York.

Osipow, S. (2000). Work. In A. Kazdin (Ed.), *Encyclopedia of psychology.* Washington, DC, New York: American Psychological Association and Oxford University Press.

Ostow, M. (2004). Psychopharmacology and psychoanalysis. *Israel Journal of Psychiatry and Related Sciences, 41,* 17–22.

Osvath, P., Voros, V., & Fekete, S. (2004). Life events and psychopathology in a group of suicide attempters. *Psychopathology, 37,* 36–40.

Otte, C., Kellner, M., Arlt, J., Jahn, H., Holsboer, F., & Wiedermann, K. (2002). Prolactin but not ACTH increases sodium lactate-induced panic attacks. *Psychiatry Research, 2,* 201–205.

Ouimette, P., Cronkite, R., Prins, A., & Moos, R. H. (2004). Posttraumatic stress disorder, anger and hostility, and health

status. *Nervous and Mental Disorders, 192,* 563–566.

Oxman, T. E., & Hall, J. G. (2001). Social support and treatment response in older depressed primary care patients. *Journal of Gerontology, 56B, No. 1,* P35–P45.

Ozen, S., & Sir, A. (2004). Frequency of PTSD in a group of search and rescue workers two months after 2003 Bingol (Turkey) earthquake. *Journal of Nervous and Mental Disorders, 192,* 573–575.

Ozer, D. J. (2001). Four principles for personality assessment. In L. A. Pervin & O. P. John (Eds.), *Handbook of personality.* New York: Guilford Press.

Ozer, D. J., & Riese, S. P. (1994). Personality assessment. *Annual Review of Psychology, 45,* 357–388.

P

Paffenbarger, R. S., Hyde, R. T., Wing, A. L., Lee, I., Jung, D. L., & Kampter, J. B. (1993). The association of changes in physical-activity level and other life-style characteristics with mortality among men. *New England Journal of Medicine, 328,* 538–545.

Pagnin, D., deQueiro, V., Pini, S., & Cassano, G. B. (2004). Efficacy of ECT in depression: A meta-analytic review. *Journal of Electroconvulsive Therapy, 20,* 10–12.

Palkovitz, R., Marks, L. D., Appleby, D. W., & Holmes, E. K. (2003). Parenting and development: Contexts, processes, and products. In L. Kuczynski (Ed.), *Handbook of dynamics in parent-child relations.* Newbury Park, CA: Sage.

Palmore, E. B., Burchett, B. M., Fillenbaum, C. G., George, L. K., & Wallman, L. M. (1985). *Retirement: Causes and consequences.* New York: Springer.

Palomo, T., Kostrzewa, R. M., Beninger, R. J., & Archer, T. (2004). Gene-environment interplay in alcoholism and other substance abuse disorders; expressions of heritability and factors influencing vulnerability. *Neurotoxicity Research, 6,* 343–361.

Paloutzian, R. F. (2000). *Invitation to the psychology of religion* (3rd ed.). Needham Heights, MA: Allyn & Bacon.

Pals, J. L. (1999). Identity consolidation in early adulthood: Relations with ego-resiliency, the context of marriage, and personality change. *Journal of Personality, 67,* 295–329.

Paludi, M. A. (2002) *Psychology of women* (2nd ed.). Upper Saddle River, NJ: Prentice Hall.

Pampallona, S., Bollini, P., Tibladi, G., Kupelnick, B., & Munizza, C. (2004). Combined pharmacotherapy and psychological treatment for depression: a systematic review. *Archives of General Psychiatry, 61,* 714–719.

Papalia, D. E., Sterns, H. L., Feldman, R. D., & Camp, C. J. (2002). *Adult development and aging* (2nd ed.). New York: McGraw-Hill.

Parati, G., & Steptoe, A. (2004). Stress reduction and blood control in hypertension: A role for transcendental meditation? *Journal of Hypertension, 22,* 2057–2060.

Pargament, K. I., Koenig, H. G., & Perez, L. (2000). The many methods of religious coping: Development and initial validation of the RCOPE. *Journal of Clinical Psychology, 56,* 519–543.

Pargament, K. I., Smith, B., Koenig, H. G., & Perez, L. (1998). Patterns of positive and negative religious coping with major life stressors. *Journal for the Scientific Study of Religion, 37,* 711–725.

Park, C. L., & Folkman, S. (1997). Meaning in the context of stress and coping. *Review of General Psychology, 1,* 115–144.

Park, K. O., Wilson, M. G., & Lee, M. S. (2004). Effects of social support at work on depression and organizational productivity. *American Journal of Health Behavior, 28,* 444–455.

Parke, R. D. (2004). Development in the family. *Annual Review of Psychology, 55.* Palo Alto, CA: Annual Reviews.

Parke, R. D., & Buriel, R. (1998). Socialization in the family. Ethnic and ecological perspectives. In W. Damon (Ed.), *Handbook of child psychology* (5th ed., Vol. 3). New York: Wiley.

Parker, P., & Arthur, M. B. (2004). Giving voice to the dual-career couple. *British Journal of Guidance and Counseling, 32,* 3–23.

Parlee, M. B. (1979, April). The friendship bond: PT's survey report on friendship in America. *Psychology Today,* pp. 43–54, 113.

Parnes, H. S., & Sommers, D. G. (1994). Shunning retirement: Work experiences of men in their seventies and early eighties. *Journal of Gerontology, 49,* 5117–5124.

Pastor, A. D., & Evans, S. M. (2003). Alcohol outcome expectancies for alcohol use problems in women with and without a family history of alcoholism. *Drug and Alcohol Dependency, 70,* 201–214.

Pate, R. H., & Bondi, A. M. (1992). Religious beliefs and practice: An integral aspect of multicultural awareness. *Counselor Education and Supervision, 32,* 108–115.

Patel, R. (2004). Antiviral agents for the prevention of sexual transmission of herpes simplex in discordant couples. *Current Opinions in Infectious Diseases, 17,* 45–48.

Patterson, C. J. (1995). Sexual orientation and human development: An overview. *Developmental Psychology, 31,* 3–11.

Patterson, C. J. (2000). Family relationships of lesbians and gay men. *Journal of Marriage and the Family, 62,* 1052–1069.

Patterson, C. J. (2002). Lesbian and gay parenthood. In M. H. Bornstein (Ed.), *Handbook of parenting* (2nd ed.). Mahwah, NJ: Erlbaum.

Patterson, M. L. (2003). Evolution and nonverbal behavior: Functions and mediating processes. *Journal of Nonverbal Behavior, 27,* 201–207.

Paunonen, S., Jackson, D., Trzebinski, J., & Forserling, F. (1992). Personality structures across cultures: A multimethod evaluation. *Journal of Personality and Social Psychology, 62,* 447–456.

Pavlov, I. P. (1906). The scientific investigation of psychical faculties or processes in the higher animals. *Science, 24,* 613–619.

Pavot, W., & Diener, E. (2003). Well-being. In R. Fernandez-Ballesteros (Ed.), *Encyclopedia of personality assessment* (Vol. 2). Thousand Oaks, CA: Sage.

Payne, V. G., & Isaacs, L. D. (2005). *Human motor development* (6th Ed.). New York: McGraw-Hill.

Payne, W. A., Hahn, D. B., & Mauer, E. B. (2005). *Understanding your health* (8th Ed.). New York: McGraw-Hill.

Pearson, J. C., Nelson, P. E., Titsworth, S., & Harter, L. (2003). *Human communication.* New York: McGraw-Hill.

Pedersen, P. B. (2004). *110 experiences for multicultural learning.* Washington, DC: American Psychological Association.

Pedersen, P. B., & Carey, J. C. (2003). *Multicultural counseling in schools* (2nd ed.). Boston: Allyn & Bacon.

Pennebaker, J. W. (1983). Accuracy of symptom perception. In A. Baum, S. E. Taylor, & J. Singer (Eds.), *Handbook of psychology and health* (Vol. 4). Hillsdale, NJ: Erlbaum.

Pennebaker, J. W. (1997). *Opening up: The healing power of expressing emotions* (Rev. ed.). New York: Guilford Press.

Pennebaker, J. W. (2001). Dealing with a traumatic emotional experience immediately after it occurs. *Advances in Mind-Body Medicine, 17,* 160–162.

Pennebaker, J. W. (2004). *Writing and health: Some practical advice.* Retrieved from http://homepage.psy.utexas.edu/homepage/faculty/pennebaker.

Pennebaker, J. W., & Beall, S. K. (1986). Confronting a traumatic event: Toward an understanding of inhibition and disease. *Journal of Abnormal Psychology, 95,* 274–281.

Pennebaker, J. W., Kiecolt-Glaser, J. D., & Glaser, G. (1988). Disclosure of traumas and immune function: Health implications for psychotherapy. *Journal of Consulting and Clinical Psychology, 56,* 239–245.

Pennebaker, J. W., & Lightner, J. M. (1980). Competition of internal and external information in an exercise setting. *Journal of Personality and Social Psychology, 39,* 165–174.

Penninx, B. W., Rejeski, W. J., Pandya, J., Miller, M. E., Di Bari, M., Applegate, W. B., & Pahor, M. (2002). Exercise and depressive symptoms: A comparison of aerobic and resistance exercise effects on emotional and physical function in older persons with high and low depressive symptomatology. *Journal of Gerontology: Psychological and Social Sciences, 57,* P124–P132.

Penza, K. M., Heim, C., & Nemeroff, C. B. (2003). Neurobiological effects of child abuse: Implications for the pathophysiology of depression and anxiety. *Archives of Women's Mental Health, 6,* 15–22.

Peplau, L. A. (2002). *Current research on gender and sexuality.* Paper presented at the meeting of the American Psychological Association, Chicago.

Peplau, L. A. (2003). Human sexuality: How do men and women differ? *Current directions in Psychological Science, 12,* 37–40.

Peplau, L. A., & Beals, K. P. (2002). Lesbians, gays, and bisexuals in relationships. In J. Worell (Ed.), *Encyclopedia of women and gender.* San Diego: Academic Press.

Peplau, L. A., & Beals, K. P. (2004). Family lives of lesbians and gay men. In A. L. Vangelisti (Ed.), *Handbook of family communication.* Mahwah, NJ: Erlbaum.

Peplau, L. A., Fingerhut, A., & Beals, K. P. (2004). Sexuality in the relationships of lesbians and gay men. In J. H. Harvey & K. Wenzel (Eds.), *The handbook of sexuality in close relationships.* Mahwah, NJ: Erlbaum.

Perault, M. C., Favreliere, S., Minet, P., & Remblier, C. (2000). Benzodiazepines and pregnancy. *Therapy, 55,* 587–595.

Perkinson, R. R. (2004). Twelve-step programs. In W. E. Craighead & C. B. Nemeroff (Eds.), *The concise Corsini encyclopedia of psychology and behavioral science.* New York: Wiley.

Perlman, D., & Peplau, L. A. (1998). Loneliness. In H. S. Friedman (Ed.), *Encyclopedia of mental health* (Vol. 2). San Diego: Academic Press.

Perls, F. (1969). *Gestalt therapy verbatim.* Lafayette, CA: Real People Press.

Perls, T., Lauerman, J. F., & Silver, M. H. (1999). *Living to 100.* New York: Basic Books.

Perrucci, C. C., Perrucci, R., & Targ, D. B. (1988). *Plant closings.* New York: Aldine.

Perry, W. G. (1970). *Forms of intellectual and ethical development in the college years.* New York: Holt, Rinehart & Winston.

Pertovaara, A., Linnankoski, I., Artchakov, D., Rama, P., & Carlson, S. (2004). A potential aphrodisiac for female macaques. *Pharmacology Biochemistry and Behavior, 79,* 137–141.

Pervin, L. A. (2000). Personality. In A. Kazdin (Ed.), *Encyclopedia of psychology.* Washington, DC, & New York: American Psychological Association and Oxford University Press.

Petersen, A. (2003). Research on men and masculinities. *Men and Masculinities, 6,* 54–69.

Peterson, B. E. (2002). Longitudinal analysis of midlife generativity, intergenerational roles, and caregiving. *Psychology and Aging, 17,* 161–168.

Peterson, C. (1988). *Personality.* Fort Worth: Harcourt Brace.

Peterson, C. (2004). Learned helplessness. In W. E. Craighead & C. B. Nemeroff (Eds.), *The concise Corsini encyclopedia of psychology and behavioral science.* New York: Wiley.

Peterson, C., & Seligman, M. E. P., & Vaillant, G. E. (1986). *Explanatory style as a risk factor for physical illness.* Unpublished manuscript, Dept. of Psychology, University of Michigan, Ann Arbor.

Peterson, C., & Steen, T. A. (2002). Optimistic explanatory style. In C. R. Snyder & S. J. Lopez (Eds.), *Handbook of positive psychology.* New York: Oxford University Press.

Peterson, M., & Wilson, J. F. (2004). Work stress in America. *International Journal of Stress Management, 11,* 91–113.

Petras, R., & Petras, K. (1994). *The 776 even stupider things ever said.* New York: Doubleday.

Pettit, R. B. (2003). Sexual teens, sexual media: Investigating media's influence on adolescent sexuality. *Journal of Social and Personal Relationships, 20,* 262–263.

Petty, R. E., & Cacioppo, J. T. (1986). The elaboration likelihood of persuasion. In L. Berkowitz (Ed.), *Advances in experimental social psychology* (Vol. 19). New York: Academic Press.

Petty, R. E., Wheeler, S. C., & Bizer, G. Y. (2000). Attitude functions and persuasion: An elaboration likelihood approach to matched versus mismatched messages. In

G. R. Maio & J. M. Olson (Eds.), *Why we evaluate.* Mahwah, NJ: Erlbaum.

Phaneuf, S., & Leeuwenburgh, C. (2001). Apoptosis and exercise. *Medical Science and Sports Exercise, 33,* 393–396.

Phares, E. J. (1984). *Personality.* Columbus, OH: Merrill.

Phelan, E. A., Anderson, L. A., Lacroix, A. Z., & Larson, E. B. (2004). Older adults' views of "successful aging"—How do they compare with researchers' definitions? *Journal of the American Geriatric Association, 52,* 211–216.

Phillips, W. T., Kiernan, R. M., & King, A. C. (2001). The effects of physical activity on physical health. In A. Baum, T. A. Revenson, & J. E. Singer (Eds.), *Handbook of health psychology.* Mahwah, NJ: Erlbaum.

Phinney, J. S. (1996). When we talk about American ethnic groups, what do we mean? *American Psychologist, 51,* 918–927.

Phinney, J. S. (2003). Ethnic identity and acculturation. In K. M. Chun, P. B. Organista, & G. Marin (Eds.), *Acculturation.* Washington, DC: American Psychological Association.

Phinney, J. S., & Alipuria, L. L. (1990). Ethnic identity in college students from four ethnic groups. *Journal of Adolescence, 13,* 171–183.

Pickering, T. G. (2001). Mental stress as a causal factor in the development of hypertension and cardiovascular disease. *Current Hypertension Reports, 3,* 249–254.

Pin, V. W. (2003). Sex and gender factors in medical studies: Implications for health and clinical practice. *Journal of the American Medical Association, 289,* 397–400.

Pines, A., & Aronson, E. (1988). *Career burnout: Causes and cures.* New York: The Free Press.

Pines, A. M., & Maslach, C. (2002). *Experiencing social psychology* (4th ed.). New York: McGraw-Hill.

Pintrich, P. R. (2003). Motivation and classroom learning. In I. B. Weiner (Ed.), *Handbook of psychology* (Vol. 7). New York: Wiley.

Pittenger, D. (2003). *Behavioral research design and analysis.* New York: McGraw-Hill.

Pittman, J. F., & Lee, C. Y. (2004). Comparing different types of child abuse and spouse abuse offenders. *Journal of Violence and Victims, 19,* 137–156.

Pittman, T. S. (1998). Motivation. In D. T. Gilbert, S. T. Fiske, & G. Lindzey (Eds.), *Handbook of social psychology* (4th ed., Vol. 1). New York: McGraw-Hill.

Plaget, J. (1952). *The origins of intelligence in children.* New York: Oxford University Press.

Plant, E. A. (2004). Responses to interracial interactions over time. *Personality and Social Psychology Bulletin, 30,* 1458–1471.

Pleck, J. H. (1983). The theory of male sex role identity: Its rise and fall, 1936–present. In M. Levin (Ed.), *In the shadow of the past: Psychology portrays the sexes.* New York: Columbia University Press.

Polivy, J., Herman, C. P., Mills, J., & Brock, H. (2003). Eating disorders in adolescence. In G. Adams & M. Berzonsky (Eds.), *Blackwell handbook of adolescence.* Malden, MA: Blackwell.

Pollock, W. (1999). *Real boys.* New York: Owl Books.

Pomerleau, O. (2000). Smoking. In A. Kazdin (Ed.), *Encyclopedia of psychology.* Washington, DC, & New York: American Psychological Association and Oxford University Press.

Porcerelli, J. H., & Hibbard, S. (2003). Projective assessment of defense mechanisms. In M. Hersen (Ed.), *Comprehensive handbook of psychological assessment* (Vol. 2). New York: Wiley.

Post, S. G., & Binstock, R. H. (Eds.). (2004). *The foundation of youth.* New York: Oxford University Press.

Powell, D. H. (2004). Behavioral treatment of debilitating test anxiety among medical students. *Journal of Clinical Psychology, 60,* 853–865.

Powell, G. N. (2004). *Managing a diverse workforce* (2nd ed.). Thousand Oaks, CA: Sage.

Powell, L. (1992). The cognitive underpinnings of coronary-prone behaviors. *Cognitive Therapy & Research, 16*(2), 123–142.

Powers, L. E., & Wampold, B. E. (1994). Cognitive-behavioral factors in adjustment to adult bereavement. *Death Studies, 18,* 1–24.

Pratt, M. W., Danso, H. A., Arnold, M. L., Norris, J. E., & Filyer, R. (2001). Adult generativity and the socialization of adolescents. *Journal of Personality, 69,* 89–120.

Presnell, K., & Stice, E. (2003). An experimental test of the effect of weight-loss dieting on bulimic pathology: Tipping the scales in a different direction. *Journal of Abnormal Psychology, 112,* 166–170.

Prins, J. B., Bos, E., Huibers, M. J., Servaes, P., Van Der Werf, S. P., Van Der Meer, J. W., & Bleijenberg, G. (2004). Social support and the persistence of complaints in chronic fatigue syndrome. *Psychotherapy and Psychosomatics, 73,* 174–182.

Probst, T. M. (2004). Economic stressors. In J. Baring, E. K. Kelloway, & M. R. Frone (Eds.), *Handbook of work stress.* Thousand Oaks, CA: Sage.

Pruchno, R., & Rosenbaum, J. (2003). Social relationships in adulthood and old age. In I. B. Weiner (Ed.), *Handbook of psychology,* Vol. VI. New York: Wiley.

Pukrop, R., Sass, H., & Steinmeyer, E. M. (2000). Circumplex models for the similarity relationships between higher-order factors of personality and personality disorders: An empirical analysis. *Contemporary Psychiatry, 41,* 438–445.

Pulkkinen, L., & Kokko, K. (2000). Identity development in adulthood: A longitudinal study. *Journal of Research in Personality, 34,* 445–470.

Purdon, C., Rowa, K., & Antony, M. M. (2005). Thought suppression and its effects on thought frequency, appraisal, and mod state in individuals with obsessive-compulsive disorder. *Behavioral Research and Therapy, 43,* 93–108.

Puri, B. K., Huttson, S. B., Saeed, N., Oatridge, A., Hajnal, J. V., Duncan, L., Chapman, M. J., Barnes, T. R., Bydder, G. M., & Joyce, E. M. (2001). A serial longitudinal quantitative MRI study of cerebral changes in first-episode schizophrenia using image segmentation and subvoxel registration. *Psychiatry Research 106,* 141–150.

Quadflieg, N., & Fichter, M. M. (2003). The course and outcome of bulimia nervosa. *European Child and Adolescent Psychiatry, 12* (Supplement 1), 1199–1209.

Rabasca, L. (1999, May). Stress caused when jobs don't meet expectations. *APA Monitor, 30,* 20–25.

Rabasca, L. (2000, June). More psychologists in the trenches. *Monitor on Psychology, 31,* 50–51.

Rabinowitz, V. C., & Sechzur, J. (1994). Feminist methodologies. In F. L. Denmark & M. A. Paludi (Eds.), *Handbook on the psychology of women.* Westport, CT: Greenwood Press.

Raffaelli, M., & Ontai, L. L. (2004). Gender socialization in Latino/a families: Results from two retrospective studies. *Sex Roles, 50,* 287–299.

Raikkonen, K., Matthews, Flory, J. D., Owens, J. F., & Gump, B. B. (1999). Effects of optimism, pessimism, and trait anxiety on ambulatory blood pressure and mood during everyday life. *Journal of Personality and Social Psychology, 76,* 104–113.

Ramadan, N. M. (2004). Prophylactic migraine therapy: Mechanisms and evidence. *Current Pain and Headache Reports, 8,* 91–95.

Rapaport, D. (1967). On the psychoanalytic theory of thinking. In M. M. Gill (Ed.), *The collected papers of David Rapaport.* New York: Basic Books.

Rapaport, S. (1994, November 28). Interview. *U.S. News and World Report,* p. 94.

Rappaport, J. L. (1989, March). The biology of obsessions and compulsions. *Scientific American,* 83–89.

Rasmussen. K. G. (1984). Nonverbal behavior, verbal behavior, resume credentials, and selection interview outcomes. *Journal of Applied Psychology, 69,* 551–556.

Ray, D., & Ksir, C. (2004). *Drugs in modern society* (10th ed.). New York: McGraw-Hill.

Ray, E. B. (2005). *Health communication in practice.* Mahwah, NJ: Erlbaum.

Ray, E. B. (Ed.). (2004). *Case studies in health communication.* Mahwah, NJ: Erlbaum.

Rayburn, C. A. (2004). Religion, spirituality, and health. *American Psychologist, 59,* 52–55.

Rector, N. A., & Beck, A. T. (2001). Cognitive behavioral therapy for schizophrenia: An empirical review. *Journal of Nervous and Mental Disorders, 189,* 278–287.

Redd, W. H. (1995). Behavioral research in cancer as a model for health psychology. *Health Psychology, 14,* 99–100.

Redinbaugh, E. M., MacCallum, J., & Kiecolt-Glaser, J. K. (1995). Recurrent syndromal depression in caregivers. *Psychology and Aging, 10,* 358–368.

Regan, P. C. (2004). Sex and the attraction process. In J. H. Harvey, A. Wenzel, & S. Sprecher (Eds.), *The handbook of sexuality in close relationships.* Mahwah, NJ: Erlbaum.

Reiche, E. M., Nunes, S. O., & Morimoto, H. K. (2004). Stress, depression, the immune system, and cancer. *Lancet Oncology, 5,* 617–625.

Reidy, D. C., & Norcross, J. C. (2004). National self-help groups and organizations. In G. P. Koocher, J. C. Norcross, & S. S. Hill (Eds.), *Psychologists' desk reference* (2nd Ed.). New York: Oxford University Press.

Reifman, A., Arnett, J. J., & Colwell, M. J. (August, 2003). *The IDEA: Inventory of Dimensions of Emerging Adulthood.* Paper presented at the meeting of the American Psychological Association, Toronto.

Reinisch, J. M. (1990). *The Kinsey Institute new report on sex: What you must know to be sexually literate.* New York: St. Martin's Press.

Religion in America. (1993). Princeton, NJ: Princeton Religious Research Center.

Renshaw, D. C. (2003). Medical research in pedophilia. *Journal of the American Medical Association, 289,* 1243–1244.

Rice, J. (2001). Family roles and patterns: Contemporary trends. In J. Worrel (Ed.), *Encyclopedia of women and gender.* San Diego: Academic Press.

Riggio, R. E. (1986). Assessment of basic social skills. *Journal of Personality and Social Psychology, 51,* 649–660.

Riley, H., & Schulte, N. S. (2004). Low emotional intelligence as a predictor of substance-use problems. *Journal of Drug Education, 33,* 391–398.

Riley, K. P., Snowdon, D. A., & Markesbery, W. R. (2002). Alzheimer's neurofibrillary pathology and the spectrum of cognitive function: Findings from the Nun Study. *Annals of Neurology, 5,* 567–577.

Ringdal, G. I., Jordhoy, M. S., Ringdal, K., & Kaasa, S. (2001). The first year of grief and bereavement in close family members to individuals who have died of cancer. *Palliative Medicine, 15,* 91–105.

Riolli, L., & Savicki, V. (2003). Optimism and coping as moderators of the relationship between chronic stress and burnout. *Psychological Reports, 92,* 1215–1226.

Ritblatt, S. N. (2003). Love, courtship, and marriage from a cross-cultural perspective. In R. R. Hamon & B. B. Ingoldsby (Eds.), *Mate selection across cultures.* Thousand Oaks, CA: Sage.

Roback, H. W., Barton, D., Castelnuovo-Tedesco, P., Gay, V., Havens, L., & Nash, J. (1999). A symposium on psychotherapy in the age of managed care. *American Journal of Psychotherapy, 53,* 1–16.

Robak, R. (2004). Grief. In W. E. Craighead & C. B. Nemeroff (Eds.), *The concise Corsini encyclopedia of psychology and behavioral science* (3rd ed.). New York: Wiley.

Robbins, G., Powers, D., & Burgess, S. (2005). *A wellness way of life* (6th Ed.). New York: McGraw-Hill.

Roberts, B. W., & Helson, R. (1997). Changes in culture, changes in personality: The influence of individualism in a longitudinal study of women. *Journal of Personality and Social Psychology, 72,* 641–651.

Roberts, B. W., & Robins, R. W. (2004). Person-environment fit and its implications for personality development: A longitudinal study. *Journal of Personality, 72,* 89–110.

Roberts, D., Anderson, B. L., & Lubaroff, A. (1994). *Stress and immunity at cancer diagnosis.* Unpublished manuscript, Dept. of

Psychology, Ohio State University, Columbus.

Roberts, J. E., Gottlib, I. H., & Kassel, J. D. (1996). Adult attachment security and symptoms of depression: The mediating roles of dysfunctional attitudes and low self-esteem. *Journal of Personality & Social Psychology, 60,* 310–320.

Robins, L. & Regier, D. (Eds.). (1991). *Psychiatric disorders in America.* New York: Free Press.

Robins, R. W., Trzesniewski, K. H., Tracey, J. L., Potter, J., & Gosling, S. D. (2002). Age differences in self-esteem from age 9 to 90. *Psychology and Aging, 17,* 423–434.

Roche, E. (2003). Do something—he's about to snap. *Harvard Business Review, 81,* 23–31, 116.

Roden, J. (2004). Revisiting the health belief model. *Nursing Health and Science, 6,* 1–10.

Rodin, J., & Langer, E. J. (1977). Long-term effects of a control-relevant intervention with the institutionalized aged. *Journal of Personality and Social Psychology, 35,* 397–402.

Roe, A. (1956). *The psychology of occupations.* New York: Wiley.

Rogers, C. R. (1961). *On becoming a person.* Boston: Houghton Mifflin.

Rogers, C. R. (1974). In retrospect: Forty-six years. *American Psychologist, 29,* 115–123.

Rogers, C. R. (1980). *A way of being.* Boston: Houghton Mifflin.

Rogers, L. E., & Escudero, V. (Eds.). (2004). *Relational communication.* Mahwah, NJ: Erlbaum.

Ronnback, L., & Hansson, E. (2004). On the potential role of glutamate transport in mental fatigue. *Journal of Neuroinflammation, 1,* 22.

Rook, K. S. (2001). Social support. In J. Worell (Ed.), *Encyclopedia of women and gender* (Vol. 2). San Diego: Academic Press.

Roose, S. P., & Pesce, V. (2004). Tricyclic antidepressants. In W. E. Craighead & C. B. Nemeroff (Eds.), *The concise Corsini encyclopedia of psychology and behavioral science.* New York: Wiley.

Roper Starch Worldwide. (2000). *Attitudes toward retirement: A poll.* New York: Author.

Rosen, G. M. (1993). Self-help or hype? Comments on psychology's failure to advance self-care. *Professional Psychology: Research and Practice, 24,* 340–345.

Rosen, R. D. (1977). *Psychobabble.* New York: Atheneum.

Rosenbaum, J. E. (1984). *Career mobility in a corporate hierarchy.* New York: Academic Press.

Rosenfeld, A. H. (1985, June). Depression: Dispelling despair. *Psychology Today,* pp. 28–34.

Rosengren, A., Hawken, S., Ounpuu, S., Silwa, K., Zubaid, M., & the INTERHEART investigators (2004). Association of psychosocial risk factors with risk of acute myocardial infarction in 11119 cases and 13648 controls from 52 countries (the INTERHEART study): case-control study. *Lancet, 364,* 953–962.

Rosenthal, R., & DiMatteo, M. R. (2001). Meta-analysis: Recent developments in quantitative methods for literature reviews. *Annual Review of Psychology, 52,* 59–62.

Rosnow R. L. & Rosenthal. R. L. (2005). *Beginning behavioral research* (5th ed.). Upper Saddle River, NJ: Prentice Hall.

Ross, C. A., & Norton, G. R. (1989). Differences between men and women with multiple personality disorder. *Hospital & Community Psychiatry, 40,* 186–188.

Rossi, A. S. (1989). A life-course approach to gender, aging, and intergenerational relations. In K. W. Schaie & C. Schooler (Eds.), *Social structure and aging.* Hillsdale, NJ: Erlbaum.

Roth, G. S., Lane, M. A., Ingram, D. K., Mattison, J. A., Elahi, D., Tobin, J. D., Muller, D., & Metter, E. J. (2002). Biomarkers of caloric restriction may predict longevity in humans. *Science, 297,* 811.

Rothwell, J. D. (2004). *In the company of others* (2nd ed.). New York: McGraw-Hill.

Rotter, J. B. (1966). Generalized expectancies for internal versus external control of reinforcement. *Psychological Monographs, 80,* (1, Whole No. 609).

Rouillon, F. (2004). Long-term therapy of generalized anxiety disorder. *European Psychiatry, 19,* 96–101.

Rowe, J. W., & Kahn, R. O. (1997). *Successful aging.* New York: Pantheon Books.

Rubenstein, L. Z., Josephson, K. R., Trueblood, P. R., Loy, S., Harker, J. O., Pietruszka, F. M., & Robbins, A. S. (2000). Effects of group exercise program on strength, mobility, and falls among fall-prone elderly men. *Journal of Gerontology: Medical Sciences, 55A,* M317–M321.

Rubenzer, S., Ones, D. Z., & Faschingbauer, T. (2000, August). *Personality traits of U.S. presidents.* Paper presented at the meeting of the American Psychological Association, Washington, DC.

Rubin, R. H. (2004). Alternative life styles today. In M. Coleman & L. Ganong (Eds.), *Handbook of contemporary families.* Thousand Oaks, CA: Sage.

Rubin, Z. (1970). Measurement of romantic love. *Journal of Personality and Social Psychology, 16,* 265–273.

Ruble, D. N. (2000). Gender constancy. In A. Kazdin (Ed.), *Encyclopedia of psychology.* Washington, DC, and New York: American Psychological Association and Oxford University Press.

Rudd, M. D., Joiner, T. E., & Rajab, M. H. (2001). *Treating suicidal behavior.* New York: Guilford.

Rueter, M., & Conger, R. (1995). Antecedents of parent-adolescent disagreements. *Journal of Marriage and the Family, 57,* 435–448.

Rugulies, R., Aust, B., & Syme, L. (2005). Epidemiology of health and illness. In S. Sutton, A. Baum, & J. Johnston (Eds.), *The SAGE handbook of health psychology.* Thousand Oaks, CA: Sage.

Rusbult, C. E., Olsen, N., Davis, J. L., & Hannon, P. A. (2001). Commitment and relationship maintenance mechanisms. In J. H. Harvey & A. Wenzel (Eds.), *Close romantic relationships.* Mahwah, NJ: Erlbaum.

Russo, N. F. (1990). Overview: Forging research priorities for women's health. *American Psychologist, 45,* 373–386.

Rutter, M. (1979). Protective factors in children's response to stress and disadvantage. In M. W. Kent & J. E. Rolf (Eds.), *Primary prevention in psychopathology* (Vol. 3). Hanover, NH: University of New Hampshire Press.

Rutter, M., & Garmezy, N. (1983). Developmental psychopathology. In P. H. Mussen (Ed.), *Handbook of child psychology* (4th ed., Vol. 4). New York: Wiley.

Ryan, M. K., & David, B. (2003). Gender differences in ways of knowing: The context dependence of the attitudes toward thinking and learning survey. *Sex Roles, 49,* 693–699.

Ryan, R. (1999, February 2). Quoted by Alfie Kohn, In pursuit of affluence, at a high price. *New York Times* (www.nytimes.com).

Ryan, R. M., & Deci, E. L. (2000). Self-determination theory and the facilitation of intrinsic motivation, social development, and well-being. *American Psychologist, 55,* 68–78.

Ryan, R. M., & Deci, E. L. (2001). On happiness and human potentials: A review of research on hedonic and eudaimonic well-being. *Annual Review of Psychology* (Vol. 52). Palo Alto, CA: Annual Reviews.

Ryckman, R. M. (2004). *Theories of personality* (8th ed.). Belmont, CA: Wadsworth.

Ryska, T. A. (2004). Enjoyment of evaluative physical activity among young participants: The role of self-handicapping and intrinsic motivation. *Child Study Journal, 33*, 213–234.

S

Saad, L. (2001, December 17). Americans' mood: Has Sept. 11 made a difference? Gallup Poll News Service (www.gallup.com/poll/releases/pr011217.asp).

Sagarin, B. J., & Cialdini, R. B. (2004). Creating critical consumers: Motivating receptivity by teaching resistance. In E. S. Knowles & J. A. Linn (Eds.), *Resistance and persuasion.* Mahwah, NJ: Erlbaum.

Salovey, P., & Birnbaum, D. (1989). Influence of mood on health-relevant cognitions. *Journal of Personality and Social Psychology, 57*, 539–551.

Salovey, P., & Mayer, J. D. (1990). Emotional intelligence. *Imagination, Cognition, and Personality, 9*, 185–211.

Salovey, P., & Rodin, J. (1989). Envy and jealousy in close relationships. In C. Hendrick (Ed.), *Close relationships.* Newbury Park, CA: Sage.

Samovar, L. A., & Porter, R. E. (2004). *Communication between cultures* (5th ed.). Belmont, CA: Wadsworth.

Santacruz, K. S., & Swagerty, D. (2001). Early diagnosis of dementia. *American Family Physician, 63*, 703–713.

Santrock, J. W. (2004). *Child development* (10th ed.). New York: McGraw-Hill.

Santrock, J. W. (2004). *Life-span development* (9th ed.). New York: McGraw-Hill.

Santrock, J. W. (2005). *Adolescence* (10th ed.). New York: McGraw-Hill.

Santrock, J. W., Minnett, A. M., & Campbell, B. D. (1994). *The authoritative guide to self-help books.* New York: Guilford.

Santrock, J. W., & Warshak, R. A. (1979). Father custody and social development in boys and girls. *Journal of Social Issues, 35*, 112–125.

Sarason, I. G., & Sarason, B. R. (2004). *Abnormal psychology* (10th ed. Updated). Upper Saddle River, NJ: Prentice-Hall.

Saraswathi, T. S., & Mistry, J. (2003). The cultural context of child development. In I. B. Weiner (Ed.), *Handbook of psychology* (Vol. VI). New York: Wiley.

Sari, Y. (2004). Serontonin (1B) receptors: from protein to physiological function and behavior. *Neuroscience and Biobehavior Review, 28*, 565–582.

Sarrel, P., & Masters, W. (1982). Sexual molestation of men by women. *Archives of Human Sexuality, 11*, 117–131.

Sarwer, D. B., Crerand, C. E., & Didie, E. R. (2003). Body dysmorphic disorder in cosmetic surgery patients. *Facial Plastic Surgery, 19*, 7–18.

Savic, I. (2002). Sex differences in hypothalamic activation by putative pheromones. *Molecular Psychiatry, 7*, 335–336.

Savin-Williams, R. C. (2001). *Mom, dad, I'm gay.* Washington, DC: American Psychological Association.

Savin-Williams, R. C., & Diamond, L. (2004). Sex. In R. Lerner & L. Steinberg (Eds.), *Handbook of adolescent psychology.* New York: Wiley.

Sax, L. J., Astin, A. W., Lindholm, J. A., Korn, W. S., Saenz, J. B., & Mahoney, K. M. (2003). *The American freshman: National norms for fall 2003.* Los Angeles: Higher Education Research Institute, UCLA.

Scanzoni, J. (2004). Household diversity. In M. Coleman & L. Ganong (Eds.), *Handbook of contemporary families.* Thousand Oaks, CA: Sage.

Schaalma, H. P., Abraham, C., Gillmore, M. R., & Kok, G. (2004). Sex education as health promotion: what does it take? *Archives of Sexual Behavior, 33*, 259–269.

Schaffer, D. V., & Gage, F. H. (2004). Neurogenesis and neuroadaptation. *Neuromolecular Medicine, 5*, 1–9.

Schaie, K. W. (1993). The Seattle longitudinal studies of adult intelligence. *Current Directions in Psychological Science, 2*, 171–175.

Schaie, K. W. (1994). The life course of adult intellectual abilities. *American Psychologist, 49*, 304–313.

Schaie, K. W. (1996). *Intellectual development in adulthood: The Seattle Longitudinal Study.* New York: Cambridge University Press.

Schaie, K. W., & Willis, S. L. (2001). *Adult development and aging* (5th ed.). Upper Saddle River, NJ: Prentice Hall.

Schaubroeck, J., Jones, J. R., & Xie, J. L. (2001). Individual differences in utilizing control to cope with job demands: Effects on susceptibility to infectious disease. *Journal of Applied Psychology, 86*, 114–120.

Scheer, S. D. (1996, March). *Adolescent to adult transitions: Social status and cognitive factors.* Paper presented at the meeting of the Society for Research on Adolescence, Boston.

Scheer, S. D., & Unger, D. G. (1994, February). *Adolescents becoming adults: Attributes for adulthood.* Paper presented at the meeting of the Society for Research on Adolescence, San Diego.

Schellenbach, C., Leadbeater, B., & Moore, K. A. (2004). Enhancing the developmental outcomes of adolescent parents and their children. In K. I. Maton, C.

J. Schellenbach, B. J. Leadbeater, & A. L. Solarz (Eds.), *Investing in children, youth, families, and communities.* Washington, DC: American Psychological Association.

Schiffman, J., & Walker, E. (1998). Schizophrenia. In H. S. Friedman (Ed.), *Encyclopedia of mental health* (Vol. 2). San Diego: Academic Press.

Schlossberg, N. K. (2004). *Retire smart, retire happy.* Washington, DC: American Psychological Association.

Schmeeckle, M., & Sprecher, S. (2004). Extended family and social networks. In A. L. Vangelisti (Ed.), *Handbook of family communication.* Mahwah, NJ: Erlbaum.

Schmelling, S. (2004). Cause for optimism. *Rehabilitation Management, 17*, 8.

Schmidt, U. (2003). Aetiology of eating disorders in the 21st century: New answers to old questions. *European Child and Adolescent Psychiatry, 12* (Supplement 1). I130–I137.

Schneider, K. J. (2002). Humanistic psychotherapy. In M. Hersen & W. H. Sledge (Eds.), *Encyclopedia of psychotherapy.* San Diego: Academic Press.

Schneider, L. S., Porsteinsson, A. P., Peskin, E. R., & Pfeiffer, E. A. (2003). Choosing treatment for Alzheimer's patients and their caregivers. *Geriatrics, 58* (Supplement 1): 3–18, 21.

Schneiderman, N., Antoni, M. H., Saab, P. G., & Ironson, G. (2001). Health psychology: Psychological and biobehavioral aspects of chronic disease management. *Annual Review of Psychology* (Vol. 52). Palo Alto, CA: Annual Reviews.

Schoka, E., & Hayslip, B. (1999, November). *Grief and the family system: The roles of communication, affect, and cohesion.* Paper presented at the meeting of the Gerontological Society of America, San Francisco.

Scholz, U., Gutiérrez-Doña, B., Sud, S., & Schwarzer, R. (2002). Is perceived self-efficacy a universal construct: Psychometric findings from 25 countries. *European Journal of Psychological Assessment, 18*, No. 3, 242–251.

Schooler, C. (2001). The intellectual effects of the demands of the work environment. In R. J. Sternberg & E. L. Grigorenko (Eds.), *Environmental effects on cognitive abilities.* Mahwah, NJ: Erlbaum.

Schroeder, J. M., & Polusny, M. A. (2004). Risk factors for adolescent alcohol use following a natural disaster. *Prehospital Disaster Medicine, 19*, 122–127.

Schulenberg, J. (June, 1999). *Binge drinking trajectories before, during, and after college: More reasons to worry from a developmental perspective.* Invited paper presented at the meeting of the American Psychological Society, Denver, Colorado.

Schultz, A., Williams, D., Israel, B., Becker, A., Parker, E., James, S. A., & Jackson, J. (2000). Unfair treatment, neighborhood effects, and mental health in the Detroit metropolitan area. *Journal of Health and Social Behavior, 41,* 314–332.

Schultz, R., & Curnow, C. (1988). Peak performance and age among super athletes: Track and field, swimming, baseball, tennis, and golf. *Journal of Gerontology, 43,* P113–P120.

Schunk, D. H. (2004). *Learning theories* (4th ed.). Upper Saddle River, NJ: Prentice Hall.

Schutzer, K. A., & Graves, B. S. (2004). Barriers and motivations to exercise in older adults. *Preventive Medicine, 39,* 1056–1061.

Schwarzer, R., & Knoll, N. (2003). Positive coping: Mastering demands and searching for meaning. In A. M. Nezu, C. M. Nezu & P A. Geller (Eds.), *Comprehensive handbook of psychology* (Vol. 9). New York: Wiley.

Schwerha, D. J., & McMullin, D. L. (2002). Prioritizing ergonomic research in aging for the 21st century American workforce. *Experimental Aging Research, 28,* 99–110.

Search Institute. (1995). *Barriers to participation in youth programs.* Unpublished manuscript, the Search Institute, Minneapolis.

Sechehaye, M. (1951). *Autobiography of a schizophrenic girl.* New York: Grune & Stratton.

Sedikides, C., Campbell, W. K., Reeder, G. D., & Elliot, A. J. (1998). The self-serving bias in relational context. *Journal of Personality and Social Psychology, 74,* 378–386.

Seeman, T. E., Crimmins, E., Huang, M. H., Singer, B., Bucur, A., Gruenewald, T., Berman, L. F., & Reuben, D. B. (2004). Cumulative biological risk and socioeconomic differences in mortality: MacArthur Studies of Successful Aging, 58, 1985–1997.

Seffge-Krenke, I. (1995). *Stress, coping, and relationships in adolescence.* Mahwah, NJ: Erlbaum.

Segal, D. L., & Coolidge, F. L. (2003). Objective assessment of personality and psychopathology: An overview. In M. Hersen (Ed.), *Comprehensive handbook of psychological assessment* (Vol. 2). New York: Wiley.

Segrin, C., & Flora, J. (2005). *Family communication.* Mahwah, NJ: Erlbaum.

Seligman, M. E. P. (1975). *Helplessness: On depression, development and death.* San Francisco: W. H. Freeman.

Seligman, M. E. P. (1978). *Helplessness: On depression, development, and death.* San Francisco: W. H. Freeman.

Seligman, M. E. P. (1989). Why is there so much depression today? The waxing of the individual and the waning of the common. In *The G. Stanley Hall Lecture Series.* Washington, DC: American Psychological Association.

Seligman, M. E. P. (1990). *Learned optimism.* New York: Knopf.

Seligman, M. E. P. (1994). *What you can change and what you can't.* New York: Knopf.

Seltzer, J. (2004). Cohabitation and family change. In M. Coleman & L. Ganong (Eds.), *Handbook of contemporary families.* Thousand Oaks, CA: Sage.

Selye, H. (1974). *Stress without distress.* Philadelphia: W. B. Saunders.

Selye, H. (1983). The stress concept: Past, present, and future. In C. I. Cooper (Ed.), *Stress research.* New York: Wiley.

Servaes, P., Vignerhoets, A., Vreugdenhil, G., Keuning, J. J., & Broekhuijsen, A. M. (1999). Inhibition of emotional expression in breast cancer patients. *Behavioral Medicine, 25,* 26–34.

Seshadri, S., Wolf, P. A., Beiser, A., Elias, M. F., Au, R., Kase, C. S., D'Agostino, R. B., & Decarli, C. (2004). Stroke risk profile, brain volume, and cognitive function: the Framington Offspring Study, *Neurology, 63,* 1591–1599.

Shadubina, A., Agam, G., & Belmaker, R. H. (2001). The mechanism of lithium: State of the art, ten years later. *Progress in Neuropsychology and Biological Psychiatry, 25,* 855–866.

Shapiro, S. L., & Walsh, R. (2003). An analysis of recent meditation research and suggestions for future directions. *Humanistic Psychologist, 31,* 86–114.

Sharkey, W. (1993). Who embarrasses whom? Relational and sex differences in the use of intentional embarrassment. In P. J. Kalbfleisch (Ed.), *Interpersonal communication.* Mahwah, NJ: Erlbaum.

Sharp, E. A., & Ganong, L. H. (2000). Awareness about expectations: Are unrealistic beliefs changed by integrative teaching. *Family Relations, 49,* 71–79.

Sharpe, S. (2004). *The way we love.* Thousand Oaks, CA: Sage.

Shaughnessy, J. J., Zechmeister, E. B., & Zechmeister, J. S. (2003). *Research methods in psychology* (6th ed.). New York: McGraw-Hill.

Shaver, P. (1986, August). *Being lonely, falling in love: Perspectives from attachment theory.* Paper presented at the meeting of the American Psychological Association Washington, DC.

Shaver, P. R., & Hazan, C. (1993). Adult romantic attachment: Theory and evidence. In W. H. Jones & D. Perlman (Eds.), *Advances in personal relationships.* London: Jessica Kingsley.

Shaw, B. A., Krause, N., Chatters, L. M., Connell, C. M., & Ingersoll-Dayton, B. (2004). Emotional support from parents early in life, aging, and health. *Psychology and Aging, 19,* 4–12.

Sheets, R. H. (2005). *Diversity pedagogy.* Boston: Allyn & Bacon.

Sheehy, G. (2003). Four 9/11 moms battle Bush. *New York Observer,* Aug. 25, p. 1.

Shelton, R. C., & Hollon, S. D. (2000). Antidepressants. In A. Kazdin (Ed.), *Encyclopedia of psychology.* Washington, DC, & New York: American Psychological Association and Oxford University Press.

Shen, Y. (2004). Relationship between suicidal behavior of psychotic patients and serontonin transporter gene in Han Chinese. *Neuroscience Letters, 372,* 94–98.

Sher, L. (2004). Daily hassles, cortisol, and the pathogenesis of depression. *Medical Hypotheses, 62,* 198–202.

Sherif-Trask, B. (2003). Love, courtship, and marriage from a cross-cultural perspective. In R. R. Hamon & B. B. Ingoldsby (Eds.), *Mate selection across cultures.* Thousand Oaks, CA: Sage.

Sherry, A., Dahlen, E., & Holaday, M. (2003). The use of sentence completion tests with adults. In M. Hersen (Ed.), *Comprehensive handbook of psychological assessment* (Vol. 2). New York: Wiley.

Sherry, S. B., Hewitt, P. L., Besser, A., McGee, B. J., & Flett, G. L. (2004). Self-oriented and socially prescribed perfectionism in the Eating Disorder Inventory perfectionism subscale. *International Journal of Eating Disorders, 22* (1), 39–57.

Sherry, S. B., Hewitt, P. L., Flett, G. L., & Harvey, M. (2003). Perfectionism dimensions, perfectionistic dysfunctional attitudes, need for approval, and depression symptoms in adult psychiatric patients and young adults. *Journal of Counseling Psychology, 50,* 373–386.

Shields, S. A. (1991). Gender in the psychology of emotion: A selective research review. In K. T. Strongman (Ed.), *International review of studies on emotion.* New York: Wiley.

Shields, S. A. (1998, August). *What* Jerry Maguire *can tell us about gender and emotion.* Paper presented at the meeting of the

International Society for Research on Emotions, Wurzburg, Germany.

Shill, M. A. (2004). Analytic neutrality, anonymity, abstinence, and elective self-disclosure. *Journal of the Psychoanalytic Association, 52,* 151–187.

Shnek, A. M., Irvine, J., Stewart, D., & Abbey, S. (2001). Psychological factors and depressive symptoms in ischemic heart disease. *Health Psychology, 20,* 141–145.

Shonk, S. M., & Cicchetti, D. (2001). Maltreatment, competency deficits, and risk for academic and behavioral maladjustment. *Developmental Psychology, 37,* 3–17.

Shorter-Gooden, K. (2004). Multiple resistance strategies: How African American women cope with racism and sexism. *Journal of Black Psychology, 30,* 406–425.

Showers, C. (1986). *The motivational consequences of negative thinking.* Paper presented at the meeting of the American Psychological Association, Washington, DC.

Shriver, J. (2003, September 11). Trade center survivors build at their own pace. *USA Today,* 1–2A.

Sidanius, J., Van Laar, C., Levin, S., & SIECUS. (1999). *Public support for sexuality education.* Washington, DC: Author.

Sim, T. (2000). Adolescent psychosocial competence. The importance and role of regard for parents. *Journal of Research on Adolescence, 10,* 49–64.

Simeon, D., Guralnik, O., Knutelska, M., & Schmeidler, J. (2002). Personality factors associated with dissociation: Temperament, defenses, and cognitive schemata. *American Journal of Psychiatry, 159,* 489–491.

Simpson, J. A. (1995). Self-monitoring and commitment to dating relationships: A classroom demonstration. In M. E. Ware & D. E. Johnson (Eds.), *Demonstrations and activities in teaching of introductory psychology.* Mahwah, NJ: Erlbaum.

Sinclair, S. (2004). Ethnic enclaves and the dynamics of social identity on the college campus: the good, the bad, and the ugly. *Journal of Personality and Social Psychology, 87,* 96–110.

Sinclair, S. L., & Monk, G. (2004). Moving beyond the blame game: toward a discursive approach to negotiating conflict within couple relationships. *Journal of Marital and Family Therapy, 30,* 335–347.

Singh, M. A. F. (2002). Exercise comes of age: Rationale and recommendations for a geriatric exercise prescription. *Journal of Gerontology: Medical Sciences, 57A,* M262–M282.

Singh, N. A., Clements, K. M., & Fiatarone, M. A. (1997). A randomized controlled trial of progressive resistance training in depressed elders. *Journal of Gerontology, 52A,* M27–M35.

Singh, R. P. (1984, January). Experimental verification of locus of control as related to conformity behavior. *Psychological Studies, 29*(1), 64–67.

Sinnott, J. D. (2003). Postformal thought and adult development: Living in balance. In J. Demick & C. Andreoletti (Eds.), *Handbook of adult development.* New York: Kluwer.

Sitzman, K. (2004). Coping with stress. *Home Healthcare Nurse, 22,* 603.

Skinner, B. F. (1938). *The behavior of organisms: An experimental analysis.* New York: Appleton-Century-Crofts.

Skoog, I., Blennow, K., & Marcusson, J. (1996). Dementia. In J. E. Birren (Ed.), *Encyclopedia of gerontology* (Vol. 1). San Diego: Academic Press.

Slade, J. M., Miszko, T. A., Laity, J. H., Agrawal, S. K., & Cress, M. E. (2002). Anaerobic power and physical function in strength-trained and non-strength-trained older adults. *Journal of Gerontology: Biological Sciences and Medical Sciences, 57,* M168–M172.

Slattery, J. M. (2004). *Counseling diverse clients.* Belmont, CA: Brooks/Cole.

Slavin, R. (1989). Cooperative learning and student achievement. In R. Slavin (Ed.), *School and classroom organization.* Mahwah, NJ: Erlbaum.

Slicker, E. K., & Thornberry, I. (2003). Older adolescent well-being and authoritative parenting. *Adolescent & Family Health, 3,* 9–19.

Sloan, D. M. (2004). Emotion regulation in action: emotional reactivity in experiential avoidance. *Behavior Research and Therapy, 42,* 1257–1270.

Small, S. A. (1990). *Preventive programs that support families with adolescents.* Washington, DC: Carnegie Council on Adolescent Development.

Smiler, A. (2004). Thirty years after the discovery of gender: Psychological concepts and measures of masculinity. *Sex Roles, 50,* 15–26.

Smith, G. C. (2003). Patterns and predictors of service use and unmet needs among aging families of adults with severe mental illness. *Psychiatric Services, 54,* 871–877.

Smith, M. B. (2001). Humanistic psychology. In W. E. Craighead & C. B. Nemeroff (Eds.), *The Corsini encyclopedia of psychology and behavioral science* (3rd ed.). New York: Wiley.

Smith, P. H., White, J. W., & Holland, L. J. (2003). A longitudinal perspective on dating violence among adolescent and college-age women. *American Journal of Public Health, 93,* 1104–1109.

Smith, T. W., & Suls, J. (2004). Introduction to the special section on the future of health psychology. *Health Psychology, 23,* 115–118.

Smolak, L., & Striegel-Moore, R. (2001). Body image concerns. In J. Worell (Ed.), *Encyclopedia of women and gender.* San Diego: Academic Press.

Smoreda, Z., & Licoppe, C. (2000). Gender-specific use of the domestic telephone. *Social Psychology Quarterly, 63,* 238–252.

Smyth, C. L., & Maclachlan, M. (2004). The context of suicide. *Journal of Mental Health, 13,* 83–92.

Snowden, L. R., & Cheung, F. K. (1990). Use of inpatient mental health services by members of ethnic minority groups. *American Psychologist, 45,* 347–355.

Snowdon, D. (2002). *Aging with grace: What the Nun Study teaches us about leading longer, healthier, and more meaningful lives.* New York: Bantam.

Snowdon, D. A. (1995). *An epidemiological study of aging in a select population and its relationship to Alzheimer's disease.* Unpublished.

Snowdon, D. A. (1997). Aging and Alzheimer's disease: Lessons from the nun study. *Gerontologist, 37,* 150–156.

Snowdon, D. A. (2003). Healthy aging and dementia: Findings from the Nun Study. *Annals of Internal Medicine, 139,* 450–454.

Snowdon, D. A., Tully, C. L., Smith, C. D., Riley, K. P., & Markesbery, W. R. (2000). Serum folate and the severity of atrophy of the neocortex in Alzheimer's disease: Findings from the Nun Study. *American Journal of Clinical Nutrition, 71,* 993–998.

Snyder, M., & Stukas, A. A. (1999). Interpersonal processes: The interplay of cognitive, motivational, and behavioral activities in social interaction. *Annual Review of Psychology* (Vol. 49). Palo Alto, CA: Annual Reviews, Inc.

Sollod, R. N. (2000). Religious and spiritual practices. In A. Kazdin (Ed.), *Encyclopedia of psychology.* Washington, DC, & New York: American Psychological Association and Oxford University Press.

Solomon, C. R., Acock, A. C., & Walker, A. J. (2004). Gender ideology and investment in housework: Postretirement. *Journal of Family Issues, 25,* 1050–1071.

Solot, D., & Miller, M. (2002). *Unmarried to each other.* New York: Marlowe.

Sommer, B. (2001). Menopause. In J. Worell (Ed.), *Encyclopedia of women and gender.* New York: Oxford University Press.

Sonnenberg, S. M., & Ursano, R. (2002). Psychoanalysis and psychoanalytic psychotherapy: Technique. In M. Hersen & W. H. Sledge (Eds.), *Encyclopedia of psychotherapy.* San Diego: Academic Press.

Souder, E., & Beck, C. (2004). Overview of Alzheimer's disease. *Nursing Clinics of North America, 39,* 545–559.

Speca, M., Carlson, L. E., Goodey, E., & Angen, M. (2000). A randomized, wait-list controlled clinical trial: The effect of a mindfulness meditation-based stress reduction program on mood and symptoms of stress in cancer outpatients. *Psychosomatic Medicine, 62,* 613–622.

Specter, M. (2002, July 15). The long ride. *The New Yorker,* pp. 48–58.

Spence, J. T., & Buckner, C. E. (2000). Instrumental and expressive traits, trait stereotypes, and sexist attitudes: What do they signify? *Psychology of Women Quarterly, 24,* 44–62.

Spence, J. T., & Helmreich, R. (1978). *Masculinity and femininity: Their psychological dimensions.* Austin: University of Texas Press.

Spencer, M. B. (2000). Ethnocentrism. In A. Kazdin (Ed.), *Encyclopedia of psychology.* Washington, DC, and New York: American Psychological Association and Oxford University Press.

Spencer, M. B., Noll, E., Stoltzfuz, J., & Harpalani, V. (2001). Identity and school adjustment: Revisiting the "acting white" assumption. *Educational Psychologist, 36,* 21–30.

Spera, S. P., Buhrfeind, E. D., & Pennebaker, J. W. (1994). Expressive writing and coping with job loss. *Academy of Management Journal, 37,* 722–733.

Spinelli, F. (2005). *The interpreted world.* Thousand Oaks, CA: Sage.

Sprei, J. E., & Courtois, C. A. (1988). The treatment of women's sexual dysfunctions arising from sexual assault. In R. A. Brown & J. R. Fields (Eds.), *Treatment of sexual problems in individual and couples therapy.* Great Neck, NY: PMA.

Sprinthall, R. C. (2003). *Basic statistical analysis* (7th ed.). Boston: Allyn & Bacon.

Srivastava, A., Locke, E. A., & Bartol, K. M. (2001). Money and subjective well-being: It's not the money, it's the motives. *Journal of Personality and Social Psychology, 80,* 959–971.

Sroufe, L. A. (2000, Spring). The inside scoop on child development: Interview. *Cutting through the hype.* Minneapolis: College of Education and Human Development, University of Minnesota.

Stafford, J., & Lynn, S. J. (2002). Cultural scripts, memories of childhood abuse, and multiple identities: A study of role-played enactments. *International Journal of Experimental Hypnosis, 50,* 67–85.

Stafford, L. (2004). Communication competencies and sociocultural priorities of middle childhood. In A. L. Vangelisti (Ed.), *Handbook of family communication.* Mahwah, NJ: Erlbaum.

Stahl, S. M. (2002). The psychopharmacology of energy and fatigue. *Journal of Clinical Psychiatry, 63,* 7–8.

Stajkovic, A. D., & Luthans, F. (1998). Self-efficacy and work-related performance: A meta-analysis. *Psychological Bulletin, 124,* 240–261.

Stanovich, K. E. (2004). *How to think straight about psychology* (7th ed.). Boston: Allyn & Bacon.

Stanton, A. L., Danoff-Burg, S., Cameron, C., & Ellis, A. P. (1994). Coping through emotional approach: Problems of conceptualization and confounding. *Journal of Personality and Social Psychology, 66,* 350–362.

Stanton, A. L., Danott-Burg, S., Cameron, C. L., Bishop, M. M., Collins, C. A., Kirk, S. B., Sworowski, L. A., & Twillman, R. (2000). Emotionally expressive coping predicts psychological and physical adjustment to breast cancer. *Journal of Consulting and Clinical Psychology, 68,* 875–882.

Stanton, A. L., Parsa, A., & Austenfeld, J. L. (2002). The adaptive potential of coping through emotional approach. In C. R. Snyder & S. J. Lopez (Eds.), *Handbook of Positive Psychology.* New York: Oxford University Press.

Staudinger, U. M. (1996). Psychologische Produktivitat und Selbstenfaltung im Alter. In M. M. Baltes & L. Montada (Eds.), *Prodktives Leben im Alter.* Frankfurt: Campus.

Staudinger, U. M. (2004). Wisdom. In W. E. Craighead & C. B. Nemeroff (Eds.), *The concise Corsini encyclopedia of psychology and behavioral science* (3rd ed.). New York: Wiley.

Staudinger, U. M., & Fleeson, W. (1996). Life investment in a sample of 20 to 105 year olds. Unpublished manuscript. Max Planck Institute for Human Development and Education, Berlin.

Steele, C. M. (1996, August). *A burden of suspicion: The role of stereotypes in shaping intellectual identity.* Paper presented at the meeting of the American Psychological Association, Toronto.

Steen, R., & Shapiro, K. (2004). Intrauterine contraceptive devices and risk of pelvic inflammatory disease: standard of care in high STI prevalence settings. *Reproductive Health Matters, 12,* 136–143.

Steiger, H., Bruce, K. R., & Israel, M. (2003). Eating disorders. In I. B. Weiner (Ed.), *Handbook of psychology* (Vol. 8). New York: Wiley.

Steinberg, L. D., & Silk, J. S. (2002). Parenting adolescents. In M. Bornstein (Ed.), *Handbook of parenting* (2nd ed., Vol. 1). Mahwah, NJ: Erlbaum.

Steiner, M., Dunn, E., & Born, L. (2003). Hormones and mood: From menarche to menopause and beyond. *Journal of Affective Disorders, 74,* 67–83.

Steinhardt, M. A., Dolbier, C. L., Bottlieb, N. H., & McCalister, K. T. (2003). The relationship between hardiness, supervisor support, group cohesion, and job stress as predictors of job satisfaction. *American Journal of Health Promotion, 17,* 382–389.

Steptoe, A., & Ayers, S. (2005). Stress, health, and illness. In S. Sutton, A. Baum, & M. Johnston (Eds.), *The SAGE handbook of health psychology.* Thousand Oaks, CA: Sage.

Stern, L., Iqbal, N., Seshadri, P., Chicano, K. L., Daily, D. A., McGrory, J., Williams, M., Gracely, E. J., & Samantha, F. F. (2004). The effects of low-carbohydrate versus conventional weight loss diets in severely obese adults: One-year follow-up of a randomized trial. *Annals of Internal Medicine, 140,* 778–785.

Sternberg, E. M., & Gold, P. W. (1996). The mind-body interaction in disease. *Mysteries of the mind.* New York: Scientific American.

Sternberg, R. J. (1988). *The triangle of love.* New York: Basic Books.

Sterns, H. L., & Huyck, H. (2001). The role of work in midlife. In M. E. Lachman (Ed.), *Handbook of midlife development.* New York: John Wiley.

Stetter, F., & Kupper, S. (2002). Autogenic training: A meta-analysis of clinical outcome studies. *Applied Psychophysiology and Biofeedback, 27,* 45–98.

Stevens, J. W. (2005). Lessons learned from poor urban African American youth. In M. Ungar (Ed.), *Handbook for working with children and youth.* Thousand Oaks, CA: Sage.

Stewart, A. J., Ostrove, J. M., & Helson, R. (2001). Middle aging in women: Patterns of personality change from the 30s to the 50s. *Journal of Adult Development, 8,* 23–37.

Stice, E., Presnell, K., & Spangler, D. (2002). Risk factors for binge eating onset in adolescent girls: A 2–year prospective investigation. *Health Psychology, 21,* 131–138.

Stice, E., & Whitenton, K. (2002). Risk factors for body dissatisfaction in adolescent girls: A longitudinal investigation. *Developmental Psychology, 38,* 669–678.

Stipek, D. (2001). *Motivation to learn* (4th ed.). Boston: Allyn & Bacon.

Stone, A. A., Cox, D. S., Valdimarsdottir, H., Jandor, L., & Neale, J. M. (1987). Evidence that secretory IgA antibody is associated with daily mood. *Journal of Personality and Social Psychology, 52,* 988–993.

Stone, A. A., Neale, J. M., Cox, D. S., Napoli, A., Valdimarsdottir, H., & Kennedy-Moore, E. (1994). Daily events are associated with secretory immune response to an oral antigen in men. *Healthy Psychology, 13,* 440–446.

Stoppler, M. C. (2003). *Stress management.* Available on the world wide web at http://stress.about.com

Story, L. B., Karney, B. R., Lawrence, E., & Bradbury, T. N. (2004). Interpersonal mediators in the intergenerational transmission of marital dysfunction. *Journal of Family Psychology, 18,* 519–529.

Stowell, J. R., McGuire, L., Glaser, R., & Kiecolt-Glaser, J. (2003). Psychoneuroimmunology. In I. B. Weiner (Ed.), *Handbook of psychology* (Vol. 9). New York: Wiley.

Strain, L. A., Grabusie, C. C., Searle, M. S., & Dunn, N. J. (2002). Continuing and ceasing leisure activities in later life: A longitudinal study. *The Gerontologist, 42,* 217–223.

Stravynski, A., Bond, S., & Amado, D. (2004). Cognitive causes of social phobia: a critical appraisal. *Clinical Psychology Review, 24,* 421–440.

Streil, J. (2001). Marriage: Still "his" and "hers"? In J. Worell (Ed.), *Encyclopedia of women and gender.* San Diego: Academic Press.

Strickland, B. (1988). Sex-related differences in health and illness. *Psychology of Women Quarterly, 12,* 381–399.

Striegel-Moore, R. H., Silberstein, L. R., & Rodin, J. (1993). The social self in bulimia nervosa: Public self-consciousness, social anxiety, and perceived fraudulence. *Journal of Abnormal Psychology, 102,* 297–303.

Strike, P. C., & Steptoe, A. (2004). Psychosocial factors in the development of coronary artery disease. *Progress in Cardiovascular Disease, 46,* 337–347.

Strong, B., Sayad, B. W., DeValut, C., & Yarber, W. L. (2005). *Human sexuality* (5th ed.). New York: McGraw-Hill.

Strupp, H. H. (1995). The psychotherapist's skills revised. *Clinical Psychology: Science and Practice, 2,* 70–74.

Stull, D. E., & Hatch, L. R. (1984). Unraveling the effects of multiple life changes. *Research on Aging, 6,* 560–571.

Stunkard, A. (2000). Obesity. In A. Kazdin (Ed.), *Encyclopedia of psychology.* Washington, DC, & New York: American Psychological Association and Oxford University Press.

Stut, R. G., & Farooque, R. S. (2003). Negative symptoms, anger, and social support: Response of an inpatient sample to news coverage of the September 11 terrorist attacks. *Psychiatry Quarterly, 74,* 237–250.

Sue, D. (2002). Culture specific psychotherapy. In M. Hersen & W. H. Sledge (Eds.), *Encyclopedia of psychotherapy.* San Diego: Academic Press.

Sue, D., & Sue, D. W. (1993). Ethnic identity: Cultural factors in the psychological development of Asians in America. In D. R. Atkinson, G. Morten, & D. W. Sue (Eds.), *Counseling American minorities.* Madison, WI: Brown & Benchmark.

Sue, S. (2000). Ethnocultural psychotherapy. In A. Kazdin (Ed.), *Encyclopedia of psychology.* Washington, DC, & New York: American Psychological Association and Oxford University Press.

Sugarman, L. (2004). *Counseling and the life course.* Thousand Oaks, CA: Sage.

Suinn, R. M. (1984). *Fundamentals of abnormal psychology.* Chicago: Nelson-Hall.

Sullivan, H. S. (1953). *The interpersonal theory of psychiatry.* New York: W. W. Norton.

Sullivan, K. T., & Christensen, A. (1998). In H. S. Friedman (Ed.), *Encyclopedia of mental health* (Vol. 1). San Diego: Academic Press.

Suls, J., & Rothman, A. (2004). Evolution of the biophychosocial model: Prospects and challenges. *Health Psychology, 23,* 119–125.

Super, D. E. (1976). *Career education and the meanings of work.* Washington, DC: U.S. Office of Education.

Super, D. E., Kowalski, R., & Gotkin, E. (1967). *Floundering and trial after high school.* Unpublished manuscript, Columbia University.

Surra, C. A., Gray, C. R., Cottle, N., & Boettcher, T. M. J. (2004). Research on mate selection and premarital relationships: What do we really know. In A. L. Vangelisti (Ed.), *Handbook of family communication.* Mahwah, NJ: Erlbaum.

Susman, E. J., & Rogol, A. (2004). Puberty and psychological development. In R. Lerner & L. Steinberg (Eds.), *Handbook of adolescent psychology.* New York: Wiley.

Sutker, P. B., & Allain, A. N. (1993). Behavior and personality assessment in men labeled adaptive sociopaths. *Journal of Behavioral Assessment, 5,* 65–79.

Sutton, S., Baum, A., & Johnston, M. (Eds.). (2005). *The SAGE handbook of health psychology.* Thousand Oaks, CA: Sage.

Suveg, C., & Zeman, J. (2004). Emotion regulation in children with anxiety disorders. *Journal of Clinical Child and Adolescent Psychology, 33,* 750–759.

Swaab, D. F., Chung, W. C., Kruijver, F. P., Hofman, M. A., & Ishunina, T. A. (2001). Structural and functional sex differences in the human hypothalamus. *Hormones and Behavior, 40,* 93–98.

Swain, S. O. (1992). Men's friendships with women. In P. Nardi (Ed.), *Gender in intimate relationships.* Belmont, CA: Wadsworth.

Swann, W. B., De La Ronde, C., & Hixon, J. G. (1994). Authenticity and positive strivings in marriage and courtship. *Journal of Personality and Social Psychology, 66,* 857–869.

Swartz-Kulstad, J. L., & Martin, W. E. (2000). Culture as an essential aspect of person-environment fit. In W. E. Martin & J. L. Swartz-Kulstad (Eds.), *Person-environment psychology and mental health.* Mahwah, NJ: Erlbaum.

T

Tajfel, H. (1978). The achievement of group differentiation. In H. Tajfel (Ed.), *Differentiation between social groups.* London: Academic Press.

Takano, A., & others. (2004). Estimation of the time-course of dopamine D-sub-2–receptor occupancy in living human brain from plasma pharmacokinetics of antipsychotics. *International Journal of Neuropsychopharmacology, 7,* 19–26.

Tan, A. (1989). *The joy luck club.* New York: Putnam.

Tanaka-Matsumi, J. (2001). Abnormal psychology and culture. In D. Matsumoto (Ed.), *The handbook of culture and psychology.* New York: Oxford University Press.

Tannen, D. (1986). *That's not what I meant!* New York: Ballentine.

Tannen, D. (1990). *You just don't understand: Women and men in conversation.* New York: Ballantine.

Tavris, C. (1989). *Anger: The misunderstood emotion* (2nd ed.). New York: Touchstone.

Tavris, C., & Wade, C. (1984). *The longest war: Sex differences in perspective* (2nd ed.). San Diego: Harcourt Brace Jovanovich.

Tay, K. W., Ward, C. M., & Hill, J. A. (1993, August). *Holland's congruence and certainty of career aspirations in Asian graduate students.* Paper presented at the meeting of the American Psychological Association, Toronto.

Taylor, M. G., & Lynch, S. M. (2004). Trajectories of impairment, social support, and depressive symptoms in later life.

Journals of Gerontology B: Psychological Sciences and Social Sciences, 59, S238–S246.

Taylor, S. (2002). Classical conditioning. In M. Hersen & W. H. Sledge (Eds.), *Encyclopedia of psychotherapy.* San Diego: Academic Press.

Taylor, S. E. (1979). Hospital patient behavior: Reactance, helplessness, or control? *Journal of Social Issues, 35,* 156–184.

Taylor, S. E. (2002). *The tending instinct.* New York: Times Books.

Taylor, S. E. (2004). Commentary in "Taylor takes on 'Fight-or-flight.'" *American Psychological Society, 17,* 21.

Taylor, S. E., & Brown, J. D. (1988). Illusion and well-being: A social psychological perspective on mental health. *Psychological Bulletin, 103,* 193–210.

Taylor, S. E., Peplau, L. A., Sears, D. O., & Peplau, A. L. (2003). *Social psychology* (11th ed.). Upper Saddle River, NJ: Prentice Hall.

Teicher, M. H., Andersen, S. L., Polcari, A., Anderson, C. M., Navalta, C. P., & Kim, D. M. (2003). The neurobiological consequences of early stress and childhood maltreatment. *Neuroscience and Biobehavioral Research, 27,* 33–44.

Tennen, H., & Affleck, G. (2002). Benefit-finding and benefit-reminding. In C. R. Snyder & S. J. Lopez (Eds.), *Handbook of positive psychology.* New York: Oxford University Press.

Tesser, A. (2000). Self-esteem. In A. Kazdin (Ed.), *Encyclopedia of psychology.* Washington, DC, & New York: American Psychological Association and Oxford University Press.

Tharp, R. G. (1991). Cultural diversity and treatment of children. *Journal of Consulting & Clinical Psychology, 59,* 799–812.

Thayer, J. F., Rossy, I., Sollers, J., Friedman, B. H., & Allen, M. T. (1996, March). *Relationships among heart period variability and cardiodynamic measures vary as a function of fitness.* Paper presented at the meeting of the American Psychosomatic Society, Williamsburg, VA.

Thiel de Bocanegra, H., & Brickman, E. (2004). Mental health impact of the World Trade Center attacks on displaced Chinese workers. *Journal of Traumatic Stress, 17,* 55–62.

Thigpen, C. H., & Cleckley, H. M. (1957). *Three faces of Eve.* New York: McGraw-Hill.

Thomas, C. B. (1983). Unpublished manuscript. Baltimore: Johns Hopkins University.

Thomas, S. P. (2003). Men's anger. *Psychology of Men and Masculinity, 4,* 163–175.

Thompson, C. E., & Isaac, K. (2004). African Americans: Treatment issues and recommendations. In D. R. Atkinson (Ed.), *Counseling American minorities* (6th Ed.). New York: McGraw-Hill.

Thompson, K. M., Crosby, R. D., Wonderlich, S. A., Mitchell, J. E., Redlin, J., Demuth, G., Smyth, J., & Haseltine, B. (2003). Psychopathology and sexual trauma in childhood and adulthood. *Journal of Traumatic Stress, 16,* 35–38.

Thompson, R., & Murachver, T. (2001). Predicting gender from electronic discourse. *British Journal of Social Psychology, 40,* 193–208.

Thompson, S. C. (2002). The role of personal control in adaptive functioning. In C. R. Snyder & S. J. Lopez (Eds.), *Handbook of positive psychology.* New York: Oxford University Press.

Thomson, E., Mosley, J., Hanson, T. L., & McLanahan, S. S. (2001). Remarriage, cohabitation, and changes in mothering behavior. *Journal of Marriage and the Family, 63,* 370–380.

Thoresen, C. E., & Harris, A. H. S. (2002). Spirituality and health: What's the evidence and what's needed? *Annals of Behavioral Medicine, 24,* 3–13.

Thorn, B. E. (2004). *Cognitive therapy for chronic pain.* New York: Guilford.

Thorne, B. M. (2001). Introversion-extraversion. In W. E. Craighead & C. B. Nemeroff (Eds.), *The Corsini encyclopedia of psychology and behavioral science* (3rd ed.). New York: Wiley.

Tolan, P., Miller, L., & Thomas, P. (1988). Perception and experience of two types of social stress and self-image among adolescents. Journal of Youth and Adolescence, 17, **147–163.**

Tovian, S. M. (2004). Health services and health care economics. *Health Psychology, 23,* 138–141.

Travis, F., & Areander, A. (2004). EEG asymmetry and mindfulness meditation. *Psychosomatic Medicine, 66,* 147–148.

Triandis, H. C. (2001). Individualism and collectivism. In D. Matsumoto (Ed.), *The handbook of culture and psychology.* New York: Oxford University Press.

Triandis, H. C., Brislin, R., & Hui, C. H. (1988). Cross-cultural training across the individualism divide. *International Journal of Intercultural Relations, 12,* 269–288.

Trinidad, D. R., & Johnson, C. A. (2002). The association between emotional intelligence and early adolescent tobacco and alcohol. *Personality and Individual Differences, 32,* 95–105.

Trindad, D. R., Unger, J. B., Chou, C. P., Azen, S. P., & Johnson, C. A. (2004). Emotional intelligence and smoking risk factors in adolescents: Interactions on smoking intentions. *Journal of Adolescent Health, 34,* 46–55.

Troen, B. R. (2003). The biology of aging. *Mt. Sanai Journal of Medicine, 70,* 3–22.

Truitner, K., & Truitner, N. (1993). Death and dying in Buddhism. In D. P. Irish & K. F. Lundquist (Eds.), *Ethnic variations in dying, death, and grief: Diversity in universality.* Washington, DC: Taylor & Francis.

Trull, T. J., & Widiger, T. A. (2003). Personality disorders. In I. B. Weiner (Ed.), *Handbook of Psychology* (Vol. 8). New York: Wiley.

Tucker, J. S., Schwartz, J. E., Clark, K. M., & Friedman, H. S. (1999). Age-related changes in the associations of social network ties with mortality risk. *Psychology and Aging, 14,* 564–571.

Tulving, E. (2000). Concepts of memory. In E. Tulving & F. I. M. Craik (Eds.), *The Oxford handbook of memory.* New York: Oxford University Press.

Turner, W. L., Wallace, B. R., Anderson, J. R., & Bird, C. (2004). The last mile of the way: understanding caregiving in African American families at the end of life. *Journal of Marital and Family Therapy, 30,* 427–438.

Twenge, J. M., Zhang, L., & Im, C. (2004). It's beyond my control: a cross-temporal meta-analysis of increasing externality in locus of control, 1960–2002. *Personality and Social Psychology Review, 8,* 308–319.

U.S. Bureau of Labor Statistics. (2003). *People.* Washington, DC: Author.

U.S. Bureau of the Census. (2003). *People: 2002 data profiles.* Washington, DC: Author.

U.S. Department of Education. (2000). *Trends in educational equity for girls and women.* Washington, DC: Author.

U.S. Department of Health and Human Services. (2003). *Child abuse and neglect statistics.* Washington, DC: U.S. Department of Health and Human Services.

U.S. Department of Health and Human Services. (2004). *Nutrition.* Washington, DC: Author.

U.S. Department of Labor. (2005). *SCANS.* Washington, DC: Author.

U.S. Surgeon General's Report (1990). *The health benefits of smoking cessation.* Bethesda, MD: U.S. Department of Health and Human Services.

Ubell, C. (1992, December 6). We can age successfully. *Parade,* pp. 14–15.

Underwood, M. (2004). Sticks and stones and social exclusion: Aggression among boys and girls. In P. K. Smith & C. H. Hart (Eds.), *Blackwell handbook of childhood social development*. Malden, MA: Blackwell.

UNESCO. (2004). *Gender equality and development*. Geneva, Swit: UNESCO.

Ungar, L., & Florian, V. (2004). What helps middle-aged widows with their psychological and social adaptation several years after their loss? *Death Studies, 28*, 621–641.

Ungar, M. (Ed.) (2005). *Handbook for working with children and youth*. Thousand Oaks, CA: Saage.

UNICEF. (2004). *The state of the world's children: 2004*. Geneva, Swit: UNICEF.

University of Buffalo Counseling Services. (2003). *Procrastination*. Buffalo, NY: Author.

University of Illinois Counseling Center. (1996). *Overcoming procrastination*. Urbana-Champaign, IL: Department of Student Affairs.

University of Texas at Austin Counseling and Mental Health Center. (1999). *Coping with perfectionism*. Austin, TX: Author.

Uppaluri, C. R., Schumm, I. P., & Lauderdale, D. S. (2001). Self-reports of stress in Asian immigrants: Effects of ethnicity and acculturation. *Ethnic Distribution 11*, 107–144.

Urdan, T., & Midgley, C. (2001). Academic self-handicapping: What we know, what more there is to learn. *Educational Psychology Review, 13*, 115–138.

V

Vaillant, G. E. (1977). *Adaptation to life*. Boston: Little, Brown.

Vaillant, G. E. (1992). Is there a natural history of addiction? In C. P. O'Brien & J. H. Jaffe (Eds.), *Addictive states*. Cambridge, MA: Harvard University Press.

Vaillant, G. E. (2002). *Aging well*. Boston: Little, Brown.

Valeri, S. M. (2003). Social factors: Isolation and loneliness versus social activity. In A. Spirito & J. C. Overholser (Eds.), *Evaluating and treating adolescent suicide attempters*. San Diego: Academic Press.

Van Ameringen, M., Mancini, C., Farvolden, P., & Oakman, A. J. (2000). The neurobiology of social phobia: From pharmacology to brain imaging. *Current Psychiatry Reports, 2*, 358–366.

Van Buren, E., & Graham, S. (2003). *Redefining ethnic identity: Its relationship to positive and negative school adjustment outcomes*

for minority youth. Paper presented at the meeting of the Society for Research in Child Development, Tampa.

Van Citters, A. D., & Bartels, S. J. (2004). A systematic review of the effectiveness of community-based mental health outreach services for older adults. *Psychiatric Services, 55*, 1237–1249.

van Eijck, K., & Mommaas, H. (2004). Leisure, lifestyle, and the new middle class. *Leisure Sciences, 26*, 373–392.

Van Elst, L. T., Ebert, D., & Trimble, M. R. (2001). Hippocampus and amygdala pathology in depression. *American Journal of Psychiatry, 158*, 652–653.

van Lankveld, J. J. D. M. (1998). Bibliotherapy in the treatment of sexual dysfunctions: A meta-analysis. *Journal of Consulting and Clinical Psychology, 66*, 702–708.

van Praag, H. M. (2000). Serotonin disturbances and suicide risk: Is aggression or anxiety an interjacent link? *Crisis, 21*, 160–162.

Vatcher, C. A., & Bogo, M. (2001). The feminist/emotionally focused therapy practice model: An integrated approach for couple therapy. *Journal of Marital and Family Therapy, 27*, 69–83.

Vega, W. A., Sribney, W. M., Augilar-Gaxiola, S., & Kolody, B. (2004). 12–month prevalence of DSM-III-R psychiatric disorders among Mexican Americans: nativity, social assimilation, and age determinants. *Journal of Nervous and Mental Disorders, 192*, 532–541

Vegas, O., Beitia, G., Sanchez-Martin, J. R., Arregi, A., & Aspiroz, A. (2004). Behavioral and neurochemical responses in mice tumors submitted to social stress. *Behavioral Brain Research, 155*, 125–134.

Vermeiren, R., Bogaerts, J., Ruchkin, V., Deboutte, D., & Schwab-Stone, M. (2004). Subtypes of self-esteem and self-concept in adolescent violent and property offenders. *Journal of Child Psychology and Psychiatry, 45*, 405–411.

Vernoy, M. W., & Kyle, D. (2003). *Behavioral statistics in action* (3rd ed.). New York: McGraw-Hill.

Versiani, M., Cassano, G., Perugi, G., Benedetti, A., Mastalli, L., Nadi, A., & Savino, M. (2002). Reboxetine, a selective norepinephrine reuptake inhibitor, is an effective and well-tolerated treatment for panic disorder. *Journal of Clinical Psychiatry, 63*, 31–37.

Viney, L. L., Henry, R., Walker, B. M., & Crooks, L. (1989). The emotional reactions of HIV antibody positive men. *British Journal of Medical Psychology, 62*(2), 153–161.

Visher, E., & Visher, J. (1989). Parenting coalitions after remarriage: Dynamics and therapeutic guidelines. *Family Relations, 38*, 65–70.

Vitaliano, P. P., Young, H. M., & Zhang, J. (2004). Is caregiving a risk factor for illness? *Current Directions in Psychological Science, 13*, 13–16.

Vogel, D. L., Wester, S. R., Heesacker, M., & Madon, S. (2003). Confirming gender stereotypes: A social role perspective. *Sex Roles, 49*, 519–530.

Vogel, M., Pfeifer, S., Schaub, R. T., Grabe, H. J., Barnow, S., Freyberger, H. J., & Cascorbi, I. (2004). Decreased levels of dopamine d (3) receptor mRNA in schizophrenic and bipolar patients. *Neuropsychobiology, 50*, 305–310.

Voydanoff, P. (1990). Economic distress and family relations: A review of the eighties. *Journal of Marriage and the Family, 52*, 1099–1115.

W

Wadden, T. A., Foser, G. D., Stunkard, A. J., & Conill, A. M. (1996). Effects of weight cycling on the resting energy expenditure and body composition of obese women. *Eating Disorders, 19*, 5–12.

Wahl, H-W., Becker, S., Gurmedi, D., & Schilling, O. (2004). The role of primary and secondary control in adaptation to age-related vision loss: A study of older adults with macular degeneration. *Psychology and Aging, 19*, 235–239.

Waldron, S., Scharf, R., Crouse, J., Firesein, S. K., Burton, A., & Hurst, D. (2004). Saying the right thing at the right time: a view through the lens of the analytic process scales (APS). *Psychoanalytic Quarterly, 73*, 1079–1125.

Walker, E. F., Bollini, A., Hochman, K., & Kestler, L. (2005). Schizophrenia. In J. E. Maddux & B. A. Winstead (Eds.), *Psychopathology*. Mahwah, NJ: Erlbaum.

Walker, E. F., Kestler, L., Bollini, A., & Hochman, K. (2004). Schizophrenia: Etiology and course. *Annual Review of Psychology, 54*. Palo Alto, CA: Annual Reviews.

Walker, L. (2000). *The Battered Woman Syndrome* (2nd ed.). Springer, New York.

Walker, L. (2001). Battering in adult relationships. In J. Worell (Ed.), *Encyclopedia of women and gender* (Vol. 1.) San Diego: Academic Press.

Wall, T. L., Shea, S. H., Chan, K. K., & Carr, L. G. (2001). A genetic association with the development of alcohol and other substance abuse behavior in Asian Americans. *Journal of Abnormal Psychology, 110,* 173–178.

Wallace, M., Mills, B., & Browning, C. (1997). Effects of cross-training on markers of insulin resistance/hyperinsulinemia. *Medical Science and Sports Exercise, 29,* 1170–1175.

Wallace, R. R., & Benson, H. (1972). The physiology of meditation. *Scientific American, 226,* 85–90.

Wallerstein, R. S. (1989). The psychotherapy research project of the Menninger Foundation: An overview. *Journal of Consulting and Clinical Psychology, 57,* 195–205.

Wallis, D. J., & Hetherington, M. M. (2004). Stress and eating: the effects of ego-threat and cognitive demand on food intake in restrained and emotional eaters. *Appetite, 43,* 39–46.

Wallston, K. A. (2001). Conceptualization and operationalization of perceived control. In A. Baum, T. A. Revenson, & J. E. Singer (Eds.), *Handbook of health psychology.* Mahwah, NJ: Erlbaum.

Walsh, L. A. (2000, Spring). The inside scoop on child development: Interview. *Cutting through the hype.* Minneapolis: College of Education & Human Development, University of Minnesota.

Walsh, W. B. (1995, August). *Person-environment psychology: Contemporary models and perspectives.* Paper presented at the meeting of the American Psychological Association, New York City.

Walters, A. (1994). Using visual media to reduce homophobia: A classroom demonstration. *Journal of Sex Education and Therapy, 20,* 92–100.

Walters, E., & Kendler, K. S. (1994). Anorexia nervosa and anorexia-like symptoms in a population based twin sample. *American Journal of Psychiatry, 152,* 62–71.

Walters, G. D. (2000). Behavioral self-control training for problem drinkers: A meta-analysis of randomized clinical studies. *Behavior Therapy, 31,* 135–149.

Ward, L. M. (2004). Wading through the stereotypes: Positive and negative associations between media use and black adolescents' conceptions of self. *Developmental Psychology, 40,* 284–294.

Ward, R. A., & Grashial, A. F. (1995). Using astrology to teach research methods to introductory psychology students. In M. E. Ware & D. E. Johnson (Eds.), *Demonstrations and activities in teaching of psychology* (Vol. 1). Mahwah, NJ: Erlbaum.

Wardlaw, G. M., Hampl, J. S., & DiSilvestro, R. A. (2004). *Perspectives in nutrition* (6th Ed.). New York: McGraw-Hill.

Warnecke, R. B., Morera, O., Turner, L., Mermelstein, R., Johnson, T. P., Parsons, J., Crittenden, K., Freels, S., & Flay, B. (2001). Changes in self-efficacy and readiness for smoking cessation among women with high school or less education. *Journal of Health and Social Behavior, 42,* 97–110.

Warner, H. (2002, September 16). Commentary. *Dallas Morning News,* p. 6F.

Warr, P. (1994). Age and employment. In M. Dunnette, L. Hough, & H. Triandis (Eds.), *Handbook of industrial and organizational psychology* (Vol. 4). Palo Alto, CA: Consulting Psychologists Press.

Warr, P. (2004). Work, well-being, and mental health. In J. Baring, E. K. Kelloway, & M. R. Frone (Eds.), *Handbook of work stress.* Thousand Oaks, CA: Sage.

Watanabe, C., Okumura, J., Chiu, T. Y., & Wakai, S. (2004). Social support and depressive symptoms among displaced older workers following the 1999 Taiwan earthquake. *Journal of Traumatic Stress, 17,* 63–67.

Waterman, A. S. (1985). Identity in the context of adolescent psychology. In A. S. Waterman (Ed.), *Identity in adolescence: Processes and contents.* San Francisco: Jossey-Bass.

Waterman, A. S. (1989). Curricula interventions for identity change: Substantive and ethical considerations. *Journal of Adolescence, 12,* 389–400.

Waterman, A. S. (1992). Identity as an aspect of optimal psychological functioning. In G. R. Adams, T. P. Gullotta, & R. Montemayor (Eds.), *Adolescent identity formation.* Newbury Park, CA: Sage.

Waterman, A. S. (1999). Identity, the identity statuses, and identity status development: A contemporary statement. *Developmental Review, 19,* 591–621.

Waters, E., Merrick, S., Albersheim, L., Treboux, D., & Crowell, J. (2000). Attachment theory from infancy to adulthood: A 20–year-longitudinal study of relations between infant Strange Situation classification and attachment representations in adulthood. *Child Development, 71,* 684–689.

Watson, A. L., & Sher, K. J. (1998). Resolution of alcohol problems without treatment: Methodological issues and future directions of natural recovery research. *Clinical Psychology: Science and Practice, 5,* 1–18.

Watson, D. L., & Tharp, R. G. (2002). *Self-directed behavior* (8th ed.). Belmont, CA: Wadsworth.

Watson, R., & DeMeo, P. (1987). Premarital cohabitation vs. traditional courtship and subsequent marital adjustment: A replication and follow-up. *Family Relations, 36,* 193–197.

Waysman, M., Schwarzwald, J., & Solomon, Z. (2001). Hardiness: An examination of its relationship with positive and negative long-term changes following trauma. *Journal of Traumatic Stress, 14,* 531–548.

Wechsler, H., Davenport, A., Sowdall, G., Moetykens, B., & Castillo, S. (1994). Health and behavioral consequences of binge drinking in college. *Journal of the American Medical Association, 272,* 1672–1677.

Wechsler, H., Lee, J. E., Kuo, M., Seibring, M., Nelson, T. F., & Lee, H. (2002). Trends in college binge drinking during a period of increased prevention efforts: Findings from 4 Harvard School of Public Health College Alcohol Study surveys: 1993–2001. *Journal of American College Health, 50,* 203–217.

Weekes, C. (1996). Bibliotherapy. In C. G. Lindemann (Ed.), *Handbook of the treatment of the anxiety disorders* (2nd ed., pp. 375–384). Northvale, NJ: Jason Aronson.

Wegener, D. T., Pelty, N. D., Smolak, N. D., & Fabrigar. L. R. (2004). Multiple routes to resisting attitude change. In E. S. Knowles & J. A. Linn (Eds.), *Resistance and persuasion.* Mahwah, NJ: Erlbaum.

Weine, S. M., Becker, D. F., McGlashan, T., H., Laub, D., Lazrove, S., Vojvoda, D., & Hyman, L. (1995). Psychiatric consequences of "ethnic cleansing": Clinical assessments and trauma testimonies of newly resettled Bosnian refugees. *American Journal of Psychiatry, 152,* 536–542.

Weiner, I. B. (2003). Rorschach assessment: Current status. In M. Hersen (Ed.), *Comprehensive handbook of psychological assessment* (Vol. 2). New York: Wiley.

Weinraub, M., Horuath, D. L., & Gringlas, M. B. (2002). Single parenthood. In M. H. Bornstein (Ed.), *Handbook of parenting* (2nd ed., Vol. 3). Mahwah, NJ: Erlbaum.

Weisfeld, G. E., & Woodward, L. (2004). Current evolutionary perspectives on adolescent romantic relationships. *Journal of the American Academy of Child and Adolescent Psychiatry, 43,* 11–19.

Weismiller, D. G. (2004). Emergency contraception. *American Journal of Family Physicians, 70,* 707–714.

Weissman, M., & Olfson, M. (1995). Depression in women: Implications for health care research. *Science, 269,* 799–801.

Wells, K., Miranda, J., Bruce, M. L., Alegria, M., & Wallerstein, N. (2004). Bridging community intervention and mental health services research. *American Journal of Psychiatry, 161,* 955–963.

Wentzel, K. R., & Erdley, C. A. (1993). Strategies for making friends: Relations to social behavior and peer acceptance in early adolescence. *Developmental Psychology, 29,* 819–826.

Wenzlaff, R. M., & Prohaska, M. L. (1989). When misery loves company: Depression, attributions, and responses to others' moods. *Journal of Experimental Social Psychology, 25,* 220–223.

Westermeyer, J. F. (2004). Predictors and characteristics of Erikson's life cycle model among men: a 32-year longitudinal study. *International Journal of Aging and Human Development, 58,* 29–48.

Wetherell, J. L., Thorp, S. R., Patterson, T. L., Golshan, S., Jeste, D. V., & Gatz, M. (2004). Quality of life in geriatric generalized anxiety disorder: A preliminary investigation. *Journal of Psychiatric Research, 38,* 305–312.

Whippie, B., Ogden, G., & Komisaruk, B. (1992). Analgesia produced in women by genital self-stimulation. *Archives of Sexual Behavior, 9,* 87–99.

White, J. W. (2001). Aggression and gender. In J. Worell (Ed.), *Encyclopedia of women and gender.* San Diego: Academic Press.

Whitehead, B. D., & Popenoe, D. (2003). *The State of our Unions.* New Brunswick, NJ: Rutgers University.

Whitfield, K. E., Weidner, G., Clark, R., & Anderson, N. B. (2003). Cultural aspects of health psychology. In I. B. Weiner (Ed.), *Handbook of psychology* (Vol. 9). New York: Wiley.

Whiting, B. B., & Edwards, C. P. (1998). *Children of different worlds.* Cambridge, MA: Harvard University Press.

Widiger, T. A. (2000). Diagnostic and statistical manual of disorders. In A. Kazdin (Ed.), *Encyclopedia of psychology.* Washington, DC, & New York: American Psychological Association and Oxford University Press.

Widiger, T. A. (2005). Classification and diagnosis: historical development and contemporary issues. In J. E. Maddux & B. A. Winstead (Eds.), *Psychopathology.* Mahwah, NJ: Erlbaum.

Wiederman, M. W., & Whitley, B. E. (Eds.). (2002). *Handbook for conducting research on human sexuality.* Mahwah, NJ: Erlbaum.

Wiggins, J. S., & Trapnell, P. D. (1997). Personality structure: The return of the big five. In R. Hogan, J. Johnson, & S. Briggs (Eds.), *Handbook of personality research.* San Diego: Academic Press.

Wild, D. (2003). Coming home from war: A literature review. *Emergency Nurse, 11,* 22–27.

Wilkinson, M. (2004). The mind-brain relationship: The emergent self. *Journal of Analytic Psychology, 49,* 83–101.

Willcox, B. J., Willcox, M. D., & Suzuki, M. (2002). *The Okinawa program.* New York: Crown.

Williams, J. E., & Best, D. L. (1982). *Measuring sex stereotypes: A thirty-nation study.* Newbury Park, CA: Sage.

Williams, J. E., & Best, D. L. (1989). *Sex and psyche: Self-concept viewed cross-culturally.* Newbury Park, CA: Sage.

Williams, M. H. (2005). *Nutrition for health, fitness, & sport* (7th Ed.). New York: McGraw-Hill.

Williams, R. B. (1995). Coronary prone behaviors, hostility, and cardiovascular health. In K. Orth-Gomer & N. Schneiderman (Eds.), *Behavioral medicine approaches to cardiovascular disease prevention.* Mahwah, NJ: Erlbaum.

Williams, R. B. (2001). Hostility (and other psychosocial risk factors): Effects on health and the potential for successful behavioral approaches to prevention and treatment. In A. Baum, T. A. Revenson, & J. E. Singer (Eds.), *Handbook of health psychology.* Mahwah, NJ: Erlbaum.

Williams, R. B. (2002). Hostility, neuroendocrine changes, and health outcomes. In H. G. Koenig & H. J. Cohen (Eds.), *The link between religion and health.* New York: Oxford University Press.

Williams, S. L. (2005). Anxiety disorders. In J. E. Maddux & B. A. Winstead (Eds.), *Psychopathology.* Mahwah, NJ: Erlbaum.

Willis, S. L., & Schaie, K. W. (1999). Intellectual functioning in midlife. In S. L. Willis & J. D. Reid (Eds.), *Life in the middle: Psychological and social development in middle age.* San Diego: Academic Press.

Wilmot, W. W., & Hocker, J. L. (2001). *Interpersonal conflict* (6th ed.). New York: McGraw-Hill.

Wilson, J. P., Friedman, M. J., & Lindy, J. D. (Eds.). (2001). *Treating psychological trauma and PTSD.* New York: Guilford.

Wineberg, H. (1994). Marital reconciliation in the United States: Which couples are successful? *Journal of Marriage and the Family, 56,* 80–88.

Wing, R. R., & Polley, B. A. (2001). Obesity. In A. Baum, T. A. Revenson, & J. E. Singer (Eds.), *Handbook of health psychology.* Mahwah, NJ: Erlbaum.

Wink, P., & Dillon, M. (2002). Spiritual development across the adult life course: Findings from a longitudinal study. *Journal of Adult Development, 9,* 79–94.

Winstead, B. A., & Sanchez, J. (2005). Gender and psychopatholgy. In J. E. Maddux & B. A. Winstead (Eds.), *Psychopathology.* Mahwah, NJ: Erlbaum.

Wolsko, P. M., Eisenberg, D. M., Davis, R. B., & Phillips, R. S. (2004). Use of mind-body medical therapies. *Journal of General Internal Medicine, 19,* 43–50.

Wong, E. H., Sonder, M. S., Amara, S. G., Tinholt, P. M., Percey, M. F., Hoffman, W. P., Hyslop, D. K., Franklin, S., Porsolt, R. D., Bondignori, A., Carfagna, N., & McArthur, R. A. (2000). Reboxetine: A pharmacologically potent, selective and specific norepinephrine inhibitor. *Biological Psychiatry, 47,* 818–829.

Wong, P. T. P., & Watt, L. M. (1991). What types of reminiscence are associated with successful aging? *Psychology and Aging, 6,* 272–279.

Wood, A. F., & Smith, M. J. (2005). *Online Communication.* Mahwah, NJ: Erlbaum.

Wood, J. T. (2000). Gender and personal relationships. In C. Hendrick & S. S. Hendrick (Eds.), *Close relationships.* Thousand Oaks, CA: Sage.

Wood, J. T. (2001). *Gendered lives* (4th ed.). Belmont, CA: Wadsworth.

Wood, J. T. (2004). *Communication mosaics* (3rd ed.). Belmont, CA: Wadsworth.

Wood, W., & Eagly, A. H. (2002). A cross-cultural analysis of the behavior of women and men: Implications for the origins of sex differences. *Psychological Bulletin, 128,* 699–727.

Woods, C. M., Tolin, D. F., & Abramowitz, J. S. (2004). Dimensionality of the obsessive beliefs questionnaire. *Journal of Psychopathology and Behavioral Assessment, 26,* 113–125.

Wooley, S. C., & Garner, D. M. (1991). Obesity treatment: The high cost of false hope. *Journal of the American Dietetic Association, 91,* 1248–1251.

Wren, T., & Mendoza C. (2004). Cultural identity and personal identity. In D. Lapsley & D. Narvaez (Eds.), *Moral development, self, and identity.* Mahwah, NJ: Erlbaum.

Wu, A. M., Tang, C. S., & Kwok, T. C. (2004). Self-efficacy, health locus of control, and psychological distress in elderly Chinese women with chronic illnesses. *Aging and Mental Health, 8,* 21–28.

Wyer, N. (2004). Value conflicts in intergroup perception: A social-cognitive perspective. In G. V. Bodenhausen & A. J.

Lambert (Eds.), *Foundations of social cognition.* Mahwah, NJ: Erlbaum.

Wyer, R. S., & Adaval, R. (2003). Message reception skills in social communication. In J. O. Greene & B. R. Burleson (Eds.), *Handbook of communication and social interactional skills.* Mahwah, NJ: Erlbaum.

Wysocki, C. J., & Preti, G. (2004). Facts, fallacies, fears, and frustrations with human pheromones. *The Anatomical Record, 281A,* 1201–1211.

Y

Yali, A. M., & Revenson, T. A. (2004). How changes in population demographics will impact health psychology: Incorporating a broader notion of cultural competence into the field. *Health Psychology, 23,* 147–155.

Yalom, I. D. (1975). *The theory and practice of group psychotherapy.* New York: Basic Books.

Yalom, I. D. (1995). *The theory and practice of group psychotherapy* (4th ed.). New York: Basic Books.

Yalom, V. J. (2004). Group psychotherapy. In G. P. Koocher, J. C. Norcross, & S. S. Hill (Eds.), *Psychologists' desk reference* (2nd Ed.). New York: Oxford University Press.

Yate, M. (2005). *Knock 'em dead.* Boston: Adams Media.

Yates, M. (1995, March). *Community service and political-moral discussions among Black urban adolescents.* Paper presented at the meeting of the Society for Research in Child Development, Indianapolis.

Yates, W. R. (2004). The link between religion and health: Psychoneuroimmunology and the faith factor. *American Journal of Psychiatry, 161,* 586.

Yehnda, R. (2004). Risk and resilience in posttraumatic stress disorder. *Journal of Clinical Psychiatry, 65* (Supplement 1), 29–36.

Yodanis, C. L. (2004). Gender inequality, violence against women, and fear: a cross-national test of the feminist theory of violence against women. *Journal of Interpersonal Violence, 19,* 655–675.

Young, E. A. (2004). Perfectionism, low self-esteem, and family factors as predictors of bulimic behavior. *Eating Behavior, 5,* 273–283.

Young, E., & Korzun, A. (1998). Psychoneuroendocrinology of depression: Hypothalamic-pituitary-gonadal axis. *Psychiatric Clinics of North America, 21,* 309–323.

Z

Zahm, S., & Gold, E. (2002). Gestalt therapy. In M. Hersen & W. H. Sledge (Eds.), *Encyclopedia of psychotherapy.* San Diego: Academic Press.

Zarit, S. H., & Knight, B. G. (Eds.). (1996). *A guide to psychotherapy and aging.* Washington, DC: American Psychological Association.

Zhou, L-Y., Dawson, M. L., Herr, C., & Stukas, S. K. (2004). American and Chinese college students' predictions of people's occupations, housework responsibilities, and hobbies as a function of cultural and gender influences. *Sex Roles, 50,* 547–563.

Zielinski, D. S., Campa, M. I., & Eckenrode, J. J. (2003, April). *Child maltreatment and the early onset of problem behaviors: A follow-up at 19 years.* Paper presented at the meeting of the Society for Research in Child Development, Tampa.

Zilbergeld, B. (1992). *The new male sexuality.* New York: Bantam Books.

Zimmer-Gembeck, M. J., & Collins, W. A. (2003). Autonomy development during adolescence. In G. Adams & M. Berzonsky (Eds.), *Blackwell handbook of adolescence.* Malden, MA: Blackwell.

Zimmerman, B. J., & Schunk, D. H. (2004). Self-regulating intellectual processes and outcomes. In D. Y. Dai & R. J. Sternberg (Eds.), *Motivation, emotion, and cognition.* Mahwah, NJ: Erlbaum.

Zucker, A. N., Ostrove, H. M., & Stewart, A. J. (2002). College educated women's personality development in adulthood: Perceptions and age differences. *Psychology and Aging, 17,* 236–244.

Zunzenegui, M., Alvarado, B. E., Del Ser, T., & Otero, A. (2003). Social networks, social integration, and social engagement determine cognitive decline in community-dwelling Spanish older adults. *Journals of Gerontology Series B: Psychological and Social Sciences, 58,* S93–S100.

Zurbriggen, E. L., & Yost, M. R. (2004). Power, desire, and pleasure in sexual fantasies. *Journal of Sex Research, 41,* 288–300.

Credits

Line Art and Text

Chapter 1

Figure 1.1: From *The Child: Development in a Social Context*, by CB Kopp/JB Krakow, © 1982 by Addison-Wesley Publishing Company, Inc. Reprinted by permission of Pearson Education, Inc. **Figure 1.2:** From Diener & Seligman, 2002, "Very Happy People," *Psychological Science*, Vol. 13, pp. 81–84. Reprinted by permission from Blackwell Publishers. **Self-Assessment 1.2:** From Deiner, F., Emmons, R.A., Earsen, R.J., & Griffin, S. (1985). *The Satisfaction with Life Scale.* Journal of Personality Assessment, 49, 71–75. **Figure 1.3:** From *Psychology,* 7e by John Santrock, Fig. 2.1. Copyright © 2003 The McGraw-Hill Companies Inc. Reprinted with permission from The McGraw-Hill Companies. **Figure 1.4:** From *Psychology,* 7e by John Santrock, Fig. 2.5. Copyright © 2003 The McGraw-Hill Companies Inc. Reprinted with permission from The McGraw-Hill Companies.

Chapter 2

Figure 2.1: From Psychology: A *Scientific Study of Human Behavior,* 5th edition by Wrightsman / Sigelman / Sanford. © 1979. Reprinted with permission of Wadsworth, a division of Thomson Learning: www.thomsonrights.com. Fax 800 730–2215. **Figure 2.2:** From *Psychology,* 7e by John Santrock, Fig. 12.2. Copyright © 2003 The McGraw-Hill Companies Inc. Reprinted with permission from The McGraw-Hill Companies. **Figure 2.3:** From *Psychology,* 7e by John Santrock, Fig. 12.3. Copyright © 2003 The McGraw-Hill Companies Inc. Reprinted with permission from The McGraw-Hill Companies. **Figure 2.4:** From *Psychology,* 7e by John Santrock, Fig. 12.4. Copyright © 2003 The McGraw-Hill Companies Inc. Reprinted with permission from The McGraw-Hill Companies. **Figure 2.5:** From *Psychology,* 7e by John Santrock, Fig. 7.2. Copyright © 2003 The McGraw-Hill Companies Inc. Reprinted with permission from The McGraw-Hill Companies. **Figure 2.6:** From *Psychology,* 7e by John Santrock, Fig. 7.4. Copyright © 2003 The McGraw-Hill Companies Inc. Reprinted with permission from The McGraw-Hill Companies. **Figure 2.7:** From *Psychology,* 7e by John Santrock, Fig. 7.12. Copyright © 2003 The McGraw-Hill Companies Inc. Reprinted with permission from the McGraw-Hill Companies. **Figure 2.8:** From *Psychology,* 7e by John Santrock, Fig. 12.6. Copyright © 2003 The McGraw-Hill Companies Inc. Reprinted with permission from The McGraw-Hill Companies. **Self-Assessment 2.1:** Schwarzer, R., & Jerusalem, M. (2000). *Generalized Self-Efficacy Scale (Rev.).* Berlin, GER: Frei Univertitat Berlin. Used by permission. **Self-Assessment 2.2:** Reprinted from H. M. Lefcourt (Ed.), *Research With the Locus of Control Construct,* Vol 2, Nowicki, S., Jr., & Duke, M.P., "The Nowicki-Strickland Life-Span Locus of Control Scales: Construct Validation," pp. 9–51, Copyright © 1983, with permission from Elsevier. **Figure 2.9:** From *Psychology,* 7e by John Santrock, Fig. 11.2. Copyright © 2003 The McGraw-Hill Companies Inc. Reprinted with permission from The McGraw-Hill Companies. **Figure 2.10:** From *Psychology,* 7e by John Santrock, Fig. 12.8. Copyright © 2003 The McGraw-Hill Companies Inc. Reprinted with permission from The McGraw-Hill Companies. **Figure 2.11:** Reprinted with permission from the H. J. Eysenck Memorial Fund. **Self-Assessment 2.3:** From *Psychology,* 7e by John Santrock, p. 498. Copyright © 2003 The McGraw-Hill Companies Inc. Reprinted with permission from The McGraw-Hill Companies. **Figure 2.12:** From *Psychology,* 7e by John Santrock, Fig. 12.11. Copyright © 2003 The McGraw-Hill Companies Inc. Reprinted with permission from The McGraw-Hill Companies. **Figure 2.14:** Reprinted by permission of the publisher from *The Thematic Apperception Test* by Henry A. Murray. Cambridge, MA: Harvard University Press. Copyright © 1943 by the President and Fellows of Harvard College. **Figure 2.15:** From *Psychology,* 7e by John Santrock, Fig. 12.17. Copyright © 2003 The McGraw-Hill Companies Inc. Reprinted with permission from The McGraw-Hill Companies.

Chapter 3

Figure 3.1: From *Human Adjustment,* 2e by Jane Halonen and John Santrock, Fig. 3.3. Copyright © 1997 The McGraw-Hill Companies Inc. Reprinted with permission of The McGraw-Hill Companies. **Self-Assessment 3.1:** Rosenberg, M. (1965). Society and the adolescent self-image. Princeton, NJ: Princeton University Press. **Figure 3.2:** From *Psychology,* 7e by John Santrock, Fig. 12.9. Copyright © 2003 The McGraw-Hill Companies Inc. Reprinted with permission of The McGraw-Hill Companies. **Figure 3.3:** From *Educational Psychology,* 2e by John Santrock, Fig. 3.7. Copyright © 2004 The McGraw-Hill Companies Inc. Reprinted with permission from The McGraw-Hill Companies. **Figure 3.4:** Sax, L.J., Astin, A.W., Lindholm, J.A., Korn, W.S., Saenz, V.B., Mahoney, K.M. (2003). *The American Freshman: National Norms for Fall 2003.* Copyright © 2003 Higher Education Research Institute, UCLA. Reprinted with permission. **Self-Assessment 3.5:** From Craig W. Ellison and Raymond F. Paloutzian, The Spiritual Well-Being Scale. Copyright © 1982 Craig W. Ellison and Raymond F. Paloutzian. Used by permission. All rights reserved. Not to be duplicated without expressed written permission from the copyright holders or from Life Advance, Inc., 81 Front Street, Nyack, NY 10960. See www.lifeadvance.com.

Chapter 4

Self-Assessment 4.1: *University of California Wellness Letter,* August 1985; Scale developers: Lyle Miller and Alma Dell Smith, Boston University Medical Center. © Health Letter Associates, 1985. Reprinted with permission. **Figure 4.1:** From *The Stress of Life* by H. Selye. Copyright © 1976 The McGraw-Hill Companies Inc. Reprinted with permission from The McGraw-Hill Companies. **Figure 4.2:** From *Psychology,* 7e by John Santrock, Fig. 15.5. Copyright © 2003 The McGraw-Hill Companies Inc. Reprinted with permission from The McGraw-Hill Companies. **Figure 4.3:** From *Psychology,* 7e by John Santrock, Fig. 15.6. Copyright © 2003 The McGraw-Hill Companies Inc. Reprinted with permission from The McGraw-Hill Companies. **Self-Assessment 4.2:** From *Psychology,* 7e by John Santrock, Fig. 15.3. Copyright © 2003 The McGraw-Hill Companies Inc. Reprinted with permission from The McGraw-Hill Companies. **Figure 4.6:** Reprinted from *Journal of Psychosomatic Research,* Vol. 29, S.C. Kobasa, S.R. Maddi, M.C. Puccette and M. Zola, Effectiveness of hardiness, exercise, and social support as a resource against illness, pp. 523–533. Copyright © 1985 Elsevier Science. With permission from Elsevier Science. **Excerpt, pg. 135:** American Psychological Association, "10 Ways to Build Resilience," from *The Road to Resilience,* Washington, D.C.: APA. As found on http://apahelpcenter.org/featuredtopics/feature. php?id=6&ch=4. Copyright © 2004 by the American Psychological Association. Reprinted with permission.

Chapter 5

Figure 5.1: From C. J. Holahan and R. H. Moos, "Personal & Contextual Determinants of Coping Strategies" in *Journal of Personality and Social Psychology,* 52:946–955. Copyright © 1987 by the American Psychological Association. Adapted with permission. **Figure 5.2:** From *Contemporary Behavior Therapy,* 2nd edition by Spiegler / Guevremont. © 1993. Reprinted with permission of Wadsworth, a division of Thomson Learning: www.thomsonrights.com. Fax 800 730–2215. **Figure 5.3:** From *Psychology,* 7e by John Santrock, Fig. 15.10. Copyright © 2003 The McGraw-Hill Companies Inc. Reprinted with permission from The McGraw-Hill Companies. **Figure 5.4:** From *Journal of the American Medical Association,* 1997, 277, 1940–1944. Copyright © 1997 American Medical Association. All rights reserved. Reprinted with permission. **Self-Assessment 5.2:** From *Educational Psychology,* 1e by John Santrock, p. 116. Copyright © 2001 The McGraw-Hill Companies Inc. Reprinted with permission from The McGraw-Hill Companies.

Chapter 6

Figure 6.1: From *Psychology,* 7e by John Santrock, Fig. 16.1. Copyright © 2003 The McGraw-Hill Companies Inc. Reprinted with permission from The McGraw-Hill Companies. **Self-Assessment 6.1:** "Self-Monitoring" from Mark Snyder, *Journal of Personality and Social Psychology,* 30:562–537. Copyright © 1974 by the American Psychological Association. Adapted with permission. **Figure 6.2:** From *Psychology,* 7e by John Santrock, Fig. 16.5. Copyright © 2003 The McGraw-Hill Companies Inc. Reprinted with permission from The McGraw-Hill Companies. **Figure 6.3:** Based on findings in "Behavioral Study of Obedience" by Stanley Milgram in *Journal of Abnormal and Social Psychology,* 67:371–378, 1963. Reprinted with permission. **Figure 6.4:** Reprinted from *Encyclopedia of Women and Gender: Sex Similarities and Differences and the Impact of Society on Gender,* 2 Volume Set, edited by Judith Worell, Copyright © 2001, with permission from Elsevier. **Excerpt, pg. 185:** Cialdini, R. (2001). Adapted from *Influence.* Boston: Allyn & Bacon, pp. 50, 96, 141, 176, 201, 231.

McGraw-Hill Companies Inc. Reprinted with permission from The McGraw-Hill Companies. **Self-Assessment 11.3:** From *The Psychology of Death, Dying and Bereavement* by Richard Schulz. Copyright © McGraw-Hill Companies Inc. Reprinted with permission. **Figure 11.8:** From *Life-Span Development,* 9e by John Santrock, Fig. 16.9. Copyright © 2004 The McGraw-Hill Companies Inc. Reprinted with permission from The McGraw-Hill Companies. **Figure 11.9:** From *Life-Span Development,* 9e by John Santrock, Fig. 2.2. Copyright © 2004 The McGraw-Hill Companies Inc. Reprinted with permission from The McGraw-Hill Companies. **Figure 11.10:** From D. Mroczek and C. M. Kolarz, "The Effect of Age in Positive and Negative Affect" in *Journal of Personality and Social Psychology,* Vol. 75, pp. 1333–1349. Copyright © 1998 by the American Psychological Association. Adapted with permission. **Figure 11.11:** From L. Carstensen, et al., "The Social Context of Emotion" in *Annual Review of Geriatrics and Gerontology* by Schaie/Lawton, 1997, Vol. 17, p. 331. Used by permission of Springer Publishing Company, New York 10012. **Figure 11.12:** From *Life-Span Development,* 9e by John Santrock, Fig. 16.1. Copyright © 2004 The McGraw-Hill Companies Inc. Reprinted with permission from The McGraw-Hill Companies.

Chapter 12

Self-Assessment 12.1: Items from survey created by Prarthana Prasad and Jonathan Baron (1996). University of Pennsylvania. In "Measurement of Gender-Role Attitudes, Beliefs, and Principles." Reprinted with permission. **Figure 12.1:** From *Child Development,* 10e by John Santrock, Fig. 13.1. Copyright © 2004 The McGraw-Hill Companies Inc. Reprinted with permission from The McGraw-Hill Companies. **Figure 12.2:** From *Child Development,* 10e by John Santrock, Fig. 13.4. Copyright © 2004 The McGraw-Hill Companies Inc. Reprinted with permission from The McGraw-Hill Companies. **Figure 12.3:** After "Use of Free Responses and Cluster Analysis to Determine Stereotypes of Eight Groups," Niemann, Y.F., Jennings, L., Rozell, R.M., Baxter, J.C., & Sullivan, E., *Personality and Social Psychology Bulletin,* 20, pp. 379–390. Copyright © 1994 by Society for Personality and Social Psychology, Inc. Reprinted by Permission of Sage Publications, Inc. **Self-Assessment 12.2:** From *Bulletin of the Psychonomic Society* 2:219–220, 1973, reprinted by permission of Psychonomic Society. **Figure 12.4:** From Janet S. Hyde et al, "Gender Differences in Mathematics Performance: A Meta-Analysis," *Psychological Bulletin,* 107:139–155, 1990. Copyright © 1990 by the American Psychological Association. Adapted with permission. **Figure 12.5:** Reproduced by special permission of the Publisher, Mind Garden, Inc., 1690 Woodside Road, #202, Redwood City, CA 94061 USA www.mindgarden.com from the Bem Sex Role Inventory by Sandra Bem. Copyright © 1978 by Consulting Psychologists Press, Inc. All rights reserved. Further reproduction is prohibited without the Publisher's written consent. **Excerpt, pg. 366:** Adapted from *Like Water for Chocolate* by Laura Esquivel. Reprinted with permission from Doubleday, a division of Random House, Inc.

Chapter 13

Figure 13.1: W. H. Masters and V. E. Johnson, *Human Sexual Response,* 1966, Little, Brown and Company. Reprinted by permission. **Figure 13.2:**

From *Human Adjustment,* 2e by Jane Halonen and John Santrock, Fig. 9.1. Copyright © 1997 The McGraw-Hill Companies Inc. Reprinted with permission from The McGraw-Hill Companies. **Figure 13.3:** From *Human Adjustment,* 2e by Jane Halonen and John Santrock, Fig. 9.2. Copyright © 1997 The McGraw-Hill Companies Inc. Reprinted with permission from The McGraw-Hill Companies. **Figure 13.4:** From *Psychology,* 7e by John Santrock, Fig. 11.9. Copyright © 2003 The McGraw-Hill Companies Inc. Reprinted with permission from The McGraw-Hill Companies. **Figure 13.5:** From A. Freeman and M.A. Reinecke, "Cognitive Therapy" in A. S. Gurman, ed., *Essential Psychotherapies,* Guilford Press, 1995. Reprinted with permission of the Guilford Press. **Self-Assessment 13.1:** Adapted from Robert F. Valois, "The Valois Sexual Attitude Questionnaire," page 52–54, *Wellness R.S.V.P.,* First Edition, 1981, Benjamin/Cummings Publishing Company, Inc, Menlo Park, CA, copyright 1992 by Valois, Kammermann & Associates and the authors. Used with permission of Valois, Kammermann & Associates and the authors. **Self-Assessment 13.2:** Reprinted from *The Journal of Sex Research,* a publication of The Society for the Scientific Study of Sex; PO Box 208, Mount Vernon, IA 52314, USA. Used with permission. **Self-Assessment 13.3:** From *Psychology,* 7e by John Santrock, Fig. 15.15. Copyright © 2003 The McGraw-Hill Companies Inc. Reprinted with permission from The McGraw-Hill Companies. **Figure 13.6:** Reproduced with the permission of The Alan Guttmacher Institute from: *Preventing Pregnancy, Protecting Health: A New Look at Birth Control Choices in the United States,* S Harlap, K Kost and JD Forrest, 1991 (126 pp. printed, perfect bound). **Figure 13.8:** Fisher and others, (2000) *The Sexual Victimization of College Women.* Washington, DC: U.S. Department of Justice. **Excerpt, pgs. 415–416:** From the brochure "Acquaintance Rape" (2004), pp. 3–7, by The Northern Michigan University Counseling & Consultation Services.

Chapter 14

Figure 14.1: From *Psychology,* 7e by John Santrock, Fig. 13.1. Copyright ©2003 The McGraw-Hill Companies Inc. Reprinted with permission from The McGraw-Hill Companies. **Figure 14.2:** From *Psychology,* 7e by John Santrock, Fig. 13.2. Copyright © 2003 The McGraw-Hill Companies Inc. Reprinted with permission from The McGraw-Hill Companies. **Figure 14.3:** From *Psychology,* 7e by John Santrock, Fig. 13.3. Copyright © 2003 The McGraw-Hill Companies Inc. Reprinted with permission from The McGraw-Hill Companies. **Figure 14.4:** From *Psychology,* 7e by John Santrock, Fig. 13.4. Copyright © 2003 The McGraw-Hill Companies Inc. Reprinted with permission from The McGraw-Hill Companies. **Self-Assessment 14.1:** From *Psychology,* 7e by John Santrock, p. 539. Copyright © 2003 The McGraw-Hill Companies Inc. Reprinted with permission from The McGraw-Hill Companies. **Figure 14.6:** Reprinted, with permission, from the *Annual Review of Neuroscience,* Volume 20 ©1997 by Annual Reviews, www.AnnualReviews.org. **Figure 14.8:** From *Psychology,* 7e by John Santrock, Fig. 13.10. Copyright © 2003 The McGraw-Hill Companies Inc. Reprinted with permission from The McGraw-Hill Companies. **Figure 14.9:** From *Science,* 269, p. 779, Figure 1. Copyright 1995, American Association for the Advancement of Science. Adapted from M. M. Weissman, et al., *World*

Psychological Association Teaching Bulletin. Depression 2, 1 (1994). Reprinted with permission.

Chapter 15

Figure 15.1: From *Psychology,* 7e by John Santrock, Fig. 14.1. Copyright © 2003 The McGraw-Hill Companies Inc. Reprinted with permission from The McGraw-Hill Companies. **Figure 15.2:** From Stephen R. Marder, M.D., et. al., *The Journal of Clinical Psychiatry,* Volume 58, pg. 538–546, 1997. Copyright © 1997, Physicians Postgraduate Press. Reprinted by permission. **Figure 15.3:** From *Psychology,* 7e by John Santrock, Fig. 14.3. Copyright © 2003 The McGraw-Hill Companies Inc. Reprinted with permission from The McGraw-Hill Companies. **Figure 15.4:** From *Psychology,* 7e by John Santrock, Fig. 14.4. Copyright © 2003 The McGraw-Hill Companies Inc. Reprinted with permission from The McGraw-Hill Companies. **Figure 15.5:** From *Psychology,* 7e by John Santrock, Fig. 14.5. Copyright © 2003 The McGraw-Hill Companies Inc. Reprinted with permission from The McGraw-Hill Companies. **Figure 15.6:** From *Psychology,* 7e by John Santrock, Fig. 14.7. Copyright © 2003 The McGraw-Hill Companies Inc. Reprinted with permission from The McGraw-Hill Companies. **Self-Assessment 15.1:** MacDonald, A., & Games, R. (1972) Ellis' irrational values. *Rational Living,* 7, 25–28. Reprinted with permission from the Institute for Rational-Emotive Therapy. **Figure 15.7:** Reprinted with permission from Michael J. Lambert, Brigham Young University. **Figure 15.8:** From "A Survival Analysis of Clinically Significant Change in Outpatient Psychotherapy" by Anderson & Lambert, from *Journal of Clinical Psychology,* 57, 875–888. Copyright © 2001 John Wiley & Sons, Inc. This material is used by permission of John Wiley & Sons, Inc. **Figure 15.9:** From *Psychology,* 7e by John Santrock, Fig. 14.14. Copyright © 2003 The McGraw-Hill Companies Inc. Reprinted with permission from The McGraw-Hill Companies. **Self-Assessment 15.2:** From *Psychology,* 7e by John Santrock, p. 595. Copyright © 2003 The McGraw-Hill Companies Inc. Reprinted with permission from The McGraw-Hill Companies. **Excerpt, pgs. 469–470:** From *Abnormal Psychology,* 6th ed. by G. C. Davision and J. M. Neale. Copyright © 1994 John Wiley & Sons, Inc. This material is used by permission of John Wiley & Sons, Inc. **Excerpt, pg. 477:** Excerpt from Beck, A. T., Rush, A. J., Shaw, B. F., & Emery, G. (1979). *Cognitive Therapy of Depression.* New York: Guilford Press, pp. 145–146. Reprinted with permission of the Guilford Press.

Chapter 16

Self-Assessment 16.1: Adapted from Allen, R., & Linde, S. (1981). *Lifegain.* Burlington, VT: Human Resources Institute, www.healthyculture.com. Reprinted with permission. **Figure 16.1:** United States Department of Agriculture. **Figure 16.2:** Alice Lictenstein, Tufts University, Drawing appeared in *USA Today,* Sept. 17, 2003, p. 5D. USA Today. Copyright © 2004. Reprinted with permission. **Figure 16.3:** From *Scientific American,* November 1997 issue, p. 44. Reprinted by permission of Slim Films. **Figure 16.4:** National Institutes of Health. **Self-Assessment 16.2:** Psychological Counseling Services, College of New Jersey. Reprinted with permission. **Figure 16.6:** From Pate, et al. *Journal of the American Medical Association,* 1995, 273, 404. Copyright © 1995 American Medical Association. All rights reserved. Reprinted by permission. **Figure 16.7:** From *The*

Photo Credits

Chapter 1

Opener: © Helen Norman/CORBIS; **p. 4 (top):** © Seanna O'Sullivan/Sygma/CORBIS; **p. 4 (bottom):** © AP/Wide World Photos; **p. 6:** © Chuck Savage/CORBIS; **p. 8:** © Jay Dickman; **p. 10:** © Bios/M. Gunter/Peter Arnold; **p. 16:** © Bob Daemmrich/Stock Boston; **p. 18:** © Bob Daemmrich; **p. 21:** © Reuters News Media/CORBIS; **p. 25:** © McGraw-Hill Higher Education, John Thoeming, photographer

Chapter 2

Opener: © Marty Loken/Stone/Getty Images; **p. 36 (top):** © National Portrait Gallery, Smithsonian Institution/Art Resource; **p. 36 (middle):** © AFP/Getty Images; **p. 36 (bottom):** © Brian Snyder/Reuters/CORBIS; **p. 38:** © Bettmann/CORBIS; **p. 42:** © CORBIS; **p. 43 (top):** © Bettmann/CORBIS; 2.4: © The Granger Collection, New York; **p. 48:** © Joe McNally; **p. 49:** Courtesy of Stanford University News Service; **p. 56:** Centers for the Study of the Person; 2.10: © David Frazier Photo Library; 2.14: Reprinted by permission of the Publishers from Henry A. Murray, "Thematic Apperception Test", Cambridge, MA: Harvard University Press. Copyright © 1943 by the President and Fellows of Harvard College. © 1971 by Henry A. Murray

Chapter 3

Opener: Artwork by Tom Stilz, reprinted permission of the Decade of Behavior; **p. 80:** AP/Wide World Photos; **p. 89:** © Bettmann/CORBIS; **p. 92:** © USA Today Library, staff photographer Robert Deutsch; **p. 98:** © Skjold Photographs; **p. 99:** © Catherine Karnow/CORBIS; **p. 103:** © Jose Luis Pelaez/The Stock Market/CORBIS

Chapter 4

Opener: © Bob Krist/The Stock Market/CORBIS; **p. 112:** © Jennifer S. Altman; 4.4: © Meckes/Ottawa/Photo Researchers; **p. 128:** © Lisette Le Bon/SuperStock; **p. 130:** © Catherine Gehm; **p. 131:** Courtesy of Vonnie McLoyd; **p. 133 (top left):** © Catherine Ursillo/Photo Researches; **p. 133 (middle):** © Monica Anderson/Stock Boston;

p. 133 (top right): © AFP/Getty Images; **p. 133 (bottom):** © Christopher Brown/Stock Boston

Chapter 5

Opener: © Philip North-Coombes/Stone/Getty; **p. 142:** © Time Life Pictures/Getty Images; **p. 146:** © Bisson Bernard/Sygma/CORBIS; **p. 156:** © Tom Stewart/CORBIS; **p. 162 (left):** © Cary Wolkinsky/Stock Boston; **p. 162 (right):** Steve Liss/ Time Life Pictures/Getty Images; **p. 164:** © Peter Gregoire Photography

Chapter 6

Opener: © Chuck Savage/The Stock Market/CORBIS; 6.1: © Jose Luis Pelaez, Inc./CORBIS; 6.2: © William Vandivert; 6.3: Copyright © 1965 by Stanley Milgram. From the film OBEDIENCE distributed by Penn State Media Sales; **p. 187 (left & right):** © Reuters NewMedia/CORBIS; **p. 188 (top right):** © Bob Daemmrich/The Image Works; **p. 188 (background):** © Larry Kolvoord/The Image Works; **p. 188 (top middle):** © Bill Gillette/Stock Boston; **p. 188 (top right):** © Spencer Grant/Index Stock; **p. 192:** © Bill Losh/Taxi/Getty Images; **p. 193:** © Mary Kate Denny/PhotoEdit

Chapter 7

Opener: © Jose Luis Pelaez/The Stock Market/CORBIS; **p. 204:** © John Burke/SuperStock; **p. 209:** © Jose l. Pelaez/The Stock Market/CORBIS; **p. 215:** © Bruce Ayres; 7.8 (top): © Vol. GA02 PhotoDisc/Getty Images; 7.8 (middle 1): © James Shaffer; 7.8 (middle 2): © James Shaffer; 7.8 (bottom): © Larry Dale Gordon

Chapter 8

Opener: © John Henley/The StockMarket/CORBIS; **p. 238 (top):** © David Young-Wolff/PhotoEdit; **p. 238 (middle):** © Tony Freeman/PhotoEdit; **p. 238 (bottom):** © James McLoughlin; **p. 243 (left):** © David Young-Wolff/PhotoEdit; **p. 243 (right):** © Michael Heller/The Stock Market/CORBIS; **p. 248:** © Carol Ford/Stone/Getty Images

Chapter 9

Opener: © Ariel Skelley/The Stock Market/CORBIS; **p. 267:** © Ronald Mackechnie/Stone/Getty Images; **p. 271:** © Michael Newman/PhotoEdit; **p. 272:** © S. Gazin/The Image Works; **p. 274:** © Michael Newman/Photo Edit; 9.7: © Spencer Grant/PhotoEdit; **p. 276:** © William Hubbell/Woodfin Camp & Associates; 9.8: © Peter Correz/Stone/Getty Images; **p. 284:** © Karen Kasmauski/Woodfin Camp & Associates

Chapter 10

Opener: © Jose Luis Pelaez/The Stock Market/CORBIS; **p. 292:** © AP/Wide World Photos; **p. 296 (left & right):** © Ellen Senisi/The Image Works; **p. 314:** © LWA-Dann Tardif/CORBIS; **p. 315:** © Ariel Skelley/CORBIS; **p. 316:** © AP/Wide World Photos; **p. 317:** © Greg Sailor; **p. 318:** © Chris Cheadle/Stone/Getty Images

Chapter 11

Opener: © Bob Torrez/Stone/Getty Images; 11.2 (25-34 yrs.): © Eyewire/Getty website; (35-54 yrs.): © PhotoDisc/Getty website; (55-65 yrs.): © CORBIS website; (70-84 yrs.): © PhotoDisc/Getty website; (85-105yrs.): © Vol. 34/CORBIS;

p. 332: © David Young-Wolff/Stone/Getty Images; **p. 335 (left):** © Bettmann/CORBIS; **p. 335 (right):** © Matthew Mendelsohn/CORBIS; **p. 338:** © USA Today, staff photographer Paul Wiseman; **p. 339:** © John Goodman; 11.7 (left & right): © Alfred Pasieka/SPL/Photo Researchers; **p. 341 (left & right):** © James Balog; **p. 344:** © Elizabeth Crews; **p. 347 (top left):** IS008-55 / CORBIS website; **p. 347 (top right):** © Ariel Skelley/CORBIS; **p. 347 (bottom):** © Vol. RFCD296/CORBIS; **p. 350:** Courtesy of Laura Carstensen; **p. 351:** © Bryan Peterson/The Stock Market; **p. 352:** © G. Wayne Floyd/Unicorn Stock Photos; **p. 355:** © Eastcott Momatinck/The Image Works; **p. 357:** Courtesy of Sara Wheeler; **p. 358:** © Patrick Ward/Stock Boston

Chapter 12

Opener: © Jose L. Pelaez/The Stock Market/CORBIS; **p. 378:** © Catherine Gehm; **p. 381:** © James Pozarik; **p. 382:** © Cindy Charles/PhotoEdit; **p. 384:** © Peter Beck/The Stock Market/CORBIS; **p. 386:** © ShootingStar

Chapter 13

Opener: © Photomorgana/CORBIS; **p. 394 (top):** © AP/Wide World Photos; **p. 394 (bottom):** © Suzanne DeChillo/The New York Times; **p. 398 (top left):** © Bob Coyle, Photographer; **p. 398 (top right):** © Anthony Mercieca/Photo Researchers; **p. 398 (bottom left):** © Seven-Olaf Lindblad/Photo Researchers; **p. 398 (bottom right):** © Jan Cannefax/EKM Nepenthe; **p. 400:** © 1996 Rob Lemine/The Stock Market/CORBIS

Chapter 14

Opener: © Howard Berman/The Image Bank/Getty Images; **p. 424:** © Theo Westenberger; **p. 426:** © AP/Wide World Photos; **p. 434 (top):** © AP/Wide World Photos; **p. 434 (bottom):** © Rex USA Ltd.; 14.5: © 1974 The Washington Post, photo by Gerald Martineau. Reprinted by permission; **p. 438:** © Erich Lessing/Art Resource, New York; 14.7: Courtesy Lewis Baxter and Michael Phelps/UCLA School of Medicine; **p. 446 (top):** © Vauthey Pierre/Sygma/CORBIS; **p. 446 (bottom):** © Bettmann/CORBIS; 14.10: © Grunnitus/Photo Researchers; **p. 451:** © Bob Daemmrich/The Image Works; **p. 452:** © AP/Wide World Photos

Chapter 15

Opener: © Tom Stewart/CORBIS; **p. 467:** © Will and Demi McIntyre/Photo Researchers; **p. 468:** © Historical Pictures/Stock Montage; **p. 472:** Courtesy of Deke Simon; **p. 473 (top):** © David Frazier Photo Library; **p. 473 (bottom):** University of Washington, Mary Levin; **p. 481:** © Bruce Ayres/Stone/Getty Images; **p. 482:** © Bob Daemmrich/Stock Boston; **p. 485:** Courtesy Dr. Stanley Su

Chapter 16

Opener: © PictureQuest; **p. 498:** © AP/Wide World Photos; **p. 504:** © John Elk III; **p. 506:** © AP/Wide World Photos; **p. 510:** © Tony Freeman/PhotoEdit; **p. 511:** Courtesy of Colin Bloor; **p. 513:** © Macduff Everton/The Image Bank/Getty Images; **p. 517:** © Joe Raelle/Newsmakers/Getty Images; **p. 522:** © Spencer Grant/Photo Edit

Name Index

D

Subject Index

S